NEW ZEALAND CRICKET

2009 C
AL NACK

62nd Edition

Edited by

Francis Payne

&

Ian Smith

Hodder Moa

The Editors welcome contributions from readers for inclusion in the *2010 Almanack*

Please correspond directly with the editors:

Francis Payne,
97 Bond Crescent,
Forrest Hill,
AUCKLAND.
Phone/Fax: (09) 410-5259
E-mail: francisp@xtra.co.nz

Ian Smith,
91 Kamahi Street,
Stokes Valley,
WELLINGTON.
Phone: (04) 9766-477
E-mail: ianelizabeth@paradise.net.nz

Front cover: Ross Taylor hits a boundary during the third test between New Zealand and India at the Basin Reserve. Andrew Cornaga/PHOTOSPORT

Back cover: Jesse Ryder celebrates the dismissal of Yuvraj Singh at the Basin Reserve. Andrew Cornaga/PHOTOSPORT

ISBN 978-1-86971-177-1

A Hodder Moa Book

Published in 2009 by Hachette Livre NZ Ltd
4 Whetu Place, Mairangi Bay, Auckland, New Zealand
Printed by 1010 Printing International Ltd., China

CONTENTS

NEW ZEALAND CRICKET

Office Bearers

2008/09

Patron
His Excellency The Hon. Sir Anand Satyanand G.N.Z.M. Q.S.O.
Governor-General of New Zealand

President
D.O. Neely, M.B.E.

Vice-Presidents
The Presidents of Major Associations

Board
A.R. Isaac *(chairman),* D.S. Currie Q.S.O, S.L. Boock,
A. Urlwin, S.A. Riddell, B.D. King, C.J.D. Moller, S. Heal

Chief Executive
J.T.C. Vaughan

Auditors
Ernst and Young, Chartered Accountants

Solicitor
L.M.C. Robinson, Saunders Robinson

Bankers
The National Bank of New Zealand

Life Members
M. Brito, C.F. Collins, O.B.E., J.H. Heslop C.B.E.,
J. Lamason, T. Macdonald, Q.S.M., P.F. McKelvey, M.B.E. C.N.Z.M.,
D.O. Neely, M.B.E., Hon. Justice B.J. Paterson, O.B.E. Q.C. C.N.Z.M.,
J.R. Reid, O.B.E., Y. Taylor, Sir Allan Wright, K.B.E.

Honorary Cricket Members
J.C. Alabaster, F.J. Cameron, M.B.E., R.O. Collinge,
B.E. Congdon, O.B.E., R.S. Cunis *(deceased)*, A.E. Dick,
G.T. Dowling, O.B.E., J.W. Guy, D.R. Hadlee, B.F. Hastings,
H.J. Howarth *(deceased)*, A.R. MacGibbon,
V. Pollard, J.R. Reid, O.B.E., B.W. Sinclair,
J.T. Sparling, E.W.T. Tindill, O.B.E..

Honorary Member
H.H. Whiting.

National Selectors
Senior: G.M. Turner *(convenor),* D.J. Nash, J.G. Wright, M.J Greatbatch *(advisor).*
Age Group: K. Patel *(convenor)*, B.L. Cairns, M.D. O'Neill, J.G. Wright
Women: G.R. Stead *(convenor),* J.E. Harris, P.D. Kinsella.

National Code of Conduct Commissioner
N.R.W. Davidson Q.C.

Statistician
F. Payne.

FROM THE EDITORS

The 62nd edition of the *New Zealand Cricket Almanack* covers yet another full year of cricketing activity at all levels. The period under review began with the New Zealand Emerging Players in Australia in July 2008 and ended with the World Twenty20 in England in June 2009.

During that time the BlackCaps toured Bangladesh and made two visits to Australia while also hosting West Indies and India for a total of five tests, ten one-day internationals and four Twenty20 internationals. The White Ferns had one of their busiest seasons with a five-match Rose Bowl series in New Zealand followed by a one-off Twenty20 international in Sydney, which was part of a double-header which also featured the Australian and New Zealand men's teams. The women returned to Australia for the ICC World Cup in March and paid a third visit in June, when they played three Twenty20 internationals en-route to the World Twenty20 in England. The New Zealand A team went to Australia and India in July 2008 and the New Zealand Under 19 side toured England in July and August.

The increase in the amount of cricket which we are now required to cover continues unabated. The forthcoming season sees the BlackCaps in Sri Lanka in August and in South Africa for the Champions Trophy in September. New Zealand were scheduled to visit Pakistan but the situation in that country has resulted in the one-day internationals being moved to the United Arab Emirates while the three tests will be played in New Zealand in December.

Bangladesh and Australia arrive after the New Year and another World Twenty20 tournament (men and women) goes ahead in West Indies in April 2010. There are also A team tours to Australia and India and New Zealand will host the Under 19 World Cup in January.

White Ferns

The best performed national side were the White Ferns. The Rose Bowl series finished 2-2 after the final match was washed out, New Zealand having led 2-0 at one stage. New Zealand then defeated Australia in the opening match of both the World Cup and the World Twenty20 but, having now got the better of their old foes, found England to be their new nemesis.

New Zealand reached the final of both ICC tournaments only to lose to England on each occasion. The White Ferns' only other loss in either competition was to England in the Super Six section of the World Cup.

The White Ferns made great strides under new coach Gary Stead and they will be looking to go one better next time. The forthcoming season has them scheduled to play Australia for the Rose Bowl and then travel to West Indies for another World Twenty20 in April.

The BlackCaps

The 2008/09 season was not a vintage one for the BlackCaps, although there were certainly a number of highlights. The only win in nine tests was a come-from-behind effort against Bangladesh, and that was almost solely due to a remarkable one-man performance from Daniel Vettori. Eighteen one-day internationals (as many as four ended in a no result) and ten Twenty20s saw a 50-50 outcome in both formats.

The ongoing search for a test match opening batting pair continued. The names of the incumbents of twelve months ago, Jamie How and Aaron Redmond, were missing when New Zealand Cricket announced their new list of contracted players. Tim McIntosh played in all five home tests, scored a very fortuitous hundred but achieved little else. He was joined by Martin Guptill who had just one first-class hundred to his name.

The decision to swap Jesse Ryder and Daniel Flynn in the batting order produced immediate success. Ryder had an outstanding summer and showed an uncanny ability to adapt seamlessly from big-hitting one-day mode to long-term test match-style batting and scored a century and a double hundred in successive tests. Ross Taylor was another whose performances provided encouragement for the future. Over the period under review he averaged 39 in tests, 45 in one-day internationals and 29 in Twenty20s, always scoring runs at a good clip. Furthermore, his best, surely, is yet to come.

As we write, Shane Bond looks set to rejoin the reliable Chris Martin as New Zealand's test match new ball pairing. Both are now aged 34, however, so how long the partnership lasts remains to be seen. On the other hand, twenty-year-old Tim Southee's fortunes fell away during the season and it is to be hoped, for New Zealand's sake, that this was just a temporary setback for a very talented cricketer.

Home and Away

New Zealand were given a stern test by Bangladesh, who won the first one-day international and could have won at least one of the other two. Daniel Vettori, as we mentioned, saved the day for his team in the first test.

After New Zealand had a successful opening day in the first test in Australia, the home side regained their composure and went on to win both matches. New Zealand returned for the Chappell-Hadlee series in February and won the first two games. Australia won the next two and the final game had to be abandoned. By coincidence, the White Ferns' Rose Bowl series had exactly the same sequence of results.

The two tests against West Indies were drawn, with neither side quite having the ability to finish the other off. The decision review system was used in these matches. The Twenty20s saw the first ever "super over" eliminator while New Zealand just edged ahead of the Duckworth/Lewis target at Napier to take the one-day series.

The much anticipated tour by India lived up to all expectations, even more so when an extra test was added to their National Bank itinerary.

After losing both Twenty20s, India showed awesome batting power in the one-dayers, but struggled at Eden Park in the one game where the bowlers had some assistance. India won the test series 1-0, their first series win in New Zealand since their first visit in 1967/68.

The test matches were again played away from "concrete jungles" and the move was once more a success. University Oval in Dunedin, however, might be seen to better advantage a little later in the summer, as was the case with the first test staged there in 2007/08.

New Zealand's final assignment for the season was the World Twenty20 in England but they were only able to record wins against Scotland (a seven-overs-a-side affair) and Ireland.

The Domestic Scene

Domestic cricket again provided a great deal of interesting cricket. Five of the six associations took part in a final (Wellington missed out while Otago reached both one-day finals). After a slow start, Auckland won three of their four games after Christmas to be the top qualifier in the State Championship and met Central Districts in what turned out to be an intriguing final.

The match had been scheduled for Lincoln, regardless of who was the top qualifier, allowing certainty in preparing a pitch in New Zealand's autumn. Daily highlights of the match were also available on New Zealand Cricket's website.

Northern Districts defeated Otago by 49 runs in the State Shield final but the Twenty20 final was rained off. Otago, as top qualifier, were named the winners and were subsequently granted a place in the Indian Champions League.

The women's competitions were dominated by Canterbury and Wellington. Canterbury won the State League title off the last possible ball of the game while Wellington won the Twenty20 title the following day. Both games were played at the Basin Reserve.

At the end of the season State Insurance announced they would not be renewing their sponsorship of domestic cricket which began in 2001/02.

Coaching Changes

There were plenty of coaching changes during the season. Andy Moles took over from John Bracewell from the West Indies series and Mark O'Donnell joined him as his assistant when India arrived. Gary Stead was the new White Ferns coach.

O'Donnell's departure from Auckland saw Paul Strang and Matt Horne take over the reins while Grant Bradburn did likewise after Moles left Northern Districts. Former New Zealand assistant coach Bob Carter took on the Canterbury coaching role and former England all-rounder Dermot Reeve had his first season with Central Districts.

Acknowledgments

We again wish to thank the associations, scorers and officials throughout the country who supplied information to us. In particular we would like to acknowledge the help of Catherine Campbell *(Women's Cricket)* and the rest of the staff at New Zealand Cricket and Chris McQuaid for his help with women's cricket.

Francis Payne & Ian Smith
June 2009

DIARY OF THE SEASON

July

3 New Zealand Cricket's umpiring manager, Brian Aldridge, retires after 11 years in the position. Aldridge stood in 26 test matches and 45 one-day internationals

5 Dermot Reeve, the former England all-rounder, is named as Central Districts' coach. Reeve moved to New Zealand in 2006 and had been living in Queenstown. He will be contracted to New Zealand Cricket under a new initiative in which all provincial cricket coaches are centrally contracted and available for wider coaching programmes outside their major associations during winter.

8 New Zealand coach John Bracewell confirms he will return for a second spell at Gloucestershire in 2008, as director of cricket, after his contract with New Zealand Cricket expires.

10 Ian Butler announces he will move from Northern Districts to Otago for the 2008/09 season.

11 Steve Jenkin, coach of the New Zealand women's team, stands down after three years in the position.

The major associations name the players offered contracts for the 2008/09 season. The only players without first-class experience are New Zealand Under 19 players Trent Boult *(Northern Districts)* and Harry Boam *(Wellington)*. Otago include 22-year-old Neil Wagner, a left-arm pace bowler who has played first-class cricket in South Africa.

25 Gary Stead is appointed as the New Zealand women's coach to replace Steve Jenkin. Stead had been High Performance Centre coach since 2004 and coached the Canterbury women's team to both domestic titles in 2007/08.

30 Chris Cairns is named as the head of the "World Future League" financed by several leading Indian companies. The league aims to get cricketers aged between 14 and 17 representing India, Pakistan and Sri Lanka in a tournament in January.

August

5 Otago announce that they have signed England all-rounder Dimitri Mascarenhas for the 2008/09 State Shield and State Twenty20 tournaments.

13 New Zealand's visit to Pakistan for a three-match one-day series prior to the Champions Trophy is cancelled. Three games in Multan and Faisalabad were scheduled from 24 to 30 August.

14 Former Zimbabwe leg-spinner Paul Strang is named as the high performance coach contracted by New Zealand Cricket to focus on a selected group of elite cricketers within the Auckland region. Strang will work with Auckland's coach Mark O'Donnell and high performance manager Kaushik Patel.

Bob Carter is appointed Canterbury coach, replacing Dave Nosworthy who is returning to South Africa.

25 The Champions Trophy, scheduled to be held in Pakistan, is postponed until 2009 due to security concerns.

26 Mathew Sinclair is named as captain of Central Districts for the 2008/09 season.

September

3 The bat that Glenn Turner used to score his 100th hundred fetches $13,937 at a charity auction organised by the Lord's Taverners.

4 Former New Zealand Rugby Union chief executive Chris Moller is named as a board member of New Zealand Cricket replacing Dennis Radford who retires by rotation. Sir John Anderson stands down after 13 years as chairman and Alan Isaac becomes the acting chairman. Don Neely will be recommended for a further and final one-year term as president at the Annual General Meeting.

5 New Zealand Cricket announces a net loss of $7.586m after distributions to major and district associations of $10.492m, including player backpays of $1.2m. NZC had budgeted for a loss of $3.03m. The major increase in expenditure was $7.367m to $12.562m for the international men's team. NZC runs its revenue based on a four-year cycle and recorded a $6.46m profit the previous year. It predicts a surplus for the four years ending 31 May, 2010. The annual report also notes that there were over 100,000 registered participants in New Zealand for the first time.

12 Stephen Cunis is named as coach of the Canterbury women's team, taking over from Gary Stead who had been appointed coach of the New Zealand women's team.

25 Chris Martin is ruled out of the one-day series in Bangladesh after suffering a hamstring injury playing for Warwickshire. He is replaced by Michael Mason. Martin later pulls out of the test matches as well and is replaced by Mark Gillespie.

29 New Zealand Cricket names Dubai-based company Dheeraj and East Coast LLC as the new sponsor of the New Zealand men's team in a three-year deal. The National Bank retain sponsorship of the home international series.

30 Carisbrook is one of two Dunedin landmarks given national recognition by the New Zealand Historic Places Trust. Carisbrook and the Dunedin Athenaeum and Mechanics Institute gained approval for a Category 1 registration status.

October

1 Matthew Bell is named as captain of the Wellington State Shield and State Championship teams for 2008/09, taking over from Michael Parlane who had returned to Northern Districts. Stephen Fleming will lead the province in the State Twenty20 championship.

4 Former South Australian wicketkeeper-batsman Shane Deitz signs as a network coach with Cricket Wellington. Deitz, who scored 3753 runs at 30.76 in 66 first-class matches, will play at club level for Naenae Old Boys.

13 Dayle Hadlee is named as one of the coaches for the ICC's Global Cricket Academy in Dubai. He will work alongside Rod Marsh, the Academy's director of coaching, to help train and develop players from across the world.

31 Canterbury appoints Shane Jurgensen as its high performance coach. Jurgensen, 32, played for three Australian states and had been Queensland's director and head coach of high performance. He has also been involved with assisting the New Zealand A and New Zealand Emerging Players sides in Australia.

November

1 New Zealand Cricket names Geoff Allott as general manager of cricket. Allott, 36, will oversee the cricket operations and coaching, management and selection of the New Zealand national side and other elite teams.

4 Jacob Oram is ruled out of New Zealand's tour to Australia due to the back injury he suffered during the first test against Bangladesh.

5 Brendon McCullum is named the National Bank Player of the Year at New Zealand Cricket's awards night. The batting awards go to Ross Taylor *(Redpath Cup)* and McCullum *(Walter Hadlee Trophy)* while the bowling awards go to Chris Martin *(Winsor Cup)* and Kyle Mills *(Walter Hadlee Trophy)*. A new award, the J.R. Reid Trophy for best all-rounder, is awarded to Jacob Oram. Nicola Browne and Helen Watson win the Ruth Martin Cup and Phyl Blackler Cup, awarded for outstanding batting and bowling, while the State Medal and State Plate, for outstanding performances in domestic cricket, go to Nathan McCullum and Sara McGlashan. Sir Richard Hadlee is awarded the Sutcliffe Medal for outstanding services to cricket.

6 A new way of measuring performances of players in domestic cricket is launched. The Most Valuable Player (MVP) system, developed by the Professional Cricketers' Association in England, uses a cumulative points system that rewards players for every run scored, every wicket taken and every catch held throughout the season. A player also achieves bonus points based on other criteria important to the outcome of the match.

11 Stuart Heal, a former chairman of Otago Cricket, is appointed as a director on the board of New Zealand Cricket. He fills the vacancy left by the retirement of Sir John Anderson who resigned at the NZC annual meeting in September. Sir John is replaced as chairman by Alan Isaac.

25 Andy Moles is named as the new men's national coach with John Bracewell stepping down after the second test against Australia. High performance manager John Wright joins the national selection panel alongside Glenn Turner and Dion Nash.

28 Grant Bradburn is appointed as coach of Northern Districts, replacing Andy Moles. Craig Ross is named as his assistant.

December

6 Shane Jurgensen, recently appointed as Canterbury's high performance coach, is named as New Zealand's men's bowling coach.

24 New Zealand Cricket names Dermot Reeve as bowling coach for New Zealand's Twenty20 matches against West Indies while Mark Greatbatch is appointed as a selection advisor.

January

5 Sir Richard Hadlee is named as one of the inaugural inductees of the ICC Cricket Hall of Fame, established by the ICC as part of its centenary year celebrations.

31 An agreement is reached between Canterbury Cricket and the three Hagley Oval-based cricket clubs, St Albans, Riccarton and Old Boys-Collegians, on the proposed use of the ground as Canterbury's new headquarters. Canterbury Cricket will inform the Christchurch City Council that its clubs are unified and that the council can look at upgrading the ground to test match standard.

February

14 Olympic team chef de mission Dave Currie is appointed manager of the New Zealand men's team for a three-year period beginning with the series against India. He succeeds Lindsay Crocker, manager for the previous five years. Currie will be released from his role to attend the Commonwealth Games and a temporary manager will be appointed at that time.

24 Mark O'Donnell is named as assistant coach of the New Zealand men's team. Auckland subsequently name Paul Strang as caretaker coach until the end of the season.

New Zealand and Zimbabwe agree to postpone New Zealand's tour of Zimbabwe, which was due to take place this July, by a year.

26 Jimad Khan, from the Onslow Cricket Club in Wellington, hits a ball 98.27 metres to win the inaugural State Big Hits competition. Khan was one of six regional finalsists who competed at the Basin Reserve against Ian Butler (94.77m) and Jacob Oram (91.89m).

March

4 New Zealand Cricket cancels New Zealand's tour to Pakistan, scheduled for later in 2009, following the terror attack on the Sri Lankan team in Lahore.

10 Iain O'Brien announces he will be playing for Leicestershire in the 2009 season and plans to be available for their opening championship game beginning on 15 April.

14 Grant Elliott signs for Surrey as their overseas player for the first part of the 2009 season. Elliott had previously played club cricket for Surrey club Weybridge.

20 James Franklin signs for Gloucestershire for the 2009 season. He had previously played for the county in 2004. He will link up with former New Zealand coach John Bracewell, Gloucestershire's director of cricket.

25 Tony Hill is appointed to the International Cricket Council's elite panel of umpires. His appointment follows the retirement of Steve Bucknor.

30 Jeetan Patel becomes the fourth Wellington player to secure a county contract for 2009 when he signs for Warwickshire.

31 Haidee Tiffen announces her retirement from international cricket after having led New Zealand to the final at the women's World Cup in Australia.

April

1 Cricket Wellington extend Anthony Stuart's coaching contract to 2011. Stuart first coached Wellington in the 2006/07 season.

6 Cricket Wellington scorers Ian Smith and Cheryl Styles are among eight Wellington-based volunteers who receive ICC Centenary Medals during the lunch break on the first day of the third test at the Basin Reserve. The others are Trevor Rigby, Mike Curtis, Patricia McKelvey, Rob Mitchell, Earle Cooper and Denis Currie.

Others to be presented with ICC centenary medals from New Zealand during the course of the year are: Chris Rapson, Christopher (Bob) Pratt, Michael Satterthwaite, Royce Riordan, Harry Findlay, Peter Moody, Dennis Radford, Stan Landon-Lane, Gary Ashworth, Colin Aitken, Russell Payne, Russell Smith, Malcolm Jones, John Heikell, Harvey King, Ted Tempero, Neil Sulzberger, Mike Cotter, Dermot Payton, Graeme Young, Tim Brownlee, John Corner, Ces Renwick, Arthur Lennan, Rex Smith, Peter McDermott, Lynda Prichard, Ray Hopkins, Chris Gillies, Derek Cockburn, Brian Bellringer, Dave Hoskin, Ian Leggat, Allan Whimp, Warren Shirley, Mike O'Connor, Peter Cameron, Lauchlin Weir, Brian Keats, Ann McKenna, Mike Dormer, Lesley Murdoch.

11 Mathew Sinclair is named as the State Most Valuable Player. He tallied 342.04 points, ahead of Graham Napier (329.54) and Neil Wagner (325.47).

27 Aimee Watkins (formerly Mason) is named as New Zealand women's captain, taking over from Haidee Tiffen who retired after the World Cup.

May

5 Grant Bradburn is confirmed as Northern Districts' coach for 2009/10, having taken over mid-season when Andy Moles left to coach New Zealand.

8 New Zealand Cricket announces a group of 27 players to prepare for the Under 19 World Cup, scheduled for Kenya in February 2010. The World Cup team will be selected following the National Under 19 championship in 2009/10. The squad is: Corey Anderson, Harry Boam, Tom Blundell, Doug Bracewell, Michael Bracewell, Craig Cachopa, Dane Cleaver, Rory Darkins, Lachlan Ferguson, Shane Gadsdon, Chamika Gajanayaka, Matt Henry, Jono Hickey, Timothy Johnston, Tom Latham, Matt McEwan, Adam Milne, James Neesham, Henry Nicholls, Bevan Small, Ben Smith, Blair Soper, Mattie Thomas, Logan van Beek, Theo van Woerkom, Ben Wheeler and Harry Wright.

25 Otago are confirmed as participants in the inaugural Champions League Twenty20 competition to be held in India from 8 to 23 October.

29 Mathew Sinclair steps down as captain of Central Districts. He says that it was an honour to captain the Stags but for personal and family reasons he is standing down to give someone else the opportunity. Jamie How subsequently takes over the role.

June

1 Former New Zealand cricketer John Morrison is made a Member of the New Zealand Order of Merit (MNZM) in the Queen's Birthday Honours List.

4 State Insurance announce they will not be renewing their sponsorship of New Zealand domestic cricket. They had been sponsors since the 2001/02 season.

11 Jesse Ryder is kept under observation in hospital in London for treatment for a groin infection. The rest of the New Zealand team travels to Nottingham for their Twenty20 international against Ireland. Aaron Redmond is called into the squad in case a replacement is required.

12 Chris Martin announces he is returning to Canterbury for the 2009/10 cricket season after a four-year stint with Auckland. Martin and his wife are expecting their first child and are heading back to Christchurch to have family around them for the arrival.

23 Canterbury name Paul Wiseman as network coach. The position, funded by New Zealand Cricket, is responsible for implementing and delivering a High Performance Programme to advance Canterbury's NZC-identified age-group elite cricketers.

26 New Zealand Cricket names the 20 players to be offered International Playing Agreements for the year 1 August 2009 to 31 July 2010. They are: Brent Arnel, Shane Bond, Neil Broom, Ian Butler, Grant Elliott, James Franklin, Daniel Flynn, Martin Guptill, Gareth Hopkins, Brendon McCullum, Tim McIntosh, Chris Martin, Kyle Mills, Iain O'Brien, Jacob Oram, Jeetan Patel, Jesse Ryder, Tim Southee, Ross Taylor and Daniel Vettori. Arnel, Broom, Butler, Elliott, Guptill and McIntosh are offered contracts for the first time while Bond returns to the list. Peter Fulton, Mark Gillespie, Jamie How, James Marshall, Michael Mason, Aaron Redmond and Scott Styris are missing from the previous year.

27 New Zealand are named to host the Under 19 World Cup in February 2010 after Kenya are stripped of its hosting rights. Kenya had been awarded the event in 2006 but the amount of work still needing to be done represented too great a risk for the successful staging of the event, according to the International Cricket Council.

PLAYERS OF THE YEAR

Jesse Ryder had a quiet return to the New Zealand side on the tour of Bangladesh. The Wellington left-hander scored 67 in three one-day internationals but in the test series showed his ability with scores of 1, 38, 91 and 39 not out in his first four innings. In Australia he scored 70 in four test innings.

The changes in fortune came in the home series against West Indies and India. New coach Andy Moles decided that Ryder and Daniel Flynn should swap places in the batting order with Flynn going to number three and Ryder to number five. There was instant success for both with Flynn scoring a career-best 95 and Ryder getting 89 in the first test at Dunedin. In the second test Ryder joined the group of players to register fifties in both innings of a test with scores of 57 and 59 not out.

This form continued in the two Twenty20 games with Ryder making 12 and 62. After scoring 67 runs in three one-dayers Ryder was omitted for the fourth game due to disciplinary reasons and then suffered an injury which forced him to miss the one-day series in Australia and some domestic games for Wellington.

Ryder returned for the series against India, scoring 1 and 26 in the BlackCaps' two Twenty20 victories and in the third one-day match at Christchurch he scored his first hundred. India had scored a New Zealand record of 392-4 but Ryder and Brendon McCullum responded with 166 off 22 overs, Ryder top scoring with 105. This was followed by 46 in the fourth game and 63 at Auckland, in New Zealand's only win. He also had career best figures of 3-29 off nine overs.

In the first test against India, Ryder made his maiden test century, scoring 102. It was his fourth test innings in a row with a score of over fifty. In the second test at Napier he became the eleventh New Zealand batsman to score a test double century, getting a deserved 201. In all nine tests he scored 771 runs, at 55.07, and was by far New Zealand's leading run scorer.

Ryder was a member of the New Zealand side at the World Twenty20 but suffered an injury and only played in the first game before returning home early. All in all he has had a great season for a player with such limited international experience.

In the past 12 months 25-year-old **Ross Taylor** has become the rock in the BlackCaps' batting line up. He has shown that he can handle this mantle in all forms of the game.

He started the season in Bangladesh and scored 103 (his third one-day international century) in the third game of the series. His only disappointments of the season came in the test series where he totalled just 40 runs in three innings. On the tour to Australia he was the only New Zealand player to score a fifty in the first test and then had scores of 44 and 1 in the second.

During the West Indies series in December, Taylor scored 65 runs in the tests and then had his highest Twenty20 score, getting 63 in the first game. When the one-day internationals came he averaged 93.50, scoring 187 runs, including two fifties. In the Chappell-Hadlee series against Australia he was New Zealand's second-highest scorer with 195 runs, including scores of 64 and 76.

Taylor had scores of 31 and 27 in the Twenty20 games against India but had a modest one day series. However, he shone during the test matches. He had an outstanding partnership with Jesse Ryder in the second test at Napier. Ryder scored 201 and Taylor achieved his second test score of over 150. In the final test, at Wellington, Taylor played a match saving innings of 107, his fourth test century.

Taylor played in the World Twenty20 Cup but injury caused him to miss two important games. In all nine tests he scored 587 runs at 39.13 and was New Zealand's leading scorer in one-day internationals with 591 runs at 45.46. Taylor has also developed into a fine first slip fieldsman, taking 15 catches in nine tests, and has now taken 27 catches in just 17 matches.

If Taylor can continue to build on this sort of form the Black Caps could well be on the road to improving their standings.

PROMISING PLAYERS

Kane Williamson played one first-class game and four one-day matches in the 2007/08 season after captaining New Zealand in the Under 19 World Cup. In 2008/09 the 19-year-old stamped his mark on the New Zealand cricket scene. He became an integral part of the Northern Districts side in all forms of the game, winning the Northern Districts *Cricketer of the Year* award.

He was the sixth highest scorer in State Championship games, with 707 runs at an average of 53.80. He scored a fifty in six of his seven appearances and got hundreds in the last two games. This included 111 and 95 against Auckland and 100 versus Wellington. Williamson also developed his bowling during the season, his off-spin accounting for 16 wickets, including 5-75 against Canterbury.

In State Shield games he scored 319 runs at 45.57, including 100 against Canterbury. He also took four wickets. Williamson played in four games in the Twenty20 competition scoring 57 runs at 14.25.

In a short period of time he has shown great maturity and seems unfazed when pressure is applied. Provided he maintains the strong performances shown during the past season he seems assured of representing New Zealand in the near future.

Martin Guptill began the 2008/09 season with a one-day career average of 42.58, including two centuries, but a first-class average of just 22.59, with a highest score of 99 made on debut.

He made a tremendous advance during the season, playing for the BlackCaps in all three forms of the game. He was injured at the start of the season and did not play in the State Championship until round four, when he made his maiden first-class century, 148 against Otago. He had earlier played for Auckland against West Indies.

Guptill was picked to bat at number three for the BlackCaps in the fourth one-day international against West Indies but when Jesse Ryder was suspended he was promoted to opener and became the first New Zealand batsman to score a century on debut, making an unbeaten 122. This was followed by 43 in the final game.

Guptill then toured Australia, scoring 136 at 34.00 in the five Chappell-Hadlee games including an unbeaten 64 in the final game. He scored 147 runs against India to finish the summer with 448 runs in twelve one-day internationals. Guptill was then selected in the test team against India and had two scores in the forties. His final outing was the World Twenty20 where he was New Zealand's second-highest scorer with 102 runs at 34.

He has immediately looked comfortable at international level and looks likely to play a major part in New Zealand cricket over the next few years.

Former Zimbabwe Under 19 representative **Colin de Grandhomme** came to New Zealand and first played for Auckland in the 2006/07 season. During the 2008/09 season he was a regular member of the side, becoming a more than useful all-rounder.

He was Auckland's second highest scorer in the State Championship with 545 runs at 51.45, including centuries against Northern Districts and Central Districts. His useful medium-paced bowling obtained 21 wickets at 24.57.

He played in six State Shield games, scoring 66 runs, and took a career best 3-38 against Canterbury. He was replaced in the final four games when international players returned. In the Twenty20 competition he played in all seven games, getting 121 runs at 17.58 and securing five wickets.

With all-rounders being an important part of the game de Grandhomme has shown that he could be a very valuable player in that role.

HAPPENINGS

Syd Ward is the oldest surviving first-class cricketer in the world and is the only one over 100 years old. Eric Tindill remains the oldest test cricketer from any country. As far as can be ascertained, the oldest New Zealand players are:

		Born
S.W. Ward	*Wellington*	5. 8.1907
E.W.T. Tindill	*Wellington*	18.12.1910
V. James	*Canterbury*	24. 8.1915
N.A. McMahon	*Auckland*	24. 5.1916
T.L. Pritchard	*Wellington*	10. 3.1917
C.A. Snedden	*Auckland*	7. 1.1918
J.L. Wyatt	*Northern Districts*	7. 3.1919
A.T. Burgess	*Canterbury*	1. 5.1920

Central Districts' oldest player is Trevor Barber (born 3.6.1925) while Otago's oldest is Ian Payne (born 18.7.1921).

• • •

Richard Jones and Kruger van Wyk led their teams in every match of the three domestic competitions in 2008/09, as they had also done the previous season.

Northern Districts and Otago used three different captains during the season. The six sides were led by:

	Official captain	***Replacement***
Auckland	Richard Jones	–
Canterbury	Kruger van Wyk	–
Central Districts	Mathew Sinclair	Jamie How
Northern Districts	James Marshall	Michael Parlane, Peter McGlashan
Otago	Craig Cumming	Nathan McCullum, Greg Todd
Wellington	Matthew Bell	Stephen Fleming

• • •

New Zealand played nine test matches during the past twelve months for one win, three losses and five draws. Jesse Ryder, in his first season, was the leading scorer with 771 runs while Daniel Vettori was the leading wicket taker with 36 victims.

Ryder and Ross Taylor each scored two hundreds while Tim McIntosh, Brendon McCullum and Vettori each made one. Ryder, Vettori, Taylor, McCullum and Iain O'Brien were the only players to appear in all nine matches..

• • •

New Zealand took part in 18 one-day internationals in the same period with seven wins, seven losses and four no results. Ross Taylor was the leading scorer with 591 runs while Kyle Mills (26) again took the most wickets. Taylor, Grant Elliott, Martin Guptill (on debut) and Jesse Ryder scored hundreds.

Jacob Oram, who appeared in eleven matches, was the most economical of the regular bowlers, conceding 3.93 runs per over. McCullum, Mills and Taylor were the only players to appear in every game.

• • •

The highest run scorer in first-class cricket over the past twelve months was Peter Ingram who totalled 957. James Franklin (914) and Mathew Sinclair (904) also scored more than 900 runs. The most first-class wickets were taken by Daniel Vettori and Iain O'Brien with 40 apiece.

The Cornwall Cricket Club in Auckland again organised the limited-overs national club competition which was played from 7-12 April 2009. Teams involved were Cadets *(Northern Districts)*, Albion *(Otago)*, Lancaster Park-Woolston *(Christchurch)*, Napier Tech Old Boys *(Central Districts)*, Hutt District *(Wellington)* and Howick-Pakuranga *(Auckland)*.

Players with first-class experience who took part were Nick Beard *(Albion)*, Jono Boult, Llorne Howell and Trent Boult *(Cadets)*, Andrew de Boorder, Gareth Hayne and Greg Morgan *(Howick-Pakuranga)*, Ash Turner *(Hutt District)*, Andrew Ellis, Ryan McCone and Martin Kain *(Lancaster Park-Woolston)* and Craig Findlay *(Napier Tech Old Boys)*.

In the final **Hutt District** 120 (D. Cudby 42, M.O. Kain 4-8) **lost to Lancaster Park-Woolston** 121-3 (K.R. Ambler 60*) by 7 wckets.

Tournament awards were: Batting – James Colson *(Hutt District)*, Bowling – Martin Kain *(Lancaster Park-Woolston)*, Player of the Tournament – Andrew Ellis *(Lancaster Park-Woolston)*.

• • •

A number of New Zealand players have a high ratio of catches per match over their first-class careers. Stephen Fleming ended his career with 340 catches in 247 first-class games while Neal Parlane, 89 (one as a wicketkeeper) in 75, Ross Taylor, 66 in 60, and Jamie How, 84 in 83, also average at least one catch per game. James Marshall has taken 109 (one as a wicketkeeper) in 111 matches.

• • •

During the season Michael Parlane overtook Chris Harris' record for the most appearances in domestic one-day cricket. Craig Cumming ended the season with 99 matches to his name.

The most games in domestic one-day cricket have now been played by:

matches		*matches*	
139	M.E. Parlane *ND, W*	112	M.S. Sinclair *CD*
137	C.Z. Harris *C*	110	G.J. Hopkins *ND, C, O, A*
129	C.J. Nevin *W*	107	C.B. Gaffaney *O*
125	M.D. Bell *ND, W*	105	L.G. Howell *CD, C, A, ND*
122	R.G Hart *ND*	103	M.D. Bailey *ND*
121	G.E. Bradburn *ND*	102	M.N. Hart *ND*
118	R.A. Jones *A, W*	101	M.W. Douglas *CD, W*
114	A.C. Barnes *A*	100	R.G. Petrie *C, W*

A total of 101 players have made 50 or more appearances.

• • •

Parlane also overtook Harris' record for most runs in domestic one-day cricket and finished the season with 3909. Harris is next with 3796 runs. Harris remains the leading wicket taker with 134 victims.

• • •

Several New Zealand provincial players continued their international careers with other countries over the past twelve months. Former Canterbury and Otago all-rounder Darron Reekers represented Netherlands in the European Championship Division One in July 2008 (which included two official one-day internationals) and in the ICC World Twenty20 qualifying series in Ireland in August.

He made 196 off 117 balls against Norway at Dublin in a European Championship match, out of a total of 474 in 50 overs. His century came off 58 balls. He also played in eight matches in the qualifying series for the ICC World Cup in South Africa in April 2009. Reekers was also a member of the Netherlands team which played in the World Twenty20 in England in June, scoring 20 off 13 balls in their famous win over England at Lord's.

Peter Borren, a former New Zealand Under 19 representative, also took part in Netherlands' historic victory, scoring 30 off 25 balls. He also played in the European Championship Division One competition and the World Cup and World Twenty20 qualifiers, as well as one one-day international and one Inter-Continental Cup match against Canada in July 2009.

• • •

Ian Billcliff played ten matches for Canada in the ICC World Cup qualifying series in South Africa in April 2009. Three of the matches were official one-day internationals. His best efforts were 61 against Namibia and 96 not out against Afghanistan.

• • •

Former Central Districts' opening batsman Geoff Barnett, who was born in Nelson but whose mother is Canadian, also played ten matches for Canada in that tournament, scoring 102 not out against Uganda. He also appeared in Inter-Continental Cup matches (first-class) against Scotland and Netherlands in July 2009.

• • •

Dannevirke-born Peter Connell made his one-day international debut for Ireland against New Zealand in July 2008. He later appeared in Inter-Continental Cup matches against Netherlands, Kenya and Namibia and the two ICC qualifying series. He was a member of the Ireland team at the World Twenty20 in June, playing in the match against New Zealand at Trent Bridge.

The former Hastings Boys' High School teacher had a remarkable debut in first-class cricket when he took ten wickets in the match, including a second-inning hat-trick, against the Netherlands in Rotterdam. He became only the 16th player in the history of first-class cricket to capture three wickets in three balls on debut.

Connell, who is teaching at Carrick Fergus Grammar School in Belfast, qualifies for his adopted country through his Irish-born grandparents.

• • •

Former Central Districts and Wellington left-arm spinner Regan West was also a member of Ireland's team at the World Twenty20. He played Inter-Continental Cup matches against Kenya and Namibia and the ICC World Cup qualifiers in South Africa in April 2009, taking 5-26 against Oman. He also appeared in three one-day internationals against Kenya in July 2009.

• • •

Sean Eathorne took a brilliant catch to dismiss Fidel Edwards while fielding as substitute in the first test against West Indies at Dunedin and joins the small list of players who have made a catch in a test for New Zealand without ever actually gaining a test cap.

The other players who have taken a catch as substitute but never gained test selection are: Tim Ritchie (v West Indies 1986/87), Mark Hastings (v Pakistan 1993/94), Marcel McKenzie (v England 2001/02), Carl Cachopa (v West Indies 2005/06), Stu Mills (v Sri Lanka 2006/07) and Nick Horsley (v England 2007/08).

• • •

Former Northern Districts player Neisha Pratt again captained the Hong Kong women's team which took part in the Asian Cricket Council's Women's Twenty20 Championship in Kuala Lumpur in July 2009.

Pratt made 60 not out against Kuwait and an unbeaten 55 against Malaysia, heading the tournament batting aggregates with 230 runs at 57.50. Hong Kong defeated Thailand by four runs in the final.

Jesse Ryder took 72 balls to reach his maiden one-day international century, against India at Christchurch. This was the third fastest for New Zealand:

balls				
67	C.D. McMillan	v Australia	Hamilton	2006/07
71	J.D.P. Oram	v Australia	Perth	2006/07
72	J.D. Ryder	v India	Christchurch	2008/09
75	C.L. Cairns	v India	Christchurch	1998/99
75	C.D. McMillan	v Pakistan	Christchurch	2000/01
81	L. Vincent	v Zimbabwe	Bulawayo	2005/06
85	C.L. Cairns	v India	Pune	1995/96
86	J.M. How	v England	Napier	2007/08
87	A.C. Parore	v South Africa	Centurion	1994/95
90	S.P. Fleming	v Bangladesh	Antigua	2006/07
93	N.J. Astle	v Pakistan	Dunedin	2000/01
94	K.R. Rutherford	v India	Baroda	1994/95
94	S.B. Styris	v Australia	Christchurch	2005/06
96	K.J. Wadsworth	v Australia	Christchurch	1973/74
96	K.R. Rutherford	v Sri Lanka	East London	1994/95
97	C.Z. Harris	v Australia	Madras	1995/96
99	C.L. Cairns	v South Africa	Brisbane	2001/02

• • •

Martin Guptill became the fifth player to score a century in his first one-day international when he made 122 not out against West Indies at Auckland. This small list is:

D.L. Amiss (103)	England v Australia	Manchester	1972
D.L. Haynes (148)	West Indies v Australia	St John's	1977/78
A. Flower (115*)	Zimbabwe v Sri Lanka	New Plymouth	1991/92
Saleem Elahi (102*)	Pakistan v Sri Lanka	Gujranwala	1995/96
M.J. Guptill (122*)	New Zealand v West Indies	Auckland	2008/09

• • •

Guptill reached his century with a six, the fourth New Zealand batsman to achieve this feat in a one-day international. The others are Craig McMillan, against Pakistan at Christchurch in 2000/01 and Australia at Hamilton in 2006/07, Lou Vincent, against Zimbabwe at Bulawayo in 2005/06, and Brendon McCullum against Ireland at Aberdeen in 2008.

• • •

New Zealand umpire Brent "Billy" Bowden officiated in eight tests and eight one-day internationals during the past 12 months.

He stood in two of South Africa's matches in England, two matches during Australia's tour to India, one match of England's series in India, one match during South Africa's tour to Australia and two matches of the return series in South Africa. He also officiated in three one-day matches in the European Championship Division One and all five games between Australia and Pakistan in Abu Dhabi.

• • •

Tony Hill, who was promoted to the Elite Panel during the year, stood in four tests and four one-day internationals during the same period. All the tests were in West Indies, two involving England (including the match at Antigua which was called off after ten deliveries) and two with Bangladesh. His four one-day internationals were in New Zealand.

Gary Baxter, who is on the International Panel, stood in eight one-day internationals during the past year. This included five matches in New Zealand and three ICC World Cup qualifiers in South Africa.

Former New Zealand captain Jeff Crowe was the ICC Match Referee in nine tests and ten one-day internationals over the last 12 months. He was involved in series in England, India, Bangladesh, Kenya, United Arab Emirates and South Africa.

• • •

Evan Watkin added a test match to his umpiring record when he took over from Billy Doctrove during the second test between New Zealand and India at Napier. Doctrove was unable to officiate after the second day because of illness. As Watkin took a full part in the game he gets credited with his third test. Chris Gaffaney took over as third umpire.

• • •

New Zealand were left to score 617 runs to win the third test against India at Wellington, the highest total they had ever been set in a test. Details of the targets of 500 or more are:

target				*result*
617	by India	Wellington	2008/09	drawn
553	by England	Napier	2007/08	lost by 121 runs
550	by England	Christchurch	2001/02	lost by 98 runs
531	by South Africa	Johannesburg	2007/08	lost by 358 runs
511	by England	Nottingham	1983	lost by 165 runs
504	by Sri Lanka	Wellington	2006/07	lost by 217 runs

• • •

New Zealand made 317-7 to defeat Bangladesh at Chittagong, only the second time they had won a test chasing more than 300. New Zealand's highest fourth innings totals are:

451	v England	Christchurch	2001/02	lost by 98 runs
440	v England	Nottingham	1973	lost by 38 runs
431	v England	Napier	2007/08	lost by 121 runs
345	v England	Nottingham	1983	lost by 165 runs
324-5	v Pakistan	Christchurch	1993/94	won by 5 wickets
317-7	v Bangladesh	Chittagong	2008/09	won by 3 wickets
311	v England	Wellington	2007/08	lost by 126 runs
304-8	v Zimbabwe	Harare	1997/98	drawn

• • •

Prior to their win in Bangladesh, the highest score New Zealand had made to win a match on the subcontinent was just 82-5, against Pakistan at Lahore in 1969. New Zealand went on to win the series, their first success overseas.

Left-arm spinners accounted for 22 wickets in the match at Chittagong, which is the second-highest in all tests. Daniel Vettori and Shakib Al Hasan each took nine wickets while Abdur Razzaq accounted for four more. In the test between India and Pakistan at Bangalore in 1986/87, Maninder Singh, Ravi Shastri and Iqbal Qasim captured 24 wickets.

• • •

During the season Michael Parlane extended his record to 6653 runs and 15 centuries in first-class cricket. Excluding players who played county cricket, both are records for a player who never represented New Zealand.

The only players who have scored more runs than Parlane, without playing for New Zealand, are Ray Hitchcock (12,473), who played just two matches in New Zealand before embarking on a long county career, and Peter Arnold (8013), who played most of his cricket for Northamptonshire.

Next on the list of most runs without playing for New Zealand are Chris Gaffaney (4711) and Scott Briasco (4390) while Parlane's brother, Neal, also features, with 4040 runs.

New Zealand services teams took part in a number of games during the past twelve months. The combined New Zealand Defence Force team also played Marlborough and Nelson.

RNZAF Inter-base Tournament

Men's Final (Wilson Memorial Trophy)

Ohakea 176 (H. Madsen 81, C. Turkington 38, M. Chadwick 3-27, K. Bevins 3-28) **defeated Auckland** 56 (G. Schofield 5-18, C. Turkington 3-15) by 120 runs

Women's Final (McCombie Cup)

Auckland 222-5 (H. Ireland 71*, R. Blucher 71) **defeated Ohakea** 122-5 (A. Hockenhull 34, K. Small 32) by 100 runs

The men's player of the tournament was Flt Lt Graham Burnnand *(Ohakea)* and Sgt Darren Grant *(Woodbourne)* while the women's player of the tournament was Sqn Ldr Rachel James *(Auckland)*.

RNZAF Women's Cricket

RNZAF 152-5 (R. Blucher 55, A. Hockenhull 30) **defeated Marian College** 71(C. Sefo 4-16, A Forbes 3-18) by 81 runs

Ashburton College 14(A. Forbes 4-3) **lost to RNZAF** 15-0 by 10 wickets

Combined Canterbury Under 15/Under 17 64 (H. Ireland 3-13) **lost to RNZAF** 65-4 (A. Forbes 27*) by 6 wickets

Inter-services Cricket

New Zealand Army 274-7 (K. Hurrell 119, R. King 50) lost to **Royal New Zealand Navy** 277 for 7 (Randall Bartholomew 83*, Greg Staines 75, Shane Goodwin 27, Greg Gatley 27, Scott MacGibbon 4-43) by 3 wickets

Royal New Zealand Air Force 328-7 (K. Bevins 142*, K. Borck 45, G. Burnnand 30, M. Lambert 3-62) **defeated Royal New Zealand Navy** 222 (B. Owens 75, G. Gatley 62) by 106 runs

Royal New Zealand Air Force 253-9 (K. Bevins 96, R. King 3-29) **defeated to New Zealand Army** 90 (S. McQuillan 34, H. Madsen 4-16, G. Schofield 3-30) by 163 runs

Royal New Zealand Air Force won the Bill Morley Cup for the ninth year in succession. Player of the tournament was Cpl Kim Bevins *(RNZAF)*.

New Zealand Defence Force

Marlborough 318-5 (M. Hood 154, A. McCaa 56, C. Cornelius 43*) **defeated New Zealand Defence Force** 151 (M. Robinson 38, N. d'Auvergne 4-25) by 167 runs

Nelson 294-7 (S. Fenemor 108, A. Coles 65, C. McLean 40, T. Horne 3-40) **defeated New Zealand Defence Force** 259 (M. Robinson 70, K. Hurrell 61, R. King 50, N. Todd 4-56, B. Hodgson 3-43) by 35 runs

Amongst the regular bowlers in the State Shield in 2008/09, Mitchell McClenaghan and Leighton Burtt were the most expensive, conceding 6.01 and 6.00 runs per over. The most expensive bowlers in domestic one-day cricket (minimum 100 overs) have been:

	Overs	*Mdns*	*Runs*	*Wkts*	*Ave*	*RPO*
H.K. Bennett *(C)*	133.5	3	776	23	33.73	5.79
J.D. Ryder *(CD, W)*	140	3	783	26	30.11	5.59
C.R. Pryor *(A, O)*	157.4	3	863	23	37.52	5.47
L.M. Burtt *(C)*	154.2	11	842	34	24.76	5.45
B.C. Hiini *(C)*	179	8	955	21	45.47	5.33

• • •

Aaron Redmond scored 100 not out from 56 balls for Otago in their Twenty20 match against Central Districts at University Oval. It was the fourth century in the four-year history of the competition but the first time that someone reaching three figures had been in the winning team. Ross Taylor (111), Chris Gaffaney (101) and Chris Harris (100) had previously all ended up on the losing side.

Redmond reached his century off the last ball of the 19th over, taking Otago to 183-5 in reply to Central's 185-6. At that stage umpires Evan Watkin and (in a twist of fate) Chris Gaffaney decided that time had expired and invoked a six run penalty against the bowling side. This took Otago's score past Central's, the match thus concluding at that stage.

• • •

The records for most first-class hundreds for each province were substantially rewritten during the season. Matthew Bell scored his 18th hundred for Wellington, taking him past Bert Sutcliffe's record of most centuries for any single province.

In addition, Tim McIntosh equalled then surpassed Trevor Franklin's record for Auckland, Michael Papps went past Chris Harris on the Canterbury table and Mathew Sinclair overtook Mark Greatbatch's Central Districts record. Craig Cumming equalled Glenn Turner's Otago tally of 13, one behind Ken Rutherford and four behind Sutcliffe. James Marshall (8) is the nearest challenger to Graeme Hick's Northern Districts record of ten (made in two seasons).

The leaders in this category are now: 20 – Matthew Bell *(Wellington)*, 18 – Mathew Sinclair *(Central Districts)*, 17 – Bert Sutcliffe *(Otago)*, 15 – Bruce Edgar *(Wellington)*, Michael Papps *(Canterbury)*, 14 – Ken Rutherford *(Otago)*, Mark Greatbatch *(Central Districts)*, 13 – John Reid *(Wellington)*, Glenn Turner *(Otago)*, Martin Crowe *(Central Districts)*, Craig Cumming *(Otago)*, Tim McIntosh *(Auckland)*.

• • •

James Franklin scored his second double century for Wellington during the season, only the fourth batsman to achieve this feat. Matthew Bell has three double centuries for Wellington while the incomparable Bert Sutcliffe scored three double and two triple centuries for Otago.

Other players with two double hundreds for one province are: Roger Blunt *(Otago)*, Peter Fulton *(Canterbury)*, Mark Greatbatch *(Central Districts)*, Chris Harris *(Canterbury)*, Syd Hiddleston *(Wellington)*, Tim McIntosh *(Auckland)*, John Reid *(Wellington)* and Mathew Sinclair *(Central Districts)*. Blunt and Fulton each had one triple and one double century.

• • •

New Zealand's score of 279 against India at Hamilton was the lowest test innings to include two individual hundreds. Jesse Ryder scored 102 and Daniel Vettori made 118. The previous record for a completed innings was 284, by Australia against West Indies in Brisbane in 1968/69, when Bill Lawry made 105 and Ian Chappell 117.

Vettori became the first player to register a score of 118 for New Zealand in test cricket. This had been the lowest score not recorded in a test for New Zealand. The lowest individual score yet to be made for New Zealand is now 131.

In the second test against Australia at Adelaide, Chris Martin recorded a record sixth pair in test cricket. Mervyn Dillon, B.S. Chandresekhar, Marvan Atapattu, Muttiah Muralitharan and Courtney Walsh have registered four apiece.

Martin extended his sequence of scoreless innings in first-class cricket (including not outs) to seven in the match against New South Wales but a pair of singles in the first test meant that Peter Visser's record of ten in a row, for Central Districts in the mid-1980s, remained intact.

However, normal service was restored and Martin reeled off another run of six before the sequence was broken in the most astonishing and unexpected fashion when he hit Harbhajan Singh back over his head for four in the third test against India at Wellington in April.

These were the first runs Martin had scored in any cricket since the first test in Australia in November. He had played 22 matches for Auckland, New Zealand and New Zealand A without getting off the mark.

Martin took 20 wickets in five tests during the summer to reach 160 test wickets, fourth-equal, with Danny Morrison, on New Zealand's all-time list.

• • •

The nineteenth Gillette Cup limited-overs competition for secondary school boys was played in Palmerston North from 11-14 December 2008. A total of 185 teams entered the competition which is organised by each major association, with one winner from each progressing to the final. The runners-up from Central Districts and Northern Districts, the two associations with the most entries, also contested the finals. Hamilton Boys' High School won the tournament, defeating Westlake Boys' High School in the final.

Adam Milne *(Palmerston North Boys' High School)* was named player of the tournament.

GROUP A

Round 1
Wanganui Collegiate 124 lost to **Westlake Boys' High School** 128-1 by 9 wickets
Tauranga Boys' College 191-7 defeated **St Bede's College** 184 by 7 runs

Round 2
Wanganui Collegiate 296-5 defeated **Tauranga Boys' College** 228 by 68 runs
St Bede's College 78 lost to **Westlake Boys' High School** 79-2 by 8 wickets.

Round 3
Wanganui Collegiate 163 defeated **St Bede's College** 157 by 6 runs
Tauranga Boys' College 228-8 defeated **Westlake Boys' High School** 150 by 78 runs

GROUP B

Round 1
Hamilton Boys' High School 61 lost to **Wellington College** 62-1 by 9 wickets
Palmerston North Boys' High School 223 defeated **Otago Boys' High School** 169 by 54 runs

Round 2
Wellington College 186 defeated **Otago Boys' High School** 115 by 71 runs
Palmerston North Boys' High School 134 lost to **Hamilton Boys' High School** 138-6 by 4 wickets

Round 3
Wellington College 143-7 lost to **Palmerston North Boys' High School** 145-4 by 6 wickets
Hamilton Boys' High School 301-5 defeated **Otago Boys' High School** 111 by 190 runs

Finals
Westlake Boys' High School 157-9 lost to **Hamilton Boys' High School** 158-8 by 2 wickets
Wellington College 124 lost to **Tauranga Boys' College** 126-6 by 4 wickets
Palmerston North Boys' High School 214-8 defeated **Wanganui Collegiate** 149 by 65 runs
Otago Boys' High School 188 lost to **St Bede's College** 189-3 by 7 wickets.

Final placings: Hamilton Boys' High School 1st, Westlake Boys' High School 2nd, Tauranga Boys' College 3rd, Wellington College 4th, Palmerston North Boys' High School 5th, Wanganui Collegiate 6th, St Bede's College 7th, Otago Boys' High School 8th.

• • •

The fifteenth national secondary schools girls competition, sponsored by New Zealand Community Trust, was played in Taupo from 15-18 December 2008.

A total of 121 schools entered the competition with eight teams represented at the finals. These were the winners from each major association plus the runners-up of the two associations with the most entries. New Plymouth Girls' High School won the tournament, defeating Epsom Girls' Grammar School in the final. Player of the Tournament was again Kate Broadmore *(New Plymouth Girls' High School)*.

Results were:

GROUP A

Round 1
Burnside High School 103-9 lost to **Epsom Girls' Grammar School** 104-8 by 2 wickets
Wellington Girls' College 109-8 lost to **Havelock North High School** 111-3 by 7 wickets

Round 2
Havelock North High School 54 lost to **Burnside High School** 58-1 by 9 wickets
Epsom Girls' Grammar School 182-7 defeated **Wellington Girls' College** 68 by 114 runs

Round 3
Burnside High School 210-9 defeated **Wellington Girls' College** 97 by 113 runs
Havelock North High School 99 lost to **Epsom Girls' Grammar School** 101-7 by 3 wickets

GROUP B

Round 1
Baradene College 53 lost to **New Plymouth Girls' High School** 54-0 by 10 wickets
Waikato Diocesan School 259-7 defeated **St Hilda's Collegiate** 113 by 146 runs

Round 2
Waikato Diocesan School 121-7 lost to **Baradene College** 122-9 by 1 wicket
New Plymouth Girls' High School 293-2 defeated **St Hilda's Collegiate** 54 by 239 runs

Round 3
St Hilda's Collegiate 114 lost to **Baradene College** 118-2 by 8 wickets
New Plymouth Girls' High School 113 defeated **Waikato Diocesan School** 18 by 95 runs

Finals
New Plymouth Girls' High School 175-4 defeated **Epsom Girls' Grammar School** 71 by 104 runs
Baradene College 67 lost to **Burnside High School** 70-3 by 7 wickets
Waikato Diocesan School 79 lost to **Havelock North High School** 80-3 by 7 wickets
St Hilda's Collegiate 133 lost to **Wellington Girls' College** 134-6 by 4 wickets

Final placings: New Plymouth Girls' High School 1st, Epsom Girls' Grammar School 2nd, Burnside High School 3rd, Baradene College 4th, Havelock North High School 5th, Waikato Diocesan School 6th, Wellington Girls' College 7th, St Hilda's Collegiate 8th.

• • •

Central Districts began the State Championship with successive outright victories against Auckland, Northern Districts and Otago. The three wins in a row equalled their best ever sequences previously recorded in 1953/54, 1966/67, 1980/81 and 2001/02.

Canterbury's Johann Myburgh was run out for 199 against Central Districts at New Plymouth. He had been on 159 when last man Hamish Bennett joined him and the pair had added 48 in 39 minutes before Myburgh was run out going for a second run which would have given him his double century.

This was the first time an individual score of 199 had been recorded in New Zealand first-class cricket. Walter Hadlee, Chris Harris and Verdun Scott were all dismissed for 198 while Sam Guillen, Bert Sutcliffe, Merv Wallace and Chris Gayle (this past season) all made 197. Grant Elliott was left on 196 not out playing for Wellington against Auckland in 2007/08.

Myburgh does have one double century to his name. He made 203 for Northerns B against Easterns in 1997/98, aged 17, breaking Graeme Pollock's record as the youngest scorer of a double century in South African first-class cricket.

• • •

Former New Zealand left-arm spinner Stephen Boock contacted us to correct a long-standing error in the record books. He wrote: "In the 1987 World Cup in India, 20th match, New Zealand against Australia in Chandigarh, my potentially match-winning innings was cut down in its adolescence when I was run out for 12 by a brilliant throw by Craig McDermott from the cover-point boundary.

"During this innings, I hit the only six of my international career – a low screamer off the back foot, still rising as it passed over the wide mid on boundary, off the bowling of Steve Waugh. To my eternal chagrin, this mighty blow has been afforded to Willie Watson. Anyone in the know should have noticed this mistake, but it has remained – strangely untouched – for some years." We have amended our records.

• • •

Brendon Diamanti produced a memorable all-round performance in Central Districts' State Championship game against Canterbury at Rangiora. Central had followed on 280 runs behind and early on the last day lost their sixth wicket at 263.

Diamanti joined Greg Hay, who were both on a king pair, having been dismissed first ball in the first innings. They proceeded to add an unbeaten 205 for the seventh wicket. Hay ended on 131 (the 200th first-class century for Central) and Diamanti finished on 135. Diamanti had taken 5-74 in Canterbury's first innings and thus became just the fourth Central player to score a century and take five wickets in an innings of the same match.

Vic Pollard and Bryan Yuile did so in 1967/68 while Martin Crowe achieved the feat twice in the 1980s. Only two other New Zealand players have performed the twin feat this century – Grant Bradburn in 2000/01 and Tama Canning in 2004/05.

Diamanti made his New Zealand debut during the season, the fifth player to gain national honours while playing in Blenheim. He followed in the footsteps of Fen Cresswell, Gary Bartlett, Lance Cairns and Carl Bulfin and is now a double international, having represented New Zealand at indoor cricket in the early 1990s.

• • •

Karori 1A cricketer William Bell is normally an opening batsman but he was late getting to his game against North City Trojans in Tawa because he had been at work. When he walked to the wicket in the 50-over match, the score was 27-9.

In no way deterred by the situation, Bell thrashed his first ball for six, over the clubrooms, took 26 off the first over he faced and went on to blast 100 not out, sharing a last wicket stand of 148 with number three batsman Baz Taniwha, who was run out in the 50th over for 49, after earlier looking like being the team's top scorer with three. North City then fell 51 runs short of Karori's 175.

To add to the bizarre events of the day, the final wicket only fell because Taniwha, who still had two balls left to score his fifty, ran himself out congratulating Bell on his century.

Daniel Vettori almost single-handedly took New Zealand to victory against Bangladesh in the first test at Chittagong. In the process he became the first player to score a half-century and take four wickets in both innings of a test. He was only the third player to score a fifty in each innings and take eight or more wickets in a match, as this short list reveals:

G.A. Faulkner	78 & 123	5-120 & 3-40	SA v E	Johannesburg	1909/10
Mushtaq Mohammad	121 & 56	5-28 & 3-69	P v WI	Port of Spain	1976/77
D.L. Vettori	55* & 76	5-59 & 4-74	NZ v B	Chittagong	2008/09

• • •

Vettori also came close to being the first player in test history to be top wicket taker in both innings and highest scorer in both innings. Aaron Redmond (79) outscored Vettori by three runs in the second innings at Chittagong to deny him a unique feat.

Being the best performer in three out of the four innings in a test match had been achieved 68 times, three of the last four by Vettori who also did it against Australia in Adelaide in 2004/05 and against Sri Lanka in Wellington in 2006/07.

• • •

New Zealand Under 19 representative Fraser Colson had an interesting Labour weekend. When his senior club match for Hutt District was rained off he changed codes and boarded the 2 pm flight to Napier to help out Western Suburbs at the national Under 19 football tournament.

Colson arrived in Napier at 3 pm, changed into his gear during the five-minute drive to the ground and was outstanding in his first game of football for seven weeks. He played two games for Wests the next day and, when they were knocked out of the tournament, he flew home in the evening to prepare for Hutt's next match against Upper Hutt at Trentham Memorial Park on Monday.

Colson was in the middle after five overs and batted for the rest of the innings, hitting 145 not out from 140 balls, with 12 fours and five sixes. He said "I was pretty tired on Monday morning but I think it helped being that tired because I knew I had to really concentrate hard when I batted. Tuesday I was dead, I didn't want to get out of bed. But looking back now it was really worthwhile because it really helps to kick off the season with a big one early. It really clicked on Monday, I felt as though I knew my game pretty well."

• • •

One of the scorers in the three-day game between Auckland and Central Districts at the National Under 19 Tournament at Lincoln was 19-year-old Fumi Kato from Japan. She came to New Zealand in April 2003 and enrolled at Craighead Diocesan School in Timaru. While at high school her friends introduced her to cricket and she eventually took up the game and played in the school team for two years and also became the team scorer.

When she graduated from high school she moved to Christchurch to attend University. She continued to further her interest in scoring and became scorer for the Old Boys-Old Collegians premier team which contains names such as Shane Bond, Todd Astle and Hamish Bennett.

• • •

Fourteen-year-old schoolboy G.J. Pike is thought to have become the youngest player to score a century in Taranaki premier grade cricket. The Francis Douglas Memorial College fourth former scored 113, including 14 fours, against Stratford in the final round of two-day matches.

His century followed a tough start to his premier grade career when he admitted to not getting into double figures for the first few matches. Cricket historian Brian Bellringer, of New Plymouth, was at a loss to come up with anyone the same age as Pike scoring a century in Taranaki premier cricket. Bellringer could only single out former New Zealand representatives Martin Donnelly and Lawrie Miller as possibilities.

Ross Taylor had a good chance to break John Reid's long-standing New Zealand record for most runs in a calendar year when he went in to the tests against West Indies requiring 119 runs to set a new mark. He scored just 65 in his three innings, however, and Reid's record remained intact. The most runs by a New Zealand batsman in a calendar year is:

	year	*tests*	*runs*	*ave*
J.R. Reid	1965	13	871	36.29
M.D. Crowe	1985	10	820	51.25
L.R.P.L. Taylor	2008	12	818	38.95
B. Sutcliffe	1955	9	769	51.26
N.J. Astle	1999	12	769	45.23
B.B. McCullum	2008	14	764	33.21
M.D. Crowe	1987	13	751	62.58
S.P. Fleming	2004	10	737	46.06
J.G. Wright	1990	7	705	78.33

• • •

Daniel Vettori captured 54 test wickets in 2008, second only to Richard Hadlee's New Zealand record of 64 in 1985. The top performers in this category are:

	year	*tests*	*wkts*	*ave*
R.J. Hadlee	1985	10	64	17.43
D.L. Vettori	2008	14	54	26.12
C.L. Cairns	1999	10	47	20.12
R.J. Hadlee	1987	7	39	20.74
D.L. Vettori	2004	9	38	32.21
R.J. Hadlee	1980	6	38	19.07
I.E. O'Brien	2008	10	38	21.57
D.L. Vettori	1999	13	37	39.83
D.J. Nash	1999	13	37	28.48
H.J. Howarth	1969	9	36	23.72
D.K. Morrison	1990	10	36	34.02

• • •

During the New Zealand A tour to India there was an error by the scorers in the first of the two first-class games against India A at Chennai. Two wickets were credited to BJ Watling (who had never bowled in a first-class match at that stage) instead of to his fellow opening batsman Aaron Redmond.

The New Zealand management alerted the scorers and the Cricinfo statistician at the time but the error was not acted upon. The two wickets correctly credited to Redmond mean he now has exactly 100 wickets in first-class cricket. Watling subsequently did get to bowl in a first-class game, sending down five balls for Northern Districts against Central Districts.

• • •

New Zealand defeated Australia in the Chappell-Hadlee series match in Perth when Daniel Vettori hit the final ball of the fiftieth over for four. Here is a list of one-day internationals involving New Zealand which were won by the team batting second off the last possible ball of the match:

NZ (213-8)	P (214-9)	Multan	1984/85
Z (258-7)	NZ (260-5)	Dhaka	1998/99
NZ (191)	SA (194-8)	Napier	1998/99
NZ (256-9)	SA (258-7)	Cape Town	2000/01
NZ (291-8)	WI (292-6)	Arnos Vale	2001/02
NZ (248-6)	SA (249-8)	Durban	2007/08
E (245)	NZ (246-9)	The Oval	2008
A (181)	NZ (182-8)	Perth	2008/09

Jesse Ryder and Brendon McCullum responded to India's massive total of 392-4, in the one-day international at Christchurch, with an opening partnership of 166. New Zealand totalled 334 but still went down by 58 runs. This meant that the partnership between Ryder and McCullum became the highest for a side batting second and losing. Here are the highest:

166	J.D. Ryder/B.B. McCullum	NZ (334) v I (392-4)	Christchurch	2008/09
165	M.E. Trescothick/N.V. Knight	E (264-7) v A (271-4)	Hobart	2002/03
160	G.C. Smith/A.B. de Villiers	SA (294) v A (377-6)	Basseterre	2006/07
150	G. Kirsten/A.J. Hall	SA (212) v SL (249-7)	Galle	2000/01

• • •

Umpire Dave Paterson was involved in an unusual happening in the State Championship game between Northern Districts and Auckland at the new Cobham Oval (which became New Zealand's 62nd first-class venue). In Northern Districts' first innings he gave twin brothers Hamish and James Marshall out lbw to consecutive balls from Daryl Tuffey.

• • •

Jeet Raval, who scored 256 for Auckland against Central Districts, began his representative career batting at number eleven. It was just Raval's second innings in first-class cricket and the third highest maiden century in New Zealand first-class cricket after Peter Fulton (301*) and Bill Carson (290).

Raval was an age group representative in Gujarat, India, before he came to New Zealand with his family in 2004. He first represented Ahmedabad District in Under 15 and Under 17 tournaments and was then selected for Gujarat Under 15 and Under 17 teams in successive seasons. At that stage he bowled right-arm medium-fast and batted at number eleven. He recalled that "One day I batted at number nine and made 21, batting all day. Next time I opened and got 100 for the state Under 15 team and I've opened ever since."

When the family moved to New Zealand, Raval made plenty of runs for Avondale College and compiled 203 for his club, Suburbs New Lynn.

Raval suffered agonising cramp before he reached his first century against Central and later strained his left groin, finishing his long innings with a runner.

• • •

Auckland leg-spinner Tarun Nethula had the distinction of being the leading wicket taker in the State Championship in his first season of first-class cricket.

Nethula was born in Kurnool, Andhra Pradesh and moved to New Zealand with his family in 1995. He had played for HYD Under 13 in the Andhra Pradesh State Tournament. He returned to India in 1997 and did his school certificate there and came back to Auckland in 1998. While in India he was amongst the probables for the state Under 16 side.

• • •

Two former umpires passed away during the last twelve months. Rex Bowden, born in Timaru on 21 October 1930, died in Christchurch on 1 February 2009. He played for South Canterbury and umpired one Hawke Cup elimination game. Bowden was also a keen cricket historian who wrote a book on South Canterbury cricket called "Green Fields of Yesteryears". He had been a Life Member of the South Canterbury Cricket Association since 1976.

Stanley Arthur Copelin, born in Mudgee, New South Wales on 23 October 1926, passed away in New Plymouth on 15 June 2009. He umpired eight first-class games between 1968/69 and 1977/78. He also umpired twelve Hawke Cup elimination games and twelve Hawke Cup challenges and stood in three women's one-day internationals during the 1982 World Cup, including one with Dickie Bird.

Ryan McCone made his first-class debut for Canterbury against Otago at Christchurch in March and found himself at the wicket shortly after lunch on the first day with the score at 101-7. He opened his account with two fours and went on to add 167 with Kruger van Wyk, a Canterbury eighth wicket record against Otago.

The ninth wicket fell one run later with McCone on 61. Hamish Bennett, however, proved a reliable last wicket partner and stayed for 35 minutes while McCone reached a century on debut with successive fours off James McMillan. McCone was just the sixth player in the entire history of first-class cricket to score a century on debut while batting at number nine. There are also four instances of players doing so at number ten. The complete list is:

J.P. O'Halloran (128*)	Victoria v South Australia	Melbourne	1896/97
F.W. Hyett (108*)	Victoria v Tasmania	Melbourne	1914/15
E.E.B. Forssberg (143)	NSW v Queensland	Sydney	1920/21
Ashraf (107)	The Rest v Hindus	Amritsar	1940/41
C. Sampath (123)	Trinidad v Barbados	Bridgetown	1948/49
J. Mitter (136)	Bengal v Bihar	Jamshedpur	1950/51
J.C. Breakey (123)	Transvaal B v NE Transvaal	Johannesburg	1970/71
K.T. Medlycott (117*)	Surrey v Cambridge U.	Banstead	1984
K. Seth (125*)	Madhya Pradesh v Vidarbha	Indore	2000/01
R.J. McCone (102)	Canterbury v Otago	Christchurch	2008/09

Hyett, Forssberg, Mitter and Seth batted at number ten

When asked about his batting, McCone said: "I have had a hundred before but that was a few years ago now at schoolboy level. So it has definitely been a while between drinks!"

• • •

There have been 17 instances of a player scoring a century in a first-class match in New Zealand when batting at number nine. Victor Trumper's record of 293 for Arthur Sims' Australians against Canterbury in 1913/14 is unlikely to be beaten. The highest by a New Zealand batsman from this position is Ian Smith's 173, for New Zealand against India at Auckland in 1989/90.

Ian Leggat (142* for Central Districts v Otago, 1952/53), Anton Murray (100* for South Africa v Canterbury, 1952/53) and Bruce Martin (113* for New Zealand A v Sri Lanka A, 2003/04) all made centuries batting at number ten.

• • •

New Zealand declared their first innings at 262-6 in the second test against Bangladesh at Mirpur. Here is a list of test matches in which the sides batting first declared their innings closed for less than 300 runs. All the matches had been influenced by the weather.

130-9d	Pakistan v England	Lord's	1974
164-7d	England v West Indies	Manchester	1939
200-9d	Australia v England	Melbourne	1936/37
207-3d	Australia v India	Delhi	1986/87
216-8d	England v Australia	Nottingham	1964
217-8d	England v Australia	Nottingham	1956
241-2d	England v Pakistan	Lord's	1971
248-8d	South Africa v England	Pretoria	1999/00
262-6d	New Zealand v Bangladesh	Mirpur	2008/09
266-7d	New Zealand v Australia	Wellington	1981/82
296-8d	India v New Zealand	Cuttack	1995/96
297-8d	West Indies v England	Georgetown	1947/48

All matches were drawn apart from Australia, who won in 1936/37, England, who won in 1999/00, and West Indies, who won in 1947/48.

One curious aspect of New Zealand's innings of 262-6 was that six different Bangladesh bowlers claimed one wicket each. It was only the second time where a side had lost six wickets in a test innings that each wicket was obtained by a different bowler. New Zealand were also involved on the other occasion. The details are (with bowlers listed in the order that they bowled):

India (255-6) v New Zealand at Christchurch, 1975/76. (R.O. Collinge, R.J. Hadlee, D.R. Hadlee, H.J. Howarth, J.M. Parker and A.D.G. Roberts).

New Zealand (262-6d) v Bangladesh at Mirpur, 2008/09. (Masrafe bin Mortaza, Mahbubul Alam, Adbur Razzaq, Shahadat Hossain, Shakib Al Hasan and Mohammad Ashraful).

• • •

An Auckland Emerging Players team visited Queensland in October. The squad was Jeet Raval, Andrew de Boorder, Brad Chemaly, Colin de Grandhomme, Craig Cachopa, Kirk Bunting, Jimmy Neesham, Tarun Nethula, Josh Tasman-Jones, Andy McKay, Colin Munro, Lochie Ferguson, Jonathon Basset-Graham. Paul Strang and Tony Sail were the coaches and national junior selector Kaushik Patel was manager. Details were:

Auckland Emerging Players 118-5 **defeated Brisbane Boys' College** 56 by 62 runs

Team Australia 157-5 **lost to Team New Zealand** 158-6 by 4 wickets *(the two sides from the first match were mixed for the second game)*

Sunshine Coast 229 (Bunting 61, McKay 5-39) **lost to Auckland Emerging Players** 230-8 (de Boorder 68) by 2 wickets

Toombul 225-9 (de Grandhomme 4-38) **lost to Auckland Emerging Players** 226-3 (de Grandhomme 65*, de Boorder 50) by 7 wickets

Auckland Emerging Players 237-7 (Bunting 68) **defeated Sunshine State** 84 (Neesham 4-19) by 153 runs

Auckland Emerging Players 315-6 (Neesham 65) **defeated Queensland Wanderers** 111 by 204 runs

• • •

New Zealand captain Daniel Vettori dismissed his opposite number Mohammad Ashraful in both innings of the first test at Chittagong. Here is a list of test matches in which the captain from one side dismissed the opposing captain in both innings. The bowling captains and their sides are listed first:

Australia v England	Lord's	1909	M.A. Noble/A.C. MacLaren
England v South Africa	Lord's	1924	A.E.R. Gilligan/H.W. Taylor
England v New Zealand	Lord's	1937	R.W.V. Robins/M.L. Page
Australia v India	Madras	1959/60	R. Benaud/G.S. Ramchand
Australia v West Indies	Sydney	1960/61	R. Benaud/F.M.M. Worrell
Australia v South Africa	Johannesburg	1966/67	R.B. Simpson/P.L. van der Merwe
West Indies v Australia	Adelaide	1968/69	G.S. Sobers/W.M. Lawry
Pakistan v New Zealand	Dacca	1969/70	Intikhab Alam/G.T. Dowling
West Indies v India	Bridgetown	1970/71	G.S. Sobers/A.L. Wadekar
India v New Zealand	Kanpur	1976/77	B.S. Bedi/G.M. Turner
South Africa v India	Johannesburg	1996/97	W.J. Cronje/S.R. Tendulkar
England v Sri Lanka	Lord's	2006	A. Flintoff/D.P.M.D. Jayawardene
New Zealand v Bangladesh	Chittagong	2008-09	D.L. Vettori/Mohammad Ashraful

Mohammad Ashraful turned the tables in the second test and dismissed Vettori, who in turn took Ashraful's wicket once again. The list of captains who dismissed each other in the same test reads:

home captain	***visiting captain***		
J.R. Reid *(New Zealand)*	D.S. Atkinson *(West Indies)*	Auckland	1955/56
R. Benaud *(Australia)*	E.R. Dexter *(England)*	Adelaide	1962/63
R. Benaud *(Australia)*	T.L. Goddard *(South Africa)*	Brisbane	1963/64
J.R. Reid *(New Zealand)*	T.L. Goddard *(South Africa)*	Wellington	1963/64
A.W. Greig *(England)*	I.M. Chappell *(Australia)*	Lord's	1975
M.A. Atherton *(England)*	Wasim Akram *(Pakistan)*	Leeds	1996
Wasim Akram *(Pakistan)*	C.A. Walsh *(West Indies)*	Karachi	1997/98
S.M. Pollock *(South Africa)*	Waqar Younis *(Pakistan)*	Durban	2002/03
Mohammad Ashraful *(Bangladesh)*	D.L. Vettori *(New Zealand)*	Mirpur	2008/09

• • •

Daniel Vettori became the first batsman to twice score a century batting at number eight on the first day of a test match when he made 118 against India in the first test at Hamilton. New Zealand's Ian Smith is the only number nine to score a hundred on the first day and was 169 not out at the close against India at Auckland in 1989/90. Here are the players who have scored a first-day hundred from number eight:

104	T.G. Evans	England v West Indies	Manchester	1950
124	B.R. Taylor	New Zealand v West Indies	Auckland	1968/69
100	M.V. Boucher	South Africa v West Indies	Centurion	1998/99
111	S.M. Pollock	South Africa v Sri Lanka	Centurion	2000/01
127	D.L. Vettori	New Zealand v Zimbabwe	Harare	2005/06
113	Kamran Akmal	Pakistan v India	Karachi	2005/06
118	D.L. Vettori	New Zealand v India	Hamilton	2008/09

The 186 run partnership between Jesse Ryder and Vettori was also a record for the seventh wicket on the first day of a test.

• • •

New Zealand were bowled out for the same total in each innings of this test, only the eighth time this had happened in test cricket. New Zealand account for half the occurrences.The full list is:

New Zealand (172 & 172) v South Africa	Wellington	1952/53
New Zealand (208 & 208) v West Indies	Wellington	1955/56
India (136 & 136) v Australia	Calcutta	1956/57
India (201 & 201) v Australia	Sydney	1980/81
New Zealand, 161 & 161v Australia	Hobart	1993/94
Sri Lanka (306 & 306) v South Africa	Cape Town	1997/98
Bangladesh (148 & 148) v Pakistan	Chittagong	2001/02
New Zealand (279 & 279) v India	Hamilton	2008/09

• • •

When Gareth Hopkins stumped Joseph Yovich from the bowling of Tarun Nethula in the State Championship game between Auckland and Northern Districts at Eden Park's Outer Oval, it was his 300th wicketkeeping dismissal in first-class cricket.

He became just the seventh New Zealand player to reach the landmark after Ian Smith (426 dismissals), Ken James (422), Erv McSweeney (385), Adam Parore (382), Warren Lees (336) and Robbie Hart (315). *(Full details in New Zealand First-class Records).*

Bevan Griggs also reached a wicketkeeping milestone during the season when he caught Richard Jones off Ewen Thompson's bowling in the State Championship final at Lincoln. It was his 200th wicketkeeping dismissal for Central Districts. He became the seventh player to make 200 dismissals for one province.

The other players who have achieved this are Erv McSweeney (328 for Wellington), Chris Nevin (269 for Wellington), Warren Lees (244 for Otago), Robbie Hart (243 for Northern Districs), Lee Germon (238 for Canterbury) and Reece Young (233 for Auckland). *(Full details in New Zealand First-class Records).*

• • •

Christchurch-born Ben Stokes had a memorable beginning to his county cricket debut. The England Under 19 all-rounder bowled former England batsman Mark Ramprakash in his first over for Durham against Surrey at The Oval in May 2009, in a Friends Provident Trophy 50-over match. Stokes, 17, was two days old when Ramprakash made his test debut in 1991.

Stokes is the son of former Kiwi prop Gerard Stokes. Stokes was 12 when his father, a former Kiwis' assistant-coach, took on the coaching job at Workington. Ben Stokes juggled both codes in Cumbria, representing his county and the North of England at rugby league. Stokes has represented England at cricket at various age-group levels and played for the England Under 19 team against Bangladesh in 2009.

• • •

During Australia's first innings of the first test against New Zealand at Brisbane, Andrew Symonds achieved the unusual feat of scoring eight runs off a single delivery. Symonds, who had almost been caught off the previous ball, hit Iain O'Brien to deep midwicket and he and Michael Clarke ran three. The throw came back to wicketkeeper Brendon McCullum who then aimed at the stumps but missed and the ball went for four overthrows.

By that stage Symonds and Michael Clarke had run another, pushing the final tally to eight. To make sure there was no further confusion umpire Rudi Koertzen held up eight fingers to the scorers to indicate how many runs they should record. Two balls later O'Brien had his revenge when he had Symonds caught behind.

• • •

Former Auckland and Canterbury player Hamish Barton was Argentina's player-coach in the ICC World Cricket League Americas Region Divison One tournament in Florida in November 2008.

Argentina came close to a famous win against Canada at Piccolo Park. Argentina posted a respectable 191-7 in their 50 overs, thanks mainly to Barton, who batted through the innings and was on 99 not out when the overs ran out. In reply, Canada slumped to 184-9 and it took their last pair to see them to victory. Barton also made 74 against USA and 68 against Suriname.

Barton also played for Argentina in the ICC World Cricket League Divison Three tournament in Buenos Aires in January 2009, scoring 33 and taking 3-12 against Afghanistan. He joined New Zealand Cricket, in May 2009, as a member of their development team.

• • •

Jesse Ryder scored 89, 57, 59 not out in his three innings against West Indies and followed this with 102 in the first innings of the first test against India. He thus became just the sixth New Zealand batsman to reach fifty in four successive test innings after Martin Donnelly, Bert Sutcliffe, Bevan Congdon (twice), Jeremy Coney and Ken Rutherford.

The record for all countries is seven, shared by Everton Weekes, Andy Flower and Shivnarine Chanderpaul. Weekes' sequence included a record five consecutive hundreds.

Ryder scored 201 in his next test and became the first New Zealand batsman to register hundreds in successive test matches since Nathan Astle in West Indies in 1995/96.

NZC

NEW ZEALAND IN BANGLADESH – 2008/09

Back row: A. Cooke *(security)*, M.D. O'Neill *(batting coach)*, T. Wilson *(fielding coach)*, R. Marsden *(physiotherapist)*, G.J. Hopkins, T.G. Southee, G.D. Elliott, J.D. Ryder, J.G. Bracewell *(coach)*, V.F. Johnson *(bowling coach)*, B. Stronach *(trainer)*, L.M. Crocker *(manager)*.
Front row: J.S. Patel, A.J. Redmond, J.M. How, B.B. McCullum, D.L. Vettori *(captain)*, K.D. Mills, L.R.P.L. Taylor, I.E. O'Brien, D.R. Flynn.

Photosport

NEW ZEALAND v INDIA — 2nd Twenty20 International

Back row: B. Stronach *(trainer)*, Z. Hitchcock *(video analyst)*, D. Currie *(manager)*, L.R.P.L. Taylor, I.E. O'Brien, E.P. Thompson, I.G. Butler, M.J. Guptill, J.D.P. Oram, G.D. Elliott, N.T. Broom, S.J. Jurgensen *(bowling coach)*, K. Stalker *(physiotherapist)*, A.J. Moles *(coach)*.
Front row: N.L. McCullum, B.B. McCullum, D.L. Vettori *(captain)*, T.G. Southee, J.D. Ryder, T. Wilson *(fielding coach)*.

Photosport

NEW ZEALAND WOMEN — Rose Bowl Series

Back row: D. Parkes *(trainer)*, R. Guy *(physiotherapist)*, G.R. Stead *(coach)*, R.H. Priest, S.J. McGlashan, S.W. Bates, A.E. Satterthwaite, N.J. Browne, S.F.M. Devine, K.L. Pulford, B.R. Blair *(assistant coach)*, C.E. Taylor *(video analyst)*, C.A. Campbell *(manager)*.
Front row: K.J. Martin, B.H. McNeill, A.K. Burrows, H.M. Tiffen *(captain)*, A.L. Mason, S.K.Tsukigawa, L.R. Doolan.

Standish & Preece

NEW ZEALAND A — 2008/09

Back row: M. Hesson *(coach)*, B. Kennedy *(video analyst)*, R. Marsden *(physiotherapist)*, V.F. Johnson *(assistant coach)*, G. Morris *(manager)*, M. Smith *(trainer)*.
Second row: B.P. Martin, E.P. Thompson, B.J. Arnel, K.S. Williamson, R.A. Young.
Front row: D.R. Flynn, P.G. Fulton, J.E.C. Franklin, J.M. How *(captain)*, C.S. Martin, A.J. Redmond.

Standish & Preece

NEW ZEALAND EMERGING PLAYERS — 2008/09

Back row: B.S. Wilson, T.T. Davis, L.J. Shaw, J.A. Raval, M.J. McClenaghan.
Second row: S.A. Deitz *(assistant coach)*, M.D. O'Neill *(coach)*, A.P. de Boorder, N.B. Beard, V. Vallabh *(physiotherapist)*, S. Cushen *(manager)*.
Front row: S.R. Allen, J.M. Brodie, T.G. McIntosh *(captain)*, B.M.K. Patton, B.C. Hiini.

CDCA

CENTRAL DISTRICTS — 2008/09

Back row: G.R. Hay, D.A.J. Bracewell, M.J. McClenaghan, G.H. Worker, R.R. Sherlock, B.M.K. Patton, T.I. Weston.

Front row: D.A. Reeve *(coach)*, P.J. Ingram, B.B.J. Griggs, M.S. Sinclair *(captain)*, J.D.P. Oram, E.P. Thompson, C.R. Tutchen *(manager/physiotherapist)*.

CDCA

CENTRAL DISTRICTS WOMEN — 2008/09

Back row: K. Strange *(coach)*, E. Lanser, R.H. Candy, K.M. Sutherland, Z.A. McWilliams, S.J. McGlashan, K.E. Broadmore, S.L. Norman *(manager)*.

Front row: K.C.R. Rangi, L.A.M. Hayes, R.H. Priest, A.L. Mason *(captain)*, K.M. Winkley, A.K. Burrows.

NDCA

NORTHERN DISTRICTS – 2008/09

Back row: S.R. Gadsdon, K.S. Williamson, T.A. Boult, T. T. Davis, A.P. Devcich, D.R. Flynn, J.J. Boult.

Second Row: S. Derry *(manager/physiotherapist)*, C.W. Ross *(assistant coach)*, G.E. Bradburn *(coach)*, B-J. Watling, B.S. Wilson, B.J. Arnel, T.G. Southee, S.L. Andrews, T.W. Andersson *(scorer/statistician)*, C.S. Stevens *(selector)*, P.J. Malcon *(selector)*.

Front Row: B.E. Scott, J.A.F. Yovich, P.D. McGlashan, J.A.H. Marshall *(captain)*, M.E. Parlane, G.W. Aldridge, B.P. Martin.

NDCA

NORTHERN DISTRICTS WOMEN – 2008/09

Back row: C.W. Dickeson *(coach)*, N.C. Dodd, H.R. Huddleston, N.P. Edwards, M.J.G. Nielsen, K.L. Pulford, B.N. Kirkbride, A.M. Peterson, H.J. Partridge *(manager)*.

Front row: E.L. Bailey, N.J. Browne, A.J. Wilkins *(captain)*, L.E. Milliken, E.M. Wilson.

WCA

WELLINGTON – 2008/09

Back row: S.R. Allen, A.R. Lamb, M.J. Tugaga, G.D. Elliott, J.M. Brodie, B-J. Crook, C.J. Nevin, S.J. Hotter *(trainer)*.

Second row: A.M. Stuart *(coach)*, D. Painter *(manager)*, K.A. Forde, S.J. Murdoch, D.J. Bowden, H.K.P. Boam, M.V. Houghton, M. Burns, L.J. Woodcock, J.D. Ryder, C. van Dyk *(assistant coach)*.

Front row: J.S. Patel, I.E. O'Brien, M.D. Bell *(captain)*, N.R. Parlane, J.E.C. Franklin, M.R. Gillespie.

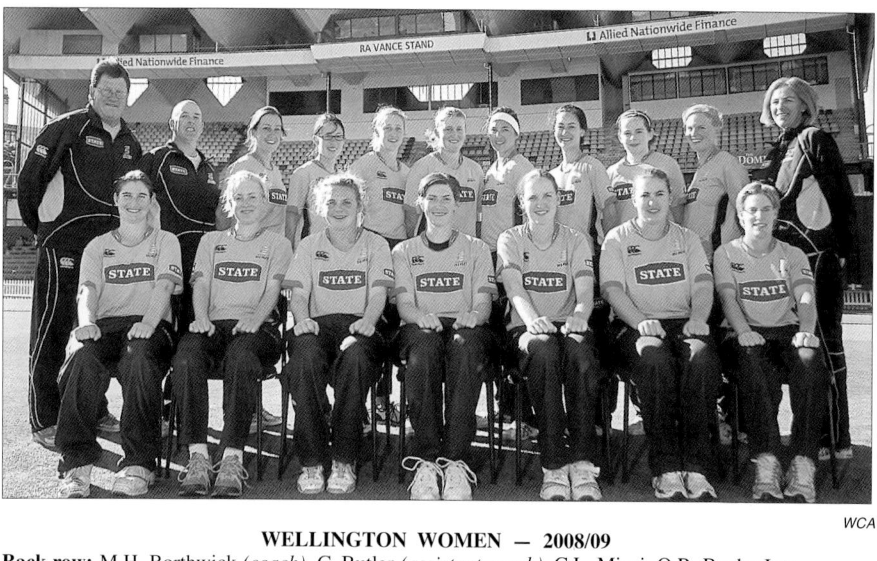

WCA

WELLINGTON WOMEN – 2008/09

Back row: M.H. Borthwick *(coach)*, G. Butler *(assistant coach)*, C.L. Mizzi, O.R. Bupha-Intr, S.F.M. Devine, E.C. Perry, K.A. Tomlinson, M.J. Hodgson, H.M. Bedford, S.J. Bradbury, W. Bedford *(manager)*.

Front row: E.J. Scurr, S.E.A. Ruck, L.R. Doolan, A.M. Dodd *(captain)*, A.E. Cooper, M.G. Wakefield, A.C. Stockwell.

Apex Photographic

HAWKE'S BAY — 2008/09

Back row: D. Smidt *(coach)*, K. Noema-Barnett, D.A.J. Bracewell, A.J. Douglas, B.S.M. McLennan, R.J. Schaw, M.S. Sinclair, J.M.K. Kuru, B. Meehan *(manager)*.

Front row: J. Mackie, J.W. de Terte, R.D. Breakwell, M.J.E. Calkin, S. Danks, L. Rukuwai, B.Z. Meehan.

NCA

The pavilion at Whangarei's Cobham Oval, which became New Zealand's 62nd first-class venue when Northern Districts met Auckland in the State Championship game from 6-9 March, 2009.

NZC

NEW ZEALAND UNDER TEAM 19 IN ENGLAND — 2008

Back row: D.N. Patel *(coach)*, G.J. Morgan, D.S. Robinson, A.W. Mathieson, H.K.P Boam, D.A.J. Bracewell, J.D.S. Needsham, F.J. Colson, K. Pulley *(manager)*.
Front row: M.D. O'Neill *(batting coach)*, T.M. Clarke, A. Verma, G.H. Worker, K.S. Williamson *(captain)*, N.B. Beard, J. Austin-Smellie, C. Cachopa, M. Payne *(physiotherapist)*.

Clive Ralph

NEW ZEALAND UNDER 17 TOURNAMENT TEAM — 2008/09

Back row: H. Wright, H. Nicholls, B. Small, C. McConchie, C. Ware, R. Darkins.
Front row: B. Wheeler, C. Cachopa, T. Latham *(captain)*, M. Henry, T. van Woerkom, A. Vodnala.

Daniel Vettori joined a short list of players have scored 500 runs and taken 50 wickets in one calendar year of test cricket. He became the seventh player to achieve the feat, Kapil Dev having done so on two occasions, as this list shows:

	year	*tests*	*runs*	*ave*	*wkts*	*ave*
J.M. Gregory (A)	1921	12	765	54.64	51	25.33
I.T. Botham (E)	1978	12	565	43.46	63	18.41
Kapil Dev (I)	1979	18	619	30.95	74	23.24
I.T. Botham (E)	1981	12	629	28.59	62	25.64
Kapil Dev (I)	1983	18	579	22.26	75	23.17
S.M. Pollock (SA)	2001	13	573	52.09	55	21.38
A. Flintoff (E)	2005	13	659	31.38	61	25.45
D.L. Vettori (NZ)	2008	14	672	35.36	54	26.13

New Zealand played 14 test matches in 2008, surpassing their previous record of 13 in 1965 and 1999. The most played by any country in one year is 18 by India in 1979 and 1983.

• • •

New Zealand won the first test against Bangladesh at Chittagong by successfully chasing a target which was higher than any of the three previous innings of the match. The three occasions when New Zealand have achieved this feat are:

v Pakistan at Dunedin 1984/85
Pakistan 274 & 223 New Zealand 220 & 278-8
New Zealand won by 2 wickets

v India at Hamilton 2002/03
India 99 & 154 New Zealand 94 & 160-6
New Zealand won by 4 wickets

Bangladesh at Chittagong 2008/09
Bangladesh 245 & 242 New Zealand 171 and 317-7
New Zealand won by 3 wickets

• • •

Virender Sehwag arrived in New Zealand with a sequence of eleven consecutive test centuries of 150 more. While his feat may well be considered as Bradman-like, this is one record which Bradman does not hold. His best sequence was six scores of 150 or more while the next best after Sehwag is seven, by his coach Gary Kirsten. Sehwag's sequence is:

195	v Australia	Melbourne	2003/04
309	v Pakistan	Multan	2004/05
155	v Australia	Chennai	2004/05
164	v South Africa	Kanpur	2004/05
173	v Pakistan	Mohali	2004/05
201	v Pakistan	Bangalore	2004/05
254	v Pakistan	Lahore	2005/06
180	v West Indies	Gros Islet	2005/06
151	v Australia	Adelaide	2007/08
319	v South Africa	Chennai	2007/08
201*	v Sri Lanka	Galle	2008/09

Sehwag scored his runs during those eleven hundreds at a strike rate of 83. He hit the first three balls he faced on tour for six but was not able to extend his test centuries record while in New Zealand. His highest score in the three tests was 48.

OBITUARIES

Wynne Pennell BRADBURN

***Born:** Thames, 24 November, 1938*

***Died:** Hamilton, 25 September, 2008*

Right-hand batsman, right-arm slow-medium bowler

Wynne Bradburn opened the batting for New Zealand in two tests against South Africa and was a member of the first Northern Districts team to win the Plunket Shield. He also accomplished the rare feat of twice carrying his bat through a completed innings.

By the age of 17 Bradburn was playing Hawke Cup cricket for Thames Valley. He had also made his first appearance for Northern Districts, in a three-day game against a Wellington side (which contained five past or future test cricketers) the season before Northern were admitted to the Plunket Shield competition.

Bradburn made his first-class debut at Carisbrook on Boxing Day 1957. He scored 33, batting at number four, and top scored in Northern's second innings of 90 before falling lbw to Jack Alabaster for 26. He also made 41 and 24 (out of totals of 111 and 117) against Auckland. The *Almanack* that year noted that Northern's emphasis was on team building and that ten of the 16 players used were new to first-class cricket. Bradburn was one of several players of whom it was said "there was definite indication that the talent is there waiting to be developed" and "they could all become leading players of the future".

As it turned out, Bradburn had little success over the next two seasons but by 1960/61 he was opening the batting and hit 71 in 227 minutes against Otago at Seddon Park. He was also selected in the New Zealand Colts team which played a two-day game against Dennis Silk's MCC side at Ashburton. He scored 43 and shared a 107 run opening partnership with Ian Hartland.

Three days later Bradburn carried his bat through Northern's first innings of 87 at the Basin Reserve. Bob Blair (7-30) routed the visitors but Bradburn remained unbeaten, finishing with 45 in 148 minutes. For good measure he made 32 before being fifth out when Northern followed on.

Twelve months later Bradburn repeated the feat in an extraordinary game at Seddon Park. Wellington had gained a 12 run first innings lead but were bowled out for just 80 in their second innings as Dave Hoskin (7-33) claimed career best figures. Needing just 93 to win (a victory which would have given them the Plunket Shield for the first time) Northern collapsed to be 33-9 when Hoskin joined Bradburn.

The number eleven stayed for 32 minutes, while 24 runs were added, before he was bowled by Bob Blair, who finished with 5-30. Bradburn ended with 37 not out, made in 113 minutes. He remains the only Northern Districts batsman to carry his bat through an innings.

Next season Northern made amends and won the Shield for the first time in their history. Bradburn, though, had a modest season and the *Almanack* said "Once again Bradburn failed to produce the form of which he is capable".

The following season saw improved form from Bradburn with 282 runs in nine innings for Northern. This included 98 in 248 minutes against a strong Wellington attack of Blair, Morrison, Reid, Taylor and Butler at Seddon Park. Bradburn also impressed with 48 in 196 minutes in a two-day game against South Africa. When Graham Dowling broke his finger in the first test, Bradburn was called upon to make his test debut at Carisbrook.

New Zealand made just 149 and 138, Bradburn scoring 32, in 119 minutes, and 14. In the third test at Auckland he scored 2 and 14. In his second innings, with the score at 49-0, Bradburn walked, after an appeal for a caught behind, without waiting for the umpire's decision, despite it turning out to be "not out".

Bradburn scored the only century of his first-class career in the 1965/66 season when he came close to carrying his bat for a third time. He made 107 in 358 minutes, with a six and eight fours, against a strong Auckland attack which included Cunis, Sutton, Sparling and Howarth. Bradburn was last man out in a total of 210 and followed up with 59 in 183 minutes in the second innings.

As it turned out, this was to be the last time that Bradburn was to reach fifty in first-class cricket, despite playing a further 25 innings. He continued playing for Waikato (later Hamilton) until 1975/76.

Bradburn's son, Grant, played a record 115 first-class games for Northern Districts and took over as coach during the 2008/09 season.

Bradburn's record in first-class cricket is:

Season	*M*	*I*	*NO*	*HS*	*Runs*	*Ave*	*100*	*50*	*ct*	*Wkts*	*Runs*	*Ave*	*Best*
1957/58	5	10	0	41	171	17.10	–	–	2	0	48	–	–
1958/59	2	3	0	5	7	2.33	–	–	–	0	4	–	–
1959/60	4	7	1	25	68	11.33	–	–	8				
1960/61	5	10	1	71	212	23.55	–	1	4				
1961/62	5	10	1	49	152	16.88	–	–	4				
1962/63	6	11	1	58*	219	21.90	–	1	5				
1963/64	7	13	0	98	344	26.46	–	2	15	6	141	23.50	2-16
1964/65	6	11	0	87	284	25.81	–	2	6	4	250	62.50	1-27
1965/66	5	9	0	107	253	28.11	1	1	7	3	52	17.33	2-13
1966/67	6	12	1	46	235	21.36	–	–	5	2	128	64.00	1-17
1967/68	2	4	0	43	56	14.00	–	–	4	3	128	42.66	1-17
1968/69	4	7	0	27	76	10.85	–	–	6	1	53	53.00	1-41
TOTAL	**57**	**107**	**5**	**107**	**2077**	**20.36**	**1**	**7**	**66**	**19**	**804**	**42.31**	**2-13**

For	*M*	*I*	*NO*	*HS*	*Runs*	*Ave*	*100*	*50*	*ct*	*Wkts*	*Runs*	*Ave*	*Best*
NZ (tests)	2	4	0	32	62	15.50	–	–	2				
ND	55	103	5	107	2015	20.56	1	7	64	19	804	42.31	2-13
TOTAL	**57**	**107**	**5**	**107**	**2077**	**20.36**	**1**	**7**	**66**	**19**	**804**	**42.31**	**2-13**

Robert Smith CUNIS

Born: *Whangarei, 5 January, 1941*

Died: *Whangarei, 9 August, 2008*

Right-hand batsman, right-arm fast-medium bowler

Bob Cunis was a lion-hearted fast-medium bowler and determined lower-order batsman. He appeared in twenty test matches and played a key role in New Zealand's first series win. He bowled with a unique, wrong-footed action and forever seemed to be rolling up his shirt sleeves as he walked back to his mark.

Cunis was in the first eleven at Whangarei Boys' High School and also represented Whangarei Colts. He attended Teachers' Training College in Auckland and joined the Eden club. It did not take him long to attract the attention of the Auckland selectors and he made an immediate impact.

Cunis made his first-class debut against Northern Districts at Seddon Park on 29 December 1960 and by the end of his third over had figures of 2-11. He finished with 6-72 from 34 overs and two weeks later played for the New Zealand Colts team against Dennis Silk's MCC side in a two-day game at Ashburton.

The following summer Cunis became a permanent fixture in the Auckland team and ended the season with 27 wickets at 14.18 in five games. He took 7-29 (which remained his best figures) from 22.5 overs against Central Districts at Eden Park, having 0-16 off 12 overs at one stage.

Another productive season followed, with 17 wickets at 17.29 in 1962/63. Cunis had now teamed up with left-arm fast bowler Bob Sutton and they formed a formidable opening attack for several seasons, with Sutton unlucky not to follow Cunis to national honours.

Auckland won the Plunket Shield in 1963/64 and Cunis' return of 23 wickets at 17.30 played a large part in their success. Thirteen of these wickets came in the opening match of the season when Cunis took 6-44 and 7-41 against Canterbury at Lancaster Park. Auckland won a thrilling game by one wicket and the *Almanack,* with some understatement, noted "Cunis had a good match with 13 wickets for 85 runs".

Cunis also made his test debut that season when he replaced Dick Motz for the third test against South Africa at Eden Park. He took 0-80 and 2-47 with Graeme Pollock and Denis Lindsay being his two victims. Later that year Cunis was a member of the New Zealand Cricket Council's team which played 42 matches in eight different countries. He was the leading wicket taker with 124 at 9.56 each.

The following season Cunis came to light with the bat. Auckland were 80-8, chasing Wellington's 289 at the Basin Reserve, when he joined Hec Schuster. The pair put on 122 for the ninth wicket which remained the Auckland record until bettered by Reece Young and Greg Morgan in 2007/08. Cunis reached his first half-century in first-class cricket and was 60 not out, after 168 minutes, when the innings ended.

Cunis returned to form with the ball in 1965/66, taking 22 wickets at 17.45 for Auckland, as well as scoring two more fifties. Now batting as high as number seven, he shared a partnership of 159 with Noel Harford for the sixth wicket against Central Districts. He played in all three tests against Mike Smith's England team, capturing seven wickets.

The following season saw Cunis in fine all-round form, averaging 32 with the bat and 21 with the ball in six games for Auckland. He took 7-30 against Northern Districts in the Plunket Shield opener and followed this with the only century of his first-class career in the next match, against Otago at Eden Park. He came in to bat with the score at 79-6 and added 78 with Graham Vivian. When the ninth wicket fell Cunis was on 73 but Hedley Howarth stayed for 68 minutes, while 60 runs were added, and Cunis was finally last man out for 111, made in 254 minutes. He hit a six and eleven fours.

Cunis came close to a second hundred eleven days later against Wellington but ran himself out when on 99, scored in 185 minutes. He also took 5-60 in Wellington's second innings.

Cunis was hampered by a knee injury in 1967/68 but returned with a vengeance the following summer, capturing 45 wickets at 19.13. Auckland won the Plunket Shield once again and Cunis was outstanding with 34 wickets at just 13.14. He took six wickets in an innings on three occasions and ten in a match once.

He also took 5-93 for North Island against the South at Pukekura Park and played in all three tests against West Indies, captained by Gary Sobers. Cunis took five wickets in the second test at Wellington, which New Zealand won by six wickets. His 3-39 in the second innings included the wickets of Seymour Nurse, Clive Lloyd and Sobers.

Cunis was an automatic selection for New Zealand's tour which followed. He captured 38 wickets at 27.76 in England, with a best of 6-54 against Sussex. This performance saw him included in the team for the third test against England. He took five wickets in the match, bowling Geoff Boycott in both innings.

New Zealand then faced six tests in quick succession in India and Pakistan. With the series against India level, New Zealand were thwarted by rain in the third test at Hyderabad. Cunis took 3-12 off 14 overs as India were bowled out for 89 in their first innings and had 3-12 from 12 overs in the second with India 76-7, chasing an improbable 268.

A five wicket win at Lahore meant New Zealand went in to the third test against Pakistan at Dacca with a 1-0 series lead, needing only a draw to secure their first ever series win. Glenn Turner's maiden test century helped New Zealand reach 273 and Pakistan responded with 290-7 before Intikhab Alam declared.

New Zealand were in dire straits on the last day when their eighth wicket fell at 101 with well over four hours remaining. Cunis joined Mark Burgess and the pair remained together for 109 minutes, adding 96 invaluable runs, before Cunis finally fell for 23. The innings ended soon after with Burgess unbeaten on 119.

Pakistan now required 184 in around 150 minutes but Cunis bowled both openers, Aftab Gul and Sadiq Mohammad, before tea. After the break he bowled Asif Iqbal and had Shafqat Rana caught to have the home side 46-4. Five more runs were added but disturbances in the crowd of nearly 40,000 caused the match to be abandoned 65 minutes early and New Zealand had won their first test series.

Cunis captured 30 wickets at 18.73 in the 1970/71 season including ten in two tests against Ray Illingworth's England team. He produced his best figures in tests with 6-76 off 24 (eight-ball) overs at Eden Park and finished with nine wickets in the match.

The following summer Cunis was the sole New Zealander named in a World team to play in Australia after the tour by South Africa was cancelled. He found conditions unsuited to his style of bowling and took just nine wickets in nine first-class games, although he did play in two of the "tests" against Australia.

Cunis found the going just as tough when New Zealand made their first tour to West Indies later in the season. He played in all five tests but his six wickets cost over 100 runs each. His finest moment on tour came with the bat.

New Zealand were 99-6 on the first day of the second test at Port of Spain but Ken Wadsworth helped Bevan Congdon add 69 for the seventh wicket. Cunis joined Congdon at 168-7 and saw a further 43 runs added before stumps. Next day the pair took their partnership to 136 before Cunis was finally dismissed for 51, made in 179 minutes. Congdon ended unbeaten on 166 as New Zealand reached 348 and the match eventually ended in a draw (as did each of the other four tests).

The West Indies tour turned out to be the last time that Cunis gained national selection. Two modest seasons for Auckland followed and his first-class career looked as though it had come to an end. However, Cunis, now based in Rotorua, returned to first-class cricket with Northern Districts in 1975/76, teaming up with Richard Collinge and taking 29 wickets in two seasons.

Cunis continued to play for Bay of Plenty and then returned to play for Northland until he was well into his forties. He was far from finished with the game, however. He moved into selection once his playing career was over, serving as a national selector and also as coach of the national team in the late 1980s. He also had a spell as a television commentator and wrote a weekly newspaper column.

Cunis is also the last person to play both first-class rugby and cricket for Auckland, a record he will probably hold for all-time. He played four games for an Auckland XV in 1965 and 1966, as first five-eighth, scored one try and kicked one dropped goal and one conversion.

He was a school teacher and, later, a principal during his working life. His son, Stephen, represented Canterbury from 1998/99 to 2005/06.

Cunis' record in first-class cricket is:

Season	*M*	*I*	*NO*	*HS*	*Runs*	*Ave*	*100*	*50*	*ct*	*Wkts*	*Runs*	*Ave*	*5W*	*10W*	*Best*
1960/61	2	3	1	12	24	12.00	–	–	–	9	185	20.55	1	–	6-72
1961/62	5	7	2	24*	47	9.40	–	–	1	27	383	14.18	1	–	7-29
1962/63	5	6	0	18	42	7.00	–	–	–	17	294	17.29	1	–	6-40
1963/64	6	8	3	20	49	9.80	–	–	–	25	525	21.00	2	1	7-41
1964/65	6	4	1	60*	109	36.33	–	1	1	18	544	30.22	–	–	3-32
1965/66	8	15	4	68	231	21.00	–	2	2	29	632	21.79	1	–	5-48
1966/67	9	14	2	111	354	29.50	1	2	1	23	634	27.56	2	–	7-30
1967/68	5	7	2	28*	101	20.20	–	–	–	7	211	30.14	–	–	3-60
1968/69	10	11	5	20*	88	14.66	–	–	3	45	861	19.13	4	1	6-39
1969 (E)	12	13	4	19*	83	9.22	–	–	5	38	1055	27.76	2	–	6-54
1969/70 (I)	3	6	1	12	30	6.00	–	–	–	9	158	17.55	–	–	3-12
1969/70 (P)	3	3	0	23	28	9.33	–	–	–	9	218	24.22	–	–	4-21
1969/70 (A)	3	2	0	18	20	10.00	–	–	–	8	208	26.00	–	–	2-27
1969/70	2	3	1	22	26	13.00	–	–	–	4	109	27.25	–	–	4-58
1970/71	7	7	4	36	123	41.00	–	–	3	30	562	18.73	3	–	6-37
1970/71 (A)	1	–	–	–	–	–	–	–	–	4	69	17.25	–	–	4-69
1971/72 (A)	9	11	2	43	129	14.33	–	–	3	9	544	60.44	–	–	2-59
1971/72	1	1	1	3*	3	–	–	–	–	2	84	42.00	–	–	1-24
1971/72 (WI)	9	9	2	51	143	20.42	–	1	1	16	970	60.62	–	–	3-37
1972/73	6	7	2	10	45	9.00	–	–	2	13	426	32.76	–	–	3-41
1973/74	6	7	3	18	76	19.00	–	–	2	15	416	27.73	1	–	5-136
1975/76	7	7	1	29	82	13.66	–	–	4	13	589	45.30	–	–	4-58
1976/77	7	6	4	8*	16	8.00	–	–	2	16	610	38.12	–	–	3-25
TOTAL	**132**	**157**	**45**	**111**	**1849**	**16.50**	**1**	**6**	**30**	**386**	**10,287**	**26.65**	**18**	**2**	**7-29**

For	M	I	NO	HS	Runs	Ave	100	50	ct	Wkts	Runs	Ave	5W	10W	Best
NZ (tests)	20	31	8	51	295	12.82	–	1	1	51	1887	37.00	1	–	6-76
NZ (others)	25	25	8	22*	230	13.52	–	–	5	63	1942	30.82	2	-	6-54
Auckland	62	75	21	111	1084	20.07	1	5	15	229	4603	20.10	14	2	7-29
ND	14	13	5	29	98	12.25	–	–	6	29	1119	41.34	-	-	4-58
World XI	9	11	2	43	129	14.33	–	–	3	9	544	60.44	-	-	2-59
NZ XI	1	1	1	12*	12	–	–	–	–	0	19	–	–	–	–
North Island	1	1	0	1	1	1.00	–	–	–	5	93	18.60	1	-	5-93
TOTAL	**132**	**157**	**45**	**111**	**1849**	**16.50**	**1**	**6**	**30**	**386**	**10,287**	**26.65**	**18**	**2**	**7-29**

Hedley John HOWARTH

Born: *Auckland, 25 December, 1943*

Died: *Auckland, 7 November, 2008*

Left-hand batsman, slow left-arm bowler

When Hedley Howarth retired he had taken more wickets than any other bowler in New Zealand first-class cricket and had captured more test wickets than any other New Zealand spin bowler.

Howarth attended Ponsonby Primary School and captained the Grafton and Districts Schoolboys' team at the annual January tournament. In the same year he led the Auckland Cricket Association Boys' representative team. He received early coaching from former test cricketers Don Cleverley and Merv Wallace and also found time to play rugby league for the Ponsonby club.

Howarth was in the Auckland Grammar first eleven from 1958 to 1961 and his team mates included Mark Burgess, Terry Jarvis, Ross Dykes and future All Black Graham Thorne. He joined the Grafton club when he left school and gained selection in the Auckland Brabin Cup side, the New Zealand Colts B team and the Auckland Under 23 team.

By 1962/63 he was a member of the Auckland Plunket Shield squad and was twelfth man for their last three matches. He did, however, make his first-class debut that season for the New Zealand Under 23 XI against the Plunket Shield winners, Northern Districts. Howarth took one wicket, that of Wynne Bradburn who was to make his test debut the following year.

The following season Howarth was a regular member of the Auckland side which won the Plunket Shield. He took 13 wickets in five matches, including 5-32 against Northern Districts when he bowled Auckland to victory in a sensational match which they won by eight runs after following on. Howarth captured the final wicket with four balls of the game remaining.

Two unspectacular seasons followed but Howarth showed improved form in 1966/67 when he captured 25 wickets at 18.84. The next season he took a career best 6-23 against Otago in a low-scoring match at Carisbrook which Auckland won by just 36 runs.

The 1968/69 season brought even better results with 36 wickets at 16.05 apiece. Howarth took 30 wickets at 13.00 for Auckland, including 6-29 against Central Districts, and 6-78 for North Island against West Indies. It was subsequently no surprise when Howarth was named in the New Zealand team which was to play nine test matches in England, India and Pakistan.

Howarth took 57 wickets in England and a further 28 in India and Pakistan. His final tally was 85 wickets at just 19.61 each. He made a compelling claim for inclusion in the New Zealand test side when he took 7-43 against Essex and followed this with 6-99 against Middlesex. He duly made his test debut, at Lord's, taking 2-24 and 3-102 off 49 overs.

New Zealand lost the first test of the Indian leg of the tour but levelled the series in the next match at Nagpur. Howarth took 4-66 and 5-34 to bowl New Zealand to an historic victory. New Zealand were thwarted by wet weather at Hyderabad in their bid for their first series win. India made 89 and 76-7 but Howarth was barely required as the New Zealand pace attack caused most of the damage.

The first test in Pakistan ended in a draw but not before Howarth had claimed another five wicket haul, taking 5-80 off 33 overs at Karachi. One of his victims was Hanif Mohammad, playing in his last test. Howarth took another five wickets in the second test, which New

Zealand won, and had figures of 4-85 in Pakistan's first innings of the third, at Dacca. A heroic rearguard action by Mark Burgess and Bob Cunis enabled New Zealand to draw the match and gain their first ever test series win. Howarth dismissed six batsmen caught and bowled during the tests on the subcontinent, including some truly remarkable efforts.

Howarth was awarded the Winsor Cup in 1970 (for the most meritorious bowling in first-class cricket over the previous twelve months). He had taken 100 wickets at 21.73, a figure still without parallel in the long history of the award.

He warmed up for New Zealand's next tour with 31 wickets in five Plunket Shield matches in the 1971/72 season, capturing at least one wicket in every innings he bowled in. At the end of the season New Zealand embarked on their first tour to West Indies where Howarth sent down 496 overs, far more than any other of the bowlers.

As a sign of things to come, prior to the first test he bowled 52 overs in the President's XI's innings at Montego Bay. There were a further 61 overs during the first test and then 42 in one innings against Trinidad. In the second test he took 3-102 off 53 overs in the first innings followed by another 20 overs in the second.

New Zealand had the chance of an historic win in the third test at Bridgetown but were held at bay by a 254 run partnership between Charlie Davis and Gary Sobers. West Indies batted out the game, scoring 564-8 off 214 overs. Howarth did his share, finishing with figures of 74-24-138-2. No other New Zealand bowler has ever sent down as many as the 444 deliveries that Howarth did in that innings.

Howarth took five wickets in the last test and also bowled 80 overs. It was just reward for his efforts that he was able to claim five wickets in each innings in the final match of the tour against Bermuda.

While Howarth remained a prolific wicket taker after the tour, there were many who felt that he was never quite the same attacking force after the stock-bowling role that he had been required to take on in West Indies, sometimes bowling as first change.

Even so, Howarth enjoyed his most prolific season at home the following season with 49 wickets at 23.38. He captured 37 wickets in five Plunket Shield matches, although only ten at 44.00 in the three tests against Pakistan. At one stage Howarth took five wickets in three successive innings and also had figures of 7-48 against Northern Districts.

Another tour to England followed but this time Howarth found wickets harder to come by, finishing with 31 at 36.74 each. Ten of these came against a combined Oxford and Cambridge Universities team. Howarth missed the first test because of injury but returned for the second at Lord's where he put in another marathon bowling performance.

In what was almost a replay of what had happened at Bridgetown, New Zealand let victory slip away and were forced to bowl and bowl as the home team made the game safe. This time England batted for 196 overs, Howarth's figures reading 70-24-144-4.

Howarth was not available for New Zealand's first test tour to Australia in 1973/74 but played a major role for Auckland with 35 wickets in six games. This included two seven wicket hauls against Otago at Carisbrook, equalling the Auckland record of 14 wickets in a match.

The next two seasons saw Howarth claim a further 72 wickets. In 1975/76 he was left out of the New Zealand test team for the first time since his debut in England in 1969, the New Zealand selectors opting for an all-pace attack for the third test against India at the Basin Reserve. Richard Hadlee, the favourite to fill the twelfth man role, took eleven wickets in the match and never looked back.

Howarth, however, was back in the team when Australia came to New Zealand the following summer. Despite another prolific season for Auckland, he did little with the ball in the two tests. He had more success with the bat, scoring a career best 61 at Lancaster Park to help New Zealand avoid the follow on in a match which eventually ended in a draw.

Howarth reached fifty only three times in 179 first-class innings, all in the 1976/77 season. His return of 296 runs at 32.88 and 34 wickets at 30.97 that summer was quite definitely in the all-rounder class.

The 1977/78 season started in promising fashion for Howarth with a five wicket haul to bowl the North Island to victory against the South at Lancaster Park. However, his output for Auckland declined and long-time rival John McIntyre was preferred for some games. With another left-arm spinner, Stephen Boock, having a very successful season the national selectors decided it was time for a change.

Howarth played four more games for Auckland the following season, passing Bob Blair's record of most wickets in New Zealand first-class cricket.

Howarth played in nine one-day internationals and took part in the first World Cup in England in 1975. It was no surprise that such a skilful practitioner of his art should adapt so well to the fifty-over game, conceding just 3.41 runs per over.

Standing over six feet tall, broad of shoulders and long of limb, Hedley Howarth could be found helping his father manage the family business of Kia Ora Fisheries on the Auckland waterfront. His working day began at 4 am and he frequently arrived to play for Auckland having already done the best part of a day's work.

His father, George, came from England and loved his cricket. The great English left-arm slow bowler Hedley Verity died in action in July 1943, five months before Howarth was born, and it was thought that George named his second son after Verity. If so, it was quite remarkable that this son also achieved cricketing fame as a left-arm slow bowler.

Don Neely remembered facing Howarth and said: "One of the secrets of his bowling could be seen, if never quite understood, and only from very close. When playing against him, balls that you thought were overtossed, suddenly dropped as the under-spun ball fell short of the anticipated length. This was the reason that of the 541 wickets that he captured in first-class cricket, 49 of them (9%) were caught and bowled, an exceptional statistic."

Neely also pointed out, "When Zealand made their first tour to West Indies they were confronted by comatose wickets that were made for batsmen of both sides to churn out runs with monotonous regularity. Bruce Taylor was the only bowler on either side to capture many wickets. Howarth's concentration, patience and stamina were put to the test as he bowled the vast number of 338 overs in five tests and conceded only 703 runs under the broiling sun against such batsmen as Gary Sobers, Lawrence Rowe, Alvin Kallicharran, Roy Fredericks and Charlie Davis. On these shirt-front wickets he perplexed and imprisoned their normal flamboyant batting skills by accuracy of length and subtlety of flight."

Summing up, Neely said, "Judged by any standard Hedley Howarth was a great bowler. Merely to watch him was to know from the balance of the run-up, the high ease of the left-arm action, the scrupulous length and the pensive variety, all proclaimed him a master of his art. Howarth was a gentleman first and a cricketer second. His character and disposition never changed amidst all his many triumphs; he just remained Hedley Howarth."

Howarth's record in first-class cricket is:

Season	*M*	*I*	*NO*	*HS*	*Runs*	*Ave*	*100*	*50*	*ct*	*Wkts*	*Runs*	*Ave*	*5W*	*10W*	*Best*
1962/63	1	2	1	23*	26	26.00	–	–	1	1	85	85.00	–	–	1-45
1963/64	6	10	2	19	74	9.25	–	–	7	18	433	24.05	1	–	5-32
1964/65	4	5	2	24*	57	19.00	–	–	2	8	282	35.25	–	–	3-51
1965/66	4	6	2	7	20	5.00	–	–	0	12	291	24.25	–	–	4-34
1966/67	6	9	5	36*	126	31.50	–	–	6	25	471	18.84	–	–	4-31
1967/68	5	7	0	24	76	10.85	–	–	2	14	223	15.92	1	–	6-23
1968/69	8	6	1	4*	7	1.40	–	–	6	36	578	16.05	4	–	6-29
1969 (E)	12	17	8	11*	59	6.55	–	–	2	57	1126	19.75	3	–	7-43
1969/70 (I)	3	5	3	17*	26	13.00	–	–	6	12	218	18.16	1	–	5-34
1969/70 (P)	3	4	1	4	6	2.00	–	–	3	16	323	20.18	1	–	5-80
1969/70 (A)	3	3	2	9*	14	14.00	–	–	2	8	258	32.25	1	–	5-32
1969/70	3	3	0	10	11	3.66	–	–	0	7	248	35.42	1	–	5-61
1970/71	7	7	2	27*	90	18.00	–	–	6	21	687	32.71	–	–	4-46
1970/71 (A)	1	1	0	0	0	0.00	–	–	1	0	58	–	–	–	–
1971/72	5	7	2	39	107	21.40	–	–	6	31	663	21.38	1	–	5-34
1971/72 (WI)	10	7	3	16	37	9.25	–	–	5	32	1102	34.43	2	1	5-32
1972/73	9	11	3	15	63	7.87	–	–	11	49	1146	23.38	4	1	7-48
1973 (E)	11	7	4	17	69	23.00	–	–	13	31	1139	36.74	2	1	5-70
1973/74	9	10	4	29*	95	15.83	–	–	20	40	1011	25.27	3	1	7-42
1974/75	8	13	3	47	170	17.00	–	–	5	38	920	24.21	1	–	5-77
1975/76	9	9	5	21	72	18.00	–	–	12	34	863	25.38	2	1	7-75
1976/77	9	13	4	61	296	32.88	–	3	13	34	1053	30.97	1	1	8-75
1977/78	5	9	1	27	72	9.00	–	–	3	9	204	22.66	1	–	5-56
1978/79	4	8	0	25	95	11.87	–	–	5	8	292	36.50	1	–	5-70
TOTAL	**145**	**179**	**58**	**61**	**1668**	**13.78**	**–**	**3**	**137**	**541**	**13,674**	**25.27**	**31**	**6**	**8-75**

For	*M*	*I*	*NO*	*HS*	*Runs*	*Ave*	*100*	*50*	*ct*	*Wkts*	*Runs*	*Ave*	*5W*	*10W*	*Best*
NZ (tests)	30	42	18	61	291	12.12	–	1	33	86	3178	36.95	2	–	5-34
NZ (others)	31	28	12	13*	161	10.06	–	–	13	111	2798	25.20	9	2	7-43
Auckland	80	103	27	56	1163	15.30	–	2	87	332	7361	22.17	18	4	8-75
North Island	3	4	0	27	27	6.75	–	–	3	11	252	22.90	2	–	6-78
NZ Under 23	1	2	1	23*	26	26.00	–	–	1	1	85	85.00	–	–	1-45
TOTAL	**145**	**179**	**58**	**61**	**1668**	**13.78**	**-**	**3**	**137**	**541**	**13,674**	**25.27**	**31**	**6**	**8-75**

AMENDMENTS

To previous editions

2008

Page 161

The fourth wicket partnership of 112 was between P.J. Ingram and T.I. Weston.

Pages 169-171

The three games were played on 30, 31 March, 1, 2 April, 2008.

NEW ZEALAND EMERGING PLAYERS IN AUSTRALIA

A New Zealand Emerging Players side took part in a tournament in Brisbane in July 2008 with the Australian Institute of Sport team, the Indian National Academy side and the South African Emerging Players. They also played three games against Queensland after the tournament.

The team was: J.D. Ryder *(captain, Wellington)*, C.J. Anderson *(Canterbury)*, B.J. Arnel *(Northern Districts)*, H.K. Bennett *(Canterbury)*, T.A. Boult *(Northern Districts)*, N.T. Broom *(Otago)*, L.M. Burtt *(Canterbury)*, B.J. Diamanti *(Central Districts)*, J.E.C. Franklin *(Wellington)*, B.B.J. Griggs *(Central Districts)*, M.J. Guptill *(Auckland)*, G.R. Hay *(Central Districts)*, B.C. Hiini *(Canterbury)*, P.J. Ingram *(Central Districts)*, R.J. Schaw *(Central Districts)*, B-J. Watling *(Northern Districts)*. Coach, A.J. Moles; Batting coach, M.D. O'Neill (until New Zealand Under 19 tour of England); Bowling Coach, V.F. Johnson; Manager, M.F. Sharpe; Trainer, M. Smith; Physiotherapist, R. Marsden.

INDIAN NATIONAL ACADEMY v SOUTH AFRICA EMERGING PLAYERS (Twenty20)

At Peter Burge Oval, Brisbane 14 July, 2008

Indian National Academy 87-7 (S. Badrinath 37, W.D. Parnell 3-15) **defeated South Africa Emerging Players** 75-8 (A. Mishra 3-11) by 12 runs

AUSTRALIAN INSTITUTE OF SPORTS v NEW ZEALAND EMERGING PLAYERS (Twenty20)

At Peter Burge Oval, Brisbane 14 July, 2008

New Zealand Emerging Players 139-8 (C.J. Anderson 53, G.J. Sullivan 3-25) **lost to Australian Institute of Sports** 141-4 (M.C. Henriques 57, P.J. Forrest 44) by 6 wickets

AUSTRALIAN INSTITUTE OF SPORTS v INDIAN NATIONAL ACADEMY

At Fred Kratzman Oval, Brisbane 15 July, 2008

Australian Institute of Sports 269-7 (M.S. Wade 115, P.J. Forrest 50, G.D. Moller 31, Pankaj Singh 3-58) **lost to Indian National Academy** 272-5 (S. Badrinath 83, S. Dhawan 75, A.M. Nayar 41) by 5 wickets

NEW ZEALAND EMERGING PLAYERS v SOUTH AFRICA EMERGING PLAYERS

At Peter Burge Oval, Brisbane 15 July, 2008

South Africa Emerging Players 93 (V.B. van Jaarsveld 34*) **lost to New Zealand Emerging Players** 94-5 (P.J. Ingram 30*, C.J.D. de Villiers 3-6) by 5 wickets

AUSTRALIAN INSTITUTE OF SPORTS v NEW ZEALAND EMERGING PLAYERS

At W.E.P. Harris Oval, Brisbane 17 July, 2008

Australian Institute of Sports 274 (P.J. Forrest 81, T.P. Doropoulos 69, S.N.J. O'Keefe 40, T.A. Boult 3-37) **defeated New Zealand Emerging Players** 237 (C.J. Anderson 73, B-J. Watling 35, A.V. Raymond 3-50) by 37 runs

INDIAN NATIONAL ACADEMY v SOUTH AFRICA EMERGING PLAYERS

At Albury Oval, Brisbane 17 July, 2008

Indian National Academy 80 (T. Tshabalala 3-11, W.D. Parnell 3-26) **lost to South Africa Emerging Players** 81-5 by 5 wickets

AUSTRALIAN INSTITUTE OF SPORTS v SOUTH AFRICA EMERGING PLAYERS
At Allan Border Field, Brisbane 19 July, 2008

South Africa Emerging Players 234 (A.M. Amla 42, D. Elgar 31, W.L. Coetsee 31, M.W. Hill 3-39) **lost to Australian Institute of Sports** 235-8 (U.T. Khawaja 74, S.N.J. O'Keefe 46, W.D. Parnell 3-33) by 2 wickets

INDIAN NATIONAL ACADEMY v NEW ZEALAND EMERGING PLAYERS
At W.E.P. Harris Oval, Brisbane 19 July, 2008

New Zealand Emerging Players 248-6 (M.J. Guptill 112, G.R. Hay 44) **lost to Indian National Academy** 251-3 (V. Kohli 120, M.K. Tiwary 60*, S. Dhawan 55) by 7 wickets

AUSTRALIAN INSTITUTE OF SPORTS v INDIAN NATIONAL ACADEMY
At Albury Oval, Brisbane 20 July, 2008

Australian Institute of Sports 371-5 (M.C. Henriques 124, T.P. Doropoulos 107, D.A. Warner 80) **defeated Indian National Academy** 352 (S.K. Raina 115, S. Badrinath 95, G.J. Sullivan 3-62, T.P. Doropoulos 3-68) by 19 runs

NEW ZEALAND EMERGING PLAYERS v SOUTH AFRICA EMERGING PLAYERS
At W.E.P. Harris Oval, Brisbane 20 July, 2008

New Zealand Emerging Players 276-9 (M.J. Guptill 65, G.R. Hay 43, J.D. Ryder 31) **defeated South Africa Emerging Players** 266-9 (I. Khan 98, D. Elgar 47, H. Davids 31, R.J. Schaw 3-40, B.C. Hiini 3-51) by 10 runs

AUSTRALIAN INSTITUTE OF SPORTS v NEW ZEALAND EMERGING PLAYERS
At Allan Border Field, Brisbane 22 July, 2008

Australian Institute of Sports 281-7 (D.A. Warner 89*, J.W. Hastings 57*, S.N.J. O'Keefe 47, J.D. Ryder 3-43) **lost to New Zealand Emerging Players** 282-5 (N.T. Broom 94, B-J. Watling 64*, C.J. Anderson 52*) by 5 wickets

INDIAN NATIONAL ACADEMY v SOUTH AFRICA EMERGING PLAYERS
At Albury Oval, Brisbane 22 July, 2008

Indian National Academy 315-5 (S. Dhawan 184*, V. Kohli 51, S.K. Raina 41, N.E. Mbhalati 3-72) **defeated South Africa Emerging Players** 314-7 (I. Khan 121, H. Davids 115, W.L. Coetsee 33*) by 1 run

NEW ZEALAND EMERGING PLAYERS v INDIAN NATIONAL ACADEMY
At Allan Border Field, Brisbane 23 July, 2008

New Zealand Emerging Players 116-8 (D.S. Kulkarni 3-14) **defeated Indian National Academy** 110 (R.A. Jadeja 42, B.J. Arnel 3-7) by 4 runs (D/L)

AUSTRALIAN INSTITUTE OF SPORTS v SOUTH AFRICA EMERGING PLAYERS
At Albury Oval, Brisbane 23 July, 2008

Australian Institute of Sports 208-1 (D.A. Warner 119*, T.P. Doropoulos 65) **defeated South Africa Emerging Players** 166-8 (D. Smit 33, I. Khan 30, S.N.J. O'Keefe 3-19) by 32 runs (D/L)

NEW ZEALAND EMERGING PLAYERS v SOUTH AFRICA EMERGING PLAYERS
At Peter Burge Oval, Brisbane 25 July, 2008

Abandoned without a ball being bowled

AUSTRALIAN INSTITUTE OF SPORTS v INDIAN NATIONAL ACADEMY
At Peter Burge Oval, Brisbane 25 July, 2008

Abandoned without a ball being bowled

INDIAN NATIONAL ACADEMY v SOUTH AFRICA EMERGING PLAYERS (3rd and 4th playoff)
At W.E.P. Harris Oval, Brisbane 26 July, 2008

Abandoned without a ball being bowled

AUSTRALIAN INSTITUTE OF SPORTS v NEW ZEALAND EMERGING PLAYERS (Final)
At Allan Border Field, Brisbane 26 July, 2008

Australian Institute of Sports 240-9 (S.N.J. O'Keefe 70, P.J. Forrest 46, D.A. Warner 35, J.D. Ryder 3-35, B.E. Scott 3-59) **lost to New Zealand Emerging Players** 243-7 (N.T. Broom 62, M.J. Guptill 41, B-J. Watling 40*, J.D. Ryder 36, G.J. Sullivan 3-50) by 3 wickets

QUEENSLAND v NEW ZEALAND EMERGING PLAYERS
At Cazaly's Stadium, Cairns 29, 30, 31 July, 2008

Queensland 310-6d (M.L. Love 107, C.T. Perren 59, C.P. Simpson 43*, A.J. Nye 33, A.A. Noffke 30) and 206-5d (R.J. Harris 60*, N.J. Kruger 43, A.J. Nye 41) **defeated New Zealand Emerging Players** 204-6d (J.D. Ryder 63, R.J. Schaw 37, B.B.J. Griggs 34*, S.A. Brant 3-24) and 248 (J.D. Ryder 68, C.J. Anderson 60, G.R. Hay 44, N.T. Broom 32, A.A. Noffke 4-56, R.J. Harris 3-33) by 64 runs

QUEENSLAND v NEW ZEALAND EMERGING PLAYERS (Twenty20)
At Cazaly's Stadium, Cairns 1 August, 2008

Queensland 172-6 (C.T. Perren 69) **defeated New Zealand Emerging Players** 161-7 (M.J. Guptill 61, N.T. Broom 36, A.J. Nye 3-24) by 11 runs

QUEENSLAND v NEW ZEALAND EMERGING PLAYERS
At Cazaly's Stadium, Cairns 3 August, 2008

New Zealand Emerging Players 301-9 (C.J. Anderson 69, M.J. Guptill 68, J.D. Ryder 54, B.C. Hiini 31) **lost to Queensland** 304-6 (N.J. Kruger 92*, L.A. Carseldine 49, N.J. Reardon 48, C.D. Hartley 35*, C.T. Perren 31, L.M. Burtt 3-58) by 4 wickets

NEW ZEALAND A IN AUSTRALIA & INDIA

New Zealand A played nine matches in Queensland and India during September and early October. There were three warm-up games in Brisbane before a tri-series with India A and Australia A and finally two first-class games against India A.

New Zealand A started off the tri-series with a good win over Australia A but then lost the next three games and failed to qualify for the final. The two first-class games saw both sides gain a convincing win.

The highlight of the tour was a splendid double of 105 and career-best bowling figures of 4-30 by Aaron Redmond in the second first-class game. In the first game Nathan McCullum took 6-90 (also his best in first-class cricket) while Brent Arnel showed good form with 4-38 in the second innings.

Peter Fulton topped the batting in the one-day section and BlackCap bowlers Mark Gillespie and Jeetan Patel took the most wickets.

The touring party was: P.G. Fulton *(Canterbury, co-captain)*, J.A.H. Marshall *(Northern Districts, co-captain)*, B.J. Arnel *(Northern Districts)*, T.A. Boult *(Northern Districts)*, N.T. Broom *(Otago)*, G.D. Elliott *(Wellington)*, M.R. Gillespie *(Wellington)*, M.J. Guptill *(Auckland)*, G.R. Hay *(Central Districts)*, N.L. McCullum *(Otago)*, M.J. Mason *(Central Districts)*, I.E. O'Brien *(Wellington)*, J.S. Patel *(Wellington)*, A.J. Redmond *(Otago)*, B.E. Scott *(Northern Districts)*, R.A. Young *(Auckland)*, B-J. Watling *(Northern Districts)*. Coach, M. Hesson; Bowling coach, D.R. Hadlee; Manager, G.M. Turner; Physiotherapist, S. Derry; Trainer, W. Frost; Security advisor, D. Maugham. Boult and O'Brien replaced Gillespie and Patel for the first-class games.

New Zealand A First-class Averages

BATTING	*M*	*I*	*NO*	*HS*	*Agg*	*Ave*	*100s*	*50s*	*Ct*	*St*
M.J. Guptill	1	2	0	80	121	60.50	-	1	2	-
A.J. Redmond	2	4	0	105	198	49.50	1	1	4	-
J.A.H. Marshall	2	4	0	51	172	43.00	-	1	3	-
P.G. Fulton	2	4	0	39	114	28.50	-	-	4	-
M.J. Mason	1	2	1	18*	28	28.00	-	-	-	-
G.R. Hay	2	4	0	49	98	24.50	-	-	-	-
R.A. Young	2	4	1	39*	66	22.00	-	-	7	-
B-J. Watling	2	4	1	34*	60	20.00	-	-	2	-
T.A. Boult	2	3	1	10	13	6.50	-	-	3	-
B.E. Scott	1	2	1	4*	4	4.00	-	-	-	-
N.L. McCullum	2	4	0	7	10	2.50	-	-	2	-
N.T. Broom	1	2	0	2	2	1.00	-	-	-	-
B.J. Arnel	1	2	0	2	2	1.00	-	-	-	-
I.E. O'Brien	1	1	0	0	0	0.00	-	-	1	-

BOWLING	*O*	*M*	*R*	*W*	*Ave*	*Best*	*5w*	*10w*
B.E. Scott	26	11	38	3	12.66	2-5	-	-
A.J. Redmond	44.1	8	178	10	17.80	4-30	-	-
I.E. O'Brien	35	13	72	4	18.00	3-30	-	-
B.J. Arnel	24	5	86	4	21.50	4-38	-	-
N.L. McCullum	124	20	346	12	28.83	6-90	1	-
T.A. Boult	48	10	124	4	31.00	2-34	-	-
M.J. Mason	25	7	48	1	48.00	1-23	-	-
M.J. Guptill	3	0	5	0	-	-	-	-
N.T. Broom	9	1	30	0	-	-	-	-

QUEENSLAND v NEW ZEALAND A

Not first-class

at W.E.P. Harris Oval, Brisbane on 3, 4, 5 September, 2008
Toss : New Zealand A. Umpires : D. Mealey & D.L. Moloney
Close of play: 1st day: New Zealand A 304-6, Young 62, McCullum 28; 2nd day: no play
No result.

New Zealand A won the toss and batted but both openers went within one run of each other. Fulton and Marshall added 142 for the third wicket with Fulton's 83 taking 146 deliveries while Marshall needed 138 for his 59. Young, in his first game back after a season-ending injury the previous summer, scored a run-a-ball 62 not out to take New Zealand A to 304-6 by the close. Unfortunately, rain prevented any further play.

NEW ZEALAND A

FIRST INNINGS	*Runs*	*Mins*	*Balls*	*6s*	*4s*
A.J.Redmond c Hartley b Cutting	10	52	37	-	2
B-J.Watling c Hartley b Cutting	11	36	28	-	-
P.G.Fulton* c Nye b Brant	83	201	146	-	13
J.A.H.Marshall lbw b Sullivan	59	153	138	-	8
G.R.Hay c Kruger b Doran	3	6	7	-	-
N.T.Broom c Doran b Sullivan	25	63	56	-	2
R.A.Young† not out	62	113	62	-	3
N.L.McCullum not out	28	74	66	-	2
J.S.Patel					
B.E.Scott					
M.J.Mason					
Extras (b 4, lb 4, w 3, nb 12)	23				
TOTAL (91 overs) (6 wkts dec)	**304**	352			

QUEENSLAND

R.A.Broad
C.T.Perren
A.J.Nye
G.D.Moller
N.J.Kruger
C.P.Simpson*
C.D.Hartley†
D.J.Doran
G.J.Sullivan
B.C.J.Cutting
S.A.Brant
L.W.Feldman

Bowling	*O*	*M*	*R*	*W*
QUEENSLAND				
Sullivan	16	5	45	2
Brant	15	3	44	1
Cutting	15	3	49	2
Doran	33	4	97	1
Feldman	12	1	61	0

Fall of Wickets

	NZA
	1st
1st	23
2nd	24
3rd	166
4th	169
5th	191
6th	225
7th	-
8th	-
9th-	-
10th	

QUEENSLAND v NEW ZEALAND A — One-day

at Albury Oval, Brisbane on 7 September, 2008
Toss : Queensland. Umpires : A.R. Curran & T.P. Laycock
New Zealand A won by 36 runs.

Queensland decided to bowl first and New Zealand A responded with an opening stand of 67 before Redmond went. Guptill and Broom both scored fifties with both batsmen facing 71 balls in their innings. Marshall scored at better than a run a ball in making 44 as New Zealand A reached 263-6 in its 50 overs.

Gillespie took an early wicket when the home side batted but Broad held the Queensland innings together with 72 from 115 balls. The only other player to reach thirty was Simpson with 44. Gillespie took 4-31 and Mason 3-45 as New Zealand A won by 36 runs

NEW ZEALAND A

	Runs	Mins	Balls	6s	4s
A.J.Redmond lbw b McDermott	25	61	49	-	5
M.J.Guptill c Rimmington b Boyce	57	89	71	1	8
N.T.Broom c Carseldine b McDermott	64	92	71	3	2
J.A.H.Marshall* c McDermott b Carseldine	44	49	39	2	1
G.R.Hay not out	22	53	36	-	1
G.D.Elliott c McDermott b Rimmington	28	24	25	1	2
R.A.Young† lbw b Rimmington	1	6	5	-	-
B-J.Watling not out	9	6	5	-	1
J.S.Patel					
M.R.Gillespie					
M.J.Mason					
B.J.Arnel					
Extras (lb 4, w 8, nb 1)	13				
TOTAL (50 overs) (6 wkts)	**263**	193			

QUEENSLAND

	Runs	Mins	Balls	6s	4s
N.J.Reardon b Gillespie	10	16	15	-	2
R.A.Broad b Broom	72	149	115	-	6
L.A.Carseldine c Young b Mason	24	37	27	-	3
G.C.Batticcotto c Young b Arnel	1	6	8	-	-
C.P.Simpson* b Gillespie	44	72	52	-	5
A.J.Bichel c Young b Gillespie	2	8	7	-	-
D.E.O'Brien† b Mason	24	36	27	-	3
N.J.Rimmington c Watling b Elliott	25	27	26	-	2
C.R.Swan c Redmond b Gillespie	9	17	11	-	-
C.J.Boyce c Guptill b Mason	9	11	7	-	1
S.Walter not out	0	2	0	-	-
A.McDermott					
Extras (lb 4, w 3)	7				
TOTAL (49.1 overs)	**227**	195			

Bowling	*O*	*M*	*R*	*W*
QUEENSLAND				
Swan	9	1	44	0
Walter	5	0	18	0
Simpson	7	0	42	0
Rimmington	10	0	47	2
McDermott	6	0	32	2
Boyce	4	0	34	1
Carseldine	5	0	29	1
Reardon	4	0	13	0
NEW ZEALAND A				
Arnel	10	1	38	1
Gillespie	9.1	2	31	4
Mason	10	0	45	3
Elliott	10	0	48	1
Patel	4.2	0	18	0
Broom	3.4	0	24	1
Redmond	2	0	19	0

Fall of Wickets	***NZA***	***Q***
1st	67	12
2nd	99	52
3rd	188	53
4th	206	155
5th	243	159
6th	250	159
7th	-	201
8th	-	210
9th	-	224
10th	-	227

QUEENSLAND v NEW ZEALAND A

One-day

at Albury Oval, Brisbane on 8 September, 2008
Toss : New Zealand A. Umpires : I.R. Barsby & J.J.P. O'Sullivan
New Zealand A won by 4 runs.

Fulton was the star of the game for scoring 139 from 139 balls. He hit 8 sixes and 10 fours in his innings. Broom and Elliott gave good support as New Zealand A reached 270-6.

Reardon went early in Queensland's reply and then Perren and Carseldine added 106 for the second wicket. Carseldine went on to score 102 from 121 balls. Nye scored 48 from 56 balls but New Zealand A restricted Queensland to 266-6 and registered a four run win. Gillespie, although expensive, was the most successful bowler.

NEW ZEALAND A

	Runs	Mins	Balls	6s	4s
B-J.Watling c Hartley b Brant	15	26	22	-	2
M.J.Guptill b Swards	6	31	25	-	1
P.G.Fulton* c Brant b Carseldine	139	142	139	8	10
G.R.Hay b Swards	0	1	1	-	-
G.D.Elliott lbw b Doran	32	79	55	-	3
N.T.Broom c Carseldine b Reardon	50	60	47	3	2
N.L.McCullum not out	15	10	8	1	1
R.A.Young† not out	1	5	3	-	-
B.E.Scott					
M.R.Gillespie					
M.J.Mason					
B.J.Arnel					
Extras (b 4, lb 4, w 4)	12				
TOTAL (50 overs) (6 wkts)	**270**	179			

QUEENSLAND

	Runs	Mins	Balls	6s	4s
C.T.Perren b Scott	39	99	54	-	4
N.J.Reardon c Watling b Gillespie	10	6	6	-	2
L.A.Carseldine b Arnel	102	153	121	2	6
A.J.Nye c Fulton b Gillespie	48	66	56	1	4
N.J.Kruger b Gillespie	5	15	6	-	-
C.P.Simpson* run out	15	24	17	-	-
W.J.Townsend not out	28	37	30	-	3
C.D.Hartley† not out	12	22	10	-	1
B.Laughlin					
S.A.Brant					
L.C.Swards					
D.J.Doran					
Extras (lb 2, w 5)	7				
TOTAL (50 overs) (6 wkts)	**266**	214			

Bowling	*O*	*M*	*R*	*W*
QUEENSLAND				
Swards	7	1	51	2
Brant	8	3	18	1
Laughlin	10	2	43	0
Doran	10	0	38	1
Simpson	7	0	33	0
Carseldine	6	0	58	1
Reardon	2	0	21	1
NEW ZEALAND A				
Mason	10	1	46	0
Gillespie	10	0	73	3
Arnel	8	0	32	1
Scott	10	0	57	1
McCullum	4	0	24	0
Elliott	7	0	27	0
Broom	1	0	5	0

Fall of Wickets	***NZA***	***Q***
1st	22	11
2nd	22	117
3rd	22	199
4th	117	205
5th	236	221
6th	258	231
7th	-	-
8th	-	-
9th	-	-
10th	-	-

AUSTRALIA A v NEW ZEALAND A — One-day

at Rajiv Gandhi International Stadium, Hyderabad on 15 September, 2008
Toss : New Zealand A. Umpires : S. Dua & V.D. Nerurkar
New Zealand A won by 129 runs.

Redmond went in the fourth over but Guptill and Fulton then added 104 for the second wicket with Fulton reaching fifty off 62 balls. He hit twelve boundaries. The Australian attack restricted the New Zealand batsmen to 235-9 after they had been 153-2 in the thirtieth over. Doherty, with 4-34, was the best of the bowlers.

When Australia batted Hughes went in the first over and they never recovered. Only two players were able to reach double figures and five players failed to score. The Wellington trio of Gillespie, Elliott and Patel bowled well, taking nine wickets between them, as New Zealand A won easily by 129 runs.

NEW ZEALAND A

	Runs	Mins	Balls	6s	4s
A.J.Redmond b Bollinger	5	18	12	-	-
M.J.Guptill lbw b Doherty	33	109	59	2	3
P.G.Fulton* c Tait b Bollinger	75	139	101	-	12
J.A.H.Marshall c Hughes b White	25	21	22	-	4
N.T.Broom c White b Siddle	30	61	42	1	1
G.D.Elliott st Ronchi b Doherty	10	24	20	-	1
N.L.McCullum b Doherty	2	7	7	-	-
R.A.Young† not out	13	31	21	-	1
J.S.Patel b Doherty	3	11	7	-	-
M.R.Gillespie b Noffke	2	4	5	-	-
B.E.Scott not out	8	7	6	-	1
Extras (b 1, lb 11, w 15, nb 2)	29				
TOTAL (50 overs) (9 wkts)	**235**	211			

AUSTRALIA A

	Runs	Mins	Balls	6s	4s
P.J.Hughes c Broom b Gillespie	8	4	5	-	2
L.Ronchi† lbw b Gillespie	27	34	21	-	6
D.J.Hussey c Young b Gillespie	0	7	2	-	-
C.L.White* run out	42	71	71	-	7
M.J.North c Young b Elliott	5	17	5	-	1
A.C.Voges c Young b Elliott	0	1	2	-	-
A.A.Noffke c Young b Patel	0	15	11	-	-
X.J.Doherty c Fulton b Patel	0	8	5	-	-
P.M.Siddle st Young b Patel	3	40	22	-	-
D.E.Bollinger b Patel	0	6	3	-	-
S.W.Tait not out	9	8	10	1	-
Extras (lb 5, w 6, nb 1)	12				
TOTAL (26.1 overs)	**106**	121			

Bowling	*O*	*M*	*R*	*W*
AUSTRALIA A				
Tait	7	0	36	0
Bollinger	7	1	26	2
Siddle	9	2	43	1
Noffke	9	1	49	1
White	9	1	35	1
Doherty	9	0	34	4
NEW ZEALAND A				
Gillespie	9	1	37	3
Scott	7	1	33	0
Elliott	4	1	15	2
Patel	6.1	1	16	4

Fall of Wickets	***NZA***	***AA***
1st	11	9
2nd	115	18
3rd	152	47
4th	170	67
5th	198	67
6th	204	73
7th	206	73
8th	218	97
9th	221	97
10th	-	106

16th September 2008
Hyderabad: **Australia A beat India A by 86 runs (D/L)**
India A 207 (49.4 overs) (Y.K.Pathan 54, P.Kumar 31, A.M.Nayar 30, A.A.Noffke 4-39, S.W. Tait 3-27);
Australia A 168 for 1 (27 overs) (L.Ronchi 108*, P.J.Hughes 47)

INDIA A v NEW ZEALAND A — One-day

at Rajiv Gandhi International Stadium, Hyderabad on 17 September, 2008
Toss : India A. Umpires : S. Dua & V.D. Nerurkar
India A won by 5 wickets.

New Zealand A struggled early and were 8-3 after 6.2 overs. Fulton and Broom then added 89 off 109 balls for the fourth wicket. Broom reached fifty from 56 balls but another collapse had New Zealand A at 110-6. Elliott and McCullum added 48 off 77 balls but the last four wickets fell for 9 runs to leave New Zealand A at 167. Chawla, with 3-43, was India A's most successful bowler.

India A lost early wickets but scored at a fast rate to be 60-4 after 12.4 overs. Badrinath and Karthik then added 68 off 99 balls as Badrinath reached fifty off 64 balls. India A won comfortably with 15.4 overs to spare.

NEW ZEALAND A

	Runs	Mins	Balls	6s	4s
B-J.Watling run out	1	10	9	-	-
M.J.Guptill c Karthik b Kumar	0	17	12	-	-
P.G.Fulton* c Raina b Pathan Y.K.	40	106	69	2	2
J.A.H.Marshall c Asnodkar b Pathan I.K.	1	9	8	-	-
N.T.Broom run out	52	77	57	2	5
G.D.Elliott not out	35	79	61	-	2
R.A.Young† b Chawla	0	3	2	-	-
N.L.McCullum run out	29	47	40	-	-
J.S.Patel lbw b Chawla	0	3	5	-	-
M.J.Mason c Karthik b Kumar	0	4	3	-	-
M.R.Gillespie lbw b Chawla	3	6	3	-	-
Extras (w 6)	6				
TOTAL (44.5 overs)	**167**	185			

INDIA A

	Runs	Mins	Balls	6s	4s
R.V.Uthappa c Fulton b Mason	24	35	23	1	4
S.A.Asnodkar b Gillespie	0	8	5	-	-
S.K.Raina c Guptill b Gillespie	4	9	4	-	1
S.Badrinath* not out	69	104	88	2	7
R.G.Sharma c Broom b Elliott	11	29	16	-	2
K.D.Karthik† c Young b Patel	22	68	52	-	3
Y.K.Pathan not out	31	24	20	3	1
I.K.Pathan					
P.Kumar					
P.P.Chawla					
D.S.Kulkarni					
Extras (b 1, lb 1, w 3, nb 2)	7				
TOTAL (34.2 overs) (5 wkts)	**168**	159			

Bowling	*O*	*M*	*R*	*W*
INDIA A				
Pathan I.K.	8	1	23	1
Kumar	8	1	17	2
Kulkarni	5	0	28	0
Chawla	9.5	0	43	3
Pathan Y.K.	9	0	38	1
Raina	5	0	18	0
NEW ZEALAND A				
Mason	7	1	41	1
Gillespie	9	2	34	2
Elliott	4	0	19	1
Patel	6	0	36	1
McCullum	6	1	24	0
Broom	2.2	0	12	0

Fall of Wickets	*NZA*	*IA*
1st	2	1
2nd	7	18
3rd	8	34
4th	97	60
5th	109	128
6th	110	-
7th	158	-
8th	159	-
9th	160	-
10th	167	-

INDIA A v NEW ZEALAND A — One-day

at M.A. Chidambaram Stadium, Chennai on 21 September, 2008
Toss : New Zealand A. Umpires : S. Das & M.R. Singh
India A won by 81 runs.

New Zealand A struck early claiming two wickets in the first three overs and after 12 overs the home team were 66-5. At that stage the Indian batsmen took charge. Pathan hit a glorious 148 off just 123 balls, with nine fours and nine sixes. He reached his fifty from 52 balls and his century from 103. The New Zealand A bowlers struggled with only Arnel conceding less than five runs per over. The Indian innings reached 305-9.

New Zealand A were always behind the run rate losing wickets at regular intervals. The top five batsmen all passed twenty but only Marshall was able to reach 50. Raina was the most successful bowler, taking 4-23. India A won comfortably by 81 runs meaning they qualified to meet Australia in the final.

INDIA A

	Runs	Mins	Balls	6s	4s
R.V.Uthappa c Young b Gillespie	0	15	10	-	-
S.A.Asnodkar run out	0	3	1	-	-
S.Badrinath* run out	22	42	30	-	4
K.D.Karthik† c Gillespie b Arnel	26	48	25	2	2
S.K.Raina run out	8	9	7	-	-
R.G.Sharma c Young b Gillespie	36	94	55	1	1
Y.K.Pathan c McCullum b Broom	148	163	123	9	9
I.K.Pathan c & b Broom	31	44	41	1	2
P.P.Chawla not out	16	29	15	1	-
P.Kumar					
D.S.Kulkarni					
Extras (lb 4, w 7, nb 7)	18				
TOTAL (50 overs) (8 wkts)	**305**	227			

NEW ZEALAND A

	Runs	Mins	Balls	6s	4s
A.J.Redmond c Badrinath b Kumar	23	41	39	-	2
B-J.Watling c sub (A.M.Nayar) b Kulkarni	23	83	47	-	2
P.G.Fulton* st Karthik b Chawla	42	63	39	1	5
J.A.H.Marshall lbw b Raina	51	66	49	2	3
N.T.Broom lbw b Raina	33	54	38	1	1
G.D.Elliott c Kulkarni b Pathan I.K.	8	14	13	-	-
N.L.McCullum c Chawla b Kumar	9	19	12	-	-
R.A.Young† c Uthappa b Raina	11	29	20	-	-
M.R.Gillespie c Kulkarni b Raina	13	7	8	1	1
J.S.Patel c Raina b Chawla	6	7	7	-	-
B.J.Arnel not out	0	2	2	-	-
Extras (lb 4, w 1)	5				
TOTAL (45.4 overs)	**224**	198			

Bowling	*O*	*M*	*R*	*W*
NEW ZEALAND A				
Gillespie	10	1	64	2
Arnel	10	2	41	1
Elliott	8	0	57	0
Patel	8	0	52	0
McCullum	5	0	28	0
Broom	9	0	59	2
INDIA A				
Pathan I.K.	8	2	29	1
Kumar	8	0	31	2
Kulkarni	9	0	59	1
Chawla	9.4	2	42	2
Pathan Y.K.	4	0	26	0
Raina	6	0	23	4
Badrinath	1	0	10	0

Fall of Wickets	*IA*	*NZA*
1st	0	34
2nd	6	76
3rd	53	97
4th	63	168
5th	66	183
6th	171	185
7th	230	199
8th	305	214
9th	-	220
10th	-	224

AUSTRALIA A v NEW ZEALAND A — One-day

at M.A. Chidambaram Stadium, Chennai on 22 September, 2008
Toss : New Zealand A. Umpires : S. Das & M.R. Singh
Australia A won by 8 wickets.

New Zealand decided to bat after winning the toss but were soon 2-2. Fulton (51 balls for his fifty) and Hay added 97 for the third wicket and the score reached 127-3 but then wickets tumbled with New Zealand A being all out for 144. Australian A captain White finished with 4-32.

Mason soon accounted for Ronchi but Hussey was in top form and went to his fifty from just 46 balls. White assisted Hughes in hitting off the required runs to give Australia A victory with 25.1 overs remaining.

NEW ZEALAND A

	Runs	Mins	Balls	6s	4s
A.J.Redmond run out	0	9	8	-	-
M.J.Guptill c North b Geeves	1	7	2	-	-
P.G.Fulton* c Hussey b White	65	125	73	4	3
G.R.Hay b Tait	36	97	75	-	3
G.D.Elliott c Ronchi b Doherty	12	30	24	-	2
N.T.Broom c & b White	6	27	16	-	-
R.A.Young† c Hussey b Doherty	0	3	2	-	-
B.E.Scott c Bailey b Tait	3	26	19	-	-
J.S.Patel lbw b White	0	1	1	-	-
M.R.Gillespie b White	6	11	5	1	-
M.J.Mason not out	0	5	2	-	-
Extras (lb 2, w 12, nb 1)	15				
TOTAL (37.3 overs)	**144**	175			

AUSTRALIA A

	Runs	Mins	Balls	6s	4s
P.J.Hughes not out	37	114	69	-	2
L.Ronchi† c Broom b Mason	2	6	4	-	-
D.J.Hussey c Mason b Patel	78	76	56	3	10
C.L.White* not out	22	30	23	1	4
M.J.North					
A.C.Voges					
G.J.Bailey					
A.A.Noffke					
B.Geeves					
X.J.Doherty					
S.W.Tait					
Extras (lb 1, w 2, nb 3)	6				
TOTAL (24.5 overs) (2 wkts)	**145**	159			

Bowling	O	M	R	W
AUSTRALIA A				
Tait	8	3	24	2
Geeves	8	0	37	1
Noffke	6	0	17	0
Doherty	8	0	32	2
White	7.3	0	32	4
NEW ZEALAND A				
Gillespie	7.5	0	49	0
Mason	5	0	24	1
Scott	3	0	19	0
Patel	7	2	35	1
Redmond	2	0	17	0

Fall of Wickets	*NZA*	*AA*
1st	2	6
2nd	2	118
3rd	99	-
4th	127	-
5th	127	-
6th	127	-
7th	138	-
8th	138	-
9th	138	-
10th	144	-

24th September 2008
Chennai: **India A beat Australia A by 3 wickets**
Australia A 272 for 6 (50 overs) (D.J.Hussey 74, P.J.Hughes 49*, M.J.North 40, G.J.Bailey 36, A.A.Noffke 33*, C.L.White 30);
India A 277 for 7 (46 overs) (R.G.Sharma 51, S.K.Raina 46, Y.K.Pathan 36, D.B. Ravi Teja 33)

26th September 2008 (Final)
Chennai: **Australia A beat India A by 156 runs**
Australia A 303 for 7 (50 overs) (D.J.Hussey 75, A.C.Voges 55*, L.Ronchi 52, C.L.White 50);
India A 147 (32 overs) (R.G.Sharma 46, B.Geeves 3-41)

INDIA A v NEW ZEALAND A First-class

at M.A. Chidambaram Stadium, Chennai on 28, 29, 30 September, 1 October 2008
Toss : India A. Umpires : K. Hariharan & S.L. Shastri
Close of play: 1st day: New Zealand A 36-0, Redmond 31, Watling 2; 2nd day: India A 27-1, Kukreja 15, Vijay 4
3rd day: New Zealand A 41-1, Redmond 25, Fulton 7
India A won by 129 runs.

India A decided to bat first after winning the toss but lost an early wicket. Seven batsmen passed twenty but no one could reach fifty as McCullum bowled well. He had career best figures of 6-90 as India A were dismissed for 248.

New Zealand A had a good start, with the openers putting on 65 for the first wicket, but only Redmond, Fulton and Marshall were able to pass thirty in a disappointing effort that saw the team dismissed for 230, conceding a lead of 18. The wickets were shared equally by the home team bowlers.

India A again lost an early wicket but then the innings was dominated by their captain Raina. He scored 146 from 212 balls, with eight sixes. He was severe on the spinners McCullum and Redmond and took 107 balls to reach his century. Arnel took four wickets at the end as India A were dismissed for 336, leaving New Zealand A 355 to win.

Watling went early and the New Zealand A batsmen again got starts but could not reach fifty. Marshall top scored with 47 as New Zealand A were dismissed for 225. Dinda took 5-60 and Mishra 3-55.

INDIA A

FIRST INNINGS	*Runs*	*Mins*	*Balls*	*6s*	*4s*	*SECOND INNINGS*	*Runs*	*Mins*	*Balls*	*6s*	*4s*
S.O.Kukreja lbw b Mason	5	20	18	-	1	c Young b Boult	41	130	110	-	4
S.Dhawan c Boult b McCullum	27	135	85	-	2	c Redmond b Boult	7	24	14	-	1
M.Vijay c Redmond b McCullum	45	98	66	-	7	c Fulton b Redmond	57	176	106	1	7
S.K.Raina* b Boult	21	73	64	-	2	c Marshall b McCullum	146	212	130	8	10
J.N.Shah c Boult b McCullum	38	85	55	-	5	c Young b Redmond	7	20	20	-	1
Y.K.Pathan c Boult b McCullum	44	79	63	2	4	c Watling b McCullum	25	48	36	-	2
W.P.Saha† c Redmond b McCullum	25	55	44	-	1	b Arnel	39	96	83	-	5
A.Mishra not out	23	41	29	-	4	lbw b Arnel	3	8	7	-	-
M.B.Pamar c Young b Redmond	2	4	3	-	-	lbw b Arnel	0	1	1	-	-
A.B.Dinda c McCullum b Redmond	5	17	18	-	-	b Arnel	0	3	4	-	-
S.Tyagi lbw b McCullum	3	11	11	-	-	not out	0	1	1	-	-
Extras (b 4, lb 2, w 2, nb 2)	10					(b 4, lb 3, w 2, nb 2)	11				
TOTAL (75.4 overs)	**248**	314				(85 overs)	**336**	368			

NEW ZEALAND A

	Runs	*Mins*	*Balls*	*6s*	*4s*		*Runs*	*Mins*	*Balls*	*6s*	*4s*
A.J.Redmond c Pathan b Mishra	51	117	82	1	8	c Shah b Mishra	37	123	85	1	3
B-J.Watling run out	10	107	66	-	1	lbw b Pamar	6	48	31	-	-
P.G.Fulton* b Pamar	37	149	98	1	5	c Saha b Mishra	39	81	62	-	7
G.R.Hay b Mishra	6	33	36	-	-	b Dinda	20	84	73	-	1
J.A.H.Marshall lbw b Dinda	51	116	107	-	6	lbw b Mishra	47	177	103	-	2
N.T.Broom c Vijay b Pamar	2	25	17	-	-	lbw b Dinda	0	2	1	-	-
N.L.McCullum b Dinda	0	6	2	-	-	c Saha b Dinda	3	26	22	-	-
R.A.Young† c Pamar b Tyagi	10	30	22	-	2	not out	39	110	87	-	6
B.J.Arnel lbw b Tyagi	2	10	7	-	-	(11) lbw b Dinda	0	1	1	-	-
M.J.Mason not out	18	52	47	-	2	(9) c Kukreja b Pamar	10	18	15	-	1
T.A.Boult c & b Pamar	10	40	29	-	1	(10) c Saha b Dinda	3	21	21	-	-
Extras (b 8, lb 10, w 1, nb 14)	33					(b 2, lb 5, w 3, nb 11)	21				
TOTAL (83.1 overs)	**230**	347				(81.4 overs)	**225**	349			

Bowling	*O*	*M*	*R*	*W*	*O*	*M*	*R*	*W*
NEW ZEALAND A								
Mason	12	4	23	1	13	3	25	0
Boult	14	0	42	1	12	4	34	2
Arnel	11	2	48	0	13	3	38	4
McCullum	30.4	1	90	6	28	3	118	2
Broom	2	0	8	0	7	1	22	0
Redmond	6	0	31	2	12	0	92	2
INDIA A								
Dinda	17	3	44	2	18.4	4	60	5
Tyagi	15	2	49	2	11	1	39	0
Mishra	22	4	61	2	25	4	55	3
Pamar	26.1	7	57	3	25	5	60	2
Pathan	3	2	1	0				
Raina					2	1	4	0

Fall of Wickets

	IA *1st*	*NZA* *1st*	*IA* *2nd*	*NZA* *2nd*
1st	8	65	12	22
2nd	79	71	73	90
3rd	88	89	156	90
4th	126	179	171	148
5th	156	179	230	148
6th	210	179	318	154
7th	216	181	329	201
8th	219	189	329	215
9th	237	202	329	225
10th	248	230	336	225

INDIA A v NEW ZEALAND A — First-class

at M.A. Chidambaram Stadium, Chennai on 3, 4, 5, 6 October, 2008
Toss : New Zealand A. Umpires : S.J. Phadkar & S. Rao
Close of play: 1st day: New Zealand A 270-3, Hay 44, Marshall 21; 2nd day: India A 162-3, Vijay 76, Pujara 49
3rd day: New Zealand A 107-3, Hay 15, Marshall 8
New Zealand won by 133 runs.

New Zealand A batted first and had an opening stand of 190 between Redmond and Guptill. Redmond reached his seventh first-class hundred from 192 balls and his innings lasted 308 minutes. Guptill looked good with his 80. Hay was dismissed just short of a fifty as New Zealand A made 315. Mishra took his 17th five wicket bag.

India A lost Kukreja in the second over but the other opener, Vijay, became the anchor. He made 98 off 250 balls before falling at 195. Former India captain Ganguly made 14 before being run out. Pujara scored 80 from 201 balls but India A were all out for 276, giving New Zealand A a lead of 39. Redmond had career best figures of 4-30.

In the second innings Redmond went early and the next five players all scored more than twenty but could not reach a fifty. New Zealand A declared at 194-7 to leave India A 234 to win.

New Zealand A struck early on and had India A in tatters at 25-5. Only Kukreja was able to reach twenty as the home team were dismissed for just 100. O'Brien, with 3-30, took most wickets and Scott, McCullum and Redmond each took two as New Zealand A squared the series with its 133 run win.

NEW ZEALAND A

FIRST INNINGS	*Runs*	*Mins*	*Balls*	*6s*	*4s*	*SECOND INNINGS*	*Runs*	*Mins*	*Balls*	*6s*	*4s*
A.J.Redmond b Singh	105	308	211	1	12	c Jadeja b Singh	5	21	15	-	1
M.J.Guptill c Pujara b Mishra	80	258	180	-	12	lbw b Raina	41	100	77	-	4
P.G.Fulton* c Saha b Mishra	5	9	6	-	1	b Mishra	33	50	34	2	4
G.R.Hay lbw b Singh	49	106	95	-	2	c Raina b Jadeja	23	71	71	-	1
J.A.H.Marshall c Jadeja b Mishra	31	141	90	-	2	c Vijay b Raina	43	76	72	-	3
B-J.Watling c Saha b Mishra	10	95	77	-	-	not out	34	68	67	-	3
R.A.Young† lbw b Jadeja	13	32	37	-	2	c Vijay b Mishra	4	17	23	-	-
N.L.McCullum lbw b Mishra	7	15	10	-	-	c sub (J.N.Shah) b Mishra	0	5	5	-	-
B.E.Scott lbw b Jadeja	0	3	4	-	-	not out	4	11	2	-	-
T.A.Boult not out	0	11	9	-	-						
I.E.O'Brien lbw b Mishra	0	3	5	-	-						
Extras (b 3, lb 7, w 1, nb 4)	15					(b 6, lb 1)	7				
TOTAL (120 overs)	**315**	475				(61 overs) (7 wkts dec)	**194**	213			

INDIA A

	Runs	*Mins*	*Balls*	*6s*	*4s*		*Runs*	*Mins*	*Balls*	*6s*	*4s*
S.O.Kukreja c Young b Boult	0	5	8	-	-	c Young b Redmond	31	170	142	-	2
M.Vijay c Fulton b McCullum	98	320	250	2	13	c Fulton b O'Brien	0	4	2	-	-
S.K.Raina* lbw b Scott	11	34	19	-	2	(5) run out	5	5	6	-	-
S.C.Ganguly run out	14	57	39	-	2	c Watling b Scott	6	26	17	-	1
C.A.Pujara c Young b O'Brien	80	288	201	-	5	(3) c McCullum b O'Brien	0	6	3	-	-
R.A.Jadeja c O'Brien b Redmond	33	171	125	-	3	c Young b Scott	4	5	6	-	-
W.P.Saha† c Guptill b McCullum	10	28	21	-	2	lbw b O'Brien	16	74	61	-	-
A.Mishra c & b Redmond	2	28	15	-	-	c Guptill b Redmond	7	53	41	-	-
R.P.Singh c Marshall b Redmond	6	27	22	-	-	lbw b McCullum	7	15	18	-	1
P.Sangwan c Fulton b Redmond	2	9	12	-	-	c Marshall b McCullum	11	29	26	-	2
A.B.Dinda not out	0	5	4	-	-	not out	10	25	18	-	2
Extras (b 14, lb 4, w 1, nb 1)	20					(lb 2, w 1)	3				
TOTAL (119.1 overs)	**276**	492				(58.2 overs)	**100**	215			

Bowling	*O*	*M*	*R*	*W*	*O*	*M*	*R*	*W*
INDIA A								
Singh	21	7	57	2	6	0	23	1
Dinda	19	4	48	0	3	2	10	0
Sangwan	15	3	55	0	2	0	17	0
Mishra	35	12	81	6	22	5	65	3
Jadeja	24	8	50	2	16	6	36	1
Raina	6	1	14	0	10	2	27	2
Ganguly					2	0	9	0
NEW ZEALAND A								
O'Brien	22	9	42	1	13	4	30	3
Boult	18	5	43	1	4	1	5	0
Scott	22	9	33	1	4	2	5	2
McCullum	44	8	105	2	21.2	8	33	2
Redmond	10.1	2	30	4	16	6	25	2
Guptill	3	0	5	0				

Fall of Wickets

	NZA *1st*	***IA*** *1st*	***NZA*** *2nd*	***IA*** *2nd*
1st	190	1	10	1
2nd	195	24	70	1
3rd	229	96	92	12
4th	275	195	129	21
5th	285	221	158	25
6th	305	236	176	56
7th	314	248	182	69
8th	315	270	-	78
9th	315	274	-	78
10th	315	276	-	100

NEW ZEALAND IN BANGLADESH

New Zealand made its second official tour of Bangladesh playing three one-day internationals and two test matches. A warm up game prior to the first one-day international was rained off.

New Zealand lost the first one-day international giving the hosts their first win in 12 attempts against New Zealand. The BlackCaps won the next two matches, however, to take the series 2-1. In the first test New Zealand had to come from behind to win by three wickets while the final test ended with New Zealand on top after the first three days were lost to rain.

In the one-day series Ross Taylor scored the only century with 103 in the third match. Jacob Oram hit fifties in each of the first two games and Jamie How scored 73 in the final match. Kyle Mills was the leading New Zealand bowler with six wickets at an average of 10.83

The test series belonged to the captain Daniel Vettori. In the first test he joined the group who have made two fifties in a test, with scores of 55 not out and 76. He also scored a fifty and took five wickets in an innings for the third time in his test career when he took 5-59 and 4-74. Aaron Redmond scored his maiden test fifty and new cap Jesse Ryder scored 91 in the second test. Vettori took 14 wickets in three innings and was ably assisted by Iain O'Brien, who took eight wickets in unhelpful conditions.

The touring party was: D.L. Vettori *(captain, Northern Districts)*, G.D. Elliott *(Wellington)*, D.R. Flynn *(Northern Districts)*, M.R. Gillespie *(Wellington)*, G.J. Hopkins *(Auckland)*, J.M. How *(Central Districts)*, M.J. Mason *(Central Districts)*, B.B. McCullum *(Otago)*, K.D. Mills *(Auckland)*, I.E. O'Brien *(Wellington)*, J.D.P. Oram *(Central Districts)*, J.S. Patel *(Wellington)*, A.J. Redmond *(Otago)*, J.D. Ryder *(Wellington)*, T.G. Southee *(Northern Districts)*, S.B. Styris *(Auckland)*, L.R.P.L. Taylor *(Central Districts)*. Coach, J.G. Bracewell; Batting coach, M.D. O'Neill; Bowling coaches, V.F. Johnson and D.R. Hadlee; Fielding coach/Video analyst, T. Wilson; Manager, L.M. Crocker; Physiotherapist, R. Marsden, Trainer, B. Stronach.

Redmond and O'Brien replaced Styris and Mason for the test matches. C.S. Martin *(Auckland)* withdrew from the original selection because of injury and was replaced by Mason (one-day games) and Gillespie (tests).

New Zealand Test Averages

BATTING	*M*	*I*	*NO*	*HS*	*Agg*	*Ave*	*100s*	*50s*	*Ct*	*St*
D.L. Vettori	2	3	1	76	153	76.50	-	2	3	-
J.D. Ryder	2	4	1	91	169	56.33	-	1	1	-
D.R. Flynn	2	3	1	49	103	51.50	-	-	1	-
A.J. Redmond	2	4	1	79	130	43.33	-	1	3	-
B.B. McCullum	2	3	0	66	93	31.00	-	1	3	3
J.M. How	2	4	0	36	68	17.00	-	-	1	-
L.R.P.L. Taylor	2	3	0	19	40	13.33	-	-	3	-
J.D.P. Oram	1	2	1	8*	8	8.00	-	-	-	-
K.D. Mills	2	2	1	4	5	5.00	-	-	1	-
I.E. O'Brien	2	1	0	5	5	5.00	-	-	-	-
J.S. Patel	2	1	0	0	0	0.00	-	-	-	-
G.D. Elliott	1	1	1	8*	8	-	-	-	-	-

BOWLING	*O*	*M*	*R*	*W*	*Ave*	*Best*	*5w*	*10w*
A.J. Redmond	4.3	1	11	1	11.00	1-8	-	-
I.E. O'Brien	53.1	21	95	8	11.87	3-31	-	-
D.L. Vettori	97	34	199	14	14.21	5-59	2	-
J.S. Patel	56.1	20	165	5	33.00	2-53	-	-
K.D. Mills	46	13	123	1	123.00	1-55	-	-
J.D. Ryder	3	1	10	0	-	-	-	-
J.D.P. Oram	28	16	33	0	-	-	-	-

Bangladesh Test Averages

BATTING	*M*	*I*	*NO*	*HS*	*Agg*	*Ave*	*100s*	*50s*	*Ct*	*St*
Shakib Al Hasan	2	3	0	71	125	41.66	-	1	1	-
Mushfiqur Rahim	2	3	0	79	118	39.33	-	1	2	-
Mehrab Hossain	2	3	0	83	96	32.00	-	1	1	-
Masrafe bin Mortaza	2	3	0	48	92	30.66	-	-	1	-
Tamim Iqbal	2	3	0	33	75	25.00	-	-	-	-
Abdur Razzaq	2	3	1	18	45	22.50	-	-	2	-
Naeem Islam	1	2	0	19	33	16.50	-	-	1	-
Rajin Saleh	2	3	0	20	26	8.66	-	-	2	-
Shahadat Hossain	2	3	2	4	4	4.00	-	-	-	-
Zunaed Siddique	2	3	0	6	10	3.33	-	-	1	-
Mohammad Ashraful	2	3	0	2	2	0.66	-	-	1	-
Mahbubul Alam	1	1	1	0*	0	-	-	-	-	-

BOWLING	*O*	*M*	*R*	*W*	*Ave*	*Best*	*5w*	*10w*
Shakib Al Hasan	95.4	29	178	10	17.80	7-36	1	-
Mohammad Ashraful	9	0	38	2	19.00	1-3	-	-
Naeem Islam	15	2	27	1	27.00	1-11	-	-
Masrafe bin Mortaza	32	10	85	3	28.33	1-14	-	-
Abdur Razzaq	97	19	224	5	44.80	3-93	-	-
Mahbubul Alam	11	1	49	1	49.00	1-37	-	-
Shahadat Hossain	36	1	140	1	140.00	1-39	-	-
Tamim Iqbal	1	0	1	0	-	-	-	-
Zunaed Siddique	2	0	2	0	-	-	-	-
Mehrab Hossain	10	0	45	0	-	-	-	-

New Zealand One-day International Averages

BATTING	*M*	*I*	*NO*	*HS*	*Agg*	*Ave*	*100s*	*50s*	*Ct*	*St*	*SR*
J.D.P. Oram	3	3	1	75*	135	67.50	-	2	3	-	85
L.R.P.L. Taylor	3	3	0	103	138	46.00	1	-	-	-	77
J.M. How	3	3	0	73	80	26.66	-	1	1	-	67
K.D. Mills	3	3	1	18*	51	25.50	-	-	-	-	69
D.L. Vettori	3	3	1	30	50	25.00	-	-	1	-	62
J.D. Ryder	3	3	0	34	67	22.33	-	-	3	-	69
T.G. Southee	3	2	1	19*	19	19.00	-	-	-	-	111
D.R. Flynn	3	3	0	25	36	12.00	-	-	-	-	45
B.B. McCullum	3	3	0	14	32	10.66	-	-	5	-	66
S.B. Styris	3	3	0	12	16	5.33	-	-	1	-	41
J.S. Patel	2	1	1	4*	4	-	-	-	-	-	28
M.R. Gillespie	1	1	1	2*	2	-	-	-	-	-	100

BOWLING	*O*	*M*	*R*	*W*	*Ave*	*Best*	*R/O*
K.D. Mills	21.4	4	65	6	10.83	3-13	3.00
J.D.P. Oram	21	4	50	4	12.50	2-16	2.38
J.S. Patel	14	3	44	2	22.00	2-29	3.14
J.D. Ryder	4	0	25	1	25.00	1-16	6.25
M.R. Gillespie	8.3	1	37	1	37.00	1-37	4.35
S.B. Styris	12	0	45	1	45.00	1-22	3.75
T.G. Southee	28	0	114	2	57.00	1-33	4.07
D.L. Vettori	28	0	112	1	112.00	1-25	4.00
D.R. Flynn	1	0	6	0	-	-	6.00

Bangladesh One-day International Averages

BATTING	*M*	*I*	*NO*	*HS*	*Agg*	*Ave*	*100s*	*50s*	*Ct*	*St*	*SR*
Mohammad Ashraful	3	3	1	60*	108	54.00	-	1	2	-	72
Naeem Islam	3	2	1	46*	46	46.00	-	-	3	-	43
Zunaed Siddique	3	3	0	85	118	39.33	-	1	3	-	55
Mushfiqur Rahim	3	3	0	30	56	18.66	-	-	1	-	45
Masrafe bin Mortaza	3	2	0	27	36	18.00	-	-	-	-	75
Tamim Iqbal	3	3	0	35	47	15.66	-	-	1	-	88
Abdur Razzaq	3	2	0	27	30	15.00	-	-	-	-	88
Shahadat Hossain	3	2	1	12*	12	12.00	-	-	1	-	75
Imrul Kayes	1	1	0	12	12	12.00	-	-	-	-	42
Shakib Al Hasan	3	3	1	10	16	8.00	-	-	-	-	42
Mahmudullah	2	1	0	8	8	8.00	-	-	2	-	38
Syed Rasel	3	1	1	0*	0	-	-	-	3	-	0

BOWLING	*O*	*M*	*R*	*W*	*Ave*	*Best*	*R/O*
Masrafe bin Mortaza	30	6	123	7	17.57	4-44	4.10
Shakib Al Hasan	30	0	91	5	18.20	2-20	3.03
Syed Rasel	22	4	81	4	20.25	3-23	3.68
Naeem Islam	22	0	104	3	34.66	2-20	4.73
Abdur Razzaq	29	0	152	4	38.00	3-33	5.24
Shahadat Hossain	15	0	82	1	82.00	1-29	5.47
Mahmudullah	2	0	8	0	-	-	4.00

BANGLADESH CRICKET BOARD XI v NEW ZEALAND One-day

at Narayanganj Osmani Stadium, Fatulla on 7 October, 2008
Abandoned without a ball being bowled.

BANGLADESH v NEW ZEALAND First One-day International

at Sher-e-Bangla National Stadium, Mirpur on 9 October, 2008
Toss : Bangladesh. Umpires : D.J. Harper & Nadir Shah
Bangladesh won by 7 wickets.

Bangladesh won the toss and decided to bowl on a wicket which gave the bowlers every encouragement. New Zealand reached 47 before the first wicket fell but then there was a collapse to 79-6 before Oram and Vettori added 70 for the seventh wicket, a New Zealand record against Bangladesh. Oram got to his fifty from 79 balls but New Zealand managed only 201-9.

Bangladesh lost an early wicket but a stand of 109 off 106 balls for the third wicket ensured that Bangladesh would win its first one-day international against New Zealand at its twelfth attempt. Siddique scored his fifty from 92 balls while Ashraful needed 46 deliveries for his fifty. The win was achieved with 27 balls to spare.

NEW ZEALAND

	Runs	Mins	Balls	6s	4s
J.D.Ryder c Mahmudullah b Mortaza	34	52	35	1	4
B.B.McCullum† c Rasel b Mortaza	14	40	21	-	3
J.M.How lbw b Mortaza	7	36	20	-	1
L.R.P.L.Taylor c Ashraful b Shahadat	2	7	4	-	-
S.B.Styris lbw b Razzaq	4	27	13	-	-
D.R.Flynn c Mahmudullah b Razzaq	6	24	20	-	-
J.D.P.Oram c Rasel b Razzaq	57	111	89	1	4
D.L.Vettori* c Naeem b Shakib	30	72	57	-	4
K.D.Mills c Shahadat b Mortaza	16	30	26	1	1
T.G.Southee not out	19	16	14	1	2
M.R.Gillespie not out	2	10	2	-	-
Extras (lb 5, w 5)	10				
TOTAL (50 overs) (9 wkts)	**201**	217			

BANGLADESH

	Runs	Mins	Balls	6s	4s
Tamim Iqbal c Styris b Mills	12	18	12	-	2
Zunaed Siddique c Oram b Gillespie	85	189	137	-	8
Mushfiqur Rahim† c Ryder b Styris	30	84	59	1	1
Mohammad Ashraful* not out	60	97	56	1	5
Shakib Al Hasan not out	5	10	9	-	-
Naeem Islam					
Mahmudullah					
Masrafe bin Mortaza					
Abdur Razzaq					
Shahadat Hossain					
Syed Rasel					
Extras (lb 6, w 4)	10				
TOTAL (45.3 overs) (3 wkts)	**202**	200			

Bowling	O	M	R	W
BANGLADESH				
Mortaza	10	3	44	4
Rasel	2	0	18	0
Shahadat	6	0	29	1
Shakib	10	0	30	1
Razzaq	10	0	33	3
Naeem	10	0	34	0
Mahmudullah	2	0	8	0
NEW ZEALAND				
Mills	7	0	28	1
Gillespie	8.3	1	37	1
Southee	9	0	41	0
Oram	5	0	11	0
Vettori	9	0	48	0
Styris	6	0	22	1
Ryder	1	0	9	0

Fall of Wickets

	NZ	*B*
1st	47	18
2nd	55	85
3rd	59	194
4th	62	-
5th	65	-
6th	79	-
7th	149	-
8th	174	-
9th	185	-
10th	-	-

BANGLADESH v NEW ZEALAND Second One-day International

at Sher-e-Bangla National Stadium, Mirpur on 11 October, 2008
Toss : Bangladesh. Umpires : D.J. Harper & Nadir Shah
New Zealand won by 75 runs.

Bangladesh again decided to put New Zealand in to bat and again had the Blackcaps in trouble. They went from 31-0 to 45-4 and at 115-7 were in dire straits. An unbroken last wicket stand of 45 got New Zealand past the 200 mark. Oram reached fifty from 56 balls.

The home side lost a wicket to the second ball of the innings and never really recovered. Only three batsmen were able to pass 25. Mills bowled well to lead the New Zealand attack, finishing with 3-13, as New Zealand won by 75 runs with 44 balls to spare and levelled the series.

NEW ZEALAND

	Runs	Mins	Balls	6s	4s
J.D.Ryder c & b Rasel	30	63	42	-	4
B.B.McCullum† c Zunaed b Rasel	12	34	15	1	1
J.M.How c Ashraful b Rasel	0	20	16	-	-
L.R.P.L.Taylor c Zunaed b Shakib	33	93	54	2	2
S.B.Styris c Zunaed b Mortaza	0	7	8	-	-
D.R.Flynn b Naeem	25	56	46	1	2
J.D.P.Oram not out	75	100	62	4	5
D.L.Vettori* c & b Naeem	1	5	6	-	-
K.D.Mills b Shakib	17	39	35	-	2
T.G.Southee run out	0	10	3	-	-
J.S.Patel not out	4	22	14	-	-
Extras (lb 12, w 2, nb 1)	15				
TOTAL (50 overs) (9 wkts)	**212**	229			

BANGLADESH

	Runs	Mins	Balls	6s	4s
Tamim Iqbal lbw b Mills	0	1	2	-	-
Zunaed Siddique c Vettori b Southee	32	117	67	-	3
Mushfiqur Rahim† b Mills	11	34	28	-	1
Mohammad Ashraful*c McCullum b Oram	40	121	86	-	2
Shakib Al Hasan c Oram b Vettori	10	17	17	-	1
Naeem Islam run out	0	2	0	-	-
Mahmudullah run out	8	29	21	-	-
Masrafe bin Mortaza c Oram b Mills	27	33	27	1	3
Abdur Razzaq b Oram	3	6	3	-	-
Shahadat Hossain run out	0	10	2	-	-
Syed Rasel not out	0	5	2	-	-
Extras (lb 5, w 1)	6				
TOTAL (42.4 overs)	**137**	192			

Bowling	*O*	*M*	*R*	*W*
BANGLADESH				
Mortaza	10	1	29	1
Rasel	10	4	23	3
Razzaq	9	0	67	0
Shahadat	7	0	41	0
Shakib	10	0	20	2
Naeem	4	0	20	2
NEW ZEALAND				
Mills	6.4	3	13	3
Southee	9	0	33	1
Oram	8	2	23	2
Styris	6	0	23	0
Patel	4	0	15	0
Vettori	9	0	25	1

Fall of Wickets

	NZ	*B*
1st	31	0
2nd	43	18
3rd	44	71
4th	45	86
5th	86	86
6th	112	106
7th	115	111
8th	156	115
9th	167	132
10th	-	137

BANGLADESH v NEW ZEALAND Third One-day International

at Chittagong Divisional Stadium on 14 October, 2008
Toss : New Zealand. Umpires : Enamul Haque & D.J. Harper
New Zealand won by 79 runs.

The third game of the series was played at Chittagong, with New Zealand deciding to bat first. Both openers were back in the pavilion after 37 balls but How and Taylor then added 125 from 155 balls for the third wicket. How reached fifty from 54 balls while Taylor scord his half-century off 74 balls and his third century from 117 deliveries. New Zealand scored 249-7, with 30 runs coming off the last three overs.

Bangladesh again lost an early wicket and struggled from then on. Only Tamim and Naeem reached thirty. The wickets were shared by the bowlers as New Zealand won by 79 runs, winning the series 2-1.

NEW ZEALAND

	Runs	Mins	Balls	6s	4s
J.D.Ryder b Rasel	3	16	20	-	-
B.B.McCullum† lbw b Mortaza	6	29	12	-	-
J.M.How lbw b Naeem	73	113	82	-	10
L.R.P.L.Taylor c Mushfiqur b Mortaza	103	175	119	4	5
S.B.Styris lbw b Shakib	12	24	18	-	1
J.D.P.Oram c Tamim b Shakib	3	12	6	-	-
D.R.Flynn c Naeem b Razzaq	5	19	14	-	-
D.L.Vettori* not out	19	32	17	1	-
K.D.Mills not out	18	16	12	1	1
T.G.Southee					
J.S.Patel					
Extras (lb 4, w 3)	7				
TOTAL (50 overs) (7 wkts)	**249**	221			

BANGLADESH

	Runs	Mins	Balls	6s	4s
Tamim Iqbal c McCullum b Patel	35	53	39	-	5
Zunaed Siddique c Ryder b Mills	1	11	7	-	-
Imrul Kayes c McCullum b Oram	12	39	28	-	1
Mohammad Ashraful* b Oram	8	14	7	-	1
Shakib Al Hasan c Ryder b Patel	1	21	12	-	-
Naeem Islam not out	46	134	106	-	5
Mushfiqur Rahim† c How b Southee	15	33	35	-	1
Masrafe bin Mortaza c McCullum b Mills	9	27	21	-	-
Abdur Razzaq c McCullum b Ryder	27	47	31	1	2
Shahadat Hossain not out	12	16	14	-	2
Syed Rasel					
Extras (w 4)	4				
TOTAL (50 overs) (8 wkts)	**170**	201			

Bowling	*O*	*M*	*R*	*W*
BANGLADESH				
Mortaza	10	2	50	2
Rasel	10	0	40	1
Razzaq	10	0	52	1
Shakib	10	0	41	2
Naeem	8	0	50	1
Shahadat	2	0	12	0
NEW ZEALAND				
Mills	8	1	24	2
Southee	10	0	40	1
Patel	10	3	29	2
Oram	8	2	16	2
Vettori	10	0	39	0
Ryder	3	0	16	1
Flynn	1	0	6	0

Fall of Wickets

	NZ	*B*
1st	5	13
2nd	13	49
3rd	138	49
4th	172	57
5th	179	59
6th	201	77
7th	219	98
8th	-	144
9th	-	-
10th	-	-

BANGLADESH v NEW ZEALAND — First Test

at Chittagong Divisional Stadium on 17, 18, 19, 20, 21 October, 2008
Toss : Bangladesh. Umpires : E.A.R. de Silva & D.J. Harper
Close of play: 1st day: Bangladesh 183-4, Mehrab 79, Mushfiqur 59; 2nd day: NZ 155-9, Vettori 48
3rd day: Bangladesh 184-8, Mortaza 5, Razzaq 0; 4th day: NZ 145-2, Redmond 62, Vettori 0
New Zealand won by 3 wickets.

Bangladesh put up a brave showing in this game. This was the first test since 14 of their players had signed with the ICL. The home team made 245, thanks mainly to a 144 run stand for the fifth wicket between Mehrab (fifty off 84 balls) and Mushfiqur (fifty off 138 balls) which was a record for Bangladesh against all countries. Vettori took his 16th five wicket haul and had good assistance from O'Brien, who took 3-36.

New Zealand struggled when they batted. Wickets fell regularly and only an unbeaten 55 from Vettori saw the visitors through to 171. His fifty came from 73 deliveries. Shakib returned the best bowling figures for Bangladesh in test cricket with his 7-36. The home side gained a handy lead of 74.

However, they were in trouble at 71-5 in the second innings before 71 from Shakib (fifty off 105 balls) saw them to 242. Vettori took 4-74 to give him nine wickets in the match. This left New Zealand 317 to win, their highest successful run chase overseas being 164-4 against Australia in 1985/86.

There was more fight in New Zealand's batting the second time. How reached 36, Redmond recorded his first test fifty, off 135 balls, and Ryder made 38. Vettori came in as night-watchman, at 145-2, and was not dismissed until the score was 298. He was ably assisted by Flynn, who was dismissed one run short of a maiden test fifty and victory. Oram suffered a back injury during the Bangladesh second innings.

BANGLADESH

FIRST INNINGS	*Runs*	*Mins*	*Balls*	*6s*	*4s*	*SECOND INNINGS*	*Runs*	*Mins*	*Balls*	*6s*	*4s*
Tamim Iqbal c McCullum b Vettori	18	123	90	-	2	c & b Vettori	33	132	100	-	5
Zunaed Siddique lbw b O'Brien	0	4	1	-	-	c Redmond b Mills	6	28	16	-	1
Rajin Saleh b O'Brien	20	151	129	-	-	lbw b Patel	6	30	23	-	1
Mohammad Ashraful* lbw b Vettori	2	39	35	-	-	c Redmond b Vettori	0	4	2	-	-
Mehrab Hossain c Redmond b O'Brien	83	228	179	-	11	c Mills b Patel	6	19	18	-	1
Mushfiqur Rahim† c How b Vettori	79	299	210	1	12	b O'Brien	32	165	121	-	4
Naeem Islam st McCullum b Patel	14	72	46	-	2	(8) lbw b Vettori	19	97	70	-	2
Shakib Al Hasan c Vettori b Patel	5	30	18	-	1	(7) c Taylor b Vettori	71	203	151	-	12
Masrafe bin Mortaza c Ryder b Vettori	0	3	3	-	-	st McCullum b Redmond	44	111	87	-	7
Abdur Razzaq c McCullum b Vettori	11	19	22	-	1	c Taylor b O'Brien	18	56	45	-	2
Shahadat Hossain not out	0	1	0	-	-	not out	0	47	17	-	-
Extras (b 12, lb 1)	13					(b 4, lb 1, nb 2)	7				
TOTAL (122.1 overs)	**245**	481				(107.3 overs)	**242**	388			

NEW ZEALAND

	Runs	*Mins*	*Balls*	*6s*	*4s*		*Runs*	*Mins*	*Balls*	*6s*	*4s*
A.J.Redmond lbw b Shakib	19	113	65	-	2	(2) c Zunaed b Shakib	79	325	237	-	10
J.M.How c Saleh b Shakib	16	74	46	-	2	(1) b Razzaq	36	132	82	1	5
J.D.Ryder c Saleh b Shakib	1	7	5	-	-	run out	38	156	101	-	4
L.R.P.L.Taylor lbw b Razzaq	12	19	22	-	2	(5) c sub (Mahbubul Alam) b Mortaza	9	39	20	-	-
B.B.McCullum† c Razzaq b Shakib	25	58	37	-	4	(6) lbw b Razzaq	2	22	9	-	-
D.R.Flynn c Mushfiqur b Naeem	19	41	42	1	2	(7) c Naeem b Shakib	49	158	126	-	6
J.D.P.Oram c Mortaza b Shakib	0	9	4	-	-	(8) not out	8	35	35	-	1
D.L.Vettori* not out	55	117	82	-	7	(4) b Razzaq	76	265	213	-	7
K.D.Mills c Mushfiqur b Shakib	4	58	44	-	-	not out	1	3	4	-	-
J.S.Patel c Shakib b Ashraful	0	38	31	-	-						
I.E.O'Brien b Shakib	5	16	12	-	-						
Extras (b 8, lb 6, nb 1)	15					(b 13, lb 3, w 3)	19				
TOTAL (64.5 overs)	**171**	276				(137.5 overs) (7 wkts)	**317**	554			

Bowling	*O*	*M*	*R*	*W*	*O*	*M*	*R*	*W*
NEW ZEALAND								
Mills	19	7	46	0	18	2	55	1
O'Brien	23	11	36	3	17	7	28	2
Oram	20	14	14	0	8	2	19	0
Ryder	3	1	10	0				
Patel	21.1	7	67	2	20	7	53	2
Vettori	36	15	59	5	42	13	74	4
Redmond					2.3	1	8	1
BANGLADESH								
Mortaza	7	4	13	0	14	4	37	1
Shahadat	11	0	35	0	11	1	46	0
Shakib	25.5	6	36	7	44.5	17	79	2
Razzaq	16	1	51	1	50	15	93	3
Mehrab	1	0	8	0	2	0	6	0
Naeem	3	0	11	1	12	2	16	0
Ashraful	1	0	3	1	4	0	24	0

Fall of Wickets	**B** *1st*	**NZ** *1st*	**B** *2nd*	**NZ** *2nd*
1st	0	27	24	55
2nd	34	29	36	145
3rd	40	46	37	185
4th	44	52	49	209
5th	188	99	71	216
6th	229	99	127	298
7th	229	100	175	316
8th	229	126	180	-
9th	245	155	220	-
10th	245	171	242	-

BANGLADESH v NEW ZEALAND — Second Test

at Shere Bangla National Stadium, Mirpur on 25, 26, 27, 28, 29 October, 2008
Toss : Bangladesh. Umpires : E.A.R. de Silva & D.J. Harper
Close of play: 1st day: no play; 2nd day: no play
3rd day: no play; 4th day: Bangladesh 13-3, Tamim 8, Mehrab 0
Match drawn.

Elliott replaced the injured Oram who returned home. The first three days' play were washed out as Dhaka recovered from a cyclone.

Bangladesh decided to field first and had both openers out with the score at 10. Ryder and McCullum added 137 for the fourth wicket. Ryder's maiden test fifty came from 78 balls while McCullum needed 86 balls for his fifty. New Zealand declared at 262-6 and had the home side 13-3 at stumps, with Vettori taking three wickets in his only over.

On the last day Bangladesh continued to struggle and slumped to 44-6 before Shakib and Mortaza added 78 for the seventh wicket. Vettori took his 17th five wicket haul and O'Brien finished with 3-31 as Bangladesh passed the 100-run follow-on target, declaring at 169-9. New Zealand batted out time, losing one wicket, and the match finished in a draw.

NEW ZEALAND

FIRST INNINGS	*Runs*	*Mins*	*Balls*	*6s*	*4s*	*SECOND INNINGS*	*Runs*	*Mins*	*Balls*	*6s*	*4s*
A.J.Redmond lbw b Mortaza	2	15	7	-	-	(2) not out	30	139	89	-	4
J.M.How b Mahbubul	8	18	11	-	2	(1) c Razzaq b Mortaza	8	20	14	-	1
J.D.Ryder c Mehrab b Razzaq	91	203	140	-	12	not out	39	118	84	-	3
L.R.P.L.Taylor b Shahadat	19	56	36	-	3						
B.B.McCullum† c Ashraful b Shakib	66	174	122	1	8						
D.R.Flynn not out	35	81	81	-	3						
D.L.Vettori* b Ashraful	22	27	34	1	2						
G.D.Elliott not out	8	25	21	-	-						
K.D.Mills											
J.S.Patel											
I.E.O'Brien											
Extras (b 6, lb 3, nb 2)	11					(b 1, nb 1)	2				
TOTAL (75 overs) (6 wkts dec)	**262**	300				(31 overs) (1 wkt dec)	**79**	139			

BANGLADESH

	Runs	Mins	Balls	6s	4s
Tamim Iqbal c Taylor b Vettori	24	98	75	-	2
Zunaed Siddique st McCullum b Vettori	4	36	25	-	-
Mohammad Ashraful* lbw b Vettori	0	2	2	-	-
Rajin Saleh lbw b Vettori	0	2	3	-	-
Mehrab Hossain lbw b Patel	7	27	23	-	1
Mushfiqur Rahim† c McCullum b O'Brien	7	34	27	-	1
Shakib Al Hasan lbw b Vettori	49	112	87	-	6
Masrafe bin Mortaza c Flynn b O'Brien	48	129	89	2	7
Abdur Razzaq not out	16	30	16	-	3
Shahadat Hossain c Vettori b O'Brien	4	5	3	-	1
Mahbubul Alam not out	0	1	0	-	-
Extras (lb 2, w 6, nb 2)	10				
TOTAL (58.1 overs) (9 wkts dec)	**169**	242			

Bowling	*O*	*M*	*R*	*W*	*O*	*M*	*R*	*W*
BANGLADESH								
Mortaza	6	1	21	1	5	1	14	1
Mahbubul	8	0	37	1	3	1	12	0
Razzaq	25	2	72	1	6	1	8	0
Shahadat	8	0	39	1	6	0	20	0
Shakib	22	6	57	1	3	0	6	0
Mehrab	3	0	20	0	4	0	11	0
Ashraful	3	0	7	1	1	0	4	0
Zunaed					2	0	2	0
Tamim					1	0	1	0
NEW ZEALAND								
Mills	9	4	22	0				
O'Brien	13.1	3	31	3				
Patel	15	6	45	1				
Vettori	19	6	66	5				
Redmond	2	0	3	0				

Fall of Wickets

	NZ 1st	*B 1st*	*NZ 2nd*
1st	10	13	8
2nd	10	13	-
3rd	49	13	-
4th	186	26	-
5th	201	44	-
6th	233	44	-
7th	-	122	-
8th	-	155	-
9th	-	169	-
10th	-	-	-

NEW ZEALAND IN AUSTRALIA

New Zealand toured Australia in November for two tests and returned in February for a five-match Chappell-Hadlee series which ended 2-2 with one game abandoned.

There were many changes between the two tours. John Bracewell coached the side for the test series but in the one-day series new coach Andy Moles guided the side. In the first-class section, the only century was Jamie How's 170 against New South Wales. In the tests only Aaron Redmond, Ross Taylor and Brendon McCullum made fifties as the side were only able to pass 250 once. In the bowling line-up Chris Martin and Iain O'Brien were the leading wicket-takers with Daniel Vettori giving good support.

Grant Elliott hit a maiden one-day international century in the Chappell-Hadlee series, with Taylor, and Martin Guptill getting fifties. O'Brien (10) and Kyle Mills (9) were the leading wicket-takers. The one-day series was notable for the introduction of new players with Ryder, Styris and Oram all unfit. Ryder was selected but withdrew due to injury.

The touring party for the tests was: D.L. Vettori *(captain, Northern Districts)*, G.D. Elliott *(Wellington)*, D.R. Flynn *(Northern Districts)*, P.G. Fulton *(Canterbury)*, M.R. Gillespie *(Wellington)*, G.J. Hopkins *(Auckland)*, J.M. How *(Central Districts)*, B.B. McCullum *(Otago)*, C.S. Martin *(Auckland)*, K.D. Mills *(Auckland)*, I.E. O'Brien *(Wellington)*, J.S. Patel *(Wellington)*, A.J. Redmond *(Otago)*, J.D. Ryder *(Wellington)*, T.G. Southee *(Northern Districts)*, L.R.P.L. Taylor *(Central Districts)*. Coach, J.G. Bracewell; Batting coach, M.D. O'Neill; Bowling coach, D.R. Hadlee; Fielding coach/Video analyst, T. Wilson; Manager, L.M. Crocker; Physiotherapist, K. Stalker, Trainer, B. Stronach.

Only thirteen of the squad originally travelled to Australia with Fulton and Hopkins remaining in New Zealand to play domestic cricket. Hopkins returned to New Zealand after the first test to play for Auckland and went back to Australia as cover for McCullum prior to the second test. Patel replaced Mills after the first test while Elliott and Gillespie returned to New Zealand during the second test to play for Wellington.

The squad for the Chappell-Hadlee series was: D.L. Vettori *(captain, Northern Districts)*, T.A. Boult *(Northern Districts)*, N.T. Broom *(Otago)*, C.D. Cumming *(Otago)*, B.J. Diamanti *(Central Districts)*, G.D. Elliott *(Wellington)*, P.G. Fulton *(Canterbury)*, M.J. Guptill *(Auckland)*, G.J. Hopkins *(Auckland)*, B.B. McCullum *(Otago)*, K.D. Mills *(Auckland)*, I.E. O'Brien *(Wellington)*, J.S. Patel *(Wellington)*, T.G. Southee *(Northern Districts)*, L.R.P.L. Taylor *(Central Districts)*. Coach, A.J. Moles; Bowling coach, S.J. Jurgensen; Fielding coach/Video analyst, T. Wilson; Manager, L.M. Crocker; Physiotherapist, K. Stalker, Trainer, B. Stronach; Nutritionist, K. Fouhy.

Cumming replaced Ryder, who withdrew because of injury. Hopkins joined the team as cover after an injury to McCullum. Boult, Cumming, Diamanti, Fulton, Hopkins and Patel were replaced by I.G. Butler *(Otago)*, J.E.C. Franklin *(Wellington)*, N.L. McCullum *(Otago)* and P.D. McGlashan *(Northern Districts)* for the Twenty20 international.

New Zealand First-class Averages

BATTING	*M*	*I*	*NO*	*HS*	*Agg*	*Ave*	*100s*	*50s*	*Ct*	*St*
J.M. How	3	6	0	170	228	38.00	1	-	2	-
B.B. McCullum	3	6	1	84*	183	36.60	-	2	11	-
L.R.P.L. Taylor	3	6	0	75	209	34.83	-	1	5	-
D.R. Flynn	3	6	1	55	145	29.00	-	1	-	-
D.L. Vettori	3	6	1	73	119	23.80	-	1	2	-
A.J. Redmond	3	6	0	83	133	22.16	-	1	5	-
P.G. Fulton	1	2	0	29	36	18.00	-	-	2	-
J.D. Ryder	3	6	0	30	96	16.00	-	-	3	-
K.D. Mills	1	2	0	17	17	8.50	-	-	-	-
T.G. Southee	3	6	1	13	41	8.20	-	-	-	-
G.D. Elliott	1	2	0	9	9	4.50	-	-	-	-
I.E. O'Brien	3	6	0	14	20	3.33	-	-	-	-
C.S. Martin	3	6	2	1	2	0.50	-	-	1	-

BOWLING	O	M	R	W	Ave	Best	5w	10w
A.J. Redmond	6	0	47	2	23.50	2-47	-	-
J.D. Ryder	16	3	54	2	27.00	2-7	-	-
C.S. Martin	101	26	309	11	28.09	3-16	-	-
I.E. O'Brien	98	17	338	11	30.72	3-73	-	-
D.L. Vettori	124.5	29	288	9	32.00	4-71	-	-
G.D. Elliott	16	5	44	1	44.00	1-15	-	-
T.G. Southee	92.4	14	336	6	56.00	4-63	-	-
K.D. Mills	29	8	86	0	-	-	-	-

New Zealand Test Averages

BATTING	M	I	NO	HS	Agg	Ave	100s	50s	Ct	St
B.B. McCullum	2	4	1	84*	125	41.66	-	1	9	-
L.R.P.L. Taylor	2	4	0	75	160	40.00	-	1	3	-
D.R. Flynn	2	4	1	39*	88	29.33	-	-	-	-
A.J. Redmond	2	4	0	83	115	28.75	-	1	2	-
P.G. Fulton	1	2	0	29	36	18.00	-	-	2	-
J.D. Ryder	2	4	0	30	70	17.50	-	-	2	-
J.M. How	2	4	0	28	58	14.50	-	-	2	-
D.L. Vettori	2	4	1	18*	43	14.33	-	-	2	-
T.G. Southee	2	4	1	12*	25	8.33	-	-	-	-
G.D. Elliott	1	2	0	9	9	4.50	-	-	-	-
I.E. O'Brien	2	4	0	3	4	1.00	-	-	-	-
C.S. Martin	2	4	0	1	2	0.50	-	-	-	-

BOWLING	O	M	R	W	Ave	Best	5w	10w
A.J. Redmond	6	0	47	2	23.50	2-47	-	-
J.D. Ryder	13	2	48	2	24.00	2-7	-	-
I.E. O'Brien	67	13	213	7	30.42	3-111	-	-
C.S. Martin	66	13	221	6	36.83	3-69	-	-
D.L. Vettori	86.4	24	197	5	39.40	2-46	-	-
G.D. Elliott	16	5	44	1	44.00	1-15	-	-
T.G. Southee	61.2	9	225	5	45.00	4-63	-	-

Australia Test Averages

BATTING	M	I	NO	HS	Agg	Ave	100s	50s	Ct	St
S.M. Katich	2	3	1	131*	164	82.00	1	-	2	-
M.J. Clarke	2	3	0	110	217	72.33	1	1	4	-
B.J. Haddin	2	3	0	169	194	64.66	1	-	5	-
M.E.K. Hussey	2	3	0	70	105	35.00	-	1	-	-
R.T. Ponting	2	3	0	79	100	33.33	-	1	5	-
S.R. Clark	2	3	2	18	32	32.00	-	-	1	-
M.G. Johnson	2	3	0	31	59	19.66	-	-	-	-
A. Symonds	2	3	0	26	46	15.33	-	-	5	-
M.L. Hayden	2	3	0	24	32	10.66	-	-	1	-
B. Lee	2	3	0	19	30	10.00	-	-	1	-
S.R. Watson	1	2	0	5	6	3.00	-	-	-	-
N.M. Hauritz	1	1	0	1	1	1.00	-	-	-	-

BOWLING	O	M	R	W	Ave	Best	5w	10w
M.G. Johnson	65.4	21	154	14	11.00	5-39	1	-
B. Lee	75.3	18	262	12	21.83	5-105	1	-
N.M. Hauritz	40	13	95	4	23.75	2-32	-	-
S.R. Clark	62	18	167	7	23.85	4-43	-	-
S.R. Watson	15	3	54	2	27.00	2-35	-	-
A. Symonds	17	2	33	1	33.00	1-17	-	-
M.J. Clarke	2	0	6	0	-	-	-	-

New Zealand One-day International Averages

BATTING	M	I	NO	HS	Agg	Ave	100s	50s	Ct	St	SR
G.D. Elliott	5	5	1	115	210	52.50	1	1	1	-	80
L.R.P.L. Taylor	5	5	0	76	195	39.00	-	2	1	-	78
M.J. Guptill	5	5	1	64*	136	34.00	-	1	2	-	81
B.B. McCullum	5	5	0	43	114	22.80	-	-	4	-	70
N.T. Broom	5	5	1	29	81	20.25	-	-	-	-	68
P.G. Fulton	5	5	0	40	95	19.00	-	-	3	-	61
D.L. Vettori	5	3	2	7*	15	15.00	-	-	5	-	88
T.G. Southee	5	3	1	17	27	13.50	-	-	-	-	135
K.D. Mills	5	4	0	26	52	13.00	-	-	1	-	69
J.S. Patel	3	2	1	9	11	11.00	-	-	1	-	100
C.D. Cumming	1	1	0	0	0	0.00	-	-	-	-	0
B.J. Diamanti	1	1	1	26*	26	-	-	-	1	-	118
I.E. O'Brien	5	1	1	0*	0	-	-	-	-	-	0

BOWLING	O	M	R	W	Ave	Best	R/O
K.D. Mills	42	3	183	9	20.33	4-35	4.36
I.E. O'Brien	45	2	253	10	25.30	3-68	5.62
G.D. Elliott	21	0	107	2	53.50	2-44	5.10
T.G. Southee	45	0	253	3	84.33	1-34	5.62
D.L. Vettori	44	0	187	2	93.50	1-24	4.25
J.S. Patel	20	0	110	1	110.00	1-47	5.50
B.J. Diamanti	2	0	25	0	-	-	12.50

Australia One-day International Averages

BATTING	M	I	NO	HS	Agg	Ave	100s	50s	Ct	St	SR
C.J. Ferguson	4	4	3	55*	102	102.00	-	1	2	-	136
B.J. Haddin	5	5	1	109	283	70.75	1	1	5	-	88
M.E.K. Hussey	5	5	1	75*	259	64.75	-	3	5	-	94
M.J. Clarke	4	4	0	98	188	47.00	-	2	2	-	75
C.L. White	4	2	1	17*	27	27.00	-	-	2	-	90
D.J. Hussey	5	5	0	79	115	23.00	-	1	1	-	72
S.E. Marsh	1	1	0	15	15	15.00	-	-	-	-	53
M.G. Johnson	5	2	0	20	21	10.50	-	-	2	-	105
J.R. Hopes	5	3	0	18	31	10.33	-	-	1	-	62
R.T. Ponting	4	4	0	16	38	9.50	-	-	1	-	57
D.J. Warner	2	2	0	7	9	4.50	-	-	-	-	31
N.W. Bracken	5	2	1	3*	3	3.00	-	-	3	-	50
S.W. Tait	1	1	1	9*	9	-	-	-	-	-	90
B.W. Hilfenhaus	4	1	1	0*	0	-	-	-	1	-	0
P.M. Siddle	1	-	-	-	-	-	-	-	-	-	-

BOWLING	O	M	R	W	Ave	Best	R/O
P.M. Siddle	3	0	13	1	13.00	1-13	4.33
S.W. Tait	10	1	40	2	20.00	2-40	4.00
J.R. Hopes	42	3	159	7	22.71	2-30	3.79
N.W. Bracken	40.1	5	218	9	24.22	3-35	5.42
C.L. White	7	0	52	2	26.00	2-10	7.43
M.G. Johnson	43	4	192	7	27.42	3-51	4.47
D.J. Hussey	9	0	43	1	43.00	1-9	4.78
B.W. Hilfenhaus	31.5	2	186	4	46.50	2-44	5.84
M.J. Clarke	24	0	103	2	51.50	1-18	4.29

NEW SOUTH WALES v NEW ZEALAND — First-class

at Sydney Cricket Ground on 13, 14, 15, 16 November, 2008
Toss : New Zealand. Umpires : G.A. Abood & P.R. Reiffel
Close of play: 1st day: NSW 15-0, Hughes 10, Khawaja 5; 2nd day: NSW 309-6, S.P.D. Smith 47, D.L.R. Smith 5
3rd day: NZ 157-5, Vettori 61, McCullum 5
New South Wales won by 6 wickets.

Elliott and Gillespie were omitted for this game. How completely dominated the New Zealand first innings innings, recording his highest score in first-class cricket. He reached his hundred off 174 balls in 203 minutes and was last man out, having scored all 29 runs of the last wicket partnership.

Martin claimed an early wicket when the home team batted but some steady batting saw them with a 43 run lead by the end of the second day. New South Wales stretched their advantage to 95 runs and then had New Zealand reeling at 35-4. With a rearranged batting order (Ryder was ill and McCullum had suffered an injury) Vettori came in at number six and helped Flynn put on 113 for the fifth wicket. McCullum hit a fifty on the last morning, leaving New South Wales 162 to win.

An excellent spell from Martin had the home team battling but the two Smiths combined in an unbroken partnership of 83 to take their side to victory.

NEW ZEALAND

FIRST INNINGS	Runs	Mins	Balls	6s	4s	*SECOND INNINGS*	Runs	Mins	Balls	6s	4s
A.J.Redmond c Smith D.L.R. b Hazlewood	5	20	16	-	1	lbw b Henriques	0	7	7	-	-
J.M.How c Thornley b Lambert	170	332	272	6	13	c Smith D.L.R. b Henriques	13	52	40	-	1
J.D.Ryder c Smith D.L.R. b Lambert	16	51	25	-	2	(8) c Hazlewood b Smith S.P.D.	10	33	25	-	2
L.R.P.L.Taylor c Forrest b Hazlewood	31	79	60	1	1	(3) c Smith D.L.R. b Henriques	18	34	33	-	2
B.B.McCullum† run out	4	13	11	-	-	(7) c Henriques b Lambert	54	152	94	2	7
D.R.Flynn c Smith D.L.R. b Lambert	2	31	7	-	-	(4) c Forrest b Henriques	55	140	123	-	7
D.L.Vettori* c Smith S.P.D. b Lambert	3	16	15	-	-	(6) b Hazlewood	73	178	139	-	3
K.D.Mills c & b Smith S.P.D.	17	60	65	-	-	(5) c Smith D.L.R. b Henriques	0	7	4	-	-
T.G.Southee b Smith S.P.D.	13	18	28	-	1	run out	3	25	16	-	-
I.E.O'Brien b Lambert	2	18	11	-	-	lbw b Hazlewood	14	50	35	-	3
C.S.Martin not out	0	18	6	-	-	not out	0	13	11	-	-
Extras (lb 1, nb 2)	3					(b 7, lb 8, w 1)	16				
TOTAL (85.3 overs)	**266**	332				(86.1 overs)	**256**	350			

NEW SOUTH WALES

	Runs	Mins	Balls	6s	4s		Runs	Mins	Balls	6s	4s
P.J.Hughes c McCullum b O'Brien	64	120	88	-	10	(2) lbw b Martin	8	19	13	-	1
U.T.Khawaja c McCullum b Martin	5	21	17	-	-	(1) b Martin	24	147	99	-	3
P.J.Forrest c Taylor b O'Brien	26	124	83	-	2	c Ryder b O'Brien	26	75	57	-	5
M.C.Henriques c Taylor b Vettori	55	114	90	-	6	c Redmond b Martin	18	24	24	-	4
D.J.Thornley* c Martin b Southee	85	207	153	1	8						
S.P.D.Smith c Redmond b Vettori	68	233	172	1	6	(5) not out	37	86	71	-	7
G.M.Lambert c Redmond b Martin	10	22	11	-	2						
D.L.R.Smith† c sub (M.R.Gillespie) b O'Brien	7	27	24	-	-	(6) not out	42	69	51	-	7
B.Casson lbw b Vettori	15	34	23	-	2						
N.M.Hauritz b Vettori	10	21	28	-	1						
J.R.Hazlewood not out	2	9	5	-	-						
Extras (b 8, lb 2, w 1, nb 3)	14					(b 4, lb 2, nb 1)	7				
TOTAL (115.1 overs)	**361**	459				(52.2 overs) (for 4 wkts)	**162**	**217**			

Bowling	O	M	R	W	O	M	R	W
NEW SOUTH WALES								
Hazlewood	18	4	53	2	11.1	4	23	2
Henriques	8	5	9	0	19	4	51	5
Lambert	16.3	5	74	5	14	1	46	1
Hauritz	16	2	44	0	7	2	15	0
Smith S.P.D.	27	4	85	2	17	3	65	1
Casson					18	4	41	0
NEW ZEALAND								
Mills	17	2	64	0	12	6	22	0
Southee	23	4	71	1	8.2	1	40	0
Vettori	29.1	4	71	4	9	1	20	0
Martin	24	8	72	2	11	5	16	3
O'Brien	22	4	73	3	9	0	52	1
Ryder					3	1	6	0

Fall of Wickets

	NZ 1st	NSW 1st	NZ 2nd	NSW 2nd
1st	10	16	2	9
2nd	57	92	30	50
3rd	121	103	33	72
4th	127	175	35	79
5th	157	276	148	-
6th	167	301	171	-
7th	217	312	196	-
8th	233	338	215	-
9th	237	352	251	-
10th	266	361	256	-

In New South Wales' first innings Redmond took over as wicketkeeper and made two catches.
In the second innings Ryder kept wicket and took a catch. He was replaced by Redmond who also took a catch.

AUSTRALIA v NEW ZEALAND — First Test

at Woolloongabba, Brisbane on 20, 21, 22, 23 November, 2008
Toss : New Zealand. Umpires : B.R. Doctrove & R.E. Koertzen
Close of play: 1st day: NZ 7-0, Redmond 3, How 2; 2nd day: Australia 131-6, Katich 67, Haddin 6
3rd day: NZ 143-6, Taylor 67
Australia won by 149 runs.

From the side that played Bangladesh, New Zealand included Southee at the expense of Mills and Martin replaced Patel. Australia played a four-man pace attack which meant that Krezja, who had taken 12 wickets on his test debut, was twelfth man.

Vettori won the toss and sent Australia in to bat and the BlackCaps had immediate success with three wickets in the first seven overs, all to Southee. Clarke became the mainstay of the innings getting fifty off 136 balls and was last man out, two short of a hundred. Southee, with 4-63, took full advantage of the conditions.

Redmond went early when New Zealand batted and only three batsmen exceeded fourteen. At one stage New Zealand were 127-5 but lost five wickets for just 29 to concede a first innings lead of 58.

Hayden went to the first ball of the Australian second innings but Katich remained steadfast as he carried his bat for the first time in a test. He got his fifty from 86 balls and his sixth test century after 179 deliveries. He received good support as the last two wickets added 82 valuable runs and set New Zealand a target of 327.

How became Lee's 300th test victim in the first over and the New Zealand batsmen again struggled with only Taylor reaching thirty. His fourth test fifty came from 79 balls but it was a lone hand as the last six wickets fell for 44 to give Australia a 149 run win. Johnson had career best figures, taking five wickets in an innings for the first time, and received good support from Clark.

AUSTRALIA

FIRST INNINGS	*Runs*	*Mins*	*Balls*	*6s*	*4s*	*SECOND INNINGS*	*Runs*	*Mins*	*Balls*	*6s*	*4s*
M.L.Hayden c Taylor b Southee	8	18	16	-	2	c McCullum b Martin	0	1	1	-	-
S.M.Katich c McCullum b Southee	10	27	17	-	1	not out	131	346	245	-	16
R.T.Ponting* c How b Southee	4	14	8	-	1	c Redmond b O'Brien	17	35	26	-	-
M.E.K.Hussey lbw b Martin	35	119	78	-	4	c McCullum b O'Brien	0	3	4	-	-
M.J.Clarke b Ryder	98	297	217	-	9	run out	9	28	15	-	1
A.Symonds c McCullum b O'Brien	26	54	33	-	3	c McCullum b Martin	20	73	48	-	3
S.R.Watson c McCullum b O'Brien	1	11	8	-	-	lbw b Martin	5	14	10	-	1
B.J.Haddin† c How b Ryder	6	22	19	-	1	b Vettori	19	65	44	-	3
B.Lee c McCullum b Southee	4	18	12	-	1	b Vettori	7	34	25	-	1
M.G.Johnson c Taylor b Vettori	5	30	15	-	1	c Vettori b Elliott	31	68	59	1	3
S.R.Clark not out	13	43	40	-	1	c Vettori b Southee	18	17	12	-	4
Extras (lb 2, w 1, nb 1)	4					(lb 10, nb 1)	11				
TOTAL (77 overs)	**214**	330				(81.2 overs)	**268**	346			

NEW ZEALAND

	Runs	*Mins*	*Balls*	*6s*	*4s*		*Runs*	*Mins*	*Balls*	*6s*	*4s*
A.J.Redmond c Ponting b Clark	3	25	19	-	-	c & b Clark	10	46	30	-	1
J.M.How b Lee	14	65	39	-	2	c Ponting b Lee	0	3	1	-	-
J.D.Ryder c Haddin b Watson	30	70	50	-	5	lbw b Johnson	24	65	50	-	3
L.R.P.L.Taylor lbw b Lee	40	77	51	-	7	c Haddin b Johnson	75	188	128	-	9
B.B.McCullum† c Ponting b Johnson	8	7	8	-	2	lbw b Clark	3	11	6	-	-
D.R.Flynn not out	39	133	80	-	7	b Johnson	29	99	69	-	5
G.D.Elliott b Watson	9	48	32	-	2	b Clark	0	15	10	-	-
D.L.Vettori* c Symonds b Johnson	2	26	12	-	-	c Symonds b Johnson	10	27	18	-	1
T.G.Southee c Symonds b Johnson	0	3	4	-	-	not out	12	19	7	2	-
I.E.O'Brien c Clarke b Johnson	1	4	3	-	-	c Clarke b Clark	3	5	7	-	-
C.S.Martin b Clark	1	8	8	-	-	b Johnson	1	5	4	-	-
Extras (lb 3, nb 6)	9					(lb 5, w 2, nb 3)	10				
TOTAL (50 overs)	**156**	240				(54.3 overs)	**177**	244			

Bowling	*O*	*M*	*R*	*W*	*O*	*M*	*R*	*W*
NEW ZEALAND								
Martin	18	4	42	1	21	5	69	3
Southee	18	3	63	4	16.2	5	62	1
O'Brien	19	6	44	2	17	1	58	2
Elliott	10	4	29	0	6	1	15	1
Vettori	8	0	27	1	19	4	46	2
Ryder	4	1	7	2	2	0	8	0
AUSTRALIA								
Lee	16	5	38	2	9	0	53	1
Clark	15	2	46	2	17	5	43	4
Watson	10	2	35	2	5	1	19	0
Johnson	8	3	30	4	17.3	6	39	5
Symonds	1	0	4	0	4	0	12	0
Clarke					2	0	6	0

Fall of Wickets

	A *1st*	***NZ*** *1st*	***A*** *2nd*	***NZ*** *2nd*
1st	13	7	0	0
2nd	22	44	40	30
3rd	23	64	40	40
4th	96	73	53	49
5th	132	108	109	133
6th	139	127	115	143
7th	152	143	156	160
8th	160	143	186	161
9th	183	149	239	164
10th	214	156	268	177

AUSTRALIA v NEW ZEALAND — Second Test

at Adelaide Oval on 28, 29, 30 November, 1 December, 2008
Toss : New Zealand. Umpires : B.R. Doctrove & R.E. Koertzen
Close of play: 1st day: NZ 262-6, McCullum 30, Vettori 12; 2nd day: Australia 241-3, Hussey 69, Clarke 43
3rd day: NZ 35-0, Redmond 15, How 13
Australia won by an innings and 62 runs.

Both sides made changes. Australia brought in Hauritz for Watson and the injured Krezja, while Fulton came into the New Zealand side at the expense of Elliott. On a good batting wicket New Zealand won the toss and decided to bat first.

All the batsmen got starts but only Redmond was able to reach fifty, coming from 80 balls. He made his highest test score before being caught on the boundary. The last five wickets again stumbled, adding only 42, with the last four going for just four runs.

Australia had a steady start before Hayden, in his 100th test, was run out. Ponting, Hussey, Clarke and Haddin then put the BlackCap attack to the sword, all reached fifties, with Clarke and Haddin going on to hundreds. Clarke's ninth century came from 108 balls while Haddin's maiden test hundred needed 133. When the innings ended Australia had a lead of 265. O'Brien was the pick of the pace bowlers while Vettori toiled away, bowling nearly 60 overs.

New Zealand batted safely through to stumps but Redmond went to the second ball of day four. Wickets fell at regular intervals and only stubborn resistance from McCullum got the score to 203. He added 50 for the ninth wicket with O'Brien, who failed to score. Martin reached a record sixth pair in tests and registered his 25th duck. Lee had career best match figures as Australia won by an innings and 62 runs to take the series 2-0. This was John Bracewell's final match as coach of the New Zealand team.

NEW ZEALAND

FIRST INNINGS	*Runs*	*Mins*	*Balls*	*6s*	*4s*	*SECOND INNINGS*	*Runs*	*Mins*	*Balls*	*6s*	*4s*
A.J.Redmond c Symonds b Hauritz	83	151	125	2	14	c Clarke b Lee	19	40	33	-	4
J.M.How c Haddin b Johnson	16	77	47	-	2	c Ponting b Lee	28	100	66	-	4
J.D.Ryder c Clarke b Hauritz	13	43	28	-	1	c Symonds b Lee	3	28	16	-	-
L.R.P.L.Taylor lbw b Clark	44	123	88	-	6	c & b Lee	1	22	20	-	-
P.G.Fulton c Katich b Symonds	29	81	71	1	3	b Johnson	7	71	55	-	-
D.R.Flynn b Lee	11	48	42	-	2	lbw b Johnson	9	36	27	-	2
B.B.McCullum† c Haddin b Lee	30	139	101	1	2	not out	84	178	134	2	14
D.L.Vettori* not out	18	100	83	-	1	c Hayden b Hauritz	13	33	32	-	3
T.G.Southee c Katich b Johnson	2	12	6	-	-	c Ponting b Hauritz	11	47	34	1	-
I.E.O'Brien c Haddin b Lee	0	5	6	-	-	lbw b Lee	0	56	38	-	-
C.S.Martin b Lee	0	8	5	-	-	b Johnson	0	12	2	-	-
Extras (b 4, lb 8, w 1, nb 11)	24					(b 7, lb 8, nb 13)	28				
TOTAL (98.3 overs)	**270**	413				(74.1 overs)	**203**	416			

AUSTRALIA

	Runs	Mins	Balls	6s	4s
M.L.Hayden run out	24	41	36	-	5
S.M.Katich c Ryder b Vettori	23	59	42	-	4
R.T.Ponting* c Fulton b O'Brien	79	152	124	-	13
M.E.K.Hussey c Redmond b Martin	70	277	183	-	8
M.J.Clarke c Ryder b O'Brien	110	331	239	-	11
A.Symonds c McCullum b Martin	0	5	3	-	-
B.J.Haddin† c Fulton b Redmond	169	300	222	2	24
B.Lee c Taylor b O'Brien	19	49	48	1	3
M.G.Johnson c McCullum b Redmond	23	44	38	-	4
N.M.Hauritz b Vettori	1	13	12	-	-
S.R.Clark not out	1	6	4	-	-
Extras (b 2, lb 8, w 1, nb 5)	16				
TOTAL (157.4 overs)	**535**	633			

Bowling	*O*	*M*	*R*	*W*	*O*	*M*	*R*	*W*
AUSTRALIA								
Lee	25.3	8	66	4	25	5	105	5
Clark	20	6	56	1	10	5	22	0
Johnson	25	5	56	2	15.1	7	29	3
Hauritz	16	2	63	2	24	11	32	2
Symonds	12	2	17	1				
NEW ZEALAND								
Martin	27	4	110	2				
Southee	27	1	100	0				
Vettori	59.4	20	124	2				
O'Brien	31	6	111	3				
Ryder	7	1	33	0				
Redmond	6	0	47	2				

Fall of Wickets

	NZ *1st*	A *1st*	NZ *2nd*
1st	46	38	39
2nd	101	49	55
3rd	130	155	58
4th	194	244	63
5th	200	247	76
6th	228	428	84
7th	266	470	105
8th	269	526	131
9th	270	532	181
10th	270	535	203

PRIME MINISTER'S XI v NEW ZEALAND — One-day

at Manuka Oval, Canberra on 29 January, 2009
Toss : Prime Minister's XI. Umpires : I.H. Lock & Y. Ramasundara
Prime Minister's XI won by 6 wickets.

This game was the only warm-up match before the one-day series. Boult played his first game for New Zealand who reached 271-5 in its fifty overs, thanks mainly to McCullum scoring 114 from 130 deliveries and Fulton getting 53 from 75 balls.

The New Zealand bowlers struggled in the hot conditions, with Bailey scoring an unbeaten 107 from 138 balls. Former test opener Langer made 72 and added 153 with Bailey. Australian Capital Territory representative Ryan Carters kept wicket due to an injury to McCullum.

NEW ZEALAND

	Runs	Mins	Balls	6s	4s
B.B.McCullum† c Ferguson b McKay	114	194	130	1	9
M.J.Guptill c Christian b McKay	16	27	18	1	1
P.G.Fulton c Paine b McKay	53	75	79	-	5
L.R.P.L.Taylor c Klinger b Henriques	38	46	41	1	4
K.D.Mills c McKay b Holland	11	17	9	1	-
G.D.Elliott not out	29	28	23	1	1
N.T.Broom not out	1	3	1	-	-
D.L.Vettori*					
J.S.Patel					
I.E.O'Brien					
T.A.Boult					
Extras (b 1, w 7, nb 1)	9				
TOTAL (50 overs) (5 wkts)	**271**	195			

PRIME MINISTER'S XI

	Runs	Mins	Balls	6s	4s
P.J.Hughes b Patel	22	45	27	-	3
M.Klinger c Broom b Boult	6	14	11	-	-
C.J.Ferguson c sub (R.G.L.Carters) b O'Brien	30	39	32	-	5
G.J.Bailey not out	107	146	138	2	9
J.L.Langer* c Guptill b Patel	72	112	67	-	5
M.C.Henriques not out	20	23	13	2	-
D.T.Christian					
T.D.Paine†					
C.J.McKay					
J.M.Holland					
J.Behrendorff					
Extras (b 3, lb 4, w 7, nb 1)	15				
TOTAL (47.5 overs) (4 wkts)	**272**	194			

Bowling	*O*	*M*	*R*	*W*
PRIME MINISTER'S XI				
McKay	10	1	52	3
Behrendorff	8	0	21	0
Henriques	10	0	70	1
Christian	9	0	55	0
Holland	10	0	53	1
Bailey	3	0	19	0
NEW ZEALAND				
Mills	8	1	36	0
Boult	6.5	0	56	1
O'Brien	8	0	48	1
Patel	10	0	51	2
Vettori	10	0	42	0
Elliott	5	0	32	0

Fall of Wickets	***NZ***	***PM***
1st	31	16
2nd	112	53
3rd	183	71
4th	212	224
5th	265	-
6th	-	-
7th	-	-
8th	-	-
9th	-	-
10th	-	-

AUSTRALIA v NEW ZEALAND — First One-day International

at Western Australia C.A. Ground, Perth on 1 February, 2009 (d/n)
Toss : Australia. Umpires : S.A. Bucknor & B.N.J. Oxenford
New Zealand won by 2 wickets.

Mills dismissed the Australian openers in his third and fourth overs and then Australia suffered two run outs to be 51-4 and then 54-5. Michael Hussey and Haddin added 61 from 95 balls to assist in a recovery but Australia were dismissed for 181 from 48.4 overs. Mills and O'Brien were the most successful bowlers but Vettori was very economical, conceding just 22 runs from his ten overs.

McCullum was dismissed with the second ball of the innings and New Zealand lost two wickets on 25. Taylor and Broom added 42 with Broom reaching his highest score. Taylor went to fifty from 83 balls but was dismissed at 170. With one ball remaining the scores were level but Vettori hit the final ball for four to give the BlackCaps a two wicket win.

AUSTRALIA

	Runs	Mins	Balls	6s	4s
S.E.Marsh c Fulton b Mills	15	25	28	-	2
D.J.Warner c Fulton b Mills	7	36	18	-	-
R.T.Ponting* run out	5	18	13	-	-
M.J.Clarke run out	12	35	27	-	1
D.J.Hussey c McCullum b Patel	13	34	26	-	1
M.E.K.Hussey c Elliott b O'Brien	49	99	65	1	1
B.J.Haddin† b Mills	31	57	54	1	1
J.R.Hopes c Vettori b O'Brien	18	35	30	-	1
M.G.Johnson b Mills	20	27	17	-	3
N.W.Bracken lbw b Southee	0	4	4	-	-
S.W.Tait not out	9	18	10	-	2
Extras (w 2)	2				
TOTAL (48.4 overs)	**181**	194			

NEW ZEALAND

	Runs	Mins	Balls	6s	4s
B.B.McCullum† lbw b Tait	0	2	2	-	-
M.J.Guptill b Bracken	13	47	33	1	1
P.G.Fulton c & b Johnson	7	58	35	-	1
L.R.P.L.Taylor c Clarke b Bracken	64	175	97	1	6
G.D.Elliott c Hussey M.E.K. b Hopes	8	43	31	-	-
N.T.Broom b Clarke	29	52	50	-	2
K.D.Mills b Tait	26	55	35	-	3
D.L.Vettori* not out	7	26	9	-	-
T.G.Southee b Bracken	3	11	6	-	-
J.S.Patel not out	2	4	2	-	-
I.E.O'Brien					
Extras (b 3, lb 9, w 11)	23				
TOTAL (50 overs) (8 wkts)	**182**	237			

Bowling	*O*	*M*	*R*	*W*
NEW ZEALAND				
Mills	9.4	0	35	4
Southee	10	0	34	1
O'Brien	10	1	43	2
Vettori	10	0	22	0
Patel	9	0	47	1
AUSTRALIA				
Tait	10	1	40	2
Bracken	10	3	35	3
Johnson	10	2	34	1
Hopes	10	1	23	1
Clarke	6	0	18	1
Hussey D.J.	4	0	20	0

Fall of Wickets	***A***	***NZ***
1st	20	0
2nd	23	25
3rd	27	25
4th	51	64
5th	54	106
6th	115	168
7th	152	170
8th	153	178
9th	154	-
10th	181	-

AUSTRALIA v NEW ZEALAND Second One-day International

at Melbourne Cricket Ground on 6 February, 2009 (d/n)
Toss : New Zealand. Umpires : S.A. Bucknor & P.R. Reiffel
New Zealand won by 6 wickets.

Ferguson made his debut for Australia. Michael Hussey was making his 100th one-day international appearance and Clarke captained Australia in Ponting's absence.

Warner went in the third over and Australia were 63-3 before Clarke and Michael Hussey added 133 for the fourth wicket from 169 balls. Clarke got fifty from 75 balls while Hussey needed 68. Australia reached 225-5.

Guptill went early but then New Zealand had some useful partnerships as the remaining batsmen all got starts. Elliott got his second fifty from 64 balls and made his highest score as the BlackCaps won with seven balls to spare and took a 2-0 lead in the series.

AUSTRALIA

	Runs	Mins	Balls	6s	4s
D.J.Warner c Vettori b Mills	2	10	1	-	-
M.J.Clarke* b O'Brien	98	197	133	-	7
B.J.Haddin† c McCullum b Southee	12	29	20	-	1
D.J.Hussey run out	10	30	22	-	1
M.E.K.Hussey c Vettori b O'Brien	75	115	94	-	4
C.L.White not out	17	22	14	-	-
C.J.Ferguson not out	6	12	6	-	-
J.R.Hopes					
M.G.Johnson					
N.W.Bracken					
B.W.Hilfenhaus					
Extras (lb 2, w 3)	5				
TOTAL (50 overs) (5 wkts)	**225**	210			

NEW ZEALAND

	Runs	Mins	Balls	6s	4s
B.B.McCullum† c Hussey M.E.K. b Hopes	43	112	75	-	3
M.J.Guptill c White b Bracken	8	17	14	-	1
P.G.Fulton c Haddin b Hopes	21	46	34	-	3
L.R.P.L.Taylor c Haddin b Johnson	47	112	74	-	3
G.D.Elliott not out	61	100	75	-	6
N.T.Broom not out	26	34	21	-	4
K.D.Mills					
D.L.Vettori*					
T.G.Southee					
J.S.Patel					
I.E.O'Brien					
Extras (lb 8, w 12)	20				
TOTAL (48.5 overs) (4 wkts)	**226**	202			

Bowling	*O*	*M*	*R*	*W*
NEW ZEALAND				
Mills	10	1	37	1
Southee	10	0	57	1
O'Brien	10	0	48	2
Vettori	10	0	35	0
Patel	8	0	38	0
Elliott	2	0	8	0
AUSTRALIA				
Bracken	9	1	34	1
Hilfenhaus	9.5	1	58	0
Johnson	10	0	43	1
Clarke	5	0	21	0
Hopes	10	1	30	2
White	3	0	18	0
Hussey D.J.	2	0	14	0

Fall of Wickets	***A***	***NZ***
1st	4	21
2nd	35	62
3rd	63	104
4th	196	176
5th	206	-
6th	-	-
7th	-	-
8th	-	-
9th	-	-
10th	-	-

AUSTRALIA v NEW ZEALAND — Third One-day International

at Sydney Cricket Ground on 8 February, 2009 (d/n)
Toss : New Zealand. Umpires : S.A. Bucknor & S.J.A. Taufel
Australia won by 32 runs.

Ponting was due to be rested for the second and third games but returned to the side after the loss in Melbourne. Australia had a new opening combination of Haddin and Clarke and they reached a century stand off 116 balls, with Clarke getting fifty from 60 balls and Haddin 54 balls. Haddin went to his maiden century after 107 balls. Michael Hussey produced a cameo with fifty from 30 balls. O'Brien had his best bowling figures but was expensive.

Guptill and Taylor were dismissed before the end of the sixth over, but Elliott, batting at number four, scored fifty from 69 balls and reached his maiden century from 108 deliveries. He and McCullum, who had injured his shoulder and did not open, added 69 from 49 balls before Elliott went at 252. The innings then folded and Australia had a 32 run win with 15 balls to spare.

AUSTRALIA

	Runs	Mins	Balls	6s	4s
B.J.Haddin† run out	109	156	114	3	8
M.J.Clarke c Guptill b Elliott	64	100	69	1	6
R.T.Ponting* c Mills b Elliott	16	26	23	-	1
D.J.Hussey c McCullum b O'Brien	7	10	7	-	1
C.L.White c Vettori b O'Brien	10	23	16	-	1
M.E.K.Hussey c Taylor b Mills	51	58	32	-	6
C.J.Ferguson lbw b Vettori	28	33	23	-	4
J.R.Hopes b O'Brien	8	14	11	-	-
M.G.Johnson c Patel b Mills	1	6	3	-	-
N.W.Bracken not out	3	6	2	-	-
B.W.Hilfenhaus not out	0	1	0	-	-
Extras (b 1, w 3)	4				
TOTAL (50 overs) (9 wkts)	**301**	220			

NEW ZEALAND

	Runs	Mins	Balls	6s	4s
M.J.Guptill c Ferguson b Bracken	6	17	16	-	1
P.G.Fulton c White b Hopes	40	85	63	1	3
L.R.P.L.Taylor lbw b Hilfenhaus	4	3	2	-	1
G.D.Elliott c Hussey M.E.K. b Hopes	115	188	124	-	8
N.T.Broom c Hilfenhaus b White	15	43	23	-	-
K.D.Mills c Bracken b Hussey D.J.	2	5	4	-	-
D.L.Vettori* c Clarke b White	2	6	4	-	-
T.G.Southee c Haddin b Johnson	17	16	10	1	1
B.B.McCullum† c Ponting b Hilfenhaus	36	55	27	1	3
J.S.Patel b Bracken	9	14	9	1	-
I.E.O'Brien not out	0	4	3	-	-
Extras (b 4, lb 11, w 8)	23				
TOTAL (47.1 overs)	**269**	220			

Bowling	*O*	*M*	*R*	*W*
NEW ZEALAND				
Mills	9	0	59	2
Southee	10	0	52	0
Vettori	10	0	52	1
O'Brien	10	1	68	3
Elliott	8	0	44	2
Patel	3	0	25	0
AUSTRALIA				
Bracken	8.1	1	65	2
Hilfenhaus	9	1	44	2
Johnson	10	2	36	1
Hopes	10	0	49	2
Clarke	5	0	41	0
Hussey D.J.	3	0	9	1
White	2	0	10	2

Fall of Wickets	***A***	***NZ***
1st	135	12
2nd	169	16
3rd	187	96
4th	200	149
5th	212	152
6th	274	157
7th	297	183
8th	297	252
9th	299	262
10th	-	269

AUSTRALIA v NEW ZEALAND — Fourth One-day International

at Adelaide Oval on 10 February, 2009 (d/n)
Toss : New Zealand. Umpires : S.A. Bucknor & S.J. Davis
Australia won by 3 wickets.

Bracken made his 100th one-day international appearance in this match. New Zealand decided to bat first after winning the toss and had an opening stand of 69 from 17.5 overs. Taylor made fifty from 58 balls but New Zealand could reach only 244.

The Australian innings was centred around the Hussey brothers. David scored fifty from 77 balls and hit his highest score, while Michael reached his half century from 50 balls. The pair added 115 from 119 balls to give Australia victory with ten balls to spare and levelled the series.

NEW ZEALAND

	Runs	Mins	Balls	6s	4s
B.B.McCullum† b Clarke	33	91	55	-	-
M.J.Guptill c Bracken b Johnson	45	70	70	1	4
P.G.Fulton c Bracken b Hopes	5	12	10	-	-
L.R.P.L.Taylor c Haddin b Johnson	76	115	71	2	6
G.D.Elliott c Hussey D.J. b Johnson	26	40	29	-	2
C.D.Cumming c Johnson b Hopes	0	4	6	-	-
N.T.Broom c Hopes b Hilfenhaus	11	28	24	-	1
K.D.Mills b Bracken	23	42	27	1	1
D.L.Vettori* not out	6	12	4	-	-
T.G.Southee not out	7	4	4	-	-
I.E.O'Brien					
Extras (lb 2, w 10)	12				
TOTAL (50 overs) (8 wkts)	**244**	217			

AUSTRALIA

	Runs	Mins	Balls	6s	4s
B.J.Haddin† run out	43	101	67	1	5
M.J.Clarke c Fulton b O'Brien	14	23	19	-	1
R.T.Ponting* c Guptill b Southee	15	37	27	-	2
D.J.Hussey b O'Brien	79	119	96	-	6
M.E.K.Hussey not out	75	80	71	2	4
C.J.Ferguson not out	13	20	11	-	2
C.L.White					
J.R.Hopes					
M.G.Johnson					
N.W.Bracken					
B.W.Hilfenhaus					
Extras (lb 1, w 6, nb 1)	8				
TOTAL (48.2 overs) (4 wkts)	**247**	194			

Bowling	O	M	R	W
AUSTRALIA				
Bracken	10	0	51	1
Hilfenhaus	10	0	56	1
Johnson	10	0	51	3
Hopes	10	1	37	2
Clarke	8	0	23	1
White	2	0	24	0
NEW ZEALAND				
Mills	9.2	2	30	0
Southee	10	0	61	1
O'Brien	10	0	54	2
Vettori	10	0	54	0
Elliott	9	0	47	0

Fall of Wickets	***NZ***	***A***
1st	69	29
2nd	83	57
3rd	86	101
4th	141	216
5th	141	-
6th	173	-
7th	226	-
8th	235	-
9th	-	-
10th	-	-

AUSTRALIA v NEW ZEALAND — Fifth One-day International

at Woolloongabba, Brisbane on 13 February, 2009 (d/n)
Toss : New Zealand. Umpires : S.A. Bucknor & R.J. Tucker
No result.

Siddle *(Australia)* and Diamanti *(New Zealand)* made their debuts. Steady rain delayed the start and the game became a 22 over match. Australia were in some trouble at 70-4 after 11.1 overs but Haddin and Ferguson added 98 off 71 balls to get Australia to 168-4. Ferguson scored his maiden fifty from 33 balls while Haddin needed 43.

There was another delay during the interval and the New Zealand innings was reduced to 20 overs with a revised target of 156. McCullum went early but then Guptill gave a great display of hitting getting fifty from just 24 balls. After 14 overs the rain set in again and the match had to be abandoned. The series was thus tied at 2-2 with Australia retaining the Chappell-Hadlee Trophy.

AUSTRALIA

	Runs	Mins	Balls	6s	4s
J.R.Hopes† c Vettori b Mills	5	10	9	-	1
B.J.Haddin not out	88	97	65	3	5
R.T.Ponting* c McCullum b Mills	2	7	3	-	-
D.J.Hussey b O'Brien	6	7	7	-	1
M.E.K.Hussey c Diamanti b Vettori	9	25	13	-	-
C.J.Ferguson not out	55	46	35	-	7
C.L.White					
M.G.Johnson					
P.M.Siddle					
N.W.Bracken					
B.W.Hilfenhaus					
Extras (w 3)	3				
TOTAL (22 overs) (4 wkts)	**168**	94			

NEW ZEALAND

	Runs	Mins	Balls	6s	4s
B.B.McCullum† b Hilfenhaus	2	1	2	-	-
M.J.Guptill not out	64	82	34	3	5
P.G.Fulton c Ferguson b Bracken	22	14	12	2	2
L.R.P.L.Taylor c Hussey M.E.K. b Johnson	4	6	3	-	1
G.D.Elliott c Haddin b Bracken	0	6	1	-	-
N.T.Broom run out	0	2	1	-	-
K.D.Mills c Hussey M.E.K. b Siddle	1	9	9	-	-
B.J.Diamanti not out	26	30	22	-	3
D.L.Vettori*					
T.G.Southee					
I.E.O'Brien					
Extras (lb 1, w 3)	4				
TOTAL (14 overs) (6 wkts)	**123**	82			

Bowling	*O*	*M*	*R*	*W*
NEW ZEALAND				
Mills	4	0	22	2
Southee	5	0	49	0
O'Brien	5	0	40	1
Diamanti	2	0	25	0
Vettori	4	0	24	1
Elliott	2	0	8	0
AUSTRALIA				
Hilfenhaus	3	0	28	1
Bracken	3	0	33	2
Johnson	3	0	28	1
Siddle	3	0	13	1
Hopes	2	0	20	0

Fall of Wickets	***A***	***NZ***
1st	9	2
2nd	20	40
3rd	30	56
4th	70	68
5th	-	68
6th	-	73
7th	-	-
8th	-	-
9th	-	-
10th	-	-

AUSTRALIA v NEW ZEALAND — Twenty20 International

at Sydney Cricket Ground on 15 February, 2008 (d/n)
Toss : Australia. Umpires : B.N.J. Oxenford & P.R. Reiffel
Australia won by 1 run.

Eight players were making their Twenty20 international debuts: Ferguson, Henriques and Siddle for Australia and Guptill, Broom, Elliott, Butler and O'Brien for New Zealand.

Australia batted first and made 150-7, Hussey top-scoring with 41 off 39 balls. New Zealand's innings was centred around Brendon McCullum who reached fifty from 41 balls but at times did not see much of the strike. Consequently the BlackCaps got behind the run rate and lost wickets. Needing 12 to win off the last two balls Nathan McCullum scored a four and a six as New Zealand lost by one run.

AUSTRALIA

	Runs	Mins	Balls	6s	4s
D.A.Warner c Vettori b O'Brien	23	19	15	-	4
B.J.Haddin*† c & b Southee	15	15	10	-	2
C.J.Ferguson b Butler	8	15	9	-	1
D.J.Hussey c Broom b Vettori	41	51	39	1	1
A.C.Voges lbw b Elliott	26	28	24	-	2
C.L.White c Vettori b O'Brien	16	16	11	1	-
J.R.Hopes not out	16	12	10	-	1
M.C.Henriques run out	1	1	2	-	-
P.M.Siddle not out	1	3	1	-	-
N.W.Bracken					
B.W.Hilfenhaus					
Extras (lb 1, w 1, nb 1)	3				
TOTAL (20 overs) (7 wkts)	**150**	87			

NEW ZEALAND

	Runs	Mins	Balls	6s	4s
B.B.McCullum† c Voges b Hilfenhaus	61	61	47	2	5
M.J.Guptill lbw b Siddle	0	2	2	-	-
P.G.Fulton c Haddin b Siddle	1	8	8	-	-
N.T.Broom c Ferguson b Hopes	36	31	26	-	6
G.D.Elliott not out	23	38	30	-	1
J.E.C.Franklin run out	3	6	3	-	-
N.L.McCullum not out	10	3	4	1	1
I.G.Butler					
D.L.Vettori*					
T.G.Southee					
I.E.O'Brien					
Extras (b 3, lb 10, w 2)	15				
TOTAL (20 overs) (5 wkts)	**149**	80			

Bowling	*O*	*M*	*R*	*W*
NEW ZEALAND				
Franklin	1	0	6	0
Southee	4	0	31	1
O'Brien	4	0	34	2
Butler	4	0	30	1
Vettori	4	0	23	1
McCullum N.L.	2	0	14	0
Elliott	1	0	11	1
AUSTRALIA				
Siddle	4	0	24	2
Bracken	4	1	16	0
Hilfenhaus	4	0	32	1
Hopes	4	0	40	1
Hussey	4	0	24	0

Fall of Wickets

	A	*NZ*
1st	34	5
2nd	38	12
3rd	52	73
4th	104	131
5th	128	137
6th	135	-
7th	138	-
8th	-	-
9th	-	-
10th	-	-

WEST INDIES IN NEW ZEALAND

West Indies made their tenth visit to New Zealand in December and January. They played two test matches, five one-day internationals, two Twenty20 internationals and a three-day game against Auckland. The tour was badly affected by rain with the elements ruining the first test at Dunedin and four of the five one-day internationals.

The test series was drawn 0-0, the Twenty20 series was shared 1-1 and the one-day series went to New Zealand 2-1 after they won the the final game on a Duckworth/Lewis result.

West Indies' captain Chris Gayle led from the front, scoring 305 runs in the tests, including 197 in the final innings, and he also scored 260 in the one-day series. Shivnarine Chanderpaul scored 202 test runs and 139 one-day runs, batting just twice. Jerome Taylor scored his maiden test century at Dunedin. On the bowling front the outstanding performance came from Fidel Edwards, who had career best figures of 7-87 in the Napier test.

Of the New Zealand players Tim McIntosh scored a century in his second test while Martin Guptill scored 122 not out in his one-day debut. Daniel Vettori, Iain O'Brien and Jeetan Patel all had five wicket hauls in the tests.

The touring party was: C.H. Gayle *(captain)*, L.S. Baker, C.S. Baugh, S.J. Benn, S. Chanderpaul, S. Chattergoon, F.H. Edwards, S.E. Findlay, L.R. Johnson, X.M. Marshall, N.O. Miller, B.P. Nash, K.A. Pollard, D.B.L. Powell, D. Ramdin, K.A.J. Roach, R.R. Sarwan, J.E. Taylor. Coach, J. Dyson; Manager, Omar Khan.

Findlay, Miller and Pollard replaced Benn, Johnson and Roach for the one-day internationals, although Benn remained for the Twenty20 games. Sarwan was originally the vice-captain but he resigned after the team arrived in New Zealand and was replaced by Ramdin.

West Indies First-class Averages

BATTING	*M*	*I*	*NO*	*HS*	*Agg*	*Ave*	*100s*	*50s*	*Ct*	*St*
C.H. Gayle	2	3	0	197	305	101.66	1	1	2	-
S. Chanderpaul	3	4	1	126*	224	74.66	1	1	2	-
R.R. Sarwan	3	4	1	158*	178	59.33	1	-	2	-
B.P. Nash	3	4	0	74	185	46.25	-	2	-	-
J.E. Taylor	2	3	0	106	131	43.66	1	-	-	-
S. Chattergoon	3	4	0	93	144	36.00	-	1	2	-
X.M. Marshall	3	4	0	47	91	22.75	-	-	3	-
D. Ramdin	3	4	1	37*	54	18.00	-	-	7	-
F.H. Edwards	3	4	1	20	38	12.66	-	-	3	-
D.B.L. Powell	2	3	0	22	28	9.33	-	-	-	-
S.J. Benn	2	3	1	4*	8	4.00	-	-	1	-
L.R. Johnson	1	1	0	3	3	3.00	-	-	-	-
L.S. Baker	2	1	1	0*	0	-	-	-	1	-
K.A.J. Roach	1	-	-	-	-	-	-	-	-	-

BOWLING	*O*	*M*	*R*	*W*	*Ave*	*Best*	*5w*	*10w*
L.R. Johnson	3	0	15	1	15.00	1-15	-	-
F.H. Edwards	96.4	14	371	14	26.50	7-87	1	-
C.H. Gayle	44	8	98	3	32.66	3-42	-	-
D.B.L. Powell	60	14	200	6	33.33	3-68	-	-
J.E. Taylor	59	15	204	5	40.80	2-67	-	-
B.P. Nash	23	3	93	1	93.00	1-69	-	-
S.J. Benn	89	14	249	2	124.50	1-54	-	-
L.S. Baker	53	8	180	1	180.00	1-95	-	-
R.R. Sarwan	4	1	13	0	-	-	-	-
X.M. Marshall	4	0	14	0	-	-	-	-
S. Chattergoon	7.1	0	44	0	-	-	-	-
K.A.J. Roach	17	4	44	0	-	-	-	-

New Zealand Test Averages

BATTING	M	I	NO	HS	Agg	Ave	100s	50s	Ct	St
J.D. Ryder	2	3	1	89	205	102.50	-	3	3	-
T.G. McIntosh	2	4	1	136	197	65.66	1	-	-	-
D.R. Flynn	2	4	1	95	189	63.00	-	2	2	-
D.L. Vettori	2	2	0	30	59	29.50	-	-	-	-
B.B. McCullum	2	3	0	31	75	25.00	-	-	8	-
L.R.P.L. Taylor	2	3	0	46	65	21.66	-	-	3	-
J.M. How	2	4	0	54	86	21.50	-	1	2	-
K.D. Mills	2	3	0	18	30	10.00	-	-	-	-
J.E.C. Franklin	2	3	1	7	9	4.50	-	-	1	-
I.E. O'Brien	2	2	1	4	4	4.00	-	-	1	-
J.S. Patel	1	1	0	2	2	2.00	-	-	1	-
M.R. Gillespie	1	1	1	16*	16	-	-	-	-	-

BOWLING	O	M	R	W	Ave	Best	5w	10w
D.L. Vettori	99	32	218	10	21.80	6-56	1	-
J.S. Patel	71	28	151	6	25.16	5-110	1	-
I.E. O'Brien	65	13	211	8	26.37	6-75	1	-
K.D. Mills	45	11	133	3	44.33	3-64	-	-
J.E.C. Franklin	48	7	179	3	59.66	2-61	-	-
J.D. Ryder	3	0	9	0	-	-	-	-
M.R. Gillespie	21	5	102	0	-	-	-	-

West Indies Test Averages

BATTING	M	I	NO	HS	Agg	Ave	100s	50s	Ct	St
C.H. Gayle	2	3	0	197	305	101.66	1	1	2	-
S. Chanderpaul	2	3	1	126*	202	101.00	1	1	2	-
B.P. Nash	2	3	0	74	162	54.00	-	2	-	-
J.E. Taylor	2	3	0	106	131	43.66	1	-	-	-
S. Chattergoon	2	3	0	25	51	17.00	-	-	1	-
X.M. Marshall	2	3	0	20	44	14.66	-	-	3	-
D.B.L. Powell	2	3	0	22	28	9.33	-	-	-	-
R.R. Sarwan	2	3	0	11	20	6.66	-	-	-	-
F.H. Edwards	2	3	0	20	20	6.66	-	-	2	-
D. Ramdin	2	3	0	6	17	5.66	-	-	6	-
S.J. Benn	1	2	1	4*	4	4.00	-	-	-	-
L.S. Baker	1	1	1	0*	0	-	-	-	1	-

BOWLING	O	M	R	W	Ave	Best	5w	10w
F.H. Edwards	67.4	10	246	11	22.36	7-87	1	
C.H. Gayle	44	8	98	3	32.66	3-42	-	
D.B.L. Powell	60	14	200	6	33.33	3-68	-	
J.E. Taylor	59	15	204	5	40.80	2-67	-	
S.J. Benn	41	7	103	1	103.00	1-54	-	
B.P. Nash	7	2	24	0	-	-	-	
L.S. Baker	25	3	85	0	-	-	-	

New Zealand One-day International Averages

BATTING	*M*	*I*	*NO*	*HS*	*Agg*	*Ave*	*100s*	*50s*	*Ct*	*St*	*SR*
M.J. Guptill	2	2	1	122*	165	165.00	1	-	1	-	94
L.R.P.L. Taylor	5	4	2	75	187	93.50	-	2	4	-	82
J.D.P. Oram	3	1	0	25	25	25.00	-	-	-	-	108
N.T. Broom	2	2	1	24*	24	24.00	-	-	-	-	133
J.D. Ryder	4	3	0	32	67	22.33	-	-	-	-	77
B.B. McCullum	5	4	0	41	86	21.50	-	-	4	-	91
D.R. Flynn	5	4	1	23*	48	16.00	-	-	-	-	64
J.M. How	3	2	0	27	27	13.50	-	-	3	-	64
K.D. Mills	5	1	0	6	6	6.00	-	-	-	-	85
M.S. Sinclair	1	1	0	2	2	2.00	-	-	-	-	18
D.L. Vettori	5	1	0	0	0	0.00	-	-	-	-	0
G.D. Elliott	5	2	2	30*	44	-	-	-	1	-	100
T.G. Southee	5	1	1	6*	6	-	-	-	-	-	150
J.S. Patel	2	-	-	-	-	-	-	-	-	-	-
M.R. Gillespie	3	-	-	-	-	-	-	-	-	-	-

BOWLING	*O*	*M*	*R*	*W*	*Ave*	*Best*	*R/O*
D.L. Vettori	34	4	119	6	19.83	4-20	3.50
M.R. Gillespie	22	2	112	5	22.40	4-58	5.09
J.S. Patel	8.4	0	47	2	23.50	1-8	5.42
K.D. Mills	38	4	168	7	24.00	3-57	4.42
J.D. Ryder	10	0	52	2	26.00	1-17	5.20
T.G. Southee	34	3	180	5	36.00	2-33	5.29
J.D.P. Oram	13	0	45	1	45.00	1-25	3.46
G.D. Elliott	6	0	42	0	-	-	7.00

West Indies One-day International Averages

BATTING	*M*	*I*	*NO*	*HS*	*Agg*	*Ave*	*100s*	*50s*	*Ct*	*St*	*SR*
S. Chanderpaul	3	2	0	94	139	69.50	-	1	-	-	82
C.H. Gayle	5	5	1	135	260	65.00	1	-	-	-	101
R.R. Sarwan	5	4	1	67*	132	44.00	-	1	1	-	73
D. Ramdin	5	4	2	28*	40	20.00	-	-	5	-	81
X.M. Marshall	3	3	1	29*	31	15.50	-	-	-	-	42
B.P. Nash	4	3	1	15	28	14.00	-	-	-	-	75
S. Chattergoon	4	4	1	17*	38	12.66	-	-	2	-	46
F.H. Edwards	5	2	0	13	14	7.00	-	-	-	-	45
K.A. Pollard	4	4	0	19	26	6.50	-	-	-	-	118
S.E. Findlay	3	2	0	8	11	5.50	-	-	2	-	39
J.E. Taylor	3	1	0	4	4	4.00	-	-	1	-	16
D.B.L. Powell	4	2	0	4	5	2.50	-	-	2	-	62
N.O. Miller	4	1	1	25*	25	-	-	-	2	-	69
L.S. Baker	3	-	-	-	-	-	-	-	1	-	-

BOWLING	*O*	*M*	*R*	*W*	*Ave*	*Best*	*R/O*
J.E. Taylor	9	0	36	2	18.00	2-26	4.00
L.S. Baker	16	1	65	3	21.66	2-29	4.06
D.B.L. Powell	32	0	160	7	22.85	3-25	5.00
N.O. Miller	15	0	93	2	46.50	2-26	6.20
F.H. Edwards	28	1	190	4	47.50	3-26	6.79
K.A. Pollard	12	0	66	1	66.00	1-40	5.50
C.H. Gayle	7.3	0	68	1	68.00	1-28	9.06
B.P. Nash	14	0	59	0	-	-	4.21

AUCKLAND v WEST INDIES

First-class

at Eden Park Outer Oval, Auckland on 5, 6, 7 December, 2008
Toss : Auckland. Umpires : B.G. Frost & D.J. Walker
Close of play: 1st day: Auckland 359-2, Jones 186, Young 56; 2nd day: West Indies 82-0, Chattergoon 31, Marshall 45
Match drawn.

Auckland won the toss and batted but soon lost Guptill. McIntosh and Jones then added 223 for the second wicket with the century stand coming from 136 balls and the two hundred partnership from 263 balls in 171 minutes. McIntosh reached fifty from 86 balls while Jones needed 79 deliveries. Jones reached his thirteenth century from 130 balls and had a 135 run stand with Young, who got fifty from 87 balls.

Jones scored his first double century from 326 balls after 394 minutes. Hopkins then controlled the rest of the innings getting his eighth first-class century off 182 deliveries. All of the visiting bowlers toiled with Edwards the most successful.

West Indies had a good opening stand before Marshall went early on the third day. Chattergoon and Sarwan then added 116 for the second wicket. Chattergoon got fifty from 167 balls while Sarwan needed 94. Sarwan reached his hundred after 144 balls and 199 minutes and retired at 336-3. Shaw, who had replaced McIntosh when the opener joined the BlackCaps in Dunedin, took two quick wickets as the tourists finished at 431-7. Raval made his first-class debut in this game.

AUCKLAND

FIRST INNINGS	*Runs*	*Mins*	*Balls*	*6s*	*4s*
T.G.McIntosh c Ramdin b Baker	78	226	139	1	10
M.J.Guptill c Chattergoon b Edwards	10	12	9	-	2
R.A.Jones* c Benn b Edwards	201	401	330	3	26
R.A.Young lbw b Edwards	61	150	121	1	5
G.J.Hopkins† not out	103	220	182	1	7
K.D.Mills c Sarwan b Benn	50	82	63	1	9
J.A.Raval c Sarwan b Nash	31	60	59	2	2
C.de Grandhomme c Edwards b Johnson	21	30	30	-	2
T.S.Nethula not out	2	8	8	-	-
D.R.Tuffey					
M.D.Bates					
L.J.Shaw					
Extras (b 13, lb 9, w 4, nb 4)	30				
TOTAL (156.1 overs) (7 wkts dec)	**587**	598			

WEST INDIES

	Runs	*Mins*	*Balls*	*6s*	*4s*
S.Chattergoon c Bates b Nethula	93	301	247	1	11
X.M.Marshall b Bates	47	155	106	2	6
R.R.Sarwan retired hurt	158	276	198	2	23
L.R.Johnson lbw b Mills	3	41	22	-	-
S.Chanderpaul c Mills b Shaw	22	102	87	-	3
B.P.Nash run out	23	38	18	-	3
D.Ramdin*† not out	37	49	45	-	7
S.J.Benn c Nethula b Shaw	4	3	4	-	1
F.H.Edwards not out	18	20	14	1	2
K.A.J.Roach					
L.S.Baker					
Extras (b 5, lb 4, w 2, nb 15)	26				
TOTAL (121 overs) (6 wkts)	**431**	496			

Bowling	*O*	*M*	*R*	*W*
WEST INDIES				
Edwards	29	4	125	3
Roach	17	4	44	0
Baker	28	5	95	1
Benn	48	7	146	1
Sarwan	4	1	13	0
Nash	16	1	69	1
Marshall	4	0	14	0
Chattergoon	7.1	0	44	0
Johnson	3	0	15	1
AUCKLAND				
Mills	24	9	58	1
Tuffey	17	3	38	0
Bates	22	3	74	1
Nethula	33	0	158	1
Guptill	11	2	42	0
de Grandhomme	7	2	8	0
Shaw	7	0	44	2

Fall of Wickets

	A	***WI***
	1st	*1st*
1st	11	90
2nd	234	206
3rd	369	248
4th	386	350
5th	457	396
6th	520	401
7th	575	-
8th	-	-
9th	-	-
10th	-	-

Shaw replaced McIntosh, who had been called in to the New Zealand team, on the third day.

NEW ZEALAND v WEST INDIES — First Test

at University Oval, Dunedin on 11, 12, 13, 14, 15 December, 2008
Toss : New Zealand. Umpires : M.R. Benson & A.M. Saheba
Close of play: 1st day: NZ 226-4, Ryder 54, McCullum 4; 2nd day: no play
3rd day: West Indies 39-0, Gayle 29, Chattergoon 9; 4th day: NZ 44-2, McIntosh 24, Flynn 4
Match drawn.

McIntosh (New Zealand) and Baker and Nash (West Indies) made their test debuts. Rain interfered with the game washing out the second and fifth days' play. During this series teams were able to refer on-field umpiring decisions to the third umpire.

How went in the sixth over and Flynn came in at number three for the first time. He reached his maiden test fifty after 77 balls in 103 minutes. He was dismissed five runs short of his century when he was given out after a referral. Ryder scored his second test fifty from 87 balls. The second day was washed out and play did not start until after lunch on the third day. Ryder went for 89 at 310 and Mills was also out after a referral as the Blackaps were dismissed for 365.

West Indies survived 14 overs until stumps but then lost two early wickets on the fourth day. Gayle got fifty from 68 balls but West Indies were in trouble at 173-6. Chanderpaul was joined by Taylor and they added 153 for the seventh wicket in 138 minutes, a record for West Indies against New Zealand.

Taylor made his first fifty from 60 balls and got his maiden test (and first-class) century after just a further 37 deliveries. After his dismissal the innings soon ended. Vettori took his 18th five wicket bag, finishing with 6-56.

How and night-watchman Mills went in successive balls late on the fourth day but rain had the final say and the match was drawn.

NEW ZEALAND

FIRST INNINGS	*Runs*	*Mins*	*Balls*	*6s*	*4s*	*SECOND INNINGS*	*Runs*	*Mins*	*Balls*	*6s*	*4s*
T.G.McIntosh c Baker b Gayle	34	138	111	-	5	not out	24	50	35	-	3
J.M.How c Chanderpaul b Powell	10	21	10	-	2	b Powell	10	35	18	-	2
D.R.Flynn lbw b Gayle	95	233	187	-	12	(4) not out	4	11	7	-	1
L.R.P.L.Taylor c Marshall b Gayle	15	37	22	-	3						
J.D.Ryder c Chanderpaul b Powell	89	239	157	-	12						
B.B.McCullum† c Ramdin b Taylor	25	110	66	-	3						
J.E.C.Franklin hit wicket b Edwards	7	23	19	-	1						
D.L.Vettori* c Marshall b Powell	30	46	43	-	4						
K.D.Mills lbw b Edwards	12	59	30	-	2	(3) b Powell	0	2	1	-	-
M.R.Gillespie not out	16	69	38	-	2						
I.E.O'Brien c & b Edwards	4	27	16	-	1						
Extras (lb 16, w 9, nb 3)	28					(b 4, lb 1, nb 1)	6				
TOTAL (116 overs)	**365**	507				(10 overs) (2 wkts)	**44**	50			

WEST INDIES

	Runs	Mins	Balls	6s	4s
C.H.Gayle* c Franklin b O'Brien	74	134	103	1	11
S.Chattergoon c O'Brien b Mills	13	78	50	-	1
R.R.Sarwan c McCullum b Mills	8	21	16	-	2
X.M.Marshall c Ryder b Vettori	20	70	51	-	4
S.Chanderpaul b Vettori	76	281	200	-	10
B.P.Nash c Ryder b Mills	23	67	60	1	3
D.Ramdin† lbw b Vettori	5	16	5	-	1
J.E.Taylor c McCullum b Vettori	106	138	107	3	17
D.B.L.Powell lbw b Vettori	0	1	1	-	-
F.H.Edwards c sub (S.W.Eathorne) b Vettori	0	8	6	-	-
L.S.Baker not out	0	9	5	-	-
Extras (b 1, lb 10, nb 4)	15				
TOTAL (100 overs)	**340**	416			

Bowling	*O*	*M*	*R*	*W*	*O*	*M*	*R*	*W*
WEST INDIES								
Taylor	23	7	61	1				
Powell	24	7	68	3	5	0	17	2
Edwards	22	4	91	3	5	0	22	0
Baker	25	3	85	0				
Gayle	21	2	42	3				
Nash	1	0	2	0				
NEW ZEALAND								
Gillespie	21	5	102	0				
Mills	24	6	64	3				
O'Brien	15	4	46	1				
Vettori	25	7	56	6				
Franklin	15	2	61	0				

Fall of Wickets

	NZ 1st	*WI 1st*	*NZ 2nd*
1st	10	66	33
2nd	97	87	33
3rd	128	114	-
4th	189	134	-
5th	278	162	-
6th	289	173	-
7th	310	326	-
8th	327	326	-
9th	347	334	-
10th	365	340	-

NEW ZEALAND v WEST INDIES — Second Test

at McLean Park, Napier on 19, 20, 21, 22, 23 December, 2008
Toss : West Indies. Umpires : A.M. Saheba & R.E. Koertzen
Close of play: 1st day: West Indies 258-6, Chanderpaul 100, Taylor 1; 2nd day: NZ 145-2, McIntosh 62, Taylor 4
3rd day: West Indies 62-2, Gayle 36, Marshall 0; 4th day: West Indies 278-7, Gayle 146, Edwards 1
Match drawn.

Both sides made one change with Patel replacing Gillespie in the BlackCaps side while Benn took the place of Baker in West Indies' team.

West Indies made a steady start but then lost four wickets for 31 to be 74-4. Nash joined Chanderpaul and they added 163 for the fifth wicket. Chanderpaul scored his fifty from 147 balls and Nash reached his maiden test fifty after 120 balls. Chanderpaul scored his century from 214 balls while O'Brien had career best test figures of 6-75.

How went early in New Zealand's innings but then McIntosh and Flynn added 118 for the second wicket. Flynn got fifty from 130 balls and McIntosh fifty from 181 balls. Ryder then joined McIntosh and they added 100 off 143 balls for the fifth wicket. McIntosh scored his maiden test hundred from 285 balls while Ryder needed 61 balls for his fifty. Vettori passed 3000 test runs and Edwards finished with career best figures of 7-87.

West Indies lost two wickets before erasing the first innings deficit of 64 and they were indebted to Gayle and Nash who added 124 for the fifth wicket. Gayle scored his fifty from 65 balls and on 88 reached 5000 test runs. His century came from 340 balls. Patel took five wickets in a test innings for the first time.

New Zealand were set 312 to win but McIntosh went in the third over. How and Ryder both scored fifties but once McCullum was dismissed the match petered out to a draw. Ryder joined the group of players who have scored two fifties in a test match.

WEST INDIES

FIRST INNINGS	*Runs*	*Mins*	*Balls*	*6s*	*4s*	*SECOND INNINGS*	*Runs*	*Mins*	*Balls*	*6s*	*4s*
C.H.Gayle* c McCullum b O'Brien	34	57	49	-	5	c McCullum b Patel	197	514	396	7	20
S.Chattergoon c How b Vettori	13	116	72	-	2	c Taylor b Patel	25	42	39	-	4
R.R.Sarwan c McCullum b Patel	11	13	19	-	2	lbw b Vettori	1	13	15	-	-
X.M.Marshall c Ryder b O'Brien	6	17	16	-	1	c Taylor b Patel	18	64	61	1	2
S.Chanderpaul not out	126	340	282	3	11	c & b Patel	0	1	1	-	-
B.P.Nash c Flynn b Franklin	74	212	162	-	12	c How b Franklin	65	200	172	-	9
D.Ramdin† b Vettori	6	27	10	-	1	c Flynn b Franklin	6	31	22	-	-
J.E.Taylor c McCullum b O'Brien	17	34	24	-	3	lbw b O'Brien	8	45	39	-	2
S.J.Benn c McCullum b O'Brien	0	2	2	-	-	(11) not out	4	13	8	-	-
D.B.L.Powell c McCullum b O'Brien	6	14	6	-	1	lbw b Vettori	22	39	37	1	2
F.H.Edwards lbw b O'Brien	0	19	7	-	-	(9) c Taylor b Patel	20	137	86	-	3
Extras (lb 6, w 1, nb 7)	14					(lb 2, w 1, nb 6)	9				
TOTAL (107 overs)	**307**	421				(145 overs)	**375**	543			

NEW ZEALAND

	Runs	*Mins*	*Balls*	*6s*	*4s*		*Runs*	*Mins*	*Balls*	*6s*	*4s*
T.G.McIntosh b Taylor	136	456	337	-	21	lbw b Taylor	3	13	9	-	-
J.M.How c Chattergoon b Edwards	12	56	27	-	1	c Gayle b Edwards	54	106	85	-	8
D.R.Flynn c & b Edwards	57	190	161	2	4	run out	33	70	50	-	6
L.R.P.L.Taylor c Ramdin b Edwards	4	26	14	-	-	lbw b Benn	46	86	50	2	3
J.D.Ryder c Ramdin b Edwards	57	103	68	-	8	not out	59	128	99	-	4
B.B.McCullum† c Ramdin b Taylor	31	87	45	1	2	c Ramdin b Taylor	19	33	21	1	1
J.E.C.Franklin c Gayle b Powell	0	17	9	-	-	not out	2	29	14	-	-
D.L.Vettori* c Ramdin b Edwards	29	68	45	-	3						
K.D.Mills lbw b Edwards	18	69	38	-	2						
J.S.Patel c Marshall b Edwards	2	20	15	-	-						
I.E.O'Brien not out	0	11	7	-	-						
Extras (lb 19, nb 6)	25					(w 2, nb 2)	4				
TOTAL (126.4 overs)	**371**	535				(51 overs) (5 wkts)	**220**	235			

Bowling	*O*	*M*	*R*	*W*	*O*	*M*	*R*	*W*
NEW ZEALAND								
Franklin	16	2	57	1	17	3	61	2
Mills	15	4	48	0	6	1	21	0
Patel	25	12	41	1	46	16	110	5
O'Brien	26	6	75	6	24	3	90	1
Vettori	22	4	71	2	52	21	91	2
Ryder	3	0	9	0				
WEST INDIES								
Taylor	23	6	76	2	13	2	67	2
Powell	26	7	85	1	5	0	30	0
Edwards	29.4	6	87	7	11	0	46	1
Gayle	18	6	33	0	5	0	23	0
Nash	6	2	22	0				
Benn	24	5	49	0	17	2	54	1

Fall of Wickets

	WI 1st	*NZ 1st*	*WI 2nd*	*NZ 2nd*
1st	43	19	58	8
2nd	54	137	61	62
3rd	63	145	106	96
4th	74	245	106	170
5th	237	316	230	203
6th	257	317	252	-
7th	279	319	272	-
8th	279	367	342	-
9th	299	368	363	-
10th	307	371	375	-

NEW ZEALAND v WEST INDIES — First Twenty20 International

at Eden Park, Auckland on 26 December, 2008 (d/n)
Toss : New Zealand. Umpires : A.L. Hill & B.F. Bowden
West Indies won the eliminator.

New Zealand won the toss and batted but lost McCullum at the end of the third over. Taylor was the only batsman to make a substantial score, getting fifty from 43 balls. Styris was hit on the thumb and suffered a fracture which would keep him out of cricket for the season.

Gayle led West Indies' reply, scoring fifty from 34 balls but had little support. West Indies lost their eighth wicket at 150 with two balls remaining but Benn came in and hit a four and then a single to level the scores. The two teams had also needed a tie-breaker when they had met at Eden Park in 2005/06.

A one-over eliminator took place, with each team naming three batsmen and one bowler. West Indies scored 25 in its over, with Gayle scoring all the runs, while the BlackCaps made 15-2.

NEW ZEALAND

	Runs	Mins	Balls	6s	4s
J.D.Ryder b Edwards	12	24	17	-	1
B.B.McCullum† c Benn b Baker	14	13	10	-	3
L.R.P.L.Taylor b Taylor	63	77	50	4	4
S.B.Styris c & b Pollard	21	21	12	1	2
J.D.P.Oram c Marshall b Benn	13	17	14	-	1
J.E.C.Franklin c & b Gayle	2	5	3	-	-
D.R.Flynn c Edwards b Gayle	10	20	7	1	-
K.D.Mills not out	10	12	6	1	-
D.L.Vettori* not out	2	3	2	-	-
T.G.Southee					
J.S.Patel					
Extras (lb 1, w 6, nb 1)	8				
TOTAL (20 overs) (7 wkts)	**155**	96			

WEST INDIES

	Runs	Mins	Balls	6s	4s
C.H.Gayle* c Taylor b Patel	67	60	41	5	5
S.Chanderpaul c & b Mills	6	9	5	-	1
X.M.Marshall b Vettori	28	27	24	1	3
R.R.Sarwan c Flynn b Vettori	4	16	12	-	-
S.E.Findlay c McCullum b Southee	19	31	17	-	2
K.A.Pollard c Patel b Vettori	7	5	4	1	-
C.S.Baugh† c McCullum b Patel	2	4	2	-	-
J.E.Taylor not out	11	22	11	-	1
F.H.Edwards run out	1	1	2	-	-
S.J.Benn not out	5	4	2	-	1
L.S.Baker					
Extras (lb 4, w 1)	5				
TOTAL (20 overs) (8 wkts)	**155**	95			

Bowling	*O*	*M*	*R*	*W*
WEST INDIES				
Baker	4	0	32	1
Taylor	4	0	33	1
Edwards	3	0	28	1
Benn	4	0	20	1
Pollard	2	0	25	1
Gayle	3	0	16	2
NEW ZEALAND				
Mills	4	0	27	1
Southee	4	0	39	1
Oram	4	0	35	0
Patel	4	0	34	2
Vettori	4	0	16	3

Fall of Wickets	*NZ*	*WI*
1st	21	19
2nd	37	82
3rd	70	109
4th	104	114
5th	112	124
6th	142	130
7th	149	149
8th	-	150
9th	-	-
10th	-	-

WEST INDIES

	Runs	Mins	Balls	6s	4s
C.H.Gayle* not out	25	6	6	3	1
X.M.Marshall run out	0	2	0	-	-
S.Chanderpaul not out	0	3	0	-	-
Extras	0				
TOTAL (1 over) (1 wkt)	**25**	6			

NEW ZEALAND

	Runs	Mins	Balls	6s	4s
J.D.P.Oram c Marshall b Benn	6	2	3	1	-
L.R.P.L.Taylor b Benn	6	4	2	1	-
B.B.McCullum† not out	0	1	0	-	-
Extras (b 2, nb 1)	3				
TOTAL (1 over) (2 wkts)	**15**	4			

Bowling	*O*	*M*	*R*	*W*
NEW ZEALAND				
Vettori	1	0	25	0
WEST INDIES				
Benn	0.4	0	13	2

Fall of Wickets	*WI*	*NZ*
1st	7	8
2nd	-	15

NEW ZEALAND v WEST INDIES Second Twenty20 International

at Seddon Park, Hamilton on 28 December, 2008 (d/n)
Toss : New Zealand. Umpires : G.A.V. Baxter & E.A. Watkin
New Zealand won by 36 runs.

Thompson made his debut for New Zealand. After Vettori had won the toss Ryder and McCullum scored 130 in 11.4 overs for New Zealand. Ryder needed 30 balls for his fifty while McCullum reached his from 28 balls. After the first wicket went the BlackCaps slumped to 191-9, with only Franklin able to reach double figures.

Thompson captured the key wicket of Gayle with his second ball and from then on the tourists never really threatened, although Sarwan reached a fifty off 30 balls. New Zealand won by 36 runs to level the series.

NEW ZEALAND

	Runs	Mins	Balls	6s	4s
J.D.Ryder c Sarwan b Gayle	62	59	41	3	7
B.B.McCullum† c Chanderpaul b Gayle	59	49	34	4	6
L.R.P.L.Taylor c Marshall b Pollard	6	6	4	-	1
J.D.P.Oram run out	9	14	1	-	-
D.R.Flynn c Ramdin b Pollard	3	5	4	-	-
J.E.C.Franklin c Findlay b Benn	20	18	11	2	1
D.L.Vettori* b Taylor	2	14	4	-	-
K.D.Mills b Taylor	6	12	7	-	-
E.P.Thompson not out	1	6	1	-	-
T.G.Southee run out	2	3	3	-	-
J.S.Patel					
Extras (b 12, lb 4, w 5)	21				
TOTAL (20 overs) (9 wkts)	**191**	91			

WEST INDIES

	Runs	Mins	Balls	6s	4s
C.H.Gayle* c Oram b Thompson	1	5	4	-	-
R.R.Sarwan c Southee b Oram	53	55	36	3	3
X.M.Marshall c Flynn b Southee	10	20	14	-	1
S.Chanderpaul c Oram b Vettori	5	7	4	-	1
S.E.Findlay b Vettori	13	15	14	-	2
K.A.Pollard c Ryder b Patel	38	33	24	2	4
D.Ramdin† c Taylor b Patel	30	26	21	-	4
J.E.Taylor not out	0	4	0	-	-
S.J.Benn not out	0	2	3	-	-
F.H.Edwards					
L.S.Baker					
Extras (lb 3, w 2)	5				
TOTAL (20 overs) (7 wkts)	**155**	88			

Bowling	O	M	R	W
WEST INDIES				
Baker	2	0	14	0
Taylor	4	0	29	2
Benn	4	0	45	1
Edwards	2	0	31	0
Gayle	4	0	27	2
Pollard	4	0	29	2
NEW ZEALAND				
Mills	4	0	35	0
Thompson	3	1	18	1
Southee	4	0	44	1
Vettori	4	0	19	2
Oram	3	0	24	1
Patel	2	1	12	2

Fall of Wickets	*NZ*	*WI*
1st	130	5
2nd	139	49
3rd	142	64
4th	152	87
5th	161	87
6th	164	155
7th	184	155
8th	189	-
9th	191	-
10th	-	-

NEW ZEALAND v WEST INDIES — First One-day International

at Queenstown Events Centre on 31 December, 2008
Toss : New Zealand. Umpires : A.L. Hill & M.R. Benson
No result.

New Zealand chose to field first after winning the toss. They had restricted the West Indies to 129-5 after 35.4 overs when it started to rain and the players never returned to the field. Mills, Vettori and Oram all had economical spells with the ball before the stoppage came.

WEST INDIES	Runs	Mins	Balls	6s	4s
C.H.Gayle* c McCullum b Mills	25	54	36	1	1
S.Chattergoon b Gillespie	14	49	35	-	2
R.R.Sarwan c McCullum b Vettori	38	66	57	-	3
X.M.Marshall not out	29	91	59	-	2
B.P.Nash b Southee	12	12	13	-	1
K.A.Pollard c McCullum b Southee	3	6	4	-	-
D.Ramdin† not out	2	9	10	-	-
J.E.Taylor					
N.O.Miller					
F.H.Edwards					
L.S.Baker					
Extras (w 6)	6				
TOTAL (35.4 overs) (5 wkts)	**129**	146			

NEW ZEALAND

J.D.Ryder
B.B.McCullum†
J.M.How
L.R.P.L.Taylor
D.R.Flynn
J.D.P.Oram
G.D.Elliott
D.L.Vettori*
K.D.Mills
T.G.Southee
M.R.Gillespie

Bowling **NEW ZEALAND**	*O*	*M*	*R*	*W*
Mills	7	0	23	1
Gillespie	7	1	31	1
Southee	7.4	0	33	2
Oram	6	0	16	0
Vettori	8	0	26	1

Fall of Wickets	***WI***
1st	42
2nd	42
3rd	102
4th	117
5th	123
6th	-
7th	-
8th	-
9th	-
10th	-

NEW ZEALAND v WEST INDIES Second One-day International

at AMI Stadium, Christchurch on 3 January, 2009 (d/n)
Toss : West Indies. Umpires : M.R. Benson & G.A.V. Baxter
West Indies won by 5 wickets.

West Indies chose to bowl after winning the toss and dismissed McCullum in the third over. After 6.5 overs rain interrupted play with New Zealand 26-1. When the match resumed it became a 28 over game. The BlackCaps reached 152-8 with Oram and Elliott playing valuable cameo innings. Oram passed 2000 runs in one-day internationals. Edwards bowled well for his 3-26.

West Indies had a revised target of 158 in 28 overs and lost an early wicket. Sarwan got fifty from 55 balls but the tourists were behind the run rate before a late flurry from Ramdin saw West Indies reach their target with one ball to spare.

NEW ZEALAND

	Runs	Mins	Balls	6s	4s
J.D.Ryder c Chattergoon b Miller	32	59	43	3	1
B.B.McCullum† c Ramdin b Edwards	1	10	2	-	-
J.M.How b Taylor	27	60	36	-	2
L.R.P.L.Taylor c Powell b Miller	13	32	20	-	-
D.R.Flynn c Ramdin b Taylor	4	6	5	-	-
J.D.P.Oram c Chattergoon b Edwards	25	29	23	1	2
G.D.Elliott not out	30	40	27	1	1
D.L.Vettori* b Edwards	0	2	1	-	-
K.D.Mills c Miller b Gayle	6	12	7	-	-
T.G.Southee not out	6	6	4	-	1
J.S.Patel					
Extras (lb 2, w 6)	8				
TOTAL (28 overs) (8 wkts)	**152**	131			

WEST INDIES

	Runs	Mins	Balls	6s	4s
C.H.Gayle* b Vettori	36	49	31	1	4
S.Chattergoon b Southee	6	15	14	-	1
R.R.Sarwan not out	67	113	65	1	3
X.M.Marshall b Oram	2	12	11	-	-
B.P.Nash b Patel	15	27	23	1	-
K.A.Pollard c Taylor b Mills	3	10	5	-	-
D.Ramdin† not out	28	28	18	-	3
J.E.Taylor					
N.O.Miller					
D.B.L.Powell					
F.H.Edwards					
Extras (lb 1)	1				
TOTAL (27.5 overs) (5 wkts)	**158**	129			

Bowling	*O*	*M*	*R*	*W*
WEST INDIES				
Edwards	6	1	26	3
Powell	5	0	18	0
Taylor	6	0	26	2
Pollard	2	0	26	0
Miller	6	0	26	2
Gayle	3	0	28	1
NEW ZEALAND				
Mills	6	0	27	1
Southee	5.5	1	38	1
Patel	5	0	39	1
Oram	5	0	25	1
Vettori	6	0	28	1

Fall of Wickets

	NZ	***WI***
1st	9	14
2nd	59	61
3rd	68	68
4th	76	96
5th	87	110
6th	114	-
7th	115	-
8th	135	-
9th	-	-
10th	-	-

NEW ZEALAND v WEST INDIES Third One-day International

at Westpac Stadium, Wellington on 7 January, 2009 (d/n)
Toss : New Zealand. Umpires : M.R. Benson & A.L. Hill
New Zealand won by 7 wickets.

This was to be the only match of the series that was not affected by rain. The West Indies batting was most disappointing and the visitors slumped to 74-8 before the last two wickets added 54. Only Chanderpaul and number ten Miller were able to reach twenty. Vettori bowled well for his 4-20 and he was ably assisted by all the other bowlers.

Chasing just 129 the BlackCaps went from 34-0 to 40-3 in eleven balls but Taylor and Flynn saw their side through without any further loss. Taylor reached fifty from 49 balls. New Zealand won with 29.3 overs left and squared the series 1-1

WEST INDIES

	Runs	Mins	Balls	6s	4s
C.H.Gayle* b Mills	18	39	24	-	3
X.M.Marshall c How b Mills	0	2	3	-	-
R.R.Sarwan c How b Southee	5	14	15	-	1
S.Chanderpaul lbw b Ryder	45	137	77	-	4
S.E.Findlay b Southee	8	42	25	-	2
D.Ramdin† lbw b Vettori	1	6	10	-	-
K.A.Pollard lbw b Vettori	1	9	5	-	-
J.E.Taylor c Taylor b Vettori	4	22	25	-	-
D.B.L.Powell b Vettori	1	5	4	-	-
N.O.Miller not out	25	50	36	-	2
F.H.Edwards c How b Patel	13	24	27	-	1
Extras (lb 3, w 3, nb 1)	7				
TOTAL (41.4 overs)	**128**	180			

NEW ZEALAND

	Runs	Mins	Balls	6s	4s
J.D.Ryder c Miller b Powell	14	26	20	-	1
B.B.McCullum† c Sarwan b Powell	18	24	14	-	3
J.M.How c Taylor b Powell	0	11	6	-	-
L.R.P.L.Taylor not out	51	74	50	3	5
D.R.Flynn not out	23	64	34	-	3
J.D.P.Oram					
G.D.Elliott					
D.L.Vettori*					
K.D.Mills					
T.G.Southee					
J.S.Patel					
Extras (b 4, lb 4, w 14, nb 1)	23				
TOTAL (20.3 overs) (3 wkts)	**129**	103			

Bowling	*O*	*M*	*R*	*W*
NEW ZEALAND				
Mills	10	2	31	2
Southee	10	2	36	2
Oram	2	0	4	0
Elliott	2	0	9	0
Vettori	10	3	20	4
Patel	3.4	0	8	1
Ryder	4	0	17	1
WEST INDIES				
Edwards	7	0	53	0
Powell	7	0	25	3
Taylor	3	0	10	0
Miller	3	0	22	0
Gayle	0.3	0	11	0

Fall of Wickets	***WI***	***NZ***
1st	1	34
2nd	15	34
3rd	35	40
4th	55	-
5th	56	-
6th	58	-
7th	70	-
8th	74	-
9th	101	-
10th	128	-

NEW ZEALAND v WEST INDIES Fourth One-day International

at Eden Park, Auckland on 10 January, 2009
Toss : West Indies. Umpires : G.A.V. Baxter & M.R. Benson
No result.

Guptill and Broom made their debuts replacing Oram (injured) and Ryder (suspended). McCullum and Guptill reached fifty off 66 balls before two wickets fell. Guptill and Taylor then added 144 for the third wicket.

Guptill got fifty from 70 balls and went on to become only the fifth player to score a century on his one-day international debut. His century came from 123 balls. Taylor scored fifty from 73 balls as New Zealand reached 275-4.

West Indies had reached 47 from 8.4 overs before rain stopped play and the match resumed with the target 235 from 40 overs. Only eleven more deliveries had been bowled, however, before rain intervened again, just after Gayle had hit Southee for four and six off consecutive balls. No further play was possible.

NEW ZEALAND

	Runs	Mins	Balls	6s	4s
B.B.McCullum† c Ramdin b Baker	26	64	50	-	3
M.J.Guptill not out	122	201	135	2	8
M.S.Sinclair c Ramdin b Baker	2	12	11	-	-
L.R.P.L.Taylor b Edwards	75	99	87	1	6
D.R.Flynn c Baker b Powell	0	3	2	-	-
N.T.Broom not out	24	20	17	2	-
G.D.Elliott					
D.L.Vettori*					
K.D.Mills					
T.G.Southee					
M.R.Gillespie					
Extras (b 8, lb 5, w 11, nb 2)	26				
TOTAL (50 overs) (4 wkts)	**275**	201			

WEST INDIES

	Runs	Mins	Balls	6s	4s
C.H.Gayle* not out	46	45	37	3	4
S.Chattergoon not out	17	45	26	-	2
R.R.Sarwan					
S.Chanderpaul					
S.E.Findlay					
B.P.Nash					
D.Ramdin†					
N.O.Miller					
D.B.L.Powell					
F.H.Edwards					
L.S.Baker					
Extras (lb 1)	1				
TOTAL (10.3 overs) (0 wkts)	**64**	45			

Bowling	*O*	*M*	*R*	*W*
WEST INDIES				
Edwards	10	0	65	1
Powell	10	0	51	1
Baker	10	1	29	2
Nash	10	0	43	0
Miller	6	0	45	0
Gayle	4	0	29	0
NEW ZEALAND				
Mills	5	0	30	0
Gillespie	5	1	23	0
Southee	0.3	0	10	0

Fall of Wickets	*NZ*	*WI*
1st	68	-
2nd	74	-
3rd	218	-
4th	219	-
5th	-	-
6th	-	-
7th	-	-
8th	-	-
9th	-	-
10th	-	-

NEW ZEALAND v WEST INDIES Fifth One-day International

at McLean Park, Napier on 13 January, 2009
Toss : New Zealand. Umpires : M.R. Benson & A.L. Hill
New Zealand won by 9 runs (D/L).

Gayle again dominated the match, scoring 135 off 129 balls. His first fifty came from 57 balls and his century after 110 deliveries. Chanderpaul was dismissed six runs short of his hundred. Gillespie had his best one-day international bowling figures and Mills took three wickets.

New Zealand batted positively from the start, reaching fifty from just 4.4 overs. All the top five batsmen reached twenty but yet again the rain interfered. Play did not get underway again and New Zealand were declared winners by nine runs, under the Duckworth/Lewis method, and took the series 2-1.

WEST INDIES

	Runs	Mins	Balls	6s	4s
C.H.Gayle† c Taylor b Mills	135	175	129	5	9
S.Chattergoon b Mills	1	10	6	-	-
R.R.Sarwan c Elliott b Gillespie	22	66	43	-	1
S.Chanderpaul c Guptill b Ryder	94	118	91	1	9
S.E.Findlay run out	3	5	3	-	-
K.A.Pollard c Taylor b Gillespie	19	10	8	2	1
D.Ramdin* b Gillespie	9	14	11	-	1
D.B.L.Powell c McCullum b Mills	4	7	4	-	-
B.P.Nash not out	1	4	1	-	-
F.H.Edwards b Gillespie	1	3	4	-	-
L.S.Baker					
Extras (lb 2, w 2)	4				
TOTAL (50 overs) (9 wkts)	**293**	205			

NEW ZEALAND

	Runs	Mins	Balls	6s	4s
J.D.Ryder c Findlay b Powell	21	29	23	1	2
B.B.McCullum† c Findlay b Baker	41	56	28	1	6
M.J.Guptill c Ramdin b Pollard	43	60	39	1	4
L.R.P.L.Taylor not out	48	107	71	-	3
D.R.Flynn c & b Powell	21	35	34	-	2
N.T.Broom lbw b Powell	0	1	1	-	-
G.D.Elliott not out	14	33	17	-	-
D.L.Vettori*					
K.D.Mills					
T.G.Southee					
M.R.Gillespie					
Extras (b 1, lb 6, w 13, nb 3)	23				
TOTAL (35 overs) (5 wkts)	**211**	164			

Bowling	*O*	*M*	*R*	*W*
NEW ZEALAND				
Mills	10	2	57	3
Gillespie	10	0	58	4
Southee	10	0	63	0
Vettori	10	1	45	0
Ryder	6	0	35	1
Elliott	4	0	33	0
WEST INDIES				
Edwards	5	0	46	0
Powell	10	0	66	3
Baker	6	0	36	1
Pollard	10	0	40	1
Nash	4	0	16	0

Fall of Wickets

	WI	*NZ*
1st	1	59
2nd	73	96
3rd	243	138
4th	247	175
5th	272	175
6th	279	-
7th	291	-
8th	291	-
9th	293	-
10th	-	-

INDIA IN NEW ZEALAND

India played ten matches in New Zealand from late February to early April. The tour consisted of two Twenty20 internationals, five one-day internationals and three test matches. The original itinerary had two tests, a fixture against New Zealand A, and one Twenty20 game. However, after their series against Pakistan was cancelled, India requested a third test and the itinerary was rearranged.

New Zealand won the two Twenty20 matches but India won the rain affected one-day series 3-1. They also won the test series 1-0, their first series win in New Zealand since their first tour in 1967/68. The Indian batting line-up was daunting, with Sehwag, Tendulkar, Dravid, Laxman and Gambhir all shining at some part of the tour. Of the bowlers, Zaheer Khan and Harbhajan Singh had good tours, consistently taking wickets.

Centuries were scored by Tendulkar (third one-day international and first test), Sehwag (fourth one-day international), Gambhir (second and third tests) and Laxman (second test). Dhoni led the side well and it was no coincidence that when he missed the second test the team had their worst performance of the tour.

Because India played only international matches, some players did not get a game. While the one-day games were taking place Dravid, Laxman, Mishra, Balaji, Vijay and Kulkarni all played one game in the State Championship.

The team was very popular with good attendances at all matches. The touring party was: M.S. Dhoni *(captain)*, V. Sehwag *(vice-captain)*, L. Balaji, R.S. Dravid, G. Gambhir, Harbhajan Singh, R.A. Jadeja, K.D. Karthik, Z. Khan, D.S. Kulkarni, P. Kumar, V.V.S. Laxman, A. Mishra, P.P. Ojha, M.M. Patel, I.K. Pathan, Y.K. Pathan, S.K. Raina, I. Sharma, R.G. Sharma, S.R. Tendulkar, M. Vijay, Yuvraj Singh. Coach, G. Kirsten; Manager, Niranjan Shah (one-day games), Rakesh Yadav (tests).

Jadeja was replaced by Tendulkar for the one-day series while Kumar, Ojha, the two Pathans, Raina and Rohit Sharma were replaced by Balaji, Dravid, Kulkarni, Laxman, Mishra and Vijay for the test section.

New Zealand Test Averages

BATTING	*M*	*I*	*NO*	*HS*	*Agg*	*Ave*	*100s*	*50s*	*Ct*	*St*
J.D. Ryder	3	5	0	201	327	65.40	2	-	2	-
L.R.P.L. Taylor	3	5	0	151	322	64.40	2	-	6	-
D.L. Vettori	3	5	1	118	220	55.00	1	1	3	-
B.B. McCullum	3	5	0	115	232	46.40	1	1	11	-
M.J. Guptill	3	5	0	49	136	27.20	-	-	-	-
J.E.C. Franklin	3	5	0	52	130	26.00	-	1	1	-
I.E. O'Brien	3	5	2	19*	61	20.33	-	-	1	-
D.R. Flynn	2	4	0	67	79	19.75	-	1	-	-
T.G. McIntosh	3	5	0	32	60	12.00	-	-	3	-
T.G. Southee	1	2	0	16	19	9.50	-	-	1	-
K.D. Mills	1	2	0	2	2	1.00	-	-	-	-
J.M. How	1	1	0	1	1	1.00	-	-	1	-
J.S. Patel	1	1	0	1	1	1.00	-	-	-	-
C.S. Martin	3	3	3	4*	4	-	-	-	2	-

BOWLING	*O*	*M*	*R*	*W*	*Ave*	*Best*	*5w*	*10w*
C.S. Martin	134.1	32	458	14	32.71	4-98	-	-
J.D. Ryder	33	14	89	2	44.50	1-3	-	-
J.S. Patel	64	12	180	4	45.00	2-60	-	-
I.E. O'Brien	125.4	29	452	9	50.22	3-103	-	-
D.L. Vettori	136.4	32	366	7	52.28	2-45	-	-
T.G. Southee	30	3	152	2	76.00	2-94	-	-
K.D. Mills	24.2	4	119	1	119.00	1-98	-	-
J.E.C. Franklin	89	17	290	1	290.00	1-38	-	-
J.M. How	1	1	0	0	-	-	-	-
L.R.P.L. Taylor	2	1	4	0	-	-	-	-

India Test Averages

BATTING	*M*	*I*	*NO*	*HS*	*Agg*	*Ave*	*100s*	*50s*	*Ct*	*St*
G. Gambhir	3	6	1	167	445	89.00	2	1	1	-
M.S. Dhoni	2	3	1	56*	155	77.50	-	2	11	1
V.V.S. Laxman	3	5	1	124*	295	73.75	1	2	4	-
S.R. Tendulkar	3	5	0	160	344	68.80	1	2	2	-
R.S. Dravid	3	6	1	83	314	62.80	-	4	4	-
Z. Khan	3	4	2	51*	110	55.00	-	1	1	-
Yuvraj Singh	3	5	1	54*	125	31.25	-	1	2	-
V. Sehwag	3	5	0	48	140	28.00	-	-	5	-
M.M. Patel	3	3	2	15*	24	24.00	-	-	1	-
Harbhajan Singh	3	4	0	60	94	23.50	-	1	-	-
I. Sharma	3	3	0	18	24	8.00	-	-	1	-
K.D. Karthik	1	1	0	6	6	6.00	-	-	1	-

BOWLING	*O*	*M*	*R*	*W*	*Ave*	*Best*	*5w*	*10w*
Harbhajan Singh	147.4	28	342	16	21.37	6-63	1	-
S.R. Tendulkar	9	0	45	2	22.50	2-45	-	-
Z. Khan	115.3	24	400	13	30.76	5-65	1	-
I. Sharma	94.2	21	334	8	41.75	4-73	-	-
M.M. Patel	84	15	290	6	48.33	3-60	-	-
Yuvraj Singh	22.3	2	84	1	84.00	1-11	-	-
V. Sehwag	22	0	116	0	-	-	-	-

New Zealand One-day International Averages

BATTING	M	I	NO	HS	Agg	Ave	100s	50s	Ct	St	SR
P.D. McGlashan	4	2	1	56*	63	63.00	-	1	8	-	123
J.D. Ryder	5	4	0	105	225	56.25	1	1	-	-	106
M.J. Guptill	5	4	1	64	147	49.00	-	2	-	-	84
B.B. McCullum	5	4	0	77	150	37.50	-	2	1	-	85
T.G. Southee	1	1	0	32	32	32.00	-	-	-	-	160
G.D. Elliott	5	3	1	35*	64	32.00	-	-	1	-	103
K.D. Mills	5	2	0	54	54	27.00	-	1	-	-	158
L.R.P.L. Taylor	5	4	1	31	71	23.66	-	-	3	-	93
I.G. Butler	3	2	0	24	24	12.00	-	-	-	-	120
J.D.P. Oram	5	3	0	7	8	2.66	-	-	-	-	57
N.T. Broom	1	1	0	2	2	2.00	-	-	-	-	28
D.L. Vettori	4	1	1	26*	26	-	-	-	-	-	173
I.E. O'Brien	4	1	1	3*	3	-	-	-	1	-	37
S.B. Styris	1	0	0	0	0	-	-	-	1	-	0
J.S. Patel	1	1	1	0*	0	-	-	-	-	-	0
E.P. Thompson	1	-	-	-	-	-	-	-	-	-	-

BOWLING	O	M	R	W	Ave	Best	R/O
I.G. Butler	20	1	117	3	39.00	1-37	5.85
J.D. Ryder	18.4	0	126	3	42.00	3-29	6.85
G.D. Elliott	11	0	89	2	44.50	1-20	8.09
D.L. Vettori	20	0	107	2	53.50	1-14	5.35
K.D. Mills	36	0	229	4	57.25	2-58	6.36
I.E. O'Brien	24.3	1	176	3	58.66	2-43	7.24
J.D.P. Oram	27.3	1	147	2	73.50	2-22	5.38
J.S. Patel	5	0	37	0	-	-	7.40
E.P. Thompson	4	0	42	0	-	-	10.50
T.G. Southee	10	0	105	0	-	-	10.50

India One-day International Averages

BATTING	M	I	NO	HS	Agg	Ave	100s	50s	Ct	St	SR
S.R. Tendulkar	3	3	1	163*	244	122.00	1	1	1	-	108
M.S. Dhoni	5	4	2	84*	184	92.00	-	2	2	1	98
V. Sehwag	5	5	1	125*	299	74.75	1	2	2	-	150
S.K. Raina	5	4	2	66	125	62.50	-	1	1	-	148
G. Gambhir	5	4	1	63*	113	37.66	-	1	1	-	77
Yuvraj Singh	5	4	0	87	100	25.00	-	1	-	-	99
Y.K. Pathan	5	3	2	20*	21	21.00	-	-	-	-	131
P. Kumar	5	1	0	6	6	6.00	-	-	1	-	50
Z. Khan	5	1	0	5	5	5.00	-	-	2	-	50
I. Sharma	2	1	0	3	3	3.00	-	-	-	-	42
Harbhajan Singh	5	1	0	1	1	1.00	-	-	1	-	20
R.G. Sharma	2	1	1	43*	43	-	-	-	1	-	58
M.M. Patel	3	-	-	-	-	-	-	-	1	-	-

BOWLING	O	M	R	W	Ave	Best	R/O
Y.K. Pathan	9.4	0	37	3	12.33	1-1	3.83
Harbhajan Singh	26	0	148	5	29.60	3-27	5.69
Yuvraj Singh	25	0	153	4	38.25	2-71	6.12
I. Sharma	15.2	1	120	3	40.00	2-57	7.82
P. Kumar	25.1	1	161	4	40.25	2-28	6.41
Z. Khan	33	2	184	4	46.00	2-65	5.58
M.M. Patel	9.2	0	93	0	-	-	9.96

NEW ZEALAND v INDIA — First Twenty20 International

at AMI Stadium, Christchurch on 25 February, 2009 (d/n)
Toss : New Zealand. Umpires : G.A.V. Baxter & E.A. Watkin
New Zealand won by 7 wickets.

Batting first, India reached 162-8 thanks mainly to a bright 61 from Raina. His fifty came from 38 balls. Sehwag hit the first three balls he faced on tour for six.

Ryder went early in reply but then all the New Zealand batsmen made good contributions with Brendon McCullum getting fifty from 46 balls. McCullum and Oram combined in an unbroken stand of 60 for the fourth wicket as the BlackCaps went on to a comfortable win by seven wickets with seven balls to spare.

INDIA

	Runs	Mins	Balls	6s	4s
G.Gambhir b O'Brien	6	8	7	-	1
V.Sehwag b O'Brien	26	14	10	4	-
S.K.Raina not out	61	74	43	5	2
R.G.Sharma c McCullum B.B. b Butler	7	9	7	1	-
Yuvraj Singh lbw b Vettori	1	4	3	-	-
M.S.Dhoni*† b Butler	2	5	6	-	-
Y.K.Pathan c Oram b McCullum N.L.	20	7	8	3	-
I.K.Pathan c McCullum N.L. b Ryder	12	13	14	-	1
Harbhajan Singh b Southee	21	25	22	-	2
Z.Khan					
I.Sharma					
Extras (lb 3, w 3)	6				
TOTAL (20 overs) (8 wkts)	**162**	83			

NEW ZEALAND

	Runs	Mins	Balls	6s	4s
J.D.Ryder lbw b Sharma I.	1	5	4	-	-
B.B.McCullum† not out	56	88	49	3	2
M.J.Guptill lbw b Harbhajan	41	26	28	3	4
L.R.P.L.Taylor b Khan	31	28	20	3	1
J.D.P.Oram not out	29	26	15	2	3
N.T.Broom					
N.L.McCullum					
D.L.Vettori*					
I.G.Butler					
T.G.Southee					
I.E.O'Brien					
Extras (w 5, nb 3)	8				
TOTAL (18.5 overs) (3 wkts)	**166**	88			

Bowling	*O*	*M*	*R*	*W*
NEW ZEALAND				
Southee	4	0	42	1
O'Brien	4	0	36	2
Butler	4	0	29	2
Vettori	4	0	18	1
McCullum N.L.	2	0	27	1
Ryder	2	0	7	1
INDIA				
Khan	4	0	20	1
Sharma I.	4	0	35	1
Pathan I.K.	3	0	38	0
Harbhajan	4	0	19	1
Pathan Y.K.	2.5	0	37	0
Yuvraj	1	0	17	0

Fall of Wickets	***I***	***NZ***
1st	25	2
2nd	32	56
3rd	54	106
4th	56	-
5th	61	-
6th	82	-
7th	101	-
8th	162	-
9th	-	-
10th	-	-

NEW ZEALAND v INDIA — Second Twenty20 International

at Westpac Stadium, Wellington on 27 February, 2009 (d/n)
Toss : New Zealand. Umpires : G.A.V. Baxter & A.L. Hill
New Zealand won by 5 wickets.

India were restricted to 149-6 by a good New Zealand bowling effort. Yuvraj struck a fifty from 32 balls but succumbed two balls later.

Brendon McCullum was again to the fore as he played a sheet anchor innings for the BlackCaps. He lost partners at regular intervals but scored fifty from 43 balls. His brother was at the non-striker's end when he struck the winning runs off the last ball to give New Zealand a 2-0 series win.

INDIA

	Runs	Mins	Balls	6s	4s
G.Gambhir c McCullum B.B. b Butler	10	29	13	1	-
V.Sehwag c Vettori b O'Brien	24	15	11	-	5
S.K.Raina c Southee b Butler	0	4	4	-	-
Yuvraj Singh c Oram b O'Brien	50	33	34	4	3
M.S.Dhoni*† not out	28	57	30	-	2
Y.K.Pathan b Vettori	0	3	2	-	-
R.A.Jadeja c Guptill b Southee	19	14	16	1	1
I.K.Pathan not out	15	13	10	1	-
Harbhajan Singh					
Z.Khan					
I.Sharma					
Extras (lb 2, w 1)	3				
TOTAL (20 overs) (6 wkts)	**149**	87			

NEW ZEALAND

	Runs	Mins	Balls	6s	4s
J.D.Ryder b Khan	26	22	15	2	3
B.B.McCullum† not out	69	94	55	1	8
M.J.Guptill lbw b Harbhajan	10	15	19	-	1
L.R.P.L.Taylor b Pathan I.K.	27	35	25	-	2
J.D.P.Oram c Dhoni b Pathan I.K.	0	1	1	-	-
N.T.Broom c Pathan I.K. b Yuvraj	5	5	3	-	1
N.L.McCullum not out	1	11	2	-	-
D.L.Vettori*					
I.G.Butler					
T.G.Southee					
I.E.O'Brien					
Extras (b 1, lb 6, w 5	12				
TOTAL (20 overs) (5 wkts)	**150**	94			

Bowling	*O*	*M*	*R*	*W*
NEW ZEALAND				
Southee	4	0	36	1
O'Brien	4	0	30	2
Butler	4	0	42	2
Vettori	4	0	21	1
Ryder	4	0	18	0
INDIA				
Pathan I.K.	4	0	41	2
Khan	4	0	30	1
Sharma	2	0	19	0
Harbhajan	4	0	15	1
Jadeja	4	0	21	0
Yuvraj	2	0	17	1

Fall of Wickets

	I	*NZ*
1st	29	53
2nd	36	69
3rd	47	125
4th	92	125
5th	94	134
6th	121	-
7th	-	-
8th	-	-
9th	-	-
10th	-	-

NEW ZEALAND v INDIA — First One-day International

at McLean Park, Napier on 3 March, 2009 (d/n)
Toss : India. Umpires : A.L. Hill & R.E. Koertzen
India won by 53 runs (D/L).

Butler was recalled to the New Zealand one-day side for the first time in over four years. Rain interfered with the first one-day international of the tour. India had made 27-0 off 4.3 overs when rain stopped play and the match was reduced to 38 overs per side. India reached 100 off 14 overs and then never looked back. Sehwag needed 37 balls to score fifty, Raina a quick 31 deliveries and Dhoni a more circumspect 66 as the tourists got to 273-4. All the New Zealand bowlers suffered at their hands.

New Zealand had a revised target of 278 from 38 overs and had reached 111-4 off 20.5 overs when more rain fell. The revised target after this stoppage was 216 from 28 overs. Guptill top scored with his fifty coming from 61 balls but New Zealand fell 53 runs short.

INDIA

	Runs	Mins	Balls	6s	4s
V.Sehwag c Taylor b Vettori	77	79	56	1	11
S.R.Tendulkar c McCullum b Butler	20	43	23	-	2
M.S.Dhoni*† not out	84	120	89	-	6
Yuvraj Singh run out	2	17	13	-	-
S.K.Raina c O'Brien b Elliott	66	49	39	4	5
Y.K.Pathan not out	20	15	10	1	2
G.Gambhir					
Harbhajan Singh					
Z.Khan					
P.Kumar					
M.M.Patel					
Extras (b 1, lb 1, nb 2)	4				
TOTAL (38 overs) (4 wkts)	**273**	164			

NEW ZEALAND

	Runs	Mins	Balls	6s	4s
J.D.Ryder c Sehwag b Kumar	11	31	25	-	1
B.B.McCullum† c Harbhajan b Kumar	0	6	5	-	-
M.J.Guptill c Gambhir b Harbhajan	64	90	70	-	5
L.R.P.L.Taylor c Tendulkar b Pathan	31	31	24	-	3
G.D.Elliott run out	11	20	11	-	-
J.D.P.Oram c Dhoni b Yuvraj	0	1	1	-	-
N.T.Broom st Dhoni b Harbhajan	2	14	7	-	-
I.G.Butler c Patel b Khan	0	5	1	-	-
K.D.Mills c Sehwag b Harbhajan	0	1	2	-	-
D.L.Vettori* not out	26	20	15	-	3
I.E.O'Brien not out	3	18	8	-	-
Extras (lb 10, w 3, nb 1)	14				
TOTAL (28 overs) (9 wkts)	**162**	121			

Bowling	O	M	R	W
NEW ZEALAND				
Mills	7	0	69	0
O'Brien	8	1	52	0
Butler	8	1	42	1
Oram	2	0	19	0
Vettori	8	0	42	1
Ryder	3	0	27	0
Elliott	2	0	20	1
INDIA				
Khan	6	1	19	1
Kumar	6	1	28	2
Patel	2	0	14	0
Yuvraj	6	0	42	1
Pathan	4	0	22	1
Harbhajan	4	0	27	3

Fall of Wickets	*I*	*NZ*
1st	69	0
2nd	121	23
3rd	131	81
4th	241	111
5th	-	111
6th	-	132
7th	-	132
8th	-	132
9th	-	132
10th	-	-

NEW ZEALAND v INDIA — Second One-day International

at Westpac Stadium, Wellington on 6 March, 2009 (d/n)
Toss : India. Umpires : E.A. Watkin & R.E. Koertzen
No result.

McCullum had injured his thumb in the first game and could play as a batsman only, allowing McGlashan to make his debut. Sehwag scored a quick fifty from 32 balls as rain interrupted the Indian innings after 19 overs.

Six overs were lost and then at 151-3, after 24 overs, another disruption reduced the game to 34 overs per side. Tendulkar got to fifty from 57 balls before a final rain break brought an end to play with India at 188-4.

INDIA

	Runs	Mins	Balls	6s	4s
V.Sehwag c McGlashan b Butler	54	60	36	1	9
S.R.Tendulkar lbw b Vettori	61	100	69	1	7
G.Gambhir c Elliott b O'Brien ...	30	65	36	-	2
Yuvraj Singh c Taylor b Mills	0	5	4	-	-
M.S.Dhoni*† not out	23	33	19	-	2
S.K.Raina not out	13	13	8	-	2
Y.K.Pathan					
Harbhajan Singh					
Z.Khan					
P.Kumar					
M.M.Patel					
Extras (lb 3, w 4)	7				
TOTAL (28.4 overs) (4 wkts)	**188**	140			

NEW ZEALAND

J.D.Ryder
B.B.McCullum
M.J.Guptill
L.R.P.L.Taylor
G.D.Elliott
J.D.P.Oram
P.D.McGlashan†
D.L.Vettori*
K.D.Mills
I.G.Butler
I.E.O'Brien

Bowling **NEW ZEALAND**	*O*	*M*	*R*	*W*
Mills	7	0	46	1
O'Brien	6	0	44	1
Butler	7	0	38	1
Oram	4	0	29	0
Vettori	3	0	14	1
Ryder	1.4	0	14	0

Fall of Wickets	***I***
1st	76
2nd	139
3rd	142
4th	166
5th	-
6th	-
7th	-
8th	-
9th	-
10th	-

NEW ZEALAND v INDIA — Third One-day International

at AMI Stadium, Christchurch on 8 March, 2009 (d/n)
Toss : New Zealand. Umpires : G.A.V. Baxter & R.E. Koertzen
India won by 58 runs

Patel and Southee came into the New Zealand side for Vettori (who had returned home for the birth of his first child) and O'Brien. McCullum captained the BlackCaps for the first time in a one-day international.

After an early success, New Zealand struggled to contain the Indian batsmen, especially Tendulkar. He reached fifty from 59 balls and his 43rd one-day century from 101 balls. His next fifty then took just 26 deliveries before he retired hurt on 163. Yuvraj scored fifty from 42 balls and Dhoni was three balls slower.

Southee suffered at their hands becoming the second New Zealand bowler to concede 100 runs in a one-day international. India's score of 392-4 was the highest score against New Zealand in a one-day international.

New Zealand started well in their chase with Ryder and McCullum putting on 166 off 22 overs for the first wicket. McCullum had fifty from 52 balls and Ryder fifty from 36 balls but McCullum's dismissal triggered a collapse as the BlackCaps went from 166-0 to 218-7. Ryder got to his maiden century off 72 deliveries. Mills scored a maiden fifty from 27 balls and Southee got some revenge getting his highest one-day score but India won by 58 runs to take a 2-0 series lead.

INDIA

	Runs	Mins	Balls	6s	4s
V.Sehwag b Mills	3	15	6	-	-
S.R.Tendulkar retired hurt	163	206	133	5	16
G.Gambhir c McGlashan b Butler	15	46	27	-	1
Yuvraj Singh c McGlashan b Elliott	87	82	60	6	10
M.S.Dhoni*† c McGlashan b Mills	68	76	58	2	5
S.K.Raina not out	38	22	18	5	-
Y.K.Pathan not out	1	6	2	-	-
Harbhajan Singh					
Z.Khan					
P.Kumar					
M.M.Patel					
Extras (lb 5, w 8, nb 4)	17				
TOTAL (50 overs) (4 wkts)	**392**	229			

NEW ZEALAND

	Runs	Mins	Balls	6s	4s
J.D.Ryder c Khan b Harbhajan	105	108	80	4	12
B.B.McCullum* run out	71	88	68	3	6
L.R.P.L.Taylor run out	7	9	6	-	1
M.J.Guptill lbw b Yuvraj	1	3	4	-	-
G.D.Elliott b Khan	18	27	24	-	1
J.D.P.Oram b Harbhajan	7	9	11	-	-
P.D.McGlashan† b Khan	7	14	9	-	-
I.G.Butler b Yuvraj	24	23	19	1	1
K.D.Mills c Khan b Pathan	54	55	32	3	6
T.G.Southee c & b Kumar	32	36	20	2	3
J.S.Patel not out	0	2	0	-	-
Extras (lb 2, w 4, nb 2)	8				
TOTAL (45.1 overs)	**334**	191			

Bowling	*O*	*M*	*R*	*W*
NEW ZEALAND				
Mills	10	0	58	2
Southee	10	0	105	0
Butler	5	0	37	1
Oram	8	1	34	0
Patel	5	0	37	0
Ryder	5	0	56	0
Elliott	7	0	60	1
INDIA				
Khan	9	0	65	2
Kumar	8.1	0	60	1
Patel	7.2	0	79	0
Yuvraj	10	0	71	2
Harbhajan	10	0	56	2
Pathan	0.4	0	1	1

Fall of Wickets	***I***	***NZ***
1st	15	166
2nd	65	179
3rd	203	182
4th	382	188
5th	-	203
6th	-	217
7th	-	218
8th	-	251
9th	-	334
10th	-	334

Tendulkar retired hurt at 338-3

NEW ZEALAND v INDIA — Fourth One-day International

at Seddon Park, Hamilton on 11 March, 2009 (d/n)
Toss : New Zealand. Umpires : G.A.V. Baxter & R.E. Koertzen
India won by 84 runs (D/L).

Vettori and O'Brien returned and Thompson made his debut, replacing Patel, Southee and Butler (who was injured). New Zealand had an opening stand of 102 with McCullum getting fifty from 66 balls but the BlackCaps had slumped to 175-5 before McGlashan and Elliott added an unbeaten 95 off 61 balls. There had been a stoppage for rain which reduced the game to 47 overs per side. McGlashan scored his maiden fifty from 38 balls to give New Zealand a total of 270-5.

India started at a frantic pace. They were 83-0 after 10 overs when rain came. Four overs were lost and the target went to 263 from 43 overs. Sehwag had scored fifty from just 31 balls as he slammed the attack. Gambhir needed 52 balls for his fifty. At 169-0 off 19.2 overs there was a further interruption and the target became 220 off 36 overs. Sehwag went to his 11th century from 60 balls.

Another shower came at 201-0 after 19.3 overs and when they were able to resume the target was 197 off 33 overs. However, India had already passed that score so they took a 3-0 lead in the series.

NEW ZEALAND

	Runs	Mins	Balls	6s	4s
J.D.Ryder c Raina b Yuvraj	46	84	57	-	6
B.B.McCullum lbw b Khan	77	129	95	2	7
L.R.P.L.Taylor c Sharma R.G. b Pathan	5	11	13	-	-
M.J.Guptill c sub (K.D.Karthik) b Sharma I.	25	55	49	-	-
J.D.P.Oram c Dhoni b Sharma I.	1	4	2	-	-
P.D.McGlashan† not out	56	65	42	1	6
G.D.Elliott not out	35	47	27	1	3
D.L.Vettori*					
K.D.Mills					
E.P.Thompson					
I.E.O'Brien					
Extras (lb 9, w 13, nb 3)	25				
TOTAL (47 overs) (5 wkts)	**270**	200			

INDIA

	Runs	Mins	Balls	6s	4s
G.Gambhir not out	63	105	67	-	6
V.Sehwag not out	125	105	74	6	14
M.S.Dhoni*†					
Yuvraj Singh					
R.G.Sharma					
S.K.Raina					
Y.K.Pathan					
Harbhajan Singh					
Z.Khan					
P.Kumar					
I.Sharma					
Extras (lb 9, w 4)	13				
TOTAL (23.3 overs) (0 wkts)	**201**	105			

Bowling	*O*	*M*	*R*	*W*
INDIA				
Khan	10	0	49	1
Kumar	7	0	51	0
Sharma I.	8	0	57	2
Yuvraj	9	0	40	1
Pathan	5	0	14	1
Harbhajan	8	0	50	0
NEW ZEALAND				
Mills	5	0	29	0
Thompson	4	0	42	0
O'Brien	3	0	37	0
Vettori	5	0	32	0
Oram	4.3	0	43	0
Elliott	2	0	9	0

Fall of Wickets	***NZ***	***I***
1st	102	-
2nd	114	-
3rd	155	-
4th	156	-
5th	175	-
6th	-	-
7th	-	-
8th	-	-
9th	-	-
10th	-	-

NEW ZEALAND v INDIA — Fifth One-day International

at Eden Park, Auckland on 14 March, 2009 (d/n)
Toss : India. Umpires : G.A.V. Baxter R.E. Koertzen
New Zealand won by 8 wickets.

Styris was recalled to the BlackCap side for the last game of the series. India put on a very disappointing batting display in front of a capacity crowd. Only Sharma and Sehwag were able to pass eleven runs in a game reduced to 43 overs due to a delayed start. Ryder had career best bowling figures and received good support from Oram.

New Zealand made light work of their target with Ryder scoring fifty from 38 balls and Guptill needing 49 for his half-century. New Zealand won with 19.4 overs to spare as they gained some consolation with their win.

INDIA

	Runs	Mins	Balls	6s	4s
G.Gambhir c McGlashan b Mills	5	23	16	-	-
V.Sehwag c McGlashan b Oram	40	57	27	3	3
S.K.Raina c Styris b Oram	8	23	19	-	1
R.G.Sharma not out	43	106	74	1	1
Yuvraj Singh c McGlashan b Ryder	11	26	24	-	-
M.S.Dhoni*† b Ryder	9	19	21	-	1
Y.K.Pathan b Ryder	0	3	4	-	-
Harbhajan Singh run out	1	8	5	-	-
Z.Khan run out	5	16	10	-	-
P.Kumar c McGlashan b O'Brien	6	11	12	-	1
I.Sharma c Taylor b O'Brien	3	7	7	-	-
Extras (lb 9, w 9)	18				
TOTAL (36.3 overs)	**149**	154			

NEW ZEALAND

	Runs	Mins	Balls	6s	4s
J.D.Ryder b Sharma I.	63	70	49	4	6
B.B.McCullum b Kumar	2	10	8	-	-
M.J.Guptill not out	57	97	50	2	7
L.R.P.L.Taylor not out	28	37	33	1	4
S.B.Styris					
J.D.P.Oram					
P.D.McGlashan†					
G.D.Elliott					
K.D.Mills					
D.L.Vettori*					
I.E.O'Brien					
Extras (w 1)	1				
TOTAL (23.2 overs) (2 wkts)	**151**	108			

Bowling	O	M	R	W
NEW ZEALAND				
Mills	7	0	27	1
O'Brien	7.3	0	43	2
Oram	9	0	22	2
Ryder	9	0	29	3
Vettori	4	0	19	0
INDIA				
Kumar	4	0	22	1
Khan	8	1	51	0
Sharma I.	7.2	1	63	1
Harbhajan	4	0	15	0

Fall of Wickets	*I*	*NZ*
1st	30	9
2nd	65	93
3rd	69	-
4th	88	-
5th	110	-
6th	111	-
7th	116	-
8th	131	-
9th	143	-
10th	149	-

NEW ZEALAND v INDIA — First Test

at Seddon Park, Hamilton on 18, 19, 20, 21 March, 2009
Toss : India. Umpires : I.J. Gould & S.J.A. Taufel
Close of play: 1st day: India 29-0, Gambhir 6, Sehwag 22; 2nd day: India 278-4, Tendulkar 70, Yuvraj 8
3rd day: NZ 75-3, Flynn 24
India won by 10 wickets.

Guptill made his test debut and Martin was recalled after missing the series against West Indies. After being put in to bat New Zealand were in dire straits at 60-6 before Ryder and Vettori added 186 for the seventh wicket, a record against India. Ryder scored fifty from 102 balls while Vettori needed 85 deliveries. Vettori reached his third test century from 139 balls. The stand of 186 came from 284 balls before Vettori edged Patel to Dhoni. O'Brien helped add 29 before he was stumped with Ryder on 98. Martin survived five balls and then Ryder hit a boundary to reach his maiden test century but was out to the next ball. Apart from the two centurions the next highest score was 18 in a disappointing batting performance. Sharma and Patel were the pick of the bowlers.

India got off to a bright start but lost Sehwag to a direct throw. Gambhir and Dravid scored fifties from 97 and 108 balls respectively but the star of the innings was Tendulkar. He reached fifty from 118 balls and his 42nd test hundred came from a further 50 balls. Zaheer got his third fifty off 45 deliveries. Only three Indian batsmen failed to score 20 as the visitors got a lead of 241. Martin and O'Brien each took three wickets.

McIntosh went in the first over to give Zaheer his 200th test wicket and wickets fell regularly without the big partnership that was needed. Flynn scored fifty from 118 balls. When Vettori went at 199-8 the BlackCaps were in danger of losing by an innings but O'Brien proved a good foil for McCullum as they added 76 for the ninth wicket in 100 minutes. McCullum scored fifty from 85 balls and Harbhajan had his 23rd five wicket bag, taking 6-63. New Zealand were dismissed for 279 and a lead of 38. India scored the runs off 32 balls for a ten wicket win and a 1-0 series lead.

NEW ZEALAND *FIRST INNINGS*	Runs	Mins	Balls	6s	4s	*SECOND INNINGS*	Runs	Mins	Balls	6s	4s
T.G.McIntosh c Sehwag b Sharma	12	75	52	-	1	c Tendulkar b Khan	0	2	3	-	-
M.J.Guptill c Dravid b Khan	14	28	20	-	2	c Sehwag b Harbhajan	48	115	86	1	7
D.R.Flynn c Dhoni b Khan	0	7	3	-	-	c Gambhir b Harbhajan	67	289	183	-	10
L.R.P.L.Taylor b Sharma	18	58	37	-	2	(5) c Sehwag b Patel	4	58	30	-	-
J.D.Ryder c Laxman b Sharma	102	269	162	-	14	(6) lbw b Harbhajan	21	36	27	1	2
J.E.C.Franklin c Dhoni b Sharma	0	3	2	-	-	(7) c Patel b Harbhajan	14	51	44	-	1
B.B.McCullum† c Laxman b Patel	3	10	8	-	-	(8) c Laxman b Yuvraj	84	168	135	-	11
D.L.Vettori* c Dhoni b Patel	118	196	164	2	14	(9) c Dhoni b Harbhajan	21	51	41	-	2
K.D.Mills b Patel	0	2	1	-	-	(4) lbw b Patel	2	20	19	-	-
I.E.O'Brien st Dhoni b Harbhajan	8	29	19	-	1	c Laxman b Harbhajan	14	100	45	-	3
C.S.Martin not out	0	5	5	-	-	not out	0	4	2	-	-
Extras (lb 1, nb 3)	4					(b 1, lb 3)	4				
TOTAL (78.2 overs)	**279**	345				(102.3 overs)	**279**	450			
INDIA											
G.Gambhir c McCullum b Martin	72	173	135	-	11	not out	30	23	18	-	6
V.Sehwag run out	24	40	21	-	5						
R.S.Dravid b O'Brien	66	182	138	-	12	(2) not out	8	23	14	-	2
S.R.Tendulkar c Taylor b O'Brien	160	397	260	-	26						
V.V.S.Laxman c Taylor b Martin	30	108	91	-	4						
Yuvraj Singh b Martin	22	72	50	-	4						
M.S.Dhoni*† c McCullum b O'Brien	47	143	123	-	7						
Harbhajan Singh c Vettori b Mills	16	34	27	1	2						
Z.Khan not out	51	62	46	-	8						
I.Sharma c McCullum b Vettori	6	26	13	-	1						
M.M.Patel c Martin b Vettori	9	22	20	-	1						
Extras (b 6, lb 3, nb 8)	17					(b 1)	1				
TOTAL (152.4 overs)	**520**	634				(5.2 overs) (0 wkts)	**39**	23			

Bowling	O	M	R	W	O	M	R	W
INDIA								
Khan	16	3	70	2	28	7	79	1
Sharma	19.2	4	73	4	22	7	62	0
Patel	18	4	60	3	17	2	60	2
Harbhajan	22	7	57	1	28	2	63	6
Sehwag	3	0	18	0				
Yuvraj					7.3	2	11	1
NEW ZEALAND								
Martin	30	9	98	3	3	0	17	0
Mills	22	4	98	1	2.2	0	21	0
O'Brien	33	7	103	3				
Franklin	23	1	98	0				
Vettori	35.4	8	90	2				
Ryder	9	5	24	0				

Fall of Wickets	NZ 1st	I 1st	NZ 2nd	I 2nd
1st	17	37	0	-
2nd	17	142	68	-
3rd	40	177	75	-
4th	51	238	110	-
5th	51	314	132	-
6th	60	429	154	-
7th	246	443	161	-
8th	246	457	199	-
9th	275	492	275	-
10th	279	520	279	-

NEW ZEALAND v INDIA — Second Test

at McLean Park, Napier on 26, 27, 28, 29, 30 March, 2009
Toss : New Zealand. Umpires : B.R. Doctrove (replaced by E.A. Watkin) & I.J. Gould
Close of play: 1st day: NZ 351-4, Ryder 137, Franklin 26; 2nd day: India 79-3, Dravid 21, Tendulkar 0
3rd day: India 47-1, Gambhir 14, Dravid 11; 4th day: India 252-2, Gambhir 102, Tendulkar 58
Match drawn.

Both sides made changes from Hamilton. Karthik replaced Dhoni, who was injured, with Sehwag taking the captaincy role. How replaced the injured Flynn while Patel replaced Mills.

New Zealand again had a disastrous start being 23-3. Taylor and Ryder then added 271 for the fourth wicket, a New Zealand record against all countries. Taylor scored his fifty from 68 balls and his third century from 151. Ryder reached fifty after 61 balls and his second hundred after 147. He then went on to his double century from 327 balls. Franklin, McCullum and Vettori all played useful hands. McCullum scored his third test century from 131 deliveries as New Zealand declared at 619-9, its third-highest score. Zaheer and Sharma each took three wickets. Harbhajan took his 600th wicket in first-class cricket when he dismissed Patel.

India had a flying start through Sehwag but were 78-3 before Dravid and Tendulkar added 87. Dravid got fifty from 110 balls and Laxman needed 101 balls for his fifty. India went from 246-4 to 305 all out to give New Zealand a lead of 314. Martin had taken his 150th test wicket.

Following on, India batted well. Apart from the opening stand every other wicket added at least 96 with the second and fourth wickets adding over a hundred. Gambhir scored his fifth hundred from 265 balls and Laxman scored his 14th hundred from 187 balls, with the game ending in a draw.

Umpire Billy Doctrove was taken ill at the start of the third day and third umpire Evan Watkin stood for the remainder of the game.

NEW ZEALAND

FIRST INNINGS	*Runs*	*Mins*	*Balls*	*6s*	*4s*	*SECOND INNINGS*	*Runs*	*Mins*	*Balls*	*6s*	*4s*
T.G.McIntosh c Karthik b Sharma	12	29	27	-	2						
M.J.Guptill c Sehwag b Khan	8	45	21	-	1						
J.M.How b Khan	1	8	11	-	-						
L.R.P.L.Taylor c Yuvraj b Harbhajan	151	262	204	1	26						
J.D.Ryder b Khan	201	489	328	1	24						
J.E.C.Franklin run out	52	180	122	-	7						
B.B.McCullum† c Tendulkar b Sharma	115	162	140	-	13						
D.L.Vettori* b Sharma	55	100	72	-	6						
J.S.Patel c Sharma b Harbhajan	1	14	9	-	-						
I.E.O'Brien not out	1	3	1	-	-						
C.S.Martin											
Extras (b 7, lb 8, nb 7)	22										
TOTAL (154.4 overs) (9 wkts dec)	**619**	650									

INDIA

	Runs	*Mins*	*Balls*	*6s*	*4s*		*Runs*	*Mins*	*Balls*	*6s*	*4s*
G.Gambhir c Vettori b Patel	16	77	53	-	1	lbw b Patel	137	643	436	-	18
V.Sehwag* c McCullum b Vettori	34	39	25	1	5	lbw b Patel	22	42	21	-	4
R.S.Dravid c McCullum b Ryder	83	282	206	-	12	c How b Vettori	62	242	20	1	6
I.Sharma lbw b Vettori	0	14	13	-	-						
S.R.Tendulkar c Taylor b Patel	49	98	65	1	7	(4) c McCullum b Martin	64	167	131	1	9
V.V.S.Laxman c McIntosh b Martin	76	197	149	-	14	(5) not out	124	262	212	-	25
Yuvraj Singh c McIntosh b Martin	0	17	11	-	-	(6) not out	54	79	63	-	10
K.D.Karthik† c Ryder b Martin	6	38	31	-	1						
Harbhajan Singh c Martin b O'Brien	18	22	11	1	2						
Z.Khan c Ryder b O'Brien	8	12	6	-	-						
M.M.Patel not out	0	1	0	-	-						
Extras (b 1, lb 7, nb 7)	15					(b 9, lb 1, nb 3)	13				
TOTAL (93.4 overs)	**305**	405				(180 overs) (4 wkts dec)	**476**	723			

Bowling	*O*	*M*	*R*	*W*	*O*	*M*	*R*	*W*
INDIA								
Khan	34	6	129	3				
Sharma	27	5	95	3				
Patel	28	3	128	0				
Harbhajan	41.4	7	120	2				
Sehwag	12	0	73	0				
Yuvraj	12	0	59	0				
NEW ZEALAND								
Martin	24	5	89	3	30	8	86	1
Franklin	15	4	34	0	21	5	48	0
Vettori	19	5	45	2	38	13	76	1
O'Brien	13.4	4	66	2	32	9	94	0
Patel	19	2	60	2	45	10	120	2
Ryder	3	1	3	1	11	5	38	0
Taylor					2	1	4	0
How					1	1	0	0

Fall of Wickets	***NZ***	***I***	***I***
	1st	*1st*	*2nd*
1st	21	48	30
2nd	22	73	163
3rd	23	78	260
4th	294	165	356
5th	415	246	-
6th	477	253	-
7th	605	270	-
8th	618	291	-
9th	619	305	-
10th	-	305	-

NEW ZEALAND v INDIA — Third Test

at Allied Nationwide Finance Basin Reserve, Wellington on 3, 4, 5, 6, 7 April, 2009
Toss : New Zealand. Umpires : D.J. Harper & S.J.A. Taufel
Close of play: 1st day: India 375-9, Sharma 15, Patel 14; 2nd day: India 51-1, Gambhir 28, Dravid 9
3rd day: India 349-5, Yuvraj 15, Dhoni 16; 4th day: NZ 167-4, Taylor 69, Franklin 26
Match drawn.

Dhoni returned to lead India, while Flynn and Southee replaced How and Patel in the New Zealand side. In India's innings only two players failed to reach double figures but Tendulkar's 62 was the highest score. He needed 67 balls for fifty while Dhoni took 86 balls and Harbhajan 58. Martin was again New Zealand's best bowler with 4-98.

New Zealand produced a disappointing batting effort with only three players able to reach 20. It was only the ninth wicket partnership that avoided the follow on with O'Brien making his highest score. Zaheer had his seventh five wicket haul.

With a first innings lead of 182 India piled on the runs. Gambhir got his sixth century from 223 balls while Dravid, Laxman and Dhoni each scored fifties. India set New Zealand 617 to win the game.

When Dravid caught McIntosh he broke Mark Waugh's test record for catches by a fieldsman. Taylor scored his fourth century from 158 balls while both Guptill and Franklin were lbw for 49. O'Brien had added 23 with Vettori when rain came half an hour after lunch. Play did not resume and consequently the game was drawn with India winning the series 1-0.

INDIA

FIRST INNINGS	*Runs*	*Mins*	*Balls*	*6s*	*4s*	*SECOND INNINGS*	*Runs*	*Mins*	*Balls*	*6s*	*4s*
G.Gambhir lbw b Franklin	23	78	47	-	2	lbw b O'Brien	167	352	257	2	16
V.Sehwag c McCullum b O'Brien	48	70	51	1	7	c Taylor b Martin	12	9	7	-	3
R.S.Dravid c Franklin b Martin	35	182	114	-	3	c McCullum b Vettori	60	187	145	-	10
S.R.Tendulkar c McCullum b Martin	62	108	85	-	11	c Taylor b Vettori	9	25	20	1	-
V.V.S.Laxman c McIntosh b Southee	4	25	16	-	-	b O'Brien	61	138	109	-	9
Yuvraj Singh lbw b Ryder	9	11	12	-	2	c Taylor b Martin	40	75	46	1	6
M.S.Dhoni*† c O'Brien b Southee	52	106	89	1	6	not out	56	108	83	-	8
Harbhajan Singh c Vettori b Martin	60	102	78	1	7	c Southee b Martin	0	3	3	-	-
Z.Khan c McCullum b O'Brien	33	41	23	-	6	not out	18	38	31	1	1
I.Sharma c McCullum b Martin	18	43	31	-	2						
M.M.Patel not out	15	25	14	-	3						
Extras (b 2, lb 8, w 3, nb 7)	20					(lb 5, w 1, nb 5)	11				
TOTAL (92.1 overs)	**379**	396				(116 overs) (7 wkts dec)	**434**	471			

NEW ZEALAND

	Runs	*Mins*	*Balls*	*6s*	*4s*		*Runs*	*Mins*	*Balls*	*6s*	*4s*
T.G.McIntosh c Yuvraj b Khan	32	116	74	-	6	c Dravid b Khan	4	48	32	-	-
M.J.Guptill b Khan	17	27	23	-	2	lbw b Harbhajan	49	137	93	2	4
D.R.Flynn c Dhoni b Khan	2	14	8	-	-	b Khan	10	43	39	-	1
L.R.P.L.Taylor c Dhoni b Harbhajan	42	139	92	-	6	b Harbhajan	107	261	165	-	16
J.D.Ryder c Dhoni b Khan	3	22	12	-	-	c Dravid b Harbhajan	0	2	2	-	-
J.E.C.Franklin c Sehwag b Harbhajan	15	52	42	-	2	lbw b Tendulkar	49	250	171	-	7
B.B.McCullum† c Dhoni b Harbhajan	24	88	56	-	2	c Dravid b Tendulkar	6	25	16	-	-
D.L.Vettori* c Dhoni b Sharma	11	13	13	1	1	not out	15	43	24	-	2
T.G.Southee c & b Khan	16	33	27	-	3	c Dhoni b Harbhajan	3	13	13	-	-
I.E.O'Brien c Dhoni b Patel	19	49	38	-	2	not out	19	19	17	-	4
C.S.Martin not out	4	5	5	-	1						
Extras (b 9, lb 3)	12					(b 10, lb 2, w 1, nb 6)	19				
TOTAL (65 overs)	**197**	290				(94.3 overs) (8 wkts)	**281**	419			

Bowling	*O*	*M*	*R*	*W*	*O*	*M*	*R*	*W*
NEW ZEALAND								
Martin	25.1	3	98	4	22	7	70	3
Southee	18	1	94	2	12	2	58	0
O'Brien	22	3	89	2	25	6	100	2
Franklin	14	4	38	1	16	3	72	0
Vettori	9	1	47	0	35	5	108	2
Ryder	4	2	3	1	6	1	21	0
INDIA								
Khan	18	2	65	5	19.3	6	57	2
Sharma	14	3	47	1	12	2	57	0
Patel	8	2	20	1	13	4	22	0
Harbhajan	23	4	43	3	33	8	59	4
Yuvraj	2	0	10	0	1	0	4	0
Sehwag					7	0	25	0
Tendulkar					9	0	45	2

Fall of Wickets

	I *1st*	*NZ* *1st*	*I* *2nd*	*NZ* *2nd*
1st	73	21	14	30
2nd	75	31	184	54
3rd	165	80	208	84
4th	173	98	314	84
5th	182	120	319	226
6th	204	125	397	244
7th	283	138	397	253
8th	315	160	-	258
9th	347	181	-	-
10th	379	197	-	-

ENGLAND LIONS IN NEW ZEALAND

The England Lions made a seven match tour of New Zealand in February and March. They played two two-day games against New Zealand Emerging Players, two four-day matches against New Zealand A, two one-day games and a Twenty20 match.

The team contained seven players who had played for the full England side at either test or one-day level. Wellington player Graham Napier joined the side for the one-day segment. Both of the four-day games were drawn although the Lions were within one wicket of winning the second. New Zealand A won both one-day games and the Twenty20 match.

The England squad was: R.W.T. Key *(captain)*, G.J. Batty, M. Davies, S.M. Davies, L.A. Dawson, J.L. Denly, R.H. Joseph, S.I. Mahmood, S.C. Moore, E.J.G Morgan, G.R. Napier, S.R. Patel, L.J. Plunkett, B.J.M. Scott, I.J.L. Trott, L.J. Wright. Coach, D. Parsons; Manager, G. Jackson.

England Lions First-class Averages

BATTING	*M*	*I*	*NO*	*HS*	*Agg*	*Ave*	*100s*	*50s*	*Ct*	*St*
I.J.L. Trott	2	4	2	138*	271	135.50	1	2	2	-
L.J. Wright	2	3	0	105	229	76.33	1	2	1	-
R.W.T. Key	2	4	1	90	198	66.00	-	2	2	-
S.R. Patel	2	3	0	101	181	60.33	1	1	2	-
S.I. Mahmood	1	2	1	52	59	59.00	-	1	1	-
B.J.M. Scott	2	3	1	47	82	41.00	-	-	4	-
G.J. Batty	2	2	0	64	66	33.00	-	1	1	-
S.C. Moore	2	4	0	43	117	29.25	-	-	2	-
L.E. Plunkett	2	2	0	29	51	25.50	-	-	-	-
E.J.G. Morgan	1	1	0	18	18	18.00	-	-	1	-
J.L. Denly	1	2	0	12	19	9.50	-	-	-	-
M. Davies	2	1	1	6*	6	-	-	-	-	-
R.H. Joseph	1	-	-	-	-	-	-	-	1	-

BOWLING	*O*	*M*	*R*	*W*	*Ave*	*Best*	*5w*	*10w*
M. Davies	55	16	160	9	17.77	4-47	-	-
I.J.L. Trott	24	8	55	2	27.50	2-33	-	-
G.J. Batty	64.4	17	204	6	34.00	3-49	-	-
S.I. Mahmood	44	6	195	5	39.00	3-118	-	-
L.E. Plunkett	55	8	197	4	49.25	2-78	-	-
R.H. Joseph	17.2	4	67	1	67.00	1-67	-	-
L.J. Wright	32	4	118	1	118.00	1-83	-	-
S.R. Patel	10	1	33	0	-	-	-	-

NZ EMERGING PLAYERS v ENGLAND LIONS — Two-day

at Bert Sutcliffe Oval, Lincoln on 22, 23 February, 2009
Toss : England Lions. Umpires : C.B. Gaffaney & E.J. Gray
Close of play: 1st day: NZ Emerging Players 321-7, Hiini 9, Davis 26
Match drawn.

Each team's first innings was limited to 90 overs each. The Emerging Players had a century opening stand with Brodie getting fifty from 99 balls. He then continued to a century after 188 deliveries as the home side reached 321-7. Former Otago player Trott was the most succesful bowler with 3-31.

England Lions reached 277 with Moore (fifty off 37 balls) and Scott (fifty off 122 balls) getting fifties. Davis was the best bowler taking 3-61.

NEW ZEALAND EMERGING PLAYERS

FIRST INNINGS	*Runs*	*Mins*	*Balls*	*6s*	*4s*
T.G.McIntosh* c Patel b Trott	43	154	136	-	6
J.M.Brodie c Davies S.M. b Plunkett	124	355	216	3	12
B.M.K.Patton c Patel b Trott	10	7	10	-	2
B.S.Wilson c Wright b Trott	25	65	64	-	4
A.P.de Boorder c Davies S.M. b Wright	7	14	14	-	1
J.A.Raval c Plunkett b Batty	20	54	41	-	3
S.R.Allen† c Davies M. b Wright	35	43	32	-	6
B.C.Hiini not out	9	38	24	-	-
T.T.Davis not out	26	25	19	-	5
N.B.Beard					
L.J.Shaw					
M.J.McClenaghan					
Extras (lb 3, w 3, nb 16)	22				
TOTAL (90 overs) (7 wkts)	**321**	381			

ENGLAND LIONS

	Runs	*Mins*	*Balls*	*6s*	*4s*
S.C.Moore c Raval b Davis	75	152	82	1	12
R.W.T.Key* c Raval b Davis	31	37	31	-	4
I.J.L.Trott b Shaw	0	3	2	-	-
S.R.Patel c Allen b Davis	6	13	14	-	-
E.J.G.Morgan c Allen b McClenaghan	31	46	37	1	4
S.M.Davies† c Wilson b Hiini	3	4	5	-	-
L.J.Wright c Wilson b McClenaghan	6	6	7	-	1
B.J.M.Scott not out	53	168	124	-	6
G.J.Batty c Patton b Beard	35	73	58	1	3
L.E.Plunkett c McIntosh b beard	2	13	10	-	-
S.I.Mahmood c Davis b Hiini	29	43	42	1	4
M.Davies					
Extras (b 1, lb 5)	6				
TOTAL (68.4 overs)	**277**	284			

Bowling	*O*	*M*	*R*	*W*
ENGLAND LIONS				
Mahmood	14	1	55	0
Davies M.	16	5	35	0
Plunkett	21	4	83	1
Wright	11	1	56	2
Batty	12	2	38	1
Trott	13	4	31	3
Patel	3	0	20	0
NZ EMERGING PLAYERS				
McClenaghan	11.3	1	68	2
Shaw	15.3	4	49	1
Davis	15	2	61	3
Hiini	12.4	1	38	2
Beard	13	2	43	2
Raval	1	0	12	0

Fall of Wickets

	EP	***EL***
	1st	*1st*
1st	101	59
2nd	111	59
3rd	150	66
4th	164	114
5th	216	117
6th	281	124
7th	286	163
8th	-	226
9th	-	230
10th	-	277

Scott was a replacement for J.L.Denly

NZ EMERGING PLAYERS v ENGLAND LIONS — Two-day

at Bert Sutcliffe Oval, Lincoln on 25, 26 February, 2009
Toss : England Lions. Umpires : P.J. Agent & J.M. Busby
Close of play: 1st day: NZ Emerging Players 12-0, McIntosh 4, Brodie 8
Match drawn.

England Lions batted first and were 8-3 before recovering to 278. Moore and Batty both scored half-centuries, from 65 and 62 balls respectively. McClenaghan troubled all the batsmen, taking 5-36, and received good support from Shaw with 3-71.

The Emerging Players were dismissed for 277 with Brodie continuing his good form with another fifty from 88 balls. Hay had an unbeaten sixty. Former England test players Mahmood and Plunkett took seven wickets between them. England Lions were 86-2 at close of play.

ENGLAND LIONS

FIRST INNINGS	Runs	Mins	Balls	6s	4s	*SECOND INNINGS*	Runs	Mins	Balls	6s	4s
J.L.Denly b McClenaghan	0	3	6	-	-	b McClenaghan	0	1	2	-	-
R.W.T.Key* c Allen b Shaw	4	7	2	-	1						
S.C.Moore b Shaw	59	132	92	-	10						
I.J.L.Trott lbw b Shaw	3	15	12	-	-	(2) not out	41	77	54	-	7
S.R.Patel lbw b Styris	31	97	69	-	5	(4) not out	41	41	40	-	6
E.J.G.Morgan c Allen b McClenaghan	38	90	56	-	7						
L.J.Wright c Allen b McClenaghan	7	30	25	-	1	(3) b Hiini	4	33	24	-	-
B.J.M.Scott† b McClenaghan	17	59	46	-	2						
G.J.Batty b McClenaghan	66	114	88	-	10						
L.E.Plunkett c McIntosh b Davis	17	35	30	-	3						
S.I.Mahmood not out	29	65	57	-	3						
M.Davies											
R.H.Joseph											
Extras (lb 5, w 1, nb 1)	7						0				
TOTAL (80.2 overs)	**278**	329				(20 overs) (2 wkts)	**86**	77			

NEW ZEALAND EMERGING PLAYERS

	Runs	Mins	Balls	6s	4s
T.G.McIntosh* b Mahmood	22	73	50	-	1
J.M.Brodie c Trott b Plunkett	57	149	103	-	5
B.M.K.Patton c Morgan b Plunkett	30	51	51	-	5
S.B.Styris c Davies b Plunkett	24	62	36	-	4
B.S.Wilson c Moore b Plunkett	5	11	12	-	1
G.R.Hay not out	60	140	82	-	5
G.H.Worker c Morgan b Batty	28	48	39	-	5
S.R.Allen† c Moore b Joseph	2	11	10	-	-
B.C.Hiini b Mahmood	6	23	24	-	-
T.T.Davis c Scott b Mahmood	15	20	18	-	2
N.B.Beard run out	9	16	11	-	-
M.J.McClenaghan					
L.J.Shaw					
Extras (b 2, w 9, nb 8)	19				
TOTAL (71.3 overs)	**277**	311			

Bowling	*O*	*M*	*R*	*W*	*O*	*M*	*R*	*W*
NZ EMERGING PLAYERS								
McClenaghan	13.2	5	36	5	3	2	9	1
Shaw	14	0	71	3	5	0	26	0
Davis	13	3	61	1	5	1	28	0
Hiini	11	7	16	0	5	1	13	1
Styris	10	4	21	1				
Beard	15	2	53	0	2	0	10	0
Worker	4	1	15	0				
ENGLAND LIONS								
Davies	9	2	34	0				
Mahmood	15.3	0	58	3				
Trott	9	2	28	0				
Plunkett	16	0	76	4				
Joseph	8	0	31	1				
Wright	7	0	29	0				
Batty	7	0	19	1				

Fall of Wickets

	EL *1st*	*EP* *1st*	*EL* *2nd*
1st	0	59	0
2nd	4	108	30
3rd	8	133	-
4th	95	143	-
5th	101	172	-
6th	126	218	-
7th	153	226	-
8th	171	243	-
9th	214	263	-
10th	278	277	-

NEW ZEALAND A v ENGLAND LIONS — First-class

at Queenstown Events Centre on 1, 2, 3, 4 March, 2009
Toss : New Zealand A. Umpires : C.B. Gaffaney & D.M. Quested
Close of play: 1st day: England Lions 123-0, Key 79, Moore 42; 2nd day: New Zealand A 22-1, How 5, Ingram 12
3rd day: New Zealand A 375-3, How 161, Franklin 83
Match drawn.

New Zealand A decided to bowl first and were soon in trouble as the England Lions' openers put together a century stand on a rain affected first day. Key got his fifty from 61 balls and Trott and Patel added 164 for the third wicket off 43 overs. Trott scored his fifty from 98 balls and his hundred from 204 deliveries while Patel's fifty took 73 balls and his hundred took 136. Wright chipped in with a 47-ball fifty as the Lions declared at 493-5.

McIntosh went early but How and Ingram added 177 for the second wicket. Ingram scored his fifty from 113 balls. How reached fifty from 72 balls and his hundred from 199. He went on to reach his highest first-class score, carrying his bat through the innings. Franklin got fifty from 55 balls in a 149 run stand for the fourth wicket. After he was dismissed six wickets fell for 45 runs. Watling was unable to bat due to a finger injury. Davies took 4-54 off 29 overs to be the most impressive bowler.

In the second innings, Moore went early but Key and Trott added an unbroken 140 before the game finished in a draw.

ENGLAND LIONS

FIRST INNINGS	*Runs*	*Mins*	*Balls*	*6s*	*4s*
R.W.T.Key* c Young b McClenaghan	90	181	127	-	10
S.C.Moore c How b Arnel	43	160	115	-	3
I.J.L.Trott not out	138	380	269	-	8
S.R.Patel c Ingram b Arnel	101	165	139	-	16
E.J.G.Morgan b McClenaghan	18	78	66	-	2
L.J.Wright c Young b Williamson	55	68	50	1	8
B.J.M.Scott† not out	34	46	34	-	4
G.J.Batty					
L.E.Plunkett					
M.Davies					
R.H.Joseph					
Extras (b 4, lb 5, w 3, nb 2)	14				
TOTAL (133 overs) (5 wkts dec)	**493**	545			

SECOND INNINGS	*Runs*	*Mins*	*Balls*	*6s*	*4s*
(2) not out	66	167	106	-	8
(1) c Arnel b McClenaghan	11	14	17	-	2
not out	75	151	127	-	10
(lb 2, nb 4)	6				
(41 overs) (1 wkt)	**158**	167			

NEW ZEALAND A

	Runs	*Mins*	*Balls*	*6s*	*4s*
T.G.McIntosh c Patel b Davies	3	13	12	-	-
J.M.How* not out	190	551	380	2	21
P.J.Ingram c Scott b Davies	73	209	161	-	11
K.S.Williamson b Batty	22	77	59	-	4
J.E.C.Franklin c Moore b Plunkett	92	173	146	1	13
R.A.Young† c Joseph b Davies	1	7	5	-	-
L.J.Woodcock c Morgan b Davies	6	77	-	1	
M.J.McClenaghan b Batty	1	19	14	-	-
B.J.Arnel b Wright	0	7	10	-	-
T.A.Boult c Scott b Joseph	8	31	24	-	2
B-J.Watling absent hurt					
Extras (lb 5, w 11, nb 18)	34				
TOTAL (133.2 overs)	**430**	551			

Bowling	*O*	*M*	*R*	*W*	*O*	*M*	*R*	*W*
NEW ZEALAND A								
Boult	21	3	62	0				
Franklin	25	1	113	0	9	0	33	0
Arnel	27	7	56	2	12	0	38	0
McClenaghan	24	1	100	2	8	0	35	1
Woodcock	22	1	90	0	9	2	35	0
Williamson	14	0	63	1	3	0	15	0
ENGLAND LIONS								
Joseph	17.2	4	67	1				
Davies	29	13	54	4				
Plunkett	26	2	96	1				
Wright	21	2	83	1				
Batty	26	7	78	2				
Trott	7	3	21	0				
Patel	7	1	26	0				

Fall of Wickets	***EL***	***NZA***	***EL***
	1st	*1st*	*2nd*
1st	130	4	18
2nd	140	181	-
3rd	304	236	-
4th	356	385	-
5th	437	386	-
6th	-	392	-
7th	-	399	-
8th	-	400	-
9th	-	430	-
10th	-	-	-

NEW ZEALAND A v ENGLAND LIONS — First-class

at Bert Sutcliffe Oval, Lincoln on 7, 8, 9, 10 March, 2009
Toss : New Zealand A. Umpires : E.J. Gray & T.J. Parlane
Close of play: 1st day: England Lions 331-9, Mahmood 40, Davies 5; 2nd day: England Lions 56-0, Moore 29, Key 25
3rd day: New Zealand A 72-1, Redmond 27, Flynn 28
Match drawn.

England Lions were in trouble at 154-6 before the last four wickets added 190. Patel scored fifty from 73 balls and then Wright got a half-century from 56 deliveries. Batty and Mahmood scored fifties from numbers eight and ten in the order. Thompson took 4-98 and was assisted by Arnel with 3-47.

The New Zealand innings was in tatters at 59-5 before Williamson, Young and Thompson gave the innings some substance and the score reached 243.Young needed 72 balls for his fifty, while Thompson scored his at a run a ball.

With a 103 run lead the Lions made a good start. Trott scored fifty from 58 deliveries but he was overshadowed by Wright who scored a 91-ball hundred. Franklin took 3-56 as England declared at 353-9, leaving New Zealand A 457 to win.

How went early and Flynn and Redmond were dismissed quickly after a 92 run stand. Redmond got fifty from 79 balls. At 223-6 the game took a twist. Robertson had been twelfth man but after Thompson was called into the New Zealand one-day squad he came into the game as a full substitute. He went on to score his second century, off 110 balls, and reached his highest score. Chris Martin helped him play out the last twenty deliveries to salvage a draw.

ENGLAND LIONS

FIRST INNINGS	*Runs*	*Mins*	*Balls*	*6s*	*4s*	*SECOND INNINGS*	*Runs*	*Mins*	*Balls*	*6s*	*4s*
S.C.Moore c Redmond b Thompson	22	85	60	-	3	c Young b Franklin	41	158	108	-	7
R.W.T.Key* c Young b Franklin	4	12	9	-	-	lbw b Arnel	38	122	86	-	5
I.J.L.Trott c Flynn b Thompson	7	28	16	-	-	c Williamson b Thompson	51	89	60	-	7
S.R.Patel c Young b Arnel	64	125	101	2	7	c & b Thompson	16	38	27	-	2
J.L.Denly c Martin B.P. b Arnel	12	63	44	-	2	b Martin B.P.	7	9	13	1	-
L.J.Wright lbw b Arnel	69	123	78	-	13	c Redmond b Martin B.P.	105	116	96	1	11
B.J.M.Scott† c Williamson b Martin B.P.	1	45	27	-	-	b Franklin	47	112	109	-	4
G.J.Batty b Thompson	64	112	94	1	10	c Young b Franklin	2	9	8	-	-
L.E.Plunkett b Martin C.S.	29	83	57	1	3	c Williamson b Arnel	22	30	28	1	1
S.I.Mahmood b Thompson	52	70	59	2	7	not out	7	6	3	-	-
M.Davies not out	6	38	25	-	-						
Extras (b 2, lb 6, nb 8)	16					(b 1, lb 8, w 4, nb 4)	17				
TOTAL (93.4 overs)	**346**	386				(89 overs) (9 wkts dec)	**353**	373			

NEW ZEALAND A

FIRST INNINGS	*Runs*	*Mins*	*Balls*	*6s*	*4s*	*SECOND INNINGS*	*Runs*	*Mins*	*Balls*	*6s*	*4s*
A.J.Redmond c Wright b Davies	0	7	7	-	-	lbw b Plunkett	55	107	87	-	10
J.M.How* c Mahmood b Davies	4	37	12	-	-	lbw b Davies	8	17	12	-	2
D.R.Flynn c Batty b Plunkett	33	94	67	-	3	c Moore b Plunkett	45	107	60	-	4
P.G.Fulton c Scott b Davies	9	25	13	-	2	c Trott b Batty	45	148	105	-	7
K.S.Williamson lbw b Batty	35	131	93	1	3	c Scott b Mahmood	48	104	88	-	6
J.E.C.Franklin c Key b Davies	2	8	6	-	-	c Key b Mahmood	1	13	8	-	-
R.A.Young† b Batty	71	139	105	-	11	b Trott	59	119	91	-	5
E.P.Thompson lbw b Batty	60	76	56	1	10						
B.P.Martin c Trott b Mahmood	0	4	3	-	-	c Patel b Mahmood	0	7	8	-	-
B.J.Arnel lbw b Mahmood	0	1	1	-	-	lbw b Trott	5	64	39	-	1
C.S.Martin not out	0	13	9	-	-	not out	0	13	8	-	-
I.A.Robertson						(8) not out	107	194	148	2	12
Extras (b 5, lb 8, w 2, nb 14)	29					(lb 19, w 1)	20				
TOTAL (59.4 overs)	**243**	261				(109 overs) (9 wkts)	**393**	450			

Bowling	*O*	*M*	*R*	*W*	*O*	*M*	*R*	*W*
NEW ZEALAND A								
Martin C.S.	19	4	58	1	16	2	64	0
Franklin	16	2	54	1	16	2	56	3
Thompson	18.4	2	98	4	14	1	72	2
Martin B.P.	17	1	63	1	27	2	113	2
Arnel	20	8	47	3	16	5	39	2
Williamson	3	0	18	0				
ENGLAND LIONS								
Mahmood	16	2	77	2	28	4	118	3
Davies	13	2	47	4	13	1	59	1
Plunkett	8	2	23	1	21	4	78	2
Trott	1	0	1	0	16	5	33	2
Wright	7	0	33	0	4	2	2	0
Batty	14.4	4	49	3	24	6	77	1
Patel					3	0	7	0

Fall of Wickets

	EL *1st*	**NZA** *1st*	**EL** *2nd*	**NZA** *2nd*
1st	8	1	82	15
2nd	24	27	102	107
3rd	51	43	149	124
4th	103	57	162	211
5th	112	59	165	217
6th	154	142	282	223
7th	219	225	291	370
8th	276	226	342	371
9th	299	226	353	393
10th	346	243	-	-

Robertson replaced Thompson who was called into the New Zealand team

NEW ZEALAND A v ENGLAND LIONS — One-day

at Fitzherbert Park, Palmerston North on 14 March, 2009
Toss : England Lions. Umpires : P.L. Gasston & K.C. Manley
New Zealand A won by 35 runs.

This game saw 711 runs scored in one day on a good batting wicket. New Zealand A set the pace with Ingram reaching his highest one-day score. His hundred came from 108 balls. Stewart got fifty from 50 balls and McCullum blasted a fifty from just 26 balls. Napier was the most successful bowler but his wickets were expensive. New Zealand A reached 373-6, the second highest one-day score in New Zealand.

England Lions made a good fist of the challenge and were 263-4 after 40.5 overs. Trott had scored fifty from 60 balls and Morgan fifty from 45 deliveries. Napier raced to fifty from just 22 balls, including seven fours and two sixes, but the Lions collapsed to 338 all out to give the home team a 35 run win. Mason and Diamanti each took three wickets.

NEW ZEALAND A

	Runs	Mins	Balls	6s	4s
A.J.Redmond c Scott b Napier	21	31	25	-	3
P.J.Ingram c Denly b Joseph	135	192	129	1	15
C.D.Cumming* c Scott b Joseph	6	20	16	-	-
J.A.H.Marshall b Trott	34	45	32	-	2
S.L.Stewart b Napier	59	59	57	1	7
G.J.Hopkins† c Trott b Napier	2	10	7	-	-
N.L.McCullum not out	50	44	26	3	5
B.J.Diamanti not out	39	21	15	2	4
G.W.Aldridge					
M.J.Mason					
W.C.McSkimming					
Extras (b 1, lb 5, w 14, nb 7)	27				
TOTAL (50 overs) (6 wkts)	**373**	214			

ENGLAND LIONS

	Runs	Mins	Balls	6s	4s
J.L.Denly b Mason	1	5	5	-	-
R.W.T.Key* run out	44	55	45	-	6
I.J.L.Trott c McSkimming b Mason	94	165	97	-	8
S.R.Patel c McCullum b Diamanti	14	28	22	-	1
E.J.G.Morgan c McCullum b Aldridge	74	70	60	2	7
G.R.Napier c Ingram b Mason	77	53	41	3	9
S.C.Moore c sub (I.P.Sandbrook) b Diamanti	8	5	4	-	2
L.E.Plunkett b McSkimming	7	14	7	-	-
S.I.Mahmood c sub (I.P.Sandbrook) b Diamanti	1	5	3	-	-
B.J.M.Scott† b Aldridge	4	14	6	-	-
R.H.Joseph not out	1	3	1	-	-
Extras (b 1, lb 3, w 7, nb 2)	13				
TOTAL (48.1 overs)	**338**	209			

Bowling	O	M	R	W
ENGLAND LIONS				
Mahmood	10	0	60	0
Napier	10	0	74	3
Plunkett	8	0	61	0
Joseph	10	0	89	2
Patel	5	0	39	0
Trott	7	1	44	1
NEW ZEALAND A				
McSkimming	10	1	53	1
Mason	8	0	61	3
Aldridge	8.1	0	63	2
McCullum	10	0	69	0
Diamanti	9	0	74	3
Cumming	3	0	14	0

Fall of Wickets	***NZA***	***EL***
1st	32	9
2nd	51	70
3rd	138	97
4th	235	226
5th	246	263
6th	300	271
7th	-	316
8th	-	319
9th	-	334
10th	-	338

NEW ZEALAND A v ENGLAND LIONS — One-day

at Fitzherbert Park, Palmerston North on 16 March, 2009
Toss : England Lions. Umpires : W.R. Knights & E.A. Watkin
New Zealand A won by 6 wickets.

In a good all-round batting effort, in which only one player in the top eight failed to reach twenty, England Lions reached 284. Denly scored fifty from 44 balls.

In reply New Zealand A were 138-4 before Marshall and Hopkins had an unbroken stand of 147 off 130 balls. Marshall scored fifty from 49 balls and took a further 50 to reach his hundred. Hopkins scored his fifty from 48 balls as the home team went to a six wicket win and won the series 2-0.

ENGLAND LIONS

	Runs	Mins	Balls	6s	4s
J.L.Denly c Thompson b McCullum	68	94	78	-	8
R.W.T.Key* c Styris b Thompson	21	24	18	-	3
I.J.L.Trott run out	48	79	51	-	6
S.R.Patel run out	27	54	36	-	1
E.J.G.Morgan b McCullum	0	7	7	-	-
S.C.Moore c Mason b Diamanti	29	51	45	-	1
G.R.Napier c Mason b McSkimming	22	22	18	2	1
B.J.M.Scott† b Diamanti	31	40	24	-	4
L.E.Plunkett lbw b Styris	8	14	11	-	-
S.I.Mahmood not out	13	21	13	-	1
R.H.Joseph not out	4	4	3	-	-
Extras (w 9, nb 4)	13				
TOTAL (50 overs) (9 wkts)	**284**	209			

NEW ZEALAND A

	Runs	Mins	Balls	6s	4s
A.J.Redmond c Denly b Napier	17	27	32	-	2
P.J.Ingram b Plunkett	38	60	37	-	6
J.A.H.Marshall not out	125	154	112	-	11
S.B.Styris c Morgan b Plunkett	21	22	21	-	2
S.L.Stewart c Scott b Trott	1	15	9	-	-
G.J.Hopkins*† not out	66	83	67	-	4
N.L.McCullum					
B.J.Diamanti					
E.P.Thompson					
M.J.Mason					
W.C.McSkimming					
Extras (lb 6, w 10, nb 1)	17				
TOTAL (46.1 overs) (4 wkts)	**285**	182			

Bowling	O	M	R	W
NEW ZEALAND A				
Thompson	8	0	50	1
Mason	9	0	71	0
McSkimming	9	0	54	1
McCullum	10	0	41	2
Diamanti	9	0	49	2
Styris	5	0	19	1
ENGLAND LIONS				
Napier	8.1	1	46	1
Mahmood	8	0	50	0
Joseph	4	0	29	0
Plunkett	7	0	33	2
Patel	10	0	57	0
Trott	7	0	44	1
Moore	1	0	11	0
Denly	1	0	9	0

Fall of Wickets	*EL*	*NZA*
1st	36	26
2nd	138	91
3rd	146	126
4th	148	138
5th	189	-
6th	208	-
7th	226	-
8th	249	-
9th	274	-
10th	-	-

NEW ZEALAND A v ENGLAND LIONS — Twenty20

at Pukekura Park, New Plymouth on 19 March, 2009
Toss : New Zealand A. Umpires : W.R. Knights & D.J. Walker
New Zealand A won by 84 runs.

New Zealand A made 227-6 from their twenty overs due mainly to Stewart's innings. He went to fifty from 25 balls and was unbeaten on 88 from 39 balls at the close.

In reply England A were always struggling with Patel the only player to make a good score. His fifty came from 26 deliveries but the Lions were dismissed for just 143. Thompson took 3-23 from his four overs. New Zealand A won by 84 runs.

NEW ZEALAND A

	Runs	Mins	Balls	6s	4s
A.J.Redmond run out	17	18	14	-	3
C.D.Cumming* b Napier	29	23	18	-	6
J.A.H.Marshall st Scott b Trott	24	24	18	1	2
S.B.Styris c Napier b Plunkett	1	2	3	-	-
S.L.Stewart not out	88	53	39	7	6
N.L.McCullum st Scott b Dawson	2	2	4	-	-
G.J.Hopkins† c Dawson b Mahmood	41	22	18	2	5
B.J.Diamanti not out	11	10	7	-	2
E.P.Thompson					
M.J.Mason					
W.C.McSkimming					
Extras (b 8, w 5, nb 1)	14				
TOTAL (20 overs) (6 wkts)	**227**	90			

ENGLAND LIONS

	Runs	Mins	Balls	6s	4s
J.L.Denly run out	7	6	6	-	1
R.W.T.Key* run out	12	10	9	-	2
I.J.L.Trott b McCullum	6	20	10	-	-
G.R.Napier c Cumming b Mason	10	3	4	1	1
S.R.Patel c Redmond b Thompson	64	40	36	5	6
E.J.G.Morgan c Mason b Styris	14	24	13	-	-
S.C.Moore b Thompson	21	13	11	2	1
B.J.M.Scott† c McCullum b Thompson	1	3	3	-	-
L.A.Dawson c Cumming b McSkimming	2	10	3	-	-
L.E.Plunkett not out	3	6	4	-	-
S.I.Mahmood b McSkimming	0	1	1	-	-
Extras (lb 2, w 1)	3				
TOTAL (16.4 overs)	**143**	73			

Bowling	*O*	*M*	*R*	*W*
ENGLAND LIONS				
Napier	4	0	43	1
Mahmood	4	0	43	1
Plunkett	4	0	27	1
Patel	4	0	53	0
Trott	2	0	34	1
Dawson	2	0	19	1
NEW ZEALAND A				
McSkimming	2.4	0	16	2
Mason	3	0	15	1
Thompson	4	0	23	3
McCullum	3	0	43	1
Diamanti	2	0	15	0
Styris	2	0	29	1

Fall of Wickets

	NZA	***EL***
1st	40	17
2nd	54	19
3rd	55	30
4th	97	48
5th	100	111
6th	196	117
7th	-	120
8th	-	139
9th	-	143
10th	-	143

ICC WORLD TWENTY20

New Zealand had a disappointing time at the World Twenty20 in England in June. Although they qualified for the second phase and won their first match at that level, their only wins were at the expense of Scotland, in a seven-overs-a-side game, and Ireland. New Zealand had lost to South Africa by one run earlier in the tournament but that was as close as they got to defeating major cricketing country. The warm up games had been heartening with five wins before a loss to Australia.

The team did suffer from injuries with Jesse Ryder having to be replaced after being hospitalised with a groin injury. Ross Taylor missed some games and Daniel Vettori played only in the last two games due to a shoulder injury.

Brendon McCullum and Ryder's replacement, Aaron Redmond, were the only players to score fifties, with some of the later batsmen failing to produce the runs expected of them. Ian Butler and Nathan McCullum bowled well with the latter opening the bowling in some games. Vettori took four wickets in his two games.

The squad was: D.L. Vettori *(captain, Northern Districts)*, B.B. McCullum *(vice-captain, Otago)*, N.T. Broom *(Otago)*, I.G. Butler *(Otago)*, B.J. Diamanti *(Central Districts)*, J.E.C. Franklin *(Wellington)*, M.J. Guptill *(Auckland)*, N.L. McCullum *(Otago)*, P.D. McGlashan *(Northern Districts)*, K.D. Mills *(Auckland)*, I.E. O'Brien *(Wellington)*, J.D.P. Oram *(Central Districts)*, A.J. Redmond *(Otago)*, J.D. Ryder *(Wellington)*, S.B. Styris *(Auckland)*, L.R.P.L. Taylor *(Central Districts)*. Coach, A.J. Moles; Assistant coach, M.R. O'Donnell; Bowling coach, S.J. Jurgensen; Fielding coach, T. Wilson; Manager, D. Currie; Video analyst; Z. Hitchcock; Physiotherapist, K. Stalker, Trainer, B. Stronach.

New Zealand Averages

BATTING	*M*	*I*	*NO*	*HS*	*Agg*	*Ave*	*100s*	*50s*	*Ct*	*St*	*SR*
M.J. Guptill	5	4	1	45*	102	34.00	-	-	1	-	129
A.J. Redmond	3	3	0	63	101	33.66	-	1	-	-	177
J.D. Ryder	1	1	0	31	31	31.00	-	-	-	-	258
S.B. Styris	5	5	2	42	81	27.00	-	-	2	-	119
L.R.P.L. Taylor	3	3	1	22	51	25.50	-	-	2	-	104
B.B. McCullum	5	5	0	57	107	21.40	-	1	4	-	115
J.E.C. Franklin	3	2	1	7*	14	14.00	-	-	2	-	70
J.D.P. Oram	5	5	0	24	59	11.80	-	-	2	-	109
D.L. Vettori	2	2	0	8	11	5.50	-	-	-	-	78
P.D. McGlashan	5	3	0	8	15	5.00	-	-	2	-	93
N.L. McCullum	5	2	0	7	9	4.50	-	-	-	-	60
K.D. Mills	4	2	0	4	4	2.00	-	-	-	-	57
N.T. Broom	2	1	0	1	1	1.00	-	-	1	-	20
I.G. Butler	5	2	2	2*	3	-	-	-	-	-	100
I.E. O'Brien	1	-	-	-	-	-	-	-	-	-	-
B.J. Diamanti	1	-	-	-	-	-	-	-	-	-	-

BOWLING	*O*	*M*	*R*	*W*	*Ave*	*Best*	*R/O*
D.L. Vettori	8	0	52	4	13.00	2-20	6.50
N.L. McCullum	12.1	0	66	5	13.20	3-15	5.42
I.G. Butler	13	0	98	6	16.33	3-19	7.54
K.D. Mills	14.4	0	115	5	23.00	2-12	7.84
S.B. Styris	6	0	48	2	24.00	1-10	8.00
I.E. O'Brien	1	0	16	0	-	-	16.00
J.D. Ryder	1	0	19	0	-	-	19.00
B.J. Diamanti	2	0	19	0	-	-	9.50
J.E.C. Franklin	6	0	48	0	-	-	8.00
J.D.P. Oram	13	0	99	0	-	-	7.62

NEW ZEALAND v SCOTLAND — Group D

at The Oval on 6 June, 2009
Toss : New Zealand. Umpires : B.R. Doctrove & D.J. Harper
New Zealand won by 7 wickets.

New Zealand's first game of the tournament was reduced to seven overs-a-side due to rain. Scotland blasted 89 runs off their seven overs with Coetzer getting 33 off just 15 balls. Butler took 3-19 off his two overs as Scotland lost three wickets at the score of 89.

New Zealand, in reply, reached the target in just six overs. Ryder got 31 from only 12 balls and Brendon McCullum 18 off just seven as the openers brought up their fifty partnership from 2.4 overs.

SCOTLAND

	Runs	Mins	Balls	6s	4s
R.R.Watson c Taylor b Butler	27	9	10	-	6
N.S.Poonia run out	27	31	15	1	2
K.J.Coetzer c McGlashan b Butler	33	17	15	2	3
J.H.Stander not out	0	1	1	-	-
C.J.O.Smith† b Butler	0	1	1	-	-
G.M.Hamilton*					
D.F.Watts					
N.F.I.McCallum					
C.M.Wright					
G.D.Drummond					
C.S.MacLeod					
Extras (lb 2)	2				
TOTAL (7 overs) (4 wkts)	**89**	33			

NEW ZEALAND

	Runs	Mins	Balls	6s	4s
B.B.McCullum* run out	18	18	7	-	4
J.D.Ryder c MacLeod b Wright	31	13	12	2	3
L.R.P.L.Taylor not out	21	16	10	2	1
J.D.P.Oram c Stander b Watson	8	3	6	-	1
S.B.Styris not out	8	8	4	1	-
M.J.Guptill					
P.D.McGlashan†					
J.E.C.Franklin					
N.L.McCullum					
I.G.Butler					
I.E.O'Brien					
Extras (w 1, nb 3)	4				
TOTAL (6 overs) (3 wkts)	**90**	31			

Bowling	*O*	*M*	*R*	*W*
NEW ZEALAND				
O'Brien	1	0	16	0
Franklin	1	0	12	0
Butler	2	0	19	3
Oram	2	0	21	0
Ryder	1	0	19	0
SCOTLAND				
MacLeod	1	0	19	0
Drummond	2	0	25	0
Wright	1	0	20	1
Watson	1	0	4	1
Stander	1	0	22	0

Fall of Wickets	*S*	*NZ*
1st	30	51
2nd	89	59
3rd	89	68
4th	89	-
5th	-	-
6th	-	-
7th	-	-
8th	-	-
9th	-	-
10th	-	-

NEW ZEALAND v BANGLADESH
At Sir Paul Getty's Ground, Wormsley 26 May, 2009

Bangladesh 146-6 (Mahmudullah 43, Shakib Al Hasan 35) **lost to New Zealand** 147-6 (M.J Guptill 61, P.D. McGlashan 35) by 4 wickets

NEW ZEALAND v IRELAND
At County Ground, Derby 27 May, 2009

Ireland 152-5 (J.P. Bray 48, J.D. Ryder 3-4) **lost to New Zealand** 153-3 (L.R.P.L. Taylor 74, M.J. Guptill 45*) by 7 wickets

NEW ZEALAND v PROFESSIONAL CRICKETERS ASSOCIATION MASTER'S XI
At Sir Paul Getty's Ground, Wormsley 29 May, 2009

New Zealand 198-3 (L.R.P.L. Taylor 74, M.J. Guptill 56*, J.D. Ryder 37 **defeated PCA Master's XI** 144-8 (S.B. Styris 51, I.E. O'Brien 3-14) by 54 runs

NEW ZEALAND v NETHERLANDS
At Sir Paul Getty's Ground, Wormsley 30 May, 2009

New Zealand 194-8 (B.B. McCullum 62, P.M. Seelaar 3-35, R.N. ten Doeschate 3-40) **defeated Netherlands** 104 (J.E.C. Franklin 3-10, D.L. Vettori 3-24) by 90 runs

GROUP A

6th June 2009
Nottingham: **India beat Bangladesh by 25 runs**
India 180 for 5 (20 overs) (G.Gambhir 50, Yuvraj Singh 41, R.G.Sharma 36);
Bangladesh 155 for 8 (20 overs) (Junaid Siddique 41, P.P.Ojha 4-21)

8th June 2009
Nottingham: **Ireland beat Bangladesh by 6 wickets**
Bangladesh 137 for 8 (20 overs) (Masrafe bin Mortaza 33*, D.T.Johnston 3-20);
Ireland 138 for 4 (18.2 overs) (N.J.O'Brien 40, K.J.O'Brien 39*)

10th June 2009
Nottingham: **India beat Ireland by 8 wickets**
Ireland 112 for 8 (18 overs) (Z.Khan 4-19);
India 113 for 2 (15.3 overs) (R.G.Sharma 52*, G.Gambhir 37)

Points: India 4, Ireland 2, Bangladesh 0

GROUP B

5th June 2009
Lord's: **Netherlands beat England by 4 wickets**
England 162 for 5 (20 overs) (L.J.Wright 71, R.S.Bopara 46);
Netherlands 163 for 6 (20 overs) (T.N.de Grooth 49, P.W.Borren 30, J.M.Anderson 3-23)

7th June 2009
The Oval: **England beat Pakistan by 48 runs**
England 185 for 5 (20 overs) (K.P.Pietersen 58, L.J.Wright 34, O.A.Shah 33);
Pakistan 137 for 7 (20 overs) (Younis Khan 46*, S.C.J.Broad 3-17)

9th June 2009
Lord's: **Pakistan beat Netherlands by 82 runs**
Pakistan 175 for 5 (20 overs) (Kamran Akmal 41, Younis Khan 36, Misbah-ul-Haq 31*, Shoaib Malik 30);
Netherlands 93 (17.3 overs) (Shahid Afridi 4-11, Saeed Ajmal 3-20)

Points: England 2, Pakistan 2, Netherlands 2

GROUP C

6th June 2009
The Oval: **West Indies beat Australia by 7 wickets**
Australia 169 for 7 (20 overs) (D.A.Warner 63);
West Indies 172 for 3 (15.5 overs) (C.H.Gayle 88, A.D.S.Fletcher 53)

8th June 2009
Nottingham: **Sri Lanka beat Australia by 6 wickets**
Australia 159 for 9 (20 overs) (B.A.W.Mendis 3-20, S.L.Malinga 3-36);
Sri Lanka 160 for 4 (19 overs) (K.C.Sangakkara 55*, T.M.Dilshan 53)

10th June 2009
Nottingham: **Sri Lanka beat West Indies by 15 runs**
Sri Lanka 192 for 5 (20 overs) (S.T.Jayasuriya 81, T.M.Dilshan 74, L.M.P.Simmons 4-19);
West Indies 177 for 5 (20 overs) (D.J.Bravo 51)

Points: Sri Lanka 4, West Indies 2, Australia 0

GROUP D

7th June 2009
The Oval: **South Africa beat Scotland by 130 runs**
South Africa 211 for 5 (20 overs) (A.B.de Villiers 79*, J.H.Kallis 48, G.C.Smith 38);
Scotland 81 (15.4 overs) (K.J.Coetzer 42)

Points: South Africa 4, New Zealand 2, Scotland 0

GROUP E

11th June 2009
Nottingham: **South Africa beat England by 7 wickets**
England 111 (19.5 overs) (O.A.Shah 38, W.D.Parnell 3-14);
South Africa 114 for 3 (18.2 overs) (J.H.Kallis 57*, H.H.Gibbs 30)

12th June 2009
Lord's: **West Indies beat India by 7 wickets**
India 153 for 7 (20 overs) (Yuvraj Singh 67, Y.K.Pathan 31, D.J.Bravo 4-38, F.H.Edwards 3-24);
West Indies 156 for 3 (18.4 overs) (D.J.Bravo 66*, L.M.P.Simmons 44)

13th June 2009
The Oval: **South Africa beat West Indies by 20 runs**
South Africa 183 for 7 (20 overs) (H.H.Gibbs 55, J.H.Kallis 45, G.C.Smith 31, J.E.Taylor 3-30);
West Indies 163 for 9 (20 overs) (L.M.P.Simmons 77, W.D.Parnell 4-13)

14th June 2009
Lord's: **England beat India by 5 runs**
England 153 for 7 (20 overs) (K.P.Pietersen 46, R.S.Bopara 37, Harbhajan Singh 3-30);
India 150 for 5 (20 overs) (Y.K.Pathan 33*, M.S.Dhoni 30*)

15th June 2009
The Oval: **West Indies beat England by 5 wickets *(D/L)***
England 161 for 6 (20 overs) (R.S.Bopara 55, K.P.Pietersen 31);
West Indies 82 for 5 (8.2 overs)

16th June 2009
Nottingham: **South Africa beat India by 12 runs**
South Africa 130 for 5 (20 overs) (A.B.de Villiers 63);
India 118 for 8 (20 overs) (J.Botha 3-16)

Points: South Africa 6, West Indies 4, England 2, India 0

GROUP F

12th June 2009
Lord's: **Sri Lanka beat Pakistan by 19 runs**
Sri Lanka 150 for 7 (20 overs) (T.M.Dilshan 46);
Pakistan 131 for 9 (20 overs) (Younis Khan 50, S.L.Malinga 3-17)

14th June 2009
Lord's: **Sri Lanka beat Ireland by 9 runs**
Sri Lanka 144 for 9 (20 overs) (D.P.M.D.Jayawardene 78, A.R.Cusack 4-18);
Ireland 135 for 7 (20 overs) (W.T.S.Porterfield 31, N.J.O'Brien 31, J.F.Mooney 31*)

15th June 2009
The Oval: **Pakistan beat Ireland by 39 runs**
Pakistan 159 for 5 (20 overs) (Kamran Akmal 57);
Ireland 120 for 9 (20 overs) (W.T.S.Porterfield 40, Saeed Ajmal 4-19)

Points: Sri Lanka 6, Pakistan 4, New Zealand 2, Ireland 0

NEW ZEALAND v SOUTH AFRICA — Group D

at Lord's on 9 June, 2009 (d/n)
Toss : New Zealand. Umpires : Asad Rauf & D.J. Harper
South Africa won by 1 run.

Diamanti made his debut and South Africa reached 128-7. Only Smith and Duminy were able to pass 20. Butler again bowled well getting 2-13 off his four overs.

Brendon McCullum gave the BlackCaps a good start getting 57 off 54 balls and adding 56 off 11 overs with Taylor. However, the run rate slowed with van der Merwe's four overs conceding just 14 runs. New Zealand needed 36 off the last 3 overs but could only manage 34. Oram was run out going for the tie, giving South Africa a one run win.

SOUTH AFRICA

	Runs	Mins	Balls	6s	4s
J.H.Kallis run out	24	36	23	1	2
G.C.Smith* b Butler	33	55	35	-	4
H.H.Gibbs c & b Styris	3	13	7	-	-
R.E.van der Merwe b McCullum N.L.	0	8	6	-	-
J.P.Duminy c Broom b Mills	29	35	23	2	1
A.B.de Villiers run out	15	9	8	-	2
M.V.Boucher† c McCullum B.B. b Butler	6	9	6	-	-
J.A.Morkel not out	10	13	10	-	-
J.Botha not out	2	4	2	-	-
D.W.Steyn					
W.D.Parnell					
Extras (lb 4, w 2)	6				
TOTAL (20 overs) (7 wkts)	**128**	98			

NEW ZEALAND

	Runs	Mins	Balls	6s	4s
B.B.McCullum* st Boucher b van der Merwe	57	74	54	-	6
M.J.Guptill c van der Merwe b Steyn	6	8	5	-	1
N.T.Broom c & b Kallis	1	4	5	-	-
L.R.P.L.Taylor b van der Merwe	22	44	31	-	2
J.D.P.Oram run out	24	27	18	-	2
S.B.Styris not out	7	16	7	-	-
P.D.McGlashan†					
N.L.McCullum					
I.G.Butler					
K.D.Mills					
B.J.Diamanti					
Extras (b 4, lb 1, w 5)	10				
TOTAL (20 overs) (5 wkts)	**127**	91			

Bowling	*O*	*M*	*R*	*W*
NEW ZEALAND				
Mills	4	0	34	1
Oram	4	0	30	0
Butler	4	0	13	2
Diamanti	2	0	19	0
McCullum N.L.	4	0	18	1
Styris	2	0	10	1
SOUTH AFRICA				
Steyn	4	0	22	1
Parnell	4	0	38	0
Kallis	3	0	17	1
Botha	3	0	17	0
Morkel	2	0	14	0
van der Merwe	4	0	14	2

Fall of Wickets

	SA	*NZ*
1st	49	19
2nd	63	26
3rd	63	82
4th	65	93
5th	85	127
6th	107	-
7th	121	-
8th	-	-
9th	-	-
10th	-	-

NEW ZEALAND v INDIA

At Lord's 1 June, 2009

New Zealand 170-7 (L.R.P.L. Taylor 41, I. Sharma 4-25) **defeated India** 257 (S.K. Raina 45, R.A. Jadeja 41, R.G. Sharma 36, D.L. Vettori 3-24) by 9 runs

NEW ZEALAND v AUSTRALIA

At The Oval 2 June, 2009

New Zealand 147 (P.D. McGlashan 49, S.B. Styris 42, M.G. Johnson 4-20) **lost to Australia** 151-3 (R.T. Ponting 56, M.J. Clarke 49*) by 7 wickets

NEW ZEALAND v IRELAND — Group F

at Trent Bridge, Nottingham on 11 June, 2009
Toss : Ireland. Umpires : E.A.R. de Silva & M. Erasmus
New Zealand won by 83 runs.

Redmond had replaced Ryder in the squad and made his Twenty20 international debut. He scored 63 off just 30 balls to give the side a good start. Guptill, with 45 not out off 32 balls, and Styris, 42 from 25, took the New Zealand side to 198-5.

Ireland were dismissed in 16.4 overs for just 114 with Nathan McCullum having career best figures of 3-15. Mills took 2-12.

NEW ZEALAND

	Runs	Mins	Balls	6s	4s
B.B.McCullum*c West b McCallan	10	21	14	1	-
A.J.Redmond lbw b Cusack	63	38	30	-	13
M.J.Guptill not out	45	60	32	4	-
S.B.Styris c O'Brien K.J. b McCallan	42	19	25	3	1
J.D.P.Oram c Botha b Cusack	15	5	7	1	1
P.D.McGlashan† b Johnston	5	4	5	-	-
J.E.C.Franklin not out	7	6	7	-	-
N.T.Broom					
N.L.McCullum					
I.G.Butler					
K.D.Mills					
Extras (b 3, lb 4, w 4)	11				
TOTAL (20 overs) (5 wkts)	**198**	82			

IRELAND

	Runs	Mins	Balls	6s	4s
W.T.S.Porterfield* run out	1	2	1	-	-
G.C.Wilson c Franklin b Styris	23	34	28	-	2
N.J.O'Brien† c Oram b Mills	3	7	4	-	-
A.C.Botha run out	28	23	17	-	5
K.J.O'Brien c Franklin b McCullum N.L.	2	9	3	-	-
J.F.Mooney run out	12	14	14	-	1
A.R.Cusack c McCullum B.B. b McCullum N.L.	20	14	12	1	1
D.T.Johnston run out	14	14	9	1	-
W.K.McCallan lbw b McCullum N.L.	0	1	2	-	-
R.M.West b Mills	8	7	8	-	1
P.Connell not out	1	3	2	-	-
Extras (lb 2, w 1)	3				
TOTAL (16.4 overs)	**115**	73			

Bowling	O	M	R	W
IRELAND				
Connell	1	0	14	0
Johnston	4	0	43	1
O'Brien K.J.	4	0	31	0
McCallan	4	0	33	2
Cusack	4	0	43	2
West	3	0	27	0
NEW ZEALAND				
Mills	2.4	0	12	2
Franklin	3	0	17	0
Butler	2	0	15	0
Oram	3	0	25	0
Styris	3	0	29	1
McCullum N.L.	3	0	15	3

Fall of Wickets	*NZ*	*I*
1st	51	1
2nd	91	15
3rd	152	57
4th	168	58
5th	176	67
6th	-	86
7th	-	104
8th	-	104
9th	-	112
10th	-	115

NEW ZEALAND v PAKISTAN — Group F

at The Oval on 13 June, 2009 (d/n)
Toss : New Zealand. Umpires : M.R. Benson & R.J. Tucker
Pakistan won by 6 wickets.

Vettori made his first appearance in the tournament after having suffered a shoulder injury. New Zealand struggled against the Pakistan attack. They slumped to 73-6 and then lost the last four wickets for 26 to be dismissed for 99 in 18.3 overs. Umar Gul became the first player to take five wickets in a Twenty20 international match, as he demolished the tail and finished with 5-6 from three overs.

Pakistan were always in control when they batted. Shahzaib, 35 from 28 balls, and Afridi, 29 not out off 18, saw Pakistan reach their target in just 13.1 overs.

NEW ZEALAND

	Runs	Mins	Balls	6s	4s
B.B.McCullum c Fawad b Razzak	12	8	6	-	2
A.J.Redmond c Gul b Aamer	15	18	14	-	2
M.J.Guptill lbw b Razzak	8	14	8	-	1
S.B.Styris c Afridi b Gul	22	33	29	1	-
J.D.P.Oram c Misbah b Afridi	5	12	11	-	-
P.D.McGlashan† lbw b Gul	8	14	8	-	1
N.L.McCullum b Gul	7	9	11	-	1
J.E.C.Franklin b Gul	7	16	13	-	-
D.L.Vettori* run out	8	11	9	-	1
K.D.Mills c Shahzaib b Gul	0	1	1	-	-
I.G.Butler not out	1	4	1	-	-
Extras (lb 4, w 2)	6				
TOTAL (18.3 overs)	**99**	79			

PAKISTAN

	Runs	Mins	Balls	6s	4s
Kamran Akmal† c Guptill b Mills	19	18	14	1	1
Shahzaib Hasan run out	35	37	28	2	4
Abdul Razzak c McGlashan b Vettori	5	13	8	-	-
Shoaib Malik c McCullum B.B. b Vettori	4	5	3	-	1
Shahid Afridi not out	29	19	18	-	3
Younis Khan* not out	6	17	9	-	-
Misbah-ul-Haq					
Fawad Alam					
Umar Gul					
Saeed Ajmal					
Mohammad Aamer					
Extras (w 1, nb 1)	2				
TOTAL (13.1 overs) (4 wkts)	**100**	57			

Bowling	O	M	R	W
PAKISTAN				
Aamer	3	0	23	1
Razzak	3.3	1	17	2
Ajmal	4	0	24	0
Afridi	4	0	17	1
Malik	1	0	8	0
Gul	3	0	6	5
NEW ZEALAND				
Mills	4	0	28	1
Franklin	2	0	19	0
Vettori	4	0	20	2
Butler	2	0	22	0
McCullum N.L.	1.1	0	11	0

Fall of Wickets

	NZ	P
1st	17	36
2nd	33	61
3rd	37	61
4th	55	71
5th	73	-
6th	73	-
7th	88	-
8th	93	-
9th	93	-
10th	99	-

NEW ZEALAND v SRI LANKA — Group F

at Trent Bridge, Nottingham on 16 June, 2009
Toss : Sri Lanka. Umpires : S.J. Davis & S.J.A. Taufel
Sri Lanka won by 48 runs.

New Zealand needed to win this game to have any chance of reaching the semi-finals. Sri Lanka reached 158-5 with the tournament's leading scorer, Dilshan, getting 48 off 37 balls. He was assisted by Jayawardene who made 41 not out from 29 balls and Sangakkara, 35 from 35. Vettori was the best bowler with 2-32.

New Zealand were 64-2 at one stage but collapsed to be 110 all out in just 17 overs. Only Guptill, 43 off 34 balls, and Redmond, 23 from 13, were able to pass 10 runs in a disappointing effort. Mendis took 3-9 and Udana 2-17.

SRI LANKA

	Runs	Mins	Balls	6s	4s
T.M.Dilshan c McCullum B.B. b Vettori	48	49	37	-	5
S.T.Jayasuriya c Taylor b McCullum N.L.	0	2	1	-	-
L.P.C.Silva c Oram b Mills	13	14	10	-	2
K.C.Sangakkara*† c Styris b Vettori	35	55	35	-	3
D.P.M.D.Jayawardene not out	41	35	29	1	6
J.Mubarak lbw b Butler	8	3	5	-	1
A.D.Mathews not out	6	6	4	-	-
I.Udana					
S.L.Malinga					
M.Muralitharan					
B.A.W.Mendis					
Extras (b 1, lb 1, w 4, nb 1)	7				
TOTAL (20 overs) (5 wkts)	**158**	85			

NEW ZEALAND

	Runs	Mins	Balls	6s	4s
B.B.McCullum c Mubarak b Udana	10	11	12	-	2
A.J.Redmond c Silva b Malinga	23	27	13	1	3
M.J.Guptill c Mathews b Jayasuriya	43	45	34	1	4
L.R.P.L.Taylor st Sangakkara b Mendis	8	8	8	-	1
S.B.Styris b Mendis	2	1	3	-	-
J.D.P.Oram b Udana	7	16	12	-	-
P.D.McGlashan† c Mubarak b Mendis	2	5	3	-	-
N.L.McCullum run out	2	5	4	-	-
D.L.Vettori* c Malinga b Muralitharan	3	6	5	-	-
K.D.Mills run out	4	8	6	-	1
I.G.Butler not out	2	5	2	-	-
Extras (lb 1, w 3)	4				
TOTAL (17 overs)	**110**	78			

Bowling	*O*	*M*	*R*	*W*
NEW ZEALAND				
McCullum N.L.	4	0	22	1
Mills	4	0	41	1
Oram	4	0	23	0
Butler	3	0	29	1
Vettori	4	0	32	2
Styris	1	0	9	0
SRI LANKA				
Udana	3	0	17	2
Jayasuriya	3	0	28	1
Muralitharan	4	0	18	1
Malinga	3	0	26	1
Mendis	3	0	9	3
Dilshan	1	0	11	0

Fall of Wickets	*SL*	*NZ*
1st	3	30
2nd	25	39
3rd	87	64
4th	137	66
5th	147	93
6th	-	95
7th	-	98
8th	-	100
9th	-	102
10th	-	110

18th June 2009 (Semi-final)
Nottingham: **Pakistan beat South Africa by 7 runs**
Pakistan 149 for 4 (20 overs) (Shahid Afridi 51, Shoaib Malik 34);
South Africa 142 for 5 (20 overs) (J.H.Kallis 64, J.P.Duminy 44*)

19th June 2009 (Semi-final)
The Oval: **Sri Lanka beat West Indies by 57 runs**
Sri Lanka 158 for 5 (20 overs) (T.M.Dilshan 96*);
West Indies 101 (17.4 overs) (C.H.Gayle 63*, A.D.Mathews 3-16, M.Muralitharan 3-29)

21st June 2009 (Final)
Lord's: **Pakistan beat Sri Lanka by 8 wickets**
Sri Lanka 138 for 6 (20 overs) (K.C.Sangakkara 64*, A.D.Mathews 35*, Abdul Razzak 3-20);
Pakistan 139 for 2 (18.4 overs) (Shahid Afridi 54*, Kamran Akmal 37)

INTERNATIONAL SUMMARY

2008/09

Test Matches

	Played	Won	Lost	Drawn
India	3	–	1	2
Bangladesh	2	1	–	1
Australia	2	–	2	–
West Indies	2	–	–	2
TOTAL	9	1	3	5

New Zealand Test Averages

BATTING	M	I	NO	HS	Agg	Ave	100s	50s	Ct	St
J.D. Ryder	9	16	2	201	771	55.07	2	4	8	-
D.L. Vettori	9	14	3	118	475	43.18	1	3	8	-
L.R.P.L. Taylor	9	15	0	151	587	39.13	2	1	15	-
D.R. Flynn	8	15	3	95	459	38.25	-	3	3	-
B.B. McCullum	9	15	1	115	525	37.50	1	3	31	3
A.J. Redmond	4	8	1	83	245	35.00	-	2	5	-
T.G. McIntosh	5	9	1	136	257	32.12	1	-	3	-
M.J. Guptill	3	5	0	49	136	27.20	-	-	-	-
J.E.C. Franklin	5	8	1	52	139	19.85	-	1	2	-
P.G. Fulton	1	2	0	29	36	18.00	-	-	2	-
J.M. How	7	13	0	54	213	16.38	-	1	6	-
T.G. Southee	3	6	1	16	44	8.80	-	-	1	-
G.D. Elliott	2	3	1	9	17	8.50	-	-	-	-
I.E. O'Brien	9	12	3	19*	74	8.22	-	-	2	-
J.D.P. Oram	1	2	1	8*	8	8.00	-	-	-	-
K.D. Mills	5	7	1	18	37	6.16	-	-	1	-
C.S. Martin	5	7	3	4*	6	1.50	-	-	2	-
J.S. Patel	4	3	0	2	3	1.00	-	-	1	-
M.R. Gillespie	1	1	1	16*	16	-	-	-	-	-

BOWLING	O	M	R	W	Ave	Best	5w	10w
A.J. Redmond	10.3	1	58	3	19.33	2-47	-	
D.L. Vettori	419.2	122	980	36	27.22	6-56	3	
I.E. O'Brien	310.5	76	971	32	30.34	6-75	1	
J.S. Patel	191.1	60	496	15	33.06	5-110	1	
C.S. Martin	200.1	45	679	20	33.95	4-98	-	
J.D. Ryder	52	17	156	4	39.00	2-7	-	
G.D. Elliott	16	5	44	1	44.00	1-15	-	
T.G. Southee	91.2	12	377	7	53.85	4-63	-	
K.D. Mills	115.2	28	375	5	75.00	3-64	-	
J.E.C. Franklin	137	24	469	4	117.25	2-61	-	
J.M. How	1	1	0	0	-	-	-	
L.R.P.L. Taylor	2	1	4	0	-	-	-	
J.D.P. Oram	28	16	33	0	-	-	-	
M.R. Gillespie	21	5	102	0	-	-	-	

One-day Internationals

	Played	Won	Lost	Tied	NR
West Indies	5	2	1	–	2
Australia	5	2	2	–	1
India	5	1	3	–	1
Bangladesh	3	2	1	–	–
TOTAL	**18**	**7**	**7**	**–**	**4**

New Zealand One-day International Averages

BATTING	*M*	*I*	*NO*	*HS*	*Agg*	*Ave*	*100s*	*50s*	*Ct*	*St*	*SR*
P.D. McGlashan	4	2	1	56*	63	63.00	-	1	8	-	123
M.J. Guptill	12	11	3	122*	448	56.00	1	3	3	-	87
G.D. Elliott	15	10	4	115	318	53.00	1	1	3	-	86
L.R.P.L. Taylor	18	16	3	103	591	45.46	1	4	8	-	81
J.D. Ryder	12	10	0	105	359	35.90	1	1	3	-	91
J.D.P. Oram	11	7	1	75*	168	28.00	-	2	3	-	86
B.B. McCullum	18	16	0	77	382	23.87	-	2	14	-	79
D.L. Vettori	17	8	4	30	91	22.75	-	-	6	-	80
J.M. How	6	5	0	73	107	21.40	-	1	4	-	66
T.G. Southee	14	7	3	32	84	21.00	-	-	-	-	137
P.G. Fulton	5	5	0	40	95	19.00	-	-	3	-	61
K.D. Mills	18	10	1	54	163	18.11	-	1	1	-	86
N.T. Broom	8	8	2	29	107	17.83	-	-	-	-	74
J.S. Patel	8	4	3	9	15	15.00	-	-	1	-	60
D.R. Flynn	8	7	1	25	84	14.00	-	-	-	-	54
I.G. Butler	3	2	0	24	24	12.00	-	-	-	-	120
S.B. Styris	4	3	0	12	16	5.33	-	-	2	-	41
M.S. Sinclair	1	1	0	2	2	2.00	-	-	-	-	18
C.D. Cumming	1	1	0	0	0	0.00	-	-	-	-	0
B.J. Diamanti	1	1	1	26*	26	-	-	-	1	-	118
I.E. O'Brien	9	2	2	3*	3	-	-	-	1	-	27
M.R. Gillespie	4	1	1	2*	2	-	-	-	-	-	100
E.P. Thompson	1	-	-	-	-	-	-	-	-	-	-

BOWLING	*O*	*M*	*R*	*W*	*Ave*	*Best*	*R/O*
K.D. Mills	137.4	11	645	26	24.80	4-35	4.68
M.R. Gillespie	30.3	3	149	6	24.83	4-58	4.88
I.E. O'Brien	69.3	3	429	13	33.00	3-68	6.17
J.D. Ryder	32.4	0	203	6	33.83	3-29	6.21
J.D.P. Oram	61.3	5	242	7	34.57	2-16	3.93
I.G. Butler	20	1	117	3	39.00	1-37	5.85
S.B. Styris	12	0	45	1	45.00	1-22	3.75
J.S. Patel	47.4	3	238	5	47.60	2-29	4.99
D.L. Vettori	126	4	525	11	47.72	4-20	4.17
G.D. Elliott	38	0	238	4	59.50	2-44	6.26
T.G. Southee	117	3	652	10	65.20	2-33	5.57
D.R. Flynn	1	0	6	0	-	-	6.00
B.J. Diamanti	2	0	25	0	-	-	12.50
E.P. Thompson	4	0	42	0	-	-	10.50

Twenty20 Internationals

	Played	Won	Lost	Tied	NR
West Indies	2	1	1	–	–
India	2	2	–	–	–
Australia	1	–	1	–	–
Scotland	1	1	–	–	–
South Africa	1	–	1	–	–
Ireland	1	1	–	–	–
Pakistan	1	–	1	–	–
Sri Lanka	1	–	1	–	–
TOTAL	**10**	**5**	**5**	–	–

New Zealand Twenty20 International Averages

BATTING	*M*	*I*	*NO*	*HS*	*Agg*	*Ave*	*100s*	*50s*	*Ct*	*St*	*SR*
B.B. McCullum	10	10	2	69*	366	45.75	-	5	8	-	127
A.J. Redmond	3	3	0	63	101	33.66	-	1	-	-	177
L.R.P.L. Taylor	7	7	1	63	178	29.66	-	1	4	-	120
J.D. Ryder	5	5	0	62	132	26.40	-	1	1	-	148
S.B. Styris	6	6	2	42	102	25.50	-	-	2	-	127
M.J. Guptill	8	7	1	45*	153	25.50	-	-	2	-	119
N.T. Broom	5	3	0	36	42	14.00	-	-	2	-	123
J.D.P. Oram	9	9	1	29*	110	13.75	-	-	6	-	115
N.L. McCullum	8	4	2	10*	20	10.00	-	-	1	-	95
J.E.C. Franklin	6	5	1	20	39	9.75	-	-	2	-	105
K.D. Mills	6	4	1	10*	20	6.66	-	-	1	-	100
D.R. Flynn	2	2	0	10	13	6.50	-	-	2	-	118
D.L. Vettori	7	4	1	8	15	5.00	-	-	3	-	75
P.D. McGlashan	5	3	0	8	15	5.00	-	-	2	-	93
T.G. Southee	5	1	0	2	2	2.00	-	-	3	-	66
P.G. Fulton	1	1	0	1	1	1.00	-	-	-	-	12
G.D. Elliott	1	1	1	23*	23	-	-	-	-	-	76
I.G. Butler	8	2	2	2*	3	-	-	-	-	-	100
E.P. Thompson	1	1	1	1*	1	-	-	-	-	-	100
J.S. Patel	2	-	-	-	-	-	-	-	1	-	-
I.E. O'Brien	4	-	-	-	-	-	-	-	-	-	-
B.J. Diamanti	1	-	-	-	-	-	-	-	-	-	-

BOWLING	*O*	*M*	*R*	*W*	*Ave*	*Best*	*R/O*
G.D. Elliott	1	0	11	1	11.00	1-11	11.00
J.S. Patel	6	1	46	4	11.50	2-12	7.67
D.L. Vettori	28	0	149	12	12.41	3-16	5.32
N.L. McCullum	16.1	0	107	6	17.83	3-15	6.62
E.P. Thompson	3	1	18	1	18.00	1-18	6.00
I.G. Butler	25	0	199	11	18.09	3-19	7.96
I.E. O'Brien	13	0	116	6	19.33	2-30	8.92
S.B. Styris	6	0	48	2	24.00	1-10	8.00
K.D. Mills	22.4	0	177	6	29.50	2-12	7.81
T.G. Southee	20	0	192	5	38.40	1-31	9.60
J.D. Ryder	7	0	44	1	44.00	1-7	6.29
J.D.P. Oram	20	0	158	1	158.00	1-24	7.90
B.J. Diamanti	2	0	19	0	-	-	9.50
J.E.C. Franklin	7	0	54	0	-	-	7.71

PROVINCIAL SUMMARIES

AUCKLAND CRICKET ASSOCIATION

Formed 1883, affiliated 1894/95.

Selectors: M.R. O'Donnell (replaced by P.A. Strang), R.M.J. Armour, K. Patel and W. Wheeler

Auckland won the State Championship, defeating Central Districts in the final. In contrast, Auckland finished last in the State Shield and third in the Twenty20 competition.

Reece Young led the scoring with 557 runs followed by Colin de Grandhomme (545) and captain Richard Jones (502). Tharan Nethula, who was the leading wicket taker in the competition, had 28 victims and was followed by Daryl Tuffey (27), Lance Shaw (26), Andy McKay (23) and de Grandhomme (21). Gareth Hopkins had 25 dismissals as wicket-keeper.

Young (312) was also the leading scorer in the State Shield while Chris Martin (12) took the most wickets. In the Twenty20 competition Jones was the top scorer with 152 runs while Azhar Abbas topped the bowling with 10 victims.

When Mark O'Donnell was appointed as New Zealand's assistant coach, Paul Strang took over the reins with assistance from Matt Horne. Contracted players were: Michael Bates, Andrew de Boorder, Colin de Grandhomme, Martin Guptill, Roneel Hira, Paul Hitchcock, Richard Jones, Tim McIntosh, Andy McKay, Rob Nicol, Lance Shaw and Reece Young.

CANTERBURY CRICKET ASSOCIATION

Formed 1877, affiliated 1894/95.

Selectors: R.M. Carter, S.J. Jurgensen and G.K. MacDonald

Canterbury came last in the State Championship but were second in both the one-day tables. They lost to Otago in the State Shield semi-final and the Twenty20 final was washed out.

Johann Myburgh (739) and Michael Papps (719) were Canterbury's leading run scorers in the Championship while Hamish Bennett (26 wickets) and Andrew Ellis (23) were the most successful bowlers.

Papps (416 runs) led the way in the State Shield, followed by Shanan Stewart (376), Peter Fulton (339) and Myburgh (324). Shane Bond (19 wickets) was by far the most successful bowler. Myburgh (328 runs) and Bond (11 wickets) were Canterbury's leading players in Twenty20.

Bob Carter took over the coaching duties after Dave Nosworthy returned to South Africa. Contracted players were: Corey Anderson, Todd Astle, Hamish Bennett, Leighton Burtt, Michael Davidson, Andrew Ellis, Brandon Hiini, Johann Myburgh, Michael Papps, Iain Robertson, Shanan Stewart, Kruger van Wyk.

CENTRAL DISTRICTS CRICKET ASSOCIATION

Formed 1950, affiliated 1954/55.

Selectors: D.A. Reeve and P.S. Briasco

Central Districts started the season with three wins in the State Championship and were always in one of the top two positions. They lost momentum after the break but still finished in second place before losing to Auckland in the final. Central struggled in the one-day programme, finishing fourth in the State Shield and fifth in the Twenty20.

Mathew Sinclair was the leading run scorer in both the Championship and the Shield. He scored 904 runs in the Championship followed by Peter Ingram (884) and Brad Patton (521). Mitchell McClenaghan was the leading bowler with 26 wickets. Bevan Griggs had 26 victims behind the stumps and Sinclair took 18 catches.

Sinclair scored 532 runs in the State Shield, followed by Ingram with 386. McClenaghan (13) was again the leading wicket taker. In Twenty20 Sinclair scored 254 runs and Michael Mason claimed nine wickets.

Dermot Reeve took over as coach. Contracted players were: Brendon Diamanti, Bevan Griggs, Greg Hay, Brett Hefford, Peter Ingram, Tim Lythe, Mitchell McClenaghan, Robbie Schaw, Richard Sherlock, Mathew Sinclair, Ewen Thompson, Tim Weston.

NORTHERN DISTRICTS CRICKET ASSOCIATION

Formed 1953, granted Plunket Shield status 1956/57

Selectors: A.J. Moles (replaced by G.E. Bradburn), P.J. Malcon and C.J. Stevens

Northern Districts won the State Shield but struggled in the other competitions, finishing fourth in the Championship and last in the Twenty20.

Kane Williamson (707) and Michael Parlane (599) were their leading run scorers in the Championship while Bruce Martin was the most successful bowler with 21 victims. In the Shield, B-J Watling top scored with 509 runs followed by skipper James Marshall (388), Parlane (338) and Williamson (320). Brent Arnel took 17 wickets with newcomer Trent Boult getting 16. Peter McGlashan top scored with 161 runs in Twenty20 while Joseph Yovich (14) and Martin (11) were the leading bowlers.

Andy Moles started the season as coach but was appointed BlackCaps' coach in December. Grant Bradburn took over and was reappointed for 2009/10.

Contracted players were: Graeme Aldridge, Steve Andrews, Brent Arnel, Trent Boult, Bruce Martin, Peter McGlashan, Cameron Merchant, Michael Parlane, Bradley Scott, B-J Watling, Kane Williamson, Joseph Yovich.

OTAGO CRICKET ASSOCIATION

Formed 1876, affiliated 1894/95.

Selectors: M. Hesson, S.F. Forde and M.A. Bracewell

Otago won the State Twenty20 competition and qualified for the Champions League. They were beaten finalists in the State Shield, after defeating second qualifier Canterbury in the semi-final but could only finish in fifth place in the Championship.

In the Championship, captain Craig Cumming scored 784 runs, followed by Neil Broom (501). Neil Wagner took 24 wickets. Wicketkeeper Derek de Boorder had 15 victims in the first four rounds but missed the rest of the season due to injury. Shaun Haig deputised. Cumming was also the top run scorer in the Shield with 421. Wagner was the competition's leading wicket taker with 24, followed by Ian Butler (18).

In the Twenty20 games Aaron Redmond led the way with 325 runs (the most in the competition) while Hamish Rutherford, in his first season, scored 220. Butler took 10 wickets.

Michael Hesson again coached the side. Contracted players were: Derek de Boorder, Neil Broom, Ian Butler, Craig Cumming, Michael Harvie, Nathan McCullum, James McMillan, Warren McSkimming, Leighton Morgan, Craig Smith, Greg Todd, Neil Wagner.

WELLINGTON CRICKET ASSOCIATION

Formed 1875, affiliated 1894/95.

Selectors: A.M. Stuart, G.M. Hooper, L.R. Dry, C. van Dyk and M.R. Heissenbuttel

Wellington was the only side not to reach a final in 2008/09, finishing third in the State Championship, fifth in the State Shield and fourth in the Twenty20.

James Franklin scored 631 runs in the Championship followed by Matthew Bell (591). Bell broke the record for most centuries for one province during the season. Luke Woodcock and Dewayne Bowden topped the bowling with 16 wickets each. Chris Nevin had 22 victims behind the stumps.

Bell (336) and Franklin (306) were the top run scorers in the Shield. Graham Napier took 21 wickets. Franklin again led the way, with 209 runs, in Twenty20 while Napier (14) and Woodcock (11) were the leading wicket-takers.

The side was again coached by Anthony Stuart. Contracted players were: Matthew Bell, Harry Boam, Dewayne Bowden, Josh Brodie, Michael Burns, B-J Crook, Grant Elliott, Kevin Forde, Mark Houghton, Chris Nevin, Neal Parlane, Luke Woodcock.

STATE CHAMPIONSHIP REVIEW 2008/09

Each side again played eight matches with the two top qualifiers meeting in the final. Auckland topped the points table meaning second placed Central Districts had to win outright to claim the title. The final was scheduled for Lincoln, regardless of who was the top qualifier, allowing certainty in preparing a pitch in New Zealand's autumn. Daily highlights of the match were available on New Zealand Cricket's website for the first time.

As in the previous four seasons, the final went into the fifth day. Central recovered from a disappointing first innings and left Auckland 188 runs for victory. The Auckland batsmen, who had scored heavily in previous outings, struggled and when the fifth wicket fell at 104, Central had every chance. Gareth Hopkins and Colin de Grandhomme ended their hopes, however, and guided Auckland to their fourth title in eight seasons, their first since 2004/05.

The competition began two days earlier than the previous season, with a single game on 10 November. Twelve games were again played prior to Christmas and before the commencement of the State Shield and the State Twenty20 competitions. The Championship resumed on 6 March (a break of almost three months) and after each team had played each other once, the remaining three rounds saw the teams placed 1, 2, and 3 in 2007/08 drawn against the sides placed 4, 5, and 6. Points were carried through from the first five rounds.

Only ten of the the 25 matches ended in an outright decision, two fewer than the previous season while two high-scoring games failed to even reach a decision on the first innings.

In round-robin play Auckland and Central each had four outright wins while Wellington and Northern Districts had two apiece. Otago and Canterbury failed to win any games outright. Central were the only side not to lose outright.

Canterbury, who won the final from second spot in 2007/08, dropped to last, swapping places with Central, who had no outright wins the previous season. Auckland rose from third to first, Wellington dropped from first to third while Otago and Northern also swapped positions. Central began with three successive outright wins but Auckland went ahead, winning their first three games after the competition resumed in March.

Playing time was again six and a half hours per day, although this was extended if the number of overs to be bowled in the day had not been completed. Teams were required to bowl 100 overs a day with no reduction for change of innings. The only penalties for slow over rates were financial and these were calculated round by round instead of over the whole season.

Points were awarded as follows:

a) six points for an outright win
b) two points for a first innings win
c) three points for a tie
d) one point each for a first innings tie (providing the team did not win outright)
e) one point each for a no result on the first innings

Final points and placings were:

	P	*OW*	*OL*	*1st Inns W*	*1st Inns L*	*NR*	*Total*
Auckland	8	4	1	2	—	1	37
Central Districts	8	4	—	—	3	1	31
Wellington	8	2	1	2	1	2	22
Northern Districts	8	2	4	1	1	—	18
Otago	8	—	2	4	2	—	8
Canterbury	8	—	4	1	3	—	4

Central Districts defeated Canterbury outright after trailing on the first innings

CANTERBURY v AUCKLAND — State Championship

at MainPower Oval, Rangiora on 10, 11, 12, 13 November, 2008
Toss : Canterbury. Umpires : G.A.V. Baxter & W.R. Knights
Close of play: 1st day: Auckland 356-6, de Grandhomme 35; 2nd day: Auckland 143-5, de Grandhomme 19, Croft 9
3rd day: Canterbury 280-9, Anderson 39, Bennett 0
***Auckland won by 73 runs.** Points: Auckland 8, Canterbury 0*

Lancashire player Croft made his first appearance for Auckland and Nethula made his first-class debut. The first day was dominated by McIntosh (century from 217 balls in 286 minutes) and Young (hundred off 149 balls in 208 minutes) who shared a second wicket partnership of 197, an Auckland record against Canterbury. McIntosh equalled Trevor Franklin's record of 12 centuries for Auckland.

The next day Canterbury finished off the Auckland innings but were then bowled out in just 43 overs. By the close Auckland's lead was already 372. The Auckland tail again offered little resistance and Canterbury were left with 405 to win in almost two days.

Canterbury's ninth wicket fell at 273 but bad light ended play shortly afterwards and the players had to return on the fourth morning. Anderson reached his fifty and was particularly severe on the new ball, taking 20 off three overs. He had reached his highest score before Shaw eventually dismissed Bennett, who had contributed just a single to the last wicket stand of 58. Auckland had won by 73 runs.

Myburgh equalled the New Zealand first-class record of five catches in an innings by a fielder and equalled the Canterbury record of six in a match.

AUCKLAND

FIRST INNINGS	*Runs*	*Mins*	*Balls*	*6s*	*4s*	*SECOND INNINGS*	*Runs*	*Mins*	*Balls*	*6s*	*4s*
T.G.McIntosh b Davidson	140	375	282	3	13	c Myburgh b Davidson	9	16	15	1	-
R.A.Jones* c Myburgh b Davidson	28	56	36	-	5	c Myburgh b Davidson	22	50	25	-	3
R.A.Young lbw b Bennett	100	213	156	-	19	c Myburgh b Astle	40	108	81	-	5
S.B.Styris b Davidson	1	11	9	-	-	lbw b Astle	28	56	35	-	6
G.J.Hopkins† lbw b Astle	27	47	38	-	6	c Myburgh b Hiini	9	49	31	-	-
C.de Grandhomme c van Wyk b Hiini	49	109	79	-	1	b Bennett	20	56	45	-	2
S.J.Croft c Fulton b Hiini	9	31	21	-	1	not out	31	95	66	-	4
T.S.Nethula lbw b Hiini	7	23	18	-	1	c Myburgh b Hiini	4	33	24	-	-
L.J.Shaw c Fulton b Bennett	3	29	23	-	-	lbw b Hiini	0	1	1	-	-
A.J.McKay not out	5	31	20	-	-	b Hiini	0	14	14	-	-
Azhar Abbas b Bennett	2	10	9	-	-	b Bennett	0	5	5	-	-
Extras (b 9, lb 14, w 3, nb 1)	27					(lb 8, w 3, nb 1)	12				
TOTAL (115 overs)	**398**	477				(56.5 overs)	**175**	251			

CANTERBURY

FIRST INNINGS	*Runs*	*Mins*	*Balls*	*6s*	*4s*	*SECOND INNINGS*	*Runs*	*Mins*	*Balls*	*6s*	*4s*
T.D.Astle c McIntosh b Shaw	0	3	5	-	-	c Young b de Grandhomme	23	105	68	-	2
M.H.W.Papps c Hopkins b Azhar	14	50	28	-	-	lbw b Shaw	26	52	39	-	4
P.G.Fulton lbw b McKay	27	82	58	-	3	c Styris b Nethula	64	154	114	1	8
J.G.Myburgh c de Grandhomme b McKay	12	47	38	-	1	lbw b de Grandhomme	67	121	99	-	9
S.L.Stewart c McIntosh b McKay	0	1	1	-	-	lbw b Nethula	0	14	17	-	-
I.A.Robertson b Shaw	8	15	8	-	2	c Hopkins b de Grandhomme	14	25	19	-	2
C.F.K.van Wyk*† not out	44	95	58	-	7	b Nethula	5	33	14	-	-
C.J.Anderson b de Grandhomme	45	69	48	3	3	not out	88	109	86	3	10
B.C.Hiini lbw b Croft	0	4	5	-	-	lbw b Croft	11	31	29	-	2
M.P.F.Davidson c Hopkins b de Grandhomme	2	4	4	-	-	lbw b Croft	10	15	14	-	2
H.K.Bennett lbw b McKay	4	9	7	-	1	c Hopkins b Shaw	1	47	18	-	-
Extras (b 4, lb 6, w 1, nb 2)	13					(b 7, lb 2, w 1, nb 12)	22				
TOTAL (43 overs)	**169**	199				(84.2 overs)	**331**	362			

Bowling	*O*	*M*	*R*	*W*	*O*	*M*	*R*	*W*
CANTERBURY								
Bennett	22	3	71	3	17.5	3	46	2
Davidson	30	12	68	3	14	3	35	2
Hiini	28	4	101	3	14	5	47	4
Anderson	12	2	38	0				
Robertson	11	1	45	0				
Astle	12	1	52	1	11	1	39	2
AUCKLAND								
Shaw	13	3	45	2	14.2	2	51	2
McKay	12	2	37	4	23	0	111	0
Azhar	8	2	30	1	7	5	9	0
de Grandhomme	7	2	30	2	12	1	37	3
Croft	3	0	17	1	7	0	31	2
Nethula					21	3	83	3

Fall of Wickets

	A *1st*	***C*** *1st*	***A*** *2nd*	***C*** *2nd*
1st	45	0	18	37
2nd	242	38	49	79
3rd	243	54	100	178
4th	288	54	109	186
5th	331	62	131	192
6th	356	70	147	208
7th	376	151	160	221
8th	379	152	160	253
9th	391	157	172	273
10th	398	169	175	331

CENTRAL DISTRICTS v AUCKLAND — State Championship

at Nelson Park, Napier on 17, 18, 19, 20 November, 2008
Toss : Auckland. Umpires : G.A.V. Baxter & C.B. Gaffaney
Close of play: 1st day: CD 191-6, Weston 15, Thompson 1; 2nd day: CD 133-2, Patton 61, Weston 33
3rd day: Auckland 159-6, Croft 12, Nethula 2
***Central Districts won by 138 runs.** Points: Central Districts 8, Auckland 0*

Eighteen-year-old Doug Bracewell (son of Brendon) made his first-class debut in this game while Sinclair captained a side at first-class level for the first time.

The home team struggled on a shortened first day with Patton, who had a previous solitary appearance in 2006/07 when he scored a duck, reaching his maiden fifty. Auckland wrapped up the innings next morning but were soon in trouble themselves and were bowled out six runs short of Central's total. Bracewell dismissed de Boorder with the last ball of his first over.

Central built up a good lead before stumps and piled on more runs the next day. Patton completed a memorable comeback by reaching his century off 201 balls in 268 minutes. Sinclair reached 10,000 first-class runs during his innings of 58.

Auckland were left to score 342 runs for victory but by stumps were 159-6. Hefford and McClenaghan soon cleaned up the remainder of the Auckland innings the next morning, the match finishing just after midday.

CENTRAL DISTRICTS

FIRST INNINGS	*Runs*	*Mins*	*Balls*	*6s*	*4s*	*SECOND INNINGS*	*Runs*	*Mins*	*Balls*	*6s*	*4s*
G.H.Worker c Young b McKay	24	90	74	-	2	b McKay	27	118	87	-	4
P.J.Ingram c Styris b McKay	37	118	64	-	5	lbw b Shaw	1	10	5	-	-
B.M.K.Patton c & b de Grandhomme	57	159	118	-	7	c McIntosh b Azhar	142	404	285	-	15
M.S.Sinclair* b Shaw	11	25	22	-	2	(5) c Styris b Croft	58	92	77	-	8
G.R.Hay lbw b de Grandhomme	1	3	5	-	-	(6) b Shaw	6	25	17	-	1
B.B.J.Griggs† run out	23	109	63	-	2	(7) b Shaw	0	1	2	-	-
T.I.Weston not out	31	86	68	-	4	(4) run out	66	107	78	-	9
E.P.Thompson c Young b Azhar	2	43	33	-	-	c Young b McKay	2	19	6	-	-
D.A.J.Bracewell c McIntosh b Azhar	0	3	5	-	-	c Azhar b McKay	4	10	11	-	1
B.E.Hefford c Styris b Azhar	0	7	4	-	-	c McIntosh b McKay	1	14	12	-	-
M.J.McClenaghan c Croft b de Grandhomme	4	22	14	-	1	not out	1	18	13	-	-
Extras (b 4, lb 9, w 7, nb 3)	23					(b 12, lb 9, nb 6)	27				
TOTAL (78 overs)	**213**	331				(97.5 overs)	**335**	403			

AUCKLAND

	Runs	*Mins*	*Balls*	*6s*	*4s*		*Runs*	*Mins*	*Balls*	*6s*	*4s*
T.G.McIntosh c Ingram b Thompson	1	34	27	-	-	lbw b McClenaghan	8	24	20	1	-
R.A.Jones* c Worker b Thompson	5	10	5		-	c Sinclair b Hefford	25	74	57	-	2
A.P.de Boorder c Patton b Bracewell	19	53	40	-	3	c Sinclair b Thompson	1	5	7	-	-
S.B.Styris b Thompson	0	1	1	-	-	lbw b Worker	71	124	81	-	11
R.A.Young† lbw b Thompson	4	9	4	-	1	lbw b Thompson	34	115	103	-	4
C.de Grandhomme lbw b Thompson	11	30	16	-	1	lbw b Worker	0	5	7	-	-
S.J.Croft c Griggs b Hefford	59	83	71	-	5	c Griggs b McClenaghan	15	60	43	-	2
T.S.Nethula c Sinclair b McClenaghan	33	87	66	-	4	run out	12	38	32	-	1
L.J.Shaw not out	40	110	57	-	5	lbw b Hefford	0	5	3	-	-
A.J.McKay c Griggs b Hefford	15	56	50	-	1	b Hefford	18	30	25	-	3
Azhar Abbas c Griggs b McClenaghan	15	37	28	-	2	not out	12	12	12	-	2
Extras (w 1, nb 4)	5					(lb 3, w 1, nb 3)	7				
TOTAL (60.1 overs)	**207**	254				(64.3 overs)	**203**	254			

Bowling	*O*	*M*	*R*	*W*	*O*	*M*	*R*	*W*
AUCKLAND								
Shaw	17	1	63	1	20	5	75	3
McKay	22	6	55	2	20	5	57	4
Azhar	22	6	52	3	12.5	4	41	1
de Grandhomme	11	6	12	3	6	1	30	0
Croft	6	2	18	0	13	4	30	1
Styris					4	1	10	0
Nethula					20	5	56	0
de Boorder					2	0	15	0
CENTRAL DISTRICTS								
Thompson	18	2	57	5	11	4	22	2
McClenaghan	18.1	3	74	2	16	1	76	2
Bracewell	14	2	41	1	5	1	23	0
Hefford	10	1	35	2	12.3	2	48	3
Sinclair					9	3	14	0
Worker					11	4	17	2

Fall of Wickets	***CD 1st***	***A 1st***	***CD 2nd***	***A 2nd***
1st	67	6	1	18
2nd	82	17	73	19
3rd	104	17	179	62
4th	105	23	272	130
5th	170	40	284	130
6th	174	42	284	154
7th	198	121	307	163
8th	198	136	311	168
9th	198	180	325	173
10th	213	207	335	203

OTAGO v NORTHERN DISTRICTS — State Championship

at University Oval, Dunedin on 17, 18, 19, 20 November, 2008
Toss : Otago. Umpires : B.G. Frost & P.D. Jones
Close of play: 1st day: ND 223-7, Aldridge 18, Scott 5; 2nd day: Otago 116-2, Cumming 69, Broom 4
3rd day: Otago 256-9, Butler 19, McMillan 7
***First innings win to Otago.** Points: Otago 2, Northern Districts 0*

Hamish Rutherford (son of Ken) made his first-class debut while Butler and Wagner played their first games for Otago and Scott and Boult did likewise for Northern. Williamson, who had played one match in 2007/08 scoring 2 and 0, provided the first day's highlight with his maiden fifty.

Northern were dismissed for 275 next day and Boult struck immediately with Rutherford being dismissed first ball. Boult proceeded to complete his first five wicket haul to leave Otago 235-9. Butler and McMillan took the score to 256 by stumps and edged past Northern's total next morning.

With little chance of a result Northern batted for 74 overs, reaching 181-7, before the match was called off at 4.57 pm.

NORTHERN DISTRICTS

FIRST INNINGS	Runs	Mins	Balls	6s	4s	SECOND INNINGS	Runs	Mins	Balls	6s	4s
B-J.Watling c de Boorder b McMillan	21	50	49	-	4	(2) c Broom b Wagner	40	108	74	-	5
C.J.Merchant c Broom b Wagner	0	2	1	-	-	(1) c Butler b Harvie	25	71	52	-	4
M.E.Parlane c de Boorder b Wagner	41	130	91	-	5	b Butler	18	60	55	-	3
J.A.H.Marshall* b Butler	12	28	19	-	2	c de Boorder b Wagner	0	3	1	-	-
K.S.Williamson c de Boorder b McCullum	82	183	139	1	7	run out	23	51	40	1	2
P.D.McGlashan† lbw b McCullum	32	99	70	-	4	c Broom b Wagner	10	52	38	-	1
B.P.Martin lbw b Butler	7	43	34	-	-	b Butler	0	2	2	-	-
G.W.Aldridge run out	21	60	47	-	2	not out	25	141	97	-	1
B.E.Scott b McCullum	29	129	118	-	1	not out	21	113	87	-	2
B.J.Arnel b Harvie	18	81	66	-	1						
T.A.Boult not out	1	10	12	-	-						
Extras (lb 7, w 3, nb 1)	11					(b 14, lb 2, w 1, nb 2)	19				
TOTAL (107.3 overs)	**275**	432				(74 overs) (7 wkts)	**181**	294			

OTAGO

FIRST INNINGS	Runs	Mins	Balls	6s	4s
C.D.Cumming* c McGlashan b Arnel	85	229	176	-	11
H.D.Rutherford b Boult	0	2	1	-	-
G.R.Todd b Boult	29	108	94	-	3
N.T.Broom b Arnel	54	292	234	-	3
S.B.Haig c Boult b Martin	2	11	10	-	-
N.L.McCullum lbw b Aldridge	23	80	60	-	2
D.C.de Boorder† lbw b Boult	16	90	68	-	-
I.G.Butler not out	37	92	69	2	3
N.Wagner c McGlashan b Boult	2	9	7	-	-
M.J.Harvie c Watling b Boult	0	2	3	-	-
J.M.McMillan not out	8	70	44	-	1
Extras (b 6, lb 13, nb 2)	21				
TOTAL (127.2 overs) (9 wkts dec)	**277**	487			

Bowling	O	M	R	W	O	M	R	W
OTAGO								
Wagner	21	6	44	2	16	5	32	3
Harvie	21	7	54	1	8	2	21	1
Butler	19	2	59	2	12	3	19	2
McMillan	18	0	65	1	10	0	45	0
McCullum	28.3	9	46	3	24	10	42	0
Cumming					3	2	6	0
Broom					1	1	0	0
NORTHERN DISTRICTS								
Boult	20	3	58	5				
Arnel	33	12	55	2				
Scott	23	10	48	0				
Aldridge	18	5	38	1				
Martin	28.2	10	48	1				
Williamson	5	0	11	0				

Fall of Wickets

	ND 1st	O 1st	ND 2nd
1st	3	1	56
2nd	34	70	78
3rd	62	142	78
4th	108	145	99
5th	187	191	118
6th	198	227	118
7th	200	229	127
8th	227	235	-
9th	269	235	-
10th	275	-	-

WELLINGTON v CANTERBURY — State Championship

at Allied Nationwide Finance Basin Reserve, Wellington on 17, 18, 19, 20 November, 2008
Toss : Wellington. Umpires : A.L. Hill & D.J. Walker
Close of play: 1st day: Wellington 155-2. Bell 88, Crook 21; 2nd day: Canterbury 45-2, Ellis 7, Stewart 21
3rd day: Canterbury 115-3, Papps 37, Davidson 1
***Wellington won by an innings and 42 runs.** Points: Wellington 8, Canterbury 0*

Lamb made his first-class debut while Napier played his first four-day game for Wellington. Only 47 overs were possible on the first day, Bell being twelve runs short of passing Bert Sutcliffe's record of most centuries for one province when stumps were drawn. The Wellington skipper duly reached the landmark next morning, after facing 163 balls in 228 minutes.

Wellington declared at 428-8 and captured two Canterbury wickets before the close. The visitors fared little better next day and had to follow on 266 runs behind. They had reached 115-3 by the close but wickets fell at regular intervals on the last day and Wellington clinched an innings victory when Woodcock dismissed Bennett at 1.26 pm.

WELLINGTON

FIRST INNINGS	*Runs*	*Mins*	*Balls*	*6s*	*4s*	*SECOND INNINGS*	*Runs*	*Mins*	*Balls*	*6s*	*4s*
M.D.Bell* c Robertson b Burtt	146	356	252	-	23						
J.M.Brodie lbw b Hiini	40	140	104	-	4						
N.R.Parlane c van Wyk b Burtt	0	12	7	-	-						
B-J.Crook c Stewart b Ellis	21	42	39	-	4						
J.E.C.Franklin c Robertson b Davidson	69	146	102	-	7						
L.J.Woodcock not out	58	194	125	-	7						
C.J.Nevin† b Bennett	27	71	60	-	2						
G.R.Napier lbw b Bennett	0	14	7	-	-						
D.J.Bowden c & b Davidson	46	75	57	1	5						
J.S.Patel not out	11	22	19		1						
A.R.Lamb											
Extras (b 1, lb 4, w 1, nb 4)	10										
TOTAL (128 overs) (8 wkts dec)	**428**	533									

CANTERBURY

	Runs	*Mins*	*Balls*	*6s*	*4s*		*Runs*	*Mins*	*Balls*	*6s*	*4s*
T.D.Astle lbw b Lamb	1	15	13	-	-	lbw b Napier	26	51	41	-	4
M.H.W.Papps c Parlane b Franklin	16	17	12	-	4	c Nevin b Franklin	40	198	153	-	2
A.M.Ellis c Bell b Patel	32	154	124	-	2	b Patel	7	38	29	-	-
S.L.Stewart c Parlane b Franklin	33	160	136	-	3	b Napier	39	68	54	-	5
I.A.Robertson lbw b Patel	0	2	1	-	-	(6) b Woodcock	36	118	75	-	6
C.J.Anderson b Patel	3	26	13	-	-	(7) c Brodie b Bowden	26	65	42	-	3
C.F.K.van Wyk*† c Bell b Lamb	13	88	56	-	-	(8) c Crook b Woodcock	23	55	49	-	1
B.C.Hiini run out	18	54	53	-	1	(9) c Crook b Woodcock	3	13	13	-	-
M.P.F.Davidson c Patel b Woodcock	8	36	15	-	-	(5) c Parlane b Napier	3	57	41	-	-
L.M.Burtt c Parlane b Franklin	27	35	49	-	4	not out	5	28	23	-	1
H.K.Bennett not out	8	39	27	-	1	c Franklin b Woodcock	3	22	18	-	-
Extras (b 2, lb 1)	3					(b 8, lb 4, nb 1)	13				
TOTAL (83.1 overs)	**162**	330				(89.3 overs)	**224**	364			

Bowling	*O*	*M*	*R*	*W*	*O*	*M*	*R*	*W*
CANTERBURY								
Burtt	21	1	87	2				
Davidson	23	4	68	2				
Hiini	26	9	93	1				
Bennett	20	5	57	2				
Ellis	20	8	40	1				
Astle	6	1	36	0				
Robertson	12	1	42	0				
WELLINGTON								
Franklin	9.1	5	22	3	14	4	34	1
Lamb	15	7	26	2	1	0	2	0
Patel	31	9	55	3	25	5	70	1
Woodcock	16	5	37	1	14.3	3	40	4
Napier	12	3	19	0	22	6	44	3
Bowden					13	4	22	1

Fall of Wickets	***W***	***C***	***C***
	1st	*1st*	*2nd*
1st	112	17	36
2nd	120	17	46
3rd	155	82	110
4th	278	82	118
5th	284	82	126
6th	317	90	180
7th	333	115	201
8th	397	117	209
9th	-	133	214
10th	-	162	224

OTAGO v CANTERBURY — State Championship

at Queen's Park, Invercargill on 24, 25, 26, 27 November, 2008
Toss : Otago. Umpires : B.G. Frost & P.D. Jones
Close of play: 1st day: Otago 211-4, Broom 48, McCullum 30; 2nd day: Otago 234-5, Broom 62, de Boorder 1
3rd day: Canterbury 145-5, Anderson 19, van Wyk 11
***First innings win to Otago.** Points: Otago 2, Canterbury 0*

Only 56 overs could be bowled on the first day, with Otago reaching 211-4 by the close. The second day was restricted to just 12.2 overs but on the third Broom finally brought up his hundred, from 189 balls in 271 minutes.

Canterbury lost five wickets before the close and declared early on the last day. Otago raced to 113 in 17 overs before declaring and leaving Canterbury a target of 292 for victory. Fifties from Ellis and Stewart almost brought them home. Ten were required when Broom started the last over but only three singles resulted, leaving Otago with a first innings win.

OTAGO

FIRST INNINGS	Runs	Mins	Balls	6s	4s	SECOND INNINGS	Runs	Mins	Balls	6s	4s
C.D.Cumming* c Papps b Ellis	31	66	50	-	5	(6) b Bennett	2	5	5	-	-
S.B.Haig c Ellis b Bennett	52	110	71	-	9	not out	28	84	30	1	2
G.R.Todd c van Wyk b Ellis	31	98	72	-	4	(7) not out	4	7	6	-	-
N.T.Broom not out	140	312	222	-	21	(3) c Papps b Bennett	21	27	26	1	1
H.D.Rutherford c Astle b Ellis	0	9	6	-	-	(1) c van Wyk b Bennett	31	24	23	2	3
N.L.McCullum c Burtt b Davidson	38	109	83	-	5	(5) b Ellis	17	11	12	1	1
D.C.de Boorder† c van Wyk b Burtt	11	24	21	-	1						
I.G.Butler b Burtt	12	46	37	-	2	(4) b Ellis	1	5	3	-	-
N.Wagner b Burtt	13	42	26	-	3						
M.J.Harvie c Stewart b Burtt	3	16	9	-	-						
J.M.McMillan lbw b Burtt	0	1	1	-	-						
Extras (b 5, lb 3, w 3, nb 10)	21					(lb 5, w 1, nb 3)	9				
TOTAL (98 overs)	**352**	417				(17 overs) (5 wkts dec)	**113**	83			

CANTERBURY

FIRST INNINGS	Runs	Mins	Balls	6s	4s	SECOND INNINGS	Runs	Mins	Balls	6s	4s
T.D.Astle lbw b Wagner	4	13	12	-	-	c de Boorder b Wagner	29	34	38	-	5
M.H.W.Papps lbw b McCullum	53	168	124	-	6	lbw b Cumming	35	156	112	-	3
A.M.Ellis c de Boorder b Wagner	30	79	67	-	4	st de Boorder b McCullum	71	202	165	-	9
J.G.Myburgh c de Boorder b Wagner	2	9	9	-	-	c Butler b McCullum	34	68	62	1	2
S.L.Stewart lbw b McCullum	19	49	41	-	3	not out	69	103	68	4	3
C.J.Anderson not out	34	106	81	-	2	c de Boorder b McMillan	5	5	7	-	1
C.F.K.van Wyk*† not out	25	90	63	-	2	c de Boorder b McMillan	8	18	12	-	-
I.A.Robertson						b Wagner	19	60	40	-	-
M.P.F.Davidson						not out	1	5	1	-	-
L.M.Burtt											
H.K.Bennett											
Extras (lb 6, nb 1)	7					(b 3, lb 5, w 5, nb 1)	14				
TOTAL (66 overs) (5 wkts dec)	**174**	259				(84 overs) (7 wkts)	**285**	324			

Bowling	O	M	R	W	O	M	R	W
CANTERBURY								
Burtt	26	2	119	5	5	0	31	0
Davidson	30	9	75	1	2	0	22	0
Bennett	13	3	65	1	6	0	36	3
Ellis	16	6	35	3	4	0	19	2
Robertson	10	3	35	0				
Astle	1	0	5	0				
Anderson	2	0	10	0				
OTAGO								
Wagner	16	1	49	3	17	2	68	2
Harvie	9	0	30	0	4	2	20	0
McMillan	12	3	27	0	10	1	38	2
McCullum	19	4	41	2	25	12	65	2
Butler	9	0	21	0	14	6	36	0
Todd	1	1	0	0				
Cumming					10.3	2	32	1
Broom					3.3	0	18	0

Fall of Wickets	O	C	O	C
	1st	*1st*	*2nd*	*2nd*
1st	72	6	44	38
2nd	106	66	80	112
3rd	141	68	81	167
4th	145	107	100	182
5th	232	114	103	187
6th	253	-	-	216
7th	286	-	-	272
8th	326	-	-	-
9th	352	-	-	-
10th	352	-	-	-

NORTHERN DISTRICTS v CENTRAL DISTRICTS

at Seddon Park, Hamilton on 24, 25, 26, 27 November, 2008
Toss : Central Districts. Umpires : B.F.Bowden & D.J. Walker
Close of play: 1st day: ND 136-2, Merchant 88, Marshall 6; 2nd day: CD 201-2, Ingram 144, Sinclair 22
3rd day: ND 83-2, Watling 33, Marshall 0
***Central Districts won by 8 wickets.** Points: Central Districts 8, Northern Districts 0*

Only 43.4 overs were bowled on the first day with Merchant dominating the scoring with 88 out of 136-2. He added just a single the next day, equalling his highest score, and it was left to Williamson and Aldridge (maiden fifty) to take Northern to 325.

When the visitors replied, Ingram and Sinclair put on 264, the highest third wicket partnership in Central's history. Sinclair reached his hundred after 274 minutes from 225 balls and passed Mark Greatbatch's record of most centuries for Central. Ingram reached his century after 139 minutes, from just 101 balls, and went to his first double century after 319 minutes and 258 balls.

He was finally dismissed for 247, the highest ever innings for Central. It was also the highest score made at Seddon Park and Central's 479-9 was their best against Northern.

Watling was last man out when Northern batted again, having reached his century after 336 minutes from 258 balls. Central needed 96 to win and reached their target at 5.35 pm.

NORTHERN DISTRICTS

FIRST INNINGS	Runs	Mins	Balls	6s	4s	SECOND INNINGS	Runs	Mins	Balls	6s	4s
B-J.Watling c Worker b Thompson	2	33	29	-	-	c Ingram b Thompson	111	382	283	-	16
C.J.Merchant lbw b Thompson	89	178	122	2	12	b Oram	7	16	13	-	1
M.E.Parlane run out	36	132	113	-	5	c Weston b Worker	41	62	54	-	8
J.A.H.Marshall* c Sinclair b Oram	15	35	23	-	2	lbw b Worker	33	149	124	-	4
K.S.Williamson c Worker b Sherlock	73	194	149	-	10	b Sherlock	5	17	7	-	1
P.D.McGlashan† c Griggs b Thompson	8	12	14	-	1	c Griggs b McClenaghan	12	16	14	-	2
G.W.Aldridge not out	73	227	158	-	12	lbw b Sherlock	4	16	9	-	1
B.E.Scott b Sherlock	1	18	12	-	-	b Worker	1	6	2	-	-
B.P.Martin b Sherlock	0	12	7	-	-	c Griggs b Oram	20	67	60	-	2
B.J.Arnel c Sinclair b Patton	1	28	25	-	-	lbw b Thompson	8	15	9	-	-
T.A.Boult c Sinclair b Patton	0	8	4	-	-	not out	0	9	2	-	-
Extras (b 8, lb 8, w 3, nb 8)	27					(b 4, lb 1, w 1, nb 1)	7				
TOTAL (108 overs)	**325**	439				(96 overs)	**249**	379			

CENTRAL DISTRICTS

FIRST INNINGS	Runs	Mins	Balls	6s	4s	SECOND INNINGS	Runs	Mins	Balls	6s	4s
G.H.Worker b Boult	11	17	20	-	2	c Boult b Williamson	22	93	72	-	2
P.J.Ingram c Parlane b Martin	247	458	356	4	31	c Watling b Aldridge	38	79	53	-	6
B.M.K.Patton c Watling b Arnel	24	71	51	-	4	not out	12	36	17	-	1
M.S.Sinclair* c Aldridge b Boult	101	275	226	1	11	not out	22	22	25	-	5
G.R.Hay b Arnel	12	31	29	-	1						
T.I.Weston st McGlashan b Martin	10	29	21	-	2						
B.B.J.Griggs† c Williamson b Martin	47	96	77	-	8						
E.P.Thompson b Martin	16	59	38	-	3						
R.R.Sherlock c Williamson b Scott	0	12	8	-	-						
M.J.McClenaghan not out	2	6	6	-	-						
J.D.P.Oram											
Extras (lb 8, w 1)	9					(lb 4, w 1)	5				
TOTAL (138.4 overs) (9 wkts dec)	**479**	526				(27.5 overs) (2 wkts)	**99**	116			

Bowling	O	M	R	W	O	M	R	W
CENTRAL DISTRICTS								
Thompson	26	8	61	3	24	8	45	2
Sherlock	19	6	52	3	12	0	68	2
Oram	18	10	22	1	18	5	34	2
McClenaghan	18	2	102	0	13	2	43	1
Patton	7	1	19	2				
Worker	12	3	33	0	28	5	54	3
Sinclair	8	1	20	0	1	1	0	0
NORTHERN DISTRICTS								
Boult	21	2	85	2	5	1	17	0
Arnel	28	7	74	2	8	2	26	0
Scott	27.4	3	113	1				
Aldridge	6	0	47	0	6	2	12	1
Martin	54	8	145	4	5	0	23	0
Williamson	2	0	7	0	3	0	12	1
Watling					0.5	0	5	0

Fall of Wickets	*ND*	*CD*	*ND*	*CD*
	1st	*1st*	*2nd*	*2nd*
1st	10	16	8	56
2nd	119	102	75	72
3rd	141	366	144	-
4th	148	390	156	-
5th	161	403	183	-
6th	296	424	193	-
7th	300	476	198	-
8th	301	477	233	-
9th	313	479	248	-
10th	325	-	249	-

AUCKLAND v WELLINGTON — State Championship

at Eden Park Outer Oval, Auckland on 24, 25, 26, 27 November, 2008
Toss : Auckland. Umpires : A.L. Hill & E.A. Watkin
Close of play: 1st day: no play; 2nd day: Wellington 247-4, Franklin 51, Woodcock 0
3rd day: Auckland 133-0, McIntosh 70, Jones 62
***No result.** Points: Auckland 1, Wellington 1*

After no play on the first day, Auckland decided to field and had some early success. Bell went to another century, from 206 balls in 284 minutes, but his dismissal only brought Woodcock to join Franklin and these two proceeded to add 282 runs for the fifth wicket, a record by any team against Auckland.

Franklin reached his century after 245 minutes from 192 balls and his double century from 280 balls after 363 minutes. He was finally dismissed for 219, his highest score and the highest by a Wellington batsman against Auckland. Woodcock went to three figures after 276 minues and 186 balls and Bell declared.

Auckland were 133-0 by the close and batted through the whole of the last day, both sides taking one point after no result on the first innings. McIntosh reached a record 13th century for Auckland after 301 minutes and 226 balls. Tuffey made his debut for Auckland in this game, playing his first first-class match since November 2006.

WELLINGTON

FIRST INNINGS	*Runs*	*Mins*	*Balls*	*6s*	*4s*
M.D.Bell* c Styris b Nethula	122	325	239	-	19
J.M.Brodie lbw b McKay	7	50	39	-	-
N.R.Parlane c & b Tuffey	11	49	27	-	1
B-J.Crook c Croft b de Grandhomme	40	115	73	-	6
J.E.C.Franklin c de Grandhomme b Tuffey	219	374	290	8	28
L.J.Woodcock not out	102	277	186	3	10
G.R.Napier not out	5	11	3	-	1
C.J.Nevin†					
D.J.Bowden					
J.S.Patel					
A.R.Lamb					
M.V.Houghton					
Extras (b 10, lb 11, w 2, nb 4)	27				
TOTAL (142.1 overs) (5 wkts dec)	**533**	603			

AUCKLAND

	Runs	*Mins*	*Balls*	*6s*	*4s*
T.G.McIntosh c Nevin b Woodcock	191	484	361	5	16
R.A.Jones* c Nevin b Napier	69	243	178	-	7
R.A.Young c Bell b Franklin	42	139	114	-	5
S.B.Styris c Nevin b Napier	1	22	14	-	-
K.D.Mills lbw b Houghton	18	86	72	1	1
S.J.Croft c Houghton b Napier	34	66	54	1	3
P.A.Hitchcock b Napier	20	61	55	1	1
C.de Grandhomme not out	43	101	91	1	8
T.S.Nethula not out	17	97	80	-	2
D.R.Tuffey					
A.J.McKay					
G.J.Hopkins†					
Extras (b 1, lb 5)	6				
TOTAL (170 overs) (7 wkts)	**441**	653			

Bowling	*O*	*M*	*R*	*W*
AUCKLAND				
Mills	32	10	58	0
Tuffey	33	9	87	2
McKay	23	1	94	1
de Grandhomme	12	2	40	1
Croft	16.1	2	77	0
Nethula	25	2	146	1
Styris	1	0	10	0
WELLINGTON				
Lamb	15	1	69	0
Franklin	24	9	43	1
Napier	32	9	52	4
Bowden	23	4	63	0
Patel	12	1	42	0
Woodcock	34	10	75	1
Houghton	29	7	91	1
Bell	1	1	0	0

Fall of Wickets	***W***	***A***
	1st	*1st*
1st	16	150
2nd	56	265
3rd	150	274
4th	239	326
5th	521	328
6th	-	381
7th	-	382
8th	-	-
9th	-	-
10th	-	-

Hopkins and Patel left the game to join the New Zealand team in Australia and were replaced by Hitchcock and Houghton for the last day

WELLINGTON v NORTHERN DISTRICTS State Championship

at Allied Nationwide Finance Basin Reserve, Wellington on 1, 2, 3, 4 December, 2008
Toss : Northern Districts. Umpires : M.P. George & D.M. Quested
Close of play: 1st day: ND 274-9, Aldridge 50, Boult 16; 2nd day: Wellington 219-4, Brodie 99, Franklin 0
3rd day: ND 3-0, Wilson 1, Merchant 2
***Wellington won by an innings and 12 runs.** Points: Wellington 8, Northern Districts 0*

Northern won the toss and batted and were 274-9 at the close. Another fifty from Aldridge was the highlight. Next morning he and Boult continued their last wicket stand which was finally worth 83 runs.

By the close of the second day Brodie (previous highest score of 40) was 99 not out and he duly reached three figures next morning after 340 minutes and 268 balls. His dismissal brought Woodcock and Franklin together and they added 121 for the sixth wicket. Nevin then assisted Franklin in a partnership of 164, a Wellington seventh wicket record against Northern. Franklin reached his century from 203 balls in 270 minutes.

Bell declared just before stumps and it was only a century from Marshall (329 minutes and 235 balls) that avoided a complete rout on the last day. Wellington completed an innings victory at 5.27 pm.

NORTHERN DISTRICTS

FIRST INNINGS	*Runs*	*Mins*	*Balls*	*6s*	*4s*	*SECOND INNINGS*	*Runs*	*Mins*	*Balls*	*6s*	*4s*
B.S.Wilson c Brodie b Houghton	36	139	108	-	6	c Parlane b Franklin	1	37	36	-	-
C.J.Merchant b Franklin	10	25	14	-	2	c Brodie b Elliott	16	74	45	-	2
M.E.Parlane c Nevin b Napier	47	153	121	-	6	c Bell b Gillespie	0	21	12	-	-
J.A.H.Marshall* c Nevin b Elliott	35	60	62	-	5	not out	105	334	240	-	12
K.S.Williamson c Nevin b Gillespie	22	67	39	-	2	c Brodie b Gillespie	0	18	14	-	-
P.D.McGlashan† c Nevin b Gillespie	9	34	22	-	1	c Parlane b Woodcock	12	82	71	-	2
G.W.Aldridge not out	67	210	157	-	7	b Napier	15	59	42	-	1
B.E.Scott c Nevin b Napier	25	45	33	-	4	c Napier b Gillespie	23	88	90	-	3
B.P.Martin lbw b Napier	0	14	13	-	-	lbw b Gillespie	4	5	5	-	1
B.J.Arnel c Parlane b Gillespie	4	15	13	-	-	lbw b Napier	8	22	16	-	1
T.A.Boult c sub (B-J.Crook) b Gillespie	35	130	107	-	6	lbw b Woodcock	2	41	18	-	-
Extras (b 8, lb 2, w 2, nb 8)	20					(b 5, lb 5, w 1, nb 1)	12				
TOTAL (113.3 overs)	**310**	450				(98 overs)	**198**	394			

WELLINGTON

	Runs	Mins	Balls	6s	4s
M.D.Bell* b Aldridge	3	36	25	-	-
J.M.Brodie c Aldridge b Arnel	110	366	289	-	11
N.R.Parlane lbw b Arnel	21	53	45	-	4
G.D.Elliott c Wilson b Boult	78	218	166	-	9
M.V.Houghton c McGlashan b Arnel	4	7	9	-	1
J.E.C.Franklin c Arnel b Boult	160	340	248	4	11
L.J.Woodcock c Marshall b Martin	53	178	139	-	3
C.J.Nevin† not out	71	114	85	-	7
G.R.Napier not out	0	1	0	-	-
D.J.Bowden					
M.R.Gillespie					
Extras (lb 14, w 2, nb 4)	20				
TOTAL (167 overs) (7 wkts dec)	**520**	653			

Bowling	*O*	*M*	*R*	*W*	*O*	*M*	*R*	*W*
WELLINGTON								
Gillespie	23.3	3	81	4	20	7	43	4
Franklin	23	2	75	1	11	4	21	1
Napier	22	6	51	3	22	10	38	2
Bowden	5	0	13	0	3	1	6	0
Elliott	18	8	29	1	13	6	19	1
Houghton	19	5	46	1	9	4	19	0
Woodcock	3	1	5	0	20	5	42	2
NORTHERN DISTRICTS								
Boult	18	4	55	2				
Arnel	27	12	66	3				
Aldridge	19	1	79	1				
Scott	30	9	66	0				
Martin	45	10	145	1				
Williamson	25	5	70	0				
Marshall	3	0	25	0				

Fall of Wickets	***ND***	***W***	***ND***
	1st	*1st*	*2nd*
1st	19	16	12
2nd	96	52	18
3rd	130	213	20
4th	150	218	21
5th	172	235	54
6th	177	356	93
7th	216	520	150
8th	218	-	154
9th	227	-	179
10th	310	-	198

CENTRAL DISTRICTS v OTAGO — State Championship

at McLean Park, Napier on 5, 6, 7, 8 December, 2008
Toss : Central Districts. Umpires : A.L. Hill & D.M. Quested
Close of play: 1st day: Otago 357 all out; 2nd day: CD 316-7, Thompson 19, Sherlock 15
3rd day: Otago 211-6, de Boorder 43, Butler 11
***Central Districts won by 8 wickets.** Points: Central Districts 8, Otago 0*

Otago were sent in and lost wickets in each of the first two overs. Cumming then added 159 with Broom and 79 with Rutherford before he was dismissed. His hundred came from 129 balls in 168 minutes. Otago were all out just before the close.

Central batted through the second day, reaching 316-7. Sinclair reached yet another hundred from 171 balls in 231 minutes. Central finished with a lead of 21 and had Otago 211-6 at stumps. Next day they were dismissed for 281, de Boorder left not out on 73.

The home side required 261 to win and had no trouble reaching their target. Patton was the star with his second hundred (158 balls and 190 minutes) as he and Sinclair shared an unbroken stand of 141 for the third wicket. The match ended at 5.42 pm.

OTAGO

FIRST INNINGS	Runs	Mins	Balls	6s	4s	SECOND INNINGS	Runs	Mins	Balls	6s	4s
C.D.Cumming* c McClenaghan b Worker	133	251	184	-	19	c Sinclair b McClenaghan	1	17	13	-	-
S.B.Haig b Thompson	0	4	2	-	-	c Griggs b McClenaghan	27	70	44	-	4
G.R.Todd c Ingram b McClenaghan	0	2	1	-	-	c Patton b Thompson	74	263	193	-	5
N.T.Broom c Griggs b McClenaghan	60	147	101	-	10	lbw b Oram	0	4	5	-	-
H.D.Rutherford c Thompson b Sinclair	41	74	51	3	2	run out	1	10	5	-	-
N.L.McCullum c Worker b Sherlock	35	85	74	1	4	b Worker	44	84	60	-	4
D.C.de Boorder† lbw b Thompson	19	85	70	-	1	not out	73	248	200	-	9
I.G.Butler b Thompson	24	42	25	-	5	b Oram	27	96	82	-	2
N.Wagner c Ingram b Thompson	2	9	5	-	-	lbw b Bracewell	4	7	5	-	1
M.J.Harvie c Griggs b Oram	11	63	50	-	2	c Griggs b Bracewell	8	16	13	-	2
J.M.McMillan not out	7	51	41	-	-	c Griggs b Bracewell	11	16	16	-	2
Extras (b 7, lb 5, w 9, nb 4)	25					(b 3, lb 6, nb 2)	11				
TOTAL (100 overs)	**357**	403				(105.4 overs)	**281**	421			

CENTRAL DISTRICTS

FIRST INNINGS	Runs	Mins	Balls	6s	4s	SECOND INNINGS	Runs	Mins	Balls	6s	4s
G.H.Worker c Rutherford b Harvie	21	98	71	-	2	b Butler	28	52	36	-	5
P.J.Ingram c Broom b Harvie	51	113	75	-	7	c de Boorder b Wagner	40	130	74	-	3
B.M.K.Patton b Wagner	32	93	69	-	3	not out	110	210	168	1	11
M.S.Sinclair* c de Boorder b Harvie	108	256	188	1	14	not out	52	130	99	-	5
T.I.Weston b McMillan	23	51	41	1	2						
J.D.P.Oram c Cumming b McCullum	28	29	31	-	5						
B.B.J.Griggs† c de Boorder b McCullum	0	1	1	-	-						
D.A.J.Bracewell b Butler	26	91	82	1	4						
E.P.Thompson c de Boorder b Harvie	36	110	75	1	1						
R.R.Sherlock not out	36	119	67	1	6						
M.J.McClenaghan c Rutherford b McMillan	0	2	2	-	-						
Extras (b 5, lb 9, w 1, nb 2)	17					(b 1, lb 25, w 4, nb 1)	31				
TOTAL (116.4 overs)	**378**	481				(62.4 overs) (2 wkts)	**261**	249			

Bowling	O	M	R	W	O	M	R	W
CENTRAL DISTRICTS								
Thompson	25	6	64	4	25	10	48	1
McClenaghan	17	3	48	2	23	3	71	2
Sherlock	12	2	63	1	5	0	22	0
Oram	18	5	50	1	17	7	30	2
Bracewell	10	0	71	0	10.4	0	51	3
Sinclair	5	2	18	1				
Worker	13	2	31	1	25	5	50	1
OTAGO								
Wagner	29	7	95	1	13	1	33	1
Harvie	26	6	73	4	10	2	42	0
McMillan	16.4	1	56	2	9	0	45	0
Butler	16	4	52	1	6	0	30	1
McCullum	26	4	78	2	20	1	67	0
Cumming	3	0	10	0				
Broom					2.4	0	9	0
Todd					2	0	9	0

Fall of Wickets

	O 1st	CD 1st	O 2nd	CD 2nd
1st	1	70	3	59
2nd	4	77	46	120
3rd	163	140	47	-
4th	242	193	48	-
5th	261	193	119	-
6th	305	272	185	-
7th	323	293	244	-
8th	329	348	249	-
9th	338	378	263	-
10th	357	378	281	-

Weston retired hurt at 146-2 on 2 and returned at 348-8.

NORTHERN DISTRICTS v CANTERBURY State Championship

at Seddon Park, Hamilton on 12, 13, 14, 15 December, 2008
Toss : Northern Districts. Umpires : C.B. Gaffaney & E.A. Watkin
Close of play: 1st day: ND 208-6, Yovich 34; 2nd day: Canterbury 62-2, Fulton 10, Myburgh 10
3rd day: ND 45-2, Parlane 12
***First innings win to Northern Districts.** Points: Northern Districts 2, Canterbury 0*

Northern won the toss and batted and were 208-6 at the end of a slow day. Williamson fell two runs short of his maiden hundred just before stumps. Runs came more freely next morning as McGlashan and Aldridge (highest score) put on 163 for the eighth wicket, a Northern record against all teams.

Canterbury lost two wickets before stumps and were dismissed next day for 265. Northern did not enforce the follow-on and rattled up 152 in 28 overs, leaving Canterbury 318 to win.

Astle reached his maiden hundred from 156 balls in 184 minutes and the visitors looked on track for victory at 259-3. Quick wickets, including three successive runs outs, put paid to their hopes, however, and they finished 24 runs short of their target.

NORTHERN DISTRICTS

FIRST INNINGS	*Runs*	*Mins*	*Balls*	*6s*	*4s*	*SECOND INNINGS*	*Runs*	*Mins*	*Balls*	*6s*	*4s*
B-J.Watling c Fulton b Burtt	19	125	90	-	3	(2) c van Wyk b Myburgh	14	54	31	-	2
C.J.Merchant c van Wyk b Bennett	9	59	39	-	1	(1) b Myburgh	15	15	14	-	2
M.E.Parlane lbw b Ellis	21	61	44	-	4	not out	36	93	66	-	3
J.A.H.Marshall* lbw b Ellis	0	7	4	-	-	c Astle b Myburgh	30	15	18	1	4
K.S.Williamson c Astle b Bennett	98	269	225	1	11	c Fulton b Myburgh	10	9	12	-	2
J.A.F.Yovich c van Wyk b Ellis	65	336	243	-	11	(7) not out	16	16	19	1	1
B.P.Martin c van Wyk b Bennett	4	6	4	-	1						
P.D.McGlashan† b Davidson	91	282	247	-	11	(6) b Hiini	15	12	12	1	2
G.W.Aldridge c van Wyk b Burtt	75	204	149	-	8						
T.G.Southee c Bennett b Davidson	3	17	9	-	-						
B.J.Arnel not out	0	3	2	-	-						
Extras (b 3, lb 24, w 6, nb 12)	45					(b 4, lb 8, nb 4)	16				
TOTAL (174 overs)	**430**	684				(28 overs) (5 wkts dec)	**152**	108			

CANTERBURY

	Runs	*Mins*	*Balls*	*6s*	*4s*		*Runs*	*Mins*	*Balls*	*6s*	*4s*
T.D.Astle c McGlashan b Aldridge	23	78	56	-	4	c Williamson b Aldridge	101	200	168	2	16
A.M.Ellis c Aldridge b Southee	12	42	30	-	2	c McGlashan b Arnel	29	148	118	-	2
P.G.Fulton c Parlane b Yovich	84	335	263	1	11	c Marshall b Martin	56	113	80	2	5
J.G.Myburgh c Merchant b Williamson	61	188	165	-	8	run out	39	82	62	1	2
S.L.Stewart b Williamson	4	7	8	-	1	c Merchant b Williamson	30	65	44	1	-
C.J.Anderson b Southee	11	19	23	-	2	run out	8	12	11	-	1
C.F.K.van Wyk*†c Watling b Williamson	15	52	39	-	3	(9) not out	2	6	3	-	-
B.C.Hiini c Yovich b Martin	19	64	53	-	2	(7) run out	2	15	7	-	-
M.P.F.Davidson c Merchant b Yovich	9	10	9	-	2	(8) c Southee b Martin	1	8	7	-	-
L.M.Burtt b Martin	4	16	15	-	1						
H.K.Bennett not out	0	6	2	-	-						
Extras (b 7, lb 12, nb 4)	23					(b 12, lb 10, nb 4)	26				
TOTAL (109.5 overs)	**265**	409				(82.4 overs) (8 wkts)	**294**	326			

Bowling	*O*	*M*	*R*	*W*	*O*	*M*	*R*	*W*
CANTERBURY								
Burtt	27	6	72	2	2	0	13	0
Davidson	25	6	43	2	2	0	7	0
Hiini	21	9	36	0	4	0	27	1
Bennett	26	8	79	3				
Ellis	22	9	44	3	7	2	37	0
Astle	24	3	75	0				
Myburgh	29	6	54	0	13	0	56	4
NORTHERN DISTRICTS								
Southee	19	8	36	2	9	1	38	0
Aldridge	11	0	33	1	6	1	29	1
Arnel	19	10	39	0	8	2	36	1
Martin	25.5	17	30	2	27	5	80	2
Williamson	27	6	67	3	25.4	6	72	1
Yovich	8	0	41	2	7	2	17	0

Fall of Wickets

	ND	***C***	***ND***	***C***
	1st	*1st*	*2nd*	*2nd*
1st	29	31	16	122
2nd	61	48	45	171
3rd	61	166	79	238
4th	63	174	100	259
5th	204	192	125	269
6th	208	224	-	286
7th	254	240	-	290
8th	417	254	-	294
9th	429	264	-	-
10th	430	265	-	-

WELLINGTON v CENTRAL DISTRICTS State Championship

at Allied Nationwide Finance Basin Reserve, Wellington on 12, 13, 14, 15 December, 2008
Toss : Wellington. Umpires : P.D. Jones & D.J. Walker
Close of play: 1st day: CD 54-0, Worker 19, Ingram 30; 2nd day: CD 452-5, Sinclair 164, Griggs 138
3rd day: Wellington 261-5, Woodcock 22
***No result.** Points: Wellington 1, Central Districts 1*

Eighteen-year-old Boam made his first-class debut in this game which saw just 24.3 overs bowled on the first day. By the end of the second day Central had amassed 452-5 with Sinclair and Griggs sharing in a partnership of 235. This was the highest sixth wicket stand by Central against any team and by any side against Wellington.

Sinclair reached his third hundred of the season from 223 balls in 266 minutes while Griggs made his highest score. His hundred took 167 minutes and 142 balls. Central were finally all out for 523, their highest total against Wellington. Boam wrapped up the innings with three wickets in eleven balls.

The home team reached 261-5 by the close and the weather ruled out any possible chance of a decision on the last day.

CENTRAL DISTRICTS

FIRST INNINGS	*Runs*	*Mins*	*Balls*	*6s*	*4s*
G.H.Worker run out	24	106	92	-	2
P.J.Ingram c Parlane b Napier	34	111	84	-	2
B.M.K.Patton c Woodcock b Bowden	36	115	79	-	3
M.S.Sinclair* c Woodcock b Lamb	164	432	341	-	16
T.I.Weston c Parlane b Patel	23	59	46	-	2
G.R.Hay b Napier	11	29	25	-	1
B.B.J.Griggs† c Boam b Lamb	143	238	191	-	19
D.A.J.Bracewell c Nevin b Boam	26	40	29	-	4
E.P.Thompson b Boam	24	43	30	-	3
M.J.McClenaghan not out	6	16	9	-	1
B.E.Hefford c Parlane b Boam	0	6	3	-	-
Extras (b 5, lb 16, w 2, nb 9)	32				
TOTAL (153.3 overs)	**523**	602			

WELLINGTON

	Runs	*Mins*	*Balls*	*6s*	*4s*
M.D.Bell* c Hay b McClenaghan	75	301	224	1	7
J.M.Brodie c Sinclair b Bracewell	23	63	46	-	4
N.R.Parlane c Griggs b McClenaghan	54	94	79	1	9
G.D.Elliott c Sinclair b Bracewell	63	184	165	-	5
L.J.Woodcock c Sinclair b Worker	59	195	130	-	5
G.R.Napier c Griggs b Hefford	20	38	31	-	3
C.J.Nevin† lbw b McClenaghan	8	39	28	-	1
H.K.P.Boam not out	45	116	103	1	5
D.J.Bowden not out	22	40	33	-	2
J.S.Patel					
A.R.Lamb					
Extras (w 2, nb 5)	7				
TOTAL (139 overs) (7 wkts)	**376**	527			

Bowling	*O*	*M*	*R*	*W*
WELLINGTON				
Lamb	20	3	66	2
Napier	27	4	90	2
Elliott	18	5	57	0
Boam	23.3	10	56	3
Bowden	17	0	68	1
Patel	30	2	116	1
Woodcock	18	4	49	0
CENTRAL DISTRICTS				
Thompson	26	7	74	0
McClenaghan	32	7	100	3
Bracewell	21	5	68	2
Hefford	29	11	59	1
Worker	30	6	74	1
Sinclair	1	0	1	0

Fall of Wickets	**CD**	**W**
	1st	*1st*
1st	63	38
2nd	64	107
3rd	139	204
4th	194	228
5th	217	261
6th	452	288
7th	465	336
8th	503	-
9th	517	-
10th	523	-

AUCKLAND v OTAGO

State Championship

at Eden Park Outer Oval, Auckland on 13, 14, 15, 16 December, 2008
Toss : Auckland. Umpires : E.J. Gray & W.R. Knights
Close of play: 1st day: Otago 350-5, Todd 83, de Boorder 84; 2nd day: Auckland 288-2, Guptill 129, Styris 70
3rd day: Otago 132-4, Haig 7, McCullum 6
***First innings win to Auckland.** Points: Auckland 2, Otago 0*

Otago were sent in and responded with 158 for the first wicket. Cumming, who went at 165, reached his hundred from 134 balls after 177 minutes and Todd fell just two runs short of three figures the following morning.

Chasing 418, Auckland were 288-2 by the end of the second day. Guptill (who made 99 on debut) had reached his maiden first-class hundred off 166 balls in 211 minutes. He and Styris continued on the third day, their partnership eventually worth 185 runs. Jones declared with a lead of 12 runs and Otago were 132-4 at stumps.

McCullum went at 182 but any hopes Auckland had were dashed by a 145 run partnership between Haig and de Boorder, an Otago sixth wicket record against Auckland. Haig reached his century from 217 balls after 286 minutes. With no possibility of a result, the match was called off at tea.

OTAGO

FIRST INNINGS	*Runs*	*Mins*	*Balls*	*6s*	*4s*	*SECOND INNINGS*	*Runs*	*Mins*	*Balls*	*6s*	*4s*
C.D.Cumming* c Guptill b Nethula	105	206	150	-	17	c Croft b Nethula	58	167	128	-	7
A.J.Redmond c Young b de Grandhomme	50	180	126	1	10	c Hopkins b Martin	1	18	12	-	-
G.R.Todd c Hopkins b McKay	98	302	201	-	15	c Hopkins b McKay	6	5	5	-	1
N.T.Broom lbw b Nethula	60	114	94	-	9	c Hopkins b de Grandhomme	47	145	99	-	6
S.B.Haig c Croft b Tuffey	31	56	35	-	5	lbw b Nethula	108	295	223	-	10
N.L.McCullum c Hopkins b Tuffey	0	3	4	-	-	c & b Nethula	25	99	81	-	3
D.C.de Boorder† c Croft b Martin	28	85	64	1	3	not out	68	221	158	-	8
W.C.McSkimming c Hopkins b de Grandhomme	21	46	31	-	5	c de Grandhomme b Nethula	11	17	16	-	2
I.G.Butler lbw b de Grandhomme	0	23	15	-	-	not out	0	10	4	-	-
M.J.Harvie c Hopkins b McKay	2	12	10	-	-						
J.M.McMillan not out	0	4	5	-	-						
Extras (b 6, lb 8, w 2, nb 7)	23					(b 2, lb 8, w 2, nb 7)	19				
TOTAL (121.2 overs)	**418**	520				(120 overs) (7 wkts)	**343**	492			

AUCKLAND

	Runs	Mins	Balls	6s	4s
M.J.Guptill c de Boorder b Harvie	148	357	306	1	25
R.A.Jones* lbw b McMillan	18	38	30	-	4
R.A.Young c Redmond b McMillan	54	110	79	-	10
S.B.Styris b McSkimming	94	200	135	-	11
G.J.Hopkins† lbw b Harvie	1	13	7	-	-
S.J.Croft b Harvie	53	91	84	-	9
C.de Grandhomme b Butler	34	36	27	2	4
T.S.Nethula not out	4	51	27	-	-
A.J.McKay b Harvie	0	2	2	-	-
D.R.Tuffey					
C.S.Martin					
Extras (b 5, lb 10, w 6, nb 3)	24				
TOTAL (115.4 overs) (8 wkts dec)	**430**	453			

Bowling	*O*	*M*	*R*	*W*	*O*	*M*	*R*	*W*
AUCKLAND								
Martin	26	8	84	1	24	4	75	1
Tuffey	27	6	81	2				
de Grandhomme	21	7	60	3	22	7	42	1
Croft	6	0	29	0	9	2	33	0
McKay	16.2	6	50	2	24	2	65	1
Styris	7	0	25	0	6	1	18	0
Nethula	18	1	75	2	35	5	100	4
OTAGO								
McSkimming	21	5	65	1				
McMillan	12	2	40	2				
Harvie	20.4	2	89	4				
Butler	20	4	87	1				
Todd	9	0	40	0				
McCullum	19	3	58	0				
Redmond	9	0	28	0				
Cumming	5	1	8	0				

Fall of Wickets

	O	*A*	*O*
	1st	*1st*	*2nd*
1st	158	36	7
2nd	165	151	16
3rd	262	336	116
4th	325	336	117
5th	325	337	182
6th	384	379	327
7th	398	430	341
8th	415	430	-
9th	418	-	-
10th	418	-	-

CANTERBURY v CENTRAL DISTRICTS State Championship

at MainPower Oval, Rangiora on 6, 7, 8, 9 March, 2009
Toss : Canterbury. Umpires : C.B. Gaffaney & K.C. Manley
Close of play: 1st day: Canterbury 388-5, Myburgh 104; 2nd day: CD 130-3, Patton 30, Sinclair 0
3rd day: CD 191-4, Weston 45, Hay 33
***First innings win to Canterbury.** Points: Canterbury 2, Central Districts 0*

Two members of the Indian touring side, Dravid and Mishra, played in this match. Canterbury won the toss and batted and by the end of the day three batsmen had registered centuries. Papps, who overtook Chris Harris as Canterbury's leading century maker, reached three figures off 119 balls after 148 minutes. Dravid (215 minutes and 160 balls) and Myburgh (193 minutes and 147 balls) followed.

Central made a reasonable reply but it was nowhere enough, in the circumstances, and they followed on 280 runs behind. Early on the last day Central lost their sixth wicket at 263, bringing Hay and Diamanti together. Both players were on a king pair. They proceeded to add an unbeaten 205 for the seventh wicket with Hay's hundred (the 200th for Central) taking 276 minutes and 211 balls while Diamanti needed 130 balls and 165 minutes.

There was now no chance of any result but McClenaghan took the opportunity of claiming a first-class hat trick by dismissing Astle with the last ball of his first over and Myburgh and Stewart in his second.

CANTERBURY

FIRST INNINGS	*Runs*	*Mins*	*Balls*	*6s*	*4s*	*SECOND INNINGS*	*Runs*	*Mins*	*Balls*	*6s*	*4s*
T.D.Astle c Sinclair b Diamanti	29	99	76	-	5	c Sinclair b McClenaghan	0	3	6	-	-
M.H.W.Papps c Patton b Diamanti	127	188	157	-	20	not out	9	37	24	-	1
R.S.Dravid c Sinclair b Diamanti	102	226	164	-	13						
J.G.Myburgh c Sinclair b Diamanti	107	222	168	2	17	(3) b McClenaghan	0	5	1	-	-
S.L.Stewart c Griggs b Diamanti	4	21	14	-	-	(4) lbw b McClenaghan	0	1	1	-	-
C.J.Anderson c Griggs b Sinclair	17	42	39	-	3	(5) not out	8	25	22	-	-
C.F.K.van Wyk*† c Hay b Mishra	92	243	167	-	11						
A.M.Ellis b Worker	43	135	112	-	5						
M.P.F.Davidson c Hay b Mishra	13	35	23	-	2						
L.M.Burtt lbw b Mishra	1	30	15	-	-						
H.K.Bennett not out	0	19	16	-	-						
Extras (b 2, lb 4, w 1, nb 1)	8					(b 2)	2				
TOTAL (158.2 overs)	**543**	629				(9 overs) (3 wkts)	**19**	37			

CENTRAL DISTRICTS

	Runs	*Mins*	*Balls*	*6s*	*4s*		*Runs*	*Mins*	*Balls*	*6s*	*4s*
P.J.Ingram run out	43	72	56	-	7	c Stewart b Bennett	24	73	60	-	4
G.H.Worker c van Wyk b Ellis	50	154	92	-	7	c Papps b Ellis	36	144	75	-	6
B.M.K.Patton c van Wyk b Astle	35	127	104	-	2	c Dravid b Astle	14	31	24	-	2
M.J.McClenaghan c van Wyk b Astle	2	13	12	-	-						
M.S.Sinclair* c Davidson b Ellis	56	132	90	-	9	(4) c Anderson b Bennett	33	30	28	-	7
T.I.Weston b Burtt	40	91	63	-	6	(5) c Davidson b Bennett	78	155	139	-	11
G.R.Hay c van Wyk b Burtt	0	1	1	-	-	(6) not out	131	395	300	-	14
B.B.J.Griggs† b Bennett	18	43	28	-	3	(7) c Anderson b Myburgh	4	16	11	-	1
B.J.Diamanti b Ellis	0	1	1	-	-	(8) not out	135	230	194	-	22
A.Mishra c van Wyk b Ellis	11	46	29	-	2						
M.J.Mason not out	1	11	4	-	-						
Extras (b 2, lb 1, nb 4)	7					(b 2, lb 5, w 3, nb 3)	13				
TOTAL (79.2 overs)	**263**	343				(138 overs) (6 wkts dec)	**468**	522			

Bowling	*O*	*M*	*R*	*W*	*O*	*M*	*R*	*W*
CENTRAL DISTRICTS								
Mason	25	6	94	0	4	2	4	0
McClenaghan	26	4	115	0	3	1	5	3
Patton	5	1	24	0				
Diamanti	32	10	74	5				
Mishra	48.2	4	155	3	2	1	8	0
Worker	15	2	51	1				
Sinclair	7	2	24	1				
CANTERBURY								
Burtt	15	0	68	2	20	0	80	0
Davidson	11	0	47	0	14	3	41	0
Ellis	19.2	8	39	4	16	4	67	1
Bennett	10	2	31	1	22	4	100	3
Myburgh	9	1	34	0	32	4	86	1
Astle	15	5	41	2	34	13	87	1

Fall of Wickets

	C	*CD*	*CD*	*C*
	1st	*1st*	*2nd*	*2nd*
1st	90	76	46	0
2nd	183	127	71	0
3rd	336	130	111	0
4th	352	145	119	-
5th	388	232	257	-
6th	395	232	263	-
7th	487	232	-	-
8th	517	232	-	-
9th	532	257	-	-
10th	543	263	-	-

OTAGO v WELLINGTON — State Championship

at University Oval, Dunedin on 6, 7, 8, 9 March, 2009
Toss : Wellington. Umpires : B.G. Frost & E.C. Hendrikse
Close of play: 1st day: Wellington 94-5, Woodcock 23; 2nd day: Otago 210-7, Wells 22, Wagner 1
3rd day: Wellington 74-2, Parlane 53, Crook 0
***First innings win to Otago.** Points: Otago 2, Wellington 0*

Tugaga made his first-class debut in this game which also featured two members of the Indian squad, Laxman and Balaji.

Wellington sent Otago in to bat and were well rewarded. The visitors were all out for 174 with number eight McSkimming top scoring with 39 not out. The home side, however, lost Bell to the first ball of the innings and were 94-5 at stumps. Otago went on to claim an unlikely 35 run advantage and reached 210-7 by the close of the second day.

A lively innings from Harvie took Otago's lead past 300 and Wellington were left to chase 322 for victory. Bell again fell cheaply and Brodie followed soon after. Parlane, Woodcock and Crook, who reached his maiden century from 234 balls in 297 minutes, showed plenty of resistance but could not quite reach the required scoring rate. When stumps were drawn at 6.39 pm, Wellington still required another 39 runs.

OTAGO

FIRST INNINGS	Runs	Mins	Balls	6s	4s	SECOND INNINGS	Runs	Mins	Balls	6s	4s
C.D.Cumming* lbw b Burns	29	115	80	-	4	c Woodcock b Burns	4	2	3	-	1
H.D.Rutherford c Nevin b Burns	0	13	9	-	-	c Parlane b Burns	2	13	4	-	-
G.R.Todd lbw b Burns	5	23	19	-	-	b Woodcock	73	223	180	-	8
V.V.S.Laxman c Boam b Burns	20	69	46	-	1	c & b Woodcock	44	123	79	-	6
S.B.Haig† c Parlane b Balaji	26	53	40	-	5	c Nevin b Woodcock	4	8	6	-	1
N.L.McCullum c Parlane b Bowden	12	24	19	-	3	b Balaji	33	83	61	-	6
S.R.Wells c Parlane b Tugaga	7	46	32	-	-	b Balaji	25	103	86	-	3
W.C.McSkimming not out	39	100	73	1	5	c Bell b Tugaga	17	74	54	-	2
N.Wagner c Nevin b Bowden	23	65	46	-	4	c Nevin b Bowden	17	39	24	-	2
M.J.Harvie b Bowden	0	6	4	-	-	not out	37	56	42	2	4
J.M.McMillan run out	0	3	3	-	-	lbw b Woodcock	17	41	29	1	2
Extras (b 1, lb 4, w 1, nb 7)	13					(lb 5, w 2, nb 6)	13				
TOTAL (60.4 overs)	**174**	253				(93.4 overs)	**286**	330			

WELLINGTON

FIRST INNINGS	Runs	Mins	Balls	6s	4s	SECOND INNINGS	Runs	Mins	Balls	6s	4s
M.D.Bell* c Wells b McSkimming	0	1	1	-	-	b Wagner	1	12	11	-	-
J.M.Brodie c McCullum b Wells	32	117	72	-	6	lbw b McCullum	17	57	42	-	2
N.R.Parlane lbw b Wagner	5	6	9	-	1	lbw b Wagner	59	89	65	-	10
B-J.Crook b Wagner	23	45	38	-	3	not out	101	304	237	2	9
L.J.Woodcock c McCullum b Harvie	36	134	94	-	5	c Rutherford b McSkimming	69	202	150	-	7
H.K.P.Boam c Haig b McCullum	10	37	29	-	1	(8) not out	12	30	24	-	3
C.J.Nevin† c Haig b Harvie	1	25	23	-	-	(6) c Haig b McSkimming	14	20	16	-	1
D.J.Bowden c Haig b McSkimming	11	31	19	-	2	(7) lbw b McSkimming	0	1	1	-	-
L.Balaji lbw b McSkimming	12	33	30	-	1						
M.J.Tugaga not out	0	25	15	-	-						
M.Burns c Haig b McSkimming	0	14	9	-	-						
Extras (lb 8, w 1)	9					(b 2, lb 7, w 1)	10				
TOTAL (56.3 overs)	**139**	236				(91 overs) (6 wkts)	**283**	356			

Bowling	O	M	R	W	O	M	R	W
WELLINGTON								
Balaji	15	4	39	1	23	11	55	2
Burns	16	2	41	4	18	3	55	2
Bowden	14.4	1	40	3	19	2	73	1
Tugaga	8	3	28	1	10	2	28	1
Boam	3	1	11	0				
Woodcock	4	1	10	0	23.4	6	70	4
OTAGO								
McSkimming	14.3	3	40	4	19	5	54	3
Wagner	15	3	46	2	13	4	35	2
McMillan	12	5	27	0	10	2	36	0
Harvie	11	6	10	2	17	2	45	0
Wells	2	1	8	1	3	1	10	0
McCullum	2	2	0	1	28	9	91	1
Cumming					1	0	3	0

Fall of Wickets	O	W	O	W
	1st	1st	2nd	2nd
1st	9	0	4	2
2nd	22	5	17	42
3rd	55	46	94	84
4th	70	73	98	237
5th	94	94	162	259
6th	101	111	166	259
7th	118	116	205	-
8th	174	134	217	-
9th	174	139	239	-
10th	174	139	286	-

NORTHERN DISTRICTS v AUCKLAND — State Championship

at Cobham Oval, Whangarei on 6, 7, 8, 9 March, 2009
Toss : Auckland. Umpires : P.D. Jones & D.G. Paterson
Close of play: 1st day: ND 4-0, Wilson 2, Devcich 2; 2nd day: Auckland 27-1, McIntosh 6, Kitchen 15
3rd day: ND 113-3, H.J.H.Marshall 43, Scott 0
***Auckland won by 22 runs.** Points: Auckland 8, Northern Districts 0*

The new Cobham Oval became New Zealand's 62nd first-class venue. Kitchen and 17-year-old Gadsdon made their first-class debuts and they were later joined by Boult (bother of Trent) when he replaced Martin.

Auckland chose to bat first and lost McIntosh in the first over. Styris and de Grandhomme hit fifties and Auckland reached 277. Northern safely faced four overs before stumps.

The home side looked likely to take first innings points at 254-6 but lost their last four wickets for just 14 runs. Auckland slumped to 134-8 the following day but were rescued by a 106 run partnership between Hopkins and Tuffey. The Auckland keeper reached his hundred from 147 balls after 206 minutes.

Northern needed 269 to win and were 113-3 at stumps. Wickets fell at regular intervals next day and the home side were 204-8. Davis hit 30 off 26 balls but went at 238 and Yovich was dismissed by a combination of his former team mates, giving Auckland a win by just 22 runs.

AUCKLAND

FIRST INNINGS	Runs	Mins	Balls	6s	4s	*SECOND INNINGS*	Runs	Mins	Balls	6s	4s
T.G.McIntosh lbw b Aldridge	0	1	3	-	-	c Yovich b Boult	31	116	81	-	5
R.A.Jones* c Devcich b Davis	9	22	20	-	1	c Gadsdon b Davis	0	5	2	-	-
A.K.Kitchen b Aldridge	7	24	13	-	1	lbw b Boult	27	92	79	-	4
S.B.Styris c Gadsdon b Scott	95	201	146	-	14	c Devcich b Boult	2	9	7	-	-
S.J.Croft c Marshall J.A.H. b Scott	47	68	57	-	8	c & b Boult	0	10	5	-	-
G.J.Hopkins† c Wilson b Yovich	10	58	36	-	-	c & b Aldridge	100	210	149	-	9
C.de Grandhomme st Gadsdon b Devcich	63	118	81	1	8	c Gadsdon b Scott	6	29	17	-	1
T.S.Nethula lbw b Aldridge	1	13	8	-	-	b Aldridge	11	27	25	-	1
L.J.Shaw c Gadsdon b Yovich	0	6	6	-	-	b Davis	11	22	21	-	1
D.R.Tuffey lbw b Devcich	22	48	47	-	2	run out	53	111	112	1	5
A.J.McKay not out	4	20	17	-	-	not out	7	14	8	-	1
Extras (b 1, lb 4, w 5, nb 9)	19					(b 4, lb 6, w 1)	11				
TOTAL (71.2 overs)	**277**	299				(84.2 overs)	**259**	332			

NORTHERN DISTRICTS

	Runs	Mins	Balls	6s	4s		Runs	Mins	Balls	6s	4s
B.S.Wilson c & b Nethula	62	221	157	-	6	c Jones b Shaw	12	36	23	-	1
A.P.Devcich c Hopkins b Shaw	14	86	64	-	-	c Hopkins b Tuffey	16	6	48	-	1
H.J.H.Marshall lbw b Tuffey	10	53	31	-	-	c Nethula b Shaw	43	108	82	-	4
J.A.H.Marshall* lbw b Tuffey	0	1	1	-	-	c de Grandhomme b Nethula	38	72	54	-	7
M.E.Parlane lbw b Nethula	75	273	185	-	6	(6) c Hopkins b McKay	8	53	31	-	-
J.A.F.Yovich run out	25	73	62	-	2	(7) c Styris b Tuffey	41	139	93	-	3
G.W.Aldridge c Croft b McKay	25	45	42	-	2	(8) lbw b de Grandhomme	14	34	25	-	2
J.J.Boult b Nethula	31	59	41	-	3	(9) c Styris b de Grandhomme	5	9	10	-	-
T.T.Davis st Hopkins b Nethula	0	10	10	-	-	(10) b de Grandhomme	30	26	26	1	5
B.E.Scott not out	10	15	9	-	1	(5) lbw b Nethula	27	110	81	-	3
S.R.Gadsdon† c de Grandhomme b Tuffey	2	10	7	-	-	not out	2	17	16	-	-
B.P.Martin											
Extras (lb 7, w 6, nb 1)	14					(b 2, lb 2, w 1, nb 5)	10				
TOTAL (101.2 overs)	**268**	432				(80.4 overs)	**246**	314			

Bowling	*O*	*M*	*R*	*W*				
NORTHERN DISTRICTS								
Aldridge	14	4	46	3	14.2	2	42	2
Davis	13	1	56	1	15	6	46	2
Yovich	12	2	56	2	8	1	27	0
Scott	16	3	59	2	10	2	31	1
Martin	8	0	35	0				
Devcich	8.2	2	20	2	9	0	25	0
Boult					28	6	78	4
AUCKLAND								
Tuffey	24.2	7	45	3	17.4	10	25	2
McKay	20	4	66	1	12	3	44	1
de Grandhomme	11	3	20	0	14	2	40	3
Shaw	13	2	43	1	8	0	27	2
Styris	7	0	15	0				
Nethula	26	3	72	4	29	1	106	2

Fall of Wickets

	A 1st	ND 1st	A 2nd	ND 2nd
1st	0	37	2	22
2nd	16	65	56	40
3rd	16	65	66	113
4th	93	114	67	114
5th	152	162	67	141
6th	229	199	84	162
7th	238	254	108	193
8th	240	256	134	204
9th	264	257	240	238
10th	277	268	259	246

Boult replaced Martin who was called into the New Zealand A team

OTAGO v AUCKLAND

State Championship

at Queenstown Events Centre on 13, 14, 15 March, 2009
Toss : Auckland. Umpires : D.M. Quested & D.J. Walker
Close of play: 1st day: Auckland 69-0, McIntosh 30, Jones 33; 2nd day: Auckland 428-5, Young 31, de Grandhomme 0
***Auckland won by an innings and 84 runs.** Points: Auckland 8, Otago 0*

Beard made his first-class debut in this game while Todd captained a side at first-class level for the first time. Auckland sent Otago in to bat and had regular success throughout the day. By the close they were 141 in arrears with all wickets intact.

The Auckland openers eventually put on 169 with Jones reaching his hundred after 261 minutes and 187 balls. Kitchen, with one previous match to his name, brought up his first hundred from 127 balls in 166 minutes and Young joined in with a century from 147 balls after 214 minutes.

Facing arrears of 324, Otago were bowled out for 240 before the end of the third day. Broom hit 79 and Beard scored 32 at number eleven.

OTAGO

FIRST INNINGS	Runs	Mins	Balls	6s	4s	SECOND INNINGS	Runs	Mins	Balls	6s	4s
L.J.Morgan c Kitchen b McKay	54	158	102	-	7	(2) c Young b de Grandhomme	18	101	72	-	1
H.D.Rutherford c Nicol b Tuffey	5	27	14	-	-	(1) lbw b McKay	37	52	35	-	6
G.R.Todd* c & b de Grandhomme	10	34	28	-	1	c Young b Martin	23	52	39	-	3
N.T.Broom c Young b Tuffey	26	67	50	-	5	c Kitchen b McKay	79	135	101	-	15
J.W.Sheed c McIntosh b Nethula	27	119	87	-	5	c Kitchen b Martin	0	8	9	-	-
S.B.Haig† lbw b Nethula	35	99	71	-	5	lbw b Martin	26	127	96	-	4
S.R.Wells c Young b Tuffey	7	22	20	-	1	c Kitchen b McKay	0	12	6	-	-
N.Wagner b Nethula	18	58	35	-	2	run out	1	4	3	-	-
M.J.Harvie c Tuffey b Nethula	17	27	22	-	3	c Croft b Nethula	11	43	13	-	1
J.M.McMillan c Young b Tuffey	1	22	19	-	-	c Nethula b McKay	4	3	4	-	1
N.B.Beard not out	0	5	1	-	-	not out	32	36	43	-	6
Extras (lb 10)	10					(b 1, lb 3, nb 5)	9				
TOTAL (74.5 overs)	**210**	328				(69.2 overs)	**240**	296			

AUCKLAND

	Runs	Mins	Balls	6s	4s
T.G.McIntosh c Beard b McMillan	74	222	184	-	10
R.A.Jones* c Wagner b Harvie	102	273	193	-	11
R.J.Nicol b Harvie	31	66	66	-	3
A.K.Kitchen c Todd b Wagner	125	199	155	4	13
S.J.Croft b Harvie	41	85	73	-	4
R.A.Young† not out	100	215	147	-	8
C.de Grandhomme c Haig b McMillan	26	70	58	-	3
T.S.Nethula lbw b Beard	2	21	13	-	-
D.R.Tuffey not out	7	24	13	-	-
A.J.McKay					
C.S.Martin					
J.A.Raval					
L.J.Shaw					
Extras (b 4, lb 11, w 8, nb 3)	26				
TOTAL (149.5 overs) (7 wkts dec)	**534**	595			

Bowling	O	M	R	W	O	M	R	W
AUCKLAND								
Martin	16	2	60	0				
Tuffey	20.5	8	32	4	18	4	55	0
de Grandhomme	10	3	22	1	8	3	23	1
McKay	15	3	47	1	14	0	58	4
Nethula	13	4	39	4	12.2	2	38	1
Croft					3	0	13	0
Shaw					14	4	49	3
OTAGO								
Wagner	35	7	124	1				
Harvie	26	4	96	3				
McMillan	27.5	2	104	2				
Wells	13	3	39	0				
Beard	42	7	133	1				
Broom	4	0	22	0				
Todd	2	1	1	0				

Fall of Wickets

	O	A	O
	1st	*1st*	*2nd*
1st	16	169	51
2nd	44	218	81
3rd	92	229	81
4th	108	331	81
5th	164	428	191
6th	169	495	191
7th	175	508	192
8th	206	-	192
9th	210	-	196
10th	210	-	240

Shaw and Raval replaced Martin and McIntosh who joined the New Zealand squad

CANTERBURY v NORTHERN DISTRICTS State Championship

at Queen Elizabeth II Park, Christchurch on 13, 14, 15, 16 March, 2009
Toss : Northern Districts. Umpires : E.C. Hendrikse & P.D. Jones
Close of play: 1st day: ND 62-1, Wilson 23, Flynn 29; 2nd day: Canterbury 8-2, Papps 2
3rd day: ND 31-1, Wilson 3, H.J.H.Marshall 21
***Northern Districts won by 6 wickets.** Points: Northern Districts 8, Canterbury 0*

Northern sent Canterbury in to bat and had early success. Myburgh and Robertson then added 112 for the fourth wicket and van Wyk hit 67 later in the innings.

Northern's reply centred around a 209 run partnership between Wilson (highest score and century off 188 balls in 234 minues) and Flynn (146 balls and 213 minutes for his hundred).

Canterbury recovered from 8-2 and had reached 267 before Fulton left. He had reached his hundred from 173 balls in 227 minutes while Papps took 211 minutes and 170 balls. Fulton scored 96 of his runs from 20 deliveries. Once the partnership was broken, however, Canterbury collapsed, leaving Northern 173 to win. Williamson was the destroyer with his first five wicket haul. The winning runs came at 1.40 pm on the fourth day.

CANTERBURY

FIRST INNINGS	*Runs*	*Mins*	*Balls*	*6s*	*4s*	*SECOND INNINGS*	*Runs*	*Mins*	*Balls*	*6s*	*4s*
T.D.Astle b Southee	18	60	45	-	1	c Devcich b Arnel	0	7	7	-	-
M.H.W.Papps c Gadsdon b Arnel	11	38	27	-	1	lbw b Williamson	128	295	244	1	18
P.G.Fulton c Gadsdon b Southee	0	14	11	-	-	(4) c Devcich b Williamson	122	255	196	8	12
J.G.Myburgh b Yovich	50	154	110	-	8	(5) c Parlane b Devcich	7	24	17	-	1
I.A.Robertson c Parlane b Southee	61	121	94	1	9	(6) not out	12	64	40	-	1
C.J.Anderson b Southee	0	3	4	-	-	(7) b Williamson	4	12	7	-	1
C.F.K.van Wyk*† b Arnel	67	137	123	-	11	(8) c Gadsdon b Williamson	2	13	10	-	-
A.M.Ellis c Parlane b Arnel	9	21	13	-	2	(9) c Southee b Martin	5	10	12	-	1
B.C.Hiini c Williamson b Southee	8	49	35	-	1	(3) c Williamson b Southee	5	13	13	-	-
L.M.Burtt not out	11	46	31	-	1	b Martin	1	6	10	-	-
H.K.Bennett c Williamson b Arnel	0	2	2	-	-	c & b Williamson	5	13	11	-	1
Extras (b 1, lb 7, nb 3)	11					(b 8, lb 2, w 2, nb 6)	18				
TOTAL (82 overs)	**246**	321				(93.3 overs)	**309**	356			

NORTHERN DISTRICTS

	Runs	*Mins*	*Balls*	*6s*	*4s*		*Runs*	*Mins*	*Balls*	*6s*	*4s*
B.S.Wilson c Astle b Bennett	109	248	203	-	14	lbw b Myburgh	40	164	109	1	3
A.P.Devcich c Burtt b Ellis	4	30	15	-	1	lbw b Bennett	1	10	4	-	-
D.R.Flynn lbw b Bennett	104	224	154	2	11						
K.S.Williamson c Robertson b Myburgh	53	117	112	1	5	lbw b Burtt	35	60	44	-	5
H.J.H.Marshall c Ellis b Burtt	48	81	81	-	5	(3) lbw b Ellis	28	37	37	-	4
M.E.Parlane* c van Wyk b Burtt	8	31	19	-	1	(5) not out	28	85	52	-	3
J.A.F.Yovich b Hiini	16	62	37	-	2	(6) not out	29	3	27	1	4
B.P.Martin c van Wyk b Hiini	1	3	3	-	-						
T.G.Southee c Astle b Myburgh	10	20	12	-	1						
S.R.Gadsdon† st van Wyk b Myburgh	9	19	19	-	2						
B.J.Arnel not out	2	6	5	-	-						
B.E.Scott											
T.T.Davis											
Extras (b 4, lb 3, w 1, nb 11)	19					(b 3, lb 2, w 1, nb 6)	12				
TOTAL (108.1 overs)	**383**	447				(45.1 overs) (4 wkts)	**173**	384			

Bowling	*O*	*M*	*R*	*W*				
NORTHERN DISTRICTS								
Southee	21	8	43	5	20	4	70	1
Arnel	18	7	38	4	2	0	4	1
Yovich	15	3	55	1	14	2	45	0
Marshall	3	0	6	0				
Martin	17	3	57	0	22	8	49	2
Williamson	8	1	39	0	25.3	8	75	5
Davis					6	0	47	0
Devcich					4	1	9	1
CANTERBURY								
Burtt	22	3	97	2	7	1	28	1
Bennett	21	6	48	2	12	2	51	1
Ellis	23	6	81	1	11	4	32	1
Hiini	20	2	56	2	7	1	26	0
Astle	2	0	23	0	3.1	0	22	0
Myburgh	20.1	2	71	3	5	2	9	1

Fall of Wickets

	C *1st*	***ND*** *1st*	***C*** *2nd*	***ND*** *2nd*
1st	23	24	3	8
2nd	29	233	8	38
3rd	32	234	267	99
4th	144	307	280	136
5th	144	329	280	-
6th	154	359	285	-
7th	172	360	295	-
8th	204	363	300	-
9th	246	380	302	-
10th	246	383	309	-

Scott and Davis replaced Flynn and Arnel who joined the New Zealand squad

CENTRAL DISTRICTS v WELLINGTON State Championship

at McLean Park, Napier on 13, 14, 15, 16 March, 2009
Toss : Wellington. Umpires : B.G. Frost & E.J. Gray
Close of play: 1st day: Wellington 222-5, Franklin 54, Nevin 36; 2nd day: CD 156-2, Vijay 64, Sinclair 57
3rd day: Wellington 201-3, Franklin 107, Woodcock 17*
***First innings win to Wellington.** Points: Wellington 2, Central Districts 0*

Rance made his first-class debut while two members of the Indian touring party, Vijay and Kulkarni, took part in this match. Wellington won the toss and batted but slumped to 131-5. Nevin then joined Franklin and the pair added 91 before bad light stopped play.

The next day Franklin went after the partnership had been worth 138. Nevin reached his hundred off 204 balls in 278 minutes and Wellington finished with 410. Central began well but were bowled out 114 runs in arrears and Wellington ended the third day 315 runs ahead. Franklin reached three figures from 136 balls after 181 minutes.

On the last day the visitors batted on and left Central an unlikely target of 414. Vijay was lbw in the third over but How and Worker then added 171 (Central's highest second wicket partnership against Wellington). The match was called off shortly after tea, two balls after How had reached his century.

WELLINGTON

FIRST INNINGS	*Runs*	*Mins*	*Balls*	*6s*	*4s*	*SECOND INNINGS*	*Runs*	*Mins*	*Balls*	*6s*	*4s*
M.D.Bell* c Rance b McClenaghan	25	32	22	-	5	(2) b Hefford	60	128	85	-	13
J.M.Brodie c Worker b Hefford	23	111	78	-	4	(1) lbw b Bracewell	12	22	16	-	2
N.R.Parlane b Sinclair	59	129	92	2	6						
B-J.Crook c Vijay b Sinclair	12	58	40	-	3	(3) c Hay b McClenaghan	0	16	11	-	-
J.E.C.Franklin c How b Hefford	76	236	198	-	9	(4) not out	107	184	141	-	17
L.J.Woodcock c How b Rance	2	41	28	-	-	(5) c Sinclair b McClenaghan	33	120	86	-	2
C.J.Nevin† c Sinclair b How	134	317	237	1	15	(7) c Bracewell b Worker	5	17	8	-	-
D.J.Bowden b Sinclair	26	60	39	-	4	(8) not out	27	20	16	1	1
M.V.Houghton c Griggs b Bracewell	23	105	87	-	2						
D.S.Kulkarni not out	13	43	27	-	2						
M.Burns c Hay b Bracewell	4	9	7	-	1						
H.K.P.Boam						(6) not out	49	64	52	-	8
Extras (lb 8, w 2, nb 3)	13					(lb 4, w 1, nb 1)	6				
TOTAL (142 overs)	**410**	560				(69 overs) (5 wkts dec)	**299**	280			

CENTRAL DISTRICTS

	Runs	Mins	Balls	6s	4s		Runs	Mins	Balls	6s	4s
J.M.How c Parlane b Franklin	18	39	25	-	3	not out	101	204	169	2	10
M.Vijay lbw b Bowden	93	283	194	1	13	lbw b Burns	3	12	9	-	-
G.H.Worker c Nevin b Franklin	8	22	20	-	1	not out	63	191	180	-	9
M.S.Sinclair* c Bell b Kulkarni	62	116	91	-	8						
T.I.Weston c Brodie b Bowden	15	46	29	-	1						
G.R.Hay c Brodie b Bowden	0	2	2	-	-						
B.B.J.Griggs† b Bowden	43	151	82	-	7						
D.A.J.Bracewell c Nevin b Kulkarni	1	11	6	-	-						
S.H.A.Rance c sub (Boam) b Franklin	31	36	33	1	5						
B.E.Hefford c Franklin b Kulkarni	0	5	4	-	-						
M.J.McClenaghan not out	0	41	37	-	-						
Extras (lb 3, w 5, nb 17)	25					(lb 2, w 1, nb 4)	7				
TOTAL (84.2 overs)	**296**	368				(59 overs) (1 wkt)	**174**	200			

Bowling	*O*	*M*	*R*	*W*	*O*	*M*	*R*	*W*
CENTRAL DISTRICTS								
McClenaghan	28	7	89	1	13	1	73	2
Bracewell	23	5	76	2	12	2	49	1
Rance	19	3	64	1	11	1	61	0
Hefford	22	8	49	2	8	4	17	1
Worker	16	0	58	0	5	0	40	1
Sinclair	23	11	31	3	9	2	8	0
Vijay	5	0	21	0				
How	6	3	14	1	11	1	47	0
WELLINGTON								
Franklin	20	3	59	3				
Kulkarni	19	2	62	3	7	1	19	0
Burns	15	4	48	0	10	3	26	1
Woodcock	11	2	50	0	10	1	37	0
Bowden	14.2	1	55	4	8	2	32	0
Houghton	5	0	19	0	24	5	58	0

Fall of Wickets	***W***	***CD***	***W***	***CD***
	1st	*1st*	*2nd*	*2nd*
1st	30	28	20	3
2nd	85	45	37	-
3rd	117	163	115	-
4th	126	190	236	-
5th	131	190	252	-
6th	269	225	-	-
7th	330	239	-	-
8th	387	275	-	-
9th	402	276	-	-
10th	410	296	-	-

Franklin retired not out at 201-3 to join the New Zealand team and replacement player Boam continued his innings

WELLINGTON v OTAGO State Championship

at Allied Nationwide Finance Basin Reserve, Wellington on 20, 21, 22, 23 March, 2009
Toss : Wellington. Umpires : E.J. Gray & E.A. Watkin
Close of play: 1st day: Wellington 7-0, Brodie 1, Bell 6; 2nd day: Wellington 242-6, Nevin 65, Bowden 85
3rd day: Otago 257-2, Todd 94, Broom 2
***First innings win to Wellington.** Points: Wellington 2, Otago 0*

Wellington sent Otago in to bat but had to wait until the score had reached 122 before they had any success. This breakthrough triggered a collapse and, despite a fifty from Morgan, Otago lost all their remaining wickets for the addition of just 148 runs and were all out just before stumps. Brodie equalled the New Zealand first-class record of five catches in an innings.

Wellington slumped to 98-6 but Bowden joined Nevin and the pair batted through to the close, adding 148 runs. Bowden went without addition next morning but Patel and Nevin added a further 76 to give Wellington first innings points.

Otago responded strongly and soon wiped off the deficit. Cumming reached his century from 158 balls in 221 minutes and Todd was six runs short of his century at the close. Unfortunately for him, however, no play was possible the next day and he was left on 94 not out.

OTAGO

FIRST INNINGS	*Runs*	*Mins*	*Balls*	*6s*	*4s*	*SECOND INNINGS*	*Runs*	*Mins*	*Balls*	*6s*	*4s*
C.D.Cumming* c Brodie b Patel	45	120	75	-	5	b Crook	118	292	199	2	9
A.J.Redmond b Woodcock	76	110	93	1	12	b Patel	28	46	30	-	5
G.R.Todd c Brodie b Woodcock	1	15	12	-	-	not out	94	251	229	-	12
N.T.Broom c Brodie b Patel	6	32	32	-	-	not out	2	5	3	-	-
L.J.Morgan lbw b Bowden	64	186	181	-	7						
S.B.Haig† c Brodie b Patel	13	75	50	-	1						
W.C.McSkimming c Brodie b Patel	0	2	2	-	-						
N.Wagner lbw b Patel	29	124	103	-	4						
N.B.Beard c Nevin b Bowden	5	31	24	-	-						
N.L.McCullum c Crook b Bowden	16	26	17	1	2						
M.J.Harvie not out	0	14	7	-	-						
Extras (lb 4, w 4, nb 7)	15					(b 7, lb 1, w 3, nb 4)	15				
TOTAL (98.1 overs)	**270**	372				(76 overs) (2 wkts)	**257**	298			

WELLINGTON

	Runs	Mins	Balls	6s	4s
J.M.Brodie lbw b McSkimming	5	23	15	-	1
M.D.Bell* lbw b Harvie	30	59	42	-	5
N.R.Parlane c Morgan b McCullum	13	43	31	-	2
G.D.Elliott c McCullum b McSkimming	21	95	81	-	1
B-J.Crook c Morgan b McCullum	4	36	32	-	1
L.J.Woodcock lbw b Wagner	11	28	27	-	1
C.J.Nevin† c Redmond b Harvie	93	204	143	-	10
D.J.Bowden c Wagner b McCullum	85	124	122	1	9
J.S.Patel c Redmond b Harvie	44	56	36	2	4
M.J.Tugaga not out	3	8	7	-	-
M.Burns					
Extras (b 5, lb 10, nb 1)	16				
TOTAL (89.1 overs) (9 wkts dec)	**325**	337			

Bowling	*O*	*M*	*R*	*W*	*O*	*M*	*R*	*W*
WELLINGTON								
Burns	9	1	34	0	6	0	41	0
Bowden	12.1	2	52	3	7	1	33	0
Elliott	7	3	20	0	6	1	14	0
Tugaga	8	1	34	0	9	1	30	0
Patel	33	8	65	5	24	3	72	1
Woodcock	29	13	61	2	22	3	57	0
Crook					2	1	2	1
OTAGO								
McSkimming	15	4	60	2				
Wagner	15	3	56	1				
Harvie	13.1	3	44	3				
McCullum	28	3	84	3				
Beard	15	2	56	0				
Cumming	3	0	10	0				

Fall of Wickets

	O	**W**	**O**
	1st	*1st*	*2nd*
1st	122	19	62
2nd	126	50	255
3rd	127	52	-
4th	142	64	-
5th	181	85	-
6th	185	98	-
7th	234	246	-
8th	250	322	-
9th	253	325	-
10th	270	-	-

AUCKLAND v NORTHERN DISTRICTS State Championship

at Eden Park Outer Oval, Auckland on 20, 21, 22 March, 2009
Toss : Auckland. Umpires : B.G. Frost & C.B. Gaffaney
Close of play: 1st day: Auckland 14-0, Croft 9, Jones 5; 2nd day: Auckland 397-6, de Grandhomme 27, Nethula 1
Auckland won by an innings and 16 runs. *Points: Auckland 8, Northern Districts 0*

Auckland sent Northern in to bat and saw Wilson and Hamish Marshall put on 59 for the first wicket. The only batsman to reach fifty was Williamson, whose maiden hundred arrived after 201 minutes from 131 balls. Northern were all out shortly before stumps.

Auckland batted throughout the second day, scoring 383 runs off 100 overs. Kitchen reached his second century after 173 minutes and 134 balls and went on to the highest score of his brief career. On the third day de Grandhomme brought up his hundred from 109 balls after 177 minutes and Auckland continued until they were all out for 540.

Facing a deficit of 234, the visitors slumped to 13-3 before Parlane and Williamson added 132 for the fourth wicket. Once Shaw removed Parlane more wickets tumbled. Williamson narrowly missed his second century of the match while Tuffey finished with figures of 6-33 against his former team.

NORTHERN DISTRICTS

FIRST INNINGS	*Runs*	*Mins*	*Balls*	*6s*	*4s*	*SECOND INNINGS*	*Runs*	*Mins*	*Balls*	*6s*	*4s*
B.S.Wilson c Nicol b Tuffey	24	90	63	-	3	c Hopkins b Tuffey	0	2	4	-	-
H.J.H.Marshall c de Grandhomme Shaw	38	65	43	-	7	c Hopkins b Tuffey	6	36	33	-	-
M.E.Parlane lbw b Nethula	34	74	37	2	4	c Kitchen b Shaw	72	176	145	1	9
J.A.H.Marshall* c Hopkins b Tuffey	3	8	6	-	-	c Croft b Tuffey	0	17	12	-	-
K.S.Williamson c de Grandhomme b Nethula	111	219	144	4	12	c Young b Tuffey	95	184	108	-	14
P.D.McGlashan† c de Grandhomme b McKay	27	54	48	-	4	b McKay	18	48	37	-	2
J.A.F.Yovich c Kitchen b Shaw	6	15	15	-	1	st Hopkins b Nethula	8	58	46	-	1
G.W.Aldridge c Nethula b de Grandhomme	16	29	30	-	3	b Nethula	4	35	23	-	-
B.P.Martin not out	24	125	124	-	2	lbw b Tuffey	5	13	6	-	-
T.G.Southee c Croft b Shaw	6	34	15	-	-	not out	0	14	9	-	-
B.J.Arnel run out	2	11	5	-	-	c Croft b Tuffey	0	2	2	-	-
Extras (b 5, lb 3, w 1, nb 6)	15					(b 1, lb 1, w 7, nb 1)	10				
TOTAL (87.2 overs)	**306**	366				(70.4 overs)	**218**	302			

AUCKLAND

	Runs	Mins	Balls	6s	4s
S.J.Croft c McGlashan b Aldridge	41	71	56	-	9
R.A.Jones* lbw b Yovich	62	146	99	1	11
R.J.Nicol c Williamson b Yovich	4	13	11	-	1
A.K.Kitchen c McGlashan b Southee	132	260	213	5	18
R.A.Young lbw b Aldridge	78	194	164	1	10
G.J.Hopkins† c Wilson b Aldridge	22	66	54	-	5
C.de Grandhomme c sub (B.E.Scott) b Williamson	104	182	113	6	8
T.S.Nethula lbw b Yovich	10	44	31	-	2
D.R.Tuffey b Yovich	15	17	13	-	3
L.J.Shaw c McGlashan b Williamson	34	41	34	-	7
A.J.McKay not out	0	15	21	-	-
Extras (b 4, lb 10, w 8, nb 16)	38				
TOTAL (132.1 overs)	**540**	529			

Bowling	*O*	*M*	*R*	*W*	*O*	*M*	*R*	*W*
AUCKLAND								
Tuffey	19.2	7	41	2	18.4	9	33	6
McKay	17	2	76	1	11	3	30	1
Shaw	17	2	57	3	13	3	31	1
de Grandhomme	14	2	55	1	5	1	20	0
Nethula	20	1	69	2	23	1	102	2
NORTHERN DISTRICTS								
Southee	29	9	99	1				
Arnel	1.4	0	4	0				
Aldridge	27.2	6	109	3				
Yovich	25	2	136	4				
Marshall H.J.H.	9	2	20	0				
Martin	25	1	90	0				
Williamson	15.1	2	68	2				

Fall of Wickets

	ND *1st*	***A*** *1st*	***ND*** *2nd*
1st	59	67	0
2nd	76	80	8
3rd	88	138	13
4th	121	337	145
5th	192	337	187
6th	199	391	206
7th	233	419	213
8th	283	457	214
9th	299	521	218
10th	306	540	218

CENTRAL DISTRICTS v CANTERBURY State Championship

at Pukekura Park, New Plymouth on 21, 22, 23, 24 March, 2009
Toss : Canterbury. Umpires : T.J. Parlane & D.J. Walker
Close of play: 1st day: Canterbury 290-4, Myburgh 96, Robertson 4; 2nd day: CD 139-5, Oram 7, Griggs 20
3rd day: CD 74-0, Ingram 34, How 35
***Central Districts won by 3 wickets.** Points: Central Districts 6, Canterbury 2*

Kain made his first-class debut in this game and watched his side reach 290-4 at the close of the first day. Myburgh soon reached his hundred next morning (167 balls and 232 minutes) and continued to pile up the runs. When the ninth wicket fell at 445 Myburgh was on 159 and found an ally in Bennett who stayed for 39 minutes. The partnership was finally broken when Myburgh was run out going for a second run which would have taken him to 200.

Central found batting much more difficult and only Thompson (fifty off 27 balls) made much impression. Canterbury chose to bat again and stretched their lead to 447 before declaring. Myburgh reached his second century of the game from 154 balls in 198 minutes.

The home team reached 74-0 off twenty overs before the close and had reached 159 before the first wicket fell. Worker helped Ingram add a further 115 runs, with the Central opener reaching his hundred off 177 balls in 263 minutes. Ingram was finally out at 366 but Weston continued aggressively and Central reached their target shortly before five o'clock, with Weston hitting Myburgh for six.

CANTERBURY

FIRST INNINGS	*Runs*	*Mins*	*Balls*	*6s*	*4s*	*SECOND INNINGS*	*Runs*	*Mins*	*Balls*	*6s*	*4s*
T.D.Astle c Weston b Mason	0	3	4	-	-	c Griggs b Thompson	0	2	6	-	-
M.H.W.Papps lbw b Mason	54	120	102	-	10	not out	63	214	166	1	7
P.G.Fulton c Thompson b Diamanti	64	187	124	1	9	b Mason	1	9	5	-	-
J.G.Myburgh run out	199	473	328	6	21	not out	101	201	160	2	15
S.L.Stewart c Sinclair b Oram	67	127	98	1	9						
I.A.Robertson c How b Mason	16	64	36	-	2						
C.F.K.van Wyk*† c Griggs b Mason	46	102	82	-	8						
A.M.Ellis lbw b Mason	3	17	13	-	-						
M.O.Kain b Thompson	24	40	34	-	5						
L.M.Burtt c How b Thompson	0	7	9	-	-						
H.K.Bennett not out	8	39	17	-	2						
Extras (b 5, lb 5, nb 2)	12					(b 3, nb 1)	4				
TOTAL (140.5 overs)	**493**	576				(56 overs) (2 wkts dec)	**169**	214			

CENTRAL DISTRICTS

	Runs	Mins	Balls	6s	4s		Runs	Mins	Balls	6s	4s
P.J.Ingram b Bennett	13	18	13	-	3	b Bennett	166	380	249	3	20
J.M.How c Kain b Bennett	0	8	2	-	-	c Bennett b Kain	93	164	143	-	18
G.H.Worker b Bennett	6	57	34	-	1	c Papps b Astle	55	119	114	-	10
M.S.Sinclair* c van Wyk b Burtt	39	92	70	-	7	c Papps b Ellis	0	21	18	-	-
T.I.Weston lbw b Kain	32	57	42	-	6	(6) not out	89	140	104	2	10
J.D.P.Oram c van Wyk b Bennett	11	61	26	-	2	(5) c Robertson b Ellis	3	14	10	-	-
B.B.J.Griggs† b Burtt	35	116	84	-	6	b Astle	6	27	16	-	1
B.J.Diamanti b Burtt	0	7	5	-	-	c van Wyk b Ellis	5	13	16	-	1
E.P.Thompson hit wicket b Ellis	51	43	28	2	8	not out	19	45	18	-	2
R.J.Schaw c van Wyk b Burtt	0	8	5	-	-						
M.J.Mason not out	3	2	1	-	-						
Extras (b 2, lb 11, nb 12)	25					(b 1, lb 9, nb 4)	14				
TOTAL (49.4 overs)	**215**	222				(114 overs) (7 wkts)	**450**	463			

Bowling	*O*	*M*	*R*	*W*	*O*	*M*	*R*	*W*
CENTRAL DISTRICTS								
Mason	29	6	83	5	4	2	11	1
Thompson	24	3	89	2	21	4	54	1
Oram	25	11	75	1				
Diamanti	24.5	4	78	1	11	2	25	0
Worker	13	3	50	0	10	3	32	0
Schaw	15	1	64	0	10	1	44	0
Sinclair	10	1	44	0				
CANTERBURY								
Burtt	114	1	48	4	18	0	81	0
Bennett	15	3	48	4	14	0	91	1
Ellis	10	3	36	1	30	7	69	3
Kain	13	1	70	1	15	2	51	1
Myburgh					15	1	60	0
Astle					22	1	88	2

Fall of Wickets

	C *1st*	*CD* *1st*	*C* *2nd*	*CD* *2nd*
1st	0	11	0	159
2nd	96	21	13	274
3rd	141	55	-	284
4th	279	104	-	294
5th	318	106	-	366
6th	392	151	-	385
7th	404	152	-	392
8th	443	212	-	-
9th	445	212	-	-
10th	493	215	-	-

CANTERBURY v OTAGO

at Queen Elizabeth II Park, Christchurch on 28, 29, 30, 31 March, 2009
Toss : Otago. Umpires : P.J. Agent & B.G. Frost
Close of play: 1st day: Otago 21-0, Cumming 14, Redmond 7; 2nd day: Otago 316-9, Harvie 12, McMillan 8
3rd day: Canterbury 233-4, Myburgh 50, van Wyk 2
***First innings win to Otago.** Points: Otago 2, Canterbury 0*

McCone made his first-class debut in this match and found himself coming to the wicket shortly after lunch on the first day with the score at 101-7. He opened his account with two fours and proceeded to add 167 with his captain, a Canterbury eighth wicket record against Otago. The ninth wicket fell one run later with McCone on 61. Bennett once again proved a reliable last wicket partner and stayed for 35 minutes while McCone reached a century on debut (168 balls and 208 minutes) with successive fours off McMillan.

Otago replied very strongly with an opening stand of 179. Cumming reached his hundred after 200 minutes and 156 balls, equalling Glenn Turner's Otago record of four centuries in one season. However, once the first wicket fell, Otago collapsed and it was left to the last pair, Harvie and McMillan, to ensure first innings points.

Papps registered another century on the third day (198 balls and 229 minutes) and Canterbury were 228 runs ahead when bad light ended play. Rain and more poor light prevented any play on the last day.

CANTERBURY

FIRST INNINGS	*Runs*	*Mins*	*Balls*	*6s*	*4s*	*SECOND INNINGS*	*Runs*	*Mins*	*Balls*	*6s*	*4s*
T.D.Astle b McSkimming	0	19	18	-	-	b Wagner	1	4	3	-	-
M.H.W.Papps c Redmond b Wagner	40	100	61	-	4	lbw b McCullum	103	248	215	-	11
P.G.Fulton b McMillan	3	19	20	-	-	c Todd b McCullum	61	132	115	1	9
J.G.Myburgh lbw b Harvie	10	28	20	-	2	not out	50	130	67	1	5
S.L.Stewart lbw b McCullum	16	45	40	-	2	c Cumming b McCullum	6	15	14	-	1
I.A.Robertson b McCullum	2	24	9	-	-						
C.F.K.van Wyk*† c sub (N.B.Beard) b Wagner	105	216	180	-	14	(6) not out	2	3	4	-	-
A.M.Ellis lbw b McMillan	4	32	29	-	-						
R.J.McCone c Redmond b McMillan	102	214	173	-	17						
L.M.Burtt lbw b McSkimming	0	5	1	-	-						
H.K.Bennett not out	2	35	25	-	-						
Extras (b 5, lb 13, nb 13)	31					(b 4, lb 1, w 1, nb 4)	10				
TOTAL (93.2 overs)	**315**	367				(69 overs) (4 wkts)	**233**	268			

OTAGO

	Runs	Mins	Balls	6s	4s
C.D.Cumming* b Ellis	173	344	264	1	24
A.J.Redmond c sub (M.O.Kain) b Astle	58	219	143	-	4
G.R.Todd c van Wyk b Ellis	19	19	16	-	4
N.T.Broom b Myburgh	6	23	26	-	1
L.J.Morgan lbw b Myburgh	6	20	20	-	-
N.L.McCullum c Stewart b Astle	7	8	7	1	-
S.B.Haig† lbw b Myburgh	1	5	4	-	-
W.C.McSkimming c McCone b Myburgh	17	48	33	-	25
N.Wagner c Burtt b Ellis	0	10	7	-	-
M.J.Harvie c Astle b Burtt	15	40	34	-	1
J.M.McMillan not out	12	33	27	-	2
Extras (b 2, nb 4)	6				
TOTAL (96.3 overs)	**320**	377			

Bowling	*O*	*M*	*R*	*W*	*O*	*M*	*R*	*W*
OTAGO								
McSkimming	18	5	50	2	13	6	22	0
Wagner	16	1	77	2	13	2	41	1
McMillan	14.2	5	27	3	2	0	20	0
Harvie	9	3	35	1	9	2	30	0
McCullum	25	5	65	2	26	2	87	3
Cumming	8	2	21	0	2	0	6	0
Todd	3	0	22	0				
Broom					1	0	5	0
Redmond					3	0	17	0
CANTERBURY								
Burtt	13.3	2	54	1				
Bennett	8	1	38	0				
McCone	10	2	33	0				
Astle	18	1	61	2				
Ellis	23	9	48	3				
Myburgh	24	1	84	4				

Fall of Wickets

	C	*O*	*C*
	1st	*1st*	*2nd*
1st	8	179	1
2nd	15	200	120
3rd	43	215	223
4th	61	231	231
5th	72	240	-
6th	82	245	-
7th	101	293	-
8th	268	293	-
9th	269	293	-
10th	315	320	-

NORTHERN DISTRICTS v WELLINGTON State Championship

at Cobham Oval, Whangarei on 28, 29, 30, 31 March, 2009
Toss : Wellington. Umpires : K.C. Manley & D.J. Walker
Close of play: 1st day: Wellington 269-7, Nevin 47, Houghton 13; 2nd day: ND 217-2, Parlane 76, Williamson 7
3rd day: Wellington 53-0, Brodie 28, Bell 23
***Northern Districts won by 8 wickets.** Points: Northern Districts 8, Wellington 0*

Bell chose to bat first and responded with a century, his twentieth for Wellington, off 164 balls in 196 minutes. Parlane and Nevin hit fifties to take Wellington to 321 on the second morning.

Northern's batsmen also enjoyed the conditions. Wilson fell six runs short of a century but Parlane (hundred from 231 balls in 295 minutes) and Williamson (163 balls and 256 minutes) made no mistake. The home team continued batting until late on the third day, finishing with the highest score in their history. The 165 run partnership between Wilson and Parlane was a Northern second wicket record against Wellington.

The visitors struggled against the spin of Martin (who took nine wickets in the match) and Williamson on the last day and were bowled out for 289. Northern needed just 65 to win and hit off the runs in ten overs for the loss of two wickets.

WELLINGTON

FIRST INNINGS	*Runs*	*Mins*	*Balls*	*6s*	*4s*	*SECOND INNINGS*	*Runs*	*Mins*	*Balls*	*6s*	*4s*
J.M.Brodie c Williamson b Southee	5	30	23	-	1	lbw b Martin	56	204	161	-	7
M.D.Bell* c Aldridge b Martin	100	211	173	-	17	lbw b Williamson	29	141	111	-	3
N.R.Parlane c Marshall H.J.H. b Martin	62	227	174	-	7	lbw b Aldridge	13	27	17	-	2
G.D.Elliott lbw b Aldridge	0	4	2	-	-	b Martin	84	189	144	2	8
H.K.P.Boam lbw b Martin	0	11	9	-	-	c McGlashan b Williamson	0	10	8	-	-
L.J.Woodcock c Wilson b Martin	11	47	34	-	2	c Scott b Martin	32	76	76	1	4
C.J.Nevin† c Scott b Williamson	72	164	118	-	10	lbw b Southee	9	41	26	-	2
D.J.Bowden c Scott b Southee	24	63	66	-	4	st McGlashan b Williamson	19	21	18	1	2
M.V.Houghton c Scott b Martin	21	94	76	-	-	not out	10	42	30	-	1
M.J.Tugaga not out	10	49	34	-	2	c Yovich b Southee	35	37	39	-	6
M.Burns b Martin	8	37	44	-	1	b Southee	0	1	1	-	-
Extras (b 2, lb 2, nb 4)	8					(w 1, nb 1)	2				
TOTAL (125 overs)	**321**	478				(105 overs)	**289**	404			

NORTHERN DISTRICTS

FIRST INNINGS	*Runs*	*Mins*	*Balls*	*6s*	*4s*	*SECOND INNINGS*	*Runs*	*Mins*	*Balls*	*6s*	*4s*
B.S.Wilson c Nevin b Burns	94	264	229	-	9	c Burns b Bowden	25	33	25	-	3
H.J.H.Marshall c Brodie b Woodcock	28	70	59	1	3	c Woodcock b Burns	0	9	5	-	-
M.E.Parlane b Bowden	103	304	237	3	5	not out	31	32	22	-	6
K.S.Williamson c Nevin b Burns	100	257	174	1	11						
J.A.H.Marshall* lbw b Burns	20	22	15	-	3	(4) not out	2	12	9	-	-
P.D.McGlashan† c Boam b Woodcock	56	86	69	-	7						
J.A.F.Yovich c Nevin b Boam	8	25	26	-	1						
G.W.Aldridge c Tugaga b Bowden	21	55	35	-	1						
B.E.Scott not out	55	85	63	2	4						
T.G.Southee c Nevin b Tugaga	3	12	5	-	-						
B.P.Martin c Nevin b Burns	30	27	17	3	1						
Extras (b 2, lb 6, w 6, nb 14)	28					(lb 1, w 5, nb 1)	7				
TOTAL (152.4 overs)	**546**	613				(10 overs) (2 wkts)	**65**	46			

Bowling	*O*	*M*	*R*	*W*				
NORTHERN DISTRICTS								
Southee	21	5	49	2	23	10	58	3
Aldridge	16	3	59	1	9	2	31	1
Scott	16	2	38	0	11	6	24	0
Yovich	3	1	16	0	3	0	9	0
Williamson	32	10	82	1	24	6	91	3
Martin	37	13	73	6	35	13	76	3
WELLINGTON								
Bowden	20	2	94	2	5	0	44	1
Burns	20.4	5	61	4	5	0	20	1
Woodcock	38	4	151	2				
Houghton	23	4	79	0				
Tugaga	14	2	58	1				
Elliott	22	7	47	0				
Boam	15	0	48	1				

Fall of Wickets

	W *1st*	***ND*** *1st*	***W*** *2nd*	***ND*** *2nd*
1st	22	38	72	10
2nd	157	203	98	52
3rd	158	269	121	-
4th	167	301	122	-
5th	179	407	187	-
6th	196	424	206	-
7th	244	430	242	-
8th	301	484	244	-
9th	303	500	289	-
10th	321	546	289	-

AUCKLAND v CENTRAL DISTRICTS — State Championship

at Eden Park Outer Oval, Auckland on 29, 30, 31 March, 1 April, 2009
Toss : Central Districts. Umpires : P.D. Jones & D.M. Quested
Close of play: 1st day: Auckland 323-4, Raval 156, Hopkins 14; 2nd day: CD 56-0, Ingram 34, Worker 19; 3rd day: CD 276-6, Sinclair 100, Bracewell 9
First innings win to Auckland. *Points: Auckland 2, Central Districts 0*

The two teams were already assured of meeting in the final but an outright win to Central would have given them the advantage of being the top qualifier. Sinclair sent Auckland in to bat and Jones was dismissed first ball but a partnership of 152 between Raval and Young put Auckland in control.

Hopkins and Raval added a further 228 before the Auckland opener was out. In his second first-class innings Raval reached his century off 227 balls in 297 minutes and his two hundred after 479 minutes from 394 balls. It was the highest individual innings for Auckland against Central.

Hopkins then went to his hundred from 205 balls after 283 minutes and de Grandhomme flogged the tired attack, hitting eight sixes and reaching three figures (with a six) from 91 balls in 110 minutes. Auckland's total was the highest by any team against Central and the highest score on the Outer Oval.

The rest of the match was largely academic. Sinclair (180 minutes and 145 balls) scored a hundred and the match was called off at 3.18 pm after Nicol had hit Worker for three successive sixes to reach his century (214 minutes and 141 balls). His unbroken partnership with Hopkins was an Auckland fourth wicket record against Central, passing the record that Raval and Young had established on the first day. Noema-Barnett made his first-class debut in this game.

AUCKLAND

FIRST INNINGS	*Runs*	*Mins*	*Balls*	*6s*	*4s*	*SECOND INNINGS*	*Runs*	*Mins*	*Balls*	*6s*	*4s*
J.A.Raval c Griggs b Patton	256	603	483	2	43						
R.A.Jones* lbw b Thompson	0	4	1	-	-	(1) lbw b McClenaghan	15	60	41	-	2
R.J.Nicol c Sinclair b Bracewell	39	121	87	-	3	(2) not out	104	214	145	4	13
A.K.Kitchen c Griggs b McClenaghan	23	33	15	-	5	(3) b Mason	3	7	5	-	-
R.A.Young c Patton b Mason	74	184	120	1	10	(4) b McClenaghan	1	5	5	-	-
G.J.Hopkins† not out	132	372	269	-	15	(5) not out	70	140	94	-	11
C.de Grandhomme not out	103	114	92	8	8						
K.D.Mills											
D.R.Tuffey											
L.J.Shaw											
M.D.Bates											
S.J.Croft											
Extras (b 17, lb 15, nb 3)	35					(lb 1, w 1, nb 3)	5				
TOTAL (177 overs) (5 wkts dec)	**662**	696				(48 overs) (3 wkts)	**198**	204			

CENTRAL DISTRICTS

	Runs	Mins	Balls	6s	4s
P.J.Ingram lbw b Mills	54	106	80	-	11
G.H.Worker b Bates	37	186	125	-	3
B.M.K.Patton c Jones b Bates	17	69	45	-	3
M.S.Sinclair* not out	131	240	184	2	19
K.Noema-Barnett c Kitchen b Bates	11	86	65	-	2
B.B.J.Griggs† c Kitchen b Nicol	5	27	18	-	1
E.P.Thompson c de Grandhomme b Tuffey	33	29	24	2	4
D.A.J.Bracewell c Nicol b Bates	13	51	37	-	3
M.J.Mason c Hopkins b Tuffey	0	10	6	-	-
M.J.McClenaghan b Shaw	3	21	16	-	-
T.I.Weston absent hurt					
Extras (b 5, lb 3, nb 6)	14				
TOTAL (99 overs)	**318**	407			

Bowling	*O*	*M*	*R*	*W*				
CENTRAL DISTRICTS								
Mason	21	6	55	1	8	4	22	1
Thompson	31	7	100	1	5	0	14	0
McClenaghan	26	3	99	1	8	1	33	2
Noema-Barnett	20	5	57	0	9	1	40	0
Bracewell	25	4	102	1	7	0	29	0
Worker	29	3	90	0	11	2	59	0
Sinclair	13	0	43	0				
Patton	12	1	84	1				
AUCKLAND								
Mills	18	3	73	1				
Tuffey	26	15	36	2				
Shaw	12	2	41	1				
Bates	25	7	82	4				
de Grandhomme	9	3	41	0				
Nicol	9	4	37	1				

Fall of Wickets

	A	CD	A
	1st	*1st*	*2nd*
1st	4	76	35
2nd	79	111	38
3rd	131	118	39
4th	283	170	-
5th	511	192	-
6th	-	255	-
7th	-	289	-
8th	-	300	-
9th	-	318	-
10th	-	-	-

Croft replaced Mills who was called into the New Zealand squad on the 4th day

AUCKLAND v CENTRAL DISTRICTS — Final

at Bert Sutcliffe Oval, Lincoln on 6, 7, 8, 9, 10 April, 2009
Toss : Auckland. Umpires : B.F. Bowden & C.B. Gaffaney
Close of play: 1st day: CD 169-8, Oram 35, Mason 1; 2nd day: Auckland 300-5, Hopkins 28, de Grandhomme 4
3rd day: CD 116-3, Ingram 60, Patton 0; 4th day: CD 349 all out
Auckland won by 5 wickets.

Auckland chose to field first but saw How and an aggressive Ingram post a fifty partnership in the twelfth over. However, once Ingram departed there was little resistance and Central were all out for 180. Shaw finished with his best figures.

Jones (203 balls in 306 minutes) and Kitchen (145 balls and 180 minutes) scored centuries for Auckland, sharing a 184 run partnership, an Auckland third wicket record against Central. The Central bowlers fought back and did well to restrict Auckland to 342, although the lead was still a substantial 162.

Ingram (90) top scored in Central's second innings and an aggressive fifty from Thompson took their score to 349. Auckland were left with 188 to score on the final day.

The in-form Auckland batting lineup struggled on the last morning and when Young was fifth man out at 104, an upset seemed possible. Hopkins and de Grandhomme, however, had other ideas and hit off the remaining 84 runs in less than 20 overs.

CENTRAL DISTRICTS

FIRST INNINGS	*Runs*	*Mins*	*Balls*	*6s*	*4s*	*SECOND INNINGS*	*Runs*	*Mins*	*Balls*	*6s*	*4s*
P.J.Ingram c Hopkins b Shaw	46	64	47	-	8	c Young b Nethula	90	227	155	-	9
J.M.How c & b de Grandhomme	9	74	47	-	1	c Hopkins b Shaw	3	18	10	-	-
G.H.Worker b Shaw	0	2	2	-	-	c Raval b Bates	14	67	58	-	1
M.S.Sinclair* b Shaw	34	88	63	-	4	c Nicol b Nethula	33	63	53	-	5
B.M.K.Patton c Nethula b de Grandhomme	18	64	51	-	3	lbw b Shaw	24	66	39	-	4
J.D.P.Oram c de Grandhomme b Tuffey	37	79	56	1	4	c Hopkins b Bates	36	47	31	-	8
B.B.J.Griggs† c Hopkins b Shaw	8	14	9	-	2	run out	44	116	100	-	4
B.J.Diamanti c Hopkins b Bates	10	17	10	-	2	lbw b Nethula	22	54	39	1	2
E.P.Thompson lbw b Shaw	0	4	3	-	-	not out	54	76	51	2	3
M.J.Mason not out	9	27	16	-	1	c & b Tuffey	1	10	7	-	-
M.J.McClenaghan c Raval b Tuffey	0	7	3	-	-	c Kitchen b Tuffey	4	40	21	-	1
Extras (lb 4, nb 5)	9					(b 10, lb 6, w 2, nb 6)	24				
TOTAL (50.2 overs)	**180**	229				(93 overs)	**349**	401			

AUCKLAND

	Runs	*Mins*	*Balls*	*6s*	*4s*		*Runs*	*Mins*	*Balls*	*6s*	*4s*
J.A.Raval c How b Mason	4	23	14	-	1	c Griggs b McClenaghan	10	34	27	-	2
R.A.Jones* c Griggs b Thompson	109	325	220	-	14	c & b McClenaghan	38	131	82	-	5
R.J.Nicol c Griggs b McClenaghan	12	27	17	-	2	c Patton b Thompson	4	6	6	-	1
A.K.Kitchen c Griggs b Diamanti	115	213	180	3	15	c Griggs b Diamanti	10	25	19	-	2
R.A.Young b Worker	12	28	37	-	2	lbw b Worker	18	138	101	-	2
G.J.Hopkins† b Diamanti	32	74	54	-	6	not out	48	154	118	-	4
C.de Grandhomme c Worker b McClenaghan	32	108	70	1	2	not out	54	79	59	1	6
D.R.Tuffey b Oram	5	41	30	-	-						
L.J.Shaw c How b McClenaghan	1	32	18	-	-						
T.S.Nethula not out	3	26	16	-	-						
M.D.Bates run out	1	15	12	-	-						
Extras (b 4, lb 5, w 2, nb 5)	16					(lb 3, w 1, nb 2)	6				
TOTAL (110.3 overs)	**342**	415				(68.2 overs) (5 wkts)	**188**	289			

Bowling	*O*	*M*	*R*	*W*	*O*	*M*	*R*	*W*
AUCKLAND								
Tuffey	15.2	4	42	2	30	4	89	2
Shaw	13	1	59	5	19	1	81	2
Bates	14	1	60	1	12	1	59	2
de Grandhomme	8	3	15	2	8	1	21	0
Nethula					24	1	83	3
CENTRAL DISTRICTS								
Mason	3.4	0	18	1				
Thompson	21	5	59	1	16.2	5	48	1
McClenaghan	21.5	2	97	3	16	1	74	2
Diamanti	25	10	51	2	14	7	17	1
Oram	19	8	48	1	10	4	24	0
Sinclair	3	1	6	0				
Worker	17	4	54	1	12	4	22	1

Fall of Wickets	***CD***	***A***	***CD***	***A***
	1st	*1st*	*2nd*	*2nd*
1st	57	15	12	16
2nd	57	39	52	21
3rd	57	223	111	41
4th	109	246	172	75
5th	116	275	181	104
6th	144	304	223	-
7th	165	326	282	-
8th	166	338	298	-
9th	178	339	311	-
10th	180	342	349	-

2008/09 FIRST-CLASS STATISTICS

REGISTER OF PLAYERS

The following players appeared in first-class cricket for New Zealand teams during the 2008/09 season.

		Born	*At*	*Type*			*First-class debut*	
Aldridge Graeme William	ND	15.11.77	Christchurch	RHB	RFM		ND v W	98/99
Anderson Corey James	C	13.12.90	Christchurch	LHB	LFM		C v CD	06/07
Arnel Brent John	ND	3. 1.79	Hamilton	RHB	RFM		ND v C	05/06
Astle Todd Duncan	C	24. 9.86	Palmerston North	RHB	RLB		C v W	05/06
Azhar Abbas	A	1. 4.75	Khanewal, Pakistan	RHB	RM		Railways v PIA	95/96
Bates Michael David	A	11.10.83	Auckland	RHB	LM		A v O	03/04
Beard Nicholas Brendan	O	16. 9.89	Dunedin	LHB	SLA		O v A	08/09
Bell Matthew David	W	25. 2.77	Dunedin	RHB	ROB	WK	ND v NZA	93/94
Bennett Hamish Kyle	C	22. 2.87	Timaru	LHB	RFM		C v W	05/06
Boam Harry Kenneth Perrott	W	15.10.90	Birmingham, England	RHB	RM		W v CD	08/09
Boult Jonathan James	ND	29.11.85	Rotorua	LHB	ROB		ND v A	08/09
Boult Trent Alexander	ND	22. 7.89	Rotorua	RHB	LFM		NZ A v India A	08/09
Bowden Dewayne Jamie	W	27. 2.82	Wellington	LHB	LFM		W v ND	05/06
Bracewell Douglas Andrew John	CD	28. 9.90	Tauranga	RHB	RM		CD v A	08/09
Brodie Joshua Michael	W	8. 6.87	Wellington	LHB			W v CD	07/08
Broom Neil Trevor	O	20.11.83	Christchurch	RHB	RM		C v W	02/03
Burns Michael	W	6. 7.79	Balclutha	RHB	RFM		W v C	06/07
Burtt Leighton McGregor	C	17. 4.84	Christchurch	RHB	RM		C v O	06/07
Butler Ian Gareth	O	24.11.81	Auckland	RHB	RFM		ND v O	01/02
Croft Steven John	A	11.10.84	Blackpool, England	RHB	RM		Lancs v OUCCE	05
Crook Brendon-John	W	29. 6.84	Lower Hutt	LHB	RM		W v A	07/08
Cumming Craig Derek	O	31. 8.75	Timaru	RHB	RM		C v CD	95/96
de Boorder Andrew Philip	A	6. 7.88	Hastings	RHB	RM		A v W	07/08
de Boorder Derek Charles	O	25.10.85	Hastings	RHB		WK	O v CD	07/08
de Grandhomme Colin	A	22. 7.86	Harare, Zimbabwe	RHB	RM		Zim A v Kenya	05/06
Davidson Michael Philip Forbes	C	24. 9.81	Christchurch	RHB	LFM		C v O	06/07
Davis Te Ahu Trevor	ND	9.12.85	Auckland	RHB	RFM		ND v O	04/05
Devcich Anton Paul	ND	28. 9.85	Hamilton	LHB	SLA		ND v O	04/05
Diamanti Brendon John	CD	30. 4.81	Blenheim	RHB	RM		CD v W	03/04
Elliott Grant David	W, NZ	21. 3.79	Johannesburg, S.Africa	RHB	RFM		Natal B v Trans B	96/97
Ellis Andrew Malcolm	C	24. 3.82	Christchurch	RHB	RFM		C v A	02/03
Flynn Daniel Raymond	ND, NZ	16. 4.85	Rotorua	LHB	SLA		ND v O	04/05
Franklin James Edwards Charles	W, NZ	7.11.80	Wellington	LHB	LFM		W v I	98/99
Fulton Peter Gordon	C, NZ	1. 2.79	Christchurch	RHB	RM		C v A	00/01
Gadsdon Shane Robert	ND	8. 4.91	Auckland	RHB		WK	ND v A	08/09
Gillespie Mark Raymond	W, NZ	17.10.79	Wanganui	RHB	RFM		W v O	99/00
Griggs Bevan Barry John	CD	29. 3.78	Palmerston North	RHB		WK	CD v O	00/01
Guptill Martin James	A, NZ	30. 9.86	Auckland	RHB	ROB		A v W	05/06
Haig Shaun Barry	O	19. 3.82	Auckland	RHB	RM	WK	O v CD	05/06
Harvie Mathew James	O	6.12.84	Dunedin	RHB	RFM		O v A	03/04
Hay Gregory Robert	CD	14. 7.84	Rotorua	RHB	ROB		CD v W	06/07
Hefford Brent Edward	CD	8. 5.78	Blenheim	LHB	RM		CD v C	99/00
Hiini Brandon Christopher	C	11.12.81	Invercargill	RHB	RM		C v CD	05/06
Hitchcock Paul Anthony	A	23. 1.75	Wellington	RHB	RM		W v ND	99/00
Hopkins Gareth James	A	24.11.76	Lower Hutt	RHB	WK		NC v CC	97/98
Houghton Mark Vincent	W	3.11.84	Upper Hutt	RHB	SLA		W v ND	07/08
How Jamie Michael	CD, NZ	19. 5.81	New Plymouth	RHB	ROB		CD v W	00/01
Ingram Peter John	CD	25.10.78	Hawera	RHB	ROB		CD v O	01/02
Jones Richard Andrew	A	22.10.73	Auckland	RHB			A v C	93/94
Kain Martin Owen	C	16. .5.88	Nelson	LHB	SLA		C v CD	08/09
Kitchen Anaru Kyle	A	21. 2.84	Auckland	RHB	SLA		A v ND	08/09
Lamb Andrew Robert	W	1. 1.78	Bathurst, Australia	RHB	RFM		W v C	08/09
Marshall Hamish John Hamilton	ND	15. 2.79	Warkworth	RHB	RM		ND v W	98/99
Marshall James Andrew Hamilton	ND	15. 2.79	Warkworth	RHB	RM		ND v W	97/98
Martin Bruce Philip	ND	25. 4.80	Whangarei	RHB	SLA		ND v CD	99/00
Martin Christopher Stewart	NZ	10.12.74	Christchurch	RHB	RFM		C v W	97/98
Mason Michael James	CD	27. 8.74	Carterton	RHB	RFM		CD v ND	97/98
McClenaghan Mitchell John	CD	11. 6.86	Hastings	LHB	LFM		CD v O	07/08
McCone Ryan James	C	5. 9.87	Christchurch	LHB	LM		C v O	08/09
McCullum Brendon Barrie	NZ	27. 9.81	Dunedin	RHB		WK	O v CD	99/00

		Born	At	Type			First-class debut	
McCullum Nathan Leslie	O	1. 9.80	Dunedin	RHB	ROB		O v W	99/00
McGlashan Peter Donald	ND	22. 6.79	Napier	RHB		WK	CD v O	00/01
McIntosh Timothy Gavin	A, NZ	4.12.79	Auckland	LHB			A v ND	98/99
McKay Andrew John	A	17. 4.80	Auckland	RHB	LFM		A v CD	02/03
McMillan James Michael	O	14. 6.78	Christchurch	RHB	RFM		O v CD	00/01
McSkimming Warren Charles	O	21. 6.79	Ranfurly	RHB	RM		O v C	99/00
Merchant Cameron John	ND	4. 1.84	Sydney, Australia	LHB	ROB		ND v O	07/08
Mills Kyle David	A, NZ	15. 3.79	Auckland	RHB	RFM		A v O	98/99
Morgan Leighton James	O	16. 2.81	Wellington	RHB	SLA		W v CD	01/02
Myburgh Johannes Gerhardus	C	22.10.80	Pretoria, South Africa	RHB	ROB		Nthn B v WP B	97/98
Napier Graham Richard	W	6. 1.80	Colchester, England	RHB	RM		Essex v Camb.U	97
Nethula Tarun Sai	A	8. 5.83	Kurnool, India	RHB	RLB		A v C	08/09
Nevin Christopher John	W	3. 8.75	Dunedin	RHB		WK	W v ND	95/96
Nicol Robert James	A	28. 5.83	Auckland	RHB	ROB		A v CD	01/02
Noema-Barnett Kieran	CD	4. 6.87	Dunedin	LHB	RM		CD v A	08/09
O'Brien Iain Edward	NZ	10. 7.76	Lower Hutt	RHB	RM		W v O	00/01
Oram Jacob David Philip	CD, NZ	28. 7.78	Palmerston North	LHB	RM		NZA v B	97/98
Papps Michael Hugh William	C	2. 7.79	Christchurch	RHB		WK	C v O	98/99
Parlane Michael Edward	ND	22. 7.72	Pukekohe	RHB			ND v A	92/93
Parlane Neal Ronald	W	9. 8.78	Whangarei	RHB			ND v CD	96/97
Patel Jeetan Shashi	W, NZ	7. 5.80	Wellington	RHB	ROB		W v A	99/00
Patton Bradley Michael King	CD	9.11.79	Hastings	LHB	RM		CD v C	06/07
Rance Seth Hayden Arnold	CD	23. 8.87	Wellington	RHB	RM		CD v W	08/09
Raval Jeet Ashok	A	22. 5.88	Ahmedabad, India	LHB	RLB		A v WI	08/09
Redmond Aaron James	O, NZ	23. 9.79	Auckland	RHB	RLB		SI v NI	99/00
Robertson Iain Anthony	C	9.11.82	Christchurch	RHB	ROB		C v CD	05/06
Rutherford Hamish Duncan	O	27. 4.89	Dunedin	LHB			O v ND	08/09
Ryder Jesse Daniel	NZ	6. 8.84	Masterton	LHB	RM		CD v ND	02/03
Schaw Robert James	CD	12. 5.84	Waipukurau	LHB	RLB		CD v ND	06/07
Scott Bradley Esmond	ND	16. 9.79	Ashburton	LHB	LFM		O v A	00/01
Shaw Lance Joseph	A	24. 8.83	Auckland	RHB	RFM		A v CD	05/06
Sheed Jordan William	O	24. 9.82	Timaru	RHB	RLB		O v C	01/02
Sherlock Richard Roland	CD	15. 9.83	Palmerston North	RHB	RFM		CD v W	03/04
Sinclair Mathew Stuart	CD	9.11.75	Katherine, Australia	RHB	RM	WK	CD v C	95/96
Southee Timothy Grant	ND, NZ	11.12.88	Whangarei	RHB	RFM		ND v O	06/07
Stewart Shanan Luke	C	21. 6.82	Christchurch	RHB	RM		C v ND	01/02
Styris Scott Bernard	A	10. 7.75	Brisbane, Australia	RHB	RM		ND v W	94/95
Taylor Luteru Ross Poutoa Lote	NZ	8. 3.84	Lower Hutt	RHB	ROB		CD v C	02/03
Thompson Ewen Paul	CD	17.12.79	Warkworth	LHB	LFM		CD v O	00/01
Todd Gregory Rex	O	17. 6.82	Masterton	LHB	RM		CD v O	00/01
Tuffey Daryl Raymond	A	11. 6.78	Milton	RHB	RFM		ND v A	96/97
Tugaga Malaesaili Julian	W	16. 2.90	Wellington	LHB	RFM		W v O	08/09
van Wyk Cornelius Francoius Kruger	C	7. 2.80	Wolmaransstad, S.Africa	RHB		WK	N v GW	00/01
Vettori Daniel Luca	NZ	27. 1.79	Auckland	RHB	SLA		ND v E	96/97
Wagner Neil	O	13. 3.86	Pretoria, S.Africa	LHB	LFM		NW v Nthns	05/06
Watling Bradley-John	ND	9. 7.85	Durban, S.Africa	RHB		WK	ND v A	04/05
Wells Samuel Raymond	O	13. 7.84	Dunedin	LHB	RM		O v CD	07/08
Weston Timothy Ian	CD	6. 6.82	Stratford	RHB		WK	CD v C	05/06
Williamson Kane Stuart	ND	8. 8.90	Tauranga	RHB	ROB		ND v A	07/08
Wilson Bradley Svend	ND	10. 4.85	Auckland	RHB	ROB		ND v O	04/05
Woodcock Luke James	W	19. 3.82	Wellington	LHB	SLA	WK	W v O	01/02
Worker George Herrick	CD	23. 8.89	Palmerston North	LHB	SLA		CD v W	07/08
Young Reece Alan	A	15. 9.79	Auckland	RHB		WK	A v C	98/99
Yovich Joseph Adam Frank	ND	15.12.76	Whangarei	LHB	RFM		ND v C	96/97

Key

RHB	right-hand batsman	*SLA*	slow left-arm	*RSM*	right slow-medium
LHB	left-hand batsman	*RLB*	right leg-break	*LFM*	left fast-medium
RM	right medium	*ROB*	right off-break	*LSM*	left slow-medium
LM	left medium	*RFM*	right fast-medium	*WK*	wicketkeeper

FIRST-CLASS UMPIRES

2008/09

Nineteen local umpires officiated in domestic competition matches. Derek Walker went to South Africa on the annual exchange programme, standing in two games, while Earl Hendrikse umpired two State Championship games. Brent Bowden was again on the Emirates Elite panel and was re-appointed for 2009/10. Tony Hill, who had been on the second tier panel, was also appointed to the Elite Panel for the first time. Gary Baxter, who had umpired the Under 19 World Cup final, was on the second tier panel and umpired in one-day internationals. Evan Watkin was on the third umpire panel and stood for most of the second test against India when Billy Doctrove was unwell.

Agent, Phillip John *(Canterbury)*. Age 48. Made his debut this season umpiring one first-class game.

Baxter, Gary Arthur Vincent *(Canterbury)*. Age 57. Debut 1998/99. On ICC second tier panel. Has umpired 56 first-class games, 27 one-day internationals, 44 one-day games, five Twenty20 internationals and ten Twenty 20 games.

Bowden, Brent Fraser *(Auckland)*. Age 46. Debut 1992/93. Member of ICC Elite panel. Has umpired more tests than any other New Zealand umpire. Has stood in 54 Tests, 117 first-class games, 132 one-day internationals, 78 one-day games, six Twenty20 internationals and seven Twenty20 games.

Busby, Jeremy Martin *(Wellington)*. Age 47. Debut in 1996/97 and has now stood in seven first-class games, nine one-day matches and two Twenty20 games.

Earl, Kevin David *(Bay of Plenty)*. Age 60. Made his debut this season standing in one Twenty20 match.

Frost, Barry George *(Auckland)*. Age 51. Debut in 1998/99 and has now officiated in 54 first-class games, 54 one-day games and ten Twenty20 matches.

Gaffaney, Christopher Blair *(Otago)*. Age 34. Former Otago player who made his umpiring debut in 2007/08. Has now stood in eight first-class matches, two one-day games and one Twenty20 game.

Gasston, Peter Louis *(Auckland)*. Age 48. Debut in 2005/06 and has now umpired five one-day games and three Twenty20 games.

George, Michael Peter *(Horowhenua-Kapiti)*. Age 50. Debut in 1999/00 and has now stood in 25 first-class games, 25 one-day matches and three Twenty20 games.

Gray, Evan John *(Wellington)*. Age 54. Former Wellington and New Zealand representative who made his umpiring debut in 2005/06. Has now umpired 12 first-class games, 15 one-day fixtures and seven Twenty20 games.

Hill, Anthony Lloyd *(Counties)*. Age 58. Debut in 1993/94. Now appointed to ICC Elite Panel. Has umpired 71 first-class games, including nine test matches. Has also stood in 63 one-day internationals,76 one-day matches, 11 Twenty20 internationals and 14 domestic Twenty20 games.

Jones, Phillip David *(Auckland)*. Age 48. Debut in 2002/03 and has now umpired 34 first-class games, 23 one-day matches and six Twenty20 games.

Knights, Wayne Roger *(Auckland)*. Age 38. Debut in 2001/02 and has now officiated in two first-class matches, 11 one-day games and two Twenty20 matches.

Manley, Kevin Charles *(Auckland)*. Age 58. Made his debut in 1999/00 and has now umpired five first-class games, five one-day matches and two Twenty20 games.

Parlane, Tim James *(Northland/South Canterbury)*. Age 52. Debut in 2001/02. Has umpired 20 first-class matches, 21 one-day games and three Twenty20 fixtures.

Paterson, David Gordon *(Marlborough)*. Age 47. Debut in 2001/02 and has now stood in two first-class games, nine one-day matches and one Twenty20 game.

Quested, David Murray *(Canterbury)*. Age 62. Debut in 1990/91. Has now umpired in 111 first-class games, including five tests. Has also stood in 31 one-day internationals, 93 one-day games and nine Twenty20 games.

Walker, Derek John *(North Otago)*. Age 49. Former Otago representative. Umpiring debut in 2004/05. Has stood in 30 first-class matches, 27 one-day games and 11 Twenty20 matches.

Watkin, Evan Allan *(Wellington)*. Age 57. Debut in 1989/90. New Zealand's longest serving umpire. Has umpired in 105 first-class games, including three tests and also 22 one-day internationals. Has officiated in 108 one-day matches, three Twenty20 internationals and 11 Twenty20 matches.

COMPLETE AVERAGES

Averages for West Indies and England Lions are on pages 76 and 102.

	M	In	NO	HS	Runs	Ave	100	50	Ct	St	O	M	R	W	Ave	5WI	10WM	Best
G.W.Aldridge	7	12	3	75	360	40.00	-	3	5	-	146.4	26	525	15	35.00	-	-	3-46
C.J.Anderson	6	12	3	88*	249	27.66	-	1	2	-	14	2	48	0	-	-	-	-
B.J.Arnel	8	12	2	18	48	4.80	-	-	2	-	219.4	72	522	20	26.10	-	-	4-38
T.D.Astle	8	16	0	101	255	15.93	1	-	6	-	148.1	26	529	10	52.90	-	-	2-39
Azhar Abbas	2	4	1	15	29	9.66	-	-	1	-	49.5	17	132	5	26.40	-	-	3-52
L.Balaji	1	1	0	12	12	12.00	-	-	-	-	38	15	94	3	31.33	-	-	2-55
M.D.Bates	3	1	0	1	1	1.00	-	-	1	-	73	12	275	8	34.37	-	-	4-82
N.B.Beard	2	3	2	32*	37	37.00	-	-	1	-	57	9	189	1	189.00	-	-	1-133
M.D.Bell	8	11	0	146	591	53.72	3	2	6	-	1	1	0	0	-	-	-	-
H.K.Bennett	8	10	5	8*	31	6.20	-	-	2	-	206.5	40	761	26	29.26	-	-	4-48
H.K.P.Boam	4	6	3	49*	116	38.66	-	-	3	-	41.3	11	115	4	28.75	-	-	3-56
J.J.Boult	1	2	0	31	36	18.00	-	-	1	-	28	6	78	4	19.50	-	-	4-78
T.A.Boult	4	6	2	35	46	11.50	-	-	2	-	85	13	277	9	30.77	1	-	5-58
D.J.Bowden	8	9	2	85	260	37.14	-	1	-	-	161.1	20	595	16	37.18	-	-	4-55
D.A.J.Bracewell	5	6	0	26	70	11.66	-	-	1	-	127.4	19	510	10	51.00	-	-	3-51
J.M.Brodie	8	11	0	110	330	30.00	1	1	12	-								
N.T.Broom	7	12	2	140*	501	50.10	1	4	4	-	12.1	1	54	0	-	-	-	-
M.Burns	4	4	0	8	12	3.00	-	-	1	-	99.4	18	326	12	27.16	-	-	4-41
L.M.Burtt	7	8	2	27	49	8.16	-	-	3	-	188.1	16	778	19	40.94	1	-	5-119
I.G.Butler	4	7	2	37*	101	20.20	-	-	2	-	96	19	304	7	43.42	-	-	2-19
S.J.Croft	8	10	1	59	330	36.66	-	2	10	-	63.1	10	248	4	62.00	-	-	2-31
B-J.Crook	5	7	1	101*	201	33.50	1	-	3	-	2	1	2	1	2.00	-	-	1-2
C.D.Cumming	7	12	0	173	784	65.33	4	2	2	-	35.3	7	96	1	96.00	-	-	1-32
M.P.F.Davidson	5	8	1	13	47	6.71	-	-	3	-	151	37	406	10	40.60	-	-	3-68
T.T.Davis	2	2	0	30	30	15.00	-	-	-	-	34	7	149	3	49.66	-	-	2-46
A.P.de Boorder	1	2	0	19	20	10.00	-	-	-	-	2	0	15	0	-	-	-	-
D.C.de Boorder	4	6	2	73*	215	53.75	-	2	14	1								
C.de Grandhomme	10	14	3	104	566	51.45	2	2	13	-	185	49	516	21	24.57	-	-	3-12
A.P.Devcich	2	4	0	16	35	8.75	-	-	4	-	21.2	3	54	3	18.00	-	-	2-20
B.J.Diamanti	3	6	1	135*	172	34.40	1	-	-	-	106.5	33	245	9	27.22	1	-	5-74
R.S.Dravid	4	7	1	102	416	69.33	1	4	5	-								
G.D.Elliott	4	5	0	84	246	49.20	-	3	-	-	84	30	186	2	93.00	-	-	1-19
A.M.Ellis	7	11	0	71	245	22.27	-	1	2	-	201.2	66	547	23	23.78	-	-	4-39
D.R.Flynn	6	11	1	104	450	45.00	1	3	3	-								
J.E.C.Franklin	11	16	2	219	865	61.78	3	4	4	-	313.1	56	979	18	54.38	-	-	3-22
P.G.Fulton	6	12	0	122	536	44.66	1	5	4	-								
S.R.Gadsdon	2	3	1	9	13	6.50	-	-	7	1								
M.R.Gillespie	2	1	1	16*	16	-	-	-	-	-	64.3	15	226	8	28.25	-	-	4-43
B.B.J.Griggs	9	13	0	143	376	28.92	1	-	26	-								
M.J.Guptill	5	7	0	148	294	42.00	1	-	1	-	11	2	42	0	-	-	-	-
S.B.Haig	8	13	1	108	353	29.41	1	1	6	-								
M.J.Harvie	8	11	2	37*	104	11.55	-	-	-	-	183.5	41	589	19	31.00	-	-	4-73
G.R.Hay	5	7	1	131*	161	26.83	1	-	5	-								
B.E.Hefford	3	4	0	1	1	0.25	-	-	-	-	81.3	26	208	9	23.11	-	-	3-48
B.C.Hiini	4	8	0	19	66	8.25	-	-	-	-	120	30	386	11	35.09	-	-	4-47
P.A.Hitchcock	1	1	0	20	20	20.00	-	-	-	-								
G.J.Hopkins	8	11	4	132*	554	79.14	3	1	23	2								
M.V.Houghton	4	4	1	23	58	19.33	-	-	1	-	109	25	312	2	156.00	-	-	1-46
J.M.How	8	14	2	190*	513	42.75	2	2	10	-	18	5	61	1	61.00	-	-	1-14
P.J.Ingram	9	15	0	247	957	63.80	2	4	5	-								
R.A.Jones	10	15	0	201	703	46.86	3	2	2	-								
M.O.Kain	1	1	0	24	24	24.00	-	-	1	-	28	3	121	2	60.50	-	-	1-51
A.K.Kitchen	5	8	0	132	442	55.25	3	-	9	-								
D.S.Kulkarni	1	1	1	13*	13	-	-	-	-	-	26	3	81	3	27.00	-	-	3-62
A.R.Lamb	3	-	-	-	-	-	-	-	-	-	51	11	163	4	40.75	-	-	2-26
V.V.S.Laxman	4	7	1	124*	359	59.83	1	2	4	-								
H.J.H.Marshall	4	8	0	48	201	25.12	-	-	1	-	12	2	26	0	-	-	-	-
J.A.H.Marshall	7	14	2	105*	293	24.41	1	-	3	-	3	0	25	0	-	-	-	-
B.P.Martin	9	13	1	30	95	7.91	-	-	1	-	373.1	91	1027	24	42.79	1	-	6-73
C.S.Martin	6	5	5	4*	4	-	-	-	2	-	235.1	52	799	17	47.00	-	-	4-98
M.J.Mason	4	5	3	9*	14	7.00	-	-	-	-	94.4	26	287	9	31.88	1	-	5-83
M.J.McClenaghan	9	11	4	6*	23	3.28	-	-	2	-	311	42	1234	29	42.55	-	-	3-5

	M	In	NO	HS	Runs	Ave	100	50	Ct	St	O	M	R	W	Ave	5WI	10WM	Best
R.J.McCone	1	1	0	102	102	102.00	1	-	1	-	10	2	33	0	-	-	-	-
B.B.McCullum	5	8	0	115	307	38.37	1	1	19	-								
N.L.McCullum	7	11	0	44	250	22.72	-	-	3	-	270.3	64	724	19	38.10	-	-	3-46
P.D.McGlashan	6	11	0	91	290	26.36	-	2	9	2								
T.G.McIntosh	12	19	1	191	792	44.00	3	2	9	-								
A.J.McKay	7	8	4	18	49	12.25	-	-	-	-	229.2	37	790	23	34.34	-	-	4-37
J.M.McMillan	7	10	4	17	60	10.00	-	-	-	-	153.5	21	530	12	44.16	-	-	3-27
W.C.McSkimming	4	6	1	39*	105	21.00	-	-	-	-	100.3	28	291	12	24.25	-	-	4-40
C.J.Merchant	4	8	0	89	171	21.37	-	1	3	-								
K.D.Mills	6	7	0	50	100	14.28	-	1	1	-	143.2	37	441	6	73.50	-	-	3-64
A.Mishra	1	1	0	11	11	11.00	-	-	-	-	50.2	5	163	3	54.33	-	-	3-155
L.J.Morgan	3	4	0	64	142	35.50	-	2	2	-								
J.G.Myburgh	7	14	2	199	739	61.58	3	4	6	-	147.1	17	454	13	34.92	-	-	4-56
G.R.Napier	4	4	2	20	25	12.50	-	-	1	-	137	38	294	14	21.00	-	-	4-52
T.S.Nethula	9	12	4	33	106	13.25	-	-	7	-	299.2	29	1127	29	38.86	-	-	4-39
C.J.Nevin	8	10	1	134	434	48.22	1	3	22	-								
R.J.Nicol	4	6	1	104*	194	38.80	1	-	4	-	9	4	37	1	37.00	-	-	1-37
K.Noema-Barnett	1	1	0	11	11	11.00	-	-	-	-	29	6	97	0	-	-	-	-
I.E.O'Brien	5	7	3	19*	65	16.25	-	-	2	-	190.5	42	663	17	39.00	1	-	6-75
J.D.P.Oram	4	5	0	37	115	23.00	-	-	-	-	125	50	283	8	35.37	-	-	2-30
M.H.W.Papps	7	14	2	128	719	59.91	3	3	5	-								
M.E.Parlane	8	16	3	103	599	46.07	1	2	5	-								
N.R.Parlane	8	10	0	62	297	29.70	-	4	15	-								
J.S.Patel	6	4	1	44	58	19.33	-	-	2	-	290	68	751	21	35.76	2	-	5-65
B.M.K.Patton	7	12	2	142	521	52.10	2	1	5	-	24	3	127	3	42.33	-	-	2-19
S.H.A.Rance	1	1	0	31	31	31.00	-	-	1	-	30	4	125	1	125.00	-	-	1-64
J.A.Raval	4	4	0	256	301	75.25	1	-	2	-								
A.J.Redmond	4	7	0	76	268	38.28	-	4	7	-	12	0	45	0	-	-	-	-
I.A.Robertson	7	10	2	107*	275	34.37	1	1	4	-	33	5	122	0	-	-	-	-
H.D.Rutherford	5	9	0	41	117	13.00	-	-	3	-								
J.D.Ryder	5	8	1	201	532	76.00	2	3	5	-	36	14	98	2	49.00	-	-	1-3
R.J.Schaw	1	1	0	0	0	0.00	-	-	-	-	25	2	108	0	-	-	-	-
B.E.Scott	6	9	3	55*	192	32.00	-	1	4	-	133.4	35	379	4	94.75	-	-	2-59
L.J.Shaw	8	8	1	40*	89	12.71	-	-	-	-	180.2	26	666	28	23.78	1	-	5-59
J.W.Sheed	1	2	0	27	27	13.50	-	-	-	-								
R.R.Sherlock	2	2	1	36*	36	36.00	-	-	-	-	48	8	205	6	34.16	-	-	3-52
M.S.Sinclair	9	15	3	164	904	75.33	4	4	18	-	89	24	209	5	41.80	-	-	3-31
T.G.Southee	5	7	1	16	41	6.83	-	-	3	-	172	48	545	16	34.06	1	-	5-43
S.L.Stewart	7	13	1	69*	287	23.91	-	2	4	-								
S.B.Styris	5	8	0	95	292	36.50	-	3	7	-	25	2	78	0	-	-	-	-
L.R.P.L.Taylor	5	8	0	151	387	48.37	2	-	9	-	2	1	4	0	-	-	-	-
E.P.Thompson	8	11	2	60	297	33.00	-	3	3	-	306	72	905	29	31.20	1	-	5-57
G.R.Todd	8	14	2	98	467	38.91	-	4	2	-	17	2	72	0	-	-	-	-
D.R.Tuffey	8	5	1	53	102	25.50	-	1	3	-	267.1	86	604	27	22.37	1	-	6-33
M.J.Tugaga	3	4	3	35	48	48.00	-	-	1	-	49	9	178	3	59.33	-	-	1-28
C.F.K.van Wyk	8	14	4	105	449	44.90	1	2	22	1								
D.L.Vettori	5	7	1	118	279	46.50	1	1	3	-	235.4	64	584	17	34.35	1	-	6-56
M.Vijay	1	2	0	93	96	48.00	-	1	1	-	5	0	21	0	-	-	-	-
N.Wagner	7	10	0	29	109	10.90	-	-	2	-	219	42	700	21	33.33	-	-	3-32
B-J.Watling	4	6	0	111	207	34.50	1	-	4	-	0.5	0	5	0	-	-	-	-
S.R.Wells	2	4	0	25	39	9.75	-	-	1	-	18	5	57	1	57.00	-	-	1-8
T.I.Weston	8	10	2	89*	407	50.87	-	3	2	-								
K.S.Williamson	9	16	0	111	812	50.75	2	5	12	-	212.2	44	690	17	40.58	1	-	5-75
B.S.Wilson	5	10	0	109	403	40.30	1	2	4	-								
L.J.Woodcock	9	12	2	102*	472	47.20	1	4	5	-	274.1	61	809	16	50.56	-	-	4-40
G.H.Worker	9	16	1	63*	426	28.40	-	3	6	-	247	46	715	12	59.58	-	-	3-54
R.A.Young	11	16	1	100*	749	49.93	2	6	18	-								
J.A.F.Yovich	5	9	2	65	214	30.57	-	1	3	-	95	13	402	9	44.66	-	-	4-136

LEADING AVERAGES

BATTING *(top 20, qualification six innings)*

	M	*I*	*NO*	*HS*	*Runs*	*Ave*	*100s*	*50s*
G.J. Hopkins	8	11	4	132*	554	79.14	3	1
J.D. Ryder	5	8	1	201	532	76.00	2	3
M.S. Sinclair	9	15	3	164	904	75.33	4	4
R.S. Dravid	4	7	1	102	416	69.33	1	4
C.D. Cumming	7	12	0	173	784	65.33	4	2
P.J. Ingram	9	15	0	247	957	63.80	2	4
J.E.C. Franklin	11	16	2	219	865	61.78	3	4
J.G. Myburgh	7	14	2	199	739	61.58	3	4
M.H.W. Papps	7	14	2	128	719	59.91	3	3
V.V.S. Laxman	4	7	1	124*	359	59.83	1	2
A.K. Kitchen	5	8	0	132	442	55.25	3	-
D.C. de Boorder	4	6	2	73*	215	53.75	-	2
M.D. Bell	8	11	0	146	591	53.72	3	2
B.M.K. Patton	7	12	2	142	521	52.10	2	1
C. de Grandhomme	10	14	3	104	566	51.45	2	2
T.I. Weston	8	10	2	89*	407	50.87	-	3
K.S. Williamson	9	16	0	111	812	50.75	2	5
N.T. Broom	7	12	2	140*	501	50.10	1	4
R.A. Young	11	16	1	100*	749	49.93	2	6
L.R.P.L. Taylor	5	8	0	151	387	48.37	2	-

BOWLING *(top 20, qualification 10 wickets)*

	Overs	*Mdns*	*Runs*	*Wkts*	*Ave*	*5WI*	*10WM*	*Best*
G.R. Napier	137	38	294	14	21.00	-	-	4-52
D.R. Tuffey	267.1	86	604	27	22.37	1	-	6-33
A.M. Ellis	201 2	66	547	23	23.78	-	-	4-39
L.J. Shaw	180.2	26	666	28	23.78	1	-	5-59
W.C. McSkimming	100.3	28	291	12	24.25	-	-	4-40
C. de Grandhomme	185	49	516	21	24.57	-	-	3-12
B.J. Arnel	219.4	72	522	20	26.10	-	-	4-38
M. Burns	99.4	18	326	12	27.16	-	-	4-41
H.K. Bennett	206.5	40	761	26	29.26	-	-	4-48
M.J. Harvie	183.5	41	589	19	31.00	-	-	4-73
E.P. Thompson	306	72	905	29	31.20	1	-	5-57
N. Wagner	219	42	700	21	33.33	-	-	3-32
T.G. Southee	172	48	545	16	34.06	1	-	5-43
A.J. McKay	229.2	37	790	23	34.34	-	-	4-37
D.L. Vettori	235.4	64	584	17	34.35	1	-	6-56
J.G. Myburgh	147.1	17	454	13	34.92	-	-	4-56
G.W. Aldridge	146.4	26	525	15	35.00	-	-	3-46
B.C. Hiini	120	30	386	11	35.09	-	-	4-47
J.S. Patel	290	68	751	21	35.76	2	-	5-65
D.J. Bowden	161.1	20	595	16	37.18	-	-	4-55

CENTURIES

There were 84 centuries scored in first-class cricket in 2008/09, passing the record of 56 made in the 2006/07 season. A total of 53 players scored hundreds, also beating the previous best of 39 in 1998/99.

C.D. Cumming and M.S.Sinclair each made four, A.K. Kitchen, G.J. Hopkins, J.E.C. Franklin, J.G. Myburgh, M.D. Bell, M.H.W. Papps, R.A. Jones and T.G. McIntosh each made three and B.M.K. Patton, C. de Grandhomme, G. Gambhir, J.D. Ryder, J.M. How, K.S. Williamson, L.R.P.L. Taylor, P.J. Ingram and R.A. Young each scored two.

The fastest hundreds of the season were scored by L.J. Wright (England Lions v New Zealand A at Lincoln) and C. de Grandhomme (Auckland v Central Districts at Auckland) who took 91 balls to reach their centuries.

†256	J.A. Raval	Auckland v Central Districts	Auckland
247	P.J. Ingram	Central Districts v Northern Districts	Hamilton
219	J.E.C. Franklin	Wellington v Auckland	Auckland
201	R.A. Jones	Auckland v West Indies	Auckland
201	J.D. Ryder	New Zealand v India *(Second Test)*	Napier
199	J.G. Myburgh	Canterbury v Central Districts	New Plymouth
197	C.H. Gayle	West Indies v New Zealand *(Second Test)*	Napier
191	T.G. McIntosh	Auckland v Wellington	Auckland
190*	J.M. How	New Zealand A v England Lions	Queenstown
173	C.D. Cumming	Otago v Canterbury	Christchurch
167	G. Gambhir	India v New Zealand *(Third Test)*	Wellington
166	P.J. Ingram	Central Districts v Canterbury	New Plymouth
164	M.S. Sinclair	Central Districts v Wellington	Wellington
160	S.R. Tendulkar	India v New Zealand *(First Test)*	Hamilton
160	J.E.C. Franklin	Wellington v Northern Districts	Wellington
158*	R.R. Sarwan	West Indies v Auckland	Auckland
156*	J.E.C. Franklin	Wellington v Central Districts	Napier
151	L.R.P.L. Taylor	New Zealand v India *(Second Test)*	Napier
†148	M.J. Guptill	Auckland v Otago	Auckland
146	M.D. Bell	Wellington v Canterbury	Wellington
143	B.B.J. Griggs	Central Districts v Wellington	Wellington
†142	B.M.K. Patton	Central Districts v Auckland	Napier
140	T.G. McIntosh	Auckland v Canterbury	Rangiora
140*	N.T. Broom	Otago v Canterbury	Invercargill
138*	I.J.L. Trott	England Lions v New Zealand A	Queenstown
137	G. Gambhir	India v New Zealand *(Second Test)*	Napier
136	T.G. McIntosh	New Zealand v West Indies *(Second Test)*	Napier
135*	B.J. Diamanti	Central Districts v Canterbury	Rangiora
134	C.J. Nevin	Wellington v Central Districts	Napier
133	C.D. Cumming	Otago v Central Districts	Napier
132*	G.J. Hopkins	Auckland v Central Districts	Auckland
132	A.K. Kitchen	Auckland v Northern Districts	Auckland
131*	M.S. Sinclair	Central Districts v Auckland	Auckland
131*	G.R. Hay	Central Districts v Canterbury	Rangiora
128	M.H.W. Papps	Canterbury v Northern Districts	Christchurch
127	M.H.W. Papps	Canterbury v Central Districts	Rangiora
126*	S. Chanderpaul	West Indies v New Zealand *(Second Test)*	Napier
†125	A.K. Kitchen	Auckland v Otago	Queenstown
124*	V.V.S. Laxman	India v New Zealand *(Second Test)*	Napier
122	P.G. Fulton	Canterbury v Northern Districts	Christchurch
122	M.D. Bell	Wellington v Auckland	Auckland
118	D.L. Vettori	New Zealand v India *(First Test)*	Hamilton
118	C.D. Cumming	Otago v Wellington	Wellington

115	B.B. McCullum	New Zealand v India *(Second Test)*	Napier
115	A.K. Kitchen	Auckland v Central Districts	Lincoln
†111	K.S. Williamson	Northern Districts v Auckland	Auckland
111	B-J. Watling	Northern Districts v Central Districts	Hamilton
†110	J.M. Brodie	Wellington v Northern Districts	Wellington
110*	B.M.K. Patton	Central Districts v Otago	Napier
109	R.A. Jones	Auckland v Central Districts	Lincoln
109	B.S. Wilson	Northern Districts v Canterbury	Christchurch
108	S.B. Haig	Otago v Auckland	Auckland
108	M.S. Sinclair	Central Districts v Otago	Napier
107	L.R.P.L. Taylor	New Zealand v India *(Third Test)*	Wellington
107	J.G. Myburgh	Canterbury v Central Districts	Rangiora
107*	I.A. Robertson	New Zealand A v England Lions	Lincoln
†106	J.E. Taylor	West Indies v New Zealand *(First Test)*	Dunedin
105	L.J. Wright	England Lions v New Zealand A	Lincoln
105*	J.A.H. Marshall	Northern Districts v Wellington	Wellington
105	C.F.K. van Wyk	Canterbury v Otago	Christchurch
105	C.D. Cumming	Otago v Auckland	Auckland
104*	R.J. Nicol	Auckland v Central Districts	Auckland
104	D.R. Flynn	Northern Districts v Canterbury	Christchurch
104	C. de Grandhomme	Auckland v Northern Districts	Auckland
103	M.H.W. Papps	Canterbury v Otago	Christchurch
103	M.E. Parlane	Northern Districts v Wellington	Whangarei
103*	G.J. Hopkins	Auckland v West Indies	Auckland
103*	C. de Grandhomme	Auckland v Central Districts	Auckland
102	R.S. Dravid	Canterbury v Central Districts	Rangiora
†102	R.J. McCone	Canterbury v Otago	Christchurch
102	R.A. Jones	Auckland v Otago	Queenstown
102*	L.J. Woodcock	Wellington v Auckland	Auckland
102	J.D. Ryder	New Zealand v India *(First Test)*	Hamilton
†101	T.D. Astle	Canterbury v Northern Districts	Hamilton
101	S.R. Patel	England Lions v New Zealand A	Queenstown
101	M.S. Sinclair	Central Districts v Northern Districts	Hamilton
101*	J.M. How	Central Districts v Wellington	Napier
101*	J.G. Myburgh	Canterbury v Central Districts	New Plymouth
†101*	B-J. Crook	Wellington v Otago	Dunedin
100	R.A. Young	Auckland v Canterbury	Rangiora
100*	R.A. Young	Auckland v Otago	Queenstown
100	M.D. Bell	Wellington v Northern Districts	Whangarei
100	K.S. Williamson	Northern Districts v Wellington	Whangarei
100	G.J. Hopkins	Auckland v Northern Districts	Whangarei

† *maiden first-class century*

CENTURY PARTNERSHIPS

There were a record 86 century partnerships in 2008/09 compared to 63 the previous season. The previous record was 73 in 2000/01.

FIRST WICKET

179	C.D.Cumming & A.J.Redmond	Otago v Canterbury	Christchurch
169	T.G.McIntosh & R.A.Jones	Auckland v Otago	Queenstown
159	P.J.Ingram & J.M.How	Central Districts v Canterbury	New Plymouth
158	C.D.Cumming & A.J.Redmond	Otago v Auckland	Auckland
150	T.G.McIntosh & R.A.Jones	Auckland v Wellington	Auckland
130	R.W.T.Key & S.C.Moore	England Lions v New Zealand A	Queenstown
122	T.D.Astle & A.M.Ellis	Canterbury v Northern Districts	Hamilton
122	C.D.Cumming & A.J.Redmond	Otago v Wellington	Wellington
112	M.D.Bell & J.M.Brodie	Wellington v Canterbury	Wellington

SECOND WICKET

223	T.G.McIntosh & R.A.Jones	Auckland v West Indies	Auckland
209	B.S.Wilson & D.R.Flynn	Northern Districts v Canterbury	Christchurch
197	T.G.McIntosh & R.A.Young	Auckland v Canterbury	Rangiora
193	C.D.Cumming & G.R.Todd	Otago v Wellington	Wellington
177	J.M.How & P.J.Ingram	New Zealand A v England Lions	Queenstown
171*	J.M.How & G.H.Worker	Central Districts v Wellington	Napier
170	G.Gambhir & R.S.Dravid	India v New Zealand *(Third Test)*	Wellington
165	B.S.Wilson & M.E.Parlane	Northern Districts v Wellington	Whangarei
140*	R.W.T.Key & I.J.L.Trott	England Lions v New Zealand A	Queenstown
135	M.D.Bell & N.R.Parlane	Wellington v Northern Districts	Whangarei
133	G.Gambhir & R.S.Dravid	India v New Zealand *(Second Test)*	Napier
119	M.H.W.Papps & P.G.Fulton	Canterbury v Otago	Christchurch
118	T.G.McIntosh & D.R.Flynn	New Zealand v West Indies *(Second Test)*	Napier
116	S.Chattergoon & R.R.Sarwan	West Indies v Auckland	Auckland
115	T.G.McIntosh & R.A.Young	Auckland v Wellington	Auckland
115	M.J.Guptill & R.A.Young	Auckland v Otago	Auckland
115	P.J.Ingram & G.H.Worker	Central Districts v Canterbury	New Plymouth
109	C.J.Merchant & M.E.Parlane	Northern Districts v Central Districts	Hamilton
105	G.Gambhir & R.S.Dravid	India v New Zealand *(First Test)*	Hamilton

THIRD WICKET

264	P.J.Ingram & M.S.Sinclair	Central Districts v Northern Districts	Hamilton
259	M.H.W.Papps & P.G.Fulton	Canterbury v Northern Districts	Christchurch
185	M.J.Guptill & S.B.Styris	Auckland v Otago	Auckland
184	R.A.Jones & A.K.Kitchen	Auckland v Central Districts	Lincoln
164	I.J.L.Trott & S.R.Patel	England Lions v New Zealand A	Queenstown
161	J.M.Brodie & G.D.Elliott	Wellington v Northern Districts	Wellington
159	C.D.Cumming & N.T.Broom	Otago v Central Districts	Napier
156*	M.H.W.Papps & J.G.Myburgh	Canterbury v Central Districts	New Plymouth
153	R.S.Dravid & J.G.Myburgh	Canterbury v Central Districts	Rangiora
141*	B.M.K.Patton & M.S.Sinclair	Central Districts v Otago	Napier
135	R.A.Jones & R.A.Young	Auckland v West Indies	Auckland
118	P.G.Fulton & J.G.Myburgh	Canterbury v Northern Districts	Hamilton
118	M.Vijay & M.S.Sinclair	Central Districts v Wellington	Napier
106	B.K.M.Patton & T.I.Weston	Central Districts v Auckland	Napier
103	M.H.W.Papps & J.G.Myburgh	Canterbury v Otago	Christchurch
100	C.D.Cumming & N.T.Broom	Otago v Auckland	Auckland

FOURTH WICKET

271	L.R.P.L.Taylor & J.D.Ryder	New Zealand v India *(Second Test)*	Napier
199	A.K.Kitchen & R.A.Young	Auckland v Northern Districts	Auckland
159*	R.J.Nicol & G.J.Hopkins	Auckland v Central Districts	Auckland
153	B-J.Crook & L.J.Woodcock	Wellington v Otago	Dunedin
152	J.A.Raval & R.A.Young	Auckland v Central Districts	Auckland
149	J.M.How & J.E.C.Franklin	New Zealand A v England Lions	Queenstown
138	J.G.Myburgh & S.L.Stewart	Canterbury v Central Districts	New Plymouth
132	M.E.Parlane & K.S.Williamson	Northern Districts v Auckland	Auckland
123	M.D.Bell & J.E.C.Franklin	Wellington v Canterbury	Wellington
112	J.G.Myburgh & I.A.Robertson	Canterbury v Northern Districts	Christchurch
106	G.Gambhir & V.V.S.Laxman	India v New Zealand *(Third Test)*	Wellington
102	A.K.Kitchen & S.J.Croft	Auckland v Otago	Queenstown
100	T.G.McIntosh & J.D.Ryder	New Zealand v West Indies *(Second Test)*	Napier

FIFTH WICKET

282	J.E.C.Franklin & L.J.Woodcock	Wellington v Auckland	Auckland
228	J.A.Raval & G.J.Hopkins	Auckland v Central Districts	Auckland
163	S.Chanderpaul & B.P.Nash	West Indies v New Zealand *(Second Test)*	Napier
142	L.R.P.L.Taylor & J.E.C.Franklin	New Zealand v India *(Third Test)*	Wellington
141	K.S.Williamson & J.A.F.Yovich	Northern Districts v Canterbury	Hamilton
138	T.I.Weston & G.R.Hay	Central Districts v Canterbury	Rangiora
124	S.Chanderpaul & B.P.Nash	West Indies v New Zealand *(Second Test)*	Napier
121	J.D.Ryder & J.E.C.Franklin	New Zealand v India *(Second Test)*	Napier
120*	V.V.S.Laxman & Yuvraj Singh	India v New Zealand *(Second Test)*	Napier
110	N.T.Broom & S.B.Haig	Otago v Auckland	Queenstown
106	K.S.Williamson & P.D.McGlashan	Northern Districts v Wellington	Whangarei

SIXTH WICKET

235	M.S.Sinclair & B.B.J.Griggs	Central Districts v Wellington	Wellington
151*	G.J.Hopkins & C.de Grandhomme	Auckland v Central Districts	Auckland
145	S.B.Haig & D.C.de Boorder	Otago v Auckland	Auckland
138	J.E.C.Franklin & C.J.Nevin	Wellington v Central Districts	Napier
135	K.S.Williamson & G.W.Aldridge	Northern Districts v Central Districts	Hamilton
121	J.E.C.Franklin & L.J.Woodcock	Wellington v Northern Districts	Wellington
117	L.J.Wright & B.J.M.Scott	England Lions v New Zealand A	Lincoln
115	S.R.Tendulkar & M.S.Dhoni	India v New Zealand *(First Test)*	Hamilton

SEVENTH WICKET

205*	G.R.Hay & B.J.Diamanti	Central Districts v Canterbury	Rangiora
186	J.D.Ryder & D.L.Vettori	New Zealand v India *(First Test)*	Hamilton
164	J.E.C.Franklin & C.J.Nevin	Wellington v Northern Districts	Wellington
153	S.Chanderpaul & J.E.Taylor	West Indies v New Zealand *(First Test)*	Dunedin
148	C.J.Nevin & D.J.Bowden	Wellington v Otago	Wellington
147	R.A.Young & I.A.Robertson	New Zealand A v England Lions	Lincoln
128	B.B.McCullum & D.L.Vettori	New Zealand v India *(Second Test)*	Napier

EIGHTH WICKET

167	C.F.K.van Wyk & R.J.McCone	Canterbury v Otago	Christchurch
163	P.D.McGlashan & G.W.Aldridge	Northern Districts v Canterbury	Hamilton

NINTH WICKET

106	G.J.Hopkins & D.R.Tuffey	Auckland v Northern Districts	Whangarei

WICKETKEEPING DISMISSALS

The following New Zealand players who appeared in 2008/09 have made at least one dismissal in first-class cricket while keeping wicket.

	ct	st	total
G.J.Hopkins	286	20	306
C.J.Nevin	270	9	279
R.A.Young	241	5	246
B.B.McCullum	218	16	234
C.F.K.van Wyk *	219	11	230
B.B.J.Griggs	201	7	208
P.D.McGlashan *	104	8	112
D.C.de Boorder *	33	6	39
M.H.W.Papps	34	4	38
B-J.Watling	26	–	26
M.S.Sinclair	11	1	12
S.R.Gadsdon *	7	1	8
S.B.Haig	6	–	6
M.D.Bell	4	–	4
L.J.Woodcock	3	–	3
A.J.Redmond	3	–	3
B-J.Crook	2	–	2
C.D.Cumming	1	–	1
J.A.H.Marshall	1	–	1
N.R.Parlane	1	–	1
J.D.Ryder	1	–	1

* *no further catches taken as fielder*

NEW ZEALANDERS IN OVERSEAS CRICKET

Andre Adams *(Nottinghamshire)*, Paul Wiseman *(Durham)*, Shane Bond *(Hampshire)*, Chris Martin *(Warwickshire)* and Craig Spearman and Hamish Marshall *(Gloucestershire)* appeared in county cricket in 2008.

At the time of going to print we were not able to include the final figures for players in county cricket in 2009 and the career records do not include performances in any of these matches.

The details for 2008 were:

	M	I	NO	HS	Runs	Ave	100	50	ct
A.R. Adams	8	11	1	58	133	13.30	-	1	4
S.E. Bond	4	5	0	17	33	6.60	-	-	-
H.J.H. Marshall	16	29	1	121	850	30.35	2	5	6
C.S. Martin	6	2	0	0	0	0.00	-	-	1
C.M. Spearman	5	9	1	95	173	21.62	-	1	2
P.J. Wiseman	16	22	2	65	479	23.95	-	3	1

	O	M	R	W	Ave	5WI	10WM	Best
A.R. Adams	230.4	64	594	31	19.16	-	-	4-39
S.E. Bond	99.1	15	365	19	19.21	2	-	7-66
H.J.H. Marshall	62	12	204	1	204.00	-	-	1-31
C.S. Martin	159.1	27	580	16	36.25	1	-	5-84
P.J. Wiseman	197	43	614	17	36.11	-	-	4-87

BOWLING PERFORMANCES

This season there were 17 instances of bowlers taking five or more wickets in an innings compared to 27 in the previous season. J.S. Patel was the only player to achieve the feat more than once. No player took ten wickets in a match. There was one hat trick, the first in domestic competition since 2004/05.

FIVE WICKETS IN AN INNINGS

7-87	F.H. Edwards	West Indies v New Zealand *(Second Test)*	Napier
6-33	D.R. Tuffey	Auckland v Northern Districts	Auckland
6-56	D.L. Vettori	New Zealand v West Indies *(First Test)*	Dunedin
6-63	Harbhajan Singh	India v New Zealand *(First Test)*	Hamilton
6-73	B.P. Martin	Northern Districts v Wellington	Whangarei
6-75	I.E. O'Brien	New Zealand v West Indies *(Second Test)*	Napier
5-43	T.G. Southee	Northern Districts v Canterbury	Christchurch
5-57	E.P. Thompson	Central Districts v Auckland	Napier
5-58	T.A. Boult	Northern Districts v Otago	Dunedin
5-59	L.J. Shaw	Auckland v Central Districts	Lincoln
5-65	J.S. Patel	Wellington v Otago	Wellington
5-65	Z. Khan	India v New Zealand *(Third Test)*	Wellington
5-74	B.J. Diamanti	Central Districts v Canterbury	Rangiora
5-75	K.S. Williamson	Northern Districts v Canterbury	Christchurch
5-83	M.J. Mason	Central Districts v Canterbury	New Plymouth
5-110	J.S. Patel	New Zealand v West Indies *(Second Test)*	Napier
5-119	L.M. Burtt	Canterbury v Otago	Invercargill

HAT TRICK

M.J. McClenaghan	Central Districts v Canterbury	Rangiora

CAREER AVERAGES

as at 1 May, 2009 for players active during the 2008/09 season

	M	In	NO	HS	Runs	Ave	100	50	Ct	St	Wkts	Runs	Ave	5WI	10WM	Best
G.W.Aldridge	70	93	30	75	1359	21.57	-	3	31	-	176	5448	30.95	5	-	5-27
C.J.Anderson	11	20	4	88*	455	28.43	-	2	4	-	3	341	113.66	-	-	1-33
B.J.Arnel	25	30	9	18	102	4.85	-	-	6	-	77	1982	25.74	2	1	6-82
T.D.Astle	31	56	2	101	1238	22.92	1	6	21	-	41	1696	41.36	-	-	4-26
Azhar Abbas	45	66	23	44*	321	7.46	-	-	12	-	154	3879	25.18	6	2	6-38
M.D.Bates	7	7	2	28	72	14.40	-	-	1	-	15	479	31.93	-	-	4-47
N.B.Beard	2	3	2	32*	37	37.00	-	-	1	-	1	189	189.00	-	-	1-133
M.D.Bell	161	273	18	265	9546	37.43	24	52	127	-	0	23	-	-	-	-
H.K.Bennett	28	29	13	27	107	6.68	-	-	7	-	73	2909	39.84	1	-	7-50
H.K.P.Boam	4	6	3	49*	116	38.66	-	-	3	-	4	115	28.75	-	-	3-56
J.J.Boult	1	2	0	31	36	18.00	-	-	1	-	4	78	19.50	-	-	4-78
T.A.Boult	6	9	3	35	59	9.83	-	-	5	-	13	401	30.84	1	-	5-58
D.J.Bowden	26	36	8	106*	990	35.35	1	4	7	-	51	1769	34.68	-	-	4-55
D.A.J.Bracewell	5	6	0	26	70	11.66	-	-	1	-	10	510	51.00	-	-	3-51
J.M.Brodie	9	13	0	110	368	28.30	1	1	13	-						
N.T.Broom	48	77	7	150	2693	38.47	5	15	32	-	5	335	67.00	-	-	1-8
M.Burns	10	11	3	8	42	5.25	-	-	4	-	27	693	25.66	-	-	4-41
L.M.Burtt	19	22	6	29*	159	9.93	-	-	6	-	59	2017	34.18	3	1	6-108
I.G.Butler	41	53	18	68	590	16.85	-	2	11	-	120	3809	31.74	2	-	6-46
B-J.Crook	9	13	1	101*	333	27.75	1	1	5	-	1	2	2.00	-	-	1-2
C.D.Cumming	117	208	17	187	6858	35.90	15	32	52	-	30	1592	53.06	-	-	3-31
M.P.F.Davidson	11	15	1	56	234	16.71	-	1	4	-	31	923	29.77	1	-	5-39
T.T.Davis	7	8	1	30	43	6.14	-	-	4	-	13	559	43.00	-	-	3-61
A.P.de Boorder	5	8	0	88	181	22.62	-	1	-	-	0	15	-	-	-	-
D.C.de Boorder	12	16	4	74	498	41.50	-	4	33	6						
C.de Grandhomme	28	44	5	109	1215	31.15	3	5	24	-	37	1079	29.16	-	-	4-65
A.P.Devcich	6	10	1	94*	209	23.22	-	1	9	-	3	142	47.33	-	-	2-20
B.J.Diamanti	23	35	5	136	691	23.03	2	1	5	-	57	1982	34.77	3	1	6-73
G.D.Elliott	48	74	4	196*	2170	31.00	5	12	29	-	63	2378	37.74	-	-	4-56
A.M.Ellis	38	60	8	78	1423	27.36	-	9	20	-	62	2160	34.83	1	-	5-63
D.R.Flynn	41	71	10	110	2077	34.04	5	8	14	-	0	87	-	-	-	-
J.E.C.Franklin	100	147	21	219	3971	31.51	6	18	35	-	328	8669	26.42	11	1	7-30
P.G.Fulton	74	124	11	301*	4961	43.90	8	28	57	-	11	399	36.27	-	-	4-49
S.R.Gadsdon	2	3	1	9	13	6.50	-	-	7	1						
M.R.Gillespie	52	6	11	81*	915	16.63	-	3	8	-	212	5170	24.38	10	-	6-42
B.B.J.Griggs	73	114	11	143	2761	26.80	2	15	206	7						
M.J.Guptill	22	37	1	148	1025	28.47	1	5	9	-	1	55	55.00	-	-	1-8
S.B.Haig	15	23	1	111	722	32.81	2	3	14	-						
M.J.Harvie	19	21	6	37*	199	13.26	-	-	3	-	41	1717	41.87	-	-	4-73
G.R.Hay	22	38	4	164*	1443	42.44	4	6	12	-						
B.E.Hefford	48	63	20	32*	358	8.32	-	-	12	-	119	3719	31.25	1	-	5-50
B.C.Hiini	23	33	9	103*	719	29.95	2	1	10	-	70	2009	28.70	2	-	5-32
P.A.Hitchcock	11	16	3	51	298	22.92	-	1	1	-	14	747	53.35	-	-	3-27
G.J.Hopkins	110	173	28	175*	4873	33.60	10	20	290	20	0	13	-	-	-	-
M.V.Houghton	9	9	1	81	192	24.00	-	1	2	-	14	612	43.71	-	-	3-20
J.M.How	83	144	11	190*	4586	34.48	11	24	84	-	20	1079	53.95	-	-	3-57
P.J.Ingram	58	105	6	247	3374	34.08	9	12	34	-	0	47	-	-	-	-
R.A.Jones	114	198	11	201	6301	33.69	15	31	99	-	1	0	0.00	-	-	1-0
M.O.Kain	1	1	0	24	24	24.00	-	-	1	-	2	121	60.50	-	-	1-51
A.K.Kitchen	5	8	0	132	442	55.25	3	-	9	-						
A.R.Lamb	3	-	-	-	-	-	-	-	-	-	4	163	40.75	-	-	2-26
H.J.H.Marshall	117	200	13	168	6547	35.01	15	30	56	-	11	723	65.72	-	-	1-6
J.A.H.Marshall	111	193	10	235	5461	29.84	10	27	109	-	4	324	81.00	-	-	1-5
B.P.Martin	85	113	30	113*	1469	17.69	1	4	35	-	215	7510	34.93	13	2	7-33
C.S.Martin	139	171	83	25	351	3.98	-	-	28	-	435	13,686	31.46	18	1	6-54
M.J.Mason	72	98	30	64*	1131	16.63	-	1	18	-	230	5716	24.85	9	1	6-56
M.J.McClenaghan	12	14	5	6*	29	3.22	-	-	3	-	32	1509	47.15	-	-	3-5
R.J.McCone	1	1	0	102	102	102.00	1	-	1	-	0	33	-	-	-	-
B.B.McCullum	84	143	8	160	4557	33.75	7	26	233	16						
N.L.McCullum	46	70	6	106*	1662	25.96	1	9	50	-	96	3820	39.79	2	-	6-90
P.D.McGlashan	46	70	7	103*	1705	27.06	1	9	104	8						
T.G.McIntosh	84	140	10	268	4425	34.03	14	15	70	-	0	80	-	-	-	-
A.J.McKay	19	21	8	36*	148	11.38	-	-	2	-	54	1648	30.51	-	-	4-37

	M	In	NO	HS	Runs	Ave	100	50	Ct	St	Wkts	Runs	Ave	5WI	10WM	Best
J.M.McMillan	37	46	23	21*	198	8.60	-	-	5	-	90	3050	33.88	1	-	7-105
W.C.McSkimming	54	79	13	111	1414	21.42	1	6	23	-	187	4595	24.57	8	1	6-39
C.J.Merchant	8	14	0	89	394	28.14	-	3	5	-	0	6	-	-	-	-
K.D.Mills	66	94	23	117*	1840	25.91	1	12	22	-	176	5059	28.74	3	1	5-33
L.J.Morgan	11	17	0	81	462	27.17	-	3	5	-						
J.G.Myburgh	64	117	18	203	4422	44.66	11	27	44	-	27	1171	43.37	-	-	4-56
T.S.Nethula	9	12	4	33	106	13.25	-	-	7	-	29	1127	38.86	-	-	4-39
C.J.Nevin	105	159	23	143*	4755	34.96	4	27	275	9	0	0	-	-	-	-
R.J.Nicol	66	102	11	160	3278	36.02	7	17	46	-	15	1070	71.33	-	-	2-26
K.Noema-Barnett	1	1	0	11	11	11.00	-	-	-	-	0	97	-	-	-	-
I.E.O'Brien	70	83	22	44	491	8.04	-	-	11	-	249	6281	25.22	10	1	8-55
J.D.P.Oram	81	129	17	155	3802	33.94	8	17	34	-	151	3956	26.19	3	-	6-45
M.H.W.Papps	100	180	15	192	6069	36.78	16	25	114	4	0	6	-	-	-	-
M.E.Parlane	126	215	12	203	6653	32.77	15	26	76	-	1	56	56.00	-	-	1-14
N.R.Parlane	75	118	10	165	4040	37.40	8	27	89	-	0	46	-	-	-	-
J.S.Patel	74	85	32	58*	921	17.37	-	2	23	-	152	6156	40.50	5	-	6-32
B.M.K.Patton	8	13	2	142	521	47.36	2	1	6	-	3	128	42.66	-	-	2-19
S.H.A.Rance	1	1	0	31	31	31.00	-	-	1	-	1	125	125.00	-	-	1-64
J.A.Raval	4	4	0	256	301	75.25	1	-	2	-						
A.J.Redmond	84	145	10	146	4381	32.45	7	27	65	-	100	4314	43.14	-	-	4-30
I.A.Robertson	21	28	7	107*	828	39.42	2	4	15	-	17	953	56.05	-	-	3-58
H.D.Rutherford	5	9	0	41	117	13.00	-	-	3	-						
J.D.Ryder	49	79	6	236	3236	44.32	7	17	41	-	45	1226	27.24	-	-	4-23
R.J.Schaw	14	21	2	34	319	16.78	-	-	7	-	26	1467	56.42	-	-	5-130
B.E.Scott	50	64	17	96	1088	23.14	-	5	18	-	149	3968	26.63	5	-	6-20
L.J.Shaw	23	28	7	52*	212	10.09	-	13	3	-	74	1897	25.63	2	-	5-59
J.W.Sheed	43	74	4	89	1513	21.61	-	11	22	-	2	196	98.00	-	-	1-30
R.R.Sherlock	12	17	5	64	164	13.66	-	1	3	-	31	1049	33.83	-	-	4-33
M.S.Sinclair	148	251	26	268	10,862	48.27	27	56	149	1	14	616	44.00	-	-	3-31
T.G.Southee	25	32	5	77*	360	13.33	-	2	4	-	83	2509	30.22	4	-	6-68
S.L.Stewart	56	99	7	149	3058	33.23	4	19	20	-	4	344	86.00	-	-	2-52
S.B.Styris	123	205	18	212*	5786	30.94	9	29	99	-	203	6353	31.29	9	1	6-32
L.R.P.L.Taylor	60	100	3	217	3696	38.10	9	17	66	-	4	330	82.50	-	-	2-34
E.P.Thompson	44	64	9	126	1544	28.07	3	8	15	-	143	4491	31.40	3	1	7-55
G.R.Todd	45	80	13	165	2502	37.34	4	13	15	-	14	909	64.92	-	-	2-26
D.R.Tuffey	78	92	21	89*	1001	14.09	-	4	33	-	264	6742	25.53	10	1	7-12
M.J.Tugaga	3	4	3	35	48	48.00	-	-	1	-	3	178	59.33	-	-	1-28
C.F.K.van Wyk	73	110	20	111	2948	32.75	3	16	219	11	1	9	9.00	-	-	1-7
D.L.Vettori	142	202	30	137*	4939	28.71	5	29	70	-	460	14,559	31.65	28	3	7-87
N.Wagner	27	31	8	43*	272	11.82	-	-	5	-	110	2329	21.17	4	-	5-28
B-J.Watling	38	70	2	153	1913	28.13	4	8	46	-	0	5	-	-	-	-
S.R.Wells	6	9	1	29	120	15.00	-	-	3	-	6	245	40.83	-	-	2-7
T.I.Weston	28	47	8	152	1627	41.71	1	12	16	-						
K.S.Williamson	10	18	0	111	814	45.22	2	5	12	-	17	690	40.58	1	-	5-75
B.S.Wilson	24	43	0	109	1094	25.44	2	5	16	-	0	26	-	-	-	-
L.J.Woodcock	61	98	10	106	2445	27.78	3	13	30	-	70	2699	38.55	-	-	4-3
G.H.Worker	13	23	1	71	602	27.36	-	4	11	-	15	898	59.86	-	-	3-54
R.A.Young	85	112	19	114	2457	26.41	4	14	244	5	0	3	-	-	-	-
J.A.F.Yovich	89	139	27	144	3143	28.06	2	17	27	-	237	7815	32.97	8	1	7-64

STATE SHIELD

2008/09

The 2008/09 State Shield competition was one of the most even with top qualifier Northern Districts winning the final by 49 runs over third placed Otago. It was Northern's first one-day title since 2004/05 while it was Otago's third successive final.

The points table saw some dramatic changes during the season. After five rounds Central Districts seemed assured of qualifying for the top three, as they were in first place with four wins, but they then won just one game in the last half of the competition and missed out. Northern were always in the top three. After losing their first game they went on to win seven of the next eight. Canterbury and Otago were always in the mix but for Wellington and Auckland it was a series to forget.

Twelve centuries were scored compared to 18 from the previous season. Martin Guptill and Matthew Bell had the highest individual score of 124. The fastest century of the season went to Shanan Stewart who scored his hundred from 82 balls against Northern Districts. Four players scored in excess of 400 runs – Mathew Sinclair was the leading run scorer with 532 followed by B-J Watling (509), Craig Cumming (421) and Michael Papps (416).

There were two instances of a team scoring 300 runs in an innings with Otago making 311-8 against Central Districts while Central scored 301-8 against Auckland.

Three players took five wickets in an innings. Neil Wagner took 5-34 against Wellington while Graeme Aldridge and Ian Butler had figures of 5-39 and 5-55 in the final. Six players took 15 wickets or more. Wagner was the leading wicket-taker with 24, followed by Graham Napier (21), Shane Bond (19), Butler (18), Brent Arnel (17) and Trent Boult (16). The format was the same as the previous season.

Final points were:

	P	*W*	*L*	*T*	*NR*	*Bonus*	*Points*
Northern Districts	10	7	3	–	–	1	29
Canterbury	10	5	4	–	1	2	24
Otago	10	4	4	–	2	4	24
Central Districts	10	5	5	–	–	2	22
Wellington	10	4	6	–	–	–	16
Auckland	10	3	6	–	1	–	14

First Round

Croft *(Auckland)*, Bracewell and Noema-Barnett *(Central Districts)*, Murdoch, Crook, Boam and Karaitiana *(Wellington)* all made their debuts.

Auckland lost wickets regularly and only an eighth wicket stand of 65 got them through to 205. Croft, the Lancashire professional, made fifty from 80 balls. Bracewell and Sinclair batted well in Central Districts' reply. Bracewell got fifty from 49 balls and Sinclair made his fifty from 53 balls as he guided them to a win and a bonus point with 63 balls to spare.

Northern lost early wickets to a spirited Wellington attack. Only Williamson, with a maiden fifity from 88 balls, was able to pass twenty. Napier, Elliott and Karaitiana bowled well. When he caught Scott, Nevin took his 150th catch in domestic one-day games. Wellington lost Murdoch in the fourth over and struggled to 77-4 after 26 overs. An unbroken stand of 72 off 105 balls gave them a win with 39 balls to spare. Bell scored his fifty from 87 deliveries.

The match between Otago and Canterbury was abandoned.

AUCKLAND v CENTRAL DISTRICTS — State Shield

at Eden Park Outer Oval, Auckland on 21 December, 2008
Toss : Auckland. Umpires : G.A.V. Baxter & B.G. Frost
Central Districts won by 5 wickets. *Points: Central Districts 5, Auckland 0*

AUCKLAND

	Runs	Mins	Balls	6s	4s
P.A.Hitchcock b Thompson	28	35	31	1	4
M.J.Guptill c & b Thompson	1	12	8	-	-
R.A.Jones* b McClenaghan	5	15	12	-	-
S.B.Styris c Griggs b Diamanti	8	24	12	-	1
R.A.Young b Noema-Barnett	32	67	38	-	3
G.J.Hopkins† c Griggs b Diamanti	3	18	5	-	-
S.J.Croft c Sinclair b Thompson	59	107	93	-	4
C.de Grandhomme c Griggs b Schaw	1	4	4	-	-
R.M.Hira c Noema-Barnett b Bracewell	41	85	77	-	3
M.D.Bates not out	15	25	14	-	2
C.S.Martin b Bracewell	0	1	1	-	-
Extras (lb 3, w 6, nb 3)	12				
TOTAL (48.4 overs)	**205**	206			

CENTRAL DISTRICTS

	Runs	Mins	Balls	6s	4s
D.A.J.Bracewell run out	55	88	70	1	8
P.J.Ingram b Martin	12	25	16	-	2
G.H.Worker b Martin	1	16	6	-	-
M.S.Sinclair* not out	84	113	77	1	11
B.B.J.Griggs† run out	1	4	7	-	-
T.I.Weston c de Grandhomme b Martin	36	52	56	1	3
E.P.Thompson not out	6	9	7	-	1
K.Noema-Barnett					
B.J.Diamanti					
R.J.Schaw					
M.J.McClenaghan					
Extras (b 4, lb 1, w 5, nb 2)	12				
TOTAL (39.3 overs) (5 wkts)	**207**	159			

Bowling	*O*	*M*	*R*	*W*
CENTRAL DISTRICTS				
Thompson	9	0	52	3
McClenaghan	8	0	31	1
Bracewell	6.4	0	33	2
Diamanti	10	0	35	2
Schaw	10	1	30	1
Noema-Barnett	5	0	21	1
AUCKLAND				
Bates	4	0	15	0
Martin	9.3	1	69	3
Hitchcock	5	0	42	0
de Grandhomme	5	0	18	0
Hira	10	3	32	0
Styris	6	0	26	0

Fall of Wickets

	A	*CD*
1st	10	23
2nd	33	45
3rd	39	109
4th	62	112
5th	68	182
6th	105	-
7th	108	-
8th	173	-
9th	205	-
10th	205	-

NORTHERN DISTRICTS v WELLINGTON — State Shield

at Cobham Oval, Whangarei on 21 December, 208
Toss : Wellington. Umpires : A.L. Hill & D.J.Walker
***Wellington won by 6 wickets.** Points: Wellington 4, Northern Districts 0*

NORTHERN DISTRICTS

	Runs	Mins	Balls	6s	4s
H.J.H.Marshall b Napier	3	7	6	-	-
B-J.Watling c Gillespie b Napier	0	18	9	-	-
M.E.Parlane c Bell b Elliott	20	71	48	1	1
J.A.H.Marshall* c Parlane b Gillespie	16	26	22	-	2
K.S.Williamson b Napier	67	148	109	-	3
P.D.McGlashan† b Woodcock	11	27	24	-	-
J.A.F.Yovich c Nevin b Karaitiana	10	39	29	-	-
B.P.Martin b Karaitiana	0	8	7	-	-
B.E.Scott c Nevin b Elliott	8	24	17	-	-
T.G.Southee lbw b Elliott	1	3	3	-	-
B.J.Arnel not out	0	8	1	-	-
Extras (lb 2, w 8, nb 2)	12				
TOTAL (45.3 overs)	**148**	194			

WELLINGTON

	Runs	Mins	Balls	6s	4s
S.J.Murdoch c Williamson b Arnel	0	15	16	-	-
M.D.Bell* not out	74	190	127	-	7
N.R.Parlane c Watling b Southee	5	30	17	-	-
G.D.Elliott c McGlashan b Yovich	19	54	41	-	1
B-J.Crook c Martin b Yovich	1	11	11	-	-
C.J.Nevin† not out	35	76	50	-	2
L.J.Woodcock					
G.R.Napier					
H.K.P.Boam					
M.R.Gillespie					
R.P.C.Karaitiana					
Extras (lb 9, w 5, nb 1)	15				
TOTAL (43.3 overs) (4 wkts)	**149**	190			

Bowling	*O*	*M*	*R*	*W*
WELLINGTON				
Gillespie	9	0	34	1
Napier	7.3	1	24	3
Elliott	10	1	32	3
Boam	5	0	17	0
Karaitiana	7	2	18	2
Woodcock	7	0	21	1
NORTHERN DISTRICTS				
Southee	9	3	29	1
Arnel	10	1	27	1
Scott	10	1	32	0
Martin	7	0	26	0
Yovich	7.3	2	26	2

Fall of Wickets	***ND***	***W***
1st	4	3
2nd	14	29
3rd	35	72
4th	54	77
5th	80	-
6th	106	-
7th	112	-
8th	135	-
9th	137	-
10th	148	-

CANTERBURY v OTAGO — State Shield

at Queen Elizabeth II Park, Christchurch on 21 December, 2008
***Abandoned without a ball being bowled.** Points: Canterbury 2, Otago 2*

Second Round

Kitchen *(Auckland)*, Boult *(Northern Districts)*, Mascarenhas and Wagner *(Otago)* made their debuts. Butler made his debut for Otago after having previously represented Northern Districts. Martin *(Northern Districts)* was playing his fiftieth game.

Central Districts lost two wickets in the second over but then Ingram and Sinclair added 100 for the third wicket. Ingram got fifty from 57 balls. When on 49 Sinclair reached 3000 runs in one-day domestic games. Wellington lost four quick wickets and then never threatened. Nevin reached 3000 runs when on 15. Napier scored 50 from 42 balls but Wellington were dismissed for 203 giving Central an 82 run win and another bonus point. Bracewell and McClenaghan had best bowling figures.

Otago had two early set-backs but Haig held the innings together. He scored his maiden fifty from 73 balls and was ninth man out. Boult had a very economical start with just ten runs conceded from eight overs. After Marshall went in the second over Watling and Parlane added an unbroken 169 from 204 balls to win the match by nine wickets with 86 balls to spare. Watling reached fifty from 88 balls, 11 more than Parlane.

After Auckland lost two quick wickets Kitchen, in his debut match, batted with maturity reaching fifty from 74 deliveries as he and Young added 107 for the fourth wicket to enable Auckland to reach 226-8. Ellis had career best bowling figures. In reply Canterbury lost three wickets to run outs but passed Auckland's total with seven balls to spare. Fulton reached fifty from 57 balls and de Grandhomme had his best bowling figures.

CENTRAL DISTRICTS v WELLINGTON — State Shield

at Trafalgar Park, Nelson on 27 December, 2008
Toss : Wellington. Umpires : C.B. Gaffaney & D.M. Quested
Central Districts won by 82 runs. *Points: Central Districts 5, Wellington 0*

CENTRAL DISTRICTS

	Runs	Mins	Balls	6s	4s
D.A.J.Bracewell c Bell b Napier	5	6	4	-	1
P.J.Ingram b Woodcock	67	89	78	-	9
J.M.How b Napier	0	1	1	-	-
M.S.Sinclair* c Woodcock b Boam	92	165	113	-	9
B.B.J.Griggs† b O'Brien	23	31	3	-	4
T.I.Weston c Boam b Napier	38	49	38	-	5
B.J.Diamanti not out	26	28	16	1	3
K.Noema-Barnett b Elliott	11	14	9	-	1
R.J.Schaw b Elliott	0	2	3	-	-
M.J.Mason not out	16	9	7	1	2
M.J.McClenaghan					
Extras (lb 3, w 4)	7				
TOTAL (50 overs) (8 wkts)	**285**	205			

WELLINGTON

	Runs	Mins	Balls	6s	4s
S.J.Murdoch lbw b McClenaghan	2	13	11	-	-
M.D.Bell* lbw b Mason	0	17	10	-	-
N.R.Parlane b Bracewell	12	31	23	-	2
G.D.Elliott lbw b Noema-Barnett	33	72	56	1	2
B-J.Crook c Griggs b Bracewell	0	1	2	-	-
C.J.Nevin† c Sinclair b Schaw	35	52	35	1	3
G.R.Napier st Griggs b Diamanti	50	48	42	4	1
L.J.Woodcock c Bracewell b Diamanti	21	49	31	1	-
H.K.P.Boam not out	21	41	32	-	2
R.P.C.Karaitiana c Griggs b Diamanti	1	8	4	-	-
I.E.O'Brien c Diamanti b McClenaghan	17	22	15	-	2
Extras (lb 2, w 8, nb 1)	11				
TOTAL (43.2 overs)	**203**	186			

Bowling	*O*	*M*	*R*	*W*
WELLINGTON				
O'Brien	8	0	41	1
Napier	10	1	47	3
Boam	8	0	53	1
Elliott	9	0	53	2
Karaitiana	7	0	43	0
Woodcock	8	1	45	1
CENTRAL DISTRICTS				
Mason	7	2	26	1
McClenaghan	7.2	2	29	2
Diamanti	10	0	45	3
Bracewell	6	1	24	2
Schaw	10	0	55	1
Noema-Barnett	3	0	22	1

Fall of Wickets	*CD*	*W*
1st	8	3
2nd	8	3
3rd	108	30
4th	148	30
5th	230	84
6th	230	102
7th	259	161
8th	259	166
9th	-	171
10th	-	203

OTAGO v NORTHERN DISTRICTS

State Shield

at Molyneux Park, Alexandra on 27 December, 2008
Toss : Northern Districts. Umpires : M.P. George & P.D. Jones
***Northern Districts won by 9 wickets.** Points: Northern Districts 5, Otago 0*

OTAGO

	Runs	Mins	Balls	6s	4s
A.J.Redmond c McGlashan b Boult	0	3	6	-	-
S.B.Haig run out	79	118	112	-	4
G.R.Todd c Watling b Boult	1	6	5	-	-
C.D.Cumming* lbw b Yovich	21	59	51	-	2
N.T.Broom c & b Williamson	4	20	11	-	-
N.L.McCullum c Martin b Yovich	26	47	43	-	2
A.D.Mascarenhas b Yovich	1	3	2	-	-
D.C.de Boorder† lbw b Martin	8	19	15	-	-
W.C.McSkimming c Scott b Arnel	0	7	4	-	-
I.G.Butler lbw b Arnel	7	15	10	-	1
N.Wagner not out	1	5	4	-	-
Extras (b 3, lb 3, w 13)	19				
TOTAL (43.5 overs)	**167**	160			

NORTHERN DISTRICTS

	Runs	Mins	Balls	6s	4s
B-J.Watling not out	83	146	119	1	10
H.J.H.Marshall lbw b Wagner	0	6	2	-	-
M.E.Parlane not out	65	139	91	2	6
J.A.H.Marshall*					
K.S.Williamson					
P.D.McGlashan†					
J.A.F.Yovich					
B.P.Martin					
B.E.Scott					
T.A.Boult					
B.J.Arnel					
Extras (b 2, lb 4, w 17)	23				
TOTAL (35.2 overs) (1 wkt)	**171**	146			

Bowling	*O*	*M*	*R*	*W*
NORTHERN DISTRICTS				
Boult	8	2	10	2
Arnel	7.5	0	33	2
Scott	5	0	29	0
Yovich	10	0	30	3
Williamson	6	0	30	1
Martin	7	0	29	1
OTAGO				
McSkimming	7	0	34	0
Wagner	7	1	48	1
Mascarenhas	6	2	14	0
Butler	6.2	0	37	0
McCullum	7	0	25	0
Cumming	2	0	7	0

Fall of Wickets	*O*	*ND*
1st	0	2
2nd	5	-
3rd	58	-
4th	74	-
5th	125	-
6th	127	-
7th	152	-
8th	154	-
9th	163	-
10th	167	-

AUCKLAND v CANTERBURY

State Shield

at Eden Park, Auckland on 27 December, 2008
Toss : Canterbury. Umpires : W.R. Knights & T.J Parlane
***Canterbury won by 3 wickets.** Points: Canterbury 4, Auckland 0*

AUCKLAND

	Runs	Mins	Balls	6s	4s
P.A.Hitchcock b Burson	1	5	5	-	-
M.J.Guptill c van Wyk b Bond	23	20	14	-	5
R.A.Jones* b Bond	0	4	4	-	-
A.K.Kitchen b Burson	69	106	104	1	7
R.A.Young lbw b Burson	43	110	82	-	3
G.J.Hopkins† c sub (C.Frauenstein) b Ellis	31	52	29	1	2
S.J.Croft c Robertson b Ellis	5	14	15	-	-
C.de Grandhomme not out	38	35	31	-	5
R.M.Hira c Hiini b Ellis	0	3	3	-	-
M.D.Bates not out	10	17	13	-	-
C.S.Martin					
Extras (lb 4, w 2)	6				
TOTAL (50 overs) (8 wkts)	**226**	192			

CANTERBURY

	Runs	Mins	Balls	6s	4s
I.A.Robertson c Hopkins b de Grandhomme	12	59	43	-	1
M.H.W.Papps c Hopkins b Martin	21	45	28	-	3
P.G.Fulton run out	60	107	78	1	4
J.G.Myburgh c Hira b de Grandhomme	2	7	8	-	-
S.L.Stewart b de Grandhomme	35	50	48	1	2
C.Z.Harris run out	17	45	36	-	2
C.F.K.van Wyk*† not out	27	44	30	-	3
A.M.Ellis run out	14	21	15	-	1
B.C.Hiini not out	16	11	8	1	1
S.E.Bond					
R.D.Burson					
Extras (lb 5, w 19, nb 1)	25				
TOTAL (48.5 overs) (7 wkts)	**229**	198			

Bowling	*O*	*M*	*R*	*W*
CANTERBURY				
Bond	10	0	57	2
Burson	10	1	41	3
Harris	10	0	31	0
Ellis	10	0	50	3
Hiini	6	0	30	0
Myburgh	4	0	13	0
AUCKLAND				
Martin	9	1	31	1
Bates	7	1	38	0
de Grandhomme	8	1	38	3
Hira	10	1	54	0
Hitchcock	6.5	1	36	0
Croft	8	0	27	0

Fall of Wickets	*A*	*C*
1st	5	32
2nd	6	51
3rd	29	63
4th	136	131
5th	145	153
6th	154	174
7th	200	204
8th	201	-
9th	-	-
10th	-	-

Third Round

Davidson *(Canterbury)* made his debut.

Auckland decided to bat but lost two quick wickets before Jones and Kitchen added 85. Kitchen reached his second successive fifty from 71 balls. Napier had his best one-day bowling figures in New Zealand. Wellington started disastrously. Parlane became Hopkins 100th catch but a maiden fifty from Crook (91 balls) and an unbeaten fifty from Nevin saw Wellington through to their first win with eleven balls to spare. Tuffey had his best bowling return.

Central Districts' form deserted them and they could make only 188 against Otago. Worker (highest score) and Sinclair were the only players to reach thirty. Otago had a good start but then lost two wickets quickly before Todd and Cumming put on an unbeaten 131 off 137 balls to give them a win and a bonus point with 70 balls to spare. Cumming reached his fifty off 60 balls.

Canterbury had a good all-round batting display with all but one player reaching double figures. Robertson (61 balls) and Fulton (64 balls) made fifties. Stewart became Yovich's 100th wicket. Hamish Marshall made his maiden hundred from 94 balls.

WELLINGTON v AUCKLAND — State Shield

at Allied Nationwide Finance Basin Reserve, Wellington on 30 December, 2008
Toss : Auckland. Umpires : E.J. Gray & D.M. Quested
Wellington won by 4 wickets. *Points: Wellington 4, Auckland 0*

AUCKLAND

	Runs	Mins	Balls	6s	4s
P.A.Hitchcock c Nevin b Franklin	12	23	15	-	1
M.J.Guptill c Murdoch b Napier	1	18	16	-	-
R.A.Jones* c Crook b Woodcock	39	91	61	-	3
A.K.Kitchen c Franklin b Woodcock	65	131	93	3	4
R.A.Young lbw b Woodcock	0	2	2	-	-
G.J.Hopkins† b Karaitiana	10	17	17	-	-
S.J.Croft c Franklin b Napier	39	76	53	-	1
C.de Grandhomme b Napier	10	22	17	-	-
R.M.Hira c Franklin b Napier	14	25	18	-	1
D.R.Tuffey not out	2	6	3	-	-
C.S.Martin run out	0	2	1	-	-
Extras (lb 1, w 3, nb 1)	5				
TOTAL (49.1 overs)	**197**	211			

WELLINGTON

	Runs	Mins	Balls	6s	4s
S.J.Murdoch c Hopkins b Tuffey	8	32	12	-	-
M.D.Bell* c Guptill b Tuffey	0	4	5	-	-
N.R.Parlane c Hopkins b Tuffey	0	6	4	-	-
B-J.Crook b Hitchcock	75	162	136	-	9
J.E.C.Franklin c Hopkins b Tuffey	38	107	66	-	3
C.J.Nevin† not out	52	66	45	-	4
G.R.Napier b Croft	13	17	14	-	-
L.J.Woodcock not out	4	14	8	-	-
M.V.Houghton					
R.P.C.Karaitiana					
I.E.O'Brien					
Extras (b 1, lb 3, w 4, nb 1)	9				
TOTAL (48.1 overs) (6 wkts)	**199**	207			

Bowling	*O*	*M*	*R*	*W*
WELLINGTON				
Napier	10	0	40	4
Franklin	9	0	31	1
Karaitiana	9	1	38	1
O'Brien	9.1	0	34	0
Houghton	4	0	26	0
Woodcock	8	2	27	3
AUCKLAND				
Tuffey	9	1	33	4
Martin	10	2	38	0
de Grandhomme	4	0	22	0
Croft	7	0	30	1
Hitchcock	8.1	0	42	1
Hira	10	0	30	0

Fall of Wickets	***A***	***W***
1st	13	1
2nd	14	3
3rd	99	17
4th	99	115
5th	122	152
6th	144	172
7th	165	-
8th	194	-
9th	197	-
10th	197	-

OTAGO v CENTRAL DISTRICTS

State Shield

at Molyneux Park, Alexandra on 30 December, 2008
Toss : Otago. Umpires : G.A.V. Baxter & D.J. Walker
***Otago won by 8 wickets.** Points: Otago 5, Central Districts 0*

CENTRAL DISTRICTS

	Runs	Mins	Balls	6s	4s
D.A.J.Bracewell c de Boorder b Wagner	14	31	23	-	2
P.J.Ingram c Cumming b Mascarenhas	17	53	35	-	2
G.H.Worker c de Boorder b McCullum	33	73	62	-	3
M.S.Sinclair* run out	31	64	55	-	1
B.B.J.Griggs† run out	3	18	16	-	-
T.I.Weston c Todd b Cumming	12	40	29	-	1
E.P.Thompson b Wagner	20	49	40	-	-
B.J.Diamanti c Broom b McSkimming	18	30	23	-	3
R.J.Schaw not out	18	23	13	1	1
M.J.Mason not out	3	7	4	-	-
B.E.Hefford					
Extras (b 2, lb 12, w 5)	19				
TOTAL (50 overs) (8 wkts)	**188**	202			

OTAGO

	Runs	Mins	Balls	6s	4s
A.J.Redmond c Sinclair b Hefford	31	64	46	-	4
S.B.Haig c Griggs b Hefford	21	53	40	-	1
G.R.Todd not out	48	112	71	-	3
C.D.Cumming* not out	70	101	733	1	7
N.T.Broom					
N.L.McCullum					
A.D.Mascarenhas					
D.C.de Boorder†					
W.C.McSkimming					
N.Wagner					
C.M.Smith					
Extras (lb 12, w 9)	21				
TOTAL (38.2 overs) (2 wkts)	**191**	166			

Bowling	O	M	R	W
OTAGO				
McSkimming	6	0	23	1
Wagner	8	0	35	2
Mascarenhas	10	0	28	1
Smith	6	0	34	0
McCullum	10	0	37	1
Cumming	10	1	17	1
CENTRAL DISTRICTS				
Mason	8	1	36	0
Thompson	8	1	44	0
Bracewell	7	0	25	0
Hefford	5	1	23	2
Schaw	5	0	22	0
Diamanti	5.2	0	29	0

Fall of Wickets	*CD*	*O*
1st	31	57
2nd	43	60
3rd	99	-
4th	107	-
5th	114	-
6th	141	-
7th	151	-
8th	175	-
9th	-	-
10th	-	-

CANTERBURY v NORTHERN DISTRICTS

State Shield

at MainPower Oval, Rangiora on 30 December, 2008
Toss : Canterbury. Umpires : B.G. Frost & P.D. Jones
***Northern Districts won by 4 wickets.** Points: Northern Districts 4, Canterbury 0*

CANTERBURY

	Runs	Mins	Balls	6s	4s
I.A.Robertson run out	54	84	62	1	8
M.H.W.Papps run out	34	91	59	-	3
P.G.Fulton c Martin b Yovich	52	83	68	1	4
J.G.Myburgh st McGlashan b Scott	25	45	41	1	1
S.L.Stewart c Boult b Yovich	40	48	34	3	1
C.Z.Harris c Aldridge b Boult	6	23	14	-	-
B.C.Hiini not out	13	20	10	-	1
C.F.K.van Wyk*† not out	15	14	12	-	1
A.M.Ellis					
S.E.Bond					
M.P.F.Davidson					
Extras (b 3, lb 2, w 9)	14				
TOTAL (50 overs) (6 wkts)	**253**	207			

NORTHERN DISTRICTS

	Runs	Mins	Balls	6s	4s
H.J.H.Marshall c Papps b Harris	113	155	105	1	14
B-J.Watling run out	17	48	31	-	3
M.E.Parlane b Bond	10	28	22	-	-
J.A.H.Marshall* c Davidson b Myburgh	51	49	50	-	4
K.S.Williamson run out	13	37	29	-	1
P.D.McGlashan† not out	27	39	27	-	3
J.A.F.Yovich c Fulton b Ellis	0	1	1	-	-
B.P.Martin not out	11	27	19	-	1
G.W.Aldridge					
B.E.Scott					
T.A.Boult					
Extras (w 14, nb 1)	15				
TOTAL (47.1 overs) (6 wkts)	**257**	195			

Bowling	O	M	R	W
NORTHERN DISTRICTS				
Boult	10	0	48	1
Aldridge	6	0	26	0
Scott	8	0	58	1
Williamson	10	1	34	0
Yovich	6	0	28	2
Martin	10	2	54	0
CANTERBURY				
Bond	10	0	72	1
Davidson	8.1	0	48	0
Harris	10	0	44	1
Hiini	6	0	30	0
Ellis	8	1	40	1
Myburgh	5	0	23	1

Fall of Wickets	*C*	*ND*
1st	92	60
2nd	96	94
3rd	154	190
4th	193	219
5th	217	221
6th	222	221
7th	-	-
8th	-	-
9th	-	-
10th	-	-

Fourth Round

Patton *(Central Districts)* and Rutherford *(Otago)* made their debuts.

Papps (fifty from 66 balls) and Myburgh (54 balls) added 105 for the third wicket. Harris (fifty from 53 balls) saw the innings through to 294-6. Myburgh's 90 was his highest score. Ingram and Sinclair added 110 for the third wicket and both players scored fifty from 48 balls. Central won with eleven balls to spare.

The game at Hamilton was reduced to 34 overs per side. Guptill scored fifty from 35 balls and his second hundred after 88 balls. This was his highest score and his 124 completely dominated the Auckland total of 197-7. Watling scored fifty from 61 balls as Northern reached the total with fourteen balls to spare.

Wellington were indebted to a 142 run stand between Parlane and Crook. Parlane needed 71 balls for his fifty and Crook 93 as Wellington went from 199-3 to 220-9. Wagner got his first five wicket haul. Otago got its first fifty from 67 balls as Redmond (fifty from 69 balls) and Todd (46 balls) showed the way. When on 27 Todd had reached 1000 runs.

CENTRAL DISTRICTS v CANTERBURY — State Shield

at Fitzherbert Park, Palmerston North on 2 January, 2009
Toss : Central Districts. Umpires : P.D. Jones & W.R. Knights
***Central Districts won by 4 wickets.** Points: Central Districts 4, Canterbury 0*

CANTERBURY

	Runs	Mins	Balls	6s	4s
I.A.Robertson b McClenaghan	5	7	7	-	1
M.H.W.Papps c Griggs b Worker	72	108	94	2	8
P.G.Fulton c Bracewell b Thompson	9	26	17	-	1
J.G.Myburgh b Hefford	90	144	85	1	12
S.L.Stewart c Weston b Diamanti	20	15	20	-	4
C.Z.Harris not out	62	86	58	1	8
B.C.Hiini b McClenaghan	13	16	12	1	-
C.F.K.van Wyk*† not out	5	13	8	-	-
A.M.Ellis					
S.E.Bond					
R.D.Burson					
Extras (b 4, lb 8, w 5, nb 1)	18				
TOTAL (50 overs) (6 wkts)	**294**	214			

CENTRAL DISTRICTS

	Runs	Mins	Balls	6s	4s
G.H.Worker c van Wyk b Bond	30	60	53	-	3
P.J.Ingram run out	91	137	96	-	11
B.M.K.Patton c Harris b Ellis	3	6	5	-	-
M.S.Sinclair* c Burson b Ellis	97	114	90	-	9
T.I.Weston lbw b Myburgh	16	12	15	-	2
B.B.J.Griggs† run out	9	14	10	-	-
E.P.Thompson not out	17	29	13	-	2
B.J.Diamanti not out	26	13	9	1	4
D.A.J.Bracewell					
B.E.Hefford					
M.J.McClenaghan					
Extras (lb 4,nb 2)	6				
TOTAL (48.1 overs) (6 wkts)	**295**	199			

Bowling	O	M	R	W
CENTRAL DISTRICTS				
Thompson	8	1	34	1
McClenaghan	10	0	52	2
Hefford	10	1	46	1
Bracewell	7	0	54	0
Diamanti	9	0	54	1
Worker	6	0	42	1
CANTERBURY				
Bond	10	1	54	1
Burson	9	0	42	0
Hiini	8	0	52	0
Ellis	9	0	72	2
Harris	8	0	47	0
Myburgh	4.1	0	24	1

Fall of Wickets	C	CD
1st	7	73
2nd	33	78
3rd	138	188
4th	163	216
5th	235	240
6th	262	255
7th	-	-
8th	-	-
9th	-	-
10th	-	-

NORTHERN DISTRICTS v AUCKLAND — State Shield

at Seddon Park, Hamilton on 2 January, 2009
Toss : Northern Districts. Umpires : B.G. Frost & D.M. Quested
***Northern Districts won by 7 wickets.** Points: Northern Districts 5, Auckland 0*

AUCKLAND

	Runs	Mins	Balls	6s	4s
M.J.Guptill c Boult b Scott	124	129	97	4	11
R.A.Young run out	0	9	5	-	-
R.A.Jones* c & b Boult	13	16	15	-	3
A.K.Kitchen b Arnel	3	21	18	-	-
G.J.Hopkins† c & b Williamson	6	13	10	-	-
S.J.Croft c Watling b Martin	17	33	34	-	-
P.A.Hitchcock not out	25	3	25	-	1
R.M.Hira run out	0	1	0	-	-
C.de Grandhomme					
D.R.Tuffey					
C.S.Martin					
Extras (b 4, lb 4, w 1)	9				
TOTAL (34 overs) (7 wkts)	**197**	134			

NORTHERN DISTRICTS

	Runs	Mins	Balls	6s	4s
B-J.Watling not out	93	134	97	-	12
H.J.H.Marshall c Martin b Croft	34	46	23	-	5
M.E.Parlane run out	22	25	19	-	3
J.A.H.Marshall* b Hitchcock	7	15	12	-	-
K.S.Williamson not out	36	45	40	-	2
P.D.McGlashan†					
J.A.F.Yovich					
B.P.Martin					
B.E.Scott					
T.A.Boult					
B.J.Arnel					
Extras (b 1, lb 1, w 3, nb 1)	6				
TOTAL (31.4 overs) (3 wkts)	**198**	131			

Bowling	*O*	*M*	*R*	*W*
NORTHERN DISTRICTS				
Boult	6	0	46	1
Arnel	7	1	39	1
Scott	6	0	39	1
Williamson	4	0	23	1
Martin	7	0	24	1
Yovich	4	0	18	0
AUCKLAND				
Martin	6	0	33	0
Tuffey	5.4	0	48	0
Croft	3	0	28	1
Hitchcock	6	0	27	1
Hira	7	0	31	0
de Grandhomme	4	0	29	0

Fall of Wickets	***A***	***ND***
1st	15	68
2nd	42	106
3rd	63	118
4th	79	-
5th	126	-
6th	195	-
7th	197	-
8th	-	-
9th	-	-
10th	-	-

WELLINGTON v OTAGO — State Shield

at Allied Nationwide Finance Basin Reserve, Wellington on 2 January, 2009
Toss : Otago. Umpires : D.G. Paterson & D.J. Walker
***Otago won by 7 wickets.** Points: Otago 5, Wellington 0*

WELLINGTON

	Runs	Mins	Balls	6s	4s
S.J.Murdoch lbw b Butler	13	51	29	-	1
M.D.Bell* b McSkimming	21	38	38	-	4
N.R.Parlane c Cumming b Wagner	82	136	93	2	3
B-J.Crook c de Boorder b Wagner	65	108	103	-	6
J.E.C.Franklin c & b Mascarenhas	12	19	12	-	1
G.R.Napier c McCullum b Wagner	6	11	9	-	-
C.J.Nevin† c Cumming b Mascarenhas	9	11	7	-	-
L.J.Woodcock lbw b Wagner	2	7	3	-	-
M.V.Houghton b Wagner	1	7	3	-	-
R.P.C.Karaitiana not out	1	4	3	-	-
I.E.O'Brien					
Extras (lb 5, w 3)	8				
TOTAL (50 overs) (9 wkts)	**220**	200			

OTAGO

	Runs	Mins	Balls	6s	4s
A.J.Redmond b Napier	64	122	79	-	7
S.B.Haig b O'Brien	46	57	45	1	8
G.R.Todd b Napier	58	102	66	3	3
C.D.Cumming* not out	43	55	36	-	7
N.L.McCullum not out	7	17	7	-	-
H.D.Rutherford					
A.D.Mascarenhas					
D.C.de Boorder†					
W.C.McSkimming					
I.G.Butler					
N.Wagner					
Extras (lb 3, w 2)	5				
TOTAL (38.5 overs) (3 wkts)	**223**	178			

Bowling	*O*	*M*	*R*	*W*
OTAGO				
Wagner	10	1	34	5
McSkimming	7	2	15	1
Butler	7	0	53	1
Mascarenhas	10	1	39	2
McCullum	10	0	39	0
Cumming	6	0	35	0
WELLINGTON				
Napier	10	2	29	2
Franklin	5.4	0	34	0
O'Brien	7.5	0	47	1
Karaitiana	3	0	22	0
Houghton	5.2	0	46	0
Woodcock	7	0	42	0

Fall of Wickets	***W***	***O***
1st	33	66
2nd	36	164
3rd	177	188
4th	199	-
5th	204	-
6th	212	-
7th	217	-
8th	219	-
9th	220	-
10th	-	-

Fifth Round

Mascarenhas stole the show for Otago, coming to the wicket at 117-5. He and de Boorder added 60 for the seventh wicket and 72 came off 29 balls for the eighth wicket, with the fifty partnership between Mascarenhas and Butler coming from 19 balls. Mascarenhas' fifty came from 44 balls and he was unbeaten on 75 after 51 balls. Tuffey had five consecutive sixes hit from his last over. Guptill and Jones both scored fifties for Auckland, Guptill needing 57 balls and Jones 69. Croft and Hitchcock put on 69 off 52 balls and Hitchcock hit a six off the last ball from Wagner to give Auckland its first win of the season.

Ellis went early but then the next four Canterbury batsmen all got starts. Myburgh (fifty from 63 balls) and Stewart (52 balls) enabled Canterbury to reach 242-9. Wellington lost Nevin early and were soon 77-7 as only Woodcock, playing his fiftieth game, was able to reach twenty. He got fifty from 81 balls as Canterbury had an easy 78 run win.

Northern Districts had a century opening stand off 103 balls. Hamish Marshall got fifty from 44 balls and Watling fifty from 59. When he was on 27 Watling reached 1000 runs. Worker had his best bowling figures as Northern totalled 256-9. Worker and Ingram set a new opening partnership record for Central with 161 coming from 177 balls. Worker reached his highest score and got his fifty from 72 balls compared to Ingram's 48. Central ended with a win and 17 deliveries to spare.

AUCKLAND v OTAGO — State Shield

at Eden Park Outer Oval, Auckland on 5 January, 2009
Toss : Auckland. Umpires : G.A.V. Baxter & A.L. Hill
***Auckland won by 3 wickets.** Points: Auckland 4, Otago 0*

OTAGO

	Runs	Mins	Balls	6s	4s
A.J.Redmond c Hopkins b Martin	12	34	20	-	2
B.B.McCullum c Hopkins b Tuffey	4	12	11	-	-
G.R.Todd c Hopkins b Hitchcock	39	75	54	-	7
C.D.Cumming* lbw b Hira	41	78	53	-	5
N.T.Broom run out	9	19	25	-	-
N.L.McCullum run out	4	19	15	-	-
A.D.Mascarenhas not out	75	90	51	6	3
D.C.de Boorder† c de Grandhomme b Croft	35	46	45	-	4
I.G.Butler c Tuffey b Martin	18	24	13	2	-
N.Wagner b Martin	0	1	1	-	-
C.M.Smith c Hopkins b Martin	0	1	3	-	-
Extras (lb 2, w 18)	20				
TOTAL (48.5 overs)	**257**	204			

AUCKLAND

	Runs	Mins	Balls	6s	4s
M.J.Guptill c Wagner b Cumming	58	87	66	-	9
R.A.Young c de Boorder b Wagner	12	26	16	-	2
R.A.Jones* b Butler	54	98	77	-	3
A.K.Kitchen b Wagner	25	59	43	-	2
G.J.Hopkins† c Smith b Butler	9	34	18	-	1
S.J.Croft c Redmond b McCullum N.L.	42	50	31	2	2
P.A.Hitchcock not out	46	54	39	2	2
C.de Grandhomme c Redmond b Wagner	11	14	9	-	1
R.M.Hira not out	1	3	1	-	-
D.R.Tuffey					
C.S.Martin					
Extras (lb 4, w 1)	5				
TOTAL (50 overs) (7 wkts)	**263**	217			

Bowling	*O*	*M*	*R*	*W*
AUCKLAND				
Tuffey	9	1	57	1
Martin	8.5	1	33	4
de Grandhomme	6	0	32	0
Hira	10	0	36	1
Hitchcock	9	0	52	1
Croft	6	0	45	1
OTAGO				
Wagner	10	0	54	3
Smith	7	1	50	0
Mascarenhas	8	0	42	0
Butler	10	0	37	2
McCullum N.L.	9	0	54	1
Cumming	6	0	22	1

Fall of Wickets

	O	*A*
1st	11	28
2nd	31	104
3rd	91	145
4th	111	157
5th	117	165
6th	125	234
7th	185	256
8th	257	-
9th	257	-
10th	257	-

CANTERBURY v WELLINGTON — State Shield

at Queen Elizabeth II Park, Christchurch on 5 January, 2009
Toss : Wellington. Umpires : P.D. Jones & D.M. Quested
Canterbury won by 78 runs. *Points: Canterbury 5, Wellington 0*

CANTERBURY

	Runs	Mins	Balls	6s	4s
A.M.Ellis b Napier	0	9	8	-	-
M.H.W.Papps c Nevin b O'Brien	46	85	63	1	4
P.G.Fulton b Woodcock	36	102	62	-	1
J.G.Myburgh b Elliott	51	74	65	1	5
S.L.Stewart c Boam b Napier	53	78	57	2	2
C.Z.Harris b Gillespie	8	34	15	-	-
B.C.Hiini c Bell b Napier	10	11	5	1	1
C.F.K.van Wyk*† c Nevin b Gillespie	4	2	2	-	1
S.E.Bond b Gillespie	5	7	8	-	-
R.D.Burson not out	5	14	7	-	-
H.K.Bennett not out	3	11	8	-	-
Extras (b 1, lb 9, w 10, nb 1)	21				
TOTAL (50 overs) (9 wkts)	**242**	218			

WELLINGTON

	Runs	Mins	Balls	6s	4s
C.J.Nevin† lbw b Bond	0	11	10	-	-
M.D.Bell* b Ellis	14	52	32	-	2
B-J.Crook run out	16	28	23	-	2
G.D.Elliott run out	2	24	15	-	-
S.J.Murdoch c van Wyk b Hiini	19	55	43	-	2
G.R.Napier c sub (I.A.Robertson) b Burson	0	1	2	-	-
L.J.Woodcock c Papps b Ellis	53	125	84	1	3
H.K.P.Boam b Hiini	0	7	8	-	-
R.P.C.Karaitiana run out	11	23	17	-	2
M.R.Gillespie st van Wyk b Harris	11	17	16	-	2
I.E.O'Brien not out	19	34	24	1	1
Extras (b 4, lb 1, w 10, nb 4)	19				
TOTAL (45.1 overs)	**164**	193			

Bowling	O	M	R	W
WELLINGTON				
Napier	10	0	44	3
Gillespie	10	1	44	3
Elliott	9	0	41	1
O'Brien	10	0	48	1
Karaitiana	6	0	26	0
Woodcock	5	0	29	1
CANTERBURY				
Bond	10	3	24	1
Burson	6	2	22	1
Ellis	7.1	2	25	2
Bennett	5	0	32	0
Harris	10	1	33	1
Hiini	7	1	23	2

Fall of Wickets	C	W
1st	5	6
2nd	79	35
3rd	103	39
4th	175	45
5th	207	45
6th	212	75
7th	217	77
8th	225	95
9th	228	122
10th	-	164

CENTRAL DISTRICTS v NORTHERN DISTRICTS — State Shield

at Fitzherbert Park, Palmerston North on 5 January, 2009
Toss : Northern Districts. Umpires : E.J. Gray & D.J. Walker
Central Districts won by 6 wickets. *Points: Central Districts 4, Northern Districts 0*

NORTHERN DISTRICTS

	Runs	Mins	Balls	6s	4s
H.J.H.Marshall c Sinclair b Schaw	57	80	54	-	7
B-J.Watling b Worker	65	111	79	1	3
D.R.Flynn c How b Diamanti	2	4	4	-	-
J.A.H.Marshall* c Griggs b Schaw	35	43	45	-	3
K.S.Williamson run out	12	11	13	-	2
P.D.McGlashan† lbw b Worker	13	32	29	-	-
J.A.F.Yovich not out	41	75	54	-	2
B.P.Martin b Mason	2	7	6	-	-
B.E.Scott run out	7	10	5	-	1
T.A.Boult c Griggs b Thompson	10	12	7	-	1
B.J.Arnel not out	7	7	5	-	1
Extras (lb 1, w 3, nb 1)	5				
TOTAL (50 overs) (9 wkts)	**256**	206			

CENTRAL DISTRICTS

	Runs	Mins	Balls	6s	4s
P.J.Ingram b Scott	67	111	75	-	9
G.H.Worker b Martin	82	123	112	1	10
J.M.How b Martin	9	20	15	-	1
L.R.P.L.Taylor c Martin b Boult	46	54	38	2	5
M.S.Sinclair* not out	27	54	35	-	1
B.B.J.Griggs† not out	9	7	8	-	2
E.P.Thompson					
B.J.Diamanti					
D.A.J.Bracewell					
R.J.Schaw					
M.J.Mason					
Extras (b 1, lb 9, w 7)	17				
TOTAL (47.1 overs) (4 wkts)	**257**	188			

Bowling	O	M	R	W
CENTRAL DISTRICTS				
Thompson	9	0	45	1
Bracewell	2	0	17	0
Mason	9	0	60	1
Schaw	10	0	47	2
Diamanti	10	0	56	1
Worker	10	0	30	2
NORTHERN DISTRICTS				
Boult	10	2	44	1
Arnel	8	0	46	0
Yovich	5	0	41	0
Williamson	6	0	36	0
Scott	8.1	0	54	1
Martin	10	3	26	2

Fall of Wickets	ND	CD
1st	110	161
2nd	113	168
3rd	142	175
4th	163	242
5th	176	-
6th	202	-
7th	208	-
8th	222	-
9th	242	-
10th	-	-

Sixth Round

Wells *(Otago)* and Dean and Lamb *(Wellington)* made their debuts.

How controlled the Central innings. He got fifty from 83 balls as Central made 263-6. When Ingram was on 27 he had reached 1000 runs. Wellington had their best start for the season with an opening stand at better than a run a ball. Bell made fifty from 62 balls and then reached his fourth hundred from 122 deliveries. He was dismissed with just two runs needed as Wellington won with 19 balls left.

Papps got fifty from 89 balls and his sixth century from 137 deliveries as Canterbury made 223-7. McIntosh, back in the Auckland one-day side, made fifty from 77 balls, the same as Hopkins. Hopkins reached 2000 runs when on 82 and Auckland won with eleven balls to spare. Frauenstein had his best bowling figures.

Haig got fifty from 53 balls as Otago got 238. Northern lost Watling to the second ball of the innings but contributions from the next six batsmen saw the side through to victory with three balls remaining. McGlashan got fifty from 55 balls.

WELLINGTON v CENTRAL DISTRICTS — State Shield

at Allied Nationwide Finance Basin Reserve, Wellington on 11 January, 2009
Toss : Wellington. Umpires : P.L. Gasston & D.M. Quested
***Wellington won by 6 wickets.** Points: Wellington 4, Central Districts 0*

CENTRAL DISTRICTS

	Runs	Mins	Balls	6s	4s
P.J.Ingram b O'Brien	33	56	37	-	5
G.H.Worker b O'Brien	29	64	45	-	4
J.M.How not out	88	157	105	1	9
M.S.Sinclair* lbw b Woodcock	32	50	37	-	5
B.B.J.Griggs† lbw b Bowden	28	47	36	-	3
E.P.Thompson b Woodcock	1	10	8	-	-
D.A.J.Bracewell b Woodcock	1	2	3	-	-
B.J.Diamanti not out	28	36	29	1	2
R.J.Schaw					
M.J.McClenaghan					
B.E.Hefford					
Extras (b 1, lb 7, w 15)	23				
TOTAL (50 overs) (6 wkts)	**263**	214			

WELLINGTON

	Runs	Mins	Balls	6s	4s
M.D.Bell* c McClenaghan b Schaw	124	199	141	-	17
G.R.Napier c Ingram b McClenaghan	36	41	21	3	3
B-J.Crook c Worker b Schaw	29	71	53	1	2
J.E.C.Franklin c Griggs b McClenaghan	33	53	39	1	2
C.J.Nevin† not out	27	34	30	-	-
L.J.Woodcock not out	0	2	0	-	-
J.J.B.Dean					
H.K.P.Boam					
D.J.Bowden					
I.E.O'Brien					
A.R.Lamb					
Extras (b 3, lb 2, w 11, nb 2)	18				
TOTAL (46.5 overs) (4 wkts)	**267**	202			

Bowling	*O*	*M*	*R*	*W*
WELLINGTON				
Napier	10	0	63	0
Bowden	10	0	38	1
O'Brien	10	0	33	2
Boam	4	0	38	0
Lamb	8	0	52	0
Woodcock	8	1	31	3
CENTRAL DISTRICTS				
Thompson	4	0	40	0
McClenaghan	10	1	50	2
Hefford	7	0	32	0
Bracewell	3	0	19	0
Schaw	9	0	54	2
Diamanti	10	0	49	0
Worker	3.5	0	18	0

Fall of Wickets	***CD***	***W***
1st	67	62
2nd	71	142
3rd	121	205
4th	179	262
5th	185	-
6th	187	-
7th	-	-
8th	-	-
9th	-	-
10th	-	-

CANTERBURY v AUCKLAND — State Shield

at Queen Elizabeth II Park, Christchurch on 11 January, 2009
Toss : Canterbury. Umpires : A.L. Hill & D.J. Walker
***Auckland won by 3 wickets.** Points: Auckland 4, Canterbury 0*

CANTERBURY

	Runs	Mins	Balls	6s	4s
A.M.Ellis c Hopkins b Martin	10	60	37	-	-
M.H.W.Papps c Kitchen b Martin	109	195	147	1	11
P.G.Fulton c & b Hira	37	61	55	-	3
J.G.Myburgh b Croft	23	36	30	-	2
S.L.Stewart c Martin b Tuffey	7	18	11	-	-
C.J.Anderson c Hira b Martin	2	8	7	-	-
C.F.K.van Wyk*† not out	13	15	9	-	1
C.Frauenstein b Hitchcock	8	7	5	1	-
S.E.Bond					
R.D.Burson					
H.K.Bennett					
Extras (lb 4, w 9, nb 1)	14				
TOTAL (50 overs) (7 wkts)	**223**	203			

AUCKLAND

	Runs	Mins	Balls	6s	4s
T.G.McIntosh run out	71	143	104	1	4
R.A.Young b Frauenstein	36	61	46	1	5
R.A.Jones* b Frauenstein	3	8	8	-	-
A.K.Kitchen c van Wyk b Frauenstein	0	3	1	-	-
G.J.Hopkins† not out	86	117	96	1	7
S.J.Croft c van Wyk b Burson	13	17	19	-	1
P.A.Hitchcock run out	7	15	8	-	1
C.de Grandhomme b Burson	6	12	7	-	1
R.M.Hira not out	0	1	0	-	-
D.R.Tuffey					
C.S.Martin					
Extras (lb 2, w 2)	4				
TOTAL (48.1 overs) (7 wkts)	**226**	192			

Bowling	*O*	*M*	*R*	*W*
AUCKLAND				
Tuffey	10	2	26	1
Martin	10	1	39	3
de Grandhomme	4	0	18	0
Hira	10	0	49	1
Hitchcock	10	0	56	1
Croft	6	0	31	1
CANTERBURY				
Bond	10	0	50	0
Burson	10	1	45	2
Ellis	8.1	0	33	0
Frauenstein	7	0	36	3
Myburgh	9	0	39	0
Bennett	4	0	21	0

Fall of Wickets	***C***	***A***
1st	35	61
2nd	115	67
3rd	160	67
4th	187	158
5th	193	176
6th	204	199
7th	223	222
8th	-	-
9th	-	-
10th	-	-

NORTHERN DISTRICTS v OTAGO — State Shield

at Cobham Oval, Whangarei on 11 January, 2009
Toss : Northern Districts. Umpires : B.F. Bowden & B.G. Frost
***Northern Districts won by 3 wickets.** Points: Northern Districts 4, Otago 0*

OTAGO

	Runs	Mins	Balls	6s	4s
A.J.Redmond b Aldridge	7	23	18	-	-
S.B.Haig c Boult b Yovich	50	89	54	-	8
G.R.Todd c Boult b Yovich	24	53	38	-	3
C.D.Cumming* c McGlashan b Yovich	0	1	1	-	-
H.D.Rutherford c Boult b Martin	19	33	30	-	2
N.L.McCullum c Watling b Martin	39	66	55	-	1
D.C.de Boorder† c Marshall J.A.H. b Scott	43	64	58	-	3
S.R.Wells lbw b Scott	13	40	24	-	-
I.G.Butler c Parlane b Boult	23	19	17	1	2
N.Wagner run out	3	4	4	-	-
J.M.McMillan not out	0	2	0	-	-
Extras (lb 11, w 6)	17				
TOTAL (49.5 overs)	**238**	202			

NORTHERN DISTRICTS

	Runs	Mins	Balls	6s	4s
B-J.Watling c Haig b Wagner	0	1	2	-	-
H.J.H.Marshall c Redmond b McMillan	21	71	24	-	2
M.E.Parlane b McMillan	44	58	53	-	3
J.A.H.Marshall* b Butler	32	71	53	-	-
K.S.Williamson c & b McCullum	43	65	58	-	2
P.D.McGlashan† c Cumming b Butler	51	79	58	-	5
J.A.F.Yovich b Butler	27	79	38	-	2
G.W.Aldridge not out	2	14	3	-	-
B.P.Martin not out	8	9	9	-	-
B.E.Scott					
T.A.Boult					
Extras (lb 1, w 9, nb 1)	11				
TOTAL (49.3 overs) (7 wkts)	**239**	227			

Bowling	*O*	*M*	*R*	*W*
NORTHERN DISTRICTS				
Boult	9.5	1	47	1
Aldridge	8	0	37	1
Scott	9	0	43	2
Yovich	6	0	37	3
Martin	10	0	30	2
Williamson	7	0	33	0
OTAGO				
Wagner	10	0	55	1
McMillan	9.3	1	51	2
Butler	10	1	34	3
Cumming	6	0	40	0
McCullum	10	0	40	1
Wells	4	0	18	0

Fall of Wickets	***O***	***ND***
1st	24	0
2nd	85	68
3rd	85	76
4th	95	145
5th	117	149
6th	174	226
7th	203	228
8th	235	-
9th	235	-
10th	238	-

Seventh Round

Wellington started briskly but then lost wickets regularly. Parlane reached 2000 runs with his first run. Franklin got fifty from 68 balls to reach his highest score. Boam also reached his highest score. Jones led the way for Auckland, getting fifty from 66 balls, as he ensured an Auckland victory with twenty balls left.

Central Districts struggled with only three players able to reach twenty. Diamanti reached fifty off 59 balls. Boult and Arnel had their best bowling figures. Hamish Marshall became Griggs' 100th dismissal. Parlane became the leading run-scorer in domestic one-day games when he reached 53. His fifth hundred needed 103 balls as he and James Marshall added 117. Marshall took 49 balls for his fifty. Northern won with 50 balls remaining. Thompson played his fiftieth game.

Otago lost three quick wickets before captain Cumming came to the rescue. He reached fifty from 81 balls and then his third century after 125 deliveries. He had good support from Nathan McCullum who made fifty from 49 balls and his highest score as Otago reached 288-7. Canterbury disappointed in their reply. Only two players reached thirty. Stewart reached 2000 runs when on 21 while Mascarenhas and Nathan McCullum both had best bowling figures as Otago won convincingly by 125 runs.

AUCKLAND v WELLINGTON — State Shield

at Eden Park Outer Oval, Auckland on 14 January, 2009
Toss : Auckland. Umpires : P.D. Jones & T.J. Parlane
Auckland won by 3 wickets. *Points: Auckland 4, Wellington 0*

WELLINGTON

	Runs	Mins	Balls	6s	4s
M.D.Bell* lbw b Nicol	23	80	47	-	4
G.R.Napier c Hopkins b Tuffey	23	37	18	1	2
B-J.Crook run out	8	27	22	-	1
N.R.Parlane lbw b Hira	21	46	34	-	2
J.E.C.Franklin c Guptill b Hitchcock	80	120	87	-	6
C.J.Nevin† c Jones b Nicol	0	4	2	-	-
L.J.Woodcock c Hopkins b Croft	20	44	39	-	-
H.K.P.Boam b Tuffey	33	43	33	-	3
D.J.Bowden c Hopkins b Tuffey	9	15	10	-	1
A.R.Lamb not out	7	10	7	-	1
I.E.O'Brien not out	6	1	1	1	-
Extras (lb 3, w 8)	11				
TOTAL (50 overs) (9 wkts)	**241**	223			

AUCKLAND

	Runs	Mins	Balls	6s	4s
T.G.McIntosh c Nevin b Woodcock	45	85	61	-	8
M.J.Guptill c Lamb b Bowden	19	39	23	-	4
R.A.Jones* c Boam b Lamb	79	150	97	1	6
R.A.Young c Nevin b Woodcock	32	42	42	1	3
G.J.Hopkins† c Crook b Woodcock	6	18	8	-	1
R.J.Nicol c Parlane b O'Brien	31	32	23	1	4
S.J.Croft not out	19	28	14	1	2
P.A.Hitchcock b Napier	1	8	6	-	-
R.M.Hira not out	5	9	6	-	1
D.R.Tuffey					
C.S.Martin					
Extras (b 2, lb 2, w 2)	6				
TOTAL (46.4 overs) (7 wkts)	**243**	213			

Bowling	*O*	*M*	*R*	*W*
AUCKLAND				
Tuffey	10	1	32	3
Martin	9	0	66	0
Hitchcock	8	0	43	1
Croft	3	0	11	1
Nicol	10	0	35	2
Hira	10	0	51	1
WELLINGTON				
Napier	9.4	0	48	1
Bowden	10	3	50	1
O'Brien	10	1	49	1
Woodcock	10	0	36	3
Lamb	5	0	47	1
Boam	2	0	9	0

Fall of Wickets	***W***	***A***
1st	41	47
2nd	57	88
3rd	66	142
4th	106	170
5th	107	215
6th	156	223
7th	217	227
8th	220	-
9th	235	-
10th	-	-

NORTHERN DISTRICTS v CENTRAL DISTRICTS State Shield

at Cobham Oval, Whangarei on 14 January, 2009
Toss : Northern Districts. Umpires : G.A.V. Baxter & D.M. Quested
***Northern Districts won by 6 wickets.** Points: Northern Districts 4, Central Districts 0*

CENTRAL DISTRICTS

	Runs	Mins	Balls	6s	4s
D.A.J.Bracewell c Martin b Boult	11	14	9	-	2
P.J.Ingram lbw b Arnel	46	55	35	-	8
G.H.Worker c McGlashan b Arnel	7	22	17	-	-
J.M.How* b Aldridge	5	24	15	-	1
B.B.J.Griggs† b Williamson	44	91	89	-	1
K.Noema-Barnett c & b Williamson	18	48	27	1	1
B.J.Diamanti c Martin b Arnel	56	76	63	-	5
E.P.Thompson b Boult	16	34	20	-	2
R.J.Schaw b Boult	13	17	11	-	1
M.J.McClenaghan not out	9	17	8	-	1
B.E.Hefford c Marshall J.A.H. b Arnel	0	5	3	-	-
Extras (lb 4, w 5, nb 1)	10				
TOTAL (49.2 overs)	**235**	206			

NORTHERN DISTRICTS

	Runs	Mins	Balls	6s	4s
H.J.H.Marshall c Griggs b McClenaghan	6	3	6	-	1
B-J.Watling c Diamanti b Thompson	35	67	50	-	5
M.E.Parlane not out	111	171	112	-	8
J.A.H.Marshall* c Griggs b McClenaghan	64	69	57	1	5
P.D.McGlashan† c Griggs b McClenaghan	2	5	4	-	-
K.S.Williamson not out	10	31	22	-	-
J.A.F.Yovich					
G.W.Aldridge					
B.P.Martin					
T.A.Boult					
B.J.Arnel					
Extras (b 1, w 6, nb 1)	8				
TOTAL (41.4 overs) (4 wkts)	**236**	175			

Bowling	*O*	*M*	*R*	*W*
NORTHERN DISTRICTS				
Boult	10	0	65	3
Aldridge	9	1	60	1
Arnel	8.2	3	26	4
Yovich	2	0	9	0
Williamson	10	1	36	2
Martin	10	0	35	0
CENTRAL DISTRICTS				
McClenaghan	10	1	72	3
Thompson	9	0	42	1
Hefford	1.4	0	8	0
Schaw	9	0	46	0
Diamanti	6	0	30	0
Worker	6	0	37	0

Fall of Wickets	***CD***	***ND***
1st	22	6
2nd	52	76
3rd	70	193
4th	70	197
5th	111	-
6th	150	-
7th	201	-
8th	210	-
9th	231	-
10th	235	-

OTAGO v CANTERBURY State Shield

at University Oval, Dunedin on 14 January, 2009
Toss : Canterbury. Umpires : B.G. Frost & D.J. Walker
***Otago won by 125 runs.** Points: Otago 5, Canterbury 0*

OTAGO

	Runs	Mins	Balls	6s	4s
S.B.Haig b Bond	1	9	7	-	-
B.B.McCullum b Bond	1	3	5	-	-
G.R.Todd c van Wyk b Burson	9	39	18	-	2
C.D.Cumming* lbw b Frauenstein	106	142	130	-	16
N.T.Broom b Frauenstein	19	51	34	1	-
N.L.McCullum run out	71	76	55	3	7
A.D.Mascarenhas c Robertson b Bond	28	32	26	1	2
I.G.Butler not out	32	25	17	2	2
D.C.de Boorder† not out	11	13	8	1	-
N.Wagner					
J.M.McMillan					
Extras (b 2, lb 4, w 4)	10				
TOTAL (50 overs) (7 wkts)	**288**	202			

CANTERBURY

	Runs	Mins	Balls	6s	4s
I.A.Robertson c Broom b McMillan	30	47	32	3	1
M.H.W.Papps b Mascarenhas	27	41	33	-	6
P.G.Fulton c McCullum B.B. b Mascarenhas	2	35	14	-	-
J.G.Myburgh c McCullum N.L. b Mascarenhas	1	5	7	-	-
S.L.Stewart lbw b Butler	22	40	38	-	2
C.J.Anderson c de Boorder b Butler	7	50	22	-	1
C.F.K.van Wyk*† c Cumming b McCullum N.L.	14	27	33	-	1
A.M.Ellis c Cumming b McCullum N.L.	32	44	28	1	4
C.Frauenstein c Butler b McMillan	9	22	17	1	-
S.E.Bond c Haig b McCullum N.L.	6	22	9	-	-
R.D.Burson not out	2	6	7	-	-
Extras (lb 6, w 4, nb 1)	11				
TOTAL (39.5 overs)	**163**	179			

Bowling	*O*	*M*	*R*	*W*
CANTERBURY				
Bond	10	1	52	3
Burson	10	1	55	1
Ellis	10	1	72	0
Frauenstein	10	0	45	2
Myburgh	7	1	40	0
Robertson	3	0	18	0
OTAGO				
Mascarenhas	10	0	42	3
Wagner	8	1	42	0
McMillan	8	0	32	2
Butler	8	1	20	2
McCullum N.L.	5.5	0	21	3

Fall of Wickets	***O***	***C***
1st	2	59
2nd	7	61
3rd	28	62
4th	93	81
5th	180	92
6th	227	109
7th	249	113
8th	-	129
9th	-	158
10th	-	163

Eighth Round

Parlane and Elliott added 162 from 156 balls for the Wellington third wicket. Parlane, who batted with a runner for most of his innings, got fifty from 64 balls and reached his maiden century after 112 balls. Elliott got fifty from 47 balls as Wellington finished at 289-9. Boult had career best bowling figures. Northern started well with the opening stand of 93 taking just 14 overs. Hamish Marshall needed just 34 balls for his fifty while Watling needed 67. James Marshall then got fifty from 59 deliveries but he went at 248-5. Northern started the last over at 280-7 and lost Southee and Boult off the first two balls. Arnel got a single off the third ball, McGlashan tried a reverse sweep off the fourth but missed so nine runs were needed off the last two balls. McGlashan hit the fifth ball out of the Basin Reserve and then repeated the dose with the last ball to give Northern a win by one wicket. Franklin played his fiftieth game.

Canterbury had a century opening stand as Papps reached fifty from 73 balls. Myburgh then hit fifty from just 37 balls to steer Canterbury to 298-6. He and Stewart added 102 off 64 balls for the fourth wicket. Noema-Barnett had his best bowling figures. Central had a poor start being 56-6 in the fifteenth over. Noema-Barnett gave the innings some substance as he reached his maiden fifty from 45 balls but it was to no avail as Central were dismissed for 166, giving Canterbury a 132 run win.

The game between Otago and Auckland was abandoned.

WELLINGTON v NORTHERN DISTRICTS — State Shield

at Allied Nationwide Finance Basin Reserve, Wellington on 17 January, 2009
Toss : Northern Districts. Umpires : G.A.V. Baxter & E.A. Watkin
Northern Districts won by 1 wicket. *Points: Northern Districts 4, Wellington 0*

WELLINGTON

	Runs	Mins	Balls	6s	4s
M.D.Bell* b Boult	11	28	21	-	2
J.D.Ryder c Arnel b Southee	28	40	28	-	3
N.R.Parlane run out	105	152	114	-	10
G.R.Napier b Boult	6	28	19	-	-
G.D.Elliott c Flynn b Boult	78	98	71	2	2
J.E.C.Franklin c Watling b Arnel	11	23	12	-	1
C.J.Nevin† b Arnel	13	18	13	-	2
L.J.Woodcock run out	5	10	5	-	-
M.R.Gillespie c Arnel b Boult	2	9	7	-	-
J.S.Patel not out	10	13	8	1	-
I.E.O'Brien not out	5	6	2	-	1
Extras (lb 8, w 7)	15				
TOTAL (50 overs) (9 wkts)	**289**	217			

NORTHERN DISTRICTS

	Runs	Mins	Balls	6s	4s
B-J.Watling b Patel	63	129	85	-	4
H.J.H.Marshall c Franklin b Patel	52	62	38	-	8
M.E.Parlane lbw b O'Brien	3	12	11	-	-
J.A.H.Marshall* c Nevin b Gillespie	74	119	82	-	5
D.R.Flynn lbw b Patel	6	8	8	-	-
K.S.Williamson c Napier b O'Brien	26	39	29	-	2
P.D.McGlashan† not out	39	59	30	3	1
B.P.Martin b O'Brien	2	5	4	-	-
T.G.Southee b Gillespie	8	27	13	-	-
T.A.Boult b Gillespie	0	1	1	-	-
B.J.Arnel not out	1	6	1	-	-
Extras (b 4, lb 4, w 9, nb 2)	19				
TOTAL (50 overs) (9 wkts)	**293**	238			

Bowling	O	M	R	W
NORTHERN DISTRICTS				
Boult	10	0	50	4
Southee	10	1	61	1
Arnel	10	1	53	2
Martin	10	0	53	0
Williamson	2	0	16	0
Flynn	8	0	48	0
WELLINGTON				
Napier	9	0	47	0
Franklin	4	0	25	0
Gillespie	8	0	71	3
O'Brien	10	0	43	3
Patel	10	0	43	3
Woodcock	4	0	25	0
Elliott	5	0	31	0

Fall of Wickets	*W*	*ND*
1st	34	93
2nd	44	98
3rd	68	167
4th	230	173
5th	245	226
6th	262	248
7th	272	251
8th	272	280
9th	276	280
10th		

CANTERBURY v CENTRAL DISTRICTS **State Shield**

at Queen Elizabeth II Park, Christchurch on 17 January, 2009
Toss : Central Districts. Umpires : B.G. Frost & D.J. Walker
***Canterbury won by 132 runs.** Points: Canterbury 5, Central Districts 0*

CANTERBURY

	Runs	Mins	Balls	6s	4s
I.A.Robertson lbw b Diamanti	46	102	73	-	6
M.H.W.Papps lbw b Worker	69	137	95	-	10
P.G.Fulton b Schaw	27	53	41	-	2
J.G.Myburgh c Thompson b Noema-Barnett	71	65	48	3	7
S.L.Stewart c How b Noema-Barnett	44	43	35	1	6
C.J.Anderson b McClenaghan	13	10	6	1	1
C.Frauenstein not out	1	9	1	-	-
C.F.K.van Wyk*† not out	1	1	1	-	-
S.E.Bond					
R.D.Burson					
L.M.Burtt					
Extras (b 1, lb 16, w 9)	26				
TOTAL (50 overs) (6 wkts)	**298**	213			

CENTRAL DISTRICTS

	Runs	Mins	Balls	6s	4s
P.J.Ingram c van Wyk b Bond	7	23	8	1	-
G.H.Worker c Fulton b Bond	2	12	11	-	-
J.M.How c van Wyk b Bond	0	1	1	-	-
M.S.Sinclair* c Frauenstein b Burson	14	24	19	-	2
L.R.P.L.Taylor b Burtt	14	46	27	-	2
B.B.J.Griggs† lbw b Burson	14	18	15	-	3
B.J.Diamanti c Myburgh b Frauenstein	20	52	36	-	2
K.Noema-Barnett c Burson b Frauenstein	63	83	56	4	5
E.P.Thompson lbw b Burson	16	29	25	-	1
R.J.Schaw b Burtt	7	9	7	-	1
M.J.McClenaghan not out	0	2	0	-	-
Extras (w 3, nb 6)	9				
TOTAL (33.1 overs)	**166**	154			

Bowling	*O*	*M*	*R*	*W*
CENTRAL DISTRICTS				
Thompson	10	2	49	0
McClenaghan	9	1	73	1
Diamanti	10	1	26	1
Schaw	10	0	53	1
Noema-Barnett	4	0	30	2
Worker	7	0	50	1
CANTERBURY				
Bond	8	0	25	3
Burtt	8	1	58	2
Burson	8	1	21	3
Frauenstein	6.1	0	43	2
Myburgh	3	0	19	0

Fall of Wickets

	C	*CD*
1st	100	11
2nd	155	11
3rd	181	20
4th	283	30
5th	284	46
6th	297	56
7th	-	119
8th	-	156
9th	-	166
10th	-	166

OTAGO v AUCKLAND **State Shield**

at University Oval, Dunedin on 17 January, 2009
***Abandoned without a ball being bowled.** Points: Otago 2, Auckland 2*

Ninth Round

After a good start Wellington crumbled to be dismissed for 217 in a game reduced to 49 overs. With Canterbury requiring 221 in 49 overs Robertson went early, but Fulton and Myburgh then took control. Fulton scored fifty from 91 balls and Myburgh fifty from 76 as Canterbury won with 28 balls left.

Otago made a solid start, Brendon McCullum getting fifty from 57 balls. Mascarenhas then hit fifty from just 25 balls to enable Otago to reach 311-8. Central had a reasonable start but once the opening stand was broken, the top order crumbled. Only Sinclair, fifty off 65 balls, and Thompson enabled Central to reach 248.

Auckland lost two wickets in the third over, when Young came to the crease. He scored fifty from 65 balls and reached his maiden century after a further 61 and Auckland were dismissed for 259. Watling and James Marshall added 155 for the third wicket. Watling scored his fifty from 63 balls and his fourth century from 110 deliveries. Marshall required 62 balls for his fifty. Northern won with 33 balls left. Tuffey took his hundredth wicket.

WELLINGTON v CANTERBURY — State Shield

at Allied Nationwide Finance Basin Reserve, Wellington on 19 January, 2009
Toss : Wellington. Umpires : P.D. Jones & D.M. Quested
***Canterbury won by 7 wickets.** Points: Canterbury 4, Wellington 0*

WELLINGTON

	Runs	Mins	Balls	6s	4s
M.D.Bell* c Burson b Frauenstein	37	106	63	-	2
J.D.Ryder b Burson	35	42	29	1	4
B-J.Crook c van Wyk b Ellis	4	11	9	-	1
G.D.Elliott c Papps b Ellis	9	17	17	-	2
J.E.C.Franklin lbw b Burtt	45	84	65	-	2
C.J.Nevin† c van Wyk b Burson	3	16	12	-	-
G.R.Napier c van Wyk b Burtt	20	44	29	-	2
L.J.Woodcock b Bond	20	37	35	-	1
J.S.Patel b Bond	11	30	14	-	-
I.E.O'Brien not out	8	17	13	-	-
M.R.Gillespie not out	12	13	8	-	2
Extras (b 4, lb 4, w 5)	13				
TOTAL (49 overs) (9 wkts)	**217**	213			

CANTERBURY

	Runs	Mins	Balls	6s	4s
I.A.Robertson c Nevin b Napier	2	27	19	-	-
M.H.W.Papps b Napier	32	36	26	-	7
P.G.Fulton not out	85	162	122	1	5
J.G.Myburgh c Napier b Patel	51	101	79	1	2
S.L.Stewart not out	30	51	29	1	2
C.F.K.van Wyk*†					
A.M.Ellis					
C.Frauenstein					
S.E.Bond					
R.D.Burson					
L.M.Burtt					
Extras (lb 13, w 8)	21				
TOTAL (45.5 overs) (3 wkts)	**221**	190			

Bowling	*O*	*M*	*R*	*W*
CANTERBURY				
Bond	10	1	19	2
Burtt	10	0	52	2
Burson	10	0	54	2
Ellis	8	1	35	2
Frauenstein	5	0	24	1
Myburgh	6	0	25	0
WELLINGTON				
Gillespie	8	0	37	0
Napier	7	0	40	2
Patel	10	0	37	1
O'Brien	8	0	25	0
Woodcock	6.5	0	48	0
Elliott	3	0	11	0
Franklin	3	0	10	0

Fall of Wickets	***W***	***C***
1st	48	31
2nd	61	50
3rd	78	144
4th	111	-
5th	126	-
6th	159	-
7th	170	-
8th	196	-
9th	197	-
10th	-	-

CENTRAL DISTRICTS v OTAGO — State Shield

at Pukekura Park, New Plymouth on 21 January, 2009
Toss : Central Districts. Umpires : B.G. Frost & P.D. Jones
***Otago won by 63 runs.** Points: Otago 5, Central Districts 0*

OTAGO

	Runs	Mins	Balls	6s	4s
B.B.McCullum c Ingram b Noema-Barnett	82	146	94	1	9
S.B.Haig b Thompson	17	41	28	-	4
G.R.Todd c Taylor b Hefford	26	43	30	-	3
C.D.Cumming* c Thompson b Worker	48	45	53	1	3
N.T.Broom c How b Thompson	39	44	37	1	3
N.L.McCullum c Diamanti b Thompson	9	18	16	-	-
A.D.Mascarenhas not out	53	46	27	3	5
D.C.de Boorder† c How b McClenaghan	2	16	6	-	-
I.G.Butler b Hefford	1	2	3	-	-
W.C.McSkimming not out	17	8	8	1	2
N.Wagner					
Extras (b 4, lb 1, w 10, nb 2)	17				
TOTAL (50 overs) (8 wkts)	**311**	205			

CENTRAL DISTRICTS

	Runs	Mins	Balls	6s	4s
G.H.Worker c McCullum B.B. b Wagner	25	35	31	-	4
P.J.Ingram b McSkimming	37	72	49	-	4
J.M.How b Wagner	0	1	1	-	-
L.R.P.L.Taylor c Broom b Butler	8	29	15	-	1
M.S.Sinclair* c Mascarenhas b Wagner	68	130	85	-	5
K.Noema-Barnett c de Boorder b Butler	3	7	6	-	-
B.J.Diamanti b Butler	0	1	2	-	-
B.B.J.Griggs† c McCullum B.B. b Mascarenhas	28	54	47	-	4
E.P.Thompson b McSkimming	40	54	38	1	2
M.J.McClenaghan not out	10	25	16	-	1
B.E.Hefford lbw b Wagner	2	19	6	-	-
Extras (lb 18, w 9)	27				
TOTAL (49.2 overs)	**248**	218			

Bowling	*O*	*M*	*R*	*W*
CENTRAL DISTRICTS				
Thompson	10	0	45	3
McClenaghan	8	0	58	1
Hefford	7	0	57	2
Diamanti	10	0	72	0
Noema-Barnett	9	0	51	1
Worker	6	0	23	1
OTAGO				
Wagner	9.2	1	39	4
Mascarenhas	10	0	44	1
McSkimming	8	0	39	2
Butler	10	1	50	3
McCullum N.L.	10	0	52	0
Cumming	2	0	6	0

Fall of Wickets	***O***	***CD***
1st	52	40
2nd	103	40
3rd	175	76
4th	185	76
5th	210	81
6th	257	81
7th	286	147
8th	287	229
9th	-	231
10th	-	248

AUCKLAND v NORTHERN DISTRICTS — State Shield

at Eden Park Outer Oval, Auckland on 21 January, 2009
Toss : Northern Districts. Umpires : D.J. Walker & E.A. Watkin
***Northern Districts won by 7 wickets.** Points: Northern Districts 4, Auckland 0*

AUCKLAND

	Runs	Mins	Balls	6s	4s
T.G.McIntosh b Scott	30	83	59	-	4
M.J.Guptill c Parlane b Southee	5	10	7	-	1
R.A.Jones* c Parlane b Southee	0	1	2	-	-
R.A.Young b Southee	119	183	134	2	11
G.J.Hopkins† c Scott b Arnel	29	38	42	-	1
R.J.Nicol c Parlane b Arnel	34	45	30	-	4
P.A.Hitchcock c Flynn b Arnel	0	2	2	-	-
S.J.Croft c Marshall J.A.H. b Scott	12	16	13	-	1
R.M.Hira run out	12	13	6	-	2
D.R.Tuffey c Marshall J.A.H. b Scott	1	3	2	-	-
C.S.Martin not out	0	2	1	-	-
Extras (b 5, lb 10, w 2)	17				
TOTAL (50 overs)	**259**	203			

NORTHERN DISTRICTS

	Runs	Mins	Balls	6s	4s
H.J.H.Marshall c sub (A.K.Kitchen) b Hira	25	48	35	-	4
B-J.Watling not out	113	184	125	1	11
M.E.Parlane c Hira b Nicol	32	20	19	-	5
J.A.H.Marshall* c Nicol b Tuffey	79	102	83	-	8
D.R.Flynn not out	2	11	6	-	-
K.S.Williamson					
P.D.McGlashan†					
B.E.Scott					
T.G.Southee					
T.A.Boult					
B.J.Arnel					
Extras (lb 3, w 8, nb 1)	12				
TOTAL (44.3 overs) (3 wkts)	**263**	184			

Bowling	*O*	*M*	*R*	*W*
NORTHERN DISTRICTS				
Southee	10	2	46	3
Boult	7	1	40	0
Scott	10	0	55	3
Arnel	10	0	47	3
Williamson	10	0	39	0
Flynn	3	0	17	0
AUCKLAND				
Tuffey	9	0	61	1
Martin	8	0	47	0
Hitchcock	8	0	50	0
Hira	7	0	42	1
Nicol	10	0	45	1
Croft	2	0	10	0
Jones	0.3	0	5	0

Fall of Wickets	***A***	***ND***
1st	5	57
2nd	5	97
3rd	84	252
4th	142	-
5th	206	-
6th	207	-
7th	233	-
8th	253	-
9th	254	-
10th	259	-

Tenth Round

Canterbury were in trouble at 74-4 before Stewart and Anderson added 139 for the fifth wicket. Stewart got fifty from 54 balls and his second hundred off 82 balls. It was his highest score. Anderson reached his maiden fifty from 55 balls. Northern were down and out at 66-5 before Williamson and McGlashan created a new sixth wicket record in domestic one-day cricket with a stand of 196 off 200 balls. Both scored maiden hundreds, Williamson taking 128 balls and McGlashan 86. It was to no avail, however, as Canterbury won by five runs to get a place in the semi-final.

Central lost Ingram early but fifties from Worker (highest score) and Sinclair enabled them to reach 301-8. The pair added 111 for the third wicket and Central scored 99 from the last 77 balls. When he reached 6 Griggs had made 1000 runs. Croft had his best figures with the ball. Guptill went early but Auckland's batsmen either got to thirty or couldn't make double figures. Mills got the only fifty (off 44 balls) as Central won by 51 runs.

Cumming and Broom scored fifties for Otago as they reached 244. Cumming required 45 balls compared to Broom's 68. Napier went early in Wellington's innings but fifties to Crook (50 balls) and Franklin (77 balls) helped. Franklin and Allen made their highest scores as they added 67 for the seventh wicket. Wellington eventually won off the last ball with nine wickets down. Todd was playing his fiftieth game.

NORTHERN DISTRICTS v CANTERBURY — State Shield

at Seddon Park, Hamilton on 25 January, 2009
Toss : Northern Districts. Umpires : B.F. Bowden & E.A. Watkin
***Canterbury won by 5 runs.** Points: Canterbury 4, Northern Districts 0*

CANTERBURY

	Runs	Mins	Balls	6s	4s
I.A.Robertson c McGlashan b Yovich	31	91	55	-	6
M.H.W.Papps lbw b Boult	1	5	5	-	-
P.G.Fulton c Yovich b Arnel	31	69	53	1	3
J.G.Myburgh c Flynn b Yovich	6	12	10	-	1
S.L.Stewart b Boult	120	123	90	5	11
C.J.Anderson c McGlashan b Arnel	71	90	70	3	4
A.M.Ellis run out	0	3	3	-	-
C.F.K.van Wyk*† not out	9	28	11	-	-
S.E.Bond b Boult	0	2	3	-	-
R.D.Burson					
L.M.Burtt					
Extras (lb 4, w 1)	5				
TOTAL (50 overs) (8 wkts)	**274**	215			

NORTHERN DISTRICTS

	Runs	Mins	Balls	6s	4s
B-J.Watling lbw b Burson	12	33	15	-	2
H.J.H.Marshall c Papps b Bond	0	2	2	-	-
M.E.Parlane c van Wyk b Bond	13	24	24	-	2
J.A.H.Marshall*c Anderson b Ellis	17	41	27	-	2
D.R.Flynn lbw b Bond	4	6	8	-	1
K.S.Williamson run out	100	162	128	2	7
P.D.McGlashan† c Papps b Bond	112	129	94	6	8
J.A.F.Yovich not out	1	5	1	-	-
B.E.Scott not out	4	1	1	-	-
T.A.Boult					
B.J.Arnel					
Extras (lb 4, w 2)	6				
TOTAL (50 overs) (7 wkts)	**269**	205			

Bowling	O	M	R	W
NORTHERN DISTRICTS				
Scott	10	1	61	0
Boult	10	0	48	3
Arnel	10	1	49	2
Yovich	10	0	56	2
Williamson	6	0	31	0
Marshall H.J.H.	4	0	25	0
CANTERBURY				
Bond	10	0	56	4
Burtt	10	0	61	0
Burson	10	0	57	1
Ellis	10	0	45	1
Myburgh	10	0	46	0

Fall of Wickets	C	ND
1st	2	1
2nd	65	26
3rd	73	28
4th	74	33
5th	213	66
6th	214	262
7th	274	265
8th	274	-
9th	-	-
10th	-	-

CENTRAL DISTRICTS v AUCKLAND — State Shield

at Pukekura Park, New Plymouth on 25 January, 2009
Toss : Auckland. Umpires : P.D. Jones & D.J. Walker
Central Districts won by 51 runs. *Points: Central Districts 4, Auckland 0*

CENTRAL DISTRICTS

	Runs	Mins	Balls	6s	4s
G.H.Worker c Young b Croft	86	153	104	3	8
P.J.Ingram c Hopkins b Martin	9	20	9	-	2
J.M.How st Hopkins b Tuffey	46	58	42	1	7
M.S.Sinclair* not out	87	135	101	1	7
K.Noema-Barnett c Guptill b Nicol	5	5	6	-	1
B.J.Diamanti c Hopkins b Mills	25	27	18	-	4
B.B.J.Griggs† b Croft	26	19	16	1	3
E.P.Thompson c Nicol b Croft	1	2	2	-	-
D.A.J.Bracewell run out	1	3	2	-	-
R.J.Schaw not out	4	1	1	-	1
M.J.McClenaghan					
Extras (b 1, lb 5, w 4, nb 1)	11				
TOTAL (50 overs) (8 wkts)	**301**	215			

AUCKLAND

	Runs	Mins	Balls	6s	4s
T.G.McIntosh c & b Diamanti	44	65	58	-	6
M.J.Guptill c Bracewell b McClenaghan	5	8	4	-	1
R.A.Jones* b Diamanti	33	73	39	1	3
R.A.Young c Diamanti b Schaw	38	44	40	1	3
G.J.Hopkins† c Griggs b Worker	3	6	6	-	-
R.J.Nicol b Diamanti	45	71	61	1	2
K.D.Mills not out	57	78	51	2	5
S.J.Croft c Worker b Thompson	3	14	8	-	-
R.M.Hira b Diamanti	0	5	4	-	-
D.R.Tuffey c Sinclair b Thompson	1	3	3	-	-
C.S.Martin b Thompson	0	2	3	-	-
Extras (lb 7, w 11, nb 3)	21				
TOTAL (45.4 overs)	**250**	**189**			

Bowling	O	M	R	W
AUCKLAND				
Martin	7	0	44	1
Mills	10	1	61	1
Tuffey	10	0	57	1
Hira	9	0	51	0
Nicol	10	0	55	1
Croft	4	0	27	3
CENTRAL DISTRICTS				
Thompson	9.4	0	46	3
McClenaghan	6	0	46	1
Diamanti	8	0	34	4
Schaw	10	0	51	1
Worker	9	0	35	1
Bracewell	3	0	31	0

Fall of Wickets	***CD***	***A***
1st	18	11
2nd	91	91
3rd	202	114
4th	209	118
5th	250	148
6th	292	234
7th	294	249
8th	296	249
9th	-	250
10th	-	250

OTAGO v WELLINGTON — State Shield

at Queen's Park, Invercargill on 25 January, 2009
Toss : Wellington. Umpires : G.A.V. Baxter & B.G. Frost
Wellington won by 1 wicket. *Points: Wellington 4, Otago 0*

OTAGO

	Runs	Mins	Balls	6s	4s
A.J.Redmond c Allen b Patel	46	82	59	1	7
S.B.Haig c O'Brien b Bowden	4	6	4	-	1
G.R.Todd run out	19	37	27	-	2
C.D.Cumming* c Patel b Franklin	54	71	50	1	5
N.T.Broom c Allen b Napier	77	120	81	2	5
N.L.McCullum run out	16	28	24	-	1
A.D.Mascarenhas lbw b Patel	4	6	6	-	1
D.C.de Boorder† c Patel b O'Brien	7	25	23	-	-
W.C.McSkimming b Napier	2	6	6	-	-
I.G.Butler b Napier	3	10	7	-	-
N.Wagner not out	6	6	4	-	1
Extras (lb 4, w 2)	6				
TOTAL (48.3 overs)	**244**	208			

WELLINGTON

	Runs	Mins	Balls	6s	4s
M.D.Bell* c & b McSkimming	32	63	50	-	4
G.R.Napier lbw b Wagner	2	3	2	-	-
B-J.Crook c de Boorder b McSkimming	52	88	52	2	6
G.D.Elliott lbw b McSkimming	4	4	5	-	1
J.E.C.Franklin not out	87	157	98	2	7
J.J.B.Dean run out	3	14	14	-	-
L.J.Woodcock c de Boorder b Butler	5	16	14	-	-
S.R.Allen† b Wagner	22	58	40	1	-
D.J.Bowden b Wagner	17	24	15	-	2
J.S.Patel c McCullum b Wagner	9	11	9	-	1
I.E.O'Brien not out	0	5	1	-	-
Extras (lb 5, w 7)	12				
TOTAL (50 overs) (9 wkts)	**245**				

Bowling	O	M	R	W
WELLINGTON				
Napier	9.3	1	55	3
Bowden	5	0	22	1
Franklin	7	1	32	1
O'Brien	9	0	48	1
Patel	10	0	41	2
Woodcock	5	0	26	0
Elliott	3	0	16	0
OTAGO				
Wagner	10	0	55	4
Mascarenhas	10	2	31	0
Butler	9	0	53	1
McSkimming	10	0	52	3
Cumming	1	0	7	0
McCullum	10	0	42	0

Fall of Wickets	***O***	***W***
1st	10	3
2nd	51	79
3rd	89	84
4th	147	101
5th	179	113
6th	185	123
7th	210	190
8th	214	230
9th	235	240
10th	244	-

CANTERBURY v OTAGO — Semi-final

at Queen Elizabeth II Park, Christchurch on 28 January, 2009
Toss : Otago. Umpires : B.F. Bowden & E.A. Watkin
Otago won by 8 wickets.

In a great bowling effort Otago dismissed Canterbury for just 86. McSkimming reached 100 wickets in the process. Only two Canterbury batsmen were able to reach double figures and extras was the third highest scorer. Despite Bond taking two quick wickets, Otago knocked the runs off in just 14 overs to reach their third successive State Shield final.

CANTERBURY

	Runs	Mins	Balls	6s	4s
M.H.W.Papps lbw b Wagner	5	34	15	-	-
I.A.Robertson b Wagner	0	2	3	-	-
C.F.K.van Wyk*† c de Boorder b Wagner	8	25	28	-	1
J.G.Myburgh c de Boorder b McSkimming	4	40	31	-	-
S.L.Stewart b Mascarenhas	5	22	17	-	-
C.J.Anderson c Todd b McCullum	23	49	35	-	3
C.Z.Harris not out	12	90	60	-	1
A.M.Ellis b Butler	8	18	18	-	1
S.E.Bond c Cumming b McCullum	7	11	10	1	-
R.D.Burson c de Boorder b McSkimming	4	17	14	-	-
L.M.Burtt b McSkimming	0	3	3	-	-
Extras (lb 5, w 5)	10				
TOTAL (39 overs)	**86**	160			

OTAGO

	Runs	Mins	Balls	6s	4s
A.J.Redmond not out	48	60	41	-	10
S.B.Haig b Bond	3	14	11	-	-
G.R.Todd b Bond	0	5	1	-	-
C.D.Cumming* not out	38	39	31	-	7
N.L.McCullum					
S.W.Eathorne					
A.D.Mascarenhas					
D.C.de Boorder†					
I.G.Butler					
W.C.McSkimming					
N.Wagner					
Extras (w 1)	1				
TOTAL (14 overs) (2 wkts)	**90**	60			

Bowling	*O*	*M*	*R*	*W*
OTAGO				
Wagner	7	3	11	3
Mascarenhas	10	1	16	1
McSkimming	8	2	13	3
McCullum	9	1	23	2
Butler	5	0	18	1
CANTERBURY				
Bond	5	0	39	2
Burtt	2	0	9	0
Burson	2	0	12	0
Harris	2	0	11	0
Ellis	3	1	19	0

Fall of Wickets	*C*	*O*
1st	0	5
2nd	13	13
3rd	14	-
4th	24	-
5th	31	-
6th	57	-
7th	68	-
8th	79	-
9th	86	-
10th	86	-

NORTHERN DISTRICTS v OTAGO — Final

at Seddon Park, Hamilton on 31 January, 2009
Toss : Otago. Umpires : G.A.V. Baxter & E.A. Watkin
Northern Districts won by 49 runs.

Northern were in trouble at 125-6 but Yovich and Aldridge added 64 off 12 overs to give the innings some substance. Both players reached their highest scores. Butler had career best figures of 5-55. and passed 50 wickets in the process.

Otago had a poor start and when Mascarenhas came to the crease the score was 78-5 with 161 needed from 178 balls. He then proceeded to score just 17 from 70 balls. The run rate went to 116 from 70 balls when he was dismissed as soon as he tried to attack. Butler hit out at the end to suggest what might have been but Northern won the State Shield for the first time since 2004/05. An interesting fact from the game was that all three slow bowlers, McCullum, Martin and Williamson each conceded 23 runs from their ten overs with the two Northern spinners bowling five maidens between them.

NORTHERN DISTRICTS

	Runs	Mins	Balls	6s	4s
H.J.H.Marshall c Haig b Wagner	8	12	16	-	1
B-J.Watling c de Boorder b Butler	28	80	55	-	3
M.E.Parlane run out	18	40	23	1	1
J.A.H.Marshall* c de Boorder b Butler	13	17	14	-	3
K.S.Williamson c Todd b McCullum	13	38	25	-	2
P.D.McGlashan† c Rutherford b Mascarenhas	17	55	38	1	-
J.A.F.Yovich not out	78	108	76	3	6
G.W.Aldridge c Todd b Butler	36	54	39	1	3
B.P.Martin c de Boorder b Butler	8	10	6	-	1
B.E.Scott b Butler	4	10	6	-	-
B.J.Arnel not out	5	5	3	-	1
Extras (b 4, lb 2, w 3, nb 1)	10				
TOTAL (50 overs) (9 wkts)	**238**	224			

OTAGO

	Runs	Mins	Balls	6s	4s
S.B.Haig b Aldridge	5	6	8	-	1
H.D.Rutherford c Yovich b Arnel	8	38	20	-	1
G.R.Todd c & b Aldridge	11	22	19	-	2
A.J.Redmond c Aldridge b Martin	29	53	39	-	6
S.W.Eathorne lbw b Martin	21	50	31	-	3
N.L.McCullum* c Williamson b Aldridge	33	68	50	-	3
A.D.Mascarenhas b Aldridge	17	48	70	-	-
W.C.McSkimming c Marshall H.J.H. b Aldridge	0	2	1	-	-
I.G.Butler c Williamson b Arnel	44	40	23	4	2
D.C.de Boorder† c Marshall H.J.H. b Scott	10	20	11	-	1
N.Wagner not out	2	2	2	-	-
Extras (lb 1, w 8)	9				
TOTAL (45.4 overs)	**189**	184			

Bowling	O	M	R	W
OTAGO				
Wagner	10	0	48	1
Mascarenhas	10	0	38	1
McSkimming	10	0	68	0
Butler	10	1	55	5
McCullum	10	1	23	1
NORTHERN DISTRICTS				
Scott	7.4	0	59	1
Aldridge	9	0	39	5
Arnel	7	2	33	2
Yovich	2	0	11	0
Martin	10	2	23	2
Williamson	10	3	23	0

Fall of Wickets

	ND	O
1st	9	6
2nd	49	25
3rd	68	31
4th	69	75
5th	94	78
6th	125	123
7th	189	123
8th	202	132
9th	221	186
10th	-	189

2008/09 STATE SHIELD AVERAGES

	M	In	NO	HS	Runs	Ave	100s	50s	Ct	St	O	M	R	W	Ave	R/O	Best
G.W.Aldridge	4	2	1	36	38	38.00	-	-	3	-	32	1	162	7	23.14	5.06	5-39
S.R.Allen	1	1	0	22	22	22.00	-	-	2	-							
C.J.Anderson	5	5	0	71	116	23.20	-	1	1	-							
B.J.Arnel	9	4	4	7*	13	-	-	-	2	-	78.1	9	353	17	20.76	4.51	4-26
M.D.Bates	2	2	2	15*	25	-	-	-	-	-	11	1	53	0	-	4.82	-
M.D.Bell	10	10	1	124	336	37.33	1	1	3	-							
H.K.Bennett	2	1	1	3*	3	-	-	-	-	-	9	0	53	0	-	5.89	-
H.K.P.Boam	5	3	1	33	54	27.00	-	-	3	-	19	0	117	1	117.00	6.16	1-53
S.E.Bond	10	4	0	7	18	4.50	-	-	-	-	93	6	448	19	23.57	4.82	4-56
T.A.Boult	9	2	0	10	10	5.00	-	-	6	-	80.5	6	398	16	24.87	4.92	4-50
D.J.Bowden	3	2	0	17	26	13.00	-	-	-	-	25	3	110	3	36.66	4.40	1-22
D.A.J.Bracewell	8	6	0	55	87	14.50	-	1	3	-	34.4	1	203	4	50.75	5.85	2-24
N.T.Broom	6	5	0	77	148	29.60	-	1	3	-							
R.D.Burson	9	3	2	5*	11	11.00	-	-	3	-	75	6	349	13	26.84	4.65	3-21
L.M.Burtt	4	1	0	0	0	0.00	-	-	-	-	30	1	180	4	45.00	6.00	2-52
I.G.Butler	9	7	1	44	128	21.33	-	-	1	-	75.2	4	357	18	19.83	4.73	5-55
S.J.Croft	9	9	1	59	209	26.12	-	1	-	-	39	0	209	8	26.12	5.36	3-27
B-J.Crook	9	9	0	75	250	27.77	-	3	2	-							
C.D.Cumming	9	9	3	106	421	70.16	1	2	7	-	33	1	134	2	67.00	4.06	1-17
M.P.F.Davidson	1	-	-	-	-	-	-	-	1	-	8.1	0	48	0	-	5.88	-
D.C.de Boorder	10	7	1	43	116	19.33	-	-	14	-							
C.de Grandhomme	6	5	1	38*	66	16.50	-	-	2	-	31	1	157	3	52.33	5.06	3-38
J.J.B.Dean	2	1	0	3	3	3.00	-	-	-	-							
B.J.Diamanti	10	8	3	56	199	39.80	-	1	5	-	88.2	1	430	12	35.83	4.86	4-34
S.W.Eathorne	2	1	0	21	21	21.00	-	-	-	-							
G.D.Elliott	6	6	0	78	145	24.16	-	1	-	-	39	1	184	6	30.66	4.72	3-32
A.M.Ellis	9	6	0	32	64	10.66	-	-	-	-	73.2	6	391	11	35.54	5.33	3-50
D.R.Flynn	4	4	1	6	14	4.66	-	-	3	-	11	0	65	0	-	5.91	-
J.E.C.Franklin	7	7	1	87*	306	51.00	-	2	4	-	28.4	1	132	2	66.00	4.60	1-31
C.Frauenstein	4	3	1	9	18	9.00	-	-	1	-	28.1	0	148	8	18.50	5.25	3-36
P.G.Fulton	9	9	1	85*	339	42.37	-	3	2	-							
M.R.Gillespie	4	3	1	12*	25	12.50	-	-	1	-	35	1	186	7	26.57	5.31	3-44
B.B.J.Griggs	10	10	1	44	185	20.55	-	-	14	1							
M.J.Guptill	8	8	0	124	236	29.50	1	1	3	-							
S.B.Haig	9	9	0	79	226	25.11	-	2	3	-							
C.Z.Harris	5	5	2	62*	105	35.00	-	1	1	-	40	1	166	2	83.00	4.15	1-33
B.E.Hefford	5	2	0	2	2	1.00	-	-	-	-	30.4	2	166	5	33.20	5.41	2-23
B.C.Hiini	4	4	2	16*	52	26.00	-	-	1	-	27	1	135	2	67.50	5.00	2-23
R.M.Hira	9	9	3	41	73	12.16	-	-	4	-	83	4	376	4	94.00	4.53	1-36
P.A.Hitchcock	8	8	2	46*	120	20.00	-	-	-	-	61	1	348	5	69.60	5.70	1-27
G.J.Hopkins	9	9	1	86*	183	22.87	-	1	15	1							
M.V.Houghton	2	1	0	1	1	1.00	-	-	-	-	9.2	0	72	0	-	7.71	-
J.M.How	7	7	1	88*	148	24.66	-	1	4	-							
P.J.Ingram	10	10	0	91	386	38.60	-	3	2	-							
R.A.Jones	9	9	0	79	226	25.11	-	2	1	-	0.3	0	5	0	-	-	-
R.P.C.Karaitiana	5	3	1	11	13	6.50	-	-	-	-	32	3	147	3	49.00	4.59	2-18
A.K.Kitchen	5	5	0	69	162	32.40	-	2	1	-							
A.R.Lamb	2	1	1	7*	7	-	-	-	1	-	13	0	99	1	99.00	7.62	1-47
H.J.H.Marshall	11	11	0	113	319	29.00	1	2	2	-	4	0	25	0	-	6.25	-
J.A.H.Marshall	11	10	0	79	388	38.80	-	4	4	-							
B.P.Martin	9	6	2	11*	31	7.75	-	-	6	-	81	7	300	8	37.50	3.70	2-23
C.S.Martin	9	4	1	0*	0	0.00	-	-	2	-	77.2	6	400	12	33.33	5.17	4-33
A.D.Mascarenhas	9	6	2	75*	178	44.50	-	2	2	-	84	6	294	9	32.66	3.50	3-42
M.J.Mason	3	2	2	16*	19	-	-	-	-	-	24	3	122	2	61.00	5.08	1-26
M.J.McClenaghan	8	3	3	10*	19	-	-	-	1	-	68.2	5	411	13	31.61	6.01	3-72
B.B.McCullum	3	3	0	82	87	29.00	-	1	3	-							
N.L.McCullum	10	8	1	71	205	29.28	-	1	4	-	90.5	2	356	9	39.55	3.91	3-21
P.D.McGlashan	11	8	2	112	272	45.33	1	1	6	1							
T.G.McIntosh	4	4	0	71	190	47.50	-	1	-	-							
J.M.McMillan	2	1	1	0*	0	-	-	-	-	-	17.3	1	83	4	20.75	4.74	2-32
W.C.McSkimming	7	4	1	17*	19	6.33	-	-	1	-	56	4	244	10	24.40	4.36	3-13
K.D.Mills	1	1	1	57*	57	-	-	1	-	-	10	1	61	1	61.00	6.10	1-61
S.J.Murdoch	5	5	0	19	42	8.40	-	-	1	-							
J.G.Myburgh	10	10	0	90	324	32.40	-	4	1	-	48.1	1	229	2	114.50	4.75	1-23
G.R.Napier	10	9	0	50	156	17.33	-	1	2	-	92.4	5	437	21	20.80	4.71	4-40
C.J.Nevin	9	9	3	52*	174	29.00	-	1	9	-							

	M	In	NO	HS	Runs	Ave	100s	50s	Ct	St	O	M	R	W	Ave	R/O	Best
R.J.Nicol	3	3	0	45	110	36.66	-	-	2	-	30	0	135	4	33.75	4.50	2-35
K.Noema-Barnett	6	5	0	63	100	20.00	-	1	1	-	21	0	124	5	24.80	5.90	2-30
I.E.O'Brien	9	6	5	19*	55	55.00	-	-	1	-	82	1	368	10	36.80	4.49	3-43
M.H.W.Papps	10	10	0	109	416	41.60	1	2	5	-							
M.E.Parlane	10	10	2	111*	338	42.25	1	1	4	-							
N.R.Parlane	6	6	0	105	225	37.50	1	1	2	-							
J.S.Patel	3	3	1	11	30	15.00	-	-	2	-	30	0	121	6	20.16	4.03	3-43
B.M.K.Patton	1	1	0	3	3	3.00	-	-	-	-							
A.J.Redmond	8	8	1	64	237	33.85	-	1	3	-							
I.A.Robertson	8	8	0	54	180	22.50	-	1	2	-	3	0	18	0	-	6.00	-
H.D.Rutherford	3	2	0	19	27	13.50	-	-	1	-							
J.D.Ryder	2	2	0	35	63	31.50	-	-	-	-							
R.J.Schaw	8	5	2	18*	42	14.00	-	-	-	-	73	1	358	8	44.75	4.90	2-47
B.E.Scott	9	4	1	8	23	7.66	-	-	2	-	73.5	2	430	9	47.77	5.82	3-55
M.S.Sinclair	9	9	3	97	532	88.66	-	5	5	-							
C.M.Smith	2	1	0	0	0	0.00	-	-	1	-	13	1	84	0	-	6.46	-
T.G.Southee	3	2	0	8	9	4.50	-	-	-	-	29	6	136	5	27.20	4.69	3-46
S.L.Stewart	10	10	1	120	376	41.77	1	1	-	-							
S.B.Styris	1	1	0	8	8	8.00	-	-	-	-	6	0	26	0	-	4.33	-
L.R.P.L.Taylor	3	3	0	46	68	22.66	-	-	1	-							
E.P.Thompson	9	8	2	40	117	19.50	-	-	3	-	76.4	4	397	12	33.08	5.17	3-45
G.R.Todd	10	10	1	58	235	26.11	-	1	4	-							
D.R.Tuffey	7	3	1	2*	4	2.00	-	-	1	-	62.4	5	314	11	28.54	5.01	4-33
C.F.K.van Wyk	10	9	6	27*	96	32.00	-	-	12	1							
N.Wagner	10	5	3	6*	12	6.00	-	-	1	-	89.2	7	421	24	17.54	4.71	5-34
B-J.Watling	11	11	3	113*	509	63.62	1	4	5	-							
S.R.Wells	1	1	0	13	13	13.00	-	-	-	-	4	0	18	0	-	4.50	-
T.I.Weston	4	4	0	38	102	25.50	-	-	1	-							
K.S.Williamson	11	9	2	100	320	45.71	1	1	6	-	71	5	301	4	75.25	4.24	2-36
L.J.Woodcock	10	9	2	53	130	18.57	-	1	1	-	68.5	4	330	12	27.50	4.79	3-27
G.H.Worker	9	9	0	86	295	32.77	-	2	2	-	47.5	0	235	6	39.16	4.91	2-30
R.A.Young	9	9	0	119	312	34.66	1	-	1	-							
J.A.F.Yovich	9	6	3	78*	157	52.33	-	1	2	-	52.3	2	256	12	21.33	4.87	3-30

HIGHEST STRIKE RATES *(qualification 150 runs)*

		Runs	Balls	S/R
H.J.H.Marshall	*ND*	319	311	102
B.J.Diamanti	*CD*	199	196	101
M.J.Guptill	*A*	236	235	100
G.R.Napier	*W*	156	156	100
S.L.Stewart	*C*	376	379	99
A.D.Mascarenhas	*O*	178	182	97
P.D.McGlashan	*ND*	272	304	89
P.J.Ingram	*CD*	386	438	88
C.D.Cumming	*O*	421	478	88
J.A.H.Marshall	*ND*	388	445	87

MOST ECONOMICAL BOWLING *(qualification 30 overs)*

		O	M	R	W	Ave	R/O
A.D.Mascarenhas	*O*	84	6	294	9	32.66	3.50
B.P.Martin	*ND*	81	7	300	8	37.50	3.70
N.L.McCullum	*O*	90.5	2	356	9	39.55	3.91
J.S.Patel	*W*	30	0	121	6	20.16	4.03
C.D.Cumming	*O*	33	1	134	2	67.00	4.06
C.Z.Harris	*C*	40	1	166	2	83.00	4.15
K.S.Williamson	*ND*	71	5	301	4	75.25	4.23
W.C.McSkimming	*O*	56	4	244	10	24.40	4.35
I.E.O'Brien	*W*	82	1	368	10	36.80	4.48
R.J.Nicol	*A*	30	0	135	4	33.75	4.50

CAREER RECORDS

	M	In	NO	HS	Runs	Ave	100s	50s	Ct	St	O	M	R	W	Ave	R/O	Best
G.W.Aldridge	81	43	22	36	325	15.47	-	-	18	-	618	42	2901	117	24.79	4.69	5-34
S.R.Allen	6	5	0	22	51	10.20	-	-	7	-							
C.J.Anderson	10	10	1	71	118	13.11	-	1	3	-							
B.J.Arnel	27	10	7	11*	47	15.66	-	-	4	-	218.2	17	1100	37	29.72	5.03	4-26
M.D.Bates	4	2	2	15*	25	-	-	-	-	-	28	1	163	0	-	5.82	-
M.D.Bell	125	119	9	124	2947	26.79	4	14	62	-	0.2	0	4	0	-	-	-
H.K.Bennett	19	4	2	3*	6	3.00	-	-	-	-	133.5	3	776	23	33.73	5.79	6-45
H.K.P.Boam	5	3	1	33	54	27.00	-	-	3	-	19	0	117	1	117.00	6.16	1-53
S.E.Bond	37	22	10	40	165	13.75	-	-	3	-	314.5	28	1446	49	29.51	4.59	4-36
T.A.Boult	9	2	0	10	10	5.00	-	-	6	-	80.5	6	398	16	24.87	4.92	4-50
D.J.Bowden	21	17	9	32*	215	26.87	-	-	5	-	152	14	638	17	37.52	4.20	2-37
D.A.J.Bracewell	8	6	0	55	87	14.50	-	1	3	-	34.4	1	203	4	50.75	5.85	2-24
N.T.Broom	44	40	7	93	1173	35.54	-	8	15	-	24	0	145	2	72.50	6.04	1-13
R.D.Burson	39	15	10	15*	92	18.40	-	-	6	-	299.2	29	1285	50	25.70	4.29	4-45
L.M.Burtt	20	6	4	8*	25	12.50	-	-	-	-	154.2	11	842	34	24.76	5.45	5-26
I.G.Butler	40	29	6	47	388	16.86	-	-	6	-	295.2	18	1469	53	27.71	4.97	5-55
S.J.Croft	9	9	1	59	209	26.12	-	1	-	-	39	0	209	8	26.12	5.36	3-27
B-J.Crook	9	9	0	75	250	27.77	-	3	2	-							
C.D.Cumming	99	94	5	112	2479	27.85	3	14	45	-	392	14	1795	39	46.02	4.58	2-18
M.P.F.Davidson	1	-	-	-	-	-	-	-	1	-	8.1	0	48	0	-	5.88	-
D.C.de Boorder	21	14	3	52*	281	25.54	-	1	26	2							
C.de Grandhomme	15	14	2	38*	174	14.50	-	-	5	-	31	1	157	3	52.33	5.06	3-38
J.J.B.Dean	2	1	0	3	3	3.00	-	-	-	-							
B.J.Diamanti	48	33	9	60	510	21.25	-	2	18	-	385.4	24	1755	65	27.00	4.55	5-58
S.W.Eathorne	5	4	2	37*	94	47.00	-	-	-	-	4	0	28	2	14.00	7.00	2-28
G.D.Elliott	32	25	6	107*	790	41.57	1	5	10	-	211.5	6	1040	41	25.36	4.90	5-34
A.M.Ellis	26	19	1	52	353	19.61	-	1	4	-	140.2	10	741	21	35.28	5.28	3-50
D.R.Flynn	33	33	3	149	867	28.90	2	4	8	-	58	0	344	6	57.33	5.93	2-45
J.E.C.Franklin	52	44	14	87*	1001	33.36	-	6	18	-	384	36	1637	54	30.31	4.26	4-30
C.Frauenstein	8	7	1	48	91	15.16	-	-	2	-	40.1	0	223	10	22.30	5.55	3-36
P.G.Fulton	48	44	5	115*	1422	36.46	1	11	17	-	3	0	24	0	-	8.00	-
M.R.Gillespie	49	32	8	26	242	10.08	-	-	8	-	396.2	23	1957	71	27.56	4.93	4-31
B.B.J.Griggs	79	63	10	74	1020	19.24	-	3	97	6							
M.J.Guptill	28	27	2	124	960	38.40	3	4	15	-							
S.B.Haig	15	15	0	79	266	17.73	-	2	5	1							
C.Z.Harris	137	126	42	107	3796	45.19	1	23	72	-	1091.3	72	4014	134	29.95	3.67	4-28
B.E.Hefford	45	20	7	16*	79	6.07	-	-	6	-	348.1	35	1584	62	25.54	4.54	3-13
B.C.Hiini	23	17	8	33	190	21.11	-	-	5	-	179	8	955	21	45.47	5.34	3-38
R.M.Hira	29	18	9	44*	149	16.55	-	-	7	-	242	13	1113	29	38.37	4.60	4-31
P.A.Hitchcock	88	80	17	108	1383	21.95	2	2	18	-	698.5	38	3391	125	27.12	4.85	5-10
G.J.Hopkins	110	95	16	130*	2042	25.84	1	8	112	20							
M.V.Houghton	9	5	2	23*	44	14.66	-	-	-	-	54.1	0	310	2	155.00	5.72	2-50
J.M.How	58	57	2	95	1614	29.34	-	14	29	-	53	2	257	7	36.71	4.85	2-15
P.J.Ingram	35	35	1	104	1105	32.50	2	6	5	-							
R.A.Jones	118	117	6	108	2877	25.91	1	15	30	-	0.3	0	5	0	-	-	-
R.P.C.Karaitiana	5	3	1	11	13	6.50	-	-	-	-	32	3	147	3	49.00	4.59	2-18
A.K.Kitchen	5	5	0	69	162	32.40	-	2	1	-							
A.R.Lamb	2	1	1	7*	7	-	-	-	1	-	13	0	99	1	99.00	7.62	1-47
H.J.H.Marshall	85	82	6	113	1842	24.23	1	12	33	-	7	0	43	1	43.00	6.14	1-14
J.A.H.Marshall	92	89	8	152*	3042	37.55	4	20	37	-	48.1	1	269	4	67.25	5.58	1-20
B.P.Martin	57	39	10	35*	371	12.79	-	-	22	-	472.2	29	1827	60	30.45	3.86	4-28
C.S.Martin	81	29	15	13	53	3.78	-	-	14	-	678.5	61	3169	116	27.31	4.66	5-43
A.D.Mascarenhas	9	6	2	75*	178	44.50	-	2	2	-	84	6	294	9	32.66	3.50	3-42
M.J.Mason	73	41	17	20	239	9.95	-	-	16	-	576	65	2398	104	23.05	4.16	6-25
M.J.McClenaghan	9	4	4	10*	23	-	-	-	1	-	73.2	5	466	13	35.84	6.35	3-72
B.B.McCullum	30	27	3	170	749	31.20	2	3	26	1							
N.L.McCullum	74	61	12	71	974	19.87	-	5	26	-	565.5	24	2427	64	37.92	4.28	3-21
P.D.McGlashan	65	59	16	112	1569	36.48	1	8	61	10							
T.G.McIntosh	22	22	0	74	513	23.31	-	3	10	-							
J.M.McMillan	36	20	13	9*	52	7.42	-	-	8	-	276.3	19	1345	50	26.90	4.86	3-30
W.C.McSkimming	79	60	18	59*	601	14.30	-	2	21	-	643.5	55	2936	101	29.06	4.56	5-9
K.D.Mills	53	45	13	57*	783	24.46	-	3	14	-	439.1	46	1833	70	26.18	4.17	4-40
S.J.Murdoch	5	5	0	19	42	8.40	-	-	1	-							
J.G.Myburgh	20	20	0	90	585	29.25	-	7	4	-	65.1	1	330	3	110.00	5.06	1-23
G.R.Napier	14	13	0	50	225	17.30	-	1	5	-	127.4	8	588	30	19.60	4.60	4-40
C.J.Nevin	129	122	9	149	3124	27.64	5	14	157	12							

	M	In	NO	HS	Runs	Ave	100s	50s	Ct	St	O	M	R	W	Ave	R/O	Best
R.J.Nicol	59	59	6	135	1588	29.96	1	9	22	-	240.5	3	1082	36	30.05	4.49	5-54
K.Noema-Barnett	6	5	0	63	100	20.00	-	1	1	-	21	0	124	5	24.80	5.90	2-30
I.E.O'Brien	33	14	11	19*	69	23.00	-	-	5	-	293	19	1318	46	28.65	4.50	5-35
M.H.W.Papps	73	73	6	137*	2738	40.86	6	15	43	2							
M.E.Parlane	139	138	10	132	3909	30.53	5	22	32	-	0.3	0	5	0	-	-	-
N.R.Parlane	94	87	6	105	2125	26.23	1	13	46	-							
J.S.Patel	30	20	7	22*	140	10.76	-	-	14	-	245.3	6	1117	29	38.51	4.54	4-47
B.M.K.Patton	1	1	0	3	3	3.00	-	-	-	-							
A.J.Redmond	68	66	6	134*	1526	25.43	2	6	21	-	140.2	1	730	19	38.42	5.20	3-40
I.A.Robertson	31	30	2	60	682	24.35	-	4	9	-	82	1	408	7	58.28	4.98	3-58
H.D.Rutherford	3	2	0	19	27	13.50	-	-	1	-							
J.D.Ryder	47	46	2	63	932	21.18	-	5	15	-	140	3	783	26	30.11	5.59	4-39
R.J.Schaw	18	10	3	18*	64	9.14	-	-	1	-	167.4	3	804	16	50.25	4.79	2-36
B.E.Scott	61	37	15	44	417	18.95	-	-	16	-	522.2	32	2485	77	32.27	4.75	4-63
M.S.Sinclair	112	109	15	110	3399	36.15	1	28	58	1	17.4	0	121	3	40.33	6.85	1-15
C.M.Smith	10	6	3	11*	29	9.66	-	-	4	-	74.1	5	378	9	42.00	5.09	3-46
T.G.Southee	8	7	0	16	52	7.42	-	-	2	-	74.3	8	382	10	38.20	5.12	3-43
S.L.Stewart	73	72	5	120	2200	32.83	3	9	13	-	6	0	51	2	25.50	8.50	2-51
S.B.Styris	86	79	19	123	2282	38.03	1	16	38	-	586.4	46	2538	100	25.38	4.32	4-19
L.R.P.L.Taylor	34	34	4	132*	1495	49.83	4	10	19	-	31	0	140	2	70.00	4.52	1-13
E.P.Thompson	53	37	10	62*	507	18.77	-	3	14	-	429.4	35	1966	86	22.86	4.57	5-45
G.R.Todd	52	49	5	95	1159	26.34	-	6	18	-	71.3	2	378	12	31.50	5.28	2-23
D.R.Tuffey	88	47	23	37	390	16.25	-	-	23	-	720.1	55	3224	101	31.92	4.47	4-33
C.F.K.van Wyk	28	27	15	85*	658	54.83	-	5	39	4							
N.Wagner	10	5	3	6*	12	6.00	-	-	1	-	89.2	7	421	24	17.54	4.71	5-34
B-J.Watling	37	37	4	116*	1289	39.06	4	8	13	-							
S.R.Wells	1	1	0	13	13	13.00	-	-	-	-	4	0	18	0	-	4.50	-
T.I.Weston	15	15	2	77*	394	30.30	-	2	5	-							
K.S.Williamson	15	13	4	100	348	38.66	1	1	7	-	71	5	301	4	75.25	4.24	2-36
L.J.Woodcock	54	42	8	71	709	20.85	-	3	13	-	295.2	8	1408	34	41.41	4.76	4-36
G.H.Worker	10	10	0	86	298	29.80	-	2	2	-	50.5	0	248	6	41.33	4.87	2-30
R.A.Young	60	49	12	119	960	25.94	1	2	63	12							
J.A.F.Yovich	93	78	20	78*	1300	22.41	-	6	27	-	508.2	26	2684	106	25.32	5.28	4-44

STATE TWENTY20

2008/09

The fourth season of domestic Twenty20 cricket saw an expanded competition with the six teams playing eight matches each prior to the final. Otago, who had finished last in 2007/08, qualified in first place while Canterbury edged out Auckland, on net run rate, for second spot. The previous season's finalists, Northern Districts and Central Districts, trailed the field with just a solitary win between them.

No play was possible in the final so Otago, by virtue of topping the points table, were declared winners with subsequent entry to the Champions League. In the event of the scores being level at the end of a match, a one over eliminator was used to find the winner.

Aaron Redmond (from 56 balls) scored the only century while the fastest fifty was made by Luke Vivian (18 balls).

Final points were:

	P	*W*	*L*	*NR*	*Points*
Otago	8	6	1	1	26
Canterbury	8	5	2	1	22
Auckland	8	5	2	1	22
Wellington	8	4	3	1	18
Central Districts	8	1	6	1	6
Northern Districts	8	–	7	1	2

OTAGO v CANTERBURY — State Twenty20

at University Oval, Dunedin on 4 February, 2009
Toss : Canterbury. Umpires : M.P. George & E.A. Watkin
***Otago won by 30 runs.** Points: Otago 4, Canterbury 0*

OTAGO

	Runs	*Mins*	*Balls*	*6s*	*4s*
A.J.Redmond c Stewart b Ellis	26	21	17	1	4
H.D.Rutherford c & b Myburgh	41	38	23	2	3
G.R.Todd c van Wyk b Ellis	4	7	6	-	-
N.L.McCullum* not out	76	50	42	7	3
A.D.Mascarenhas not out	57	41	35	2	6
S.W.Eathorne					
D.C.de Boorder†					
W.C.McSkimming					
I.G.Butler					
N.Wagner					
M.D.C.Craig					
Extras (lb 14, w 1, nb 3)	18				
TOTAL (20 overs) (3 wkts)	**222**	82			

CANTERBURY

	Runs	*Mins*	*Balls*	*6s*	*4s*
I.A.Robertson lbw b Craig	32	23	24	2	3
M.H.W.Papps c & b McSkimming	6	13	9	-	1
J.G.Myburgh not out	73	67	42	3	8
S.L.Stewart c McSkimming b Butler	18	10	9	1	2
C.J.Anderson c Rutherford b McCullum	0	5	6	-	-
D.J.Broom c McCullum b Wagner	20	13	16	-	3
C.Frauenstein c Craig b Butler	0	3	1	-	-
C.F.K.van Wyk*† not out	31	22	16	3	1
A.M.Ellis					
M.P.F.Davidson					
L.M.Burtt					
Extras (lb 3, w 6, nb 3)	12				
TOTAL (20 overs) (6 wkts)	**192**	84			

Bowling	*O*	*M*	*R*	*W*
CANTERBURY				
Burtt	4	0	60	0
Davidson	4	0	26	0
Ellis	4	0	42	2
Frauenstein	4	0	53	0
Myburgh	4	0	27	1
OTAGO				
Wagner	4	0	47	1
McSkimming	4	0	37	1
Craig	3	0	22	1
Butler	4	0	31	2
McCullum	3	0	38	1
Mascarenhas	2	0	14	0

Fall of Wickets

	O	*C*
1st	60	31
2nd	69	47
3rd	82	80
4th	-	87
5th	-	127
6th	-	133
7th	-	-
8th	-	-
9th	-	-
10th	-	-

CENTRAL DISTRICTS v WELLINGTON — State Twenty20

at McLean Park, Napier on 4 February, 2009 (d/n)
Toss : Central Districts. Umpires : P.D. Jones & D.M. Quested
Wellington won by 19 runs (D/L). *Points: Wellington 4, Central Districts 0*

WELLINGTON

	Runs	Mins	Balls	6s	4s
C.J.Nevin† c Sinclair b Thompson	16	19	15	-	2
S.P.Fleming* b Mason	1	8	3	-	-
M.D.Bell c Worker b Noema-Barnett	32	44	34	-	3
J.J.B.Dean run out	0	5	2	-	-
D.J.Bowden c Mason b Noema-Barnett	15	15	13	-	1
J.E.C.Franklin not out	50	45	28	3	-
G.R.Napier run out	1	3	3	-	-
B-J.Crook b Calkin	9	7	7	-	1
L.J.Woodcock not out	29	21	16	-	3
H.K.P.Boam					
M.V.Houghton					
Extras (lb 4, w 2, nb 1)	7				
TOTAL (20 overs) (7 wkts)	**160**	85			

CENTRAL DISTRICTS

	Runs	Mins	Balls	6s	4s
P.J.Ingram c Bell b Houghton	28	28	21	-	3
G.H.Worker c Dean b Franklin	8	15	9	-	-
J.M.How run out	3	8	4	-	-
M.S.Sinclair* b Napier	17	23	17	1	-
K.Noema-Barnett not out	4	21	7	-	-
M.J.E.Calkin not out	1	2	2	-	-
T.I.Weston					
E.P.Thompson					
B.B.J.Griggs†					
R.J.Schaw					
M.J.Mason					
Extras (w 2)	2				
TOTAL (10 overs) (4 wkts)	**63**	50			

Bowling	O	M	R	W
CENTRAL DISTRICTS				
Thompson	4	0	32	1
Mason	4	0	20	1
Noema-Barnett	4	0	26	2
Worker	4	0	47	0
How	2	0	12	0
Calkin	2	0	19	1
WELLINGTON				
Bowden	2	0	14	0
Franklin	4	0	34	1
Napier	2	0	7	1
Houghton	2	0	8	1

Fall of Wickets	W	CD
1st	8	23
2nd	21	37
3rd	27	43
4th	54	62
5th	83	-
6th	84	-
7th	96	-
8th	-	-
9th	-	-
10th	-	-

AUCKLAND v NORTHERN DISTRICTS — State Twenty20

at Eden Park Outer Oval, Auckland on 4 February, 2009
Toss : Auckland. Umpires : B.F. Bowden & D.J. Walker
Auckland won by 5 wickets. *Points: Auckland 4, Northern Districts 0*

NORTHERN DISTRICTS

	Runs	Mins	Balls	6s	4s
H.J.H.Marshall c Young b Azhar	2	1	3	-	-
J.A.H.Marshall* c Jones b Martin	1	8	5	-	-
D.R.Flynn c Young b Azhar	1	11	5	-	-
P.D.McGlashan† run out	52	47	34	3	4
M.E.Parlane c Kitchen b de Grandhomme	30	33	33	-	4
B-J.Watling c Kitchen b Morgan	16	18	14	-	1
J.A.F.Yovich c & b de Grandhomme	0	2	1	-	-
G.W.Aldridge run out	8	4	5	-	1
B.E.Scott not out	22	15	13	1	2
B.P.Martin not out	10	13	7	-	1
B.J.Arnel					
Extras (b 4, lb 1, w 2)	7				
TOTAL (20 overs) (8 wkts)	**149**	84			

AUCKLAND

	Runs	Mins	Balls	6s	4s
R.A.Jones* b Scott	20	14	13	-	4
C.de Grandhomme st McGlashan b Martin	36	29	20	2	4
R.A.Young† c Flynn b Martin	15	17	13	-	3
L.J.Vivian c Watling b Martin	2	9	5	-	-
S.J.Croft c Marshall J.A.H. b Yovich	1	4	3	-	-
G.J.Hopkins not out	38	36	26	1	3
A.K.Kitchen not out	33	34	32	1	3
G.J.Morgan					
R.M.Hira					
Azhar Abbas					
C.S.Martin					
Extras (b 1, lb 3, w 1)	5				
TOTAL (18.4 overs) (5 wkts)	**150**	77			

Bowling	O	M	R	W
AUCKLAND				
Azhar	4	0	24	2
Martin	3	0	14	1
de Grandhomme	4	0	34	2
Morgan	4	0	25	1
Croft	3	0	24	0
Hira	2	0	23	0
NORTHERN DISTRICTS				
Arnel	3.4	0	35	0
Aldridge	3	0	30	0
Scott	3	0	28	1
Martin	4	0	16	3
Yovich	3	0	24	1
Flynn	2	0	13	0

Fall of Wickets	ND	A
1st	2	35
2nd	4	71
3rd	5	76
4th	81	79
5th	104	79
6th	106	-
7th	116	-
8th	117	-
9th	-	-
10th	-	-

CENTRAL DISTRICTS vAUCKLAND

State Twenty20

at Pukekura Park, New Plymouth on 6 February, 2009
Toss : Auckland. Umpires : B.G. Frost & P.L. Gasston
***Auckland won by 6 wickets.** Points: Auckland 4, Central Districts 0*

CENTRAL DISTRICTS

	Runs	Mins	Balls	6s	4s
P.J.Ingram c Hopkins b Azhar	36	21	19	-	7
G.H.Worker run out	7	29	11	-	1
J.M.How* c Hira b de Grandhomme	32	26	17	1	4
M.J.E.Calkin c Hopkins b de Grandhomme	1	6	5	-	-
K.Noema-Barnett run out	0	1	1	-	-
T.I.Weston run out	2	5	3	-	-
E.P.Thompson b Azhar	59	39	37	3	5
B.B.J.Griggs† c Jones b Croft	13	28	17	-	-
R.J.Schaw not out	19	12	9	1	2
M.J.Mason b Martin	1	2	2	-	-
M.J.McClenaghan not out	2	4	2	-	-
Extras (lb 4, w 6, nb 3)	13				
TOTAL (20 overs) (9 wkts)	**185**	90			

AUCKLAND

	Runs	Mins	Balls	6s	4s
R.A.Jones* c Mason b McClenaghan	63	78	46	3	5
C.de Grandhomme b Thompson	17	5	7	2	1
R.A.Young c McClenaghan b Thompson	10	15	14	-	1
A.K.Kitchen c Noema-Barnett b Calkin	31	32	30	1	2
L.J.Vivian not out	55	22	18	6	2
G.J.Hopkins† not out	0	1	0	-	-
S.J.Croft					
G.J.Morgan					
R.M.Hira					
Azhar Abbas					
C.S.Martin					
Extras (b 1, lb 4, w 6, nb 1)	12				
TOTAL (18.5 overs) (4 wkts)	**188**	79			

Bowling	*O*	*M*	*R*	*W*
AUCKLAND				
Azhar	4	0	43	2
Martin	4	0	32	1
Morgan	4	0	30	0
de Grandhomme	3	0	36	2
Croft	2	0	22	1
Hira	3	0	18	0
CENTRAL DISTRICTS				
Mason	4	0	48	0
Thompson	4	0	37	2
McClenaghan	2.5	0	27	1
Schaw	2	0	15	0
Noema-Barnett	3	0	20	0
Worker	1	0	12	0
Calkin	2	0	24	1

Fall of Wickets

	CD	*A*
1st	45	22
2nd	62	44
3rd	69	121
4th	69	180
5th	80	-
6th	87	-
7th	160	-
8th	175	-
9th	176	-
10th	-	-

WELLINGTON v OTAGO

State Twenty20

at Allied Nationwide Finance Basin Reserve, Wellington on 6 February, 2009
Toss : Wellington. Umpires : G.A.V. Baxter & D.J. Walker
***Otago won by 117 runs.** Points: Otago 4, Wellington 0*

OTAGO

	Runs	Mins	Balls	6s	4s
A.J.Redmond c Napier b Woodcock	32	47	32	-	3
H.D.Rutherford b Woodcock	87	49	38	6	8
A.D.Mascarenhas c Nevin b Napier	1	5	4	-	-
N.L.McCullum* b Napier	24	22	13	1	3
G.R.Todd b Woodcock	30	13	14	2	2
I.G.Butler c Bell b Napier	15	13	11	2	-
W.C.McSkimming not out	19	12	10	2	1
D.C.de Boorder† not out	0	3	0	-	-
S.W.Eathorne					
N.Wagner					
M.D.C.Craig					
Extras (lb 5, nb 2)	7				
TOTAL (20 overs) (6 wkts)	**215**	88			

WELLINGTON

	Runs	Mins	Balls	6s	4s
C.J.Nevin† c de Boorder b McSkimming	10	3	5	1	1
S.P.Fleming* b Wagner	0	6	2	-	-
J.J.B.Dean c & b McSkimming	20	34	20	-	1
M.D.Bell run out	0	1	2	-	-
J.E.C.Franklin c Todd b McSkimming	31	27	21	-	5
G.R.Napier c de Boorder b Mascarenhas	2	7	4	-	-
B-J.Crook b McCullum	21	18	13	1	2
L.J.Woodcock c Craig b McCullum	7	9	9	-	-
D.J.Bowden c McSkimming b Butler	2	4	3	-	-
H.K.P.Boam not out	2	6	5	-	-
M.V.Houghton c Butler b Wagner	0	4	1	-	-
Extras (lb 1, w 2)	3				
TOTAL (14.1 overs)	**98**	69			

Bowling	*O*	*M*	*R*	*W*
WELLINGTON				
Bowden	4	0	45	0
Franklin	4	0	35	0
Napier	4	0	31	3
Houghton	2	0	36	0
Woodcock	4	0	45	3
Boam	2	0	18	0
OTAGO				
McSkimming	4	0	28	3
Wagner	2.1	0	6	2
Butler	2	0	13	1
Craig	3	0	24	0
Mascarenhas	2	0	23	1
McCullum	1	0	3	2

Fall of Wickets

	O	*W*
1st	125	10
2nd	125	10
3rd	131	10
4th	175	63
5th	188	63
6th	205	67
7th	-	93
8th	-	96
9th	-	96
10th	-	98

CANTERBURY v NORTHERN DISTRICTS — State Twenty20

at Queen Elizabeth II Park, Christchurch on 6 February, 2009
Toss : Canterbury. Umpires : W.R. Knights & D.M. Quested
***Canterbury won by 4 wickets.** Points: Canterbury 4, Northern Districts 0*

NORTHERN DISTRICTS

	Runs	Mins	Balls	6s	4s
M.E.Parlane c Frauenstein b Bond	10	11	14	-	1
H.J.H.Marshall c Astle b Davidson	1	6	3	-	-
D.R.Flynn run out	2	18	8	-	-
J.A.H.Marshall* b Davidson	1	2	2	-	-
P.D.McGlashan† run out	2	5	6	-	-
B-J.Watling c van Wyk b Ellis	48	42	41	1	6
K.S.Williamson c Astle b Frauenstein	30	47	34	2	-
J.A.F.Yovich b Ellis	4	2	2	-	1
G.W.Aldridge not out	15	9	8	1	1
B.P.Martin not out	1	2	2	-	-
B.J.Arnel					
Extras (b 2, lb 2, w 1)	5				
TOTAL (20 overs) (8 wkts)	**119**	76			

CANTERBURY

	Runs	Mins	Balls	6s	4s
I.A.Robertson c Marshall J.A.H. b Yovich	13	15	10	-	3
M.H.W.Papps b Arnel	8	10	5	-	2
J.G.Myburgh c Marshall H.J.H. b Yovich	36	48	34	1	4
S.L.Stewart lbw b Yovich	0	1	1	-	-
C.J.Anderson b Martin	11	13	14	-	2
C.F.K.van Wyk*† st McGlashan b Martin	23	34	25	-	1
A.M.Ellis not out	11	18	12	-	1
C.Frauenstein not out	10	11	10	-	-
T.D.Astle					
M.P.F.Davidson					
S.E.Bond					
Extras (b 4, lb 2, w 4)	10				
TOTAL (18.3 overs) (6 wkts)	**122**	78			

Bowling	*O*	*M*	*R*	*W*
CANTERBURY				
Bond	4	0	32	1
Davidson	4	0	9	2
Ellis	4	0	21	2
Astle	3	0	22	0
Myburgh	2	0	11	0
Frauenstein	3	0	20	1
NORTHERN DISTRICTS				
Arnel	3.3	0	18	1
Aldridge	3	0	30	0
Yovich	4	1	23	3
Martin	4	0	25	2
Williamson	4	0	20	0

Fall of Wickets	***ND***	***C***
1st	4	23
2nd	11	23
3rd	12	23
4th	15	39
5th	17	88
6th	97	98
7th	101	-
8th	114	-
9th	-	-
10th	-	-

AUCKLAND v CANTERBURY — State Twenty20

at Eden Park Outer Oval, Auckland on 8 February, 2009
Toss : Canterbury. Umpires : B.F. Bowden & B.G. Frost
***Canterbury won by 2 wickets.** Points: Canterbury 4, Auckland 0*

AUCKLAND

	Runs	Mins	Balls	6s	4s
R.A.Jones* c Papps b Bond	0	1	1	-	-
C.de Grandhomme c Robertson b Davidson	18	16	11	2	-
A.K.Kitchen c Astle b Bond	0	1	2	-	-
S.J.Croft c Myburgh b Bond	50	61	42	1	4
S.B.Styris c Bond b Myburgh	35	34	28	2	3
L.J.Vivian c Anderson b Ellis	30	26	21	3	1
G.J.Hopkins† run out	15	10	10	-	2
R.M.Hira not out	1	4	3	-	-
G.J.Morgan not out	1	2	2	-	-
Azhar Abbas					
C.S.Martin					
Extras (lb 3, w 6)	9				
TOTAL (20 overs) (7 wkts)	**159**	85			

CANTERBURY

	Runs	Mins	Balls	6s	4s
I.A.Robertson c Vivian b Hira	31	43	34	1	3
M.H.W.Papps c Croft b Martin	1	9	4	-	-
J.G.Myburgh c Hopkins b Azhar	0	1	1	-	-
S.L.Stewart c Hopkins b Morgan	36	36	26	1	5
C.J.Anderson c Hira b Croft	23	25	13	2	1
C.F.K.van Wyk*† run out	21	26	19	-	3
C.Frauenstein c Hopkins b Martin	27	21	16	2	1
A.M.Ellis run out	1	8	2	-	-
T.D.Astle not out	6	9	3	-	1
M.P.F.Davidson not out	1	2	1	-	-
S.E.Bond					
Extras (lb 6, w 10)	16				
TOTAL (20 overs) (8 wkts)	**163**	98			

Bowling	*O*	*M*	*R*	*W*
CANTERBURY				
Bond	4	1	26	3
Davidson	4	0	29	1
Ellis	4	0	44	1
Astle	2	0	17	0
Frauenstein	3	0	17	0
Myburgh	3	0	23	1
AUCKLAND				
Azhar	4	0	24	1
Martin	4	0	23	2
de Grandhomme	4	0	40	0
Hira	4	0	30	1
Morgan	3	0	25	1
Croft	1	0	15	1

Fall of Wickets	***A***	***C***
1st	0	14
2nd	0	14
3rd	31	69
4th	98	75
5th	138	121
6th	156	128
7th	157	144
8th	-	158
9th	-	-
10th	-	-

CENTRAL DISTRICTS v OTAGO — State Twenty20

at Pukekura Park, New Plymouth on 8 February, 2009
Toss : Otago. Umpires : G.A.V. Baxter & E.J. Gray
***Otago won by 23 runs.** Points: Otago 4, Central Districts 0*

OTAGO

	Runs	Mins	Balls	6s	4s
A.J.Redmond c Noema-Barnett b Worker	67	68	46	2	7
H.D.Rutherford lbw b Schaw	35	29	21	1	6
G.R.Todd run out	31	24	19	1	3
N.L.McCullum* not out	40	30	22	4	1
A.D.Mascarenhas c Weston b Schaw	22	7	9	2	2
I.G.Butler not out	4	8	3	-	-
S.W.Eathorne					
D.C.de Boorder†					
W.C.McSkimming					
N.Wagner					
M.D.C.Craig					
Extras (lb 2, w 5)	7				
TOTAL (20 overs) (4 wkts)	**206**	85			

CENTRAL DISTRICTS

	Runs	Mins	Balls	6s	4s
P.J.Ingram b Mascarenhas	27	29	16	-	5
J.M.How c de Boorder b McSkimming	4	3	2	-	1
M.S.Sinclair* c Redmond b Mascarenhas	61	51	42	2	7
K.Noema-Barnett b Butler	38	19	18	4	-
T.I.Weston c Eathorne b McCullum	5	9	5	-	1
E.P.Thompson c Redmond b McSkimming	10	9	9	1	-
B.B.J.Griggs† c Rutherford b Butler	13	25	16	-	1
G.H.Worker b McSkimming	0	1	1	-	-
R.J.Schaw not out	16	19	10	1	1
M.J.Mason not out	0	1	1	-	-
B.E.Hefford					
Extras (b 1, lb 6, w 2)	9				
TOTAL (20 overs) (8 wkts)	**183**	87			

Bowling	O	M	R	W
CENTRAL DISTRICTS				
Mason	4	0	33	0
Thompson	3	0	41	0
Schaw	3	0	27	2
Noema-Barnett	3	0	32	0
Hefford	4	0	41	0
Worker	3	0	30	1
OTAGO				
McSkimming	3	0	33	3
Wagner	4	0	24	0
Craig	2	0	28	0
Butler	4	0	25	2
Mascarenhas	4	0	38	2
McCullum	3	0	28	1

Fall of Wickets	O	CD
1st	56	13
2nd	118	73
3rd	159	126
4th	186	139
5th	-	145
6th	-	154
7th	-	154
8th	-	183
9th	-	-
10th	-	-

WELLINGTON v NORTHERN DISTRICTS — State Twenty20

at Allied Nationwide Finance Basin Reserve, Wellington on 8 February, 2009
Toss : Wellington. Umpires : J.M. Busby & D.J. Walker
***Wellington won by 6 wickets.** Points: Wellington 4, Northern Districts 0*

NORTHERN DISTRICTS

	Runs	Mins	Balls	6s	4s
H.J.H.Marshall c Nevin b Napier	0	1	1	-	-
M.E.Parlane c Napier b Boam	28	24	18	1	4
D.R.Flynn c Nevin b Napier	0	3	2	-	-
J.A.H.Marshall* not out	58	76	52	-	6
P.D.McGlashan† c Dean b Woodcock	27	18	19	1	1
B-J.Watling c & b Woodcock	5	6	6	-	-
J.A.F.Yovich c Dean b Woodcock	8	7	7	-	1
G.W.Aldridge b Bowden	22	21	14	1	2
B.E.Scott not out	1	1	1	-	-
B.P.Martin					
B.J.Arnel					
Extras (b 4, lb 4, w 6)	14				
TOTAL (20 overs) (7 wkts)	**163**	82			

WELLINGTON

	Runs	Mins	Balls	6s	4s
C.J.Nevin† c Aldridge b Martin	29	44	28	-	4
S.P.Fleming* c Scott b Yovich	28	25	18	1	5
J.E.C.Franklin not out	64	53	31	5	3
G.R.Napier c McGlashan b Yovich	5	4	4	-	1
B-J.Crook c & b Aldridge	8	12	11	-	1
L.J.Woodcock not out	23	16	12	1	3
M.D.Bell					
J.J.B.Dean					
D.J.Bowden					
H.K.P.Boam					
M.V.Houghton					
Extras (b 4, lb 2, w 1)	7				
TOTAL (17.2 overs) (4 wkts)	**164**	79			

Bowling	O	M	R	W
WELLINGTON				
Napier	4	0	25	2
Bowden	4	0	42	1
Boam	4	0	32	1
Houghton	4	0	29	0
Woodcock	4	0	27	3
NORTHERN DISTRICTS				
Aldridge	3.2	0	38	1
Martin	4	0	50	1
Scott	3	0	27	0
Arnel	3	0	19	0
Yovich	4	0	24	2

Fall of Wickets	ND	W
1st	1	54
2nd	4	91
3rd	47	97
4th	91	124
5th	107	-
6th	121	-
7th	162	-
8th	-	-
9th	-	-
10th	-	-

NORTHERN DISTRICTS v CENTRAL DISTRICTS State Twenty20

at Seddon Park, Hamilton on 11 February, 2009 (d/n)
Toss : Northern Districts. Umpires : P.D. Jones & E.A. Watkin
***Central Districts won by 2 runs.** Points: Central Districts 4, Northern Districts 0*

CENTRAL DISTRICTS

	Runs	Mins	Balls	6s	4s
P.J.Ingram c McGlashan b Aldridge	13	7	7	-	2
M.J.E.Calkin† c McGlashan b Yovich	26	29	18	2	2
J.M.How c Williamson b Yovich	5	12	9	-	1
M.S.Sinclair* c Marshall b Yovich	52	44	41	1	5
K.Noema-Barnett c Aldridge b Williamson	17	8	8	2	1
T.I.Weston c Williamson b Scott	34	33	27	-	3
E.P.Thompson not out	7	12	7	-	-
R.J.Schaw run out	12	5	4	1	1
M.J.Mason					
B.E.Hefford					
M.J.McClenaghan					
Extras (lb 4, w 1, nb 1)	6				
TOTAL (20 overs) (7 wkts)	**172**	82			

NORTHERN DISTRICTS

	Runs	Mins	Balls	6s	4s
M.E.Parlane c Weston b McClenaghan	19	31	25	-	2
H.J.H.Marshall c Noema-Barnett b Thompson	2	6	5	-	-
D.R.Flynn c Ingram b Thompson	7	7	5	-	1
B-J.Watling c Sinclair b McClenaghan	33	42	28	-	3
P.D.McGlashan*† lbw b Noema-Barnett	47	34	27	3	3
K.S.Williamson run out	10	15	10	-	-
J.A.F.Yovich not out	33	23	16	2	3
G.W.Aldridge b Thompson	3	10	3	-	-
B.E.Scott c Calkin b Thompson	0	1	1	-	-
B.P.Martin not out	0	2	0	-	-
B.J.Arnel					
Extras (lb 6, w 10)	16				
TOTAL (20 overs) (8 wkts)	**170**	94			

Bowling	*O*	*M*	*R*	*W*
NORTHERN DISTRICTS				
Arnel	3	0	29	0
Aldridge	3	0	22	1
Yovich	4	0	34	3
Scott	4	0	33	1
Williamson	2	0	21	1
Martin	4	0	29	0
CENTRAL DISTRICTS				
Mason	4	0	27	0
Thompson	4	0	31	4
Schaw	3	0	19	0
McClenaghan	4	0	22	2
Hefford	3	0	33	0
Noema-Barnett	2	0	32	1

Fall of Wickets	***CD***	***ND***
1st	16	8
2nd	41	17
3rd	55	54
4th	82	99
5th	146	127
6th	156	137
7th	172	160
8th	-	160
9th	-	-
10th	-	-

OTAGO v AUCKLAND State Twenty20

at University Oval, Dunedin on 13 February, 2009
Toss : Auckland. Umpires : D.M. Quested & D.J. Walker
***Auckland won by 3 runs.** Points: Auckland 4, Otago 0*

AUCKLAND

	Runs	Mins	Balls	6s	4s
R.A.Jones* c McCullum b McSkimming	14	13	10	-	2
C.de Grandhomme c Craig b Mascarenhas	24	19	17	2	1
R.A.Young† c Craig b Mascarenhas	8	13	6	-	1
S.B.Styris b McSkimming	6	11	14	-	-
S.J.Croft b Butler	16	27	22	-	1
L.J.Vivian lbw b McCullum	13	14	14	-	1
R.J.Nicol not out	26	32	17	2	-
R.M.Hira b Wagner	28	23	20	2	-
G.J.Morgan					
Azhar Abbas					
C.S.Martin					
Extras (lb 5, w 2)	7				
TOTAL (20 overs) (7 wkts)	**142**	83			

OTAGO

	Runs	Mins	Balls	6s	4s
A.J.Redmond c Styris b Martin	19	18	19	-	3
H.D.Rutherford c Nicol b Martin	11	25	10	-	1
G.R.Todd b Hira	39	43	35	-	4
N.L.McCullum* c Hira b Morgan	19	14	12	2	1
S.W.Eathorne c Styris b Hira	4	7	6	-	-
A.D.Mascarenhas c Styris b Hira	14	22	17	-	-
I.G.Butler not out	15	20	14	1	-
W.C.McSkimming not out	8	11	7	-	1
D.C.de Boorder†					
M.D.C.Craig					
N.Wagner					
Extras (b 2, w 8)	10				
TOTAL (20 overs) (6 wkts)	**139**	86			

Bowling	*O*	*M*	*R*	*W*
OTAGO				
Wagner	4	0	34	1
McSkimming	4	0	14	2
Butler	4	0	39	1
Mascarenhas	4	0	26	2
McCullum	3	0	15	1
Craig	1	0	9	0
AUCKLAND				
Azhar	3	0	17	0
Martin	4	0	33	2
de Grandhomme	2	0	16	0
Nicol	4	0	29	0
Morgan	3	0	21	1
Hira	4	0	21	3

Fall of Wickets	***A***	***O***
1st	33	25
2nd	48	36
3rd	54	72
4th	57	89
5th	76	111
6th	90	118
7th	142	-
8th	-	-
9th	-	-
10th	-	-

CANTERBURY v WELLINGTON — State Twenty20

at Queen Elizabeth II Park, Christchurch on 13 February, 2009
Toss : Wellington. Umpires : G.A.V. Baxter & K.C. Manley
***Wellington won by 6 wickets.** Points: Wellington 4, Canterbury 0*

CANTERBURY

	Runs	Mins	Balls	6s	4s
I.A.Robertson c Bell b Woodcock	28	33	24	1	2
M.H.W.Papps b Woodcock	46	46	43	-	5
J.G.Myburgh b Woodcock	15	21	17	-	-
S.L.Stewart st Nevin b Houghton	2	3	3	-	-
C.J.Anderson c Bell b Houghton	0	1	3	-	-
C.F.K.van Wyk*† run out	17	22	14	-	1
C.Frauenstein c Nevin b Napier	8	6	6	-	1
A.M.Ellis c Napier b Bowden	7	9	8	-	-
T.D.Astle not out	1	2	2	-	-
S.E.Bond					
M.P.F.Davidson					
Extras (w 2)	2				
TOTAL (20 overs) (8 wkts)	**126**	75			

WELLINGTON

	Runs	Mins	Balls	6s	4s
C.J.Nevin† c Frauenstein b Davidson	4	8	5	-	-
S.P.Fleming*c Frauenstein b Davidson	0	5	6	-	-
M.D.Bell lbw b Bond	46	36	28	1	6
J.J.B.Dean c Davidson b Ellis	26	38	26	1	2
J.E.C.Franklin not out	28	32	20	-	4
B-J.Crook not out	17	27	25	-	3
D.J.Bowden					
G.R.Napier					
L.J.Woodcock					
H.K.P.Boam					
M.V.Houghton					
Extras (lb 1, w 6, nb 1)	8				
TOTAL (18.1 overs) (4 wkts)	**129**	75			

Bowling	*O*	*M*	*R*	*W*
WELLINGTON				
Bowden	4	0	24	1
Franklin	4	0	24	0
Napier	4	0	25	1
Houghton	4	0	25	2
Woodcock	4	0	28	3
CANTERBURY				
Bond	4	0	11	1
Davidson	4	0	28	2
Frauenstein	1.1	0	23	0
Ellis	4	0	20	1
Myburgh	4	0	31	0
Astle	1	0	15	0

Fall of Wickets	*C*	*W*
1st	61	4
2nd	87	4
3rd	92	76
4th	92	80
5th	93	-
6th	104	-
7th	119	-
8th	126	-
9th	-	-
10th	-	-

OTAGO v NORTHERN DISTRICTS — State Twenty20

at University Oval, Dunedin on 15 February, 2009
Toss : Northern Districts. Umpires : G.A.V. Baxter & D.J. Walker
***Otago won by 21 runs.** Points: Otago 4, Northern Districts 0*

OTAGO

	Runs	Mins	Balls	6s	4s
A.J.Redmond c Williamson b Martin	80	63	51	4	7
H.D.Rutherford c Wilson b Yovich	27	27	16	1	4
C.D.Cumming* c Watling b Martin	11	11	10	1	-
A.D.Mascarenhas c Watling b Yovich	55	39	30	3	5
G.R.Todd not out	10	22	11	-	-
W.C.McSkimming not out	1	6	3	-	-
S.W.Eathorne					
M.D.C.Craig					
D.C.de Boorder†					
N.Wagner					
J.M.McMillan					
Extras (b 1, lb 2, w 3, nb 1)	7				
TOTAL (20 overs) (4 wkts)	**191**	86			

NORTHERN DISTRICTS

	Runs	Mins	Balls	6s	4s
B.S.Wilson b Cumming	91	60	53	3	9
B-J.Watling† c Eathorne b McMillan	8	17	13	-	-
M.E.Parlane* c Eathorne b Mascarenhas	18	18	14	1	1
H.J.H.Marshall c & b Cumming	3	10	7	-	-
D.R.Flynn not out	35	37	21	3	1
J.A.F.Yovich st de Boorder b Cumming	0	1	1	-	-
K.S.Williamson c Mascarenhas b Wagner	3	4	4	-	-
T.T.Davis run out	0	1	0	-	-
B.E.Scott st de Boorder b Cumming	5	4	4	-	1
B.P.Martin not out	4	9	4	-	-
B.J.Arnel					
Extras (lb 2, nb 1)	3				
TOTAL (20 overs) (8 wkts)	**170**	89			

Bowling	*O*	*M*	*R*	*W*
NORTHERN DISTRICTS				
Yovich	4	0	35	2
Scott	4	0	31	0
Davis	2	0	30	0
Arnel	3	0	28	0
Williamson	1	0	10	0
Martin	4	0	34	2
Flynn	2	0	20	0
OTAGO				
Wagner	4	0	21	1
McSkimming	3	0	25	0
McMillan	3	0	38	1
Craig	3	0	26	0
Mascarenhas	4	0	34	1
Cumming	3	0	24	4

Fall of Wickets	*O*	*ND*
1st	63	27
2nd	90	68
3rd	155	90
4th	188	129
5th	-	129
6th	-	134
7th	-	134
8th	-	145
9th	-	-
10th	-	-

CANTERBURY v CENTRAL DISTRICTS — State Twenty20

at Queen Elizabeth II Park, Christchurch on 15 February, 2009
Toss : Central Districts. Umpires : D.G. Paterson & D.M. Quested
***Canterbury won by 13 runs.** Points: Canterbury 4, Central Districts 0*

CANTERBURY

	Runs	Mins	Balls	6s	4s
I.A.Robertson c McClenaghan b Mason	4	7	8	-	-
M.H.W.Papps c Calkin b Worker	32	41	29	1	1
J.G.Myburgh b Schaw	28	23	25	1	2
S.L.Stewart c Worker b Mason	50	46	33	-	6
C.J.Anderson run out	2	11	6	-	-
C.Frauenstein c Calkin b McClenaghan	6	6	6	-	-
C.F.K.van Wyk*† c Worker b McClenaghan	13	12	10	-	1
A.M.Ellis c How b Mason	0	2	2	-	-
S.E.Bond not out	1	3	1	-	-
T.D.Astle not out	0	1	0	-	-
M.P.F.Davidson					
Extras (lb 7, w 5)	12				
TOTAL (20 overs) (8 wkts)	**148**	80			

CENTRAL DISTRICTS

	Runs	Mins	Balls	6s	4s
P.J.Ingram c & b Frauenstein	7	20	14	-	1
M.J.E.Calkin† c Ellis b Bond	0	3	1	-	-
J.M.How c Ellis b Bond	62	6	50	1	6
M.S.Sinclair* c van Wyk b Astle	21	15	14	-	4
K.Noema-Barnett b Frauenstein	12	16	12	-	1
E.P.Thompson c sub (R.J.McCone) b Astle	6	5	4	-	1
T.I.Weston c van Wyk b Bond	7	23	10	-	-
R.J.Schaw b Ellis	3	4	4	-	-
G.H.Worker b Bond	6	5	4	-	1
M.J.Mason c Bond b Frauenstein	1	4	2	-	-
M.J.McClenaghan not out	2	2	1	-	-
Extras (lb 1, w 6, nb 1)	8				
TOTAL (19.1 overs)	**135**	86			

Bowling	O	M	R	W
CENTRAL DISTRICTS				
Thompson	4	0	22	0
Mason	4	0	22	3
Schaw	4	0	27	1
Worker	4	0	32	1
Noema-Barnett	2	0	24	0
McClenaghan	2	0	14	2
CANTERBURY				
Bond	4	0	19	4
Davidson	4	0	30	0
Frauenstein	3.1	0	20	3
Ellis	4	0	30	1
Astle	2	0	12	2
Myburgh	2	0	23	0

Fall of Wickets	***C***	***CD***
1st	7	2
2nd	59	20
3rd	73	52
4th	96	93
5th	110	104
6th	143	117
7th	144	122
8th	147	132
9th	-	133
10th	-	135

AUCKLAND v WELLINGTON — State Twenty20

at Eden Park Outer Oval, Auckland on 15 February, 2009
Toss : Auckland. Umpires : B.F. Bowden & K.C. Manley
***Auckland won by 3 wickets.** Points: Auckland 4, Wellington 0*

WELLINGTON

	Runs	Mins	Balls	6s	4s
C.J.Nevin† c Styris b Azhar	3	9	8	-	-
S.P.Fleming* c Croft b Azhar	13	20	14	-	1
D.J.Bowden b Martin	14	16	12	1	-
J.D.Ryder run out	0	7	1	-	-
B-J.Crook c Hira b Nicol	19	14	15	2	-
H.K.P.Boam c Styris b Hira	2	6	6	-	-
G.R.Napier c de Grandhomme b Nicol	5	12	11	-	-
M.D.Bell not out	42	38	32	1	4
L.J.Woodcock not out	25	31	23	1	1
M.V.Houghton					
J.S.Patel					
Extras (lb 1, w 2, nb 2)	5				
TOTAL (20 overs) (7 wkts)	**128**	84			

AUCKLAND

	Runs	Mins	Balls	6s	4s
R.A.Jones* b Napier	32	48	37	-	4
C.de Grandhomme c Bowden b Napier	26	13	13	-	6
S.J.Croft c Crook b Napier	0	1	2	-	-
S.B.Styris c Nevin b Patel	13	26	23	-	-
L.J.Vivian b Ryder	22	25	16	1	1
G.J.Hopkins† retired hurt	9	17	9	-	1
R.J.Nicol c Bowden b Patel	15	14	9	1	-
R.M.Hira run out	4	10	7	-	-
G.J.Morgan not out	2	4	2	-	-
Azhar Abbas not out	6	2	1	1	-
C.S.Martin					
Extras (lb 3)	3				
TOTAL (19.5 overs) (7 wkts)	**132**	87			

Bowling	O	M	R	W
AUCKLAND				
Azhar	4	0	24	2
Martin	4	0	26	1
Nicol	4	0	25	2
Hira	4	0	19	1
Morgan	3	0	15	0
de Grandhomme	0.5	0	18	0
Styris	0.1	0	0	0
WELLINGTON				
Bowden	2	0	15	0
Napier	4	0	29	3
Houghton	4	0	19	0
Patel	3.5	0	22	2
Woodcock	2	0	14	0
Ryder	4	0	30	1

Fall of Wickets	***W***	***A***
1st	6	34
2nd	22	34
3rd	31	72
4th	31	74
5th	44	105
6th	54	124
7th	60	125
8th	-	-
9th	-	-
10th	-	-

Hopkins retired hurt at 105-4

NORTHERN DISTRICTS v CANTERBURY — State Twenty20

at Seddon Park, Hamilton on 18 February, 2009 (d/n)
Toss : Northern Districts. Umpires : B.G. Frost & P.L. Gasston
***Canterbury won the eliminator.** Points: Canterbury 4, Northern Districts 0*

CANTERBURY

	Runs	Mins	Balls	6s	4s
P.G.Fulton c McGlashan b Yovich	1	9	4	-	-
M.H.W.Papps c Boult b Davis	39	47	33	2	4
J.G.Myburgh c Scott b Martin	40	26	24	2	4
S.L.Stewart b Martin	19	19	13	1	2
C.J.Anderson c McGlashan b Davis	22	23	17	2	-
C.F.K.van Wyk*† run out	23	29	18	-	2
C.Frauenstein c Wilson b Yovich	6	3	2	1	-
A.M.Ellis run out	20	12	9	2	-
S.E.Bond not out	0	1	0	-	-
M.P.F.Davidson					
L.M.Burtt					
Extras (w 1)	1				
TOTAL (20 overs) (8 wkts)	**171**	93			

NORTHERN DISTRICTS

	Runs	Mins	Balls	6s	4s
B.S.Wilson b Bond	12	9	12	-	2
B-J.Watling c van Wyk b Davidson	8	15	5	-	2
M.E.Parlane* b Ellis	14	7	7	-	3
P.D.McGlashan† run out	3	8	7	-	-
H.J.H.Marshall c Stewart b Burtt	49	48	34	-	4
D.R.Flynn c Burtt b Ellis	47	51	35	3	4
J.A.F.Yovich not out	18	22	11	-	2
B.P.Martin st van Wyk b Frauenstein	19	12	9	1	2
T.T.Davis					
B.E.Scott					
T.A.Boult					
Extras (nb 1)	1				
TOTAL (20 overs) (7 wkts)	**171**	93			

Bowling	*O*	*M*	*R*	*W*
NORTHERN DISTRICTS				
Yovich	4	0	28	2
Boult	4	0	41	0
Scott	4	0	48	0
Davis	4	0	33	2
Martin	4	0	21	2
CANTERBURY				
Bond	4	0	33	1
Davidson	4	0	34	1
Ellis	4	0	24	2
Burtt	3	0	26	1
Myburgh	2	0	22	0
Frauenstein	3	0	32	1

Fall of Wickets

	C	*ND*
1st	20	20
2nd	79	34
3rd	92	34
4th	104	39
5th	130	131
6th	138	144
7th	170	171
8th	171	-
9th	-	-
10th	-	-

Eliminator: Northern Districts 6-1, Canterbury 7-0

OTAGO v CENTRAL DISTRICTS — State Twenty20

at University Oval, Dunedin on 18 February, 2009
Toss : Central Districts. Umpires : C.B. Gaffaney & E.A. Watkin
***Otago won by 5 wickets.** Points: Otago 4, Central Districts 0*

CENTRAL DISTRICTS

	Runs	Mins	Balls	6s	4s
J.M.How c Craig b Butler	27	18	19	3	-
P.J.Ingram c & b McCullum	24	30	17	1	2
M.S.Sinclair* lbw b McCullum	18	12	11	-	2
K.Noema-Barnett c McCullum b Cumming	3	9	8	-	-
J.D.P.Oram c de Boorder b Cumming	51	25	27	5	2
M.J.E.Calkin† not out	37	38	26	3	1
B.J.Diamanti b Butler	13	18	10	-	2
E.P.Thompson not out	6	4	2	1	-
G.R.Hay					
R.J.Schaw					
M.J.Mason					
Extras (b 1, lb 4, w 1)	6				
TOTAL (20 overs) (6 wkts)	**185**	83			

OTAGO

	Runs	Mins	Balls	6s	4s
A.J.Redmond not out	100	88	56	7	6
H.D.Rutherford b Mason	2	11	7	-	-
N.T.Broom c Hay b Diamanti	22	26	20	-	3
N.L.McCullum c Schaw b How	5	6	7	-	1
C.D.Cumming* c Schaw b Thompson	34	25	16	3	1
A.D.Mascarenhas c Schaw b Noema-Barnett	4	8	6	-	-
I.G.Butler not out	1	6	2	-	-
M.D.C.Craig					
D.C.de Boorder†					
N.Wagner					
J.M.McMillan					
Extras (b 4, lb 1, w 10, pen 6)	21				
TOTAL (19 overs) (5 wkts)	**189**	90			

Bowling	*O*	*M*	*R*	*W*
OTAGO				
Wagner	4	0	30	0
Mascarenhas	2	0	22	0
Butler	4	0	29	2
McMillan	1	0	20	0
McCullum	4	0	24	2
Cumming	4	0	44	2
Craig	1	0	11	0
CENTRAL DISTRICTS				
Mason	4	0	38	1
Thompson	3	0	27	1
Diamanti	4	0	21	1
Schaw	2	0	25	0
How	2	0	23	1
Noema-Barnett	3	0	31	1
Calkin	1	0	13	0

Fall of Wickets

	CD	*O*
1st	39	19
2nd	68	77
3rd	70	82
4th	82	148
5th	136	163
6th	177	-
7th	-	-
8th	-	-
9th	-	-
10th	-	-

Sinclair kept wicket from the 18th over

WELLINGTON v AUCKLAND — State Twenty20

at Allied Nationwide Finance Basin Reserve, Wellington on 18 February, 2009
Toss : Auckland. Umpires : T.J. Parlane & D.M. Quested
Auckland won by 5 wickets. *Points: Auckland 4, Wellington 0*

WELLINGTON

	Runs	Mins	Balls	6s	4s
C.J.Nevin† c de Grandhomme b Azhar	0	1	2	-	-
S.P.Fleming* b Morgan	57	61	35	1	9
G.R.Napier c Vivian b Morgan	9	19	12	-	2
M.D.Bell c Guptill b Nicol	22	21	18	1	2
J.D.Ryder b Morgan	16	14	14	1	-
J.E.C.Franklin c Morgan b Nicol	9	18	11	-	-
L.J.Woodcock b Styris	3	7	5	-	-
B-J.Crook c Styris b Nicol	7	11	8	-	-
D.J.Bowden st Young b Nicol	1	3	2	-	-
J.S.Patel not out	8	11	9	-	-
M.V.Houghton not out	6	9	5	-	-
Extras (b 3, lb 1, w 2, nb 1)	7				
TOTAL (20 overs) (9 wkts)	**145**	97			

AUCKLAND

	Runs	Mins	Balls	6s	4s
M.J.Guptill b Houghton	43	21	21	3	5
C.de Grandhomme c Bowden b Franklin	0	8	3	-	-
R.A.Jones* c Bell b Napier	22	34	30	-	2
S.B.Styris c Crook b Franklin	26	27	19	1	2
L.J.Vivian c Patel b Napier	3	9	6	-	-
R.J.Nicol not out	28	28	21	2	1
S.J.Croft not out	20	24	16	1	1
R.A.Young†					
G.J.Morgan					
Azhar Abbas					
C.S.Martin					
Extras (b 1, lb 3)	4				
TOTAL (19.2 overs) (5 wkts)	**146**	81			

Bowling	*O*	*M*	*R*	*W*
AUCKLAND				
Azhar	4	0	34	1
Martin	4	0	18	0
Morgan	4	0	16	3
Nicol	4	0	37	4
Styris	4	0	36	1
WELLINGTON				
Bowden	2	0	8	0
Franklin	4	0	35	2
Napier	4	0	36	2
Houghton	4	0	26	1
Patel	3	0	16	0
Woodcock	2	0	11	0
Ryder	0.2	0	10	0

Fall of Wickets	***W***	***A***
1st	0	12
2nd	32	50
3rd	77	87
4th	109	97
5th	112	100
6th	118	-
7th	130	-
8th	130	-
9th	132	-
10th	-	-

CANTERBURY v AUCKLAND — State Twenty20

at Queen Elizabeth II Park, Christchurch on 20 February, 2009
Abandoned without a ball being bowled. *Points: Canterbury 2, Auckland 2*

WELLINGTON v CENTRAL DISTRICTS — State Twenty20

at Allied Nationwide Finance Basin Reserve, Wellington on 20 February, 2009
Abandoned without a ball being bowled. *Points: Wellington 2, Central Districts 2*

NORTHERN DISTRICTS v OTAGO — State Twenty20

at Blake Park, Mt Maunganui on 20 February, 2009
Abandoned without a ball being bowled. *Points: Northern Districts 2, Otago 2*

AUCKLAND v OTAGO

State Twenty20

at Eden Park Outer Oval, Auckland on 22 February, 2009
Toss : Auckland. Umpires : B.G. Frost & E.A. Watkin
***Otago won by 42 runs.** Points: Otago 4, Auckland 0*

OTAGO

	Runs	Mins	Balls	6s	4s
A.J.Redmond c Styris b Azhar	1	3	3	-	-
B.B.McCullum c Guptill b Hira	26	42	18	2	1
H.D.Rutherford b Azhar	17	17	16	1	2
C.D.Cumming* c Martin b de Grandhomme	76	50	46	5	6
N.T.Broom c Croft b Morgan	8	10	10	-	1
N.L.McCullum c Croft b Morgan	1	5	4	-	-
A.D.Mascarenhas c de Grandhomme b Martin	10	20	11	-	1
I.G.Butler not out	17	12	11	1	-
D.C.de Boorder† run out	0	2	1	-	-
N.Wagner not out	0	1	0	-	-
M.J.Harvie					
Extras (b 1, lb 2, w 4)	7				
TOTAL (20 overs) (8 wkts)	**163**	89			

AUCKLAND

	Runs	Mins	Balls	6s	4s
M.J.Guptill c Cumming b Mascarenhas	6	26	12	1	-
C.de Grandhomme b Wagner	0	1	2	-	-
R.A.Jones* c Mascarenhas b Harvie	1	3	2	-	-
S.B.Styris c & b Harvie	0	1	2	-	-
S.J.Croft b Butler	55	68	50	-	8
R.A.Young† c Cumming b Butler	0	3	3	-	-
L.J.Vivian b McCullum N.L.	16	25	24	1	-
R.M.Hira not out	18	27	20	-	1
G.J.Morgan not out	6	7	5	-	1
Azhar Abbas					
C.S.Martin					
Extras (lb 5, w 14)	19				
TOTAL (20 overs) (7 wkts)	**121**	88			

Bowling	O	M	R	W
AUCKLAND				
Azhar	4	0	20	2
Martin	4	0	33	1
Styris	3	0	37	0
Hira	4	0	32	1
Morgan	4	0	31	2
de Grandhomme	1	0	7	1
OTAGO				
Wagner	4	0	29	1
Harvie	3	0	15	2
Butler	4	0	24	2
Mascarenhas	4	0	24	1
McCullum N.L.	4	1	16	1
Cumming	1	0	8	0

Fall of Wickets	*O*	*A*
1st	2	1
2nd	22	3
3rd	75	3
4th	100	46
5th	105	47
6th	138	77
7th	155	107
8th	162	-
9th	-	-
10th	-	-

CENTRAL DISTRICTS v CANTERBURY

State Twenty20

at Fitzherbert Park, Palmerston North on 22 February, 2009
Toss : Central Districts. Umpires : G.A.V. Baxter & M.P. George
***Canterbury won by 3 wickets.** Points: Canterbury 4, Central Districts 0*

CENTRAL DISTRICTS

	Runs	Mins	Balls	6s	4s
P.J.Ingram c Fulton b Davidson	2	4	4	-	-
J.M.How c van Wyk b Davidson	12	13	11	-	2
M.J.E.Calkin† c Ellis b Davidson	0	1	1	-	-
J.D.P.Oram c Anderson b Burtt	14	35	22	-	-
M.S.Sinclair* not out	85	69	61	3	5
K.Noema-Barnett c Myburgh b Frauenstein	3	11	6	-	-
G.R.Hay c & b Bond	7	9	6	-	1
E.P.Thompson not out	17	17	11	1	-
B.J.Diamanti					
R.J.Schaw					
M.J.Mason					
Extras (lb 2, nb 2)	4				
TOTAL (20 overs) (6 wkts)	**144**	86			

CANTERBURY

	Runs	Mins	Balls	6s	4s
M.H.W.Papps c Thompson b Mason	1	2	2	-	-
P.G.Fulton c Sinclair b Mason	11	12	11	-	2
J.G.Myburgh b Diamanti	36	44	35	-	4
S.L.Stewart c Ingram b Diamanti	22	26	19	1	2
C.J.Anderson c Sinclair b Mason	18	31	14	1	-
C.F.K.van Wyk*† run out	40	33	27	1	2
C.Frauenstein c Calkin b Mason	0	1	1	-	-
A.M.Ellis not out	4	9	3	-	-
S.E.Bond not out	0	1	0	-	-
M.P.F.Davidson					
L.M.Burtt					
Extras (lb 2, w 10, nb 1)	13				
TOTAL (18.3 overs) (7 wkts)	**145**	87			

Bowling	O	M	R	W
CANTERBURY				
Bond	4	0	37	1
Davidson	3	0	22	3
Burtt	4	0	19	1
Ellis	4	0	28	0
Frauenstein	3	0	20	1
Myburgh	2	0	16	0
CENTRAL DISTRICTS				
Mason	3.3	0	23	4
Thompson	4	0	36	0
Oram	4	0	24	0
Diamanti	3	0	16	2
Schaw	2	0	23	0
Noema-Barnett	2	0	21	0

Fall of Wickets	*CD*	*C*
1st	7	2
2nd	8	16
3rd	15	68
4th	61	76
5th	76	124
6th	96	125
7th	-	144
8th	-	-
9th	-	-
10th	-	-

NORTHERN DISTRICTS v WELLINGTON — State Twenty20

at Blake Park, Mt Maunganui on 22 February, 2009
Toss : Northern Districts. Umpires : K.D. Earl & D.M. Quested
***Wellington won by 7 wickets.** Points: Wellington 4, Northern Districts 0*

NORTHERN DISTRICTS

	Runs	Mins	Balls	6s	4s
P.D.McGlashan† c Franklin b Houghton	30	31	20	3	-
M.E.Parlane* c Elliott b Franklin	4	12	15	-	-
K.S.Williamson c Franklin b Patel	14	29	20	-	1
A.P.Devcich b Woodcock	30	29	24	1	1
B-J.Watling c & b Houghton	1	1	2	-	-
H.J.H.Marshall c Franklin b Houghton	7	5	6	-	1
J.A.F.Yovich st Nevin b Patel	2	4	4	-	-
G.W.Aldridge b Napier	3	17	8	-	-
B.P.Martin st Nevin b Woodcock	6	9	10	-	1
T.A.Boult not out	3	3	2	-	-
B.J.Arnel b Napier	0	1	2	-	-
Extras (lb 6, w 4)	10				
TOTAL (18.5 overs)	**110**	80			

WELLINGTON

	Runs	Mins	Balls	6s	4s
C.J.Nevin† c Williamson b Yovich	15	15	14	-	2-
S.P.Fleming* not out	46	73	44	-	6
G.R.Napier c Watling b Martin	20	21	14	1	2
J.E.C.Franklin c Watling b Aldridge	27	28	25	1	3
G.D.Elliott not out	0	3	2	-	-
M.D.Bell					
H.K.P.Boam					
L.J.Woodcock					
M.V.Houghton					
J.S.Patel					
I.E.O'Brien					
Extras (lb 1, w 2)	3				
TOTAL (16.3 overs) (3 wkts)	**111**	73			

Bowling	*O*	*M*	*R*	*W*
WELLINGTON				
Napier	3.5	1	9	2
Franklin	3	0	21	1
O'Brien	2	0	9	0
Houghton	4	0	28	3
Patel	4	0	27	2
Woodcock	2	0	10	2
NORTHERN DISTRICTS				
Boult	2	0	11	0
Yovich	3.3	0	26	1
Arnel	3	0	18	0
Aldridge	2	0	12	1
Martin	4	0	29	1
Williamson	2	0	14	0

Fall of Wickets	***ND***	***W***
1st	8	23
2nd	47	65
3rd	67	105
4th	69	-
5th	83	-
6th	88	-
7th	97	-
8th	106	-
9th	106	-
10th	110	-

OTAGO v CANTERBURY — State Twenty20 Final

at University Oval, Dunedin on 1 March, 2009
Abandoned without a ball being bowled.

2008/09 STATE TWENTY20 AVERAGES

	M	In	NO	HS	Runs	Ave	100s	50s	Ct	St	O	M	R	W	Ave	R/O	Best
G.W.Aldridge	5	5	1	22	51	12.75	-	-	3	-	14.2	0	132	3	44.00	9.21	1-12
C.J.Anderson	7	7	0	23	76	10.86	-	-	2	-							
B.J.Arnel	6	1	0	0	0	0.00	-	-	-	-	19.1	0	147	1	147.00	7.67	1-18
T.D.Astle	4	3	3	6*	7	-	-	-	3	-	8	0	66	2	33.00	8.25	2-12
Azhar Abbas	7	1	1	6*	6	-	-	-	-	-	27	0	186	10	18.60	6.89	2-20
M.D.Bell	7	5	1	46	142	35.50	-	-	5	-							
H.K.P.Boam	6	2	1	2*	4	4.00	-	-	-	-	6	0	50	1	50.00	8.33	1-32
S.E.Bond	6	3	3	1*	1	-	-	-	3	-	24	1	158	11	14.36	6.58	4-19
T.A.Boult	2	1	1	3*	3	-	-	-	1	-	6	0	52	0	-	8.67	-
D.J.Bowden	6	4	0	15	32	8.00	-	-	3	-	18	0	148	2	74.00	8.22	1-24
D.J.Broom	1	1	0	20	20	20.00	-	-	-	-							
N.T.Broom	2	2	0	22	30	15.00	-	-	-	-							
L.M.Burtt	3	-	-	-	-	-	-	-	1	-	11	0	105	2	52.50	9.55	1-19
I.G.Butler	6	5	4	17*	52	52.00	-	-	1	-	22	0	161	10	16.10	7.32	2-24
M.J.E.Calkin	6	6	2	37*	65	16.25	-	-	4	-	5	0	56	2	28.00	11.20	1-19
M.D.C.Craig	6	-	-	-	-	-	-	-	5	-	13	0	120	1	120.00	9.23	1-22
S.J.Croft	7	6	1	55	142	28.40	-	2	4	-	6	0	61	2	30.50	10.17	1-15
B-J.Crook	6	6	1	21	81	16.20	-	-	2	-							
C.D.Cumming	3	3	0	76	121	40.33	-	1	3	-	8	0	76	6	12.66	9.50	4-24
M.P.F.Davidson	7	1	1	1*	1	-	-	-	1	-	27	0	178	9	19.77	6.59	3-22
T.T.Davis	2	1	0	0	0	0.00	-	-	-	-	6	0	63	2	31.50	10.50	2-33
D.C.de Boorder	7	2	1	0*	0	0.00	-	-	4	2							
C.de Grandhomme	7	7	0	36	121	17.28	-	-	4	-	14.5	0	151	5	30.20	10.18	2-34
J.J.B.Dean	4	3	0	26	46	15.33	-	-	3	-							
A.P.Devcich	1	1	0	30	30	30.00	-	-	-	-							
B.J.Diamanti	2	1	0	13	13	13.00	-	-	-	-	7	0	37	3	12.33	5.29	2-16
S.W.Eathorne	5	1	0	4	4	4.00	-	-	3	-							
G.D.Elliott	1	1	1	0*	0	-	-	-	1	-							
A.M.Ellis	7	6	2	20	43	10.75	-	-	3	-	28	0	209	9	23.22	7.46	2-21
S.P.Fleming	7	7	1	57	145	24.16	-	1	-	-							
D.R.Flynn	6	6	1	47	92	18.40	-	-	1	-	4	0	33	0	-	8.25	-
J.E.C.Franklin	6	6	3	64*	209	69.66	-	2	3	-	19	0	149	4	37.25	7.84	2-35
C.Frauenstein	7	7	1	27	57	9.50	-	-	4	-	20.2	0	185	6	30.83	9.09	3-20
P.G.Fulton	2	2	0	11	12	6.00	-	-	1	-							
B.B.J.Griggs	3	2	0	13	26	13.00	-	-	-	-							
M.J.Guptill	2	2	0	43	49	24.50	-	-	2	-							
M.J.Harvie	1	-	-	-	-	-	-	-	1	-	3	0	15	2	7.50	5.00	2-15
G.R.Hay	2	1	0	7	7	7.00	-	-	1	-							
B.E.Hefford	2	-	-	-	-	-	-	-	-	-	7	0	74	0	-	10.57	-
R.M.Hira	6	4	2	28	51	25.50	-	-	4	-	21	0	143	6	23.83	6.81	3-21
G.J.Hopkins	4	4	3	38*	62	62.00	-	-	5	-							
M.V.Houghton	7	2	1	6*	6	6.00	-	-	1	-	24	0	171	7	24.42	7.13	3-28
J.M.How	7	7	0	62	145	20.71	-	1	1	-	4	0	35	1	35.00	8.75	1-23
P.J.Ingram	7	7	0	36	137	19.57	-	-	2	-							
R.A.Jones	7	7	0	63	152	21.71	-	1	2	-							
A.K.Kitchen	3	3	1	33*	64	32.00	-	-	2	-							
H.J.H.Marshall	7	7	0	49	64	9.14	-	-	2	-							
J.A.H.Marshall	3	3	1	58*	60	30.00	-	1	2	-							
B.P.Martin	7	6	4	19	40	20.00	-	-	-	-	28	0	204	11	18.54	7.29	3-16
C.S.Martin	7	-	-	-	-	-	-	-	1	-	27	0	179	8	22.37	6.63	2-23
A.D.Mascarenhas	7	7	1	57*	163	27.16	-	2	2	-	22	0	181	7	25.85	8.23	2-26
M.J.Mason	7	3	1	1	2	1.00	-	-	2	-	27.3	0	211	9	23.44	7.67	4-23
M.J.McClenaghan	3	2	2	2*	4	-	-	-	2	-	8.5	0	63	5	12.60	7.13	2-14
B.B.McCullum	1	1	0	26	26	26.00	-	-	-	-							
N.L.McCullum	6	6	2	76*	165	41.25	-	1	4	-	18	1	124	8	15.50	6.89	2-3
P.D.McGlashan	6	6	0	52	161	26.83	-	1	5	2							
J.M.McMillan	2	-	-	-	-	-	-	-	-	-	4	0	58	1	58.00	14.50	1-38
W.C.McSkimming	5	3	3	19*	28	-	-	-	4	-	18	0	137	9	15.22	7.61	3-28
G.J.Morgan	7	3	3	6*	9	-	-	-	1	-	25	0	163	8	20.37	6.52	3-16
J.G.Myburgh	7	7	1	73*	228	38.00	-	1	3	-	19	0	153	2	76.50	8.05	1-23
G.R.Napier	7	6	0	20	42	7.00	-	-	3	-	25.5	1	162	14	11.57	6.27	3-29
C.J.Nevin	7	7	0	29	77	11.00	-	-	5	3							
R.J.Nicol	3	3	2	28*	69	69.00	-	-	1	-	12	0	91	6	15.16	7.58	4-37
K.Noema-Barnett	7	7	1	38	77	12.83	-	-	3	-	19	0	186	4	46.50	9.79	2-26
I.E.O'Brien	1	-	-	-	-	-	-	-	-	-	2	0	9	0	-	4.50	-
J.D.P.Oram	2	2	0	51	65	32.50	-	1	-	-	4	0	24	0	-	6.00	-

	M	In	NO	HS	Runs	Ave	100s	50s	Ct	St	O	M	R	W	Ave	R/O	Best
M.H.W.Papps	7	7	0	46	133	19.00	-	-	1	-							
M.E.Parlane	7	7	0	30	123	17.57	-	-	-	-							
J.S.Patel	3	1	1	8*	8	-	-	-	1	-	10.5	0	65	4	16.25	6.00	2-22
A.J.Redmond	7	7	1	100*	325	54.16	1	2	2	-							
I.A.Robertson	5	5	0	32	108	21.60	-	-	1	-							
H.D.Rutherford	7	7	0	87	220	31.42	-	1	2	-							
J.D.Ryder	2	2	0	16	16	8.00	-	-	-	-	4.2	0	40	1	40.00	9.23	1-30
R.J.Schaw	7	4	2	19*	50	25.00	-	-	3	-	16	0	136	3	45.33	8.50	2-27
B.E.Scott	5	4	2	22*	28	14.00	-	-	2	-	18	0	167	2	83.50	9.28	1-28
M.S.Sinclair	6	6	1	85*	254	50.80	-	3	4	-							
S.L.Stewart	7	7	0	50	147	21.00	-	1	2	-							
S.B.Styris	5	5	0	35	80	16.00	-	-	7	-	7.1	0	73	1	73.00	10.19	1-36
E.P.Thompson	7	6	3	59	105	35.00	-	1	1	-	26	0	226	8	28.25	8.69	4-31
G.R.Todd	5	5	1	39	114	28.50	-	-	1	-							
C.F.K.van Wyk	7	7	1	40	168	28.00	-	-	6	1							
L.J.Vivian	7	7	1	55*	141	23.50	-	1	2	-							
N.Wagner	7	1	1	0*	0		-	-	-	-	26.1	0	191	6	31.83	7.30	2-6
B-J.Watling	7	7	0	48	119	17.00	-	-	5	-							
T.I.Weston	5	4	0	34	48	12.00	-	-	2	-							
K.S.Williamson	4	4	0	30	57	14.25	-	-	4	-	9	0	65	1	65.00	7.22	1-21
B.S.Wilson	2	2	0	91	103	51.50	-	1	2	-							
L.J.Woodcock	7	5	3	29*	87	43.50	-	-	1	-	18	0	135	11	12.27	7.50	3-27
G.H.Worker	4	4	0	8	21	5.25	-	-	3	-	12	0	121	2	60.50	10.08	1-30
R.A.Young	5	4	0	15	33	8.25	-	-	2	1							
J.A.F.Yovich	7	7	2	33*	65	13.00	-	-	-	-	26.3	1	194	14	13.85	7.59	3-23

CAREER RECORDS

	M	In	NO	HS	Runs	Ave	100s	50s	Ct	St	O	M	R	W	Ave	R/O	Best
G.W.Aldridge	16	10	4	22	66	11.00	-	-	6	-	53.2	0	433	18	24.05	8.11	4-19
C.J.Anderson	9	7	0	23	76	10.86	-	-	2	-	8	0	45	4	11.25	5.63	3-15
B.J.Arnel	17	4	1	1*	2	0.66	-	-	2	-	57.1	0	442	9	49.11	7.73	2-18
T.D.Astle	4	3	3	6*	7	-	-	-	3	-	8	0	66	2	33.00	8.25	2-12
Azhar Abbas	7	1	1	6*	6	-	-	-	-	-	27	0	186	10	18.60	6.89	2-20
M.D.Bell	10	7	2	46	157	31.40	-	-	7	-							
H.K.P.Boam	6	2	1	2*	4	4.00	-	-	-	-	6	0	50	1	50.00	8.33	1-32
S.E.Bond	12	5	3	7	10	5.00	-	-	4	-	48	1	342	17	20.11	7.13	4-19
T.A.Boult	2	1	1	3*	3	-	-	-	1	-	6	0	52	0	-	8.67	-
D.J.Bowden	16	10	2	17*	84	10.50	-	-	7	-	47	0	344	7	49.14	7.32	2-13
D.J.Broom	1	1	0	20	20	20.00	-	-	-	-							
N.T.Broom	14	14	1	33	178	13.69	-	-	3	-	20	0	195	5	39.00	9.75	1-5
L.M.Burtt	12	1	0	1	1	1.00	-	-	5	-	42	0	354	12	29.50	8.43	2-16
I.G.Butler	11	10	4	21	89	14.83	-	-	4	-	34	0	270	12	22.50	7.94	2-24
M.J.E.Calkin	6	6	2	37*	65	16.25	-	-	4	-	5	0	56	2	28.00	11.20	1-19
M.D.C.Craig	6	-	-	-	-	-	-	-	5	-	13	0	120	1	120.00	9.23	1-22
S.J.Croft	7	6	1	55	142	28.40	-	2	4	-	6	0	61	2	30.50	10.17	1-15
B-J.Crook	6	6	1	21	81	16.20	-	-	2	-							
C.D.Cumming	15	15	0	76	333	22.20	-	1	7	-	19.5	0	150	13	11.53	7.56	4-24
M.P.F.Davidson	7	1	1	1*	1	-	-	-	1	-	27	0	178	9	19.77	6.59	3-22
T.T.Davis	2	1	0	0	0	0.00	-	-	-	-	6	0	63	2	31.50	10.50	2-33
D.C.de Boorder	12	6	3	3*	8	2.66	-	-	5	4							
C.de Grandhomme	8	7	0	36	121	17.28	-	-	4	-	14.5	0	151	5	30.20	10.18	2-34
J.J.B.Dean	4	3	0	26	46	15.33	-	-	3	-							
A.P.Devcich	6	6	0	30	85	14.16	-	-	-	-	5	0	43	0	-	8.60	-
B.J.Diamanti	15	9	3	36*	114	19.00	-	-	3	-	55	0	427	25	17.08	7.76	3-14
S.W.Eathorne	5	1	0	4	4	4.00	-	-	3	-							
G.D.Elliott	11	11	4	57	233	33.28	-	2	3	-	18.3	0	166	6	27.66	8.97	2-25
A.M.Ellis	17	13	4	20	104	11.55	-	-	8	-	43.4	1	320	16	20.00	7.32	2-18
S.P.Fleming	12	12	1	57	219	19.90	-	1	1	-							
D.R.Flynn	19	19	2	47	306	18.00	-	-	2	-	14	0	99	0	-	7.07	-
J.E.C.Franklin	7	7	3	64*	250	62.50	-	2	5	-	22	0	188	4	47.00	8.55	2-35
C.Frauenstein	17	13	1	27	125	10.41	-	-	7	-	27.2	0	246	8	30.75	9.00	3-20
P.G.Fulton	10	10	1	39	153	17.00	-	-	3	-							
B.B.J.Griggs	16	9	1	34	119	14.87	-	-	6	4							
M.J.Guptill	12	11	1	55	312	31.20	-	1	8	-							
M.J.Harvie	4	3	1	14*	26	13.00	-	-	1	-	14	0	123	5	24.60	8.79	2-15
G.R.Hay	13	11	5	62*	227	37.83	-	1	5	-							
B.E.Hefford	9	1	1	0*	0	-	-	-	1	-	31	0	297	4	74.25	9.58	2-26
R.M.Hira	11	6	3	28	51	17.00	-	-	6	-	35	0	257	10	25.70	7.34	3-21
G.J.Hopkins	16	15	6	47	282	31.33	-	-	8	2							
M.V.Houghton	11	3	2	18*	24	24.00	-	-	3	-	36.3	0	261	10	26.10	7.15	3-24
J.M.How	20	20	2	78*	642	35.66	-	5	9	-	14	0	135	5	27.00	9.64	1-12
P.J.Ingram	14	13	1	36	180	15.00	-	-	2	-							
R.A.Jones	21	20	4	75	377	23.56	-	2	5	-							
A.K.Kitchen	3	3	1	33*	64	32.00	-	-	2	-							
H.J.H.Marshall	9	9	0	49	82	9.11	-	-	4	-							
J.A.H.Marshall	16	16	3	58*	382	29.38	-	3	4	-	4	0	31	0	-	7.75	-
B.P.Martin	16	11	5	19	74	12.33	-	-	2	-	62	0	452	23	19.65	7.29	3-16
C.S.Martin	20	-	-	-	-	-	-	-	6	-	78	0	616	17	36.23	7.90	2-23
A.D.Mascarenhas	7	7	1	57*	163	27.16	-	2	2	-	22	0	181	7	25.85	8.23	2-26
M.J.Mason	14	3	1	1	2	1.00	-	-	4	-	54.3	0	417	17	24.52	7.65	4-23
M.J.McClenaghan	3	2	2	2*	4	-	-	-	2	-	8.5	0	63	5	12.60	7.13	2-14
B.B.McCullum	9	9	0	62	277	30.77	-	2	5	-							
N.L.McCullum	18	18	4	76*	447	31.92	-	2	8	-	56.4	1	403	24	16.79	7.11	4-16
P.D.McGlashan	19	19	2	94	496	29.17	-	2	9	6							
J.M.McMillan	8	1	1	0*	0	-	-	-	1	-	24.1	0	170	7	24.28	7.03	3-15
W.C.McSkimming	13	6	5	19*	50	50.00	-	-	7	-	45	1	361	13	27.76	8.02	3-28
G.J.Morgan	7	3	3	6*	9	-	-	-	1	-	25	0	163	8	20.37	6.52	3-16
J.G.Myburgh	12	12	2	73*	343	34.30	-	2	3	-	20	0	164	2	82.00	8.20	1-23
G.R.Napier	10	7	1	48*	90	15.00	-	-	3	-	36.3	1	265	15	17.66	7.26	3-29
C.J.Nevin	18	16	1	87*	289	19.26	-	1	9	4							
R.J.Nicol	16	10	5	78*	316	63.20	-	1	8	-	33	0	286	12	23.83	8.67	4-37
K.Noema-Barnett	12	12	1	38	121	11.00	-	-	3	-	19	0	186	4	46.50	9.79	2-26
I.E.O'Brien	8	2	1	1*	1	1.00	-	-	-	-	26	0	182	9	20.22	7.00	3-21

	M	In	NO	HS	Runs	Ave	100s	50s	Ct	St	O	M	R	W	Ave	R/O	Best
J.D.P.Oram	10	10	1	57	230	25.55	-	2	3	-	25.3	0	220	4	55.00	8.62	2-26
M.H.W.Papps	19	17	0	66	380	22.35	-	2	3	-							
M.E.Parlane	17	17	0	48	304	17.88	-	-	4	-							
J.S.Patel	10	4	2	12	26	13.00	-	-	2	-	33.5	1	201	8	25.12	5.94	3-17
A.J.Redmond	18	15	1	100*	455	32.50	1	3	6	-	18.1	0	149	7	21.28	8.20	4-24
I.A.Robertson	15	12	0	32	150	12.50	-	-	3	-	21	0	165	3	55.00	7.86	1-23
H.D.Rutherford	7	7	0	87	220	31.42	-	1	2	-							
J.D.Ryder	12	12	2	66	248	24.80	-	2	3	-	33.2	1	309	4	77.25	9.27	1-12
R.J.Schaw	17	7	4	19*	71	23.66	-	-	4	-	47.2	0	428	16	26.75	9.04	3-21
B.E.Scott	17	13	8	22*	108	21.60	-	-	5	-	55.3	0	467	13	35.92	8.41	3-9
M.S.Sinclair	19	19	2	85*	498	29.29	-	5	11	-	1	0	13	0	-	13.00	-
S.L.Stewart	14	12	1	66*	261	23.72	-	2	2	-							
S.B.Styris	16	16	0	62	340	21.25	-	2	8	-	29.2	0	266	8	33.25	9.06	2-35
E.P.Thompson	18	15	6	59	212	23.55	-	1	4	-	65	0	498	24	20.75	7.66	5-32
G.R.Todd	16	16	4	39	341	28.41	-	-	5	-							
C.F.K.van Wyk	16	13	3	40	240	24.00	-	-	9	2							
L.J.Vivian	8	8	2	55*	143	23.83	-	1	4	-							
N.Wagner	7	1	1	0*	0	-	-	-	-	-	26.1	0	191	6	31.83	7.30	2-6
B-J.Watling	13	12	4	48	204	25.50	-	-	5	-							
T.I.Weston	5	4	0	34	48	12.00	-	-	2	-							
K.S.Williamson	4	4	0	30	57	14.25	-	-	4	-	9	0	65	1	65.00	7.22	1-21
B.S.Wilson	2	2	0	91	103	51.50	-	1	2	-							
L.J.Woodcock	15	10	5	36*	180	36.00	-	-	1	-	40	0	332	16	20.75	8.30	3-27
G.H.Worker	4	4	0	8	21	5.25	-	-	3	-	12	0	121	2	60.50	10.08	1-30
R.A.Young	14	7	2	26	73	14.60	-	-	5	2							
J.A.F.Yovich	14	13	4	33*	131	14.55	-	-	1	-	42.3	1	365	16	22.81	8.58	3-23

PROVINCIAL A TEAM COMPETITION

The Provincial A competition took place from 21-27 January at Lincoln. In a change of format, one full round-robin of one-day matches was played with the top two teams meeting in the final. The remaining four sides were due to play two Twenty 20 matches on that day but rain meant that no play was possible while the fifty-over final was reduced to 22 overs each. Final points were: Northern Districts 18, Auckland 16, Otago 14, Canterbury 13, Wellington 4, Central Districts 0.

CANTERBURY v NORTHERN DISTRICTS *Northern Districts won by 35 runs*
At Bert Sutcliffe Oval *21 January, 2009*

Northern Districts 289-6 (B.S. Wilson 70, I.A. Page 68, S.J.M. McLeod 50)

Canterbury 254 (C.J. Anderson 64, A.W. Robertson 58*, D.J. Broom 40, T.T. Davis 5-41)

AUCKLAND v OTAGO *Auckland won by 6 wickets*
At Lincoln No.3 *21 January, 2009*

Otago 258-6 (H.D. Rutherford 64, A.J. Redmond 54, J.W. Sheed 53*)

Auckland 262-4 (J.A. Raval 82, A.P. de Boorder 38*, C. Munro 34, M. Turner 30, D.N. Hakaraia 30)

CENTRAL DISTRICTS v WELLINGTON *Wellington won by 15 runs*
At Lincoln Green *21 January, 2009*

Wellington 308-4 (F.J. Colson 121, J.M. Brodie 93, H.K.P. Boam 43*)

Central Districts 293-8 (M.J.E. Calkin 72, D.L. Rayner 53*, T.I. Lythe 47)

AUCKLAND v CENTRAL DISTRICTS *Auckland won by 8 runs*
At Bert Sutcliffe Oval *22 January, 2009*

Auckland 283-9 (M. Turner 82, A.P. de Boorder 50, J.A. Raval 37, D.N. Hakaraia 33, G.R. Hay 4-44, T.I. Lythe 3-48)

Central Districts 275 (J.W. de Terte 59, J.M.K. Kuru 51, L. Rukuwai 32, L.J. Shaw 4-76)

CANTERBURY v WELLINGTON *Canterbury won by 6 wickets*
At Lincoln No.3 *22 January, 2009*

Wellington 265-6 (J.M. Brodie 110, H.K. Bennett 3-56)

Canterbury 267-4 (T.D. Astle 85, D.J. Broom 70*, C.J. Anderson 51)

NORTHERN DISTRICTS v OTAGO *Otago won by 6 wickets*
At Lincoln Green *22 January, 2009*

Northern Districts 198 (B.S. Wilson 46, K.G. Bettley 43, N.B. Beard 3-34

Otago 202-4 (J.W. Sheed 52, S.W. Eathorne 49, S.R. Wells 42*)

AUCKLAND v CANTERBURY *Auckland won by 4 wickets*
At Lincoln Green *23 January, 2009*

Canterbury 256-8 (L. van Beek 75*, T.R. Muir 40, A.W. Robertson 34)

Auckland 257-6 (D.N. Hakaraia 112*, M. Turner 45, C. Munro 32)

OTAGO v CENTRAL DISTRICTS *Otago won by 96 runs*
At Lincoln No.3 23 January, 2009

Otago 260 (S.R. Wells 87, M.D.C. Craig 70, H.D. Rutherford 39, D.L. Rayner 6-46)

Central Districts 164 (J.W. de Terte 51, D. Meiring 37, M.D.C. Craig 3-48)

WELLINGTON v NORTHERN DISTRICTS *Northern Districts won by 32 runs*
At Bert Sutcliffe Oval 23 January, 2009

Northern Districts 302-6 (B.S. Wilson 150, S.J.M. McLeod 67, J.J. Boult 31)

Wellington 270 (D.J. Bowden 80, H.K.P. Boam 39, S.J. Murdoch 36, G.W. Aldridge 3-54)

CANTERBURY v OTAGO *Canterbury won by 9 wickets*
At Bert Sutcliffe Oval 25 January, 2009

Otago 173 (A.D. Bullick 46, S.R. Wells 39, M.P.F. Davidson 3-32)

Canterbury 175-1 (B.J. Rae 82, T.D. Astle 73*)

CENTRAL DISTRICTS v NORTHERN DISTRICTS *Northern won by 3 wickets*
At Lincoln Green 25 January, 2009

Central Districts 206 (T.I. Lythe 43, D. Meiring 38, T.T. Davis 4-34)

Northern Districts 210-7 (B.S. Wilson 49, C.J. Merchant 43, I.A. Page 39)

WELLINGTON v AUCKLAND *Auckland won by 6 wickets*
At Lincoln No.3 25 January, 2009

Wellington 261-9 (J.M. Brodie 66, J. Sewell 61, M. Pollard 30, G.J. Morgan 3-41, A.P. de Boorder 3-48)

Auckland 262-4 (D.N. Hakaraia 99*, M. Turner 50, J.A. Raval 37, S. McCann 36*, J. Sewell 3-40)

OTAGO v WELLINGTON *Otago won by 9 runs*
At Bert Sutcliffe Oval 26 January, 2009

Otago 234-8 (M.D.C. Craig 54, S.W. Eathorne 49, J.W. Sheed 40, S.M. Fitzgibbon 36)

Wellington 225-7 (S.J. Murdoch 85, F.J. Colson 36, M.D.C. Craig 3-38, W.E.R. Somerville 3-50)

AUCKLAND v NORTHERN DISTRICTS *Northern Districts won by 63 runs*
At Lincoln No.3 26 January, 2009

Northern Districts 205-9 (I.A. Page 73, C.J. Merchant 36)

Auckland 142 (D.N. Hakaraia 42, K.G. Bettley 3-16)

CANTERBURY v CENTRAL DISTRICTS *Canterbury won by 5 wickets*
At Lincoln Green 26 January, 2009

Central Districts 285-7 (M.J.E. Calkin 46, G.R. Hay 44, D.L. Rayner 39, M. Gardner 38, M.O. Kain 3-30)

Canterbury 289-5 (D.J. Broom 140*, S. Noster 46)

FINAL

AUCKLAND v NORTHERN DISTRICTS *Auckland won by 14 runs*
At Bert Sutcliffe Oval 27 January, 2009

Auckland 202-4 (D.N. Hakaraia 88, J.A. Raval 61)

Northern Districts 188-6 (B.S. Wilson 100, C.J. Merchant 41, B. Singh 5-28)

TWENTY20 MATCHES

OTAGO v CANTERBURY *Abandoned*
At Lincoln No.3 27 January, 2009

WELLINGTON v CENTRAL DISTRICTS *Abandoned*
At Lincoln Green 27 January, 2009

OTAGO v WELLINGTON *Abandoned*
At Lincoln No.3 27 January, 2009

CANTERBURY v CENTRAL DISTRICTS *Abandoned*
At Lincoln Green 27 January, 2009

NEW ZEALAND UNDER 19 IN ENGLAND

The New Zealand Under 19 team toured England in July and August 2008. England won the two-test series 1-0 while the five-match one-day series finished 1-1, with two no results and a tie.

The squad was: K.S. Williamson *(captain)*, T.M. Clarke, A.W. Mathieson A. Verma *(Northern Districts)*, J. Austin-Smellie, H.K.P Boam, F.J. Colson *(Wellington)*, N.B. Beard, M.G. Bracewell *(Otago)*, D.A.J. Bracewell, D.S. Robinson, G.H. Worker *(Central Districts)*, C. Cachopa, G.J. Morgan, J.D.S. Needsham *(Auckland)*. Coach, D.N. Patel; Batting coach, M.D. O'Neill; Manager, K. Pulley; Physiotherapist, M. Payne.

New Zealand Test Averages

BATTING	*M*	*I*	*NO*	*HS*	*Agg*	*Ave*	*100s*	*50s*	*Ct*	*St*
K.S. Williamson	1	2	0	151	226	113.00	1	1	3	-
G.H. Worker	2	4	0	96	202	50.50	-	2	1	-
G.J. Morgan	2	4	0	81	121	30.25	-	1	3	-
H.K.P. Boam	2	4	0	68	116	29.00	-	1	-	-
T.M. Clarke	1	2	0	36	38	19.00	-	-	-	-
J.D.S. Needsham	1	2	0	30	35	17.50	-	-	-	-
N.B. Beard	2	4	0	25	66	16.50	-	-	-	-
C. Cachopa	1	2	0	15	27	13.50	-	-	2	-
F.J. Colson	2	4	0	42	48	12.00	-	-	2	-
D.S. Robinson	2	4	0	29	48	12.00	-	-	-	-
A. Verma	2	4	1	15	32	10.66	-	-	-	-
J. Austin-Smellie	1	2	1	8*	8	8.00	-	-	1	1
D.A.J. Bracewell	2	4	0	10	18	4.50	-	-	-	-
A.W. Mathieson	1	2	2	7*	8	-	-	-	-	-

BOWLING	*O*	*M*	*R*	*W*	*Ave*	*Best*	*5w*	*10w*
N.B. Beard	83.1	13	239	7	34.14	5-64	1	-
H.K.P.Boam	38	7	115	3	38.33	1-28	-	-
J.D.S. Needsham	20	2	80	2	40.00	2-80	-	-
D.A.J. Bracewell	37	4	175	4	43.75	3-73	-	-
G.J. Morgan	60.1	14	193	4	48.25	2-110	-	-
G.H. Worker	18	1	76	1	76.00	1-45	-	-
A.W. Mathieson	25	5	82	1	82.00	1-62	-	-
A. Verma	26	4	109	1	109.00	1-46	-	-
K.S. Williamson	15	1	48	0	-	-	-	-

New Zealand One-day Averages

BATTING	*M*	*I*	*NO*	*HS*	*Agg*	*Ave*	*100s*	*50s*	*Ct*	*St*	*SR*
G.J. Morgan	5	4	2	32	106	53.00	-	-	2	-	108
M.G. Bracewell	5	4	0	61	160	40.00	-	1	1	-	88
N.B. Beard	5	2	1	23	34	34.00	-	-	1	-	113
K.S. Williamson	5	4	0	52	106	26.50	-	1	5	-	58
D.A.J. Bracewell	5	3	1	20*	46	23.00	-	-	1	-	63
G.H. Worker	5	4	0	45	86	21.50	-	-	-	-	76
H.K.P. Boam	5	3	0	41	63	21.00	-	-	2	-	42
F.J. Colson	5	4	0	32	80	20.00	-	-	2	-	65
C. Cachopa	4	3	0	16	33	11.00	-	-	5	-	54
J.D.S. Needsham	5	2	0	16	19	9.50	-	-	2	-	79
T.M. Clarke	1	1	1	19*	19	-	-	-	-	-	70
J. Austin-Smellie	2	1	1	12*	12	-	-	-	1	-	33
A.W. Mathieson	2	1	1	0*	0	-	-	-	-	-	0
A. Verma	1	-	-	-	-	-	-	-	-	-	-

BOWLING	*O*	*M*	*R*	*W*	*Ave*	*Best*	*R/O*
G.H. Worker	8	0	38	4	9.50	3-14	4.75
N.B. Beard	28.1	1	130	6	21.66	4-35	4.61
G.J. Morgan	29	2	179	7	25.57	5-38	6.17
J.D.S. Needsham	26.5	1	112	3	37.33	1-20	4.17
D.A.J. Bracewell	22	1	135	3	45.00	2-51	6.14
H.K.P. Boam	31	0	136	3	45.33	2-26	4.39
A. Verma	8	0	47	1	47.00	1-47	5.88
K.S. Williamson	8	0	50	1	50.00	1-28	6.25
A.W. Mathieson	8	1	52	1	52.00	1-35	6.50

ECB UNDER 17 v NEW ZEALAND UNDER 19 *New Zealand Under 19 won by 2 wkts*
At Sleaford Cricket Club Ground 21 July, 2008

ECB Under 17 313-6 (J. Manuel 107, J. Butler 77*)

New Zealand Under 19 315-8 (C. Cachopa 70, D.A.J. Bracewell 53, H.K.P. Boam 47, F.J. Colson 38, D.S. Robinson 32)

ECB UNDER 17 v NEW ZEALAND UNDER 19 *Match drawn*
At Sleaford Cricket Club Ground 22, 23 July, 2008

ECB Under 17 257 (C. Jones 49, J. Butler 45, L. Wells 40, J. Burke 33, G.J. Morgan 3-39, A. Verma 3-47) and 181-3d (J. Manuel 86, J. Goodman 62)

New Zealand Under 19 309 (G.H. Worker 111, D.S. Robinson 39, F.J. Colson 32, J.D.S. Needsham 30, R. Patel 5-93) and 116-2 (T.M. Clarke 61*, D.A.J. Bracewell 52*)

ENGLAND v NEW ZEALAND — First Test

at County Ground, Taunton on 26, 27, 28, 29 July, 2008
Toss : England. Umpires : P.J. Hartley & R.T. Robinson
Close of play: 1st day: England 305-3, Redfern 130, Smith 123; 2nd day: NZ 111-4, Worker 68, Morgan 27*
3rd day: NZ 102-2, Colson 35, Boam 17
England won by an innings and 130 runs.

ENGLAND

FIRST INNINGS	*Runs*	*Mins*	*Balls*	*6s*	*4s*	*SECOND INNINGS*	*Runs*	*Mins*	*Balls*	*6s*	*4s*
A.D.Hales c Worker b Bracewell	31	67	48	-	5						
J.W.A.Taylor lbw b Morgan	4	17	9	-	-						
T.Westley* c Austin-Smellie b Needsham	3	34	34	-	-						
D.J.Redfern run out	151	336	267	-	18						
G.P.Smith c Morgan b Boam	157	367	308	-	21						
L.A.Dawson c Morgan b Beard	100	117	97	2	13						
B.C.Brown† b Needsham	3	21	21	-	-						
C.R.Woakes st Austin-Smellie b Worker	40	45	43	1	6						
L.J.Fletcher not out	2	4	2	-	-						
W.A.T.Beer											
I.D.Saxelby											
Extras (b 6, lb 6, w 5, nb 4)	21										
TOTAL (137.3 overs) (8 wkts dec)	**512**	512									

NEW ZEALAND

	Runs	Mins	Balls	6s	4s		Runs	Mins	Balls	6s	4s
D.S.Robinson lbw b Woakes	0	3	4	-	-	lbw b Dawson	13	94	83	-	1
G.H.Worker* c Brown b Woakes	72	229	175	-	13	c & b Beer	33	100	82	-	5
F.J.Colson lbw b Woakes	6	37	24	-	-	lbw b Beer	42	94	89	-	4
H.K.P.Boam lbw b Saxelby	5	28	22	-	-	c Brown b Beer	17	70	68	-	1
D.A.J.Bracewell lbw b Saxelby	0	4	2	-	-	c Saxelby b Beer	10	38	41	-	1
G.J.Morgan c Smith b Fletcher	38	202	128	-	4	c Redfern b Beer	2	8	8	-	-
T.M.Clarke b Beer	36	64	48	-	5	c Taylor b Dawson	2	8	7	-	-
J.D.S.Needsham b Saxelby	30	91	73	-	5	c Westley b Beer	5	31	34	-	-
J.Austin-Smellie† c Brown b Beer	0	2	1	-	-	not out	8	54	56	-	1
N.B.Beard c Westley b Saxelby	20	96	65	-	1	c Fletcher b Dawson	4	14	12	-	-
A.Verma not out	12	25	22	-	2	c Saxelby b Dawson	3	12	14	-	-
Extras (b 4, lb 7, w 1, nb 3)	15					(b 6, lb 3)	9				
TOTAL (93.3 overs)	**234**	395				(82.2 overs)	**148**	266			

Bowling	*O*	*M*	*R*	*W*	*O*	*M*	*R*	*W*
NEW ZEALAND								
Morgan	25	4	66	1				
Verma	11	2	54	0				
Needsham	20	2	80	2				
Bracewell	15	1	77	1				
Beard	38.3	4	122	1				
Boam	19	2	56	1				
Worker	9	0	45	1				
ENGLAND								
Woakes	21	7	30	3	3	2	6	0
Fletcher	16	1	67	1	4	0	17	0
Beer	24	9	46	2	34	13	53	6
Saxelby	21.3	5	47	4	5	2	10	0
Dawson	7	2	17	0	34.2	15	39	4
Westley	2	0	14	0	2	0	14	0
Redfern	2	0	2	0				

Fall of Wickets

	E	*NZ*	*NZ*
	1st	*1st*	*2nd*
1st	16	0	50
2nd	37	16	52
3rd	53	32	102
4th	340	32	117
5th	400	116	121
6th	423	155	124
7th	510	174	124
8th	512	174	129
9th	-	217	140
10th	-	234	148

ENGLAND v NEW ZEALAND — Second Test

at County Ground, Worcester on 1, 2, 3, 4 August, 2008
Toss : England. Umpires : S.A. Garratt & N.A. Mallender
Close of play: 1st day: NZ 323-7, Morgan 47, Beard 13; 2nd day: England 278-5, Smith 104, Brown 8
3rd day: NZ 186-4, Williamson 108, Boam 50
Match drawn.

NEW ZEALAND

FIRST INNINGS	*Runs*	*Mins*	*Balls*	*6s*	*4s*	*SECOND INNINGS*	*Runs*	*Mins*	*Balls*	*6s*	*4s*
D.S.Robinson c Woakes b Dawson	29	75	57	-	5	lbw b Saxelby	6	51	30	-	-
G.H.Worker c Brown b Saxelby	96	171	134	-	14	b Saxelby	1	17	11	-	-
K.S.Williamson* lbw b Saxelby	75	122	111	-	11	c Westley b Saxelby	151	255	198	-	15
F.J.Colson run out	0	6	4	-	-	b Meaker	0	6	4	-	-
C.Cachopa† c Woakes b Dawson	12	53	37	-	1	c Taylor b Meaker	15	24	24	-	3
H.K.P.Boam c Brown b Dawson	26	78	63	-	4	c Westley b Woakes	68	142	137	1	6
D.A.J.Bracewell c Taylor b Dawson	8	8	12	-	1	lbw b Woakes	0	9	8	-	-
G.J.Morgan c & b Dawson	81	170	140	2	8	run out	0	3	1	-	-
N.B.Beard b Saxelby	17	99	60	-	1	lbw b Beer	25	85	52	1	-
A.Verma run out	2	10	12	-	-	c Smith b Beer	15	21	18	-	2
A.W.Mathieson not out	7	24	20	-	1	not out	1	7	4	-	-
Extras (lb 13, nb 6)	19					(lb 17, w 1, nb 2)	20				
TOTAL (107.2 overs)	**372**	417				(80.5 overs)	**302**	315			

ENGLAND

FIRST INNINGS	*Runs*	*Mins*	*Balls*	*6s*	*4s*	*SECOND INNINGS*	*Runs*	*Mins*	*Balls*	*6s*	*4s*
A.D.Hales b Boam	52	74	67	-	12	lbw b Beard	66	102	79	-	12
J.W.A.Taylor lbw b Morgan	0	11	7	-	-	c Williamson b Beard	13	93	68	-	1
T.Westley* c Cachopa b Verma	24	87	62	-	4	c sub (J.Austin-Smellie) b Beard	15	57	55	-	1
D.J.Redfern c Williamson b Beard	29	62	41	1	4	not out	79	165	127	-	12
G.P.Smith not out	150	333	288	-	26	c Williamson b Beard	0	5	2	-	-
L.A.Dawson run out	43	99	81	-	5	lbw b Beard	13	15	13	-	1
B.C.Brown† lbw b Bracewell	49	109	77	-	9	c Colson b Boam	29	64	67	-	1
C.R.Woakes c Colson b Bracewell	10	11	11	-	1	c Cachopa b Morgan	5	8	6	-	1
W.A.T.Beer c Morgan b Bracewell	10	31	26	-	2	not out	4	24	20	-	-
S.C.Meaker b Mathieson	4	13	14	-	1						
I.D.Saxelby lbw b Morgan	6	11	8	-	1						
Extras (b 8, lb 4, w 4, nb 9)	25					(b 12, lb 7, w 2, nb 1)	22				
TOTAL (112.1 overs)	**402**	380				(72.4 overs) (7 wkts)	**246**	274			

Bowling	*O*	*M*	*R*	*W*	*O*	*M*	*R*	*W*
ENGLAND								
Woakes	26	4	96	0	19	1	54	2
Meaker	13	3	44	0	11	0	52	2
Saxelby	28	4	106	3	20	3	68	3
Dawson	26.2	3	74	5	23	1	73	0
Beer	14	2	39	0	7.5	0	38	2
NEW ZEALAND								
Morgan	23.1	5	110	2	12	5	17	1
Mathieson	20	3	62	1	5	2	20	0
Bracewell	18	3	73	3	4	0	25	0
Verma	13	1	46	1	2	1	9	0
Boam	10	3	31	1	9	2	28	1
Beard	21	3	53	1	23.4	6	64	5
Worker	4	0	11	0	5	1	20	0
Williamson	3	0	4	0	12	1	44	0

Fall of Wickets

	NZ 1st	*E 1st*	*NZ 2nd*	*E 2nd*
1st	89	6	5	83
2nd	200	82	38	88
3rd	201	82	41	133
4th	212	145	65	141
5th	238	243	236	173
6th	246	344	238	235
7th	276	358	238	240
8th	339	380	269	-
9th	342	387	293	-
10th	372	402	302	-

ENGLAND v NEW ZEALAND First One-day International

at St Lawrence Ground, Canterbury on 8 August, 2008
Toss : England. Umpires : N.L. Bainton & P. Willey
England won by 6 wickets (D/L).

NEW ZEALAND

	Runs	Mins	Balls	6s	4s
M.G.Bracewell c Westley b Sanderson	39	82	50	-	7
G.H.Worker b Saxelby	0	10	7	-	-
K.S.Williamson* c Sanderson b Riazuddin	12	27	24	-	1
F.J.Colson run out	20	31	28	-	4
C.Cachopa† b Dawson	16	47	22	-	-
H.K.P.Boam c Smith b Saxelby	41	102	81	-	1
D.A.J.Bracewell b Fletcher	20	54	38	1	-
J.D.S.Needsham run out	16	24	17	-	2
G.J.Morgan not out	24	21	15	1	2
N.B.Beard not out	11	11	8	-	1
A.W.Mathieson					
Extras (b 1, lb 12, w 13, nb 6)	32				
TOTAL (48 overs) (8 wkts)	**231**	213			

ENGLAND

	Runs	Mins	Balls	6s	4s
A.G.Wakely c Cachopa b Needsham	44	44	37	2	6
A.D.Hales c & b Boam	35	57	39	1	6
G.P.Smith c Williamson b Bracewell D.A.J.	14	51	28	-	-
D.J.Redfern c Williamson b Boam	3	8	3	-	-
T.Westley* not out	46	57	46	1	3
L.A.Dawson not out	27	27	21	-	3
B.C.Brown†					
L.J.Fletcher					
B.W.Sanderson					
I.D.Saxelby					
H.Riazuddin					
Extras (lb 3, w 3, nb 1)	7				
TOTAL (28.5 overs) (4 wkts)	**176**	126			

Bowling	*O*	*M*	*R*	*W*
ENGLAND				
Saxelby	10	0	62	2
Fletcher	10	1	38	1
Riazuddin	9	1	46	1
Sanderson	5	0	23	1
Westley	6	0	16	0
Dawson	8	0	33	1
NEW ZEALAND				
Mathieson	3	1	17	0
Morgan	5	0	39	0
Bracewell D.A.J.	6	0	44	1
Needsham	5.5	0	21	1
Boam	6	0	26	2
Worker	1	0	8	0
Beard	2	0	18	0

Fall of Wickets	***NZ***	***E***
1st	3	77
2nd	44	89
3rd	78	93
4th	99	121
5th	129	-
6th	169	-
7th	185	-
8th	206	-
9th	-	-
10th	-	-

ENGLAND v NEW ZEALAND Second One-day International

at St Lawrence Ground, Canterbury on 9 August, 2008
Toss : New Zealand. Umpires : N.L. Bainton & P. Willey
No result.

ENGLAND

	Runs	Mins	Balls	6s	4s
A.G.Wakely c Cachopa b Needsham	57	52	41	1	9
A.D.Hales run out	6	20	13	-	1
G.P.Smith c Cachopa b Verma	81	121	90	1	8
D.J.Redfern c Needsham b Boam	0	13	6	-	-
T.Westley* c Williamson b Morgan	27	40	37	-	4
L.A.Dawson c Cachopa b Beard	18	15	19	-	2
B.C.Brown† not out	30	43	34	1	2
H.Riazuddin c Bracewell D.A.J. b Beard	2	9	10	-	-
J.A.R.Harris c Colson b Morgan	7	12	11	-	1
L.J.Fletcher not out	2	5	2	-	-
B.W.Sanderson					
Extras (lb 1, w 8)	9				
TOTAL (44 overs) (8 wkts)	**239**	173			

NEW ZEALAND

M.G.Bracewell
G.H.Worker
K.S.Williamson*
F.J.Colson
C.Cachopa†
H.K.P.Boam
D.A.J.Bracewell
J.D.S.Needsham
G.J.Morgan
N.B.Beard
A.Verma

Bowling NEW ZEALAND	*O*	*M*	*R*	*W*
Morgan	8	0	57	2
Verma	8	0	47	1
Needsham	5	0	42	1
Boam	8	0	30	1
Bracewell D.A.J.	5	0	25	0
Beard	10	0	37	2

Fall of Wickets	*E*
1st	40
2nd	96
3rd	105
4th	155
5th	180
6th	205
7th	211
8th	232
9th	-
10th	-

ENGLAND v NEW ZEALAND — Third One-day International

at County Ground, Hove on 11 August, 2008 (d/n)
Toss : England. Umpires : R.A. Kettleborough & N.J. Llong
Match tied.

ENGLAND

	Runs	Mins	Balls	6s	4s
A.G.Wakely c Cachopa b Mathieson	64	56	47	1	12
A.D.Hales b Beard	77	93	64	1	11
G.P.Smith run out	3	12	10	-	-
D.J.Redfern c Colson b Needsham	23	40	27	-	2
T.Westley* c & b Beard	12	36	33	-	1
L.A.Dawson lbw b Beard	1	3	3	-	-
B.C.Brown† c Needsham b Worker	36	62	52	-	2
H.Riazuddin lbw b Beard	1	4	6	-	-
J.A.R.Harris b Worker	7	26	25	-	1
L.J.Fletcher c Bracewell M.G. b Worker	3	6	6	-	-
W.A.T.Beer not out	4	7	5	-	1
Extras (b 1, w 4, nb 1)	6				
TOTAL (46.1 overs)	**237**	177			

NEW ZEALAND

	Runs	Mins	Balls	6s	4s
M.G.Bracewell b Beer	47	46	41	-	7
G.H.Worker c Fletcher b Beer	41	54	53	-	6
K.S.Williamson* c Wakely b Beer	28	62	51	-	1
F.J.Colson c Brown b Dawson	24	50	50	1	-
C.Cachopa† lbw b Dawson	5	14	12	-	-
H.K.P.Boam lbw b Dawson	15	18	25	1	-
D.A.J.Bracewell c Wakely b Dawson	6	10	9	-	1
G.J.Morgan c Riazuddin b Fletcher	32	40	30	1	2
J.D.S.Needsham c Riazuddin b Dawson	3	6	7	-	-
N.B.Beard b Fletcher	23	30	22	2	-
A.W.Mathieson not out	0	1	0	-	-
Extras (lb 10, w 2, nb 1)	13				
TOTAL (49.5 overs)	**237**	186			

Bowling	*O*	*M*	*R*	*W*
NEW ZEALAND				
Mathieson	5	0	35	1
Morgan	6	0	45	0
Williamson	2	0	22	0
Bracewell D.A.J.	2	0	15	0
Boam	7	0	50	0
Beard	10	1	35	4
Needsham	10	1	20	1
Worker	4.1	0	14	3
ENGLAND				
Harris	9	0	44	0
Fletcher	3.5	0	38	2
Riazuddin	8	2	34	0
Westley	9	0	37	0
Beer	10	0	35	3
Dawson	10	1	39	5

Fall of Wickets

	E	**NZ**
1st	110	88
2nd	123	99
3rd	165	148
4th	175	150
5th	177	167
6th	194	172
7th	196	177
8th	220	185
9th	236	236
10th	237	237

ENGLAND v NEW ZEALAND — Fourth One-day International

at County Ground, Northampton on 14 August, 2008
Toss : England. Umpires : S.A. Garratt & B. Leadbeater
No result.

NEW ZEALAND

	Runs	Mins	Balls	6s	4s
M.G.Bracewell run out	13	26	23	-	2
G.H.Worker c & b Harris	0	2	1	-	-
C.Cachopa c Brown b Harris	12	34	27	-	1
K.S.Williamson* lbw b Sanderson	14	43	24	-	2
F.J.Colson c Dawson b Saxelby	4	10	9	-	-
H.K.P.Boam c & b Dawson	7	47	42	-	-
G.J.Morgan lbw b Dawson	21	32	26	-	3
J.Austin-Smellie† not out	12	40	36	-	-
D.A.J.Bracewell not out	20	32	25	-	3
J.D.S.Needsham					
N.B.Beard					
Extras (lb 4, w 2)	6				
TOTAL (35.3 overs) (7 wkts)	**109**	140			

ENGLAND

A.G.Wakely
A.D.Hales
G.P.Smith
D.J.Redfern
T.Westley*
L.A.Dawson
B.C.Brown†
B.W.Sanderson
J.A.R.Harris
I.D.Saxelby
W.A.T.Beer

Bowling	*O*	*M*	*R*	*W*
ENGLAND				
Harris	8	2	24	2
Saxelby	8	2	20	1
Sanderson	7	1	25	1
Dawson	8.3	0	25	2
Beer	4	0	11	0

Fall of Wickets	***NZ***
1st	6
2nd	24
3rd	34
4th	39
5th	49
6th	69
7th	78
8th	-
9th	-
10th	-

ENGLAND v NEW ZEALAND — Fifth One-day International

at County Ground, Northampton on 15 August, 2008
Toss : New Zealand. Umpires : S.A. Garratt & R.T. Robinson
New Zealand won by 6 wickets.

ENGLAND

	Runs	Mins	Balls	6s	4s
A.G.Wakely c Austin-Smellie b Morgan	13	11	15	-	2
A.D.Hales b Morgan	11	45	16	-	2
G.P.Smith b Morgan	8	24	21	-	1
D.J.Redfern c Williamson b Bracewell D.A.J.	0	7	7	-	-
T.Westley* c Morgan b Williamson	85	119	117	-	8
L.A.Dawson c Williamson b Worker	50	95	58	-	7
B.C.Brown† c Morgan b Bracewell D.A.J.	31	42	34	-	2
J.A.R.Harris c Boam b Morgan	20	16	22	1	1
B.W.Sanderson b Morgan	6	7	4	-	1
W.A.T.Beer not out	5	9	4	-	-
I.D.Saxelby not out	1	5	2	-	-
Extras (b 1, lb 5, w 2)	8				
TOTAL (50 overs) (9 wkts)	**238**	199			

NEW ZEALAND

	Runs	Mins	Balls	6s	4s
G.H.Worker c Brown b Sanderson	45	56	51	-	8
M.G.Bracewell c & b Dawson	61	100	66	1	6
K.S.Williamson* run out	52	100	81	1	2
F.J.Colson c Westley b Beer	32	40	35	-	4
T.M.Clarke not out	19	40	27	-	2
G.J.Morgan not out	29	24	27	1	4
H.K.P.Boam					
D.A.J.Bracewell					
J.D.S.Needsham					
J.Austin-Smellie†					
N.B.Beard					
Extras (lb 1, w 1)	2				
TOTAL (47.5 overs) (4 wkts)	**240**	184			

Bowling	*O*	*M*	*R*	*W*
NEW ZEALAND				
Morgan	10	2	38	5
Bracewell D.A.J.	9	1	51	2
Boam	10	0	30	0
Needsham	6	0	29	0
Beard	6.1	0	40	0
Worker	2.5	0	16	1
Williamson	6	0	28	1
ENGLAND				
Harris	7	1	32	0
Saxelby	10	0	45	0
Sanderson	8	0	46	1
Beer	10	0	48	1
Dawson	8.5	1	50	1
Westley	2	0	11	0
Redfern	2	1	7	0

Fall of Wickets

	E	*NZ*
1st	14	80
2nd	32	142
3rd	33	187
4th	33	203
5th	151	-
6th	189	-
7th	222	-
8th	227	-
9th	236	-
10th	-	-

NATIONAL UNDER 19 TOURNAMENT

The Under 19 tournament was held from 21 December to 11 January. Each team played two three-day games and four-one day matches with points from all matches being combined. A further round of finals matches was then played. The first round featured nearest neighbours while the other games were played at Lincoln. Final placings were: Auckland, Canterbury, Otago, Wellington, Northern Districts, Central Districts.

FIRST ROUND

AUCKLAND v NORTHERN DISTRICTS *Auckland won by an innings and 91 runs*

Auckland 400-8 dec (C. Cachopa 122, A. Manning 113, M. Barry 32, A. Mathieson 3-96)

Northern Districts 170 (F. Kilgour 59, Z. Scott 32) and 139 (T. Clark 37, J. Coughlan 4-7, R. Bezuidenhout 3-31)

WELLINGTON v CENTRAL DISTRICTS *First innings win to Central Districts*

Central Districts 304-8 dec (B.J. Barnett 62*, A. Dodd 57, B. Smith 55, D. Robinson 51) and 194-7 dec (E. Bolstad 54, A. Dodd 52, R. Pepperall 4-22)

Wellington 155 (H. Wright 71, B.J Barnett 3-16, S. Smidt 3-23) and 231-5 (M. Pollard 101*, V. Ward 37, T. Blundell 32)

OTAGO v CANTERBURY *Canterbury won by 155 runs*

Canterbury 300 (L. Bartholomeusz 82, T. Latham 57, J. Winchester 50, M. Laffey 31, N. Beard 5-92, B. Soper 3-32) and 160-2 dec (W. Walsh 71, T. Latham 38)

Otago 164 (N. Beard 59, M. Bracewell 30, J. Reeves 4-32) and 141 (M. Bracewell 31, N. Beard 30, M. Farrant 4-31)

SECOND ROUND

WELLINGTON v CANTERBURY *Canterbury won by an innings and 27 runs*

Canterbury 395-6 dec (T. Latham 148, L. Bartholomeusz 108, M. Laffey 61*)

Wellington 198 (M. Pollard 54, M. Tugaga 31, M. Farrant 4-21) and 170 (T. Blundell 60, V. Ward 40, M. Farrant 3-16, L. van Beek 3-42)

OTAGO v NORTHERN DISTRICTS *Otago won by 64 runs*

Otago 176 (N. Beard 53, J. Hickey 3-66) and 229-8 dec (G. Spittle 100, S. Paulin 49, T. Clarke 4-56)

Northern Districts 167 (A. Verma 31, N. Beard 5-26, B. Soper 3-42) and 174 (A. Verma 51, B. Popli 44, N. Beard 5-37, B. Soper 3-38)

AUCKLAND v CENTRAL DISTRICTS *First innings win to Central Districts*

Central Districts 292-6 dec (D. Robinson 134*, D. McKeefry 62, A. MacDuff 4-39) and 186 (A. Dodd 47, E. Bolstad 46, B. Schmulian 3-17)

Auckland 253 (C. Cachopa 85, B. Schmulian 63, J. Bassett-Graham 30, D. McKeefry 4-42) and 145-6 (V. Davies 40, J. Needsham 33, B.J Barnett 4-45)

THIRD ROUND

AUCKLAND v OTAGO *Auckland won by 4 wickets*

Otago 198 (M. Bracewell 46, G. Scott 44, L. Ferguson 5-31, J. Neesham 3-27)

Auckland 199-6 (K. Bunting 74)

CENTRAL DISTRICTS v WELLINGTON *Wellington won by 3 wickets*

Central Districts 173 (B.J. Barnett 49)

Wellington 174-7 (M. Pollard 76, A. Dodd 3-25)

NORTHERN DISTRICTS v CANTERBURY *Canterbury won by 129 runs*

Canterbury 252-9 (M. Laffey 72, L. van Beek 49)

Northern Districts 123 (A. Herwels 29*)

FOURTH ROUND

CENTRAL DISTRICTS v NORTHERN DISTRICTS *Central won by 31 runs*

Central Districts 255-6 (B. Smith 96*, B.J. Barnett 63, E. Bolstad 31)

Northern Districts 224 (A. Herwels 64, S. Martin 48, A. Verma 41, D. McKeefry 3-22)

WELLINGTON v AUCKLAND *Wellington won by 63 runs*

Wellington 208 (H. Boam 66, C. Gajanayaka 52, A. MacDuff 4-25, J. Coughlan 3-49)

Auckland 145 (A. MacDuff 42, M. Tugaga 4-26, H. Boam 3-10)

CANTERBURY v OTAGO *Canterbury won by 4 wickets*

Otago 176 (N. Eathorne 65, M. McEwan 4-19)

Canterbury 177-6 (M. Laffey 56*, W. Walsh 33, L. Bartholomeusz 39)

FIFTH ROUND

AUCKLAND v NORTHERN DISTRICTS *Auckland won by 63 runs*

Auckland 249 (J. Tasman-Jones 72, A. Herwels 3-54)

Northern Districts 186 (S. Martin 94, B. Schmulian 4-25)

WELLINGTON v OTAGO *Wellington won by 8 wickets*

Otago 144 (J. Simpson 51, J. Fuller 33, M. Tugaga 3-17, H. Boam 3-21)

Wellington 145-2 (J. Hindley 59*, H. Boam 51*)

CANTERBURY v CENTRAL DISTRICTS *Central Districts won by 1 run*

Central Districts 230-7 (E. Bolstad 69*, D. Robinson 51, A. Dodd 51, M. Farrant 3-37)

Canterbury 229-9 (W. Walsh 57, L. Bartholomeusz 39, A. Dodd 3-41)

SIXTH ROUND

OTAGO v CENTRAL DISTRICTS *Otago won by 7 wickets*

Central Districts 225-9 (A. Dodd 69, B. Meehan 51*, B. Smith 30)

Otago 228-3 (G. Spittle 100*, G. Scott 61, M. Bracewell 38)

NORTHERN DISTRICTS v WELLINGTON *Wellington won by 103 runs*

Wellington 181-8 (C. Gajanayaka 42*, T. Blundell 37)

Northern Districts 78 (J. Matthews 33*, M. Tugaga 4-14)

AUCKLAND v CANTERBURY *Auckland won by 3 wickets*

Canterbury 241-7 (B. Walsh 80, T. Latham 33)

Auckland 242-7 (T. Manning 99*, J. Bassett-Graham 39, M. Barry 35, M. Farrant 3-45, M. McEwan 3-49)

FINALS

AUCKLAND v CANTERBURY *Auckland won by 5 wickets*

Canterbury 209 (L. van Beek 64, L. Bartholomeusz 38, J. Neesham 3-39)

Auckland 211-5 (J. Needsham 69, K. Bunting 62, T. Manning 34*)

OTAGO v WELLINGTON *Otago won by 7 runs*

Otago 231-9 (J. Simpson 70, T. Pere 4-44)

Wellington 224 (C. Gajanayaka 64, M. Pollard 48, N. Beard 3-11, J. Fuller 3-61)

CENTRAL DISTRICTS v NORTHERN DISTRICTS *Northern won by 5 wickets*

Central Districts 229-6 (A. Dodd 68, B. Smith 64, A. Verma 3-48)

Northern Districts 230-5 (F. Kilgour 52, A. Herwels 51*, B.J. Barnett 3-32)

NEW ZEALAND UNDER 19 INTERNAL TOUR

The New Zealand Under 19 team toured the North Island in February. The touring party was: C. Cachopa *(Auckland, captain)*, B-J. Barnett *(Central Districts)*, J. Bassett-Graham *(Auckland)*, N. Beard *(Otago)*, M. Farrant *(Canterbury)*, J. Fuller *(Otago)*, T. Latham *(Canterbury)*, A. Mathieson *(Northern Districts)*, J. Needsham *(Auckland)*, M. Pollard *(Wellington)*, D. Robinson *(Central Districts)*, M. Tugaga *(Wellington)*, L. van Beek *(Canterbury)*, A. Verma *(Northern Districts)*. Coach, M.D. O'Neill; Assistant coaches, M.J. Horne, S.A. Deitz; Selector/Bowling advisor, B.L. Cairns; Manager, K. Pulley; Physiotherapist, M. Payne.

NEW ZEALAND UNDER 19 v WELLINGTON A
At Karori Park, Wellington 3, 4, 5 February, 2009

Wellington A 236 (S. Rhodes 71, T. Blundell 40, J. Sewell 34, J. Fuller 4-18, M. Tugaga 3-36) **drew with New Zealand Under 19** 182-3 (T. Latham 82, M. Pollard 59*)

NEW ZEALAND UNDER 19 v NORTHERN DISTRICTS A
At Owen Delaney Park, Taupo 8, 9, 10 February, 2009

Northern Districts A 298 (K. Bettley 104, I. Page 100, A. Verma 4-43) and 201 (T. Davis 44, K. Bettley 35, N. Beard 5-55) **drew with New Zealand Under 19** 303-7 dec (C. Cachopa 76, T Latham 42) and 39-4 (T. Davis 3-23)

NEW ZEALAND UNDER 19 v WELLINGTON A
At Karori Park, Wellington 11 February, 2009

New Zealand Under 19 291 (L. van Beek 63*, J. Needsham 63, C. Cachopa 56) **defeated Wellington A** 257 (S. Allen 71, V. Ward 55, F. Colson 38, J. Needsham 3-62) by 34 runs

NEW ZEALAND UNDER 19 v AUCKLAND A
At Cornwall Park, Auckland 12 February, 2009

Auckland A 257 (D. Hakaraia 62, T. Nethula 51, J. Raval 42, M.Tugaga 3-33, N. Beard 3-47) **defeated New Zealand Under 19** 210 (C. Cachopa 63, T. Latham 55, B. Singh 3-22) by 47 runs

NEW ZEALAND UNDER 19 v AUCKLAND A
At Cornwall Park, Auckland 13 February, 2009

New Zealand Under 19 248-6 (T. Latham 84, D. Robinson 53, M. Bates 3-32) **defeated Auckland A** 155 (J. Raval 68, A. de Boorder 42, N. Beard 5-21) by 93 runs.

NATIONAL UNDER 17 TOURNAMENT

The National Under 17 tournament was held in Napier from 14 to 22 January. Canterbury again won the title with 26 points followed by Central Districts (13), Northern Districts (13), Wellington (11), Otago (8) and Auckland (2).

A tournament team was selected at the completion of the fifth round. It was T. Latham *(Canterbury, captain)*, C. Cachopa *(Auckland)*, H. Nicholls, C. McConchie, M. Henry, T. van Woerkom *(Canterbury)*, B. Wheeler, B. Small *(Central Districts)*, R. Darkins, A. Vodnala *(Northern Districts)*, C. Ware *(Otago)*, H. Wright *(Wellington)*.

FIRST ROUND

AUCKLAND v WELLINGTON *Auckland won by 63 runs*

Auckland 103 (D. Burney 37, T. Gibson 3-20, C. McLean 3-21) and 176 (T. Ellis 42, H. Wright 5-45, T. Gibson 3-35)

Wellington 127 (S. Lawson 42, J. Morris 3-27) and 89 (M. Taylor 37, I. Sodhi 4-15, J. Morris 3-10)

NORTHERN DISTRICTS v OTAGO *First innings win to Northern Districts*

Otago 240 (A. Simpson 71, J. Horrel 40, R. Darkins 4-88, J. Wilkinson 3-17)

Northern Districts 321-9 (E. McKillop 43, A. Vodal 42, S. Davey 39)

CANTERBURY v CENTRAL DISTRICTS *First innings win to Canterbury*

Canterbury 339-7d (C. McConchie 151, T. Latham 58, H. Nicholls 47)

Central Districts 173 (D. Cleaver 80, T. van Woerkom 5-34, C. Johnston 3-29) and 200-4 (B. Wheeler 101*, T. Richards 40*)

SECOND ROUND

OTAGO v CANTERBURY *Canterbury won by 81 runs*

Canterbury 214-9 (H. Nicholls 75, M. Henry 57, D.Dukes 3-48)

Otago 133 (T. van Woerkom 3-12)

CENTRAL DISTRICTS v WELLINGTON *Central Districts won by 150 runs*

Central Districts 275-8 (B. Wheeler 86, S. McConville 30, H. Wright 3-27)

Wellington 125 (B. Small 5-36)

AUCKLAND v NORTHERN DISTRICTS *Northern Districts won by 65 runs*

Northern Districts 207-9 (E. McKillop 42, R. Fitzjohns 35*, I. Sodhi 3-17)

Auckland 142 (R. Darkins 3-13, M. Thomas 3-23)

THIRD ROUND

CENTRAL DISTRICTS v NORTHERN DISTRICTS *First innings win to Central*

Central Districts 194 (J. Steward 51, B. Wheeler 35, W. Young 33, M. Thomas 5-17)

Northern Districts 53 (B. Small 4-9) and 278-6 (A. Vodnala 117, A. Abraham 64)

OTAGO v AUCKLAND *First innings win to Otago*

Otago 291 (B. Cant 63, M. Hunter 58, M. Collins 40, T. Ellis 3-59)

Auckland 81 (C. Ware 4-33) and 289-9 (C. Cachopa 140*, C. Elton 69*)

CANTERBURY v WELLINGTON *Canterbury won by 32 runs*

Canterbury 283 (T. Latham 120, M. Henry 49, H. Nicholls 43, L. Boydajian 3-60) and 110-1d (B. Ward 46*, C. McConchie 35*)

Wellington 175-9d (S. Lawson 62*, M. Taylor 31, M. Henry 3-47) and 186 (N. Ward 58, J. Joseph 35 T. van Woerkom 7-76)

FOURTH ROUND

AUCKLAND v CANTERBURY *Canterbury won by 9 wickets*

Canterbury 369-7d (T. Latham 93, J. Richards 77, C. McConchie 52) and 46-1

Auckland 138-9d and 102 (H. Blackwell 31, M. Henry 3-15)

CENTRAL DISTRICTS v OTAGO *First innings win to Otago*

Otago 242 (C. McMeeken 76, L. Edwards 54, T. Haggas 5-64)

Central Districts 241 (B. Wheeler 79, I. West 43, T. Richards 38, C. Ware 4-71)

WELLINGTON v NORTHERN DISTRICTS *Wellington won by 4 wickets*

Northern Districts 167 (M. Gurrey 47, T. Gibson 4-45) and 172-7d (T. Beehre 32, M. Gurry 31)

Wellington 72 (R. Darkins 9-32) and 268-6 (N. Ward 100, S. Lawson 53*)

FIFTH ROUND

AUCKLAND v CENTRAL DISTRICTS *Central Districts won by 4 wickets*

Auckland 203-8 (D. Burrey 80*, H. Blackwell 34, B. Wheeler 3-41, T. Richards 3-55)

Central Districts 207-6 (S. McConville 79, W. Young 58)

NORTHERN DISTRICTS v CANTERBURY *Canterbury won by 8 wickets*

Northern Districts 157-9 (M. Henry 3-33)

Canterbury 160-2 (C. McConchie 45, H. Nicholls 43*, J. Richards 35*)

OTAGO v WELLINGTON *Wellington won by 5 wickets*

Otago 135 (B. Cant 48, L. Boydajian 3-31)

Wellington 136-5 (H. Wright 51, M. Taylor 35)

HAWKE CUP

The major competition for the District (formerly Minor) Associations reverted to the Hawke Cup from 1999/00. The Fuji Xerox Cup since 1995/96, it was renamed the National District Championship in 1998/99. The competition was for the U-Bix Cup from 1985/86 to 1994/95.

Apart from tournaments in 1910/11, 1912/13 and 2000/01, the competition has always been on a challenge basis. To reduce the number of challenges received by the holders it was decided to pair off all the Minor Associations. This scheme commenced in the 1924/25 season, when the first three elimination matches were played. Since then numerous elimination matches have been staged to determine the right to challenge the holders of the cup.

At the end of 1999/00 it was decided to exclude the teams from the four major centres who had taken part in the tournament in recent seasons. As Dunedin Metropolitan held the trophy at the time, a national zonal tournament was held to find a new holder and the challenge format resumed in 2001/02.

Holders

Southland, 1910/11; won the tournament of six matches.

Southland, March 14, 1911, to March 25, 1913; resisted one challenge.

South Auckland, 1912/13; won the tournament of four matches.

	Challenges resisted
Wanganui, December 26, 1913, to March 28, 1919	5
Poverty Bay, March 28, 1919, to February 15, 1921	4
Wairarapa, February 15, 1921, to December 26, 1921	1
Rangitikei, December 26, 1921, to January 3, 1922	—
Nelson, January 3, 1922, to April 1, 1922	2
Wanganui, April 1, 1922, to January 22, 1924	7
Nelson, January 22, 1924, to February 2, 1926	7
Wanganui, February 2, 1926, to December 6, 1926	2
Taranaki, December 6, 1926, to December 20, 1927	3
Wanganui, December 20, 1927, to February 23, 1928	2
Manawatu, February 23, 1928, to March 29, 1930	9
Rangitikei, March 29, 1930, to December 15, 1930	—
Waikato, December 15, 1930, to January 2, 1933	11
Nelson, January 2, 1933, to December 27, 1933	2
Taranaki, December 27, 1933, to December 27, 1934	3
Manawatu, December 27, 1934, to February 14, 1938	15
Waikato, February 14, 1938, to January 30, 1940	7
Manawatu, January 30, 1940, to April 7, 1947	9
Hawke's Bay, April 7, 1947, to February 14, 1948	1
Wanganui, February 14, 1948, to December 13, 1948	1
Hutt Valley, December 13, 1948, to April 11, 1950	7
Hawke's Bay, April 11, 1950, to January 3, 1951	2
Wairarapa, January 3, 1951, to March 12, 1951	1
Waikato, March 12, 1951, to December 10, 1951	—
Nelson, December 10, 1951, to December 30, 1952	6
Wanganui, December 30, 1952, to December 28, 1955	13
Hutt Valley, December 28, 1955, to January 2, 1956	—
Northland, January 2, 1956, to December 8, 1956	2
Waikato, December 8, 1956, to December 8, 1958	9
Nelson, December 8, 1958, to February 1, 1965	28
Manawatu, February 1, 1965, to January 24, 1967	9
North Canterbury, January 24, 1967, to February 27, 1967	—
Nelson, February 27, 1967, to December 17, 1967	—
Hutt Valley, December 17, 1967, to January 7, 1968	1
Marlborough, January 7, 1968, to March 3, 1968	1
Hawke's Bay, March 3, 1968, to February 23, 1969	4

	Challenges resisted
Waikato, February 23, 1969, to February 7, 1970	3
Southland, February 7, 1970, to December 29, 1970	1
Taranaki, December 29, 1970, to March 12, 1973	12
Southland, March 12, 1973, to February 27, 1977	14
Wairarapa, February 27, 1977, to February 5, 1979	6
Nelson, February 5, 1979, to February 21, 1983	14
Northland, February 21, 1983, to March 14, 1983	2
Hawke's Bay, March 14, 1983, to February 20, 1984	2
Northland, February 20, 1984, to February 27, 1984	—
Nelson, February 27, 1984, to February 24, 1986	8
Hawke's Bay, February 24, 1986, to March 18, 1986	1
Bay of Plenty, March 18, 1986, to February 23, 1987	2
Hawke's Bay, February 23, 1987, to March 16, 1987	—
Bay of Plenty, March 16, 1987, to March 23, 1987	—
Southland, March 23, 1987, to March 15, 1988	4
North Canterbury, March 15, 1988, to March 22, 1988	—
Taranaki, March 22, 1988, to February 13, 1989	—
Northland, February 13, 1989, to February 27, 1989	—
Southland, February 27, 1989, to February 24, 1992	15
Northland, February 24, 1992, to March 23, 1992	1
Nelson, March 23, 1992, to March 15, 1993	3
Canterbury Country, March 15, 1993, to March 29, 1993	—
Manawatu, March 29, 1993, to February 28, 1994	2
Marlborough, February 28, 1994 to March 14, 1994	—
Taranaki, March 14, 1994 to January 29, 1996	7
Central Otago, January 29, 1996 to February 12, 1996	—
Nelson, February 12, 1996 to February 26, 1996	—
Hutt Valley, February 26, 1996 to January 20, 1997	2
Nelson, January 20, 1997 to February 17, 1997	1
Auckland-Manukau, February 17, 1997 to March 3, 1997	—
Bay of Plenty, March 3, 1997 to January 26, 1998	1
Wellington City, January 26, 1998 to February 9, 1998	—
Manawatu, February 9, 1998 to February 23, 1998	—
Auckland-Waitakere, February 23, 1998 to March 9, 1998	—
Northland, March 9, 1998 to February 8, 1999	2
Wellington City, February 8, 1999 to February 22, 1999	—
Canterbury Country, February 22, 1999 to January 24, 2000	2
South Canterbury, January 24, 2000 to February 7, 2000	—
Dunedin Metropolitan, February 7, 2000 to March 26, 2001	3
Hamilton, March 26, 2001 to March 25, 2002	4
Manawatu, March 25, 2002 to February 17, 2003	—
Hawke's Bay, February 17, 2003 to 3 March, 2003	—
Northland, 3 March, 2003 to 16 February, 2004	2
Mid-Canterbury, 16 February, 2004 to 7 February, 2005	1
Canterbury Country, 7 February, 2005 to 7 March, 2005	1
Hamilton, 7 March, 2005 to 12 March, 2007	5
Taranaki, 12 March, 2007 to 18 February, 2008	—
Canterbury Country, 18 February 2008 to 17 March, 2008	1
Hamilton, 17 March, 2008 to 16 February, 2009	—
Hawke's Bay, 16 February, 2009	2

Career Aggregates

BATTING	M	I	NO	HS	Runs	Ave
Leggat I.B. *(Nelson)*, 1948-68	38	56	1	130	1968	35.78
Reade L.B. *(Nelson)*, 1958-73	35	57	2	117	1951	35.47
Lowans G.E. *(Nelson)*, 1958-73	30	48	1	148	1811	38.53
Anderson R.W. *(Northland and Southland)*, 1970-77	16	31	6	255	1773	70.92
McVicar C.C. *(Manawatu)*, 1935-54	28	44	1	180	1754	40.79
Spence D.V. *(Hawkes Bay and Nelson)*, 1949-67	34	51	8	151	1574	36.60
Hoskin R.N.*(Southland and Central Otago)*, 1978-96	31	35	4	162	1429	46.09
Pierce R.A. *(Nelson)*, 1969-89	24	31	2	150	1426	49.17
Congdon B.E. *(Nelson)*, 1959-65	19	28	2	133	1413	54.34
Gallichan N. *(Manawatu)*, 1925-47	29	48	5	142	1409	32.76
Hampton B.L. *(Nelson)*, 1960-75	21	32	3	236	1391	49.26
Hodgson W.G. *(Nelson)*, 1978-86	24	29	2	265	1348	49.92
Norris W.E. *(Manawatu)*, 1926-47	42	61	6	84	1242	22.58
Orton R.W. *(Rangitikei and Wanganui)*, 1911-26	20	33	1	204	1222	38.18
Hayward R.E. *(Nelson)*, 1979-89	23	26	2	113	1115	46.45
Holland C.A. *(Wanganui)*, 1912-28	24	38	4	111	1060	31.17
Edwards G.N. *(Nelson)*, 1972-86	24	30	2	236	1038	37.07
Toynbee M.H. *(Nelson)*, 1974-81	13	17	3	200*	1031	73.64

BOWLING	M	Runs	Wkts	Ave
Holland C.A. *(Wanganui)*, 1912-28	24	2202	189	11.65
Gallichan N. *(Manawatu)*, 1925-47	29	2053	177	11.59
Leggat I.B. *(Nelson)*, 1948-67	38	2149	134	16.03
Spence D.V. *(Hawkes Bay and Nelson)*, 1949-67	34	1697	110	15.42
Alabaster G.D. *(Thames Valley and Southland)*, 1961-79	20	1508	102	14.78
Newman J. *(Nelson)*, 1922-46	20	1348	97	13.89
Alabaster J.C. *(Southland)*, 1955-74	14	1223	92	13.29
Bernau E.H.L. *(Wanganui and Hawkes Bay)*, 1912-28	14	1009	90	11.21

Highest Individual Innings

272*	Kinzett C.A.	Nelson v Marlborough	Nelson	1933/34
268	Robinson G.G.	Hamilton v Northland	Hamilton	2005/06
265	Hodgson W.G.	Nelson v Taranaki	Nelson	1983/84
264	Everest J.K.	Waikato v Manawatu	Hamilton	1956/57
255	Anderson R.W.	Southland v Ashburton County	Invercargill	1976/77
236	Hampton B.L.	Nelson v Waikato	Nelson	1963/64
236	Edwards G.N.	Nelson v North Canterbury	Nelson	1984/85
229	Douglas M.W.	Nelson v Southland	Nelson	1992/93

Best Bowling in an Innings

10-35	Holland C.A.	Wanganui v South Taranaki	Wanganui	1922/23
9-103	Jordan A.B.	Taranaki v Hutt Valley	New Plymouth	1971/72
8-9	Clough R.	Waikato v Bay of Plenty	Hamilton	1938/39
8-20	Andrews S.L.	Hamilton v Northland	Hamilton	2001/02
8-25	Smith J.D.	Waikato v Horowhenua	Hamilton	1969/70
8-25	Jordan A.B.	Taranaki v Franklin	New Plymouth	1971/72
8-26	Haycock R.S.	Nelson v Marlborough	Nelson	1924/25

Best Bowling in a Match

14-79	Holland C.A.	Wanganui v South Taranaki	Wanganui	1922/23
14-89	Jordan A.B.	Taranaki v Franklin	New Plymouth	1971/72
14-133	Upston I.A.	Hutt Valley v Wanganui	Wanganui	1955/56
14-149	Sulzberger G.P.	Taranaki v Manawatu	New Plymouth	1994/95

HAMILTON v HAWKE'S BAY — Hawke Cup

at Galloway Park, Hamilton on 14, 15, 16 February, 2009
Toss : Hamilton. Umpires : C.B. Gaffaney & W.R. Knights
Close of play: 1st day: Hamilton 13-2, Shutte 6, Daley 5; 2nd day: Hawke's Bay 236-4, de Terte 68, Taiaroa 58
Hawke's Bay won by 123 runs

HAWKE'S BAY

FIRST INNINGS	*Runs*	*Mins*	*Balls*	*6s*	*4s*	*SECOND INNINGS*	*Runs*	*Mins*	*Balls*	*6s*	*4s*
T.I.Lythe c Shutte b Baker	3	38	39	-	-	c McLeod b Mathieson	1	25	20	-	-
B.Z.Meehan c Daley b Mathieson	21	97	78	-	4	run out	28	131	113	-	4
A.M.Dodd b Shutte	20	70	52	-	2	c Graafhuis b Verma	18	42	46	-	1
B.M.K.Patton* c Daley b Mathieson	14	25	22	-	3	lbw b Baker	41	91	73	-	3
J.W.de Terte lbw b Shutte	0	1	1	-	-	not out	102	219	181	1	17
M.P.Taiaroa† b Baker	18	80	68	-	2	lbw b Baker	59	126	131	-	9
D.A.J.Bracewell c Verma b Bettley	91	157	141	1	9	lbw b Baker	4	2	3	-	1
R.D.Breakwell lbw b Bettley	17	36	32	-	3	lbw b Baker	0	13	12	-	-
A.J.Douglas lbw b Bettley	3	25	25	-	-	b Mathieson	1	8	6	-	-
J.M.K.Kuru c Baker b Bettley	11	11	12	1	1	b Baker	0	13	13	-	-
B.S.M.McLennan not out	0	13	8	-	-	b Baker	1	13	5	-	-
Extras (b 3, lb 2, w 4, nb 3)	12					(b 2, lb 6, w 3, nb 12)	23				
TOTAL (79.1 overs)	**210**	286				(98.3 overs)	**278**	351			

HAMILTON

	Runs	*Mins*	*Balls*	*6s*	*4s*		*Runs*	*Mins*	*Balls*	*6s*	*4s*
F.Graafhuis b Kuru	0	10	7	-	-	c Taiaroa b McLennan	12	19	18	-	2
K.G.Bettley c Taiaroa b McLennan	0	5	5	-	-	(8) lbw b Patton	14	54	38	-	-
R.R.Shutte b Lythe	56	124	95	-	8	lbw b McLennan	14	26	17	-	1
N.M.Daley*† c Bracewell b McLennan	14	45	32	-	1	(9) b Patton	4	6	5	-	-
G.G.Robinson b Bracewell	28	76	58	-	3	(4) c Breakwell b McLennan	11	37	19	-	1
A.P.Devcich b McLennan	7	23	16	-	1	(5) c Taiaroa b Douglas	21	40	35	-	2
B.J.Hatwell b Lythe	4	13	14	-	1	lbw b McLennan	18	39	35	-	2
S.J.M.McLeod lbw b Douglas	9	35	37	-	-	(6) c Patton b McLennan	110	168	121	-	16
A.Verma c sub (S.R.Bussell) b Douglas	11	46	34	1	-	(2) c Meehan b McLennan	0	3	2	-	-
J.D.Baker b Douglas	2	2	4	-	-	b Bracewell	10	22	22	-	1
A.W.Mathieson not out	5	13	9	-	1	not out	0	29	15	-	-
Extras (b 2, lb 6, nb 1)	9					(lb 4, nb 2)	6				
TOTAL (51.4 overs)	**145**	205				(54.1 overs)	**220**	231			

Bowling	*O*	*M*	*R*	*W*	*O*	*M*	*R*	*W*
HAMILTON								
Baker	20	8	38	2	23.3	10	39	6
Verma	14	7	32	0	12	7	22	1
Shutte	16	6	46	2	7	0	25	0
Mathieson	16	2	52	2	19	9	50	2
Bettley	11.1	1	17	4	21	1	78	0
McLeod	2	0	20	0	9	2	25	0
Devcich					7	1	31	0
HAWKE'S BAY								
Kuru	9	2	30	1	13	1	46	0
McLennan	15	4	35	3	16.1	1	62	6
Bracewell	10	5	15	1	13	3	51	1
Douglas	5.4	0	31	3	5	1	24	1
Lythe	12	4	26	2				
Patton					7	0	33	2

Fall of Wickets	***HB***	***H***	***HB***	***H***
	1st	*1st*	*2nd*	*2nd*
1st	8	2	2	1
2nd	45	4	32	22
3rd	55	38	82	29
4th	55	102	108	50
5th	64	104	238	61
6th	111	113	242	108
7th	152	113	242	154
8th	176	130	247	164
9th	198	132	252	191
10th	210	145	278	220

HAWKE'S BAY v NORTHLAND

Hawke Cup

at Nelson Park, Napier on 28 February, 1, 2 March, 2009
Toss : Hawke's Bay. Umpires : P.L Gasston & E.J. Gray
Close of play: 1st day: no play; 2nd day: Northland 281-9, Child 4, Darkins 8
No result

NORTHLAND

FIRST INNINGS	*Runs*	*Mins*	*Balls*	*6s*	*4s*
B.S.Wilson* b Noema-Barnett	39	114	75	-	5
T.Duffin c Calkin b McLennan	82	207	153	-	10
M.E.Parlane run out	28	52	48	1	4
I.A.Page c Sinclair b Kuru	11	42	31	-	1
J.A.F.Yovich b Bracewell	25	65	54	-	1
B.L.Hood† c Calkin b Kuru	9	9	7	-	2
C.J.Page c Lythe b Bracewell	33	61	43	-	3
T.Saati c de Terte b Noema-Barnett	16	22	19	-	-
M.J.Tulloch run out	2	4	3	-	-
J.S.Child not out	4	11	4	-	-
R.J.Darkins not out	8	3	4	-	1
Extras (b 8, lb 7, w 6, nb 3)	24				
TOTAL (73 overs) (9 wkts dec)	**281**	304			

HAWKE'S BAY

	Runs	*Mins*	*Balls*	*6s*	*4s*
T.I.Lythe lbw b Child	12	70	57	-	2
B.Z.Meehan lbw b Child	6	32	25	-	-
B.M.K.Patton* lbw b Yovich	6	6	7	-	1
J.W.de Terte c Darkins b Yovich	2	11	7	-	-
M.S.Sinclair not out	141	282	207	-	25
M.J.E.Calkin† lbw b Saati	62	113	98	-	9
D.A.J.Bracewell c & b Saati	7	21	21	-	1
K.Noema-Barnett c Duffin b Page C.J.	3	27	21	-	-
R.J.Schaw not out	11	98	87	-	2
J.M.K.Kuru					
B.S.M.McLennan					
Extras (b 5, lb 1, w 1, nb 4)	11				
TOTAL (87.4 overs) (7 wkts)	**261**	337			

Bowling	*O*	*M*	*R*	*W*
HAWKE'S BAY				
McLennan	16	3	47	1
Kuru	10	0	29	2
Noema-Barnett	10	3	30	2
Schaw	13	0	66	0
Bracewell	14	2	56	2
Lythe	7	1	33	0
Sinclair	3	0	5	0
NORTHLAND				
Yovich	23	8	53	2
Saati	16	3	42	2
Child	15.4	2	62	2
Darkins	11	0	49	0
Tulloch	5	1	16	0
Page C.J.	11	3	29	1
Duffin	2	1	1	0
Parlane	4	1	3	0

Fall of Wickets	***N***	***HB***
	1st	*1st*
1st	118	17
2nd	158	24
3rd	174	30
4th	174	34
5th	188	153
6th	235	167
7th	247	182
8th	258	-
9th	271	-
10th	-	-

HAWKE'S BAY v CANTERBURY COUNTRY — Hawke Cup

at Nelson Park, Napier on 14, 15, 16 March, 2009
Toss : Hawke's Bay. Umpires : C.B. Gaffaney & T.J. Parlane
Close of play: 1st day: Hawke's Bay 139-4, de Terte 36, Calkin 31; 2nd day: Canterbury Country 73-3, Robertson 15, Frew 10
Hawke's Bay won by an innings and 100 runs

CANTERBURY COUNTRY

FIRST INNINGS	Runs	Mins	Balls	6s	4s	SECOND INNINGS	Runs	Mins	Balls	6s	4s
L.D.Bartholomeusz c Patton b McLennan	0	10	12	-	-	c Patton b McLennan	9	42	35	-	1
C.G.Bartholomuesz lbw b Kuru	0	21	14	-	-	c Taiaroa b Patton	28	75	48	-	4
P.W.Carey c Taiaroa b Noema-Barnett	22	73	62	-	3	c de Terte b Patton	0	11	9	-	-
A.W.Robertson* c Findlay b Kuru	0	17	11	-	-	c de Terte b Douglas	39	122	109	-	4
R.M.Frew c Taiaroa b Douglas	10	43	30	-	1	c Taiaroa b Douglas	33	91	62	-	5
D.H.Fulton† c Taiaroa b Calkin	1	41	31	-	-	c Taiaroa b Calkin	23	40	25	-	3
M.R.Laffey c Findlay b Patton	39	146	112	-	3	lbw b Noema-Barnett	1	4	3	-	-
J.S.Winchester lbw b Patton	43	105	82	1	6	b Patton	27	39	25	-	6
S.L.Langrope not out	9	18	13	-	1	c Calkin b Patton	0	5	5	-	-
W.D.Bell c Douglas b Patton	0	7	2	-	-	c Calkin b Patton	9	21	16	-	1
B.D.Bellamy lbw b Noema-Barnett	1	3	4	-	-	not out	16	13	16	1	1
Extras (b 10, lb 10, w 10)	30					(b 5, lb 6, w 1, nb 5)	17				
TOTAL (62.2 overs)	**155**	301				(58.3 overs)	**202**	242			

HAWKE'S BAY

	Runs	Mins	Balls	6s	4s
T.I.Lythe b Langrope	31	47	40	-	5
R.J.Schaw c Carey b Langrope	0	2	3	-	-
B.M.K.Patton* lbw b Langrope	30	87	65	-	4
J.W.de Terte c Fulton b Bartholomeusz L.D.	118	280	230	-	18
M.P.Taiaroa† c Bartholomuesz C.G. b Bellamy	0	14	10	-	-
M.J.E.Calkin lbw b Langrope	51	70	57	-	7
C.O.Findlay c Fulton b Langrope	91	116	123	3	9
K.Noema-Barnett c Bellamy b Bartholomeusz L.D.	37	78	58	1	6
A.J.Douglas b Laffey	34	71	63	1	4
J.M.K.Kuru not out	50	58	49	2	6
B.S.M.McLennan c Bartholomeusz L.D. b Bell	0	3	1	-	-
Extras (b 1, lb 7, w 3, nb 4)	15				
TOTAL (115.5 overs)	**457**	422			

Bowling	O	M	R	W	O	M	R	W
HAWKE'S BAY								
McLennan	12	6	32	1	11	4	31	1
Kuru	12	7	22	2	10	2	26	0
Douglas	12	3	25	1	9	0	36	2
Noema-Barnett	10.2	4	8	2	8	2	24	1
Calkin	6	4	10	1	2	1	6	1
Schaw	5	0	25	0				
Patton	5	1	13	3	11.3	2	49	5
Lythe					5	2	11	0
de Terte					2	0	8	0
CANTERBURY COUNTRY								
Langrope	27	4	98	5				
Bellamy	17	2	73	1				
Bartholomeusz L.D.	17	3	62	2				
Bell	29.5	4	94	1				
Bartholomuesz C.G.	13	1	63	0				
Laffey	9	1	36	1				
Frew	3	0	23	0				

Fall of Wickets

	CC 1st	HB 1st	CC 2nd
1st	0	1	29
2nd	6	50	34
3rd	12	80	55
4th	40	87	123
5th	44	167	129
6th	51	301	132
7th	145	366	171
8th	150	373	172
9th	152	450	183
10th	155	457	202

WOMEN'S CRICKET

Compiled by Catherine Campbell

The past year has been a very significant one for women's cricket in New Zealand. The White Ferns competed in two ICC events and reached the final in both. In March 2009 they were defeated by England in the ICC Women's World Cup final in Sydney and in June they went down to England, again, in the ICC World Twenty20 at Lord's.

In other international cricket the Rose Bowl, played in New Zealand, was tied at 2-2 with the last match being abandoned without a ball being bowled. The White Ferns then went to Australia to play a one-off Twenty20 ahead of the BlackCaps v Australia Twenty20 match at the Sydney Cricket Ground.

En route to the ICC World Twenty20 the White Ferns played a three-match Twenty20 series against Australia, losing 2-1.

In domestic cricket the State Canterbury Magicians and State Wellington Blaze met in both the State League and State League Twenty20 finals with Canterbury winning the State League and Wellington the Twenty20 competition.

Auckland won the women's national development tournament at Lincoln University and New Plymouth Girls' High School won the NZCT Cup for a record sixth successive year. Raroa Normal Intermediate from Wellington won the Milo Shield.

White Ferns' captain Haidee Tiffen announced her retirement from all cricket at the conclusion of the ICC Women's World Twenty20 and Aimee Watkins (formerly Mason, who married in March) was named as her successor.

PLAYER OF THE YEAR

Kate Pulford is the 2008/09 Player of the Year. In the domestic State League competition, playing for the State Northern Spirit, Pulford scored 333 runs at an average of 33.30 and took 17 wickets at an economy rate of 3.19. In the State League Twenty20 competition she scored 193 runs at an average of 64.33 and took two wickets at an economy rate of 5.64.

After thoroughly deserving a recall to the White Ferns (she last played for New Zealand in 2003) she was a key figure with her right-arm pace bowling in all the international series played during the season.

In the home Rose Bowl series she took two wickets at an economy rate of 3.95. At the World Cup she made an immediate impact in the opening match against Australia where she removed the three key Australian batsmen. She went on to take six wickets during the tournament at an economy rate of 3.5 and was selected in the tournament team.

At the ICC World Twenty20 she took five wickets at an economy rate of 4.55. Over the whole of the summer Pulford repeatedly demonstrated her ability as the leading White Ferns bowler. Whenever she was introduced into the attack something always happened.

PROMISING PLAYER

Sian Ruck is the Promising Player of the Year. In the 2008/09 season, playing for the State Wellington Blaze, she took nine wickets in the State League at an economy rate of 3.72 and in the State League Twenty20 competition she took four wickets at an economy rate of 5.82.

The left-arm medium-pace bowler was selected for the White Ferns for the ICC World Twenty20 in England in June 2009. During the tournament Ruck took seven wickets at an economy rate of 4.77. Opening the bowling, she repeatedly took wickets in her opening spell and deservedly gained selection in the tournament team.

ROSE BOWL

New Zealand Cricket hosted the annual Rose Bowl series in 2008/09. For the first time in a number of years the matches were played in the North Island.

New Zealand won the first two matches at Cobham Oval but Australia fought back to win the next two matches at Seddon Park only for the fifth and deciding match at the Basin Reserve to be abandoned without a ball being bowled.

As current holders of the Rose Bowl, Australia retained the trophy for another year. Shelley Nitschke was named Player of the Series. She scored 144 runs at an average of 36 and had an economy rate of 4.10 with her left-arm orthodox spin bowling.

The team was: Haidee Tiffen *(captain)*, Beth McNeill, Amy Satterthwaite *(Canterbury)*, Sophie Devine, Lucy Doolan *(Wellington)*, Nicola Browne, Kate Pulford *(Northern Districts)*, Abby Burrows, Sara McGlashan, Aimee Mason, Rachel Priest *(Central Districts)*, Suzie Bates, Katey Martin, Sarah Tsukigawa *(Otago)*. Coach, Gary Stead; Assistant Coach, Bruce Blair; Manager, Catherine Campbell; Physiotherapist, Rachelle Guy; Trainer, Deanne Parkes; Video Analyst, Clare Taylor.

New Zealand Averages

BATTING	*M*	*I*	*NO*	*HS*	*Agg*	*Ave*	*100s*	*50s*	*Ct*	*St*	*SR*
A.E. Satterthwaite	3	3	1	67	136	68.00	-	1	-	-	72
H.M. Tiffen	4	4	1	64*	103	34.33	-	1	1	-	54
L.R. Doolan	4	4	1	34	98	32.66	-	-	2	-	75
N.J. Browne	3	3	0	45	75	25.00	-	-	2	-	64
A.L. Mason	3	3	0	34	74	24.66	-	-	-	-	86
S.J. Tsukigawa	3	3	0	45	63	21.00	-	-	-	-	80
S.W. Bates	3	3	0	33	61	20.33	-	-	-	-	84
S.J. McGlashan	3	3	0	18	34	11.33	-	-	-	-	52
K.L. Pulford	3	3	0	19	32	10.66	-	-	1	-	55
S.F.M. Devine	3	3	0	17	27	9.00	-	-	2	-	65
K.J. Martin	3	3	0	8	17	5.66	-	-	2	-	38
R.H. Priest	3	3	1	7	11	5.50	-	-	2	1	40
B.H. McNeill	3	2	1	4	5	5.00	-	-	-	-	62
A.K. Burrows	3	1	1	1*	1	-	-	-	-	-	100

BOWLING	*O*	*M*	*R*	*W*	*Ave*	*Best*	*R/O*
S.W. Bates	29	2	123	6	20.50	3-40	4.24
A.K. Burrows	17	0	81	3	27.00	2-15	4.76
N.J. Browne	27	2	120	4	30.00	2-29	4.44
B.H. McNeill	30	2	128	4	32.00	2-52	4.27
K.L. Pulford	20	0	79	2	39.50	1-24	3.95
L.R. Doolan	24	2	110	2	55.00	1-22	4.58
S.J. Tsukigawa	15	1	77	1	77.00	1-36	5.13
A.E. Satterthwaite	3	0	23	0	-	-	7.67
A.L. Mason	9	0	57	0	-	-	6.33
S.F.M. Devine	26	3	114	0	-	-	4.38

Australia Averages

BATTING	*M*	*I*	*NO*	*HS*	*Agg*	*Ave*	*100s*	*50s*	*Ct*	*St*	*SR*
J.M. Fields	2	2	1	52	62	62.00	-	1	-	-	62
L.K. Ebsary	2	2	0	86	116	58.00	-	1	-	-	94
K.L. Rolton	4	4	1	62	111	37.00	-	1	1	-	70
S. Nitschke	4	4	0	73	144	36.00	-	2	-	-	75
L.J. Poulton	3	3	0	81	89	29.66	-	1	-	-	68
A.J. Blackwell	4	4	0	59	115	28.75	-	1	5	-	72
L.C. Sthalekar	4	3	0	72	79	26.33	-	1	2	-	58
J.E. Cameron	3	3	0	26	65	21.66	-	-	3	-	77
E.A. Perry	3	3	1	29	40	20.00	-	-	1	-	48
R.M. Farrell	2	2	1	13*	20	20.00	-	-	-	-	105
E.M. Sampson	3	1	0	6	6	6.00	-	-	1	-	100
L.A. Coleman	2	2	0	6	6	3.00	-	-	1	2	120
E.A. Osborne	4	2	2	4*	7	-	-	-	2	-	46
S.J. Andrews	2	-	-	-	-	-	-	-	1	-	-
D.M. Kimmince	2	-	-	-	-	-	-	-	3	-	-

BOWLING	*O*	*M*	*R*	*W*	*Ave*	*Best*	*R/O*
R.M. Farrell	13	1	61	4	15.25	3-26	4.69
E.M. Sampson	21	1	93	6	15.50	3-34	4.43
L.C. Sthalekar	32.3	4	135	7	19.28	3-16	4.15
E.A. Osborne	39	5	130	5	26.00	3-32	3.33
S. Nitschke	29	0	119	4	29.75	1-14	4.10
S.J. Andrews	14	1	69	2	34.50	1-17	4.93
D.M. Kimmince	16	1	83	2	41.50	1-33	5.19
E.A. Perry	192		77	1	77.00	1-26	4.05

AUSTRALIA v NEW ZEALAND — Rose Bowl

at Cobham Oval, Whangarei on 1 February, 2009
Toss : New Zealand. Umpires : B.F. Bowden & D.J. Walker
New Zealand won by 2 wickets.

New Zealand won the toss and elected to field. Nitschke was the first to be dismissed, giving Burrows a wicket on debut. All the New Zealand bowlers bowled well and at 65-6 Australia were in trouble. Fields and Perry put on 61 for the seventh wicket and there were useful contributions from the lower order. Burrows and Bates took two wickets each.

In reply New Zealand was in trouble at 28-5 but Tsukigawa and Satterthwaite batted sensibly and Doolan scored 34 off 62 balls batting at number nine. Satterthwaite saw the team to victory with an unbeaten 49 off 91 balls including six fours. New Zealand won with 26 balls remaining to go one-up in the series.

AUSTRALIA

	Runs	Mins	Balls	6s	4s
A.J.Blackwell b Pulford	10	39	31	-	1
S.Nitschke c Priest b Burrows	9	32	29	-	1
L.C.Sthalekar run out	1	19	8	-	-
K.L.Rolton* lbw b Burrows	2	5	4	-	-
J.M.Fields† run out	52	125	94	-	6
L.J.Poulton c Devine b Bates	4	10	15	-	-
J.E.Cameron c Martin b Doolan	16	42	35	-	3
E.A.Perry c Devine b Bates	29	56	62	-	2
R.M.Farrell not out	13	17	14	-	1
E.A.Osborne not out	4	9	8	-	-
E.M.Sampson					
Extras (lb 3, w 7)	10				
TOTAL (50 overs) (8 wkts)	**150**	185			

NEW ZEALAND

	Runs	Mins	Balls	6s	4s
K.J.Martin lbw b Sampson	8	11	12	-	2
K.L.Pulford b Farrell	9	34	23	-	1
S.W.Bates c Cameron b Sampson	0	1	1	-	-
H.M.Tiffen* c Cameron b Farrell	1	9	5	-	-
S.J.McGlashan c Sampson b Farrell	5	18	16	-	1
S.J.Tsukigawa lbw b Osborne	18	40	31	-	4
A.E.Satterthwaite not out	49	134	91	-	6
S.F.M.Devine c Blackwell b Nitschke	7	20	22	-	1
L.R.Doolan run out	34	70	62	-	3
R.H.Priest† not out	2	9	11	-	-
A.K.Burrows					
Extras (b 2, lb 7, w 9)	18				
TOTAL (45.4 overs) (8 wkts)	**151**	177			

Bowling	*O*	*M*	*R*	*W*
NEW ZEALAND				
Devine	10	3	27	0
Burrows	7	0	15	2
Pulford	9	0	24	1
Bates	10	0	38	2
Doolan	10	1	29	1
Tsukigawa	4	1	14	0
AUSTRALIA				
Sampson	8	0	26	2
Farrell	8	1	26	3
Perry	9	1	36	0
Osborne	10	3	19	1
Sthalekar	5.4	0	21	0
Nitschke	5	0	14	1

Fall of Wickets	***A***	***NZ***
1st	24	10
2nd	26	10
3rd	30	18
4th	35	22
5th	39	28
6th	65	56
7th	126	74
8th	138	148
9th	-	-
10th	-	-

AUSTRALIA v NEW ZEALAND
Rose Bowl

at Cobham Oval, Whangarei on 3 February, 2009
Toss : New Zealand. Umpires : G.A.V. Baxter & B.G. Frost
New Zealand won by 4 runs.

New Zealand again won the toss and batted on this occasion. All the top order made starts but captain Tiffen was the only player to pass 50, being 64 not out off 103 balls, including three fours. At the end of 50 overs New Zealand were 218-7.

In reply the Australian innings was held together by Sthalekar and Rolton who put on 113 for the third wicket. Sthalekar scored 72 off 116 balls, including four fours, and Rolton made 62 off 86 balls, including ten fours. Cameron hit 26 off 27 balls but New Zealand took regular wickets. In an exciting last over New Zealand held their nerve and won by four runs. Bates took three wickets and Browne took two.

NEW ZEALAND

	Runs	Mins	Balls	6s	4s
K.L.Pulford c Perry b Nitschke	19	55	31	-	2
A.L.Mason c Blackwell b Sampson	10	26	19	-	1
S.W.Bates c Cameron b Perry	28	25	29	-	2
S.J.McGlashan run out	18	48	35	-	3
H.M.Tiffen* not out	64	132	103	-	3
N.J.Browne c Coleman b Sthalekar	15	26	38	-	1
A.E.Satterthwaite c Rolton b Sthalekar	20	25	20	-	2
R.H.Priest† c Osborne b Andrews	7	11	8	-	1
L.R.Doolan not out	29	21	17	-	3
B.H.McNeill					
A.K.Burrows					
Extras (w 8)	8				
TOTAL (50 overs) (7 wkts)	**218**	188			

AUSTRALIA

	Runs	Mins	Balls	6s	4s
S.Nitschke c Priest b Burrows	4	8	9	-	-
A.J.Blackwell b Browne	9	18	13	-	1
L.C.Sthalekar b Bates	72	172	116	-	4
K.L.Rolton* c Pulford b Bates	62	105	86	-	10
L.J.Poulton lbw b Browne	4	22	18	-	-
J.E.Cameron run out	26	39	27	-	2
E.A.Perry c Browne b Bates	6	17	15	-	-
L.A.Coleman† run out	6	5	4	-	-
E.A.Osborne not out	3	15	7	-	-
E.M.Sampson st Priest b McNeill	6	9	6	-	-
S.J.Andrews					
Extras (b 1, lb 6, w 9)	16				
TOTAL (50 overs) (9 wkts)	**214**	209			

Bowling	*O*	*M*	*R*	*W*
AUSTRALIA				
Sampson	7	1	33	1
Andrews	10	0	52	1
Nitschke	8	0	34	1
Perry	5	0	26	1
Osborne	10	1	33	0
Sthalekar	10	2	40	2
NEW ZEALAND				
Browne	10	1	29	2
Burrows	5	0	21	1
McNeill	10	1	35	1
Pulford	5	0	24	0
Doolan	5	0	31	0
Mason	3	0	14	0
Satterthwaite	2	0	13	0
Bates	10	1	40	3

Fall of Wickets	***NZ***	***A***
1st	20	11
2nd	59	16
3rd	60	129
4th	99	140
5th	120	191
6th	160	194
7th	179	201
8th	-	206
9th	-	214
10th	-	-

AUSTRALIA v NEW ZEALAND — Rose Bowl

at Seddon Park, Hamilton on 6 February, 2009 (d/n)
Toss : New Zealand. Umpires : P.D. Jones & E.A. Watkin
Australia won by 104 runs.

New Zealand won the toss for the third time in a row and fielded in this day/night match. Australian openers Blackwell and Nitschke put on 148 for the first wicket with Blackwell making 59 off 79 balls, including six fours, and Nitschke 73 off 85 balls, including twelve fours. The middle order of Ebsary, Rolton and Cameron all chipped in and at the end of the 50 overs Australia had made 258-8.

In New Zealand's reply Martin was dismissed early and Mason, Bates and Tiffen all got underway but did not carry on. New Zealand was all out in 39.5 overs for 154. The two Australian off spinners Osborne and Sthalekar did the damage with three wickets each. Australia won by 104 runs.

AUSTRALIA

	Runs	Mins	Balls	6s	4s
A.J.Blackwell c Doolan b Browne	59	106	79	-	6
S.Nitschke c Martin b Doolan	73	112	85	-	12
L.C.Sthalekar b Browne	6	16	11	-	-
L.K.Ebsary run out	30	63	47	-	4
K.L.Rolton* c Browne b McNeill	28	64	49	-	6
J.E.Cameron c Tiffen b Bates	23	18	22	-	4
L.A.Coleman† run out	0	2	1	-	-
E.A.Perry not out	5	9	5	-	-
R.M.Farrell run out	7	5	5	-	1
E.A.Osborne					
D.M.Kimmince					
Extras (lb 5, w 18, nb 4)	27				
TOTAL (50 overs) (8 wkts)	**258**	201			

NEW ZEALAND

	Runs	Mins	Balls	6s	4s
K.J.Martin b Farrell	8	32	26	-	-
A.L.Mason c Blackwell b Kimmince	34	55	32	-	6
S.W.Bates st Coleman b Nitschke	33	49	42	-	4
H.M.Tiffen* lbw b Sthalekar	30	67	61	1	1
N.J.Browne b Osborne	15	31	32	-	1
S.J.McGlashan c & b Osborne	11	20	14	-	1
S.J.Tsukigawa c & b Sthalekar	0	1	3	-	-
L.R.Doolan st Coleman b Sthalekar	4	14	12	-	-
R.H.Priest† run out	2	12	8	-	-
S.F.M.Devine lbw b Osborne	3	2	5	-	-
B.H.McNeill not out	1	4	4	-	-
Extras (lb 3, w 10)	13				
TOTAL (39.5 overs)	**154**	178			

Bowling

	O	M	R	W
NEW ZEALAND				
Browne	10	0	51	2
Bates	9	1	45	1
Devine	6	0	40	0
McNeill	10	1	41	1
Tsukigawa	6	0	27	0
Mason	4	0	27	0
Doolan	5	1	22	1
AUSTRALIA				
Perry	5	1	15	0
Farrell	5	0	35	1
Kimmince	6	0	33	1
Nitschke	7	0	20	1
Osborne	9	1	32	3
Sthalekar	7.5	2	16	3

Fall of Wickets

	A	NZ
1st	148	33
2nd	149	59
3rd	159	93
4th	216	125
5th	236	138
6th	237	138
7th	246	146
8th	258	148
9th	-	151
10th	-	154

AUSTRALIA v NEW ZEALAND — Rose Bowl

at Seddon Park, Hamilton on 8 February, 2009
Toss : Australia. Umpires : D.M. Quested & E.A. Watkin
Australia won by 44 runs.

Australia won their first toss of the series and batted. All the top order scored runs with Australia reaching 307-4 off 50 overs. Ebsary top scored with 86 off 76 balls, including nine fours. In the Australian innings a total of 37 fours were hit. All the New Zealand bowlers came under pressure. McNeill was the most successful with 2-52 off her ten overs.

When New Zealand replied Martin was dismissed in the second over but Doolan, Satterthwaite, Mason, Browne and Tsukigawa all got underway with bright innings. However, in chasing such a large total wickets fell at regular intervals. New Zealand was all out for 263 in 48 overs giving Australia victory by 44 runs. The series was now level at 2-2 with one match to play.

AUSTRALIA

	Runs	Mins	Balls	6s	4s
S.Nitschke b Tsukigawa	58	97	69	-	9
L.J.Poulton c Doolan b Pulford	81	130	97	-	11
L.K.Ebsary b McNeill	86	98	76	-	9
A.J.Blackwell b McNeill	37	40	35	-	4
K.L.Rolton* not out	19	30	19	-	2
J.M.Fields† not out	10	5	6	-	2
L.C.Sthalekar					
E.A.Osborne					
D.M.Kimmince					
E.M.Sampson					
S.J.Andrews					
Extras (b 1, lb 1, w 12, nb 2)	16				
TOTAL (50 overs) (4 wkts)	**307**	202			

NEW ZEALAND

	Runs	Mins	Balls	6s	4s
K.J.Martin† c Kimmince b Andrews	1	7	6	-	-
L.R.Doolan run out	31	45	38	1	4
A.E.Satterthwaite c Blackwell b Sthalekar	67	102	76	-	7
H.M.Tiffen* c Sthalekar b Kimmince	8	15	20	-	1
A.L.Mason c Kimmince b Nitschke	30	36	35	-	2
N.J.Browne c Andrews b Sampson	45	67	46	1	4
S.J.Tsukigawa c Kimmince b Osborne	45	43	44	2	2
S.F.M.Devine c Blackwell b Sthalekar	17	15	14	-	1
K.L.Pulford b Sampson	4	6	4	-	-
B.H.McNeill b Sampson	4	7	4	-	1
A.K.Burrows not out	1	4	1	-	-
Extras (b 1, lb 6, w 3)	10				
TOTAL (48 overs)	**263**	178			

Bowling	*O*	*M*	*R*	*W*
NEW ZEALAND				
Devine	10	0	47	0
Pulford	6	0	31	1
Burrows	5	0	45	0
Mason	2	0	16	0
McNeill	10	0	52	2
Browne	7	1	40	0
Tsukigawa	5	0	36	1
Doolan	4	0	28	0
Satterthwaite	1	0	10	0
AUSTRALIA				
Sampson	6	0	34	3
Andrews	4	1	17	1
Kimmince	10	1	50	1
Nitschke	9	0	51	1
Osborne	10	0	46	1
Sthalekar	9	0	58	2

Fall of Wickets

	A	*NZ*
1st	121	5
2nd	175	60
3rd	256	71
4th	297	130
5th	-	147
6th	-	218
7th	-	247
8th	-	256
9th	-	257
10th	-	263

AUSTRALIA v NEW ZEALAND — Rose Bowl

at Allied Nationwide Finance Basin Reserve, Wellington on 12 February, 2009
Abandoned without a ball being bowled.

ICC WORLD CUP

Australia hosted the ICC Women's World Cup in March 2009. The matches were played in New South Wales with Australia, England, New Zealand, India, West Indies, South Africa, Sri Lanka and Pakistan participating.

New Zealand went into the tournament ranked third in the world and was in the same group as Australia, West Indies and South Africa. The White Ferns were unbeaten in group play but lost to England in the Super Six stage having won their other Super Six matches against India and Pakistan.

The final was played at North Sydney Oval with England emerging as World Cup Champions. Kate Pulford and Suzie Bates were selected in the Tournament Team with Sophie Devine selected as 12th man.

The team was: Haidee Tiffen *(captain)*, Beth McNeill, Amy Satterthwaite *(Canterbury)*, Sophie Devine, Lucy Doolan *(Wellington)*, Nicola Browne, Kate Pulford *(Northern Districts)*, Abby Burrows, Sara McGlashan, Aimee Mason, Rachel Priest *(Central Districts)*, Suzie Bates, Katey Martin, Sarah Tsukigawa *(Otago)*. Coach, Gary Stead; Assistant Coach, Bruce Blair; Manager, Catherine Campbell; Physiotherapist, Rachelle Guy; Trainer, Jason Wheadon; Video Analyst, Maia Lewis.

New Zealand Averages

BATTING	*M*	*I*	*NO*	*HS*	*Agg*	*Ave*	*100s*	*50s*	*Ct*	*St*	*SR*
H.M. Tiffen	6	6	0	100	279	46.50	1	2	2	-	53
S.W. Bates	7	7	1	168	275	45.83	1	-	2	-	99
N.J. Browne	7	7	3	51*	142	35.50	-	1	2	-	64
S.J. McGlashan	7	7	1	88*	174	29.00	-	1	2	-	71
A.E. Satterthwaite	6	6	0	73	162	27.00	-	1	2	-	72
S.J. Tsukigawa	7	5	2	41*	70	23.33	-	-	1	-	81
L.R. Doolan	6	4	1	48	63	21.00	-	-	2	-	79
K.L. Pulford	6	6	0	71	115	19.16	-	1	-	-	66
A.L. Mason	7	7	0	38	105	15.00	-	-	1	-	71
R.H. Priest	6	4	2	14*	29	14.50	-	-	7	1	126
K.J. Martin	2	2	0	7	13	6.50	-	-	1	-	30
S.F.M. Devine	6	4	0	13	17	4.25	-	-	2	-	89
A.K. Burrows	2	1	1	3*	3	-	-	-	2	-	42
B.H. McNeill	2	-	-	-	-	-	-	-	1	-	-

BOWLING	*O*	*M*	*R*	*W*	*Ave*	*Best*	*R/O*
L.R. Doolan	36	12	95	9	10.55	3-21	2.64
A.L. Mason	48.1	5	157	11	14.27	4-2	3.25
S.F.M. Devine	45.4	3	167	8	20.87	2-19	3.65
K.L. Pulford	36	4	126	6	21.00	3-32	3.50
S.J. Tsukigawa	32	7	102	3	34.00	2-8	3.19
N.J. Browne	42	3	139	4	34.75	2-24	3.31
S.W. Bates	32.1	2	150	4	37.50	4-7	4.60
A.K. Burrows	12.1	1	43	1	43.00	1-28	3.53
A.E. Satterthwaite	2	0	14	0	-	-	7.00
B.H. McNeill	13	2	34	0	-	-	2.62

GROUP A

8th March 2009
Newcastle: **West Indies beat South Africa by 2 wickets**
South Africa 116 (45.2 overs) (A.E.Smith 46, S.R.Taylor 4-17);
West Indies 117 for 8 (48.4 overs)

10th March 2009
Newcastle: **Australia beat South Africa by 61 runs**
Australia 258 for 4 (50 overs) (K.L.Rolton 96*, S.Nitschke 87, A.E.Smith 3-42);
South Africa 197 (49.3 overs) (T.Chetty 58, M.du Preez 37, C.Brits 36, S.Nitschke 3-43)

12th March 2009
Sydney: **Australia beat West Indies by 47 runs**
Australia 211 for 7 (50 overs) (A.J.Blackwell 46*, S.Nitschke 45, J.M.Fields 42, E.A.Perry 36);
West Indies 164 for 7 (50 overs) (D.J.S.Dottin 51, S.R.Taylor 32)

Points: New Zealand 6, Australia 4, West Indies 2, South Africa 0

GROUP B

7th March 2009
Canberra: **England beat Sri Lanka by 100 runs**
England 277 for 5 (50 overs) (S.C.Taylor 101, C.M.G.Atkins 50, S.J.Taylor 38, L.S.Greenway 32);
Sri Lanka 177 for 7 (50 overs) (S.P.de Alwis 37, L.A.Marsh 3-31)

7th March 2009
Bowral: **India beat Pakistan by 10 wickets**
Pakistan 57 (29 overs) (R.Dhar 3-7);
India 58 for 0 (10 overs)

9th March 2009
Canberra: **Pakistan beat Sri Lanka by 57 runs**
Pakistan 161 for 7 (50 overs)
Sri Lanka 104 (39.4 overs) (H.A.S.D.Siriwardene 58, Qanita Jalil 3-33)

10th March 2009
Sydney: **England beat India by 9 wickets**
India 169 (48.4 overs) M.Raj 59, A.Sharma 33, A.A.Deshpande 32, H.L.Colvin 3-22, J.L.Gunn 3-50);
England 172 for 1 (38.4 overs) (C.M.G.Atkins 69*, S.C.Taylor 69*)

12th March 2009
Sydney: **England beat Pakistan by 8 wickets**
Pakistan 78 (39.5 overs) (L.A.Marsh 5-15);
England 82 for 2 (23.1 overs) (C.M.Edwards 32*)

12th March 2009
Sydney: **India beat Sri Lanka by 35 runs**
India 137 for 7 (50 overs) (M.Raj 75*);
Sri Lanka 102 (44.2 overs) (A.Sharma 3-19)

Points: England 6, India 4, Pakistan 2, Sri Lanka 0

SUPER SIX

14th March 2009
Sydney: **India beat Australia by 16 runs**
India 234 for 5 (50 overs) (A.Chopra 76, A.A.Deshpande 45, M.Raj 44, A.Sharma 31*, L.C. Sthalekar 3-52);
Australia 218 for 7 (50 overs) (A.J.Blackwell 54, J.M.Fields 43, L.K.Ebsary 39*)

14th March 2009
Sydney: **Pakistan beat West Indies by 4 wickets**
West Indies 132 for 9 (50 overs) (S.R.Taylor 55, Almas Akram 3-7);
Pakistan 134 for 6 (47.5 overs) (Armaan Khan 43*)

16th March 2009
Sydney: **Australia beat Pakistan by 107 runs**
Australia 229 for 6 (50 overs) (S.Nitschke 56, L.K.Ebsary 51, L.J.Poulton 47, J.M.Fields 36);
Pakistan 122 (45.1 overs) (Asmavia Iqbal 36)

17th March 2009
Sydney: **England beat West Indies by 146 runs**
England 236 for 8 (50 overs) (S.J.Taylor 78, S.C.Taylor 65, C.M.G.Atkins 50, S.F.Daley 3-31);
West Indies 90 (38.2 overs) (L.A.Marsh 3-17)

19th March 2009
Sydney: **Australia beat England by 8 wickets**
England 161 (49.3 overs) (S.C.Taylor 49, S.J.Andrews 3-35);
Australia 163 for 2 (33.5 overs) (K.L.Rolton 41*, A.J.Blackwell 38*, L.J.Poulton 38, S.Nitschke 37)

19th March 2009
Sydney: **India beat West Indies by 8 wickets**
West Indies 84 (44.4 overs) (P.Roy 4-14);
India 85 for 2 (17.5 overs) (S.Naik 39*, M.Raj 33*)

Points: New Zealand 8, England 8, India 6, Australia 6, Pakistan 2, West Indies 0

NEW ZEALAND v AUSTRALIA — Group A

at North Sydney Oval, Sydney on 8 March, 2009
Toss : Australia. Umpires : S.S. Prasad & Shahul Hameed
New Zealand won by 13 runs (D/L).

Australia won the toss and chose to field. Pulford was dismissed early but Tiffen, who scored 57 off 113 balls, including six fours, and Bates, 29 off 24 balls, including six fours, enjoyed a promising partnership. Satterthwaite joined the captain and hit 38 off 53 balls (six fours). When she was dismissed, with the score at 109-3, New Zealand were well placed and entering the last 20 overs they were 171/4. Wickets then fell regularly and New Zealand collapsed to be all out for 205 in 48 overs.

In reply, Australia lost wickets in reach of victory as rain was imminent. Pulford took the key wickets of Nitschke, Rolton and Sthalekar in an inspired spell and when the rain finally brought an end to the match New Zealand had won by 13 runs under the Duckworth/Lewis method.

NEW ZEALAND

	Runs	Mins	Balls	6s	4s
K.L.Pulford run out	3	14	12	-	-
H.M.Tiffen* c Cameron b Osborne	57	151	113	-	6
S.W.Bates b Farrell	29	32	24	-	6
A.E.Satterthwaite c Rolton b Sthalekar	38	53	51	-	6
S.J.McGlashan c Fields b Perry	29	62	54	-	3
A.L.Mason c Nitschke b Sthalekar	0	2	2	-	-
N.J.Browne b Osborne	3	4	2	-	-
S.J.Tsukigawa c & b Sampson	2	11	9	-	-
R.H.Priest† c Sthalekar b Perry	7	11	9	-	1
S.F.M.Devine c Rolton b Perry	13	16	7	-	2
A.K.Burrows not out	3	10	7	-	-
Extras (lb 3, w 16, nb 2)	21				
TOTAL (48 overs)	**205**	188			

AUSTRALIA

	Runs	Mins	Balls	6s	4s
S.Nitschke lbw b Pulford	27	65	42	1	2
A.J.Blackwell c Mason b Devine	4	10	7	-	-
K.L.Rolton* c McGlashan b Pulford	21	29	28	1	3
L.C.Sthalekar c Priest b Pulford	6	9	12	-	1
J.M.Fields† not out	26	82	53	-	1
J.E.Cameron c Browne b Devine	15	27	27	-	3
L.K.Ebsary c Priest b Mason	1	3	5	-	-
E.A.Perry not out	17	35	27	-	1
E.M.Sampson					
R.M.Farrell					
E.A.Osborne					
Extras (lb 3, w 10, nb 2)	15				
TOTAL (33 overs) (6 wkts)	**132**	136			

Bowling	*O*	*M*	*R*	*W*
AUSTRALIA				
Sampson	9	0	33	1
Farrell	7	1	20	1
Perry	6	1	40	3
Nitschke	6	0	37	0
Osborne	10	0	37	2
Sthalekar	10	1	35	2
NEW ZEALAND				
Devine	7	2	19	2
Burrows	3	0	15	0
Browne	7	0	25	0
Pulford	7	0	32	3
Mason	6	1	21	1
Bates	3	0	17	0

Fall of Wickets	***NZ***	***A***
1st	6	12
2nd	42	49
3rd	109	58
4th	171	71
5th	171	98
6th	174	100
7th	176	-
8th	180	-
9th	187	-
10th	205	-

NEW ZEALAND v PAKISTAN

At Manly Oval, Sydney 3 March, 2009

New Zealand 303-9 (S.W.Bates 80, S.J. McGlashan 63, H.M. Tiffen 33) **defeated Pakistan** 177-8 (Bismah Mahroof 39, Nain Abidi 38, Sania Khan 36, Sana Mir 34, S.K. Tsukigawa 3-23) by 126 runs

NEW ZEALAND v INDIA

At Old King's Oval, Sydney 4 March, 2009

India 168-6 (A. Chopra 73, P. Roy 44) **defeated New Zealand** 141 (A.L. Mason 39*, S.W. Bates 34) by 27 runs

NEW ZEALAND v WEST INDIES Group A

at Bankstown Oval, Sydney on 10 March, 2009
Toss : New Zealand. Umpires : N.D. Harrison & A.P. Ward
New Zealand won by 56 runs.

On a very slow Bankstown wicket and outfield New Zealand was in early trouble and only some lusty hitting by Tsukigawa, with 41 not out off 35 balls (five fours and a six) and Priest, with 14 off four balls, got them to the modest total of 192-8 off 50 overs.

In response, New Zealand bowled well, particularly the off-spinners Mason and Doolan, who finished with three wickets each. At the end of 50 overs West Indies had made 136-8 to give New Zealand a hard fought win by 56 runs.

NEW ZEALAND

	Runs	Mins	Balls	6s	4s
K.J.Martin lbw b Alexander	6	32	34	-	-
L.R.Doolan run out	10	39	19	-	-
S.W.Bates c Jack b Lewis	11	48	41	-	1
A.E.Satterthwaite b Taylor	37	82	63	-	1
S.J.McGlashan c Taylor b Mohammed	14	60	44	-	-
A.L.Mason* c Taylor b Dottin	38	62	53	-	2
N.J.Browne b Taylor	1	9	7	-	-
S.J.Tsukigawa not out	41	42	35	1	5
S.F.M.Devine b Alexander	4	6	2	-	1
R.H.Priest† not out	14	2	4	-	3
B.H.McNeill					
Extras (lb 7, w 6, nb 3)	16				
TOTAL (50 overs) (8 wkts)	**192**	195			

WEST INDIES

	Runs	Mins	Balls	6s	4s
S.R.Taylor c McGlashan b Mason	38	82	73	-	4
D.J.S.Dottin lbw b Devine	0	2	1	-	-
P.Y.Lavine c Bates b Mason	40	123	97	-	2
A.S.S.Fletcher run out	12	35	42	-	1
C.P.Jack c Priest b Doolan	4	21	15	-	-
S.A.C.A.King b Mason	0	8	7	-	-
D.A.Lewis not out	14	39	29	-	-
M.R.Aguilleira*† b Doolan	6	17	21	-	-
K.N.Alexander c Satterthwaite b Doolan	0	1	3	-	-
A.Mohammed not out	7	14	13	-	-
S.C.Selman					
Extras (lb 3, w 11, nb 1)	15				
TOTAL (50 overs) (8 wkts)	**136**	175			

Bowling	*O*	*M*	*R*	*W*
WEST INDIES				
Selman	5	1	14	0
Lewis	10	1	26	1
Alexander	10	2	37	2
Lavine	6	0	31	0
Taylor	10	1	33	2
Mohammed	8	1	31	1
Dottin	1	0	13	1
NEW ZEALAND				
Devine	8	1	24	1
McNeill	5	1	17	0
Tsukigawa	8	1	14	0
Browne	4	0	15	0
Mason	10	2	26	3
Doolan	10	3	21	3
Bates	5	0	16	0

Fall of Wickets	***NZ***	***WI***
1st	19	1
2nd	21	62
3rd	48	100
4th	85	106
5th	99	106
6th	104	108
7th	161	123
8th	178	123
9th	-	-
10th	-	-

NEW ZEALAND v SOUTH AFRICA — Group A

at Bradman Oval, Bowral on 12 March, 2009
Toss : South Africa. Umpires : M.D. Martell & A.P. Ward
New Zealand won by 199 runs.

With New Zealand moving out of Sydney to the picturesque Bradman Oval in Bowral, South Africa won the toss and chose to field. Pulford and Bates were out early to have New Zealand 4-2.

The highlights of the innings were Satterthwaite's 73 off 76 balls (11 fours) and McGlashan's 88 not out off 76 balls (nine fours and one six). Browne scored 51 not out off 74 balls (seven fours) and New Zealand posted a healthy 250-5 off 50 overs.

New Zealand bowled particularly well and were backed up by an excellent fielding display. Bates bowled five overs and took 4-7 and Mason had 4-2 off 4.1 overs. South Africa suffered a dramatic collapse and went from 44-2 to be all out for 51 in just 22.1 overs, giving New Zealand a comprehensive victory.

NEW ZEALAND

	Runs	Mins	Balls	6s	4s
K.L.Pulford b van der Westhuizen C.	1	6	8	-	-
H.M.Tiffen* run out	16	86	57	-	2
S.W.Bates c Kilowan b van der Westhuizen C.	0	1	1	-	-
A.E.Satterthwaite b Smith	73	90	76	-	11
S.J.McGlashan not out	88	106	76	1	9
A.L.Mason c Chetty b Smith	3	7	9	-	-
N.J.Browne not out	51	85	74	-	7
S.J.Tsukigawa					
L.R.Doolan					
R.H.Priest†					
S.F.M.Devine					
Extras (lb 9, w 8, nb 1)	18				
TOTAL (50 overs) (5 wkts)	**250**	193			

SOUTH AFRICA

	Runs	Mins	Balls	6s	4s
Y.van der Westhuizen lbw b Devine	1	7	8	-	-
T.Chetty† b Pulford	8	30	20	-	-
C.Z.Brits c Priest b Bates	25	42	46	-	1
M.du Preez c Browne b Mason	7	21	12	-	1
A.E.Smith* c & b Bates	0	8	6	-	-
S.M.Benade c Devine b Bates	0	10	7	-	-
M.Knapp c Tsukigawa b Mason	0	3	5	-	-
A.P.C.Kilowan not out	3	19	13	-	-
C.van der Westhuizen b Bates	0	1	1	-	-
S.Ismail st Priest b Mason	2	9	13	-	-
M.Letsoalo lbw b Mason	0	5	3	-	-
Extras (lb 1, w 3, nb 1)	5				
TOTAL (22.1 overs)	**51**	83			

Bowling	*O*	*M*	*R*	*W*
SOUTH AFRICA				
Kilowan	10	0	52	0
van der Westhuizen C.	10	4	18	2
Benade	6	0	37	0
Ismail	8	1	48	0
Smith	10	0	58	2
Letsoalo	6	0	28	0
NEW ZEALAND				
Devine	5	0	14	1
Pulford	6	1	15	1
Browne	2	0	12	0
Bates	5	2	7	4
Mason	4.1	2	2	4

Fall of Wickets	***NZ***	***SA***
1st	4	3
2nd	4	22
3rd	88	44
4th	107	44
5th	111	44
6th	-	45
7th	-	45
8th	-	45
9th	-	50
10th	-	51

NEW ZEALAND v ENGLAND — Super Six

at Bankstown Oval, Sydney on 14 March, 2009
Toss : England. Umpires : Shahul Hameed & T.H. Wijewardene
England won by 31 runs.

England won the toss and chose to bat. Sarah Taylor was out early but the rest of the England order chipped in to help them reach 201-5 in 50 overs.

In New Zealand's reply, Tiffen top scored with 53 off 111 balls (four fours) and Browne and Tsukigawa had a bright partnership towards the end of the innings. However, New Zealand were always behind the required run rate and were all out for 170 in 48.4 overs, their first defeat of the tournament. England captain Edwards inflicted most of the damage with 4-37 off her 8.4 overs.

ENGLAND

	Runs	Mins	Balls	6s	4s
S.J.Taylor† c Doolan b Devine	7	23	25	-	-
C.M.G.Atkins lbw b Tsukigawa	36	83	56	-	2
S.C.Taylor c Doolan b Browne	19	49	37	-	1
C.M.Edwards* b Devine	57	91	79	-	5
L.S.Greenway run out	8	35	28	-	-
B.L.Morgan not out	37	69	59	-	2
J.L.Gunn not out	22	23	16	1	-
H.L.Colvin					
L.A.Marsh					
I.T.Guha					
K.H.Brunt					
Extras (lb 6, w 9)	15				
TOTAL (50 overs) (5 wkts)	**201**	189			

NEW ZEALAND

	Runs	Mins	Balls	6s	4s
K.L.Pulford c Taylor S.J. b Brunt	8	31	23	-	1
H.M.Tiffen* c Guha b Edwards	53	141	111	-	4
S.W.Bates c Guha b Gunn	18	28	34	-	3
A.E.Satterthwaite c Edwards b Marsh	2	12	14	-	-
S.J.McGlashan b Marsh	0	12	12	-	-
A.L.Mason c Atkins b Colvin	23	37	44	-	2
S.F.M.Devine c Guha b Edwards	0	3	5	-	-
N.J.Browne b Edwards	14	20	18	1	-
S.J.Tsukigawa not out	23	22	21	-	2
L.R.Doolan c Atkins b Brunt	2	3	2	-	-
R.H.Priest† b Edwards	8	10	9	-	-
Extras (b 1, w 17, nb 1)	19				
TOTAL (48.4 overs)	**170**	164			

Bowling	*O*	*M*	*R*	*W*
NEW ZEALAND				
Devine	8	0	45	2
Pulford	6	1	11	0
Bates	6	0	37	0
Tsukigawa	10	2	30	1
Browne	7	2	11	1
Mason	5	0	26	0
Doolan	6	2	21	0
Satterthwaite	2	0	14	0
ENGLAND				
Brunt	8	2	25	2
Guha	5	0	21	0
Gunn	5	2	17	1
Marsh	10	1	21	2
Colvin	10	2	31	1
Edwards	8.4	1	37	4
Morgan	2	0	17	0

Fall of Wickets	***E***	***NZ***
1st	20	24
2nd	62	53
3rd	68	60
4th	96	69
5th	158	107
6th	-	109
7th	-	126
8th	-	147
9th	-	150
10th	-	170

NEW ZEALAND v INDIA — Super Six

at North Sydney Oval, Sydney on 17 March, 2009
Toss : India. Umpires : S.J. Davis & Shahul Hameed
New Zealand won by 5 wickets.

India won the toss and elected to bat. Pulford and Devine both made early breakthroughs at the top of the order while Chopra and Malhotra provided the bulk of the runs for India. Devine and Pulford each took two wickets as India were all out for 207 in 49.4 overs.

In New Zealand's innings, Pulford and Tiffen put on 78 for the first wicket. Pulford top scored with 71 off 88 balls, including ten fours, and Bates, batting at number three, was 47 not out when the win came after 47.4 overs.

INDIA

	Runs	Mins	Balls	6s	4s
A.A.Deshpande† c Priest b Pulford	8	15	14	-	1
A.Chopra lbw b Mason	52	151	106	-	3
P.Roy lbw b Devine	3	18	14	-	-
M.Raj c Priest b Browne	21	49	45	-	2
R.Dhar b Pulford	5	18	12	-	1
J.Goswami* run out	4	27	18	-	-
R.Malhotra not out	59	63	52	-	8
A.Sharma run out	14	17	16	-	1
H.Kaur run out	13	19	16	-	1
S.K.Naidu run out	2	3	3	-	-
G.Sultana c Tiffen b Devine	1	3	2	-	-
Extras (lb 3, w 21, nb 1)	25				
TOTAL (49.4 overs)	**207**	197			

NEW ZEALAND

	Runs	Mins	Balls	6s	4s
K.L.Pulford st Deshpande b Roy	71	94	88	-	10
H.M.Tiffen* lbw b Naidu	23	6	54	-	2
S.W.Bates not out	47	104	65	-	3
A.E.Satterthwaite c Sharma b Sultana	12	13	17	-	2
S.J.McGlashan c & b Roy	11	20	28	-	-
A.L.Mason c Sharma b Dhar	23	16	16	1	2
N.J.Browne not out	15	23	19	-	2
S.J.Tsukigawa					
L.R.Doolan					
R.H.Priest†					
S.F.M.Devine					
Extras (lb 4, w 4)	8				
TOTAL (47.4 overs) (5 wkts)	**210**	171			

Bowling	*O*	*M*	*R*	*W*
NEW ZEALAND				
Devine	8.4	0	35	2
Pulford	10	2	38	2
Browne	10	0	28	1
Bates	9	0	52	0
Mason	7	0	24	1
Tsukigawa	5	1	27	0
INDIA				
Goswami	6	1	16	0
Dhar	7	1	43	1
Sultana	10	0	32	1
Sharma	5	0	22	0
Naidu	4	0	14	1
Roy	10	0	59	2
Malhotra	5.4	0	20	0

Fall of Wickets

	I	*NZ*
1st	14	78
2nd	26	109
3rd	62	126
4th	83	147
5th	108	175
6th	126	-
7th	153	-
8th	197	-
9th	204	-
10th	207	-

NEW ZEALAND v PAKISTAN — Super Six

at Drummoyne Oval, Sydney on 19 March, 2009
Toss : New Zealand. Umpires : S.J. Davis & L. Oala
New Zealand won by 223 runs.

New Zealand won the toss and batted with the highlights coming from Tiffen and Bates, who each scored centuries. It was Tiffen's maiden one-day international century and she was dismissed for exactly 100 (128 balls, three fours).

Bates continued on and was eventually dismissed for 168 off 105 balls, including 19 fours and six sixes. The pair had put on 262 runs for the second wicket. At the end of 50 overs New Zealand had reached a massive 373-7.

In reply, Pakistan batted bravely but were well behind the run rate throughout. They were all out for 150 in 48.1 overs. Doolan was the most successful of the New Zealand bowlers with 3-30 off ten overs. New Zealand won by 223 runs and confirmed their place in the World Cup final.

NEW ZEALAND

	Runs	Mins	Balls	6s	4s
K.L.Pulford c Armaan b Asmavia	24	17	18	-	5
H.M.Tiffen* c Armaan b Nazir	100	171	128	-	3
S.W.Bates c Jalil b Mir	168	130	105	6	19
S.J.McGlashan lbw b Sajjida	11	10	10	1	-
A.L.Mason lbw b Nazir	5	4	5	-	-
N.J.Browne not out	33	24	22	2	2
S.J.Tsukigawa c Nazir b Sajjida	2	4	3	-	-
K.J.Martin† run out	7	10	8	-	-
L.R.Doolan not out	3	1	1	-	-
B.H.McNeill					
A.K.Burrows					
Extras (b 2, lb 2, w 16)	20				
TOTAL (50 overs) (7 wkts)	**373**	189			

PAKISTAN

	Runs	Mins	Balls	6s	4s
Nain Abidi b Doolan	52	108	104	-	7
Bismah Maroof c Martin b Browne	14	50	40	-	1
Asmavia Iqbal b Browne	7	7	6	-	1
Armaan Khan† c Burrows b Doolan	1	2	2	-	-
Sana Mir c Burrows b Doolan	8	16	15	-	2
Urooj Mumtaz* b Burrows	27	86	62	-	2
Sajjida Shah run out	4	9	7	-	-
Javeria Khan c McNeill b Tsukigawa	2	3	5	-	-
Sania Khan lbw b Tsukigawa	4	13	11	-	-
Qanita Jalil run out	10	4	9	-	2
Naila Nazir not out	5	23	28	-	-
Extras (w 16)	16				
TOTAL (48.1 overs)	**150**	165			

Bowling	*O*	*M*	*R*	*W*
PAKISTAN				
Asmavia	6	0	58	1
Jalil	5	0	26	0
Mir	10	0	53	1
Sania	4	0	38	0
Nazir	8	0	48	2
Javeria	7	0	46	0
Sajjida	9	0	80	2
Mumtaz	1	0	20	0
NEW ZEALAND				
Burrows	9.1	1	28	1
Pulford	4	0	13	0
Browne	5	0	24	2
Doolan	10	3	30	3
McNeill	8	1	17	0
Mason	7	0	30	0
Tsukigawa	5	2	8	2

Fall of Wickets	***NZ***	***P***
1st	34	42
2nd	296	54
3rd	314	55
4th	321	65
5th	329	95
6th	337	106
7th	370	108
8th	-	124
9th	-	135
10th	-	150

NEW ZEALAND v ENGLAND — Final

at North Sydney Oval, Sydney on 22 March, 2009
Toss : New Zealand. Umpires : S.J. Davis & B.G. Jerling
England won by 4 wickets.

New Zealand won the toss and batted. Wickets fell regularly, however, and the White Ferns were in trouble at 101-7 after 29 overs. Doolan came to the rescue, scoring 48 off 57 balls (including eight fours) batting at number nine but New Zealand were all out for 166 in 47.2 overs.

In reply, England reached their target with 23 balls remaining. Sarah Taylor and Atkins put on 74 for the first wicket and although the New Zealanders kept fighting, and took some quick wickets in the middle stages, England were always in control. Doolan completed a fine match with 3-23 off her ten overs of off-spin. England won the World Cup final by four wickets.

NEW ZEALAND

	Runs	Mins	Balls	6s	4s
K.L.Pulford c Taylor S.C. b Guha	8	29	23	-	1
H.M.Tiffen* c Taylor S.J. b Shaw	30	62	56	-	4
S.W.Bates c Atkins b Shaw	2	15	7	-	-
A.E.Satterthwaite c Taylor S.J. b Shaw	0	1	1	-	-
S.J.McGlashan c Greenway b Colvin	21	25	20	-	4
A.L.Mason b Marsh	13	28	18	-	2
N.J.Browne lbw b Shaw	25	98	78	-	2
S.J.Tsukigawa c Taylor S.J. b Brunt	2	16	18	-	-
L.R.Doolan st Taylor S.J. b Marsh	48	54	57	-	8
S.F.M.Devine lbw b Edwards	0	4	5	-	-
R.H.Priest† not out	0	3	1	-	-
Extras (lb 2, w 15)	17				
TOTAL (47.2 overs)	**166**	172			

ENGLAND

	Runs	Mins	Balls	6s	4s
S.J.Taylor† c Tiffen b Doolan	39	64	45	-	6
C.M.G.Atkins c Devine b Doolan	40	96	85	-	2
S.C.Taylor b Mason	21	27	30	-	4
C.M.Edwards* c Priest b Doolan	10	16	19	-	1
L.S.Greenway c Satterthwaite b Mason	8	33	34	-	1
B.L.Morgan run out	9	35	27	-	2
N.J.Shaw not out	17	30	27	-	3
H.L.Colvin not out	5	15	10	-	-
L.A.Marsh					
K.H.Brunt					
I.T.Guha					
Extras (lb 1, w 17)	18				
TOTAL (46.1 overs) (6 wkts)	**167**	161			

Bowling	*O*	*M*	*R*	*W*
ENGLAND				
Brunt	10	3	33	1
Guha	5	0	24	1
Shaw	8.2	0	34	4
Colvin	10	1	26	1
Marsh	10	3	34	2
Edwards	4	1	13	1
NEW ZEALAND				
Devine	9	0	30	0
Pulford	3	0	17	0
Browne	7	1	24	0
Bates	4.1	0	21	0
Doolan	10	4	23	3
Tsukigawa	4	1	23	0
Mason	9	0	28	2

Fall of Wickets	***NZ***	***E***
1st	26	74
2nd	49	109
3rd	49	111
4th	62	121
5th	74	139
6th	92	149
7th	101	-
8th	164	-
9th	166	-
10th	166	-

14th March 2009 (Seventh place playoff)
Sydney: **South Africa beat Sri Lanka by 9 wickets**
Sri Lanka 75 (39 overs) (D.van Nierkerk 3-11);
South Africa 76 for 1 (28.3 overs) (T.Chetty 41*, C.Brits 31*)

21st March 2009 (Fifth place playoff)
Sydney: **West Indies beat Pakistan by 3 wickets**
Pakistan 131 (46.3 overs) (Bismah Maroof 33, S.F.Daley 4-29);
West Indies 135 for 7 (46.3 overs)

21st March 2009 (Third place playoff)
Sydney: **India beat Australia by 3 wickets (D/L)**
Australia 142 (44.4 overs) (K.L.Rolton 52, L.C.Sthalekar 30);
India 145 for 7 (43.5 overs) (L.C.Sthalekar 3-27)

NEW ZEALAND IN AUSTRALIA

New Zealand played a one-off Twenty20 international in Sydney in February, as part of a double-header with the men's team, and a three-match Twenty20 series in Brisbane in June, on their way to the World Twenty20 in England. New Zealand won the first match but Australia took the series 2-1.

The squad for the game in Sydney was the same as that for the Rose Bowl series in New Zealand in February.

AUSTRALIA v NEW ZEALAND — Twenty20 International

at Sydney Cricket Ground, Sydney on 15 February, 2009
Toss : Australia. Umpires : M.G. Kumutat & P.J. Tate
Australia won by 9 wickets.

This was part of a double-header Twenty20 featuring the New Zealand and Australian men's and women's teams, and was played at the conclusion of the New Zealand-based Rose Bowl Series.

With rain imminent Australia won the toss and elected to field. With several rain stoppages the New Zealand innings never gathered momentum and when the innings closed, after 14 overs, New Zealand had scored 91-5. Pulford top scored with 29 off 24 balls, including four fours.

Australia's target, under the Duckworth/Lewis system, was 82 off 12 overs. The Australians scored 83-1 off 10.1 overs, winning with eleven balls to spare. Nitschke was unbeaten on 54 off 33 balls (eight fours) and Sthalekar was not out on 23 off 25 balls.

NEW ZEALAND

	Runs	Mins	Balls	6s	4s
R.H.Priest† run out	2	10	5	-	-
K.L.Pulford c Osborne b Nitschke	29	28	24	-	4
S.W.Bates st Fields b Nitschke	7	22	11	-	-
S.J.McGlashan c Sampson b Sthalekar	8	20	14	-	-
S.F.M.Devine st Fields b Sthalekar	23	17	16	-	2
S.J.Tsukigawa not out	6	11	5	-	-
N.J.Browne not out	13	9	9	-	-
L.R.Doolan					
B.H.McNeill					
H.M.Tiffen*					
A.E.Satterthwaite					
Extras (lb 1, w 2)	3				
TOTAL (14 overs) (5 wkts)	**91**	64			

AUSTRALIA

	Runs	Mins	Balls	6s	4s
L.J.Poulton c Browne b Devine	1	1	3	-	-
S.Nitschke not out	54	51	33	-	8
L.C.Sthalekar not out	23	49	25	-	2
J.E.Cameron					
L.K.Ebsary					
J.M.Fields†					
E.A.Perry					
A.J.Blackwell					
E.A.Osborne					
K.L.Rolton*					
E.M.Sampson					
Extras (b 1, w 4)	5				
TOTAL (10.1 overs) (1 wkt)	**83**	51			

Bowling	*O*	*M*	*R*	*W*
AUSTRALIA				
Sampson	3	0	19	0
Perry	2	0	14	0
Nitschke	3	0	16	2
Osborne	3	0	13	0
Sthalekar	3	0	28	2
NEW ZEALAND				
Devine	3	0	17	1
Pulford	1	0	5	0
McNeill	1	0	12	0
Bates	1.1	0	13	0
Tsukigawa	2	0	14	0
Doolan	1	0	7	0
Browne	1	0	14	0

Fall of Wickets

	NZ	***A***
1st	17	6
2nd	37	-
3rd	41	-
4th	68	-
5th	72	-
6th	-	-
7th	-	-
8th	-	-
9th	-	-
10th	-	-

AUSTRALIA v NEW ZEALAND First Twenty20 International

at Allan Border Field, Brisbane on 1 June, 2009
Toss : New Zealand. Umpires : N.S. McNamara & D.B. Mealey
New Zealand won by 4 runs.

New Zealand won the toss and decided to bat. Captain Watkins was dismissed in the second over but debutant Lind and Bates put on 52 for the second wicket. Bates top scored with 38 off 28 balls, including five fours and the team was all out for 115 in 19 overs. Opening pace bowler Farrell took three wickets for Australia as did off-spinner Sthalekar.

Australia made a disastrous start and were 15-4 before a partnership of 58 between Fields and Rolton steadied the innings. However, at the end of 20 overs they were four runs short of New Zealand's score. Debutant Ruck took two wickets.

NEW ZEALAND

	Runs	Mins	Balls	6s	4s
A.L.Watkins* b Farrell	5	10	6	-	1
V.J.Lind b Perry	20	36	24	-	1
S.W.Bates c Ebsary b Sthalekar	38	33	28	-	5
S.J.McGlashan c Fields b Sthalekar	7	17	11	-	1
A.E.Satterthwaite run out	7	4	4	1	-
L.R.Doolan run out	0	1	3	-	-
S.J.Tsukigawa b Sthalekar	2	9	4	-	-
K.J.Martin† c Andrews b Farrell	15	18	13	-	2
K.L.Pulford c Cameron b Nitschke	3	6	6	-	-
S.F.M.Devine not out	4	10	8	-	-
S.E.A.Ruck lbw b Farrell	1	7	7	-	-
Extras (b 1, lb 7, w 5)	13				
TOTAL (19 overs)	**115**	85			

AUSTRALIA

	Runs	Mins	Balls	6s	4s
S.Nitschke lbw b Devine	1	12	13	-	-
L.J.Poulton c Devine b Pulford	4	28	13	-	-
L.K.Ebsary b Ruck	0	4	3	-	-
L.C.Sthalekar b Ruck	0	1	1	-	-
J.M.Fields† not out	32	66	37	-	3
K.L.Rolton* run out	36	33	31	1	5
J.E.Cameron c Devine b Watkins	15	15	11	-	2
A.J.Blackwell not out	11	10	11	-	-
E.A.Perry					
R.M.Farrell					
S.J.Andrews					
Extras (lb 1, w 10, nb 1)	12				
TOTAL (20 overs) (6 wkts)	**111**	91			

Bowling	*O*	*M*	*R*	*W*
AUSTRALIA				
Farrell	4	0	13	3
Andrews	3	0	22	0
Nitschke	4	0	27	1
Perry	4	0	33	1
Sthalekar	4	1	12	3
NEW ZEALAND				
Ruck	4	0	13	2
Devine	3	1	9	1
Pulford	3	0	15	1
Doolan	2	0	19	0
Watkins	4	0	15	1
Bates	1	0	15	0
Tsukigawa	3	0	24	0

Fall of Wickets	***NZ***	***A***
1st	15	6
2nd	67	7
3rd	80	7
4th	88	15
5th	88	73
6th	88	96
7th	100	-
8th	108	-
9th	110	-
10th	115	-

AUSTRALIA v NEW ZEALAND Second Twenty20 International

at Allan Border Field, Brisbane on 2 June, 2009
Toss : New Zealand. Umpires : A.R. Curran & D.B. Mealey
Australia won by 8 wickets.

In a match affected by rain New Zealand won the toss and elected to bat. Martin was dismissed early and there were several short interruptions for rain and the innings never gained any momentum. At the end of 20 overs New Zealand were 80-7 with Tsukigawa top scoring with 16.

Australia's openers, Poulton and Nitschke, put on 54 for the first wicket and this took the Australians to their target of 74 in 18 overs with five overs to spare.

NEW ZEALAND

	Runs	Mins	Balls	6s	4s
K.J.Martin c Fields b Andrews	3	7	6	-	-
A.L.Watkins* st Fields b Sthalekar	12	27	16	-	1
S.W.Bates c Blackwell b Sthalekar	11	45	27	-	-
S.J.McGlashan c Andrews b Sthalekar	1	6	6	-	-
A.E.Satterthwaite c Fields b Nitschke	10	27	21	-	-
S.J.Tsukigawa c Fields b Andrews	16	32	26	-	-
S.F.M.Devine c Ebsary b Perry	11	12	11	-	2
R.H.Priest† not out	3	9	6	-	-
K.L.Pulford not out	1	1	1	-	-
S.M.Bullen					
S.E.A.Ruck					
Extras (lb 1, w 11)	12				
TOTAL (20 overs) (7 wkts)	**80**	90			

AUSTRALIA

	Runs	Mins	Balls	6s	4s
L.J.Poulton c Pulford b Watkins	33	35	31	1	3
S.Nitschke run out	25	44	29	-	2
L.K.Ebsary not out	9	15	14	-	1
L.C.Sthalekar not out	3	4	4	-	-
J.M.Fields†					
K.L.Rolton*					
A.J.Blackwell					
J.E.Cameron					
E.A.Perry					
R.M.Farrell					
S.J.Andrews					
Extras (lb 2, w 2)	4				
TOTAL (13 overs) (2 wkts)	**74**	51			

Bowling	*O*	*M*	*R*	*W*
AUSTRALIA				
Farrell	4	0	26	0
Andrews	4	0	19	2
Nitschke	4	0	14	1
Sthalekar	4	0	11	3
Perry	4	0	9	1
NEW ZEALAND				
Pulford	2	0	8	0
Ruck	2	0	14	0
Devine	1	0	7	0
Bullen	3	0	19	0
Watkins	2	0	10	1
Tsukigawa	2	0	14	0
Bates	1	1	0	0

Fall of Wickets

	NZ	***A***
1st	8	54
2nd	25	67
3rd	29	-
4th	42	-
5th	55	-
6th	69	-
7th	77	-
8th	-	-
9th	-	-
10th	-	-

AUSTRALIA v NEW ZEALAND Third Twenty20 International

at Allan Border Field, Brisbane on 3 June, 2009
Toss : New Zealand. Umpires : J.J. Kangur & D. Maloney
Australia won by 32 runs.

New Zealand won their third toss in a row and elected to field in the deciding match. Sthalekar top scored for the home side with 34 off 29 balls, including three fours, and after 20 overs Australia were 124-6. Watkins was the most successful of the New Zealand bowlers with 2-26 off four overs.

New Zealand lost wickets regularly and were all out for 92 in 18 overs. Andrews took three wickets and Farrell and Sthalekar two wickets each to give Australia a win by 32 runs and a series win 2-1.

AUSTRALIA

	Runs	Mins	Balls	6s	4s
E.J.Villani c Bates b Devine	11	10	14	-	2
L.J.Poulton st Priest b Watkins	30	46	27	-	4
L.K.Ebsary c & b Watkins	8	21	17	-	-
L.C.Sthalekar lbw b Pulford	34	31	29	-	3
J.M.Fields† not out	22	28	23	-	2
K.L.Rolton* run out	2	4	5	-	-
A.J.Blackwell run out	10	5	5	-	2
E.A.Osborne					
R.M.Farrell					
K.E.Pike					
S.J.Andrews					
Extras (b 1, lb 2, w 4)	7				
TOTAL (20 overs) (6 wkts)	**124**	79			

NEW ZEALAND

	Runs	Mins	Balls	6s	4s
A.L.Watkins* run out	6	17	10	-	1
V.J.Lind c Sthalekar b Andrews	9	14	17	-	1
S.W.Bates c Blackwell b Osborne	16	26	17	-	1
S.J.McGlashan c Fields b Pike	9	16	16	-	1
A.E.Satterthwaite c Rolton b Farrell	14	2	16	-	1
S.J.Tsukigawa c Rolton b Sthalekar	9	13	11	-	-
S.F.M.Devine b Andrews	10	16	7	1	-
K.J.Martin lbw b Farrell	0	1	1	-	-
R.H.Priest† c Poulton b Andrews	9	9	7	-	-
L.R.Doolan not out	2	4	4	-	-
K.L.Pulford c Rolton b Sthalekar	2	2	3	-	-
Extras (lb 3, w 3)	6				
TOTAL (18 overs)	**92**	69			

Bowling	*O*	*M*	*R*	*W*
NEW ZEALAND				
Devine	3	0	12	1
Bates	4	0	26	0
Pulford	4	0	22	1
Watkins	4	0	26	2
Doolan	4	0	28	0
Tsukigawa	1	0	7	0
AUSTRALIA				
Farrell	3	0	10	2
Andrews	3	0	16	3
Sthalekar	4	0	25	2
Pike	4	0	17	1
Osborne	4	0	21	1

Fall of Wickets	***A***	***NZ***
1st	12	17
2nd	43	17
3rd	73	42
4th	106	46
5th	110	67
6th	124	68
7th	-	69
8th	-	87
9th	-	89
10th	-	92

ICC WOMEN'S WORLD TWENTY20

In June 2009 the top eight women's countries participated in the ICC World Twenty20 in England. The groupings were the same as in the recently staged ICC Women's World Cup in Sydney. The Twenty20 group matches were based at the Somerset County Ground in Taunton while the semi-finals and final were played as double-headers with the men's matches at Trent Bridge, The Oval and Lord's.

New Zealand won their three group matches against Australia, West Indies and South Africa then travelled to Nottingham where they beat India in their semi-final. England defeated Australia in the other semi-final. The final at Lord's preceded the men's Sri Lanka v Pakistan final.

Unfortunately for New Zealande, they were outplayed in the final by England who, with their win, had won both the major ICC events. The next ICC World Twenty20 will be played in West Indies in April/May 2010 and the eight top women's countries will once again participate.

The team was: Aimee Watkins *(captain)*, Sara McGlashan, Rachel Priest *(Central Districts)*, Saskia Bullen, Victoria Lind *(Auckland)*, Amy Satterthwaite *(Canterbury)*, Sophie Devine, Lucy Doolan, Sian Ruck *(Wellington)*, Nicola Browne, Kate Pulford *(Northern Districts)*, Suzie Bates, Katey Martin, Sarah Tsukigawa *(Otago)*. Coach, Gary Stead; Assistant Coach, Maia Lewis; Manager, Catherine Campbell; Physiotherapist, Rachelle Guy; Trainer, Deanne Parkes; Video Analyst, Mark Borthwick.

New Zealand Averages

BATTING	*M*	*I*	*NO*	*HS*	*Agg*	*Ave*	*100s*	*50s*	*Ct*	*St*	*SR*
A.L. Watkins	5	5	2	89*	200	66.66	-	2	1	-	136
S.W. Bates	5	5	1	60	136	34.00	-	1	3	-	107
S.J. Tsukigawa	4	2	1	21*	26	26.00	-	-	1	-	130
S.F.M. Devine	3	2	1	14*	24	24.00	-	-	1	-	171
L.R. Doolan	5	5	0	41	80	16.00	-	-	-	-	88
K.L. Pulford	5	1	0	14	14	14.00	-	-	-	-	140
N.J. Browne	5	4	1	24*	38	12.66	-	-	-	-	88
S.J. McGlashan	5	4	1	14*	32	10.66	-	-	3	-	86
A.E. Satterthwaite	5	4	0	19	39	9.75	-	-	1	-	52
R.H. Priest	5	2	1	9*	9	9.00	-	-	3	2	100
S.E.A. Ruck	5	1	1	0*	0	-	-	-	-	-	0
K.J. Martin	2	-	-	-	-	-	-	-	-	-	-
S.M. Bullen	1	-	-	-	-	-	-	-	-	-	-

BOWLING	*O*	*M*	*R*	*W*	*Ave*	*Best*	*R/O*
S.M. Bullen	4	0	20	2	10.00	2-20	5.00
S.E.A. Ruck	18	0	86	7	12.28	3-12	4.78
K.L. Pulford	18	1	82	5	16.40	1-8	4.56
L.R. Doolan	13	1	76	4	19.00	3-16	5.85
A.E. Satterthwaite	6	0	40	2	20.00	2-20	6.67
S.F.M. Devine	11	0	54	2	27.00	1-12	4.91
S.W. Bates	9	0	63	2	31.50	1-20	7.00
N.J. Browne	7	0	47	1	47.00	1-18	6.71
S.J. Tsukigawa	3	0	16	0	-	-	5.33
A.L. Watkins	8	0	40	0	-	-	5.00

POOL A

11th June 2009
Taunton: **West Indies beat South Africa by 3 runs**
West Indies 123-7 (20 overs) (S.R.Taylor 50);
South Africa 120 (19.4 overs) (M.du Preez 38)

14th June 2009
Taunton: **Australia beat West Indies by 8 wickets**
West Indies 135 for 8 (20 overs) (D.J.S.Dottin 53);
Australia 136 for 2 (17.2 overs) (S.Nitschke 56, L.C.Sthalekar 34, R.M.Farrell 31*)

16th June 2009
Taunton: **Australia beat South Africa by 24 runs**
Australia 164 for 6 (18 overs) (K.L.Rolton 43, A.J.Blackwell 40*, S.Ismail 3-27);
South Africa 140 for 7 (15.3 overs) (S.A.Fritz 39, T.Chetty 36, S.Nitschke 4-21)

Points: New Zealand 6, Australia 4, West Indies 2, South Africa 0

POOL B

11th June 2009
Taunton: **England beat India by 10 wickets**
India 112 for 8 (20 overs) (H.L.Colvin 3-20);
England 113 for 0 (15.4 overs) (C.M.Edwards 61*, S.J.Taylor 50*)

12th June 2009
Taunton: **Sri Lanka beat Pakistan by 4 wickets**
Pakistan 104 for 7 (20 overs) (Bismah Maroof 50, L.E.Kaushalya 3-16);
Sri Lanka 105 for 6 (18.2 overs) (S.I.Galagedara 37)

13th June 2009
Taunton: **India beat Pakistan by 5 wickets**
Pakistan 75 (19.5 overs) (P.Roy 5-16, R.Dhar 3-13);
India 78-5 (17.4 overs) (A.Chopra 37*)

14th June 2009
Taunton: **England beat Sri Lanka by 71 runs**
England 140 for 7 (20 overs) (S.C.Taylor 75*, L.E.Kaushalya 4-18);
Sri Lanka 69 for 8 (20 overs)

15th June 2009
Taunton: **India beat Sri Lanka by 5 wickets**
Sri Lanka 94 for 6 (18 overs);
India 95 for 5 (16.5 overs) (M.Raj 32*, P.G.Raut 30)

16th June 2009
Taunton: **England beat Pakistan by 63 runs**
Engand 123 (20 overs) (C.M.Edwards 43);
Pakistan 60 (16.5 overs) (H.L.Colvin 3-18)

Points: England 6, India 4, Sri Lanka 2, Pakistan 0

NEW ZEALAND v AUSTRALIA — Pool A

at County Ground, Taunton on 12 June, 2009
Toss : Australia. Umpires : I.J. Gould & N.J. Llong
New Zealand won by 9 wickets.

Australia won the toss and decided to bat. The New Zealand bowlers struck early with left-armer Ruck impressing with 3-12 off four overs. Sthalekar provided some resistance in the middle order with 46 off 36 balls, including seven fours. At the end of 20 overs Australia were 123-8.

When New Zealand batted Doolan was run out in the second over but that was the only wicket lost as Bates and Watkins took their team to victory. Bates was unbeaten on 41 off 42 balls (five fours) and Watkins was not out on 73 off 51 balls (twelve fours and a six) to give New Zealand a comfortable victory in 16.2 overs.

AUSTRALIA

	Runs	Mins	Balls	6s	4s
L.J.Poulton b Ruck	2	7	8	-	-
S.Nitschke c Priest b Ruck	18	22	17	-	3
L.K.Ebsary lbw b Ruck	0	1	1	-	-
J.M.Fields† run out	3	15	12	-	-
K.L.Rolton* b Pulford	6	16	12	-	1
L.C.Sthalekar st Priest b Bates	46	38	36	-	7
J.E.Cameron st Priest b Doolan	1	1	4	-	-
A.J.Blackwell run out	19	25	19	-	2
R.M.Farrell not out	13	8	8	-	2
E.A.Perry not out	4	2	3	-	-
S.J.Andrews					
Extras (b 1, lb 3, w 7)	11				
TOTAL (20 overs) (8 wkts)	**123**	76			

NEW ZEALAND

	Runs	Mins	Balls	6s	4s
L.R.Doolan run out	3	4	5	-	-
S.W.Bates not out	41	60	42	-	5
A.L.Watkins* not out	73	56	51	1	12
A.E.Satterthwaite					
N.J.Browne					
S.J.McGlashan					
K.J.Martin					
S.F.M.Devine					
R.H.Priest†					
K.L.Pulford					
S.E.A.Ruck					
Extras (b 3, lb 4, w 3)	10				
TOTAL (16.2 overs) (1 wkt)	**127**	60			

Bowling	*O*	*M*	*R*	*W*
NEW ZEALAND				
Devine	4	0	25	0
Ruck	4	0	12	3
Pulford	4	1	21	1
Doolan	4	1	23	1
Browne	2	0	15	0
Bates	2	0	23	1
AUSTRALIA				
Nitschke	4	0	23	0
Farrell	3	0	23	0
Perry	3	0	31	0
Andrews	3	0	25	0
Sthalekar	3.2	0	18	0

Fall of Wickets	*A*	*NZ*
1st	5	9
2nd	6	-
3rd	25	-
4th	25	-
5th	50	-
6th	51	-
7th	99	-
8th	112	-
9th	-	-
10th	-	-

NEW ZEALAND v ENGLAND

At King's College Ground, Taunton   8 June, 2009

New Zealand 122-8 (A.L. Watkins 38) **lost to England** 126-3 (C.M. Edwards 55*, S.J. Taylor 44) by 7 wickets

NEW ZEALAND v INDIA

At Taunton Vale Sports Club Ground, Taunton   9 June, 2009

New Zealand 123-5 (A.L. Watkins 60, A.E. Satterthwaite 34) **defeated India** 106 (P. Roy 28) by 17 runs

NEW ZEALAND v WEST INDIES — Pool A

at County Ground, Taunton on 13 June, 2009
Toss : New Zealand. Umpires : N.J. Llong & S.J.A. Taufel
New Zealand won by 52 runs.

New Zealand won the toss and batted. Bates and Doolan put on 94 for the first wicket. Bates scored 60 off 39 balls, including eleven fours, and Doolan 41 off 38, balls, including two fours and three sixes. The innings fell away in the latter stages but Tsukigawa hit an aggressive 21 not out off 11 balls. At the end of 20 overs New Zealand had made 158-6.

West Indies started well but the introduction of off-spinner Doolan slowed momentum and she completed a fine double, taking 3-16 off her four overs. At the end of their 20 overs West Indies had made 106-7, giving New Zealand victory by 52 runs.

NEW ZEALAND

	Runs	Mins	Balls	6s	4s
S.W.Bates lbw b Daley	60	38	39	-	11
L.R.Doolan run out	41	59	38	3	2
N.J.Browne c Nero b Taylor	8	2	5	-	2
A.L.Watkins* c Aguilleira b Taylor	1	4	4	-	-
A.E.Satterthwaite c Selman b Mohammed	10	13	14	-	-
S.J.McGlashan b Lavine	5	6	5	-	-
R.H.Priest† not out	9	17	16	1	-
S.J.Tsukigawa not out	21	14	11	-	3
K.J.Martin					
K.L.Pulford					
S.E.A.Ruck					
Extras (w 1, nb 2)	3				
TOTAL (20 overs) (6 wkts)	**158**	81			

WEST INDIES

	Runs	Mins	Balls	6s	4s
S.R.Taylor not out	58	67	56	-	6
P.Lavine lbw b Pulford	11	15	13	-	2
D.A.Lewis run out	2	6	8	-	-
J.B.Nero run out	5	5	5	-	1
D.J.S.Dottin c Satterthwaite Doolan	0	1	1	-	-
M.R.Aguilleira*† c Bates b Doolan	8	9	14	-	1
S.A.C.A.King b Doolan	0	1	1	-	-
K.N.Alexander run out	11	8	10	-	1
S.F.Daley not out	9	14	12	-	-
A.Mohammed					
S.C.Selman					
Extras (lb 1, w 1)	2				
TOTAL (20 overs) (7 wkts)	**106**	67			

Bowling	*O*	*M*	*R*	*W*
WEST INDIES				
Selman	2	0	15	0
Lewis	2	0	33	0
Lavine	4	0	32	1
Mohammed	4	0	34	1
Taylor	4	0	25	2
Daley	4	0	19	1
NEW ZEALAND				
Bates	1	0	12	0
Ruck	4	0	21	0
Pulford	2	0	8	1
Doolan	4	0	16	3
Watkins	4	0	12	0
Tsukigawa	3	0	16	0
Satterthwaite	2	0	20	0

Fall of Wickets

	NZ	***WI***
1st	94	32
2nd	103	36
3rd	106	44
4th	121	45
5th	125	60
6th	128	61
7th	-	78
8th	-	-
9th	-	-
10th	-	-

NEW ZEALAND v SOUTH AFRICA — Pool A

at County Ground, Taunton on 15 June, 2009
Toss : New Zealand. Umpires : D.J. Harper & A.M. Saheba
New Zealand won by 6 wickets.

South Africa won the toss and batted with New Zealand opening the bowling with two left-armers. Pace bowler Ruck took 1-18 off two overs and orthodox spinner Bullen took 2-20 off her four overs. Brits batted positively for 57 not out off 51 balls. At the end of 20 overs South Africa had scored 124-4.

In reply, New Zealand reached their target for the loss of four wickets. Captain Watkins top scored with 35 off 28 balls and the unbroken fifth wicket partnership of 33 runs, between Browne and McGlashan, took their team to victory.

SOUTH AFRICA

	Runs	Mins	Balls	6s	4s
S.A.Fritz c Priest b Ruck	10	8	11	-	2
T.Chetty† b Bullen	7	12	8	-	1
C.Z.Brits not out	57	54	51	-	5
M.du Preez b Bullen	4	4	3	-	1
S.M.Benade c Tsukigawa b Pulford	44	43	46	-	5
A.E.Smith not out	0	1	1	-	-
D.van Niekerk					
S.Loubser*					
C.van der Westhuizen					
S.Ismail					
A.P.C.Kilowan					
Extras (lb 1, w 1)	2				
TOTAL (20 overs) (4 wkts)	**124**	63			

NEW ZEALAND

	Runs	Mins	Balls	6s	4s
L.R.Doolan c van der Westhuizen b Ismail	19	16	22	-	3
S.W.Bates c Ismail b Loubser	24	40	27	-	3
A.L.Watkins* c Brits b Ismail	35	42	28	-	5
A.E.Satterthwaite b van Niekerk	0	2	2	-	-
N.J.Browne not out	24	30	20	-	1
S.J.McGlashan not out	14	15	11	-	2
K.L.Pulford					
S.J.Tsukigawa					
R.H.Priest†					
S.M.Bullen					
S.E.A.Ruck					
Extras (lb 1, w 9, nb 1)	11				
TOTAL (18.1 overs) (4 wkts)	**127**	59			

Bowling	*O*	*M*	*R*	*W*
NEW ZEALAND				
Ruck	2	0	18	1
Bullen	4	0	20	2
Pulford	4	0	16	1
Browne	2	0	14	0
Doolan	4	0	27	0
Watkins	4	0	28	0
SOUTH AFRICA				
Kilowan	3	0	24	0
van der Westhuizen	3.1	0	22	0
Ismail	4	1	26	2
Smith	1	0	11	0
Loubser	4	0	27	1
van Niekerk	3	0	16	1

Fall of Wickets

	SA	*NZ*
1st	16	26
2nd	22	65
3rd	30	66
4th	121	94
5th	-	-
6th	-	-
7th	-	-
8th	-	-
9th	-	-
10th	-	-

NEW ZEALAND v INDIA — Semi-final

at Trent Bridge, Nottingham on 18 June, 2009
Toss : New Zealand. Umpires : Asad Rauf & M.R. Benson
New Zealand won by 52 runs.

New Zealand won the toss and batted. Doolan was out early and Bates was dismissed in the sixth over. Watkins was the backbone of the innings with a magnificent, unbeaten 89 off 58 balls, including ten fours and two sixes. At the end of their 20 overs New Zealand had made 145-5.

In their reply, India lost wickets regularly to be 93-9 at the end of their 20 overs. Ruck and Satterthwaite each took two wickets while the New Zealanders fielded brilliantly to thoroughly outplay India and gain a place in the final.

NEW ZEALAND

	Runs	Mins	Balls	6s	4s
L.R.Doolan c Chopra b Dhar	3	6	6	-	-
S.W.Bates c Kaur b Sharma	10	28	15	-	1
A.L.Watkins* not out	89	71	58	2	10
A.E.Satterthwaite run out	10	13	16	-	1
N.J.Browne st Naik b Roy	5	15	9	-	-
S.J.McGlashan b Sharma	4	8	8	-	-
S.F.M.Devine not out	14	7	8	1	-
K.L.Pulford					
S.J.Tsukigawa					
R.H.Priest†					
S.E.A.Ruck					
Extras (lb 2, w 8)	10				
TOTAL (20 overs) (5 wkts)	**145**	78			

INDIA

	Runs	Mins	Balls	6s	4s
P.G.Raut c Devine b Ruck	5	5	6	-	1
A.Chopra c Bates b Pulford	15	24	24	-	1
M.Raj c McGlashan b Satterthwaite	20	35	2	-	2
H.Kaur b Ruck	0	1	1	-	-
R.Malhotra run out	4	6	10	-	-
A.Sharma c Watkins b Satterthwaite	24	21	27	1	2
S.Naik† c McGlashan b Bates	2	6	3	-	-
R.Dhar c Bates b Devine	4	11	5	-	-
P.Roy run out	5	6	7	-	-
J.Goswami* not out	9	9	14	-	-
G.Sultana not out	2	2	2	-	-
Extras (lb 1, w 1, nb 1)	3				
TOTAL (20 overs) (9 wkts)	**93**	72			

Bowling	O	M	R	W
INDIA				
Goswami	4	0	22	0
Dhar	4	1	35	1
Sharma	4	0	21	2
Kaur	1	0	14	0
Raut	3	0	17	0
Sultana	3	0	28	0
Roy	1	0	6	1
NEW ZEALAND				
Devine	4	0	17	1
Ruck	4	0	18	2
Pulford	4	0	17	1
Satterthwaite	4	0	20	2
Bates	4	0	20	1

Fall of Wickets	NZ	I
1st	5	7
2nd	45	30
3rd	69	30
4th	96	42
5th	120	49
6th	-	58
7th	-	76
8th	-	77
9th	-	87
10th	-	-

19th June 2009 (Semi-final)
The Oval: **England beat Australia by 8 wickets**
Australia 163 for 5 (20 overs) (L.J.Poulton 39, K.L.Rolton 38, S.Nitschke 37);
England 165 for 2 (19 overs) (S.C.Taylor 76*, B.L.Morgan 46*)

NEW ZEALAND v ENGLAND — Final

at Lord's on 21 June, 2009
Toss : England. Umpires : Aleem Dar & R.E. Koertzen
England won by 6 wickets.

England won the toss and chose to field. New Zealand made a disastrous start losing the in-form Bates and Watkins by the third over. Satterthwaite top scored with 19 off 42 balls with England's pace bowler Brunt inflicting the damage with 3-6 off her four overs. New Zealand were all out for just 85, the last wicket falling to the last ball of the twentieth over.

In reply, England made a safe start and the two Taylors, Sarah and Claire, took the team to within reach of victory before a late flurry of wickets. It was not enough for New Zealand, though, and England reached the target in 17 overs with six wickets in hand.

NEW ZEALAND

	Runs	Mins	Balls	6s	4s
S.W.Bates st Taylor S.J. b Marsh	1	3	4	-	-
L.R.Doolan c Taylor S.J. b Brunt	14	26	19	-	2
A.L.Watkins* b Brunt	2	8	6	-	-
A.E.Satterthwaite c Taylor S.C. b Shaw	19	55	42	-	-
R.H.Priest† c & b Brunt	0	1	3	-	-
N.J.Browne b Shaw	1	9	9	-	-
S.J.McGlashan c Greenway b Gunn	9	14	13	-	-
S.J.Tsukigawa c Taylor S.J. b Gunn	5	6	9	-	-
S.F.M.Devine run out	10	14	16	-	1
K.L.Pulford c Taylor S.C. b Edwards	14	9	10	-	2
S.E.A.Ruck not out	0	1	0	-	-
Extras (b 1, lb 4, w 4, nb 1)	10				
TOTAL (20 overs)	**85**	82			

ENGLAND

	Runs	Mins	Balls	6s	4s
S.J.Taylor† c Priest b Pulford	23	31	33	-	3
C.M.Edwards* b Ruck	9	13	10	-	2
S.C.Taylor not out	39	47	32	-	4
B.L.Morgan c McGlashan b Browne	6	18	17	-	-
L.S.Greenway b Devine	3	3	7	-	-
J.L.Gunn not out	2	4	3	-	-
C.M.G.Atkins					
N.J.Shaw					
K.H.Brunt					
H.L.Colvin					
L.A.Marsh					
Extras (lb 1, w 3)	4				
TOTAL (17 overs) (4 wkts)	**86**	61			

Bowling	O	M	R	W
ENGLAND				
Marsh	4	0	16	1
Brunt	4	2	6	3
Shaw	4	0	17	2
Colvin	4	0	16	0
Gunn	3	0	19	2
Edwards	1	0	6	1
NEW ZEALAND				
Devine	3	0	12	1
Ruck	4	0	17	1
Pulford	4	0	20	1
Bates	2	0	8	0
Browne	3	0	18	1
Doolan	1	0	10	0

Fall of Wickets	*NZ*	*E*
1st	2	19
2nd	10	39
3rd	23	70
4th	23	74
5th	31	-
6th	48	-
7th	58	-
8th	62	-
9th	84	-
10th	85	-

STATE LEAGUE

2008/09

The State Canterbury Magicians won the 2008/09 State League competition. State Wellington Blaze had led the competition throughout and had been the dominant team. The last round of matches was exciting with three teams vying for a place in the final.

Northern Districts all-rounder Nicola Browne was the leading run scorer in the competition with 449 runs at an average of 64.14 and Otago's leg spinner Emma Campbell was the leading wicket taker with 24 wickets at 9.50 and an economy rate of 3.38. There were two centuries scored, by Browne and Wellington's Megan Wakefield. Amanda Cooper, also from Wellington, returned the best bowling figures of 6-9.

Final points were:

	P	*W*	*L*	*T*	*NR*	*Bonus*	*Points*
Wellington	10	8	2	–	–	4	36
Canterbury	10	5	4	–	1	3	25
Central Districts	10	5	4	–	1	1	23
Otago	10	5	4	–	1	1	23
Northern Districts	10	3	7	–	–	–	12
Auckland	10	2	7	–	1	–	10

CENTRAL DISTRICTS v CANTERBURY — State League

at Pukekura Park, New Plymouth on 6 December, 2008
Toss : Canterbury. Umpires : K.C. Manley & E.A. Watkin
***Central Districts won by 3 wickets.** Points: Central Districts 4, Canterbury 0*

CANTERBURY

	Runs	Mins	Balls	6s	4s
M.F.Fahey run out	4	15	16	-	-
F.L.Mackay run out	7	44	23	-	1
A.E.Satterthwaite lbw b Candy	2	8	12	-	-
H.M.Tiffen* lbw b Mason	32	76	65	-	5
J.C.Brehaut c Rangi b Broadmore	20	38	35	-	1
A.C.Boyce run out	13	35	22	-	3
R.C.Milburn† c Priest b Sim	3	5	10	-	-
B.H.McNeill not out	10	55	38	-	-
E.M.Bermingham b Sim	9	14	13	-	1
S.K.Burke b Winkley	11	22	23	-	1
M.L.Mitchell lbw b Winkley	0	5	3	-	-
L.M.M.Tahuhu					
Extras (lb 3, w 18)	21				
TOTAL (43.2 overs)	**132**	163			

CENTRAL DISTRICTS

	Runs	Mins	Balls	6s	4s
K.M.Sutherland lbw b McNeill	0	6	8	-	-
A.L.Mason c Fahey b Bermingham	41	92	68	1	4
M.A.Frey lbw b Burke	1	3	3	-	-
S.J.McGlashan c Milburn b Mackay	18	65	44	-	3
Z.A.McWilliams lbw b Burke	14	66	73	-	1
R.H.Priest*† lbw b McNeill	12	55	47	-	1
K.E.Broadmore b Burke	6	28	21	-	-
R.H.Candy not out	18	26	13	-	3
K.C.R.Rangi not out	4	2	3	-	1
C.J.Sim					
K.M.Winkley					
A.K.Burrows					
Extras (lb 2, w 17)	19				
TOTAL (46.4 overs) (7 wkts)	**133**	175			

Bowling	*O*	*M*	*R*	*W*
CENTRAL DISTRICTS				
Candy	10	2	27	1
Burrows	8	3	15	0
Broadmore	10	4	26	1
McWilliams	3	0	17	0
Mason	4	0	13	1
Sim	5	0	21	2
Winkley	3.2	1	10	2
CANTERBURY				
Burke	9.4	1	25	3
McNeill	8	1	25	2
Satterthwaite	7	1	35	0
Tahuhu	2	0	17	0
Mackay	10	3	10	1
Bermingham	10	2	19	1

Fall of Wickets	*C*	*CD*
1st	9	1
2nd	11	2
3rd	27	67
4th	67	73
5th	92	103
6th	95	103
7th	101	129
8th	115	-
9th	132	-
10th	132	-

NORTHERN DISTRICTS v WELLINGTON — State League

at Blake Park, Mt Maunganui on 6 December, 2008
Toss : Northern Districts. Umpires : P.D. Jones & W.R. Knights
***Wellington won by 6 wickets.** Points: Wellington 4, Northern Districts 0*

NORTHERN DISTRICTS

	Runs	Mins	Balls	6s	4s
K.L.Pulford st Stockwell b Dodd	96	91	71	-	13
N.C.Dodd b Perry	1	40	30	-	-
A.J.Wilkins* c Stockwell b Doolan	27	75	59	-	2
N.J.Browne b Doolan	6	15	16	-	-
A.M.Peterson c Stockwell b Doolan	3	22	15	-	-
L.E.Milliken run out	15	30	27	-	1
H.R.Huddleston c Wakefield b Perry	22	35	38	-	2
M.J.G.Nielsen not out	28	38	30	-	2
E.M.Wilson not out	16	19	16	-	1
A.Swart†					
N.P.Edwards					
E.L.Bailey					
Extras (b 1, lb 2, w 17, nb 2)	22				
TOTAL (50 overs) (7 wkts)	**236**	186			

WELLINGTON

	Runs	Mins	Balls	6s	4s
L.R.Doolan lbw b Pulford	2	2	3	-	-
S.J.Bradbury c Swart b Pulford	14	46	25	-	3
A.E.Cooper not out	85	169	124	-	8
M.G.Wakefield c & b Nielsen	67	80	70	-	11
S.F.M.Devine c Wilkins b Browne	15	20	44	-	2
M.J.Hodgson not out	11	23	24	-	1
S.E.A.Ruck					
A.M.Dodd*					
E.C.Perry					
K.A.Tomlinson					
A.C.Stockwell†					
S.M.P.Sim					
Extras (lb 14, w 23, nb 6)	43				
TOTAL (43 overs) (4 wkts)	**237**	172			

Bowling	*O*	*M*	*R*	*W*
WELLINGTON				
Devine	10	0	45	0
Ruck	8	1	41	0
Dodd	10	0	49	1
Perry	7	0	31	2
Doolan	10	0	40	3
Cooper	5	0	27	0
NORTHERN DISTRICTS				
Pulford	6	1	34	2
Huddleston	4	1	24	0
Edwards	4	0	19	0
Milliken	10	0	30	0
Browne	10	0	57	1
Bailey	4	0	30	0
Dodd	2	0	10	0
Nielsen	3	0	19	1

Fall of Wickets	*ND*	*W*
1st	50	2
2nd	127	63
3rd	145	180
4th	146	206
5th	161	-
6th	181	-
7th	199	-
8th	-	-
9th	-	-
10th	-	-

OTAGO v AUCKLAND — State League

at Molyneux Park, Alexandra on 6 December, 2008
Toss : Otago. Umpires : C.B. Gaffaney & R.S. Kinsey
Auckland won by 2 wickets. *Points: Auckland 4, Otago 0*

OTAGO

	Runs	Mins	Balls	6s	4s
S.W.Bates c Lind b Scripps	22	24	24	-	4
K.J.Martin† c Lind b Mistry	0	6	4	-	-
M.J.Kane b Mistry	12	27	25	-	-
S.J.Tsukigawa* c Barriball b Tremaine	73	138	85	-	7
L.M.Grant run out	2	14	16	-	-
A.S.M.Kitchin c Scripps b Gruber	2	2	4	-	-
A.M.Te Wake c Scripps b Gruber	2	26	25	-	-
K.J.Crowley run out	9	33	47	-	-
E.M.Campbell run out	24	54	47	-	2
T.J.Morrison c Gruber b Mistry	0	9	5	-	-
L.M.M.Foote not out	2	4	4	-	-
T.R.Hopkinson					
Extras (b 4, lb 3, w 7)	14				
TOTAL (47.4 overs)	**162**	171			

AUCKLAND

	Runs	Mins	Balls	6s	4s
M.L.Lynch run out	69	150	118	1	4
V.J.Lind† c Te Wake b Tsukigawa	23	16	15	-	4
M.P.Murphy c Crowley b Campbell	27	45	46	-	3
K.T.Perkins c Foote b Bates	7	20	17	-	-
S.R.H.Barriball run out	1	9	7	-	-
W.L.Horneman lbw b Campbell	12	19	17	-	2
S.A.P.Hopkins run out	8	20	17	-	1
M.A.Tremaine not out	3	2	12	-	-
P.Mistry b Tsukigawa	1	17	3	-	-
S.M.Bullen not out	1	4	6	-	-
P.A.Gruber*					
N.Scripps					
Extras (lb 2, w 9)	11				
TOTAL (43 overs) (8 wkts)	**163**	155			

Bowling	O	M	R	W
AUCKLAND				
Scripps	9	0	39	1
Mistry	8.4	1	18	3
Tremaine	10	0	44	1
Gruber	10	1	20	2
Bullen	10	1	34	0
OTAGO				
Bates	10	0	44	1
Hopkinson	4	1	21	0
Tsukigawa	10	2	27	2
Morrison	7	0	25	0
Campbell	10	2	32	2
Foote	2	0	12	0

Fall of Wickets	*O*	*A*
1st	9	35
2nd	31	90
3rd	40	103
4th	46	114
5th	48	138
6th	73	152
7th	96	153
8th	158	162
9th	160	-
10th	162	-

CENTRAL DISTRICTS v CANTERBURY — State League

at Pukekura Park, New Plymouth on 7 December, 2008
Toss : Canterbury. Umpires : K.C. Manley & E.A. Watkin
Canterbury won by 21 runs. *Points: Canterbury 4, Central Districts 0*

CANTERBURY

	Runs	Mins	Balls	6s	4s
M.F.Fahey c Priest b Candy	0	1	3	-	-
F.L.Mackay c Sutherland b Broadmore	25	57	55	-	2
A.E.Satterthwaite c Mason b Burrows	3	5	5	-	-
H.M.Tiffen* run out	69	158	115	-	5
J.C.Brehaut c Frey b Broadmore	2	7	12	-	-
A.C.Boyce c Frey b Broadmore	3	9	7	-	-
R.C.Milburn† c Mason b Broadmore	1	15	20	-	-
B.H.McNeill b Burrows	39	81	77	-	2
E.M.Bermingham not out	7	24	5	-	-
M.L.Mitchell not out	13	3	4	1	-
S.K.Burke					
L.M.M.Tahuhu					
Extras (b 2, lb 5, w 14, nb 3)	24				
TOTAL (50 overs) (8 wkts)	**186**	177			

CENTRAL DISTRICTS

	Runs	Mins	Balls	6s	4s
K.M.Sutherland st Milburn b Satterthwaite	12	52	40	-	1
A.L.Mason c Bermingham b Mackay	11	47	28	-	1
M.A.Frey b Mackay	6	48	39	-	-
S.J.McGlashan b Burke	69	122	97	-	5
Z.A.McWilliams run out	0	3	6	-	-
R.H.Priest*† c Burke b Satterthwaite	14	28	31	-	2
R.H.Candy c Burke b Satterthwaite	3	10	7	-	-
K.C.R.Rangi c Burke b Satterthwaite	7	25	18	-	-
K.E.Broadmore c Mitchell b Burke	0	3	1	-	-
K.M.Winkley not out	8	25	9	-	-
A.K.Burrows c Mitchell b McNeill	18	20	19	-	1
C.J.Sim					
Extras (b 4, lb 2, w 11)	17				
TOTAL (49.1 overs)	**165**	196			

Bowling	O	M	R	W
CENTRAL DISTRICTS				
Candy	10	1	36	1
Burrows	10	0	50	2
Broadmore	10	4	11	4
Mason	10	2	20	0
Sim	4	0	18	0
Winkley	6	0	44	0
CANTERBURY				
Burke	10	0	41	2
McNeill	9.1	1	33	1
Satterthwaite	10	0	31	4
Mackay	10	2	21	2
Bermingham	10	0	33	0

Fall of Wickets	*C*	*CD*
1st	0	35
2nd	5	36
3rd	50	71
4th	55	72
5th	63	98
6th	69	110
7th	161	137
8th	172	139
9th	-	140
10th	-	165

NORTHERN DISTRICTS v WELLINGTON — State League

at Blake Park, Mt Maunganui on 7 December, 2008
Toss : Northern Districts. Umpires : M.P. George & W.R. Knights
***Wellington won by 5 wickets.** Points: Wellington 4, Northern Districts 0*

NORTHERN DISTRICTS

	Runs	Mins	Balls	6s	4s
K.L.Pulford b Tomlinson	51	59	42	-	8
N.C.Dodd st Stockwell b Dodd	58	149	125	-	4
A.J.Wilkins* run out	39	57	63	-	3
N.J.Browne not out	53	63	53	2	4
M.J.G.Nielsen c Wakefield b Dodd	5	14	8	-	-
L.E.Milliken not out	16	16	13	-	1
A.M.Peterson					
H.R.Huddleston					
A.Swart†					
E.M.Wilson					
N.P.Edwards					
E.L.Bailey					
Extras (b 2, lb 2, w 14, nb 5)	23				
TOTAL (50 overs) (4 wkts)	**245**	181			

WELLINGTON

	Runs	Mins	Balls	6s	4s
L.R.Doolan run out	26	38	37	-	5
S.J.Bradbury b Pulford	4	67	38	-	-
A.E.Cooper c Browne b Milliken	33	58	48	-	4
M.G.Wakefield c Swart b Edwards	44	56	49	-	4
S.F.M.Devine not out	83	78	61	-	13
E.C.Perry run out	26	46	43	-	2
M.J.Hodgson not out	0	4	0	-	-
S.E.A.Ruck					
A.M.Dodd*					
K.A.Tomlinson					
A.C.Stockwell†					
C.K.Mizzi					
Extras (b 2, lb 6, w 22, nb 2)	32				
TOTAL (45.4 overs) (5 wkts)	**248**	176			

Bowling	O	M	R	W
WELLINGTON				
Devine	10	2	34	0
Ruck	8	0	44	0
Perry	9	2	34	0
Tomlinson	2	0	20	1
Doolan	10	3	32	0
Dodd	9	0	56	2
Cooper	2	0	21	0
NORTHERN DISTRICTS				
Pulford	10	0	41	1
Browne	3	0	14	0
Wilson	10	1	43	0
Milliken	8	0	42	1
Edwards	5	0	36	1
Bailey	5	0	22	0
Dodd	2	0	8	0
Huddleston	2.4	0	34	0

Fall of Wickets	***ND***	***W***
1st	73	44
2nd	140	66
3rd	180	104
4th	197	157
5th	-	232
6th	-	-
7th	-	-
8th	-	-
9th	-	-
10th	-	-

OTAGO v AUCKLAND — State League

at Molyneux Park, Alexandra on 7 December, 2009
Toss : Auckland. Umpires : C.B. Gaffaney & R.S. Kinsey
***Otago won by 6 wickets.** Points: Otago 4, Auckland 0*

AUCKLAND

	Runs	Mins	Balls	6s	4s
M.L.Lynch c Morrison b Hopkinson	10	36	29	-	1
V.J.Lind† c Tsukigawa b Bates	91	150	12	-	12
M.P.Murphy c Hopkinson b Campbell	16	43	39	-	1
K.T.Perkins c Hopkinson b Morrison	0	9	7	-	-
S.R.H.Barriball st Martin b Campbell	13	25	33	-	2
W.L.Horneman c & b Hopkinson	2	8	9	-	-
S.A.P.Hopkins lbw b Campbell	0	3	3	-	-
M.A.Tremaine c Morrison b Campbell	1	10	9	-	-
P.A.Gruber* not out	14	38	20	-	-
P.Mistry b Tsukigawa	9	13	15	-	-
S.M.Bullen not out	5	16	14	-	-
N.Scripps					
Extras (b 1, lb 4, w 11)	16				
TOTAL (50 overs) (9 wkts)	**177**	181			

OTAGO

	Runs	Mins	Balls	6s	4s
S.W.Bates c Tremaine b Scripps	5	20	17	-	1
K.J.Martin† c Murphy b Gruber	50	86	63	-	7
M.J.Kane b Bullen	26	60	52	-	3
S.J.Tsukigawa* lbw b Bullen	4	2	4	-	1
A.S.M.Kitchin not out	45	93	96	-	4
E.M.Campbell not out	22	91	58	-	1
L.M.Grant					
A.M.Te Wake					
K.J.Crowley					
T.J.Morrison					
L.M.M.Foote					
T.Hopkinson					
Extras (b 1, lb 1, w 23, nb 1)	26				
TOTAL (48.2 overs) (4 wkts)	**178**	178			

Bowling	O	M	R	W
OTAGO				
Bates	10	1	42	1
Hopkinson	10	0	41	2
Tsukigawa	10	1	30	1
Morrison	10	0	25	1
Campbell	10	0	34	4
AUCKLAND				
Mistry	10	3	30	0
Scripps	10	2	36	1
Tremaine	2	0	14	0
Murphy	5	0	16	0
Bullen	10	1	40	2
Gruber	10	2	27	1
Lynch	1	0	11	0

Fall of Wickets	***A***	***O***
1st	39	24
2nd	85	96
3rd	96	100
4th	122	100
5th	136	-
6th	137	-
7th	141	-
8th	147	-
9th	158	-
10th	-	-

AUCKLAND v WELLINGTON — State League

at Melville Park, Auckland on 20 December, 2008
Toss : Wellington. Umpires : P.L. Gasston & D.G. Paterson
***Wellington won by 3 runs.** Points: Wellington 4, Auckland 0*

WELLINGTON

	Runs	Mins	Balls	6s	4s
L.R.Doolan b Scripps	0	3	6	-	-
S.J.Bradbury c Murphy b Mistry	0	6	5	-	-
A.E.Cooper lbw b Scripps	12	64	52	-	-
M.G.Wakefield c & b Mistry	6	22	14	-	-
S.F.M.Devine c Mistry b Bullen	11	7	8	-	2
M.J.Hodgson c & b Bullen	13	24	35	-	-
E.C.Perry c Scripps b Mistry	18	18	18	-	2
K.A.Tomlinson not out	32	101	71	-	4
A.C.Stockwell† lbw b Mistry	0	8	6	-	-
A.M.Dodd* c Barriball b Coetzee	25	69	64	-	4
S.E.A.Ruck c Barriball b Coetzee	4	9	8	-	1
O.R.Bupha-Intr					
Extras (w 4, nb 1)	5				
TOTAL (47.4 overs)	**126**	170			

AUCKLAND

	Runs	Mins	Balls	6s	4s
M.L.Lynch lbw b Devine	2	2	5	-	-
M.P.Murphy st Stockwell b Dodd	30	63	49	-	4
S.R.H.Barriball lbw b Ruck	2	19	16	-	-
K.T.Perkins b Devine	0	9	5	-	-
S.M.Bullen lbw b Ruck	1	11	9	-	-
W.L.Horneman c Perry b Dodd	18	63	59	-	1
N.Scripps c Hodgson b Dodd	0	17	17	-	-
V.J.Lind† lbw b Doolan	23	57	46	-	3
P.Mistry c Wakefield b Ruck	7	14	19	-	1
S.Coetzee not out	7	41	30	-	1
P.A.Gruber* lbw b Cooper	5	25	17	-	-
M.A.Tremaine					
Extras (b 6, lb 1, w 19, nb 2)	28				
TOTAL (45.1 overs)	**123**	165			

Bowling	*O*	*M*	*R*	*W*
AUCKLAND				
Scripps	10	4	21	2
Mistry	9	2	27	4
Bullen	10	3	27	2
Coetzee	4.4	1	12	2
Gruber	7	0	25	0
Tremaine	7	4	14	0
WELLINGTON				
Devine	10	2	18	2
Ruck	9	2	20	3
Perry	2	0	16	0
Dodd	10	4	21	3
Doolan	10	1	29	1
Cooper	4.1	0	12	1

Fall of Wickets	***W***	***A***
1st	0	2
2nd	0	19
3rd	15	27
4th	26	28
5th	44	57
6th	48	63
7th	63	84
8th	67	93
9th	117	103
10th	126	123

CANTERBURY v OTAGO — State League

at MainPower Oval, Rangiora on 20 December, 2008
***Abandoned without a ball being bowled.** Points: Canterbury 2, Otago 2*

NORTHERN DISTRICTS v CENTRAL DISTRICTS State League

at Blake Park, Mt Maunganui on 20 December, 2008
Toss : Central Districts. Umpires : M.P. George & W.R. Knights
***Central Districts won by 10 runs.** Points: Central Districts 4, Northern Districts 0*

CENTRAL DISTRICTS

	Runs	Mins	Balls	6s	4s
A.L.Mason c Peterson b Edwards	16	27	23	-	3
K.M.Sutherland c Dodd b Edwards	8	20	19	-	1
K.E.Broadmore run out	12	49	30	-	1
S.J.McGlashan lbw b Milliken	15	23	23	-	2
Z.A.McWilliams c Wilkins b Milliken	4	28	30	-	-
R.H.Candy run out	22	37	29	-	3
R.H.Priest*† b Edwards	64	89	67	-	8
K.C.R.Rangi run out	11	9	7	-	2
M.A.Frey not out	42	70	57	-	3
K.M.Winkley b Milliken	11	10	11	-	1
A.K.Burrows not out	3	7	5	-	-
L.A.M.Hayes					
Extras (b 2, lb 2, w 23)	27				
TOTAL (50 overs) (9 wkts)	**235**	189			

NORTHERN DISTRICTS

	Runs	Mins	Balls	6s	4s
K.L.Pulford b Hayes	22	25	26	-	3
N.C.Dodd b Burrows	0	2	3	-	-
A.J.Wilkins*† c McGlashan b Mason	43	66	56	-	8
N.J.Browne c Mason b Broadmore	98	153	111	2	7
A.M.Peterson b Winkley	19	48	53	-	2
L.E.Milliken lbw b Winkley	0	1	2	-	-
M.J.G.Nielsen b Burrows	0	5	4	-	-
H.R.Huddleston run out	14	29	28	-	-
E.M.Wilson run out	1	5	1	-	-
A.Swart lbw b Broadmore	7	14	8	-	-
N.P.Edwards not out	1	1	1	-	-
E.L.Bailey					
Extras (lb 1, w 18, nb 1)	20				
TOTAL (48.4 overs)	**225**	179			

Bowling	*O*	*M*	*R*	*W*
NORTHERN DISTRICTS				
Pulford	10	0	49	0
Edwards	10	1	43	3
Wilson	10	1	29	0
Milliken	10	1	46	3
Browne	4	0	35	0
Bailey	6	0	29	0
CENTRAL DISTRICTS				
Burrows	9	1	42	2
Hayes	7	0	37	1
McWilliams	5	2	17	0
Broadmore	7.4	0	47	2
Mason	10	0	48	1
Winkley	10	2	33	2

Fall of Wickets	***CD***	***ND***
1st	24	3
2nd	30	29
3rd	50	90
4th	62	152
5th	76	152
6th	112	153
7th	137	186
8th	207	191
9th	228	224
10th	-	225

AUCKLAND v WELLINGTON State League

at Melville Park, Auckland on 21 December, 2008
Toss : Auckland. Umpires : P.L. Gasston & D.G. Paterson
***Wellington won by 92 runs.** Points: Wellington 5, Auckland 0*

WELLINGTON

	Runs	Mins	Balls	6s	4s
L.R.Doolan st Lind b Scripps	0	1	3	-	-
S.J.Bradbury run out	11	63	60	-	1
A.E.Cooper c Tremaine b Mistry	11	37	31	-	-
M.G.Wakefield c Perkins b Scripps	120	142	119	-	13
S.F.M.Devine b Mistry	32	48	36	-	4
M.J.Hodgson c Barriball b Tremaine	7	38	29	-	-
E.C.Perry b Scripps	9	19	12	-	-
K.A.Tomlinson not out	4	15	7	-	-
A.M.Dodd* not out	2	4	4	-	-
A.C.Stockwell†					
S.E.A.Ruck					
O.R.Bupha-Intr					
Extras (b 4, lb 2, w 7, nb 1)	14				
TOTAL (50 overs) (7 wkts)	**210**	187			

AUCKLAND

	Runs	Mins	Balls	6s	4s
M.L.Lynch c Stockwell b Dodd	33	69	60	-	2
V.J.Lind† c Stockwell b Doolan	20	51	34	-	3
W.L.Horneman c Stockwell b Doolan	0	6	4	-	-
M.P.Murphy b Doolan	20	38	33	-	1
K.T.Perkins lbw b Devine	12	47	41	-	1
S.Coetzee c Cooper b Devine	5	11	12	-	-
S.M.Bullen not out	6	41	23	-	1
P.A.Gruber* b Devine	2	9	12	-	-
P.Mistry c Stockwell b Cooper	5	17	10	-	1
N.Scripps c Stockwell b Ruck	2	5	7	-	-
S.R.H.Barriball absent hurt					
M.A.Tremaine					
Extras (w 11, nb 2)	13				
TOTAL (39 overs)	**118**	151			

Bowling	*O*	*M*	*R*	*W*
AUCKLAND				
Scripps	10	2	35	3
Mistry	10	2	37	2
Bullen	10	2	26	0
Coetzee	6	1	29	0
Tremaine	8	0	46	1
Gruber	6	0	31	0
WELLINGTON				
Devine	8	1	30	3
Ruck	8	1	32	1
Doolan	10	1	22	3
Dodd	7	0	26	1
Cooper	6	2	8	1

Fall of Wickets	***W***	***A***
1st	0	50
2nd	23	52
3rd	43	56
4th	112	91
5th	140	98
6th	178	100
7th	203	104
8th	-	115
9th	-	118
10th	-	-

CANTERBURY v OTAGO — State League

at MainPower Oval, Rangiora on 21 December, 2008
Toss : Canterbury. Umpires : J.M. Busby & D.W. Reid
***Canterbury won by 6 wickets.** Points: Canterbury 5, Otago 0*

OTAGO

	Runs	Mins	Balls	6s	4s
K.J.Martin† b Satterthwaite	3	34	24	-	-
S.W.Bates c Mitchell b McNeill	9	29	21	-	-
M.J.Kane c Mackay b Bermingham	26	64	43	1	-
S.J.Tsukigawa* b Mackay	15	23	25	-	2
A.S.M.Kitchin c Mitchell b Mackay	3	6	7	-	-
L.M.Grant lbw b Mitchell	3	17	12	-	-
E.M.Campbell lbw b Bermingham	0	5	5	-	-
A.M.Te Wake b Burke	6	24	25	-	-
K.J.Crowley c Mackay b McNeill	8	24	19	-	-
T.J.Morrison b McNeill	6	19	9	-	1
L.M.M.Foote not out	0	14	11	-	-
T.R.Hopkinson					
Extras (lb 2, w 11, nb 3)	16				
TOTAL (33.1 overs)	**95**	134			

CANTERBURY

	Runs	Mins	Balls	6s	4s
F.L.Mackay c Te Wake b Tsukigawa	12	21	23	-	1
M.L.Mitchell c Martin b Bates	21	33	20	-	3
A.E.Satterthwaite not out	36	65	47	-	2
H.M.Tiffen* c Foote b Campbell	3	21	14	-	-
A.C.Boyce lbw b Campbell	5	9	8	-	-
J.C.Brehaut not out	9	21	22	-	1
E.M.Bermingham					
R.C.Milburn†					
B.H.McNeill					
S.K.Burke					
K.A.Neilson					
L.M.M.Tahuhu					
Extras (lb 2, w 10)	12				
TOTAL (22.2 overs) (4 wkts)	**98**	87			

Bowling	*O*	*M*	*R*	*W*
CANTERBURY				
Burke	7	3	11	1
McNeill	6.1	1	11	3
Satterthwaite	3	0	12	1
Tahuhu	4	0	18	0
Mackay	3	0	13	2
Bermingham	6	0	14	2
Mitchell	4	0	14	1
OTAGO				
Bates	7	0	27	1
Tsukigawa	7	1	27	1
Campbell	4	0	17	2
Hopkinson	4	0	20	0
Morrison	0.2	0	5	0

Fall of Wickets	*O*	*C*
1st	12	25
2nd	14	42
3rd	42	57
4th	49	69
5th	65	-
6th	67	-
7th	70	-
8th	86	-
9th	86	-
10th	95	-

NORTHERN DISTRICTS v CENTRAL DISTRICTS — State League

at Blake Park, Mt Maunganui on 21 December, 2008
Toss : Central Districts. Umpires : M.P. George & W.R. Knights
***Central Districts won by 18 runs**. Points: Central Districts 4, Northern Districts 0*

CENTRAL DISTRICTS

	Runs	Mins	Balls	6s	4s
A.L.Mason run out	42	81	55	-	3
K.M.Sutherland c Wilkins b Pulford	5	19	18	-	1
K.E.Broadmore lbw b Dodd	47	101	81	-	5
S.J.McGlashan c & b Bailey	55	70	68	-	4
K.C.R.Rangi b Dodd	2	14	9	-	-
R.H.Priest*† not out	49	48	40	2	2
R.H.Candy c Huddleston b Milliken	21	19	22	-	1
Z.A.McWilliams c Pulford b Milliken	4	7	4	-	-
K.M.Winkley not out	6	4	4	-	-
A.K.Burrows					
M.A.Frey					
L.A.M.Hayes					
Extras (b 3, lb 6, w 24, nb 1)	34				
TOTAL (50 overs) (7 wkts)	**265**	185			

NORTHERN DISTRICTS

	Runs	Mins	Balls	6s	4s
K.L.Pulford lbw b Winkley	22	42	42	-	1
N.C.Dodd lbw b Hayes	8	19	15	-	2
A.J.Wilkins*† lbw b Winkley	27	51	49	-	3
N.J.Browne run out	101	134	94	-	9
A.M.Peterson c & b McWilliams	28	36	39	-	1
L.E.Milliken run out	0	2	0	-	-
M.J.G.Nielsen b Burrows	18	34	26	-	-
H.R.Huddleston b Hayes	17	38	24	-	-
E.M.Wilson run out	0	1	1	-	-
A.Swart not out	11	8	9	-	-
E.L.Bailey not out	2	2	2	-	-
N.P.Edwards					
Extras (lb 5, w 7, nb 1)	13				
TOTAL (50 overs) (9 wkts)	**247**	188			

Bowling	*O*	*M*	*R*	*W*
NORTHERN DISTRICTS				
Pulford	10	2	24	1
Browne	1	0	5	0
Edwards	8	0	60	0
Wilson	3	0	19	0
Huddleston	4	0	22	0
Milliken	8	1	31	2
Dodd	9	0	47	2
Bailey	7	0	48	1
CENTRAL DISTRICTS				
Burrows	10	0	44	1
Hayes	9	0	53	2
Winkley	10	0	43	2
Broadmore	10	0	43	0
Mason	4	0	19	0
McWilliams	7	0	40	1

Fall of Wickets	***CD***	***ND***
1st	19	21
2nd	89	42
3rd	145	72
4th	157	130
5th	192	130
6th	227	182
7th	250	227
8th		227
9th		240
10th		

AUCKLAND v CENTRAL DISTRICTS — State League

at Melville Park, Auckland on 28 December, 2008
Toss : Central Districts. Umpires : E.J. Gray & R.S. Kinsey
***Central Districts won by 61 runs.** Points: Central Districts 5, Auckland 0*

CENTRAL DISTRICTS

	Runs	Mins	Balls	6s	4s
K.M.Sutherland c Mistry b Bullen	6	46	50	-	-
A.L.Mason* c Lind b Scripps	4	10	7	-	-
K.E.Broadmore c Scripps b Coetzee	5	19	11	-	-
S.J.McGlashan b Mistry	82	143	97	-	6
M.A.Frey run out	1	10	7	-	-
R.H.Priest† c Bullen b Murphy	36	38	62	-	3
Z.A.McWilliams run out	13	19	22	-	-
R.H.Candy run out	5	7	5	-	1
S.L.Norman c Lind b Mistry	1	8	7	-	-
K.M.Winkley not out	9	12	10	-	1
A.K.Burrows run out	0	1	0	-	-
L.A.M.Hayes					
Extras (b 1, lb 2, w 16)	19				
TOTAL (46.2 overs)	**181**	176			

AUCKLAND

	Runs	Mins	Balls	6s	4s
M.L.Lynch lbw b Burrows	1	13	13	-	-
V.J.Lind† lbw b Candy	4	15	11	-	-
R.J.Kember st Priest b Mason	34	94	73	-	2
M.P.Murphy c Priest b Hayes	11	36	34	-	1
K.T.Perkins run out	0	5	5	-	-
M.A.Tremaine c Norman b Mason	20	43	40	-	1
P.M.Yates c McGlashan b Mason	2	15	12	-	-
S.Coetzee c Hayes b Winkley	1	4	7	-	-
P.Mistry c Broadmore b McWilliams	28	34	35	-	5
S.M.Bullen b Burrows	3	14	19	-	-
P.A.Gruber* not out	2	14	3	-	-
N.Scripps					
Extras (lb 5, w 9)	14				
TOTAL (41.5 overs)	**120**	148			

Bowling	O	M	R	W
AUCKLAND				
Scripps	8.2	0	41	1
Mistry	8	3	31	2
Coetzee	7	1	31	1
Bullen	10	2	24	1
Gruber	8	2	25	0
Murphy	5	0	26	1
CENTRAL DISTRICTS				
Candy	7	1	22	1
Burrows	7	0	16	2
Broadmore	8	1	21	0
Hayes	4	1	12	1
Mason	10	3	18	3
Winkley	4	2	11	1
McWilliams	1.5	0	15	1

Fall of Wickets

	CD	A
1st	6	7
2nd	18	7
3rd	22	33
4th	27	37
5th	121	83
6th	141	85
7th	155	86
8th	161	89
9th	180	93
10th	181	120

CANTERBURY v NORTHERN DISTRICTS — State League

at Queen Elizabeth II Park, Christchurch on 28 December, 2008
Toss : Northern Districts. Umpires : P.J. Agent & K. Cross
***Northern Districts won by 7 wickets.** Points: Northern Districts 4, Canterbury 0*

CANTERBURY

	Runs	Mins	Balls	6s	4s
M.F.Fahey b Pulford	5	24	23	-	1
F.L.Mackay lbw b Pulford	17	73	60	-	1
A.E.Satterthwaite c Milliken b Dodd	21	53	32	-	3
H.M.Tiffen* run out	30	79	71	-	1
J.C.Brehaut lbw b Wilson	15	29	29	-	2
A.C.Boyce run out	0	3	5	-	-
R.C.Milburn† c Swart b Bailey	3	15	15	-	
B.H.McNeill c Swart b Wilson	9	27	27	-	1
M.L.Mitchell lbw b Milliken	12	15	11	1	-
E.M.Bermingham not out	14	17	13	-	1
S.K.Burke lbw b Wilson	1	4	4	-	-
L.M.M.Tahuhu					
Extras (b 5, lb 5, w 20, nb 2)	32				
TOTAL (48 overs)	**159**	174			

NORTHERN DISTRICTS

	Runs	Mins	Balls	6s	4s
K.L.Pulford lbw b Bermingham	35	64	42	-	3
N.C.Dodd st Milburn b McNeill	0	5	2	-	-
A.J.Wilkins*† c Tiffen b McNeill	51	126	118	-	8
N.J.Browne not out	54	84	74	-	7
A.M.Peterson not out	4	16	13	-	-
L.E.Milliken					
H.R.Huddleston					
M.J.G.Nielsen					
A.Swart					
E.M.Wilson					
E.L.Bailey					
N.P.Edwards					
Extras (b 1, lb 2, w 12, nb 1)	16				
TOTAL (41.2 overs) (3 wkts)	**160**	149			

Bowling	O	M	R	W
NORTHERN DISTRICTS				
Pulford	10	5	16	2
Browne	5	2	14	0
Edwards	4	0	21	0
Dodd	5	1	19	1
Milliken	9	1	20	1
Wilson	10	2	39	3
Bailey	5	1	20	1
CANTERBURY				
Burke	10	2	24	0
McNeill	8.2	0	32	2
Satterthwaite	2	0	19	0
Mackay	10	0	33	0
Bermingham	8	0	28	1
Mitchell	2	0	14	0
Tahuhu	1	0	7	0

Fall of Wickets

	C	ND
1st	17	6
2nd	55	67
3rd	61	143
4th	92	-
5th	93	-
6th	100	-
7th	129	-
8th	132	-
9th	156	-
10th	159	-

WELLINGTON v OTAGO

State League

at Karori Park, Wellington on 28 December, 2008
Toss : Wellington. Umpires : R. Allen & B.G. Frost
Wellington won by 58 runs. *Points: Wellington 5, Otago 0*

WELLINGTON

	Runs	Mins	Balls	6s	4s
L.R.Doolan c Campbell b Morrison	42	96	89	-	3
S.J.Bradbury lbw b Bates	1	27	17	-	-
A.E.Cooper b Askew	21	49	48	-	-
M.G.Wakefield lbw b Morrison	7	20	22	-	1
S.F.M.Devine c Kitchin b Morrison	25	26	27	-	5
E.C.Perry st Martin b Campbell	14	21	22	-	2
K.A.Tomlinson c Tsukigawa b Campbell	0	6	4	-	-
M.J.Hodgson not out	14	32	31	-	1
A.C.Stockwell† st Martin b Campbell	1	15	11	-	-
A.M.Dodd* c Martin b Campbell	0	6	5	-	-
S.E.A.Ruck lbw b Bates	1	8	6	-	-
R.J.M.Moffitt					
Extras (b 1, lb 1, w 6)	8				
TOTAL (47.2 overs)	**134**	162			

OTAGO

	Runs	Mins	Balls	6s	4s
K.J.Martin† c Dodd b Cooper	24	41	41	-	4
S.W.Bates c & b Cooper	19	46	33	-	1
M.J.Kane c Tomlinson b Cooper	3	20	22	-	-
S.J.Tsukigawa* run out	0	11	11	-	-
A.S.M.Kitchin c Stockwell b Dodd	0	7	6	-	-
L.R.F.Askew lbw b Cooper	1	7	4	-	-
L.M.Grant lbw b Cooper	3	20	20	-	-
E.M.Campbell b Cooper	1	9	12	-	-
K.J.Crowley b Dodd	0	10	9	-	-
T.J.Morrison not out	12	22	23	-	2
L.M.M.Foote lbw b Doolan	4	18	13	-	1
T.R.Hopkinson					
Extras (lb 3, w 6)	9				
TOTAL (32.2 overs)	**76**	115			

Bowling	*O*	*M*	*R*	*W*
OTAGO				
Bates	9.2	3	14	2
Hopkinson	5	2	6	0
Askew	10	1	27	1
Tsukigawa	4	0	21	0
Morrison	10	1	29	3
Campbell	9	1	35	4
WELLINGTON				
Devine	6	0	21	0
Ruck	4	0	15	0
Dodd	10	4	18	2
Cooper	10	6	9	6
Doolan	2.2	1	10	1

Fall of Wickets	***W***	***O***
1st	12	49
2nd	57	52
3rd	77	53
4th	77	53
5th	112	53
6th	116	55
7th	116	57
8th	122	58
9th	124	58
10th	134	76

AUCKLAND v CENTRAL DISTRICTS

State League

at Melville Park, Auckland on 29 December, 2008
Toss : Central Districts. Umpires : E.J. Gray & R.S. Kinsey
No result. *Points: Auckland 2, Central Districts 2*

AUCKLAND

	Runs	Mins	Balls	6s	4s
V.J.Lind† not out	14	23	20	-	2
R.J.Kember b Burrows	0	5	3	-	-
M.P.Murphy not out	14	17	15	-	2
M.L.Lynch					
S.R.H.Barriball					
M.A.Tremaine					
P.M.Yates					
S.Coetzee					
P.Mistry					
S.M.Bullen					
P.A.Gruber*					
N.Scripps					
Extras (lb 1)	1				
TOTAL (6.2 overs) (1 wkt)	**29**	23			

CENTRAL DISTRICTS

K.M.Sutherland
A.L.Mason*
K.E.Broadmore
S.J.McGlashan
M.A.Frey
R.H.Priest†
Z.A.McWilliams
S.L.Norman
R.H.Candy
K.M.Winkley
A.K.Burrows
L.A.M.Hayes

Bowling	*O*	*M*	*R*	*W*
CENTRAL DISTRICTS				
Candy	3.2	0	18	0
Burrows	3	0	10	1

Fall of Wickets	***A***
1st	2
2nd	-
3rd	-
4th	-
5th	-
6th	-
7th	-
8th	-
9th	-
10th	-

CANTERBURY v NORTHERN DISTRICTS — State League

at Queen Elizabeth II Park, Christchurch on 29 December, 2008
Toss : Canterbury. Umpires : P.J. Agent & K. Cross
***Northern Districts won by 4 wickets**. Points: Northern Districts 4, Canterbury 0*

CANTERBURY

	Runs	Mins	Balls	6s	4s
M.F.Fahey c Wilkins b Pulford	7	10	12	-	1
K.A.Neilson c Swart b Pulford	19	71	40	-	1
A.E.Satterthwaite lbw b Pulford	2	17	15	-	-
H.M.Tiffen* b Dodd	11	25	23	-	1
B.H.McNeill lbw b Dodd	0	1	2	-	-
J.C.Brehaut c & b Milliken	40	104	84	-	5
R.C.Milburn† run out	4	18	17	-	-
A.C.Boyce c Bailey b Wilson	0	8	8	-	-
E.M.Bermingham b Wilson	5	12	13	-	-
M.L.Mitchell lbw b Milliken	4	10	8	-	-
S.K.Burke not out	13	37	31	-	1
F.L.Mackay					
Extras (lb 10, w 21)	31				
TOTAL (42.1 overs)	**136**	161			

NORTHERN DISTRICTS

	Runs	Mins	Balls	6s	4s
K.L.Pulford c Satterthwaite b Burke	0	4	6	-	-
N.C.Dodd b Satterthwaite	18	75	61	-	1
A.J.Wilkins*† not out	54	173	121	-	3
N.J.Browne lbw b Bermingham	25	52	58	-	1
M.J.G.Nielsen c Boyce b Bermingham	0	12	7	-	-
A.M.Peterson b Satterthwaite	0	1	3	-	-
L.E.Milliken b Burke	19	27	29	-	3
E.M.Wilson not out	0	6	4	-	-
H.R.Huddleston					
A.Swart					
E.L.Bailey					
N.P.Edwards					
Extras (lb 4, w 16, nb 1)	21				
TOTAL (48 overs) (6 wkts)	**137**	178			

Bowling	*O*	*M*	*R*	*W*
NORTHERN DISTRICTS				
Pulford	10	1	23	3
Browne	6	0	20	0
Edwards	2	0	12	0
Dodd	6	0	28	2
Bailey	8	2	16	0
Wilson	6	0	15	2
Milliken	3.1	1	8	2
Huddleston	1	0	4	0
CANTERBURY				
Burke	9	2	27	2
Mackay	10	5	8	0
McNeill	10	3	26	0
Satterthwaite	9	1	30	2
Bermingham	8	0	30	2
Boyce	2	0	12	0

Fall of Wickets	*C*	*ND*
1st	11	0
2nd	23	40
3rd	47	83
4th	47	97
5th	60	97
6th	73	129
7th	76	-
8th	87	-
9th	97	-
10th	136	-

WELLINGTON v OTAGO — State League

at Karori Park, Wellington on 29 December, 2008
Toss : Wellington. Umpires : R. Allen & B.G. Frost
***Wellington won by 68 runs.** Points: Wellington 5, Otago 0*

WELLINGTON

	Runs	Mins	Balls	6s	4s
L.R.Doolan c Tsukigawa b Askew	22	40	39	-	1
S.J.Bradbury lbw b Tsukigawa	16	64	51	-	-
A.E.Cooper c Bates b Tsukigawa	1	9	10	-	-
M.G.Wakefield lbw b Morrison	25	43	41	-	3
S.F.M.Devine c Campbell b Morrison	7	23	11	-	-
E.C.Perry c Askew b Campbell	2	15	16	-	-
K.A.Tomlinson run out	23	76	68	-	2
M.J.Hodgson lbw b Morrison	0	8	7	-	-
A.C.Stockwell† b Bates	2	14	14	-	-
A.M.Dodd* b Morrison	11	30	27	-	1
S.E.A.Ruck not out	0	10	10	-	-
O.R.Bupha-Intr					
Extras (lb 1, w 10)	11				
TOTAL (49 overs)	**120**	175			

OTAGO

	Runs	Mins	Balls	6s	4s
K.J.Martin† c Stockwell b Devine	10	35	34	-	-
L.R.F.Askew c Hodgson b Devine	2	15	9	-	-
S.W.Bates c Doolan b Ruck	1	24	26	-	-
M.J.Kane lbw b Ruck	0	11	9	-	-
S.J.Tsukigawa* lbw b Dodd	1	15	15	-	-
A.S.M.Kitchin b Dodd	1	23	19	-	-
C.E.Taylor b Doolan	13	71	71	-	2
E.M.Campbell c & b Dodd	3	33	30	-	-
T.J.Morrison lbw b Perry	7	33	24	-	-
K.J.Crowley b Doolan	1	7	7	-	-
L.M.M.Foote not out	0	3	4	-	-
T.R.Hopkinson					
Extras (lb 2, w 11)	13				
TOTAL (41.1 overs)	**52**	144			

Bowling	*O*	*M*	*R*	*W*
OTAGO				
Bates	10	3	22	1
Hopkinson	4	0	17	0
Askew	10	3	19	1
Tsukigawa	9	1	34	2
Morrison	10	4	16	4
Campbell	6	1	11	1
WELLINGTON				
Devine	7	4	6	2
Ruck	10	5	12	2
Dodd	10	6	12	3
Cooper	6	5	1	0
Perry	4.1	0	10	1
Doolan	4	0	9	2

Fall of Wickets	*W*	*O*
1st	36	8
2nd	40	17
3rd	51	17
4th	77	18
5th	79	18
6th	85	20
7th	85	33
8th	96	49
9th	116	51
10th	120	52

CANTERBURY v AUCKLAND — State League

at Redwood Park, Christchurch on 3 January, 2009
Toss : Canterbury. Umpires : P.L. Gasston & P.B. Spall
***Canterbury won by 58 runs (D/L).** Points: Canterbury 5, Auckland 0*

CANTERBURY

	Runs	Mins	Balls	6s	4s
F.L.Mackay run out	7	71	43	-	1
K.A.Neilson b Bullen	23	47	43	-	1
A.E.Satterthwaite run out	76	107	93	-	10
H.M.Tiffen* c Kember b Scripps	56	97	70	-	2
M.F.Fahey c Mistry b Scripps	26	39	23	-	2
M.L.Mitchell c & b Scripps	25	16	12	2	2
E.M.Bermingham st Lind b Mistry	13	5	6	-	3
J.C.Brehaut b Mistry	10	9	6	-	1
R.C.Milburn† not out	9	6	6	-	1
B.H.McNeill					
S.K.Burke					
L.M.M.Tahuhu					
Extras (b 6, lb 4, w 9, nb 3)	22				
TOTAL (50 overs) (8 wkts)	**267**	202			

AUCKLAND

	Runs	Mins	Balls	6s	4s
M.L.Lynch c Milburn b Tahuhu	14	34	27	-	1
V.J.Lind† c Fahey b Mackay	25	52	35	-	3
R.J.Kember c Burke b Tahuhu	1	6	7	-	-
P.Mistry c Satterthwaite b Mackay	13	30	29	-	-
M.P.Murphy c Brehaut b Bermingham	31	31	32	-	4
S.R.H.Barriball not out	10	24	22	-	1
W.L.Horneman not out	1	12	4	-	-
M.A.Tremaine					
S.Coetzee					
N.Scripps					
S.M.Bullen					
P.A.Gruber*					
Extras (w 5)	5				
TOTAL (26 overs) (5 wkts)	**100**	97			

Bowling	*O*	*M*	*R*	*W*
AUCKLAND				
Scripps	10	1	58	3
Mistry	10	0	62	2
Tremaine	9	1	27	0
Bullen	10	1	49	1
Gruber	4	0	21	0
Coetzee	1	0	9	0
Murphy	6	0	31	0
CANTERBURY				
Burke	4	0	15	0
McNeill	4	0	18	0
Tahuhu	4	0	6	2
Mackay	9	0	36	2
Bermingham	4	0	23	1
Satterthwaite	1	0	2	0

Fall of Wickets	***C***	***A***
1st	35	34
2nd	54	36
3rd	161	46
4th	192	70
5th	229	90
6th	243	-
7th	247	-
8th	267	-
9th	-	-
10th	-	-

WELLINGTON v CENTRAL DISTRICTS — State League

at Karori Park, Wellington on 3 January, 2009
Toss : Wellington. Umpires : K. Cross & D.J. Ellwood
***Central Districts won by 9 runs.** Points: Central Districts 4, Wellington 0*

CENTRAL DISTRICTS

	Runs	Mins	Balls	6s	4s
K.M.Sutherland b Devine	11	35	30	-	1
A.L.Mason* c Hodgson b Cooper	52	89	70	-	8
K.E.Broadmore c Stockwell b Perry	0	14	12	-	-
S.J.McGlashan lbw b Doolan	34	77	63	-	3
Z.A.McWilliams c Stockwell b Doolan	7	47	47	-	-
R.H.Priest† st Stockwell b Doolan	7	25	24	-	1
E.Lanser c Dodd b Devine	21	30	24	-	4
R.H.Candy c Dodd b Devine	9	12	13	-	2
K.M.Winkley not out	19	15	12	-	2
M.A.Frey not out	6	14	10	-	-
A.K.Burrows					
L.A.M.Hayes					
Extras (lb 10, w 25, nb 5)	40				
TOTAL (50 overs) (8 wkts)	**206**	187			

WELLINGTON

	Runs	Mins	Balls	6s	4s
L.R.Doolan st Priest b Broadmore	31	60	47	-	3
S.J.Bradbury c Sutherland b Burrows	6	22	26	-	-
A.E.Cooper b Mason	22	41	45	-	-
M.G.Wakefield c Lanser b Burrows	47	103	70	-	5
S.F.M.Devine c Broadmore b McWilliams	23	23	28	1	3
A.M.Dodd* run out	28	44	45	-	3
E.C.Perry b McWilliams	4	8	8	-	-
K.A.Tomlinson b Burrows	0	3	5	-	-
M.J.Hodgson b Broadmore	6	18	15	-	-
H.M.Bedford b Broadmore	1	4	4	-	-
S.E.A.Ruck not out	2	5	3	-	-
A.C.Stockwell†					
Extras (lb 3, w 24)	27				
TOTAL (49.2 overs)	**197**	175			

Bowling	*O*	*M*	*R*	*W*
WELLINGTON				
Devine	10	3	25	3
Ruck	10	0	59	0
Perry	5	0	41	1
Dodd	5	0	26	0
Cooper	10	3	25	1
Doolan	10	1	20	3
CENTRAL DISTRICTS				
Candy	8	0	31	0
Burrows	10	2	30	3
Hayes	4	0	15	0
Broadmore	9.2	2	29	3
Mason	6	0	31	1
Winkley	2	0	17	0
McWilliams	10	0	41	2

Fall of Wickets	***CD***	***W***
1st	29	17
2nd	39	63
3rd	102	78
4th	137	114
5th	145	169
6th	156	178
7th	178	179
8th	178	190
9th	-	192
10th	-	197

OTAGO v NORTHERN DISTRICTS — State League

at Queen's Park, Invercargill on 3 January, 2009
Toss : Northern Districts. Umpires : R.S. Kinsey & D.W. Reid
***Otago won by 1 wicket.** Points: Otago 4, Northern Districts 0*

NORTHERN DISTRICTS

	Runs	Mins	Balls	6s	4s
N.C.Dodd b Campbell	43	122	113	-	4
K.L.Pulford c Campbell b Askew	18	35	31	-	2
A.J.Wilkins*† c Campbell b Tsukigawa	18	44	44	-	3
N.J.Browne lbw b Campbell	28	58	45	-	3
L.E.Milliken c Grant b Askew	8	12	9	-	-
M.J.G.Nielsen c Bates b Askew	7	7	7	-	1
H.R.Huddleston not out	20	35	18	-	2
A.M.Peterson c Campbell b Tsukigawa	6	9	10	-	-
E.M.Wilson b Campbell	15	17	19	-	1
A.Swart st Martin b Campbell	0	1	2	-	-
E.L.Bailey not out	1	1	2	-	-
N.P.Edwards					
Extras (lb 1, w 23)	24				
TOTAL (50 overs) (9 wkts)	**188**	180			

OTAGO

	Runs	Mins	Balls	6s	4s
K.J.Martin† c Wilkins b Pulford	22	31	36	-	1
L.R.F.Askew c Wilkins b Browne	4	14	8	-	-
S.W.Bates c Wilkins b Milliken	22	66	39	-	-
M.J.Kane b Browne	1	3	2	-	-
S.J.Tsukigawa* c & b Wilson	66	111	93	-	7
A.S.M.Kitchin b Nielsen	25	93	79	-	2
L.M.Grant b Nielsen	12	32	34	-	1
E.M.Campbell c Wilson b Milliken	0	9	6	-	-
T.J.Morrison not out	1	9	5	-	-
K.J.Crowley run out	0	1	1	-	-
L.M.M.Foote not out	0	2	1	-	-
T.R.Hopkinson					
Extras (b 4, lb 8, w 20, nb 4)	36				
TOTAL (50 overs) (9 wkts)	**189**	195			

Bowling	O	M	R	W
OTAGO				
Bates	8	1	37	0
Hopkinson	6	0	24	0
Askew	10	1	35	3
Tsukigawa	9	1	40	2
Morrison	7	1	20	0
Campbell	10	0	31	4
NORTHERN DISTRICTS				
Pulford	10	1	31	1
Browne	10	0	39	2
Huddleston	3	0	16	0
Milliken	8	1	21	2
Edwards	4	0	15	0
Wilson	7	0	29	1
Dodd	2	0	7	0
Bailey	1.4	0	13	0
Nielsen	4.2	1	6	2

Fall of Wickets	ND	O
1st	44	17
2nd	80	41
3rd	118	42
4th	138	90
5th	141	165
6th	145	184
7th	154	187
8th	187	187
9th	187	187
10th	-	-

CANTERBURY v AUCKLAND — State League

at Redwood Park, Christchurch on 4 January, 2009
Toss : Auckland. Umpires : P.L. Gasston & P.B. Spall
***Canterbury won by 6 wickets.** Points: Canterbury 4, Auckland 0*

AUCKLAND

	Runs	Mins	Balls	6s	4s
M.L.Lynch b Mitchell	65	111	97	-	5
V.J.Lind† lbw b McNeill	8	22	13	-	-
R.J.Kember b McNeill	46	95	66	-	4
M.P.Murphy lbw b McNeill	39	76	39	-	4
S.R.H.Barriball run out	12	27	26	-	1
P.Mistry b Satterthwaite	0	7	4	-	-
W.L.Horneman c Milburn b Bermingham	4	10	11	-	-
M.A.Tremaine run out	0	2	1	-	-
S.Coetzee c Bermingham b Burke	2	7	5	-	-
S.M.Bullen not out	3	14	9	-	-
N.Scripps b McNeill	0	2	2	-	-
P.A.Gruber*					
Extras (lb 4, w 21, nb 1)	26				
TOTAL (45.3 overs)	**205**	191			

CANTERBURY

	Runs	Mins	Balls	6s	4s
F.L.Mackay run out	55	61	52	-	11
K.A.Neilson st Lind b Bullen	11	28	27	-	1
A.E.Satterthwaite c & b Tremaine	20	46	24	-	3
H.M.Tiffen* not out	43	117	86	-	2
M.F.Fahey c Lynch b Gruber	8	15	14	-	1
J.C.Brehaut not out	60	87	81	-	8
B.H.McNeill					
R.C.Milburn†					
M.L.Mitchell					
E.M.Bermingham					
S.K.Burke					
L.M.M.Tahuhu					
Extras (b 1, lb 2, w 8, nb 1)	12				
TOTAL (47.1 overs) (4 wkts)	**209**	179			

Bowling	O	M	R	W
CANTERBURY				
Burke	7	0	24	1
McNeill	8.3	0	34	4
Tahuhu	3	0	20	0
Mackay	10	0	41	0
Satterthwaite	8	0	29	1
Bermingham	6	0	38	1
Mitchell	3	0	15	1
AUCKLAND				
Scripps	10	1	31	0
Mistry	6	0	55	0
Bullen	7	1	25	1
Tremaine	6	1	24	1
Coetzee	3	0	12	0
Murphy	8.1	1	30	0
Gruber	7	1	29	1

Fall of Wickets	A	C
1st	27	38
2nd	136	84
3rd	141	90
4th	172	106
5th	174	-
6th	188	-
7th	188	-
8th	198	-
9th	205	-
10th	205	-

WELLINGTON v CENTRAL DISTRICTS — State League

at Karori Park, Wellington on 4 January, 2009
Toss : Wellington. Umpires : K. Cross & D.J. Ellwood
Wellington won by 69 runs. *Points: Wellington 5, Central Districts 0*

WELLINGTON

	Runs	Mins	Balls	6s	4s
L.R.Doolan c Candy b Broadmore	19	29	30	-	3
S.J.Bradbury c Candy b Burrows	5	25	18	-	-
A.E.Cooper run out	1	11	4	-	-
M.G.Wakefield run out	35	66	60	-	3
S.F.M.Devine c Mason b McWilliams	42	69	64	1	3
A.M.Dodd* b Burrows	10	47	40	-	1
E.C.Perry st Priest b Broadmore	44	59	62	-	4
M.J.Hodgson not out	14	27	19	-	1
K.A.Tomlinson not out	2	2	3	-	-
A.C.Stockwell†					
S.E.A.Ruck					
H.M.Bedford					
Extras (lb 3, w 14)	17				
TOTAL (50 overs) 7 wkts)	**189**	175			

CENTRAL DISTRICTS

	Runs	Mins	Balls	6s	4s
K.M.Sutherland lbw b Ruck	7	16	14	-	-
A.L.Mason* c Doolan b Devine	7	32	22	-	-
K.E.Broadmore run out	8	20	16	-	1
S.J.McGlashan run out	8	23	17	-	-
Z.A.McWilliams lbw b Dodd	17	57	49	-	1
R.H.Priest† c & b Dodd	11	10	16	-	2
E.Lanser not out	26	64	69	-	3
R.H.Candy b Doolan	6	4	6	-	1
S.L.Norman lbw b Doolan	0	5	6	-	-
K.M.Winkley c Hodgson b Devine	6	14	13	-	1
A.K.Burrows c Wakefield b Doolan	5	11	9	-	1
L.A.M.Hayes					
Extras (b 1, w 16, nb 2)	19				
TOTAL (39 overs)	**120**	137			

Bowling	O	M	R	W
CENTRAL DISTRICTS				
Candy	5	0	23	0
Burrows	10	1	37	2
Broadmore	10	1	30	2
Hayes	3	0	14	0
Winkley	10	0	39	0
Mason	2	0	15	0
McWilliams	10	1	28	1
WELLINGTON				
Ruck	6	0	24	1
Devine	9	0	32	2
Dodd	10	3	19	2
Cooper	5	0	18	0
Doolan	9	2	26	3

Fall of Wickets	*W*	*CD*
1st	26	13
2nd	26	31
3rd	34	33
4th	111	48
5th	118	62
6th	152	77
7th	187	84
8th	-	84
9th	-	103
10th	-	120

OTAGO v NORTHERN DISTRICTS — State League

at Queen's Park, Invercargill on 4 January, 2009
Toss : Otago. Umpires : R.S. Kinsey & D.W. Reid
Otago won by 111 runs. *Points: Otago 5, Northern Districts 0*

OTAGO

	Runs	Mins	Balls	6s	4s
K.J.Martin† b Pulford	8	23	24	-	-
L.R.F.Askew c Peterson b Wilson	43	88	82	-	2
S.W.Bates b Edwards	89	140	93	-	10
S.J.Tsukigawa* c Pulford b Milliken	57	86	79	-	3
M.J.Kane b Milliken	3	12	6	-	-
L.M.Grant not out	12	13	8	-	2
E.M.Campbell run out	11	9	8	-	-
T.J.Morrison not out	0	1	0	-	-
A.S.M.Kitchin					
K.J.Crowley					
L.M.M.Foote					
T.R.Hopkinson					
Extras (b 2, lb 2, w 12)	16				
TOTAL (50 overs) (6 wkts)	**239**	192			

NORTHERN DISTRICTS

	Runs	Mins	Balls	6s	4s
K.L.Pulford c Askew b Tsukigawa	24	47	48	-	2
N.C.Dodd b Hopkinson	2	12	9	-	-
A.J.Wilkins*† b Morrison	30	85	65	-	4
N.J.Browne lbw b Askew	23	27	26	-	4
A.M.Peterson c Foote b Askew	3	11	11	-	-
L.E.Milliken lbw b Campbell	5	17	14	-	-
H.R.Huddleston c Kitchin b Campbell	9	23	25	-	1
M.J.G.Nielsen c Bates b Campbell	1	9	5	-	-
E.M.Wilson c Tsukigawa b Morrison	3	14	10	-	-
A.Swart b Bates	6	18	26	-	-
N.P.Edwards not out	2	10	7	-	-
E.L.Bailey					
Extras (b 1, lb 1, w 18)	20				
TOTAL (41 overs)	**128**	146			

Bowling	O	M	R	W
NORTHERN DISTRICTS				
Pulford	8	0	34	1
Browne	6	1	25	0
Nielsen	6	0	29	0
Milliken	10	0	61	2
Bailey	2	0	12	0
Dodd	6	1	23	0
Wilson	5	0	19	1
Edwards	7	0	32	1
OTAGO				
Bates	10	0	23	1
Hopkinson	3	0	22	1
Tsukigawa	7	1	19	1
Askew	7	0	36	2
Morrison	10	1	20	2
Campbell	4	0	6	3

Fall of Wickets	*O*	*ND*
1st	15	12
2nd	90	46
3rd	202	80
4th	216	92
5th	216	103
6th	235	105
7th	-	111
8th	-	117
9th	-	123
10th	-	128

CENTRAL DISTRICTS v OTAGO — State League

at Fitzherbert Park, Palmerston North on 17 January, 2009
Toss : Central Districts. Umpires : K.C. Manley & T.J. Parlane
Otago won by 1 wicket. *Points: Otago 4, Central Districts 0*

CENTRAL DISTRICTS

	Runs	Mins	Balls	6s	4s
A.L.Mason* c Foote b Taylor	36	34	31	-	6
Z.A.McWilliams c Martin b Tsukigawa	7	31	20	-	-
K.E.Broadmore c Foote b Campbell	21	60	60	-	2
S.J.McGlashan b Taylor	5	11	12	-	1
K.C.R.Rangi lbw b Tsukigawa	0	3	3	-	-
R.H.Priest† lbw b Campbell	19	41	36	-	3
K.M.Sutherland b Bates	22	49	45	-	4
E.Lanser b Bates	13	26	27	-	1
R.H.Candy c Te Wake b Bates	5	15	16	-	-
K.M.Winkley c Morrison b Campbell	29	25	20	1	3
A.K.Burrows not out	6	20	17	-	1
L.A.M.Hayes					
Extras (b 1, lb 2, w 6)	9				
TOTAL (47.5 overs)	**172**	163			

OTAGO

	Runs	Mins	Balls	6s	4s
K.J.Martin† run out	20	27	22	-	-
K.J.Crowley b Burrows	0	5	2	-	-
S.W.Bates run out	53	124	100	-	2
S.J.Tsukigawa* b McWilliams	51	58	56	-	7
A.S.M.Kitchin run out	1	3	4	-	-
L.M.Grant b Burrows	13	24	31	-	2
C.E.Taylor run out	18	29	28	-	3
E.M.Campbell c Priest b Winkley	4	16	9	-	1
T.J.Morrison b Burrows	0	7	5	-	-
A.M.Te Wake not out	0	15	15	-	-
L.M.M.Foote not out	5	11	11	-	-
T.R.Hopkinson					
Extras (lb 2, w 6)	8				
TOTAL (47.1 overs) (9 wkts)	**173**	164			

Bowling	*O*	*M*	*R*	*W*
OTAGO				
Bates	10	2	39	3
Hopkinson	4	0	22	0
Tsukigawa	7	1	26	2
Taylor	9	2	32	2
Morrison	10	2	23	0
Campbell	7.5	2	27	3
CENTRAL DISTRICTS				
Candy	10	1	38	0
Burrows	10	2	19	3
Hayes	3	0	21	0
Broadmore	7.1	0	33	0
McWilliams	5	0	21	1
Mason	8	0	35	0
Winkley	4	3	4	1

	CD	***O***
1st	46	3
2nd	46	34
3rd	56	114
4th	57	115
5th	93	138
6th	93	150
7th	126	168
8th	134	168
9th	135	168
10th	172	-

NORTHERN DISTRICTS v AUCKLAND — State League

at Cobham Oval, Whangarei on 17 January, 2009
Toss : Northern Districts. Umpires : C.B. Gaffaney & P.L. Gasston
Auckland won by 1 wicket. *Points: Auckland 4, Northern Districts 0*

NORTHERN DISTRICTS

	Runs	Mins	Balls	6s	4s
K.L.Pulford c Cox b Mistry	15	20	21	-	3
N.C.Dodd c Kember b Cox	19	76	52	-	2
A.J.Wilkins*† lbw b Tremaine	5	13	13	-	1
N.J.Browne b Cox	22	73	65	-	2
H.R.Huddleston c & b Cox	3	11	15	-	-
A.M.Peterson run out	4	8	10	-	-
L.E.Milliken run out	37	73	63	-	4
M.J.G.Nielsen c Kember b Cox	0	5	2	-	-
E.M.Wilson lbw b Mistry	14	50	37	-	2
N.P.Edwards b Mistry	0	2	1	-	-
E.L.Bailey not out	4	25	22	-	-
B.N.Kirkbride					
Extras (b 1, lb 3, w 15, nb 1)	20				
TOTAL (50 overs)	**143**	183			

AUCKLAND

	Runs	Mins	Balls	6s	4s
M.L.Lynch lbw b Pulford	2	1	2	-	-
V.J.Lind*† c Peterson b Pulford	2	23	15	-	-
R.J.Kember c Wilkins b Browne	0	5	7	-	-
M.P.Murphy run out	9	57	39	-	1
S.R.H.Barriball c Browne b Pulford	9	34	25	-	1
K.T.Perkins not out	53	142	81	-	6
W.L.Horneman c Dodd b Edwards	13	35	44	-	2
M.A.Tremaine run out	0	4	4	-	-
P.Mistry c Wilkins b Edwards	0	17	13	-	-
S.M.Bullen lbw b Browne	1	22	21	-	-
N.Scripps not out	23	53	47	-	-
R.Cox					
Extras (b 1, lb 6, w 24, nb 1)	32				
TOTAL (49.3 overs) (9 wkts)	**144**	201			

Bowling	*O*	*M*	*R*	*W*
AUCKLAND				
Scripps	4	0	8	0
Mistry	10	2	38	3
Murphy	8	2	23	0
Tremaine	8	1	26	1
Bullen	10	4	14	0
Cox	10	0	30	4
NORTHERN DISTRICTS				
Pulford	10	2	21	3
Browne	10	4	18	2
Edwards	10	1	24	2
Wilson	6	1	21	0
Dodd	3	0	8	0
Bailey	3	0	13	0
Kirkbride	4	1	14	0
Nielsen	3.3	0	18	0

Fall of Wickets

	ND	***A***
1st	21	2
2nd	29	5
3rd	57	8
4th	64	32
5th	70	37
6th	79	62
7th	79	66
8th	117	75
9th	121	87
10th	143	-

Milliken retired hurt at 117-7 on 21 and resumed at 121-9

WELLINGTON v CANTERBURY — State League

at Trentham Memorial Park, Upper Hutt on 17 January, 2009
Toss : Canterbury. Umpires : K. Cross & D.G Paterson
***Wellington won by 3 wickets.** Points: Wellington 4, Canterbury 0*

CANTERBURY

	Runs	Mins	Balls	6s	4s
F.L.Mackay c Cooper b Doolan	41	83	71	-	7
K.A.Neilson† c Cooper b Devine	11	39	34	-	2
A.E.Satterthwaite* c Wakefield b Doolan	52	69	57	-	8
B.H.McNeill lbw b Cooper	0	10	8	-	-
M.F.Fahey c & b Doolan	9	24	19	-	2
H.M.Watson run out	0	3	2	-	-
A.C.Boyce b Dodd	20	43	31	-	3
E.M.Bermingham c Ruck b Dodd	27	47	44	-	5
M.L.Mitchell c Tomlinson b Dodd	0	1	1	-	-
S.K.Burke not out	1	10	5	-	-
L.M.M.Tahuhu run out	4	2	2	-	1
S.J.Gurnsey					
Extras (b 1, lb 1, w 17)	19				
TOTAL (45.4 overs)	**184**	175			

WELLINGTON

	Runs	Mins	Balls	6s	4s
L.R.Doolan c Neilson b McNeill	37	54	42	-	6
S.J.Bradbury c Burke b Watson	3	11	13	-	-
A.E.Cooper run out	0	5	4	-	-
M.G.Wakefield c Neilson b McNeill	7	30	23	-	1
S.F.M.Devine c Mitchell b McNeill	12	25	16	-	1
A.M.Dodd* c Mitchell b Bermingham	23	53	49	-	2
E.J.Scurr not out	49	101	83	-	6
M.J.Hodgson run out	5	35	20	-	1
E.C.Perry not out	19	31	23	-	2
K.A.Tomlinson					
A.C.Stockwell†					
S.E.A.Ruck					
Extras (b 1, lb 3, w 25, nb 2)	31				
TOTAL (45.1 overs) (7 wkts)	**186**	180			

Bowling	O	M	R	W
WELLINGTON				
Devine	8	1	28	1
Ruck	8	1	17	0
Perry	5	0	28	0
Dodd	4.4	0	35	3
Doolan	10	2	36	3
Cooper	10	1	38	1
CANTERBURY				
Burke	10	1	44	0
Watson	10	2	31	1
Mackay	10	0	43	0
McNeill	7.1	1	27	3
Bermingham	6	1	23	1
Satterthwaite	2	0	14	0

Fall of Wickets	C	W
1st	25	8
2nd	87	13
3rd	98	50
4th	121	55
5th	126	69
6th	126	111
7th	170	147
8th	170	-
9th	180	-
10th	184	-

CENTRAL DISTRICTS v OTAGO — State League

at Fitzherbert Park, Palmerston North on 18 January, 2009
Toss : Central Districts. Umpires : K.C. Manley & T.J. Parlane
***Otago won by 1 run.** Points: Otago 4, Central Districts 0*

OTAGO

	Runs	Mins	Balls	6s	4s
K.J.Martin† c Rangi b Broadmore	24	33	33	-	2
K.J.Crowley b Candy	14	37	28	-	1
S.W.Bates not out	74	85	71	-	6
S.J.Tsukigawa* st Priest b Burrows	74	76	78	1	7
L.M.Grant not out	3	8	6	-	-
C.E.Taylor					
A.S.M.Kitchin					
A.M.Te Wake					
T.J.Morrison					
E.M.Campbell					
L.M.M.Foote					
T.R.Hopkinson					
Extras (lb 2, w 11)	13				
TOTAL (36 overs) (3 wkts)	**202**	119			

CENTRAL DISTRICTS

	Runs	Mins	Balls	6s	4s
Z.A.McWilliams run out	58	103	84	-	2
A.L.Mason* c Campbell b Taylor	11	16	9	-	1
S.J.McGlashan c Martin b Bates	50	61	51	2	3
R.H.Priest† b Campbell	21	26	26	1	-
K.M.Winkley c Campbell b Morrison	5	16	7	-	-
R.H.Candy c Kitchin b Morrison	18	12	14	2	-
E.Lanser not out	9	21	9	-	-
K.E.Broadmore c Bates b Taylor	16	10	9	1	-
K.C.R.Rangi b Tsukigawa	1	5	2	-	-
K.M.Sutherland st Martin b Tsukigawa	0	1	1	-	-
A.K.Burrows st Martin b Tsukigawa	0	1	2	-	-
L.A.M.Hayes					
Extras (lb 1, w 11)	12				
TOTAL (35.4 overs)	**201**	143			

Bowling	O	M	R	W
CENTRAL DISTRICTS				
Candy	7	1	27	1
Burrows	8	0	50	1
Broadmore	5	1	30	1
Winkley	5	0	21	0
Mason	5	0	40	0
McWilliams	6	0	32	0
OTAGO				
Taylor	8	1	52	2
Hopkinson	1	0	12	0
Tsukigawa	5.4	0	19	3
Morrison	7	0	39	2
Bates	7	0	43	1
Campbell	7	0	35	1

Fall of Wickets	O	CD
1st	41	21
2nd	42	117
3rd	172	150
4th	-	153
5th	-	175
6th	-	175
7th	-	197
8th	-	201
9th	-	201
10th	-	201

NORTHERN DISTRICTS v AUCKLAND — State League

at Cobham Oval, Whangarei on 18 January, 2009
Toss : Northern Districts. Umpires : C.B. Gaffaney & P.L. Gasston
***Northern Districts won by 6 wickets.** Points: Northern Districts 4, Auckland 0*

AUCKLAND

	Runs	Mins	Balls	6s	4s
M.L.Lynch c Browne b Pulford	1	9	9	-	-
V.J.Lind*† b Pulford	5	19	18	-	-
R.J.Kember c Bailey b Kirkbride	32	88	67	-	2
M.P.Murphy b Browne	2	18	15	-	-
S.R.H.Barriball run out	37	104	83	-	4
K.T.Perkins lbw b Browne	2	17	14	-	-
W.L.Horneman st Huddleston b Wilson	41	57	49	-	6
P.Mistry b Browne	15	43	28	-	1
M.A.Tremaine run out	0	1	2	-	-
S.M.Bullen c Bailey b Pulford	1	12	4	-	-
N.Scripps not out	0	1	0	-	-
R.Cox					
Extras (b 4, lb 2, w 18)	24				
TOTAL (48.1 overs)	**160**	154			

NORTHERN DISTRICTS

	Runs	Mins	Balls	6s	4s
K.L.Pulford c Lind b Cox	50	90	64	-	6
N.C.Dodd lbw b Cox	16	38	37	-	2
H.R.Huddleston† run out	8	34	25	-	1
N.J.Browne not out	39	80	60	1	5
A.M.Peterson lbw b Scripps	29	57	59	-	3
L.E.Milliken not out	2	5	3	-	-
A.J.Wilkins*					
M.J.G.Nielsen					
E.M.Wilson					
E.L.Bailey					
B.N.Kirkbride					
N.P.Edwards					
Extras (lb 1, w 15, nb 1)	17				
TOTAL (41.1 overs) (4 wkts)	**161**	154			

Bowling	*O*	*M*	*R*	*W*
NORTHERN DISTRICTS				
Pulford	9.1	3	25	3
Browne	9	4	12	3
Kirkbride	10	1	29	1
Edwards	5	0	28	0
Bailey	9	0	34	0
Dodd	5	0	17	0
Wilson	1	0	9	1
AUCKLAND				
Mistry	8	1	43	0
Scripps	7.1	1	35	1
Cox	10	1	26	2
Tremaine	3	0	15	0
Bullen	10	1	35	0
Murphy	3	1	6	0

Fall of Wickets

	A	***ND***
1st	2	47
2nd	7	80
3rd	13	91
4th	69	148
5th	84	-
6th	94	-
7th	148	-
8th	148	-
9th	160	-
10th	160	-

WELLINGTON v CANTERBURY — State League

at Trentham Memorial Park, Upper Hutt on 18 January, 2009
Toss : Wellington. Umpires : K. Cross & D.G Paterson
***Canterbury won by 39 runs**. Points: Canterbury 5, Wellington 0*

CANTERBURY

	Runs	Mins	Balls	6s	4s
F.L.Mackay b Ruck	14	40	34	-	3
K.A.Neilson† c Hodgson b Ruck	5	12	6	-	1
A.E.Satterthwaite* b Doolan	61	107	74	-	7
M.F.Fahey b Cooper	17	26	25	-	3
J.C.Brehaut c Wakefield b Perry	19	31	36	-	3
B.H.McNeill not out	24	46	35	-	2
A.C.Boyce st sub b Cooper	25	27	21	1	3
M.L.Mitchell					
E.M.Bermingham					
S.K.Burke					
L.M.M.Tahuhu					
H.M.Watson					
Extras (b 6, lb 2, w 16, nb 3)	27				
TOTAL (38 overs) (6 wkts)	**192**	151			

WELLINGTON

	Runs	Mins	Balls	6s	4s
L.R.Doolan c Tahuhu b Mackay	13	14	12	-	2
S.J.Bradbury c Boyce b Burke	10	31	23	-	-
A.E.Cooper c Satterthwaite b Mackay	7	13	14	-	1
M.G.Wakefield run out	4	23	11	-	-
S.F.M.Devine c McNeill b Mackay	2	5	7	-	-
A.M.Dodd*† retired hurt	24	76	53	-	-
E.J.Scurr b Satterthwaite	14	28	23	-	-
E.C.Perry run out	47	68	52	-	4
M.J.Hodgson b McNeill	8	24	12	-	-
K.A.Tomlinson c McNeill b Satterthwaite	4	7	6	-	-
S.E.A.Ruck not out	0	1	1	-	-
A.C.Stockwell†					
Extras (b 9, lb 3, w 7, nb 1)	20				
TOTAL (35.3 overs)	**153**	154			

Bowling	*O*	*M*	*R*	*W*
WELLINGTON				
Devine	8	1	57	0
Ruck	8	2	24	2
Dodd	3	0	20	0
Cooper	7	0	39	2
Doolan	8	0	32	1
Perry	4	0	12	1
CANTERBURY				
Burke	7	1	32	1
Mackay	6	0	25	3
McNeill	8	1	27	1
Bermingham	7	0	28	0
Satterthwaite	4.3	0	16	2
Tahuhu	3	0	13	0

Fall of Wickets

	C	***W***
1st	15	17
2nd	44	30
3rd	82	30
4th	122	33
5th	144	45
6th	192	67
7th	-	140
8th	-	153
9th	-	153
10th	-	-

Dodd retired hurt at 109-6

WELLINGTON v CANTERBURY — State League Final

at Allied Nationwide Finance Basin Reserve, Wellington on 24 January, 2009
Toss : Wellington. Umpires : E.J. Gray & D.M. Quested
Canterbury won by 2 wickets.

Wellington won the toss and chose to bat. Openers Doolan and Bradbury put on 42 for the first wicket. Wakefield scored 41 off 58 balls (two fours and one six) batting at number four and Perry and Dodd both made useful contributions in the lower order. Satterthwaite took 3-32 off nine overs and McNeill 2-35 off ten. At the end of their 50 overs Wellington had made 197-8.

In reply Canterbury made a cautious start and were in trouble at 103-6 following the dismissal of Tiffen who had scored 30 off 64 balls. With Canterbury falling behind the run rate Boyce played a brilliant cameo, making an unbeaten 30 off 15 balls, including two fours and a six. She and McNeill, who scored 31 off 32 balls, pushed Canterbury towards victory and it was left to Boyce and Milburn, with an unbeaten 21 off 29 balls, to achieve an exciting win off the last ball of the fiftieth over.

WELLINGTON

	Runs	Mins	Balls	6s	4s
L.R.Doolan lbw b Satterthwaite	19	49	40	-	2
S.J.Bradbury c & b Tahuhu	33	94	74	-	4
A.E.Cooper b Satterthwaite	3	20	14	-	-
M.G.Wakefield c & b Burke	41	67	58	1	2
S.F.M.Devine c Tahuhu b Bermingham	3	16	17	-	-
E.J.Scurr b Satterthwaite	11	42	24	-	-
E.C.Perry st Milburn b McNeill	30	48	34	-	4
A.M.Dodd* not out	29	45	30	-	3
K.A.Tomlinson st Milburn b McNeill	4	8	7	-	-
S.E.A.Ruck not out	0	2	2	-	-
M.J.Hodgson					
A.C.Stockwell†					
Extras (b 4, lb 7, w 13)	24				
TOTAL (50 overs) (8 wkts)	**197**	204			

CANTERBURY

	Runs	Mins	Balls	6s	4s
M.F.Fahey c Doolan b Perry	7	52	38	-	-
f.L.Mackay st Stockwell b Dodd	18	40	30	-	3
A.E.Satterthwaite c & b Dodd	4	15	12	-	-
H.M.Tiffen* b Devine	30	76	64	-	1
J.C.Brehaut c Tomlinson b Cooper	27	60	69	-	3
M.L.Mitchell b Devine	2	5	3	-	-
R.C.Milburn† not out	21	70	29	-	-
B.H.McNeill st Stockwell b Cooper	31	28	32	-	2
E.M.Bermingham c Perry b Devine	12	12	12	-	1
A.C.Boyce not out	30	21	15	1	2
S.K.Burke					
L.M.M.Tahuhu					
Extras (b 4, lb 3, w 5, nb 4)	16				
TOTAL (50 overs) (8 wkts)	**198**	198			

Bowling	O	M	R	W
CANTERBURY				
Burke	10	0	40	1
McNeill	10	0	35	2
Satterthwaite	9	1	32	3
Mackay	10	2	42	0
Bermingham	6	0	26	1
Tahuhu	5	0	11	1
WELLINGTON				
Devine	10	2	29	3
Ruck	4	0	21	0
Dodd	10	3	17	2
Perry	8	0	38	1
Doolan	9	0	48	0
Cooper	9	0	38	2

Fall of Wickets	W	C
1st	42	30
2nd	52	38
3rd	82	40
4th	99	96
5th	124	100
6th	139	103
7th	188	145
8th	194	160
9th	-	-
10th	-	-

REGISTER OF PLAYERS

		Born	*At*	*Type*	
Anderson Nicola Marie	ND	18. 5.92	Whangarei	RHB	RM
Askew Lynsey Riann Frances	O	3. 9.86	Bromley, England	RHB	RM
Bailey Emily Louise	ND	19. 8.92	Papakura	RHB	ROB
Barriball Samantha Rae Haereakau	A	28.10.85	Auckland	RHB	RLB
Bates Suzannah Wilson	O, NZ	16. 9.87	Dunedin	RHB	RM
Bedford Hannah Moana	W	22. 8.87	New Plymouth	RHB	RM
Bermingham Erin Margaret	C	18. 4.88	Greymouth	RHB	RLB
Blackwell Kathryn Anne	A	31. 8.83	Wagga Wagga, Aust.	RHB	RM
Boyce Amber Christina	C	23.10.84	Blenheim	RHB	RM
Bradbury Sarah Jane	W	18. 7.85	Wellington	RHB	RLB
Brehaut Janet Catherine	C	24. 7.88	Timaru	RHB	RM
Broadmore Kate Ellan	CD	11.11.91	New Plymouth	RHB	RM
Browne Nicola Jane	ND, NZ	14. 9.83	Matamata	RHB	RM
Bullen Saskia Mary	A, NZ	20. 7.83	Auckland	RHB	SLA
Bupha-Intr Olivia Raynoo	W	11. 9.86	Wellington	RHB	RM
Burke Sarah Kate	C	2. 1.82	Christchurch	RHB	RM
Burrows Abby Kirstyn	CD, NZ	29. 1.77	Kawerau	RHB	RM
Campbell Emma Maree	O	18. 2.82	Timaru	RHB	RLB
Candy Rachel Helen	CD	23. 7.86	Palmerston North	RHB	RM
Charteris Selena Eloise	C	5. 6.81	Timaru	RHB	ROB
Coetzee Shanna	A	11. 2.83	Cape Town, S.Africa	RHB	RM
Cooper Amanda Ellen	W	15. 5.83	Wellington	RHB	RM
Cox Roseanne Erin	A	29. 6.90	Auckland	LHB	LM
Crowley Kylie Jane	O	20.12.90	Dunedin	LHB	WK
Devine Sophie Frances Monique	W, NZ	1. 9.89	Wellington	RHB	RM
Dodd Anna Maree	W	24.10.80	Foxton	RHB	ROB
Dodd Natalie Claire	ND	22.11.92	Hamilton	RHB	ROB
Doolan Lucy Rose	W, NZ	11.12.87	Lower Hutt	LHB	ROB
Edwards Natalie Patricia	ND	1. 2.89	Hamilton	RHB	RM
Fahey Maria Frances	C	5. 3.84	Timaru	LHB	ROB
Foote Lucy	O	23. 7.90	Christchurch	RHB	RM
Fraser Janice Mary	ND	3. 2.79	Tokoroa	RHB	RM
Frey Michele Alexandra	CD	21.11.81	Innsbruck, Austria	RHB	ROB
Grant Lisa Margaret	O	28.11.88	Timaru	RHB	RM
Gregory Kathryn Leigh	O	21. 9.88	Invercargill	RHB	RM
Gruber Paula Anne	A	30.11.74	Waiouru	RHB	ROB
Gurnsey Sophie Jane	C	2. 4.86	Christchurch	RHB	RM
Hayes Lisa Avryll Margaret	CD	2.10.87	Hastings	RHB	RM
Hodgson Melinda Jane	W	8. 7.88	Innisfail, Australia	RHB	RM
Hopkins Sarah Anne Phelps	A	7.10.79	Auckland	RHB	
Hopkinson Tessa Rose	O	23. 4.91	Oamaru	RHB	RM
Horneman Wendy Lee	A	9. 3.84	Auckland	RHB	WK
Huddleston Holly Rachael	ND	11.10.87	Springs, South Africa	RHB	RM
Kane Megan Joanna	O	1. 8.82	Tapanui	RHB	ROB
Kember Rosamond Jane	A	28. 1.85	Auckland	RHB	RLB
Kirkbride Brooke Nicole	ND	3. 7.93	Cambridge	RHB	RM
Kitchin Abigail Samantha Maria	O	18. 6.81	Palmerston North	RHB	ROB
Lanser Esther	CD	6. 1.84	Masterton	RHB	RM
Lind Victoria Jayne	A, NZ	15. 5.85	Auckland	RHB	WK
Lynch Michelle Louise	A	16.10.75	Auckland	RHB	
Martin Katey Jane	O, NZ	7. 2.85	Dunedin	RHB	WK
Mason Aimee Louise	CD, NZ	11.10.82	New Plymouth	RHB	ROB
McGlashan Sara Jade	CD, NZ	28. 3.82	Napier	RHB	WK
Mackay Frances Louise	C	1. 6.90	Christchurch	RHB	ROB
McNeill Beth Hannah	C, NZ	10.11.82	Wellington	RHB	RM
McWilliams Zara Ann	CD	29.11.83	Hastings	RHB	RM
Milburn Rowan Claire	C, NZ	18. 6.77	Mosgiel	RHB	WK
Milliken Louise Elizabeth	ND	19. 9.83	Morrinsville	RHB	RMF
Mistry Prashilla	A	16. 3.87	Auckland	RHB	RM
Mitchell Michelle Leigh	C	8. 5.87	Christchurch	RHB	LM
Mizzi Charlotte Kate	W	17. 9.86	Wellington	RHB	WK
Moffitt Renee Janice Moia	W	6. 7.90	Hawera	LHB	ROB
Morrison Tanya Jeanette	O	1. 7.85	Gore	RHB	ROB
Murphy Megan Patricia	A	22.11.87	Rotorua	RHB	RM
Neilson Krista Anne	C	15. 5.86	Christchurch	RHB	RM
Nielsen Morna Jessie Godwin	ND	24. 2.90	Tauranga	RHB	LM

		Born	At	Type	
Norman Sarah Luba	CD	17. 5.83	Wellington	RHB	RSM
Perkins Katie Teresa	A	7. 7.88	Auckland	RHB	RM
Perry Elizabeth Cecelia	W	22.11.87	Taumarunui	RHB	RM
Peterson Anna Michelle	ND	12. 9.90	Auckland	RHB	RM
Priest Rachel Holly	CD, NZ	13. 6.85	New Plymouth	RHB	WK
Pulford Katherine Louise	ND, NZ	27. 8.80	Nelson	RHB	RM
Rangi Kelly Corrina Rangimarie	CD	21.12.91	Masterton	LHB	RLB
Ruck Sian Elizabeth Ansley	W, NZ	8.12.83	Auckland	RHB	LM
Satterthwaite Amy Ella	C, NZ	7.10.86	Christchurch	LHB	RM
Scripps Natalee	A	9.12.78	Auckland	RHB	RM
Scurr Elizabeth Jessica	W	26. 7.83	Dunedin	RHB	ROB
Sim Courtney Jayne	CD	20. 2.87	New Plymouth	RHB	RM
Sim Sarah Monique Patricia	W	24. 5.88	Whakatane	LHB	RM
Stockwell Andrea Catherine	W	14.11.83	Palmerston North	LHB	WK
Sutherland Kelly Marie	A	7.10.82	Hastings	RHB	RM
Tahuhu Lea-Marie Maureen	C	23. 9.90	Christchurch	RHB	RM
Taylor Clare Elizabeth	O	22. 5.65	Huddersfield, England	RHB	RM
Te Wake Ariana Michelle	O	30. 9.87	Hamilton	RHB	RM
Tiffen Haidee Maree	C, NZ	4. 9.79	Timaru	RHB	RM
Tomlinson Kerry-Anne	W	19. 1.90	Gisborne	RHB	RM
Tremaine Megan Anne	A	27. 3.84	Auckland	LHB	RM
Tsukigawa Sarah Jane	O, NZ	16. 6.82	Balclutha	RHB	RM
Wakefield Megan Gwenda	W	22. 9.82	Christchurch	RHB	RM
Watson Helen Maree	C, NZ	17. 2.72	Ashburton	RHB	RM
Wilkins Anna Jane	ND	21. 5.80	Hamilton	RHB	WK
Wilson Emily Mary	ND	15.10.84	Ashburton	RHB	RM
Winkley Kelly Marie	CD	16. 6.84	Napier	RHB	ROB
Yates Pamela Melissa	A	26. 9.81	Auckland	LHB	LM

2008/09 STATE LEAGUE AVERAGES

	M	*In*	*NO*	*HS*	*Runs*	*Ave*	*100s*	*50s*	*Ct*	*St*	*O*	*M*	*R*	*W*	*Ave*	*R/O*	*Best*
L.R.F.Askew	4	4	0	43	50	12.50	-	-	2	-	37	5	117	7	16.71	3.16	3-35
E.L.Bailey	10	3	3	4*	7	-	-	-	4	-	50.4	3	237	2	118.50	4.67	1-20
S.R.H.Barriball	9	7	1	37	84	14.00	-	-	4	-							
S.W.Bates	9	9	1	89	294	36.75	-	3	4	-	81.2	10	291	11	26.45	3.58	3-39
H.M.Bedford	2	1	0	1	1	1.00	-	-	-	-							
E.M.Bermingham	10	7	2	27	87	17.40	-	-	2	-	71	3	262	10	26.20	3.69	2-14
A.C.Boyce	8	8	1	30*	96	13.71	-	-	2	-	2	0	12	0	-	6.00	-
S.J.Bradbury	11	11	0	33	103	9.36	-	-	-	-							
J.C.Brehaut	9	9	2	60*	202	28.85	-	1	1	-							
K.E.Broadmore	10	9	0	47	115	12.77	-	-	2	-	77.1	13	270	13	20.76	3.50	4-11
N.J.Browne	10	10	3	101	449	64.14	1	3	3	-	64	11	239	8	29.87	3.73	3-12
S.M.Bullen	10	8	4	6*	21	5.25	-	-	2	-	87	16	274	7	39.14	3.15	2-27
O.R.Bupha-Intr	3	-	-	-	-	-	-	-	-	-							
S.K.Burke	10	4	2	13*	26	13.00	-	-	6	-	83.4	10	283	11	25.72	3.39	3-25
A.K.Burrows	10	6	2	18	32	8.00	-	-	-	-	85	9	313	17	18.41	3.68	3-19
E.M.Campbell	9	8	1	24	65	9.28	-	-	7	-	67.5	6	228	24	9.50	3.38	4-31
R.H.Candy	10	9	1	22	107	13.37	-	-	2	-	60.2	6	222	4	55.50	3.69	1-22
S.Coetzee	6	4	1	7*	15	5.00	-	-	-	-	21.4	3	93	3	31.00	4.35	2-12
A.E.Cooper	11	11	1	85*	196	19.60	-	1	4	-	74.1	17	236	14	16.85	3.18	6-9
R.Cox	2	-	-	-	-	-	-	-	2	-	20	1	56	6	9.33	2.80	4-30
K.J.Crowley	9	7	0	14	32	4.57	-	-	1	-							
S.F.M.Devine	11	11	1	83*	255	25.50	-	1	-	-	96	16	325	16	20.31	3.39	3-25
A.M.Dodd	11	9	3	29*	152	25.33	-	-	6	-	88.4	20	299	19	15.73	3.38	3-12
N.C.Dodd	10	10	0	58	165	16.50	-	1	2	-	40	2	167	5	33.40	4.18	2-28
L.R.Doolan	11	11	0	42	211	19.18	-	-	4	-	92.2	11	304	20	15.20	3.30	3-20
N.P.Edwards	10	3	2	2*	3	3.00	-	-	-	-	59	2	290	7	41.42	4.91	3-43
M.F.Fahey	9	9	0	26	83	9.22	-	-	2	-							
L.M.M.Foote	9	6	5	5*	11	11.00	-	-	5	-	2	0	12	0	-	6.00	-
M.A.Frey	7	5	2	42*	56	18.66	-	-	2	-							
L.M.Grant	8	7	2	13	48	9.60	-	-	1	-							
P.A.Gruber	8	4	2	14*	23	11.50	-	-	1	-	52	6	178	4	44.50	3.42	2-20
L.A.M.Hayes	8	-	-	-	-	-	-	-	1	-	30	1	152	4	38.00	5.06	2-53
S.J.Gurnsey	1	-	-	-	-	-	-	-	-	-							
M.J.Hodgson	11	10	4	14*	78	13.00	-	-	5	-							
S.A.P.Hopkins	2	2	0	8	8	4.00	-	-	-	-							
T.R.Hopkinson	9	-	-	-	-	-	-	-	3	-	41	3	185	3	61.66	4.51	2-41
W.L.Horneman	8	8	1	41	91	13.00	-	-	-	-	0.2	0	2	0	-	-	-
H.R.Huddleston	10	7	1	22	93	15.50	-	-	1	1	14.4	1	100	0	-	6.81	-
M.J.Kane	7	7	0	26	71	10.14	-	-	-	-							
R.J.Kember	6	6	0	46	113	18.83	-	-	3	-							
B.N.Kirkbride	2	-	-	-	-	-	-	-	-	-	14	2	43	1	43.00	3.07	1-29
A.S.M.Kitchin	9	7	1	45*	77	12.83	-	-	3	-							
E.Lanser	4	4	2	26*	69	34.50	-	-	1	-							
V.J.Lind	10	10	1	91	215	23.88	-	1	6	3							
M.L.Lynch	10	9	0	69	197	21.88	-	2	1	-	1	0	11	0	-	11.00	-
F.L.Mackay	10	9	0	55	196	21.77	-	1	2	-	88	12	272	10	27.20	3.09	3-25
K.J.Martin	9	9	0	50	161	17.88	-	1	5	6							
A.L.Mason	10	9	0	52	220	24.44	-	1	4	-	59	5	239	6	39.83	4.05	3-18
S.J.McGlashan	10	9	0	82	336	37.33	-	4	2	-							
B.H.McNeill	10	7	2	39	113	22.60	-	-	2	-	79.2	8	268	18	14.88	3.38	4-34
Z.A.McWilliams	10	9	0	58	124	13.77	-	1	1	-	47.5	3	211	6	35.16	4.44	2-41
R.C.Milburn	8	6	2	21*	41	10.25	-	-	4	4							
L.E.Milliken	10	9	2	37	102	14.57	-	-	2	-	66.1	5	259	13	19.92	3.92	3-46
P.Mistry	10	9	0	28	78	8.66	-	-	4	-	79.4	14	341	16	21.31	4.29	4-27
M.L.Mitchell	10	8	1	25	77	11.00	-	-	6	-	9	0	43	2	21.50	4.78	1-14
C.K.Mizzi	1	-	-	-	-	-	-	-	-	-							
R.J.M.Moffitt	1	-	-	-	-	-	-	-	-	-							
T.J.Morrison	9	7	3	12*	26	6.50	-	-	3	-	71.2	9	202	12	16.83	2.84	4-16
M.P.Murphy	10	10	1	39	199	22.11	-	-	2	-	35.1	4	132	1	132.00	3.76	1-26
K.A.Neilson	6	5	0	23	69	13.80	-	-	2	-							
M.J.G.Nielsen	10	8	1	28*	59	8.42	-	-	1	-	16.5	1	72	3	24.00	4.36	2-6
S.L.Norman	3	2	0	1	1	0.50	-	-	1	-							
K.T.Perkins	7	7	1	53*	74	12.33	-	1	1	-							
E.C.Perry	11	10	1	47	213	23.66	-	-	2	-	44.1	2	210	6	35.00	4.76	2-31
A.M.Peterson	10	9	1	29	96	12.00	-	-	3	-							
R.H.Priest	10	9	1	64	233	29.12	-	1	4	4							

	M	In	NO	HS	Runs	Ave	100s	50s	Ct	St	O	M	R	W	Ave	R/O	Best
K.L.Pulford	10	10	0	96	333	33.30	-	3	2	-	93.1	15	298	17	17.52	3.20	3-21
K.C.R.Rangi	6	6	1	11	25	5.00	-	-	2	-							
S.E.A.Ruck	11	6	4	4	7	3.50	-	-	1	-	83	12	309	9	34.33	3.72	3-20
A.E.Satterthwaite	10	10	1	76	277	30.77	-	3	3	-	55.3	3	220	13	16.92	3.98	4-31
N.Scripps	10	5	2	23*	25	8.33	-	-	5	-	78.3	11	304	12	25.33	3.87	3-35
E.J.Scurr	3	3	1	49*	74	37.00	-	-	-	-							
C.J.Sim	2		-	-	-	-	-	-	-	-	9	0	39	2	19.50	4.33	2-21
S.M.P.Sim	1	-	-	-	-	-	-	-	-	-							
A.C.Stockwell	11	3	0	2	3	1.00	-	-	11	7							
K.M.Sutherland	10	9	0	22	71	7.88	-	-	2	-							
A.Swart	8	4	1	11*	24	8.00	-	-	5	-							
L.M.M.Tahuhu	9	1	0	4	4	4.00	-	-	3	-	22	0	92	3	30.66	4.18	2-6
C.E.Taylor	3	2	0	18	31	15.50	-	-	-	-	17	3	84	4	21.00	4.94	2-32
A.M.Te Wake	5	3	1	6	8	4.00	-	-	3	-							
H.M.Tiffen	8	8	1	69	274	39.14	-	2	1	-							
K.A.Tomlinson	11	8	3	32*	69	13.80	-	-	3	-	2	0	20	1	20.00	10.00	1-20
M.A.Tremaine	10	6	1	20	24	4.80	-	-	3	-	53	7	210	4	52.50	3.96	1-24
S.J.Tsukigawa	9	9	0	74	341	37.88	-	5	4	-	68.4	8	243	14	17.35	3.55	3-19
M.G.Wakefield	11	11	0	120	403	36.63	1	1	6	-							
H.M.Watson	1	1	0	0	0	0.00	-	-	-	-	10	2	31	1	31.00	3.10	1-31
A.J.Wilkins	10	9	1	54*	294	36.75	-	2	9	-							
E.M.Wilson	10	7	2	16*	49	9.80	-	-	2	-	58	5	223	8	27.87	3.84	3-39
K.M.Winkley	10	8	4	29	93	23.25	-	-	-	-	54.2	8	222	8	27.75	4.10	2-10
P.M.Yates	2	1	0	2	2	2.00	-	-	-	-							

HIGHEST STRIKE RATES *(qualification 100 runs)*

		Runs	Balls	S/R
S.F.M.Devine	*W*	255	289	88
R.H.Candy	*CD*	107	125	85
K.L.Pulford	*ND*	333	393	84
S.J.Tsukigawa	*O*	341	446	76
M.G.Wakefield	*W*	403	528	76
A.E.Satterthwaite	*C*	277	371	74
N.J.Browne	*ND*	449	602	74
E.C.Perry	*W*	213	290	73
S.J.McGlashan	*CD*	336	472	71
A.L.Mason	*CD*	220	313	70

MOST ECONOMICAL BOWLING *(qualification 30 overs)*

		O	M	R	W	Ave	R/O
T.J.Morrison	*O*	71.2	9	202	12	16.83	2.83
F.L.Mackay	*C*	88	12	272	10	27.20	3.09
S.M.Bullen	*A*	87	16	274	7	39.14	3.14
L.R.F.Askew	*O*	37	5	117	7	16.71	3.16
A.E.Cooper	*W*	74.1	17	236	14	16.85	3.18
K.L.Pulford	*ND*	93.1	15	298	17	17.52	3.19
L.R.Doolan	*W*	92.2	11	304	20	15.20	3.29
E.M.Campbell	*O*	67.5	6	228	24	9.50	3.36
A.M.Dodd	*W*	88.4	20	299	19	15.73	3.37
B.H.McNeill	*C*	79.2	8	268	18	14.88	3.37

CAREER RECORDS

	M	In	NO	HS	Runs	Ave	100s	50s	Ct	St	O	M	R	W	Ave	R/O	Best
L.R.F.Askew	4	4	0	43	50	12.50	-	-	2	-	37	5	117	7	16.71	3.16	3-35
E.L.Bailey	10	3	3	4*	7	-	-	-	4	-	50.4	3	237	2	118.50	4.67	1-20
S.R.H.Barriball	13	9	1	37	84	10.50	-	-	4	-	1	0	16	0	-	16.00	-
S.W.Bates	50	46	3	183*	1020	23.72	1	5	14	-	356.2	48	1410	39	36.15	3.96	3-39
H.M.Bedford	2	1	0	1	1	1.00	-	-	-	-							
E.M.Bermingham	26	16	5	27	158	14.36	-	-	2	-	87	5	325	10	32.50	3.74	2-14
A.C.Boyce	8	8	1	30*	96	13.71	-	-	2	-	2	0	12	0	-	6.00	-
S.J.Bradbury	22	21	1	33	169	8.45	-	-	-	-							
J.C.Brehaut	12	11	2	60*	220	24.44	-	1	1	-	0.2	0	4	0	-	-	-
K.E.Broadmore	30	21	1	47	208	10.40	-	-	8	-	214.1	36	782	24	32.58	3.65	4-11
N.J.Browne	89	84	13	101	2206	31.07	1	16	29	-	654.1	60	2664	96	27.75	4.07	4-38
S.M.Bullen	53	18	11	19*	72	10.28	-	-	14	-	374	52	1331	39	334.12	3.55	3-10
O.R.Bupha-Intr	14	2	1	3	4	4.00	-	-	-	-	40	0	211	5	42.20	5.27	2-16
S.K.Burke	91	51	16	27	340	9.71	-	-	28	-	696.5	103	2366	100	23.66	3.39	4-28
A.K.Burrows	76	28	10	18	68	3.77	-	-	13	-	564.1	72	1966	81	24.27	3.48	4-28
E.M.Campbell	27	12	1	24	76	6.90	-	-	10	-	177.2	17	635	51	12.45	3.58	4-31
R.H.Candy	53	21	8	22	196	15.07	-	-	7	-	322.1	44	1121	37	30.29	3.47	5-24
S.Coetzee	33	15	6	9	56	6.22	-	-	4	-	173.2	8	760	19	40.00	4.38	2-12
A.E.Cooper	88	70	13	85*	946	16.59	-	2	25	-	524	75	1944	100	19.44	3.71	6-9
R.Cox	2	-	-	-	-	-	-	-	2	-	20	1	56	6	9.33	2.80	4-30
K.J.Crowley	17	14	1	14	73	5.61	-	-	3	-							
S.F.M.Devine	53	39	7	83*	524	16.37	-	1	13	-	394.4	53	1354	64	21.15	3.43	5-23
A.M.Dodd	88	60	11	46	667	13.61	-	-	27	-	667.4	139	1985	90	22.05	2.97	5-7
N.C.Dodd	20	14	1	58	178	13.69	-	1	4	-	100.3	4	411	12	34.25	4.08	2-28
L.R.Doolan	42	40	1	59*	723	18.53	-	4	11	-	279.1	29	1041	49	21.24	3.73	3-20
N.P.Edwards	15	3	2	2*	3	3.00	-	-	-	-	94.3	2	479	10	47.90	5.06	3-43
M.F.Fahey	80	74	7	91	1723	25.71	-	13	24	-	112.2	11	429	18	23.83	3.81	4-21
L.M.M.Foote	11	7	6	5*	15	15.00	-	-	5	-	2	0	12	0	-	6.00	-
M.A.Frey	7	5	2	42*	56	18.66	-	-	2	-							
L.M.Grant	15	14	2	19	101	8.41	-	-	2	-							
P.A.Gruber	57	24	11	25	152	11.69	-	-	17	-	397.3	45	1357	61	22.24	3.41	4-15
S.J.Gurnsey	1	-	-	-	-	-	-	-	-	-							
L.A.M.Hayes	8	-	-	-	-	-	-	-	-	1	30	1	152	4	38.00	5.06	2-53
M.J.Hodgson	32	25	9	52	282	17.62	-	1	14	-							
S.A.P.Hopkins	6	5	0	8	20	4.00	-	-	-	-							
T.R.Hopkinson	9	-	-	-	-	-	-	-	-	3	41	3	185	3	61.66	4.51	2-41
W.L.Horneman	22	20	2	41	199	11.05	-	-	4	1	0.2	0	2	0	-	-	-
H.R.Huddleston	35	21	7	48*	230	16.42	-	-	5	1	144.3	9	671	9	74.55	4.64	1-21
M.J.Kane	94	86	3	65*	974	11.73	-	3	9	-	259.1	16	1061	30	35.36	4.09	4-21
R.J.Kember	71	65	1	94	1462	22.84	-	8	22	-	5.4	0	43	1	43.00	7.59	1-22
B.N.Kirkbride	2	-	-	-	-	-	-	-	-	-	14	2	43	1	43.00	3.07	1-29
A.S.M.Kitchin	41	34	1	51	301	9.12	-	1	7	-	44	2	206	9	22.88	4.68	4-18
E.Lanser	4	4	2	26*	69	34.50	-	-	1	-							
V.J.Lind	51	47	4	91	922	21.44	-	3	14	4							
M.L.Lynch	49	46	2	69	751	17.06	-	4	12	-	1	0	11	0	-	11.00	-
F.L.Mackay	16	15	0	55	306	20.40	-	1	2	-	116	16	340	13	26.15	2.93	3-25
K.J.Martin	75	70	7	74	1265	20.07	-	7	43	39							
A.L.Mason	92	84	13	116	2027	28.54	1	7	44	-	751.3	93	2584	112	23.07	3.44	5-25
S.J.McGlashan	82	74	11	111*	2005	31.82	2	13	23	6							
B.H.McNeill	94	69	22	51*	911	19.38	-	1	25	-	714.2	95	2541	122	20.82	3.56	6-31
Z.A.McWilliams	70	54	16	69	747	19.65	-	3	14	-	419.1	39	1799	72	24.98	4.29	4-27
R.C.Milburn	106	91	14	82	1275	16.55	-	2	76	36							
L.E.Milliken	72	65	22	60*	589	13.69	-	1	18	-	543	46	2061	71	29.02	3.80	4-34
P.Mistry	39	28	3	28	187	7.48	-	-	8	-	327.3	56	1288	59	21.83	3.93	5-23
M.L.Mitchell	38	19	3	32	165	10.31	-	-	10	-	93.4	9	400	14	28.57	4.27	2-27
C.K.Mizzi	12	7	0	4	13	1.85	-	-	3	-							
R.J.M.Moffitt	5	3	1	25	36	18.00	-	-	1	-	24	1	110	1	110.00	4.58	1-24
T.J.Morrison	55	27	11	12*	73	4.56	-	-	4	-	415.4	73	1321	43	30.72	3.17	4-16
M.P.Murphy	55	46	12	94*	785	23.08	-	3	9	-	297.5	22	1317	33	39.90	4.42	4-36
K.A.Neilson	16	14	0	35	214	15.28	-	-	4	-							
M.J.G.Nielsen	14	9	2	28*	74	10.57	-	-	1	-	45.2	6	217	5	43.40	4.80	2-6
S.L.Norman	52	51	5	62	620	13.47	-	1	10	-							
K.T.Perkins	21	20	1	53*	250	13.15	-	1	5	-	12	0	85	1	85.00	7.08	1-26
E.C.Perry	56	41	8	47	518	15.69	-	-	16	-	205.5	16	967	25	38.68	4.71	3-4
A.M.Peterson	16	13	1	29	143	11.91	-	-	3	-	12	0	68	1	68.00	5.66	1-30
R.H.Priest	59	53	6	64	764	16.25	-	1	45	16							

	M	In	NO	HS	Runs	Ave	100s	50s	Ct	St	O	M	R	W	Ave	R/O	Best
K.L.Pulford	80	78	10	153*	1998	29.38	2	13	20	-	546.2	59	1975	79	25.00	3.62	3-21
K.C.R.Rangi	14	12	2	20	69	6.90	-	-	3	-							
S.E.A.Ruck	32	14	6	12	36	4.50	-	-	3	-	266	46	894	37	2416	3.36	3-20
A.E.Satterthwaite	62	45	13	95*	739	23.09	-	5	19	-	305.4	30	1157	53	21.83	3.78	4-15
N.Scripps	78	37	14	30	250	10.86	-	-	11	-	661.4	96	2111	136	15.52	3.19	6-18
E.J.Scurr	66	60	9	71	907	17.78	-	4	8	-	88.4	10	342	7	48.85	3.87	3-22
C.J.Sim	3	1	0	0	0	0.00	-	-	-	-	11	1	45	2	22.50	4.09	2-21
S.M.P.Sim	11	10	0	18	64	6.40	-	-	-	-							
A.C.Stockwell	35	26	2	49	241	10.04	-	-	23	7							
K.M.Sutherland	34	25	3	49	272	12.36	-	-	6	-	33	1	159	4	39.75	4.81	3-35
A.Swart	8	4	1	11*	24	8.00	-	-	5	-							
L.M.M.Tahuhu	9	1	0	4	4	4.00	-	-	3	-	22	0	92	3	30.66	4.18	2-6
C.E.Taylor	67	60	16	65*	1065	24.20	-	5	15	-	472.3	71	1726	61	28.29	3.65	4-25
A.M.Te Wake	18	13	3	14	68	6.80	-	-	5	-	3.2	0	43	0	-	12.90	-
H.M.Tiffen	105	96	25	97	2692	37.91	-	15	49	-	251	29	889	55	16.16	3.54	5-51
K.A.Tomlinson	34	20	4	32*	155	9.68	-	-	6	-	86.5	8	423	10	42.30	4.87	2-13
M.A.Tremaine	21	16	3	44*	90	6.92	-	-	3	-	118	14	450	15	30.00	3.81	4-22
S.J.Tsukigawa	88	81	11	108	1455	20.78	1	7	26	-	453.5	57	1728	74	23.35	3.81	5-13
M.G.Wakefield	77	71	10	120	1694	27.77	1	9	25	1	11	0	43	2	21.50	3.91	2-26
H.M.Watson	101	85	34	101	1873	36.72	1	7	28	-	732.5	130	2263	110	20.57	3.08	5-18
A.J.Wilkins	91	87	5	54*	1472	17.95	-	2	24	-	36.2	3	221	3	73.66	6.08	1-8
E.M.Wilson	10	7	2	16*	49	9.80	-	-	2	-	58	5	223	8	27.87	3.84	3-39
K.M.Winkley	31	17	5	29	147	12.25	-	-	4	-	191.5	25	681	25	27.24	3.55	4-27
P.M.Yates	2	1	0	2	2	2.00	-	-	-	-							

PROVINCIAL COMPETITION

The symbol of supremacy in women's provincial cricket has been the Hallyburton Johnstone Shield (1935/36 to 1981/82), Hansells Cup (1982/83 to 1989/90), Pub Charities National Tournament (1990/91 to 1997/98), State Insurance Cup (1998/99 to 2000/01) and State League (2001/02 to date).

WINNERS

1935/36	Wellington
1936/37	Wellington
1937/38	Wellington
1938/39	Wellington
1939/40	Auckland
1940/41	Auckland
1941/42	no competition
1942/43	Auckland
1943/44	Canterbury
1944/45	Canterbury
1945/46	Canterbury
1946/47	Auckland
1947/48	Auckland
1948/49	Auckland
1949/50	Wellington
1950/51	Wellington
1951/52	Auckland
1952/53	Wellington
1953/54	Wellington
1954/55	Auckland
1955/56	Canterbury
1956/57	Auckland
1957/58	Auckland
1958/59	Wellington
1959/60	Wellington
1960/61	Canterbury
1961/62	Canterbury
1962/63	Otago
1963/64	Canterbury
1964/65	Auckland
1965/66	Auckland
1966/67	Canterbury
1967/68	Wellington
1968/69	North Shore
1969/70	Wellington
1970/71	North Shore
1971/72	North Shore
1972/73	Canterbury
1973/74	Wellington
1974/75	Wellington
1975/76	Canterbury
1976/77	Wellington
1977/78	Wellington
1978/79	Canterbury
1979/80	Canterbury
1980/81	Canterbury
1981/82	Canterbury
1982/83	Canterbury
1983/84	Canterbury
1984/85	Canterbury
1985/86	Canterbury
1986/87	Canterbury
1987/88	Canterbury
1988/89	Canterbury
1989/90	Wellington
1990/91	Canterbury
1991/92	Canterbury
1992/93	Canterbury
1993/94	Canterbury
1994/95	Canterbury
1995/96	Canterbury
1996/97	Canterbury
1997/98	Canterbury
1998/99	Canterbury
1999/00	Auckland
2000/01	Auckland
2001/02	Auckland
2002/03	Auckland
2003/04	Canterbury
2004/05	Canterbury/Wellington
2005/06	Central Districts
2006/07	Canterbury
2007/08	Canterbury
2008/09	Canterbury

TEAM RECORDS

Highest Totals

302-5	Canterbury v Otago	Christchurch	1998/99
298-4	Canterbury v Wellington	Christchurch	1999/00
296-8	Otago v Northern Districts	Dunedin	2006/07
291-7	Central Districts v Wellington	New Plymouth	2007/08
288-5	Auckland v Central Districts	Auckland	2000/01
285-4	Auckland v Otago	Queenstown	2004/05

Lowest Totals

43	Central Districts v Auckland	Wanganui	1999/00
46	Northern Districts v Wellington	Wellington	1999/00
51	Northern Districts v Otago	Dunedin	2004/05
52	Otago v Wellington	Wellington	2008/09
59	Otago v Canterbury	Christchurch	2000/01

INDIVIDUAL RECORDS

Centuries

183*	S.W. Bates	Otago v Auckland	Auckland	2005/06
153*	K.L. Pulford	Central Districts v Canterbury	Christchurch	1999/00
141	D.A. Hockley	Canterbury v Auckland	Rangiora	1998/99
141	K.L. Pulford	Central Districts v Otago	Palmerston North	2000/01
128	D.A. Hockley	Canterbury v Wellington	Christchurch	1999/00
120	C.M. Edwards	Northern Districts v Wellington	Hamilton	2002/03
120	M.G. Wakefield	Wellington v Auckland	Auckland	2008/09
119*	C.M. Edwards	Northern Districts v Canterbury	Christchurch	2000/01
118	E.C. Drumm	Auckland v Central Districts	Auckland	2000/01
118	R.J. Rolls	Auckland v Otago	Queenstown	2004/05
117*	N. Payne	Canterbury v Wellington	Christchurch	1999/00
117	D.A. Hockley	Canterbury v Otago	Christchurch	1998/99
116	E.C. Drumm	Northern Districts v Otago	Hamilton	2005/06
116	A.L. Mason	Central Districts v Wellington	Wanganui	2005/06
115	E.C. Drumm	Northern Districts v Auckland	Auckland	2005/06
114*	E.C. Drumm	Auckland v Central Districts	Wanganui	1999/00
112*	E.C. Drumm	Auckland v Northern Districts	Auckland	2001/02
111*	R.J. Rolls	Auckland v Otago	Auckland	2003/04
111*	S.J. McGlashan	Central Districts v Canterbury	Palmerston North	2006/07
110	P.B. Flannery	Otago v Auckland	Queenstown	2004/05
110	R.J. Rolls	Auckland v Otago	Auckland	2005/06
108	S.J. Tsukigawa	Otago v Northern Districts	Dunedin	2006/07
106	R.J. Rolls	Auckland v Northern Districts	Auckland	2006/07
105*	S.J. McGlashan	Central Districts v Canterbury	Christchurch	2005/06
104*	P.B. Flannery	Canterbury v Otago	Christchurch	2000/01
104	M.K. Tyler	Auckland v Otago	Auckland	1999/00
104	A.M. Smith	Wellington v Northern Districts	Upper Hutt	2005/06
102*	N.A. Pratt	Northern Districts v Otago	Hamilton	1999/00
101	D.A. Hockley	Canterbury v Central Districts	Palmerston North	1998/99
101	H.M. Watson	Auckland v Otago	Dunedin	2000/01
101	A.M. Smith	Wellington v Otago	Wellington	2006/07
101	N.J. Browne	Northern Districts Central Districts	Mt Maunganui	2008/09
100*	M.A.M. Lewis	Wellington v Auckland	Wellington	2003/04
100*	T.M. Gould	Northern Districts v Central Districts	Mt Maunganui	2004/05
100	A.J. Blackwell	Otago v Northern Districts	Dunedin	2006/07

Five Wickets in an Innings

7.1-1-19-7	M.F. Tunupopo	Auckland v Central Districts	Wanganui	1999/00
10-6-8-6	R.J. Steele	Canterbury v Auckland	Auckland	2005/06
10-6-9-6	A.E. Cooper	Wellington v Otago	Wellington	2008/09
10-3-18-6	N. Scripps	Auckland v Northern Districts	Auckland	2003/04
9.2-2-19-6	N. Scripps	Auckland v Wellington	Auckland	2002/03
9-1-20-6	D.M. Trow	Central Districts v Northern Districts	Wanganui	2003/04
9.5-1-31-6	B.H. McNeill	Canterbury v Auckland	Auckland	2001/02
6-1-7-5	A.M. Dodd	Wellington v Otago	Dunedin	2005/06
5.5-1-12-5	C.A. Campbell	Canterbury v Northern Districts	Hamilton	1999/00
9-3-13-5	S.J. Tsukigawa	Otago v Northern Districts	Dunedin	2006/07
8.2-0-15-5	A.E. Cooper	Wellington v Auckland	Auckland	2006/07
10-3-18-5	H.M. Watson	Canterbury v Otago	Invercargill	2007/08
10-2-19-5	H.R. Daly	Canterbury v Northern Districts	Rangiora	2002/03
7-1-20-5	C.A. Campbell	Canterbury v Wellington	Wellington	1998/99
8.3-2-21-5	A.E. Cooper	Wellington v Northern Districts	Hamilton	2004/05
10-2-23-5	S.F.M. Devine	Wellington v Northern Districts	Hamilton	2006/07
10-2-23-5	P. Mistry	Auckland v Central Districts	Palmerston North	2007/08
8-1-24-5	H.J. Rae	Canterbury v Wellington	Lower Hutt	2000/01
10-3-24-5	R.H. Candy	Canterbury v Central Districts	Christchurch	2007/08
10-1-25-5	A.L. Mason	Central Districts v Wellington	Wanganui	1999/00
10-0-27-5	A.M. Little	Wellington v Otago	Wellington	2002/03
10-1-31-5	B.H. McNeill	Canterbury v Otago	Timaru	2002/03
10-0-31-5	S.E. Charteris	Canterbury v Otago	Alexandra	2005/06
10-1-33-5	S.F.M. Devine	Canterbury v Auckland	Auckland	2007/08
10-1-34-5	H.J. Partridge	Northern Districts v Auckland	Auckland	1999/00
8.3-1-37-5	N. Scripps	Auckland v Canterbury	Christchurch	2000/01
9-0-38-5	K.M. Spence	Otago v Northern Districts	Hamilton	2005/06
10-1-51-5	H.M. Tiffen	Canterbury v Auckland	Christchurch	2000/01

Wicketkeeping

DISMISSALS IN AN INNINGS

	(ct/st)				
6	(6/0)	S.J. Hill	Wellington v Northern Districts	Hamilton	2006/07
5	(2/3)	R.J. Rolls	Auckland v Canterbury	Christchurch	2000/01
5	(4/1)	R.C. Milburn	Canterbury v Auckland	Auckland	2003/04
5	(0/5)	K.J. Martin	Otago v Wellington	Dunedin	2007/08
5	(5/0)	A.C. Stockwell	Wellington v Auckland	Auckland	2008/09
4	(0/4)	R.J. Rolls	Auckland v Wellington	Auckland	1998/99
4	(1/3)	R.C. Milburn	Otago v Wellington	Dunedin	1999/00
4	(0/4)	J.L. Strachan	Canterbury v Northern Districts	Christchurch	2000/01
4	(4/0)	R.C. Milburn	Canterbury v Auckland	Christchurch	2002/03
4	(3/1)	S.J. McGlashan	Central Districts v Canterbury	Palmerston North	2002/03
4	(2/2)	K.J. Martin	Otago v Central Districts	Palmerston North	2002/03
4	(2/2)	S.J. McGlashan	Central Districts v Otago	Palmerston North	2002/03
4	(3/1)	R.J. Rolls	Auckland v Canterbury	Christchurch	2002/03
4	(3/1)	R.C. Milburn	Canterbury v Wellington	Christchurch	2003/04
4	(3/1)	S.J. Hill	Wellington v Otago	Dunedin	2003/04
4	(4/0)	R.H. Priest	Central Districts v Auckland	Napier	2003/04
4	(4/0)	R.C. Milburn	Canterbury v Central Districts	Christchurch	2005/06
4	(3/1)	R.C. Milburn	Canterbury v Central Districts	Christchurch	2005/06
4	(4/0)	J.C. Ullyett	Northern Districts v Central Districts	Palmerston North	2005/06
4	(4/0)	K.J. Martin	Otago v Canterbury	Timaru	2006/07
4	(4/0)	A.C. Stockwell	Wellington v Canterbury	Christchurch	2007/08
4	(1/3)	K.J. Martin	Otago v Canterbury	Invercargill	2007/08

Fielding

CATCHES IN AN INNINGS

4	M.M. Graham	Central Districts v Northern Districts	Wanganui	1999/00
4	S.J. Tsukigawa	Otago v Canterbury	Dunedin	2003/04
4	E.C. Drumm	Auckland v Central Distyricts	Auckland	2004/05

RECORD PARTNERSHIPS

AUCKLAND

1st	187	R.J. Rolls & R.J. Kember	v Otago	Auckland	2005/06
2nd	136	M.K. Fruin & E.C. Drumm	v Central Districts	Auckland	2000/01
3rd	151*	R.J. Rolls & I. Cronin-Knight	v Otago	Dunedin	2006/07
4th	† 157	M.K. Fruin & H.M. Watson	v Otago	Dunedin	2000/01
5th	120	R.J. Rolls & K. Perkins	v Northern Districts	Auckland	2006/07
6th	79	K. Perkins & M.A. Tremaine	v Northern Districts	Auckland	2006/07
7th	90	K.A. Ramel & A. Soma	v Wellington	Auckland	1998/99
8th	52	C.M. Nicholson & Z.A.A. Plummer	v Central Districts	Auckland	1998/99
9th	35	E.C. Drumm & S.E.M. Cowlrick	v Canterbury	Christchurch	1998/99
10th	† 57*	K.T. Perkins & N. Scripps	v Northern Districts	Whangarei	2008/09

CANTERBURY

1st	163	D.A. Hockley & P.B. Flannery	v Central Districts	Christchurch	1999/00
2nd	† 227	D.A. Hockley & N. Payne	v Wellington	Christchurch	1999/00
3rd	† 168*	A.E. Satterthwaite & H.M. Tiffen	v Northern Districts	Mt Maunganui	2007/08
4th	144	H.M. Tiffen & J.A. Lawler	v Central Districts	P. North	2000/01
5th	103*	H.M. Tiffen & J.C. Brehaut	v Auckland	Christchurch	2008/09
6th	87	S.C. Taylor & B.H. McNeill	v Auckland	Christchurch	2004/05
7th	92	H.M. Tiffen & B.H. McNeill	v Central Districts	New Plymouth	2008/09
8th	53	H.M. Tiffen & E.M. Bermingham	v Northern Districts	Mt Maunganui	2007/08
9th	38*	R.C. Milburn & A.C. Boyce	v Wellington	Wellington	2008/09
10th	39	J.C. Brehaut & S.K. Burke	v Northern Districts	Christchurch	2008/09

CENTRAL DISTRICTS

1st	179*	P.K. Gerrish & C.L. Forsyth	v Wellington	Wellington	2000/01
2nd	96	Z.A. McWilliams & S.J. McGlashan	v Otago	P. North	2008/09
3rd	143	N.M. Thessman & A.L. Mason	v Wellington	Wanganui	2005/06
4th	152	S.J. McGlashan & A.L. Mason	v Auckland	P. North	2007/08
5th	112	A.L. Mason & Z.A. McWilliams	v Wellington	New Plymouth	2007/08
6th	83	M.M. Graham & S.J. McGlashan	v Otago	Dunedin	1998/99
7th	86	A.L. Mason & E.A. Travers	v Canterbury	P. North	2000/01
8th	70	R.H. Priest & M.A. Frey	v Northern Districts	Mt Maunganui	2008/09
9th	67*	N.M. Thessman & K.M. Sutherland	v Otago	Dunedin	2001/02
10th	37	K.M. Winkley & A.K. Burrows	v Otago	P. North	2008/09

NORTHERN DISTRICTS

1st	91	T.M. Gould & M.C. Godliman	v Otago	Mt Maunganui	2007/08
2nd	77	K.L. Pulford & A.J. Wilkins	v Wellington	Mt Maunganui	2008/09
3rd	157*	T.M. Gould & M.P. Murphy	v Central Districts	Mt Maunganui	2004/05
4th	137	E.C. Drumm & N.J. Browne	v Canterbury	Hamilton	2005/06
5th	82	N.J.Browne & M.P. Murphy	v Auckland	Auckland	2006/07
6th	138*	N.J. Browne & L.E. Milliken	v Auckland	Auckland	2005/06
7th	66	A.J. Wilkins & K.J. Gibson	v Wellington	Wellington	1999/00
8th	46	M.J. Hannay & J.C. Ullyett	v Canterbury	Christchurch	2004/05
9th †	69	N.J. Browne & K.A. Tomlinson	v Wellington	Wellington	2007/08
10th	52	H.R. Huddleston & M.A. Taylor	v Otago	Mt Maunganui	2007/08

OTAGO

1st †	199	E.J. Scurr & P.B. Flannery	v Auckland	Queenstown	2004/05
2nd	94	R.J. Pullar & S.K Helmore	v Central Districts	Dunedin	2001/02
	94	R.C. Milburn & P.J. te Beest	v Canterbury	Oamaru	2001/02
3rd	164	A.J. Blackwell & S.W. Bates	v Northern Districts	Dunedin	2006/07
4th	86	S.W. Bates & K.J. Martin	v Auckland	Auckland	2005/06
5th	109*	S.W. Bates & C.E. Taylor	v Auckland	Auckland	2005/06
6th	68	K.J. Martin & A.L. Kane	v Wellington	Wellington	2006/07
7th †	106	E.J. Scurr & S.W. Bates	v Auckland	Auckland	2003/04
8th †	80	C.E. Taylor & K.M. Spence	v Northern Districts	Hamilton	2005/06
9th	56	S.K. Helmore & A.L. Kane	v Auckland	Auckland	2003/04
10th	25	K.J. Martin & T.J. Morrison	v Central Districts	Dunedin	2003/04

WELLINGTON

1st	147	A.M. Smith & L.R. Doolan	v Northern Districts	Upper Hutt	2005/06
2nd	173*	L.R.V.S. Harford & M.A.M. Lewis	v Auckland	Wellington	2003/04
3rd	159	L.R.V.S. Harford & M.A.M. Lewis	v Canterbury	Christchurch	1999/00
4th	98*	M.A.M. Lewis & F.S. King	v Otago	Lower Hutt	2000/01
5th †	133	M.G. Wakefield & M.J. Hodgson	v Northern Districts	Wellington	2007/08
6th †	144*	M.A.M. Lewis & M.G. Wakefield	v Auckland	Auckland	2002/03
7th	56	M.A.M. Lewis & A.M. Corbin	v Central Districts	Napier	2001/02
8th	55	A.E. Cooper & S.F.M Devine	v Auckland	Auckland	2006/07
9th	50	K.A. Tomlinson & A.M. Dodd	v Auckland	Auckland	2008/09
10th	44	A.M. Corbin & A.J. Green	v Central Districts	Lower Hutt	2000/01

† *record for all teams*

CAREER RECORDS

BATTING	M	In	NO	HS	Runs	Ave	100s	50s
E.C. Drumm	80	78	16	118	2993	48.27	5	17
H.M. Tiffen	104	96	25	97	2692	37.91	-	15
R.J. Rolls	90	88	7	118	2591	31.98	4	14
N.J. Browne	89	84	13	101	2206	31.07	1	16
A.L. Mason	92	84	13	116	2027	28.54	1	7
S.J. McGlashan	82	74	11	111*	2005	31.82	2	13
K.L. Pulford	80	78	10	153*	1998	29.38	2	13
H.M. Watson	101	85	34	101	1873	36.72	1	7
P.B. Flannery	57	56	7	110	1765	36.02	2	7
M.A.M. Lewis	60	56	11	100*	1755	39.00	1	11
N.M. Thessman	77	75	11	85*	1733	27.07	-	8
M.F. Fahey	80	74	7	91	1723	25.71	-	13
M.G. Wakefield	77	71	10	120	1694	27.77	1	9
A.M. Smith	55	53	5	104	1663	34.64	2	9
N. Payne	49	47	7	117*	1614	40.35	1	12
M.C. Godliman	55	52	2	87	1538	30.76	-	13

BOWLING	M	O	M	R	W	Ave	R/O	Best
N. Scripps	78	661.4	96	2111	136	15.52	3.19	6-18
B.H. McNeill	94	714.2	95	2541	122	20.82	3.56	6-31
A.L. Mason	92	751.3	93	2584	112	23.07	3.44	5-25
H.M. Watson	101	732.5	130	2263	110	20.57	3.08	5-18
S.K. Burke	91	696.5	103	2366	100	23.66	3.39	4-28
A.E. Cooper	88	524	75	1944	100	19.44	3.71	6-9
N.J. Browne	89	654.1	60	2664	96	27.75	4.07	4-38
A.M. Dodd	88	667.4	139	1985	90	22.05	2.97	5-7
A.K. Burrows	76	564.1	72	1966	81	24.27	3.48	4-28
K.L. Pulford	80	546.2	59	1975	79	25.00	3.62	3-21
S.J.Tsukigawa	88	453.5	57	1728	74	23.35	3.81	5-13
Z.A. McWilliams	70	419.1	39	1799	72	24.98	4.29	4-27
L.E. Milliken	72	543	46	2061	71	29.02	3.80	4-34

WICKETKEEPING	ct	st	Total
R.J. Rolls	86	48	134
R.C. Milburn	76	36	112
K.J. Martin	40	38	78
S.J. Hill	35	21	56
R.H. Priest	40	16	56
E.A. Travers	29	19	48
J.C. Ullyett	25	2	27
A.C. Stockwell	19	7	26

FIELDING	ct
H.M. Tiffen	49
A.L. Mason	44
I. Cronin-Knight	29
N.J. Browne	29
H.M. Watson	28
S.K. Burke	28
A.M. Dodd	27
M.A.M. Lewis	26
S.J. Tsukigawa	26

NATIONAL DEVELOPMENT TOURNAMENT

The National Development Tournament was held at Lincoln University from 8 to 13 December, 2008. Canterbury defeated Auckland in the final. The tournament began with a round of Twenty20 matches followed by five rounds of 50-over games.

FIRST ROUND

Auckland 94 lost to **Canterbury** 96-2 by 8 wickets
Central Districts 173-4 defeated **Otago** 91-6 by 82 runs
Northern Districts 109-7 defeated **Wellington** 78-8 by 31 runs

SECOND ROUND

Auckland v **Northern Districts**
Otago v **Wellington**
Canterbury v **Central Districts**
all matches abandoned

THIRD ROUND

Northern Districts 173 lost to **Wellington** 174-5 by 5 wickets
Otago 82 lost to **Canterbury** 83-1 by 9 wickets
Auckland 241-8 defeated **Central Districts** 108-9 by 133 runs

FOURTH ROUND

Auckland 144-9 defeated **Welington** 124 by 20 runs
Canterbury 228-6 defeated **Northern Districts** 113 by 115 runs
Central Districts 246-8 defeated **Otago** 141 by 105 runs

FIFTH ROUND

Northern Districts 137 lost to **Central Districts** 138-8 by 2 wickets
Otago 91-7 lost to **Auckland** 92-2 by 8 wickets
Wellington 109 lost to **Canterbury** 110-2 by 8 wickets

SIXTH ROUND

Wellington 172-9 defeated **Central Districts** 151 by 21 runs
Auckland 246-5 defeated **Canterbury** 116 by 130 runs
Northern Districts 198-8 defeated **Otago** 103 by 95 runs

Final placings: Auckland 1, Canterbury 2, Central Districts 3, Northern Districts 4, Wellington 5, Otago 6.

TEST CAREER RECORDS

	M	In	NO	HS	Runs	Ave	100	50	Ct	St	Wkts	Runs	Ave	5WI	10WM	Best
E.P.Allan	4	6	4	29*	87	43.50	-	-	1	-	5	138	27.60	-	-	3-38
T.L.Anderson	2	3	0	63	108	36.00	-	1	-	-						
E.A.Badham	3	6	1	42	121	24.20	-	-	7	-	10	275	27.50	-	-	4-46
D.Bailey	1	2	0	5	6	3.00	-	-	-	-						
H.R.Bastion	1	-	-	-	-	-	-	-	-	-	0	59	-	-	-	-
K.E.Batty	4	7	1	24	67	11.16	-	-	6	-	2	78	39.00	-	-	1-18
L.I.Bayliss	1	-	-	-	-	-	-	-	-	-	5	70	14.00	1	-	5-28
B.L.Bevege	5	10	1	100*	400	44.44	1	2	3	-	0	70	-	-	-	-
M.C.Bishop	1	2	0	27	27	13.50	-	-	2	-	0	33	-	-	-	-
E.Blackie	1	2	1	13*	21	21.00	-	-	3	1						
P.Blackler	12	21	0	68	371	17.66	-	1	5	-	18	527	29.27	-	-	4-22
B.A.Brentnall	10	16	2	84*	301	21.50	-	1	16	12						
K.D.Brown	3	2	2	50*	52	-	-	1	4	-	7	160	22.85	-	-	3-47
S.H.Brown	6	9	3	19	59	9.83	-	-	1	-	9	432	48.00	-	-	3-64
N.Browne	1	2	2	5*	5	-	-	-	1	-	0	77	-	-	-	-
N.J.Browne	2	2	0	24	23	12.00	-	-	2	-	1	83	83.00	-	-	1-43
D.K.Brownlee	1	2	0	12	17	8.50	-	-	-	-						
H.Buck	1	2	0	16	16	8.00	-	-	-	-						
S.K.Burke	1	1	1	1*	1	-	-	-	-	-	1	57	57.00	-	-	1-57
J.A.Burley	6	9	0	46	110	12.22	-	-	3	-	21	553	26.33	1	-	7-41
V.E.Burt	3	5	0	15	40	8.00	-	-	-	-	0	28	-	-	-	-
V.L.Burtt	4	8	0	39	101	12.62	-	-	5	-						
C.A.Campbell	9	5	1	29	55	13.75	-	-	2	-	18	720	40.00	-	-	4-94
P.F.Carrick	7	11	3	21	63	7.87	-	-	4	-	21	489	23.28	1	-	6-29
J.Clark	11	18	0	79	482	26.77	-	2	7	-	0	5	-	-	-	-
A.L.Clough	1	1	0	0	0	0.00	-	-	-	-	1	70	70.00	-	-	1-70
W.J.Coe	3	5	1	34	83	20.75	-	-	-	-	6	222	37.00	-	-	2-30
M.C.Corby	1	2	0	12	13	6.50	-	-	-	-	0	36	-	-	-	-
D.A.Costello	1	1	0	0	0	0.00	-	-	-	-	2	104	52.00	-	-	2-77
J.M.Coulston	5	8	1	24	76	10.85	-	-	3	-	19	341	17.94	-	-	4-38
V.R.Coutts	6	11	0	41	136	12.36	-	-	1	-						
S.D.Cowles	7	14	0	46	324	23.14	-	-	6	-	0	13	-	-	-	-
J.Currie	3	5	2	3*	7	2.33	-	-	2	-	3	170	56.66	-	-	3-36
E.J.Dickson	2	4	0	65	114	28.50	-	1	-	-						
J.D.Doull	11	22	4	103	779	43.27	1	5	6	-	0	34	-	-	-	-
E.C.Drumm	5	6	3	161*	433	144.33	2	2	-	-	2	175	87.50	-	-	1-24
B.M.Duncan	2	3	3	1*	1	-	-	-	1	-	2	115	57.50	-	-	1-3
M.H.Dunlop	2	2	0	5	5	2.50	-	-	-	-	3	123	41.00	-	-	1-5
J.R.Dunning	6	12	2	71	320	32.00	-	2	5	-	6	170	28.33	-	-	2-1
A.E.Ell	1	2	0	1	2	1.00	-	-	-	-	0	55	-	-	-	-
M.F.Fahey	2	4	1	60*	125	41.66	-	1	1	-						
V.H.M.Farrell	3	4	0	5	12	3.00	-	-	5	3						
P.B.Flannery	1	2	0	46	64	32.00	-	-	-	-	0	5	-	-	-	-
K.E.Flavell	6	7	0	204	473	67.57	1	2	2	-						
J.W.Francis	5	7	1	19	46	7.66	-	-	2	-	14	362	25.85	-	-	4-7
L.M.Fraser	3	-	-	-	-	-	-	-	-	-	4	210	52.50	-	-	2-6
M.K.Fruin	6	8	0	80	188	23.50	-	2	3	1						
J.A.Fryer	3	1	1	7*	7	-	-	-	1	-	5	154	30.80	-	-	4-3
J.Fulford	1	2	0	10	12	6.00	-	-	-	-	2	46	23.00	-	-	2-4
S.M.Gilchrist	5	3	2	7*	12	12.00	-	-	5	-	14	384	27.42	-	-	3-4
G.P.Gooder	1	2	0	11	11	5.50	-	-	-	-	8	73	9.12	1	-	6-4
K.V.Gunn	9	12	0	49	194	16.16	-	-	6	1	11	429	39.00	-	-	3-4
J.E.Harris	10	7	3	9	26	6.50	-	-	1	-	15	691	46.06	-	-	4-1
J.C.Hatcher	4	7	0	23	79	11.28	-	-	-	-						
C.E.Henshilwood	1	2	0	41	48	24.00	-	-	-	-	0	14	-	-	-	-
D.A.Hockley	19	29	4	126*	1301	52.04	4	7	9	-	5	146	29.20	-	-	2-9
M.Hollis	1	2	0	24	26	13.00	-	-	-	-	1	81	81.00	-	-	1-8
S.L.Illingworth	6	7	3	40*	120	30.00	-	-	5	5						
I.C.P.Jagersma	9	13	5	52	271	33.87	-	1	10	2	4	38	9.50	-	-	4-3
Y.Kainuku	1	1	1	23*	23	-	-	-	-	-	1	50	50.00	-	-	1-5
K.M.Keenan	5	3	2	26*	32	32.00	-	-	4	-	15	348	23.20	1	-	6-7
P.D.Kinsella	6	8	0	53	131	16.37	-	1	3	-						
I.M.Lamason	4	6	2	37*	86	21.50	-	-	-	-	2	136	68.00	-	-	2-2
J.G.Lamason	4	8	0	24	87	10.87	-	-	-	-	8	264	33.00	-	-	4-5
B.J.Legg	3	4	1	26	30	10.00	-	-	-	-	4	149	37.25	-	-	2-5
M.A.M.Lewis	9	12	0	65	252	21.00	-	2	6	-						

	M	In	NO	HS	Runs	Ave	100	50	Ct	St	Wkts	Runs	Ave	5WI	10WM	Best
J.Lord	15	22	3	39*	258	13.57	-	-	5	-	55	1049	19.07	4	1	6-119
E.J.Maker	3	4	0	5	10	2.50	-	-	1	-	5	156	31.20	-	-	3-34
C.E.Marett	7	13	4	49	304	33.77	-	-	3	-	9	268	29.77	-	-	2-16
M.Marks	2	4	1	23	30	10.00	-	-	-	-						
K.J.Martin	1	2	0	46	49	24.50	-	-	-	-						
A.L.Mason	2	2	0	14	15	7.50	-	-	2	-	3	105	35.00	-	-	2-68
K.McDonald	1	1	0	1	1	1.00	-	-	-	-						
S.J.McGlashan	2	2	0	14	20	10.00	-	-	-	-						
P.F.McKelvey	15	26	2	155*	699	29.12	2	1	8	-						
A.McKenna	7	14	1	97*	465	35.76	-	3	7	-	0	6	-	-	-	-
R.U.McKenzie	7	13	0	61	295	22.69	-	2	3	-	8	214	26.75	-	-	4-18
S.McLauchlan	4	4	0	4	4	1.00	-	-	1	-	2	83	41.50	-	-	1-7
E.L.Miller	3	6	0	32	92	15.33	-	-	1	-						
H.Miller	1	2	0	11	11	5.50	-	-	-	-	1	77	77.00	-	-	1-77
L.E.Milliken	2	2	0	6	10	5.00	-	-	-	-	2	73	36.50	-	-	2-49
K.S.Molloy	2	1	1	1*	1	-	-	-	2	-	5	91	18.20	-	-	2-24
P.Moore	2	3	1	47*	80	40.00	-	-	3	-	0	31	-	-	-	-
L.J.Murdoch	6	10	0	72	253	25.30	-	1	1	-						
K.J.Musson	1	-	-	-	-	-	-	-	-	-						
C.M.Nicholson	4	5	0	46	140	28.00	-	-	1	-	5	170	34.00	-	-	2-25
A.M.O'Leary	1	1	0	27	27	27.00	-	-	1	-						
J.B.Olson	1	1	0	0	0	0.00	-	-	-	-	0	48	-	-	-	-
C.M.Oyler	5	8	2	67*	212	35.33	-	1	2	-						
E.A.Paton	4	8	1	77*	180	25.71	-	1	4	-	9	160	17.77	-	-	4-35
K.V.Plummer	4	6	0	13	28	4.66	-	-	2	-						
.J.Powell	7	13	2	63	272	24.72	-	1	9	1						
L.Powell	4	7	0	66	145	20.71	-	1	1	-	0	8	-	-	-	-
L.M.Prichard	1	2	0	38	43	21.50	-	-	1	-						
K.L.Pulford	1	2	0	0	0	0.00	-	-	1	-	2	15	7.50	-	-	2-15
S.J.Rattray	9	17	2	59	412	27.46	-	4	1	-	19	461	24.26	1	-	5-76
D.Robinson	1	1	1	2*	2	-	-	-	-	-	1	16	16.00	-	-	1-16
R.J.Rolls	1	2	1	71	71	71.00	-	1	1	-						
E.F.Rouse	1	2	0	35	36	18.00	-	-	-	-						
M.T.Rouse	2	4	2	15*	18	9.00	-	-	-	-						
.A.Russell	1	1	0	39	39	39.00	-	-	-	-	1	37	37.00	-	-	1-14
E.M.Ryan	5	8	4	10	38	9.50	-	-	3	11						
.M.Saulbrey	11	16	4	62	198	16.50	-	1	6	-	35	951	27.17	1	-	5-32
P.Savin	1	2	0	15	18	9.00	-	-	-	-						
.Scripps	1	1	1	10*	10	-	-	-	-	-	0	57	-	-	-	-
.A.Signal	6	6	2	55*	82	20.50	-	1	3	-	8	325	40.62	-	-	2-34
.J.Signal	1	2	1	8*	8	8.00	-	-	-	-	0	21	-	-	-	-
.J.Simpson	1	2	0	4	6	3.00	-	-	-	-						
.M.Sinclair	2	4	1	10	26	8.66	-	-	2	-						
.Sinton	1	2	0	10	14	7.00	-	-	-	-						
.E.Stead	9	18	2	95	433	27.06	-	3	3	-						
.J.Steele	2	3	0	12	16	5.33	-	-	3	-	8	141	17.62	1	-	5-79
.M.Stonell	4	8	0	47	127	15.87	-	-	2	-						
.Sutherland	3	6	0	22	66	11.00	-	-	1	-	2	86	43.00	-	-	1-29
.E.Symons	1	1	0	5	5	5.00	-	-	1	-	2	71	35.50	-	-	2-71
.J.Taylor	1	2	0	3	3	1.50	-	-	-	-	1	62	62.00	-	-	1-62
.M.Thompson	1	2	1	17*	17	17.00	-	-	1	-	0	18	-	-	-	-
.I.Thorner	3	6	1	37	76	15.20	-	-	-	-	4	78	19.50	-	-	2-33
.M.Tiffen	2	4	3	66*	124	124.00	-	1	1	-						
.A.Turner	6	8	1	11*	30	4.28	-	-	2	-	19	469	24.68	-	-	3-42
.J.Turner	6	9	2	65*	208	29.71	-	2	1	-						
.M.Webb	4	8	0	42	110	13.75	-	-	-	-	6	66	11.00	-	-	3-32
.White	3	5	0	17	33	6.60	-	-	-	-	2	85	42.50	-	-	1-5
.Wickham	2	4	0	34	40	10.00	-	-	-	-	3	76	25.33	-	-	2-33
.M.Williams	4	5	1	35*	70	17.50	-	-	1	-	3	158	52.66	-	-	2-19
.Woodbury	2	3	3	7*	7	-	-	-	-	-	4	100	25.00	-	-	2-29

TEAM RECORDS

Highest Totals

517-8	v England	Scarborough	1996
403-8d	v India	Nelson	1994/95
362-5d	v England	Guildford	1996
359	v Australia	Wellington	1974/75
335	v Australia	Melbourne	1971/72

Lowest Totals

44	v England	Christchurch	1934/35
61	v England	Auckland	1948/49
63	v England	Worcester	1954
78	v Australia	Adelaide	1978/79
87	v Australia	Wellington	1947/48

INDIVIDUAL RECORDS

Centuries

204	K.E. Flavell v England at Scarborough	1996
161*	E.C. Drumm v Australia at Christchurch	1994/95
155*	P.F. McKelvey v England at Wellington	1968/69
126*	D.A. Hockley v Australia at Auckland	1989/90
117*	P.F. McKelvey v South Africa at Cape Town	1971/72
115	D.A. Hockley v England at Worcester	1996
112*	E.C. Drumm v England at Guildford	1996
107*	D.A. Hockley v England at Canterbury	1984
107	D.A. Hockley v India at Nelson	1994/95
103	J.D. Doull v England at Christchurch	1968/69
100*	B.L. Bevege v India at Dunedin	1976/77

Five Wickets in an Innings

7-41	J.A. Burley v England at The Oval	1966
6-29	P.F. Carrick v Australia at Melbourne	1971/72
6-42	G.P. Gooder v England at Auckland	1948/49
6-73	K.M. Keenan v England at Worcester	1996
6-119	J. Lord v Australia at Melbourne	1978/79
5-24	J. Lord v South Africa at Durban	1971/72
5-28	L.I. Bayliss v Australia at Dunedin	1960/61
5-32	J.M. Saulbrey v South Africa at Durban	1971/72
5-40	J. Lord v India at Dunedin	1976/77
5-76	S.J. Rattray v India at Cuttack	1984/85
5-78	J. Lord v Australia at Adelaide	1978/79
5-79	R.J. Steele v India at Vapi	2003/04

Ten Wickets in a Match

10-137	J. Lord v Australia at Melbourne	1978/79

Wicketkeeping

DISMISSALS IN AN INNINGS

	(ct/st)				
6	(2/4)	B.A. Brentnall	v South Africa	Johannesburg	1971/72
5	(3/2)	B.A. Brentnall	v England	Auckland	1968/69
4	(1/3)	V.H.M. Farrell	v England	Worcester	1954
4	(4/0)	V.H.M. Farrell	v England	The Oval	1954
4	(1/3)	E.M. Ryan	v Australia	Melbourne	1978/79

DISMISSALS IN A MATCH

	(ct/st)				
7	(3/4)	B.A. Brentnall	v South Africa	Johannesburg	1971/72
7	(2/5)	E.M. Ryan	v Australia	Melbourne	1978/79
6	(4/2)	B.A. Brentnall	v England	Auckland	1968/69
5	(3/2)	B.A. Brentnall	v South Africa	Durban	1971/72
5	(2/3)	S.L. Illingworth	v England	Guildford	1996

Fielding

CATCHES IN AN INNINGS

3	K.E. Batty	v England	Auckland	1948/49
3	P. Moore	v England	The Oval	1966
3	E.A. Badham	v Australia	Sydney	1978/79
3	M.A. M.Lewis	v England	Wanganui	1991/92
3	D.A. Hockley	v England	Scarborough	1996

CATCHES IN A MATCH

4	S.M. Gilchrist	v India	Ahmedabad	1984/85
4	M.A.M. Lewis	v England	Wanganui	1991/92

RECORD PARTNERSHIPS

1st	150	M.K. Fruin & D.A. Hockley	v England	Guildford	1996
2nd	146	M.K. Fruin & K.E. Flavell	v England	Scarborough	1996
3rd	106	K.E. Flavell & E.C. Drumm	v England	Guildford	1996
4th	94	I.J. Powell & R.U. McKenzie	v Australia	Dunedin	1960/61
5th	94*	E.C. Drumm & D.A. Hockley	v England	Guildford	1996
6th	83	D.A. Hockley & K.V. Gunn	v Australia	Christchurch	1989/90
7th	90	B.A. Brentnall & J.A. Burley	v England	Birmingham	1966
8th	87	C.E. Marett & J.M. Saulbrey	v Australia	Wellington	1974/75
9th	60*	K.E. Flavell & K.D. Brown	v England	Scarborough	1996
10th	55*	C.M. Oyler & J. Lord	v England	The Oval	1966

SUMMARY OF TEST CAREER RECORDS

Most Matches

D.A. Hockley	19	P. Blackler	12	J. Clark	11
P.F. McKelvey	15	J.D. Doull	11	J.E. Harris	10
J. Lord	15	J.M. Saulbrey	11	B.A. Brentnall	10

Most Runs

D.A. Hockley	1301	K.E. Flavell	473	J.E. Stead	433
J.D. Doull	779	A. McKenna	465	S.J. Rattray	412
P.F. McKelvey	699	E.C. Drumm	433	B.L. Bevege	400
J. Clark	482				

Most Wickets

J. Lord	55	J.M. Coulston	19	P. Blackler	18
J.M. Saulbrey	35	J.A. Turner	19	K.M. Keenan	15
J.A. Burley	21	S.J. Rattray	19	J.E. Harris	15
P.F. Carrick	21	C.A. Campbell	18		

Most Wicketkeeping Dismissals

	Ct	*St*	*Total*
B.A. Brentnall	15	12	27
E.M. Ryan	3	11	14
I.C.P. Jagersma	10	2	12
S.L. Illingworth	5	5	10

Most Catches

D.A. Hockley	9
P.F. McKelvey	8
E.A. Badham	7
A. McKenna	7
J. Clark	7

ONE-DAY INTERNATIONAL CAREER RECORDS

	M	In	NO	HS	Runs	Ave	100s	50s	Ct	St	O	M	R	W	Ave	R/O	Best
E.P.Allan	7	6	1	17	42	8.40	-	-	2	-	59	8	162	3	54.00	2.75	1-22
T.L.Anderson	26	25	0	85	440	17.60	-	2	9	-							
L.M.Astle	1	-	-	-	-	-	-	-	-	-							
E.A.Badham	13	10	1	30	86	9.55	-	-	5	-	135.3	33	290	12	24.16	2.14	2-14
H.R.Bastion	3	-	-	-	-	-	-	-	1	-	20	2	57	2	28.50	2.85	1-12
S.W.Bates	26	24	1	168	771	33.52	2	2	7	-	124.4	8	579	24	24.12	4.64	4-7
B.L.Bevege	16	16	1	101	488	32.53	1	3	3	-	22.2	7	48	3	16.00	2.16	3-17
B.A.Brentnall	5	3	0	18	40	13.33	-	-	3	3							
K.D.Brown	14	6	3	9*	19	6.33	-	-	4	-	86.4	14	252	10	25.20	2.90	2-8
S.H.Brown	18	9	4	17*	59	11.80	-	-	5	-	170	63	308	19	16.21	1.81	2-3
N.J.Browne	89	71	23	61	1456	30.33	-	8	22	-	529.2	47	2014	60	33.56	3.80	4-20
S.K.Burke	36	18	9	10*	73	8.11	-	-	3	-	256	27	1019	25	40.76	3.98	3-17
J.A.Burley	2	1	0	7	7	7.00	-	-	-	-	13	3	28	0	-	2.15	-
A.K.Burrows	5	2	2	3*	4	-	-	-	2	-	29.1	1	124	4	31.00	4.25	2-15
V.L.Burtt	9	8	0	46	168	21.00	-	-	4	-	6	0	31	2	15.50	5.17	2-31
D.Caird	4	4	1	45	72	24.00	-	-	-	-							
C.A.Campbell	85	30	15	12	69	4.60	-	-	15	-	753	150	2018	78	25.87	2.68	3-15
R.H.Candy	7	5	4	2*	3	3.00	-	-	-	-	35	4	144	3	48.00	4.11	1-25
P.F.Carrick	3	2	1	6*	7	7.00	-	-	1	-	29	1	106	6	17.66	3.66	3-43
S.E.Charteris	5	3	1	20*	20	10.00	-	-	-	-	16	0	102	1	102.00	6.07	1-32
J.Clark	31	31	1	85	875	29.16	-	7	5	-							
D.A.Costello	7	2	1	1	1	1.00	-	-	1	-	56.4	8	139	2	69.50	2.45	2-37
S.D.Cowles	5	5	0	46	93	18.60	-	-	2	-	5	0	24	0	-	4.80	-
I.Cronin-Knight	3	3	0	36	41	13.66	-	-	-	-							
S.F.M.Devine	30	24	6	40	237	13.16	-	-	10	-	233.3	17	992	27	36.74	4.24	3-38
A.M.Dodd	31	20	11	20*	155	17.22	-	-	10	-	207.1	24	755	28	26.96	3.64	3-13
L.R.Doolan	16	12	4	48	227	28.37	-	-	5	-	98.3	15	385	17	22.64	3.90	3-21
J.D.Doull	5	5	0	42	64	12.80	-	-	2	-							
E.C.Drumm	101	94	13	116	2844	35.11	2	19	24	-	257	53	778	37	21.02	3.03	4-31
J.R.Dunning	22	21	4	89	346	20.35	-	1	4	-	157	12	527	13	40.53	3.36	3-29
M.F.Fahey	45	44	2	91	1217	28.97	-	12	12	-							
P.B.Flannery	17	17	2	49*	258	17.20	-	-	3	-							
K.E.Flavell	38	33	9	54	719	29.95	-	2	5	-	70	15	156	7	22.28	2.23	2-5
D.L.Ford	3	2	0	35	46	23.00	-	-	1	-	6	0	32	0	-	5.33	-
F.E.Fraser	5	3	2	54*	94	94.00	-	1	1	-							
L.M.Fraser	13	7	1	8	31	5.16	-	-	2	-	117	20	294	12	24.50	2.51	3-21
M.K.Fruin	23	23	4	51	385	20.26	-	1	4	1							
J.A.Fryer	7	1	1	1*	1	-	-	-	-	-	33	9	115	10	11.50	3.48	3-8
S.M.Gilchrist	8	5	1	12	19	4.75	-	-	4	-	77	21	202	7	28.85	2.62	3-20
A.J.Green	14	8	5	17*	23	7.66	-	-	3	-	108.3	17	392	12	32.66	3.61	5-15
P.A.Gruber	2	1	0	0	0	0.00	-	-	-	-	10	3	35	0	-	3.50	-
K.V.Gunn	45	34	9	52	461	18.44	-	1	14	-	458.5	110	1113	53	21.00	2.42	5-22
K.Hadlee	1	1	0	14	14	14.00	-	-	-	-							
L.R.V.S.Harford	3	3	0	9	20	6.66	-	-	-	-	7	0	30	0	-	4.29	-
J.E.Harris	45	24	12	19*	99	8.25	-	-	9	-	414.2	98	1124	61	18.42	2.71	4-8
S.A.Harris	2	1	1	1*	1	-	-	-	-	-	3	0	19	0	-	6.33	-
C.E.Henshilwood	2	1	1	15*	15	-	-	-	-	-							
D.A.Hockley	118	115	18	117	4064	41.89	4	34	41	-	253.4	41	853	20	42.65	3.36	3-49
S.L.Illingworth	37	29	7	51	342	15.54	-	1	27	21							
I.C.P.Jagersma	34	27	4	58*	453	19.69	-	2	24	9	22	5	48	4	12.00	2.18	2-14
Y.Kainuku	2	2	0	4	4	2.00	-	-	-	-	12	2	49	0	-	4.08	-
K.M.Keenan	55	36	9	57*	348	12.88	-	1	9	-	452	72	1253	70	17.90	2.77	4-5
R.J.Kember	10	10	0	64	155	15.50	-	1	3	-							
F.S.King	15	10	3	31	81	11.57	-	-	2	-	108.1	14	404	21	19.23	3.73	4-24
P.D.Kinsella	20	20	3	57	443	26.05	-	2	-	-							
K.Le Comber	15	14	4	135*	442	44.20	1	2	2	-							
B.J.Legg	18	13	3	17	79	7.90	-	-	2	-	199.4	62	394	20	19.70	1.97	3-4
M.A.M.Lewis	78	73	12	105	1372	22.49	1	4	30	-	5	0	32	0	-	6.40	-
L.Lindsay	2	1	0	27	27	27.00	-	-	-	-	13	0	42	2	21.00	3.23	2-26
J.Lord	15	13	0	25	101	7.76	-	-	2	-	132.3	25	318	25	12.72	2.40	6-10
M.L.Lynch	6	6	0	29	105	17.50	-	-	-	-							
C.E.Marett	14	12	2	24	149	14.90	-	-	-	-	126.5	24	310	16	19.37	2.44	3-14
K.J.Martin	18	18	2	79	302	18.87	-	1	6	3							

	M	In	NO	HS	Runs	Ave	100s	50s	Ct	St	O	M	R	W	Ave	R/O	Best
E.T.McDonald	3	-	-	-	-	-	-	-	1	-	24	4	50	5	10.00	2.08	2-17
K.McDonald	6	6	0	34	80	13.33	-	-	1	-							
S.J.McGlashan	80	76	13	97*	1455	23.09	-	5	17	-							
P.F.McKelvey	15	14	4	42	214	21.40	-	-	2	-							
A.McKenna	14	13	0	39	214	16.46	-	-	-	-							
S.McLauchlan	29	21	5	34*	137	8.56	-	-	6	-	227.5	47	665	19	35.00	2.91	2-6
B.H.McNeill	23	18	8	88*	193	19.30	-	1	8	-	175.1	20	680	23	29.56	3.88	6-32
R.C.Milburn	15	14	1	71	237	18.23	-	1	7	5							
L.E.Milliken	48	18	8	21	110	11.00	-	-	13	-	370	45	1409	59	23.88	3.81	5-25
K.S.Molloy	5	2	1	0*	0	0.00	-	-	2	-	36	8	99	4	24.75	2.75	2-16
S.R.M.Morris	8	1	0	5	5	5.00	-	-	-	-	69	12	175	7	25.00	2.54	2-13
L.J.Murdoch	25	22	3	69	417	21.94	-	1	4	-							
K.J.Musson	13	10	2	31	86	10.75	-	-	3	-	87.2	12	253	10	25.30	2.89	3-22
C.M.Nicholson	35	22	10	73*	195	16.25	-	1	13	-	272.4	62	707	38	18.60	2.59	4-18
A.M.O'Leary	19	18	3	91*	497	33.13	-	3	3	-							
J.B.Olson	4	4	1	9*	17	5.66	-	-	-	-	27	9	52	4	13.00	1.93	3-16
G.L.Page	2	1	0	5	5	5.00	-	-	-	-	17.2	3	46	6	7.66	2.65	6-20
N.Payne	65	64	7	93	1178	20.66	-	4	17	-	158	48	407	20	20.35	2.57	3-20
M.H.Peters	16	12	5	24	79	11.28	-	-	3	-	155.5	63	291	19	15.31	1.86	2-3
K.V.Plummer	11	10	1	32	100	11.11	-	-	2	-	10	0	36	0	-	3.60	-
L.M.Powell	5	4	0	70	73	18.25	-	1	1	-							
R.H.Priest	20	16	6	42	232	23.20	-	-	14	8							
K.L.Pulford	39	34	0	95	674	19.82	-	3	9	-	152.1	10	584	22	26.54	3.83	4-5
R.J.Pullar	51	32	11	27*	253	12.04	-	-	14	-	430.1	80	1215	74	16.41	2.82	5-7
K.A.Ramel	47	37	7	41	519	17.30	-	-	13	-	204.3	26	729	35	20.82	3.56	3-26
S.J.Rattray	15	15	7	60*	305	38.12	-	1	1	-	123.1	16	399	11	36.27	3.23	2-33
R.J.Rolls	104	91	3	114	2201	25.01	2	12	90	43							
E.F.Rouse	3	3	0	48	90	30.00	-	-	-	-							
J.A.Russell	5	4	1	8*	8	2.66	-	-	-	-	26	3	84	1	84.00	3.23	1-20
E.M.Ryan	15	5	1	6*	17	4.25	-	-	13	8							
J.M.Saulbrey	5	5	3	22*	75	37.50	-	-	-	-	43	12	100	4	25.00	2.33	2-32
A.E.Satterthwaite	25	23	2	73	525	25.00	-	2	4	-	29	4	127	1	127.00	4.38	1-27
N.Scripps	7	3	3	9*	12	-	-	-	-	-	50.2	6	206	6	34.33	4.09	2-17
V.S.Sexton	2	2	0	9	12	6.00	-	-	-	-							
E.A.Signal	19	12	5	28*	79	11.28	-	-	5	-	130.3	23	496	7	70.85	3.80	2-26
R.J.Signal	6	3	1	8	12	6.00	-	-	2	-	27	2	89	2	44.50	3.30	1-10
L.J.Simpson	12	11	1	23*	95	9.50	-	-	1	-							
R.J.Steele	32	12	6	8*	41	6.83	-	-	6	-	293	57	831	34	24.44	2.84	3-10
H.M.Tiffen	117	111	16	100	2919	30.72	1	18	32	-	276	43	955	49	19.48	3.46	4-43
E.A.Travers	3	-	-	-	-	-	-	-	-	-							
D.M.Trow	2	1	1	1*	1	-	-	-	1	-	12	3	18	4	4.50	1.50	3-8
S.J.Tsukigawa	42	39	6	78*	730	22.12	-	2	9	-	255.5	19	1121	35	32.02	4.38	4-43
M.F.Tunupopo	3	-	-	-	-	-	-	-	2	-	18	4	57	0	-	3.17	-
J.A.Turner	30	14	2	15	54	4.50	-	-	6	-	265.2	42	695	28	24.82	2.61	5-5
N.J.Turner	28	26	2	114	624	26.00	1	2	4	-							
A.L.Watkins	84	75	5	111	1511	21.58	2	4	29	-	612.2	64	2353	76	30.96	3.84	4-2
H.M.Watson	66	48	10	115*	580	15.26	1	-	20	-	414.3	67	1287	54	23.83	3.10	3-14
N.M.Williams	19	13	2	21*	80	7.27	-	-	1	-	110.5	19	374	15	24.93	3.37	3-37

TEAM RECORDS

Highest Totals

455-5	v Pakistan	Christchurch	1996/97
373-7	v Pakistan	Sydney	2008/09
335-4	v Netherlands	Amstelveen	2002
297-5	v Netherlands	Sydney	1988/89
291-6	v England	Chennai	2006/07

Lowest Totals

58	v Australia	Melbourne	1984/85
61	v Australia	Wellington	1998/99
72	v England	Blackpool	2007
73	v India	Indore	1984/85
80	v India	Auckland	1981/82

INDIVIDUAL RECORDS

Centuries

168	S.W. Bates v Pakistan at Sydney	2008/09
135*	K. LeComber v Ireland at Dublin	1996
122	S.W. Bates v India at Chennai	2006/07
117	D.A. Hockley v England at Chester-le-Street	1996
116	E.C. Drumm v England at Oamaru	2000/01
115*	H.M. Watson v Ireland at Dublin	2004
114	N.J. Turner v Netherlands at Sydney	1988/89
114	R.J. Rolls v Australia at Lincoln	2001/02
111	A.L. Mason v England at Blackpool	2007
108*	E.C. Drumm v South Africa at Lincoln	2000/01
105	M.A.M. Lewis v Pakistan at Christchurch	1996/97
104*	R.J. Rolls v Australia at Chennai	2006/07
102	A.L. Mason v Australia at Darwin	2007/08
101	B.L. Bevege v International XI at Auckland	1981/82
100*	D.A. Hockley v Sri Lanka at Chandigarh	1997/98
100	D.A. Hockley v West Indies at Chandigarh	1997/98
100	D.A. Hockley v Australia at Melbourne	1999/00
100	H.M. Tiffen v Pakistan at Sydney	2008/09

Five Wickets in an Innings

6-10	J. Lord v India at Auckland	1981/82
6-20	G.L. Page v Trinidad & Tobago at St Albans	1973
6-32	B.H. McNeill v England at Lincoln	2007/08
5-5	J.A. Turner v Netherlands at Lindfield	1993
5-7	R.J. Pullar v South Africa at Hamilton	1998/99
5-10	R.J. Pullar v India at St Saviour	2002
5-15	A.J Green v Ireland at Dublin	2004
5-22	K.V. Gunn v Australia at Wellington	1989/90
5-25	L.E. Milliken v India, Pretoria	2004/05

Hat-tricks

7.1-1-18-3	J.E. Harris	v West Indies	Chiswick	1993
8-2-22-3	E.C. Drumm	v Australia	Adelaide	1995/96

Most Economical Bowling

10-7-3-0	C.A. Campbell	v Netherlands	Christchurch	2000/01
12-9-4-3	B.J. Legg	v Netherlands	Melbourne	1988/89
12-9-5-3	J.E. Harris	v Netherlands	Lindfield	1993
11.2-7-5-5	J.A. Turner	v Netherlands	Lindfield	1993
10-6-5-4	K.M. Keenan	v West Indies	Chandigarh	1997/98

Most Expensive Bowling

9-1-68-1	L.E. Milliken	v Australia	Auckland	2003/04
8-0-64-0	A.L. Mason	v Australia	Brisbane	2006/07
7-0-63-0	F.S. King	v Australia	Lincoln	2001/02
10-0-60-2	L.E. Milliken	v England	Chennai	2006/07
10-0-59-1	J.E. Harris	v Australia	Auckland	1996/97

Wicketkeeping

DISMISSALS IN AN INNINGS

	(ct/st)				
6	(4/2)	S.L. Illingworth	v Australia	Beckenham	1993
4	(2/2)	E.M. Ryan	v International XI	Auckland	1981/82
4	(2/2)	I.C.P. Jagersma	v Netherlands	Sydney	1988/89
4	(3/1)	S.L. Illingworth	v India	Ealing	1993
4	(3/1)	R.J. Rolls	v England	Oamaru	2000/01
4	(2/2)	R.J. Rolls	v England	Lincoln	2000/01
4	(4/0)	R.J. Rolls	v Australia	Lincoln	2001/02
4	(4/0)	R.J. Rolls	v India	Durham	2002
4	(4/0)	R.J. Rolls	v Sri Lanka	Pretoria	2004/05
4	(3/1)	R.J. Rolls	v Ireland	Pretoria	2004/05
4	(2/2)	R.J. Rolls	v India	Lincoln	2005/06

Fielding

CATCHES IN AN INNINGS

3	S.H. Brown	v England	Hastings	1984
3	S.M. Gilchrist	v India	Indore	1984/85
3	D.A. Hockley	v Australia	Melbourne	1990/91
3	K.A. Ramel	v Netherlands	Ghaziabad	1997/98
3	D.A. Hockley	v Sri Lanka	Chandigarh	1997/98
3	H.M. Watson	v Netherlands	Christchurch	2000/01
3	H.M. Tiffen	v England	Lincoln	2002/03
3	S.W. Bates	v England	Taunton	2007
3	S.J. Tsukigawa	v England	Lincoln	2007/08

RECORD PARTNERSHIPS

1st	180	B.L. Bevege & L.J. Murdoch	v International XI	Auckland	1981/82
2nd	262	H.M.Tiffen & S.W. Bates	v Pakistan	Sydney	2008/09
3rd	138	D.A. Hockley & M.A.M. Lewis	v Australia	Wellington	1996/97
4th	116	D.A. Hockley & E.C. Drumm	v Australia	Sydney	1997/98
5th	108*	R.J. Rolls & S.J. Tsukigawa	v Australia	Chennai	2006/07
6th	139*	S.J. McGlashan & N.J. Browne	v South Africa	Bowral	2008/09
7th	104*	S.J. Tsukigawa & N.J. Browne	v England	Chennai	2006/07
8th	74	A.E.Satterthwaite & L.R.Doolan	v Australia	Whangarei	2008/09
9th	58	K.V. Gunn & S. McLauchlan	v Australia	Wellington	1991/92
10th	33	E.C. Drumm & C.A. Campbell	v Australia	Wellington	1996/97

SUMMARY OF ONE-DAY INTERNATIONAL CAREER RECORDS

Most Matches

D.A. Hockley	118	N.J. Browne	89	M.A.M. Lewis	78
H.M. Tiffen	117	C.A. Campbell	85	H.M. Watson	66
R.J. Rolls	104	A.L. Watkins	84	K.M. Keenan	55
E.C. Drumm	101	S.J. McGlashan	80	R.J. Pullar	51

Most Runs

D.A. Hockley	4064	A.L. Watkins	1511	M.F. Fahey	1217
H.M. Tiffen	2919	N.J. Browne	1456	J. Clark	875
E.C. Drumm	2844	S.J. McGlashan	1455	S.W. Bates	771
R.J. Rolls	2201	M.A.M. Lewis	1372	S.J.Tsukigawa	730

Most Wickets

C.A. Campbell	78	J.E. Harris	61	K.V. Gunn	53
A.L. Watkins	76	N.J. Browne	60	H.M. Tiffen	49
R.J. Pullar	74	L.E. Milliken	59	C.M. Nicholson	38
K.M. Keenan	70	H.M. Watson	54	E.C. Drumm	37

Most Wicketkeeping Dismissals

	Ct	*St*	*Total*
R.J. Rolls	90	43	133
S.L. Illingworth	26	21	47
I.C.P. Jagersma	24	9	33
R.H. Priest	14	8	22
E.M. Ryan	13	8	21

Most Catches

D.A. Hockley	41
H.M. Tiffen	32
M.A.M. Lewis	30
A.L. Watkins	29
E.C. Drumm	24
N.J. Browne	22
H.M. Watson	20

TWENTY20 INTERNATIONAL CAREER RECORDS

	M	*In*	*NO*	*HS*	*Runs*	*Ave*	*100s*	*50s*	*Ct*	*St*	*O*	*M*	*R*	*W*	*Ave*	*R/O*	*Best*
S.W.Bates	13	13	1	62	344	28.66	-	2	4	-	28.1	1	199	4	49.75	7.06	1-20
N.J.Browne	14	13	5	32	122	15.25	-	-	4	-	30	0	190	9	21.11	6.33	3-14
S.M.Bullen	2	-	-	-	-	-	-	-	-	-	7	0	39	2	19.50	5.57	2-20
S.K.Burke	7	2	1	3*	6	6.00	-	-	-	-	23	1	149	7	21.28	6.48	3-15
R.H.Candy	1	-	-	-	-	-	-	-	-	-	2	0	18	0	-	9.00	-
S.E.Charteris	2	1	1	5*	5	-	-	-	1	-	4	0	17	1	17.00	4.25	1-17
S.F.M.Devine	10	8	2	23	73	12.16	-	-	5	-	33	1	176	8	22.00	5.33	1-9
L.R.Doolan	9	8	1	41	102	14.57	-	-	-	-	24	1	146	5	29.20	6.08	3-16
M.F.Fahey	2	2	0	43	60	30.00	-	-	-	-							
P.B.Flannery	1	1	0	18	18	18.00	-	-	-	-							
A.J.Green	1	1	0	3	3	3.00	-	-	-	-	4	0	20	2	10.00	5.00	2-20
R.J.Kember	3	3	0	15	22	7.33	-	-	-	-							
M.A.M.Lewis	1	1	0	25	25	25.00	-	-	-	-							
V.J.Lind	2	2	0	20	29	14.50	-	-	-	-							
K.J.Martin	6	4	0	15	18	4.50	-	-	-	-							
S.J.McGlashan	16	15	1	44	162	11.57	-	-	4	-							
B.H.McNeill	2	-	-	-	-	-	-	-	-	-	5	0	30	0	-	6.00	-
R.C.Milburn	2	1	1	1*	1	-	-	-	-	1							
L.E.Milliken	1	-	-	-	-	-	-	-	-	-	4	0	28	1	28.00	7.00	1-28
R.H.Priest	13	8	2	18	54	9.00	-	-	4	5							
K.L.Pulford	9	5	1	29	49	12.25	-	-	1	-	28	1	132	7	18.85	4.71	1-8
R.J.Rolls	2	2	0	41	80	40.00	-	-	2	1							
S.E.A.Ruck	7	2	1	1	1	1.00	-	-	-	-	24	0	113	9	12.55	4.71	3-12
A.E.Satterthwaite	13	11	2	25	115	12.77	-	-	2	-	10	0	57	8	7.12	5.70	6-17
R.J.Steele	1	-	-	-	-	-	-	-	2	-	4	0	14	0	-	3.50	-
H.M.Tiffen	9	8	1	30	121	17.28	-	-	6	-							
S.J.Tsukigawa	15	13	2	22	118	10.72	-	-	2	-	25	0	170	5	34.00	6.80	2-19
A.L.Watkins	15	15	3	89*	391	32.58	-	3	4	-	30	0	180	7	25.71	6.00	3-27
H.M.Watson	8	3	2	9*	16	16.00	-	-	2	-	28	2	152	7	21.71	5.43	3-13

Highest Totals

186-7	v South Africa	Taunton	2007
158-6	v West Indies	Taunton	2009
152-6	v England	Bath	2007
150-6	v England	Taunton	2007

Highest Individual Scores

89*	A.L. Watkins v India at Nottingham	2009
73*	A.L. Watkins v Australia at Taunton	2009
62	S.W. Bates v South Africa at Taunton	2007
60	S.W. Bates v West Indies at Taunton	2009
54*	A.L. Watkins v England at Bath	2007

Best Bowling in an Innings

6-17	A.E. Satterthwaite v England at Taunton	2007

STATE LEAGUE TWENTY20

2008/09

In a change from the inaugural season the 2008/09 competition culminated in a final. The two teams in the State League final were also the top two teams in the Twenty20 competition and the two finals were staged at the Basin Reserve on successive days.

Wellington's Lucy Doolan was the leading run scorer in the Twenty20 competition with 212 runs at an average of 53.00 and Amanda Cooper, also from Wellington, was the leading wicket taker with nine wickets at an economy rate of 6.20.

Final points were:

	P	*W*	*L*	*NR*	*Points*
Canterbury	5	4	1	–	16
Wellington	5	3	1	1	14
Central Districts	5	2	2	1	10
Auckland	5	2	3	–	8
Northern Districts	5	1	3	1	6
Otago	5	1	3	1	6

CENTRAL DISTRICTS v CANTERBURY — State League T20

at Pukekura Park, New Plymouth on 5 December, 2008
Toss : Canterbury. Umpires : K.C. Manley & E.A. Watkin
***Central Districts won by 10 runs.** Points: Central Districts 4, Canterbury 0*

CENTRAL DISTRICTS

	Runs	Mins	Balls	6s	4s
K.M.Sutherland c & b Satterthwaite	13	37	17	-	-
A.L.Mason* lbw b Burke	21	16	18	2	-
R.H.Priest† c Milburn b Burke	0	1	1	-	-
S.J.McGlashan c Milburn b Satterthwaite	1	4	8	-	-
R.H.Candy c Fahey b Bermingham	50	32	32	1	6
K.E.Broadmore c Bermingham b McNeill	18	31	24	-	2
K.C.R.Rangi not out	11	20	15	-	-
K.M.Winkley not out	6	7	5	-	-
M.A.Frey					
C.J.Sim					
A.K.Burrows					
C.J.Sim					
Extras (w 5)	5				
TOTAL (20 overs) (6 wkts)	**125**	77			

CANTERBURY

	Runs	Mins	Balls	6s	4s
F.L.Mackay b Burrows	7	10	9	-	1
M.L.Mitchell st Priest b Broadmore	11	12	11	-	2
M.F.Fahey run out	13	27	19	-	-
H.M.Tiffen* c Broadmore b Burrows	50	53	49	-	5
A.E.Satterthwaite run out	1	4	7	-	-
A.C.Boyce b Burrows	10	13	11	-	1
R.C.Milburn† not out	13	13	10	-	-
E.M.Bermingham b Sim	0	1	2	-	-
J.C.Brehaut not out	5	2	2	-	1
B.H.McNeill					
S.K.Burke					
L.M.M.Tahuhu					
Extras (b 2, lb 1, w 2)	5				
TOTAL (20 overs) (7 wkts)	**115**	71			

Bowling	*O*	*M*	*R*	*W*
CANTERBURY				
Burke	4	0	17	2
McNeill	4	0	24	1
Satterthwaite	4	1	14	2
Mackay	3	0	28	0
Mitchell	1	0	19	0
Bermingham	4	0	23	1
CENTRAL DISTRICTS				
Burrows	4	0	26	3
Broadmore	4	0	6	1
Candy	4	0	26	0
Mason	4	1	25	0
Sim	4	0	29	1

Fall of Wickets	***CD***	***C***
1st	26	19
2nd	26	19
3rd	27	58
4th	52	60
5th	92	87
6th	110	106
7th	-	108
8th	-	-
9th	-	-
10th	-	-

NORTHERN DISTRICTS v WELLINGTON — State League T20

at Blake Park, Mt Maunganui on 5 December, 2008
Toss : Wellington. Umpires : P.D. Jones & W.R. Knights
***Wellington won by 33 runs.** Points: Wellington 4, Northern Districts 0*

WELLINGTON

	Runs	Mins	Balls	6s	4s
L.R.Doolan not out	57	77	59	-	4
S.M.P.Sim c Fraser b Dodd	4	17	11	-	-
S.F.M.Devine c Huddleston b Milliken	40	31	28	1	3
M.G.Wakefield† run out	27	20	15	-	4
E.C.Perry not out	16	6	7	-	2
S.J.Bradbury					
M.J.Hodgson					
A.E.Cooper*					
S.E.A.Ruck					
A.M.Dodd					
K.A.Tomlinson					
A.C.Stockwell					
Extras (b 1, lb 8, w 18)	27				
TOTAL (20 overs) (3 wkts)	**171**	77			

NORTHERN DISTRICTS

	Runs	Mins	Balls	6s	4s
K.L.Pulford st Wakefield b Doolan	30	24	26	-	4
J.M.Fraser lbw b Cooper	23	44	29	-	3
A.J.Wilkins* b Perry	54	44	38	-	7
N.J.Browne b Cooper	0	1	1	-	-
A.M.Peterson lbw b Cooper	0	1	1	-	-
L.E.Milliken run out	4	3	2	-	1
H.R.Huddleston not out	19	25	19	-	2
M.J.G.Nielsen not out	1	8	7	-	-
N.C.Dodd					
A.Swart†					
E.M.Wilson					
E.L.Bailey					
Extras (w 3, nb 4)	7				
TOTAL (20 overs) (6 wkts)	**138**	78			

Bowling	*O*	*M*	*R*	*W*
NORTHERN DISTRICTS				
Browne	4	0	19	0
Pulford	3	0	18	0
Dodd	2	0	16	1
Huddleston	2	0	23	0
Milliken	4	0	25	1
Wilson	3	0	34	0
Peterson	2	0	27	0
WELLINGTON				
Devine	4	0	17	0
Ruck	4	0	31	0
Doolan	2	0	16	1
Dodd	4	0	19	0
Cooper	4	0	40	3
Perry	2	0	15	1

Fall of Wickets	***W***	***ND***
1st	22	44
2nd	100	86
3rd	149	86
4th	-	86
5th	-	94
6th	-	129
7th	-	-
8th	-	-
9th	-	-
10th	-	-

Cooper peformed the hat trick when she dismissed Fraser, Browne and Peterson with the 2nd, 3rd and 4th balls of her 3rd over.

OTAGO v AUCKLAND — State League T20

at Molyneux Park, Alexandra on 5 December, 2008
Toss : Otago. Umpires : C.B. Gaffaney & R.S. Kinsey
***Auckland won by 6 wickets.** Points: Auckland 4, Otago 0*

OTAGO

	Runs	Mins	Balls	6s	4s
S.W.Bates c Bullen b Scripps	20	12	16	-	3
K.J.Martin† c Perkins b Bullen	28	32	20	-	3
M.J.Kane st Lind b Tremaine	6	9	10	-	-
S.J.Tsukigawa* st Lind b Mistry	25	35	28	-	2
L.M.Grant lbw b Gruber	2	7	5	-	-
L.M.M.Foote st Lind b Gruber	1	6	5	-	-
E.M.Campbell c Barriball b Murphy	5	5	7	-	-
K.J.Crowley st Lind b Mistry	6	15	11	-	-
T.J.Morrison run out	6	8	8	-	-
A.M.Te Wake not out	0	3	3	-	-
T.R.Hopkinson lbw b Mistry	0	1	1	-	-
A.S.M.Kitchin					
Extras (b 5, w 1)	6				
TOTAL (19 overs)	**105**	71			

AUCKLAND

	Runs	Mins	Balls	6s	4s
W.L.Horneman c Campbell b Bates	13	9	12	-	2
V.J.Lind† run out	28	33	26	1	3
M.P.Murphy b Campbell	27	34	28	-	3
K.T.Perkins not out	26	27	28	-	3
M.L.Lynch b Morrison	6	11	9	-	-
S.R.H.Barriball not out	1	5	2	-	-
S.M.Bullen					
M.A.Tremaine					
P.Mistry					
P.A.Gruber*					
N.Scripps					
S.A.P.Hopkins					
Extras (lb 2, w 3)	5				
TOTAL (17.2 overs) (4 wkts)	**106**	62			

Bowling	*O*	*M*	*R*	*W*
AUCKLAND				
Mistry	4	0	27	3
Scripps	3	0	12	1
Tremaine	2	0	17	1
Gruber	4	0	17	2
Bullen	4	0	19	1
Murphy	2	0	8	1
OTAGO				
Bates	4	0	20	1
Hopkinson	1	0	14	0
Morrison	4	0	22	1
Tsukigawa	3.2	0	16	0
Campbell	4	0	23	1
Foote	1	0	9	0

Fall of Wickets	***O***	***A***
1st	28	16
2nd	45	62
3rd	70	78
4th	81	93
5th	87	-
6th	93	-
7th	95	-
8th	105	-
9th	105	-
10th	105	-

CANTERBURY v OTAGO

at Queen Elizabeth II Park, Christchurch on 19 December, 2008
Toss : Otago. Umpires : J.M. Busby & T.J. Parlane
***Canterbury won by 45 runs.** Points: Canterbury 4, Otago 0*

CANTERBURY

	Runs	Mins	Balls	6s	4s
H.M.Tiffen* run out	15	21	23	-	2
M.L.Mitchell b Bates	0	8	3	-	-
A.C.Boyce c Bates b Kitchin	31	37	28	1	1
A.E.Satterthwaite run out	18	26	22	-	-
E.M.Bermingham lbw b Kitchin	0	3	1	-	-
R.C.Milburn c Kitchin b Bates	10	21	14	-	-
J.C.Brehaut b Tsukigawa	18	14	17	-	1
K.A.Neilson† c Morrison b Tsukigawa	5	7	4	-	-
B.H.McNeill run out	5	6	5	-	-
S.K.Burke not out	5	3	3	-	-
F.L.Mackay					
L.M.M.Tahuhu					
Extras (b 1, lb 5, w 6)	12				
TOTAL (20 overs) (9 wkts)	**119**	77			

OTAGO

	Runs	Mins	Balls	6s	4s
K.J.Martin† b McNeill	2	6	5	-	-
S.W.Bates run out	9	22	17	-	-
M.J.Kane not out	32	67	52	-	-
S.J.Tsukigawa* c Tiffen b Satterthwaite	8	2	4	-	2
A.S.M.Kitchin b Burke	12	43	37	-	-
L.M.Grant not out	1	4	5	-	-
A.M.Te Wake					
K.J.Crowley					
T.J.Morrison					
L.M.M.Foote					
T.R.Hopkinson					
E.M.Campbell					
Extras (b 2, lb 1, w 7)	10				
TOTAL (20 overs) (4 wkts)	**74**	74			

Bowling	*O*	*M*	*R*	*W*
OTAGO				
Bates	4	0	15	2
Hopkinson	4	0	30	0
Tsukigawa	4	0	23	2
Kitchin	4	0	21	2
Morrison	4	0	24	0
CANTERBURY				
Burke	4	0	9	1
McNeill	4	0	17	1
Satterthwaite	4	0	21	1
Bermingham	4	1	12	0
Mackay	4	0	12	0

Fall of Wickets	***C***	***O***
1st	12	5
2nd	33	15
3rd	70	23
4th	72	70
5th	72	-
6th	101	-
7th	107	-
8th	111	-
9th	119	-
10th	-	-

NORTHERN DISTRICTS v CENTRAL DISTRICTS

at Blake Park, Mt Maunganui on 19 December, 2008
Toss : Northern Districts. Umpires : M.P. George & W.R. Knights
***Northern Districts won by 7 runs.** Points: Northern Districts 4, Central Districts 0*

NORTHERN DISTRICTS

	Runs	Mins	Balls	6s	4s
J.M.Fraser b Winkley	13	31	20	-	-
K.L.Pulford c Sutherland b Winkley	61	49	47	-	7
A.J.Wilkins*† c Rangi b McWilliams	50	30	34	1	5
N.J.Browne not out	15	19	14	-	1
L.E.Milliken not out	8	6	5	-	1
A.M.Peterson					
H.R.Huddleston					
N.C.Dodd					
M.J.G.Nielsen					
A.Swart					
E.M.Wilson					
E.L.Bailey					
Extras (w 5)	5				
TOTAL (20 overs) (3 wkts)	**152**	69			

CENTRAL DISTRICTS

	Runs	Mins	Balls	6s	4s
A.L.Mason* lbw b Pulford	2	9	5	-	-
K.M.Sutherland c Browne b Wilson	33	37	33	-	4
S.J.McGlashan lbw b Wilson	27	29	22	-	4
R.H.Candy c Browne b Wilson	1	6	4	-	-
R.H.Priest† st Wilkins b Bailey	21	20	19	-	2
K.E.Broadmore c Pulford b Milliken	25	28	21	-	2
K.M.Winkley c Pulford b Bailey	1	1	2	-	-
Z.A.McWilliams not out	15	15	10	-	2
K.C.R.Rangi not out	6	4	54	-	-
A.K.Burrows					
C.J.Sim					
M.A.Frey					
Extras (lb 4, w 9, nb 1)	14				
TOTAL (20 overs) (7 wkts)	**145**	78			

Bowling	*O*	*M*	*R*	*W*
CENTRAL DISTRICTS				
Mason	4	0	24	0
Burrows	4	0	29	0
McWilliams	4	0	37	1
Winkley	4	0	21	2
Broadmore	4	0	41	0
NORTHERN DISTRICTS				
Pulford	4	1	14	1
Huddleston	3	0	26	0
Wilson	4	0	38	3
Browne	4	0	20	0
Milliken	4	0	36	1
Bailey	1	0	7	2

Fall of Wickets	***ND***	***CD***
1st	62	8
2nd	107	65
3rd	134	67
4th	-	71
5th	-	108
6th	-	112
7th	-	134
8th	-	-
9th	-	-
10th	-	-

AUCKLAND v WELLINGTON — State League T20

at Eden Park Outer Oval, Auckland on 19 December, 2008
Toss : Wellington. Umpires : P.L. Gasston & D.G. Paterson
***Wellington won by 58 runs.** Points: Wellington 4, Auckland 0*

WELLINGTON

	Runs	Mins	Balls	6s	4s
L.R.Doolan b Bullen	37	36	34	-	6
E.C.Perry c Horneman b Coetzee	33	52	39	-	3
S.F.M.Devine c Lynch b Mistry	50	34	28	2	7
M.G.Wakefield run out	10	7	8	-	1
K.A.Tomlinson b Scripps	12	8	8	-	2
A.E.Cooper not out	2	3	3	-	-
M.J.Hodgson not out	1	1	1	-	-
S.J.Bradbury					
A.C.Stockwell†					
A.M.Dodd*					
S.E.A.Ruck					
O.R.Bupha-Intr					
Extras (lb 1, w 1, nb 1)	3				
TOTAL (20 overs) (5 wkts)	**148**	73			

AUCKLAND

	Runs	Mins	Balls	6s	4s
W.L.Horneman c Stockwell b Devine	6	7	7	-	1
V.J.Lind† c Cooper b Ruck	5	11	9	-	1
M.P.Murphy c Dodd b Devine	1	10	4	-	-
K.T.Perkins st Stockwell b Doolan	15	26	27	-	1
M.L.Lynch c Hodgson b Dodd	3	8	4	-	-
P.M.Yates run out	2	4	3	-	-
S.Coetzee c Ruck b Perry	17	19	17	-	2
S.R.H.Barriball lbw b Dodd	12	9	13	-	1
N.Scripps run out	8	10	9	-	1
P.Mistry not out	8	14	7	-	1
P.A.Gruber* b Devine	8	7	10	-	1
S.M.Bullen					
Extras (w 4, nb 1)	5				
TOTAL (18.1 overs)	**90**	67			

Bowling	*O*	*M*	*R*	*W*
AUCKLAND				
Scripps	4	0	21	1
Mistry	4	0	37	1
Coetzee	4	0	33	1
Gruber	4	0	38	0
Bullen	4	0	18	1
WELLINGTON				
Devine	3.1	0	12	3
Ruck	3	0	8	1
Doolan	4	0	24	1
Dodd	4	0	19	2
Perry	2	0	13	1
Cooper	2	0	14	0

Fall of Wickets	*W*	*A*
1st	63	10
2nd	107	12
3rd	123	17
4th	144	24
5th	146	32
6th	-	38
7th	-	63
8th	-	64
9th	-	78
10th	-	90

CANTERBURY v NORTHERN DISTRICTS — State League T20

at Queen Elizabeth II Park, Christchurch on 27 December, 2008
Toss : Northern Districts. Umpires : P.J. Agent & K. Cross
***Canterbury won by 8 wickets.** Points: Canterbury 4, Northern Districts 0*

NORTHERN DISTRICTS

	Runs	Mins	Balls	6s	4s
K.L.Pulford lbw b Satterthwaite	19	30	23	-	2
M.J.G.Nielsen b Burke	0	9	9	-	-
A.J.Wilkins*† c Neilson b Burke	5	7	5	-	1
N.J.Browne c Neilson b Satterthwaite	5	22	11	-	-
L.E.Milliken run out	0	7	10	-	-
A.M.Peterson c Brehaut b Mackay	12	27	28	-	-
H.R.Huddleston run out	8	11	10	-	-
E.M.Wilson b McNeill	8	17	14	-	-
A.Swart run out	1	1	1	-	-
N.C.Dodd not out	5	5	5	-	-
N.P.Edwards not out	1	3	5	-	-
E.L.Bailey					
Extras (b 2, lb 2, w 1, nb 1)	6				
TOTAL (20 overs) (9 wkts)	**70**	74			

CANTERBURY

	Runs	Mins	Balls	6s	4s
M.F.Fahey not out	38	46	40	-	7
M.L.Mitchell c Wilkins b Browne	5	9	8	-	-
H.M.Tiffen* b Wilson	10	18	18	-	1
A.E.Satterthwaite not out	4	17	13	-	-
A.C.Boyce					
E.M.Bermingham					
R.C.Milburn†					
J.C.Brehaut					
B.H.McNeill					
S.K.Burke					
F.L.Mackay					
K.A.Neilson					
Extras (lb 6, w 9, nb 1)	16				
TOTAL (13 overs) (2 wkts)	**73**	46			

Bowling	*O*	*M*	*R*	*W*
CANTERBURY				
Burke	4	1	13	2
McNeill	4	0	11	1
Satterthwaite	4	0	14	2
Bermingham	4	0	15	0
Mackay	4	0	13	1
NORTHERN DISTRICTS				
Browne	3	0	9	1
Pulford	3	0	19	0
Milliken	4	0	16	0
Wilson	3	0	23	1

Fall of Wickets	*ND*	*C*
1st	5	11
2nd	15	39
3rd	29	-
4th	32	-
5th	32	-
6th	47	-
7th	61	-
8th	62	-
9th	63	-
10th	-	-

AUCKLAND v CENTRAL DISTRICTS — State League T20

at Melville Park, Auckland on 27 December, 2008
Toss : Auckland. Umpires : E.J. Gray & R.S. Kinsey
***Central Districts won by 7 wickets.** Points: Central Districts 4, Auckland 0*

AUCKLAND

	Runs	Mins	Balls	6s	4s
M.L.Lynch c McGlashan b McWilliams	16	19	18	-	3
V.J.Lind† c Norman Broadmore	1	7	6	-	-
M.P.Murphy c Norman b Broadmore	3	7	9	-	-
K.A.Blackwell run out	15	18	19	-	1
K.T.Perkins st Priest b Winkley	16	26	20	-	1
W.L.Horneman st Priest b Winkley	3	8	5	-	-
S.Coetzee not out	8	20	10	-	-
P.Mistry c McGlashan b Winkley	5	4	4	-	1
M.A.Tremaine c McGlashan b Winkley	8	6	10	-	1
P.A.Gruber* run out	0	2	2	-	-
N.Scripps b Burrows	0	1	4	-	-
S.M.Bullen					
Extras (b 1, lb 3, w 4, nb 1)	9				
TOTAL (17.4 overs)	**84**	64			

CENTRAL DISTRICTS

	Runs	Mins	Balls	6s	4s
K.M.Sutherland run out	2	12	12	-	-
A.L.Mason* c Blackwell b Gruber	22	48	45	-	1
K.E.Broadmore lbw b Bullen	9	10	7	-	1
S.J.McGlashan not out	19	41	17	-	1
R.H.Candy not out	28	16	18	-	5
R.H.Priest†					
K.M.Winkley					
S.L.Norman					
Z.A.McWilliams					
A.K.Burrows					
L.A.M.Hayes					
M.A.Frey					
Extras (w 5)	5				
TOTAL (16.3 overs) (3 wkts)	**85**	65			

Bowling	O	M	R	W
CENTRAL DISTRICTS				
Broadmore	4	0	16	2
McWilliams	4	0	18	1
Hayes	2	0	15	0
Mason	2	0	9	0
Winkley	3	0	10	4
Burrows	2.4	0	12	1
AUCKLAND				
Scripps	3.3	0	21	0
Bullen	4	1	7	1
Gruber	4	0	17	1
Mistry	3	0	20	0
Coetzee	1	0	9	0
Tremaine	1	0	11	0

Fall of Wickets

	A	*CD*
1st	3	3
2nd	16	19
3rd	21	49
4th	48	-
5th	61	-
6th	63	-
7th	73	-
8th	81	-
9th	84	-
10th	84	-

WELLINGTON v OTAGO — State League T20

at Karori Park, Wellington on 27 December, 2008
Toss : Otago. Umpires : R. Allen & B.G. Frost
***Wellington won by 69 runs.** Points: Wellington 4, Otago 0*

WELLINGTON

	Runs	Mins	Balls	6s	4s
L.R.Doolan st Martin b Tsukigawa	28	31	22	-	5
E.C.Perry b Bates	8	8	6	-	1
S.F.M.Devine b Askew	2	9	4	-	-
M.G.Wakefield b Askew	61	49	44	1	6
A.E.Cooper lbw b Morrison	15	24	20	-	1
K.A.Tomlinson run out	6	21	15	-	-
M.J.Hodgson run out	0	3	4	-	-
A.M.Dodd* not out	6	6	5	-	-
S.J.Bradbury					
A.C.Stockwell†					
S.E.A.Ruck					
O.R.Bupha-Intr					
Extras (b 1, lb 3, w 7)	11				
TOTAL (20 overs) (7 wkts)	**137**	83			

OTAGO

	Runs	Mins	Balls	6s	4s
K.J.Martin† run out	0	1	1	-	-
S.W.Bates c & b Doolan	35	43	38	-	1
M.J.Kane b Ruck	7	7	6	-	-
S.J.Tsukigawa* run out	4	7	6	-	-
A.S.M.Kitchin st Stockwell b Dodd	0	4	4	-	-
L.R.F.Askew b Cooper	12	25	20	-	2
E.M.Campbell c Wakefield b Doolan	0	3	3	-	-
K.J.Crowley c Perry b Doolan	3	11	11	-	-
T.J.Morrison not out	1	12	8	-	-
L.M.M.Foote b Cooper	0	1	1	-	-
T.R.Hopkinson b Cooper	0	2	3	-	-
L.M.Grant					
Extras (lb 1, w 4, nb 1)	6				
TOTAL (16.4 overs)	**68**	67			

Bowling	O	M	R	W
OTAGO				
Bates	4	0	29	1
Hopkinson	2	0	14	0
Askew	4	0	25	2
Tsukigawa	4	0	30	1
Morrison	4	0	24	1
Campbell	2	0	11	0
WELLINGTON				
Devine	2	0	12	0
Ruck	4	0	18	1
Dodd	4	0	25	1
Doolan	4	1	12	3
Cooper	2.4	2	0	3

Fall of Wickets

	W	*O*
1st	16	0
2nd	37	13
3rd	57	20
4th	106	25
5th	126	64
6th	128	64
7th	137	64
8th	-	68
9th	-	68
10th	-	68

CANTERBURY v AUCKLAND — State League T20

at Redwood Park, Christchurch on 2 January, 2009
Toss : Auckland. Umpires : P.L. Gasston & P.B. Spall
***Canterbury won by 1 wicket.** Points: Canterbury 4, Auckland 0*

AUCKLAND

	Runs	Mins	Balls	6s	4s
V.J.Lind† c Bermingham b Satterthwaite	11	20	17	-	1
P.Mistry c Bermingham b McNeill	70	62	50	1	8
M.P.Murphy c McNeill b Mackay	25	24	16	-	3
R.J.Kember run out	10	27	14	-	1
M.L.Lynch c Tiffen b Bermingham	3	5	5	-	-
S.R.H.Barriball not out	12	14	9	-	1
W.L.Horneman not out	9	9	9	-	-
M.A.Tremaine					
S.Coetzee					
P.A.Gruber*					
N.Scripps					
S.M.Bullen					
Extras (b 3, lb 1, w 6)	10				
TOTAL (20 overs) (5 wkts)	**150**	83			

CANTERBURY

	Runs	Mins	Balls	6s	4s
M.F.Fahey b Tremaine	52	58	38	2	5
H.M.Tiffen* run out	29	31	28	-	3
A.E.Satterthwaite run out	2	3	2	-	-
J.C.Brehaut lbw b Coetzee	0	1	1	-	-
K.A.Neilson† c Horneman b Scripps	29	44	24	-	1
A.C.Boyce b Tremaine	13	9	9	1	1
E.M.Bermingham b Bullen	8	8	7	-	1
M.L.Mitchell run out	1	2	1	-	-
R.C.Milburn not out	8	11	7	-	1
B.H.McNeill run out	1	1	1	-	-
F.L.Mackay not out	1	7	1	-	-
S.K.Burke					
Extras (b 2, lb 4, w 1)	7				
TOTAL (20 overs) (9 wkts)	**151**	92			

Bowling	*O*	*M*	*R*	*W*
CANTERBURY				
McNeill	4	0	22	1
Burke	4	0	31	0
Satterthwaite	4	0	23	1
Mackay	4	0	45	1
Bermingham	4	0	25	1
AUCKLAND				
Scripps	4	0	19	1
Bullen	4	0	32	1
Gruber	4	0	34	0
Mistry	4	0	27	0
Coetzee	2	0	15	1
Tremaine	2	0	18	2

Fall of Wickets	***A***	***C***
1st	31	61
2nd	80	63
3rd	115	64
4th	125	102
5th	136	122
6th	-	136
7th	-	141
8th	-	141
9th	-	142
10th	-	-

WELLINGTON v CENTRAL DISTRICTS — State League T20

at Karori Park, Wellington on 2 January, 2009
***Abandoned without a ball being bowled.** Points: Wellington 2, Central Districts 2*

OTAGO v NORTHERN DISTRICTS — State League T20

at Queen's Park, Invercargill on 2 January, 2009
***Abandoned without a ball being bowled.** Points: Otago 2, Northern Districts 2*

CENTRAL DISTRICTS v OTAGO — State League T20

at Fitzherbert Park, Palmerston North on 16 January, 2009
Toss : Otago. Umpires : K.C. Manley & T.J. Parlane
Otago won by 6 runs. *Points: Otago 4, Central Districts 0*

OTAGO

	Runs	Mins	Balls	6s	4s
K.J.Martin† c Priest b Broadmore	94	60	65	-	13
S.W.Bates not out	70	66	50	-	7
S.J.Tsukigawa* c Hayes b Burrows	9	4	5	-	1
A.S.M.Kitchin not out	0	1	0	-	-
M.J.Kane					
K.J.Crowley					
T.J.Morrison					
K.L.Gregory					
E.M.Campbell					
L.M.Grant					
T.R.Hopkinson					
L.Foote					
Extras (lb 2, w 3)	5				
TOTAL (20 overs) (2 wkts)	**178**	68			

CENTRAL DISTRICTS

	Runs	Mins	Balls	6s	4s
A.L.Mason* st Martin b Morrison	21	17	18	-	3
R.H.Priest† c Tsukigawa b Bates	83	71	53	1	9
S.J.McGlashan b Tsukigawa	43	39	34	1	3
R.H.Candy c Hopkinson b Kitchin	1	8	3	-	-
K.C.R.Rangi b Bates	8	7	6	-	-
K.M.Winkley not out	8	7	6	-	-
K.E.Broadmore not out	1	3	1	-	-
K.M.Sutherland					
Z.A.McWilliams					
E.Lanser					
A.K.Burrows					
L.A.M.Hayes					
Extras (b 1, lb 1, w 4, nb 1)	7				
TOTAL (20 overs) (5 wkts)	**172**	78			

Bowling	*O*	*M*	*R*	*W*
CENTRAL DISTRICTS				
Broadmore	3	0	28	1
McWilliams	3	0	23	0
Hayes	2	0	12	0
Burrows	4	0	41	1
Candy	3	0	23	0
Mason	3	0	31	0
Winkley	2	0	18	0
OTAGO				
Bates	4	0	29	2
Hopkinson	2	0	20	0
Morrison	4	0	17	1
Tsukigawa	4	0	42	1
Campbell	3	0	30	0
Kitchin	3	0	32	1

Fall of Wickets	***O***	***CD***
1st	160	37
2nd	174	140
3rd	-	152
4th	-	160
5th	-	164
6th	-	-
7th	-	-
8th	-	-
9th	-	-
10th	-	-

WELLINGTON v CANTERBURY — State League T20

at Trentham Memorial Park, Upper Hutt on 16 January, 2009
Toss : Canterbury. Umpires : K. Cross & D.G. Paterson
Canterbury won by 9 runs. *Points: Canterbury 4, Wellington 0*

CANTERBURY

	Runs	Mins	Balls	6s	4s
F.L.Mackay c Cooper b Ruck	12	30	17	-	2
M.F.Fahey c Dodd b Ruck	27	22	24	-	4
A.C.Boyce c Stockwell b Doolan	3	11	8	-	-
A.E.Satterthwaite* not out	30	49	31	-	2
M.L.Mitchell c Cooper b Dodd	21	13	14	2	2
E.M.Bermingham run out	19	18	20	1	-
H.M.Watson not out	14	12	8	-	2
K.A.Neilson					
J.C.Brehaut					
B.H.McNeill					
R.C.Milburn†					
S.K.Burke					
Extras (lb 2, w 4, nb 2)	8				
TOTAL (20 overs) (5 wkts)	**134**	83			

WELLINGTON

	Runs	Mins	Balls	6s	4s
L.R.Doolan lbw b Bermingham	27	38	32	-	4
E.C.Perry b Burke	11	16	13	-	2
S.F.M.Devine b Burke	51	51	47	-	7
M.G.Wakefield b McNeill	20	32	19	-	3
A.E.Cooper c Satterthwaite b Burke	3	8	3	-	-
K.A.Tomlinson run out	1	8	4	-	-
A.M.Dodd* not out	3	4	3	-	-
M.J.Hodgson not out	0	1	0	-	-
S.J.Bradbury					
A.C.Stockwell†					
S.E.A.Ruck					
E.J.Scurr					
Extras (b 1, lb 2, w 5, nb 1)	9				
TOTAL (20 overs) (6 wkts)	**125**	85			

Bowling	*O*	*M*	*R*	*W*
WELLINGTON				
Devine	4	0	33	0
Ruck	4	0	19	2
Doolan	4	0	23	1
Dodd	4	0	24	1
Cooper	2	0	17	0
Perry	2	0	16	0
CANTERBURY				
McNeill	4	0	37	1
Burke	4	0	23	3
Watson	4	0	21	0
Mackay	4	0	18	0
Bermingham	4	0	23	1

Fall of Wickets	***C***	***W***
1st	39	27
2nd	44	62
3rd	46	112
4th	78	116
5th	108	122
6th	-	123
7th	-	-
8th	-	-
9th	-	-
10th	-	-

NORTHERN DISTRICTS v AUCKLAND — State League T20

at Cobham Oval, Whangarei on 16 January, 2009
Toss : Northern Districts. Umpires : C.B. Gaffaney & P.L. Gasston
***Auckland won by 4 wickets.** Points: Auckland 4, Northern Districts 0*

NORTHERN DISTRICTS

	Runs	Mins	Balls	6s	4s
K.L.Pulford not out	83	73	62	-	9
N.C.Dodd c Bullen b Coetzee	30	26	27	-	2
A.J.Wilkins*†b Cox	6	6	6	-	-
N.J.Browne c Horneman b Mistry	13	23	19	-	-
M.J.G.Nielsen run out	3	13	6	-	-
H.R.Huddleston not out	1	1	1	-	-
A.M.Peterson					
E.M.Wilson					
N.P.Edwards					
E.L.Bailey					
B.N.Kirkbride					
N.M.Anderson					
Extras (lb 3, w 1, nb 1)	5				
TOTAL (20 overs) (4 wkts)	**141**	73			

AUCKLAND

	Runs	Mins	Balls	6s	4s
V.J.Lind*† c Bullen b Edwards	60	63	49	1	6
P.Mistry b Pulford	5	13	11	-	-
M.P.Murphy b Nielsen	51	44	36	-	7
R.J.Kember c Wilson b Edwards	1	7	6	-	-
M.A.Tremaine not out	6	21	10	-	-
S.R.H.Barriball c Wilson b Browne	1	5	2	-	-
K.T.Perkins run out	2	6	4	-	-
W.L.Horneman not out	1	5	3	-	-
S.Coetzee					
S.M.Bullen					
R.E.Cox					
N.Scripps					
Extras (lb 1, w 12, nb 2)	15				
TOTAL (19.5 overs) (6 wkts)	**142**	85			

Bowling	O	M	R	W
AUCKLAND				
Scripps	4	0	42	0
Bullen	4	0	26	0
Coetzee	4	0	22	1
Cox	3	0	19	1
Tremaine	2	0	11	0
Mistry	3	0	18	1
NORTHERN DISTRICTS				
Pulford	4	0	28	1
Browne	3.5	0	21	1
Wilson	2	0	22	0
Bailey	3	0	24	0
Dodd	2	0	19	0
Nielsen	2	0	15	1
Edwards	3	0	12	2

Fall of Wickets	***ND***	***A***
1st	53	19
2nd	64	116
3rd	101	124
4th	138	125
5th	-	131
6th	-	139
7th	-	-
8th	-	-
9th	-	-
10th	-	-

WELLINGTON v CANTERBURY — State League T20 Final

at Allied Nationwide Finance Basin Reserve, Wellington on 25 January, 2009
Toss : Canterbury. Umpires : E.J. Gray & D.M. Quested
Wellington won by 4 wickets.

CANTERBURY

	Runs	Mins	Balls	6s	4s
F.L.Mackay c Dodd b Doolan	20	30	24	-	3
M.F.Fahey b Dodd	37	34	25	1	6
H.M.Tiffen* st Stockwell b Doolan	12	22	19	-	1
A.C.Boyce c Perry b Dodd	7	5	5	-	1
E.M.Bermingham c & b Cooper	16	23	13	-	1
A.E.Satterthwaite b Perry	2	7	4	-	-
R.C.Milburn† c Dodd b Cooper	5	11	11	-	-
M.L.Mitchell lbw b Devine	8	16	8	-	-
B.H.McNeill c Doolan b Cooper	1	1	2	-	-
J.C.Brehaut c Bradbury b Devine	4	2	2	-	1
S.K.Burke not out	0	1	0	-	-
L.M.M.Tahuhu					
Extras (b 2, lb 3, w 4, nb 2)	11				
TOTAL (18.3 overs)	**123**	85			

WELLINGTON

	Runs	Mins	Balls	6s	4s
L.R.Doolan st Milburn b Mackay	63	61	51	-	8
E.J.Scurr run out	3	21	9	-	-
M.G.Wakefield b Satterthwaite	8	14	13	-	-
S.F.M.Devine c Mitchell b Bermingham	6	12	9	-	-
A.E.Cooper c Tiffen b Mackay	1	3	3	-	-
E.C.Perry run out	22	24	23	-	-
A.M.Dodd* not out	8	19	8	-	-
M.J.Hodgson not out	3	1	1	-	-
S.J.Bradbury					
K.A.Tomlinson					
S.E.A.Ruck					
A.C.Stockwell†					
Extras (lb 1, w 9)	10				
TOTAL (19.3 overs) (6 wkts)	**124**	84			

Bowling	O	M	R	W
WELLINGTON				
Devine	3.3	0	15	2
Ruck	2	0	23	0
Perry	2	0	19	1
Dodd	3	0	13	2
Doolan	4	0	28	2
Cooper	4	0	20	3
CANTERBURY				
Burke	3	0	22	0
Mackay	4	0	32	2
Satterthwaite	4	0	15	1
McNeill	3.3	0	23	0
Bermingham	4	0	17	1
Mitchell	1	0	14	0

Fall of Wickets	***C***	***W***
1st	57	42
2nd	64	58
3rd	74	78
4th	95	82
5th	104	91
6th	107	119
7th	115	-
8th	117	-
9th	123	-
10th	123	-

2008/09 STATE LEAGUE TWENTY20 AVERAGES

	M	In	NO	HS	Runs	Ave	100s	50s	Ct	St	O	M	R	W	Ave	R/O	Best
N.M.Anderson	1	-	-	-	-	-	-	-	-	-							
L.R.F.Askew	1	1	0	12	12	12.00	-	-	-	-	4	0	25	2	12.50	6.25	2-25
E.L.Bailey	4	-	-	-	-	-	-	-	-	-	4	0	31	2	15.50	7.75	2-7
S.R.H.Barriball	4	4	2	12*	26	13.00	-	-	1	-							
S.W.Bates	4	4	1	70*	134	44.66	-	1	1	-	16	0	93	6	15.50	5.81	2-15
E.M.Bermingham	6	5	0	19	43	8.60	-	-	3	-	24	1	115	4	28.75	4.79	1-17
K.A.Blackwell	1	1	0	15	15	15.00	-	-	1	-							
A.C.Boyce	6	5	0	31	64	12.80	-	-	-	-							
S.J.Bradbury	5	-	-	-	-	-	-	-	1	-							
J.C.Brehaut	6	4	1	18	27	9.00	-	-	1	-							
K.E.Broadmore	4	4	1	25	53	17.66	-	-	1	-	15	0	91	4	22.75	6.07	2-16
N.J.Browne	4	4	1	15*	33	11.00	-	-	2	-	14.5	0	69	2	34.50	4.65	1-9
S.M.Bullen	5	-	-	-	-	-	-	-	2	-	20	1	102	4	25.50	5.10	1-7
O.R.Bupha-Intr	2	-	-	-	-	-	-	-	-	-							
S.K.Burke	6	2	2	5*	5	-	-	-	-	-	23	1	115	8	14.37	5.00	3-23
A.K.Burrows	4	-	-	-	-	-	-	-	-	-	14.4	0	108	5	21.60	7.36	3-26
E.M.Campbell	4	2	0	5	5	2.50	-	-	1	-	9	0	64	1	64.00	7.11	1-23
R.H.Candy	4	4	1	50	80	26.66	-	1	-	-	7	0	49	0	-	7.00	-
S.Coetzee	4	2	1	17	25	25.00	-	-	-	-	11	0	79	3	26.33	7.18	1-15
A.E.Cooper	5	4	1	15	21	7.00	-	-	4	-	14.4	2	91	9	10.11	6.20	3-0
R.E.Cox	1	-	-	-	-	-	-	-	-	-	3	0	19	1	19.00	6.33	1-19
K.J.Crowley	4	2	0	6	9	4.50	-	-	-	-							
S.F.M.Devine	5	5	0	51	149	29.80	-	2	-	-	16.4	0	89	5	17.80	5.34	3-12
A.M.Dodd	5	3	3	8*	17	-	-	-	4	-	19	0	100	6	16.66	5.26	2-13
N.C.Dodd	4	2	1	30	35	35.00	-	-	-	-	4	0	35	1	35.00	8.75	1-16
L.R.Doolan	5	5	1	63	212	53.00	-	2	2	-	18	1	103	8	12.87	5.72	3-12
N.P.Edwards	2	1	1	1*	1	-	-	-	-	-	3	0	12	2	6.00	4.00	2-12
M.F.Fahey	5	5	1	52	167	41.75	-	1	1	-							
L.M.M.Foote	4	2	0	1	1	0.50	-	-	-	-	1	0	9	0	-	9.00	-
J.M.Fraser	2	2	0	23	36	18.00	-	-	1	-							
M.A.Frey	3	-	-	-	-	-	-	-	-	-							
L.M.Grant	4	2	1	2	3	3.00	-	-	-	-							
K.L.Gregory	1	-	-	-	-	-	-	-	-	-							
P.A.Gruber	4	2	0	8	8	4.00	-	-	-	-	16	0	106	3	35.33	6.63	2-17
L.A.M.Hayes	2	-	-	-	-	-	-	-	1	-	4	0	27	0	-	6.75	-
M.J.Hodgson	5	4	3	3*	4	4.00	-	-	1	-							
S.A.P.Hopkins	1	-	-	-	-	-	-	-	-	-							
T.R.Hopkinson	4	2	0	0	0	0.00	-	-	1	-	9	0	78	0	-	8.67	-
W.L.Horneman	5	5	2	13	32	10.66	-	-	3	-							
H.R.Huddleston	4	3	2	19*	28	28.00	-	-	1	-	5	0	49	0	-	9.80	-
M.J.Kane	4	3	1	32*	45	22.50	-	-	-	-							
R.J.Kember	2	2	0	10	11	5.50	-	-	-	-							
B.N.Kirkbride	1	-	-	-	-	-	-	-	-	-							
A.S.M.Kitchin	4	3	1	12	12	6.00	-	-	1	-	7	0	53	3	17.66	7.57	2-21
E.Lanser	1	-	-	-	-	-	-	-	-	-							
V.J.Lind	5	5	0	60	105	21.00	-	1	-	4							
M.L.Lynch	4	4	0	16	28	7.00	-	-	1	-							
F.L.Mackay	6	4	1	20	40	13.33	-	-	-	-	23	0	148	4	37.00	6.43	2-32
K.J.Martin	4	4	0	94	124	31.00	-	1	-	2							
A.L.Mason	4	4	0	22	66	16.50	-	-	-	-	13	1	89	0	-	6.85	-
S.J.McGlashan	4	4	1	43	90	30.00	-	-	3	-							
B.H.McNeill	6	3	0	5	7	2.33	-	-	1	-	23.3	0	134	5	26.80	5.70	1-11
Z.A.McWilliams	3	1	1	15*	15	-	-	-	-	-	11	0	78	2	39.00	7.09	1-18
R.C.Milburn	6	4	2	13*	36	18.00	-	-	2	1							
L.F.Milliken	3	3	1	8*	12	6.00	-	-	-	-	12	0	77	2	38.50	6.42	1-25
P.Mistry	5	4	1	70	88	29.33	-	1	-	-	18	0	129	5	25.80	7.17	3-27
M.L.Mitchell	6	6	0	21	46	7.66	-	-	1	-	2	0	33	0	-	16.50	-
T.J.Morrison	4	2	1	6	7	7.00	-	-	1	-	16	0	87	3	29.00	5.44	1-17
M.P.Murphy	5	5	0	51	107	21.40	-	1	-	-	2	0	8	1	8.00	4.00	1-8
K.A.Neilson	4	2	0	29	34	17.00	-	-	2	-							
M.J.G.Nielsen	4	3	1	3	4	2.00	-	-	-	-	2	0	15	1	15.00	7.50	1-15
S.L.Norman	1	-	-	-	-	-	-	-	2	-							
K.T.Perkins	4	4	1	26*	59	19.66	-	-	1	-							
E.C.Perry	5	5	1	33	90	22.50	-	-	2	-	8	0	63	3	21.00	7.88	1-13

	M	In	NO	HS	Runs	Ave	100s	50s	Ct	St	O	M	R	W	Ave	R/O	Best
A.M.Peterson	4	2	0	12	12	6.00	-	-	-	-	2	0	27	0	-	13.50	-
R.H.Priest	4	3	0	83	104	34.66	-	1	1	3							
K.L.Pulford	4	4	1	83*	193	64.33	-	2	2	-	14	1	79	2	39.50	5.64	1-14
K.C.R.Rangi	3	3	2	11*	25	25.00	-	-	1	-							
S.E.A.Ruck	5	-	-	-	-	-	-	-	1	-	17	0	99	4	24.75	5.82	2-19
A.E.Satterthwaite	6	6	2	30*	57	14.25	-	-	2	-	20	1	87	7	12.42	4.35	2-14
N.Scripps	5	2	0	8	8	4.00	-	-	-	-	18.3	0	115	3	38.33	6.21	1-12
E.J.Scurr	2	1	0	3	3	3.00	-	-	-	-							
C.J.Sim	3	-	-	-	-	-	-	-	-	-	4	0	29	1	29.00	7.25	1-29
S.M.P.Sim	1	1	0	4	4	4.00	-	-	-	-							
A.C.Stockwell	5	-	-	-	-	-	-	-	2	3							
K.M.Sutherland	4	3	0	33	48	16.00	-	-	1	-							
A.Swart	3	1	0	1	1	1.00	-	-	-	-							
L.M.M.Tahuhu	3	-	-	-	-	-	-	-	-	-							
A.M.Te Wake	2	1	1	0*	0	-	-	-	-	-							
H.M.Tiffen	5	5	0	50	116	23.20	-	1	3	-							
K.A.Tomlinson	5	3	0	12	19	6.33	-	-	-	-							
M.A.Tremaine	4	2	1	8	14	14.00	-	-	-	-	7	0	57	3	19.00	8.14	2-18
S.J.Tsukigawa	4	4	0	25	46	11.50	-	-	1	-	15.2	0	111	4	27.75	7.24	2-23
M.G.Wakefield	5	5	0	61	126	25.20	-	1	1	1							
H.M.Watson	1	1	1	14*	14	-	-	-	-	-	4	0	21	0	-	5.25	-
A.J.Wilkins	4	4	0	54	115	28.75	-	2	1	1							
E.M.Wilson	4	1	0	8	8	8.00	-	-	2	-	12	0	117	4	29.25	9.75	3-38
K.M.Winkley	4	3	2	8*	15	15.00	-	-	-	-	9	0	49	6	8.16	5.44	4-10
P.M.Yates	1	1	0	2	2	2.00	-	-	-	-							

CAREER RECORDS

	M	In	NO	HS	Runs	Ave	100s	50s	Ct	St	O	M	R	W	Ave	R/O	Best
N.M.Anderson	1	-	-	-	-	-	-	-	-	-							
L.R.F.Askew	1	1	0	12	12	12.00	-	-	-	-	4	0	25	2	12.50	6.25	2-25
E.L.Bailey	4	-	-	-	-	-	-	-	-	-	3	0	24	0	-	8.00	-
S.R.H.Barriball	7	6	3	12*	34	11.33	-	-	1	-							
S.W.Bates	5	5	1	70*	156	39.00	-	1	2	-	20	0	108	6	18.00	5.40	2-15
E.M.Bermingham	10	8	1	19	64	9.14	-	-	4	-	28	1	142	4	35.50	5.07	1-17
K.A.Blackwell	1	1	0	15	15	15.00	-	-	1	-							
A.C.Boyce	6	5	0	31	64	12.80	-	-	-	-							
S.J.Bradbury	10	4	1	30	67	22.33	-	-	1	-							
J.C.Brehaut	6	4	1	18	27	9.00	-	-	1	-							
K.E.Broadmore	9	6	1	29	83	16.60	-	-	1	-	31	0	172	8	21.50	5.55	2-14
N.J.Browne	9	8	3	56*	154	30.80	-	1	2	-	34.5	2	164	6	27.33	4.70	2-17
S.M.Bullen	10	2	1	5	7	7.00	-	-	2	-	40	1	220	7	31.42	5.50	1-7
O.R.Bupha-Intr	4	-	-	-	-	-	-	-	-	-	4	0	26	0	-	6.50	-
S.K.Burke	9	2	2	5*	5	-	-	-	-	-	31	1	167	12	13.91	5.38	3-23
A.K.Burrows	9	-	-	-	-	-	-	-	-	-	30.4	0	211	7	30.14	6.88	3-26
E.M.Campbell	8	5	0	18	36	7.20	-	-	1	-	20	0	122	5	24.40	6.10	2-23
R.H.Candy	9	7	2	50	86	17.20	-	1	-	-	23	1	139	2	69.50	6.04	1-11
S.Coetzee	6	4	1	17	36	12.00	-	-	-	-	17	0	118	5	23.60	6.94	1-15
A.E.Cooper	10	9	2	22*	50	7.14	-	-	6	-	32.4	2	210	17	12.35	6.42	4-21
R.E.Cox	1	-	-	-	-	-	-	-	-	-	3	0	19	1	19.00	6.33	1-19
K.J.Crowley	6	3	1	9*	18	9.00	-	-	-	-							
S.F.M.Devine	9	9	2	67*	257	36.71	-	3	-	-	28.4	0	148	9	16.44	5.16	3-12
A.M.Dodd	5	3	3	8*	17	-	-	-	4	-	19	0	100	6	16.66	5.26	2-13
N.C.Dodd	7	2	1	30	35	35.00	-	-	-	-	10	0	62	6	10.33	6.20	3-16
L.R.Doolan	10	10	1	63	331	36.77	-	2	2	-	36	1	239	11	21.72	6.64	3-12
N.P.Edwards	4	2	2	1*	1	-	-	-	-	-	9	0	55	3	18.33	6.11	2-12
M.F.Fahey	5	5	1	52	167	41.75	-	1	1	-							
L.M.M.Foote	4	2	0	1	1	0.50	-	-	-	-	1	0	9	0	-	9.00	-
J.M.Fraser	2	2	0	23	36	18.00	-	-	1	-							
M.A.Frey	3	-	-	-	-	-	-	-	-	-							
L.M.Grant	5	3	2	19*	22	22.00	-	-	-	-							
K.L.Gregory	1	-	-	-	-	-	-	-	-	-							
P.A.Gruber	9	4	2	16*	25	12.50	-	-	2	-	36	1	203	11	18.45	5.64	2-12
L.A.M.Hayes	2	-	-	-	-	-	-	-	1	-	2	0	15	0	-	7.50	-
M.J.Hodgson	10	9	4	16*	42	8.40	-	-	2	-							
S.A.P.Hopkins	2	-	-	-	-	-	-	-	-	-							
T.R.Hopkinson	4	2	0	0	0	0.00	-	-	1	-	9	0	78	0	-	8.67	-
W.L.Horneman	10	8	3	35*	92	18.40	-	-	3	-							
H.R.Huddleston	9	4	2	19*	30	15.00	-	-	1	-	23	0	144	1	144.00	6.26	1-15
M.J.Kane	8	7	1	32*	57	9.50	-	-	-	-							
R.J.Kember	7	7	0	36	121	17.28	-	-	1	-							
B.N.Kirkbride	1	-	-	-	-	-	-	-	-	-							
A.S.M.Kitchin	8	7	2	21*	55	11.00	-	-	2	-	11	0	85	4	21.25	7.73	2-21
E.Lanser	1	-	-	-	-	-	-	-	-	-							
V.J.Lind	9	9	0	78	194	21.55	-	2	6	4							
M.L.Lynch	4	4	0	16	28	7.00	-	-	1	-							
F.L.Mackay	7	4	1	20	40	13.33	-	-	-	-	23	0	148	4	37.00	6.43	2-32
K.J.Martin	8	8	0	94	193	24.12	-	1	2	5							
A.L.Mason	9	9	1	66	273	34.12	-	1	2	-	31	1	191	7	27.28	6.16	2-9
S.J.McGlashan	9	9	4	91*	321	64.20	-	2	4	-							
B.H.McNeill	10	4	0	5	9	2.25	-	-	2	-	33.3	0	200	7	28.57	5.97	2-16
Z.A.McWilliams	7	3	3	15*	26	-	-	-	-	-	23	0	171	3	57.00	7.43	1-18
R.C.Milburn	9	5	3	13*	40	20.00	-	-	6	4							
L.E.Milliken	3	3	1	8*	12	6.00	-	-	-	-	12	0	77	2	38.50	6.42	1-25
P.Mistry	10	6	2	70	106	26.50	-	1	1	-	36.5	0	278	7	39.71	7.50	3-27
M.L.Mitchell	10	9	0	59	122	13.55	-	1	1	-	12.3	1	95	4	23.75	7.60	2-13
T.J.Morrison	8	5	2	6	8	2.66	-	-	1	-	30	1	140	6	23.33	4.67	2-12
M.P.Murphy	9	8	1	51	135	19.28	-	1	2	-	16	0	128	3	42.66	8.00	1-8
K.A.Neilson	6	3	0	40	74	24.66	-	-	2	-							
M.J.G.Nielsen	6	5	1	13	22	5.50	-	-	-	-	4	0	31	1	31.00	7.75	1-15
S.L.Norman	3	2	0	34	34	17.00	-	-	2	-							
K.T.Perkins	9	8	1	40	136	19.42	-	-	2	-							
E.C.Perry	10	9	3	33	114	19.00	-	-	4	-	24	0	175	7	25.00	7.29	3-14
A.M.Peterson	6	3	1	12	15	7.50	-	-	-	-	5	0	47	1	47.00	9.40	1-20
R.H.Priest	9	7	0	83	154	22.00	-	1	4	5							

	M	In	NO	HS	Runs	Ave	100s	50s	Ct	St	O	M	R	W	Ave	R/O	Best
K.L.Pulford	7	7	1	83*	247	41.16	-	2	3	-	26	1	149	5	29.80	5.73	1-14
K.C.R.Rangi	5	4	2	11*	26	13.00	-	-	1	-							
S.E.A.Ruck	10	2	1	2*	4	4.00	-	-	2	-	34	1	195	7	27.85	5.74	2-19
A.E.Satterthwaite	10	9	2	40	139	19.85	-	-	5	-	25	1	122	8	15.25	4.88	2-14
N.Scripps	5	2	0	8	8	4.00	-	-	-	-	18.3	0	115	3	38.33	6.21	1-12
E.J.Scurr	6	6	0	20	63	10.50	-	-	2	-	4	0	46	0	-	11.50	-
C.J.Sim	3	-	-	-	-	-	-	-	-	-	4	0	29	1	29.00	7.25	1-29
S.M.P.Sim	2	2	1	31*	35	35.00	-	-	-	-							
A.C.Stockwell	8	2	1	7*	8	8.00	-	-	2	4							
K.M.Sutherland	4	3	0	33	48	16.00	-	-	1	-							
A.Swart	3	1	0	1	1	1.00	-	-	-	-							
L.M.M.Tahuhu	3	-	-	-	-	-	-	-	-	-							
A.M.Te Wake	4	3	1	2	2	1.00	-	-	-	-							
H.M.Tiffen	8	8	2	76*	245	40.83	-	2	4	-							
K.A.Tomlinson	9	6	0	13	33	5.50	-	-	1	-	5	0	36	4	9.00	7.20	3-11
M.A.Tremaine	5	3	2	13*	27	27.00	-	-	-	-	11	0	99	3	33.00	9.00	2-18
S.J.Tsukigawa	8	8	0	29	106	13.25	-	-	2	-	30.2	3	171	8	21.37	5.63	2-17
M.G.Wakefield	10	10	0	61	285	28.50	-	2	1	2							
H.M.Watson	5	3	2	15*	39	39.00	-	-	-	-	20	0	71	0	-	3.55	-
A.J.Wilkins	9	9	1	67*	214	26.75	-	3	7	1	1	0	7	2	3.50	7.00	2-7
E.M.Wilson	4	1	0	8	8	8.00	-	-	2	-	12	0	117	4	29.25	9.75	3-38
K.M.Winkley	4	3	2	8*	15	15.00	-	-	-	-	9	0	49	6	8.16	5.44	4-10
P.M.Yates	1	1	0	2	2	2.00	-	-	-	-							

NEW ZEALAND FIRST-CLASS RECORDS

to 1 July, 2009

FIRST-CLASS MATCH DEFINED

The six countries represented at Imperial Cricket Conference on 19 May 1947 reached agreement in regard to definition of a first-class match. This did not have effect retrospectively.

A match of three or more days' duration between two sides of eleven players officially adjudged first-class shall be regarded as a first-class fixture. Matches in which either team has more than eleven players or which are scheduled for less than three days shall not be regarded as first-class. The governing body in each country shall decide the status of teams.

The records have been compiled on the following basis:

(1) Otago and Canterbury from 1863/64 to date
(2) Wellington and Auckland from 1873/74 to date
(3) Nelson from 1873/74 to 1891/92 inclusive
(4) West Coast (North Island) 1879/80
(5) Taranaki from 1882/83 to 1897/98 inclusive
(6) Hawke's Bay from 1883/84 to 1920/21 inclusive
(7) Southland from 1914/15 to 1920/21 inclusive
(8) Central Districts from 1950/51 to date
(9) Northern Districts from 1956/57 to date

Notes:

• Games played by the Melbourne Cricket Club teams of 1899/1900, 1905/1906 and 1926/27, are not treated as first-class in accordance with a decision of the New Zealand Cricket Council.

• Although set down for only two days each, the return matches played by A. Sims' Australian XI in 1913/14 against Canterbury and Wellington are included in these records; so is the match An Australian XI v Minor Associations, 1920/21, and MCC v Wellington, 1932/33.

• From 1933/34 season onwards, only games for which at least three days have been set down are treated as first-class.

• There have now been 2104 first-class matches in New Zealand.

• Unless otherwise stated, the first-class records relate to first-class matches in New Zealand and by New Zealand touring teams overseas. Apart from the games which have taken place in New Zealand, there are a further 579 played by New Zealand overseas as follows:

in Australia	1898/99 to 2008/09	86
in England	1927 to 2008	301
in South Africa	1953/54 to 2007/08	55
in Pakistan	1955/56 to 2001/02	33
in India	1955/56 to 2003/04	44
in West Indies	1971/72 to 2001/02	26
in Sri Lanka	1983/84 to 2002/03	16
in Zimbabwe	1992/93 to 2005/06	12
in Bangladesh	2004/05 to 2008/09	4

plus four games by Young New Zealand in Zimbabwe in 1984/85, three games by New Zealand Young Internationals in Zimbabwe 1988/89, one match by Wellington in Australia 1990/91, one match by Canterbury in South Africa 1993/94, three matches by New Zealand Academy in South Africa 1997/98, six games by New Zealand A in England 2000, three matches by New Zealand A in South Africa in 2004/05, three matches by New Zealand A in Sri Lanka in 2005/06, one match by New Zealand White in Australia 2006/07 and two matches by New Zealand A in India 2008/09.

GROUNDS

	Ground	No of matches	First and most recent match		Highest and lowest team totals				Highest Innings Best Bowling			
1	South Dunedin	9	O v C	1863/64	C	272	v O	1875/76	75	H.W. Moore	C v O	1877/78
	Recreation Ground		O v C	1877/78	MCC	34	v O	1863/64	8-28	W. Hendley	O v C	1869/70
2	Hagley Park *(old)*	1	C v O	1864/65	C	80	v O	1864/65	22	J. Fulton	O v C	1864/65
	Christchurch		only match		O	61	v C	1864/65	5-17	J.W. Stevens	C v O	1864/65
3	Hagley Park *(new)*	34	C v O	1866/67	SC	554	v Pk A	1998/99	301*	P.G. Fulton	C v A	2002/03
	Christchurch		C v W	2004/05	C	25	v O	1866/67	10-28	A.E. Moss	C v W	1889/90
4	Basin Reserve *	394	W v A	1873/74	NZ	671-4	v SL	1990/91	299	M.D. Crowe	NZ v SL	1990/91
	Wellington		NZ v I	2008/09	W	22	v C	1903/04	9-43	T. Eden	N v W	1875/76
5	Victory Square	7	N v W	1874/75	N	150	v A	1882/83	31	C.A. Knapp	W v N	1874/75
	Nelson		N v W	1887/88	W	19	v N	1885/86	8-26	F.H. Cooke	N v W	1887/88
6	Domain	33	A v C	1877/78	A	579	v O	1909/10	151*	Harold B. Lusk	C v A	1910/11
	Auckland		A v C	1912/13	A	13	v C	1877/78	9-75	R. Neill	A v C	1891/92
7	Caledonian Ground	4	O v C	1879/80	O	297	v W	1904/05	88	H.G. Seideberg	O v W	1904/05
	Dunedin		O v W	1904/05	A	48	v O	1889/90	8-36	A.W. Rees	A v O	1889/90
8	Lancaster Park §	334	C v A	1882/83	C	777	v O	1996/97	385	B. Sutcliffe	O v C	1952/53
	Christchurch		NZ v SL	2006/07	O	35	v A	1884/85	9-72	F.H. Cooke	O v C	1884/85
9	Botanical Gardens	1	N v W	1883/84	N	56	v W	1883/84	17	L. Fowler	N v W	1883/84
	Nelson		only match		W	30	v N	1883/84	5-10	G. Fowler	N v W	1883/84
10	Carisbrook	252	O v Tas	1883/84	NSW	752-8d	v O	1923/24	355	B. Sutcliffe	O v A	1949/50
	Dunedin		O v C	2007/08	C	27	v O	1896/97	9-50	A.H. Fisher	O v Q'ld	1896/97
11	Recreation Ground	20½	HB v W	1884/85	MCC	394	v HB	1906/07	188	C.G. Wilson	O v HB	1908/09
	Napier		HB v A	1912/13	HB	42	v C	1897/98	9-47	T.H. Dent	HB v W	1900/01
12	Farndon Park	4½	HB v T	1891/92	Q'ld	492	v HB	1896/97	135	O.W. Cowley	Q'ld v HB	1896/97
	Napier		HB v Q'ld	1896/97	T	39	v HB	1891/92	8-14	S.W Austin	NSW v HB	1893/94
13	King Edward Park	2	T v HB	1891/92	T	135	v Fiji	1894/95	62	Hugh B. Lusk	HB v T	1891/92
	Hawera		T v Fiji	1894/95	T	29	v HB	1891/92	7-?	C.R. Smith	HB v T	1891/92
14	Bayly Park	2	T v HB	1896/97	C	260	v T	1897/98	106	W.J. Crawshaw	T v HB	1896/97
	Hawera		T v C	1897/98	HB	100	v T	1896/97	6-43	D. Reese	C v T	1897/98
15	Victoria Park	3	A v C	1908/09	A	470	v HB	1910/11	88	W. Carlton	C v A	1909/10
	Auckland		A v HB	1910/11	HB	28	v A	1910/11	7-42	A.E. Relf	A v C	1908/09
16	Nelson Cricket Ground	3	HB v W	1913/14	C	337	v HB	1914/15	111	V.S. Ransford	Aust v HB	1913/14
	Hastings		HB v C	1914/15	HB	89	v C	1914/15	8-51	A.A. Mailey	Aust v HB	1913/14
17	Eden Park	233	A v Aust	1913/14	A	693-9d	v C	1939/40	336*	W.R. Hammond	E v NZ	1932/33
	Auckland		NZ v WI	2005/06	NZ	26	v E	1954/55	9-36	A.F. Wensley	A v O	1929/30
18	Rugby Park	5	S v O	1914/15	Aust	195	v S	1920/21	71	A. Galland	O v S	1919/20
	Invercargill		S v Aust	1920/21	C	37	v S	1920/21	8-84	D.J. McBeath	S v C	1920/21
19	Nelson Park	6	HB v W	1919/20	Aust	405-8d	v HB	1920/21	243*	M.S. Sinclair	CD v O	2007/08
	Napier		CD v A	2008/09	CD	405-5d	v O	2007/08	5-51	F.S. Middleton	W v HB	1919/20
					CD	153	v W	1985/86				
20	Wellington College	1	W v A	1923/24	W	569	v A	1923/24	163	J.S. Hiddleston	W v A	1923/24
	Ground		only match		A	280	v W	1923/24	6-172	S.G. Smith	A v W	1923/24
21	Sportsground †	51	CD v C	1950/51	W	590-8d	v CD	2004/05	236	J.D. Ryder	W v CD	2004/05
	Palmerston North		CD v W	2007/08	A	71	v CD	2001/02	7-31	H.B. Cave	CD v A	1952/53
22	Pukekura Park	52	CD v A	1950/51	O	543-8d	v CD	1978/79	242	M.D. Crowe	CD v O	1989/90
	New Plymouth		CD v C	2008/09	CD	59	v A	1958/59	9-100	B.W. Yuile	CD v C	1965/66
23	McLean Park	67	CD v O	1951/52	O	624	v CD	2006/07	265	M.D. Bell	W v CD	2007/08
	Napier		NZ v I	2008/09	CD	63	v W	2003/04	7-31	Abdul Qadir	P v Shell XI	1988/89
24	Trafalgar Park	28	N v W	1891/92	CD	448-3d	v O	1968/69	202*	B.E. Congdon	CD v O	1968/69
	Nelson		CD v ND	1996/97	CD	65	v W	1995/96	7-23	B.A. Bolton	C v CD	1961/62
25	Cook's Gardens	17	CD v WI	1955/56	MCC	376-7d	v CD	1960/61	138	M.G. Burgess	A v CD	1976/77
	Wanganui		CD v YNZ	1979/80	CD	71	v ND	1962/63	8-37	D.B. Clarke	ND v CD	1962/63

† now Fitzherbert Park *§ now AMI Stadium* ** now Allied Nationwide Finance Basin Reserve*

	Ground	No of matches	First and most recent match		Highest and lowest team totals				Highest Innings Best Bowling			
26	Seddon Park Hamilton	155	ND v A NZ v I	1956/57 2008/09	W ND	608-9d 32	v ND v A	1998/99 1996/97	247 9-48	P.J. Ingram A.R. Tait	CD v ND ND v A	2008/09 1996/97
27	Tauranga Domain Tauranga *(Inner)*	1	ND v CD only match	1965/66	CD ND	232 163	v ND v CD	1965/66 1965/66	64 5-41	G.V. Giles B.W. Yuile	ND v CD CD v ND	1965/66 1965/66
28	Tauranga Domain Tauranga *(Outer)*	6	ND v C ND v A	1978/79 1985/86	ND O	370 90	v O v ND	1982/83 1982/83	127 6-75	J.G. Gibson D.A. Stirling	ND v C CD v ND	1978/79 1981/82
29	Cobham Oval Whangarei	11	ND v A ND v C	1966/67 2000/01	ND ND	363 127	v CD v A	1983/84 1966/67	195 7-30	J.M. Parker R.S. Cunis	ND v C A v ND	1972/73 1966/67
30	Queen Elizabeth Park Masterton	12	CD v A CD v W	1966/67 2002/03	CD CD	414-7d 86	v A v A	1998/99 1966/67	189 6-33	M.S. Sinclair A.J. Penn	CD v W W v CD	1996/97 2002/03
31	Smallbone Park Rotorua	17	ND v O ND v CD	1968/69 1995/96	CD A	456 72	v ND v ND	1995/96 1991/92	237* 7-74	R.T. Latham G.D. Alabaster	C v ND O v ND	1990/91 1968/69
32	Cornwall Park Auckland	3	A v U23 A v W	1970/71 2000/01	A A A	274-8d 274-9d 75	v U23 v U23 v W	1970/71 1976/77 2000/01	102 8-75	R.W. Morgan H.J. Howarth	A v U23 A v U23	1970/71 1976/77
33	Horton Park Blenheim	10	CD v ND CD v A	1972/73 2002/03	CD ND	538 100	v C v CD	2000/01 2001/02	212* 7-36	D.P. Kelly A.M. Schwass	CD v C CD v ND	2000/01 2001/02
34	Harry Barker Reserve Gisborne	25	ND v O ND v A	1974/75 2007/08	ND O	516 77	v CD v ND	2006/07 1999/00	161* 6-32	V.R. Brown S.B. Styris	C v ND ND v O	1986/87 1999/00
35	Eden Park No. 2 † Auckland	96	A v CD A v CD	1975/76 2008/09	A CD CD	662-5d 61 61	v CD v A v A	2008/09 1996/97 2007/08	268 7-27	T.G. McIntosh N.A. Mallender	A v C O v A	2007/08 1984/85
36	Queen's Park Invercargill	15	O v CD O v C	1975/76 2008/09	ND O	410-9d 68	v O v C	2007/08 1977/78	162 8-31	B.A. Edgar D.G. Sewell	W v O O v CD	1989/90 1996/97
37	Bledisloe Park Pukekohe	2	ND v A ND v W	1976/77 1989/90	W ND	297-5d 152	v ND v W	1989/90 1989/90	123 5-27	R.H. Vance G.R. Larsen	W v ND W v ND	1989/90 1989/90
38	Hutt Recreation Ground Lower Hutt	14	W v ND W v C	1976/77 1985/86	W W	316 93	v O v WI	1983/84 1979/80	145* 8-24	J.G. Wright E.J. Chatfield	ND v W W v ND	1978/79 1979/80
39	Logan Park Dunedin	3	O v U23 O v C	1977/78 1979/80	O O	313 127	v U23 v C	1977/78 1979/80	106 6-44	J.M. Parker P.J. Petherick	ND v O O v U23	1978/79 1977/78
40	Temuka Oval Temuka	1	YNZ v E only match	1977/78	E YNZ	310 139	v YNZ v E	1977/78 1977/78	104 6-71	D.W. Randall G. Miller	E v YNZ E v YNZ	1977/78 1977/78
41	Molyneux Park Alexandra	28	O v CD O v SL A	1978/79 2003/04	CD O	444-8d 81	v O v CD	2001/02 2001/02	179 8-27	K.R. Rutherford J.T.C. Vaughan	O v CD A v O	1988/89 1996/97
42	University Oval Dunedin	21	O v Pak O v W	1978/79 2008/09	O O	404 46	v ND v Pak	2006/07 1978/79	221* 6-20 6-20	P.G. Fulton R.J. Webb B.E. Scott	C v O O v C O v A	2004/05 1983/84 2007/08
43	Maidstone Park Upper Hutt	1	W v CD only match	1979/80	W CD	216 50	v CD v W	1979/80 1979/80	63 6-17	B.R. Taylor J.V. Coney	W v CD W v CD	1979/80 1979/80
44	Dudley Park Rangiora	15	C v W C v W	1984/85 2002/03	C C	543-8d 62	v CD v A	1996/97 1998/99	251* 7-17	C.Z. Harris S.J. Maguiness	C v CD W v C	1996/97 1984/85
45	Centennial Park Oamaru	9	O v CD O v W	1984/85 1998/99	O C	430 94	v CD v O	1984/85 1994/95	182 6-36	K.R. Rutherford S.W. Duff	O v W CD v O	1987/88 1985/86
46	Levin Domain Levin	3	CD v C CD v W	1985/86 1987/88	W C	435-5d 68	v CD v CD	1987/88 1985/86	205* 6-28	E.B. McSweeney P.J. Visser	W v CD CD v C	1987/88 1985/86
47	Recreational Ground Morrinsville	2	ND v CD ND v W	1986/87 1988/89	CD ND	368-3d 198	v ND v CD	1986/87 1986/87	151 5-71	M.D. Crowe K.W. Martin	CD v ND CD v ND	1986/87 1986/87
48	Albert Park Te Awamutu	1	ND v CD only match	1987/88	ND CD	259 135	v CD v ND	1987/88 1987/88	94 4-41	B.A. Young B.J. Barrett	ND v CD ND v CD	1987/88 1987/88
49	Victoria Park Wanganui	11	CD v ND CD v O	1990/91 2002/03	W CC	506-4d 103	v CD v SC	1993/94 1997/98	203* 6-20	M.S. Sinclair B.C. Strang	CD v ND Z v NZ XI	1998/99 1995/96
50	Burnside Park Christchurch	1	C v CD only match	1991/92	C C	189-7 124	v CD v CD	1991/92 1991/92	63 6-67	T.E. Blain D.J. Leonard	CD v C CD v C	1991/92 1991/92
51	Petone Recreation Ground, Lower Hutt	2	W v O W v A	1991/92 1998/99	O W	300-8d 142	v W v O	1991/92 1991/92	107 5-37	E.B. McSweeney N.A. Mallender	W v O O v W	1991/92 1991/92
52	Sunnyvale Dunedin	1	O v A only match	1992/93	O A	193 105	v A v O	1992/93 1992/93	51 4-21	I.S. Billcliff N.A. Mallender	O v A O v A	1992/93 1992/93

† now Eden Park Outer Oval

	Ground	No of matches	First and most recent match	Highest and lowest team totals	Highest Innings Best Bowling
53	Lincoln Green Lincoln	5	NZA v B 1997/98 NZA v SA 1998/99	NZA 459-8d v PkA 1998/99 B 130 v NZA 1997/98	190 M.E. Parlane NZA v B 1997/98 6-69 Fazal-e-Akber Pk A v NZA 1998/99
54	Aorangi Park Timaru	4	C v Z 1997/98 C v O 2003/04	Z 422-8d v C 1997/98 C 100 v Z 1997/98	196 A.D.R. Campbell Z v C 1997/98 6-56 M.J. Mason CD v C 2002/03
55	Owen Delany Park Taupo	6	ND v O 1998/99 ND v W 2002/03	WI 450 v NZ A 1999/00 A 131 v ND 1999/00	216* S. Chanderpaul WI v NZ A 1999/00 7-33 B.P. Martin ND v A 1999/00
56	Colin Maiden Park Auckland	6	A v ND 1998/99 A v CD 2002/03	A 478 v ND 2002/03 A 182 v ND 1999/00	175* G.J. Hopkins C v A 2002/03 5-64 A.R. Adams A v ND 1999/00
57	Queen Elizabeth II Park Christchurch	29	C v O 1998/99 C v O 2008/09	W 614-8 v C 2006/07 C 114 v O 1998/99	235 J.A.H. Marshall ND v C 2001/02 9-13 P.J. Wiseman C v CD 2004/05
58	BIL Oval † Lincoln	8	NI v E A 1999/00 A v CD 2008/09	A 627-7d v O 2006/07 Pak 100 v NZ A 2000/01	205 T.G.McIntosh A v O 2006/07 6-70 A. Sheriyar E A v NZ A 1999/00
59	Queenstown Events Centre	8	O v E 2001/02 O v A 2008/09	NZ A 597-9d v SL A 2003/04 C 114 v O 2005/06	190* J.M. How NZ A v Lions 2008/09 6-32 J.S. Patel W v O 2004/05
60	North Harbour Stadium Auckland	1	A v O 2002/03 only match	A 289 v O 2002/03 O 185 v A 2002/03	157 T.G. McIntosh A v O 2002/03 4-34 S.B. O'Connor O v A 2002/03
61	Rangiora Recreation * Ground	5	C v CD 2003/04 C v CD 2008/09	C 543 v CD 2008/09 C 169 v A 2008/09	140 T.G. McIntosh A v C 2008/09 5-35 W.A. Wisneski C v CD 2003/04
62	Cobham Oval *(new)* Whangarei	2	ND v A 2008/09 ND v W 2008/09	ND 546 v W 2008/09 ND 246 v A 2008/09	103 M.E. Parlane ND v W 2008/09 6-73 B.P. Martin ND v W 2008/09

† *now Bert Sutcliffe Oval* * *now MainPower Oval*

PROVINCIAL CAREER RECORDS

Performances for the following teams are not included in the Provincial Career Records:

Team	*Opponent*	
D. Reese's Canterbury XI	Wellington	1913/14
Canterbury/Otago	MCC	1936/37
Auckland/Wellington	MCC	1936/37
Auckland XI	New Zealand	1957/58
ND/CD	MCC	1958/59
Otago Invitation XI	MCC	1962/63
Canterbury XI	New Zealand Touring Team	1967/68

Most Games for One Province

158 players have now represented their province on 50 or more occasions in first-class cricket.

120	Gray E.J.	W
119	Vance R.H.	W
115	Bradburn G.E.	ND
108	Lees W.K.	O
104	Roberts A.D.G.	ND
103	McEwan P.E.	C
102	McSweeney E.B.	W
101	Latham R.T.	C
99	White D.J.	ND
99	Nevin C.J.	W
97	Shrimpton M.J.F.	CD
95	Hart M.N.	ND
93	Young B.A.	ND
90	Blair B.R.	O
90*	Dickeson C.W.	ND
90	Morgan R.W.	A
90	McGregor S.N.	O
90	O'Sullivan D.R.	CD
90	Marshall J.A.H.	ND
89	Morrison J.F.M.	W
88	Boock S.L.	O
88	Franklin T.J.	A
88	Priest M.W.	C
88	Stead G.R.	C
88	Yovich J.A.F.	ND
87	Edgar B.A.	W
86	Bell M.D.	W
85	Duff S.W.	CD
85	Hart R.G.	ND
84	Chatfield E.J.	W
83	Blain T.E.	CD
82	Dunning B.	ND
82	Hadlee B.G.	C
82	Kuggeleijn C.M.	ND
81	Blair W.L.	O
81	Briasco P.S.	CD
81	Harris C.Z.	C
81	Young R.A.	A
80	Howarth H.J.	A
80	Hoskin R.N.	O
80	Sinclair M.S.	CD
79	Larsen G.R.	W
78	Mallender N.A.	O
78	Robertson G.K.	CD
78	Bailey M.D.	ND
77	McIntyre J.M.	A
77	Stead D.W.	C
76	Germon L.K.	C
76	Douglas M.W.	CD
76	Papps M.H.W.	C
75	Parker J.M.	ND
75*	McCullum S.J.	O
75	Gaffaney C.B.	O
74	Coney J.V.	W
74	Sulzberger G.P.	CD
73	Sparling J.T.	A
73	Barnes A.C.	A
73	Martin B.P.	ND
72	Hastings B.F.	C
72	Troup G.B.	A
72	Wells J.D.	W
72	McIntosh T.G.	A
72	Parlane M.E.	ND
72	Griggs B.B.J.	CD
69	Alabaster G.D.	O
69	Reid J.F.	A
69*	Boyle D.J.	C
69	Jones R.A.	A
68	Burgess M.G.	A
68	Cameron F.J.	O
68	Sinclair B.W.	W
68	Rutherford K.R.	O
68	Aldridge G.W.	ND
67	Edwards G.N.	CD
67	Harris R.M.	A
67	Patel D.N.	A
66	Puna N.	ND
66	Lawson R.A.	O
66	Cumming C.D.	O
65	Alabaster J.C.	O
65	Brown V.R.	C
65	Hunt A.J.	A
65	Webb P.N.	A
65*	Wright M.J.E.	ND
65	Nicol R.J.	A
64	Murray B.A.G.	W
63	Rutherford I.A.	O
63*	Stott L.W.	A
62	Cunis R.S.	A
62	Hadlee R.J.	C
62*	Smith C.J.P.	CD
62*	Cooper B.G.	ND
62	Patel J.S.	W
61	Yuile B.W.	CD
61	Campbell K.O.	O
61	Greatbatch M.J.	CD
61	Walker B.G.K.	A
60	Milburn B.D.	O
60	Newdick G.A.	W
60	Parsons A.E.W.	A
60	Sutcliffe B.	O
60	Roberts S.J.	C
60	Mason M.J.	CD
60	Woodcock L.J.	W
60	Parlane N.R.	W
59	Blair R.W.	W
59	Crowe J.J.	A
59	Smith I.D.S.	CD
59	Turner G.M.	O
59	Hartland B.R.	C
59	Smith L.D.	O
59	Marshall H.J.H.	ND
58	Dowling G.T.	C
58	Howarth G.P.	ND
58	Patrick W.R.	C
58	Reid J.R.	W
58	Ritchie T.D.	W
58	Thomson K.	C
58	Vivian G.E.	A
57	Bull C.L.	C

57	Burns K.J.	O	55	Sewell D.G.	O	53	Watson W.	A
57	Petrie E.C.	ND	54	Bilby G.P.	W	53	Franklin J.E.C.	W
57	Hamilton L.J.	CD	54*	Crocker L.M.	ND	52*	Cederwall B.W.	W
57	Ingram P.J.	CD	54	Cromb I.B.	C	52	McSkimming W.C.	O
56	Brice A.W.S.	W	54	McGirr H.M.	W	51*	Knight A.R.	O
56	Motz R.C.	C	54	Moir A.M.	O	51	Brown S.W.	A
56	Canning T.K.	A	54	Sutton R.E.	A	51	Thomson S.A.	ND
56*	Stewart S.L.	C	54	Ward J.T.	C	50	Boxshall C.	C
55	Bradburn W.P.	ND	54	Dobbs P.W.	O	50	Butler L.C.	W
55	Congdon B.E.	CD	53	Colquhoun I.A.	CD	50	Horne M.J.	A
55	Jordan A.B.	CD	53*	Pierce R.A.	CD	50	Adams A.R.	A
55	Mills G.H.	O	53*	Schofield R.M.	CD	50	Fulton P.G.	C
55	Snedden M.C.	A	53	Toynbee M.H.	CD			

** entire first-class career*

Longest Careers for One Province

Seasons			
34	Read R.J.	Canterbury	1904/05-1937/38
31	Reese T.W.	Canterbury	1887/88-1917/18
29	Luckie M.M.F.	Wellington	1891/92-1919/20
27	Fowke J.N.	Canterbury	1880/81-1906/07
27	Downes A.D.	Otago	1887/88-1913/14
27	Dempster C.S.	Wellington	1921/22-1947/48
26	Reese D.	Canterbury	1895/96-1920/21
26	Knight A.R.	Otago	1918/19-1943/44

Most Consecutive Games for One Province

74	White D.J.	Northern Districts	1985/86-1992/93
73	Hart R.G.	Northern Districts	1992/93-2002/03
70	O'Sullivan D.R.	Central Districts	1974/75-1982/83
64	Germon L.K.	Canterbury	1987/88-1993/94
63	Stead D.W.	Canterbury	1975/76-1983/84
60	Smith C.J.P.	Central Districts	1984/85-1990/91
59	Puna N.	Northern Districts	1957/58-1968/69
57	Edwards G.N.	Central Districts	1975/76-1981/82
56	Young B.A.	Northern Districts	1983/84-1989/90
54*	Cromb I.B.	Canterbury	1929/30-1946/47
54	Roberts A.D.G.	Northern Districts	1970/71-1978/79
54	Burns K.J.	Otago	1984/85-1990/91
53	Alabaster G.D.	Otago	1963/64-1972/73
52	Smith L.D.	Otago	1940/41-1955/56
52	Duff S.W.	Central Districts	1989/90-1994/95
51	Morrison J.F.M.	Wellington	1975/76-1982/83
51	Reid J.F.	Auckland	1976/77-1982/83
51	McEwan P.E.	Canterbury	1984/85-1990/91

** his complete career*

Most Centuries for One Province

	Province	*100s*		*Province*	*100s*		*Province*	*100s*
Bell M.D.	W	20	Turner G.M.	O	13	Scott V.J.	A	11
Sinclair M.S.	CD	18	Crowe M.D.	CD	13	Crowe J.J.	A	11
Sutcliffe B.	O	17	Cumming C.D.	O	13	McEwan P.E.	C	11
Edgar B.A.	W	15	McIntosh T.G.	A	13	Hick G.A.	ND	10
Papps M.H.W.	C	15	Franklin T.J.	A	12	Hadlee W.A.	C	10
Rutherford K.R.	O	14	Vance R.H.	W	12	Burgess M.G.	A	10
Greatbatch M.J.	CD	14	Harris C.Z.	C	12	Stead G.R.	C	10
Reid J.R.	W	13						

Most Runs for One Province

	Province	M	In	NO	HS	Runs	Ave	100
Edgar B.A.	W	87	160	3	162	6494	44.17	15
Vance R.H.	W	119	205	18	254*	6440	34.43	12
Sinclair M.S.	CD	80	137	15	243*	6333	51.90	18
Bell M.D.	W	86	149	11	265	6230	45.47	20
Sutcliffe B.	O	60	110	8	385*	6028	59.09	17
McEwan P.E.	C	103	185	11	155	5940	34.13	11
Latham R.T.	C	101	176	17	237*	5919	37.22	8
Roberts A.D.G.	ND	104	192	35	128*	5533	35.24	7
Harris C.Z.	C	81	121	31	251*	5293	58.81	12
Papps M.H.W.	C	76	136	12	192	5275	42.54	15
Blair B.R.	O	90	154	5	143	5057	33.93	7
Franklin T.J.	A	88	157	14	181	5051	35.25	12
Rutherford K.R.	O	68	121	7	226*	5051	44.30	14
Morrison J.F.M.	W	89	160	22	180*	4694	34.01	6
White D.J.	ND	99	173	15	209	4656	29.46	7
Bradburn G.E.	ND	115	188	23	148*	4614	27.96	4
Parker J.M.	ND	75	139	19	195	4611	38.42	7
Nevin C.J.	W	99	150	23	143*	4579	36.05	4
Shrimpton M.J.F.	CD	97	171	15	150	4551	29.17	5
Blain T.E.	CD	83	145	15	161	4547	34.97	7
Reid J.R.	W	58	102	8	296	4538	48.27	13
Marshall J.A.H.	ND	90	157	9	235	4457	30.11	8
Turner G.M.	O	59	109	14	186*	4439	46.72	13
Hadlee B.G.	C	82	151	11	163*	4429	31.63	6
Stead G.R.	C	88	146	10	190	4410	32.42	10
Greatbatch M.J.	CD	61	107	8	202*	4363	44.07	14
Gaffaney C.B.	O	75	138	11	194	4326	34.06	7
Cumming C.D.	O	66	117	11	173	4313	40.68	13
Briasco P.S.	CD	81	146	16	157	4301	33.08	6
McSweeney E.B.	W	102	153	23	205*	4296	33.04	5
McGregor S.N.	O	90	167	13	114*	4259	27.65	3
Crowe J.J.	A	59	95	9	156	4245	49.36	11
Gray E.J.	W	120	181	38	128*	4228	29.56	5
Burgess M.G.	A	68	116	13	146	4228	41.04	10
Morgan R.W.	A	90	154	8	166	4162	28.50	7
McIntosh T.G.	A	72	120	9	268	4116	37.08	13

Highest Averages

2000 RUNS/45.00 AVE	Province	M	In	NO	HS	Runs	Ave	100
Hick G.A.	ND	17	30	4	211*	2055	79.03	10
Crowe M.D.	CD	32	55	7	242	3299	68.72	13
Scott V.J.	A	44	74	15	204	3546	60.10	11
Sutcliffe B.	O	60	110	8	385	6028	59.09	17
Harris C.Z.	C	81	121	31	251*	5293	58.81	12
Jones A.H.	W	39	67	11	181*	2978	53.17	7
Sinclair M.S.	CD	80	137	15	243*	6333	51.90	18
Wallace W.M.	A	47	73	5	211	3409	50.13	9
Crowe J.J.	A	59	95	9	156	4245	49.36	11
Reid J.R.	W	58	102	8	296	4538	48.27	13
Fulton P.G.	C	50	90	10	301*	3837	47.96	7
Turner G.M.	O	59	109	14	186*	4439	46.72	13
Hiddleston J.S.	W	41	75	1	212	3413	46.12	8
Bell M.D.	W	86	149	11	265	6230	45.47	20

Most Wickets for One Province

	Province	M	Wkts	Runs	Ave	5WI	10WM	Best
Chatfield E.J.	W	84	403	7531	18.68	23	7	8-24
Boock S.L.	O	88	399	8235	20.63	28	5	8-57
O'Sullivan D.R.	CD	90	392	9560	24.38	21	3	6-40
Gray E.J.	W	120	357	9778	27.38	13	3	8-37
Howarth H.J.	A	80	332	7361	22.17	18	4	8-75
Blair R.W.	W	59	330	5004	15.16	30	10	9-72
Priest M.W.	C	88	290	8501	29.31	12	3	9-95
Downes A.D.	O	44	287	3902	13.59	33	13	8-35
Hadlee R.J.	C	62	285	4600	16.14	19	2	7-49
Moir A.M.	O	54	282	5926	21.01	20	5	8-37
Dickeson C.W.	ND	90	282	8242	29.22	9	2	7-79
Mallender N.A.	O	78	268	5433	20.27	14	3	7-27
Alabaster J.C.	O	65	264	5738	21.73	14	3	6-39
Cameron F.J.	O	68	258	5204	20.17	9	—	6-21

Most Dismissals for One Province

WICKETKEEPING	Province	M	Caught	Stumped	Total
McSweeney E.B.	W	102	289	39	328
Nevin C.J.	W	99	260	9	269
Lees W.K.	O	108	208	36	244
Hart R.G.	ND	85	228	15	243
Germon L.K.	C	76	217	21	238
Young R.A.	A	81	228	5	233
Griggs B.B.J	CD	72	195	7	202
Young B.A.	ND	93	179	11	190
Milburn B.D.	O	60	148	17	165
Ward J.T.	C	54	136	17	153
Kelly P.J.	A	48	140	12	152
Blain T.E.	CD	83	124	19	143
Croy M.G.	O	42	127	4	131
Colquhoun I.A.	CD	53	102	28	130
Smith I.D.S.	CD	59	119	11	130
Sigley M.A.	CD	44	124	4	128
Schofield R.M.	CD	53	107	15	122
Robinson S.A.	O	45	117	5	122
Wright M.J.E.	ND	65	104	17	121
Petrie E.C.	ND	57	90	22	112
Mills G.H.	O	55	78	29	107
Boxshall C.	C	50	70	36	106
Hopkins G.J.	C	41	91	10	101
Therkleson I.J.	W	39	93	7	100

Represented Most Provinces

5	Guy J.W.	CD, C, O, W, ND
4	Anderson R.W.	C, ND, O, CD
	Congdon B.E.	CD, W, O, C
	Crawshaw W.J.	O, C, W, T
	Hopkins G.J.	ND, C, O, A
	Hounsell A.R.	C, W, A, ND
	Howell L.G.	C, CD, A, ND
	McGregor P.B.	A, ND, W, CD
	Worker R.V. de R.	A, C, O, W
3	Alabaster G.D.	O, C, ND
	Allcott C.F.W.	HB, A, O
	Alpe S.	A, C, W
	Andrews B.	C, CD, O
	Beard D.D.	W, CD, ND
	Billcliff I.S.	O, W, A
	Bracewell B.P.	CD, O, ND
	Cairns B.L.	CD, O, ND
	Clark L.A.	W, O, A
	Collinge R.O.	CD, W, ND
	Crowe M.D.	A, CD, W
	D'Arcy J.W.	C, O, W
	Frith W.	C, O, W
	Hastings B.F.	W, CD, C
	Holland P.J.	CD, ND, W
3	Hussey J.M.	HB, O, A
	Jones A.H.	CD, O, W
	King R.T.	O, A, CD
	Lane M.E.L.	W, CD, C
	Lusk Harold B.	A, C, W
	McBeath D.J.	O, C, S
	McGlashan P.D.	CD, O, ND
	Macleod D.N.	CD, W, C
	Mills G.	A, HB, O
	Moloney D.A.R.	O, W, C
	Neutze P.S.	O, A, ND
	Paterson J.L.	C, HB, A
	Riley J.D.	C, W, A
	Sampson H.C.	CD, O, C
	Salmon W.J.	W, HB, T
	Stephenson F.C.	O, W, C
	Sutcliffe B.	A, O, ND
	Tracy S.R.	A, C, O
	Twose R.G.	ND, CD, W
	Uttley K.F.M.	O, C, W
	Watson H.C.	O, C, W
	Wiseman P.J.	A, O, C
	Wright E.	A, W, C
	Wright J.G.	ND, C, A

T *Taranaki* S *Southland* HB *Hawke's Bay*

PROVINCIAL RECORDS

MOST WINS IN SUCCESSION

8	Canterbury	1873/74 to 1880/81
7	Canterbury	1912/13 to 1913/14
7	Wellington	1960/61 to 1961/62
6	Canterbury	1910/11 to 1911/12
6	Auckland	1939/40 to 1943/44
6	Wellington	1962/63 to 1963/64
6	Canterbury	1996/97

MOST LOSSES IN SUCCESSION

10	Otago	1961/62 to 1963/64
8	Otago	1929/30 to 1931/32
7	Otago	1874/75 to 1880/81
7	Otago	1920/21 to 1922/23
7	Otago	1926/27 to 1927/28
7	Auckland	1997/98 to 1998/99
7	Otago	2001/02

MOST DRAWS IN SUCCESSION

9	ND	1974/75 to 1975/76
8	Wellington	1974/75 to 1975/76
7	ND	1968/69 to 1969/70
7	CD	1991/92 to 1992/93
7	Wellington	1992/93

MOST GAMES WITHOUT A WIN

38	CD	1973/74 to 1978/79
36	Otago	1960/61 to 1965/66
24	ND	1972/73 to 1975/76
21	ND	1966/67 to 1970/71

MOST GAMES WITHOUT A LOSS

24	Wellington	1984/85 to 1986/87
23	Auckland	1978/79 to 1981/82
22	Auckland	1934/35 to 1943/44
18	Auckland	1961/62 to 1964/65
18	Canterbury	1966/67 to 1969/70

MOST GAMES WITHOUT A DRAW

42	Canterbury	1896/97 to 1909/10
30	Otago	1894/95 to 1907/08
22	Canterbury	1869/70 to 1883/84
20	Canterbury	1919/20 to 1924/25

Highest Individual Innings

for and against the major sides in NZ

	For		*Against*	
Auckland	290	W.N. Carson v Otago at Dunedin, 1936/37	355	B. Sutcliffe for Otago at Dunedin, 1949/50
Canterbury	301*	P.G. Fulton v Auckland at Christchurch, 2002/03	385	B. Sutcliffe for Otago at Christchurch, 1952/53
Central Dist.	243*	M.S. Sinclair v Otago at Napier, 2007/08	265	M.D. Bell for Wellington at Napier, 2007/08
Northern Dist.	235	J.A.H. Marshall v Canterbury at Chch, 2001/02	296	J.R. Reid for Wellington at Wellington, 1962/63
Otago	385	B. Sutcliffe v Canterbury at Christchurch, 1952/53	290	W.N. Carson for Auckland at Dunedin, 1936/37
Wellington	296	J.R. Reid v Northern Dist. at Wellington, 1962/63	207	R.T. Hart for Central Dist. at Wellington, 1985/86
MCC/England	336*	W.R. Hammond v NZ at Auckand, 1932/33	222	N.J. Astle for NZ at Christchurch, 2001/02
Australia	293	V.T. Trumper v Canterbury at Christchurch 1913/14	198	W.A. Hadlee for Otago at Dunedin, 1945/46
South Africa	275*	D.J. Cullinan v NZ at Auckland, 1998/99	170	S.B. Styris for NZ at Auckland, 2003/04
West Indies	258	S.M. Nurse v NZ at Christchurch, 1968/69	214	M.S. Sinclair for NZ at Wellington, 1999/00
Pakistan	271	Javed Miandad v NZ at Auckland, 1988/89	204	M.S. Sinclair for NZ at Christchurch, 2000/01
India	192	M. Azharuddin v NZ at Auckand, 1989/90	239	G.T. Dowling for NZ at Christchurch, 1967/68
Sri Lanka	267	P.A. de Silva v NZ at Wellington, 1990/91	299	M.D. Crowe for NZ at Wellington, 1990/91
New Zealand	299	M.D. Crowe v Sri Lanka at Wellington, 1990/91	336*	W.R. Hammond for England at Auckland, 1932/33
Zimbabwe	196	A.D.R. Campbell v Canterbury at Timaru, 1997/98	157	M.J. Horne for NZ at Auckland, 1997/98
Bangladesh	102	Al Sahariar v Southern at Dunedin, 1997/98	190	M.E. Parlane for NZ Academy at Lincoln, 1997/98

Best Bowling

for and against the major sides in NZ

	For		Against	
Auckland	9-36	A.F. Wensley v Otago at Auckland, 1929/30	9-48	A.R. Tait v Auckland at Hamilton, 1996/97
Canterbury	10-28	A.E. Moss v Wellington at Christchurch, 1889/90	9-72	F.H. Cooke for Otago at Christchurch, 1884/85
Central Dist.	9-100	B.W. Yuile v Canterbury at New Plymouth, 1965/66	9-13	P.J. Wiseman for Canterbury at Christchurch, 2004/05
Northern Dist.	9-48	A.R. Tait v Auckland at Hamilton, 1996/97	9-93	P.J. Petherick for Otago at Dunedin, 1975/76
Otago	9-50	A.H. Fisher v Queensland at Dunedin, 1896/97	9-36	A.E. Wensley for Auckland at Auckland, 1929/30
Wellington	9-67	A.W.S. Brice v Auckland at Wellington, 1918/19	10-28	A.E. Moss for Canterbury at Christchurch, 1889/90
MCC/England	8-45	F.S. Trueman v Otago at Dunedin, 1958/59	7-50	H.W. Monaghan for Wellington at Wellington, 1906/07
Australia	8-27	W.J. Whitty v Auckland at Auckland, 1909/10	8-66	G.O. Rabone for Auckland at Auckland, 1956/57
South Africa	6-47	P.M. Pollock v NZ at Wellington, 1963/64	7-75	C.F.W. Allcott for Auckland at Auckland, 1931/32
West Indies	7-37	C.A. Walsh v NZ at Wellington, 1994/95	7-27	C.L. Cairns for NZ at Hamilton, 1999/00
Pakistan	7-16	Farooq Hamid v Wellington at Wellington, 1964/65	7-95	N.A. Huxford for Wellington at Wellington, 1964/65
India	8-76	E.A.S. Prasanna v NZ at Auckland, 1975/76	7-23	R.J. Hadlee for NZ at Wellington, 1975/76
Sri Lanka	6-79	C.P.H. Ramanayake v Wellington at Wellington, 1990/91	7-130	D.L. Vettori for New Zealand at Wellington, 2006/07
New Zealand	8-100	G.F. Cresswell v Australia B at Dunedin, 1949/50	8-33	H.S.T.L. Hendry for NSW at Wellington, 1923/24
Zimbabwe	6-20	B.C. Strang v NZ XI at Wanganui, 1995/96	5-16	A.R. Tait for NZ A at Dunedin, 1997/98
Bangladesh	6-143	Hasibul Hussain v Northern at Hamilton, 1997/98	7-53	C.L. Cairns for NZ at Hamilton, 2001/02

Highest Totals

for and against the major sides in NZ

	For		Against	
Auckland	693-9 dec	v Canterbury at Auckland, 1939/40	658	by Australians at Auckland, 1913/14
Canterbury	777	v Otago at Christchurch, 1996/97	693-9 dec	by Auckland at Auckland, 1939/40
Central Dist.	594-8 dec	v Auckland at Auckland, 1995/96	662-5 dec	by Auckland at Auckland, 2008/09
Northern Dist.	546	v Wellington at Whangarei, 2008/09	608-9 dec	by Wellington at Hamilton, 1998/99
Otago	624	v Central Districts at Napier, 2006/07	777	by Canterbury at Christchurch, 1996/97
Wellington	614-8	v Canterbury at Christchurch, 2006/07	613-7d	by Canterbury at Christchurch, 2006/07
MCC/England	653-5 dec	v New Zealand at Dunedin, 1935/36	537	by New Zealand at Wellington, 1983/84
Australia	663	v New Zealand at Auckland, 1920/21	484	by New Zealand at Wellington, 1973/74
South Africa	621-5 dec	v New Zealand at Auckland, 1998/99	595	by New Zealand at Auckland, 2003/04
West Indies	660-5 dec	v New Zealand at Wellington, 1994/95	587-7d	by Auckland at Auckland, 2008/09
Pakistan	616-5 dec	v New Zealand at Auckland, 1988/89	563	by New Zealand at Hamilton, 2003/04
India	520	v New Zealand at Hamilton, 2008/09	619-9d	by New Zealand at Napier, 2008/09
Sri Lanka	498	v New Zealand at Napier, 2004/05	671-4	by New Zealand at Wellington, 1990/91
New Zealand	671-4	v Sri Lanka at Wellington, 1990/91	663	by Australia at Auckland, 1920/21
Zimbabwe	422-8 dec	v Canterbury at Timaru, 1997/98	487-7d	by New Zealand at Wellington, 2000/01
Bangladesh	286-9 dec	v Southern at Dunedin, 1997/98	495	by Auckland at Auckland, 2001/02

Lowest Totals

for and against the major sides in NZ

	For		Against	
Auckland	13	v Canterbury at Auckland, 1877/78	28	by Hawke's Bay at Auckland, 1910/11
Canterbury	25	v Otago at Christchurch, 1866/67	13	by Auckland at Auckland, 1877/78
Central Dist.	50	v Wellington at Upper Hutt, 1979/80	68	by Canterbury at Levin, 1985/86
Northern Dist.	32	v Auckland at Hamilton, 1996/97	51	by Central Dist. at Hamilton, 1957/58
Otago	34	v Wellington at Dunedin, 1956/57	25	by Canterbury at Christchurch, 1866/67
Wellington	19	v Nelson at Nelson, 1885/86	32	by Hawke's Bay at Wellington, 1883/84
MCC/England	64	v New Zealand at Wellington, 1977/78	26	by New Zealand at Auckland, 1954/55
Australia	103	v New Zealand at Auckland, 1985/86	42	by New Zealand at Wellington, 1945/46
South Africa	165	v NZ Academy XI at Nelson, 1994/95	73	by Canterbury at Christchurch, 1963/64
West Indies	77	v New Zealand at Auckland, 1955/56	74	by New Zealand at Dunedin, 1955/56
Pakistan	100	v New Zealand A at Lincoln, 2000/01	46	by Otago at Dunedin, 1978/79
India	81	v New Zealand at Wellington, 1975/76	94	by New Zealand at Hamilton, 2002/03
Sri Lanka	93	v New Zealand at Wellington, 1982/83	109	by New Zealand at Napier, 1994/95
New Zealand	26	v England at Auckland, 1954/55	64	by England at Wellington, 1977/78
Zimbabwe	67	v New Zealand A at Dunedin, 1997/98	100	by Canterbury at Timaru, 1997/98
Bangladesh	108	v New Zealand at Hamilton, 2001/02	311	by Central at Wellington, 1997/98

AUCKLAND

Highest Totals

693-9 dec	v Canterbury	Auckland	1939/40
662-5 dec	v Central Districts	Auckland	2008/09
643	v Canterbury	Auckland	1919/20
627-7d	v Otago	Lincoln	2006/07
590	v Canterbury	Auckland	1937/38
587-7 dec	v West Indies	Auckland	2008/09
579	v Otago	Auckland	1909/10
550-5 dec	v Otago	Auckland	1936/37
547-8 dec	v Northern Districts	Auckland	2000/01
540	v Northern Districts	Auckland	2008/09

Lowest Totals

13	v Canterbury	Auckland	1877/78
48	v Otago	Dunedin	1889/90
48	v Wellington	Wellington	1889/90
53	v Wellington	Wellington	1873/74
55	v Otago	Dunedin	1900/01
56	v Canterbury	Auckland	1931/32
69	v Northern Districts	Auckland	1963/64
71	v Central Districts	Palmerston North	2001/02
72	v Lord Hawke's XI	Auckland	1902/03
72	v Northern Districts	Rotorua	1991/92

Most Appearances

90	Morgan R.W.	69	Jones R.A.	60	Parsons A.E.W.
88	Franklin T.J.	68	Burgess M.G.	59	Crowe J.J.
81	Young R.A.	67	Harris R.M.	58	Vivian G.E.
80	Howarth H.J.	67	Patel D.N.	56	Canning T.K.
77	McIntyre J.M.	65	Hunt A.J.	55	Snedden M.C.
73	Sparling J.T.	65	Webb P.N.	54	Sutton R.E.
73	Barnes A.C.	65	Nicol R.J.	53	Watson W.
72	Troup G.B.	63	Stott L.W.	51	Brown S.W.
72	McIntosh T.G.	62	Cunis R.S.	50	Horne M.J.
69	Reid J.F.	61	Walker B.G.K.	50	Adams A.R.

Longest Careers

Seasons			*Seasons*		
25	Garrard D.R.	1917/18-1941/42	21	Cleverley D.C.	1930/31-1950/51
24	Wallace W.M.	1933/34-1956/57	20	Stemson W.I.	1889/90-1908/09
22	Anthony A.	1909/10-1930/31	20	Horspool E.	1909/10-1928/29
22	McIntyre J.M.	1961/62-1982-83	20	Weir G.L.	1927/28-1946/47
21	Yates R.J.	1873/74-1893/94	20	Morgan R.W.	1957/58-1976/77

Benefits

Troup G.B.	1986/87	Watson W.	1994/95
Snedden M.C.	1989/90	Patel D.N.	1995/96
Crowe J.J.	1990/91	Morrison D.K.	1996/97
Franklin T.J.	1991/92	Pringle C.	1998/99
Hunt A.J.	1992/93	Barnes A.C.	2002/03

Batting

2000 RUNS	Career	M	In	NO	HS	Runs	Ave	100
Franklin T.J.	1980/81-1992/93	88	157	14	181	5051	35.25	12
Crowe J.J.	1982/83-1991/92	59	95	9	156	4245	49.36	11
Burgess M.G.	1966/67-1979/80	68	116	13	146	4228	41.04	10
Morgan R.W.	1957/58-1976/77	90	154	8	166	4162	28.50	7
McIntosh T.G.	1998/99-2008/09	72	120	9	268	4116	37.08	13
Reid J.F.	1975/76-1987/88	69	117	17	173	3733	37.33	5
Patel D.N.	1985/86-1994/95	67	102	9	204	3648	39.22	8
Harris R.M.	1955/56-1973/74	67	119	4	157	3598	31.28	3
Jones R.A.	1993/94-2008/09	69	120	7	201	3768	33.34	8
Scott V.J.	1937/38-1952/53	44	74	15	204	3546	60.10	11
Wallace W.M.	1933/34-1956/57	47	73	5	211	3409	50.13	9
Webb P.N.	1976/77-1986/87	65	114	18	136	3307	34.44	5
Nicol R.J.	2001/02-2008/09	65	100	11	160	3187	35.80	7
Horne M.J.	1992/93-2005/06	50	80	4	209*	3184	41.89	9
Sparling J.T.	1956/57-1970/71	73	123	17	105	2977	28.08	2
Barnes A.C.	1993/94-2004/05	73	113	10	134*	2893	28.08	4
Parsons A.E.W.	1973/74-1982/83	60	113	8	132	2820	26.85	3
Hemus L.G.	1904/05-1921/22	39	71	4	148	2701	40.31	8
Weir G.L.	1927/28-1946/47	42	67	6	191	2625	43.03	7
Whitelaw P.E.	1928/29-1946/47	42	68	4	195	2417	37.76	5
Jarvis T.W.	1964/65-1976/77	46	80	3	118*	2403	31.20	2
Horne P.A.	1979/80-1990/91	40	67	6	209	2380	39.01	4
Vivian G.E.	1966/67-1978/79	58	98	16	111*	2327	28.37	2
Vaughan J.T.C.	1989/90-1996/97	48	81	14	127	2269	33.86	2
Young R.A.	1998/99-2008/09	81	105	18	114	2260	25.97	4
Gedye S.G.	1956/57-1964/65	40	73	4	104	2169	31.43	3
Vincent L.	1997/98-2006/07	40	61	5	185*	2132	38.07	4
Mills J.E.	1925/26-1937/38	35	63	1	185	2126	34.29	3
Hunt A.J.	1981/82-1992/93	65	99	15	102*	2069	24.63	1
Canning T.K.	1999/00-2006/07	56	82	10	115	2067	28.70	3
Redmond R.E.	1969/70-1975/76	29	55	4	141*	2004	39.29	4

CENTURY ON DEBUT FOR PROVINCE

† 112*	Brook-Smith W.	v Hawke's Bay	Auckland	1904/05
157	Relf A.E.	v Canterbury	Christchurch	1907/08
† 119	Snedden C.A.	v Hawke's Bay	Auckland	1920/21
† 122	Scott V.J.	v Canterbury	Auckland	1937/38
† 122	Kerr A.C.	v Wellington	Auckland	1941/42
174	Patel D.N.	v Canterbury	Christchurch	1985/86
† 106* & 1	Vaughan J.T.C.	v Wellington	Wellington	1989/90

† indicates player was making his first-class debut

MOST RUNS IN A SEASON

		Runs	Ave
Crowe J.J.	1991/92	1063	62.52
McIntosh T.G.	2002/03	820	58.57
Crowe M.D.	1982/83	736	52.57
Patel D.N.	1986/87	723	55.61
Jones R.A.	2008/09	703	46.86

HIGHEST INDIVIDUAL INNINGS

290	Carson W.N.	v Otago	Dunedin	1936/37
268	McIntosh T.G.	v Canterbury	Auckland	2007/08
256	Smith S.G.	v Canterbury	Auckland	1919/20
256	Raval J.A.	v Central Districts	Auckland	2008/09

211	Wallace W.M.	v Canterbury	Auckland	1939/40
209*	Brown S.W.	v Canterbury	Christchurch	1990/91
209*	Horne M.J.	v Northern Districts	Auckland	2003/04
209	Horne P.A.	v Northern Districts	Auckland	1988/89
205	McIntosh T.G.	v Otago	Lincoln	2006/07
204	Scott V.J.	v Otago	Dunedin	1947/48
204	Patel D.N.	v Northern Districts	Auckland	1991/92
201	Jones R.A.	v West Indies	Auckland	2008/09

MOST CENTURIES IN A SEASON

4	Franklin T.J.	1987/88
4	Crowe J.J.	1991/92

TOTAL NUMBER OF CENTURIES		**293**
Most in one season	18	2008/09
1st	Mills G. 106* v Wellington	1895/96
100th	Playle W.R. 102* v Central Districts	1957/58
200th	Crowe J.J. 102 v Otago	1991/92

Bowling

150 WICKETS	*Career*	*M*	*Wkts*	*Runs*	*Ave*	*5WI*	*10WM*	*Best*
Howarth H.J.	1963/64-1978/79	80	332	7361	22.17	18	4	8-75
Sparling J.T.	1956/57-1970/71	73	248	5327	21.47	17	3	7-49
McIntyre J.M.	1961/62-1982/83	77	238	5447	22.88	8	1	6-84
Cunis R.S.	1960/61-1973/74	62	229	4603	20.10	14	2	7-29
Adams A.R.	1997/98-2007/08	50	221	4549	20.58	11	2	6-25
Snedden M.C.	1977/78-1989/90	55	217	4631	21.34	10	2	7-49
Stott L.W.	1969/70-1983/84	63	214	5341	24.95	8	–	6-68
Troup G.B.	1974/75-1986/87	72	200	5213	26.06	4	–	6-48
Canning T.K.	1999/00-2006/07	56	196	4822	24.60	6	–	6-44
Patel D.N.	1985/86-1994/95	67	184	4298	23.35	8	2	7-83
Watson W.	1984/85-1994/95	53	176	4110	23.35	7	–	7-60
Bracewell J.G.	1982/83-1989/90	42	168	4189	24.93	8	2	7-65
Morrison D.K.	1985/86-1996/97	49	168	4034	24.01	7	–	7-82
Cowie J.	1932/33-1949/50	34	154	3379	21.94	6	–	6-44
Sutton R.E.	1958/59-1973/74	54	152	3364	22.13	6	–	7-64

MOST WICKETS IN A SEASON

		Wkts	*Ave*
Canning T.K.	2002/03	46	21.97
Bracewell J.G.	1986/87	43	20.90
Hayes J.A.	1957/58	42	11.38
Lankham W.	1882/83	41	6.31

BEST IN AN INNINGS

9-36	Wensley A.F.	v Otago	Auckland	1929/30
9-75	Neill R.	v Canterbury	Auckland	1891/92
9-86	Neill R.	v Canterbury	Auckland	1897/98
8-27	Vaughan J.T.C.	v Otago	Alexandra	1996/97
8-36	Rees A.W.	v Otago	Dunedin	1889/90
8-51	Neill R.	v Wellington	Auckland	1895/96
8-51	Garrard D.R.	v Canterbury	Auckland	1921/22
8-55	Smith S.G.	v Wellington	Auckland	1919/20
8-65	Smith S.G.	v Otago	Auckland	1923/24
8-66	Rabone G.O.	v Australia	Auckland	1956/57
8-75	Cleverley D.C.	v Wellington	Wellington	1945/46
8-75	Howarth H.J.	v NZ Under 23 XI	Auckland	1976/77

BEST IN A MATCH

14-63	Rees A.W.	v Otago	Dunedin	1889/90
14-65	Hayes J.A.	v Wellington	Auckland	1957/58
14-94	Howarth H.J.	v Otago	Dunedin	1973/74
14-119	Pringle C.	v Otago	Dunedin	1993/94
13-35	Lankham W.	v Taranaki	Auckland	1882/83
13-85	Cunis R.S.	v Canterbury	Christchurch	1963/64
13-104	Oliff C.	v Wellington	Auckland	1912/13
13-107	Smith S.G.	v Wellington	Auckland	1919/20

Wicketkeeping

100 DISMISSALS	*Career*	*M*	*Caught*	*Stumped*	*Total*
Young R.A.	1998/99-2008/09	81	228	5	233
Kelly P.J.	1981/82-1988/89	48	140	12	152

MOST DISMISSALS IN A SEASON

35	(33ct/2st)	Young R.A.	2001/02
35	(35ct)	Young R.A.	2002/03

MOST DISMISSALS IN A MATCH

8	(2ct/6st)	Kent L.A.W. v Wellington	Wellington	1944/45
8	(8ct)	Smith I.D.S. v Central Districts	Nelson	1988/89
8	(8ct)	Vincent L. v Central Districts	Palmerston North	2000/01

MOST DISMISSALS IN AN INNINGS

6	(6ct)	Young R.A.v Wellington	Wellington	2002/03

MOST CATCHES IN A MATCH

8	Smith I.D.S. v Central Districts	Nelson	1988/89
8	Vincent L. v Central Districts	Palmerston North	2000/01

MOST CATCHES IN AN INNINGS

6	Young R.A.v Wellington	Wellington	2002/03

Fielding

MOST CATCHES IN A MATCH

6	Williams N.T. v Hawke's Bay	Napier	1894/95
6	Jarvis T.W. v Northern Districts	Hamilton	1968/69

MOST CATCHES IN AN INNINGS

5	Williams N.T. v Hawkes Bay	Napier	1894/95
5	Crowe J.J. v Canterbury	Auckland	1988/89

Record Partnerships

FOR

Wicket	*Score*	*Batsmen*	*Against*	*At*	*Date*
1st	286	B. Sutcliffe & D.D. Taylor	Canterbury	Auckland	1948/49
2nd	241	T.J. Franklin & J.J. Crowe	Wellington	Wellington	1988/89
3rd	445	P.E. Whitelaw & W.N. Carson	Otago	Dunedin	1936/37
4th	280	J.J. Crowe & D.N. Patel	ND	Auckland	1991/92
5th	347*	M.J. Horne & A.C. Barnes	ND	Auckland	2003/04
6th	209*	A.C. Parore & A.P. O'Dowd	Otago	Dunedin	1991/92
7th	224	V.J. Scott & A.M. Matheson	Canterbury	Auckland	1937/38
8th	189	W.N. Carson & A.M. Matheson	Wellington	Auckland	1938/39
9th	151	R.A. Young & G.J. Morgan	ND	Auckland	2007/08
10th	119	W.N. Carson & J. Cowie	Otago	Auckland	1937/38

AGAINST

Wicket	Score	Batsmen	For	At	Date
1st	373	B. Sutcliffe & L. Watt	Otago	Auckland	1950/51
2nd	287	M.D. Bell & J.D. Wells	Wellington	Auckland	1997/98
3rd	261*	M.P. Maynard & S.A. Thomson	ND	Hamilton	1990/91
4th	252	S.A. Thomson & B.A. Young	ND	Auckland	1990/91
5th	282	J.E.C. Franklin & L.J. Woodcock	Wellington	Auckland	2008/09
6th	220	M.H. Toynbee & I.D.S. Smith	CD	Napier	1982/83
7th	165	R.K. Brown & M.E.L. Lane	CD	Palmerston Nth	1993/94
8th	166	R.J. Hadlee & D.R. Hadlee	Canterbury	Christchurch	1983/84
9th	208	W.C. McSkimming & B.E. Scott	Otago	Auckland	2004/05
10th	133	G.A. Bartlett & I.A. Colquhoun	CD	Auckland	1959/60

CANTERBURY

Highest Totals

777	v Otago	Christchurch	1996/97
613-7d	v Wellington	Christchurch	2006/07
559	v Central Districts	Christchurch	1993/94
549	v Northern Districts	Christchurch	1996/97
547-5 dec	v Wellington	Christchurch	1953/54
543-8 dec	v Central Districts	Rangiora	1996/97
543	v Central Districts	Rangiora	2008/09
537	v Central Districts	Blenheim	1996/97
534	v Central Districts	Palmerston North	1994/95
526-8 dec	v Wellington	Wellington	1931/32

Lowest Totals

25	v Otago	Christchurch	1886/87
27	v Otago	Dunedin	1896/97
32	v Otago	Christchurch	1866/67
34	v Otago	Dunedin	1863/64
37	v Southland	Invercargill	1920/21
37	v Wellington	Wellington	1925/26
38	v Otago	Dunedin	1873/74
42	v Otago	Dunedin	1863/64
42	v Otago	Dunedin	1992/93
44	v Otago	Dunedin	1883/84

Most Appearances

103	McEwan P.E.	72	Hastings B.F.	58	Thomson K.
101	Latham R.T.	69	Boyle D.J.	57	Bull C.L.
88	Priest M.W.	65	Brown V.R.	56	Motz R.C.
88	Stead G.R.	62	Hadlee R.J.	56	Stewart S.L.
82	Hadlee B.G.	60	Roberts S.J.	54	Cromb I.B.
81	Harris C.Z.	59	Hartland B.R.	54	Ward J.T.
77	Stead D.W.	58	Patrick W.R.	50	Boxshall C.
76	Germon L.K.	58	Dowling G.T.	50	Fulton P.G.
76	Papps M.W.H.				

Longest Careers

Seasons		
34	Read R.J.	1904/05-1937/38
31	Reese T.W.	1887/88-1917/18
27	Fowke J.N.	1880/81-1906/07
26	Reese D.	1895/96-1920/21
25	Moorhouse H.M.	1883/84-1907/08
22	Wheatley J.	1882/83-1903/04
22	Patrick W.R.	1905/06-1926/27
21	Stevens E.C.J.	1863/64-1883/84
21	Wilding F.	1881/82-1901/02
21	Ridley A.E.	1889/90-1909/10
20	Harman T.D.	1882/83-1901/02
20	Hadlee B.G.	1961/62-1980/81

Benefits

McEwan P.E.	1988/89
Hadlee R.J.	1989/90
Latham R.T.	1992/93
Germon L.K./Priest M.W.	1997/98
Harris C.Z.	1998/99
Cairns C.L.	1999/00

Batting

2000 RUNS	Career	M	In	NO	HS	Runs	Ave	100
McEwan P.E.	1977/78-1990/91	103	185	11	155	5940	34.13	11
Latham R.T.	1980/81-1994/95	101	176	17	237*	5919	37.22	8
Harris C.Z.	1989/90-2006/07	81	121	31	251*	5293	58.81	12
Papps M.H.W.	1998/99-2008/09	76	136	12	192	5275	42.54	15
Hadlee B.G.	1961/62-1980/81	82	151	11	163*	4429	31.63	6
Stead G.R.	1993/94-2005/06	88	146	10	190	4410	32.42	10
Fulton P.G.	2000/01-2008/09	50	90	10	301*	3837	47.96	7
Dowling G.T.	1958/59-1971/72	58	100	7	206	3690	39.67	8
Hastings B.F.	1961/62-1976/77	72	122	8	226	3540	31.05	7
Priest M.W.	1984/85-1998/99	88	130	21	119	3457	31.71	4
Boyle D.J.	1980/81-1994/95	69	121	12	149	3216	29.50	3
Hadlee W.A.	1933/34-1951/52	44	80	7	194	3183	43.60	10
Stead D.W.	1969/70-1985/86	77	133	11	193*	3169	25.97	1
Stewart S.L.	2001/02-2008/09	56	99	7	149	3058	33.23	4
Cromb I.B.	1929/30-1946/47	54	96	5	171	2986	32.81	3
Brown V.R.	1978/79-1986/87	65	111	11	161*	2872	28.72	5
Patrick W.R.	1905/06-1926/27	58	108	7	129*	2803	27.75	2
Hartland B.R.	1986/87-1996/97	59	103	8	150	2771	29.16	5
Coman P.G.	1968/69-1977/78	44	78	4	104	2603	35.17	2
Thomson K.	1959/60-1973/74	58	103	11	136*	2543	27.64	4
Page M.L.	1920/21-1936/37	41	75	2	206	2424	33.20	2
Leggat J.G.	1944/45-1955/56	35	66	6	166	2391	39.85	5
Chapple M.E.	1949/50-1960/61	44	79	9	165	2364	33.77	3
Germon L.K.	1987/88-1997/98	76	101	25	160*	2336	30.73	3
McMillan C.D.	1994/95-2006/07	40	65	9	159	2332	41.64	6
Kerr J.L.	1929/30-1939/40	32	61	3	196	2228	38.41	3
Guillen S.C.	1952/53-1960/61	42	73	5	197	2186	32.14	3
Reese D.	1895/96-1920/21	47	85	4	111	2066	25.50	2
Ryan M.L.	1965/66-1978/79	45	78	8	129	2041	29.15	2
Hadlee R.J.	1971/72-1988/89	62	100	22	93	2012	25.79	—
Roberts A.W.	1927/28-1940/41	35	60	8	181	2004	38.53	2

CENTURY ON DEBUT FOR PROVINCE

† 175	Watson G.	v Otago	Christchurch	1880/81
† 108 & 18	Wood B.B.	v Wellington	Wellington	1907/08
† 105	Talbot R.O.	v Otago	Dunedin	1922/23
5 & 112*	Newman J.A.	v Otago	Christchurch	1927/28
149	Hastings B.F.	v Central Districts	Nelson	1961/62
8 & 135	Parker N.M.	v Wellington	Wellington	1973/74
115	Hopkins G.J.	v Central Districts	Christchurch	1998/99

102	Dravid R.S.	v Central Districts	Rangiora	2008/09
† 102	McCone R.J.	v Otago	Christchurch	2008/09

† indicates player was making his first-class debut

HIGHEST INDIVIDUAL INNINGS

301*	Fulton P.G.	v Auckland	Christchurch	2002/03
251*	Harris C.Z.	v Central Districts	Rangiora	1996/97
237*	Latham R.T.	v Northern Districts	Rotorua	1990/91
226	Hastings B.F.	v NZ Under 23 XI	Christchurch	1964/65
221*	Fulton P.G.	v Otago	Dunedin	2004/05
206	Page M.L.	v Wellington	Wellington	1931/32
206	Dowling G.T.	v Wellington	Christchurch	1962/63
206	Harris C.Z.	v Central Districts	Blenheim	1996/97
204	Cox A.	v Otago	Christchurch	1925/26
199	Myburgh J.G.	v Central Districts	New Plymouth	2008/09

MOST RUNS IN A SEASON

		Runs	*Ave*
Papps M.H.W.	2006/07	1005	91.36
Stead G.R.	2000/01	852	50.11
Fulton P.G.	2004/05	828	69.00
McMillan C.D.	1996/97	809	73.54
Papps M.H.W.	2001/02	793	52.86
Wright J.G.	1986/87	780	60.00
McEwan P.E.	1988/89	758	44.58
Latham R.T.	1988/89	757	58.23
Harris C.Z.	1996/97	748	187.00
Myburgh J.G.	2008/09	739	61.58
Englefield J.I.	2000/01	724	38.10
Papps M.H.W.	2008/09	719	59.91
McEwan P.E.	1983/84	713	59.41

MOST CENTURIES IN A SEASON

4 Papps M.H.W. 2006/07

TOTAL NUMBER OF CENTURIES		**285**
Most in one season	11	2006/07, 2008/09
1st	Watson G. 175 v Otago	1880/81
100th	Hastings B.F. 136 v Auckland	1964/65
200th	Germon L.K. 114 v Central Districts	1993/94

Bowling

150 WICKETS	*Career*	*M*	*Wkts*	*Runs*	*Ave*	*5WI*	*10WM*	*Best*
Priest M.W.	1984/85-1998/99	88	290	8501	29.31	12	3	9-95
Hadlee R.J.	1971/72-1988/89	62	285	4600	16.14	19	2	7-49
Burtt T.B.	1943/44-1954/55	46	241	4991	20.70	16	3	8-35
Motz R.C.	1957/58-1968/69	56	239	4589	19.20	12	3	8-61
Bennett J.H.	1898/99-1919/20	40	205	3367	16.43	17	4	7-35
Hadlee D.R.	1969/70-1983/84	49	195	3918	20.09	10	3	7-55
Roberts S.J.	1985/86-1995/96	60	193	5738	29.73	6	–	5-56
Read R.J.	1904/05-1937/38	44	184	4704	25.56	11	1	7-24
Reese D.	1895/96-1920/21	48	168	3040	18.09	10	1	6-43
Stead D.W.	1969/70-1985/86	77	167	5009	29.99	6	—	7-99
Brown V.R.	1978/79-1986/87	65	159	4393	27.62	4	2	7-28
Merritt W.E.	1926/27-1935/36	24	154	3559	23.11	15	4	8-105
Wisneski W.A.	1996/97-2003/04	44	154	4092	26.57	7	—	7-151

BEST IN AN INNINGS

10-28	Moss A.E.	v Wellington	Christchurch	1889/90
9-13	Wiseman P.J.	v Central Districts	Christchurch	2004/05
9-56	McBeath D.J.	v Auckland	Christchurch	1918/19
9-95	Priest M.W.	v Otago	Dunedin	1989/90

9-98	Robertson W.	v Wellington	Christchurch	1894/95
8-18	Frith W.	v Otago	Christchurch	1880/81
8-33	Callaway S.T.	v Hawkes Bay	Napier	1903/04
8-35	Burtt T.B.	v Otago	Dunedin	1953/54
8-41	Callaway S.T.	v Otago	Dunedin	1900/01
8-59	Robertson W.	v Auckland	Christchurch	1893/94
8-61	Mulcock E.	v Otago	Christchurch	1937/38
8-61	Motz R.C.	v Wellington	Christchurch	1966/67
8-75	Edser H.	v Wellington	Wellington	1883/84
8-96	McBeath D.J.	v Auckland	Auckland	1921/22
8-99	Thomas A.W.	v Auckland	Auckland	1914/15
8-105	Merritt W.E.	v Auckland	Auckland	1931/32

BEST IN A MATCH

15-60	Callaway S.T.	v Hawkes Bay	Napier	1903/04
15-168	McBeath D.J.	v Auckland	Christchurch	1918/19
14-59	Read R.J.	v Southland	Invercargill	1920/21
14-107	Robertson W.	v Auckland	Christchurch	1893/94
13-72	Moss A.E.	v Wellington	Christchurch	1889/90
13-82	Howell W.B.	v Wellington	Christchurch	1902/03
13-90	Frankish F.S.	v Wellington	Wellington	1901/02
13-140	Edser H.	v Wellington	Wellington	1883/84
13-163	Robertson W.	v Wellington	Christchurch	1894/95
13-181	Merritt W.E.	v Otago	Wellington	1935/36

MOST WICKETS IN A SEASON

		Wkts	*Ave*			*Wkts*	*Ave*
Boock S.L.	1977/78	56	15.66	Hadlee R.J.	1981/82	45	14.31
Callaway S.T.	1903/04	47	8.49	Hadlee R.J.	1986/87	45	12.91

Wicketkeeping

100 DISMISSALS	*Career*	*M*	*Caught*	*Stumped*	*Total*
Germon L.K.	1987/88-1997/98	76	217	21	238
Ward J.T.	1957/58-1970/71	54	136	17	153
Boxshall C.	1897/98-1914/15	50	70	36	106
Hopkins G.J.	1998/99-2002/03	41	91	10	101

MOST DISMISSALS IN A SEASON

34 (31ct/3st) Germon L.K. 1991/92

MOST DISMISSALS IN A MATCH

9	(9ct)	Germon L.K. v Northern Districts	Christchurch	1992/93

MOST DISMISSALS IN AN INNINGS

6	(6ct)	Germon L.K. v Northern Districts	Christchurch	1992/93
6	(5ct/1st)	Papps M.H.W. v Northern Districts	Gisborne	2004/05

MOST CATCHES IN A MATCH

9	Germon L.K. v Northern Districts	Christchurch	1992/93

MOST CATCHES IN AN INNINGS

6	Germon L.K. v Northern Districts	Christchurch	1992/93

Fielding

MOST CATCHES IN A MATCH

6	Cromb I.B. v Otago	Christchurch	1937/38
6	MacDonald G.K. v Pakistan	Christchurch	1984/85
6	Latham R.T. v Otago	Oamaru	1994/95
6	Myburgh J.G. v Auckland	Rangiora	2008/09

MOST CATCHES IN AN INNINGS

5	MacDonald G.K. v Pakistan	Christchurch	1984/85
5	Harris C.Z. v England	Christchurch	2001/02
5	Myburgh J.G. v Auckland	Rangiora	2008/09

Record Partnerships

FOR

Wicket	*Score*	*Batsmen*	*Against*	*At*	*Date*
1st	306	L.A. Cuff & J.D. Lawrence	Auckland	Christchurch	1893/94
2nd	254*	M.H.W. Papps & J.G. Myburgh	CD	Napier	2007/08
3rd	394*	P.G. Kennedy & R.T. Latham	ND	Rotorua	1990/91
4th	278	M.L. Page & A.W. Roberts	Wellington	Wellington	1931/32
5th	290	G.R. Stead & C.Z. Harris	CD	Blenheim	1996/97
6th	293*	P.G. Fulton & N.T. Broom	Otago	Dunedin	2004/05
7th	265	J.L. Powell & N. Dorreen	Otago	Christchurch	1929/30
8th	220	P.J. Wiseman & B.C. Hiini	ND	Hamilton	2005/06
9th	182*	L.K. Germon & R.M. Ford	Wellington	Christchurch	1989/90
10th	160	L.K. Germon & W.A. Wisneski	ND	Rangiora	1997/98

AGAINST

Wicket	*Score*	*Batsmen*	*For*	*At*	*Date*
1st	286	B. Sutcliffe & D.D. Taylor	Auckland	Auckland	1948/49
2nd	317	R.T. Hart & P.S. Briasco	CD	New Plymouth	1983/84
3rd	278	T.J. Franklin & D.N. Patel	Auckland	Christchurch	1985/86
4th	282	W.A.C. Wilkinson & A.P.F. Chapman	MCC	Christchurch	1922/23
5th	235*	G.P. Sulzberger & J.D. Ryder	CD	Napier	2002/03
6th	184	G.D. Elliott & S.M. Mills	Wellington	Christchurch	2006/07
7th	261	A.D.R. Campbell & P.A. Strang	Zimbabwe	Timaru	1997/98
8th	433	A. Sims & V.T. Trumper	Australia	Christchurch	1913/14
9th	134	J.W. Wilson & N.A. Mallender	Otago	Christchurch	1992/93
10th	184	R.C. Blunt & W. Hawksworth	Otago	Christchurch	1931/32

CENTRAL DISTRICTS

Highest Totals

594-8 dec	v Auckland	Auckland	1995/96
549-8 dec	v Canterbury	Christchurch	1998/99
542-4 dec	v Canterbury	Napier	2002/03
538	v Canterbury	Blenheim	2000/01
526	v Otago	Napier	1995/96
523	v Wellington	Wellington	2008/09
499	v Canterbury	New Plymouth	2004/05
497	v Wellington	Palmerston North	2004/05
486	v Wellington	Napier	2007/08
485-7 dec	v Wellington	Wellington	1964/65

Lowest Totals

50	v Wellington	Upper Hutt	1979/80
51	v Northern Districts	Hamilton	1957/58
59	v Auckland	New Plymouth	1958/59
61	v Auckland	Auckland	1996/97
61	v Auckland	Auckland	2007/08
63	v Wellington	Napier	2003/04
65	v Wellington	Nelson	1995/96
71	v Northern Districts	Wanganui	1962/63
72	v Auckland	Palmerston North	2001/02
74	v Otago	Invercargill	1996/97

Most Appearances

97	Shrimpton M.J.F.	74	Sulzberger G.P.	57	Hamilton L.J.
90	O'Sullivan D.R.	72	Griggs B.B.J.	57	Ingram P.J.
85	Duff S.W.	67	Edwards G.N.	55	Congdon B.E.
83	Blain T.E.	62	Smith C.J.P.	55	Jordan A.B.
81	Briasco P.S.	61	Greatbatch M.J.	53	Colquhoun I.A.
80	Sinclair M.S.	61	Yuile B.W.	53	Toynbee M.H.
78	Robertson G.K.	60	Mason M.J.	53	Schofield R.M.
76	Douglas M.W.	59	Smith I.D.S.	53	Pierce R.A.

Longest Careers

Seasons			*Seasons*		
19	Shrimpton M.J.F.	1961/62-1979/80	16	Schofield R.M.	1959/60-1974/75
17	Jones A.H.	1979/80-1995/96	16	Snook I.R.	1972/73-1987/88
16	Chapple M.E.	1950/51-1965/66	15	Coutts P.J.C.	1958/59-1972/73

Benefits

O'Sullivan D.R.	1984/85	Duff S.W.	1995/96
Robertson G.K.	1989/90	Greatbatch M.J.	1996/97
Briasco P.S.	1991/92	Douglas M.W.	2000/01
Blain T.E.	1994/95		

Batting

2000 RUNS	*Career*	*M*	*In*	*NO*	*HS*	*Runs*	*Ave*	*100*
Sinclair M.S.	1995/96-2008/09	80	137	15	243*	6333	51.90	18
Shrimpton M.J.F.	1961/62-1979/80	97	171	15	150	4551	29.17	5
Blain T.E.	1982/83-1994/95	83	145	15	161	4547	34.97	7
Greatbatch M.J.	1986/87-1999/00	61	107	8	202*	4363	44.07	14
Briasco P.S.	1982/83-1991/92	81	146	16	157	4301	33.08	6
Douglas M.W.	1987/88-2000/01	76	132	19	144	3838	33.96	7
Edwards G.N.	1973/74-1984/85	67	122	5	177*	3709	31.70	5
Sulzberger G.P.	1995/96-2004/05	74	120	12	159	3505	32.45	8
Smith C.J.P.	1983/84-1990/91	62	118	9	160*	3499	32.10	7
Ingram P.J.	2001/02-2008/09	57	104	6	247	3301	33.63	9
Crowe M.D.	1983/84-1989/90	32	55	7	242	3299	68.72	13
Duff S.W.	1985/86-1995/96	85	129	29	164*	3079	30.79	1
Spearman C.M.	1996/97-2003/04	44	76	3	144	2951	40.42	5
How J.M.	2000/01-2008/09	47	85	8	169	2868	37.24	9
Congdon B.E.	1960/61-1970/71	55	93	8	202*	2807	33.02	3
Griggs B.B.J	2000/01-2008/09	72	113	11	143	2750	26.96	2
Payton D.H.	1965/66-1976/77	49	92	4	145	2459	27.94	3
Pierce R.A.	1971/72-1984/85	53	98	5	100*	2296	24.68	1

	Career	M	In	NO	HS	Runs	Ave	100
Smith I.D.S.	1977/78-1986/87	59	95	12	145	2265	27.28	3
Hart R.T.	1982/83-1990/91	37	68	3	207	2222	34.18	5
Yuile B.W.	1959/60-1971/72	61	90	10	146	2190	27.37	1
Taylor L.R.P.L.	2002/03-2007/08	34	53	1	217	2110	40.57	4

CENTURY ON DEBUT FOR PROVINCE

† 117	Macleod D.N.	v Wellington	Wanganui	1956/57
† 25 & 119	Sampson H.C.	v Wellington	Wellington	1970/71
119 & 0	Crowe M.D.	v Northern Districts	Whangarei	1983/84
112 & 21	Wilson S.W.J.	v Otago	Blenheim	1990/91
124 & 7*	Smith B.F.	v Otago	Wanganui	2000/01

† *indicates player was making his first-class debut*

HIGHEST INDIVIDUAL INNINGS

247	Ingram P.J.	v Northern Districts	Hamilton	2008/09
243*	Sinclair M.S.	v Otago	Napier	2007/08
242	Crowe M.D.	v Otago	New Plymouth	1989/90
217	Taylor L.R.P.L.	v Otago	Napier	2006/07
212*	Kelly D.P.	v Canterbury	Blenheim	2000/01
207	Hart R.T.	v Wellington	Wellington	1985/86
203*	Sinclair M.S.	v Northern Districts	Wanganui	1998/99
202*	Congdon B.E.	v Otago	Nelson	1968/69
202*	Greatbatch M.J.	v Otago	Palmerston North	1988/89
202	Greatbatch M.J.	v Northern Districts	Rotorua	1995/96
201*	Smith B.F.	v Canterbury	New Plymouth	2001/02

MOST RUNS IN A SEASON

		Runs	Ave
Crowe M.D.	1986/87	1348	103.69
Smith B.F.	2000/01	939	58.68
Sinclair M.S.	2008/09	904	75.33
Ingram P.J.	2008/09	884	63.14
Sinclair M.S.	2005/06	723	51.64
Sinclair M.S.	1996/97	722	48.13
Douglas M.W.	1991/92	714	44.62
Briasco P.S.	1990/91	708	41.64
How J.M.	2002/03	704	44.00

MOST CENTURIES IN A SEASON

6 Crowe M.D. 1986/87

TOTAL NUMBER OF CENTURIES		**203**
Most in one season	12	2008/09
1st	Hunter A.A. 108 v Otago	1951/52
100th	Blain T.E. 103* v Otago	1990/91
200th	Hay G.R. v Canterbury	2008/09

Bowling

150 WICKETS	Career	M	Wkts	Runs	Ave	5WI	10WM	Best
O'Sullivan D.R.	1972/73-1984/85	90	392	9560	24.38	21	3	6-40
Yuile B.W.	1959/60-1971/72	61	233	4485	19.24	11	2	9-100
Robertson G.K.	1979/80-1989/90	78	228	6573	28.78	8	1	6-47
Beard D.D.	1950/51-1960/61	49	213	4531	21.27	8	2	7-56
Duff S.W.	1985/86-1995/96	85	208	6856	32.96	4	2	6-36
Mason M.J.	1997/98-2008/09	60	205	4863	23.72	8	1	6-56
Hamilton L.J.	1996/97-2006/07	57	198	5104	25.77	7	–	6-32
Jordan A.B.	1968/69-1979/80	55	157	4431	28.22	7	–	7-82
Cave H.B.	1950/51-1958/59	37	150	2962	19.74	7	1	7-31

BEST IN AN INNINGS

9-100	Yuile B.W.	v Canterbury	New Plymouth	1965/66
7-28	Yuile B.W.	v Northern Districts	Hamilton	1967/68
7-31	Cave H.B.	v Auckland	Palmerston North	1952/53
7-33	Cave H.B.	v Northern Districts	New Plymouth	1956/57
7-36	Yuile B.W.	v Otago	Nelson	1962/63
7-36	Schwass A.M.	v Northern Districts	Blenheim	2001/02

BEST IN A MATCH

13-64	Cave H.B.	v Auckland	Palmerston North	1952/53
11-99	Beard D.D.	v Otago	Dunedin	1956/57
11-115	Mason M.J.	v Canterbury	Timaru	2002/03
11-134	Robertson G.K.	v Northern Districts	Nelson	1986/87
11-138	Kay D.J.	v Canterbury	Palmerston North	1976/77

MOST WICKETS IN A SEASON

		Wkts	*Ave*
O'Sullivan D.R.	1978/79	52	19.01
Schwass A.M.	2001/02	45	14.73
O'Sullivan D.R.	1977/78	44	20.22
Blair R.W.	1955/56	42	17.28
Hamilton L.J.	2001/02	42	18.40
O'Sullivan D.R.	1980/81	40	22.00
Mason M.J.	2002/03	40	19.67

Wicketkeeping

100 DISMISSALS	*Career*	*M*	*Caught*	*Stumped*	*Total*
Griggs B.B.J	2000/01-2008/09	72	195	7	202
Blain T.E.	1982/83-1994/95	83	124	19	143
Colquhoun I.A.	1953/54-1963/64	53	102	28	130
Smith I.D.S.	1977/78-1986/87	59	119	11	130
Sigley M.A.	1994/95-2002/03	44	124	4	128
Schofield R.M.	1959/60-1974/75	53	107	15	122

MOST DISMISSALS IN A SEASON

36 (35ct/1st)) Griggs B.B.J. 2005/06

MOST DISMISSALS IN A MATCH

9	(9ct)	Schofield R.M. v Wellington	Wellington	1964/65

MOST DISMISSALS IN AN INNINGS

7	(7ct)	Schofield R.M. v Wellington	Wellington	1964/65
7	(7ct)	Griggs B.B.J. v Northern Districts	Hamilton	2007/08

MOST CATCHES IN A MATCH

9	Schofield R.M. v Wellington	Wellington	1964/65

MOST CATCHES IN AN INNINGS

7	Schofield R.M. v Wellington	Wellington	1964/65
7	Griggs B.B.J. v Northern Districts	Hamilton	2007/08

Fielding

MOST CATCHES IN A MATCH

5	Congdon B.E.v Wellington	Wellington	1964/65
5	Congdon B.E. v Otago	New Plymouth	1970/71
5	Smith I.D.S. v Auckland	New Plymouth	1978/79
5	Edwards G.N. v Otago	Palmerston North	1979/80
5	Briasco P.S. v Canterbury	Christchurch	1984/85

5	Douglas M.W. v Otago	Palmerston North	1988/89
5	How J.M. v Canterbury	Palmerston North	2003/04

MOST CATCHES IN AN INNINGS

4	Congdon B.E. v New Zealand XI	New Plymouth	1962/63
4	Neal D.W. v Auckland	Wanganui	1976/77
4	Unwin P.D. v Wellington	New Plymouth	1988/89

Record Partnerships

FOR

Wicket	*Score*	*Batsmen*	*Against*	*At*	*Date*
1st	250	R.T. Hart & C.J.P. Smith	Wellington	Wellington	1985/86
2nd	317	R.T. Hart & P.S. Briasco	Canterbury	New Plymouth	1983/84
3rd	264	P.J. Ingram & M.S. Sinclair	ND	Hamilton	2008/09
4th	276*	M.D. Crowe & P.S. Briasco	Canterbury	Christchurch	1986/87
5th	301	J.I. Englefield & L.R.P.L. Taylor	Wellington	P. North	2004/05
6th	235	M.S. Sinclair & B.B.J. Griggs	Wellington	Wellington	2008/09
7th	219	B.W. Yuile & B.L. Hampton	Canterbury	Napier	1967/68
8th	173	I.D.S. Smith & G.K. Robertson	ND	Hamilton	1982/83
9th	239	H.B. Cave & I.B. Leggat	Otago	Dunedin	1952/53
10th	133	G.A. Bartlett & I.A. Colquhoun	Auckland	Auckland	1959/60

AGAINST

Wicket	*Score*	*Batsmen*	*For*	*At*	*Date*
1st	316	M.H. Austen & R.T. Hart	Wellington	Wanganui	1993/94
2nd	254*	M.H.W. Papps & J.G. Myburgh	Canterbury	Napier	2007/08
3rd	227	K.R. Rutherford & B.R. Blair	Otago	Alexandra	1988/89
4th	310	J.D. Ryder & N.R. Parlane	Wellington	P. North	2004/05
5th	341	G.R. Larsen & E.B. McSweeney	Wellington	Levin	1987/88
6th	322	M.G. Orchard & J.A.F. Yovich	CD	Napier	2005/06
7th	192	S.W. Brown & A.C. Parore	Auckland	Auckland	1990/91
8th	143	C.M. Presland & C.W. Dickeson	ND	Whangarei	1983/84
9th	113	G.J. Hopkins & S.J. Cunis	Canterbury	Christchurch	1998/99
10th	89	M.J.E. Wright & S.J. Scott	ND	Wanganui	1978/79

NORTHERN DISTRICTS

Highest Totals

546	v Wellington	Whangarei	2008/09
523-7 dec	v Otago	Hamilton	2006/07
520-8 dec	v Otago	Hamilton	1987/88
518-4 dec	v Canterbury	Christchurch	1996/97
516	v CD	Gisborne	2006/07
498-6 dec	v Central Districts	Napier	1992/93
496-8 dec	v Canterbury	Christchurch	2001/02
492	v Auckland	Auckland	1990/91
474	v Wellington	Gisborne	1996/97
472	v Otago	Hamilton	1995/96

Lowest Totals

32	v Auckland	Hamilton	1996/97
52	v Canterbury	Hamilton	1966/67
57	v Wellington	Hamilton	1961/62
59	v Canterbury	Hamilton	1960/61
64	v Otago	Dunedin	1971/72
64	v Auckland	Auckland	1987/88
69	v Australia	Hamilton	1973/74
69	v England	Hamilton	1996/97
77	v Auckland	Auckland	2000/01
79	v Auckland	Auckland	1989/90

Most Appearances

115	Bradburn G.E.
104	Roberts A.D.G.
99	White D.J.
95	Hart M.N.
93	Young B.A.
90	Dickeson C.W.
90	Marshall J.A.H.
88	Yovich J.A.F.
85	Hart R.G.
82	Kuggeleijn C.M.
82	Dunning B.
78	Bailey M.D.
75	Parker J.M.
73	Martin B.P.
72	Parlane M.E.
68	Aldridge G.W.
66	Puna N.
65	Wright M.J.E.
62	Cooper B.G.
59	Marshall H.J.H.
58	Howarth G.P.
57	Petrie E.C.
55	Bradburn W.P.
54	Crocker L.M.
51	Thomson S.A.

Longest Careers

Seasons		
17	Dunning B.	1961/62-1977/78
17	Roberts A.D.G.	1967/68-1983/84
17	Bradburn G.E.	1985/86-2001/02
17	Parlane M.E.	1992/93-2008/09
16	Kuggeleijn C.M.	1975/76-1990/91
15	Giles G.V.	1961/62-1975/76
15	Cooper B.G.	1980/81-1994/95
15	Young B.A.	1983/84-1997/98
15	Hart M.N.	1990/91-2004/05
14	Dickeson C.W.	1973/74-1986/87
14	White D.J.	1979/80-1992/93

Benefits

Kuggeleijn C.M.	1990/91
White D.J.	1992/93
Cooper B.G.	1995/96
Young B.A.	1997/98

Batting

2000 RUNS	*Career*	*M*	*In*	*NO*	*HS*	*Runs*	*Ave*	*100*
Roberts A.D.G.	1967/68-1983/84	104	192	35	128*	5533	35.24	7
White D.J.	1979/80-1992/93	99	173	15	209	4656	29.46	7
Bradburn G.E.	1985/86-2001/02	115	188	23	148*	4614	27.96	4
Parker J.M.	1972/73-1983/84	75	139	19	195	4611	38.42	7
Marshall J.A.H.	1997/98-2008/09	90	157	9	235	4457	30.11	8
Dunning B.	1961/62-1977/78	82	148	10	142	3898	28.24	3
Young B.A.	1983/84-1997/98	93	148	36	138*	3853	34.40	5
Parlane M.E.	1992/93-2008/09	72	123	9	146	3557	31.20	7
Bailey M.D.	1989/90-2001/02	78	122	8	180*	3468	30.42	6
Kuggeleijn C.M.	1975/76-1990/91	82	138	12	116	3457	27.43	3
Hart M.N.	1990/91-2004/05	95	140	15	201*	3398	27.18	4
Wright J.G.	1975/76-1983/84	43	84	3	145*	3301	40.75	5
Yovich J.A.F.	1996/97-2008/09	88	138	27	144	3143	28.31	2
Howarth G.P.	1974/75-1985/86	58	105	6	151	3122	31.53	5
Cooper B.G.	1980/81-1994/95	62	110	4	116*	2982	28.13	4

	Career	M	In	NO	HS	Runs	Ave	100
Marshall H.J.H.	1998/99-2008/09	59	104	8	153	2816	29.33	3
Crocker L.M.	1982/83-1988/89	54	100	3	126	2663	27.45	2
Wright M.J.E.	1972/73-1983/84	65	114	10	115	2632	25.30	1
Gibson J.G.	1968/69-1980/81	49	92	5	128	2580	29.65	4
Thomson S.A.	1987/88-1996/97	51	80	20	167	2530	42.16	5
Hart R.G.	1992/93-2003/04	85	119	19	102*	2135	21.35	1
Hick G.A.	1987/88-1988/89	17	30	4	211*	2055	79.03	10
Wealleans K.A.	1988/89-1994/95	43	74	4	112*	2053	29.33	4
Bradburn W.P.	1957/58-1968/69	55	103	5	107	2015	20.56	1
Horsley N.K.W.	2002/03-2007/08	35	60	3	159	2003	35.14	2

CENTURY ON DEBUT FOR PROVINCE

118	McGregor P.B.	v Auckland	Hamilton	1962/63
† 127*	Mitchell W.J.	v Pakistan	Hamilton	1964/65
14 & 153*	Maynard M.P.	v Auckland	Hamilton	1990/91

† indicates player was making his first-class debut

HIGHEST INDIVIDUAL INNINGS

235	Marshall J.A.H.	v Canterbury	Christchurch	2001/02
212*	Styris S.B.	v Otago	Hamilton	2001/02
211*	Hick G.A.	v Auckland	Auckland	1988/89
209	White D.J.	v Central Districts	Hamilton	1985/86
201*	Hart M.N.	v Auckland	Auckland	2002/03
195	Parker J.M.	v Canterbury	Whangarei	1972/73
195	Maynard M.P.	v Auckland	Auckland	1991/92
194*	White D.J.	v Central Districts	Wanganui	1990/91
180*	Bailey M.D.	v Otago	Hamilton	1997/98
177*	Turner G.M.	v Central Districts	Napier	1976/77

MOST RUNS IN A SEASON

		Runs	Ave
Hick G.A.	1988/89	1228	94.46
Maynard M.P.	1991/92	893	68.69
Hick G.A.	1987/88	827	63.61
Marshall H.J.H.	2006/07	766	54.71
Bradburn G.E.	1989/90	726	36.30
Wealleans K.A.	1989/90	721	36.05
Williamson K.S.	2008/09	707	54.38
Marshall J.A.H.	2001/02	706	39.22

MOST CENTURIES IN A SEASON

6 Hick G.A. 1988/89

TOTAL NUMBER OF CENTURIES 156

Most in one season	9	1988/89
1st	Everest J.K. 104 v Canterbury	1956/57
100th	Parlane M.E. 132* v Canterbury	1995/96

Bowling

150 WICKETS	Career	M	Wkts	Runs	Ave	5WI	10WM	Best
Dickeson C.W.	1973/74-1986/87	90	282	8242	29.22	9	2	7-79
Yovich J.A.F.	1996/97-2008/09	88	237	7815	32.97	8	1	7-64
Bradburn G.E.	1985/86-2001/02	115	231	7302	31.61	3	—	6-56
Puna N.	1956/57-1968/69	66	224	5314	23.72	11	—	6-25
Martin B.P.	1999/00-2008/09	73	187	6435	34.41	12	2	7-33
Aldridge G.W.	1998/99-2008/09	68	172	5419	31.50	5	—	5-27
de Groen R.P.	1990/91-1995/96	38	157	3320	21.14	8	2	7-50

BEST IN AN INNINGS

9-48	Tait A.R.	v Auckland	Hamilton	1996/97
8-21	Langdon M.C.	v Auckland	Auckland	1963/64
8-30	Alabaster G.D.	v NZ Under 23 XI	Hamilton	1962/63
8-37	Clarke D.B.	v Central Districts	Wanganui	1962/63
8-49	Kennedy K.D.	v Central Districts	Hamilton	1969/70

BEST IN A MATCH

16-130	Tait A.R.	v Auckland	Hamilton	1996/97
13-99	de Groen R.P.	v Otago	Alexandra	1992/93
12-55	Martin B.P.	v Auckland	Taupo	1999/00
12-109	Lissette A.F.	v Otago	Dunedin	1959/60
11-66	Tuffey D.R.	v Wellington	Hamilton	2000/01

MOST WICKETS IN A SEASON

		Wkts	*Ave*
Tait A.R.	1996/97	53	16.32
de Groen R.P.	1992/93	46	16.84
Yovich J.A.F.	2001/02	40	26.45

Wicketkeeping

100 DISMISSALS	*Career*	*M*	*Caught*	*Stumped*	*Total*
Hart R.G.	1992/93-2003/04	85	228	15	243
Young B.A.	1983/84-1997/98	93	179	11	190
Wright M.J.E.	1972/73-1983/84	65	104	17	121
Petrie E.C.	1956/57-1966/67	57	90	22	112

MOST DISMISSALS IN A SEASON

34 (33ct/1st) Hart R.G. 2001/02

MOST DISMISSALS IN A MATCH

9 (9ct) Young B.A. v Canterbury Christchurch 1986/87

MOST DISMISSALS IN AN INNINGS

7 (7ct) Young B.A. v Canterbury Christchurch 1986/87

MOST CATCHES IN A MATCH

9 Young B.A. v Canterbury Christchurch 1986/87

MOST CATCHES IN AN INNINGS

7 Young B.A. v Canterbury Christchurch 1986/87

Fielding

MOST CATCHES IN A MATCH

6 Young B.A. v Wellington Wellington 1995/96

MOST CATCHES IN AN INNINGS

4	Pairaudeau B.H. v Central Districts	Wanganui	1962/63
4	Harris S.J. (sub) v Otago	Dunedin	1965/66
4	Barton P.H. v Canterbury	Hamilton	1974/75
4	Young B.A. v Wellington	Wellington	1995/96
4	Bailey M.D. v Otago	Alexandra	1996/97

Record Partnerships

FOR

Wicket	*Score*	*Batsmen*	*Against*	*At*	*Date*
1st	165	J.G. Wright & G.M. Turner	Wellington	Lower Hutt	1976/77
2nd	237	J.G. Gibson & C.M. Kuggeleijn	Canterbury	Hamilton	1980/81
3rd	261*	M.P. Maynard & S.A. Thomson	Auckland	Hamilton	1990/91
4th	259	G.E. Bradburn & M.E. Parlane	Canterbury	Christchurch	1996/97
5th	155*	J.A.H. Marshall & N.K.W. Horsley	Canterbury	Hamilton	2005/06
6th	322	M.G. Orchard & J.A.F. Yovich	CD	Napier	2005/06
7th	136	D.J. Nash & A.R. Tait	CD	Masterton	1997/98
8th	163	P.D.McGlashan & G.W.Aldridge	Canterbury	Hamilton	2008/09
9th	188	N.R. Parlane & D.R. Tuffey	Wellington	Wellington	1999/00
10th	113*	P.D. McGlashan & G.W. Aldridge	Wellington	Wellington	2005/06

AGAINST

Wicket	*Score*	*Batsmen*	*For*	*At*	*Date*
1st	310	R.H. Vance & B.A. Edgar	Wellington	Wellington	1988/89
2nd	263	M.J. Greatbatch & M.D. Crowe	CD	Morrinsville	1986/87
3rd	394*	P.G. Kennedy & R.T. Latham	Canterbury	Rotorua	1990/91
4th	280	J.J. Crowe & D.N. Patel	Auckland	Auckland	1991/92
5th	347*	M.J. Horne & A.C. Barnes	Auckland	Auckland	2003/04
6th	175	S.P. Fleming & L.K. Germon	Canterbury	Hamilton	1993/94
7th	205	L.K. Germon & M.W. Priest	Canterbury	Christchurch	1991/92
8th	220	P.J. Wiseman & B.C. Hiini	Canterbury	Hamilton	2005/06
9th	151	R.A. Young & G.J. Morgan	Auckland	Auckland	2007/08
10th	160	L.K. Germon & W.A. Wisneski	Canterbury	Rangiora	1997/98

OTAGO

Highest Totals

624	v Central Districts	Napier	2006/07
602-8 dec	v Canterbury	Dunedin	1928/29
601-9d	v Canterbury	Christchurch	2006/07
589	v Canterbury	Christchurch	1931/32
571-8	v Central Districts	Napier	1995/96
558-8 dec	v Auckland	Dunedin	1949/50
548-7 dec	v Auckland	Dunedin	1996/97
543-8 dec	v Central Districts	New Plymouth	1978/79
521-7 dec	v Auckland	Auckland	1950/51
505	v Central Districts	Palmerston North	1999/00

Lowest Totals

34	v Wellington	Dunedin	1956/57
35	v Auckland	Christchurch	1884/85
36	v New South Wales	Dunedin	1889/90
40	v Canterbury	Dunedin	1869/70
41	v Auckland	Dunedin	1873/74
42	v Canterbury	Dunedin	1871/72
43	v Canterbury	Christchurch	1872/73
44	v Canterbury	Dunedin	1904/05
46	v Pakistan	Dunedin	1978/79
47	v Canterbury	Christchurch	1888/89

Most Appearances

108	Lees W.K.	68	Cameron F.J.	59	Smith L.D.
90	Blair B.R.	68	Rutherford K.R.	59	Turner G.M.
90	McGregor S.N.	66	Lawson R.A.	57	Burns K.J.
88	Boock S.L.	66	Cumming C.D.	55	Mills G.H.
81	Blair W.L.	65	Alabaster J.C.	55	Sewell D.G.
80	Hoskin R.N.	63	Rutherford I.A.	54	Moir A.M.
78	Mallender N.A.	61	Campbell K.O.	54	Dobbs P.W.
75	McCullum S.J.	60	Sutcliffe B.	52	McSkimming W.C.
75	Gaffaney C.B.	60	Milburn B.D.	51	Knight A.R.
69	Alabaster G.D.				

Longest Careers

Seasons			*Seasons*		
27	Downes A.D.	1887/88-1913/14	22	McGregor S.N.	1947/48-1968/69
26	Knight A.R.	1918/19-1943/44	21	Groves L.J.	1929/30-1949/50
24	Siedeberg H.G.	1898/99-1921/22	21	Alabaster G.D.	1955/56-1975/76
24	Blair W.L.	1967/68-1990/91	20	Fisher A.H.	1890/91-1909/10
23	Torrance R.C.	1905/06-1927/28	20	Watt L.	1943/44-1962/63
23	Smith L.D.	1934/35-1956/57	20	Milburn B.D.	1963/64-1982/83
23	Mills G.H.	1935/36-1957/58			

Benefits

Lees W.K. 1987/88 — Boock S.L. 1989/90 — Mallender N.A. 1992/93

Batting

2000 RUNS	*Career*	*M*	*In*	*NO*	*HS*	*Runs*	*Ave*	*100*
Sutcliffe B.	1946/47-1961/62	60	110	8	385	6028	59.09	17
Blair B.R.	1977/78-1989/90	90	154	5	143	5057	33.93	7
Rutherford K.R.	1982/83-1994/95	68	121	7	226*	5051	44.30	14
Turner G.M.	1964/65-1982/83	59	109	14	186*	4439	46.72	13
Gaffaney C.B.	1995/96-2004/05	75	138	11	194	4326	34.06	7
Cumming C.D.	2000/01-2008/09	66	117	11	173	4313	40.68	13
McGregor S.N.	1947/48-1968/69	90	167	13	114*	4259	27.65	3
Lees W.K.	1972/73-1987/88	108	179	31	124	3754	25.36	4
Blair W.L.	1967/68-1990/91	81	149	9	140	3654	26.10	2
Hoskin R.N.	1980/81-1992/93	80	138	6	157	3573	27.06	6
McCullum S.J.	1976/77-1990/91	75	131	1	134	3174	24.41	2
Rutherford I.A.	1974/75-1983/84	63	115	3	222	3122	27.87	4
Richardson M.H.	1992/93-2000/01	49	89	10	166	3089	39.10	8
Lawson R.A.	1992/93-2003/04	66	120	5	200	2890	25.13	2
Burns K.J.	1980/81-1991/92	57	98	6	136	2699	29.33	3
Campbell K.O.	1963/64-1978/79	61	108	17	111	2613	28.71	3
Dobbs P.W.	1988/89-1994/95	54	99	6	144*	2606	28.02	3
Alabaster G.D.	1955/56-1975/76	69	108	16	108	2340	25.43	3
Smith L.D.	1934/35-1956/57	59	108	16	109	2277	24.75	1
Knight A.R.	1918/19-1943/44	51	97	3	152	2245	23.88	1

CENTURY ON DEBUT FOR PROVINCE

107 & 38	Patrick W.R.	v Canterbury	Christchurch	1917/18
† 157*	McMullan J.J.M.	v Southland	Dunedin	1917/18
172 & 16	Worker R.V.de R.	v Canterbury	Christchurch	1923/24
35 & 133	Blamires E.O.	v Canterbury	Christchurch	1923/24
† 15 & 105	Watt D.G.	v Canterbury	Christchurch	1943/44
157	Hadlee W.A.	v Auckland	Dunedin	1945/46

197 & 128	Sutcliffe B.	v MCC	Dunedin	1946/47
124 & 90	Horne M.J.	v Central Districts	Wanganui	1996/97

† indicates player was making his first-class debut

HIGHEST INDIVIDUAL INNINGS

385	Sutcliffe B.	v Canterbury	Christchurch	1952/53
355	Sutcliffe B.	v Auckland	Dunedin	1949/50
338*	Blunt R.C.	v Canterbury	Christchurch	1931/32
275	Sutcliffe B.	v Auckland	Auckland	1950/51
264	Sutcliffe B.	v Central Districts	Dunedin	1959/60
241	Horne M.J.	v Auckland	Auckland	1997/98
226*	Rutherford K.R.	v India	Dunedin	1989/90
222	Rutherford I.A.	v Central Districts	New Plymouth	1978/79
221	Blunt R.C.	v Canterbury	Dunedin	1928/29
201	Reid J.R.	v Canterbury	Dunedin	1957/58
201	Sutcliffe B.	v Northern Districts	Hamilton	1960/61
200	Lawson R.A.	v Central Districts	Napier	1995/96

MOST RUNS IN A SEASON

		Runs	*Ave*
Turner G.M.	1975/76	1027	85.58
Cumming C.D.	2008/09	784	65.33
Blair B.R.	1989/90	759	47.43
Cumming C.D.	2002/03	751	46.93
Rutherford K.R.	1989/90	747	67.90
Sutcliffe B.	1952/53	709	78.77
Turner G.M.	1974/75	703	78.11

MOST CENTURIES IN A SEASON

4	Turner G.M.	1974/75
4	Turner G.M.	1975/76
4	Cumming C.D.	2008/09

TOTAL NUMBER OF CENTURIES		**218**
Most in one season	10	2002/03
1st	Baker J.C. 103 v Hawke's Bay	1901/02
100th	Cairns B.L. 110 v Wellington	1979/80
200th	Hopkins G.J. 139* v Auckland	2006/07

Bowling

150 WICKETS	*Career*	*M*	*Wkts*	*Runs*	*Ave*	*5WI*	*10WM*	*Best*
Boock S.L.	1973/74-1989/90	88	399	8235	20.63	28	5	8-57
Downes A.D.	1887/88-1913/14	44	287	3902	13.59	33	13	8-35
Moir A.M.	1949/50-1961/62	54	282	5926	21.01	20	5	8-37
Mallender N.A.	1983/84-1992/93	78	268	5433	20.27	14	3	7-27
Alabaster J.C.	1956/57-1971/72	65	264	5738	21.73	14	3	6-39
Cameron F.J.	1953/54-1966/67	68	258	5204	20.17	9	—	6-21
Alabaster G.D.	1955/56-1975/76	69	205	4774	23.28	13	1	7-74
McSkimming W.C.	1999/00-2008/09	52	185	4553	24.61	8	1	6-39
Sewell D.G.	1995/96-2005/06	55	178	5198	29.20	7	1	8-31
Fisher A.H.	1890/91-1909/10	40	176	2766	15.71	9	1	9-50
O'Connor S.B.	1994/95-2002/03	35	160	3321	20.75	11	2	6-31

BEST IN AN INNINGS

9-50	Fisher A.H.	v Queensland	Dunedin	1896/97
9-72	Cooke F.H.	v Canterbury	Christchurch	1884/85
9-93	Petherick P.J.	v Northern Districts	Dunedin	1975/76
8-28	Hendley W.	v Canterbury	Dunedin	1869/70
8-31	Sewell D.G.	v Central Districts	Invercargill	1996/97

8-35	Downes A.D.	v Canterbury	Dunedin	1891/92
8-37	Moir A.M.	v Northern Districts	Hamilton	1958/59
8-46	Cairns B.L.	v Wellington	Invercargill	1978/79
8-55	Moir A.M.	v Canterbury	Dunedin	1951/52
8-57	Boock S.L.	v Auckland	Dunedin	1989/90
8-59	Boock S.L.	v Wellington	Invercargill	1978/79
8-61	Cooke F.H.	v Canterbury	Christchurch	1882/83
8-66	Wiseman P.J.	v Wellington	Wellington	1996/97
8-70	Hay W.A.	v Southland	Dunedin	1917/18
8-99	Blunt R.C.	v Auckland	Dunedin	1930/31
8-119	Moir A.M.	v Central Districts	New Plymouth	1953/54
8-136	Shacklock F.J.	v Canterbury	Christchurch	1903/04

BEST IN A MATCH

15-94	Cooke F.H.	v Canterbury	Christchurch	1882/83
15-104	Boock S.L.	v Auckland	Dunedin	1989/90
15-203	Moir A.M.	v Central Districts	New Plymouth	1953/54
14-93	Torrance R.C.	v Hawke's Bay	Napier	1908/09
14-103	Downes A.D.	v Hawke's Bay	Dunedin	1893/94
14-126	Moir A.M.	v Canterbury	Dunedin	1951/52
13-111	Downes A.D.	v Hawke's Bay	Dunedin	1901/02
13-144	Boock S.L.	v Northern Districts	Whangarei	1980/81

MOST WICKETS IN A SEASON

		Wkts	*Ave*
Boock S.L.	1978/79	54	18.51
Mallender N.A.	1991/92	49	12.30
Boock S.L.	1986/87	48	15.48
Petherick P.J.	1977/78	45	17.15
Petherick P.J.	1975/76	42	20.16
O'Connor S.B.	2002/03	42	18.71
Moir A.M.	1953/54	41	17.58
Boock S.L.	1980/81	41	18.46
Boock S.L.	1987/88	41	21.82
Webb M.G.	1973/74	40	14.65
Cairns B.L.	1978/79	40	22.70

Wicketkeeping

100 DISMISSALS	*Career*	*M*	*Caught*	*Stumped*	*Total*
Lees W.K.	1972/73-1987/88	108	208	36	244
Milburn B.D.	1963/64-1982/83	60	148	17	165
Croy M.G.	1994/95-2001/02	42	127	4	131
Robinson S.A.	1984/85-1996/97	45	117	5	122
Hopkins G.J.	2003/04-2006/07	33	111	3	114
Mills G.H.	1935/36-1957/58	55	78	29	107

MOST DISMISSALS IN A SEASON

38 (37ct/1st) Hopkins G.J. 2004/05

MOST DISMISSALS IN A MATCH

10 (10ct) Hopkins G.J. v Canterbury Dunedin 2004/05

MOST DISMISSALS IN AN INNINGS

7 (7ct) Croy M.G. v Auckland Auckland 2001/02

MOST CATCHES IN A MATCH

10 Hopkins G.J. v Canterbury Dunedin 2004/05

MOST CATCHES IN AN INNINGS

7 Croy M.G. v Auckland Auckland 2001/02

Fielding

MOST CATCHES IN A MATCH

6	McCullum N.L. v Central Districts	Napier	2006/07

MOST CATCHES IN AN INNINGS

4	Geddes A.E. v Canterbury	Christchurch	1903/04
4	Watson E.A. v Canterbury	Dunedin	1953/54
4	Campbell K.O. v Auckland	Dunedin	1969/70
4	Blair W.L. v Canterbury	Invercargill	1977/78
4	Blair W.L. v Northern Districts	Dunedin	1978/79
4	McCullum S.J. v Auckland	Dunedin	1987/88
4	Dobbs P.W. v India	Dunedin	1989/90
4	Burns K.J. v Northern Districts	Dunedin	1990/91
4	Gaffaney C.B. v Wellington	Wellington	1996/97
4	McCullum N.L. v Auckland	Dunedin	2004/05
4	McCullum N.L. v Central Districts	Napier	2006/07

Record Partnerships

FOR

Wicket	*Score*	*Batsmen*	*Against*	*At*	*Date*
1st	373	B. Sutcliffe & L. Watt	Auckland	Auckland	1950/51
2nd	254	K.J. Burns & K.R. Rutherford	Wellington	Oamaru	1987/88
3rd	227	K.R. Rutherford & B.R. Blair	CD	Alexandra	1988/89
4th	235	K.J. Burns & R.N. Hoskin	ND	Hamilton	1987/88
5th	266	B. Sutcliffe & W.S. Haig	Auckland	Dunedin	1949/50
6th	165	G.M. Turner & W.K. Lees	Wellington	Wellington	1975/76
7th	182	B. Sutcliffe & A.W. Gilbertson	Canterbury	Christchurch	1952/53
8th	165*	J.N. Crawford & A.G. Eckhold	Wellington	Wellington	1914/15
9th	208	W.C. McSkimming & B.E. Scott	Auckland	Auckland	2004/05
10th	184	R.C. Blunt & W. Hawksworth	Canterbury	Christchurch	1931/32

AGAINST

Wicket	*Score*	*Batsmen*	*For*	*At*	*Date*
1st	299	M.D. Bell & R.A. Jones	Wellington	Dunedin	2001/02
2nd	279	M.D. Bell & M.E. Parlane	Wellington	Dunedin	2006/07
3rd	445	P.E. Whitelaw & W.N. Carson	Auckland	Dunedin	1936/37
4th	274	R.A. Jones & S.R. Mather	Wellington	Wellington	2000/01
5th	255	B.R. Taylor & J.V. Coney	Wellington	Dunedin	1972/73
6th	293*	P.G. Fulton & N.T. Broom	Canterbury	Dunedin	2004/05
7th	265	J.L. Powell & N. Dorreen	Canterbury	Christchurch	1929/30
8th	215	J.R. Murray & A.C. Cummins	West Indies	Dunedin	1994/95
9th	239	H.B. Cave & I.B. Leggat	CD	Dunedin	1952/53
10th	138	K.C. James & A.W.S. Brice	Wellington	Wellington	1926/27

WELLINGTON

Highest Totals

614-8	v Canterbury	Christchurch	2006/07
608-9 dec	v Northern Districts	Hamilton	1998/99
595	v Auckland	Wellington	1927/28
590-8 dec	v Central Districts	Palmerston North	2004/05
575-7 dec	v Otago	Wellington	1951/52
569	v Auckland	Wellington	1923/24
560	v Otago	Dunedin	1923/24
553	v Canterbury	Wellington	1931/32
547-8d	v Auckland	Wellington	2005/06
544	v Canterbury	Christchurch	1997/98

Lowest Totals

19	v Nelson	Nelson	1885/86
22	v Canterbury	Wellington	1903/04
29	v Nelson	Nelson	1879/80
30	v Nelson	Nelson	1883/84
31	v Nelson	Nelson	1887/88
34	v Canterbury	Wellington	1886/87
35	v Auckland	Wellington	1873/74
36	v Nelson	Nelson	1885/86
37	v Nelson	Nelson	1876/77
42	v New South Wales	Wellington	1895/96
42	v Otago	Wellington	1945/46

Most Appearances

120	Gray E.J.
119	Vance R.H.
102	McSweeney E.B.
99	Nevin C.J.
89	Morrison J.F.M.
87	Edgar B.A.
86	Bell M.D.
84	Chatfield E.J.
79	Larsen G.R.
74	Coney J.V.
72	Wells J.D.
68	Sinclair B.W.
64	Murray B.A.G.
62	Patel J.S.
60	Newdick G.A.
60	Parlane N.R.
60	Woodcock L.J.
59	Blair R.W.
58	Reid J.R.
58	Ritchie T.D.
56	Brice A.W.S.
54	Bilby G.P.
54	McGirr H.M.
53	Franklin J.E.C.
52	Cederwall B.W.
50	Butler L.C.

Longest Careers

Seasons		
29	Luckie M.M.F.	1891/92-1919/20
27	Dempster C.S.	1921/22-1947/48
25	Tucker K.H.	1895/96-1919/20
24	James K.C.	1923/24-1946/47
22	Hutchings J.H.	1903/04-1924/25
22	Collins D.C.	1905/06-1926/27
22	Reaney T.P.L.	1927/28-1948/49
20	McGirr H.M.	1913/14-1932/33
20	Lamason J.R.	1927/28-1946/47

Benefits

Morrison J.F.M.	1983/84
Chatfield E.J.	1985/86
Coney J.V.	1986/87
Edgar B.A.	1987/88
Gray E.J.	1989/90
Vance R.H.	1990/91
McSweeney E.B.	1991/92
Larsen G.R.	1996/97

Batting

2000 RUNS	Career	M	In	NO	HS	Runs	Ave	100
Edgar B.A.	1975/76-1989/90	87	160	13	162	6494	44.17	15
Vance R.H.	1976/77-1990/91	119	205	18	254*	6440	34.43	12
Bell M.D.	1997/98-2008/09	86	149	11	265	6230	45.47	20
Morrison J.F.M.	1967/68-1983/84	89	160	22	180*	4694	34.01	6
Nevin C.J.	1995/96-2008/09	99	150	23	143*	4579	36.05	4
Reid J.R.	1947/48-1964/65	58	102	8	296	4538	48.27	13
McSweeney E.B.	1981/82-1993/94	102	153	23	205*	4296	33.04	5
Gray E.J.	1975/76-1991/92	120	181	38	128*	4228	29.56	5
Murray B.A.G.	1958/59-1972/73	64	116	9	213	3753	35.07	3
Sinclair B.W.	1955/56-1970/71	68	116	14	148	3583	35.12	2
Hiddleston J.S.	1913/14-1928/29	41	75	1	212	3413	46.12	8
Parlane N.R.	2002/03-2008/09	60	92	8	165	3359	39.98	7
Coney J.V.	1971/72-1986/87	74	126	21	120*	3251	30.96	4
Newdick G.A.	1970/71-1980/81	60	112	6	143	3236	30.52	4
McGirr H.M.	1913/14-1932/33	54	97	4	141	3032	32.60	5
Wells J.D.	1989/90-2000/01	72	113	18	115	3016	31.74	5
Jones A.H.	1985/86-1993/94	39	67	11	181*	2978	53.17	7
Larsen G.R.	1984/85-1998/99	79	118	25	161	2938	31.59	2
Bilby G.P.	1962/63-1976/77	54	95	11	161	2852	33.95	3
Dempster C.S.	1921/22-1947/48	40	76	3	154	2602	35.64	4
Franklin J.E.C.	1998/99-2008/09	53	77	10	219	2563	38.25	5
Ritchie T.D.	1982/83-1990/91	58	92	14	106	2494	31.97	3
Tindill E.W.T.	1932/33-1949/50	39	73	5	149	2442	35.91	6
Woodcock L.J.	2001/02-2008/09	60	97	10	106	2439	28.03	3
Parlane M.E.	2003/04-2007/08	40	69	3	203	2397	36.31	7
Jones R.A.	2000/01-2003/04	36	63	4	188	2343	39.71	7
Burnett G.P.	1987/88-1992/93	44	80	13	203*	2029	30.28	1

CENTURY ON DEBUT FOR PROVINCE

163	Williams A.B.	v Canterbury	Christchurch	1896/97
110 & 5*	Crawford J.N.	v Auckland	Auckland	1917/18
113 & 53	Kortlang H.H.L.	v Auckland	Wellington	1922/23
117 & 6	Bernau E.H.L.	v Auckland	Wellington	1922/23
† 106 & 0	Tindill E.W.T.	v Auckland	Auckland	1932/33
† 110	Ongley J.A.	v Otago	Wellington	1938/39
† 27 &141*	Smith K.F.H.	v Central Districts	Wellington	1953/54
† 132 & 2*	Bilby G.P.	v Central Districts	Wellington	1962/63
† 39 & 156*	Aiken J.M.	v Canterbury	Christchurch	1989/90
115	Fleming S.P.	v Central Districts	Wellington	2001/02

† indicates player was making his first-class debut

HIGHEST INDIVIDUAL INNINGS

296	Reid J.R.	v Northern Districts	Wellington	1962/63
283	Reid J.R.	v Otago	Wellington	1952/53
265	Bell M.D.	v Central Districts	Napier	2007/08
254*	Vance R.H.	v Northern Districts	Wellington	1988/89
236	Ryder J.D.	v Central Districts	Palmerston North	2004/05
222*	Midlane F.A.	v Otago	Wellington	1914/15
219	Bell M.D.	v Northern Districts	Hamilton	1998/99
219	Franklin J.E.C.	v Auckland	Auckland	2008/09
216	Bell M.D.	v Auckland	Auckland	1997/98
214*	Kortlang H.H.L.	v Auckland	Wellington	1921/26
213	Murray B.A.G.	v Otago	Dunedin	1968/69

212	Hiddleston J.S.	v Canterbury	Wellington	1925/26
208	Franklin J.E.C.	v Auckland	Wellington	2005/06
205*	McSweeney E.B.	v Central Districts	Levin	1987/88
204	Hiddleston J.S.	v Auckland	Wellington	1925/26
203*	Burnett G.P.	v Northern Districts	Hamilton	1991/92
203	Parlane M.E.	v Auckland	Auckland	2004/05
202	Austen M.H.	v Central Districts	Wanganui	1993/94

MOST RUNS IN A SEASON

		Runs	Ave
Vance R.H.	1988/89	888	80.72
Jones R.A.	2000/01	849	47.16
Bell M.D.	2000/01	844	52.75
Parlane N.R.	2007/08	809	57.78
Edgar B.A.	1988/89	762	63.50
Bell M.D.	2007/08	731	73.10
Edgar B.A.	1978/79	728	45.50
Jones R.A.	2002/03	726	45.37
Edgar B.A.	1989/90	720	40.00
Twose R.G.	1994/95	720	80.00
Jones A.H.	1988/89	701	87.62

MOST CENTURIES IN A SEASON

5 Bell M.D. 2000/01

TOTAL NUMBER OF CENTURIES **282**

Most in one season	10 1988/89, 1994/95, 2000/01, 2007/08, 2008/09	
1st	Heenan G.C. 146* v Hawke's Bay	1886/87
100th	Sinclair B.W. 102* v Northern Districts	1963/64
200th	Chandler P.J.B. 177 v Auckland	1996/97

Bowling

150 WICKETS	Career	M	Wkts	Runs	Ave	5WI	10WM	Best
Chatfield E.J.	1973/74-1989/90	84	403	7531	18.68	23	7	8-24
Gray E.J.	1975/76-1991/92	120	357	9778	27.38	13	3	8-37
Blair R.W.	1951/52-1964/65	59	330	5004	15.16	30	10	9-72
Brice A.W.S.	1902/03-1927/28	56	229	4684	20.45	17	7	9-67
Upham E.F.	1892/93-1909/10	40	227	3393	14.94	17	2	7-24
Gillespie M.R.	1999/00-2008/09	47	193	4592	23.79	9	—	6-42
Franklin J.E.C.	1998/99-2008/09	53	175	4019	22.96	6	1	7-30
O'Brien I.E.	2000/01-2007/08	44	173	3864	22.33	9	1	8-55
Reid J.R.	1947/48-1964/65	58	172	3115	18.11	10	—	7-29
McGirr H.M.	1913/14-1932/33	54	166	4326	26.06	7	1	7-45
Morrison B.D.	1953/54-1964/65	45	163	3858	23.66	7	2	7-42

BEST IN AN INNINGS

9-67	Brice A.W.S.	v Auckland	Wellington	1918/19
9-72	Blair R.W.	v Auckland	Wellington	1956/57
9-75	Blair R.W.	v Canterbury	Wellington	1956/57
8-13	Firth J.P.	v Hawke's Bay	Wellington	1883/84
8-21	Penn A.J.	v Canterbury	Wellington	2001/02
8-24	Chatfield E.J.	v Northern Districts	Lower Hutt	1979/80
8-34	Fisher F.E.	v Canterbury	Wellington	1952/53
8-36	Blair R.W.	v Otago	Dunedin	1952/53
8-37	Gray E.J.	v Canterbury	Lower Hutt	1985/86
8-50	Butler L.C.	v NZ Under 23 XI	Wellington	1965/66
8-55	O'Brien I.E.	v Auckland	Wellington	2006/07
8-58	Ashbolt F.L.	v Hawke's Bay	Napier	1897/98
8-59	Hiddleston J.S.	v Canterbury	Christchurch	1918/19
8-64	Collinge R.O.	v Auckland	Auckland	1967/68
8-78	Gray E.J.	v Auckland	Wellington	1989/90
8-83	Chatfield E.J.	v Otago	Dunedin	1986/87

BEST IN A MATCH

14-136	Blair R.W.	v Canterbury	Wellington	1956/57
14-151	Gray E.J.	v Canterbury	Lower Hutt	1985/86
13-58	Salmon I.J.	v Nelson	Wellington	1873/74
13-86	Chatfield E.J.	v West Indies	Lower Hutt	1979/80
13-91	Gore A.H.	v Hawke's Bay	Napier	1886/87
13-92	Middleton F.S.	v Hawke's Bay	Wellington	1919/20
13-97	Ashbolt F.L.	v Hawke's Bay	Napier	1897/98
13-117	O'Brien I.E.	v Auckland	Wellington	2006/07
13-157	Tucker K.H.	v Auckland	Wellington	1900/01
13-176	Brice A.W.S.	v Auckland	Wellington	1920/21

MOST WICKETS IN A SEASON

		Wkts	*Ave*
Chatfield E.J.	1979/80	49	10.51
Gray E.J.	1984/85	48	21.75
Chatfield E.J.	1981/82	47	16.87
Blair R.W.	1956/57	46	9.47
Walker M.D.J.	2002/03	45	18.00
Gillespie M.R.	2005/06	43	23.16
Saunders J.V.	1913/14	41	17.58
Chatfield E.J.	1976/77	41	19.48
O'Brien I.E.	2000/01	41	19.68
Penn A.J.	2001/02	40	18.30

Wicketkeeping

100 DISMISSALS	*Career*	*M*	*Caught*	*Stumped*	*Total*
McSweeney E.B.	1981/82-1993/94	102	289	39	328
Nevin C.J.	1995/95-2008/09	99	260	9	269
Therkleson I.J.	1966/67-1973/74	39	93	7	100

MOST DISMISSALS IN A SEASON

46 (46ct) Nevin C.J. 2000/01

MOST DISMISSALS IN A MATCH

10	(10ct)	Nevin C.J. v Otago	Dunedin	1995/96

MOST DISMISSALS IN AN INNINGS

6	(6ct)	Vance R.H. v Otago	Wellington	1977/78
6	(5ct 1st)	Nevin C.J. v Central Districts	Nelson	1995/96

MOST CATCHES IN A MATCH

10	Nevin C.J. v Otago	Dunedin	1995/96

MOST CATCHES IN AN INNINGS

6	Vance R.H. v Otago	Wellington	1977/78

Fielding

MOST CATCHES IN A MATCH

7	Morrison J.F.M. v Northern Districts	Wellington	1980/81

MOST CATCHES IN AN INNINGS

5	Lamason J.R. v Otago	Dunedin	1937/38
5	Morrison J.F.M. v Northern Districts	Wellington	1980/81
5	Brodie J.M. v Otago	Wellington	2008/09

Record Partnerships

FOR

Wicket	*Score*	*Batsmen*	*Against*	*At*	*Date*
1st	333	B.A. Edgar & A.H. Jones	Auckland	Wellington	1988/89
2nd	287	M.D. Bell & J.D. Wells	Auckland	Auckland	1997/98
3rd	346	G.P. Burnett & R.A. Verry	ND	Hamilton	1991/92
4th	310	J.D. Ryder & N.R. Parlane	CD	P. North	2004/05
5th	341	G.R. Larsen & E.B. McSweeney	CD	Levin	1987/88
6th	226	E.J. Gray & R.W. Ormiston	CD	Wellington	1981/82
7th	250	C.J. Nevin & M.D.J. Walker	Otago	Wellington	2003/04
8th	180	R.G. Twose & M.C. Goodson	Otago	Dunedin	1994/95
9th	127	F.L.H. Mooney & R.A. Buchan	Auckland	Wellington	1943/44
10th	138	K.C. James & A.W.S. Brice	Otago	Wellington	1926/27

AGAINST

Wicket	*Score*	*Batsmen*	*For*	*At*	*Date*
1st	287	B.R. Hartland & G.R. Stead	Canterbury	Christchurch	1994/95
2nd	254	K.J. Burns & K.R. Rutherford	Otago	Oamaru	1987/88
3rd	213	G.M. Turner & B.E. Congdon	Otago	Dunedin	1972/73
4th	278	A.W. Roberts & M.L. Page	Canterbury	Wellington	1931/32
5th	301	J.I. Englefield & L.R.P.L. Taylor	CD	P. North	2004/05
6th	235	M.S. Sinclair & B.B.J. Griggs	CD	Wellington	2008/09
7th	241	N.J. Astle & M.W. Priest	Canterbury	Christchurch	1994/95
8th	189	W.N. Carson & A.M. Matheson	Auckland	Auckland	1938/39
9th	188	N.R. Parlane & D.R. Tuffey	ND	Wellington	1999/00
10th	113*	P.D. McGlashan & G.W. Aldridge	Wellington	Wellington	2005/06

INTER-PROVINCIAL RECORDS

AUCKLAND v CANTERBURY

First match	*Played*	*Won by Auckland*	*Won by Canterbury*	*Drawn*
1873/74	126	46	40	40

Highest totals	**A**	693-9 dec		Auckland	1939/40
	C	514-6 dec		Christchurch	2002/03
Lowest totals	**A**	13		Auckland	1877/78
	C	62		Rangiora	1998/99
Highest innings	**A**	268	T.G. McIntosh	Auckland	2007/08
	C	301*	P.G. Fulton	Christchurch	2002/03
Best bowling *(innings)*	**A**	9-75	R. Neill	Auckland	1891/92
	C	9-56	D.J. McBeath	Christchurch	1918/19
Best bowling *(match)*	**A**	13-85	R.S. Cunis	Christchurch	1963/64
	C	15-168	D.J. McBeath	Christchurch	1918/19

Record Partnerships

AUCKLAND

1st	286	B. Sutcliffe & D.D. Taylor	Auckland	1948/49
2nd	197	T.G. McIntosh & R.A. Jones	Rangiora	2008/09
3rd	278	T.J. Franklin & D.N. Patel	Christchurch	1985/86
4th	206	T.G. McIntosh & L. Vincent	Christchurch	2000/01
5th	161*	B. Sutcliffe & D.D. Taylor	Auckland	1946/47
6th	160	P.N. Webb & P.J. Kelly	Auckland	1985/86
7th	224	V.J. Scott & A.M. Matheson	Auckland	1937/38
8th	153	R.J. Nicol & R.A. Young	Auckland	2001/02
9th	96	C. Pringle & D.K. Morrison	Rangiora	1995/96
10th	83	S.W. Brown & C. Pringle	Christchurch	1990/91

CANTERBURY

1st	306	L.A. Cuff & J.D. Lawrence	Christchurch	1893/94
2nd	179	B.G. Hadlee & N.M. Parker	Auckland	1978/79
3rd	183	G.R. Stead & C.Z. Harris	Christchurch	2000/01
4th	147	M.L. Page & R.O. Talbot	Christchurch	1930/31
5th	158	P.G. Kennedy & M.W. Priest	Christchurch	1991/92
6th	172	L.A. Butterfield & R.C.S.A. Shand	Christchurch	1945/46
7th	142	G.J. Hopkins & P.J. Wiseman	Auckland	2002/03
8th	166	R.J. Hadlee & D.R. Hadlee	Christchurch	1983/84
9th	115	G.J. Hopkins & A.M. Ellis	Auckland	2002/03
10th	83	H.C. Wilson & H.W. Monaghan	Christchurch	1913/14
	83	M. Graham & A.P. Cobden	Auckland	1935/36

AUCKLAND v CENTRAL DISTRICTS

First match	Played	Won by Auckland	Won by Central Districts	Drawn
1950/51	79	30	20	29

Highest totals	**A**	662-5 dec	Auckland	2008/09
	CD	594-8 dec	Auckland	1995/96
Lowest totals	**A**	71	Palmerston North	2001/02
	CD	59	New Plymouth	1958/59
Highest innings	**A**	256 J.A. Raval	Auckland	2008/09
	CD	166 M.S. Sinclair	Masterton	1998/99
Best bowling *(innings)*	**A**	7-29 R.S. Cunis	Auckland	1961/62
	CD	7-31 H.B. Cave	Palmerston North	1952/53
Best bowling *(match)*	**A**	12-146 K.W. Hough	Auckland	1959/60
	CD	13-64 H.B. Cave	Palmerston North	1952/53

Record Partnerships

AUCKLAND

1st	172	R.A. Jones & M.J. Horne	Auckland	2004/05
2nd	167	G.O. Rabone & D.D. Coleman	Auckland	1951/52
3rd	184	R.A. Jones & A.K. Kitchen	Lincoln	2008/09
4th	159*	R.J. Nicol & G.J. Hopkins	Auckland	2008/09
5th	234*	V.J. Scott & J.B. Morris	Auckland	1951/52
6th	165	J.J. Crowe & J.G. Bracewell	Auckland	1987/88
7th	192	S.W. Brown & A.C. Parore	Auckland	1990/91
8th	111	L. Vincent & R.A. Young	Auckland	2004/05
9th	104*	R.A. Young & C.J. Drum	Auckland	2000/01
10th	86*	L.J. Shaw & A.J. McKay	Auckland	2007/08

CENTRAL DISTRICTS

1st	172	C.J.P. Smith & P.S. Briasco	New Plymouth	1985/86
2nd	207*	R.G. Twose & M.W. Douglas	Auckland	1991/92
3rd	224	M.S. Sinclair & C.M. Spearman	Auckland	2003/04
4th	155	R.T. Hart & T.E. Blain	Masterton	1989/90
5th	168	B.B.J. Griggs & T.I. Weston	Auckland	2006/07
6th	220	M.H. Toynbee & I.D.S. Smith	Napier	1982/83
7th	165	R.K. Brown & M.E.L. Lane	Palmerston North	1993/94
8th	94	S.W. Duff & D.J. Leonard	Wanganui	1991/92
9th	82	R.J. Schaw & G.J.T. Hegglun	Auckland	2006/07
10th	133	G.A. Bartlett & I.A. Colquhoun	Auckland	1959/60

AUCKLAND v NORTHERN DISTRICTS

First match	*Played*	*Won by Auckland*	*Won by Northern Districts*	*Drawn*
1956/57	73	26	17	30

Highest totals	**A**	547-8 dec		Auckland	2000/01
	ND	492		Auckland	1990/91
Lowest totals	**A**	69		Auckland	1963/64
	ND	32		Hamilton	1996/97
Highest innings	**A**	209	P.A. Horne	Auckland	1988/89
		209*	M.J. Horne	Auckland	2003/04
	ND	211*	G.A. Hick	Auckland	1988/89
Best bowling	**A**	7-28	K.P. Walmsley	Hamilton	2004/05
(innings)	**ND**	9-48	A.R. Tait	Hamilton	1996/97
Best bowling	**A**	11-71	J.A. Hayes	Auckland	1957/58
(match)	**ND**	16-130	A.R. Tait	Hamilton	1996/97

Record Partnerships

AUCKLAND

1st	197	T.J. Franklin & P.A. Horne	Auckland	1985/86
2nd	175	B.A. Pocock & J.M. Aiken	Auckland	2000/01
3rd	152	T.J. Franklin & J.J. Crowe	Rotorua	1983/84
4th	280	J.J. Crowe & D.N. Patel	Auckland	1991/92
5th	347*	M.J. Horne & A.C. Barnes	Auckland	2003/04
6th	157	J.F. Reid & J.R. Wiltshire	Auckland	1977/78
7th	136	T.K. Canning & B.G.K. Walker	Hamilton	2004/05
8th	93	G.J. Hopkins & R.M. Hira	Gisborne	2007/08
9th	151	R.A. Young & G.J. Morgan	Auckland	2007/08
10th	103	P.J. Kelly & G.B. Troup	Auckland	1985/86

NORTHERN DISTRICTS

1st	156	J.A.H. Marshall & N.K.W. Horsley	Auckland	2003/04
2nd	167	M.D. Bell & G.E. Bradburn	Hamilton	1994/95
3rd	261*	M.P. Maynard & S.A. Thomson	Hamilton	1990/91
4th	252	S.A. Thomson & B.A. Young	Auckland	1990/91
5th	142	M.P. Maynard & B.A. Young	Auckland	1991/92
6th	146*	G.A. Hick & S.A. Thomson	Auckland	1988/89
7th	127	C.M. Kuggeleijn & S.A. Thomson	Auckland	1988/89
8th	90	R.G. Hart & M.E. Parlane	Hamilton	1994/95
9th	185	M.P. Maynard & S.B. Doull	Auckland	1991/92
10th	82	S.B. Doull & B.P. Martin	Taupo	1999/00

AUCKLAND v OTAGO

First match	Played	Won by Auckland	Won by Otago	Drawn
1873/74	116	59	25	32

Highest totals	**A**	627		Lincoln	2006/07
	O	558-8 dec		Dunedin	1949/50
Lowest totals	**A**	48		Dunedin	1889/90
	O	35		Christchurch	1884/85
Highest innings	**A**	290	W.N. Carson	Dunedin	1936/37
	O	355	B. Sutcliffe	Dunedin	1949/50
Best bowling *(innings)*	**A**	9-36	A.F. Wensley	Auckland	1929/30
	O	8-57	S.L. Boock	Dunedin	1989/90
Best bowling *(match)*	**A**	14-63	A.W. Rees	Dunedin	1889/90
	O	15-104	S.L. Boock	Dunedin	1989/90

Record Partnerships

AUCKLAND

1st	240	T.G. McIntosh & M.J. Horne	Dunedin	2001/02
2nd	170	L.G. Hemus & A.E. Relf	Auckland	1909/10
3rd	445	P.E. Whitelaw & W.N. Carson	Dunedin	1936/37
4th	273	T.G. McIntosh & R.J. Nicol	Lincoln	2006/07
5th	197	C.C.R. Dacre & C.F.W. Allcott	Dunedin	1926/27
6th	209*	A.C. Parore & A.P. O'Dowd	Dunedin	1991/92
7th	177*	A.C. Barnes & J.M. Mills	Alexandra	1995/96
8th	140	J.G. Kemp & J.M. McIntyre	Dunedin	1969/70
9th	82	M.Y. Pasupati & P.B. Erasmus	Dunedin	2006/07
10th	119	W.N. Carson & J. Cowie	Auckland	1937/38

OTAGO

1st	373	B. Sutcliffe & L. Watt	Auckland	1950/51
2nd	227	P.W. Dobbs & M.J. Lamont	Dunedin	1990/91
3rd	199	W.S. Haig & B. Sutcliffe	Auckland	1954/55
4th	177	M.J. Lamont & M.H. Richardson	Alexandra	1995/96
5th	266	B. Sutcliffe & W.S. Haig	Dunedin	1949/50
6th	145	M.J. Horne & M.G. Croy	Auckland	1997/98
	145	S.B. Haig & D.C. de Boorder	Auckland	2008/09
7th	164	A. Galland & A.R. Knight	Auckland	1925/26
8th	84	L.R. Pearson & J.C. Alabaster	Auckland	1964/65
9th	208	W.C. McSkimming & B.E. Scott	Auckland	2004/05
10th	60	L.D. Smith & G.W.F. Overton	Auckland	1946/47

AUCKLAND v WELLINGTON

First match	Played	Won by Auckland	Won by Wellington	Drawn
1873/74	135	56	33	46

Highest totals	**A**	522		Wellington	1918/19
	W	595		Wellington	1927/28
Lowest totals	**A**	48		Wellington	1889/90
	W	35		Wellington	1873/74
Highest innings	**A**	194	W.N. Carson	Auckland	1936/37
	W	219	J.E.C. Franklin	Auckland	2008/09
Best bowling *(innings)*	**A**	8-51	R. Neill	Auckland	1895/96
	W	9-67	A.W.S. Brice	Wellington	1918/19
Best bowling *(match)*	**A**	14-65	J.A. Hayes	Auckland	1957/58
	W	13-117	I.E. O'Brien	Wellington	2006/07

Record Partnerships

AUCKLAND

1st	201	A. Anthony & E. Horspool	Auckland	1924/25
2nd	241	T.J. Franklin & J.J. Crowe	Wellington	1988/89
3rd	203*	B.A. Pocock & A.C. Parore	Auckland	1997/98
4th	180	A.N.C. Snedden & C.C.R. Dacre	Wellington	1922/23
5th	174	R.W. Morgan & J.G. Kemp	Auckland	1967/68
6th	176	V.J. Scott & O.C. Cleal	Auckland	1940/41
7th	131	G.L. Weir & C.C.R. Dacre	Wellington	1927/28
8th	189	W.N. Carson & A.M. Matheson	Auckland	1938/39
9th	122	H.T. Schuster & R.S. Cunis	Wellington	1964/65
10th	97	A.C. Kerr & H.C. Nottman	Auckland	1941/42

WELLINGTON

1st	333	B.A. Edgar & A.H. Jones	Wellington	1988/89
2nd	287	M.D. Bell & J.D. Wells	Auckland	1997/98
3rd	246	N.R. Parlane & G.D. Elliott	Auckland	2007/08
4th	207	F.T. Badcock & T.C. Lowry	Wellington	1927/28
5th	282	J.E.C. Franklin & L.J. Woodcock	Auckland	2008/09
6th	134	K.C. James & H.M. McGirr	Wellington	1926/27
7th	144	J.R. Reid & P.T. Barton	Auckland	1959/60
8th	137	F.L.H. Mooney & F.E. Fisher	Wellington	1952/53
9th	127	F.L.H. Mooney & R.A. Buchan	Wellington	1943/44
10th	113	F.L.H. Mooney & E.C.V. Knapp	Wellington	1943/44

CANTERBURY v CENTRAL DISTRICTS

First match	Played	Won by Canterbury	Won by Central Districts	Drawn
1950/51	80	27	20	33

Highest totals	**C**	559		Christchurch	1993/94
	CD	549-8 dec		Christchurch	1998/99
Lowest totals	**C**	68		Levin	1985/86
	CD	91		Christchurch	1954/55
Highest innings	**C**	251*	C.Z. Harris	Rangiora	1996/97
	CD	212*	D.P. Kelly	Blenheim	2000/01
Best bowling *(innings)*	**C**	9-13	P.J. Wiseman	Christchurch	2004/05
	CD	9-100	B.W. Yuile	New Plymouth	1965/66
Best bowling *(match)*	**C**	12-86	P.J. Wiseman	Christchurch	2004/05
	CD	11-115	M.J. Mason	Timaru	2002/03

Record Partnerships

CANTERBURY

1st	185	B.R. Hartland & D.J. Murray	Palmerston North	1994/95
2nd	254*	M.H.W. Papps & J.G. Myburgh	Napier	2007/08
3rd	208	M.H.W. Papps & C.D. McMillan	Christchurch	2006/07
4th	204	T.W. Jarvis & K. Thomson	Wanganui	1969/70
5th	290	C.Z. Harris & G.R. Stead	Blenheim	1996/97
6th	149	M.W. Priest & L.K. Germon	Christchurch	1988/89
7th	184*	C.L. Bull & B.P. Isherwood	Nelson	1971/72
8th	136	G.R. Stead & C.J. Anderson	Christchurch	2000/01
9th	113	G.J. Hopkins & S.J. Cunis	Christchurch	1998/99
10th	85	G.T. Dowling & A.F. Rapley	Christchurch	1958/59

CENTRAL DISTRICTGS

1st	178	P.J. Ingram & J.M. How	Napier	2002/03
2nd	317	R.T. Hart & P.S. Briasco	New Plymouth	1983/84
3rd	197	M.J. Greatbatch & M.D. Crowe	New Plymouth	1986/87
4th	276*	M.D. Crowe & P.S. Briasco	Christchurch	1986/87
5th	235*	G.P. Sulzberger & J.D. Ryder	Napier	2002/03
6th	141	B.B.J. Griggs & E.P. Thompson	Christchurch	2004/05
7th	219	B.W. Yuile & B.L. Hampton	Napier	1967/68
8th	159	B.J. Diamanti & R.R. Sherlock	Napier	2007/08
9th	89	S.W. Duff & D.J. Leonard	Christchurch	1993/94
10th	98	I.A. Rutherford & D.J. Kay	Napier	1977/78

CANTERBURY v NORTHERN DISTRICTS

First match	Played	Won by Canterbury	Won by Northern Districts	Drawn
1956/57	72	27	14	31

Highest totals	C	549		Christchurch	1996/97
	ND	518-4 dec		Christchurch	1996/97
Lowest totals	C	83		Christchurch	1961/62
	ND	52		Hamilton	1966/67
Highest innings	C	237*	R.T. Latham	Rotorua	1990/91
	ND	235	J.A.H. Marshall	Christchurch	2001/02
Best bowling (innings)	C	7-24	J.W. Kiddey	Hamilton	1960/61
	ND	7-58	R.P. de Groen	Hamilton	1995/96
Best bowling (match)	C	12-81	R.J. Hadlee	Christchurch	1986/87
	ND	11-129	R.P. de Groen	Hamilton	1995/96

Record Partnerships

CANTERBURY

1st	214	B.A. Bolton & G.T. Dowling	Christchurch	1959/60
2nd	243	M.H.W. Papps & S.L. Stewart	Hamilton	2006/07
3rd	394*	P.G. Kennedy & R.T. Latham	Rotorua	1990/91
4th	181	V.R. Brown & R.T. Latham	Gisborne	1986/87
5th	252*	R.T. Latham & M.W. Priest	Christchurch	1988/89
6th	175	S.P. Fleming & L.K. Germon	Hamilton	1993/94
7th	205	L.K. Germon & M.W. Priest	Christchurch	1991/92
8th	220	P.J. Wiseman & B.C. Hiini	Hamilton	2005/06
9th	76	C.R.W. Dickel & K.I. Ferries	Hamilton	1974/75
10th	160	L.K. Germon & W.A. Wisneski	Rangiora	1997/98

NORTHERN DISTRICTS

1st	136	B.A. Pocock & M.D. Bell	Christchurch	1996/97
2nd	237	J.G. Gibson & C.M. Kuggeleijn	Hamilton	1980/81
3rd	150	R.D. Broughton & A.D.G. Roberts	Christchurch	1980/81
4th	259	G.E. Bradburn & M.E. Parlane	Christchurch	1996/97
5th	155*	J.A.H. Marshall & N.K.W. Horsley	Hamilton	2005/06
6th	180	S.A. Thomson & M.N. Hart	Hamilton	1992/93
7th	111	J.A.F. Yovich & R.G. Hart	Gisborne	2003/04
8th	163	P.D. McGlashan & G.W. Aldridge	Hamilton	2008/09
9th	69	M.N. Hart & S.B. Doull	Rangiora	2000/01
10th	62	M.N. Hart & G.W. Aldridge	Rangiora	2000/01

CANTERBURY v OTAGO

First match	Played	Won by Canterbury	Won by Otago	Drawn
1863/64	170	78	60	32

Highest totals	**C**	777	Christchurch	1996/97
	O	602-8 dec	Dunedin	1928/29
Lowest totals	**C**	25	Christchurch	1866/67
	O	40	Dunedin	1869/70
Highest innings	**C**	221* P.G. Fulton	Dunedin	2004/05
	O	385 B. Sutcliffe	Christchurch	1952/53
Best bowling *(innings)*	**C**	9-95 M.W. Priest	Dunedin	1989/90
	O	9-72 F.H. Cooke	Christchurch	1884/85
Best bowling *(match)*	**C**	13-181 W.E. Merritt	Christchurch	1935/36
	O	15-94 F.H. Cooke	Christchurch	1882/83

Record Partnerships

CANTERBURY

1st	226*	W.A. Hadlee & J.G. Leggat	Christchurch	1948/49
2nd	210	W.A. Hadlee & F.P. O'Brien	Christchurch	1940/41
3rd	178	R.M. Frew & M.H.W. Papps	Christchurch	2000/01
4th	187	P.G. Fulton & J.G. Myburgh	Christchurch	2007/08
5th	236	C.Z. Harris & N.J. Astle	Christchurch	1996/97
6th	293*	P.G. Fulton & N.T. Broom	Dunedin	2004/05
7th	265	J.L. Powell & N. Dorreen	Christchurch	1929/30
8th	167	C.F.K. van Wyk & R.J. McCone	Christchurch	2008/09
9th	109	J.H. Bennett & A.W. Thomas	Dunedin	1913/14
10th	98	S.A. Orchard & C. Boxshall	Dunedin	1908/09

OTAGO

1st	209	B. Sutcliffe & L. Watt	Dunedin	1947/48
2nd	170	C.C. Hopkins & G.G. Austin	Christchurch	1911/12
3rd	221	R.C. Blunt & J.J.M. McMullan	Dunedin	1928/29
4th	168	K.F.M. Uttley & V.J.T. Chettleburgh	Dunedin	1936/37
5th	147	K.J. Burns & D.J. Walker	Christchurch	1985/86
6th	118	P.C. Semple & G.D. Alabaster	Christchurch	1969/70
7th	182	B. Sutcliffe & A.W. Gilbertson	Christchurch	1952/53
8th	146	M.H. Austen & P.J. Wiseman	Christchurch	1996/97
9th	134	J.W. Wilson & N.A. Mallender	Christchurch	1992/93
10th	184	R.C. Blunt & W. Hawksworth	Christchurch	1931/32

CANTERBURY v WELLINGTON

First match	*Played*	*Won by Canterbury*	*Won by Wellington*	*Drawn*	*Tied*
1883/84	141	48	52	40	1

Highest totals	**C**	613-7 dec		Christchurch	2006/07
	W	614-8		Christchurch	2006/07
Lowest totals	**C**	37		Wellington	1925/26
	W	22		Wellington	1903/04
Highest innings	**C**	206	M.L. Page	Wellington	1931/32
		206	G.T. Dowling	Christchurch	1962/63
	W	212	J.S. Hiddleston	Wellington	1925/26
Best bowling *(innings)*	**C**	10-28	A.E. Moss	Christchurch	1889/90
	W	9-75	R.W. Blair	Wellington	1956/57
Best bowling *(match)*	**C**	13-72	A.E. Moss	Christchurch	1889/90
	W	14-136	R.W. Blair	Wellington	1956/57

Record Partnerships

CANTERBURY

1st	287	B.R. Hartland & G.R. Stead	Christchurch	1994/95
2nd	174	G.T. Dowling & J.W. Burtt	Wellington	1967/68
3rd	187*	C.D. McMillan & R.T. Latham	Christchurch	1994/95
4th	278	M.L. Page & A.W. Roberts	Wellington	1931/32
5th	183	C.Z. Harris & C.D. McMillan	Christchurch	1996/97
6th	209	C.Z. Harris & A.J. Redmond	Rangiora	2001/02
7th	241	N.J. Astle & M.W. Priest	Christchurch	1994/95
8th	114	A.W. Thomas & H.B. Whitta	Christchurch	1919/20
9th	182*	L.K. Germon & R.M. Ford	Christchurch	1989/90
10th	85	A.W. Hart & C.H. Thiele	Rangiora	1984/85

WELLINGTON

1st	239	C.S. Dempster & W.H. Dustin	Wellington	1931/32
2nd	209*	A.H. Jones & M.D. Crowe	Christchurch	1992/93
3rd	206	A.H. Preston & J.E.F. Beck	Christchurch	1955/56
4th	187	H.M. McGirr & T.C. Lowry	Christchurch	1930/31
5th	134*	J.F.M. Morrison & R.W. Ormiston	Christchurch	1981/82
6th	184	G.D. Elliott & S.M. Mills	Christchurch	2006/07
7th	176	S.M. Mills & C.J. Nevin	Christchurch	2006/07
8th	154	K.C. James & F.T. Badcock	Christchurch	1926/27
9th	115	E.H.L. Bernau & K.C. James	Wellington	1923/24
10th	87	N.R. Hoar & R. Allen	Christchurch	1944/45

CENTRAL DISTRICTS v NORTHERN DISTRICTS

First match	Played	Won by Central Districts	Won by Northern Districts	Drawn
1956/57	71	21	19	31

Highest totals	**CD**	479		Napier	2004/05
		479		Hamilton	2008/09
	ND	516		Gisborne	2006/07
Lowest totals	**CD**	51		Hamilton	1957/58
	ND	86		New Plymouth	1956/57
Highest innings	**CD**	247	P.J. Ingram	Hamilton	2008/09
	ND	209	D.J. White	Hamilton	1985/86
Best bowling *(innings)*	**CD**	7-28	B.W. Yuile	Hamilton	1967/68
	ND	8-37	D.B. Clarke	Wanganui	1962/63
Best bowling *(match)*	**CD**	11-134	G.K. Robertson	Nelson	1986/87
	ND	10-78	D.B. Clarke	Wanganui	1962/63

Record Partnerships

CENTRAL DISTRICTS

1st	215	J.M. How & M.S. Sinclair	Napier	2004/05
2nd	263	M.J. Greatbatch & M.D. Crowe	Morrinsville	1986/87
3rd	264	P.J. Ingram & M.S. Sinclair	Hamilton	2008/09
4th	161	L.G. Howell & M.J. Greatbatch	Rotorua	1995/96
5th	199	M.D. Crowe & M.W. Douglas	Rotorua	1989/90
6th	132*	T.E. Blain & S.W. Duff	Wanganui	1990/91
7th	179	B.B.J. Griggs & C.J.M. Furlong	Hamilton	2001/02
8th	173	I.D.S. Smith & G.K. Robertson	Hamilton	1982/83
9th	116	V. Pollard & R.O. Collinge	Palmerston North	1964/65
10th	48	M.J. Mason & L.J. Hamilton	Blenheim	2001/02

NORTHERN DISTRICTS

1st	167	M.E. Parlane & M.D. Bell	New Plymouth	1994/95
2nd	199	R.E.W. Mawhinney & D.J. White	Hamilton	1985/86
3rd	142	D.J. White & G.W. McKenzie	Hamilton	1985/86
4th	169	D.J. White & B.S. Oxenham	Wanganui	1990/91
5th	128	D.J. White & B.G. Cooper	Nelson	1986/87
6th	322	M.G. Orchard & J.A.F. Yovich	Napier	2005/06
7th	136	D.J. Nash & A.R. Tait	Masterton	1997/98
8th	143	C.M. Presland & C.W. Dickeson	Whangarei	1983/84
9th	107	R.G. Hart & A.R. Tait	Rotorua	1995/96
10th	89	M.J.E. Wright & S.J. Scott	Wanganui	1978/79

CENTRAL DISTRICTS v OTAGO

First match	*Played*	*Won by Central Districts*	*Won by Otago*	*Drawn*
1950/51	77	25	23	29

Highest totals	**CD**	526		Napier	1995/96
	O	624		Napier	2006/07
Lowest totals	**CD**	74		Invercargill	1996/97
	O	73		Dunedin	1986/87
Highest innings	**CD**	243*	M.S. Sinclair	Napier	2007/08
	O	264	B. Sutcliffe	Dunedin	1959/60
Best bowling *(innings)*	**CD**	7-36	B.W. Yuile	Nelson	1962/63
	O	8-31	D.G. Sewell	Invercargill	1996/97
Best bowling *(match)*	**CD**	11-99	D.D. Beard	Dunedin	1956/57
	O	15-203	A.M. Moir	New Plymouth	1953/54

Record Partnerships

CENTRAL DISTRICTS

1st	137	T.E. Blain & R.T. Hart	Oamaru	1984/85
2nd	242*	J.M. How & M.S. Sinclair	New Plymouth	2005/06
3rd	223	C.J.P. Smith & S.W.J. Wilson	Blenheim	1990/91
4th	207	G.P. Sulzberger & A.J. Penn	Napier	1995/96
5th	168	B.F. Smith & M.W. Douglas	Alexandra	2000/01
6th	184*	M.S. Sinclair & T.I. Lythe	Napier	2007/08
7th	123	I.D.S. Smith & S.J. Gill	Napier	1981/82
8th	113	L.R.P.L. Taylor & R.J. Schaw	Napier	2006/07
9th	239	H.B. Cave & I.B. Leggat	Dunedin	1952/53
10th	60*	B.L. Cairns & A.B. Jordan	Wanganui	1975/76

OTAGO

1st	305	R.A. Lawson & M.G. Croy	Napier	1995/96
2nd	169	G.M. Turner & R.W. Anderson	Dunedin	1974/75
3rd	227	K.R. Rutherford & B.R. Blair	Alexandra	1988/89
4th	200	B.R. Blair & G.J. Dawson	Dunedin	1982/83
5th	192	M.H. Richardson & I.S. Billcliff	Napier	1994/95
6th	147	R.N. Hoskin & J.K. Lindsay	Oamaru	1985/86
7th	121*	W.K. Lees & B. Abernethy	Napier	1981/82
8th	102	W.C. McSkimming & B.E. Scott	New Plymouth	2005/06
9th	92	D.E.C. McKechnie & B.L. Cairns	Dunedin	1976/77
10th	78	C.B. Gaffaney & D.G. Sewell	Palmerston North	1999/00

CENTRAL DISTRICTS v WELLINGTON

First match	Played	Won by Central Districts	Won by Wellington	Drawn
1950/51	78	15	28	35

Highest totals	**CD**	523		Wellington	2008/09
	W	590-8 dec		Palmerston North	2004/05
Lowest totals	**CD**	50		Upper Hutt	1979/80
	W	88		Wellington	1991/92
Highest innings	**CD**	207	R.T. Hart	Wellington	1985/86
	W	265	M.D. Bell	Napier	2007/08
Best bowling *(innings)*	**CD**	7-55	E.P. Thompson	Napier	2003/04
	W	7-30	J.E.C. Franklin	Wellington	2005/06
Best bowling *(match)*	**CD**	11-149	E.P. Thompson	Napier	2003/04
	W	10-103	B.D. Morrison	Wellington	1955/56

Record Partnerships

CENTRAL DISTRICTS

1st	250	R.T. Hart & C.J.P. Smith	Wellington	1985/86
2nd	171*	J.M. How & G.H. Worker	Napier	2008/09
3rd	180	C.D. Ingham & M.J. Greatbatch	Napier	1994/95
4th	172*	P.S. Briasco & M.W. Douglas	Palmerston North	1990/91
5th	301	J.I. Englefield & L.R.P.L. Taylor	Palmerston North	2004/05
6th	235	M.S. Sinclair & B.B.J. Griggs	Wellington	2008/09
7th	134	M.W. Douglas & S.W. Duff	Napier	1991/92
8th	84	P.M. Blackbourn & G.K. Robertson	Palmerston North	1983/84
9th	73	G.R. Hay & E.J. McInnis	Napier	2007/08
10th	52	D.J. Leonard & A.J. Alcock	Wellington	1992/93

WELLINGTON

1st	316	M.H. Austen & R.T. Hart	Wanganui	1993/94
2nd	215	M.D. Bell & M.E. Parlane	Napier	2004/05
3rd	186	J.D. Wells & S.J. Blackmore	New Plymouth	1999/00
4th	310	J.D. Ryder & N.R. Parlane	Palmerston North	2004/05
5th	341	G.R. Larsen & E.B. McSweeney	Levin	1987/88
6th	226	E.J. Gray & R.W. Ormiston	Wellington	1981/82
7th	161	S.P. Fleming & M.D.J. Walker	Wellington	2001/02
8th	135	G.R. Larsen & J.E.C. Franklin	Wellington	1998/99
9th	83	T. Vaikvee & R.O. Collinge	New Plymouth	1973/74
10th	81	L.C. Butler & R.E. Reid	Wanganui	1959/60

NORTHERN DISTRICTS v OTAGO

First match	*Played*	*Won by Northern Districts*	*Won by Otago*	*Drawn*
1956/57	69	24	19	26

Highest totals	**ND**	523-7 dec		Hamilton	2006/07
	O	457		Hamilton	1987/88
Lowest totals	**ND**	64		Dunedin	1971/72
	O	77		Gisborne	1999/00
Highest innings	**ND**	212*	S.B. Styris	Hamilton	2001/02
	O	201	B. Sutcliffe	Hamilton	1960/61
Best bowling	**ND**	7-42	K. Treiber	Hamilton	1985/86
(innings)	**O**	9-93	P.J. Petherick	Dunedin	1975/76
Best bowling	**ND**	13-99	R.P. de Groen	Alexandra	1992/93
(match)	**O**	13-144	S.L. Boock	Whangarei	1980/81

Record Partnerships

NORTHERN DISTRICTS

1st	151	G.P. Howarth & R.W. Fulton	Gisborne	1974/75
2nd	222	L.M. Crocker & C.M. Kuggeleijn	Hamilton	1983/84
3rd	190	B-J. Watling & J.A.H. Marshall	Hamilton	2007/08
4th	203	S.A. Thomson & M.P. Maynard	Hamilton	1991/92
5th	117	W.J. Mitchell & P.D. Stone	Hamilton	1966/67
6th	191	S.B. Styris & R.G. Hart	Hamilton	2001/02
7th	131	D.R. Flynn & P.D. McGlashan	Gisborne	2005/06
8th	102	J.A.F. Yovich & B.P. Martin	Dunedin	2005/06
9th	96	R.G. Hart & B.P. Martin	Dunedin	2001/02
	96	A.P. Devcich & G.W. Aldridge	Gisborne	2004/05
10th	97	R.G. Hart & G.L. West	Hamilton	2002/03

OTAGO

1st	260	R.A. Lawson & Mohammad Wasim	Dunedin	2002/03
2nd	220	M.H. Richardson & C.D. Cumming	Hamilton	2000/01
3rd	150	K.B.K. Ibadulla & K.J. Burns	Gisborne	1989/90
4th	235	K.J. Burns & R.N. Hoskin	Hamilton	1987/88
5th	123	R. Hendry & L.R. Pearson	Dunedin	1961/62
6th	146	G.J. Hopkins & N.L. McCullum	Dunedin	2006/07
7th	152*	N.L. McCullum & W.C. McSkimming	Hamilton	2007/08
8th	129	B. Sutcliffe & T. Flaws	Hamilton	1960/61
9th	39	P.W. Hills & S.L. Boock	Gisborne	1988/89
10th	59	P.W. Hills & V.F. Johnson	Gisborne	1988/89

NORTHERN DISTRICTS v WELLINGTON

First match	Played	Won by Northern Districts	Won by Wellington	Drawn
1956/57	73	13	34	26

Highest totals	**ND**	546		Whangarei	2008/09
	W	608-9 dec		Hamilton	1998/99
Lowest totals	**ND**	57		Hamilton	1961/62
	W	78		Hamilton	2000/01
Highest innings	**ND**	151	G.P. Howarth	Hamilton	1979/80
	W	296	J.R. Reid	Wellington	1962/63
Best bowling *(innings)*	**ND**	7-12	D.R. Tuffey	Hamilton	2000/01
	W	8-24	E.J. Chatfield	Lower Hutt	1979/80
Best bowling *(match)*	**ND**	11-66	D.R. Tuffey	Hamilton	2000/01
	W	12-39	E.J. Chatfield	Lower Hutt	1979/80

Record Partnerships

NORTHERN DISTRICTS

1st	165	G.M. Turner & J.G. Wright	Lower Hutt	1976/77
2nd	165	B.S. Wilson & M.E. Parlane	Whangarei	2008/09
3rd	169	J.M. Parker & A.D.G. Roberts	Wellington	1983/84
4th	208	S.A. Thomson & M.P. Maynard	Hamilton	1991/92
5th	149	K.A. Wealleans & B.A. Young	Wellington	1991/92
6th	170	E.C. Petrie & R.J. McPherson	Hamilton	1959/60
7th	94	J.A.F. Yovich & P.D. McGlashan	Hamilton	2005/06
8th	152	J.A.H. Marshall & M.G. Orchard	Hamilton	2006/07
9th	188	N.R. Parlane & D.R. Tuffey	Wellington	1999/00
10th	113*	P.D. McGlashan & G.W. Aldridge	Wellington	2005/06

WELLINGTON

1st	310	B.A. Edgar & R.H. Vance	Wellington	1988/89
2nd	215	M.D. Bell & J.D. Wells	Hamilton	1998/99
3rd	346	G.P. Burnett & R.A. Verry	Hamilton	1991/92
4th	179	P.T. Barton & J.R. Reid	Wellington	1964/65
5th	147*	J.V. Coney & G.P. Bilby	Lower Hutt	1976/77
6th	139	J.F.M. Morrison & R.W. Smith	Wellington	1972/73
7th	164	J.E.C. Franklin & C.J. Nevin	Wellington	2008/09
8th	80	M.D.J. Walker & L.J. Woodcock	Hamilton	2003/04
9th	87	I.J. Therkleson & R.O. Collinge	Whangarei	1973/74
10th	74	M.D.J. Walker & J.S. Patel	Hamilton	2003/04

OTAGO v WELLINGTON

First match	Played	Won by Otago	Won by Wellington	Drawn
1892/93	113	29	53	31

Highest totals	**O**	495	Dunedin	1923/24
	W	575-7 dec	Wellington	1951/52
Lowest totals	**O**	34	Dunedin	1956/57
	W	42	Wellington	1945/46
Highest innings	**O**	182 K.R. Rutherford	Oamaru	1987/88
	W	283 J.R. Reid	Wellington	1951/52
Best bowling *(innings)*	**O**	8-46 B.L. Cairns	Invercargill	1978/79
	W	8-36 R.W. Blair	Dunedin	1952/53
Best bowling *(match)*	**O**	12-277 A.W. Alloo	Dunedin	1923/24
	W	12-87 E.J. Chatfield	Wellington	1973/74

Record Partnerships

OTAGO

1st	193	M.H. Richardson & M.J. Horne	Wellington	2000/01
2nd	254	K.J. Burns & K.R. Rutherford	Oamaru	1987/88
3rd	213	G.M. Turner & B.E. Congdon	Dunedin	1972/73
4th	211*	K.J. Burns & A.H. Jones	Wellington	1984/85
5th	134	C.B. Gaffaney & G.J. Hopkins	Dunedin	2003/04
6th	165	G.M. Turner & W.K. Lees	Wellington	1975/76
7th	143	T.C. Fraser & C.D.G. Toomey	Dunedin	1939/40
8th	165*	J.N. Crawford & A.G. Eckhold	Wellington	1914/15
9th	80	G.H. Mills & L.J. Groves	Dunedin	1937/38
10th	90	B.L. Cairns & G.B. Thomson	Lower Hutt	1979/80

WELLINGTON

1st	299	M.D. Bell & R.A. Jones	Dunedin	2001/02
2nd	279	M.D. Bell & M.E. Parlane	Dunedin	2006/07
3rd	246	B.A.G. Murray & J.F.M. Morrison	Dunedin	1968/69
4th	274	R.A. Jones & S.R. Mather	Wellington	2000/01
5th	255	B.R. Taylor & J.V. Coney	Dunedin	1972/73
6th	184	H.M. McGirr & D.C. Collins	Dunedin	1923/24
7th	250	C.J. Nevin & M.D.J. Walker	Wellington	2003/04
8th	180	R.G. Twose & M.C. Goodson	Dunedin	1994/95
9th	72	F.T. Badcock & K.C. James	Wellington	1926/27
10th	138	K.C. James & A.W.S. Brice	Wellington	1926/27

PROVINCIAL COMPETITION

Plunket Shield

1921/22 – 1974/75

Awarded by the Governor of New Zealand, Lord Plunket, the Shield was given to Canterbury as the association with the best record in the 1906/07 season. From 1907/08 to 1920/21 the trophy was competed for under a challenge system but thereafter on a competition basis.

HOLDERS	*Tenure*	*Challenges resisted*
Canterbury	17 December, 1907	—
Auckland	17 December, 1907 to 1 February, 1911	7
Canterbury	1 February, 1911 to 12 February, 1912	2
Auckland	12 February, 1912 to 31 January, 1913	1
Canterbury	31 January, 1913 to 27 December, 1918	9
Wellington	27 December, 1918 to 24 January, 1919	—
Canterbury	24 January, 1919 to 4 January, 1920	2
Auckland	4 January, 1920 to 10 January, 1921	3
Wellington	10 January, 1921	—

Shell Series

1975/76-2000/01

In 1975/76, a new competition, sponsored by Shell, was established. For the first four seasons this was played under a two-stage system — the first round of 15 games (all teams playing each other) was for the Shell Cup*, while the second round (on a knock-out basis culminating in a final) carried the season's major prize, the Shell Trophy.

From 1979/80, only the Shell Trophy was competed for. The Shell Cup was reallocated to the limited-over competition in 1980/81, while the Plunket Shield was reserved for matches between the North and South Islands.

WINNERS

1921/22	Auckland
1922/23	Canterbury
1923/24	Wellington
1924/25	Otago
1925/26	Wellington
1926/27	Auckland
1927/28	Wellington
1928/29	Auckland
1929/30	Wellington
1930/31	Canterbury
1931/32	Wellington
1932/33	Otago
1933/34	Auckland
1934/35	Canterbury
1935/36	Wellington
1936/37	Auckland
1937/38	Auckland
1938/39	Auckland
1939/40	Auckland
1945/46	Canterbury
1946/47	Auckland
1947/48	Otago
1948/49	Canterbury
1949/50	Wellington
1950/51	Otago
1951/52	Canterbury
1952/53	Otago
1953/54	Central Districts
1954/55	Wellington
1955/56	Canterbury
1956/57	Wellington
1957/58	Otago
1958/59	Auckland
1959/60	Canterbury
1960/61	Wellington
1961/62	Wellington
1962/63	Northern Districts
1963/64	Auckland
1964/65	Canterbury
1965/66	Wellington
1966/67	Central Districts
1967/68	Central Districts
1968/69	Auckland
1969/70	Otago
1970/71	Central Districts
1971/72	Otago
1972/73	Wellington
1973/74	Wellington
1974/75	Otago
1975/76	Canterbury *Canterbury**
1976/77	Otago *Northern Districts**
1977/78	Auckland *Canterbury**
1978/79	Otago *Otago**
1979/80	Northern Districts
1980/81	Auckland
1981/82	Wellington
1982/83	Wellington
1983/84	Canterbury
1984/85	Wellington
1985/86	Otago
1986/87	Central Districts
1987/88	Otago
1988/89	Auckland
1989/90	Wellington
1990/91	Auckland
1991/92	Central Districts & Northern Districts
1992/93	Northern Districts
1993/94	Canterbury
1994/95	Auckland
1995/96	Auckland
1996/97	Canterbury
1997/98	Canterbury
1998/99	Central Districts
1999/00	Northern Districts
2000/01	Wellington

State Championship

from 2001/02

State Insurance took over the sponsorship of the competition in 2001/02. The format remained unchanged.

WINNERS

2001/02	Auckland	2002/03	Auckland	2003/04	Wellington
2004/05	Auckland	2005/06	Central Districts	2006/07	Northern Districts
2007/08	Canterbury	2008/09	Auckland		

TEAM RECORDS

Playing Record of the First-class Sides in New Zealand

	P	*W*	*L*	*D*
Canterbury	642	235	215	192*
Wellington	615	223	194	198†
Otago	594	169	263	162
Auckland	586	231	157	198
Central Districts	412	104	135	173*
Northern Districts	378	88	139	151
New Zealand	233	50	77	106
England/MCC	132	63	10	59*
Australia	109	59	7	43
Hawke's Bay	53	9	34	10
Pakistan	51	20	6	25
West Indies	40	11	10	19
India	36	11	8	17
New South Wales	23	16	2	5
South Africa	22	9	1	12
Sri Lanka	22	4	7	11
Nelson	17	9	6	2*
North Island	16	6	5	5
Fiji	15	5	8	2
South Island	15	4	8	3
New Zealand A	13	7	1	5
New Zealand U23 XI	12	—	9	3
Zimbabwe	10	2	3	5
President's XI	9	—	3	6
NZ Academy XI	9	3	3	3
Bangladesh	9	—	9	—
Southland	8	1	5	2
Taranaki	8	1	6	1
Southern	8	4	1	3
Northern	7	2	1	4
Central	7	2	3	2
The Rest	6	1	3	2
Victoria	6	1	1	4
NZ XI	6	—	3	3
Young New Zealand	5	—	2	3
Queensland	5	3	1	1
England A	7	3	—	4
Pakistan A	5	—	1	4
Tasmania	4	—	3	1
Sri Lanka A	4	—	3	1
Shell XI	3	1	1	1
Emerging Players	3	—	1	2
Governor General's XI	2	1	1	—
Commonwealth XI	2	2	—	—
D.H. Robins' XI	2	—	—	2
NZ Major Association XI	2	—	—	2
U-Bix XI	1	—	—	1
West Coast (NI)	1	1	—	—
D. Reese's XI	1	—	1	—
Minor Associations	1	—	1	—
Sir Julien Cahn's XI	1	—	—	1
South Island Army	1	1	—	—
North Island Army	1	—	1	—
New Zealand Army	1	1	—	—
New Zealand Air Force	1	—	1	—
New Zealand Services	1	—	—	1
Canterbury/Otago	1	—	—	1
Auckland/Wellington	1	—	1	—
ND/CD	1	—	—	1
Auckland XI	1	—	—	1
Otago Invitation XI	1	—	1	—
Canterbury XI	1	—	—	1
Board XI	1	—	1	—
Australian Academy XI	1	1	—	—
TOTALS	**4208**	**1366**	**1366**	**1476**

** includes a tie* † *includes two ties*

Highest Match Aggregates

Runs-Wickets			
1945-18	Canterbury v Wellington	Christchurch	1994/95
1905-40	Otago v Wellington	Dunedin	1923/24
1567-37	Auckland v Wellington	Auckland	1936/37
1554-40	Wellington v Auckland	Wellington	1922/23
1531-39	Wellington v Auckland	Wellington	1923/24
1513-34	Central Districts v Otago	Napier	2006/07
1505-25	New Zealand v India	Auckland	1989/90
1501-37	Canterbury v Otago	Christchurch	1931/32

Highest Team Totals

by any first-class team in New Zealand

777	Canterbury v Otago at Christchurch	1996/97
752-8 dec	NSW v Otago at Dunedin	1923/24
693-9 dec	Auckland v Canterbury at Auckland	1939/40
671-4	New Zealand v Sri Lanka at Wellington	1990/91
663	Australia v New Zealand at Auckland	1920/21
662-5 dec	Auckland v Central Districts at Auckland	2008/09
660-5 dec	West Indies v New Zealand at Wellington	1994/95
658	Australians v Auckland at Auckland	1913/14
653-5 dec	MCC v New Zealand at Dunedin	1935/36
653	Australians v Canterbury at Christchurch	1913/14
643	Auckland v Canterbury at Auckland	1919/20
627-7d	Auckland v Otago at Lincoln	2006/07
624	Otago v Central Districts at Napier	2006/07
621-5 dec	South Africa v New Zealand at Auckland	1998/99
619-9 dec	New Zealand v India at Napier	2008/09
616-5 dec	Pakistan v New Zealand at Auckland	1988/89
614-8	Wellington v Canterbury at Christchurch	2006/07
613-7d	Canterbury v Wellington at Christchurch	2006/07
610-6 dec	Australia v New Zealand at Auckland	1913/14
608-9 dec	Wellington v Northern Districts at Hamilton	1998/99
602-8 dec	Otago v Canterbury at Dunedin	1928/29
601-9d	Otago v Canterbury at Christchurch	2006/07

Most Runs in a Match by One Side

Runs-Wickets				
1025-20	560 & 465	Wellington v Otago	Dunedin	1923/24
973-6	498-2d & 475-4	Wellington v Canterbury	Christchurch	1994/95
972-12	496 & 476-2d	Canterbury v Wellington	Christchurch	1994/95
971-14	511-6d & 460-8	Australia v New Zealand	Wellington	1973/74
948-20	569 & 379	Wellington v Auckland	Wellington	1923/24
880-20	385 & 495	Otago v Wellington	Dunedin	1923/24
875-18	273 & 602-8d	Otago v Canterbury	Dunedin	1928/29
874-15	391 & 483-5d	New Zealand v India	Auckland	1989/90
860-8	662-5d & 198-3	Auckland v Central Districts	Auckland	2008/09
855-20	595 & 260	Wellington v Auckland	Wellington	1927/28
851-18	280 & 571-8	Otago v Central Districts	Napier	1995/96

Lowest Match Aggregates

completed matches, i.e. not drawn

Runs-Wickets			
151-30	Canterbury v Otago	Christchurch	1866/67
153-31	Otago v Canterbury	Dunedin	1896/97
156-30	Nelson v Wellington	Nelson	1885/86
159-31	Nelson v Wellington	Nelson	1887/88
176-32	Otago v Tasmania	Dunedin	1883/84
183-40	Nelson v Wellington	Nelson	1883/84
192-30	Taranaki v Hawke's Bay	Hawera	1891/92

The lowest aggregates since 1900 are:

Runs-Wickets			
241-30	Otago v Southland	Dunedin	1919/20
278-40	Southland v Otago	Invercargill	1918/19
295-28	New Zealand v Australia	Wellington	1945/46

Lowest Match Aggregates by One Side

55	36 & 19	Wellington v Nelson	Nelson	1885/86
57	25 & 32	Canterbury v Otago	Christchurch	1866/67
64	35 & 29	Taranaki v Hawke's Bay	Hawera	1891/92
72	30 & 42	Wellington v Nelson	Nelson	1883/84
76	34 & 42	Canterbury v Otago	Dunedin	1863/64
76	27 & 49	Canterbury v Otago	Dunedin	1896/97
79	31 & 48	Wellington v Nelson	Nelson	1887/88
80	51 & 29	Wellington v Nelson	Nelson	1879/80
87	40 & 47	Tasmania v Otago	Dunedin	1883/84
95	43 & 52	Otago v Canterbury	Christchurch	1872/73
96	41 & 55	Southland v Otago	Invercargill	1918/19
96	42 & 54	New Zealand v Australia	Wellington	1945/46
97	37 & 60	Wellington v Nelson	Christchurch	1876/77
99	65 & 34	Wellington v Canterbury	Wellington	1886/87

Lowest Team Totals

by any first-class team in New Zealand

13	Auckland v Canterbury at Auckland (included 8 extras)	1877/78
19	Wellington v Nelson at Nelson	1885/86
22	Wellington v Canterbury at Wellington	1903/04
25	Canterbury v Otago at Christchurch	1866/67
26	NZ v England at Auckland	1954/55
27	Canterbury v Otago at Dunedin	1896/97
28	Hawke's Bay v Auckland at Auckland (included 13 extras)	1910/11
29	Wellington v Nelson at Nelson	1879/80
29	Taranaki v Hawke's Bay at Hawera	1891/92

Highest Second Innings Totals

671-4	New Zealand v Sri Lanka	Wellington	1990/91
602-8	Otago v Canterbury	Dunedin	1928/29
589	Otago v Canterbury	Christchurch	1931/32
575-7 dec	Wellington v Otago	Wellington	1951/52
571-8 dec	Otago v Central Districts	Napier	1995/96
539	Auckland v Otago	Dunedin	1926/27
537	Auckland v Canterbury	Christchurch	1930/31
537	New Zealand v England	Wellington	1983/84
526-8 dec	Canterbury v Wellington	Wellington	1931/32
519	Canterbury v Wellington	Christchurch	1930/31

Highest Fourth Innings Totals without Loss for Victory

226-0	Canterbury v Otago	Christchurch	1948/49
175-0	Otago v Central Districts	Masterton	1971/72
174-0	Otago v Northern Districts	Alexandra	1985/86
147-0	Wellington v Otago	Dunedin	2005/06
138-0	Auckland v Otago	Auckland	1937/38
130-0	Wellington v Otago	Wellington	1921/22
130-0	Canterbury v Auckland	Christchurch	1951/52

Highest Fourth Innings Totals

495	lost 145 runs	Otago v Wellington	Dunedin	1923/24
475-4	and won	Wellington v Canterbury	Christchurch	1994/95
473-6	and won	Canterbury v Auckland	Christchurch	1930/31
458	lost 276 runs	Auckland v Wellington	Wellington	1927/28
453-8	and won	Northern Districts v Wellington	Wellington	1995/96
451	lost 98 runs	New Zealand v England	Christchurch	2001/02
450-7	and won	Central Districts v Canterbury	New Plymouth	2008/09
431	lost 121 runs	New Zealand v England	Napier	2007/08
429-8	and won	Northern Districts v Central Districts	Lincoln	2006/07
400-9	and won	Northern Districts v Central Districts	Napier	2004/05

Large Victories

BY AN INNINGS AND

364 runs	Sims' Australian XI defeated Canterbury	Christchurch	1913/14
358 runs	Australia defeated New Zealand	Wellington	1904/05
356 runs	Australia defeated Otago	Dunedin	1949/50
354 runs	Auckland defeated Hawke's Bay	Auckland	1920/21
332 runs	Wellington defeated Canterbury	Wellington	1925/26
327 runs	NSW defeated Otago	Dunedin	1923/24
322 runs	Wellington defeated Hawkes Bay	Wellington	1905/06
322 runs	West Indies defeated New Zealand	Wellington	1994/95

BY A RUNS MARGIN

512 runs	Wellington defeated Auckland	Wellington	1925/26
446 runs	Wellington defeated Otago	Wellington	1926/27
438 runs	Auckland defeated Wellington	Auckland	1934/35
425 runs	Central Districts defeated Otago	Alexandra	2001/02
382 runs	Auckland defeated Canterbury	Christchurch	1920/21
365 runs	Wellington defeated Auckland	Wellington	1923/24
355 runs	Wellington defeated Canterbury	Christchurch	1926/27

Tied Matches

Wellington v Nelson	Wellington	1873/74
New Zealand v T.N. Pearce's XI	Scarborough	1958
Central Districts v England XI	New Plymouth	1977/78
Victoria v New Zealand	Melbourne	1982/83
Wellington v Canterbury	Wellington	1988/89

Close Finishes

VICTORY BY 1 WICKET

Canterbury defeated Tasmania	Christchurch	1883/84
Otago defeated Canterbury	Christchurch	1890/91
Wellington defeated Nelson	Nelson	1891/92
Auckland defeated Wellington	Wellington	1893/94
Canterbury defeated Wellington	Wellington	1899/00
Auckland defeated Wellington	Wellington	1911/12
Canterbury defeated Auckland	Auckland	1914/15
Wellington defeated Otago	Wellington	1924/25
Auckland defeated Otago	Auckland	1946/47
Fiji defeated Wellington	Wellington	1947/48
Otago defeated Wellington	Dunedin	1948/49
Auckland defeated Canterbury	Auckland	1950/51
Central Districts defeated Wellington	Wellington	1951/52
Otago defeated Wellington	Dunedin	1952/53
MCC defeated Canterbury	Christchurch	1960/61
Auckland defeated Canterbury	Christchurch	1963/64
Wellington defeated NZ Under-23 XI	Wellington	1965/66
Canterbury defeated Auckland	Auckland	1974/75
Northern Districts defeated Central Districts	Gisborne	1979/80
New Zealand defeated West Indies	Dunedin	1979/80
Otago defeated Wellington	Alexandra	1980/81
Otago defeated Canterbury	Christchurch	1990/91
Otago defeated Wellington	Dunedin	1991/92
Central Districts defeated Auckland	Auckland	1994/95
Canterbury defeated Northern Districts	Christchurch	1994/95
Southern defeated Central	Wanganui	1997/98
Wellington defeated Northern Districts	Hamilton	2001/02
Northern Districts defeated Central Districts	Napier	2004/05

VICTORY BY 10 RUNS OR LESS

1 run	Northern Districts defeated Central Districts	Rotorua	1989/90
2 runs	Auckland defeated Canterbury	Auckland	1903/04
	Wellington defeated Canterbury	Wellington	1935/36
3 runs	Otago defeated Wellington	Wellington	1953/54
	Central Districts defeated Wellington	Wellington	1970/71
	Central Districts defeated Otago	New Plymouth	1970/71
	Canterbury defeated Central Districts	Napier	1979/80
	Auckland defeated Otago	Dunedin	2004/05
4 runs	Auckland defeated Nelson	Nelson	1882/83
	Canterbury defeated Otago	Christchurch	1882/83
	Auckland defeated Wellington	Auckland	1977/78
5 runs	Central Districts defeated Otago	New Plymouth	1953/54
	Northern Districts defeated Central Districts	Napier	1976/77
6 runs	Canterbury defeated Tasmania	Christchurch	1883/84

	Auckland defeated Canterbury	Auckland	1952/53
	South Island XI defeated North Island XI	Wellington	1957/58
	Northern Districts defeated Central Districts	Hamilton	1977/78
	Northern Districts defeated Otago	Dunedin	1978/79
	Central Districts defeated Northern Districts	Napier	1988/89
	Canterbury defeated Auckland	Auckland	2006/07
7 runs	Auckland defeated Canterbury	Christchurch	1873/74
8 runs	Auckland defeated Wellington	Wellington	1945/46
	Auckland defeated Northern Districts	Auckland	1963/64
	Central Districts defeated Auckland	Napier	1982/83
	Auckland defeated Central Districts	Auckland	1999/00
9 runs	Central Districts defeated Auckland	Nelson	1983/84
10 runs	Northern Districts defeated Canterbury	Hamilton	1960/61
	Wellington defeated Central Districts	New Plymouth	1973/74
	Otago defeated Auckland	Dunedin	1975/76

Victory after Follow-on

Auckland (180 & 302)	beat Canterbury (392 & 84)	Auckland	1952/53
Northern Districts (165 & 275)	beat Otago (320-9d & 105)	Dunedin	1961/62
Auckland (69 & 303)	beat Northern Districts (224 & 140)	Auckland	1963/64
Canterbury (166 & 360)	beat Auckland (351-9d & 149)	Christchurch	1973/74
Auckland (101 & 278)	beat Otago (268 & 108)	Dunedin	2004/05

Matches Abandoned without a Ball Being Bowled

these matches are not included in any first-class records

Hawke's Bay v Australia	Napier	1909/10
Central Districts v Northern Districts	Napier	1970/71
†Wellington v Australia	Wellington	1973/74
Central Districts v Australia	Napier	1973/74
†New Zealand v Pakistan	Dunedin	1988/89
†New Zealand President's XI v Australia	Nelson	1992/93
New Zealand A v Sri Lanka	Gisborne	1996/97
Wellington v Canterbury	Wellington	1996/97
†Northern v Pakistan A	Auckland	1998/99
†New Zealand v India	Dunedin	1998/99

† replaced with a limited-overs match

Matches Completed in One Day

Otago v Canterbury	Dunedin	11. 2.1868
Wellington v Auckland	Wellington	29.11.1874
Nelson v Wellington	Nelson	26.12.1887
Otago v Auckland	Dunedin	27.12.1889
Hawke's Bay v Taranaki	Napier	9. 1.1892
Auckland v New South Wales*	Auckland	20. 1.1894
Ireland v New Zealand	Dublin	11. 9.1937
Auckland v Fiji†	Auckland	9. 3.1954

** no play on first day* *† after no play on first two days and three declarations on third*

Most Extras in an Innings

Extras	*B*	*LB*	*NB*	*W*				
† 66	2	9	54	1	NZ Academy XI (459-8d)	v Pakistan A	Lincoln	1998/99
62	25	21	13	3	England (562)	v New Zealand	Leeds	2004

† 60	18	17	20	5	Central Districts (460-4d)	v Wellington	Wellington	1997/98
58	41	14	3	—	Wellington (380-5)	v Auckland	Wellington	1929/30
†58	6	14	30	8	Auckland (322-4d)	v Wellington	Auckland	1993/94
58	4	12	33	9	New Zealand (563)	v Pakistan	Hamilton	2003/04
57	31	16	10	—	New Zealand (387)	v England	Auckland	1929/30
54	35	14	1	4	Auckland (200-8d)	v Wellington	Auckland	1973/74
54	5	16	33	—	New Zealand A (597-9d)	v Sri Lanka A	Queenstown	2003/04
53	26	10	17	—	Canterbury (473-6)	v Auckland	Christchurch	1930/31
†53	4	2	46	1	Wellington (498-2d)	v Canterbury	Christchurch	1994/95
52					Wellington (370)	v Canterbury	Christchurch	1922/23
52	12	7	33	—	New Zealand (468)	v Pakistan	Karachi	1976/77
52	1	27	33	1	Auckland (423-7d)	v Wellington	Wellington	1992/93
† 52	1	15	32	4	Canterbury (537)	v Central Districts	Blenheim	1996/97
52	21	28	3	1	New Zealand (630-6d)	v India	Mohali	2003/04
52	7	9	28	8	Central Districts (499)	v Canterbury	N.Plymouth	2004/05
51	10	11	30	—	Auckland (369)	v West Indies	Auckland	1999/00
51	5	23	13	10	New Zealand (393)	v Bangladesh	Wellington	2007/08
50					Otago (602-8d)	v Canterbury	Dunedin	1928/29
50	13	24	11	2	Wellington (356)	v Canterbury	Wellington	1981/82
† 50	3	11	36	—	Southern (554)	v Pakistan A	Christchurch	1998/99

† no balls counted as two extras, regardless of whether runs were scored from the bat

Longest Matches in New Zealand

before 1900

FOUR DAYS

Otago v Canterbury	Dunedin	1875/76
Canterbury v Tasmania	Christchurch	1883/84
Otago v Canterbury	Dunedin	1884/85

since 1900

SIX DAYS

New Zealand v England	Christchurch	1974/75
New Zealand v India	Christchurch	1975/76
* New Zealand v England	Auckland	1977/78
New Zealand v Pakistan	Napier	1978/79
New Zealand v West Indies	Auckland	1979/80
New Zealand v India	Christchurch	1980/81

** the only match where play took place on all six days*
The other instances involved the rest day being used after a day's play was lost

FIVE DAYS

Canterbury v Otago	Christchurch	1911/12
Canterbury v Wellington	Christchurch	1922/23
Otago v Wellington	Dunedin	1923/24
Canterbury v Auckland	Christchurch	1924/25
Wellington v Otago	Wellington	1926/27
Northern Districts v Auckland	Taupo	1999/00
Auckland v Wellington	Auckland	2004/05
Wellington v Central Districts	Wellington	2005/06
Northern Districts v Canterbury	Hamilton	2006/07
Wellington v Canterbury	Wellington	2007/08
Auckland v Central Districts	Lincoln	2008/09

All other matches of five days duration since 1926/27 have been test matches. A complete list of these up to 1993/94 is on pages 288 and 289 of the 1994 Almanack. *The 1998/99 Shell Trophy final between Central Districts and Otago at Napier was scheduled for five days but completed in three.*

INDIVIDUAL RECORDS

BATTING

Highest Individual Scores

385	Sutcliffe B.	Otago v Canterbury	Christchurch	1952/53
355	Sutcliffe B.	Otago v Auckland	Dunedin	1949/50
338*	Blunt R.C.	Otago v Canterbury	Christchurch	1931/32
336*	Hammond W.R.	England v New Zealand	Auckland	1932/33
317	Rutherford K.R.	New Zealand v D.B. Close's XI	Scarborough	1986
306	Richardson M.H.	New Zealand v Zimbabwe A	Kwekwe	2000/01
301*	Fulton P.G.	Canterbury v Auckland	Christchurch	2002/03
299	Crowe M.D.	New Zealand v Sri Lanka	Wellington	1990/91
296	Reid J.R.	Wellington v Northern Districts	Wellington	1962/63
293	Trumper V.T.	Sims' Australian XI v Canterbury	Christchurch	1913/14
290	Carson W.N.	Auckland v Otago	Dunedin	1936/37
284	Woodfull W.M.	Australia v New Zealand	Auckland	1927/28
283	Reid J.R.	Wellington v Otago	Wellington	1951/52
275*	Cullinan D.J.	South Africa v New Zealand	Auckland	1998/99
275	Sutcliffe B.	Otago v Auckland	Auckland	1950/51
274*	Fleming S.P.	New Zealand v Sri Lanka	Colombo	2002/03
271	Javed Miandad	Pakistan v New Zealand	Auckland	1988/89
268	Sinclair M.S.	New Zealand A v South Africa A	Potchefstroom	2004/05
268	McIntosh T.G.	Auckland v Canterbury	Auckland	2007/08
267*	Young B.A.	New Zealand v Sri Lanka	Dunedin	1996/97
267	de Silva P.A.	Sri Lanka v New Zealand	Wellington	1990/91
265	Bell M.D.	Wellington v Central Districts	Napier	2007/08
264	Sutcliffe B.	Otago v Central Districts	Dunedin	1959/60
262	Fleming S.P.	New Zealand v South Africa	Cape Town	2005/06
259	Turner G.M.	New Zealand v Guyana	Georgetown	1971/72
259	Turner G.M.	New Zealand v West Indies	Georgetown	1971/72
258	Nurse S.M.	West Indies v New Zealand	Christchurch	1968/69
256	Smith S.G.	Auckland v Canterbury	Auckland	1919/20
256	Raval J.A.	Auckland v Central Districts	Auckland	2008/09
255*	McGlew D.J.	South Africa v New Zealand	Wellington	1952/53
254*	Vance R.H.	Wellington v Northern Districts	Wellington	1988/89
251*	Harris C.Z.	Canterbury v Central Districts	Rangiora	1996/97
250	Walters K.D.	Australia v New Zealand	Christchurch	1976/77
247*	Chappell G.S.	Australia v New Zealand	Wellington	1973/74
247	Ingram P.J.	Central Districts v Northern Districts	Hamilton	2008/09
243*	Sinclair M.S.	Central Districts v Otago	Napier	2007/08
243	Sutcliffe B.	New Zealand v Essex	Southend	1949
242*	Crowe M.D.	New Zealand v South Australia	Adelaide	1985/86
242	Crowe M.D.	Central Districts v Otago	New Plymouth	1989/90
241	Horne M.J.	Otago v Auckland	Auckland	1997/98
239	Dowling G.T.	New Zealand v India	Christchurch	1967/68
237*	Latham R.T.	Canterbury v Northern Districts	Rotorua	1990/91
236	Ryder J.D.	Wellington v Central Districts	Palmerston North	2004/05
235	Marshall J.A.H.	Northern Districts v Canterbury	Christchurch	2001/02
230*	Sutcliffe B.	New Zealand v India	New Delhi	1955/56
227	Hammond W.R.	England v New Zealand	Christchurch	1932/33
226*	Rutherford K.R.	Otago v India	Dunedin	1989/90
226	Hastings B.F.	Canterbury v NZ Under 23 XI	Christchurch	1964/65
225*	Blunt R.C.	New Zealand v Gentlemen	Eastbourne	1931
224	Vincent L.	New Zealand v Sri Lanka	Wellington	2004/05

223*	Turner G.M.	New Zealand v West Indies	Kingston	1971/72
223	Astle N.J.	New Zealand v Queensland	Brisbane	2001/02
222*	Midlane F.A.	Wellington v Otago	Wellington	1914/15
222	Rutherford I.A.	Otago v Central Districts	New Plymouth	1978/79
222	Astle N.J.	New Zealand v England	Christchurch	2001/02
221*	Fulton P.G.	Canterbury v Otago	Dunedin	2004/05
221	Macartney C.G.	NSW v Canterbury	Christchurch	1923/24
221	Blunt R.C.	Otago v Canterbury	Dunedin	1928/29
219	Bell M.D.	Wellington v Northern Districts	Hamilton	1998/99
219	Franklin J.E.C.	Wellington v Auckland	Auckland	2008/09
217	Taylor L.R.P.L.	Central Districts v Otago	Napier	2006/07
216	Fletcher K.W.R.	England v New Zealand	Auckland	1974/75
216	Bell M.D.	Wellington v Auckland	Auckland	1997/98
216*	Chanderpaul S.	West Indies v New Zealand A	Taupo	1999/00
214*	Kortlang H.H.L.	Wellington v Auckland	Wellington	1925/26
214*	Booth B.C.	Australia B v Central Districts	Palmerston North	1966/67
214	Sinclair M.S.	New Zealand v West Indies	Wellington	1999/00
213	Murray B.A.G.	Wellington v Otago	Dunedin	1968/69
213	Trimble S.C.	Australia B v New Zealand	Wellington	1969/70
213	Greenidge C.G.	West Indies v New Zealand	Auckland	1986/87
212*	Woodfull W.M.	Victoria v Canterbury	Christchurch	1924/25
212*	Richardson M.H.	New Zealand A v Sussex	Hove	2000
212*	Kelly D.P.	Central Districts v Canterbury	Blenheim	2000/01
212*	Styris S.B.	Northern Districts v Otago	Hamilton	2001/02
212	Hiddleston J.S.	Wellington v Canterbury	Wellington	1925/26
212	Dempster C.S.	New Zealand v Essex	Leyton	1931
211*	Hick G.A.	Northern Districts v Auckland	Auckland	1988/89
211*	Gibbs H.H.	South Africa v New Zealand	Christchurch	1998/99
211	Warner P.F.	Lord Hawke's XI v Otago	Dunedin	1902/03
211	Wallace W.M.	Auckland v Canterbury	Auckland	1939/40
209*	Brown S.W.	Auckland v Canterbury	Christchurch	1990/91
209*	Horne M.J.	Auckland v Northern Districts	Auckland	2003/04
209	White D.J.	Northern Districts v Central Districts	Hamilton	1985/86
209	Horne P.A.	Auckland v Northern Districts	Auckland	1988/89
208*	Sutcliffe B.	North Island v South Island	Dunedin	1947/48
208	Franklin J.E.C.	Wellington v Auckland	Wellington	2005/06
207	Hart R.T.	Central Districts v Wellington	Wellington	1985/86
206	Page M.L.	Canterbury v Wellington	Wellington	1931/32
206	Donnelly M.P.	New Zealand v England	Lord's	1949
206	Dowling G.T.	Canterbury v Wellington	Christchurch	1962/63
206	Harris C.Z	Canterbury v Central Districts	Blenheim	1996/97
205*	Lloyd C.H.	West Indies v South Island	Dunedin	1968/69
205*	McSweeney E.B.	Wellington v Central Districts	Levin	1987/88
205	McIntosh T.G.	Auckland v Otago	Lincoln	2006/07
204*	Sinclair M.S.	New Zealand v Pakistan	Christchurch	2000/01
204	Cox A.	Canterbury v Otago	Christchurch	1925/26
204	Hiddleston J.S.	Wellington v Auckland	Wellington	1925/26
204	Scott V.J.	Auckland v Otago	Dunedin	1947/48
204	Patel D.N.	Auckland v Northern Districts	Auckland	1991/92
203*	Burnett G.P.	Wellington v Northern Districts	Hamilton	1991/92
203*	Sinclair M.S.	Central Districts v Northern Districts	Wanganui	1998/99
203	Scott V.J.	New Zealand v Combined Services	Gillingham	1949
203	Reid J.R.	New Zealand v Western Province	Cape Town	1961/62
203	Edgar B.A.	Young New Zealand v Zimbabwe	Bulawayo	1984/85
203	Parlane M.E.	Wellington v Auckland	Auckland	2004/05
202*	Congdon B.E.	Central Districts v Otago	Nelson	1968/69

202*	Greatbatch M.J.	Central Districts v Otago	Palmerston North	1988/89
202	Turner G.M.	New Zealand v President's XI	Montego Bay	1971/72
202	Austen M.H.	Wellington v Central Districts	Wanganui	1993/94
202	Greatbatch M.J.	Central Districts v Northern Districts	Rotorua	1995/96
202	Fleming S.P.	New Zealand v Bangladesh	Chittagong	2004/05
201*	Hart M.N.	Northern Districts v Auckland	Auckland	2002/03
201*	Smith B.F.	Central Districts v Canterbury	New Plymouth	2001/02
201	Reid J.R.	Otago v Canterbury	Dunedin	1957/58
201	Sutcliffe B.	Otago v Northern Districts	Hamilton	1960/61
201	Mushtaq Mohammad	Pakistan v New Zealand	Dunedin	1972/73
201	Jones R.A.	Auckland v West Indies	Auckland	2008/09
201	Ryder J.D.	New Zealand v India	Napier	2008/09
200*	MacLaren A.C.	MCC v New Zealand	Wellington	1922/23
200*	Bardsley W.	NSW v Auckland	Auckland	1923/24
200*	Thorpe G.P.	England v New Zealand	Christchurch	2001/02
200	Lawson R.A.	Otago v Central Districts	Napier	1995/96

Most Runs in a Season in New Zealand

		M	*I*	*NO*	*HS*	*Runs*	*Ave*	*100*
Crowe M.D.	1986/87	11	21	3	175*	1676	93.11	8
Turner G.M.	1975/76	11	20	4	177*	1244	77.75	5
Hick G.A.	1988/89	8	16	3	211*	1228	94.46	6
Bell M.D.	2000/01	13	21	0	134	1092	52.00	6
Crowe J.J.	1991/92	10	19	2	142*	1063	62.52	4
Vance R.H.	1988/89	10	18	2	254*	1037	64.81	4
Richardson M.H.	2000/01	11	19	2	166	1035	60.88	2
Wright J.G.	1986/87	11	21	2	192	1019	53.63	3
Bell M.D.	2007/08	12	21	2	265	1016	53.47	3
Papps M.H.W.	2006/07	7	11	0	188	1005	91.36	4
Sinclair M.S.	1999/00	14	26	2	214	1004	41.83	3
Vincent L.	2004/05	10	16	2	224	999	71.35	3
Dowling G.T.	1967/68	10	18	1	239	968	56.94	4
Ingram P.J.	2008/09	9	15	0	247	957	63.80	2
Edgar B.A.	1978/79	12	23	0	134	944	41.04	2
Weekes E. de C.	1955/56	8	10	1	156	940	104.44	6
Rutherford K.R.	1989/90	13	19	2	226*	940	55.29	3
Smith B.F.	2000/01	10	17	1	168	939	58.68	2
Edgar B.A.	1981/82	11	19	1	161	934	51.88	3
Sutcliffe B.	1947/48	5	10	1	208*	911	101.22	4
Sinclair M.S.	2008/09	9	15	3	164	904	75.33	4

Most Runs in a Season for New Zealand

		M	*I*	*NO*	*HS*	*Runs*	*Ave*	*100*
Sutcliffe B.	1949	29	49	5	243	2627	59.70	7
Donnelly M.P.	1949	29	45	8	206	2287	61.81	5
Reid J.R.	*1961/62	20	36	2	203	2083	61.26	7

** includes South Africa & Australia*

Most Runs in Season of First-class Debut

			M	*I*	*NO*	*HS*	*Runs*	*Ave*
Hay G.R.	CD	2006/07	8	14	1	106	593	45.61
Cooper B.G.	ND	1980/81	7	13	0	105	520	40.00
Briasco P.S.	CD	1982/83	8	15	1	95	519	37.07
Carson W.N.	Auckland	1936/37	3	4	0	290	500	125.00

Highest Average in a Season in New Zealand

		M	I	NO	HS	Runs	Ave	100
Hammond W.R.	1932/33	3	3	1	336*	621	310.50	2
Woodfull W.M.	1924/25	6	9	5	212*	710	177.50	3
Greatbatch M.J.	1995/96	5	6	2	202	623	155.75	4
Javed Miandad	1988/89	4	5	1	271	597	149.25	3
Harris C.Z.	1996/97	5	7	1	251*	835	139.16	3
Woodfull W.M.	1927/28	6	9	3	284	781	130.16	3
Carson W.N.	1936/37	3	4	0	290	500	125.00	2
Bardsley W.	1923/24	6	7	2	200*	623	124.60	1
Cullinan D.J.	1998/99	5	7	2	275*	553	110.60	3
Hiddleston J.S.	1925/26	3	5	0	212	537	107.40	2
Weekes E. de C.	1955/56	8	10	1	156	940	104.44	6
Sutcliffe B.	1946/47	6	8	1	197	722	103.14	3
Parker J.M.	1981/82	7	13	7	117	618	103.00	2
Sutcliffe B.	1947/48	5	10	1	208*	911	101.22	4

minimum 500 runs

Centuries

George Watson registered the first century in New Zealand first-class cricket on 24 February, 1881 when he made 175 for Canterbury v Otago at Hagley Park, Christchurch.

To date, 1995 centuries have been scored in New Zealand with 56 in 2006/07 being the record for one season. A further 371 have been recorded for New Zealand teams overseas.

The following NZ players have made 15 or more centuries during their first-class careers:

Turner G.M.	103	Greatbatch M.J.	24	Wallace W.M.	17
Crowe M.D.	71	Horne M.J.	24	Scott V.J.	16
Wright J.G.	59	Bell M.D.	24	Dowling G.T.	16
Sutcliffe B.	44	Donnelly M.P.	23	Jones A.H.	16
Reid J.R.	39	Congdon B.E.	23	McMillan C.D.	16
Dempster C.S.	35	Crowe J.J.	22	Papps M.H.W.	16
Rutherford K.R.	35	Parker J.M.	21	Hastings B.F.	15
Fleming S.P.	35	Burgess M.G.	20	Blunt R.C.	15
Howarth G.P.	32	Richardson M.H.	20	Franklin T.J.	15
Spearman C.M.	30	Astle N.J.	19	Parlane M.E.	15
Sinclair M.S.	27	Lowry T.C.	18	Cumming C.D.	15
Patel D.N.	26	Hadlee W.A.	18	Jones R.A.	15
Dacre C.C.R.	24	Twose R.G.	18	Marshall H.J.H.	15
Edgar B.A.	24				

Most Centuries in a Season in New Zealand

8	Crowe M.D.	1986/87	4	Franklin T.J.	1987/88
6	Weekes E. de C.	1955/56	4	Hick G.A.	1987/88
6	Hick G.A.	1988/89	4	Vance R.H.	1988/89
6	Bell M.D.	2000/01	4	Jones A.H.	1990/91
5	Turner G.M.	1975/76	4	Crowe J.J.	1991/92
4	Sutcliffe B.	1947/48	4	Maynard M.P.	1991/92
4	Hadlee W.A.	1947/48	4	Greatbatch M.J.	1995/96
4	Sutcliffe B.	1950/51	4	Ingram P.J.	2006/07
4	Dowling G.T.	1967/68	4	Papps M.H.W.	2006/07
4	Hastings B.F.	1968/69	4	Cumming C.D.	2008/09
4	Turner G.M.	1974/75	4	Sinclair M.S.	2008/09
4	Wright J.G.	1981/82			

Five Centuries in Consecutive Innings

Player	Score	Match	Venue	Season
Weekes E. de C.	156	West Indies v Auckland	Auckland	1955/56
	148	West Indies v Canterbury	Auckland	
	123	West Indies v New Zealand	Dunedin	
	119*	West Indies v Wellington	Wellington	
	103	West Indies v New Zealand	Christchurch	

Three Centuries in Consecutive Innings

Player	Score	Match	Venue	Season
Macartney C.G.	120	NSW v Wellington	Wellington	1923/24
	120	NSW v Otago	Dunedin	
	221	NSW v Canterbury	Christchurch	
Sutcliffe B.	103	Otago v Auckland	Auckland	1947/48
	118 125	Otago v Canterbury	Dunedin	
Sutcliffe B.	141 135	Auckland v Canterbury	Auckland	1948/49
	140	New Zealand XI v The Rest	Christchurch	
Reid J.R.	101 118*	New Zealand v Orange Free State	Bloemfontein	1961/62
	165	New Zealand v South African Colts XI	East London	
Chappell I.M.	128	Australia v Northern Districts	Hamilton	1973/74
	145 121	Australia v New Zealand	Wellington	
Crowe M.D.	151	Central Districts v Northern Districts	Morrinsville	1986/87
	144 151	Central Districts v Canterbury	New Plymouth	
Hick G.A.	211*	Northern Districts v Auckland	Auckland	1988/89
	144 132	Northern Districts v Wellington	Morrinsville	
Jones A.H.	186	New Zealand v Sri Lanka	Wellington	1990/91
	122 100*	New Zealand v Sri Lanka	Hamilton	
Maynard M.P.	142	Northern Districts v Otago	Hamilton	1991/92
	195 110	Northern Districts v Auckland	Auckland	
Greatbatch M.J.	115	Central Districts v Canterbury	Christchurch	1995/96
	202	Central Districts v Northern Districts	Rotorua	
	162*	Central Districts v Auckland	Auckland	
Campbell S.L.	112 109*	West Indies v Auckland	Auckland	1999/00
	170	West Indies v New Zealand	Hamilton	
Wells J.D.	143	Wellington v Canterbury	Wellington	1999/00
	107 132*	Wellington v Central Districts	New Plymouth	
How J.M.	105 108*	Central Districts v Otago	Queenstown	2004/05
	121	Central Districts v Northern Districts	Napier	
Sinclair M.S.	121 103*	Central Districts v Otago	New Plymouth	2005/06
	101	Central Districts v Auckland	Palmerston North	
Ingram P.J.	119 166*	Central Districts v Canterbury	Christchurch	2006/07
	105	Central Districts v Auckland	Napier	

Century on First-class Debut

† Watson G.	175	Canterbury v Otago	Christchurch	1880/81
Brook-Smith W.	112*	Auckland v Hawke's Bay	Auckland	1904/05
† Wood B.B.	108 & 18	Canterbury v Wellington	Wellington	1907/08
McMullan J.J.M.	157*	Otago v Southland	Dunedin	1917/18
† Snedden C.A.	119	Auckland v Hawke's Bay	Auckland	1920/21
Talbot R.O.	105	Canterbury v Otago	Dunedin	1922/23
Tindill E.W.T.	106 & 0	Wellington v Auckland	Auckland	1932/33
Scott V.J.	122	Auckland v Canterbury	Auckland	1937/38
† Ongley J.A.	110	Wellington v Otago	Wellington	1938/39
† Kerr A.C.	122	Auckland v Wellington	Auckland	1941/42
† Watt D.G.	15 & 105	Otago v Canterbury	Christchurch	1943/44
Smith K.F.H.	27 & 141*	Wellington v Central Districts	Wellington	1953/54
Macleod D.N.	117	Central Districts v Wellington	Wanganui	1956/57
Bilby G.P.	132 & 2*	Wellington v Central Districts	Wellington	1962/63
† Mitchell W.J.	127*	Northern Districts v Pakistan	Hamilton	1964/65
† Sampson H.C.	25 & 119	Central Districts v Wellington	Wellington	1970/71
Vaughan J.T.C.	106* & 1	Auckland v Wellington	Wellington	1989/90
Aiken J.M.	39 & 156*	Wellington v Canterbury	Christchurch	1989/90
† McCone R.J.	102	Canterbury v Otago	Christchurch	2008/09

† *only century in first-class cricket*

B.R. Williams scored 103 in his fourth first-class match, not having batted in his first three matches, for Wellington v Central Districts at Wellington, 1989/90.*

Century on First-class Debut in Other Countries

In ENGLAND

Dacre C.C.R.	107	New Zealand v MCC	Lord's	1927
Crowe M.D.	104	D.B. Close's XI v Pakistan	Scarborough	1982
Horne M.J.	133	New Zealand v British Universities	Oxford	1999
Spearman C.M.	111	Gloucestershire v Worcestershire	Worcester	2002
Adams A.R.	124	Essex v Leicestershire	Leicester	2004
Marshall H.J.H.	102	Gloucestershire v Worcestershire	Bristol	2006

J.D.P. Oram scored 103 for New Zealand v Worcestershire at Worcester in 2004 in his first innings in England after not batting in his first game*

In AUSTRALIA

Sutcliffe B.	142	New Zealand v Western Australia	Perth	1953/54
Miller L.S.M.	142	New Zealand v South Australia	Adelaide	1953/54
Patel D.N.	105	New Zealand v Western Australia	Perth	1987/88
How J.M.	170	New Zealand v New South Wales	Sydney	2008/09

In SOUTH AFRICA

Reid J.R.	111	New Zealand v Western Province	Cape Town	1953/54
Kasper R.J.	122*	Natal B v Transvaal B	Pietermaritzburg	1970/71
Harris C.Z.	118*	Canterbury v Eastern Province	Grahamstown	1993/94
Richardson M.H.	173*	New Zealand v Boland	Paarl	2000/01
McCullum B.B.	101	New Zealand v Rest of South Africa	Benoni	2005/06

In WEST INDIES

Hastings B.F.	100*	New Zealand v Jamaica	Kingston	1971/72
Crowe M.D.	118	New Zealand v Shell Award XI	Kingston	1984/85
Styris S.B.	107	New Zealand v West Indies	St George's	2001/02

In INDIA

Taylor B.R.	105	New Zealand v India	Calcutta	1964/65
Burgess M.G.	102	Prime Minister's XI v President's XI	Bombay	1967/68
Parker J.M.	104	New Zealand v India	Bombay	1976/77
Wright J.G.	104	New Zealand v West Zone	Rajkot	1988/89
Crowe M.D.	101*	New Zealand v President's XI	Rajkot	1995/96
Oram J.D.P.	101*	New Zealand v India A	Rajkot	2003/04

M.H. Richardson scored 128 for New Zealand v India at Rajkot in 2003/04 in his first innings in India after not batting in his first game.*

In PAKISTAN

Reid J.R.	105*	NZ v Chief Commissioner's XI	Karachi	1955/56
Anderson R.W.	103*	NZ v NWFP Chief Minister's XI	Peshawar	1976/77

In SRI LANKA

Dempster C.S.	112*	Sir Julien Cahn's XI v Ceylon	Colombo	1936/37
Rutherford K.R.	108	NZ v Board President's XI	Galle	1986/87
Fulton P.G.	101	New Zealand A v Sri Lanka A	Kandy	2005/06

In ZIMBABWE

Franklin T.J.	153*	Young New Zealand v Zimbabwe	Harare	1984/85
Horne M.J.	181	New Zealand v Mashonaland	Harare	1997/98
Sinclair M.S.	100*	New Zealand v President's XI	Mutare	2000/01

In BANGLADESH

McCullum B.B.	143	New Zealand v Bangladesh	Dhaka	2004/05

Century in Last First-class Match

† Phillips J.	110*	Canterbury v Wellington	Christchurch	1898/99
Midlane F.A.	126 & 4	Auckland v Wellington	Wellington	1918/19
† Beechey E.M.	180 & 5	Wellington vAuckland	Wellington	1918/19
† Watt D.G.	15 & 105	Otago v Canterbury	Christchurch	1943/44
Redmond R.E.	103 & 22	Auckland v Otago	Auckland	1975/76
Wadsworth K.J.	117	Canterbury v Otago	Christchurch	1975/76
Parker J.M.	1* & 100	Northern Districts v Wellington	Wellington	1983/84
† Snook I.R.	100*	Central Dists v Northern Dists	Palmerston North	1987/88
Dempsey D.A.	121 & 44	Canterbury v Otago	Dunedin	1987/88
Reid J.F.	112	Auckland v Northern Districts	Hamilton	1987/88
Mawhinney R.E.W.	9* & 108	Otago v Canterbury	Christchurch	1990/91
Twose R.G.	108 & 6	Wellington v Auckland	Wellington	2000/01
Nash D.J.	118 & 11*	Auckland v Otago	Dunedin	2001/02

† only first-class century of career. (D.G. Watt was making his only appearance in first-class cricket. J. Phillips was playing his 124th first-class match and 203rd innings).
J.D. Riley scored 34, 121, 26 and 94 (run out) in his final two first-class matches, for Auckland in 1976/77.*

Century in Each Innings of a Match

Dacre C.C.R.	127* & 101*	Auckland v Victoria	Auckland	1924/25
† Whitelaw P.E.	115 & 155	Auckland v Wellington	Auckland	1934/35
Uttley K.F.M.	132 & 138	Otago v Auckland	Auckland	1937/38
Sutcliffe B.	197 & 128	Otago v MCC	Dunedin	1946/47
Sutcliffe B.	118 & 125	Otago v Canterbury	Dunedin	1947/48
Sutcliffe B.	141 & 135	Auckland v Canterbury	Auckland	1948/49
Sutcliffe B.	243 & 100*	New Zealand v Essex	Southend	1949
Reid J.R.	101 & 118*	New Zealand v Orange Free State	Bloemfontein	1961/62
† Gedye S.G.	104 & 101	Auckland v Central Districts	Auckland	1963/64

† Thomson K.	102 & 102*	Canterbury v Otago	Dunedin	1966/67
Chappell G.S.	247* & 133	Australia v New Zealand	Wellington	1973/74
Chappell I.M.	145 & 121	Australia v New Zealand	Wellington	1973/74
Turner G.M.	101 & 110*	New Zealand v Australia	Christchurch	1973/74
Turner G.M.	135 & 108	Otago v Northern Districts	Gisborne	1974/75
Turner G.M.	105 & 186*	Otago v Central Districts	Dunedin	1974/75
Howarth G.P.	122 & 102	New Zealand v England	Auckland	1977/78
Wright J.G.	113 & 105	Northern Districts v Auckland	Auckland	1981/82
Parker J.M.	117 & 102*	Northern Districts v Central Districts	Tauranga	1981/82
Rutherford K.R.	105 & 104*	Otago v Northern Districts	Alexandra	1985/86
Border A.R.	140 & 114*	Australia v New Zealand	Christchurch	1985/86
Cooper B.G.	105 & 100	Northern Districts v Canterbury	Gisborne	1986/87
Crowe M.D.	144 & 151	Central Districts v Canterbury	New Plymouth	1986/87
Vance R.H.	116* & 123	Wellington v Central Districts	New Plymouth	1988/89
Hick G.A.	144 & 132	Northern Districts v Wellington	Morrinsville	1988/89
Jones A.H.	122 & 100*	New Zealand v Sri Lanka	Hamilton	1990/91
Gurusinha A.P.	119 & 102	Sri Lanka v New Zealand	Hamilton	1990/91
Maynard M.P.	195 & 110	Northern Districts v Auckland	Auckland	1991/92
Crowe M.D.	152 & 137*	Wellington v Canterbury	Christchurch	1992/93
Dravid R.S.	190 & 103*	India v New Zealand	Hamilton	1998/99
Rhodes J.N.	101* & 106*	South Africa v New Zealand A	Lincoln	1998/99
Campbell S.L.	112 & 109*	West Indies v Auckland	Auckland	1999/00
Wells J.D.	107 & 132*	Wellington v Central Districts	New Plymouth	1999/00
Spearman C.M.	100 & 115	New Zealand v North West	Potchefstroom	2000/01
Hopkins G.J.	113 & 175*	Canterbury v Auckland	Auckland	2002/03
Horne M.J.	118 & 209*	Auckland v Northern Districts	Auckland	2003/04
How J.M.	105 & 108*	Central Districts v Otago	Queenstown	2004/05
Sinclair M.S.	121 & 103*	Central Districts v Otago	New Plymouth	2005/06
Ingram P.J.	119 & 166*	Central Districts v Canterbury	Christchurch	2006/07
Jones R.A.	143 & 120	Auckland v Central Districts	Auckland	2006/07
Todd G.R.	110 & 165	Otago v Wellington	Wellington	2007/08
Myburgh J.G.	199 & 101*	Canterbury v Central Districts	New Plymouth	2008/09

† *maiden first-class century*

Highest Maiden Centuries

301*	Fulton P.G.	Canterbury v Auckland	Christchurch	2002/03
290	Carson W.N.	Auckland v Otago	Dunedin	1936/37
256	Raval J.A.	Auckland v Central Districts	Auckland	2008/09
209	White D.J.	Northern Districts v Central Districts	Hamilton	1985/86
204	Cox A.	Canterbury v Otago	Christchurch	1925/26
203*	Burnett G.P.	Wellington v Northern Districts	Hamilton	1991/92
196	Kerr J.L.	Canterbury v Wellington	Christchurch	1932/33
194	Gaffaney C.B.	Otago v Auckland	Dunedin	1996/97
193*	Stead D.W.	Canterbury v Central Districts	Christchurch	1980/81
190	Moloney D.A.R.	Wellington v Auckland	Auckland	1936/37
189	Sinclair M.S.	Central Districts v Wellington	Masterton	1996/97
184	Taylor L.R.P.L.	Central Districts v Wellington	Palmerston North	2004/05
183	Gillespie H.D.	Auckland v Canterbury	Auckland	1929/30
182	McIntosh T.G.	Auckland v Canterbury	Christchurch	2000/01
180	Beechey E.M.	Wellington v Auckland	Wellington	1918/19
180	Dempster C.S.	New Zealand v Warwickshire	Birmingham	1927
180	Mooney F.L.H.	Wellington v Auckland	Wellington	1943/44
179	Ormiston R.W.	Wellington v Central Districts	New Plymouth	1982/83
177	Chandler P.J.B.	Wellington v Auckland	Wellington	1996/97
176	Cuff L.A.	Canterbury v Auckland	Christchurch	1893/94

175	Watson G.	Canterbury v Otago	Christchurch	1880/81
175	Astle N.J.	Canterbury v Northern Districts	Hamilton	1994/95
175	Orchard M.G.	Northern Districts v Central Districts	Napier	2005/06
172	Worker R.V. de R.	Otago v Canterbury	Dunedin	1923/24
172	Englefield J.I.	Canterbury v Central Districts	Blenheim	2000/01
171	Mills S.M.	Wellington v Canterbury	Christchurch	2006/07
167*	Hart R.T.	Central Districts v Canterbury	New Plymouth	1983/84
167	Lawrence J.D.	Canterbury v Auckland	Christchurch	1893/94
165	Redgrave W.P.	Wellington v Hawkes Bay	Wellington	1905/06
165	Chapple M.E.	Canterbury v South Africans	Christchurch	1952/53
165	Truscott P.B.	NZ Under-23 v Auckland	Auckland	1963/64
164*	Duff S.W.	Central Districts v Auckland	Wanganui	1991/92
164	Powell J.L.	Canterbury v Otago	Christchurch	1929/30
163*	How J.M.	Central Districts v Northern Districts	Hamilton	2002/03
163	Menzies R.E.J.	Canterbury v Wellington	Christchurch	1938/39
163	Williams A.B.	Wellington v Canterbury	Christchurch	1896/97
163	Reade L.B.	Central Districts v Northern Districts	Palmerston North	1960/61
161	Larsen G.R.	Wellington v Central Districts	Levin	1987/88
159*	Kennedy P.G.	Canterbury v Northern Districts	Rotorua	1990/91
159	Vincent L.	Auckland v Northern Districts	Auckland	1998/99
158*	Papps M.H.W.	Canterbury v Otago	Christchurch	2001/02
158	Harford N.S.	New Zealand v Oxford University	Oxford	1958
157*	McMullan J.J.M.	Otago v Southland	Dunedin	1917/18
157	Briasco P.S.	Central Districts v Canterbury	New Plymouth	1983/84
156*	Aiken J.M.	Wellington v Canterbury	Christchurch	1989/90
155*	James V.	Canterbury v Otago	Dunedin	1940/41
155*	Parore A.C.	Auckland v Otago	Dunedin	1991/92
155	Badcock F.T.	Wellington v Canterbury	Christchurch	1926/27
155	Oram J.D.P.	Central Districts v Canterbury	Christchurch	1998/99
154	Meuli E.M.	Central Districts v Auckland	Palmerston North	1952/53
153	Watling B-J.	Northern Districts v Otago	Dunedin	2006/07
152	Knight A.R.	Otago v Canterbury	Dunedin	1940/41
152	Kemp R.J.	Wellington v Auckland	Auckland	1947/48
152	Coutts P.J.C.	Central Districts v Canterbury	Christchurch	1966/67
152	Lees W.K.	New Zealand v Pakistan	Karachi	1976/77
152	Brown S.W.	Auckland v Central Districts	Auckland	1990/91
152	Weston T.I.	Central Districts v Auckland	Auckland	2006/07
151	Petrie E.C.	Auckland v Wellington	Auckland	1953/54
150	Crowe M.D.	Auckland v Central Districts	New Plymouth	1981/82

Watson, McMullan and Aiken scored their centuries on their debut in first-class cricket. Beechey was playing in his last first-class game. Carson (aged 20 years 168 days) and Cox (21 years 19 days) were both playing only their second first-class innings and remain the youngest players to score a double-century in New Zealand first-class cricket.

One Hundred Runs before Lunch

Runs	Mins				
* 110	120	Smith S.G.	Auckland v Canterbury	Auckland	1919/20
112	113	Macartney C.G.	NSW v Wellington	Wellington	1923/24
* 116	120	† Punch A.T.E.	NSW v Otago	Dunedin	1923/24
* 101	91	Macartney C.G.	NSW v Otago	Dunedin	1923/24
103	110	Hiddleston J.S.	Wellington v Canterbury	Wellington	1925/26
105	102	Dacre C.C.R.	Auckland v Otago	Dunedin	1926/27
103	103	† Vorrath W.	Otago v Wellington	Dunedin	1927/28
* 106	120	Blunt R.C.	Otago v Canterbury	Christchurch	1928/29
164	130	† Powell J.L.	Canterbury v Otago	Christchurch	1929/30
105	105	Badcock F.T.	Otago v Canterbury	Christchurch	1931/32
* 111	120	Hammond W.R.	England v New Zealand	Auckland	1932/33
102	120	Whitelaw P.E.	Auckland v Wellington	Auckland	1934/35

115	110	Wallace W.M.	New Zealand v Somerset	Taunton	1937
* 110	120	Wallace W.M.	New Zealand v Sussex	Hove	1937
* 103	120	Smith F.B.	Canterbury v Auckland	Auckland	1948/49
100	117	Sutcliffe B.	New Zealand v Essex	Southend	1949
* 100	120	Reid J.R.	Wellington v Otago	Wellington	1951/52
* 122	111	Guillen S.C.	Canterbury v Fiji	Christchurch	1953/54
* 100	126	Smith K.F.H.	Central Districts v Wellington	Wanganui	1959/60
* 108	131	Sutcliffe B.	Otago v Central Districts	Dunedin	1959/60
* 100	140	Sutcliffe B.	Otago v Northern Districts	Wellington	1960/61
* 174	140	Reid J.R.	Wellington v Northern Districts	Wellington	1962/63
120	125	Reid J.R.	Wellington v Northern Districts	Wellington	1964/65
103	120	Murray B.A.G.	New Zealand v President's XI	Rawalpindi	1969/70
* 109	141	Dunning B.	Northern Dist. v Central Dist.	Blenheim	1972/73
111	150	Dempsey D.A.	Canterbury v Otago	Christchurch	1980/81
102	147	† Crowe M.D.	Auckland v Central Districts	New Plymouth	1981/82
* 100	107	Chappell G.S.	Australia v New Zealand	Christchurch	1981/82
* 100	150	Crowe J.J.	Auckland v Northern Districts	Rotorua	1983/84
101	103	Rutherford K.R.	New Zealand v DB Close's XI	Scarborough	1986
* 101	144	Jones A.H.	Wellington v Otago	Wellington	1986/87
* 112	149	McSweeney E.B.	Wellington v Central Districts	Levin	1987/88
* 122	150	Crowe J.J.	Auckland v Wellington	Wellington	1988/89
* 117	160	Greatbatch M.J.	Central Districts v Otago	Palmerston North	1988/89
101	127	Blain T.E.	Central Districts v Wellington	New Plymouth	1988/89
107	136	† Reid R.B.	Auckland v Central Districts	Masterton	1989/90
* 116	136	Thomson S.A.	Northern Districts v Auckland	Auckland	1990/91
141	144	Maynard M.P.	Northern Districts v Auckland	Auckland	1991/92
* 139	92	Patel D.N.	Auckland v Northern Districts	Auckland	1991/92
104	140	Spearman C.M.	Central Districts v Wellington	Wellington	1997/98
101	137	Cairns C.L.	Southern v Central	Wellington	1998/99
103	140	How J.M.	Central Districts v Northern Districts	Napier	2004/05
105	140	Fulton P.G.	Canterbury v Otago	Christchurch	2004/05
106	122	Taylor L.R.P.L.	Central Districts v Northern Districts	Napier	2007/08

** batsman had been not out overnight*
† maiden first-class hundred. Punch, Vorrath, Powell and Reid did not score another century in first-class cricket

Scores of Ninety-nine

	Johnson P.R.	MCC v New Zealand	Christchurch	1906/07
†	Snedden A.N.C.	Auckland v Canterbury	Auckland	1921/22
§	Elmes C.J.	New Zealand v MCC	Auckland	1935/36
*	Whitelaw P.E.	Auckland/Wellington v MCC	Auckland	1936/37
	Sutcliffe B.	Otago v Auckland	Dunedin	1947/48
	Taylor D.D.	Auckland v Canterbury	Auckland	1948/49
†	Leggat J.G.	Canterbury v Auckland	Christchurch	1951/52
	Rae A.F.	West Indies v New Zealand	Auckland	1951/52
	O'Malley P.W.	Canterbury v Wellington	Christchurch	1953/54
†	Beck J.E.F.	New Zealand v South Africa	Cape Town	1953/54
	Hunter A.A.	Central Districts v Auckland	Auckland	1953/54
†	Leggat J.G.	Canterbury v MCC	Christchurch	1954/55
	Sutcliffe B.	Rest v New Zealand XI	Christchurch	1957/58
	Sutcliffe B.	New Zealand v Sussex	Hove	1958
§*	Bartlett G.A.	Central Districts v Auckland	Auckland	1959/60
	McGregor S.N.	Otago v Canterbury	Christchurch	1963/64
†	Cunis R.S.	Auckland v Wellington	Wellington	1966/67
	Surti R.F.	India v New Zealand	Auckland	1967/68
	Turner G.M.	New Zealand v Tasmania	Hobart	1969/70
	Burtt J.W.	Canterbury v Central Districts	Christchurch	1970/71

	Name	Match	Venue	Season
	Dowling G.T.	Canterbury v Northern Districts	Hamilton	1970/71
	Murray B.A.G.	Wellington v Northern Districts	Wellington	1970/71
	Dowling G.T.	New Zealand v Western Australia	Perth	1970/71
§*	O'Keeffe K.J.	Australia v Auckland	Auckland	1973/74
	Edwards G.N.	Central Districts v Australia	Nelson	1976/77
	Blair W.L.	Otago v Auckland	Auckland	1978/79
	Crowe M.D.	Auckland v Northern Districts	Auckland	1981/82
	Hadlee R.J.	New Zealand v England	Christchurch	1983/84
†	Lees W.K.	Otago v Northern Districts	Hamilton	1983/84
	Vance R.H.	Wellington v Canterbury	Wellington	1984/85
	Coney J.V.	New Zealand v President's XI	St Lucia	1984/85
	Jones A.H.	Wellington v Auckland	Auckland	1985/86
§*	Robertson G.K.	Central Districts v Otago	Oamaru	1985/86
	Wright J.G.	New Zealand v Australia	Melbourne	1987/88
	Crocker L.M.	Northern Districts v Wellington	Hamilton	1987/88
	Moxon M.D.	England v New Zealand	Auckland	1987/88
	McEwan P.E.	Canterbury v Wellington	Christchurch	1988/89
	Hart R.T.	Central Districts v Auckland	Masterton	1989/90
	Wright J.G.	New Zealand v Worcestershire	Worcester	1990
†	Patel D.N.	New Zealand v England	Christchurch	1991/92
+	Wright J.G.	New Zealand v England	Christchurch	1991/92
	Douglas M.W.	Central Districts v Auckland	Wanganui	1991/92
	McSweeney E.B.	Wellington v Canterbury	Wellington	1993/94
	Twose R.G.	Central Districts v Auckland	Palmerston North	1993/94
†	Jones R.A.	Auckland v Otago	Dunedin	1996/97
*	Sinclair M.S.	Central Districts v Northern Districts	Hamilton	1996/97
	Twose R.G.	Wellington v India	Wellington	1998/99
	Yovich J.A.F.	Northern Districts v Auckland	Taupo	1999/00
	Richardson M.H.	New Zealand v Zimbabwe	Harare	2000/01
	Fleming S.P.	New Zealand v South Africa	Bloemfontein	2000/01
	Gaffaney C.B.	Otago v Auckland	Auckland	2000/01
	Nevin C.J.	Wellington v Otago	Wellington	2000/01
	Sinclair M.S.	Central Districts v South Africa	Napier	2003/04
	Gaffaney C.B.	Otago v Wellington	Wellington	2004/05
	McCullum B.B.	New Zealand v Sri Lanka	Napier	2004/05
	Redmond A.J.	Otago v Northern Districts	Gisborne	2005/06
§	Guptill M.J.	Auckland v Wellington	Auckland	2005/06
	Marshall H.J.H.	Northern Districts v Auckland	Auckland	2006/07
	Marshall J.A.H.	Northern Districts v Central Districts	Gisborne	2006/07
	Vettori D.L.	New Zealand v SA Inviation XI	Bloemfontein	2007/08
	Marshall J.A.H.	Northern Districts v Central Districts	Hamilton	2007/08
	Hay G.R.	Central Districts v Northern Districts	Hamilton	2007/08
	Hopkins G.J.	Auckland v Northern Districts	Gisborne	2007/08

** not out   † batsman was run out   + batsman was stumped   § highest score in first-class cricket*

Carried Bat Through a Complete Innings

	Name	Score	Total	Match	Venue	Season
	Harris L.M.	41*	65	Otago v Tasmania	Dunedin	1883/84
	Gatehouse G.H.	54*	146	Tasmania v Otago	Dunedin	1883/84
	Mills I.	88*	156	Auckland v Otago	Dunedin	1893/94
†	Collins J.C.	128*	187	Fiji v Hawke's Bay	Napier	1894/95
	Cobcroft L.T.	85*	239	NSW v Wellington	Wellington	1895/96
	Mills G.	106*	235	Auckland v Wellington	Auckland	1895/96
	Collins D.C.	53*	131	Wellington v Canterbury	Christchurch	1906/07
§	Midlane F.A.	14*	60	Wellington§ v Canterbury	Christchurch	1910/11
	Gibbes W.R.L.	75*	193	Wellington v Canterbury	Christchurch	1911/12

† Midlane F.A.	222*	498	Wellington v Otago	Wellington	1914/15
Blunt R.C.	137*	336	Canterbury v Wellington	Wellington	1919/20
† Bardsley W.	200*	352	NSW v Auckland	Auckland	1923/24
Blunt R.C.	131*	204	Otago v Canterbury	Dunedin	1926/27
Dempster C.S.	167*	345	New Zealand v Glamorgan	Cardiff	1927
Kerr J.L.	146*	243	Canterbury v MCC	Christchurch	1935/36
Whitelaw P.E.	99*	183	Auckland/Wellington v MCC	Auckland	1936/37
Tindill E.W.T.	47*	111	Wellington v Otago	Dunedin	1946/47
† Miller L.S.M.	81*	154	Wellington v Otago	Dunedin	1956/57
Playle W.R.	89*	139	Auckland v Northern Districts	Auckland	1959/60
Bradburn W.P.	45*	87	Northern Districts v Wellington	Wellington	1960/61
Bradburn W.P.	37*	57	Northern Districts v Wellington	Hamilton	1961/62
Holloway R.A.	61*	122	Otago v Central Districts	Nelson	1962/63
Turner G.M.	43*	131	New Zealand v England	Lord's	1969
Turner G.M.	223*	386	New Zealand v West Indies	Kingston	1971/72
Redpath I.R.	159*	346	Australia v New Zealand	Auckland	1973/74
Wettimuny S.	63*	144	Sri Lanka v New Zealand	Christchurch	1982/83
† Franklin T.J.	153*	311	Young NZ v Zimbabwe	Harare	1984/85
Rutherford K.R.	89*	241	Otago v Auckland	Dunedin	1984/85
Boon D.C.	58*	103	Australia v New Zealand	Auckland	1985/86
Wright J.G.	149*	307	Canterbury v Auckland	Auckland	1988/89
Smith C.J.P.	90*	154	Central Dists v Northern Dists	Rotorua	1989/90
Murray D.J.	106*	233	Canterbury v Northern Dists	Hamilton	1992/93
Dobbs P.W.	81*	177	Otago v Canterbury	Oamaru	1994/95
Atherton M.A.	94*	228	England v New Zealand	Christchurch	1996/97
Kelly D.P.	212*	538	Central Districts v Canterbury	Blenheim	2000/01
Ingram P.J.	105*	201	Central Districts v Auckland	Auckland	2003/04
† How J.M.	190*	430	New Zealand A v England Lions	Queenstown	2008/09

† player was on the field for every ball of the match *§ one man absent*

Longest Individual Batting in a Match

Mins	*Runs*				
954	274* & 69*	Fleming S.P.	New Zealand v Sri Lanka	Colombo	2002/03
876	76 & 146*	Greatbatch M.J.	New Zealand v Australia	Perth	1989/90
835	122 & 102	Howarth G.P.	New Zealand v England	Auckland	1977/78
828	75 & 138	Wright J.G.	New Zealand v West Indies	Wellington	1986/87
813	93 & 101	Richardson M.H.	New Zealand v England	Lord's	2004
770	166* & 82	Congdon B.E.	New Zealand v West Indies	Port-of-Spain	1971/72

Longest Individual Innings

Mins	*Runs*				
741	306	Richardson M.H.	New Zealand v Zimbabwe A	Kwekwe	2000/01
720	163	Shoaib Mohammad	Pakistan v New Zealand	Wellington	1988/89
704	259	Turner G.M.	New Zealand v West Indies	Georgetown	1971/72
685	180	Reid J.F.	New Zealand v Sri Lanka	Colombo	1983/84
671	212*	Richardson M.H.	New Zealand A v Sussex	Hove	2000
659	211*	Gibbs H.H.	South Africa v New Zealand	Christchurch	1998/99
658	275*	Cullinan D.J.	South Africa v New Zealand	Auckland	1998/99
655	146*	Greatbatch M.J.	New Zealand v Australia	Perth	1989/90
655	274*	Fleming S.P.	New Zealand v Sri Lanka	Colombo	2002/03
648	158	Radley C.T.	England v New Zealand	Auckland	1977/78
647	251*	Harris C.Z.	Canterbury v Central Districts	Rangiora	1996/97
643	137	Gambhir G.	India v New Zealand	Napier	2008/09
636	170*	Jones A.H.	New Zealand v India	Auckland	1989/90

625	222	Rutherford I.A.	Otago v Central Districts	New Plymouth	1978/79
610	299	Crowe M.D.	New Zealand v Sri Lanka	Wellington	1990/91
609	120*	Crowe J.J.	New Zealand v Sri Lanka	Colombo	1986/87
605	267*	Young B.A.	New Zealand v Sri Lanka	Dunedin	1996/97
603	259	Turner G.M.	New Zealand v Guyana	Georgetown	1971/72
603	256	Raval J.A.	Auckland v Central Districts	Auckland	2008/09

Fastest Centuries

Mins	*Balls*				
52	45	Cairns B.L.	Otago v Wellington	Lower Hutt	1979/80
52	66	Cooper B.G.	Northern Districts v Canterbury	Gisborne	1986/87
53	63	Motz R.C.	Canterbury v Otago	Christchurch	1967/68

Slowest Centuries

Mins	*Balls*				
516	331	Crowe J.J.	New Zealand v Sri Lanka	Colombo	1986/87
487	397	Radley C.T.	England v New Zealand	Auckland	1977/78
464	390	Austen M.H.	Otago v Canterbury	Christchurch	1996/97
462	341	Greatbatch M.J.	New Zealand v Australia	Perth	1989/90
461	265	Crowe M.D.	New Zealand v Pakistan	Lahore	1990/91
458	341	Astle N.J.	New Zealand v Zimbabwe	Wellington	2000/01
455	307	Howarth G.P.	New Zealand v England	Auckland	1977/78

Most Boundaries in an Innings

	6s	*4s*		*Runs*			
53	8	45	Rutherford K.R.	317	New Zealand v D.B. Close's XI	Scarborough	1986
50	15	35	Reid J.R.	296	Wellington v Northern Districts	Wellington	1962/63
49	3	46	Sutcliffe B.	385	Otago v Canterbury	Christchurch	1952/53
48	3	45	Fulton P.G.	301*	Canterbury v Auckland	Christchurch	2002/03
47	3	44	Trumper V.T.	293	Sims' Australian XI v Canterbury	Christchurch	1913/14
45	2	43	Raval J.A.	256	Auckland v Central Districts	Auckland	2008/09
43	10	33	Hammond W.R.	336*	England v New Zealand	Auckland	1932/33
43	–	43	Richardson M.H.	306	New Zealand v Zimbabwe A	Kwekwe	2000/01
43	3	40	McIntosh T.G.	268	Auckland v Canterbury	Auckland	2007/08
42	1	41	Reid J.R.	283	Wellington v Otago	Wellington	1951/52
42	1	41	Crowe M.D.	242*	New Zealand v South Australia	Adelaide	1985/86
42	3	39	Crowe M.D.	242	Central Districts v Otago	New Plymouth	1989/90
41	–	41	Blunt R.C.	338*	Otago v Canterbury	Christchurch	1931/32
40	–	40	de Silva P.A.	267	Sri Lanka v New Zealand	Wellington	1990/91

Most Sixes in an Innings

Sixes		*Runs*			
15	Reid J.R.	296	Wellington v Northern Districts	Wellington	1962/63
12	Patel D.N.	204	Auckland v Northern Districts	Auckland	1991/92
11	Astle N.J.	222	New Zealand v England	Christchurch	2001/02
11	Spearman C.M.	133	Central Districts v Auckland	Auckland	2003/04
10	Hammond W.R.	336*	England v New Zealand	Auckland	1932/33
10	Robinson R.T.	166	England XI v Northern Districts	Hamilton	1987/88
10	Styris S.B.	212*	Northern Districts v Otago	Hamilton	2001/02
9	Cairns B.L.	110	Otago v Wellington	Lower Hutt	1979/80
9	Botham I.T.	80	England XI v Central Districts	Palmerston North	1983/84
9	Cairns C.L.	120	New Zealand v Zimbabwe	Auckland	1995/96
9	Southee T.G.	77*	New Zaland v England	Napier	2007/08
8	Taylor L.R.P.L.	152	Central Districts v Northern Districts	Napier	2007/08
8	Dacre C.C.R.	176	New Zealand v Derbyshire	Derby	1927

8	Bula I.L.	102	Fiji v Canterbury	Christchurch	1953/54
8	Rutherford K.R.	317	New Zealand v DB Close's XI	Scarborough	1986
8	Germon L.K.	160*	Canterbury v Wellington	Christchurch	1989/90
8	Parore A.C.	111*	Auckland v Wellington	Auckland	1997/98
8	Horne M.J.	209*	Auckland v Northern Districts	Auckland	2003/04
8	Adams A.R.	117*	Auckland v Otago	Lincoln	2006/07
8	Franklin J.E.C.	219	Wellington v Auckland	Auckland	2008/09
8	Fulton P.G.	122	Canterbury v Northern Districts	Christchurch	2008/09
8	de Grandhomme C.	103*	Auckland v Central Districts	Auckland	2008/09

Five Sixes off Consecutive Balls

Germon L.K.	off Vance R.H.	Canterbury v Wellington	Christchurch	1989/90

(Full tosses and deliberate no-balls were provided for him to hit).

Four Sixes off Consecutive Balls

Rutherford K.R.	off Doshi D.R.	New Zealand v DB Close's XI	Scarborough	1986

Three Sixes off Consecutive Balls

Hill C.	off Ollivier K.M.	Australia v New Zealand	Wellington	1904/05
Hammond W.R.	off Newman J.	England v New Zealand	Auckland	1932/33
McRae D.A.N.	off Burke C.	Canterbury v Auckland	Auckland	1937/38
Pritchard T.L.	off Groves L.J.	Wellington v Otago	Dunedin	1937/38
Edwards R.M.	off Carew M.C.	Governor General's XI v West Indies	Auckland	1968/69
Burgess M.G.	off Anderson R.W.	Auckland v Central Districts	Wanganui	1977/78
Stirling D.A.	off Brown V.R.	Central Districts v Canterbury	New Plymouth	1986/87
Thomson S.A.	off Bracewell J.G.	Northern Districts v Auckland	Auckland	1987/88
Hick G.A.	off Duff S.W.	England XI v Central Districts	New Plymouth	1991/92
Astle N.J.	off Wells J.D.	Canterbury v Wellington	Christchurch	1994/95
Vincent L.	off Vettori D.L.	Auckland v Northern Districts	Auckland	1998/99
Astle N.J.	off Caddick A.R.	New Zealand v England	Christchurch	2001/02
Spearman C.M.	off Nicol R.J.	Central Districts v Auckland	Auckland	2003/04
Adams A.R.	off Bowden D.J.	Auckland v Wellington	Wellington	2005/06
Nicol R.J.	off Worker G.H.	Auckland v Central Districts	Auckland	2008/09

Most Ducks in Succession

5	Hayes J.A.	(C, NZ 1954/55)	17,0 / dnb / 0,0 / 0,0
5	Bateman S.N.	(C 1982/83)	5*,0 / 0,0 / 0,0
4	Frith W.	(C 1882/83-1887/88)	0,0 / 0,0
4	Silver R.C.D.	(O 1936/37-1937/38)	12,0 / 0,0 / 0,11
*4	Langdon M.C.	(ND 1957/58)	25,0 / 0,0 / 0,5
4	Hastings B.F.	(C 1963/64)	1,0 / 0,0 / 0,35
4	Steele H.K.C.	(A 1974/75)	0,0 / 0,0
4	Bracewell B.P.	(NZ 1978)	0 / dnb / 0,0 / 0,0*
4	Bradburn G.E.	(ND 1987/88)	0 / 0,0 / 0
4	Morrison D.K.	(NZ 1993/94)	0 / 0,0 / 0,20*
4	Davis H.T.	(NZ, W 1997/98)	7*,0 / 0,0 / 0,21
4	Young R.A.	(A 1999/00)	0,0 / 0,0
4	Martin C.S.	(C NZ 2000/01)	5,0 / 0,0 / 0
4	Gaffaney C.B.	(O 2001/02)	31,0 / 0,0 / 0,56
4	Hamilton L.J.	(CD 2004/05)	11,0 / 0,0 / 0,2
4	Astle T.D.	(C 2008/09)	18,0 / 0,0 / 0,1

** first three games in first-class cricket*

Most Scoreless Innings in Succession

10	Visser P.J.	(CD 1984/85-1985/86)	0 / 0,0 / dnb / 0*,0 / dnb / 0*,0* 0,0 / dnb / 0
7	Hamilton L.J.	(CD 1999/00)	0,0* / 0 / 0*,0 / 0 / 0
7	Martin C.S.	(NZ 2008, NZ 2008/09))	0*,dnb / 0,0* / 0*,0 / 0*,0*
6	Hayes J.A.	(C, NZ 1954/55-1955/56)	17,0 / dnb / 0,0 / 0,0 / 0*
6	de Groen R.P.	(A 1988/89-1989/90)	1,0* / dnb / 0,0 / 0* / 0*,0*
6	Martin C.S.	(NZ, NZ A 2008/09))	0,0 / 0*,0* / 0*,0*
5	Frith W.	(O, C 1881/82-1887/8)	1,0* / 0,0 / 0,0
*5	Moss A.E.	(C 1889/90)	0,0* / 0,0 / 0*,4*
5	Burrows J.T.	(C 1932/33)	0*,0* / 0* / 0*,0*
5	Hill J.	(O 1961/62-1962/63)	0*,0* / 0* / 0*,0*
5	Unka H.	(ND 1968/69-1971/72)	0* / 0*,0* / dnb / 0*,0
5	Bracewell B.P.	(NZ 1978)	0 / dnb / 0,0 / 0,0*
5	Webb R.J.	(O 1980/81)	1,0 / dnb,0 / 0*,dnb / 0,0*
5	Troup G.B.	(A, NZ 1980/81-1981/82)	0,0* / 0,0 / dnb / 0
5	Bateman S.N.	(C 1982/83)	5*,0 / 0,0 / 0,0

** first five innings in first-class cricket*

UNUSUAL DISMISSALS

HANDLED THE BALL

Benson E.T.	MCC v Auckland	Auckland	1929/30
Gilbertson A.W.	Otago v Auckland	Auckland	1952/53
Vaughan J.T.C.	NZ Emerging Players v England XI	Hamilton	1991/92

OBSTRUCTING THE FIELD

Hayes J.A.	Canterbury v Central Districts	Christchurch	1954/55

RUN OUT BY THE BOWLER *(while backing up before the ball had been bowled)*

Reese T.W. by Downes A.D.	Canterbury v Otago	Christchurch	1894/95
Smith J. by Allen R.	Canterbury v Wellington	Wellington	1943/44
Randall D.W. by Chatfield E.J.	England v New Zealand	Christchurch	1977/78

STUMPED BY A SUBSTITUTE

Pervez Sajjad by Congdon B.E.	Pakistan v New Zealand	Lahore	1964/65
Congdon B.E. by Burge P.J.P.	Central Districts v Australia	Palmerston North	1966/67

RETIRED (out)

Ransford V.S.	Australia v Hawke's Bay	Napier	1920/21
Chappell G.S.	Australia v Wellington	Wellington	1976/77
Saeed Anwar	Pakistan v New Zealand XI	Napier	1993/94
Basit Ali	Pakistan v New Zealand XI	Napier	1993/94
Inzamam-ul-Haq	Pakistan v New Zealand XI	Napier	1993/94
Spearman C.M.	New Zealand v North West	Potchefstroom	2000/01
Strauss A.J.	England v Major Association XI	Dunedin	2007/08
Taylor L.R.P.L.	New Zealand v Northamptonshire	Northampton	2007/08

REPRESENTED TWO PROVINCES IN ONE SEASON

Sutcliffe B.	Auckland and Otago	1946/47
Sutcliffe B.	Otago and Auckland	1947/48
Clark L.A.	Otago and Auckland	1959/60
Andrews B.	Canterbury and Central Districts	1966/67

On each occasion, the second province was represented in a match against a non-provincial side. No player has played for two provinces in inter-provincial matches in the same season.

REPLACEMENT PLAYERS

Substitute	*Player replaced*			
Lawrence —	Bell A.	Wellington v Nelson	Wellington	1873/74
Cotterill C.N.	White G.	Hawke's Bay v NSW	Napier	1893/94
unknown	Ratu Epeli	Fiji v Auckland	Auckland	1894/95
Kilgour W.A.	*Wilson C.G.	Otago v Auckland	Auckland	1907/08
Bryden J.S.	*Siedeberg H.G.	Otago v Canterbury	Dunedin	1913/14
Graham W.H.	Middleton F.S.	Auckland v Wellington	Wellington	1917/18
Whitta H.B.	*Foster P.S.	Canterbury v Wellington	Christchurch	1919/20
Samuels B.	*Brice A.W.S.	Wellington v Auckland	Auckland	1919/20
Wilson E.S.	Eastman L.C.	Otago v Wellington	Wellington	1927/28
Kubunavanua P.	Logavatu I.T.	Fiji v Canterbury	Christchurch	1947/48
Abernethy B.	Webb R.J.	Otago v Auckland	Dunedin	1982/83
Neutze P.S.	Brown V.R.	Auckland v Wellington	Auckland	1987/88
Brown R.K.	Greatbatch M.J.	CD v Otago	Palmerston North	1991/92
Lee C.D.	Larsen G.R.	Wellington v ND	Hamilton	1991/92
Fleming S.P.	Harris C.Z.	Canterbury v Auckland	Auckland	1991/92
Lee C.D.	*Patel D.N.	Auckland v Otago	Dunedin	1994/95
Garner C.D.	Spearman C.M.	CD v ND	Nelson	1996/97
Cooper D.M.	Howell L.G.	CD v ND	Nelson	1996/97
Lamont M.J.	Horne M.J.	Otago v Auckland	Dunedin	1996/97
Morland N.D.	Wiseman P.J.	Otago v Auckland	Dunedin	1996/97
Sewell D.G.	Kennedy R.J.	Otago v Auckland	Dunedin	1996/97
Irving R.J.R.	Mills J.M.	Auckland v Otago	Dunedin	1996/97
Weenink S.W.	Chandler P.J.B.	Wellington v Canterbury	Christchurch	1996/97
Jonas G.R.	Davis H.T.	Wellington v Canterbury	Christchurch	1996/97
Hartland B.R.	Murray D.J.	Canterbury v Wellington	Christchurch	1996/97
Frew R.M.	Harris C.Z.	Canterbury v Wellington	Christchurch	1996/97
Sharpe M.F.	Allott G.I.	Canterbury v Wellington	Christchurch	1996/97
Hotter S.J.	Davis H.T.	Wellington v CD	Masterton	1996/97
Muir G.A.	Priest M.W.	Canterbury v Zimbabwe	Timaru	1997/98
Pawson S.J.	Priest M.W.	Canterbury v Otago	Dunedin	1997/98
Dry L.R.	Bell M.D.	Wellington v ND	Hamilton	1998/99
Morland N.D.	*Wiseman P.J.	Otago v Auckland	Dunedin	1999/00
Spearman C.M.	Sinclair M.S.	CD v Otago	Palmerston North	1999/00
Todd G.R.	Oram J.D.P.	CD v Wellington	Napier	2000/01
McCullum N.L.	Wiseman P.J.	Otago v Canterbury	Alexandra	2000/01
Robinson G.G.	*Marshall J.A.H.	ND v Canterbury	Gisborne	2004/05
O'Brien I.E.	Rasmussen S.	Wellington v Otago	Dunedin	2006/07
Hitchcock P.A.	*Hopkins G.J.	Auckland v Wellington	Auckland	2008/09
Houghton M.V.	Patel J.S.	Wellington v Auckland	Auckland	2008/09
Shaw L.J.	McIntosh T.G.	Auckland v West Indies	Auckland	2008/09
Boult J.J.	Martin B.P.	ND v Auckland	Whangarei	2008/09
Robertson I.A.	Thompson E.P.	N.Zealand A v England Lions	Lincoln	2008/09
Raval J.A.	McIntosh T.G.	Auckland v Otago	Queenstown	2008/09
Shaw L.J.	Martin C.S.	Auckland v Otago	Queenstown	2008/09
Davis T.T.	Arnel B.J.	ND v Canterbury	Christchurch	2008/09
Scott B.E.	Flynn D.R.	ND v Canterbury	Christchurch	2008/09
Boam H.K.P.	Franklin J.E.C.	Wellington v CD	Napier	2008/09
Croft S.J.	Mills K.D.	Auckland v CD	Auckland	2008/09

** indicates player did not bat or bowl before being replaced*

BOWLING

Ten Wickets in an Innings

	Overs	Maidens	Runs	Wickets			
* Moss A.E.	21.3	10	28	10	Canterbury v Wellington	Christchurch	1889/90

** on debut – the only instance in first-class cricket*

Nine Wickets in an Innings

	Overs	Maidens	Runs	Wickets			
Wiseman P.J.	16.4	9	13	9	Canterbury v CD	Christchurch	2004/05
Wensley A.F.	24	13	36	9	Auckland v Otago	Auckland	1929/30
Eden T.	15.2	0	43	9	Nelson v Wellington	Wellington	1875/76
Dent T.H.	28	11	47	9	Hawke's Bay v Wellington	Napier	1900/01
Tait A.R.	24.5	8	48	9	ND v Auckland	Hamilton	1996/97
Fisher A.H.	25.2	4	50	9	Otago v Queensland	Dunedin	1896/97
Hadlee R.J.	23.4	4	52	9	New Zealand v Australia	Brisbane	1985/86
Hadlee R.J.	24	5	55	9	New Zealand v West Zone	Rajkot	1988/89
McBeath D.J.	24	7	56	9	Canterbury v Auckland	Christchurch	1918/19
Brice A.W.S.	25.5	5	67	9	Wellington v Auckland	Wellington	1918/19
Cooke F.H.	56	24	73	9	Otago v Canterbury	Christchurch	1884/85
Blair R.W.	35	9	72	9	Wellington v Auckland	Wellington	1956/57
Neill R.	31	7	75	9	Auckland v Canterbury	Auckland	1891/92
Blair R.W.	29.5	9	75	9	Wellington v Canterbury	Wellington	1956/57
Neill R.	24.2	1	86	9	Auckland v Canterbury	Auckland	1897/98
Petherick P.J.	35	10	93	9	Otago v ND	Dunedin	1975/76
Priest M.W.	28.5	5	95	9	Canterbury v Otago	Dunedin	1989/90
Robertson W.	39.3	8	98	9	Canterbury v Wellington	Christchurch	1894/95
Yuile B.W.	45	19	100	9	CD v Canterbury	New Plymouth	1965/66

Sixteen Wickets in a Match

16-130	Tait A.R.	24.5-8-48-9/38.4-13-82-7	Northern Dists v Auckland, Hamilton	1996/97

Fifteen Wickets in a Match

15-60	Callaway S.T.	23.3-10-33-8/17-7-27-7	Canterbury v Hawke's Bay, Napier	1903/04
15-94	Cooke F.H.	40.3-16-61-8/33.3-14-33-7	Otago v Canterbury, Christchurch	1882/83
15-104	Boock S.L.	29.3-13-47-7/34.3-16-57-8	Otago v Auckland, Dunedin	1989/90
15-123	Hadlee R.J.	23.4-4-52-9/28.5-9-71-6	NZ v Australia, Brisbane	1985/86
15-168	McBeath D.J.	24-7-56-9/37-4-112-6	Canterbury v Auckland, Christchurch	1918/19
15-175	Callaway S.T.	35-14-77-7/43.4-11-98-8	NSW v New Zealand, Christchurch	1895/96
15-203	Moir A.M.	24.1-4-84-7/35.1-3-119-8	Otago v Central Dists, New Plymouth	1953/54

Fourteen Wickets in a Match

14-59	Read R.J.	13-3-35-7/14-5-24-7	Canterbury v Southland, Invercargill	1920/21
14-63	Eden T.	15.2-0-43-9/15.5-7-20-5	Nelson v Wellington, Wellington	1875/76
* 14-63	Rees A.W.	13-4-27-6/15.3-3-36-8	Auckland v Otago, Dunedin	1889/90
14-65	Callaway S.T.	36.3-18-47-7/18.2-7-18-7	NSW v Wellington, Wellington	1895/96
14-65	Hayes J.A.	18.2-6-28-7/12.1-3-37-7	Auckland v Wellington, Auckland	1957/58
14-93	Torrance R.C.	23-6-51-7/19-5-42-7	Otago v Hawke's Bay, Napier	1908/09
14-94	Howarth H.J.	22.1-5-42-7/23-6-52-7	Auckland v Otago, Dunedin	1973/74
14-103	Downes A.D.	30-12-32-7/30-8-71-7	Otago v Hawke's Bay, Dunedin	1893/94
* 14-107	Robertson W.	28.2-8-59-8/20.4-7-48-6	Canterbury v Auckland, Christchurch	1893/94
14-119	Pringle C.	27.4-10-63-7/23.5-5-56-7	Auckland v Otago, Dunedin	1993/94
14-126	Moir A.M.	18-1-55-8/25-6-71-6	Otago v Canterbury, Dunedin	1951/52
14-136	Blair R.W.	29.5-9-75-9/26-8-61-5	Wellington v Canterbury, Wellington	1956/57
14-151	Gray E.J.	50-19-114-6/26.1-12-37-8	Wellington v Canterbury, Lower Hutt	1985/86

** on debut*

Four Wickets with Consecutive Balls

Downes A.D.	Otago v Auckland	Dunedin	1893/94

Hat Tricks

Salmon I.J.	Wellington v Nelson	Wellington	1873/74
Lankham W.	Auckland v Taranaki	Auckland	1882/83
Frith C.	Otago v Canterbury	Dunedin	1884/85
Fannin H.A.	Hawkes Bay v Taranaki	Napier	1897/98
Barclay F.	Auckland v Canterbury	Auckland	1903/04
Orchard S.A.	Canterbury v Auckland	Auckland	1909/10
Bennett J.H.	Canterbury v Wellington	Wellington	1911/12
Olliff C.	Auckland v Wellington	Auckland	1912/13
Middleton F.S.	Wellington v Hawke's Bay	Wellington	1919/20
Allom M.J.C.*	England v New Zealand	Christchurch	1929/30
Mulcock E.	Canterbury v Otago	Christchurch	1937/38
Overton G.W.F.	Otago v Canterbury	Christchurch	1946/47
Murray R.M.	Wellington v Otago	Wellington	1949/50
Moir A.M.	Otago v Canterbury	Christchurch	1950/51
Jones J.F.	Wellington v Central Districts	Wellington	1953/54
Reid R.E.	Wellington v Otago	Dunedin	1958/59
Bartlett G.A.	Central Districts v Northern Districts	Hamilton	1959/60
Cameron F.J.	Otago v Northern Districts	Hamilton	1962/63
Blair R.W.	Wellington v Northern Districts	Wellington	1962/63
Alabaster G.D.	Northern Districts v Canterbury	Hamilton	1962/63
Furlong B.D.M.	NZ Under 23 XI v Canterbury	Christchurch	1964/65
Hadlee R.J.	Canterbury v Central Districts	Nelson	1971/72
Petherick P.J.	New Zealand v Pakistan	Lahore	1976/77
Toynbee M.H.	Central Districts v Northern Districts	Gisborne	1979/80
Visser P.J.	Central Districts v Auckland	Nelson	1983/84
Maguiness S.J.	Wellington v Northern Districts	Wellington	1983/84
Beard D.A.	Northern Districts v Central Districts	Nelson	1989/90
Gale A.J.	Otago v Canterbury	Dunedin	1992/93
Harris C.Z.	New Zealand v Orange Free State	Bloemfontein	1994/95
Hayes R.L.	Northern Districts v Central Districts	Rotorua	1995/96
Hotter S.J.	Wellington v Otago	Wellington	1996/97
Anderson T.R.	Central Districts v Auckland	Masterton	1998/99
Canning T.K.	Auckland v Central Districts	Auckland	1999/00
Orchard M.G.	Northern Districts v Canterbury	Gisborne	2003/04
Franklin J.E.C.	New Zealand v Bangladesh	Dhaka	2004/05
Sidebottom R.J.	England v New Zealand	Hamilton	2007/08
McClenaghan M.J.	Central Districts v Canterbury	Rangiora	2008/09

** Allom captured 4 wickets with 5 balls in the same over*

Most Wickets in a Single Day's Play in New Zealand

14	Rees A.W.	Auckland v Otago	Dunedin	1889/90
13	Lankham W.	Auckland v Taranaki	Auckland	1882/83
13	Smith C.R.	Hawke's Bay v Taranaki	Hawera	1891/92
13	Cave H.B.	Central Districts v Auckland	Palmerston North	1952/53

Outstanding Analyses

TEN WICKETS IN AN INNINGS

21.3	11	28	10	Moss A.E.	Canterbury v Wellington	Christchurch	1889/90

NINE WICKETS IN AN INNINGS

16.4	9	13	9	Wiseman P.J.	Canterbury v CD	Christchurch	2004/05
24	13	36	9	Wensley A.F.	Auckland v Otago	Auckland	1929/30
15.2	0	43	9	Eden T.	Nelson v Wellington	Wellington	1875/76
28	11	47	9	Dent T.H.	Hawke's Bay v Wellington	Napier	1900/01

EIGHT WICKETS IN AN INNINGS

13	6	13	8	Firth J.P.	Wellington v Hawke's Bay	Wellington	1883/84
19	12	14	8	Austin S.W.	NSW v Hawke's Bay	Napier	1893/94
29	21	18	8	Frith W.	Canterbury v Otago	Christchurch	1880/81
14.5	7	19	8	Fannin H.A.	Hawke's Bay v Auckland	Auckland	1897/98

SEVEN WICKETS IN AN INNINGS

10.1	6	9	7	Bracewell J.G.	Otago v Canterbury	Dunedin	1981/82
13	9	11	7	Fisher A.H.	Otago v Canterbury	Christchurch	1896/97
25.3	16	12	7	Downes A.D.	Otago v Canterbury	Dunedin	1896/97
16	8	12	7	Tuffey D.R.	Northern Districts v Wellington	Hamilton	2000/01
32.1	24	13	7	Lankham W.	Auckland v Taranaki	Auckland	1882/83
10.4	5	16	7	Farooq Hamid	Pakistan v Wellington	Wellington	1964/65
17	10	17	7	Armstrong W.W.	Australia v Wellington	Wellington	1913/14
14.2	7	17	7	Maguiness S.J.	Wellington v Canterbury	Rangiora	1984/85
18.2	7	18	7	Callaway S.T.	NSW v Wellington	Wellington	1895/96

SIX WICKETS IN AN INNINGS

8	5	3	6	Cowie J.	New Zealand v Ireland	Dublin	1937
8	5	4	6	Callaway S.T.	Canterbury v Wellington	Wellington	1903/04
9.2	3	5	6	Bennett A.P.	Nelson v Wellington	Nelson	1885/86
16	11	6	6	Haskell W.J.R.	Wellington v Otago	Wellington	1967/68
14	10	7	6	Dunlop D.	Canterbury v Wellington	Wellington	1886/87
18	14	7	6	Hampton B.L.	Central Districts v Otago	Dunedin	1963/64
15	10	8	6	Downes W.F.	Otago v Canterbury	Christchurch	1866/67
11.2	6	9	6	Fowler G.	Nelson v Wellington	Nelson	1887/88
9.3	6	10	6	Pearson F.A.	Auckland v Hawke's Bay	Auckland	1910/11

FIVE WICKETS IN AN INNINGS

15.2	13	2	5	Ashby D.A.	Canterbury v Auckland	Auckland	1877/78
5	3	3	5	Allcott C.F.W.	New Zealand v Somerset	Taunton	1927
10.3	6	5	5	Bright R.J.	Australia v Central Districts	Nelson	1976/77
9	6	6	5	Parker T.S.	Otago v Canterbury	Christchurch	1866/67
21	18	8	5	Frith C.	Otago v Tasmania	Dunedin	1883/84
4	2	8	5	Burnup C.J.	Lord Hawke's XI v NZ	Wellington	1902/03
8	4	8	5	McBeath D.J.	Southland v Canterbury	Invercargill	1920/21
9	3	9	5	Bennett J.H.	Canterbury v Wellington	Christchurch	1910/11
12	5	9	5	Butterfield L.A.	South Island v North Island	Auckland	1944/45
9.1	5	9	5	Boock S.L.	New Zealand v Middlesex	Lord's	1978

FOUR WICKETS IN AN INNINGS

3.2	2	1	4	Snedden C.A.	Auckland v Hawke's Bay	Auckland	1920/21
6.4	5	2	4	Puna N.	Northern Dists v Central Dists	Hamilton	1957/58
7	6	3	4	Carrington S.M.	Northern Districts v Otago	Tauranga	1982/83
6.5	5	3	4	Woodcock L.J.	Wellington v Otago	Wellington	2001/02

THREE WICKETS IN AN INNINGS

3	3	0	3	Smith K.F.H.	Central Districts v Canterbury	Nelson	1959/60
2.1	2	0	3	Barnes S.G.	Australia v Canterbury	Christchurch	1945/46

5	5	0	3	Gray E.J.	Wellington v Canterbury	Christchurch	1985/86
1.4	0	1	3	Bolton B.A.	Canterbury v Central Districts	Christchurch	1958/59
2	1	1	3	Thomson S.A.	Northern Districts v Canterbury	Christchurch	1992/93
1.4	0	2	3	Anthony A.	Canterbury v Wellington	Christchurch	1908/09
3.3	1	2	3	Thomas A.W.	Canterbury v Otago	Christchurch	1917/18
4	2	2	3	Sparling J.T.	Auckland v Wellington	Auckland	1957/58
5	2	3	3	Cowlishaw W.P.	Canterbury v Otago	Christchurch	1864/65
15	12	3	3	Frith W.	Canterbury v Auckland	Auckland	1877/78
2.3	1	3	3	Richardson G.	Nelson v Wellington	Wellington	1886/87
3	2	3	3	Dowson E.M.	Lord Hawke's XI v Otago	Dunedin	1902/03
5	2	3	3	Pollard V.	New Zealand v England	Auckland	1965/66

Seven Wickets in an Innings on First-class Debut

10-28	Moss A.E.	Canterbury v Wellington	Christchurch	1889/90
8-35	Wilson R.	Queensland v Auckland	Auckland	1896/97
† 8-36	Rees A.W.	Auckland v Otago	Dunedin	1889/90
8-37	Hole H.	Nelson v Wellington	Nelson	1874/75
8-48	O'Connell W.J.	Hawke's Bay v Wellington	Wellington	1919/20
8-59	Robertson W.	Canterbury v Auckland	Christchurch	1893/94
8-70	Hay W.A.	Otago v Southland	Dunedin	1917/18
7-31	Lynch D.	Auckland v Canterbury	Auckland	1877/78
7-36	Mills G.	Auckland v Wellington	Auckland	1886/87
7-39	Lankham W.	Auckland v Canterbury	Christchurch	1882/83
† 7-42	Morrison B.D.	Wellington v Otago	Wellington	1953/54
† 7-46	Stephens W.B.	Auckland v Otago	Auckland	1899/00
7-46	Doig J.A.	Southland v Otago	Invercargill	1914/15
† 7-50	Badcock F.T.	Wellington v Canterbury	Christchurch	1924/25
† 7-54	Turnbull J.A.	Auckland v Central Districts	Auckland	1955/56
7-61	Merrin R.C.	Canterbury XI v NZ Touring Team	Christchurch	1967/68
† 7-95	Noonan D.J.	New South Wales v Canterbury	Christchurch	1895/96
7-95	Huxford N.A.	Wellington v Pakistan	Wellington	1964/65

† *2nd innings*

Ten Wickets in a Match on First-class Debut

14-63	Rees A.W.	Auckland v Otago	Dunedin	1889/90
14-107	Robertson W.	Canterbury v Auckland	Christchurch	1893/94
13-72	Moss A.E.	Canterbury v Wellington	Christchurch	1889/90
12-18	Bennett A.P.	Nelson v Wellington	Nelson	1885/86
12-90	Mills W.	Taranaki v Fiji	Hawera	1894/95
12-118	Hay W.A.	Otago v Southland	Dunedin	1917/18
11-43	Fuller E.T.A.	Canterbury v Otago	Christchurch	1872/73
11-97	Wilson R.	Queensland v Auckland	Auckland	1896/97
11-99	Lankham W.	Auckland v Canterbury	Christchurch	1882/83
11-112	Morrison B.D.	Wellington v Otago	Wellington	1953/54
11-126	Noonan D.J.	New South Wales v Canterbury	Christchurch	1895/96
10-30	Lawson H.	Wellington v Nelson	Nelson	1883/84
10-31	MacDonald F.	Otago v Canterbury	Dunedin	1863/64
10-39	Holderness H.V.A.	Otago v Southland	Invercargill	1918/19
10-61	Hole H.	Nelson v Wellington	Nelson	1874/75
10-70	Mills G.	Auckland v Wellington	Auckland	1886/87
10-71	Lawton J.C.	Otago v Canterbury	Christchurch	1890/91
10-90	Brown C.M.	Auckland v Canterbury	Rangiora	1993/94
10-105	Frame W.D.	Otago v Canterbury	Dunedin	1955/56
10-122	Badcock F.T.	Wellington v Canterbury	Christchurch	1924/25
10-133	Leonard D.J.	Central Districts v Northern Districts	Rotorua	1989/90

Ten Wickets in Last First-class Match

† 10-31	MacDonald F.	Otago v Canterbury	Dunedin	1863/64
† 10-61	Hole H.	Nelson v Wellington	Nelson	1874/75
10-91	Downes W.F.	Otago v Canterbury	Dunedin	1875/76
12-114	Lankham W.	Auckland v Canterbury	Auckland	1883/84
13-140	Edser H.	Canterbury v Wellington	Wellington	1883/84
11-25	Fowler G.	Nelson v Wellington	Nelson	1887/88
11-77	Carson W.	Otago v Canterbury	Dunedin	1887/88
† 10-39	Holderness H.V.A.	Otago v Southland	Invercargill	1918/19
10-108	Vivian H.G.	Auckland v Wellington	Auckland	1938/39
11-129	de Groen R.P.	Northern Districts v Canterbury	Hamilton	1995/96

† this was the player's only first-class appearance

Most Wickets in a Season

		Matches	Wkts	Runs	Ave	5WI	10WM	Best
Boock S.L.	1977/78	13	66	1088	16.48	6	—	7-57
Hadlee R.J.	1986/87	11	62	935	15.08	8	1	7-49
Hadlee R.J.	1981/82	10	59	867	14.69	7	—	6-26
Boock S.L.	1978/79	12	58	1238	21.34	4	1	8-59
Thompson G.J.	1902-03	7	57	668	11.71	6	3	8-124
Boock S.L.	1986/87	10	55	920	16.72	6	1	6-62
Callaway S.T.	1903/04	5	54	474	8.77	8	4	8-33
Blair R.W.	1956/57	8	53	784	14.79	6	4	9-72
Tait A.R.	1996/97	9	53	865	16.32	4	1	9-48
Drum C.J.	2001/02	9	53	827	15.60	3	2	6-34
Martin C.S.	2003/04	12	53	1144	21.58	6	1	6-76
Austin S.W.	1893/94	7	52	606	11.65	6	1	8-14
Armstrong W.W.	1913/14	8	52	789	15.17	7	1	7-17
O'Sullivan D.R.	1978/79	9	52	989	19.01	3	—	6-51
Chatfield E.J.	1981/82	10	51	868	17.01	2	—	5-29
Hadlee R.J.	1978/79	10	50	909	18.18	4	—	6-28
Douglas J.W.H.T.	1906/07	9	50	663	13.26	5	1	7-49

Most Wickets in a Season for New Zealand Overseas

		Matches	Wkts	Runs	Ave	5WI	10WM	Best
Burtt T.B.	1949	27	128	2929	22.28	11	2	7-102
Cowie J.	1937	24	114	2275	19.95	6	1	6-3
Merritt W.E.	1927	25	107	2530	23.64	5	1	6-38

Most Wickets in a Season of First-class Debut

			Overs	Mdns	Runs	Wkts	Ave
Robertson W.	Canterbury & NZ	1893/94	*1534	balls	570	47	12.12
Gillespie S.R.	Northern Districts	1979/80	384.5	98	998	45	22.17
Petherick P.J.	Otago	1975/76	286	57	847	42	20.16
Lankham W.	Auckland	1882/83	†1006	balls	259	41	6.31
O'Brien I.E.	Wellington	2000/01	319.1	81	807	41	19.68

** Robertson bowled 222.2 6-ball overs and 40 5-ball overs † Lankham bowled 96.2 5-ball overs and 131 4-ball overs*

Most Balls Bowled in an Innings

444	Howarth H.J.	74-24-138-2	NZ v West Indies	Bridgetown	1971/72
426	Tufnell P.C.R.	71-22-147-2	England v New Zealand	Wellington	1991/92
426	Vettori D.L.	71-24-171-2	New Zealand v India	Mohali	1999/00
420	Howarth H.J.	70-24-144-4	NZ v England	Lord's	1973
420	Boock S.L.	70-10-229-1	NZ v Pakistan	Auckland	1988/89
417	O'Sullivan D.R.	52.1-15-125-4	CD v Otago	New Plymouth	1978/79
414	Doshi D.R.	69-34-79-2	India v New Zealand	Auckland	1980/81

414	Tauseef Ahmed	69-28-106-1	Pakistan v New Zealand	Auckland	1988/89
414	Hick G.A.	69-27-126-4	England v New Zealand	Wellington	1991/92
408	Morgan H.A.	51-16-108-3	Wellington v Otago	Dunedin	1968/69
408	Wiseman P.J.	68-21-123-4	Otago v ND	Hamilton	1995/96
407	Boock S.L.	67.5-31-75-4	Otago v CD	Alexandra	1988/89
399	Cook N.G.B.	66.3-26-153-3	England v NZ	Wellington	1983/84
396	Puna N.	66-23-131-4	ND v Auckland	Hamilton	1964/65
396	Nadkarni R.G.	66-34-114-2	India v NZ	Christchurch	1967/68
390	Chatfield E.J.	65-14-158-1	NZ v Pakistan	Auckland	1988/89

Most Balls Bowled in a Match

629	Badcock F.T.	104.5-44-178-9	Otago v Canterbury	Christchurch	1933/34
624	Dickeson C.W.	104-45-142-11	ND v Wellington	Hamilton	1979/80
618	Gray E.J.	103-39-214-6	Wellington v Otago	Wellington	1984/85
600	Allcott C.F.W.	75-23-161-5	Auckland v Canterbury	Christchurch	1924/25
600	Butler L.C.	100-46-122-4	Wellington v Auckland	Auckland	1965/66

Most Runs Conceded in a Match

304	2-173, 0-131	Dickinson G.R.	Otago v Wellington	Dunedin	1923/24
300	6-172, 4-128	Smith S.G.	Auckland v Wellington	Wellington	1923/24
277	6-136, 6-141	Alloo A.W.	Otago v Wellington	Dunedin	1923/24
266	6-185, 2-81	Merritt W.E.	New Zealand v Kent	Canterbury	1927
251	1-105, 1-146	Schaw R.J.	CD v Canterbury	Napier	2007/08
243	1-58, 3-185	Lythe T.I.	CD v Wellington	Napier	2007/08
243	6-128, 7-115	Grimmett C.V.	Australia v Canterbury	Christchurch	1927/28
241	2-99, 5-142	Brice A.W.S.	Wellington v Otago	Dunedin	1923/24
241	3-123, 1-118	Prabhakar M.	India v New Zealand	Auckland	1989/90
239	6-112, 3-127	McBeath D.J.	Otago v Auckland	Dunedin	1922/23
239	1-60, 4-179	Lambert H.N.	Wellington v Canterbury	Wellington	1931/32
237	0-99, 0-138	Bracewell J.G.	New Zealand v Sussex	Hove	1990
237	4-158, 0-79	Vettori D.L.	New Zealand v South Africa	Hamilton	2003/04
236	2-83, 2-153	Newman J.A.	Canterbury v Otago	Dunedin	1928/29
234	3-86, 4-148	Merritt W.E.	Canterbury v Otago	Dunedin	1928/29
234	4-165, 2-69	Vettori D.L.	New Zealand v Zimbabwe	Bulawayo	1997/98
233	6-117, 4-116	Patel D.N.	Auckland v ND	Auckland	1991/92

Most Runs Conceded in an Innings

70	10	229	1	Boock S.L.	New Zealand v Pakistan	Auckland	1988/89
23.2	0	218	5	Merritt W.E.	New Zealand v NSW	Sydney	1927/28
34	1	206	1	Alloo A.W.	Otago v NSW	Dunedin	1923/24
59	12	204	4	Furlong C.J.M.	CD v Canterbury	Palmerston Nth	1994/95
57	5	200	4	Vettori D.L.	New Zealand v India	Ahmedabad	1999/00
51.2	11	198	5	Pringle C.	Auckland v CD	Auckland	1995/96
41	3	194	3	Callaway S.T.	New Zealand v Australia	Wellington	1904/05
32	1	186	2	Torrance R.C.	Otago v NSW	Dunedin	1923/24
43.1	1	185	6	Merritt W.E.	New Zealand v Kent	Canterbury	1927
38.3	6	185	3	Lythe T.I.	CD v Wellington	Napier	2007/08
46	4	181	0	Hart M.N.	New Zealand v W. Indies	Wellington	1994/95
34	2	180	5	O'Connell W.J.	Hawke's Bay v Auckland	Auckland	1920/21

ALL ROUND CRICKET

500 Runs and 25 Wickets in the Same Season

		Runs	Ave	Wkts	Ave
Reid J.R.	1954/55	505	38.84	30	16.53
Sparling J.T.	1959/60	705	37.11	36	19.50
Reid J.R.	1960/61	549	34.31	37	14.78
Pollard V.	1967/68	537	31.58	31	24.74
Taylor B.R.	1968/69	518	39.84	30	28.06
Cairns B.L.	1975/76	538	41.38	27	25.66
Hadlee R.J.	1981/82	500	33.33	59	14.69
Brown V.R.	1984/85	540	38.57	31	31.35
Gray E.J.	1985/86	545	49.54	34	22.00
Priest M.W.	1988/89	603	43.07	28	40.14
Bradburn G.E.	1989/90	842	38.27	30	30.93
Patel D.N.	1990/91	679	52.23	41	28.09
Patel D.N.	1991/92	574	44.15	32	26.78
Duff S.W.	1991/92	559	46.58	28	27.64
Styris S.B.	2001/02	662	44.13	28	17.03
Wiseman P.J.	2003/04	535	38.21	31	31.00

A Century and Five Wickets in Each Innings of the Same Match

Armstrong W.W.	126*	5-27 & 5-25	Australia v New Zealand	Christchurch	1904/05
Crawford J.N.	110 & 4*	5-90 & 5-53	Wellington v Auckland	Auckland	1917/18

A Century and Ten Wickets in the Same Match

but not five in each innings

Woolley F.E.	132	6-50 & 4-38	MCC v Otago	Dunedin	1929/30
Patel D.N.	6 & 204	6-117 & 4-116	Auckland v ND	Auckland	1991/92

A Century and Five Wickets in One Innings of the Same Match

Wilding F.	104	6-55 & 0-4	Canterbury v Auckland	Christchurch	1884/85
Redgrave W.P.	165	5-37	Wellington v Hawke's Bay	Wellington	1905/06
Relf A.E.	157	6-64 & 2-48	Auckland v Canterbury	Christchurch	1907/08
Armstrong W.W.	110*	6-47 & 0-25	Australia v New Zealand	Auckland	1913/14
Crawford J.N.	6 & 178*	5-149	Otago v Wellington	Wellington	1914/15
Snedden A.N.C.	139	5-13 & 2-21	Auckland v Hawke's Bay	Auckland	1920/21
Andrews T.J.E.	111*	5-41	NSW v Canterbury	Christchurch	1923/24
McGirr H.M.	106	5-17 & 0-22	Wellington v Canterbury	Wellington	1925/26
Bellamy F.W.J.	113 & 22*	5-31 & 1-39	Canterbury v Wellington	Christchurch	1934/35
Cromb I.B.	171	5-66 & 0-56	Canterbury v Wellington	Wellington	1939/40
Reid J.R.	0 & 283	5-35 & 1-34	Wellington v Otago	Wellington	1951/52
Reid J.R.	150*	7-28 & 1-15	NZ v Chief Commissioner's XI	Karachi	1955/56
Sutcliffe B.	152*	5-102	Otago v ND	Hamilton	1956/57
Sparling J.T.	105 & 51	7-98 & 2-13	Auckland v Canterbury	Christchurch	1959/60
Reid J.R.	165	5-50 & 1-28	Wellington v Auckland	Auckland	1959/60
Butler L.C.	101*	5-34	Wellington v CD	New Plymouth	1961/62
Alabaster G.D.	108 & 35	1-34 & 5-49	Otago v CD	Wanganui	1964/65
Taylor B.R.	105 & 0*	5-86	NZ v India	Calcutta	1964/65
Pollard V.	146 & 16*	3-66 & 6-53	CD v Otago	Dunedin	1967/68
Motz R.C.	103*	3-41 & 6-57	Canterbury v Otago	Christchurch	1967/68
Yuile B.W.	146	6-68 & 1-13	CD v Canterbury	Napier	1967/68
nverarity R.J.	108	5-28	Australia B v Otago	Dunedin	1969/70

Morgan R.W.	102 & 52	5-42 & 3-48	Auckland v NZ U 23 XI	Auckland	1970/71
Taylor B.R.	10 & 129*	5-37 & 2-34	Wellington v Canterbury	Wellington	1971/72
Mushtaq Mohammad	201	2-15 & 5-49	Pakistan v New Zealand	Dunedin	1972/73
Morrison J.F.M.	8 & 106	0-4 & 5-69	Wellington v Auckland	Auckland	1977/78
Botham I.T.	103 & 30*	5-73 & 3-38	England v New Zealand	Christchurch	1977/78
Hadlee R.J.	48 & 103	5-61 & 1-76	NZ v Queensland	Brisbane	1980/81
Stead D.W.	2 & 193*	6-79 & 1-67	Canterbury v CD	New Plymouth	1980/81
Crowe M.D.	17 & 151	0-20 & 5-18	CD v Auckland	Auckland	1983/84
Botham I.T.	138	5-59 & 1-137	England v New Zealand	Wellington	1983/84
Crowe M.D.	20 & 143	1-54 & 5-51	CD v ND	New Plymouth	1984/85
Gray E.J.	108	5-54 & 4-52	NZ v Minor Counties	Norwich	1986
Rutherford K.R.	11 & 146	5-72	Otago v Wellington	Wellington	1989/90
Astle N.J.	160	6-22 & 0-45	Canterbury v Otago	Christchurch	1996/97
Nash D.J.	135* & 62	7-39 & 0-22	NZ v Hampshire	Southampton	1999
Bradburn G.E.	35 & 104	5-114	ND v Wellington	Wellington	2000/01
Canning T.K.	115	6-44 & 2-28	Auckland v ND	Hamilton	2004/05
Diamanti B.J.	0 & 135*	5-74	CD v Canterbury	Rangiora	2008/09

WICKETKEEPING

Most Dismissals in a Season

49	49/0	Nevin C.J.	2000/01
41	31/10	McSweeney E.B.	1984/85
41	35/6	McSweeney E.B.	1989/90
38	37/1	Hopkins G.J.	2004/05
36	32/4	Smith I.D.S.	1990/91
36	35/1	Griggs B.B.J.	2005/06
35	30/5	Smith I.D.S.	1979/80
35	33/2	Young R.A.	2001/02
35	33/2	Griggs B.B.J.	2007/08
35	35/0	Young R.A.	2002/03
34	29/5	Lees W.K.	1978/79
34	32/2	Smith I.D.S.	1986/87
34	31/3	Germon L.K.	1991/92
34	33/1	Nevin C.J.	1995/96
34	34/0	Hart R.G.	1997/98
34	33/1	Hart R.G.	2001/02
33	32/1	Wadsworth K.J.	1975/76
33	31/2	McCullum B.B.	2003/04
32	28/4	Smith I.D.S.	1983/84
32	28/4	McSweeney E.B.	1983/84
32	28/4	Robinson S.A.	1990/91
32	31/1	Nevin C.J.	2002/03
32	30/2	Hart R.G.	2003/04
32	31/1	Hopkins G.J.	2005/06
31	30/1	Kelly P.J.	1983/84
31	28/3	Kelly P.J.	1986/87
31	31/0	McSweeney E.B.	1990/91
31	30/1	Young B.A.	1991/92
31	28/3	Blain T.E.	1991/92
31	30/1	Croy M.G.	1998/99
31	31/0	Griggs B.B.J.	2001/02
31	31/0	Young R.A.	2004/05
30	23/7	Murray J.T.	1960/61
30	28/2	Germon L.K.	1992/93
30	29/1	Baker G.R.	1994/95
30	29/1	van Wyk C.F.K.	2007/08

Most Dismissals in a Match

10	10/0	Nevin C.J., Wellington v Otago	Wellington	1995/96
	10/0	Gilchrist A.C., Australia v New Zealand	Hamilton	1999/00
	10/0	Hopkins G.J., Otago v Canterbury	Dunedin	2004/05
	8/2	Hopkins G.J., New Zealand A v Sri Lanka A	Kandy	2005/06
	9/1	McCullum B.B., New Zealand v S.African Invitation XI	Bloemfontein	2007/08
9	9/0	Schofield R.M., Central Districts v Wellington	Wellington	1964/65
	9/0	Vance R.H., Wellington v Otago	Wellington	1977/78
	8/1	McSweeney E.B., Wellington v Otago	Lower Hutt	1983/84
	9/0	Young B.A., Northern Districts v Canterbury	Christchurch	1986/87
	9/0	Germon L.K., Canterbury v Northern Districts	Christchurch	1992/93
	9/0	Rashid Latif., Pakistan v New Zealand	Auckland	1993/94
	9/0	Hopkins G.J., Otago v Wellington	Queenstown	2004/05
	9/0	Hopkins G.J., Otago v Northern Districts	Dunedin	2005/06

8	3/5	James K.C., NZ v Derbyshire	Derby	1927
	1/7	Jackman C.K.Q., Canterbury v Wellington	Wellington	1935/36
	2/6	Kent L.A.W., Auckland v Wellington	Wellington	1944/45
	8/0	Curtis W.M., North Island XI v South Island XI	Wellington	1957/58
	8/0	Petrie E.C., NZ v Sussex	Hove	1958
	5/3	Dick A.E., NZ v Griqualand West	Kimberley	1961/62
	8/0	Parks J.M., England v NZ	Christchurch	1965/66
	7/1	Therkleson, I.J., Wellington v Northern Districts	Whangarei	1973/74
	8/0	Marsh R.W., Australia v NZ	Christchurch	1976/77
	8/0	Lees W.K., NZ v Sri Lanka	Wellington	1982/83
	4/4	McSweeney E.B., Wellington v Northern Districts	Wellington	1984/85
	8/0	Smith I.D.S., Auckland v Central Districts	Nelson	1988/89
	8/0	Smith I.D.S., NZ v Sri Lanka	Hamilton	1990/91
	7/1	Hart R.G., Northern Districts v Canterbury	Hamilton	1994/95
	7/1	Germon L.K., Canterbury v Central Districts	Palmerston North	1994/95
	7/1	Nevin C.J., Wellington v Central Districts	Nelson	1995/96
	8/0	Vincent L., Auckland v Central Districts	Palmerston North	2000/01
	8/0	Howell G.A., Wellington v Northern Districts	Hamilton	2001/02
	7/1	McCullum B.B., Canterbury v Northern Districts	Christchurch	2003/04
	7/1	Papps M.W.H., Canterbury v Northern Districts	Gisborne	2004/05
	8/0	van Wyk C.F.K., Canterbury v Auckland	Auckland	2006/07
	8/0	McGlashan P.D., Northern Districts v Auckland	Auckland	2006/07
	8/0	Griggs B.B.J., Central Districts v Northern Districts	Hamilton	2007/08

Most Dismissals in an Innings

7	7/0	Schofield R.M., Central Districts v Wellington	Wellington	1964/65
	7/0	Wasim Bari, Pakistan v NZ	Auckland	1978/79
	7/0	Young B.A., Northern Districts v Canterbury	Christchurch	1986/87
	7/0	Smith I.D.S., NZ v Sri Lanka	Hamilton	1990/91
	7/0	Croy M.G., Otago v Auckland	Auckland	2001/02
	7/0	Hopkins G.J., New Zealand A v South Africa A	Centurion	2004/05
	5/2	Hopkins G.J., New Zealand A v Sri Lanka A	Kandy	2005/06
	7/0	Griggs B.B.J., Central Districts v Northern Districts	Hamilton	2007/08
6	4/2	Mooney F.L.H., NZ v Warwickshire	Birmingham	1949
	5/1	Wadsworth K.J., NZ v Surrey	The Oval	1973
	6/0	Downes L.W., Central Districts v Canterbury	Nelson	1975/76
	5/1	Kirmani S.M.H., India v NZ	Christchurch	1975/76
	6/0	Vance R.H., Wellington v Otago	Wellington	1977/78
	6/0	Downton P.R., England XI v Otago	Dunedin	1977/78
	6/0	Germon L.K., Canterbury v Northern Districts	Christchurch	1992/93
	5/1	Hart R.G., Northern Districts v Canterbury	Hamilton	1994/95
	5/1	Nevin C.J., Wellington v Central Districts	Nelson	1995/96
	6/0	Parore A.C., New Zealand A v Pakistan A	Hamilton	1998/99
	6/0	Young R.A., Auckland v Wellington	Wellington	2002/03
	6/0	Hopkins G.J., Otago v Canterbury	Dunedin	2004/05
	5/1	Papps M.H.W., Canterbury v Northern Districts	Gisborne	2004/05
	6/0	McGlashan P.D., Northern Districts v Auckland	Auckland	2006/07
	6/0	Watling B-J., Northern Districts v Central Districts	Gisborne	2006/07
	6/0	Dhoni M.S., India v New Zealand	Wellington	2008/09

Most Catches in a Season

49	Nevin C.J.	2000/01	31	McSweeney E.B.	1984/85
37	Hopkins G.J.	2004/05	31	McSweeney E.B.	1990/91
35	McSweeney E.B.	1989/90	31	Germon L.K.	1991/92
35	Young R.A.	2002/03	31	Griggs B.B.J.	2001/02
35	Griggs B.B.J.	2005/06	31	Nevin C.J.	2002/03
34	Hart R.G.	1997/98	31	McCullum B.B.	2003/04
33	Nevin C.J.	1995/96	31	Young R.A.	2004/05
33	Hart R.G.	2001/02	31	Hopkins G.J.	2005/06
33	Young R.A.	2001/02	30	Smith I.D.S.	1979/80
33	Griggs B.B.J.	2007/08	30	Kelly P.J.	1983/84
32	Wadsworth K.J.	1975/76	30	Young B.A.	1991/92
32	Smith I.D.S.	1986/87	30	Croy M.G.	1998/99
32	Smith I.D.S.	1990/91	30	Hart R.G.	2003/04

Most Catches in a Match

10	Nevin C.J., Wellington v Otago	Wellington	1995/96
	Gilchrist A.C., Australia v New Zealand	Hamilton	1999/00
	Hopkins G.J., Otago v Canterbury	Dunedin	2004/05
9	Schofield R.M., Central Districts v Wellington	Wellington	1964/65
	Vance R.H., Wellington v Otago	Wellington	1977/78
	Young B.A., Northern Districts v Canterbury	Christchurch	1986/87
	Germon L.K., Canterbury v Northern Districts	Christchurch	1992/93
	Rashid Latif., Pakistan v New Zealand	Auckland	1993/94
	Hopkins G.J., Otago v Wellington	Queenstown	2004/05
	Hopkins G.J., Otago v Northern Districts	Dunedin	2005/06
	McCullum B.B., New Zealand v South African Invitation XI	Bloemfontein	2007/08
8	Curtis W.M., North Island XI v South Island XI	Wellington	1957/58
	Petrie E.C., NZ v Sussex	Hove	1958
	Parks J.M., England v NZ	Christchurch	1965/66
	Marsh R.W., Australia v NZ	Christchurch	1976/77
	Lees W.K., NZ v Sri Lanka	Wellington	1982/83
	McSweeney E.B., Wellington v Otago	Lower Hutt	1983/84
	Smith I.D.S., Auckland v Central Districts	Nelson	1988/89
	Smith I.D.S., NZ v Sri Lanka	Hamilton	1990/91
	Vincent L., Auckland v Central Districts	Palmerston North	2000/01
	Howell G.A., Wellington v Northern Districts	Hamilton	2001/02
	van Wyk C.F.K., Canterbury v Auckland	Auckland	2006/07
	McGlashan P.D., Northern Districts v Auckland	Auckland	2006/07
	Hopkins G.J., New Zealand A v Sri Lanka A	Kandy	2005/06
	Griggs B.B.J., Central Districts v Northern Districts	Hamilton	2007/08

Most Catches in an Innings

7	Schofield R.M., Central Districts v Wellington	Wellington	1964/65
	Wasim Bari, Pakistan v NZ	Auckland	1978/79
	Young B.A., Northern Districts v Canterbury	Christchurch	1986/87
	Smith I.D.S., NZ v Sri Lanka	Hamilton	1990/91
	Croy M.G., Otago v Auckland	Auckland	2001/02
	Hopkins G.J., New Zealand A v South Africa A	Centurion	2004/05
	Griggs B.B.J., Central Districts v Northern Districts	Hamilton	2007/08
6	Downes L.W., Central Districts v Canterbury	Nelson	1975/76
	Vance R.H., Wellington v Otago	Wellington	1977/78
	Downton P.R., England XI v Otago	Dunedin	1977/78
	Germon L.K., Canterbury v Northern Districts	Christchurch	1992/93
	Parore A.C., New Zealand A v Pakistan A	Hamilton	1998/99

	Young R.A., Auckland v Wellington	Wellington	2002/03
	Hopkins G.J., Otago v Canterbury	Dunedin	2004/05
	McGlashan P.D., Northern Districts v Auckland	Auckland	2006/07
	Watling B-J., Northern Districts v Central Districts	Gisborne	2006/07
	Dhoni M.S., India v New Zealand	Wellington	2008/09

Most Stumpings in a Season

13	Jackman C.K.Q.	1935/36	13	Kent L.A.W.	1944/45

Most Stumpings in a Match

7	Jackman C.K.Q., Canterbury v Wellington	Wellington	1935/36
6	Kent L.A.W., Auckand v Wellington	Wellington	1944/45
5	James K.C., NZ v Surrey	The Oval	1927
	James K.C., NZ v Derbyshire	Derby	1927
	Burns R.C., Canterbury v Otago	Dunedin	1928/29
	Mills A.S., Otago v Fiji	Dunedin	1947/48

Most Stumpings in an Innings

4	Jackman C.K.Q., Canterbury v Wellington	Wellington	1935/36
	Tindill E.W.T., NZ v Glamorgan	Cardiff	1937
	Kent L.A.W., Auckland v Wellington	Wellington	1944/45
	Mills A.S., Otago v Fiji	Dunedin	1947/48
	McSweeney E.B., Wellington v Northern Districts	Wellington	1984/85

FIELDING

Most Catches in a Season

23	Murray B.A.G.	1967/68	16	Harris C.Z.	2006/07
22	Coney J.V.	1977/78	16	Parlane N.R.	2007/08
20	Howarth H.J.	1973/74	15	Playle W.R.	1958/59
18	Sinclair M.S.	2001/02	15	Bradburn W.P.	1963/64
18	Sinclair M.S.	2008/09	15	Turner G.M.	1975/76
17	Crowe M.D.	1986/87	15	Blair W.L.	1978/79
17	Boyle D.J.	1990/91	15	Crowe J.J.	1990/91
17	Parlane N.R.	2002/03	15	Knight N.V.	1996/97
16	Burgess M.G.	1977/78	15	Vincent L.	1999/00
16	Edgar B.A.	1978/79	15	Bradburn G.E.	2000/01
16	Crowe M.D.	1981/82	15	How J.M.	2003/04
16	Crowe M.D.	1983/84	15	Bell M.D.	2004/05
16	Fleming S.P.	1993/94	15	Parlane N.R.	2008/09

Most Catches in a Match

7	Morrison J.F.M., Wellington v Northern Districts	Wellington	1980/81
	Fleming S.P., New Zealand v Zimbabwe	Harare	1997/98
6	Marchant J.W.A., Wellington v Nelson	Wellington	1873/74
	Williams N.T., Auckland v Hawke's Bay	Napier	1894/95
	Cromb I.B., Canterbury v Otago	Christchurch	1937/38
	Ikin J.T., MCC v Auckland	Auckland	1946/47
	Reid J.R., NZ v South Zone	Bangalore	1955/56
	Jarvis T.W., Auckland v Northern Districts	Hamilton	1968/69
	Anderson R.W., Rest v NZ	New Plymouth	1974/75

	MacDonald G.K., Canterbury v Pakistan	Christchurch	1984/85
	Young B.A., New Zealand v Pakistan	Auckland	1993/94
	Latham R.T., Canterbury v Otago	Oamaru	1994/95
	Young B.A., Northern Districts v Wellington	Wellington	1995/96
	Chandler P.J.B., New Zealand A v England	Wanganui	1996/97
	McHardy D.S., Wellington v Northern Districts	Hamilton	1996/97
	Fleming S.P., New Zealand v Australia	Brisbane	1997/98
	Bell M.D., Wellington v Canterbury	Wellington	2003/04
	Fleming S.P., New Zealand v West Indies	Wellington	2005/06
	McCullum N.L., Otago v Central Districts	Napier	2006/07
	Myburgh J.G., Canterbury v Auckland	Rangiora	2008/09

Most Catches in an Innings

5	Williams N.T., Auckand v Hawke's Bay	Napier	1894/95
	Lamason J.R., Wellington v Otago	Dunedin	1937/38
	Lamason J.R., NI Army v SI Army	Wellington	1942/43
	Ikin J.T., MCC v Auckland	Auckland	1946/47
	Rabone G.O., NZ v Oxford University	Oxford	1949
	Reid J.R., NZ v South Zone	Bangalore	1955/56
	Morrison J.F.M., Wellington v Northern Districts	Wellington	1980/81
	MacDonald G.K., Canterbury v Pakistan	Christchurch	1984/85
	Crowe J.J., Auckland v Canterbury	Auckland	1988/89
	Fleming S.P., New Zealand v Zimbabwe	Harare	1997/98
	Harris C.Z., Canterbury v England	Christchurch	2001/02
	Myburgh J.G., Canterbury v Auckland	Rangiora	2008/09
	Brodie J.M., Wellington v Otago	Wellington	2008/09

OLDEST PLAYERS

AGE Years/days			
52/189	Boxshall C.	Canterbury v Wellington	1914/15
51/216	Read R.J.	Canterbury v Auckland	1937/38
51/203	Lyttelton C.J. †	Governor-General's XI v MCC	1960/61
51/87	Wilson C.G.	Wellington v Hawke's Bay	1919/20
51/32	MacLaren A.C.	MCC v New Zealand	1922/23
50/284	Wilson E.S.	Otago v Wellington	1927/28
50/269	Hay T.D.B.	New Zealand v Royal Navy	1927
50/184	Reese T.W.	Canterbury v Otago	1917/18
50/86	Dufaur F.E.	Auckland v Wellington	1882/83
49/88	Allcott C.F.W.	Otago v Auckland	1945/46
49/48	Wilding F.	Canterbury v Hawke's Bay	1901/02
48/96	Hartley J.C.	MCC v Auckland	1922/23
48/40	Hallamore R.G.	Southland v Otago	1918/19
48/26	Badcock F.T.	New Zealanders v H.D.G. Leveson-Gower's XI	1945
47/357	Board J.H.	Hawke's Bay v Wellington	1914/15
47/325	Rowntree R.W.	Auckland v South Africa	1931/32
47/177	Fox R.H.	New Zealand v Civil Service	1927
47/151	Jones S.P.	Auckland v Otago	1908/09
47/114	Hughes W.J.	Hawke's Bay v Wellington	1905/06
47/98	Brice A.W.S.	Wellington v Australia	1927/28
47/70	Fowke J.N.	Canterbury v MCC	1906/07
46/319	Kortlang H.H.L.	Wellington v Auckland	1926/27
46/149	Stevens E.C.J.	Canterbury v Otago	1883/84
46/125	Allen R.	Wellington v Fiji	1953/54
46/14	Downes A.D.	Otago v Canterbury	1913/14
45/364	Blackie D.D.	Australia v New Zealand	1927/28
45/292	Handford A.	Southland v Otago	1914/15
45/270	Wynyard E.G.	MCC v Wellington	1906/07
45/241	Blamires E.O.	Otago v Canterbury	1926/27
45/39	Smith S.G.	Auckland v Wellington	1925/26
45/6	Beard D.D.	Northern Districts v Wellington	1964/65
44/349	Levers W.C.S.	Hawke's Bay v Wellington	1908/09
44/338	Knight A.R.	Otago v Canterbury	1943/44
44/308	Chadwick C.S.	Otago v Auckland	1924/25
44/226	Tucker K.H.	Wellington v Hawke's Bay	1919/20
44/182	Anthony A.	Auckland v Wellington	1930/31
44/178	Siedeberg H.G.	Otago v Wellington	1921/22
44/126	Garrard D.R.	Auckland v Wellington	1941/42
44/105	Newman J.A.	Canterbury v Otago	1928/29
44/75	Cate W.A.	New Zealand v MCC	1922/23
44/70	Wallace W.M.	Governor General's XI v MCC	1960/61
44/59	Dempster C.S.	Wellington v Auckland	1947/48
44/7	Wheatley J.	Canterbury v Hawke's Bay	1903/04

† *Lord Cobham*

YOUNGEST PLAYERS

AGE Years/days			
15/224	Dacre C.C.R.	Auckland v Wellington	1914/15
15/272	Midlane F.A.	Wellington v Hawke's Bay	1898/99
15/319	Ollivier A.M.	Canterbury v Otago	1866/67
16/36	Hartland J.F.	Canterbury v Otago	1877/78
16/84	Broad C.H.	Nelson v Wellington	1888/89
16/86	McGregor S.N.	Otago v Fiji	1947/48

AGE Years/days			
16/87	Dacre L.M.	Auckland v Wellington	1912/13
16/89	Anderson C.J.	Canterbury v Central Districts	2006/07
16/130	Coutts H.D.	Taranaki v Auckland	1882/83
16/147	Puna K.N.	New Zealand Under 23 XI v Otago	1971/72
16/173	Aaqib Javed	Pakistan v President's XI	1988/89
16/242	Collins J.U.	Nelson v Wellington	1884/85
16/250	Taylor L.G.	Auckland v Hawke's Bay	1910/11
16/273	Tendulkar S.R.	India v President's XI	1989/90
16/285	Reese D.	Canterbury v Wellington	1895/96
16/311	Hale H.	Tasmania v Otago	1883/84
16/325	Morgan R.W.	Auckland v Northern Districts	1957/58
16/330	Maunder P.A.	Central Districts v Auckland	1961/62
17/4	Wallace W.M.	Auckland v Wellington	1933/34
17/5	Frater R.E.	Auckland v Wellington	1918/19
17/12	Bell M.D.	Northern Districts v New Zealand Academy XI	1993/94
17/49	Williams A.B.	Otago v Canterbury	1886/87
17/52	Blunt R.C.	Canterbury v Otago	1917/18
17/65	Mitchell W.J.	Northern Districts v Pakistan	1964/65
17/66	Wilding A.F.	Canterbury v Auckland	1900/01
17/77	Clarke D.B.	Auckland v Central Districts	1950/51
17/93	Hay T.D.B.	Auckland v Wellington	1893/94
17/107	Rutherford K.R.	Otago v Auckland	1982/83
17/110	Cooke F.H.	Otago v Canterbury	1879/80
17/112	Barron J.R.	Otago v Canterbury	1917/18
17/119	Crowe M.D.	Auckland v Canterbury	1979/80
17/124	MacNeil H.	Otago v Canterbury	1877/78
17/124	Williamson K.S.	Northern Districts v Auckland	2007/08
17/152	Butler L.C.	Wellington v Auckland	1951/52
17/174	McIntyre J.M.	Auckland v Canterbury	1961/62
17/179	Rutherford I.A.	Otago v Canterbury	1974/75
17/182	Robin T.P.	Central Districts v Canterbury	1999/00
17/185	Robinson S.A.	Otago v Northern Districts	1984/85
17/213	Turner G.M.	Otago v Canterbury	1964/65
17/222	Hemi R.C.	Auckland v Wellington	1950/51
17/244	Ghulam Abbas	Pakistan v Auckland	1964/65
17/258	Rose G.A.	Central Districts v Northern Districts	1958/59
17/268	Snedden A.N.C.	Auckland v Wellington	1909/10
17/268	Beuth J.A.	Northern Districts v New Zealand Under 23 XI	1962/63
17/274	Ashbolt F.L.	Wellington v Auckland	1893/94
17/276	Collinge R.O.	Central Districts v Auckland	1963/64
17/278	Nicholls J.G.	Otago v Canterbury	1876/77
17/286	Hickmott R.G.	Canterbury v Wellington	1911/12
17/291	Bennett J.H.	Canterbury v Otago	1898/99
17/294	Cairns A.E.	Otago v Canterbury	1867/68
17/305	Gill M.F.	Central Districts v Wellington	1974/75
17/307	Currie E.W.	Otago v New South Wales	1893/94
17/307	Hastings B.F.	Wellington v Canterbury	1957/58
17/325	Bartlett G.A.	Central Districts v Northern Districts	1958/59
17/328	Cushen J.A.J.	Otago v Canterbury	1967/68
17/329	West R.M.	Central Districts v Northern Districts	1996/97
17/332	Gadsdon S.R.	Northern Districts v Auckland	2008/09
17/336	Lambert H.N.	Wellington v Canterbury	1917/18
17/352	Motz R.C.	Canterbury v Northern Districts	1957/58
17/355	Tarrant D.R.	Central Districts v Auckland	1954/55
17/362	Vettori D.L.	Northern Districts v England	1996/97

CAREER RECORDS

The following career records cover the complete first-class careers of New Zealand players. Matches for other than New Zealand teams e.g. county sides, are included.
To qualify for inclusion a player must have appeared in first-class cricket in New Zealand while a bona fide resident of the country — professional coaches and the like thus being excluded.

Batting

3000 RUNS	*Career*	*M*	*In*	*NO*	*HS*	*Runs*	*Ave*	*100*
Turner G.M.	1964/65-1982/83	455	792	101	311*	34,346	49.70	103
Wright J.G.	1975/76-1992/93	366	636	44	192	25,073	42.35	59
Crowe M.D.	1979/80-1995/96	247	412	62	299	19,608	56.02	71
Sutcliffe B.	1941/42-1965/66	233	407	39	385	17,447	47.41	44
Howarth G.P.	1968/69-1985/86	338	584	42	183	17,294	31.90	32
Fleming S.P.	1991/92-2007/08	247	406	32	274*	16,409	43.87	35
Reid J.R.	1947/48-1965	246	418	28	296	16,128	41.35	39
Patel D.N.	1976-1996/97	358	558	51	204	15,188	29.95	26
Rutherford K.R.	1982/83-1999/00	220	383	33	317	13,974	39.92	35
Congdon B.E.	1960/61-1978	241	416	40	202*	13,101	34.84	23
Spearman C.M.	1993/94-2008	195	351	16	341	12,815	38.25	30
Hitchcock R.E.	1947/48-1964	323	519	71	153*	12,473	27.84	13
Dacre C.C.R.	1914/15-1936	269	439	20	223	12,230	29.18	24
Dempster C.S.	1921/22-1947/48	184	306	36	212	12,145	44.98	35
Hadlee R.J.	1971/72-1990	342	473	93	210*	12,052	31.71	14
Edgar B.A.	1975/76-1989/90	175	307	26	203	11,304	40.22	24
Parker J.M.	1971-1983/84	207	362	39	195	11,254	34.84	21
Smith S.G.	1899/00-1925/26	211	379	30	256	10,920	31.28	14
Sinclair M.S.	1995/96-2008/09	148	251	26	268	10,862	48.27	27
Cairns C.L.	1988-2005/06	217	341	38	158	10,702	35.32	13
Burgess M.G.	1963/64-1980/81	192	322	35	146	10,281	35.82	20
Crowe J.J.	1977/78-1991/92	180	304	34	159	10,233	37.90	22
Richardson M.H.	1989/90-2004/05	157	264	31	306	9994	42.89	20
Greatbatch M.J.	1982/83-1999/00	170	292	31	202*	9890	37.89	24
Twose R.G.	1989-2000/01	178	300	35	277*	9802	36.98	18
Bell M.D.	1993/94-2008/09	161	273	18	265	9546	37.43	24
Lowry T.C.	1917/18-1937/38	198	322	20	181	9421	31.19	18
Dowling G.T.	1958/59-1971/72	158	282	13	239	9399	34.94	16
Astle N.J.	1991/92-2006/07	171	272	24	223	9321	37.58	19
Donnelly M.P.	1936/37-1960/61	131	221	26	208*	9250	47.43	23
Jones A.H.	1979/80-1995/96	145	254	33	186	9180	41.53	16
Horne M.J.	1992/93-2005/06	128	219	11	241	8501	40.87	24
Arnold P.A.	1953/54-1960	174	306	15	122	8013	27.53	7
Blunt R.C.	1917/18-1935	123	209	15	338*	7953	40.99	15
Coney J.V.	1970/71-1986/87	165	272	48	174*	7872	35.14	8
McMillan C.D.	1994/95-2007	138	226	27	168*	7817	39.28	16
Franklin T.J.	1980/81-1992/93	148	254	20	181	7794	33.30	15
Wallace W.M.	1933/34-1960/61	121	192	17	211	7757	44.32	17
Hastings B.F.	1957/58-1976/77	163	273	32	226	7685	31.89	15
Hadlee W.A.	1933/34-1951/52	117	203	17	198	7523	40.44	18
Young B.A.	1983/84-1998/99	163	276	43	267*	7489	32.14	10
Harris C.Z.	1989/90-2006/07	128	200	42	251*	7228	45.75	14
Vance R.H.	1976/77-1990/91	135	230	18	254*	6955	32.80	12
Cumming C.D.	1995/96-2008/09	117	208	17	187	6858	35.90	15
Parore A.C.	1988/89-2001/02	163	252	43	155*	6826	32.66	10

	Career	M	In	NO	HS	Runs	Ave	100
McEwan P.E.	1976/77-1990/91	115	206	15	155	6677	34.95	12
Parlane M.E.	1992/93-2008/09	126	215	12	203	6653	32.77	15
McGregor S.N.	1947/48-1968/69	148	274	16	114*	6573	25.47	5
Marshall H.J.H.	1998/99-2008/09	117	200	13	168	6547	35.01	15
James K.C.	1923/24-1946/47	204	330	41	109*	6413	22.19	7
Jones R.A.	1993/94-2008/09	114	198	11	201	6301	33.69	15
Latham R.T.	1980/81-1994/95	108	189	19	237*	6298	37.05	9
Murray B.A.G.	1958/59-1972/73	102	187	11	213	6257	35.55	6
Morrison J.F.M.	1965/66-1983/84	126	225	25	180*	6142	30.71	7
Sinclair B.W.	1955/56-1970/71	118	204	18	148	6114	32.87	6
Papps M.H.W.	1998/99-2008/09	100	180	15	192	6069	36.78	16
Blair B.R.	1977/78-1989/90	110	190	6	143	5995	32.58	7
Morgan R.W.	1957/58-1976/77	136	229	13	166	5940	27.50	8
Roberts A.D.G.	1967/68-1983/84	112	206	37	128*	5865	34.70	7
Page M.L.	1920/21-1942/43	132	213	17	206	5857	29.88	9
Shrimpton M.J.F.	1961/62-1979/80	122	218	23	150	5812	29.80	7
Styris S.B.	1994/95-2008/09	123	205	18	212*	5786	30.94	9
Blain T.E.	1982/83-1994/95	118	199	30	161	5749	34.02	8
Reid J.F.	1975/76-1987/88	101	170	22	180	5650	38.17	11
Scott V.J.	1937/38-1952/53	80	130	17	204	5620	49.73	16
Anderson R.W.	1967/68-1981/82	111	197	14	155	5609	30.65	8
Smith I.D.S.	1977/78-1991/92	178	250	42	173	5570	26.77	6
Gray E.J.	1975/76-1991/92	162	241	51	128*	5472	28.80	6
Marshall J.A.H.	1997/98-2008/09	111	193	10	235	5461	29.84	10
Chapple M.E.	1949/50-1971/72	119	201	16	165	5344	28.88	4
Pollard V.	1964/65-1974/75	130	207	33	146	5314	30.54	6
Mills J.E.	1925/26-1937/38	97	161	8	185	5025	32.84	11
Graham H.	1892/93-1906/07	113	200	9	124	5023	26.29	7
Weir G.L.	1927/28-1946/47	107	172	16	191	5022	32.19	10
Stead G.R.	1991/92-2005/06	101	165	10	190	4984	32.15	10
Bradburn G.E.	1985/86-2001/02	127	206	27	148*	4978	27.81	4
Fulton P.G.	2000/01-2008/09	74	124	11	301*	4961	43.90	8
McSweeney E.B.	1979/80-1993/94	121	177	30	205*	4947	33.65	6
Vettori D.L.	1996/97-2008/09	142	202	30	137*	4939	28.71	5
Lees W.K.	1970/71-1987/88	146	243	43	152	4932	24.66	5
Pairaudeau B.H.	1946/47-1966/67	89	159	5	163	4930	32.01	11
White D.J.	1979/80-1993/94	106	187	17	209	4926	28.98	7
Hopkins G.J.	1997/98-2008/09	110	173	28	175*	4873	33.60	10
Kerr J.L.	1929/30-1942/43	89	157	7	196	4829	32.19	8
Douglas M.W.	1987/88-2000/01	94	160	23	144	4808	35.09	9
Miller L.S.M.	1950/51-1959/60	82	142	15	144	4777	37.61	5
Nevin C.J.	1995/96-2008/09	105	159	23	143*	4755	34.96	4
Grimmett C.V.	1911/12-1940/41	248	321	54	71*	4720	17.67	—
Gaffaney C.B.	1995/96-2004/05	83	152	11	194	4711	33.41	8
Pocock B.A.	1990/91-2000/01	100	176	16	167	4699	29.36	10
Jarvis T.W.	1964/65-1976/77	97	167	8	182	4666	29.34	6
Vincent L.	1997/98-2007/08	86	139	10	224	4650	36.04	10
Sparling J.T.	1956/57-1970/71	127	215	26	105	4606	24.11	2
Edwards G.N.	1973/74-1984/85	92	164	8	177*	4589	29.41	5
How J.M.	2000/01-2008/09	83	144	11	190*	4586	34.48	11
Taylor B.R.	1963/64-1979/80	141	210	25	173	4579	24.75	4
McCullum B.B.	1999/00-2008/09	84	143	8	160	4557	33.75	7
Hadlee B.G.	1961/62-1980/81	84	155	11	163*	4539	31.52	6

	Career	M	In	NO	HS	Runs	Ave	100
Vivian H.G.	1930/31-1938/39	85	143	15	165	4443	34.71	6
McIntosh T.G.	1998/99-2008/09	84	140	10	268	4425	34.03	14
Myburgh J.G.	1997/98-2008/09	64	117	18	203	4422	44.66	11
Hart M.N.	1990/91-2004/05	135	198	26	201*	4418	25.68	4
Briasco P.S.	1982/83-1991/92	83	148	16	157	4390	33.25	6
Redmond A.J.	1999/00-2008/09	84	145	10	146	4381	32.45	7
Bracewell J.G.	1978/79-1990	149	208	40	110*	4354	25.91	4
Wiseman P.J.	1991/92-2008	186	254	51	130	4254	20.95	2
Thomson S.A.	1987/88-1996/97	90	148	38	167	4209	38.26	6
Cairns B.L.	1971/72-1988	148	226	25	110	4165	20.72	1
Parlane N.R.	1996/97-2008/09	75	118	10	165	4040	37.40	8
McGirr H.M.	1913/14-1932/33	88	146	7	141	3992	28.71	5
Franklin J.E.C.	1998/99-2008/09	100	147	21	219	3971	31.51	6
Cromb I.B.	1929/30-1946/47	88	148	12	171	3950	29.04	3
Priest M.W.	1984/85-1998/99	109	154	25	119	3945	30.58	4
Dunning B.	1961/62-1977/78	83	150	10	142	3929	28.06	3
Guy J.W.	1953/54-1972/73	90	165	13	115	3923	25.80	3
Bailey M.D.	1989/90-2001/02	89	138	9	180*	3882	30.09	8
Harris R.M.	1955/56-1973/74	73	130	5	157	3863	30.90	3
Yuile B.W.	1959/60-1971/72	123	187	31	146	3850	24.67	1
Parsons A.E.W.	1971/72-1982/83	82	156	10	141	3847	26.34	4
Sulzberger G.P.	1995/96-2004/05	83	135	12	159	3836	31.18	8
Hiddleston J.S.	1909/10-1928/29	52	97	1	212	3818	39.77	8
Oram J.D.P.	1997/98-2008/09	81	129	17	155	3802	33.94	8
Rutherford I.A.	1974/75-1983/84	79	144	4	222	3794	27.10	5
Taylor D.D.	1946/47-1960/61	95	168	6	143	3772	23.28	1
Hartland B.R.	1986/87-1996/97	83	150	8	150	3753	26.42	5
Kuggeleijn C.M.	1975/76-1990/91	89	151	15	116	3747	27.55	4
MacGibbon A.R.	1947/48-1961/62	124	206	20	94	3699	19.88	—
Blair W.L.	1967/68-1990/91	82	151	9	140	3698	26.04	2
Taylor L.R.P.L.	2002/03-2008/09	60	100	3	217	3696	38.10	9
Webb P.N.	1976/77-1986/87	75	130	19	136	3671	33.07	5
Wadsworth K.J.	1968/69-1975/76	118	164	23	117	3664	25.98	2
Roberts A.W.	1927/28-1950/51	84	135	17	181	3645	30.88	3
Leggat J.G.	1944/45-1955/56	57	106	9	166	3634	37.46	7
Austen M.H.	1982/83-1996/97	66	120	8	202*	3619	32.31	6
Howell L.G.	1990/91-2004/05	83	143	16	181	3586	28.23	3
Hoskin R.N.	1980/81-1992/93	81	140	7	157	3580	26.91	6
Nash D.J.	1990/91-2001/02	120	168	37	135*	3555	27.13	5
Patrick W.R.	1905/06-1926/27	74	138	8	143	3536	27.20	4
Smith C.J.P.	1983/84-1990/91	62	118	9	160*	3499	32.10	7
Motz R.C.	1957/58-1969	142	225	21	103*	3494	17.12	1
Larsen G.R.	1984/85-1998/99	103	157	35	161	3491	28.61	2
Brown V.R.	1978/79-1989/90	83	136	17	161*	3485	29.28	6
Rabone G.O.	1940/41-1960/61	82	135	14	125	3425	28.30	3
Ingram P.J.	2001/02-2008/09	58	105	6	247	3374	34.08	9
Pritchard T.L.	1937/38-1956	200	293	41	81	3363	13.34	—
Newdick G.A.	1970/71-1980/81	61	114	6	143	3292	30.48	4
Lawson R.A.	1992/93-2003/04	73	133	6	200	3278	25.81	3
Nicol R.J.	2001/02-2008/09	66	102	11	160	3278	36.02	7
Vivian G.E.	1964/65-1978/79	88	140	25	137*	3259	28.33	3
Ryder J.D.	2002/03-2008/09	49	79	6	236	3236	44.32	7
Moloney D.A.R.	1929/30-1940/41	64	119	7	190	3219	28.74	2

	Career	M	In	NO	HS	Runs	Ave	100
Boyle D.J.	1980/81-1994/95	69	121	12	149	3216	29.50	3
Stead D.W.	1968/69-1985/86	80	139	11	193*	3205	25.03	1
Alabaster G.D.	1955/56-1975/76	96	154	20	108	3200	23.88	3
Reese D.	1895/96-1920/21	72	134	8	148	3186	25.28	4
McCullum S.J.	1976/77-1990/91	75	131	1	134	3174	24.41	2
Duff S.W.	1985/86-1995/96	88	134	29	164*	3167	30.16	1
Vaughan J.T.C.	1989/90-1996/97	70	120	20	127	3159	31.59	2
Harford N.S.	1953/54-1966/67	74	122	8	158	3149	27.62	3
Merritt W.E.	1926/27-1946	125	191	33	87	3147	19.91	—
Mooney F.L.H.	1941/42-1954/55	91	150	14	180	3143	23.11	2
Yovich J.A.F.	1996/97-2008/09	89	139	27	144	3143	28.06	2
Redmond R.E.	1963/64-1975/76	53	100	7	141*	3134	33.69	5
Thomson K.	1959/60-1973/74	71	125	14	136*	3134	28.23	5
Tindill E.W.T.	1932/33-1949/50	69	116	13	149	3127	30.35	6
Harris P.G.Z.	1949/50-1964/65	69	120	9	118	3126	28.16	5
Germon L.K.	1987/88-2001/02	103	142	35	160*	3123	29.18	4
Englefield J.I.	1998/99-2005/06	55	97	7	172	3113	34.58	3
Wells J.D.	1989/90-2000/01	73	115	18	143	3058	31.52	5
Stewart S.L.	2001/02-2008/09	56	99	7	149	3058	33.23	4
Ryan M.L.	1965/66-1978/79	66	113	9	129	3023	29.06	3
Barnes A.C.	1993/94-2004/05	78	121	10	134*	3006	27.08	4

Bowling

200 WICKETS	Career	M	Wkts	Runs	Ave
Hadlee R.J.	1971/72-1990	342	1490	26,998	18.11
Grimmett C.V.	1911/12-1940/41	248	1424	31,740	22.28
Smith S.G.	1899/00-1925/26	211	955	17,272	18.08
Pritchard T.L.	1937/38-1956	200	818	19,062	23.30
Patel D.N.	1976-1996/97	358	654	21,737	33.23
Cairns C.L.	1988-2005/06	217	647	18,322	28.31
Boock S.L.	1973/74-1989/90	164	640	14,314	22.36
Chatfield E.J.	1973/74-1989/90	157	587	13,429	22.87
Saunders J.V.	1899/00-1913/14	107	553	12,065	21.81
Howarth H.J.	1962/63-1978/79	145	541	13,674	25.27
Blair R.W.	1951/52-1964/65	119	537	9961	18.54
Merritt W.E.	1926/27-1946	125	536	13,669	25.50
Collinge R.O.	1963/64-1978	163	524	12,793	24.41
O'Sullivan D.R.	1971-1984/85	136	523	13,554	25.91
Bracewell J.G.	1978/79-1990	149	522	13,919	26.66
Motz R.C.	1957/58-1969	142	518	11,769	22.72
Alabaster J.C.	1955/56-1971/72	143	500	12,688	25.37
Cairns B.L.	1971/72-1988	148	473	12,544	26.52
Reid J.R.	1947/48-1965	246	466	10,535	22.60
Wiseman P.J.	1991/92-2008	186	466	15,727	33.74
Vettori D.L.	1996/97-2008/09	142	460	14,559	31.65
Cameron F.J.	1952/53-1966/67	119	447	9658	21.60
Gray E.J.	1975/76-1991/92	162	444	12,522	28.20
Morrison D.K.	1985/86-1996/97	142	440	13,298	30.22
Martin C.S.	1997/98-2008/09	139	435	13,686	31.46
Taylor B.R.	1963/64-1979/80	141	422	10,605	25.13
Burtt T.B.	1943/44-1954/55	84	408	9054	22.19

	Career	M	Wkts	Runs	Ave
Snedden M.C.	1977/78-1990	118	387	9918	25.62
Cunis R.S.	1960/61-1976/77	132	386	10,287	26.65
Yuile B.W.	1959/60-1971/72	123	375	8209	21.89
Moir A.M.	1949/50-1961/62	97	368	9040	24.56
Cave H.B.	1945/46-1958/59	117	362	8663	23.93
Cowie J.	1932/33-1949/50	86	359	8002	22.28
MacGibbon A.R.	1947/48-1961/62	124	356	9301	26.12
Hadlee D.R.	1966/67-1983/84	111	351	8853	25.22
McIntyre J.M.	1961/62-1982/83	113	336	7917	23.56
Priest M.W.	1984/85-1998/99	109	329	10,478	31.84
Franklin J.E.C.	1998/99-2008/09	100	328	8669	26.42
Adams A.R.	1997/98-2007/08	82	321	7764	24.18
Callaway S.T.	1888/89-1906/07	62	320	5460	17.06
Sparling J.T.	1956/57-1970/71	127	318	7226	22.72
Downes A.D.	1888/89-1913/14	51	311	4564	14.67
Hayes J.A.	1946/47-1960/61	78	292	6759	23.14
Dickeson C.W.	1973/74-1986/87	90	282	8242	29.22
Beard D.D.	1945/46-1964/65	66	278	6000	21.58
O'Connor S.B.	1994/95-2002/03	73	278	6582	23.67
Alabaster G.D.	1955/56-1975/76	96	275	6388	23.22
Troup G.B.	1974/75-1986/87	100	272	7541	27.72
Watson W.	1984/85-1994/95	93	272	7485	27.52
Upham E.F.	1892/93-1909/10	49	265	4414	16.65
Tuffey D.R.	1996/97-2008/09	78	264	6742	25.53
Nash D.J.	1990/91-2001/02	120	255	7165	28.09
Walmsley K.P	1994/95-2005/06	67	253	6302	24.90
Robertson G.K.	1979/80-1989/90	88	252	7469	29.59
Penn A.J.	1994/95-2003/04	66	252	5806	23.03
Bradburn G.E.	1985/86-2001/02	127	250	8174	32.69
Doull S.B.	1989/90-2001/02	99	250	7233	28.93
O'Brien I.E.	2000/01-2008/09	70	249	6281	25.22
Wisneski W.A.	1992/93-2003/04	71	248	6467	26.07
Brice A.W.S.	1902/03-1927/28	61	247	5260	21.29
Bennett J.H.	1898/99-1919/20	52	241	4476	18.58
McGirr H.M.	1913/14-1932/33	88	239	6571	27.49
Yovich J.A.F.	1996/97-2008/09	89	237	7815	32.97
Mason M.J.	1997/98-2008/09	72	230	5716	24.85
Puna N.	1956/57-1968/69	70	229	5597	24.44
Dunning J.A.	1923/24-1937/38	60	228	6290	27.58
Pollard V.	1964/65-1974/75	130	224	6931	30.94
Vivian H.G.	1930/31-1938/39	85	223	6160	27.62
Cromb I.B.	1929/30-1946/47	88	222	6152	27.71
Badcock F.T.	1924/25-1945	53	221	5211	23.57
Allcott C.F.W.	1920/21-1945/46	82	220	5882	26.73
Sewell D.G.	1995/96-2005/06	67	218	6260	28.71
Duff S.W.	1985/86-1995/96	88	217	7051	32.49
Davis H.T.	1991/92-2003/04	71	215	6693	31.13
Martin B.P.	1999/00-2008/09	85	215	7510	34.93
Blunt R.C.	1917/18-1935	123	214	6638	31.01
Stott L.W.	1969/70-1983/84	63	214	5341	24.95
Hart M.N.	1990/91-2004/05	135	212	7424	35.01
Hamilton L.J.	1996/97-2006/07	60	212	5391	25.42
Gillespie M.R.	1999/00-2008/09	52	212	5170	24.38
de Groen R.P.	1987/88-1995/96	60	210	5266	25.07

	Career	M	Wkts	Runs	Ave
Stirling D.A.	1981/82-1991/92	84	206	6948	33.72
Canning T.K.	1998/99-2006/07	61	206	5042	24.47
Congdon B.E.	1960/61-1978	241	204	6125	30.02
Roberts S.J.	1985/86-1995/96	63	203	6001	29.56
Styris S.B.	1994/95-2008/09	123	203	6353	31.29
Burke C.	1937/38-1953/54	60	200	5199	25.99

Wicketkeeping

100 DISMISSALS	Career	M	Caught	Stumped	Total
Smith I.D.S.	1977/78-1991/92	178	390	36	426
James K.C.	1923/24-1946/47	204	310	112	422
McSweeney E.B.	1979/80-1993/94	121	340	45	385
Parore A.C.	1988/89-2001/02	163	358	24	382
Lees W.K.	1970/71-1987/88	146	292	44	336
Hart R.G.	1992/93-2003/04	110	298	17	315
Hopkins G.J.	1997/98-2008/09	110	286	20	306
Wadsworth K.J.	1968/69-1975/76	118	256	26	282
Germon L.K.	1987/88-2001/02	103	256	26	282
Nevin C.J.	1995/96-2008/09	105	270	9	279
Ward J.T.	1957/58-1970/71	95	227	27	254
Young R.A.	1998/99-2008/09	85	241	5	246
McCullum B.B.	1999/00/2008/09	84	218	16	234
Petrie E.C.	1950/51-1966/67	115	194	37	231
van Wyk C.F.K.	2000/01-2008/09	73	219	11	230
Mooney F.L.H.	1941/42-1954/55	91	164	54	218
Blain T.E.	1982/83-1994/95	118	190	26	216
Griggs B.B.J.	2000/01/2008/09	73	201	7	208
Croy M.G.	1994/95-2001/02	65	183	14	197
Young B.A.	1983/84-1997/98	163	185	11	196
Milburn B.D.	1963/64-1982/83	75	176	19	195
Dick A.E.	1956/57-1968/69	78	133	21	154
Kelly P.J.	1980/81-1988/89	49	140	13	153
Colquhoun I.A.	1953/54-1963/64	57	108	28	136
Guillen S.C.	1947/48-1960/61	66	100	34	134
Sigley M.A.	1994/95-2002/03	44	124	4	128
Boxshall C.	1897/98-1914/15	65	81	43	124
Schofield R.M.	1964/65-1974/75	53	107	15	122
Robinson S.A.	1984/85-1996/97	45	117	5	122
Wright M.J.E.	1972/73-1983/84	65	104	17	121
Mills G.H.	1935/36-1957/58	59	85	34	119
Tindill E.W.T.	1932/33-1949/50	69	85	33	118
McGlashan P.D.	2000/01-2008/09	46	104	8	112
Edwards G.N.	1973/74-1984/85	92	88	16	104
Therkleson I.J.	1966/67-1973/74	39	93	7	100

Leading Career Averages

BATTING *(qualification 3000 runs)*	*M*	*In*	*NO*	*HS*	*Runs*	*Ave*
Crowe M.D.	247	412	62	299	19,608	56.02
Scott V.J.	80	130	17	204	5620	49.73
Turner G.M.	455	792	101	311*	34,346	49.70
Sinclair M.S.	148	251	26	268	10,862	48.27
Donnelly M.P.	131	221	26	208*	9250	47.43
Sutcliffe B.	233	407	39	385	17,447	47.41
Harris C.Z.	128	200	42	251*	7228	45.75
Dempster C.S.	184	306	36	212	12,145	44.98
Wallace W.M.	121	192	17	211	7757	44.32
Fulton P.G.	74	124	11	301*	4961	43.90
Fleming S.P.	247	406	32	274*	16,409	43.87
Richardson M.H.	157	264	31	306	9994	42.89
Wright J.G.	366	636	44	192	25,073	42.35
Jones A.H.	145	254	33	186	9180	41.53
Reid J.R.	246	418	28	296	16,128	41.35
Blunt R.C.	123	209	15	338*	7953	40.99
Horne M.J.	128	219	11	241	8501	40.87
Hadlee W.A.	117	203	17	198	7523	40.44
Edgar B.A.	175	307	26	203	11,304	40.22

BOWLING *(qualification 200 wickets)*	*M*	*Wkts*	*Runs*	*Ave*
Downes A.D.	51	311	4564	14.67
Upham E.F.	49	265	4414	16.65
Callaway S.T.	62	320	5460	17.06
Smith S.G.	211	955	17,272	18.08
Hadlee R.J.	342	1490	26,998	18.11
Blair R.W.	119	537	9961	18.54
Bennett J.H.	52	241	4476	18.58

(C.J. Drum took 199 wickets at 19.46)

HIGHEST PARTNERSHIPS

FIRST WICKET

387	Turner G.M.	Jarvis T.W.	NZ v West Indies	Georgetown	1971/72
373	Sutcliffe B.	Watt L.	Otago v Auckland	Auckland	1950/51
333	Edgar B.A.	Jones A.H.	Wellington v Auckland	Wellington	1988/89
316	Austen M.H.	Hart R.T.	Wellington v Central Districts	Wanganui	1993/94
310	Edgar B.A.	Vance R.H.	Wellington v Northern Districts	Wellington	1988/89
306	Cuff L.A.	Lawrence J.D.	Canterbury v Auckland	Christchurch	1893/94
305	Lawson R.A.	Croy M.G.	Otago v Central Districts	Napier	1995/96
299	Bell M.D.	Jones R.A.	Wellington v Otago	Dunedin	2001/02
287	Hartland B.R.	Stead G.R.	Canterbury v Wellington	Christchurch	1994/95
286	Sutcliffe B.	Taylor D.D.	Auckland v Canterbury	Auckland	1948/49
276	Dempster C.S.	Mills J.E.	NZ v England	Wellington	1929/30
276	Griffith A.F.G.	Campbell S.L.	West Indies v NZ	Hamilton	1999/00
268	Turner G.M.	Dowling G.T.	NZ v President's XI	Montego Bay	1971/72
260	Lawson R.A.	Mohammad Wasim	Otago v Northern Districts	Dunedin	2002/03
259	Austen M.H.	Aiken J.M.	Wellington v Otago	Wellington	1994/95
253	Bell M.D.	Woodcock L.J.	Wellington v Central Districts	Napier	2007/08
252	Sutcliffe B.	Scott V.J.	NZ v Rest	Christchurch	1948/49
250	Hart R.T.	Smith C.J.P.	Central Districts v Wellington	Wellington	1985/86
247	Sutcliffe B.	Scott V.J.	NZ v Combined Services	Gillingham	1949
244	Richardson M.H.	Papps M.H.W.	NZ v Kent	Canterbury	2004
240	McIntosh T.G.	Horne M.J.	Auckland v Otago	Dunedin	2001/02
239	Dempster C.S.	Dustin W.H.	Wellington v Canterbury	Wellington	1931/32
239	Smith D.	Parks J.H.	MCC v Otago	Dunedin	1935/36
235	Hadlee W.A.	Page M.L.	Canterbury v Wellington	Christchurch	1936/37
231	Richardson M.H.	Vincent L.	NZ v India	Mohali	2003/04
230	Murray B.A.G.	Turner G.M.	NZ v President's XI	Rawalpindi	1969/70
229	Sutcliffe B.	Scott V.J.	NZ v Surrey	Oval	1949
226*	Hadlee W.A.	Leggat J.G.	Canterbury v Otago	Christchurch	1948/49
225	Richardson P.E.	Watson W.	MCC v Wellington	Wellington	1958/59
225	Greenidge C.G.	Haynes D.L.	West Indies v NZ	Christchurch	1979/80
220	Sutcliffe B.	Taylor D.D.	Auckland v Canterbury	Auckland	1948/49
220	Bell M.D.	Jones R.A.	Wellington v Canterbury	Christchurch	2000/01
219*	Edgar B.A.	Vance R.H.	Wellington v Central Districts	Wellington	1987/88
218	Hadlee W.A.	Leggat J.G.	Canterbury v Wellington	Christchurch	1947/48
218	Dempsey D.A.	Hadlee B.G.	Canterbury v Otago	Christchurch	1980/81
215	Sinclair M.S.	How J.M.	Central Districts v Northern Districts	Napier	2004/05
214	Woodfull W.M.	Ponsford W.H.	Australia v Otago	Dunedin	1927/28
214	Bolton B.A.	Dowling G.T.	Canterbury v Northern Districts	Christchurch	1959/60
214	Spearman C.M.	Twose R.G.	NZ v Zimbabwe	Auckland	1995/96
213	Lawson R.A.	Bell M.D.	NZ Academy XI v Zimbabwe	Whangarei	1995/96
213	Gaffaney C.B.	Parlane M.E.	NZ Academy XI v Bangladesh	Christchurch	1997/98
211	Turner G.M.	Parker J.M.	NZ v MCC	Lord's	1973
211	Bell M.D.	Donaldson G.T.	Wellington v Central Districts	Wellington	2003/04
209	Sutcliffe B.	Watt L.	Otago v Canterbury	Dunedin	1947/48
209	Harris B.Z.	Boyle D.J.	Canterbury v Otago	Christchurch	1991/92
208	Blunt R.C.	Worker R.V. de R.	Canterbury v MCC	Christchurch	1922/23
208	Athey C.W.J.	Robinson R.T.	England XI v Northern Districts	Hamilton	1987/88
207	Sadiq Mohammad	Zaheer Abbas	Pakistan v Wellington	Wellington	1972/73
201	Anthony A.	Horspool E.	Auckland v Wellington	Auckland	1924/25
201	Astle T.D.	Papps M.H.W.	Canterbury v Wellington	Christchurch	2006/07

SECOND WICKET

317	Hart R.T.	Briasco P.S.	Central Districts v Canterbury	New Plymouth	1983/84
315*	Gibbs H.H.	Kallis J.H.	South Africa v NZ	Christchurch	1998/99
303	Dempster C.S.	Allcott C.F.W.	NZ v Warwickshire	Birmingham	1927
287	Bell M.D.	Wells J.D.	Wellington v Auckland	Auckland	1997/98
279	Bell M.D.	Parlane M.E.	Wellington v Otago	Dunedin	2006/07
263	Greatbatch M.J.	Crowe M.D.	Central Districts v Northern Districts	Morrinsville	1986/87

256	Anderson R.W.	Edgar B.A.	NZ v Scotland	Dundee	1978
254*	Papps M.H.W.	Myburgh J.G.	Canterbury v Central Districts	Napier	2007/08
254	Burns K.J.	Rutherford K.R.	Otago v Wellington	Oamaru	1987/88
252	Baker W.A.	Beechey E.M.	Wellington v Auckland	Wellington	1918/19
250	Bell M.D.	Sinclair M.S.	New Zealand A v Sri Lanka A	Queenstown	2003/04
248	Horne M.J.	Fleming S.P.	Southern v Pakistan A	Christchurch	1998/99
245	Horne M.J.	Fleming S.P.	NZ v British Universities	Oxford	1999
244	Spearman C.M.	Sinclair M.S.	Central Districts v Northern Districts	Wanganui	1998/99
243	Papps M.H.W.	Stewart S.L.	Canterbury v Northern Districts	Hamilton	2006/07
242*	How J.M.	Sinclair M.S.	Central Districts v Otago	New Plymouth	2005/06
241	Franklin T.J.	Crowe J.J.	Auckland v Wellington	Wellington	1988/89
241	Wright J.G.	Jones A.H.	NZ v England	Wellington	1991/92
237	Gibson J.G.	Kuggeleijn C.M.	Northern Districts v Canterbury	Hamilton	1980/81
231	Carew M.C.	Nurse S.M.	West Indies v NZ	Christchurch	1968/69
229	Hemus L.G.	Midlane F.A.	Auckland v Wellington	Wellington	1918/19
227	Baker W.A.	Kortlang H.H.L.	Wellington v Otago	Dunedin	1923/24
227	Dobbs P.W.	Lamont M.J.	Otago v Auckland	Dunedin	1990/91
223	McIntosh T.G.	Jones R.A.	Auckland v West Indies	Auckland	2008/09
222	Warner P.F.	Fane F.L.	Lord Hawke's XI v Otago	Dunedin	1902/03
222	Crocker L.M.	Kuggeleijn C.M.	Northern Districts v Otago	Hamilton	1983/84
222	McCullum B.B.	Cumming C.D.	Otago v Auckland	Dunedin	2001/02
220	Macartney C.G.	Punch A.T.E.	NSW v Otago	Dunedin	1923/24
220	Richardson M.H.	Cumming C.D.	Otago v Northern Districts	Hamilton	2000/01
215	Bell M.D.	Wells J.D.	Wellington v Northern Districts	Hamilton	1998/99
215	Bell M.D.	Parlane M.E.	Wellington v Central Districts	Napier	2004/05
213	Barnett G.E.F.	Sinclair M.S.	Central Districts v Otago	New Plymouth	2005/06
212	Horspool E.	Snedden A.N.C.	Auckland v Victoria	Auckland	1924/25
210	Hadlee W.A.	O'Brien F.P.	Canterbury v Otago	Christchurch	1940/41
210	Howarth G.P.	Crowe J.J.	NZ v West Indies	Kingston	1984/85
209*	Jones A.H.	Crowe M.D.	Wellington v Canterbury	Christchurch	1992/93
209	Wilson B.S.	Flynn D.R.	Northern Districts v Canterbury	Christchurch	2008/09
207*	Twose R.G.	Douglas M.W.	Central Districts v Auckland	Auckland	1991/92
207	Mills J.E.	Blunt R.C.	NZ v H.D.G. Leveson-Gower's XI	Scarborough	1927
207	Vaughan M.P.	Hussain N.	England v Canterbury	Christchurch	2001/02
206	Raman W.V.	Gursharan Singh	India v Otago	Dunedin	1989/90
204	Gavaskar S.M.	Amarnath S.	India v NZ	Auckland	1975/76
202	Naushad Ali	Saeed Ahmed	Pakistan v Canterbury	Christchurch	1964/65
200	Smith R.W.	Bilby G.P.	Wellington v Northern Districts	Whangarei	1973/74

THIRD WICKET

467	Jones A.H.	Crowe M.D.	New Zealand v Sri Lanka	Wellington	1990/91
445	Whitelaw P.E.	Carson W.N.	Auckland v Otago	Dunedin	1936/37
394*	Kennedy P.G.	Latham R.T.	Canterbury v Northern Districts	Rotorua	1990/91
346	Burnett G.P.	Verry R.A.	Wellington v Northern Districts	Hamilton	1991/92
278	Franklin T.J.	Patel D.N.	Auckland v Canterbury	Christchurch	1985/86
265	Horne M.J.	Barnes A.C.	Auckland v Bangladesh	Auckland	2001/02
264	Chappell I.M.	Chappell G.S.	Australia v NZ	Wellington	1973/74
264	Ingram P.J.	Sinclair M.S.	Central Districts v Northern Districts	Hamilton	2008/09
261*	Maynard M.P.	Thomson S.A.	Northern Districts v Auckland	Hamilton	1990/91
259	Papps M.H.W.	Fulton P.G.	Canterbury v Northern Districts	Christchurch	2008/09
255	Lloyd C.H.	Davis C.A.	West Indies v South Island	Dunedin	1968/69
252*	Howarth G.P.	Roberts A.D.G.	Northern Districts v Pakistan	Gisborne	1978/79
248	Shoaib Mohammad	Javed Miandad	Pakistan v New Zealand	Auckland	1988/89
246	Rabone G.O.	Reid J.R.	NZ v Nottinghamshire	Nottingham	1949
246	Murray B.A.G.	Morrison J.F.M.	Wellington v Otago	Dunedin	1968/69
246	Parlane N.R.	Elliott G.D.	Wellington v Auckland	Auckland	2007/08
245	Crowe M.D.	Coney J.V.	NZ v South Australia	Adelaide	1985/86
244	Nicol R.J.	Vincent L.	Auckland v Otago	Auckland	2004/05
241	Wright J.G.	Crowe M.D.	New Zealand v West Indies	Wellington	1986/87
229	Miller L.S.M.	Sutcliffe B.	NZ v South Australia	Adelaide	1953/54
227	Rutherford K.R.	Blair B.R.	Otago v Central Districts	Alexandra	1988/89

226	Haynes D.L.	Richardson R.B.	West Indies v Shell XI	Napier	1986/87
224	Reid J.F.	Crowe M.D.	NZ v Australia	Brisbane	1985/86
224	Sinclair M.S.	Spearman C.M.	Central Districts v Auckland	Auckland	2003/04
223	Smith C.J.P.	Wilson S.W.J.	Central Districts v Otago	Blenheim	1990/91
222*	Sutcliffe B.	Reid J.R.	NZ v India	New Delhi	1955/56
222	Snedden A.N.C.	Smith S.G.	Auckland v Hawke's Bay	Auckland	1920/21
221	Blunt R.C.	McMullan J.J.M.	Otago v Canterbury	Dunedin	1928/29
221	Lara B.C.	Adams J.C.	West Indies v New Zealand	Wellington	1994/95
220	Shoaib Mohammad	Javed Miandad	Pakistan v New Zealand	Wellington	1988/89
218	Woodfull W.M.	Schneider K.J.	Australia v NZ	Auckland	1927/28
217	Dobbs P.W.	Rutherford K.R.	Otago v Central Districts	Blenheim	1990/91
216	Hemus L.G.	Smith S.G.	Auckland v Canterbury	Auckland	1919/20
214	Anthony A.	Gillespie H.D.	Auckland v Canterbury	Auckland	1929/30
213	Turner G.M.	Congdon B.E.	Otago v Wellington	Dunedin	1972/73
213	Jones A.H.	Crowe M.D.	NZ v Australia	Adelaide	1987/88
212	Booth B.C.	Burge P.J.P.	Australia B v NZ	Auckland	1966/67
210	Howarth G.P.	Crowe M.D.	NZ v Essex	Chelmsford	1983
210	Edgar G.A.	Crowe M.D.	NZ v England	Lord's	1986
210	Smith B.F.	Douglas M.W.	Central Districts v Northern Districts	Taupo	2000/01
209	McCosker R.G.	Chappell G.S.	Australia v Wellington	Wellington	1976/77
208	Papps M.H.W.	McMillan C.D.	Canterbury v Central Districts	Christchurch	2006/07
206	Preston A.H.	Beck J.E.F.	Wellington v Canterbury	Christchurch	1955/56
204	Harford N.S.	Reid J.R.	NZ v Oxford University	Oxford	1958
204	Twose R.G.	Crowe M.D.	NZ v Indian Colts XI	Hyderabad	1995/96
204	Fleming S.P.	Styris S.B.	NZ v Bangladesh	Chittagong	2004/05
203*	Pocock B.A.	Parore A.C.	Auckland v Wellington	Auckland	1997/98
201	McLeod E.G.	Lamason J.R.	Wellington v Auckland	Wellington	1935/36

FOURTH WICKET

350	Mushtaq Mohammad	Asif Iqbal	Pakistan v NZ	Dunedin	1972/73
324	Reid J.R.	Wallace W.M.	NZ v Cambridge University	Cambridge	1949
310	Ryder J.D.	Parlane N.R.	Wellington v Central Districts	Palmerston North	2004/05
299	Wallace W.M.	Donnelly M.P.	NZ v Leicestershire	Leicester	1949
282	Wilkinson W.A.C.	Champman A.P.F.	MCC v Canterbury	Christchurch	1922/23
280	Crowe J.J.	Patel D.N.	Auckland v Northern Districts	Auckland	1991/92
278	Roberts A.W.	Page M.L.	Canterbury v Wellington	Wellington	1931/32
276*	Crowe M.D.	Briasco P.S.	Central Districts v Canterbury	Christchurch	1986/87
274	Jones R.A.	Mather S.R.	Wellington v Otago	Wellington	2000/01
273	McIntosh T.G.	Nicol R.J.	Auckland v Otago	Lincoln	2006/07
271	Taylor L.R.P.L.	Ryder J.D.	New Zealand v India	Napier	2008/09
266	Denness M.H.	Fletcher K.W.R.	England v NZ	Auckland	1974/75
259	Bradburn G.E.	Parlane M.E.	Northern Districts v Canterbury	Christchurch	1996/97
254	Reid J.R.	Miller L.S.M.	NZ v Natal	Durban	1953/54
252	Thomson S.A.	Young B.A.	Northern Districts v Auckland	Auckland	1990/91
243	Horne M.J.	Astle N.J.	New Zealand v Zimbabwe	Auckland	1997/98
240	Fleming S.P.	McMillan C.D.	New Zealand v Sri Lanka	Colombo	1997/98
235	Burns K.J.	Hoskin R.N.	Otago v Northern Districts	Hamilton	1987/88
229	Congdon B.E.	Hastings B.F.	NZ v Australia	Wellington	1973/74
219	Vivian H.G.	Page M.L.	NZ v Oxford University	Oxford	1931
218	Crowe J.J.	Coney J.V.	NZ v Glamorgan	Swansea	1986
214	Ransford V.S.	Lampard A.W.	Australia v NZ	Auckland	1920/21
211*	Jones A.H.	Burns K.J.	Otago v Wellington	Wellington	1984/85
211	White D.J.	Young B.A.	Northern Districts v Auckland	Auckland	1992/93
208	Thomson S.A.	Maynard M.P.	Northern Districts v Wellington	Hamilton	1991/92
207	Midlane F.A.	Richardson C.A.	Wellington v Otago	Wellington	1899/00
207	Badcock F.T.	Lowry T.C.	Wellington v Auckland	Wellington	1927/28
207	Sulzberger G.P.	Penn A.J.	Central Districts v Otago	Napier	1995/96
206	McCullum S.J.	Dawson G.J.	Otago v Northern Districts	Dunedin	1983/84
206	Stewart A.J.	Hussain N.	England v New Zealand XI	Palmerston North	1996/97
206	McIntosh T.G.	Vincent L.	Auckland v Canterbury	Christchurch	2000/01
204	Harvey R.N.	Simpson R.B.	Australia B v Otago	Dunedin	1956/57
204	Jarvis T.W.	Thomson K.	Canterbury v Central Districts	Wanganui	1969/70

204	Redmond A.J.	Broom N.T.	Otago v Northern Districts	Hamilton	2006/07
203	Thomson S.A.	Maynard M.P.	Northern Districts v Otago	Hamilton	1991/92
200	Blair B.R.	Dawson G.J.	Otago v Central Districts	Dunedin	1982/83

FIFTH WICKET

347*	Horne M.J.	Barnes A.C.	Auckland v Northern Districts	Auckland	2003/04
341	Larsen G.R.	McSweeney E.B.	Wellington v Central Districts	Levin	1987/88
319	Rutherford K.R.	Gray E.J.	NZ v DB Close's XI	Scarborough	1986
301	Englefield J.I.	Taylor L.R.P.L.	Central Districts v Wellington	Palmerston North	2004/05
290	Harris C.Z.	Stead G.R.	Canterbury v Central Districts	Blenheim	1996/97
282	Franklin J.E.C.	Woodcock L.J.	Wellington v Auckland	Auckland	2008/09
266	Sutcliffe B.	Haig W.S.	Otago v Auckland	Dunedin	1949/50
258	Salim Malik	Inzamam-ul-Haq	Pakistan v New Zealand	Wellington	1993/94
255	Taylor B.R.	Coney J.V.	Wellington v Otago	Dunedin	1972/73
252*	Latham R.T.	Priest M.W.	Canterbury v Northern Districts	Christchurch	1988/89
244	Reid J.R.	Chapple M.E.	NZ v Western Province	Cape Town	1962/63
242	Hammond W.R.	Ames L.E.G.	England v NZ	Christchurch	1932/33
236	Harris C.Z.	Astle N.J.	Canterbury v Otago	Christchurch	1996/97
235*	Woodfull W.M.	Ransford V.S.	Victoria v NZ	Christchurch	1924/25
235*	Sulzberger G.P.	Ryder J.D.	Central Districts v Canterbury	Napier	2002/03
234*	Scott V.J.	Morris J.B.	Auckland v Central Districts	Auckland	1951/52
233	Moloney D.A.R.	Kerr J.L.	NZ v England XI	Folkestone	1937
228	Raval J.A.	Hopkins G.J.	Auckland v Central Districts	Auckland	2008/09
222	Astle N.J.	McMillan C.D.	New Zealand v Zimbabwe	Wellington	2000/01
219	Broom N.T.	Hopkins G.J.	Otago v Auckland	Lincoln	2006/07
216	Parlane N.R.	Franklin J.E.C.	Wellington v Auckland	Wellington	2005/06
213	Ritchie G.M.	Matthews G.R.J.	Australia v NZ	Wellington	1985/86
203	Booth B.C.	Davies G.R.	Australia B v Central Districts	Palmerston North	1966/67
201	Alexander W.C.	Richardson V.Y.	Australia v Auckland	Auckland	1927/28
201	Burgess M.G.	Jarvis T.W.	Auckland v Central Districts	Auckland	1971/72

SIXTH WICKET

322	Orchard M.G.	Yovich J.A.F.	Northern Districts v Central Districts	Napier	2005/06
293*	Fulton P.G.	Broom N.T.	Canterbury v Otago	Dunedin	2004/05
281	Thorpe G.P.	Flintoff A.	England v New Zealand	Christchurch	2001/02
269	Trumper V.T.	Hill C.	Australia v NZ	Wellington	1904/05
256	Martyn D.R.	Gilchrist A.C.	Australia v New Zealand	Wellington	2004/05
246*	Crowe J.J.	Hadlee R.J.	NZ v Sri Lanka	Colombo	1986/87
240	Parfitt P.H.	Knight B.R.	England v NZ	Auckland	1962/63
238	McDonald R.	Cowley O.W.	Queensland v Hawke's Bay	Napier	1896/97
235	Sinclair M.S.	Griggs B.B.J.	Central Districts v Wellington	Wellington	2008/09
233	Crawford J.N.	Armstrong W.W.	Australia v NZ	Auckland	1913/14
232	Botham I.T.	Randall D.W.	England v New Zealand	Wellington	1983/84
226	Gray E.J.	Ormiston R.W.	Wellington v Central Districts	Wellington	1981/82
220	Turner G.M.	Wadsworth K.J.	NZ v West Indies	Kingston	1971/72
220	Toynbee M.H.	Smith I.D.S.	Central Districts v Auckland	Napier	1982/83
216	Hart M.N.	Marshall H.J.H.	Northern Districts v Central Districts	Napier	2004/05
212*	McMillan C.D.	Parore A.C.	New Zealand v President's XI	Jodhpur	1999/00
209*	Parore A.C.	O'Dowd A.P.	Auckland v Otago	Dunedin	1991/92
209	Harris C.Z.	Redmond A.J.	Canterbury v Wellington	Rangiora	2001/02
203	Ormiston R.W.	Coney J.V.	Wellington v Central Districts	New Plymouth	1982/83
201	Harris C.Z.	Parore A.C	New Zealand v Orange Free State	Bloemfontein	1994/95
201	Tendulkar S.R.	Mongia N.R.	India v Central Districts	Napier	1998/99

SEVENTH WICKET

265	Powell J.L.	Dorreen N.	Canterbury v Otago	Christchurch	1929/30
261	Campbell A.D.R.	Strang P.A.	Zimbabwe v Canterbury	Timaru	1997/98
250	Nevin C.J.	Walker M.D.J.	Wellington v Otago	Wellington	2003/04
248	Yousuf Youhana	Saqlain Mushtaq	Pakistan v New Zealand	Christchurch	2000/01
246	McGlew D.J.	Murray A.R.A.	South Africa v NZ	Wellington	1952/53
244	Patrick W.R.	Allcott C.F.W.	NZ v NSW	Sydney	1925/26

241	Astle N.J.	Priest M.W.	Canterbury v Wellington	Christchurch	1994/95
229	Schneider K.J.	Oldfield W.A.S.	Australia v Canterbury	Christchurch	1927/28
225	Cairns C.L.	Oram J.D.P.	NZ v South Africa	Auckland	2003/04
224	Scott V.J.	Matheson A.M.	Auckland v Canterbury	Auckland	1937/38
219	Yuile B.W.	Hampton B.L.	Central Districts v Canterbury	Napier	1967/68
217	Walters K.D.	Gilmour G.J.	Australia v NZ	Christchurch	1976/77
212	Katich S.M.	Gilchrist A.C.	Australia v New Zealand	Christchurch	2004/05
205	Germon L.K.	Priest M.W.	Canterbury v Northern Districts	Christchurch	1991/92
205*	Hay G.R.	Diamanti B.J.	Central Districts v Canterbury	Rangiora	2008/09
192	Brown S.W.	Parore A.C.	Auckland v Central Districts	Auckland	1990/91
191	Wright J.G.	Smith I.D.S.	NZ v Western Australia	Perth	1989/90
186	Lees W.K.	Hadlee R.J.	NZ v Pakistan	Karachi	1976/77
186	Leggat R.I.	Hadlee D.R.	Canterbury v Sri Lanka	Christchurch	1982/83
186	Ryder J.D.	Vettori D.L.	New Zealand v India	Hamilton	2008/09
184*	Bull C.L.	Isherwood B.P.	Canterbury v Central Districts	Nelson	1971/72
183	Oram J.D.P.	Vettori D.L.	New Zealand v South Africa	Centurion	2005/06
182	Sutcliffe B.	Gilbertson A.W.	Otago v Canterbury	Christchurch	1952/53
182	Weston T.I.	Thompson E.P.	Central Districts v Canterbury	Christchurch	2005/06
179	Griggs B.B.J.	Furlong C.J.M.	Central Districts v Northern Districts	Hamilton	2001/02
177*	Barnes A.C.	Mills J.M.	Auckland v Otago	Alexandra	1995/96
176	Rabone G.O.	Mooney F.L.H.	NZ v MCC	Lord's	1949
176	Mills S.M.	Nevin C.J.	Wellington v Canterbury	Christchurch	2006/07

EIGHTH WICKET

433†	Trumper V.T.	Sims A.	Sims' Australian XI v Canterbury	Christchurch	1913/14
256	Fleming S.P.	Franklin J.E.C.	New Zealand v South Africa	Cape Town	2005/06
253	Astle N.J.	Parore A.C.	New Zealand v Australia	Perth	2001/02
220	Wiseman P.J.	Hiini B.C.	Canterbury v Northern Districts	Hamilton	2005/06
215	Murray J.R.	Cummins A.C.	West Indies v Otago	Dunedin	1994/95
210	Stead G.R.	Bond S.E.	Canterbury v Northern Districts	Christchurch	2004/05
190*	Mills J.E.	Allcott C.F.W.	NZ v Civil Service	Chiswick	1927
189	Carson W.N.	Matheson A.M.	Auckland v Wellington	Auckland	1938/39
185	Nash D.J.	Mills K.D.	Auckland v Wellington	Wellington	2000/01
180	Twose R.G.	Goodson M.C.	Wellington v Otago	Dunedin	1994/95
173	Smith I.D.S.	Robertson G.K.	Central Districts v Northern Districts	Hamilton	1982/83
172*	Walker B.G.K.	Mills K.D.	Auckland v Wellington	Auckland	1999/00
167	van Wyk C.F.K.	McCone R.J.	Canterbury v Otago	Christchurch	2008/09
166	Hadlee R.J.	Hadlee D.R.	Canterbury v Auckland	Christchurch	1983/84
165*	Eckhold A.G.	Crawford J.N.	Otago v Wellington	Wellington	1914/15
163	McGlashan P.D.	Aldridge G.W.	Northern Districts v Canterbury	Hamilton	2008/09
161	McSweeney E.B.	Snedden M.C.	Shell XI v West Indies	Napier	1986/87
159	Diamanti B.J.	Sherlock R.R.	Central Districts v Canterbury	Napier	2007/08
157	McLaren A.C.	McLean J.F.	MCC v NZ	Wellington	1922/23
154	James K.C.	Badcock F.T.	Wellington v Canterbury	Christchurch	1926/27
153	Nicol R.J.	Young R.A.	Auckland v Canterbury	Auckland	2001/02
152	Bradburn G.E.	Doull S.B.	Northern Districts v Canterbury	Christchurch	1991/92
152	Marshall J.A.H.	Orchard M.G.	Northern Districts v Wellington	Hamilton	2006/07

† *world record*

NINTH WICKET

239	Cave H.B.	Leggat I.B.	Central Districts v Otago	Dunedin	1952/53
209	Wiseman P.J.	Martin B.P.	New Zealand A v Sri Lanka A	Christchurch	2003/04
208	McSkimming W.C.	Scott B.E.	Otago v Auckland	Auckland	2004/05
188	Parlane N.R.	Tuffey D.R.	Northern Districts v Wellington	Wellington	1999/00
185	Maynard M.P.	Doull S.B.	Northern Districts v Auckland	Auckland	1991/92
182*	Germon L.K.	Ford R.M.	Canterbury v Wellington	Christchurch	1989/90
170*	Hart M.N.	Yovich J.A.F.	Northern Districts v South Africa	Hamilton	1998/99
163*	Cowdrey M.C.	Smith A.C.	England v NZ	Wellington	1962/63
151	Young R.A.	Morgan G.J.	Auckland v Northern Districts	Auckland	2007/08
139	Hart R.G.	Tait A.R.	Northern Districts v Wellington	Gisborne	1996/97
136	Smith I.D.S.	Snedden M.C.	NZ v India	Auckland	1989/90

135	Hart R.G.	Penn A.J.	Central v Northern	Rangiora	1998/99
134	Wilson J.W.	Mallender N.A.	Otago v Canterbury	Christchurch	1992/93
127	Mooney F.L.H.	Buchan R.A.	Wellington v Auckland	Wellington	1943/44
122	Schuster H.T.	Cunis R.S.	Auckland v Wellington	Wellington	1964/65
121	Cheetham J.E.	Murray A.R.A.	South Africa v Canterbury	Christchurch	1952/53
118	Coney J.V.	Cairns B.L.	NZ v England	Wellington	1983/84
116	Nevin C.J.	Davis H.T.	Wellington v Auckland	Auckland	1995/96
115	Robertson G.K.	Hart R.T.	Central Districts v Otago	Oamaru	1985/86
115	Hopkins G.J.	Ellis A.M.	Canterbury v Auckland	Auckland	2002/03

TENTH WICKET

184	Blunt R.C.	Hawksworth W.	Otago v Canterbury	Christchurch	1931/32
160	Germon L.K.	Wisneski W.A.	Canterbury v Northern Districts	Rangiora	1997/98
151	Hastings B.F.	Collinge R.O.	NZ v Pakistan	Auckland	1972/73
138	James K.C.	Brice A.W.S.	Wellington v Otago	Wellington	1926/27
133	Bartlett G.A.	Colquhoun I.A.	Central Districts v Auckland	Auckland	1959/60
124	Bracewell J.G.	Boock S.L.	NZ v Australia	Sydney	1985/86
123	Brice A.W.S.	Beard T.	Wellington v Otago	Wellington	1927/28
119	Carson W.N.	Cowie J.	Auckland v Otago	Auckland	1937/38
118	Astle N.J.	Cairns C.L.	New Zealand v England	Christchurch	2001/02
113	Mooney F.L.H.	Knapp E.C.V.	Wellington v Auckland	Wellington	1943/44
113*	McGlashan P.D.	Aldridge G.W.	Northern Districts v Wellington	Wellington	2005/06
107	Motz R.C.	Cameron F.J.	NZ v Worcestershire	Worcester	1965
106*	Astle N.J.	Morrison D.K.	New Zealand v England	Auckland	1996/97
105	Cherry R.W.	Torrance R.C.	Otago v Canterbury	Christchurch	1925/26
104	James K.C.	Massey H.B.	Wellington v Australia	Wellington	1927/28
103	Kelly P.J.	Troup G.B.	Auckland v Northern Districts	Auckland	1985/86
101	Astle N.J.	Owens M.B.	Canterbury v Northern Districts	Hamilton	1994/95
100	Lee C.D.	Brown C.M.	Auckland v Otago	Dunedin	1994/95

Hundred Partnership for the First Wicket in Both Innings

154 & 155	Shepherd J.S.F.	Worker R.V. de.R.	Otago v Wellington	Dunedin	1923/24
220 & 286	Taylor D.D.	Sutcliffe B.	Auckland v Canterbury	Auckland	1948/49
102 & 155	Blair W.L.	Turner G.M.	Otago v Auckland	Auckland	1972/73
172 & 148	Briasco P.S.	Smith C.J.P.	Central Districts v Auckland	New Plymouth	1985/86
107	Broad B.C.	Moxon M.D.	England XI v Northern Districts	Hamilton	1987/88
208	Athey C.W.J.	Robinson R.T.			
109 & 111	Wealleans K.A.	White D.J.	Northern Districts v India	Hamilton	1989/90
116 & 102	Greatbatch M.J.	Latham R.T.	New Zealand v Zimbabwe	Bulawayo	1992/93
145 & 131	Lawson R.A.	Gaffaney C.B.	Otago v Wellington	Wellington	1996/97
118* & 179	Twose R.G.	Bell M.D.	Wellington v Central Districts	Wellington	1997/98
102 & 112	Spearman C.M.	Kelly D.P.	Central Districts v Wellington	New Plymouth	1999/00
220	Bell M.D.	Jones R.A.	Wellington v Canterbury	Christchurch	2000/01
127	Nevin C.J.	Jones R.A.			
141	Cumming C.D.	Mohammad Wasim	Otago v Wellington	Wellington	2002/03
147	Gaffaney C.B.	Cumming C.D.			
104 & 118	Richardson M.H.	McIntosh T.G.	Auckland v Northern Districts	Auckland	2002/03

FAMILIES IN FIRST-CLASS CRICKET

Great-grandfather and Great-grandson

Orchard S.A.	(C)	Orchard M.G.	(ND)

Three Generations

Anderson W.M.	(C)	Anderson R.W.	(C, ND, O, CD)	Anderson T.R.	(CD)
*Blair J.R.	(O)	Blair R.A.J.	(O)	Blair W.L.	(O)
				Blair B.R.	(O, ND)
Burton H.G.E.L.	(W)	Burton H.E.L.	(W, A)	Burton J.E.L.	(W)
*Burtt N.V.	(C)	Burtt J.W.	(C, CD)	Burtt L.M.	(C)
Smith F.A.	(C)	Smith F.B.	(C)	Smith G.B.	(C)
*Carson W.	(O)	Carson W.N.	(A)	Carson J.R.	(A, ND)
Snedden A.N.C.	(A)	Snedden W.N.	(A)	Snedden M.C.	(A)

** J.R. Blair is the uncle of R.A.J. Blair. The Carsons are uncles and nephews. J.W. Burtt is the uncle of L.M. Burtt.*

Grandfather and Grandson

Milnes L.A.	(O)	Milnes G.S.	(CD)
Roberts H.	(W)	du Chateau V.H.	(W)

Father and Three Sons

Cotterill A.J.	(C)	Cotterill A.K.	(HB)	Cotterill B.W.	(HB)	Cotterill G.R.	(HB)
Hadlee W.A.	(C, O)	Hadlee B.G.	(C)	Hadlee D.R.	(C)	Hadlee R.J.	(C)

Father and Two Sons

Blacklock J.W.	(W)	Blacklock C.P.	(W)	Blacklock J.P.	(W)
Blair R.A.J.	(O)	Blair W.L.	(O)	Blair B.R.	(O, ND)
Crowe D.W.	(W,C)	Crowe M.D.	(A, CD, W)	Crowe J.J.	(A, SA)
Garrard C.W.	(C)	Garrard W.R.	(A)	Garrard D.R.	(A)
Furlong B.D.M.	(CD)	Furlong J.B.M.	(CD)	Furlong C.J.M.	(CD)
Harris P.G.Z.	(C)	Harris B.Z.	(C, O)	Harris C.Z.	(C)
Howell J.H.	(CD)	Howell L.G.	(C, CD, A, ND)	Howell G.A.	(C, W)
McCullum S.J.	(O)	McCullum B.B.	(O, C)	McCullum N.L.	(O)
McVicar A.C.	(Minor Assocs)	McVicar S.A.	(W)	McVicar C.C.	(CD)
Puna N.	(ND)	Puna K.N.	(ND)	Puna A.	(ND)
Reaney P.S.	(HB)	Reaney H.E.I.	(W)	Reaney T.P.L.	(W, CD)

Father and One Son

Airey W.F.	(W)	Airey D.M.L.	(W)
Aldridge C.W.	(C)	Aldridge G.W.	(ND)
Allen R.	(W)	Allen G.S.	(W)
Andrews S.	(C)	Andrews B.	(C, CD, O)
Astle A.M.	(CD)	Astle T.D.	(C)
Baker J.C.	(O)	Clark J.B.	(O)
Barclay W.S.	(W)	Barclay C.W.	(CD)
Barton P.H.	(ND, O)	Barton H.D.	(A, C)
Barry R.W.	(C)	Barry R.	(C)
Beard D.D.	(W, CD, ND)	Beard D.A.	(ND)
Blackmore J.H.	(ND)	Blackmore S.J.	(W)
Bracewell B.P.	(CD, O, ND)	Bracewell D.A.J.	(CD)
Bradburn W.P.	(ND)	Bradburn G.E.	(ND)
Burgess G.C.	(A)	Burgess M.G.	(A)
Burtt N.V.	(C)	Burtt J.W.	(C, CD)
Cairns B.L.	(CD, O, ND)	Cairns C.L.	(ND, C)

Campbell K.O.	(O)	Campbell P.A.	(O)
Child E.L.	(A, ND)	Child M.J.	(ND)
Clark L.G.	(O)	Clark L.A.	(W, O, A)
Collins W.E.	(W)	Collins D.C.	(W)
Cuff L.A.	(C, A)	Cuff A.G.	(Tasmania)
Cunis R.S.	(A, ND)	Cunis S.J.	(C)
Douglas G.W.	(CD)	Douglas M.W.	(CD, W)
Edgar A.J.	(W)	Edgar B.A.	(W)
Freeman T.A.	(O)	Freeman B.T.	(O)
Fulton F.	(O, HB)	Fulton P.R.	(HB)
Gasson E.A. snr	(C)	Gasson E.A. jnr	(C)
Gearry G.N.	(C)	Gearry R.M.	(C, CD)
Gedye A.E.	(W)	Gedye S.G.	(A)
Gilbertson J.	(S)	Gilbertson A.W.	(O)
Hartland I.R.	(C)	Hartland B.R.	(C)
Hastings B.F.	(W, CD, C)	Hastings M.A.	(C)
Hay W.P.C.	(A)	Hay S.C.	(A)
Hill A.J.	(CD)	Hill J.V.	(CD)
Hill J.	(O)	Hill R.J.	(O)
Holden W.J.	(O)	Holden A.C.	(O)
Howden C.E.	(O)	Howden C.P.	(O)
Ibadulla K.	(O)	Ibadulla K.B.K.	(O)
Jefferson R.G.	(O, W)	Jefferson M.R.	(W, ND)
Kelly J.W.H.	(W)	Kelly P.J.	(A)
Kerr A.	(A)	Kerr A.C.	(A)
Lankham G.	(A)	Lankham W.	(A)
Lowry T.H.	(HB)	Lowry T.C.	(A, W)
McGirr W.P.	(W)	McGirr H.M.	(W)
McKnight S.G.	(O)	McKnight K.J.	(O)
McKenzie N.M.	(O)	McKenzie M.N.	(C, O)
Mills G.	(A, HB, O)	Mills J.E.	(A)
Morgan H.A.	(W)	Morgan R.G.	(ND, A)
Murdoch D.H.	(O)	Murdoch G.H.	(O)
Newman A.	(W)	Newman P.A.	(CD)
O'Brien J.J.	(HB)	O'Brien M.A.	(W)
Oakley J.H.	(W)	Oakley D.F.	(W)
Ollivier A.M.	(C)	Ollivier K.M.	(C)
Ongley A.M.	(HB)	Ongley J.A.	(W, CD)
Parker N.M.	(O, C)	Parker M.M.	(O)
Postles A.J.	(A)	Postles B.J.	(A)
Redmond R.E.	(W, A)	Redmond A.J.	(C, O)
Rees W.L.	(A)	Rees A.W.	(A, HB)
Reese T.W.	(C)	Reese D.W.	(C)
Reid J.R.	(W, O)	Reid R.B.	(W, A)
Roberts A.	(W)	Roberts S.A.	(A)
Roberts H.	(W)	Roberts E.J.	(W)
Rutherford K.R.	(O)	Rutherford H.D.	(O)
Sale E.V.	(A)	Sale V.S.	(A)
Standidge J.A.	(W)	Standidge P.H.	(W)
Stead D.W.	(C)	Stead G.R.	(C)
Tindill E.W.T.	(W)	Tindill P.	(W)
Vance R.A.	(W)	Vance R.H.	(W)
Vivian H.G.	(A)	Vivian G.E.	(A)
Wallace W.M.	(A)	Wallace G.M.	(A)
Ward J.T.	(C)	Ward B.J.	(C)
Wilding F.	(C)	Wilding A.F.	(C)
Wright G.T.	(C)	Wright J.G.	(ND, C, A)

Father and Son in Same First-class Match

Reese T.W. & Reese D.W.	Canterbury v Otago	Dunedin	1917/18

Five Brothers

Cotterill A.J. (C) Cotterill C.N. (HB) Cotterill E.J. (C, A) Cotterill H. (C) Cotterill W.J. (C)

Four Brothers

Bayly A. (T)	Bayly F. (T)	Bayly G.T. (T)	Bayly H. (T)
Bracewell B.P. (CD, O, ND)	Bracewell D.W. (CD, C)	Bracewell J.G. (O, A)	Bracewell M.A. (O)
Mills E. (A)	Mills G. (A, HB, O)	Mills I. (A)	Mills W. (T, A)

Three Brothers

Alloo A.P.	(O)	Alloo A.W.	(O)	Alloo H.C.	(O)
Blacklock A.	(W)	Blacklock J.W.	(W)	Blacklock R.V.	(W)
Carlton W.	(A, C)	Carlton A.R.	(Vic)	Carlton J.	(Vic)
Cotterill A.K.	(HB)	Cotterill B.W.	(HB)	Cotterill G.R.	(HB)
Eden J.	(N)	Eden T.	(N)	Eden W.	(N)
Fowler G.	(N)	Fowler L.	(N)	Fowler S.	(N)
Gore A.H.	(W, HB)	Gore C.S.	(W)	Gore R.	(W)
Hadlee B.G.	(C)	Hadlee D.R.	(C)	Hadlee R.J.	(C)
Harman A.F.G.	(C)	Harman R.D.	(C)	Harman T.D.	(C)
Knapp C.	(N)	Knapp H.	(N)	Knapp K.	(N)
Lusk Hugh B.	(A, HB)	Lusk R.B.	(T)	Lusk W.N.B.	(A)
Mace C.	(O)	Mace H.	(W)	Mace J.	(O)
Meldrum A.L.	(A)	Meldrum D.	(A)	Meldrum W.	(A)
Newman A.	(W)	Newman J.	(C, W)	Newman S.	(W)
Parker K.J.	(A)	Parker J.M.	(ND)	Parker N.M.	(O, C)
Reese D.	(C)	Reese J.B.	(C)	Reese T.W.	(C)
Ridley A.E.	(C)	Ridley H.C.	(C)	Ridley R.	(C)
Salmon I.J.	(W)	Salmon J.A.N.	(W)	Salmon W.J.	(W, HB, T)

Two Brothers

Aberhart D.C.	(CD, C)	Aberhart W.M.	(W)
Alabaster G.D.	(O, C, ND)	Alabaster J.C.	(O)
Austin G.G.	(O)	Austin T.T.L.	(O)
Baker G.H.	(W)	Baker W.A.	(W)
Bannerman J.W.H.	(S)	Bannerman W.E.	(O)
Barton P.H.	(ND, O)	Barton R.H.	(ND)
Beal C.E.	(O, C)	Beal W.M.	(O)
Beuth D.	(CD)	Beuth A.J.	(ND)
Billcliff I.S.	(O, W, A)	Billcliff M.R.	(O)
Bishop H.A.	(HB, C)	Bishop R.E.	(HB)
Blacklock C.P.	(W)	Blacklock J.P.	(W)
Blair B.R.	(O, ND)	Blair W.L.	(O)
Blakely D.J.	(O)	Blakely J.W.	(O)
Blamires E.O.	(W, O)	Blamires H.L.	(HB)
Boddington E.R.	(N, W)	Boddington H.A.	(N, O)
Boult J.J.	(ND)	Boult T.A.	(ND)
Boyle D.J.	(C)	Boyle J.G.	(W, C)
Burtt N.V.	(C)	Burtt T.B.	(C)
Cairns A.E.	(O)	Cairns H.W.	(O)
Cameron D.S.	(O)	Cameron H.R.	(O)

Cederwall B.W.	(W)	Cederwall G.N.	(W)
Chadwick C.S.	(O)	Chadwick L.N.	(O)
Clarke D.B.	(A, ND)	Clarke D.S.	(ND)
Collins J.U.	(N, C)	Collins W.E.	(W)
Coney C.J.	(W)	Coney J.V.	(W)
Cornelius C.J.	(C)	Cornelius W.A.	(C)
Cresswell A.E.	(W, CD)	Cresswell G.F.	(W, CD)
Cross C.S.	(N, W)	Cross H.	(N)
Crowe J.J.	(A, South Australia)	Crowe M.D.	(A, CD, W)
Dacre C.C.R.	(A)	Dacre L.M.	(A)
Doull L.J.	(W)	Doull S.B.	(ND)
Dryden C.H.	(W)	Dryden W.E.	(W)
Farrant A.J.	(C)	Farrant D.G.	(C)
Fisher A.H.	(O)	Fisher R.L.	(C)
Frankish E.H.	(C)	Frankish F.S.	(C)
Frith C.	(C, O)	Frith W.	(C, O, W)
Fulton F.	(O, HB)	Fulton J.C.	(O)
Furlong C.J.M.	(CD)	Furlong J.B.M.	(CD)
Garrard D.R.	(A)	Garrard W.R.	(A)
Gatenby D.J.	(C)	Gatenby P.R.	(Tasmania)
Gilbertson J.	(S)	Gilbertson J.H.	(S)
Graham A.C.	(O)	Graham C.G.	(O)
Hamilton A.J.	(S)	Hamilton D.C.	(S)
Hampton B.L.	(CD)	Hampton I.R.	(CD)
Harris B.Z.	(C, O)	Harris C.Z.	(C)
Hart M.N.	(ND)	Hart R.G.	(ND)
Hatch K.	(W)	Hatch R.J.	(W)
Hay T.D.B.	(A)	Hay W.P.C.	(A)
Hickson H.C.	(W)	Hickson W.R.S.	(W)
Holdship A.R.	(W)	Holdship W.E.	(Middlesex)
Horne M.J.	(A, O)	Horne P.A.	(A)
Howarth G.P.	(A, ND)	Howarth H.J.	(A)
Howell L.G.	(C, CD, A, ND)	Howell G.A.	(C, W)
Howden A.M.	(A)	Howden C.E.	(O)
Lynch D.	(A)	Lynch R.F.	(W)
Lynch R.K.	(A)	Lynch S.M.	(A)
McCullum B.B.	(O, C)	McCullum N.L.	(O)
McVicar S.A.	(W)	McVicar C.C.	(CD)
Marshall J.A.H.	(ND)	Marshall H.J.H.	(ND)
Martin J.H.	(HB)	Martin H.	(HB)
Matthias H.R.	(C)	Matthias R.B.	(C)
Morris J.B.	(A)	Morris P.P.W.	(A)
Naughton D.	(W)	Naughton M.P.	(W)
Neill R.	(A)	Neill T.	(A)
Nicholson C.R.	(C, O)	Nicholson K.A.	(O)
O'Rourke M.H.	(A)	O'Rourke P.W.	(W)
Ollivier A.M.	(C)	Ollivier F.M.	(C)
Ormiston I.W.	(W)	Ormiston R.W.	(CD, W)
Papps M.H.W.	(C)	Papps T.J.T.	(C)
Parlane M.E.	(ND, W)	Parlane N.R.	(ND, W)
Powell J.L.	(C)	Powell R.F.J.	(C)
Powys A.L.	(C)	Powys R.A.N.	(C)
Puna A.	(ND)	Puna K.N.	(ND)
Reaney H.E.I.	(W)	Reaney T.P.L.	(W, CD)
Richardson C.A.	(W)	Richardson W.A.	(NSW)
Ritchie A.W.	(A)	Ritchie D.C.	(A)
Robertson G.K.	(CD)	Robertson S.P.	(CD)

Rutherford I.A.	(O, CD)	Rutherford K.R.	(O)
Schofer J.W.J.	(W)	Schofer P.J.	(W)
Scott A.H.	(A)	Scott V.J.	(A)
Shaw G.S.	(A, O)	Shaw L.J.	(A)
Snedden A.N.C.	(A)	Snedden Cyril A.	(A)
Snedden Colin A.	(A)	Snedden W.N.	(A)
Sorenson B.J.	(A)	Sorenson R.G.	(A)
Toomey C.D.G.	(O)	Toomey F.J.	(O)
Thomson K.	(C)	Thomson W.A.	(C)
Tucker K.H.	(W)	Tucker S.G.	(W)
Turnbull A.J.	(O)	Turnbull P.J.	(O)
Wallace G.F.	(A)	Wallace W.M.	(A)
Watson E.A.	(O)	Watson L.F.	(O)
Watson H.C.	(O)	Watson L.C.	(O)
Webb M.G.	(O, C)	Webb R.J.	(O)
Weir A.F.	(A)	Weir G.L.	(A)
West G.L.	(CD, ND)	West R.M.	(CD, W)
Westbrook K.R.	(Tasmania)	Westbrook R.A.	(O)
White N.M.	(HB)	White P.C.	(HB)
Williams P.F.C.	(Gloucestershire)	Williams J.N.	(HB)
Wilson A.C.	(C)	Wilson W.C.	(C)
Wyatt I.E.	(A)	Wyatt J.L.	(ND)

Uncle and Nephew

instances not included in previous lists

Bailey J.F.	(ND)	Bailey M.D.	(ND)
Burtt J.W.	(C, CD)	Burtt L.M.	(C)
CarltonW.	(A, C)	Carlton T.A.	(C, O)
Carson W.	(O)	Carson W.N.	(A)
Carson W.N.	(A)	Carson J.R.	(A, ND)
Crawford C.G.	(C)	Playle W.R.	(A)
Cunningham W.H.R.	(C)	Anderson G.F.	(C)
Dacre C.C.R. (A) & Dacre L.M.	(A)	Coleman D.D.	(A)
Fulton J.	(O)	{ Fulton F.	(O, HB)
		Fulton J.C. }	(O)
Fulton R.W.	(C, ND)	Fulton P.G.	(C)
Griffiths B.G.	(W)	Maguiness S.J.	(W)
Pocock M.G.	(ND)	Pocock B.A.	(A, ND)
Roberts B.L.	(ND)	Cairns C.L.	(ND, C)
Westbrook N.R.	(Tasmania)	Westbrook R.A.	(O)
Wilson R.S.	(O)	Paul J.M.	(O)
Wilson T.J.	(O)	Wilson J.W.	(O)

Cousins

Bateman G.C.	(C)	Bateman S.N.	(C)
Hoskin R.N.	(O)	Lamont M.J.	(O)
Hotter S.J.	(W)	Verry R.A.	(W)
Leggat I.B.	(CD)	Leggat J.G.	(C)
Lusk Harold B.	(A, C, W)	{ Lusk Hugh B.	(A, HB)
		Lusk R.B.	(T)
		Lusk W.N.B. }	(A)
McMillan C.D.	(C)	McMillan J.M.	(O)
Pringle M.R.	(A)	Webb P.N.	(A)
Reid B.A.	(WA)	Reid J.F.	(A)
Talbot G.L.	(C)	Talbot R.O.	(C, O)
Vettori D.L.	(ND)	Hill J.V.	(CD)

REDPATH CUP

Presented by Mr David Redpath

Awarded to the New Zealand batsman whose performances in first-class cricket have been, in the opinion of the Board of Control, the most meritorious since the award was last made.

HOLDERS

Season's first-class figures

		Team	In	NO	HS	Runs	Ave
1920/21	Anthony A.	Auckland	5	1	113	251	62.75
1921/22	Hiddleston J.S.	Wellington	8	1	118	396	56.57
1922/23	Blunt R.C.	Canterbury	12	1	174	583	53.00
1923/24	Hiddleston J.S.	Wellington	12	—	163	619	51.58
1924/25	Worker R.V. de R.	Otago	12	2	121*	491	49.10
1925/26	Allcott C.F.W.	Auckland	9 †	2	116	359	51.28
1926/27	Blunt R.C.	Otago	12 §	1	187	758	69.80
1927/28	Dempster C.S.	Wellington	12	1	145	616	56.00
1928/29	Weir G.L.	Auckland	4	2	106*	262	131.00
1929/30	Dempster C.S.	Wellington	10	4	141*	559	93.16
1930/31	Dempster C.S.	Wellington	42 †	6	212	1901	52.80
1931/32	Roberts A.W.	Canterbury	10	1	181	476	52.88
1932/33	Dempster C.S.	Wellington	9	2	83*	336	48.00
1933/34	Vivian H.G.	Auckland	5	—	64	263	52.60
1934/35	Whitelaw P.E.	Auckland	7	—	155	472	67.42
1935/36	Kerr J.L.	Canterbury	13 †	2	146	655	59.54
1936/37	Whitelaw P.E.	Auckland	6	1	195	410	82.00
1937/38	Uttley K.F.M.	Otago	6	—	138	420	70.00
1938/39	Wallace W.M.	Auckland	6	1	105	270	54.00
1939/40	Donnelly M.P.	Canterbury	5	1	104	302	75.50
1940-45	no award						
1945/46	Hadlee W.A.	Otago	7	—	198	449	66.14
1946/47	Sutcliffe B.	Auckland & Otago	8	1	197	722	103.14
1947/48	Sutcliffe B.	Otago	10	1	208*	911	101.22
1948/49	Sutcliffe B.	Auckland	6	—	141	511	85.16
1949/50	Sutcliffe B.	Otago	9	—	355	695	77.55
1950/51	Sutcliffe B.	Otago	12	—	275	798	66.50
1951/52	Scott V.J.	Auckland	10	2	151*	459	57.37
1952/53	Miller L.S.M.	Central Districts	9	3	128*	545	90.83
1953/54	Sutcliffe B.	Otago	34 †	2	196	1691	52.84
1954/55	Reid J.R.	Wellington	15	2	106	505	38.84
1955/56	Reid J.R.	New Zealand	33 †	6	150*	1227	45.44
1956/57	Miller L.S.M.	Wellington	13	3	83	559	55.90
1957/58	Miller L.S.M.	Wellington	14	1	95	549	42.23
1958/59	Pairaudeau B.H.	Northern Districts	11	1	80	456	45.60
1959/60	Reid J.R.	Wellington	16	1	165	724	48.26
1960/61	Harris P.G.Z.	Canterbury	14	2	108	597	49.75
1961/62	Reid J.R.	Wellington	40 †	2	203	2188	57.57
1962/63	Reid J.R.	Wellington	14	1	296	681	52.38
1963/64	Sinclair B.W.	Wellington	15	1	138	641	45.78
1964/65	Pollard V.	Central Districts	43 †	6	85	1081	29.21
1965/66	Sinclair B.W.	Wellington	17	2	114	700	56.66
1966/67	Dowling G.T.	Canterbury	18	2	102*	871	46.66
1967/68	Dowling G.T.	Canterbury	18	1	239	968	56.94
1968/69	Hastings B.F.	Canterbury	15	4	117*	872	79.27
1969/70	Murray B.A.G.	Wellington	51 †	3	157	2079	43.31

		Team	In	NO	HS	Runs	Ave
1970/71	Dowling G.T.	Canterbury	16	1	102	667	44.66
1971/72	Turner G.M.	Otago	27 †	5	259	1708	77.63
1972/73	Congdon B.E.	Otago	38 †	6	126	1728	54.00
1973/74	Turner G.M.	Otago	17 †	2	110*	714	47.60
1974/75	Turner G.M.	Otago	15	1	186*	838	59.85
1975/76	Turner G.M.	Otago	20	4	177*	1244	77.75
1976/77	Burgess M.G.	Auckland	28 †	1	138	1064	39.40
1977/78	Howarth G.P.	Northern Districts	22	1	122	685	32.61
1978/79	Howarth G.P.	Northern Districts	11	1	147*	505	50.50
1979/80	Howarth G.P.	Northern Districts	22	2	151	767	38.35
1980/81	Reid J.F.	Auckland	18	4	173	817	58.35
1981/82	Edgar B.A.	Wellington	19	1	161	934	51.88
1982/83	Edgar B.A.	Wellington	30 †	5	146	1116	44.64
1983/84	Coney J.V.	Wellington	19 †	4	174*	736	49.06
1984/85	Coney J.V.	Wellington	26 †	4	111*	877	39.86
1985/86	Crowe M.D.	Central Districts	31 †	9	242*	1667	75.77
1986/87	Crowe M.D.	Central Districts	22 †	3	175*	1703	89.63
1987/88	Crowe M.D.	Central Districts	16 †	2	144	1064	76.00
1988/89	Jones A.H.	Wellington	25 †	2	181*	1079	46.91
1989/90	Wright J.G.	Auckland	32 †	5	185	1641	60.77
1990/91	Crowe M.D.	Wellington	15 †	3	299	847	70.58
1991/92	Wright J.G.	Auckland	14	0	116	518	37.00
1992/93	Rutherford K.R.	Otago	26 †	3	105	907	39.43
1993/94	Jones A.H.	Wellington	20 †	0	143	934	46.70
1994/95	Parore A.C.	New Zealand	36 †	7	127*	1050	36.20
1995/96	Twose R.G.	New Zealand	10 †	2	119*	452	56.50
1996/97	Fleming S.P.	Canterbury	16 †	1	129	629	41.93
1997/98	Horne M.J.	Otago	22 †	1	241	1114	53.04
1998/99	Horne M.J.	Otago	19	2	132	887	52.17
1999/00	Cairns C.L.	New Zealand	26 †	3	109	903	39.26
2000/01	Richardson M.H.	Otago	45 †	5	306	2672	66.80
2001/02	Astle N.J.	Canterbury	15 †	3	223	899	74.91
2002/03	Richardson M.H.	Auckland	25 †	2	113	885	38.47
2003/04	Styris S.B.	Northern Districts	17 †	1	170	663	41.43
2004/05	Marshall H.J.H.	Northern Districts	16 †	0	160	730	45.62
2005/06	Sinclair M.S.	Central Districts	18 †	2	121	848	53.00
2006/07	Papps M.H.W.	Canterbury	18 †	0	188	1141	63.38
2007/08	Taylor L.R.P.L.	Central Districts	19 †	0	152	717	42.17

† including matches for New Zealand teams overseas

§ these figures include Blunt's scores for Otago and New Zealand against the Melbourne Cricket Club

WINSOR CUP

Presented by Sir Arthur Donnelly to perpetuate the memory of Mr W.H. Winsor

Presented to the New Zealand bowler whose performances in first-class cricket have been, in the opinion of the Board of Control, the most meritorious since the award was last made.

HOLDERS

Season's first-class figures

		Team	*Matches*	*O*	*M*	*R*	*W*	*Ave*
1938/39	Cowie J.	Auckland	4	150	20	444	21	21.14
1939/40	Pritchard T.L.	Wellington	3	113.3	9	404	23	17.56
1940-45	no award							
1945/46	Cowie J.	Auckland	5	209	69	433	24	18.04
1946/47	Cowie J.	Auckland	5	257.4	61	578	26	22.23
1947/48	Burtt T.B.	Canterbury	4	256	57	666	26	25.61
1948/49	Cresswell A.E.	Wellington	4	152	27	343	22	15.59
1949/50	Cresswell G.F.	Wellington	4	235	111	304	20	15.20
1950/51	Burtt T.B.	Canterbury	6	363.2	151	673	44	15.29
1951/52	Burtt T.B.	Canterbury	6	317	120	643	37	17.37
1952/53	Rabone G.O.	Auckland	5	174	44	405	23	17.60
1953/54	MacGibbon A.R.	Canterbury†	17	463.7	98	1271	63	20.17
1954/55	Reid J.R.	Wellington	8	279.1	121	496	30	16.53
1955/56	Cave H.B.	Central Districts*	18	673.4	271	1259	50	25.18
1956/57	Cave H.B.	Central Districts	9	358.3	138	685	41	16.70
1957/58	Hayes J.A.	Auckland	6	244.3	49	568	48	11.83
1958/59	Hough K.W.	Auckland	8	411.3	151	701	46	15.23
1959/60	Alabaster J.C.	Otago	9	313	78	824	47	17.53
1960/61	Alabaster J.C.	Otago	10	426.3	125	964	49	19.61
1961/62	Blair R.W.	Wellington	6	252	96	535	44	12,15
1962/63	Blair R.W.	Wellington	7	244.2	77	562	32	17.56
1963/64	Blair R.W.	Wellington	9	408.1	135	856	49	17.46
1964/65	Motz R.C.	Canterbury*	26	890	272	2179	93	23.43
1965/66	Puna N.	Northern Districts	8	338	126	706	38	18.57
1966/67	Pollard V.	Central Districts	11	345.4	141	672	41	16.39
1967/68	Motz R.C.	Canterbury	10	369.2	115	907	47	19.29
1968/69	Motz R.C.	Canterbury	9	265.2	54	880	40	22.00
1969/70	Howarth H.J.	Auckland*	24	991.4	355	2173	100	21.73
1970/71	Collinge R.O.	Wellington	9	230.6	46	677	37	18.29
1971/72	Taylor B.R.	Wellington*	15	560.5	118	1474	69	21.36
1972/73	Collinge R.O.	Wellington*	23	659.2	149	1806	83	21.75
1973/74	Hadlee D.R.	Canterbury*	13	336.3	35	1451	38	38.18
1974/75	Alabaster G.D.	Otago	6	182.2	26	684	34	20.11
1975/76	Collinge R.O.	Northern Districts	9	215.3	39	623	43	14.48
1976/77	Hadlee R.J.	Canterbury	15	418.2	41	1768	49	36.08
1977/78	Hadlee R.J.	Canterbury	10	266.1	56	860	42	20.47
1978/79	Hadlee R.J.	Canterbury	10	299.1	56	909	50	18.18
1979/80	Hadlee R.J.	New Zealand	3	161.3	50	361	19	19.00
1980/81	Hadlee R.J.	New Zealand*	8	349	89	855	37	23.10
1981/82	Hadlee R.J.	Canterbury	10	424.2	135	868	59	14.74
1982/83	Hadlee R.J.	Canterbury*	12	498	147	1132	59	19.18
1983/84	Hadlee R.J.	Canterbury*	10	310.4	111	587	48	12.22
1984/85	Hadlee R.J.	Canterbury*	12	429.5	119	1061	53	20.01
1985/86	Hadlee R.J.	Canterbury*	11	553.1	129	1314	72	18.25
1986/87	Hadlee R.J.	Canterbury*	12	446.1	116	1047	66	15.86
1987/88	Chatfield E.J.	Wellington*	9	355.1	114	672	24	28.00

		Team	Matches	O	M	R	W	Ave
1988/89	Hadlee R.J.	Canterbury*	7	247.5	59	541	34	15.91
1989/90	Hadlee R.J.	New Zealand*	9	349	71	1014	43	23.58
1990/91	Watson W.	New Zealand	8	333.3	92	807	26	31.03
1991/92	Cairns C.L.	Canterbury	8	294	67	872	42	20.76
1992/93	Morrison D.K.	Auckland	8	263.2	66	598	38	15.73
1993/94	Morrison D.K.	Auckland*	9	327.3	59	1021	28	36.46
1994/95	Morrison D.K.	Auckland*	11	368.5	82	1016	40	25.40
1995/96	Cairns C.L.	New Zealand*	8	232.4	62	631	26	24.26
1996/97	Doull S.B.	New Zealand*	8	255.3	67	715	33	21.66
1997/98	Cairns C.L.	Canterbury*	12	399	113	1124	51	22.03
1998/99	Penn A.J.	Central Districts	9	288	76	763	40	19.07
1999/00	Cairns C.L.	New Zealand*	17	508.5	124	1541	67	23.00
2000/01	Tuffey D.R.	Northern Districts*	12	396.5	118	1104	54	20.44
2001/02	Drum C.J.	Auckland	9	317.3	96	827	53	15.60
2002/03	Bond S.E.	Canterbury*	6	183.5	44	600	30	20.00
2003/04	Martin C.S.	Canterbury	12	448	141	1144	53	21.68
2004/05	Vettori D.L.	Northern Districts*	8	395.5	102	1052	40	26.30
2005/06	Martin C.S.	Auckland*	13	386.3	90	1199	50	23.98
2006/07	Martin C.S.	Auckland*	13	452	94	1424	52	27.38
2007/08	Martin C.S.	Auckland*	9	311.2	74	975	38	25.65

† including 16 matches for New Zealand overseas   ** includes matches for New Zealand teams overseas*

TOURING TEAMS IN NEW ZEALAND

		FIRST-CLASS MATCHES				ALL MATCHES			
		P	W	L	D	P	W	L	D
1863/64	G. Parr's England Team	—	—	—	—	4	3	—	1
1876/77	J. Lillywhite's England Team	—	—	—	—	8	6	—	2
1877/78	Australia	—	—	—	—	7	5	1	1
1880/81	Australia	—	—	—	—	10	6	1	3
1881/82	A. Shaw's England Team	—	—	—	—	7	5	—	2
1883/84	Tasmania	4	—	3	1	7	2	3	2
1886/87	Australia	—	—	—	—	5	2	—	3
1887/88	C.A. Smith's England Team	—	—	—	—	3	—	—	3
1888/89	English Footballers	—	—	—	—	1	—	—	1
1889/90	New South Wales	5	4	—	1	7	6	—	1
1893/94	New South Wales	7	4	1	2	8	4	1	3
1894/95	Fiji	6	2	2	2	8	4	2	2
1895/96	New South Wales	5	3	1	1	5	3	1	1
1896/97	Australia	—	—	—	—	5	3	—	2
1896/97	Queensland	5	3	1	1	8	4	1	3
1899/00	Melbourne Cricket Club	—	—	—	—	7	6	—	1
1902/03	Lord Hawke's England Team	7	7	—	—	18	18	—	—
1904/05	Australia	4	3	—	1	6	4	—	2
1905/06	Melbourne Cricket Club	—	—	—	—	10	8	—	2
1906/07	MCC	11	6	2	3	16	10	2	4
1909/10	Australia	6	5	—	1	9	7	—	2
1913/14	A. Sims' Australian Team	8	6	—	2	16	8	—	8
1920/21	Australia	9	6	—	3	15	12	—	3
1922/23	MCC	8	6	—	2	14	11	—	3
1923/24	New South Wales	6	5	—	1	12	8	—	4
1924/25	Victoria	6	1	1	4	12	4	1	7
1926/27	Melbourne Cricket Club	—	—	—	—	13	5	—	8
1927/28	Australia	6	4	—	2	13	6	—	7
1929/30	MCC	8	2	—	6	17	9	—	8
1930/31	West Indies	—	—	—	—	1	—	—	1
1931/32	South Africa	3	3	—	—	3	3	—	—
1932/33	MCC	3	—	—	3	3	—	—	3
1935/36	MCC	8	2	1	5	18	5	1	12
1936/37	MCC	3	1	—	2	3	1	—	2
1938/39	Sir Julien Cahn's XI	1	—	—	1	10	2	—	8
1945/46	Australia	5	5	—	—	5	5	—	—
1946/47	MCC	4	2	—	2	4	2	—	2
1947/48	Fiji	5	2	3	—	17	6	3	8
1949/50	Australia B	5	3	—	2	14	9	—	5
1950/51	MCC	4	3	—	1	4	3	—	1
1951/52	West Indies	4	2	—	2	5	3	—	2
1952/53	South Africa	4	1	—	3	5	1	—	4
1953/54	Fiji	4	1	3	—	17	8	6	3
1954/55	MCC	4	4	—	—	4	4	—	—
1955/56	West Indies	8	6	1	1	15	11	1	3
1956/57	Australia B	7	5	—	2	12	7	—	5
1958/59	MCC	5	3	—	2	5	3	—	2
1959/60	Australia B	6	2	—	4	9	4	—	5

		FIRST-CLASS MATCHES				ALL MATCHES			
		P	W	L	D	P	W	L	D
1960/61	MCC	10	4	1	5	21	11	1	9
1961/62	Fiji	—	—	—	—	22	9	9	4
1961/62	R.A. Roberts' Commonwealth XI	2	2	—	—	3	2	—	1
1962/63	MCC	4	4	—	—	4	4	—	—
1963/64	South Africa	4	1	—	3	7	1	—	6
1964/65	Pakistan	10	2	—	8	12	4	—	8
1965/66	MCC	4	—	—	4	4	—	—	4
1966/67	Australia B	9	1	2	6	10	2	2	6
1967/68	Fiji	—	—	—	—	25	12	7	6
1967/68	India	6	4	1	1	6	4	1	1
1968/69	West Indies	6	1	2	3	7	1	2	4
1969/70	Australia B	8	2	—	6	8	2	—	6
1970/71	MCC	2	1	—	1	5	3	1	1
1972/73	Pakistan	8	5	1	2	11	6	3	2
1973/74	Australia	7	2	1	4	11	6	1	4
1974/75	MCC	3	1	—	2	5	1	—	4
1975/76	India	6	3	1	2	9	3	4	2
1976/77	Australia	6	5	—	1	8	5	2	1
1977/78	Fiji	—	—	—	—	15	5	4	6
1977/78	England	8	3	1	4†	9	4	1	4†
1978/79	Pakistan	8	5	—	3	10	6	1	3
1979/80	West Indies	5	—	2	3	8	2	3	3
1979/80	D.H. Robins' XI	2	—	—	2	8	5	1	2
1980/81	India	5	1	1	3	7	1	3	3
1981/82	Australia	5	1	1	3	11	4	4	3
1982/83	England	—	—	—	—	3	—	3	—
1982/83	Sri Lanka	4	—	3	1	9	1	7	1
1983/84	England	7	1	1	5	11	4	2	5
1984/85	Pakistan	5	1	2	2	9	1	5	3
1985/86	Australia	5	1	1	3	11	5	3	3
1986/87	West Indies	5	1	1	3	9	5	1	3
1987/88	England	7	2	1	4	12	5	3	4
1988/89	Pakistan	5	1	—	4	12	2	5	5
1989/90	India	6	1	1	4	10	2	4	4
1989/90	Australia	1	—	1	—	6	5	1	—
1990/91	Sri Lanka	7	1	—	6	10	1	3	6
1990/91	England	—	—	—	—	3	1	2	—
1991/92	England	7	4	—	3	11	8	—	3
1991/92	Zimbabwe	—	—	—	—	3	1	2	—
1991/92	Australia	—	—	—	—	1	1	—	—
1991/92	Sri Lanka	—	—	—	—	1	1	—	—
1992/93	Pakistan	1	1	—	—	4	2	2	—
1992/93	Australia	4	2	1	1	10	5	4	1
1993/94	Pakistan	5	2	1	2	11	6	2	3†
1993/94	India	3	—	—	3	7	2	2	3
1994/95	West Indies	3	1	—	2	8	6	—	2
1994/95	Australia	—	—	—	—	4	3	1	—
1994/95	South Africa	2	2	—	—	6	3	2	1†
1994/95	India	—	—	—	—	4	2	2	—
1994/95	Sri Lanka	4	2	—	2	9	4	2	3
1994/95	Australian Academy	1	1	—	—	5	5	—	—

		FIRST-CLASS MATCHES				ALL MATCHES			
		P	W	L	D	P	W	L	D
1995/96	Pakistan	1	1	—	—	5	3	2	—
1995/96	Zimbabwe	4	1	—	3	8	3	2	3
1996/97	England	6	4	1	1	12	6	3	3†
1996/97	Sri Lanka	2	—	2	—	6	2	3	1
1997/98	Bangladesh	4	—	4	—	7	—	6	1
1997/98	Zimbabwe	4	1	3	—	10	3	7	—
1998/99	Pakistan A	5	—	1	4	10	1	4	5
1998/99	India	4	1	2	1	10	3	5	2
1998/99	South Africa	5	1	—	4	13	5	2	6
1999/00	England A	5	3	—	2	10	7	—	3
1999/00	West Indies	4	—	2	2	10	—	8	2
1999/00	Australia	5	4	—	1	11	8	1	2
2000/01	Zimbabwe	2	—	—	2	6	3	1	2
2000/01	Sri Lanka	—	—	—	—	6	4	2	—
2000/01	Pakistan	5	1	2	2	10	3	5	2
2001/02	Bangladesh	3	—	3	—	4	—	3	1
2001/02	England	5	1	1	3	12	4	5	3
2002/03	India	3	—	2	1	11	2	8	1
2003/04	Pakistan	3	1	—	2	9	3	4	2
2003/04	South Africa	4	1	1	2	11	3	6	2
2003/04	Sri Lanka A	4	—	3	1	6	—	5	1
2004/05	Sri Lanka	3	—	1	2	5	—	2	3
2004/05	FICA World XI	—	—	—	—	3	1	2	—
2004/05	Australia	3	2	—	1	9	8	—	1
2005/06	Australia	—	—	—	—	3	2	1	—
2005/06	Sri Lanka	—	—	—	—	4	1	3	—
2005/06	West Indies	3	—	2	1	9	1	7	1
2006/07	Sri Lanka	2	1	1	—	10	4	4	2
2006/07	Australia	—	—	—	—	3	—	3	—
2007/08	Bangladesh	2	—	2	—	9	1	7	1
2007/08	England	4	2	1	1	14	7	4	3†
2008/09	West Indies	3	—	—	3	10	2	3	5
2008/09	India	3	1	—	2	10	4	3	3
2008/09	England Lions	2	—	—	2	7	—	3	4

† includes a tie

NB: From 1900 the basis for the inclusion is any of the following:

a) First-class matches were played.
b) The touring side was its country's official team.
c) The touring side played an official New Zealand team.
d) Matches in the 1992 World Cup are not included, although preliminary games played by Zimbabwe, Australia and Sri Lanka are.

NEW ZEALAND TOURING TEAMS

		FIRST-CLASS MATCHES				ALL MATCHES			
		P	*W*	*L*	*D*	*P*	*W*	*L*	*D*
1898/99	Australia	2	—	2	—	4	1	2	1
1913/14	Australia	4	1	2	1	9	5	2	2
1925/26	Australia	4	—	1	3	9	3	1	5
1927	Great Britain	26	7	5	14	38	12	5	21
	Ceylon	—	—	—	—	1	—	—	1
1927/28	Australia	1	—	1	—	1	—	1	—
1931	Great Britain	32	6	3	23	36	7	3	26
1937	Great Britain	32	9	9	14	38	14	9	15
	Ceylon	—	—	—	—	1	—	—	1
1937/38	Australia	3	—	3	—	3	—	3	—
1949	Great Britain	32	13	1	18	35	14	1	20
	West Germany	—	—	—	—	1	1	—	—
1953/54	South Africa	16	3	4	9	17	3	4	10
	Australia	3	2	—	1	3	2	—	1
1955/56	Pakistan	6	1	3	2	6	1	3	2
	India	10	2	3	5	10	2	3	5
1958	Great Britain	31	7	6	18 †	35	7	6	22
1961/62	South Africa	18	5	2	11	24	7	2	15
	Australia	3	—	2	1	3	—	2	1
1964/65	India	4	—	1	3	4	—	1	3
	Pakistan	3	—	2	1	3	—	2	1
1965	Great Britain	19	3	6	10	21	4	6	11
	Holland	—	—	—	—	1	—	—	1
	Bermuda	—	—	—	—	2	—	—	2
	USA	—	—	—	—	1	1	—	—
1967/68	Australia	4	—	2	2	7	2	2	3
1969	Great Britain	18	4	3	11	22	5	4	13
1969/70	India	5	1	1	3	5	1	1	3
1969/70	Pakistan	4	1	—	3	4	1	—	3
1969/70	Australia	3	—	—	3	8	3	—	5
1970/71	Australia	1	—	—	1	2	—	1	1
1971/72*	Australia	—	—	—	—	2	1	—	1
1971/72	West Indies	13	1	—	12	16	4	—	12
1972/73	Australia	1	—	—	1	3	2	—	1
1973	Great Britain	19	3	2	14	23	4	3	16
1973/74	Australia	9	2	5	2	13	5	6	2
1974/75	Australia	—	—	—	—	3	3	—	—
1975	England *(Prudential Cup)*	—	—	—	—	4	2	2	—
1976/77	Pakistan	6	1	3	2	7	2	3	2
	India	3	—	2	1	3	—	2	1
1978	Great Britain	16	5	4	7	20	5	8	7
1979	Great Britain *(Prudential Cup)*	—	—	—	—	4	2	2	—
1980/81	Australia	7	1	2	4	29	14	9	6
1982/83	Australia	2	—	—	2 †	4	1	1	2 †
1982/83	Australia	—	—	—	—	18	12	6	—
1983	England	13	7	3	3	21	11	6	4
1983/84	Sri Lanka	5	2	—	3	8	4	1	3
1984/85	Sri Lanka	—	—	—	—	2	1	1	—
	Pakistan	5	—	2	3	9	1	5	3
1984/85	Australia *(WCC)*	—	—	—	—	4	1	2	1
1984/85	West Indies	7	—	2	5	12	—	7	5
1985/86	Australia	6	2	1	3	8	2	1	5

		FIRST-CLASS MATCHES				ALL MATCHES			
		P	W	L	D	P	W	L	D
1985/86	Australia	—	—	—	—	11	3	6	2
1985/86	Sri Lanka	—	—	—	—	2	1	1	—
	Sharjah	—	—	—	—	2	—	2	—
	Hong Kong	—	—	—	—	2	2	—	—
1986	England	15	4	—	11	18	5	1	12
	Holland	—	—	—	—	2	1	1	—
1986/87	Sri Lanka	2	—	—	2	2	—	—	2
1987/88	India *(Reliance World Cup)*	—	—	—	—	6	2	4	—
1987/88	Australia	6	1	2	3	19	8	8	3
1987/88	Sharjah	—	—	—	—	4	2	2	—
1988/89	India	6	1	2	3	10	1	6	3
1988/89	Australia	—	—	—	—	1	—	1	—
1989/90	Australia	3	—	—	3	4	—	1	3
1990	Sharjah	—	—	—	—	3	1	2	—
	England	12	4	2	6	19	8	5	6
1990/91	Pakistan	5	—	3	2	8	—	6	2
1990/91	Australia	—	—	—	—	10	3	7	—
1991/92	Australia	—	—	—	—	6	4	2	—
1992/93	Zimbabwe	3	2	—	1	6	5	—	1
	Sri Lanka	2	—	1	1	7	—	5	2
1993/94	Australia	7	2	3	2	16	5	9	2
1994	Sharjah	—	—	—	—	3	1	2	—
	Great Britain	12	1	3	8	21	8	5	8
1994/95	India	—	—	—	—	4	—	3	1
	South Africa	7	2	3	2	16	3	9	4
1995/96	India	6	—	1	5	11	2	4	5
1995/96	India & Pakistan *(Wills World Cup)*	—	—	—	—	6	3	3	—
1995/96	West Indies	4	1	2	1	13	7	5	1
1996/97	Sharjah	—	—	—	—	5	1	3	1†
1996/97	Pakistan	3	1	1	1	6	2	3	1
1996/97	India *(Independence Cup)*	—	—	—	—	3	1	2	—
1997/98	Kenya	—	—	—	—	3	2	—	1
	Zimbabwe	3	—	—	3	7	2	1	4†
1997/98	Australia	6	—	5	1	21	5	13	3†
1997/98	Sharjah	—	—	—	—	4	1	3	—
1997/98	Sri Lanka	5	1	2	2	11	3	4	4
1998	Malaysia *(Commonwealth Games)*	—	—	—	—	5	4	1	—
1998/99	Bangladesh *(Wills International Cup)*	—	—	—	—	2	1	1	—
1999	England	10	5	2	3	26	14	8	4
1999/00	India	6	—	2	4	11	2	5	4
2000/01	Singapore	—	—	—	—	2	—	2	—
2000/01	Zimbabwe	4	2	—	2	8	4	2	2
2000/01	Kenya	—	—	—	—	3	3	—	—
2000/01	South Africa	6	2	2	2	14	4	7	3
2000/01	Sharjah	—	—	—	—	4	1	3	—
2001/02	Sri Lanka	—	—	—	—	7	3	4	—
2001/02	Australia	5	—	1	4	21	6	8	7
2001/02	Sharjah	—	—	—	—	4	1	3	—
2001/02	Pakistan	1	—	1	—	4	—	4	—
2001/02	West Indies	2	1	—	1	8	3	3	2
2002/03	Australia	—	—	—	—	4	4	—	—
2002/03	Sri Lanka *(ICC Champions Trophy)*	—	—	—	—	4	2	2	—
2002/03	South Africa *(World Cup)*	—	—	—	—	11	7	4	—
2002/03	Sri Lanka	2	—	—	2	9	3	2	4

		FIRST-CLASS MATCHES				ALL MATCHES			
		P	W	L	D	P	W	L	D
2003/04	India	4	—	—	4	10	1	4	5
2003/04	Pakistan	—	—	—	—	5	—	5	—
2003/04	England	7	1	4	2	16	7	5	4
2004	England *(ICC Champions Trophy)*	—	—	—	—	2	1	1	—
2004/05	Bangladesh	2	2	—	—	6	5	—	1
2004/05	Australia	3	—	3	—	6	2	4	—
2005/06	{ Namibia	—	—	—	—	2	2	—	—
2005/06	{ Zimbabwe	2	2	—	—	8	7	1	—
2005/06	South Africa	—	—	—	—	8	3	4	1
2005/06	South Africa	4	—	2	2	4	—	2	2
2006/07	India *(ICC Champions Trophy)*	—	—	—	—	6	4	2	—
2006/07	Australia	—	—	—	—	8	2	6	—
2006/07	West Indies *(World Cup)*	—	—	—	—	12	8	4	—
2007/08	South Africa *(Twenty20 World Championship)*	—	—	—	—	6	3	3	—
2007/08	{ South Africa	4	1	3	—	8	2	6	—
2007/08	{ Australia	—	—	—	—	5	—	4	1
2008	England	7	1	2	4	17	4	4	6
2008/09	Bangladesh	2	1	—	1	5	3	1	1
2008/09	Australia	3	—	3	—	3	—	3	—
2008/09	Australia	—	—	—	—	7	2	4	1
2009	Engand *(ICC World Twenty20)*	—	—	—	—	5	2	3	—

NB: 1) All tours refer to those undertaken by official New Zealand sides. Unofficial practice matches have not been included in the totals.

2) The first team from New Zealand to tour overseas was Canterbury who visited Victoria and Tasmania in 1878/79. This was the first tour ever undertaken by a domestic association from any country. (None of the games are ranked as first-class.)

3) Where countries are bracketed it indicates this represented a single tour. Where there is more than one entry for the same season but countries are not bracketed, the tours were not connected.

4) The 1974/75, second 1982/83, 1990/91, 1993/94 and 1997/98 tours to Australia included a return trip after the teams had come back to New Zealand. They are all listed as single tours for the purposes of this article.

5) The 1986/87 tour to Sri Lanka was scheduled for 8 matches. The team returned home after 2 matches due to unrest in Sri Lanka.

Ninety-four official New Zealand sides have toured overseas since the first in February, 1899. The teams were as follows:

1) **1898/99 to Australia**
L.T. Cobcroft *(captain)*, F.L. Ashbolt, J.C. Baker, C. Boxshall, A.D. Downes, A.H. Fisher, F.S. Frankish, Hugh B. Lusk, G. Mills, I. Mills, D. Reese, A. Sims, E.F. Upham.

2) **1913/14 to Australia**
D. Reese *(captain)*, J.H. Bennett, C. Boxshall, T.A. Carlton, L.G. Hemus, R.G. Hickmott, W.R. Patrick, C.W. Robinson, D.M. Sandman, R.C. Somervell, A.N.C. Snedden, L.G. Taylor, B.J. Tuckwell, H.J. Tattersall.

3) **1925/26 to Australia**
W.R. Patrick *(captain)*, C.F.W. Allcott, A.W. Alloo, R.C. Blunt, C.G. Crawford, W.H.R. Cunningham, C.C.R. Dacre, H.D. Gillespie, R.W. Hope, K.C. James, T.C. Lowry, D.J. McBeath, C.J. Oliver, R.V. de R. Worker.

4) **1927 to Great Britain, Ceylon and Australia**
T.C. Lowry *(captain)*, C.F.W. Allcott, E.H.L. Bernau, E.D. Blundell*, R.C. Blunt, W.H.R. Cunningham, C.C.R. Dacre, C.S. Dempster, R.H. Fox*, T.D.B. Hay*, M. Henderson, K.C. James, H.M. McGirr, W.E. Merritt, J.E. Mills, C.J. Oliver, M.L. Page.

5) **1931 to Great Britain**
T.C. Lowry *(captain)*, C.F.W. Allcott, R.C. Blunt, I.B. Cromb, C.S. Dempster, K.C. James, J.L. Kerr, A.M. Matheson, W.E. Merritt, J.E. Mills, M.L. Page, R.O. Talbot, H.G. Vivian, G.L. Weir.

6) **1937 to Great Britain, Ceylon and Australia**
M.L. Page *(captain)*, W.N. Carson, J. Cowie, M.P. Donnelly, J.A. Dunning, N. Gallichan, W.A. Hadlee, J.L. Kerr, J.R. Lamason, T.C. Lowry, D.A.R. Moloney, C.K. Parsloe*, A.W. Roberts, E.W.T. Tindill, H.G. Vivian, W.M. Wallace, G.L. Weir.

7) **1949 to Great Britain and West Germany**
W.A. Hadlee *(captain)*, C. Burke, T.B. Burtt, H.B. Cave, J. Cowie, G.F. Cresswell, M.P. Donnelly, J.A. Hayes, F.L.H. Mooney, G.O. Rabone, J.R. Reid, V.J. Scott, F.B. Smith, B. Sutcliffe, W.M. Wallace.

8) **1953/54 to South Africa and Australia**
G.O. Rabone *(captain)*, J.E.F. Beck, W. Bell, R.W. Blair, M.E. Chapple, E.W. Dempster, J.G. Leggat*, I.B. Leggat, A.R. MacGibbon, L.S.M. Miller, F.L.H. Mooney, G.W.F. Overton, M.B. Poore, J.R. Reid, B. Sutcliffe.

9) **1955/1956 to Pakistan and India**
H.B. Cave *(captain)*, J.C. Alabaster, J.W. Guy, J.A. Hayes, N.S. Harford, P.G.Z. Harris, J.G. Leggat, A.R. MacGibbon, S.N. McGregor, T.G. McMahon, A.M. Moir, E.C. Petrie, M.B. Poore, J.R. Reid, B. Sutcliffe.

10) **1958 to Great Britain**
J.R. Reid *(captain)*, J.C. Alabaster, R.W. Blair, H.B. Cave, J.W. D'Arcy, N.S. Harford, J.A. Hayes, T. Meale, A.R. MacGibbon, L.S.M. Miller, A.M. Moir, E.C. Petrie, W.R. Playle, J.T. Sparling, B. Sutcliffe, J.T. Ward.

11) **1961/62 to South Africa and Australia**
J.R. Reid *(captain)*, J.C. Alabaster, G.A. Bartlett, P.T. Barton, F.J. Cameron, M.E. Chapple, A.E. Dick, G.T. Dowling, J.W. Guy, P.G.Z. Harris, S.N. McGregor, R.C. Motz, J.T. Sparling, J.T. Ward, B.W. Yuile.

12) **1964/65 to India, Pakistan, Great Britain, Holland, Bermuda and USA**
J.R. Reid *(captain)*, F.J. Cameron, R.O. Collinge, B.E. Congdon, A.E. Dick*, G.T. Dowling, T.W. Jarvis, R.C. Motz, R.W. Morgan, V. Pollard, B.W. Sinclair, B. Sutcliffe, B.R. Taylor, G.E. Vivian, J.T. Ward, B.W. Yuile.

13) **1967/68 to Australia**
B.W. Sinclair *(captain)*, J.C. Alabaster, M.G. Burgess, R.O. Collinge, B.E. Congdon, R.I. Harford, T.W. Jarvis, R.C. Motz, B.A.G. Murray, V. Pollard, B.R. Taylor, K. Thomson, B.W. Yuile.

14) **1969 to Great Britain, India and Pakistan**
G.T. Dowling *(captain)*, M.G. Burgess, R.O. Collinge, B.E. Congdon, R.S. Cunis, D.R. Hadlee, B.F. Hastings, H.J. Howarth, B.A.G. Murray, B.D. Milburn, V. Pollard, B.R. Taylor, D.G. Trist*, G.M. Turner, K.J. Wadsworth, B.W. Yuile.

15) **1969/70 to Australia**
G.T. Dowling *(captain)*, M.G. Burgess, R.O. Collinge, B.E. Congdon, R.S. Cunis, D.R. Hadlee, B.F. Hastings, H.J. Howarth, R.W. Morgan*, B.W. Sinclair, G.M. Turner, G.E. Vivian, K.J. Wadsworth.

16) **1970/1971 to Australia**
G.T. Dowling *(captain)*, M.G. Burgess, B.E. Congdon, R.O. Collinge, R.S. Cunis, H.J. Howarth, T.W. Jarvis, R.W. Morgan, B.R. Taylor, G.M. Turner, G.E. Vivian, K.J. Wadsworth.

17) **1971/72 to Australia**
R.W. Morgan *(captain)*, B. Andrews, R.W. Anderson, B. Dunning, B.G. Hadlee, R.J. Hadlee, W.A. Greenstreet, G.A. Newdick, R.E. Redmond, M.L. Ryan, M.J.F. Shrimpton, D.G. Trist.

18) **1971/72 to West Indies**
G.T. Dowling *(captain)*, J.C. Alabaster, M.G. Burgess, K.O. Campbell, M.E. Chapple*, R.O. Collinge, B.E. Congdon, R.S. Cunis, B.F. Hastings, H.J. Howarth, T.W. Jarvis, R.W. Morgan*, B.R. Taylor, G.M. Turner, G.E. Vivian, K.J. Wadsworth, M.G. Webb.

19) **1972/73 to Australia**
B.E. Congdon *(captain)*, B. Andrews, R.S. Cunis, B. Dunning, R.J. Hadlee, B.F. Hastings, A.B. Jordan, D.R. O'Sullivan, R.E. Redmond, G.M. Turner, G.E. Vivian, K.J. Wadsworth.

20) **1973 to Great Britain**
B.E. Congdon *(captain)*, R.W. Anderson, M.G. Burgess, R.O. Collinge, E.K. Gillott, D.R. Hadlee, R.J. Hadlee, B.F. Hastings, H.J. Howarth, J.M. Parker, V. Pollard, R.E. Redmond, B.R. Taylor, G.M. Turner, K.J. Wadsworth.

21) **1973/74 to Australia**
B.E. Congdon *(captain)*, G.D. Alabaster, B. Andrews, K.O. Campbell, B.L. Cairns, J.V. Coney*, D.R. Hadlee, R.J. Hadlee, B.F. Hastings, J.F.M. Morrison, D.R. O'Sullivan, J.M. Parker, M.J.F. Shrimpton, G.M. Turner, K.J. Wadsworth.

22) **1974/75 to Australia**
B.E. Congdon *(captain)*, B.L. Cairns, E.J. Chatfield, R.O. Collinge, G.N. Edwards, D.R. Hadlee, B.F. Hastings, G.P. Howarth, H.J. Howarth, J.F.M. Morrison, J.M. Parker, G.M. Turner, K.J. Wadsworth.

23) **1975 to England** *(World Cup)*
G.M. Turner *(captain)*, B.L. Cairns, R.O. Collinge, B.G. Hadlee, D.R. Hadlee, R.J. Hadlee, B.F. Hastings, G.P. Howarth, H.J. Howarth, B.J. McKechnie, J.F.M. Morrison, D.R. O'Sullivan, J.M. Parker, K.J. Wadsworth.

24) **1976/77 to Pakistan and India**
G.M. Turner *(captain)*, R.W. Anderson, M.G. Burgess, B.L. Cairns, R.O. Collinge, R.J. Hadlee, G.P. Howarth, W.K. Lees, J.F.M. Morrison, D.R. O'Sullivan, J.M. Parker, N.M. Parker, P.J. Petherick, A.D.G. Roberts, G.B. Troup.

25) **1978 to Great Britain**
M.G. Burgess *(captain)*, R.W. Anderson, S.L. Boock, B.P. Bracewell, B.L. Cairns, R.O. Collinge*, B.E. Congdon, B.A. Edgar, G.N. Edwards, D.R. Hadlee, R.J. Hadlee, G.P. Howarth, J.M. McIntyre, J.M. Parker, G.B. Thomson, G.B. Troup*, J.G. Wright.

26) **1979 to England** *(World Cup)*
M.G. Burgess *(captain)*, B.L. Cairns, E.J. Chatfield, J.V. Coney, B.A. Edgar, R.J. Hadlee, G.P. Howarth, W.K. Lees, B.J. McKechnie, J.F.M. Morrison, L.W. Stott, G.B. Troup, G.M. Turner, J.G. Wright.

27) **1980/81 to Australia**
G.P. Howarth *(captain)*, B.P. Bracewell*, J.G. Bracewell, S.L. Boock, M.G. Burgess, B.L. Cairns, E.J. Chatfield, J.V. Coney, B.A. Edgar, R.J. Hadlee, W.K. Lees, P.E. McEwan, B.J. McKechnie*, J.M. Parker, I.D.S. Smith, M.C. Snedden, G.B. Troup, J.G. Wright.

28) **1982/83 to Australia**
G.P. Howarth *(captain)*, B.R. Blair, S.M. Carrington, E.J. Chatfield, J.V. Coney, M.D. Crowe, B.A. Edgar, W.K. Lees, J.F.M. Morrison, J.F. Reid, G.K. Robertson, M.C. Snedden, G.B. Troup.

29) **1982/83 to Australia**
G.P. Howarth *(captain)*, B.L. Cairns, E.J. Chatfield, J.V. Coney, J.J. Crowe, M.D. Crowe*, B.A. Edgar, T.J. Franklin*, R.J. Hadlee, W.K. Lees, J.F.M. Morrison, M.C. Snedden, G.B. Troup, G.M. Turner, P.N. Webb, R.J. Webb*, J.G. Wright.

30) **1983 to England**
G.P. Howarth *(captain)*, J.G. Bracewell, B.L. Cairns, E.J. Chatfield, J.V. Coney, J.J. Crowe, M.D. Crowe, B.A. Edgar, T.J. Franklin, E.J. Gray, R.J. Hadlee, W.K. Lees, I.D.S. Smith, M.C. Snedden, S.R. Tracy*, G.M. Turner, J.G. Wright.

31) **1983/84 to Sri Lanka**
G.P. Howarth *(captain)*, S.L. Boock, J.G. Bracewell, B.L. Cairns, E.J. Chatfield, J.V. Coney, J.J. Crowe, M.D. Crowe, B.A. Edgar, R.J. Hadlee, J.F. Reid, I.D.S. Smith, D.A. Stirling, J.G. Wright.

32) **1984/85 to Pakistan and Sri Lanka**
J.V. Coney *(captain)*, S.L. Boock, J.G. Bracewell, B.L. Cairns, E.J. Chatfield, J.J. Crowe, M.D. Crowe, B.A. Edgar, E.J. Gray, P.E. McEwan, J.F. Reid, I.D.S. Smith, M.C. Snedden, D.A. Stirling, J.G. Wright.

33) **1984/85 to Australia** *(World Championship of Cricket)*
G.P. Howarth *(captain)*, B.P. Bracewell, J.G. Bracewell, B.L. Cairns, E.J. Chatfield, J.V. Coney, J.J. Crowe, M.D. Crowe, R.J. Hadlee, P.E. McEwan, J.F. Reid, I.D.S. Smith, M.C. Snedden, J.G. Wright.

34) **1984/85 to West Indies**
G.P. Howarth *(captain)*, S.L. Boock, J.G. Bracewell, B.L. Cairns, E.J. Chatfield, J.V. Coney, J.J. Crowe, M.D. Crowe, R.J. Hadlee, R.T. Hart, K.R. Rutherford, I.D.S. Smith, D.A. Stirling, G.B. Troup, J.G. Wright.

35) **1985/86 to Australia**
J.V. Coney *(captain)*, S.L. Boock, J.G. Bracewell*, V.R. Brown, B.L. Cairns, E.J. Chatfield, J.J. Crowe, M.D. Crowe, B.A. Edgar, T.J. Franklin, R.J. Hadlee, E.B. McSweeney*, J.F. Reid, I.D.S. Smith, M.C. Snedden, J.G. Wright.

36) **1985/86 to Australia**
J.V. Coney *(captain)*, B.R. Blair, S.L. Boock, J.G. Bracewell, E.J. Chatfield, J.J. Crowe, M.D. Crowe, B.A. Edgar, S.R. Gillespie, R.J. Hadlee, E.B. McSweeney, J.F. Reid, M.C. Snedden, J.G. Wright.

37) **1985/86 to Sri Lanka, Sharjah and Hong Kong**
J.G. Wright *(captain)*, T.E. Blain, B.R. Blair, J.G. Bracewell, E.J. Chatfield, J.J. Crowe, M.D. Crowe, E.J. Gray, E.B. McSweeney, G.K. Robertson, K.R. Rutherford, M.C. Snedden, W. Watson.

38) **1986 to England and Holland**
J.V. Coney *(captain)*, B.J. Barrett, T.E. Blain, J.G. Bracewell, E.J. Chatfield, J.J. Crowe, M.D. Crowe, B.A. Edgar, T.J. Franklin, E.J. Gray, R.J. Hadlee, K.R. Rutherford, I.D.S. Smith, D.A. Stirling, W. Watson, J.G. Wright.

39) **1986/87 to Sri Lanka**
J.J. Crowe *(captain)*, J.G. Bracewell, E.J. Chatfield, M.D. Crowe, E.J. Gray, R.J. Hadlee, P.A. Horne, A.H. Jones, E.B. McSweeney, D.K. Morrison, D.N. Patel, K.R. Rutherford, I.D.S. Smith, M.C. Snedden.

40) **1987/88 to India** *(World Cup)*
J.J. Crowe *(captain)*, S.L. Boock, J.G. Bracewell, E.J. Chatfield, M.D. Crowe, P.A. Horne, A.H. Jones, D.K. Morrison, D.N. Patel, K.R. Rutherford, I.D.S. Smith, M.C. Snedden, W. Watson, J.G. Wright.

41) **1987/88 to Australia**
J.J. Crowe *(captain)*, T.E. Blain*, J.G. Bracewell, V.R. Brown*, E.J. Chatfield, M.D. Crowe, S.R. Gillespie*, E.J. Gray, R.J. Hadlee, P.A. Horne, A.H. Jones, D.K. Morrison, D.N. Patel, K.R. Rutherford, I.D.S. Smith, M.C. Snedden, W. Watson, J.G. Wright.

42) **1987/88 to Sharjah**
J.G. Wright *(captain)*, T.E. Blain, E.J. Chatfield, M.J. Greatbatch, R.J. Hadlee, A.H. Jones, C.M. Kuggeleijn, D.K. Morrison, D.N. Patel, K.R. Rutherford, I.D.S. Smith, R.H. Vance, W. Watson.

43) **1988/89 to India**
J.G. Wright *(captain)*, T.E. Blain, J.G. Bracewell, E.J. Chatfield, T.J. Franklin, E.J. Gray, M.J. Greatbatch, R.J. Hadlee, A.H. Jones, C.M. Kuggeleijn, D.K. Morrison, K.R. Rutherford, I.D.S. Smith, M.C. Snedden, R.H. Vance, W. Watson*.

44) **1988/89 to Australia**
J.G. Wright *(captain)*, E.J. Chatfield, J.J. Crowe, M.D. Crowe, M.J. Greatbatch, A.H. Jones, C.M. Kuggeleijn, D.K. Morrison, I.D.S. Smith, M.C. Snedden, R.H. Vance, W. Watson.

45) **1989/90 to Australia**
J.G. Wright *(captain)*, B.P. Bracewell, J.G. Bracewell, C.L. Cairns*, J.J. Crowe, M.D. Crowe, M.J. Greatbatch, A.H. Jones, D.K. Morrison, D.N. Patel*, G.K. Robertson, I.D.S. Smith, M.C. Snedden, R.H. Vance, W. Watson.

46) **1990 to Sharjah and England**
J.G. Wright *(captain)*, J.G. Bracewell, J.J. Crowe, M.D. Crowe, T.J. Franklin, M.J. Greatbatch, Sir R.J. Hadlee, A.H. Jones, J.P. Millmow, D.K. Morrison, A.C. Parore, M.W. Priest, C. Pringle*, K.R. Rutherford, I.D.S. Smith, M.C. Snedden, S.A. Thomson, W. Watson*.

47) **1990/91 to Pakistan**
M.D. Crowe *(captain)*, G.E. Bradburn, T.J. Franklin, M.J. Greatbatch, P.A. Horne, D.K. Morrison, A.C. Parore, D.N. Patel, M.W. Priest, C. Pringle, S.J. Roberts, K.R. Rutherford, I.D.S. Smith, W. Watson, D.J. White.

48) **1990/91 to Australia**
M.D. Crowe *(captain)*, G.E. Bradburn, M.J. Greatbatch, C.Z. Harris, A.H. Jones, G.R. Larsen*, R.T. Latham, D.K. Morrison, R.G. Petrie, C. Pringle, R.B. Reid*, K.R. Rutherford, I.D.S. Smith, W. Watson, J.G. Wright, B.A. Young.

49) **1991/92 to Australia**
M.D. Crowe *(captain)*, G.E. Bradburn, C.L. Cairns, M.J. Greatbatch, C.Z. Harris, T.J. Franklin, A.H. Jones, D.K. Morrison, D.N. Patel, A.C. Parore, C. Pringle, I.D.S. Smith, S.A. Thomson, W. Watson, K.A. Wealleans.

50) **1992/93 to Zimbabwe and Sri Lanka**
M.D. Crowe *(captain)*, G.E. Bradburn*, S.B. Doull, M.J. Greatbatch, M.J. Haslam, C.Z. Harris, B.R. Hartland, A.H. Jones, G.R. Larsen, R.T. Latham, D.J. Nash, M.B. Owens*, D.N. Patel, A.C. Parore, C. Pringle*, K.R. Rutherford, M.L. Su'a, J.T.C. Vaughan*, W. Watson, J.G. Wright*.

51) **1993/94 to Australia**
M.D. Crowe *(captain)*, T.E. Blain, C.L. Cairns, S.B. Doull, R.P. de Groen*, M.J. Greatbatch, C.Z. Harris*, M.J. Haslam, A.H. Jones, R.T. Latham*, G.R. Larsen*, D.K. Morrison, D.N. Patel, B.A. Pocock, C. Pringle*, K.R. Rutherford, M.L. Su'a, S.A. Thomson*, W. Watson, D.J. White*, B.A. Young.

52) **1994 to Sharjah and England**
K.R. Rutherford *(captain)*, M.D. Crowe, H.T. Davis, M.W. Douglas, S.B. Doull, S.P. Fleming, M.J. Greatbatch, M.N. Hart, B.R. Hartland, C.Z. Harris, G.R. Larsen, D.K. Morrison, D.J. Nash, M.B. Owens*, A.C. Parore, B.A. Pocock, C. Pringle, S.A. Thomson, S.J. Roberts*, B.A. Young. (Harris and Douglas were selected only for Sharjah but Douglas re-appeared as an additional player during the England tour. Larsen captained the team in Sharjah as Rutherford was not available for that part of the tour).

53) **1994/95 to India and South Africa**
K.R. Rutherford *(captain)*, M.D. Crowe, R.P. de Groen, S.B. Doull, S.P. Fleming, L.K. Germon, C.Z. Harris, M.N. Hart, B.R. Hartland, D.K. Morrison*, D.J. Murray, D.J. Nash, A.C. Parore, M.W. Priest*, C. Pringle, M.L. Su'a, S.A. Thomson, B.A. Young.

54) **1995/96 to India**
L.K. Germon *(captain)*, N.J. Astle*, C.L. Cairns, M.D. Crowe, S.B. Doull, S.P. Fleming, A.J. Gale, M.J. Greatbatch, M.N. Hart, M.J. Haslam, G.R. Larsen*, D.K. Morrison, D.J. Nash, A.C. Parore, S.A. Thomson, R.G. Twose, B.A. Young.

55) **1995/96 to India and Pakistan** *(World Cup)*
L.K. Germon *(captain)*, N.J. Astle, C.L. Cairns, S.P. Fleming, C.Z. Harris, R.J. Kennedy, G.R. Larsen, D.K. Morrison, D.J. Nash, A.C. Parore, D.N. Patel, C.M. Spearman, S.A. Thomson, R.G. Twose.

56) **1995/96 to West Indies**
L.K. Germon *(captain)*, N.J. Astle, M.D. Bailey*, C.L. Cairns, S.P. Fleming, C.Z. Harris, M.J. Haslam*, R.J. Kennedy, G.R. Larsen, D.K. Morrison, D.J. Nash, A.C. Parore, D.N. Patel, C.M. Spearman, S.A. Thomson, R.G. Twose, J.T.C. Vaughan*.

57) **1996/97 to Sharjah and Pakistan**
L.K. Germon *(captain)*, N.J. Astle, C.L. Cairns, S.B. Doull, S.P. Fleming, M.J. Greatbatch, C.Z. Harris, M.N. Hart*, M.J. Haslam, G.R. Jonas*, R.J. Kennedy*, G.R. Larsen, D.K. Morrison, A.C. Parore, D.N. Patel, C.M. Spearman, J.T.C. Vaughan, P.J. Wiseman*, B.A. Young.

58) **1996/97 to India** *(Independence Cup)*
S.P. Fleming *(captain)*, N.J. Astle, C.L. Cairns, H.T. Davis, C.Z. Harris, M.J. Horne, G.R. Larsen, C.D. McMillan, S.B. O'Connor, A.C. Parore, D.N. Patel, A.J. Penn, D.L. Vettori, B.A. Young.

59) **1997/98 to Kenya & Zimbabwe**
S.P. Fleming *(captain)*, N.J. Astle, C.L. Cairns, H.T. Davis, C.Z. Harris, M.J. Horne, G.R. Larsen, C.D. McMillan, S.B. O'Connor, A.C. Parore, B.A. Pocock, D.G. Sewell, C.M. Spearman, D.L. Vettori, P.J. Wiseman.

60) **1997/98 to Australia**
S.P. Fleming *(captain)*, G.I. Allott, N.J. Astle, C.L. Cairns, H.T. Davis, S.B. Doull, C.J. Drum*, C.Z. Harris*, M.J. Horne, G.R. Larsen*, C.D. McMillan, D.J. Nash*, S.B. O'Connor, A.C. Parore, B.A. Pocock, C.M. Spearman*, R.G. Twose*, D.L. Vettori, B.A. Young.

61) **1997/98 to Sharjah**
S.P. Fleming *(captain)*, N.J. Astle, C.L. Cairns, S.B. Doull, C.Z. Harris, M.J. Horne, L.G. Howell, C.D. McMillan, D.J. Nash, S.B. O'Connor, A.C. Parore, M.W. Priest, P.J. Wiseman.

62) **1997/98 to Sri Lanka**
S.P. Fleming *(captain)*, N.J. Astle, C.L. Cairns, S.B. Doull, C.Z. Harris, M.J. Horne, C.D. McMillan, D.J. Nash, S.B. O'Connor, A.C. Parore, M.W. Priest, C.M. Spearman, A.R. Tait*, D.L. Vettori, P.J. Wiseman, B.A. Young.

63) **1998 to Malaysia** *(Commonwealth Games)*
S.P. Fleming *(captain)*, G.I. Allott, N.J. Astle, M.D. Bailey, M.D. Bell, C.J. Drum, C.Z. Harris, M.J. Horne, C.D. McMillan, S.B. O'Connor, A.C. Parore, A.R. Tait, D.L. Vettori, P.J. Wiseman.

64) **1998/99 to Bangladesh** *(Wills International Cup)*
S.P. Fleming *(captain)*, G.I. Allott, N.J. Astle, M.D. Bailey, M.D. Bell, S.B. Doull, C.Z. Harris, M.J. Horne, C.D. McMillan, S.B. O'Connor, A.C. Parore, A.R. Tait, D.L. Vettori, P.J. Wiseman.

65) **1999 to England**
S.P. Fleming *(captain)*, G.I. Allott, N.J. Astle, M.D. Bell*, C.E. Bulfin, C.L. Cairns, M.G. Croy*, S.B. Doull, C.Z. Harris, M.N. Hart, M.J. Horne, G.R. Larsen, C.D. McMillan, D.J. Nash, S.B. O'Connor*, A.C. Parore, A.J. Penn*, R.G. Twose, D.L. Vettori, B.G.K. Walker*.

66) **1999/00 to India**
S.P. Fleming *(captain)*, N.J. Astle, M.D. Bell, C.L. Cairns, C.J. Drum, C.Z. Harris, M.J. Horne, C.D. McMillan, D.J. Nash, S.B. O'Connor, A.C. Parore, A.J. Penn, C.M. Spearman, G.R. Stead*, S.B. Styris*, A.R. Tait*, R.G. Twose*, D.L. Vettori, P.J. Wiseman.

67) **2000/01 to Singapore, Zimbabwe, Kenya & South Africa**
S.P. Fleming *(captain)*, G.I. Allott, N.J. Astle, C.L. Cairns, C.Z. Harris, M.J. Horne, C.D. McMillan, H.J.H. Marshall, C.S. Martin, D.J. Nash, C.J. Nevin, S.B. O'Connor, A.C. Parore, A.J. Penn, M.H. Richardson, M.S. Sinclair, C.M. Spearman, S.B. Styris, G.P. Sulzberger, D.R. Tuffey, R.G. Twose, D.L. Vettori, B.G.K. Walker, K.P. Walmsley, P.J. Wiseman. (Apart from a number of players being replaced because of injury, this party was reselected and changed several times depending on the nature of the matches being played).

68) **2000/01 to Sharjah**
C.D. McMillan *(captain)*, A.R. Adams, M.D. Bell, G.E. Bradburn, J.E.C. Franklin, C.Z. Harris, K.D. Mills, C.J. Nevin, J.D.P. Oram, M.S. Sinclair, D.R.Tuffey, L. Vincent, B.G.K. Walker.

69) **2001/02 to Sri Lanka**
S.P. Fleming *(captain)*, N.J. Astle, G.E. Bradburn, J.E.C. Franklin, C.Z. Harris, K.D. Mills, C.D. McMillan, D.J. Nash, J.D.P. Oram, A.C. Parore, M.S. Sinclair, D.R.Tuffey, D.L. Vettori, L. Vincent.

70) **2001/02 to Australia**
S.P. Fleming *(captain)*, A.R. Adams, N.J. Astle, M.D. Bell, S.E. Bond*, C.L. Cairns, C.J. Drum*, J.E.C. Franklin, C.Z. Harris, B.B. McCullum, C.D. McMillan, C.S. Martin, D.J. Nash, S.B. O'Çonnor, A.C. Parore, M.H. Richardson, M.S. Sinclair, S.B. Styris, G.P. Sulzberger, D.R. Tuffey, D.L. Vettori, L. Vincent, P.J. Wiseman*.

71) **2001/02 to Sharjah & Pakistan**
S.P. Fleming *(captain)*, A.R. Adams, N.J. Astle, I.G. Butler, J.E.C. Franklin, C.Z. Harris, R.G. Hart, M.J. Horne, C.D. McMillan, C.S. Martin, C.J. Nevin, J.D.P. Oram, M.H. Richardson, M.S. Sinclair, S.B. Styris, D.R. Tuffey, D.L. Vettori, L. Vincent, B.G.K. Walker.

72) **2001/02 to West Indies**
S.P. Fleming *(captain)*, N.J. Astle, S.E. Bond, I.G. Butler, C.Z. Harris, M.N. Hart, R.G. Hart, P.A. Hitchcock, M.J. Horne, C.D. McMillan, C.S. Martin, C.J. Nevin, J.D.P. Oram, M.H. Richardson, S.B. Styris, D.R. Tuffey, D.L. Vettori, L. Vincent.

73) **2002/03 to Australia & Sri Lanka** *(ICC Champions Trophy)*
S.P. Fleming *(captain)*, N.J. Astle, S.E. Bond, I.G. Butler*, C.Z. Harris, M.N. Hart*, P.A. Hitchcock, M.J. Horne*, C.D. McMillan*, K.D. Mills, C.J. Nevin, J.D.P. Oram, M.S. Sinclair, S.B. Styris, G.P. Sulzberger, D.R. Tuffey, D.L. Vettori, L. Vincent, B.G.K. Walker*, J.A.F. Yovich*.

74) **2002/03 to South Africa** *(World Cup)*
S.P. Fleming *(captain)*, C.L. Cairns, A.R. Adams, N.J. Astle, S.E. Bond, C.Z. Harris, B.B. McCullum, C.D. McMillan, K.D. Mills, J.D.P. Oram, M.S. Sinclair, S.B. Styris, D.R. Tuffey, D.L. Vettori, L. Vincent.

75) **2002/03 to Sri Lanka**
S.P. Fleming *(captain)*, A.R. Adams, S.E. Bond, I.G. Butler, C.L. Cairns, C.Z. Harris, R.G. Hart, M.J. Horne, R.A. Jones, B.B. McCullum, K.D. Mills, C.J. Nevin, J.D.P. Oram, M.H. Richardson, M.S. Sinclair, S.B. Styris, D.R. Tuffey, D.L. Vettori, L. Vincent, P.J. Wiseman.

76) **2003/04 to India**
S.P. Fleming *(captain)*, N.J. Astle, I.G. Butler, C.L. Cairns*, C.Z. Harris*, R.G. Hart, P.A. Hitchcock*, R.A. Jones, B.B. McCullum*. C.D. McMillan, M.J. Mason, K.D. Mills*, C.J. Nevin*, J.D.P. Oram, M.H. Richardson, S.B. Styris, D.R. Tuffey, D.L. Vettori, L. Vincent, P.J. Wiseman.

77) **2003/04 to Pakistan**
C.L. Cairns *(captain)*, D.L. Vettori, T.K. Canning, C.D. Cumming, C.Z. Harris, P.A. Hitchcock, R.A. Jones, B.B. McCullum, H.J.H. Marshall, M.J. Mason, J.D.P. Oram, M.S. Sinclair, D.R. Tuffey, M.D.J. Walker, K.P. Walmsley.

78) **2004 to England**
S.P. Fleming *(captain)*, A.R. Adams*, N.J. Astle, S.E. Bond, I.G. Butler*, C.L. Cairns, J.E.C. Franklin*, C.Z. Harris*, G.J. Hopkins*, B.B. McCullum, C.D. McMillan, H.J.H Marshall*, C.S. Martin, K.D. Mills, J.D.P. Oram, M.H.W Papps, M.H. Richardson, S.B. Styris, D.R. Tuffey, D.L. Vettori.

79) **2004 to England** *(Champions Trophy)*
S.P. Fleming *(captain)*, N.J. Astle, I.G. Butler, C.L. Cairns, C.Z. Harris, B.B. McCullum, C.D. McMillan, H.J.H. Marshall, K.D. Mills, J.D.P Oram, M.H.W. Papps, S.B. Styris, D.R. Tuffey, D.L. Vettori.

80) **2004/05 to Bangladesh**
S.P. Fleming *(captain)*, A.R. Adams*, N.J. Astle, I.G. Butler, C.L. Cairns*, J.E.C. Franklin, P.G.Fulton*, C.Z. Harris*, B.B. McCullum, C.D. McMillan*, H.J.H. Marshall, C.S. Martin, K.D. Mills, J.D.P. Oram, M.H. Richardson, M.S. Sinclair, S.B. Styris, D.L. Vettori, P.J. Wiseman.

81) **2004/05 to Australia**
S.P. Fleming *(captain)*, A.R. Adams*, N.J. Astle, I.G. Butler, C.L. Cairns*, T.K. Canning*, J.E.C. Franklin, C.Z. Harris*, G.J.Hopkins*, B.B. McCullum, C.D. McMillan*, H.J.H. Marshall, C.S. Martin, K.D. Mills, J.D.P.Oram, M.H. Richardson, M.S. Sinclair, S.B. Styris, D.L. Vettori, P.J. Wiseman.

82) **2005/06 to Namibia and Zimbabwe**

S.P. Fleming *(captain)*, A.R. Adams*, N.J. Astle, S.E. Bond, C.L. Cairns*, C.D. Cumming, J.E.C. Franklin, B.B. McCullum, C.D. McMillan*, H.J.H. Marshall, J.A.H. Marshall, C.S. Martin, K.D. Mills, J.D.P. Oram, J.S. Patel*, S.B. Styris, D.L. Vettori, L. Vincent, P.J. Wiseman.

83) **2005/06 to South Africa**

S.P. Fleming *(captain)*, A.R. Adams, N.J. Astle, S.E. Bond, J.E.C. Franklin, H.J.H. Marshall, J.A.H. Marshall, B.B. McCullum, C.D. McMillan, K.D. Mills, J.D.P. Oram, J.S. Patel, S.B. Styris, D.L. Vettori, L. Vincent.

84) **2005/06 to South Africa**

S.P. Fleming *(captain)*, N.J. Astle, S.E. Bond, P.G. Fulton, J.E.C. Franklin, J.M. How, B.B. McCullum, H.J.H Marshall, C.S. Martin, M.J. Mason*, K.D. Mills, J.D.P. Oram, M.H.W. Papps, J.S. Patel, S.B. Styris, D.L. Vettori

85) **2006/07 to India** *(ICC Champions Trophy)*

S.P. Fleming *(captain)*, N.J. Astle, S.E. Bond, J.E.C. Franklin, P.G. Fulton, M.R. Gillespie, B.B. McCullum, H.J.H. Marshall, K.D. Mills, J.D.P. Oram, J.S. Patel, S.B. Styris, L.R.P.L. Taylor*, D.L. Vettori, L. Vincent.

86) **2006/07 to Australia**

S.P. Fleming *(captain)*, A.R. Adams, N.J. Astle, S.E. Bond, J.E.C. Franklin, P.G. Fulton, M.R. Gillespie, B.B. McCullum, C.D. McMillan, H.J.H. Marshall, M.J. Mason, K.D. Mills*, J.D.P. Oram*, J.S. Patel, S.B. Styris*, L.R.P.L. Taylor, D.L. Vettori, L. Vincent*.

87) **2006/07 to West Indies** *(World Cup)*

S.P. Fleming *(captain)*, S.E. Bond, J.E.C. Franklin, P.G. Fulton, M.R. Gillespie, B.B. McCullum, C.D. McMillan, H.J.H. Marshall*, C.S. Martin*, M.J. Mason, J.D.P. Oram, J.S. Patel, S.B. Styris, L.R.P.L. Taylor, D.R. Tuffey, D.L. Vettori, L. Vincent.

88) **2007/08 to South Africa** *(Twenty20 World Championship)*

D.L. Vettori *(captain)*, S.E. Bond, P.G. Fulton, M.R. Gillespie, G.J. Hopkins, C.S. Martin, C.D. McMillan, B.B. McCullum, N.L. McCullum, J.D.P. Oram, J.S. Patel, B.E. Scott, S.B. Styris, L.R.P.L. Taylor, L. Vincent.

89) **2007/08 to South Africa and Australia**

D.L. Vettori *(captain)*, S.E. Bond, C.D.Cumming, S.P. Fleming, M.R. Gillespie, G.J. Hopkins*, J.M. How*, B.B. McCullum, C.S. Martin, M.J. Mason, K.D. Mills*, I.E. O'Brien, J.D.P. Oram, M.H.W. Papps, J.S. Patel, M.S. Sinclair*, S.B. Styris, L.R.P.L. Taylor, L. Vincent.

90) **2008 to England**

D.L. Vettori *(captain)*, G.D. Elliott*, D.R. Flynn, P.G. Fulton, M.R. Gillespie*, G.J. Hopkins, J.M. How, B.B. McCullum, J.A.H. Marshall, C.S. Martin, M.J. Mason, K.D. Mills, I.E. O'Brien, J.D.P. Oram, J.S. Patel, A.J. Redmond, T.G. Southee, S.B. Styris*, L.R.P.L. Taylor.

91) **2008/09 to Bangladesh**

D.L. Vettori *(captain)*, G.D. Elliott, D.R. Flynn, M.R. Gillespie, G.J. Hopkins, J.M. How, M.J. Mason, B.B. McCullum, K.D. Mills, I.E. O'Brien*, J.D.P. Oram, J.S. Patel, A.J. Redmond*, J.D. Ryder, T.G. Southee, S.B. Styris, L.R.P.L. Taylor.

92) **2008/09 to Australia**

D.L. Vettori *(captain)*, G.D. Elliott, D.R. Flynn, P.G. Fulton, M.R. Gillespie, G.J. Hopkins, J.M. How, B.B. McCullum, C.S. Martin, K.D. Mills, I.E. O'Brien, J.S. Patel*, A.J. Redmond, J.D. Ryder, T.G. Southee, L.R.P.L. Taylor.

93) **2008/09 to Australia**

D.L. Vettori *(captain)*, T.A. Boult, N.T. Broom, I.G. Butler*, C.D. Cumming, B.J. Diamanti, G.D. Elliott, J.E.C. Franklin*, P.G. Fulton, M.J. Guptill, G.J. Hopkins*, B.B. McCullum, N.L. McCullum*, P.D. McGlashan*, K.D. Mills, I.E. O'Brien, J.S. Patel, T.G. Southee, L.R.P.L. Taylor.

94) **2009 to England** *(ICC World Twenty20)*

D.L. Vettori *(captain)*, B.B. McCullum, N.T. Broom, I.G. Butler, B.J. Diamanti, J.E.C. Franklin, M.J. Guptill, N.L. McCullum, P.D. McGlashan, K.D. Mills, I.E. O'Brien, J.D.P. Oram, A.J. Redmond*, J.D. Ryder, S.B. Styris, L.R.P.L. Taylor.

** replacement or temporary addition to the touring party*

NEW ZEALAND TEST RECORDS

REGISTER OF PLAYERS

	Born	*Died*	*Type*		*Test Career*
Adams Andre Ryan	17/7/1975 Auckland		RHB	RFM	2001/02
Alabaster John Chaloner	11/7/1930 Invercargill		RHB	RLB	1955/56-1971/72
Allcott Cyril Francis Walter	7/10/1896 Lower Moutere	19/11/1973 Auckland	LHB	LM	1929/30-1931/32
Allott Geoffrey Ian	24/12/1971 Christchurch		RHB	LFM	1995/96-1999
Anderson Robert Wickham	2/10/1948 Christchurch		RHB	RLB	1976/77-1978
Anderson William McDougall	8/10/1919 Westport	21/12/1979 Christchurch	LHB	RLBG	1945/46
Andrews Bryan	4/4/1945 Christchurch		RHB	RFM	1973/74
Astle Nathan John	15/9/1971 Christchurch		RHB	RM	1995/96-2006/07
Badcock Frederick Theodore	9/8/1897 Abbottabad, India	19/9/1982 Perth	RHB	RM	1929/30-1932/33
Barber Richard Trevor	3/6/1925 Otaki		RHB	WK	1955/56
Bartlett Gary Alex	3/2/1941 Blenheim		RHB	RF	1961/62-1967/68
Barton Paul Thomas	9/10/1935 Wellington		RHB	SLA	1961/62-1962/63
Beard Donald Derek	14/1/1920 Palmerston North	15/7/1982 Lancaster	RHB	RM	1951/52-1955/56
Beck John Edward Francis	1/8/1934 Wellington	23/4/2000 Waikanae	LHB		1953/54-1955/56
Bell Matthew David	25/2/1977 Dunedin		RHB		1998/99-2007/08
Bell William	5/9/1931 Dunedin	23/7/2002 Auckland	RHB	RLB	1953/54
Bilby Grahame Paul	7/5/1941 Wellington		RHB		1965/66
Blain Tony Elston	17/2/1962 Nelson		RHB	WK	1986-1993/94
Blair Robert William	23/6/1932 Petone		RHB	RFM	1952/53-1963/64
Blunt Roger Charles	3/11/1900 Durham, England	22/6/1966 London	RHB	RLBG	1929/30-1931/32
Bolton Bruce Alfred	31/5/1935 Christchurch		RHB	RLB	1958/59
Bond Shane Edward	7/6/1975 Christchurch		RHB	RF	2001/02-2007/08
Boock Stephen Lewis	20/9/1951 Dunedin		RHB	SLA	1977/78-1988/89
Bracewell Brendon Paul	14/9/1959 Auckland		RHB	RFM	1978-1984/85
Bracewell John Garry	15/4/1958 Auckland		RHB	ROB	1980/81-1990
Bradburn Grant Eric	26/5/1966 Hamilton		RHB	ROB	1990/91-2000/01
Bradburn Wynne Pennell	24/11/1938 Thames	25/9/2008 Hamilton	RHB	RSM	1963/64
Brown Vaughan Raymond	3/11/1959 Christchurch		LHB	ROB	1985/86
Burgess Mark Gordon	17/7/1944 Auckland		RHB	ROB	1967/68-1980/81

	Born	Died	Type		Test Career
Burke	22/3/1914	4/8/1997	RHB	RLB	1945/46
Cecil	Auckland	Auckland			
Burtt	22/1/1915	24/5/1988	RHB	SLA	1946/47-1952/53
Thomas Browning	Christchurch	Christchurch			
Butler	24/11/1981		RHB	RF	2001/02-2004/05
Ian Gareth	Auckland				
Butterfield	29/8/1913	5/7/1999	RHB	RM	1945/46
Leonard Arthur	Christchurch	Christchurch			
Cairns	10/10/1949		RHB	RM	1973/74-1985/86
Bernard Lance	Picton				
Cairns	13/6/1970		RHB	RFM	1989/90-2004
Christopher Lance	Picton				
Cameron	1/6/1932		RHB	RFM	1961/62-1965
Francis James	Dunedin				
Cave	10/10/1922	15/9/1989	RHB	RM	1949-1958
Henry Butler	Wanganui	Wanganui			
Chapple	25/7/1930	31/7/1985	RHB	SLA	1952/53-1965/66
Murray Ernest	Christchurch	Hamilton			
Chatfield	3/7/1950		RHB	RM	1974/75-1988/89
Ewen John	Dannevirke				
Cleverley	23/12/1909	16/2/2004	LHB	RFM	1931/32-1945/46
Donald Charles	Oamaru	Southport, Aust.			
Collinge	2/4/1946		RHB	LFM	1964/65-1978
Richard Owen	Wellington				
Colquhoun	8/6/1924	26/2/2005	RHB	WK	1954/55
Ian Alexander	Wellington	Paraparaumu Beach			
Coney	21/6/1952		RHB	RSM	1973/74-1986/87
Jeremy Vernon	Wellington				
Congdon	11/2/1938		RHB	RM	1964/65-1978
Bevan Ernest	Motueka				
Cowie	30/3/1912	3/6/1994	RHB	RFM	1937-1949
John	Auckland	Lower Hutt			
Cresswell	22/3/1915	10/1/1966	LHB	RM	1949-1950/51
George Fenwick	Wanganui	Blenheim			
Cromb	25/6/1905	6/3/1984	RHB	RM	1931-1931/32
Ian Burns	Christchurch	Christchurch			
Crowe	14/9/1958		RHB		1982/83-1989/90
Jeffrey John	Auckland				
Crowe	22/9/1962		RHB	RM	1981/82-1995/96
Martin David	Auckland				
Cumming	31/8/1975		RHB	RM	2004/05-2007/08
Craig Derek	Timaru				
Cunis	5/1/1941	9/8/2008	RHB	RFM	1963/64-1971/72
Robert Smith	Whangarei	Whangarei			
D'Arcy	23/4/1936		RHB		1958
John William	Christchurch				
de Groen	5/8/1962		RHB	RM	1993/94-1994/95
Richard Paul	Otorohanga				
Davis	30/11/1971		RHB	RF	1994-1997/98
Heath Te-Ihi-O-Te-Rangi	Lower Hutt				
Dempster	15/11/1903	12/2/1974	RHB		1929/30-1932/33
Charles Stewart	Wellington	Wellington			
Dempster	25/1/1925		LHB	SLA	1952/53-1953/54
Eric William	Wellington				
Dick	10/10/1936		RHB	WK	1961/62-1965
Arthur Edward	Middlemarch				
Dickinson	11/3/1903	17/3/1978	RHB	RF	1929/30-1931/32
George Ritchie	Dunedin	Lower Hutt			
Donnelly	17/10/1917	22/10/1999	LHB	SLA	1937-1949
Martin Paterson	Ngaruawahia	Sydney			
Doull	6/8/1969		RHB	RM	1992/93-1999/00
Simon Blair	Pukekohe				
Dowling	4/3/1937		RHB		1961/62-1971/72
Graham Thorne	Christchurch				
Drum	10/7/1974		RHB	RFM	2000/01-2001/02
Christopher James	Auckland				

	Born	Died	Type		Test Career
Dunning John Angus	6/2/1903 Omaha	24/6/1971 Adelaide	RHB	RM	1932/33-1937
Edgar Bruce Adrian	23/11/1956 Wellington		LHB	WK	1978-1986
Edwards Graham Neil	27/5/1955 Nelson		RHB	WK	1976/77-1980/81
Elliott Grant David	21/3/1979 Johanesburg, S. Africa		RHB	RM	2007/08-2008/09
Emery Raymond William George	28/3/1915 Auckland	18/12/1982 Auckland	RHB	RM	1951/52
Fisher Frederick Eric	28/7/1924 Johnsonville	19/6/1996 Palmerston North	RHB	LM	1952/53
Fleming Stephen Paul	1/4/1973 Christchurch		LHB		1993/94-2007/08
Flynn Daniel Raymond	16/4/1985 Rotorua		LHB	SLA	2008
Foley Henry	28/1/1906 Wellington	16/10/1948 Brisbane	LHB		1929/30
Franklin James Edward Charles	7/11/1980 Wellington		LHB	LFM	2000/01-2008/09
Franklin Trevor John	18/3/1962 Auckland		RHB	RM	1983-1990/91
Freeman Douglas Linford	8/9/1914 Sydney	31/5/1994 Sydney	RHB	RLBG	1932/33
Fulton Peter Gordon	1/2/1979 Christchurch		RHB	RM	2005/06-2008/09
Gallichan Norman	3/6/1906 Palmerston North	25/3/1969 Taupo	RHB	SLA	1937
Gedye Sidney Graham	2/5/1929 Otahuhu		RHB		1963/64-1964/65
Germon Lee Kenneth	4/11/1968 Christchurch		RHB	WK	1995/96-1996/97
Gillespie Mark Raymond	17/10/1979 Wanganui		RHB	RFM	2007/08-2008/09
Gillespie Stuart Ross	2/3/1957 Wanganui		RHB	RFM	1985/86
Gray Evan John	18/11/1954 Wellington		RHB	SLA	1983-1988/89
Greatbatch Mark John	11/12/1963 Auckland		LHB		1987/88-1996/97
Guillen Simpson Clairmonte	24/9/1924 Port of Spain, Trinidad		RHB	WK	1955/56
Guptill Martin James	30/9/1986 Auckland		RHB	ROB	2008/09
Guy John William	29/8/1934 Nelson		LHB		1955/56-1961/62
Hadlee Dayle Robert	6/1/1948 Christchurch		RHB	RM	1969-1977/78
Hadlee Richard John	3/7/1951 Christchurch		LHB	RFM	1972/73-1990
Hadlee Walter Arnold	4/6/1915 Lincoln	29/9/2006 Christchurch	RHB		1937-1950/51
Harford Noel Sherwin	30/8/1930 Winton	30/3/1981 Auckland	RHB	RM	1955/56-1958
Harford Roy Ivan	30/5/1936 London, England		LHB	WK	1967/68
Harris Chris Zinzan	20/11/1969 Christchurch		LHB	RM	1992/93-2001/02
Harris Parke Gerald Zinzan	18/7/1927 Christchurch	1/12/1991 Christchurch	RHB	ROB	1955/56-1964/65
Harris Roger Meredith	27/7/1933 Otahuhu		RHB	RM	1958/59
Hart Matthew Norman	16/5/1972 Hamilton		LHB	SLA	1993/94-1995/96
Hart Robert Garry	2/12/1974 Hamilton		RHB	WK	2001/02-2003/04

	Born	*Died*	*Type*			*Test Career*
Hartland Blair Robert	22/10/1966 Christchurch		RHB			1991/92-1994
Haslam Mark James	26/9/1972 Bury, England		LHB	SLA		1992/93-1995/96
Hastings Brian Frederick	23/3/1940 Wellington		RHB			1968/69-1975/76
Hayes John Arthur	11/1/1927 Auckland	25/12/2007 Auckland	RHB	RF		1950/51-1958
Henderson Matthew	2/8/1895 Auckland	17/6/1970 Wellington	LHB	LFM		1929/30
Hopkins Gareth James	24/11/1976 Lower Hutt		RHB	WK		2008
Horne Matthew Jeffery	5/12/1970 Auckland		RHB	RM		1996/97-2002/03
Horne Philip Andrew	21/1/1960 Upper Hutt		LHB			1986/87-1990/91
Hough Kenneth William	24/10/1928 Sydney		RHB	RM		1958/59
How Jamie Michael	19/5/1981 New Plymouth		RHB	ROB		2005/06-2008/09
Howarth Geoffrey Philip	29/3/1951 Auckland		RHB	ROB		1974/75-1984/85
Howarth Hedley John	25/12/1943 Auckland	7/11/2008 Auckland	LHB	SLA		1969-1976/77
James Kenneth Cecil	12/3/1904 Wellington	21/8/1976 Palmerston North	RHB	WK		1929/30-1932/33
Jarvis Terrence Wayne	29/7/1944 Auckland		RHB			1964/65-1972/73
Jones Andrew Howard	9/5/1959 Wellington		RHB	ROB		1986/87-1994/95
Jones Richard Andrew	22/10/1973 Auckland		RHB			2003/04
Kennedy Robert John	3/6/1972 Dunedin		RHB	RFM		1995/96
Kerr John Lambert	28/12/1910 Dannevirke	27/5/2007 Christchurch	RHB			1931-1937
Kuggeleijn Christopher Mary	10/5/1956 Auckland		RHB	ROB		1988/89
Larsen Gavin Rolf	27/9/1962 Wellington		RHB	RM		1994-1995/96
Latham Rodney Terry	12/6/1961 Christchurch		RHB			1991/92-1992/93
Lees Warren Kenneth	19/3/1952 Dunedin		RHB	WK		1976/77-1983
Leggat Ian Bruce	7/6/1930 Invercargill		RHB	RM		1953/54
Leggat John Gordon	27/5/1926 Wellington	9/3/1973 Christchurch	RHB			1951/52-1955/56
Lissette Allen Fisher	6/11/1919 Morrinsville	24/1/1973 Hamilton	RHB	SLA		1955/56
Loveridge Greg Riaka	15/1/1975 Palmerston North		RHB	RLB		1995/96
Lowry Thomas Coleman	17/2/1898 Fernhill	20/7/1976 Hastings	RHB	ROB	WK	1929/30-1931
McCullum Brendon Barrie	27/9/1981 Dunedin		RHB		WK	2003/04-2008/09
McEwan Paul Ernest	19/12/1953 Christchurch		RHB	RM		1979/80-1984/85
MacGibbon Anthony Roy	28/8/1924 Christchurch		RHB	RFM		1950/51-1958
McGirr Herbert Mendelson	5/11/1891 Wellington	14/4/1964 Nelson	RHB	RFM		1929/30
McGregor Spencer Noel	18/12/1931 Dunedin	21/11/2007 Christchurch	RHB			1954/55-1964/65
McIntosh Timothy Gavin	4/12/1979 Auckland		LHB			2008/09

	Born	Died	Type		Test Career
McLeod Edwin George	14/10/1900 Auckland	14/9/1989 Wellington	LHB	RLB	1929/30
McMahon Trevor George	8/11/1929 Wellington		RHB	WK	1955/56
McMillan Craig Douglas	13/9/1976 Christchurch		RHB	RM	1997/98-2004/05
McRae Donald Alexander Noel	25/12/1912 Christchurch	10/8/1986 Christchurch	LHB	LM	1945/46
Marshall Hamish John Hamilton	15/2/1979 Warkworth		RHB	RM	2000/01-2005/06
Marshall James Andrew Hamilton	15/2/1979 Warkworth		RHB	RM	2004/05-2008
Martin Christopher Stewart	10/12/1974 Christchurch		RHB	RFM	2000/01-2008/09
Mason Michael James	27/8/1974 Carterton		RHB	RFM	2003/04
Matheson Alexander Malcolm	27/2/1906 Omaha	31/12/1985 Auckland	RHB	RFM	1929/30-1931
Meale Trevor	11/11/1928 Auckland		LHB		1958
Merritt William Edward	18/8/1908 Sumner	9/6/1977 Christchurch	RHB	RLBG	1929/30-1931
Meuli Edgar Milton	20/2/1926 Hawera	15/4/2007 Auckland	RHB	RLB	1952/53
Milburn Barry Douglas	24/11/1943 Dunedin		RHB	WK	1968/69
Miller Lawrence Somerville Martin	31/3/1923 New Plymouth	17/12/1996 Kapiti	LHB	LSM	1952/53-1958
Mills John Ernest	3/9/1905 Dunedin	11/12/1972 Hamilton	LHB		1929/30-1932/33
Mills Kyle David	15/3/1979 Auckland		RHB	RFM	2004-2008/09
Moir Alexander McKenzie	17/7/1919 Dunedin	17/6/2000 Dunedin	RHB	RLB	1950/51-1958/59
Moloney Denis Andrew Robert	11/8/1910 Dunedin	15/7/1942 El Alamein	RHB	RLB	1937
Mooney Francis Leonard Hugh	26/5/1921 Wellington	8/3/2004 Wellington	RHB	WK	1949-1953/54
Morgan Ross Winston	12/2/1941 Auckland		RHB	ROB	1964/65-1971/72
Morrison Bruce Donald	17/12/1933 Lower Hutt		LHB	RM	1962/63
Morrison Daniel Kyle	3/2/1966 Auckland		RHB	RFM	1987/88-1996/97
Morrison John Francis MacLean	27/8/1947 Wellington		RHB	SLA	1973/74-1981/82
Motz Richard Charles	12/1/1940 Christchurch	29/4/2007 Christchurch	RHB	RFM	1961/62-1969
Murray Bruce Alexander Grenfell	18/9/1940 Wellington		RHB	RLB	1967/68-1970/71
Murray Darrin James	4/9/1967 Christchurch		RHB		1994/95
Nash Dion Joseph	20/11/1971 Auckland		RHB	RFM	1992/93-2001/02
Newman Jack	3/7/1902 Brightwater	23/9/1996 Nelson	RHB	LM	1931/32-1932/33
O'Brien Iain Edward	10/7/1976 Lower Hutt		RHB	RM	2004/05-2008/09
O'Connor Shayne Barry	15/11/1973 Hastings		LHB	LFM	1997/98-2001/02
Oram Jacob David Philip	28/7/1978 Palmerston North		LHB	RM	2002/03-2008/09
O'Sullivan David Robert	16/11/1944 Palmerston North		RHB	SLA	1972/73-1976/77

	Born	*Died*	*Type*			*Test Career*
Overton Guy William Fitzroy	8/6/1919 Dunedin	7/9/1993 Winton	LHB	RFM		1953/54
Owens Michael Barry	11/11/1969 Christchurch		RHB	RFM		1992/93-1994
Page Milford Laurenson	8/5/1902 Lyttelton	13/2/1987 Christchurch	RHB	ROB		1929/30-1937
Papps Michael Hugh William	2/7/1979 Christchurch		RHB			2003/04-2007/08
Parker John Morton	21/2/1951 Dannevirke		RHB	WK		1972/73-1980/81
Parker Norman Murray	28/8/1948 Dannevirke		RHB	RLB		1976/77
Parore Adam Craig	23/1/1971 Auckland		RHB	WK		1990-2001/02
Patel Dipak Narshibhai	25/10/1958 Nairobi, Kenya		RHB	ROB		1986/87-1996/97
Patel Jeetan Shashi	7/5/1980 Wellington		RHB	ROB		2005/06-2008/09
Petherick Peter James	25/9/1942 Ranfurly		RHB	ROB		1976/77
Petrie Eric Charlton	22/5/1927 Ngaruawahia	14/8/2004 Omokoroa	RHB	WK		1955/56-1965/66
Playle William Rodger	1/12/1938 Palmerston North		RHB			1958-1962/63
Pocock Blair Andrew	18/6/1971 Papakura		RHB			1993/94-1997/98
Pollard Victor	7/9/1945 Burnley, England		RHB	ROB		1964/65-1973
Poore Matt Beresford	1/6/1930 Christchurch		RHB	ROB		1952/53-1955/56
Priest Mark Wellings	12/8/1961 Greymouth		LHB	SLA		1990-1997/98
Pringle Christopher	26/1/1968 Auckland		RHB	RFM		1990/91-1994/95
Puna Narotam	28/10/1929 Surat, India	7/6/1996 Hamilton	RHB	ROB		1965/66
Rabone Geoffrey Osborne	6/11/1921 Gore	19/1/2006 Auckland	RHB	ROB		1949-1954/55
Redmond Aaron James	23/9/1979 Auckland		RHB	RLB		2008-2008/09
Redmond Rodney Ernest	29/12/1944 Whangarei		LHB	SLA		1972/73
Reid John Fulton	3/3/1956 Auckland		LHB	RLB	WK	1978/79-1985/86
Reid John Richard	3/6/1928 Auckland		RHB	RFM	WK	1949-1965
Richardson Mark Hunter	11/6/1971 Hastings		LHB	SLA		2000/01-2004/05
Roberts Andrew Duncan Glenn	6/5/1947 Te Aroha	26/10/1989 Wellington	RHB	RM		1975/76-1976/77
Roberts Albert William	20/8/1909 Christchurch	13/5/1978 Christchurch	RHB	RM		1929/30-1937
Robertson Gary Keith	15/7/1960 New Plymouth		RHB	RFM		1985/86
Rowe Charles Gordon	30/6/1915 Glasgow, Scotland	9/6/1995 Palmerston North	RHB			1945/46
Rutherford Kenneth Robert	26/10/1965 Dunedin		RHB	RM		1984/85-1994/95
Ryder Jesse Daniel	6/8/1984 Masterton		LHB	RM		2008/09
Scott Roy Hamilton	6/3/1917 Clyde	5/8/2005 Christchurch	RHB	RM		1946/47
Scott Verdun John	31/7/1916 Devonport	2/8/1980 Devonport	RHB	RM		1945/46-1951/52
Sewell David Graham	20/10/1977 Christchurch		RHB	LFM		1997/98

	Born	Died	Type		Test Career
Shrimpton Michael John Froud	23/6/1940 Feilding		RHB	RLBG	1962/63-1973/74
Sinclair Barry Whitley	23/10/1936 Wellington		RHB		1962/63-1967/68
Sinclair Ian McKay	1/6/1933 Rangiora		LHB	ROB	1955/56
Sinclair Mathew Stuart	9/11/1975 Katherine, Australia		RHB		1999/00-2007/08
Smith Frank Brunton	13/3/1922 Rangiora	6/7/1997 Christchurch		RHB	1946/47-1951/52
Smith Horace Dennis	8/1/1913 Toowoomba, Aust	25/1/1986 Christchurch	RHB	RFM	1932/33
Smith Ian David Stockley	28/2/1957 Nelson		RHB	WK	1980/81-1991/92
Snedden Colin Alexander	7/1/1918 Auckland		RHB	ROB	1946/47
Snedden Martin Colin	23/11/1958 Auckland		LHB	RFM	1980/81-1990
Southee Timothy Grant	11/12/1988 Whangarei		RHB	RFM	2007/08-2008/09
Sparling John Trevor	24/7/1938 Auckland		RHB	ROB	1958-1963/64
Spearman Craig Murray	4/7/1972 Auckland		RHB		1995/96-2000/01
Stead Gary Raymond	9/1/1972 Christchurch		RHB	RLB	1998/99-1999/00
Stirling Derek Alexander	5/10/1961 Upper Hutt		RHB	RFM	1984/85-1986
Styris Scott Bernard	10/7/1975 Brisbane, Aust		RHB	RM	2001/02-2007/08
Su'a Murphy Logo	7/11/1966 Wanganui		LHB	LFM	1991/92-1994/95
Sutcliffe Bert	17/11/1923 Auckland	20/4/2001 Auckland	LHB	SLA	1946/47-1965
Taylor Bruce Richard	12/7/1943 Timaru		LHB	RFM	1964/65-1973
Taylor Donald Dougald	2/3/1923 Auckland	5/12/1980 Auckland	RHB	RLBG	1946/47-1955/56
Taylor Luteru Ross Poutoa Lote	8/3/1984 Lower Hutt		RHB	ROB	2007/08-2008/09
Thomson Keith	26/2/1941 Methven		RHB		1967/68
Thomson Shane Alexander	27/1/1969 Hamilton		RHB	ROB	1989/90-1995/96
Tindill Eric William Thomas	18/12/1910 Nelson		LHB	WK	1937-1946/47
Troup Gary Bertram	3/10/1952 Taumarunui		RHB	LFM	1976/77-1985/86
Truscott Peter Bennetts	14/8/1941 Pahiatua		RHB		1964/65
Tuffey Daryl Raymond	11/6/1978 Milton		RHB	RFM	1999/00-2004
Turner Glenn Maitland	26/5/1947 Dunedin		RHB		1968/69-1982/83
Twose Roger Graham	17/4/1968 Torquay, England		LHB	RM	1995/96-1999
Vance Robert Howard	31/3/1955 Wellington		RHB		1987/88-1989/90
Vaughan Justin Thomas Caldwell	30//8/1967 Hereford, England		LHB	RM	1992/93-1996/97
Vettori Daniel Luca	27/1/1979 Auckland		LHB	SLA	1996/97-2008/09
Vincent Lou	11/11/1978 Warkworth		RHB	WK	2001/02-2007/08

	Born	Died	Type		Test Career
Vivian Graham Ellery	28/2/1946 Auckland		LHB	RLB	1964/65-1971/72
Vivian Henry Gifford	4/11/1912 Auckland	12/8/1983 Auckland	LHB	SLA	1931-1937
Wadsworth Kenneth John	30/11/1946 Nelson	19/8/1976 Nelson	RHB	WK	1969-1975/76
Walker Brooke Graeme Keith	25/3/1977 Auckland		RHB	RLB	2000/01-2001/02
Wallace Walter Mervyn	19/12/1916 Auckland	21/3/2008 Auckland	RHB		1937-1952/53
Walmsley Kerry Peter	23/8/1973 Dunedin		RHB	RFM	1994/95-2000/01
Ward John Thomas	11/3/1937 Timaru		RHB	WK	1963/64-1967/68
Watson William	31/8/1965 Auckland		RHB	RFM	1986-1993/94
Watt Leslie	17/9/1924 Waitati	15/11/1996 Dunedin	RHB		1954/55
Webb Murray George	22/6/1947 Invercargill		RHB	RFM	1970/71-1973/74
Webb Peter Neil	14/7/1957 Auckland		RHB	WK	1979/80
Weir Gordon Lindsay	2/6/1908 Auckland	31/10/2003 Auckland	RHB	RM	1929/30-1937
White David John	26/6/1961 Gisborne		RHB	ROB	1990/91
Whitelaw Paul Erskine	10/2/1910 Auckland	28/8/1988 Auckland	RHB		1932/33
Wiseman Paul John	4/5/1970 Auckland		RHB	ROB	1997/98-2004/05
Wright John Geoffrey	5/7/1954 Darfield		LHB	RM	1977/78-1992/93
Young Bryan Andrew	3/11/1964 Whangarei		RHB	WK	1993/94-1998/99
Yuile Bryan William	29/10/1941 Palmerston North		RHB	SLA	1962/63-1969/70

TEST UMPIRES

The following is the complete list of New Zealand test umpires:

Umpire	Tests	Umpire	Tests	Umpire	Tests
Bowden B.F.	54*	Harris J.C.	4	Clark L.G.	2
Dunne R.S.	39*	Morris G.C.	4	Dumbleton D.P.	2
Aldridge B.L.	26*	Cobcroft L.T.	3	Page W.P.	1
Goodall F.R.	24	McLellan J.M.	3	Burgess T.W.	1
Woodward S.J.	24	Pearce T.M.	3	Torrance R.C.	1
Cowie D.B.	22*	Cowie J.	3	Gourlay H.W.	1
Martin W.T.	15	Gwynne W.J.C.	3	Montgomery O.R.	1
Copps D.E.A.	13	Kinsella D.A.	3	Brook E.G.	1
Gardiner W.R.C.	9	McHarg R.L.	3	Vine B.W.	1
Shortt R.W.R.	9	King C.E.	3	Jelley A.E.	1
Hill A.L.	9*	Watkin E.A.	3	Tindill E.W.T.	1
MacKintosh E.C.A.	8	Butler W.P.	2	Johnston L.C.	1
Hastie J.B.R.	7	Forrester J.T.	2	Burns D.C.	1
Cave K.H.	6	Brown J.M.A.	2	Cassie H.B.	1
Monteith R.L.	6	Tomkinson S.B.	2	Bricknell B.A.	1
Quested D.M.	5	Currie R.G.	2	Higginson I.C.	1
Pengelly M.F.	4				

* *includes test matches overseas*

The following overseas umpires have stood in test matches in New Zealand:

Umpire	Tests	Umpire	Tests	Umpire	Tests
Harper D.J. *(Aus)*	11	Venkataraghavan S. *(Ind)*	3	Gould I.J. *(England)*	2
Koertzen R.E. *(SA)*	7	Benson M.R. *(Eng)*	3	Robinson I.D. *(Zim)*	1
de Silva E.A.R. *(SL)*	6	Ramaswamy V.K. *(Ind)*	2	Nichols E.A. *(WI)*	1
Hair D.B. *(Aus)*	5	Cooray B.C. *(SL)*	2	Plews N.T. *(Eng)*	1
Bucknor S.A. *(WI)*	4	Francis K.T. *(SL)*	2	Riazuddin *(Pak)*	1
Davis S.J. *(Aus)*	4	Mahboob Shah *(Pak)*	2	Jayaprakash A.V. *(Ind)*	1
Taufel S.J.A. *(Aus)*	4	Bird H.D. *(Eng)*	2	Khizar Hayat *(Pak)*	1
Randell S.G. *(Aus)*	3	Jerling B.G. *(SA)*	2	Elliott C.S. *(Eng)*	1
Orchard D.L. *(SA)*	3	Llong N.J. *(England)*	2	Barker L.H. *(WI)*	1
Tiffin R.B. *(Zim)*	3	Parker P.D. *(Australia)*	2	Lloyds J.W. *(Eng)*	1
Shepherd D.R. *(Eng)*	3	Saheba A.M. *(India)*	2	Howell I.L *(SA)*	1
Aleem Dar *(Pak)*	3			Doctrove B.R. *(WI)*	1

The following pairs of umpires have stood together in the most tests:

Pair	Tests	Pair	Tests
Goodall F.R. & Woodward S.J.	10	MacKintosh E.C.A. & Shortt R.W.R.	4
Aldridge B.L. & Dunne R.S.	7	Harris J.C. & Pearce T.M.	3
Aldridge B.L. & Woodward S.J.	6	MacKintosh E.C.A. & Martin W.T.	3
Copps D.E.A. & Gardiner W.R.C.	5	Cobcroft L.T. & Cave K.H.	3
Copps D.E.A. & Martin W.T.	4	Dunne R.S. & Woodward S.J.	3

These umpires have stood in every test of a series *(minimum 3 matches)*:

Cave K. (4)	v England	1929/30
Martin W.T. (3)	v England	1965/66
MacKintosh E.C.A. (3)	v West Indies	1968/69
Goodall F.R. (3)	v England	1983/84
Woodward S.J. (3)	v England	1983/84
Aldridge B.L. (3)	v Sri Lanka	1990/91
Aldridge B.L. (3)	v England	1991/92
Dunne R.S. (3)	v England	1991/92

TEAM RECORDS

New Zealand's Test Victories

1) **v West Indies** at Auckland 1955/56
NZ 255 & 157-9d WI 145 & 77
NZ won by 190 runs

2) **v South Africa** at Cape Town 1961/62
NZ 385 & 212-9d SA 190 & 335
NZ won by 72 runs

3) **v South Africa** at Port Elizabeth 1961/62
NZ 275 & 228 SA 190 & 273
NZ won by 40 runs

4) **v India** at Christchurch 1967/68
NZ 502 & 88-4 I 288 & 301
NZ won by 6 wickets

5) **v West Indies** at Wellington 1968/69
WI 297 & 148 NZ 282 & 166-4
NZ won by 6 wickets

6) **v India** at Nagpur 1969/70
NZ 319 & 214 I 257 & 109
NZ won by 167 runs

7) **v Pakistan** at Lahore 1969/70
P114 & 208 NZ 241 & 82-5
NZ won by 5 wickets

8) **v Australia** at Christchurch 1973/74
A 223 & 259 NZ 255 & 230-5
NZ won by 5 wickets

9) **v India** at Wellington 1975/76
I 220 & 81 NZ 334
NZ won by an innings and 33 runs

10) **v England** at Wellington 1977/78
NZ 228 & 123 E 215 & 64
NZ won by 72 runs

11) **v West Indies** at Dunedin 1979/80
WI 140 & 212 NZ 249 & 104-9
NZ won by 1 wicket

12) **v India** at Wellington 1980/81
NZ 375 & 100 I 233 & 190
NZ won by 62 runs

13) **v Australia** at Auckland 1981/82
A 210 & 280 NZ 387 & 109-5
NZ won by 5 wickets

14) **v Sri Lanka** at Christchurch 1982/83
NZ 344 SL 144 & 175
NZ won by an innings and 25 runs

15) **v Sri Lanka** at Wellington 1982/83
SL 240 & 93 NZ 201 & 134-4
NZ won by 6 wickets

16) **v England** at Leeds 1983
E 225 & 252 NZ 377 & 103-5
NZ won by 5 wickets

17) **v England** at Christchurch 1983/84
NZ 307 E 82 & 93
NZ won by an innings and 132 runs

18) **v Sri Lanka** at Kandy 1983/84
NZ 276 & 201-8d SL 215 & 97
NZ won by 165 runs

19) **v Sri Lanka** at Colombo 1983/84
SL 225 & 142 NZ 459
NZ won by an innings and 61 runs

20) **v Pakistan** at Auckland 1984/85
P 169 & 183 NZ 451-9d
NZ won by an innings and 99 runs

21) **v Pakistan** at Dunedin 1984/85
P274 & 223 NZ 220 & 278-8
NZ won by 2 wickets

22) **v Australia** at Brisbane 1985/86
A 179 & 333 NZ 553-7d
NZ won by an innings and 41 runs

23) **v Australia** at Perth 1985/86
A 203 & 259 NZ 299 & 164-4
NZ won by 6 wickets

24) **v Australia** at Auckland 1985/86
A 314 & 103 NZ 258 & 160-2
NZ won by 8 wickets

25) **v England** at Nottingham 1986
E 256 & 230 NZ 413 & 77-2
NZ won by 8 wickets

26) **v West Indies** at Christchurch 1986/87
WI 100 & 264 NZ 332-9d & 33-5
NZ won by 5 wickets

27) **v India** at Bombay 1988/89
NZ 236 & 279 I 234 & 145
NZ wonby 136 runs

28) **v India** at Christchurch 1989/90
NZ 459 & 2-0 I 164 & 296
NZ won by 10 wickets

29) **v Australia** at Wellington 1989/90
A 110 & 269 NZ 202 & 181-1
NZ won by 9 wickets

30) **v Zimbabwe** at Harare 1992/93
NZ 335 & 262-5d Z 283-9d & 137
NZ won by 177 runs

31) **v Australia** at Auckland 1992/93
A 139 & 285 NZ 224 & 201-5
NZ won by 5 wickets

32) **v Pakistan** at Christchurch 1993/94
P 344 & 179 NZ 200 & 324-5
NZ won by 5 wickets

33) v **South Africa** at Johannesburg 1994/95
NZ 411 & 194 SA 179 & 289
NZ won by 137 runs

34) v **Pakistan** at Lahore 1996/97
NZ 155 & 311 P 191 & 231
NZ won by 44 runs

35) v **Sri Lanka** at Dunedin 1996/97
NZ 586-7d SL 222 & 328
NZ won by an innings & 36 runs

36) v **Sri Lanka** at Hamilton 1996/97
NZ 222 & 273 SL 170 & 205
NZ won by 120 runs

37) v **Zimbabwe** at Wellington 1997/98
Z 180 & 250 NZ 411 & 20-0
NZ won by 10 wickets

38) v **Zimbabwe** at Auckland 1997/98
Z 170 & 277 NZ 460
NZ won by an innings and 13 runs

39) v **Sri Lanka** at Colombo 1997/98
NZ 305 & 444-6d SL 285 & 297
NZ won by 167 runs

40) v **India** at Wellington 1998/99
I 208 & 356 NZ 352 & 215-6
NZ won by 4 wickets

41) v **England** at Lord's 1999
E 186 & 229 NZ 358 & 60-1
NZ won by 9 wickets

42) v **England** at The Oval 1999
NZ 236 & 162 E 153 & 162
NZ won by 83 runs

43) v **West Indies** at Hamilton 1999/00
WI 365 & 97 NZ 393 & 70-1
NZ won by 9 wickets

44) v **West Indies** at Wellington 1999/00
NZ 518-9d WI 179 & 234
NZ won by an innings and 105 runs

45) v **Zimbabwe** at Bulawayo 2000/01
Z 350 & 119 NZ 338 & 132-3
NZ won by 7 wickets

46) v **Zimbabwe** at Harare 2000/01
NZ 465 & 74-2 Z 166 & 370
NZ won by 8 wickets

47) v **Pakistan** at Hamilton 2000/01
P 104 & 118 NZ 407-4d
NZ won by an innings & 185 runs

48) v **Bangladesh** at Hamilton 2001/02
NZ 365-9d B 205 & 108
NZ won by an innings and 52 runs

49) v **Bangladesh** at Wellington 2001/02
B 132 & 135 NZ 341-6d
NZ won by an innings and 74 runs

50) v **England** at Auckland 2001/02
NZ 202 & 269-9d E 160 & 233
NZ won by 78 runs

51) v **West Indies** at Bridgetown 2001/02
NZ 337 & 243 WI 107 & 269
NZ won by 204 runs

52) v **India** at Wellington 2002/03
I 161 & 121 NZ 247 & 36-0
NZ won by 10 wickets

53) v **India** at Hamilton 2002/03
I 99 & 154 NZ 94 & 160-6
NZ won by 4 wickets

54) v **South Africa** at Auckland 2003/04
SA 296 & 349 NZ 595 & 53-1
NZ won by 9 wickets

55) v **Bangladesh** at Dhaka 2004/05
B 177 & 126 NZ 402
NZ won by an innings and 99 runs

56) v **Bangladesh** at Chittagong 2004/05
NZ 545-6d B 182 & 262
NZ won by an innings and 101 runs

57) v **Sri Lanka** at Wellington 2004/05
SL 211 & 273 NZ 522-9d
NZ won by an innings and 38 runs

58) v **Zimbabwe** at Harare 2005/06
NZ 452-9d Z 59 & 99
NZ won by an innings and 294 runs

59) v **Zimbabwe** at Bulawayo 2005/06
Z 231 & 207 NZ 484
NZ won by an innings and 46 runs

60) v **West Indies** at Auckland 2005/06
NZ 275 & 272 WI 257 & 263
NZ won by 27 runs

61) v **West Indies** at Wellington 2005/06
WI 192 & 215 NZ 372 & 37-0
NZ won by 10 wickets

62) v **Sri Lanka** at Christchurch 2006/07
SL 154 & 179 NZ 206 & 119-5
NZ won by 5 wickets

63) v **Bangladesh** at Dunedin 2007/08
B 137 & 254 NZ 357 & 39-1
NZ won by 9 wickets

64) v **Bangladesh** at Wellington 2007/08
B 143 & 113 NZ 393
NZ won by an innings and 137 runs

65) v **England** at Hamilton 2007/08
NZ 470 & 177-9d E 348 & 110
NZ won by 189 runs

66) v **Bangladesh** at Chittagong 2008/09
B 245 & 242 NZ 171 and 317-7
NZ won by 3 wickets

Test Record by Series

		TOTAL			Cumulative					
								BY OPPONENT		
Season	Opponent	Won	Lost	Drawn	Won	Lost	Drawn	Won	Lost	Drawn
1929/30	England*	—	1	3	—	1	3	—	1	3
1931	England	—	1	2	—	2	5	—	2	5
1931/32	South Africa*	—	2	—	—	4	5	—	2	—
1932/33	England*	—	—	2	—	4	7	—	2	7
1937	England	—	1	2	—	5	9	—	3	9
1945/46	Australia*	—	1	—	—	6	9	—	1	—
1946/47	England*	—	—	1	—	6	10	—	3	10
1949	England	—	—	4	—	6	14	—	3	14
1950/51	England*	—	1	1	—	7	15	—	4	15
1951/52	West Indies*	—	1	1	—	8	16	—	1	1
1952/53	South Africa*	—	1	1	—	9	17	—	3	1
1953/54	South Africa	—	4	1	—	13	18	—	7	2
1954/55	England*	—	2	—	—	15	18	—	6	15
1955/56	Pakistan	—	2	1	—	17	19	—	2	1
1955/56	India	—	2	3	—	19	22	—	2	3
1955/56	West Indies*	1	3	—	1	22	22	1	4	1
1958	England	—	4	1	1	26	23	—	10	16
1958/59	England*	—	1	1	1	27	24	—	11	17
1961/62	South Africa	2	2	1	3	29	25	2	9	3
1962/63	England*	—	3	—	3	32	25	—	14	17
1963/64	South Africa*	—	—	3	3	32	28	2	9	6
1964/65	Pakistan*	—	—	3	3	32	31	—	2	4
1964/65	India	—	1	3	3	33	34	—	3	6
1964/65	Pakistan	—	2	1	3	35	35	—	4	5
1965	England	—	3	—	3	38	35	—	17	17
1965/66	England*	—	—	3	3	38	38	—	17	20
1967/68	India*	1	3	—	4	41	38	1	6	6
1968/69	West Indies*	1	1	1	5	42	39	2	5	2
1969	England	—	2	1	5	44	40	—	19	21
1969/70	India	1	1	1	6	45	41	2	7	7
1969/70	Pakistan	1	—	2	7	45	43	1	4	7
1970/71	England*	—	1	1	7	46	44	—	20	22
1971/72	West Indies	—	—	5	7	46	49	2	5	7
1972/73	Pakistan*	—	1	2	7	47	51	1	5	9
1973	England	—	2	1	7	49	52	—	22	23
1973/74	Australia	—	2	1	7	51	53	—	3	1
1973/74	Australia*	1	1	1	8	52	54	1	4	2
1974/75	England*	—	1	1	8	53	55	—	23	24
1975/76	India*	1	1	1	9	54	56	3	8	8
1976/77	Pakistan	—	2	1	9	56	57	1	7	10
1976/77	India	—	2	1	9	58	58	3	10	9
1976/77	Australia*	—	1	1	9	59	59	1	5	3
1977/78	England*	1	1	1	10	60	60	1	24	25
1978	England	—	3	—	10	63	60	1	27	25
1978/79	Pakistan*	—	1	2	10	64	62	1	8	12
1979/80	West Indies*	1	—	2	11	64	64	3	5	9
1980/81	Australia	—	2	1	11	66	65	1	7	4
1980/81	India*	1	—	2	12	66	67	4	10	11
1981/82	Australia*	1	1	1	13	67	68	2	8	5
1982/83	Sri Lanka*	2	—	—	15	67	68	2	—	—

Season	Opponent	TOTAL Won	TOTAL Lost	TOTAL Drawn	Cumulative Won	Cumulative Lost	Cumulative Drawn	BY OPPONENT Won	BY OPPONENT Lost	BY OPPONENT Drawn
1983	England	1	3	—	16	70	68	2	30	25
1983/84	England*	1	—	2	17	70	70	3	30	27
1983/84	Sri Lanka	2	—	1	19	70	71	4	—	1
1984/85	Pakistan	—	2	1	19	72	72	1	10	13
1984/85	Pakistan*	2	—	1	21	72	73	3	10	14
1984/85	West Indies	—	2	2	21	74	75	3	7	11
1985/86	Australia	2	1	—	23	75	75	4	9	5
1985/86	Australia*	1	—	2	24	75	77	5	9	7
1986	England	1	—	2	25	75	79	4	30	29
1986/87	West Indies*	1	1	1	26	76	80	4	8	12
1986/87	Sri Lanka	—	—	1	26	76	81	4	—	2
1987/88	Australia	—	1	2	26	77	83	5	10	9
1987/88	England*	—	—	3	26	77	86	4	30	32
1988/89	India	1	2	—	27	79	86	5	12	11
1988/89	Pakistan*	—	—	2	27	79	88	3	10	16
1989/90	Australia	—	—	1	27	79	89	5	10	10
1989/90	India*	1	—	2	28	79	91	6	12	13
1989/90	Australia*	1	—	—	29	79	91	6	10	10
1990	England	—	1	2	29	80	93	4	41	34
1990/91	Pakistan	—	3	—	29	83	93	3	13	16
1990/91	Sri Lanka*	—	—	3	29	83	96	4	—	5
1991/92	England*	—	2	1	29	85	97	4	33	35
1992/93	Zimbabwe	1	—	1	30	85	98	1	—	1
1992/93	Sri Lanka	—	1	1	30	86	99	4	1	6
1992/93	Pakistan*	—	1	—	30	87	99	3	14	16
1992/93	Australia*	1	1	1	31	88	100	7	11	11
1993/94	Australia	—	2	1	31	90	101	7	13	12
1993/94	Pakistan*	1	2	—	32	92	101	4	16	16
1993/94	India*	—	—	1	32	92	102	6	12	14
1994	England	—	1	2	32	93	104	4	34	37
1994/95	South Africa	1	2	—	33	95	104	3	11	6
1994/95	West Indies*	—	1	1	33	96	105	4	9	13
1994/95	South Africa*	—	1	—	33	97	105	3	12	6
1994/95	Sri Lanka*	—	1	1	33	98	106	4	2	7
1995/96	India	—	1	2	33	99	108	6	13	16
1995/96	Pakistan*	—	1	—	33	100	108	4	17	16
1995/96	Zimbabwe*	—	—	2	33	100	110	1	—	3
1995/96	West Indies	—	1	1	33	101	111	4	10	14
1996/97	Pakistan	1	1	—	34	102	111	5	18	16
1996/97	England*	—	2	1	34	104	112	4	36	38
1996/97	Sri Lanka*	2	—	—	36	104	112	6	2	7
1997/98	Zimbabwe	—	—	2	36	104	114	1	—	5
1997/98	Australia	—	2	1	36	106	115	7	15	13
1997/98	Zimbabwe*	2	—	—	38	106	115	3	—	5
1997/98	Sri Lanka	1	2	—	39	108	115	7	4	7
1998/99	India*	1	—	1	40	108	116	7	13	17
1998/99	South Africa*	—	1	2	40	109	118	3	13	8
1999	England	2	1	1	42	110	119	6	37	39
1999/00	India	—	1	2	42	111	121	7	14	19
1999/00	West Indies*	2	—	—	44	111	121	6	10	14
1999/00	Australia*	—	3	—	44	114	121	7	18	13
2000/01	Zimbabwe	2	—	—	46	114	121	5	—	5

		Cumulative								
		TOTAL						BY OPPONENT		
Season	Opponent	Won	Lost	Drawn	Won	Lost	Drawn	Won	Lost	Drawn
2000/01	South Africa	—	2	1	46	116	122	3	15	9
2000/01	Zimbabwe*	—	—	1	46	116	123	5	—	6
2000/01	Pakistan*	1	1	1	47	117	124	6	19	17
2001/02	Australia	—	—	3	47	117	127	7	18	16
2001/02	Bangladesh*	2	—	—	49	117	127	2	—	—
2001/02	England*	1	1	1	50	118	128	7	38	40
2001/02	Pakistan	—	1	—	50	119	128	6	20	17
2001/02	West Indies	1	—	1	51	119	129	7	10	15
2002/03	India*	2	—	—	53	119	129	9	14	19
2002/03	Sri Lanka	—	—	2	53	119	131	7	4	9
2003/04	India	—	—	2	53	119	133	9	14	21
2003/04	Pakistan*	—	1	1	53	120	134	6	21	18
2003/04	South Africa*	1	1	1	54	121	135	4	16	10
2004	England	—	3	—	54	124	135	7	41	40
2004/05	Bangladesh	2	—	—	56	124	135	4	—	—
2004/05	Australia	—	2	—	56	126	135	7	20	16
2004/05	Australia*	—	2	1	56	128	136	7	22	17
2004/05	Sri Lanka*	1	—	1	57	128	137	8	4	10
2005/06	Zimbabwe	2	—	—	59	128	137	7	—	6
2005/06	West Indies*	2	—	1	61	128	138	9	10	16
2005/06	South Africa	—	2	1	61	130	139	4	18	11
2006/07	Sri Lanka*	1	1	—	62	131	139	9	5	10
2007/08	South Africa	—	2	—	62	133	139	4	20	11
2007/08	Bangladesh*	2	—	—	64	133	139	6	—	—
2007/08	England*	1	2	—	65	135	139	8	43	40
2008	England	—	2	1	65	137	140	8	45	41
2008/09	Bangladesh	1	—	1	66	137	141	7	—	1
2008/09	Australia	—	2	—	66	139	141	7	24	17
2008/09	West Indies*	—	—	2	66	139	143	9	10	18
2008/09	India*	—	1	2	66	140	145	9	15	23

** home series*

Summary of Results

	Played	Won	Lost	Drawn
v England	94	8	45	41
v Australia	48	7	24	17
v India	47	9	15	23
v Pakistan	45	6	21	18
v West Indies	37	9	10	18
v South Africa	35	4	20	11
v Sri Lanka	24	9	5	10
v Zimbabwe	13	7	—	6
v Bangladesh	8	7	—	1
Total	**351**	**66**	**140**	**145**

Decade by Decade

	Played	Won	Lost	Drawn
1929/30 to 1937	14	–	5	9
1945/46 to 1954/55	19	–	10	9
1955/56 to 1964/65	43	3	23	17
1965/66 to 1974/75	40	5	15	20
1975/76 to 1984/85	54	13	21	20
1985/86 to 1994/95	67	12	24	31
1995/96 to 2004/05	85	24	30	31
2005/06 to 2008	29	9	12	8
Total	**351**	**66**	**140**	**145**

Highest Totals

For

671-4	v Sri Lanka	Wellington	1990/91
630-6d	v India	Mohali	2003/04
619-9d	v India	Napier	2008/09
595	v South Africa	Auckland	2003/04
593-8d	v South Africa	Cape Town	2005/06
586-7d	v Sri Lanka	Dunedin	1996/97
563	v Pakistan	Hamilton	2003/04
561	v Sri Lanka	Napier	2004/05
553-7d	v Australia	Brisbane	1985/86
551-9d	v England	Lord's	1973
545-6d	v Bangladesh	Chittagong	2004/05
543-3d	v West Indies	Georgetown	1971/72
537	v England	Wellington	1983/84
534-9d	v Australia	Perth	2001/02
522-9d	v Sri Lanka	Wellington	2004/05
518-9d	v West Indies	Wellington	1999/00
515-7d	v Sri Lanka	Colombo	2002/03
512-6d	v England	Wellington	1987/88
509	v South Africa	Hamilton	2003/04
505	v South Africa	Cape Town	1953/54
502	v India	Christchurch	1967/68

Against

660-5d	by West Indies	Wellington	1994/95
643	by Pakistan	Lahore	2001/02
621-5d	by South Africa	Auckland	1998/99
616-5d	by Pakistan	Auckland	1988/89
607-6d	by Australia	Brisbane	1993/94
593-6d	by England	Auckland	1974/75
585	by Australia	Brisbane	2004/05
583-7d	by India	Ahmedabad	1999/00
580-9d	by England	Christchurch	1991/92
575-8d	by Australia	Adelaide	2004/05
571-8d	by Pakistan	Christchurch	2000/01
570-8d	by Australia	Wellington	2004/05
567-8d	by England	Nottingham	1994
565-9d	by Pakistan	Karachi	1976/77
564-8	by West Indies	Bridgetown	1971/72
562-7d	by England	Auckland	1962/63
561	by Pakistan	Lahore	1955/56
560-8d	by England	Christchurch	1932/33

558-8d	by Australia	Hobart	2001/02
552	by Australia	Christchurch	1976/77
550	by England	Christchurch	1950/51

Lowest Totals

For

26	v England	Auckland	1954/55
42	v Australia	Wellington	1945/46
47	v England	Lord's	1958
54	v Australia	Wellington	1945/46
65	v England	Christchurch	1970/71
67	v England	Leeds	1958
67	v England	Lord's	1978
70	v Pakistan	Dacca	1955/56
73	v Pakistan	Lahore	2001/02
74	v West Indies	Dunedin	1955/56
74	v England	Lord's	1958
76	v Australia	Brisbane	2004/05
79	v South Africa	Johannesburg	1953/54
79	v Pakistan	Rawalpindi	1964/65
85	v England	Manchester	1958
89	v England	Auckland	1962/63
93	v Pakistan	Hamilton	1992/93
94	v England	Birmingham	1958
94	v West Indies	Bridgetown	1984/85
94	v India	Hamilton	2002/03
97	v England	Nottingham	1973

Against

59	by Zimbabwe	Harare	2005/06
64	by England	Wellington	1977/78
77	by West Indies	Auckland	1955/56
81	by India	Wellington	1975/76
82	by England	Christchurch	1983/84
83	by India	Mohali	1999/00
88	by India	Bombay	1964/65
89	by India	Hyderabad	1969/70
93	by Sri Lanka	Wellington	1982/83
93	by England	Christchurch	1983/84
97	by Sri Lanka	Kandy	1983/84
97	by West Indies	Hamilton	1999/00
99	by India	Hamilton	2002/03
99	by Zimbabwe	Harare	2005/06

Longest Innings

Mins	*Runs*			
851	671-4	v Sri Lanka	Wellington	1990/91
815	459	v Sri Lanka	Colombo	1983/84
802	630-6 dec	v India	Mohali	2003/04
790	406-5	v Sri Lanka	Colombo	1986/87
784	512-6 dec	v England	Wellington	1987/88
780	543-3 dec	v West Indies	Georgetown	1971/72
768	551-9 dec	v England	Lord's	1973
760	482-6 dec	v Pakistan	Lahore	1964/65
753	487-7 dec	v Zimbabwe	Wellington	2000/01

738	492	v Pakistan	Wellington	1984/85
732	447	v Pakistan	Wellington	1988/89
724	537	v England	Wellington	1983/84
713	403	v Pakistan	Auckland	1988/89
710	484	v Australia	Wellington	1973/74
709	440	v England	Nottingham	1973
705	593-8d	v South Africa	Cape Town	2005/06

Largest First Innings Leads

*393	v Zimbabwe	Harare	2005/06
*374	v Australia	Brisbane	1985/86
*364	v Sri Lanka	Dunedin	1996/97
*363	v Bangladesh	Chittagong	2004/05
*339	v West Indies	Wellington	1999/00
314	v India	Napier	2008/09
*311	v Sri Lanka	Wellington	2004/05
*303	v Pakistan	Hamilton	2000/01
*299	v Zimbabwe	Harare	2000/01
*299	v South Africa	Auckland	2003/04
298	v England	Lord's	1973
297	v England	Manchester	1999
*295	v India	Christchurch	1989/90
*290	v Zimbabwe	Auckland	1997/98
289	v West Indies	Bridgetown	1971/72
*282	v Pakistan	Auckland	1984/85
*253	v Zimbabwe	Bulawayo	2005/06

** New Zealand won the match*

Opposition Following-on

South Africa	Cape Town	1953/54
India	Bombay	1964/65
*India	Christchurch	1967/68
*Sri Lanka	Christchurch	1982/83
*England	Christchurch	1983/84
*India	Christchurch	1989/90
*Sri Lanka	Dunedin	1996/97
*West Indies	Wellington	1999/00
*Zimbabwe	Harare	2000/01
*Bangladesh	Hamilton	2001/02
India	Mohali	2003/04
*Bangladesh	Chittagong	2004/05
*Zimbabwe	Harare	2005/06
India	Napier	2008/09

** New Zealand won the match*

NB: *New Zealand did not enforce the follow-on v South Africa at Cape Town, 1961/62 and v West Indies at Bridgetown in 2001/02 although they could have done so. They eventually won both games.*

GROUNDS

Results by Grounds

In New Zealand	P	W	L	D
Eden Park, Auckland	47	9	15	23
Lancaster Park, Christchurch	40	8	16	16
Basin Reserve, Wellington	49	14	16	19
Carisbrook, Dunedin	10	3	4	3
McLean Park, Napier	8	—	2	6
Seddon Park, Hamilton	15	6	3	6
University Oval, Dunedin	2	1	—	1
Total	**171**	**41**	**56**	**74**
In Australia				
Melbourne Cricket Ground	3	—	1	2
Sydney Cricket Ground	2	—	1	1
Adelaide Oval	3	—	3	1
WACA Ground, Perth	6	1	2	3
Woolloongabba, Brisbane	7	1	6	1
Bellerive Oval, Hobart	3	—	1	2
Total	**24**	**2**	**14**	**10**
In Sri Lanka				
Kandy, Asgiriya Stadium	2	1	—	1
Sinhalese Sports Club Ground, Colombo	3	—	2	1
Colombo C.C. Ground, Colombo	2	1	—	1
Tyrone Fernando Stadium, Moratuwa	1	—	—	1
R. Premadasa Stadium, Colombo	1	1	—	—
Galle International Stadium	1	—	1	—
P. Saravanamuttu Stadium	1	—	—	1
Total	**11**	**3**	**3**	**5**
In West Indies				
Queen's Park Oval, Port of Spain	3	—	—	3
Sabina Park, Kingston	2	—	1	1
Kensington Park, Bridgetown	4	1	2	1
Bourda, Georgetown	2	—	—	2
St Johns Recreation Ground, Antigua	1	—	—	1
Queen's Park, Grenada	1	—	—	1
Total	**13**	**1**	**3**	**9**
In Zimbabwe				
Bulawayo Athletic Club	1	—	—	1
Harare Sports Club, Harare	4	3	—	1
Queens Sports Club, Bulawayo	3	2	—	1
Total	**8**	**5**	**—**	**3**
In Bangladesh				
National Stadium, Dhaka	1	1	—	—
Chittagong Stadium	2	2	—	—
National Stadium, Mirpur	1	—	—	1
Total	**4**	**3**	**—**	**1**

In Pakistan	P	W	L	D
National Stadium, Karachi	6	—	3	3
Bagh-e-Jinnah, Lahore	1	—	1	—
Dacca Stadium, Dacca	2	—	—	2
Niaz Stadium, Hyderabad	2	—	2	—
Rawalpindi Club Ground	1	—	1	—
Lahore (Gaddafi) Stadium	7	2	4	1
Iqbal Stadium, Faisalabad	1	—	1	—
Rawalpindi Cricket Stadium	1	—	1	—
Total	**21**	**2**	**13**	**6**
In South Africa				
Kingsmead, Durban	3	—	3	—
Ellis Park, Johannesburg	2	—	2	—
New Wanderers, Johannesburg	6	1	3	2
Newlands, Cape Town	4	1	1	2
St George's Park, Port Elizabeth	3	1	2	—
Goodyear Park, Bloemfontein	1	—	1	—
SuperSport Park, Centurion	2	—	2	—
Total	**21**	**3**	**14**	**4**
In England				
Lord's, London	15	1	6	8
Oval, London	9	1	4	4
Headingley, Leeds	6	1	4	1
Trent Bridge, Nottingham	9	1	6	2
Old Trafford, Manchester	7	—	3	4
Egbaston, Birmingham	4	—	4	—
Total	**50**	**4**	**27**	**19**
In India				
Brabourne Stadium, Bombay	3	—	2	1
Wankhede Stadium, Bombay	2	1	1	—
Fateh Maidan, (Lal Bahadur Stadium) Hyderabad	3	—	1	2
Feroz Shah Kotla, Delhi	2	—	1	1
Eden Gardens, Calcutta	2	—	—	2
Corporation Stadium, Madras	2	—	1	1
Chepauk, (Chidambaram Stadium) Madras	2	—	1	1
VCA Ground, Nagpur	1	1	—	—
Green Park, Kanpur	2	—	1	1
Chinnaswamy Stadium, Bangalore	2	—	2	—
Barabati Stadium, Cuttack	1	—	—	1
Punjab C.A. Stadium, Mohali	2	—	—	2
Sardar Patel Stadium, Ahmedabad	2	—	—	2
Total	**26**	**2**	**10**	**14**

Record Performances in Tests on Each NZ Ground v All Countries

Venue	***Highest Total*** *by NZ* *v NZ*	***Lowest Total*** *by NZ* *v NZ*	***Highest Individual Innings*** *by NZ* *v NZ*	***Best Bowling*** *by NZ* *v NZ*
Auckland 47 Tests	595 2003/04 v South Africa 621-5d 1998/99 by South Africa	26 1954/55 v England 77 1955/56 by West Indies	173 Smith I.D.S. 1989/90 v India 336* Hammond W.R. 1932/33 for England	7-87 Vettori D.L. 1999/00 v Australia 8-76 Prasanna E.A.S. 1975/76 for India
Christchurch 40 Tests	502 1967/68 v India 580-9d 1991/92 by England	65 1970/71 v England 82 1983/84 by England	239 Dowling G.T. 1967/68 v India 258 Nurse S.M. 1968/69 for West Indies	7-116 Hadlee R.J. 1985/86 v Australia 7-47 Tufnell P.C.R. 1991/92 for England
Carisbrook, Dunedin 10 Tests	586-7d 1996/97 v Sri Lanka 507-6d 1972/73 by Pakistan	74 1955/56 v West Indies 140 1979/80 by West Indies	267* Young B.A. 1996/97 v Sri Lanka 201 Mushtaq Mohammad 1972/73 for Pakistan	6-51 Hadlee R.J. 1984/85 v Pakistan 7-52 Intikhab Alam 1972/73 for Pakistan
Wellington 49 Tests	671-4 1990/91 v Sri Lanka 660-5d 1994/95 by West Indies	42 1945/46 v Australia 64 1977/78 by England	299 Crowe M.D. 1990/91 v Sri Lanka 267 de Silva P.A. 1990/91 for Sri Lanka	7-23 Hadlee R.J. 1975/76 v India 7-37 Walsh C.A. 1994/95 for West Indies
Napier 8 Tests	619-9d 2008/09 v India 498 2004/05 by Sri Lanka	109 1994/95 v Sri Lanka 183 1994/95 by Sri Lanka	201 Ryder J.D. 2008/09 v India 177 Strauss A.J. 2007/08 for England	5-55 Southee T.G. 2007/08 v England 7-47 Sidebottom R.J. 2007/08 for England
Hamilton 15 Tests	563 2003/04 v Pakistan 520 2008/09 by India	93 1992/93 v Pakistan 97 1999/00 by West Indies	192 Fleming S.P. 2003/04 v Pakistan 190 Dravid R.S. 1998/99 for India	7-27 Cairns C.L. 1999/00 v West Indies 6-49 Sidebottom R.J. 2007/08 for England
University Oval, Dunedin 2 Tests	365 2008/09 v West Indies 340 2008/09 by West Indies	357 2007/08 v Bangladesh 137 2007/08 by Bangladesh	117 Oram J.D.P. 2007/08 v Bangladesh 106 Taylor J.E. 2008/09 for West Indies	6-56 Vettori D.L. 2008/09 v West Indies 4-74 Masrafe Mortaza 2007/08 for Bangladesh
ALL TESTS IN NZ 171 Tests	671-4 1990/91 v Sri Lanka Wellington 660-5d 1994/95 by West Indies Wellington	26 1954/55 v England Auckland 64 1977/78 by England Wellington	299 Crowe M.D. 1990/91 v Sri Lanka Wellington 336* Hammond W.R. 1932/33 for England Auckland	7-23 Hadlee R.J. 1975/76 v India Wellington 8-76 Prasanna E.A.S. 1975/76 for India Auckland

Record Performances in Tests v All Opponents

Opponent	*Highest Total* *by NZ* *v NZ*	*Lowest Total* *by NZ* *v NZ*	*Highest Individual Innings* *by NZ* *v NZ*	*Best Bowling* *by NZ* *v NZ*
England	551-9d Lord's 1973 593-6 Auckland 1974/75	26 Auckland 1954/55 64 Wellington 1977/78	222 Astle N.J. Christchurch, 2001/02 336* Hammond W.R. Auckland, 1932/33	7-74 Cairns B.L. Leeds, 1983 7-32 Underwood D.L. Lord's, 1969
Australia	553-7d Brisbane 1985/1986 607-6d Brisbane 1993/94	42 Wellington 1945/46 103 Auckland 1985/86	188 Crowe M.D. Brisbane, 1985/86 250 Walters K.D. Christchurch, 1977/78	9-52 Hadlee R.J. Brisbane, 1985/86 6-31 Warne S.K. Hobart 1993/94
South Africa	595 Auckland 2003/04 621-5d Auckland 1998/99	79 Johannesburg 1953/54 148 Johannesburg 1953/54	262 Fleming S.P. Cape Town, 2005/06 275* Cullinan D.J. Auckland, 1998/99	6-60 Reid J.R. Dunedin, 1963/64 8-53 Lawrence G.B. Johannesburg, 1961/62
West Indies	543-3d Georgetown 1971/72 660-5d Wellington 1994/95	74 Dunedin 1955/56 77 Auckland 1955/56	259 Turner G.M. Georgetown, 1971/72 258 Nurse S.M. Christchurch, 1968/69	7-27 Cairns C.L. Hamilton, 1999/00 7-37 Walsh C.A. Wellington, 1994/95
India	630-6d Mohali 2003/04 583-7d Ahmedabad 1999/00	94 Hamilton 2002/03 81 Wellington 1975/76	239 Dowling G.T. Christchurch, 1967/68 231 Mankad M.H. Madras, 1955/56	7-23 Hadlee R.J. Wellington, 1975/76 8-72 Venkataraghavan S. Delhi, 1964/65
Pakistan	563 Hamilton 2003/04 643 Lahore 2001/02	70 Dacca 1955/56 102 Faisalabad 1990/91	204* Sinclair M.S. Christchurch, 2000/01 329 Inzamam-ul-Haq Lahore, 2001/02	7-52 Pringle C. Faisalabad 1990/91 7-52 Intikhab Alam. Dunedin, 1972/73
Sri Lanka	671-4 Wellington 1990/91 498 Napier 2004/05	102 Colombo 1992/93 93 Wellington 1982/83	299 Crowe M.D. Wellington, 1990/91 267 de Silva P.A. Wellington, 1990/91	7-130 Vettori D.L. Wellington 2006/07 6-72 Dharmasena H.D.P.K. Galle, 1997/98
Zimbabwe	487-7d Wellington 2000/01 461 Bulawayo 1997/98	207 Harare 1997/98 59 Harare 2005/06	157 Horne M.J. Auckland, 1997/98 203* Whittall G.J. Bulawayo, 1997/98	6-50 Patel D.N. Harare, 1992/93 8-109 Strang P.A. Bulawayo, 2000/0
Bangladesh	545-6d Chittagong 2004/05 171 Chittagong 2008/09	341-6d Wellington 2001/02 108 Hamilton 2001/02	202 Fleming S.P. Chittagong, 2004/05 84 Tamim Iqbal Dunedin, 2007/08	7-53 Cairns C.L. Hamilton, 2001/02 7-36 Shakib Al Hasan Chittagong, 2008/09

INDIVIDUAL RECORDS

BATTING

Test Centuries

(212 instances)

299	Crowe M.D. v Sri Lanka at Wellington	1990/91
274*	Fleming S.P. v Sri Lanka at Colombo	2002/03
267*	Young B.A. v Sri Lanka at Dunedin	1996/97
262	Fleming S.P. v South Africa at Cape Town	2005/06
259	Turner G.M. v West Indies at Georgetown	1971/72
239	Dowling G.T. v India at Christchurch	1967/68
230*	Sutcliffe B. v India at New Delhi	1955/56
224	Vincent L. v Sri Lanka at Wellington	2004/05
223*	Turner G.M. v West Indies at Kingston	1971/72
222	Astle N.J. v England at Christchurch	2001/02
214	Sinclair M.S. v West Indies at Wellington	1999/00
206	Donnelly M.P. v England at Lord's	1949
204*	Sinclair M.S. v Pakistan at Christchurch	2000/01
202	Fleming S.P. v Bangladesh at Chittagong	2004/05
201	Ryder J.D. v India at Napier	2008/09
192	Fleming S.P. v Pakistan at Hamilton	2003/04
188	Crowe M.D. v West Indies at Georgetown	1984/85
188	Crowe M.D. v Australia at Brisbane	1985/86
186	Jones A.H. v Sri Lanka at Wellington	1990/91
185	Wright J.G. v India at Christchurch	1989/90
182	Jarvis T.W. v West Indies at Georgetown	1971/72
180	Reid J.F. v Sri Lanka at Colombo	1983/84
176	Congdon B.E. v England at Nottingham	1973
175	Congdon B.E. v England at Lord's	1973
174*	Coney J.V. v England at Wellington	1983/84
174*	Fleming S.P. v Sri Lanka at Colombo	1997/98
174	Crowe M.D. v Pakistan at Wellington	1988/89
173	Smith I.D.S. v India at Auckland	1989/90
170*	Jones A.H. v India at Auckland	1989/90
170	Styris S.B. v South Africa at Auckland	2003/04
166*	Congdon B.E. v West Indies at Port of Spain	1971/72
161	Edgar B.A. v Australia at Auckland	1981/82
160	Marshall H.J.H. v Sri Lanka at Napier	2004/05
158*	Reid J.F. v Pakistan at Auckland	1984/85
158	Cairns C.L. v South Africa at Auckland	2003/04
157	Horne M.J. v Zimbabwe at Auckland	1997/98
156*	Astle N.J. v Australia at Perth	2001/02
154*	Taylor L.R.P.L. v England at Manchester	2008
152	Lees W.K. v Pakistan at Karachi	1976/77
151*	Sutcliffe B. v India at Calcutta	1964/65
151*	Hadlee R.J. v Sri Lanka at Colombo	1986/87
151	Taylor L.R.P.L. v India at Napier	2008/09
150	Jones A.H. v Australia at Adelaide	1987/88
150	Sinclair M.S. v South Africa at Port Elizabeth	2000/01
148	Reid J.F. v Pakistan at Wellington	1984/85
147	Howarth G.P. v West Indies at Christchurch	1979/80
146*	Greatbatch M.J. v Australia at Perth	1989/90

146	Marshall H.J.H. v Australia at Christchurch	2004/05
145	Richardson M.H. v India at Mohali	2003/04
143	Dowling G.T. v India at Dunedin	1967/68
143	Crowe M.D. v England at Wellington	1987/88
143	Jones A.H. v England at Wellington	1991/92
143	Jones A.H. v Australia at Perth	1993/94
143	Richardson M.H. v Bangladesh at Hamilton	2001/02
143	McCullum B.B. v Bangladesh at Dhaka	2004/05
142	Reid J.R. v South Africa at Johannesburg	1961/62
142	Crowe M.D. v England at Lord's	1994
142	McMillan C.D. v Sri Lanka at Colombo	1997/98
142	McMillan C.D. v Zimbabwe at Wellington	2000/01
141	Wright J.G. v Australia at Christchurch	1981/82
141	Astle N.J. v Zimbabwe at Wellington	2000/01
140	Crowe M.D. v Zimbabwe at Harare	1992/93
139	McMillan C.D. v Zimbabwe at Wellington	1997/98
138	Sinclair B.W. v South Africa at Auckland	1963/64
138	Wright J.G. v West Indies at Wellington	1986/87
137*	Sutcliffe B. v India at Hyderabad	1955/56
137*	Howarth G.P. v India at Wellington	1980/81
137*	Vettori D.L. v Pakistan at Hamilton	2003/04
137	Crowe M.D. v Australia at Christchurch	1985/86
137	Crowe M.D. v Australia at Adelaide	1987/88
136	Dempster C.S. v England at Wellington	1929/30
136	McIntosh T.G. v West Indies at Napier	2008/09
135	Reid J.R. v South Africa at Cape Town	1953/54
133	Greatbatch M.J. v Pakistan at Hamilton	1992/93
133	Horne M.J. v Australia at Hobart	1997/98
133	Oram J.D.P. v South Africa at Centurion	2005/06
132	Congdon B.E. v Australia at Wellington	1973/74
130	Sinclair B.W. v Pakistan at Lahore	1964/65
130	Wright J.G. v England at Auckland	1983/84
130	Fleming S.P. v West Indies at Bridgetown	2001/02
129	Dowling G.T. v India at Bombay	1964/65
129	Edgar B.A. v Pakistan at Christchurch	1978/79
129	Fleming S.P. v England at Auckland	1996/97
128	Reid J.R. v Pakistan at Karachi	1964/65
128	Crowe J.J. v England at Auckland	1983/84
128	Astle N.J. v Zimbabwe at Bulawayo	2005/06
127	Edgar B.A. v West Indies at Auckland	1979/80
127	Vettori D.L. v Zimbabwe at Harare	2005/06
126*	Oram J.D.P. v Australia at Brisbane	2004/05
126	Congdon B.E. v West Indies at Bridgetown	1971/72
126	Cairns C.L. v India at Hamilton	1998/99
125	Astle N.J. v West Indies at Bridgetown	1995/96
124	Taylor B.R. v West Indies at Auckland	1968/69
124	Cairns C.L. v Zimbabwe at Harare	2000/01
123*	Reid J.F. v India at Christchurch	1980/81
123	Howarth G.P. v England at Lord's	1978
122*	Franklin J.E.C. v South Africa at Cape Town	2005/06
122	Howarth G.P. v England at Auckland	1977/78
122	Jones A.H. v Sri Lanka at Hamilton	1990/91
121	Parker J.M. v England at Auckland	1974/75
120*	Crowe J.J. v Sri Lanka at Colombo	1986/87
120*	Thomson S.A. v Pakistan at Christchurch	1993/94
120	Dempster C.S. v England at Lord's	1931

120	Reid J.R. v India at Calcutta	1955/56
120	Young B.A. v Pakistan at Christchurch	1993/94
120	Cairns C.L. v Zimbabwe at Auckland	1995/96
120	Taylor L.R.P.L. v England at Hamilton	2007/08
119*	Reid J.R. v India at Delhi	1955/56
119*	Burgess M.G. v Pakistan at Dacca	1969/70
119*	Oram J.D.P. v South Africa at Hamilton	2003/04
119	Wright J.G. v England at The Oval	1986
119	Crowe M.D. v West Indies at Wellington	1986/87
119	Latham R.T. v Zimbabwe at Bulawayo	1992/93
119	Styris S.B. v India at Mohali	2003/04
118	Vettori D.L. v India at Hamilton	2008/09
117*	Hastings B.F. v West Indies at Christchurch	1968/69
117*	Wright J.G. v Australia at Wellington	1989/90
117	Mills J.E. v England at Wellington	1929/30
117	Morrison J.F.M. v Australia at Sydney	1973/74
117	Turner G.M. v India at Christchurch	1975/76
117	Fleming S.P. v England at Nottingham	2004
117	Oram J.D.P. v Bangladesh at Dunedin	2007/08
116	Hadlee W.A. v England at Christchurch	1946/47
116	Sutcliffe B. v England at Christchurch	1950/51
116	Pollard V. v England at Nottingham	1973
116	Wright J.G. v England at Wellington	1991/92
115	Crowe M.D. v England at Manchester	1994
115	McCullum B.B. v India at Napier	2008/09
114	Sinclair B.W. v England at Auckland	1965/66
114	Howarth G.P. v Pakistan at Napier	1978/79
114	Astle N.J. v Zimbabwe at Auckland	1997/98
114	Astle N.J. v Sri Lanka at Napier	2004/05
113*	Smith I.D.S. v England at Auckland	1983/84
113*	Wright J.G. v India at Napier	1989/90
113	Turner G.M. v India at Kanpur	1976/77
113	Crowe M.D. v India at Auckland	1989/90
112	Crowe J.J. v West Indies at Kingston	1984/85
112	Spearman C.M. v Zimbabwe at Auckland	1995/96
111*	Coney J.V. v Pakistan at Dunedin	1984/85
111	McGregor S.N. v Pakistan at Lahore	1955/56
111	Burgess M.G. v Pakistan at Lahore	1976/77
111	McCullum B.B. v Zimbabwe at Harare	2005/06
110*	Turner G.M. v Australia at Christchurch	1973/74
110	Turner G.M. v Pakistan at Dacca	1969/70
110	Hastings B.F. v Pakistan at Auckland	1972/73
110	Wright J.G. v India at Auckland	1980/81
110	Bracewell J.G. v England at Nottingham	1986
110	Horne M.J. v Zimbabwe at Bulawayo	2000/01
110	Parore A.C. v Australia at Perth	2001/02
109	Barton P.T. v South Africa at Port Elizabeth	1961/62
109	Cairns C.L. v Australia at Wellington	1999/00
108*	Crowe M.D. v Pakistan at Lahore	1990/91
108	Parker J.M. v Australia at Sydney	1973/74
108	Reid J.F. v Australia at Brisbane	1985/86
108	Styris S.B. v England at Nottingham	2004
107*	Congdon B.E. v Australia at Christchurch	1976/77
107*	Greatbatch M.J. v England at Auckland	1987/88
107*	Rutherford K.R. v England at Wellington	1987/88
107*	McMillan C.D. v England at Manchester	1999

107	Rabone G.O. v South Africa at Durban	1953/54
107	Redmond R.E. v Pakistan at Auckland	1972/73
107	Wright J.G. v Pakistan at Karachi	1984/85
107	Crowe M.D. v Sri Lanka at Colombo	1992/93
107	Styris S.B. v West Indies at St George's	2001/02
107	Bell M.D. v Bangladesh at Dunedin	2007/08
107	Taylor L.R.P.L. v India at Wellington	2008/09
106	Reid J.F. v Pakistan at Hyderabad	1984/85
106	Crowe M.D. v England at Lord's	1986
106	Richardson M.H. v Pakistan at Hamilton	2000/01
106	McMillan C.D. v Bangladesh at Hamilton	2001/02
106	Vincent L. v India at Mohali	2003/04
105*	Pollard V. v England at Lord's	1973
105	Taylor B.R. v India at Calcutta	1964/65
105	Hastings B.F. v West Indies at Bridgetown	1971/72
105	Burgess M.G. v England at Lord's	1973
105	Rutherford K.R. v Sri Lanka at Moratuwa	1992/93
105	Bell M.D. v Pakistan at Hamilton	2000/01
105	Fleming S.P. v Australia at Perth	2001/02
104	Page M.L. v England at Lord's	1931
104	Congdon B.E. v England at Christchurch	1965/66
104	Burgess M.G. v England at Auckland	1970/71
104	Parker J.M. v India at Bombay	1976/77
104	Crowe M.D. v West Indies at Auckland	1986/87
104	Vincent L. v Australia at Perth	2001/02
103*	Styris S.B. v West Indies at Auckland	2005/06
103	Hadlee R.J. v West Indies at Christchurch	1979/80
103	Wright J.G. v England at Auckland	1987/88
103	Astle N.J. v West Indies at St John's	1995/96
103	Astle N.J. v India at Ahmedabad	2003/04
102*	Astle N.J. v England at Auckland	1996/97
102	Guy J.W. v India at Hyderabad	1955/56
102	Howarth G.P. v England at Auckland	1977/78
102	Rutherford K.R. v Australia at Christchurch	1992/93
102	Ryder J.D. v India at Hamilton	2008/09
101*	Coney J.V. v Australia at Wellington	1985/86
101	Sutcliffe B. v England at Manchester	1949
101	Harris P.G.Z. v South Africa at Cape Town	1961/62
101	Burgess M.G. v West Indies at Kingston	1971/72
101	Hastings B.F. v Australia at Wellington	1973/74
101	Turner G.M. v Australia at Christchurch	1973/74
101	Franklin T.J. v England at Lord's	1990
101	Wright J.G. v Sri Lanka at Hamilton	1990/91
101	Astle N.J. v England at Manchester	1999
101	Richardson M.H. v England at Lord's	2004
101	Oram J.D.P. v England at Lord's	2008
100*	Jones A.H. v Sri Lanka at Hamilton	1990/91
100*	Parore A.C. v West Indies at Christchurch	1994/95
100*	McMillan C.D. v India at Mohali	2003/04
100	Vivian H.G. v South Africa at Wellington	1931/32
100	Reid J.R. v England at Christchurch	1962/63
100	Crowe M.D. v England at Wellington	1983/84
100	Horne M.J. v England at Lord's	1999

Century on Test Debut

117 & 7	Mills J.E. v England at Wellington	1929/30
105 & 0*	Taylor B.R. v India at Calcutta	1964/65
107 & 56	Redmond R.E. v Pakistan at Auckland	1972/73
11 & 107*	Greatbatch M.J. v England at Auckland	1987/88
214	Sinclair M.S. v West Indies at Wellington	1999/00
104 & 54	Vincent L. v Australia at Perth	2001/02
107 & 69*	Styris S.B. v West Indies at St George's	2001/02

Centuries in Both Innings of a Test

101 & 110*	Turner G.M. v Australia at Christchurch	1973/74
122 & 102	Howarth G.P. v England at Auckland	1977/78
122 & 100*	Jones A.H. v Sri Lanka at Hamilton	1990/91

NB: *In the same match that Jones achieved this feat A.P. Gurusinha (119 & 102) also scored a century in each innings. This is only the second occasion that a player from each side has scored centuries in each innings of a test (A.R. Morris and D.C.S. Compton, Australia v England, Adelaide, 1946/47).*

200 Runs in a Test

343	Fleming S.P. (274* & 69*) v Sri Lanka at Colombo	2002/03
329	Crowe M.D. (30 & 299) v Sri Lanka at Wellington	1990/91
267	Young B.A. (267*) v Sri Lanka at Dunedin	1996/97
262	Fleming S.P. (262) v South Africa at Cape Town	2005/06
259	Turner G.M. (259) v West Indies at Georgetown	1971/72
254	Sinclair M.S. (204* & 50*) v Pakistan at Christchurch	2000/01
252	Fleming S.P. (78 & 174*) v Sri Lanka at Colombo	1997/98
248	Congdon B.E. (166* & 82) v West Indies at Port of Spain	1971/72
244	Dowling G.T. (239 & 5) v India at Christchurch	1967/68
244	Turner G.M. (223* & 21) v West Indies at Kingston	1971/72
232	Astle N.J. (10 & 222) v England at Christchurch	2001/02
230	Sutcliffe B. (230*) v India at Delhi	1955/56
224	Howarth G.P. (122 & 102) v England at Auckland	1977/78
224	Vincent L. (224) v Sri Lanka at Wellington	2004/05
222	Greatbatch M.J. (76 & 146*) v Australia at Perth	1989/90
222	Jones A.H. (122 & 100*) v Sri Lanka at Hamilton	1990/91
216	Dempster C.S. (136 & 80*) v England at Wellington	1929/30
214	Jones A.H. (150 & 64) v Australia at Adelaide	1987/88
214	Sinclair M.S. (214) v West Indies at Wellington	1999/00
213	Wright J.G. (75 & 138) v West Indies at Wellington	1986/87
211	Turner G.M. (101 & 110*) v Australia at Christchurch	1973/74
206	Donnelly M.P. (206) v England at Lord's	1949
204	Reid J.R. (128 & 76) v Pakistan at Karachi	1964/65
202	Reid J.R. (60 & 142) v South Africa at Johannesburg	1961/62
202	Fleming S.P. (202) v Bangladesh at Chittagong	2004/05
201	Coney J.V. (27 & 174*) v England at Wellington	1983/84
201	Crowe M.D. (140 & 61) v Zimbabwe at Harare	1992/93
201	Ryder J.D. (201) v India at Napier	2008/09

A Century and a Fifty in a Test

136 & 80*	Dempster C.S. v England at Wellington	1929/30
52 & 120	Dempster C.S. v England at Lord's	1931
100 & 73	Vivian H.G. v South Africa at Wellington *(aged 19)*	1931/32
107 & 68	Rabone G.O. v South Africa at Durban	1953/54
60 & 142	Reid J.R. v South Africa at Johannesburg	1961/62

74 & 100	Reid J.R. v England at Christchurch	1962/63
128 & 76	Reid J.R. v Pakistan at Karachi	1964/65
59 & 119*	Burgess M.G. v Pakistan at Dacca	1969/70
166* & 82	Congdon B.E. v West Indies at Port of Spain	1971/72
107 & 56	Redmond R.E. v Pakistan at Auckland	1972/73
75 & 138	Wright J.G. v West Indies at Wellington	1986/87
150 & 64	Jones A.H. v Australia at Adelaide	1987/88
76 & 146*	Greatbatch M.J. v Australia at Perth	1989/90
140 & 61	Crowe M.D. v Zimbabwe at Harare	1992/93
105 & 53	Rutherford K.R. v Sri Lanka at Moratuwa	1992/93
57 & 102	Rutherford K.R. v Australia at Christchurch	1992/93
70 & 115	Crowe M.D. v England at Manchester	1994
57 & 120	Cairns C.L. v Zimbabwe at Auckland	1995/96
54 & 125	Astle N.J. v West Indies at Bridgetown	1995/96
78 & 174*	Fleming S.P. v Sri Lanka at Colombo	1997/98
109 & 69	Cairns C.L. v Australia at Wellington	1999/00
141 & 51*	Astle N.J. v Zimbabwe at Wellington	2000/01
204 & 50*	Sinclair M.S. v Pakistan at Christchurch	2000/01
104 & 54	Vincent L. v Australia at Perth	2001/02
107 & 69*	Styris S.B. v West Indies at St George's	2001/02
274* & 69*	Fleming S.P. v Sri Lanka at Colombo	2002/03
103 & 51	Astle N.J. v India at Ahmedabad	2003/04
93 & 101	Richardson M.H. v England at Lord's	2004

NB: *Redmond's feat of scoring a century and a fifty in his only test is unique. Only he and A.G. Ganteaume (112 WI v England, Port of Spain 1947/48) have made a century in their only test.*

Centuries in Three Successive Test Innings

Jones A.H. 186, Wellington, 122 and 100* Hamilton v Sri Lanka 1990/91

Centuries in Two Successive Test Innings

Reid J.R. 119*, Delhi and 120, Calcutta v India 1955/56
Burgess M.G. 119*, Dacca v Pakistan 1969/70 and 104, Auckland v England 1970/71
Congdon B.E. 176, Nottingham and 175, Lord's v England 1973
Pollard V. 116, Nottingham and 105*, Lord's v England 1973
Turner G.M. 101 and 110*, Christchurch v Australia 1973/74
Howarth G.P. 122 and 102, Auckland v England 1977/78 – 94 v England, Oval 1978
Crowe M.D. 143, Wellington v England 1987/88 and 174, Wellington v Pakistan 1988/89
Wright J.G. 185, Christchurch and 113* Napier v India 1989/90
Astle N.J. 125, Bridgetown and 103, St Johns v West Indies 1995/96

NB: *M.G. Burgess scored centuries in three successive tests – all played in different countries! He followed the two centuries above with 15 & 101 v West Indies at Kingston, 1971/72.*

B.E .Congdon scored centuries in successive tests v West Indies 1971/72 – 166 & 82 at Port of Spain and 126 at Bridgetown.*

G.T. Dowling did likewise with 143 & 10 at Dunedin and 239 & 5 at Christchurch v India 1967/68.

In successive tests v Pakistan 1984/85 J.F. Reid scored 106 & 21 at Hyderabad, 97 at Karachi, 148 & 3 at Wellington and 158 at Auckland.*

Fifty on Test Debut

3 & 51	Vivian H.G. v England at The Oval *(aged 18)*	1931
52 & 56	Wallace W.M. v England at Lord's	1937
64 & 0	Moloney D.A.R. v England at Lord's	1937
58	Sutcliffe B. v England at Christchurch	1946/47
50 & 25	Reid J.R. v England at Manchester	1949
93 & 64	Harford N.S. v Pakistan at Lahore	1955/56
54 & 23	Barton P.T. v South Africa at Durban	1961/62
74 & 58	Dowling G.T. v South Africa at Johannesburg	1961/62
64 & 1	Yuile B.W. v England at Auckland	1962/63
10 & 52	Gedye S.G. v South Africa at Wellington	1963/64

66 & 5	Morgan R.W. v Pakistan at Auckland	1964/65
17 & 54	Murray B.A.G. v India at Dunedin	1967/68
50 & 39	Burgess M.G. v India at Dunedin	1967/68
69 & 0*	Thomson K. v India at Christchurch	1967/68
6 & 51*	Howarth G.P. v England at Auckland	1974/75
14 & 92	Anderson R.W. v Pakistan at Lahore	1976/77
55 & 19	Wright J.G. v England at Wellington	1977/78
56 & 0*	Harris C.Z. v Sri Lanka at Moratuwa	1992/93
38 & 53	Young B.A. v Australia at Brisbane	1993/94
16 & 92	Fleming S.P. v India at Hamilton	1993/94
54 & 0	McMillan C.D. v Australia at Brisbane	1997/98
59 & 12	Papps M.H.W. v South Africa at Hamilton	2003/04
57 & 19*	McCullum B.B. v South Africa at Hamilton	2003/04
74 & 7	Cumming C.D. v Australia at Christchurch	2004/05
5 & 77*	Southee T.G. v England at Napier	2007/08

NB: *H.M. McGirr scored 51 in his first (and only) test innings but it was his second test appearance.*

Two Fifties in a Test

52 & 56	†Wallace W.M. v England at Lord's	1937
58 & 50	Vivian H.G. v England at Old Trafford	1937
96 & 54*	Smith F.B. v England at Headingley	1949
75 & 80	Donnelly M.P. v England at Old Trafford	1949
88 & 54	Sutcliffe B. v England at The Oval	1949
55 & 58	Wallace W.M. v England at The Oval	1949
93 & 64	†Harford N.S. v Pakistan at Lahore	1955/56
74 & 58	†Dowling G.T. v South Africa at Johannesburg	1961/62
55 & 55	Pollard V. v England at Lord's *(aged 19)*	1965
66 & 60	Burgess M.G. v India at Wellington	1967/68
58 & 58	Morrison J.F.M. v England at Auckland	1974/75
54 & 54	Congdon B.E. v India at Auckland	1975/76
55 & 54	Edwards G.N. v England at Auckland	1977/78
62 & 76	Edgar B.A. v England at Nottingham	1983
62 & 60	Howarth G.P. v Sri Lanka at Kandy	1983/84
57 & 84	Crowe M.D. v Pakistan at Dunedin	1984/85
50 & 52	Edgar B.A. v Australia at Sydney	1985/86
56 & 59	Wright J.G. v Australia at Auckland	1985/86
82 & 79	Crowe M.D. v Australia at Melbourne	1987/88
87 & 88	Greatbatch M.J. v Zimbabwe at Bulawayo	1992/93
74 & 89	Rutherford K.R. v Zimbabwe at Harare	1992/93
63 & 59	Rutherford K.R. v India at Hamilton	1993/94
79 & 53	Fleming S.P. v South Africa at Cape Town	1994/95
59 & 51*	Twose R.G. v Pakistan at Christchurch	1995/96
57 & 52	Cairns C.L. v England at Christchurch	1996/97
92 & 84	McMillan C.D. v India at Hamilton	1998/99
93 & 60	Horne M.J. v South Africa at Auckland	1998/99
57 & 99	Fleming S.P. v South Africa at Bloemfontein	2000/01
57 & 71	Vincent L. v England at Wellington	2001/02
95 & 71	Richardson M.H. v West Indies at St George's	2001/02
55 & 55	Richardson M.H. v Sri Lanka at Kandy	2002/03
54 & 83*	McMillan C.D. v India at Ahmedabad	2003/04
53 & 55	Taylor L.R.P.L. v England at Wellington	2007/08
59 & 66	Fleming S.P. v England at Napier	2007/08
55 & 76*	Vettori D.L. v Bangladesh at Chittagong	2008/09
57 & 59*	Ryder J.D. v West Indies at Napier	2008/09

† *on debut*

Fifties in Successive Test Innings

The following reached 50 in four successive test innings:

Donnelly M.P. 62, 206, 75 & 80 v England, 1949
Sutcliffe B. 101, 88, 54 v England 1949 and 116 v England 1950/51
Congdon B.E. 166*, 82, 126 and 61* v West Indies 1971/72
54, 54, 58 & 52 v India 1975/76
Coney J.V. 101*, 98, 93 v Australia 1985/86 and 51 v England 1986
Rutherford K.R. 74, 89 v Zimbabwe and 105, 53 v Sri Lanka 1992/93
Ryder J.D. 89, 57, 59* v West Indies and 102 v India 2008/09

Highest Score in Each Batting Position

Position in batting order					
1 or 2	267*	Young B.A.	v Sri Lanka	Dunedin	1996/97
3	274*	Fleming S.P.	v Sri Lanka	Colombo	2002/03
4	299	Crowe M.D.	v Sri Lanka	Wellington	1990/91
5	222	Astle N.J.	v England	Christchurch	2001/02
6	174*	Coney J.V.	v England	Wellington	1983/84
7	158	Cairns C.L.	v South Africa	Auckland	2003/04
8	127	Vettori D.L.	v Zimbabwe	Harare	2005/06
9	173	Smith I.D.S.	v India	Auckland	1989/90
10	83*	Bracewell J.G.	v Australia	Sydney	1985/86
11	68*	Collinge R.O.	v Pakistan	Auckland	1972/73

Century Partnership for The First Wicket

					Final innings total
276	Dempster C.S. Mills J.E.	v England	Wellington	1929/30	440
133	Sutcliffe B. Hadlee W.A.	v England	Christchurch	1946/47	345-9d
112	Sutcliffe B. Scott V.J	v England	Leeds	1949	195-2
121	Sutcliffe B. Scott V.J.	v England	The Oval	1949	345
126	Rabone G.O. Chapple M.E.	v South Africa	Cape Town	1953/54	505
101	McGregor S.N. Leggat J.G.	v India	Delhi	1955/56	112-1
136	Dowling G.T. Jarvis T.W.	v Pakistan	Lahore	1964/65	482-6d
126	Dowling G.T. Murray B.A.G.	v India	Christchurch	1967/68	502
112	Dowling G.T. Turner G.M.	v West Indies	Auckland	1968/69	297-8d
115	Dowling G.T. Turner G.M.	v West Indies	Christchurch	1968/69	367-6
106	Dowling G.T. Murray B.A.G.	v India	Hyderabad	1969/70	181

387	Turner G.M. Jarvis T.W.	v West Indies	Georgetown	1971/72	543-3d
159	Redmond R.E. Turner G.M.	v Pakistan	Auckland	1972/73	402
107	Parker J.M. Turner G.M.	v Australia	Auckland	1973/74	158
100	Wright J.G. Edgar B.A.	v Australia	Sydney	1985/86	193
117	Wright J.G. Franklin T.J.	v England	Auckland	1987/88	350-7d
149	Wright J.G. Franklin T.J.	v India	Napier	1989/90	178-1
185	Wright J.G. Franklin T.J.	v England	Lord's	1990	462-9d
134	Franklin T.J. Wright J.G.	v Sri Lanka	Wellington	1990/91	671-4
161	Franklin T.J. Wright J.G.	v Sri Lanka	Hamilton	1990/91	374-6d
116	Greatbatch M.J. Latham R.T.	v Zimbabwe	Bulawayo	1992/93	325-3d
102	Greatbatch M.J. Latham R.T.	v Zimbabwe	Bulawayo	1992/93	222-5d
110	Hartland B.R. Wright J.G.	v Sri Lanka	Moratuwa	1992/93	195-5
110	Greatbatch M.J. Hartland B.R.	v Pakistan	Hamilton	1992/93	264
111	Greatbatch M.J. Wright J.G.	v Australia	Wellington	1992/93	329
214	Spearman C.M. Twose R.G.	v Zimbabwe	Auckland	1995/96	441-5d
107	Young B.A. Horne M.J.	v South Africa	Christchurch	1998/99	127-1
131	Horne M.J. Stead G.R.	v India	Ahmedabad	1999/00	252-2
102	Richardson M.H. Bell M.D.	v Pakistan	Christchurch	2000/01	476
181	Richardson M.H. Bell M.D.	v Pakistan	Hamilton	2000/01	407-4d
104	Richardson M.H. Horne M.J.	v Bangladesh	Wellington	2001/02	341-6d
117	Richardson M.H. Vincent L.	v West Indies	St George's	2001/02	256-5
231	Richardson M.H. Vincent L.	v India	Mohali	2003/04	630-6d
163	Richardson M.H. Fleming S.P.	v England	Nottingham	2004	384

Pairs in Test Matches Involving New Zealand

By New Zealand *(55)*

*James K.C. v England at Christchurch	1929/30
*Badcock F.T. v England at Christchurch	1929/30
Cowie J. v England at Manchester	1937
*Rowe C.G. v Australia at Wellington	1945/46
*Butterfield L.A. v Australia at Wellington	1945/46
Miller L.S.M. v South Africa at Johannesburg	1953/54
Poore M.B. v England at Auckland	1954/55
Colquhoun I.A. v England at Auckland	1954/55
Hayes J.A. v England at Auckland	1954/55
Blair R.W. v West Indies at Dunedin	1955/56
Cave H.B. v West Indies at Dunedin	1955/56
MacGibbon A.R. v India at Madras	1955/56
Harford N.S. v England at Leeds	1958
Motz R.C. v South Africa at Cape Town	1961/62
Blair R.W. v England at Christchurch	1962/63
Blair R.W. v South Africa at Auckland	1963/64
Shrimpton M.J.F. v South Africa at Auckland	1963/64
Dick A.E. v Pakistan at Rawalpindi	1964/65
Bartlett G.A. v England at Christchurch	1965/66
Jarvis T.W. v Pakistan at Wellington	1972/73
Lees W.K. v England at Christchurch	1977/78
*Bracewell B.P. v England at The Oval	1978
Cairns B.L. v Australia at Brisbane	1980/81
Edgar B.A. v Australia at Perth	1980/81
Troup G.B. v India at Wellington	1980/81
Coney J.V. v Australia at Christchurch	1981/82
Smith I.D.S. v Australia at Christchurch	1981/82
Bracewell J.G. v Pakistan at Hyderabad	1984/85
*Rutherford K.R. v West Indies at Port of Spain	1984/85
Wright J.G. v England at Lord's	1986
Morrison D.K. v Australia at Melbourne	1987/88
*Kuggeleijn C.M. v India at Bangalore	1988/89
Snedden M.C. v India at Hyderabad	1988/89
Morrison D.K. v Sri Lanka at Hamilton	1990/91
Hartland B.R. v England at Auckland	1991/92
Su'a M.L. v Pakistan at Hamilton	1992/93
Morrison D.K. v Australia at Hobart	1993/94
Doull S.B. v West Indies at Wellington	1994/95
Nash D.J. v Sri Lanka at Napier	1994/95
Harris C.Z. v West Indies at Bridgetown	1995/96
Patel D.N. v England at Auckland	1996/97
Doull S.B. v England at Wellington	1996/97
Fleming S.P. v Australia at Hobart	1997/98
Vettori D.L. v Sri Lanka at Galle	1997/98
Wiseman P.J. v India at Wellington	1998/99
Twose R.G. v England at Edgbaston	1999
Wiseman P.J. v India at Kanpur	1999/00
O'Connor S.B. v Australia at Hamilton	1999/00
*Franklin J.E.C. v Pakistan at Auckland	2000/01
Martin C.S. v Pakistan at Auckland	2000/01
Martin C.S. v Pakistan at Lahore	2001/02
Martin C.S. v Australia at Brisbane	2004/05
Martin C.S. v West Indies at Auckland	2005/06

Martin C.S. v South Africa at Johannesburg	2007/08
*Gillespie M.R. v South Africa at Centurion	2007/08
O'Brien I.E. v South Africa at Centurion	2007/08
O'Brien I.E. v Australia at Adelaide	2008/09
Martin C.S. v Australia at Adelaide	2008/09

Against New Zealand *(28)*

Javed Burki for Pakistan at Wellington	1964/65
Jaisimha M.L. for India at Hyderabad	1969/70
Knott A.P.E. for England at Lord's	1973
Stackpole K.R. for Australia at Auckland	1973/74
Chandrasekhar B.S. for India at Wellington	1975/76
Hendrick M. for England at Wellington	1977/78
Kallicharran A.I. for West Indies at Dunedin	1979/80
Wood G.M. for Australia at Perth	1980/81
Holland R.G. for Australia at Brisbane	1985/86
*Patel R.G. for India at Bombay	1988/89
Malcolm D.E. for England at Birmingham	1990
Waqar Younis for Pakistan at Faisalabad	1990/91
Aamer Sohail for Pakistan at Hamilton	1992/93
Langer J.L. for Australia at Auckland	1992/93
Streak H.H. for Zimbabwe at Harare	1997/98
Rennie G.J. for Zimbabwe at Auckland	1997/98
Mbangwa M. for Zimbabwe at Auckland	1997/98
Walsh C.A. for West Indies at Wellington	1999/00
Nkala M.L. for Zimbabwe at Harare	2000/01
Monjurul Islam for Bangladesh at Wellington	2001/02
Laxman V.V.S. for India at Wellington	2002/03
Khan Z. for India at Hamilton	2002/03
Tareq Aziz for Bangladesh at Dhaka	2004/05
Mohammad Ashraful for Bangladesh at Chittagong	2004/05
Mpofu C.B. for Zimbabwe at Harare	2005/06
*Silva L.P.C. for Sri Lanka at Christchurch	2006/07
Malinga S.L. for Sri Lanka at Wellington	2006/07
Muralitharan M. for Sri Lanka at Wellington	2006/07
Aftab Ahmed for Bangladesh at Dunedin	2007/08
Shahadat Hossain for Bangladesh at Dunedin	2007/08

** on debut*

BOWLING

Ten Wickets in a Match

(22 instances)

15-123	Hadlee R.J. v Australia at Brisbane	1985/86
12-149	Vettori D.L. v Australia at Auckland	1999/00
12-170	Vettori D.L. v Bangladesh at Chittagong	2004/05
11-58	Hadlee R.J. v India at Wellington	1975/76
11-102	Hadlee R.J. v West Indies at Dunedin	1979/80
11-152	Pringle C. v Pakistan at Faisalabad	1990/91
11-155	Hadlee R.J. v Australia at Perth	1985/86
11-169	Nash D.J. v England at Lord's	1994
11-180	Martin C.S. v South Africa at Auckland	2003/04
10-88	Hadlee R.J. v India at Bombay	1988/89
10-99	Bond S.E. v Zimbabwe at Bulawayo	2005/06
10-100	Hadlee R.J. v England at Wellington	1977/78
10-100	Cairns C.L. v West Indies at Hamilton	1999/00
10-102	Hadlee R.J. v Sri Lanka at Colombo	1983/84
10-106	Bracewell J.G. v Australia at Auckland	1985/86
10-124	Chatfield E.J. v West Indies at Port of Spain	1984/85
10-140	Cowie J. v England at Manchester	1937
10-140	Hadlee R.J. v England at Nottingham	1986
10-144	Cairns B.L. v England at Leeds	1983
10-166	Troup G.B. v West Indies at Auckland	1979/80
10-176	Hadlee R.J. v Australia at Melbourne	1987/88
10-183	Vettori D.L. v Sri Lanka at Wellington	2006/07

Five Wickets in an Innings

(173 instances)

9-52	Hadlee R.J. v Australia at Brisbane	1985/86
7-23	Hadlee R.J. v India at Wellington	1975/76
7-27	Cairns C.L. v West Indies at Hamilton	1999/00
7-52	Pringle C. v Pakistan at Faisalabad	1990/91
7-53	Cairns C.L. v Bangladesh at Hamilton	2001/02
7-65	Doull S.B. v India at Wellington	1998/99
7-74	Taylor B.R. v West Indies at Bridgetown	1971/72
7-74	Cairns B.L. v England at Leeds	1983
7-87	Boock S.L. v Pakistan at Hyderabad	1984/85
7-87	Vettori D.L. v Australia at Auckland	1999/00
7-89	Morrison D.K. v Australia at Wellington	1992/93
7-116	Hadlee R.J. v Australia at Christchurch	1985/86
7-130	Vettori D.L. v Sri Lanka at Wellington	2006/07
7-143	Cairns B.L. v England at Wellington	1983/84
6-26	Hadlee R.J. v England at Wellington	1977/78
6-27	Nash D.J. v India at Mohali	1999/00
6-28	Vettori D.L. v Bangladesh at Dhaka	2004/05
6-32	Bracewell J.G. v Australia at Auckland	1985/86
6-37	Morrison D.K. v Australia at Auckland	1992/93
6-38	Bartlett G.A. v India at Christchurch	1967/68
6-40	Cowie J. v Australia at Wellington	1945/46
6-46	Butler I.G. v Pakistan at Wellington	2003/04
6-49	Hadlee R.J. v India at Bombay	1988/89
6-50	Hadlee R.J. v West Indies at Christchurch	1986/87
6-50	Patel D.N. v Zimbabwe at Harare	1992/93

6-51	Hadlee R.J. v Pakistan at Dunedin	1984/85
6-51	Bracewell J.G. v India at Bombay	1988/89
6-51	Bond S.E. v Zimbabwe at Bulawayo	2005/06
6-52	Cairns C.L. v England at Auckland	1991/92
6-53	Hadlee R.J. v England at The Oval	1983
6-54	Tuffey D.R. v England at Auckland	2001/02
6-54	Martin C.S. v Sri Lanka at Wellington	2004/05
6-56	Vettori D.L. v West Indies at Dunedin	2008/09
6-57	Hadlee R.J. v Australia at Melbourne	1980/81
6-60	Reid J.R. v South Africa at Dunedin	1963/64
6-63	Motz R.C. v India at Christchurch	1967/68
6-63	Collinge R.O. v India at Christchurch	1975/76
6-64	Vettori D.L. v Sri Lanka at Colombo	1997/98
6-67	Cowie J. v England at Manchester	1937
6-68	Rabone G.O. v South Africa at Cape Town	1953/54
6-68	Hadlee R.J. v West Indies at Dunedin	1979/80
6-69	Motz R.C. v West Indies at Wellington	1968/69
6-69	Morrison D.K. v West Indies at Christchurch	1994/95
6-70	Vettori D.L. v Bangladesh at Chittagong	2004/05
6-71	Hadlee R.J. v Australia at Brisbane	1985/86
6-73	Chatfield E.J. v West Indies at Port of Spain	1984/85
6-75	O'Brien I.E. v West Indies at Napier	2008/09
6-76	Cunis R.S. v England at Auckland	1970/71
6-76	Nash D.J. v England at Lord's	1994
6-76	Martin C.S. v South Africa at Auckland	2003/04
6-77	Cairns C.L. v England at Lord's	1999
6-78	Watson W. v Pakistan at Lahore	1990/91
6-80	Hadlee R.J. v England at Lord's	1986
6-80	Hadlee R.J. v England at Nottingham	1986
6-83	Cowie J. v England at Christchurch	1946/47
6-85	Cairns B.L. v West Indies at Christchurch	1979/80
6-85	Bracewell J.G. v Australia at Wellington	1989/90
6-87	Vettori D.L. v Australia at Perth	2001/02
6-90	Hadlee R.J. v Australia at Perth	1985/86
6-95	Troup G.B. v West Indies at Auckland	1979/80
6-100	Hadlee R.J. v Australia at Christchurch	1981/82
6-100	Vettori D.L. v Bangladesh at Chittagong	2004/05
6-105	Hadlee R.J. v West Indies at Auckland	1986/87
6-113	Patel D.N. v Zimbabwe at Bulawayo	1992/93
6-119	Franklin J.E.C v Australia at Auckland	2004/05
6-127	Vettori D.L. v India at Kanpur	1999/00
*6-155	Moir A.M. v England at Christchurch	1950/51
6-162	Burtt T.B. v England at Manchester	1949
*6-168	Cresswell G.F. v England at The Oval	1949
5-26	Taylor B.R. v India at Bombay	1964/65
5-28	Hadlee R.J. v England at Christchurch	1983/84
5-28	Boock S.L. v Sri Lanka at Kandy	1983/84
5-28	Franklin J.E.C v Bangladesh at Dhaka	2004/05
5-29	Hadlee R.J. v Sri Lanka at Colombo	1983/84
5-31	Cairns C.L. v England at The Oval	1999
5-31	Cairns C.L. v Zimbabwe at Bulawayo	2000/01
5-33	Cairns B.L. v India at Wellington	1980/81
5-34	Cameron F.J. v Pakistan at Auckland	1964/65
5-34	Howarth H.J. v India at Nagpur	1969/70
5-34	Hadlee R.J. v West Indies at Dunedin	1979/80

5-37	Martin C.S. v South Africa at Johannesburg	2005/06
5-39	Hadlee R.J. v Australia at Wellington	1989/90
5-41	Taylor B.R. v West Indies at Port of Spain	1971/72
5-41	Morrison D.K. v Pakistan at Hamilton	1992/93
5-44	Cairns C.L. v West Indies at Wellington	1999/00
5-46	Doull S.B. v Pakistan at Lahore	1996/97
5-47	Hadlee R.J. v India at Christchurch	1980/81
5-48	Cameron F.J. v South Africa at Cape Town	1961/62
5-50	Cairns C.L. v Zimbabwe at Harare	1997/98
5-51	O'Connor S.B. v Australia at Hamilton	1999/00
5-53	Hadlee R.J. v England at Birmingham	1990
5-53	Franklin J.E.C. v West Indies at Wellington	2005/06
5-55	Cairns B.L. v India at Madras	1976/77
5-55	Martin C.S. v South Africa at Wellington	2003/04
*5-55	Southee T.G. v England at Napier	2007/08
5-58	Doull S.B. v Sri Lanka at Dunedin	1996/97
5-59	Vettori D.L. v Bangladesh at Chittagong	2008/09
5-61	Morrison D.K. v West Indies at St Johns	1995/96
5-62	Moir A.M. v England at Auckland	1954/55
5-62	Hadlee R.J. v Pakistan at Christchurch	1978/79
5-62	Cairns C.L. v Sri Lanka at Colombo	1997/98
5-62	Vettori D.L. v Australia at Auckland	1999/00
5-63	Hadlee R.J. v Australia at Auckland	1981/82
5-63	Chatfield E.J. v Sri Lanka at Colombo	1983/84
5-63	Davis H.T. v Sri Lanka at Hamilton	1996/97
5-64	MacGibbon A.R. v England at Birmingham	1958
5-65	Congdon B.E. v India at Auckland	1975/76
5-65	Hadlee R.J. v Australia at Sydney	1985/86
5-65	Hadlee R.J. v Australia at Perth	1985/86
5-65	Hadlee R.J. v India at Bangalore	1988/89
5-65	Martin C.S. v Bangladesh at Wellington	2007/08
5-66	Doull S.B. v Pakistan at Auckland	1993/94
5-66	Vettori D.L. v England at Manchester	2008
5-66	Vettori D.L. v Bangaldesh at Mirpur	2008/09
5-67	Boock S.L. v England at Auckland	1977/78
5-67	Hadlee R.J. v Australia at Melbourne	1987/88
5-68	Snedden M.C. v West Indies at Christchurch	1986/87
5-68	Hadlee R.J. v Australia at Adelaide	1987/88
5-69	Burtt T.B. v West Indies at Christchurch	1951/52
5-69	Morrison D.K. v England at Christchurch	1987/88
5-69	Bond S.E. v West Indies at Auckland	2005/06
5-69	Vettori D.L. v England at Lord's	2008
5-71	Martin C.S. v Zimbabwe at Wellington	2000/01
5-73	Hadlee R.J. v Sri Lanka at Colombo	1983/84
5-73	Su'a M.L. v Pakistan at Hamilton	1992/93
5-73	Doull S.B. v South Africa at Durban	1994/95
5-74	Collinge R.O. v England at Leeds	1973
5-75	Bracewell J.G. v India at Auckland	1980/81
5-75	Morrison D.K. v India at Christchurch	1989/90
5-75	Cairns C.L. v Sri Lanka at Auckland	1990/91
5-75	Doull S.B. v England at Wellington	1996/97
5-77	Hart M.N. v South Africa at Johannesburg	1994/95
5-78	Bond S.E. v West Indies at Bridgetown	2001/02
5-79	Cairns C.L. v England at Nottingham	2004
5-80	Howarth H.J. v Pakistan at Karachi	1969/70

5-82	Collinge R.O. v Australia at Auckland	1973/74
*5-82	Wiseman P.J. v Sri Lanka at Colombo	1997/98
5-83	Cameron F.J. v South Africa at Johannesburg	1961/62
5-84	Hadlee R.J. v England at Lord's	1978
5-84	Vettori D.L. v Sri Lanka at Hamilton	1996/97
5-85	Su'a M.L. v Zimbabwe at Harare	1992/93
*5-86	Taylor B.R. v India at Calcutta	1964/65
5-86	Motz R.C. v India at Dunedin	1967/68
5-87	Cairns B.L. v Australia at Brisbane	1980/81
5-87	Hadlee R.J. v Australia at Perth	1980/81
5-87	Tuffey D.R. v Pakistan at Hamilton	2003/04
5-90	Wiseman P.J. v Zimabwe at Bulawayo	2000/01
5-93	Hadlee R.J. v England at Lord's	1983
5-93	Patel D.N. v Australia at Auckland	1992/93
5-93	Nash D.J. v England at Lord's	1994
5-95	Chatfield E.J. v England at Leeds	1983
5-97	Burtt T.B. v England at Leeds	1949
5-98	Morrison D.K. v India at Napier	1989/90
5-104	Hadlee R.J. v Pakistan at Auckland	1978/79
5-104	Bond S.E. v West Indies at St George's	2001/02
5-104	Martin C.S. v South Africa at Auckland	2003/04
5-106	Vettori D.L. v Australia at Christchurch	2004/05
5-108	Motz R.C. v England at Birmingham	1965
5-109	Hadlee R.J. v Australia at Melbourne	1987/88
5-110	Patel J.S. v West Indies at Napier	2008/09
5-113	Motz R.C. v West Indies at Christchurch	1968/69
5-117	Boock S.L. v Pakistan at Wellington	1984/85
5-121	Hadlee R.J. v Pakistan at Lahore	1976/77
5-127	Cowie J. v England at Leeds	1949
*5-136	Gillespie M.R. v South Africa at Centurion	2007/08
5-137	Cairns C.L. v Pakistan at Rawalpindi	1996/97
5-138	Vettori D.L. v Australia at Hobart	2001/02
5-145	Morrison D.K. v India at Auckland	1989/90
5-146	Cairns C.L. v Australia at Brisbane	2001/02
5-148	O'Sullivan D.R. v Australia at Adelaide	1973/74
5-152	Martin C.S. v Australia at Brisbane	2004/05
5-152	Vettori D.L. v Australia at Adelaide	2004/05
5-153	Morrison D.K. v Sri Lanka at Wellington	1990/91

** on debut*

Hat-tricks

Petherick P.J. v Pakistan at Lahore	1976/77
Franklin J.E.C. v Bangladesh at Dhaka	2004/05

All Round Cricket

Rabone G.O. 56 and 6-68 & 1-16 v South Africa at Cape Town	1953/54
Taylor B.R. 105 & 0 and 5-86 v India at Calcutta	1964/65
Congdon B.E. 54 & 54 and 5-65 v India at Auckland	1975/76
Hadlee R.J. 54* & 5 and 5-104 & 0-8 v Pakistan at Auckland	1978/79
Hadlee R.J. 51 & 17 and 5-34 & 6-68 v West Indies at Dunedin	1979/80
Hadlee R.J. 84 & 11 and 6-53 & 2-99 v England at The Oval	1983
Cairns B.L. 3 & 64 and 7-143 v England at Wellington	1983/84
Hadlee R.J. 99 and 3-16 & 5-28 v England at Christchurch	1983/84
Hadlee R.J. 54 and 9-52 & 6-71 v Australia at Brisbane	1985/86
Hadlee R.J. 68 and 6-80 & 4-60 v England at Nottingham	1986

Bracewell J.G. 52 & 32 and 2-81 & 6-51 v India at Bombay	1988/89
Patel D.N. 6 & 58* and 2-81 & 6-50 v Zimbabwe at Harare	1992/93
Nash D.J. 56 and 6-76 & 5-93 v England at Lord's	1994
Cairns C.L. 12 & 71* and 5-50 & 0-44 v Zimbabwe at Harare	1997/98
Cairns C.L. 11 & 80 and 5-31 & 1-50 v England at The Oval	1999
Cairns C.L. 72 and 3-73 & 7-27 v West Indies at Hamilton	1999/00
Cairns C.L. 61 & 43 and 5-146 & 1-29 v Australia at Brisbane	2001/02
Vettori D.L. 20 & 59 and 5-152 & 1-35 v Australia at Adelaide	2004/05
Vettori D.L. 0 & 51 and 3-53 & 7-130 v Sri Lanka at Wellington	2006/07
Southee T.G. 5 & 77 and 5-55 & 0-84 v England at Napier	2007/08
Vettori D.L. 55 & 76* and 5-59 & 4-74 v Bangladesh at Chittagong	2008/09

** On debut. Taylor is the only player from any country to score a century and take five wickets in an innings on debut.*

WICKETKEEPING AND FIELDING

MOST DISMISSALS IN AN INNINGS BY A WICKETKEEPER

7*	Smith I.D.S. v Sri Lanka at Hamilton *(all caught)*	1990/91
5	Harford R.I. v India at Wellington *(all caught)*	1967/68
5	Wadsworth K.J. v Pakistan at Auckland *(all caught)*	1972/73
5	Lees W.K. v Sri Lanka at Wellington *(all caught)*	1982/83
5	Smith I.D.S. v England at Auckland *(4ct 1st)*	1983/84
5	Smith I.D.S. v Sri Lanka at Auckland *(all caught)*	1990/91
5	Parore A.C. v England at Auckland *(all caught)*	1991/92
5	Parore A.C. v Sri Lanka at Colombo *(4ct 1st)*	1992/93
5	Parore A.C. v Zimbabwe at Harare *(all caught)*	2000/01
5	Parore A.C. v Pakistan at Auckland *(all caught)*	2000/01
5	McCullum B.B. v England at Hamilton *(all caught)*	2007/08
5	McCullum B.B. v West Indies at Napier *(all caught)*	2008/09

** equals world test record*

MOST DISMISSALS IN A MATCH BY A WICKETKEEPER

8	Lees W.K. v Sri Lanka at Wellington *(all caught)*	1982/83
8	Smith I.D.S. v Sri Lanka at Hamilton *(all caught)*	1990/91
7	Dick A.E. v South Africa at Durban *(6ct 1st)*	1961/62
7	Harford R.I. v India at Wellington *(all caught)*	1967/68
7	Smith I.D.S. v India at Wellington *(all caught)*	1980/81
7	Smith I.D.S. v England at Leeds *(all caught)*	1983
7	Parore A.C. v Pakistan at Auckland *(all caught)*	2000/01
7	Parore A.C. v Pakistan at Hamilton *(all caught)*	2000/01
7	McCullum B.B. v Australia at Brisbane *(all caught)*	2008/09

MOST STUMPINGS IN AN INNINGS

2	Mooney F.L.H. v England at Leeds	1949
2	Milburn B.D. v West Indies at Christchurch	1968/69
2	Lees W.K. v Pakistan at Hyderabad	1976/77
2	Lees W.K. v Pakistan at Karachi	1976/77
2	Lees W.K. v India at Madras	1976/77

MOST STUMPINGS IN A MATCH

2	5 instances as above plus	
	Smith I.D.S. v Australia at Sydney	1985/86
	Parore A.C. v Australia at Auckland	1999/00
	McCullum B.B. v Zimbabwe at Harare	2005/06

MOST CATCHES IN AN INNINGS BY A FIELDER

5	Fleming S.P. v Zimbabwe at Harare	1997/98
4	Crowe J.J. v West Indies at Bridgetown	1984/85
4	Crowe M.D. v West Indies at Kingston	1984/85
4	Fleming S.P. v Australia at Brisbane	1997/98
4	Fleming S.P. v Zimbawe at Harare	2005/06
4	Fleming S.P. v West Indies at Wellington	2005/06

MOST CATCHES IN A MATCH BY A FIELDER

7	Fleming S.P. v Zimbabwe at Harare	1997/98
6	Young B.A. v Pakistan at Auckland	1993/94
6	Fleming S.P. v Australia at Brisbane	1997/98
6	Fleming S.P. v West Indies at Wellington	2005/06
5	Harris C.Z. v Zimbabwe at Bulawayo	1997/98
5	Fleming S.P. v India at Wellington	1998/99
5	Sinclair M.S. v Bangladesh at Chittagong	2004/05

REPLACEMENT WICKETKEEPERS IN TEST MATCHES

Wicketkeeper	*Replacement*	*Dismissal*			
Mooney F.L.H.	Sutcliffe B.	—	v South Africa	Port Elizabeth	1953/54
Petrie E.C.	Reid J.R.	Richardson P.E. *(st)*	v England	Manchester	1958
Petrie E.C.	Reid J.R.	—	v England	Christchurch	1958/59
Ward J.T.	Morgan R.W.	Jaisimha M.L. *(c)*	v India	Calcutta	1964/65
Ward J.T.	Congdon B.E.	Hanumant Singh *(c)*	v India	Delhi	1964/65
Dick A.E.	Reid J.R.	—	v Pakistan	Lahore	1964/65
Dick A.E.	Congdon B.E. (sub)	Pervez Sajjad *(st)*	v Pakistan	Lahore	1964/65
Lees W.K.	Anderson R.W.	—	v Pakistan	Hyderabad	1976/77
Smith I.D.S.	Edgar B.A.	Laird B.M. *(c)*	v Australia	Christchurch	1981/82
Smith I.D.S.	Crowe M.D.	—	v West Indies	Kingston	1984/85
Smith I.D.S.	Horne P.A.	—	v Australia	Melbourne	1987/88
Smith I.D.S.	Blain T.E.	—	v India	Hyderabad	1988/89
Smith I.D.S.	Horne P.A.	—	v Pakistan	Faisalabad	1990/91
Smith I.D.S.	Parore A.C. (sub)	Shoaib Mohammad *(c)* Aaqib Javed *(c)*	v Pakistan	Faisalabad	1990/91
McCullum B.B.	Sinclair M.S.	Jayawardene D.P.M.D.	v Sri Lanka	Wellington	2006/07

RECORD PARTNERSHIPS

NEW ZEALAND v ALL COUNTRIES

For

1st	387	Turner G.M. & Jarvis T.W. v West Indies	Georgetown	1971/72
2nd	241	Wright J.G. & Jones A.H. v England	Wellington	1991/92
3rd	467	Jones A.H. & Crowe M.D. v Sri Lanka	Wellington	1990/91
4th	271	Taylor L.R.P.L. & Ryder J.D. v India	Napier	2008/09
5th	222	Astle N.J. & McMillan C.D. v Zimbabwe	Wellington	2000/01
6th	246*	Crowe J.J. & Hadlee R.J. v Sri Lanka	Colombo	1986/87
7th	225	Cairns C.L. & Oram J.D.P. v South Africa	Auckland	2003/04
8th	256	Fleming S.P. & Franklin J.E.C. v South Africa	Cape Town	2005/06
9th	136	Smith I.D.S. & Snedden M.C. v India	Auckland	1989/90
10th	151	Hastings B.F. & Collinge R.O. v Pakistan	Auckland	1972/73

Against

1st	413	Mankad M.H. & Roy P. for India	Madras	1955/56
2nd	369	Edrich J.H. & Barrington K.F. for England	Leeds	1965
3rd	330	Amla H.M. & Kallis J.H. for South Africa	Johannesburg	2007/08
4th	350	Mushtaq Mohammad & Asif Iqbal for Pakistan	Dunedin	1972/73
5th	281	Javed Miandad & Asif Iqbal for Pakistan	Lahore	1976/77
6th	281	Thorpe G.P. & Flintoff A. for England	Christchurch	2001/02
7th	308	Waqar Hassan & Imtiaz Ahmed for Pakistan	Lahore	1955/56
8th	246	Ames L.E.G. & Allen G.O.B. for England	Lord's	1931
9th	163*	Cowdrey M.C. & Smith A.C. for England	Wellington	1962/63
10th	114	Gillespie J.N. & McGrath G.D. for Australia	Brisbane	2004/05

NEW ZEALAND v ENGLAND

New Zealand

1st	276	Dempster C.S. & Mills J.E.	Wellington	1929/30
2nd	241	Wright J.G. & Jones A.H.	Wellington	1991/92
3rd	210	Edgar B.A. & Crowe M.D.	Lord's	1986
4th	155	Crowe M.D. & Greatbatch M.J.	Wellington	1987/88
5th	180	Crowe M.D. & Thomson S.A.	Lord's	1994
6th	141	Crowe M.D. & Parore A.C.	Manchester	1994
7th	148	Taylor L.R.P.L. & Vettori D.L.	Hamilton	2007/08
8th	104	Roberts A.W. & Moloney D.A.R.	Lord's	1937
9th	118	Coney J.V. & Cairns B.L.	Wellington	1983/84
10th	118	Astle N.J. & Cairns C.L.	Christchurch	2001/02

England

1st	223	Fowler G. & Tavare C.J.	The Oval	1983
2nd	369	Edrich J.H. & Barrington K.F.	Leeds	1965
3rd	245	Hammond W.R. & Hardstaff J.	Lord's	1937
4th	266	Denness M.H. & Fletcher K.W.R.	Auckland	1974/75
5th	242	Hammond W.R. & Ames L.E.G.	Christchurch	1932/33
6th	281	Thorpe G.P. & Flintoff A.	Christchurch	2001/02
7th	149	Knott A.P.E. & Lever P.	Auckland	1970/71
8th	246	Ames L.E.G. & Allen G.O.B.	Lord's	1931
9th	163*	Cowdrey M.C. & Smith A.C.	Wellington	1962/63
10th	59	Knott A.P.E. & Gifford N.	Nottingham	1973

NEW ZEALAND v AUSTRALIA

New Zealand

1st	111	Greatbatch M.J. & Wright J.G.	Wellington	1992/93
2nd	132	Horne M.J. & Parore A.C.	Hobart	1997/98
3rd	224	Reid J.F. & Crowe M.D.	Brisbane	1985/86
4th	229	Congdon B.E. & Hastings B.F.	Wellington	1973/74
5th	97	Fleming S.P. & McMillan C.D.	Hobart	2001/02
6th	110	Fleming S.P. & Cairns C.L.	Wellington	1999/00
7th	132*	Coney J.V. & Hadlee R.J.	Wellington	1985/86
8th	253	Astle N.J. & Parore A.C.	Perth	2001/02
9th	73	Howarth H.J. & Hadlee D.R.	Christchurch	1976/77
10th	124	Bracewell J.G. & Boock S.L.	Sydney	1985/86

Australia

1st	224	Langer J.L. & Hayden M.L.	Brisbane	2001/02
2nd	235	Slater M.J. & Boon D.C.	Hobart	1993/94
3rd	264	Chappell I.M. & Chappell G.S.	Wellington	1973/74
4th	184	Langer J.L. & Lehmann D.S.	Adelaide	2004/05
5th	213	Ritchie G.M. & Matthews G.R.J.	Wellington	1985/86
6th	256	Martyn D.R. & Gilchrist A.C.	Wellington	2004/05
7th	217	Walters K.D. & Gilmour G.J.	Christchurch	1976/77
8th	135	Gilchrist A.C. & Lee B.	Brisbane	2001/02
9th	74	Gilchrist A.C. & Kasprowicz M.S.	Auckland	2004/05
10th	114	Gillespie J.N. & McGrath G.D.	Brisbane	2004/05

NEW ZEALAND v SOUTH AFRICA

New Zealand

1st	126	Rabone G.O. & Chapple M.E.	Cape Town	1953/54
2nd	90	Horne M.J. & Astle N.J.	Auckland	1998/99
3rd	125	Richardson M.H. & Styris S.B.	Auckland	2003/04
4th	171	Sinclair B.W. & McGregor S.N.	Auckland	1963/64
5th	176	Reid J.R. & Beck J.E.F.	Cape Town	1953/54
6th	100	Vivian H.G. & Badcock F.T.	Wellington	1931/32
7th	225	Cairns C.L. & Oram J.D.P.	Auckland	2003/04
8th	256	Fleming S.P. & Franklin J.E.C.	Cape Town	2005/06
9th	87	Oram J.D.P. & Wiseman P.J.	Hamilton	2003/04
10th	57	Doull S.B. & de Groen R.P.	Johannesburg	1994/95

South Africa

1st	196	Mitchell B. & Christy J.A.H.	Christchurch	1931/32
2nd	315*	Gibbs H.H. & Kallis J.H.	Christchurch	1998/99
3rd	330	Amla H.M. & Kallis J.H.	Johannesburg	2007/08
4th	171	Smith G.C. & Kirsten G.	Wellington	2003/04
5th	141	Cullinan D.J. & Rhodes J.N.	Auckland	1998/99
6th	126*	Cullinan D.J. & Pollock S.M.	Auckland	1998/99
7th	246	McGlew D.J. & Murray A.R.A.	Wellington	1952/53
8th	136	McKenzie N.D. & Boje N.	Port Elizabeth	2000/01
9th	60	Pollock P.M. & Adcock N.A.T.	Port Elizabeth	1961/62
10th	47	McGlew D.J. & Bromfield H.D.	Port Elizabeth	1961/62

NEW ZEALAND v WEST INDIES

New Zealand

1st	387	Turner G.M. & Jarvis T.W.	Georgetown	1971/72
2nd	210	Howarth G.P. & Crowe J.J.	Kingston	1984/85
3rd	241	Wright J.G. & Crowe M.D.	Wellington	1986/87
4th	189	Sinclair M.S. & Astle N.J.	Wellington	1999/00
5th	144	Astle N.J. & Vaughan J.T.C.	Bridgetown	1995/96
6th	220	Turner G.M. & Wadsworth K.J.	Kingston	1971/72
7th	143	Crowe M.D. & Smith I.D.S.	Georgetown	1984/85
8th	136	Congdon B.E. & Cunis R.S.	Port of Spain	1971/72
9th	62*	Pollard V. & Cunis R.S.	Auckland	1968/69
	62	McCullum B.B. & Bond S.E.	Auckland	2005/06
10th	45	Morrison D.K. & Kennedy R.J.	Bridgetown	1995/96

West Indies

1st	276	Griffith A.F.G. & Campbell S.L.	Hamilton	1999/00
2nd	269	Fredericks R.C. & Rowe L.G.	Kingston	1971/72
3rd	221	Lara B.C. & Adams J.C.	Wellington	1994/95
4th	162	Weekes E.D. & Smith O.G.	Dunedin	1955/56
	162	Greenidge C.G. & Kallicharan A.I.	Christchurch	1979/80
5th	189	Worrell F.M.M. & Walcott C.L.	Auckland	1951/52
6th	254	Sobers G.S. & Davis C.A.	Bridgetown	1971/72
7th	153	Chanderpaul S. & Taylor J.E.	Dunedin	2008/09
8th	83	Richards I.V.A. & Marshall M.D.	Bridgetown	1984/85
9th	70	Marshall M.D. & Garner J.	Bridgetown	1984/85
10th	31	Findlay T.M. & Shillingford G.C.	Bridgetown	1971/72

NEW ZEALAND v INDIA

New Zealand

1st	231	Richardson M.H. & Vincent L.	Mohali	2003/04
2nd	155	Dowling G.T. & Congdon B.E.	Dunedin	1967/68
3rd	222*	Sutcliffe B. & Reid J.R.	New Delhi	1955/56
4th	271	Taylor L.R.P.L. & Ryder J.D.	Napier	2008/09
5th	142	Taylor L.R.P.L. & Franklin J.E.C.	Wellington	2008/09
6th	137	McMillan C.D. & Cairns C.L.	Wellington	1998/99
7th	186	Ryder J.D. & Vettori D.L.	Hamilton	2008/09
8th	137	Nash D.J. & Vettori D.L.	Wellington	1998/99
9th	136	Smith I.D.S. & Snedden M.C.	Auckland	1989/90
10th	61	Ward J.T. & Collinge R.O.	Madras	1964/65

India

1st	413	Mankad M.H. & Roy P.	Madras	1955/56
2nd	204	Gavaskar S.M. & Amarnath S.	Auckland	1975/76
3rd	238	Umrigar P.R. & Manjrekar V.L.	Hyderabad	1955/56
4th	281	Tendulkar S.R. & Ganguly S.C.	Ahmedabad	1999/00
5th	182	Dravid R.S. & Ganguly S.C.	Ahmedabad	2003/04
6th	193*	Sardesai D.N. & Hanumant Singh	Bombay	1964/65
7th	128	Tendulkar S.R. & More K.S.	Napier	1989/90
8th	144	Dravid R.S. & Srinath J.	Hamilton	1998/99
9th	105	Kirmani S.M.H. & Bedi B.S.	Bombay	1976/77
	105	Kirmani S.M.H. & Yadav N.S.	Auckland	1980/81
10th	57	Desai R.B. & Bedi B.S.	Dunedin	1967/68

NEW ZEALAND v PAKISTAN

New Zealand

1st	181	Richardson M.H. & Bell M.D.	Hamilton	2000/01
2nd	195	Wright J.G. & Howarth G.P.	Napier	1978/79
3rd	178	Sinclair B.W. & Reid J.R.	Lahore	1964/65
4th	147	McMillan C.D. & Fleming S.P.	Hamilton	2000/01
5th	183	Burgess M.G. & Anderson R.W.	Lahore	1976/77
6th	145	Reid J.F. & Hadlee R.J.	Wellington	1984/85
7th	186	Lees W.K. & Hadlee R.J.	Karachi	1976/77
8th	125	Fleming S.P. & Vettori D.L.	Hamilton	2003/04
9th	99	Vettori D.L. & Tuffey D.R.	Hamilton	2003/04
10th	151	Hastings B.F. & Collinge R.O.	Auckland	1972/73

Pakistan

1st	172	Rameez Raja & Shoaib Mohammad	Karachi	1990/91
2nd	262	Saeed Anwar & Ijaz Ahmed	Rawalpindi	1996/97
3rd	248	Shoaib Mohammad & Javed Miandad	Auckland	1988/89
4th	350	Mushtaq Mohammad & Asif Iqbal	Dunedin	1972/73
5th	281	Javed Miandad & Asif Iqbal	Lahore	1976/77
6th	217	Hanif Mohammad & Majid Khan	Lahore	1964/65
7th	308	Waqar Hassan & Imtiaz Ahmed	Lahore	1955/56
8th	89	Anil Dalpat & Iqbal Qasim	Karachi	1984/85
9th	78	Inzamam-ul-Haq & Shoaib Akhtar	Lahore	2001/02
10th	65	Salah-ud-din & Mohammad Farooq	Rawalpindi	1964/65

NEW ZEALAND v SRI LANKA

New Zealand

1st	161	Franklin T.J. & Wright J.G.	Hamilton	1990/91
2nd	172	Richardson M.H. & Fleming S.P.	Colombo	2002/03
3rd	467	Jones A.H. & Crowe M.D.	Wellington	1990/91
4th	240	Fleming S.P. & McMillan C.D.	Colombo	1997/98
5th	151	Rutherford K.R. & Harris C.Z.	Moratuwa	1992/93
6th	246*	Crowe J.J. & Hadlee R.J.	Colombo	1986/87
7th	75	Fleming S.P. & Vettori D.L.	Christchurch	2006/07
8th	98	Vincent L. & Mills K.D.	Wellington	2004/05
9th	59	Vincent L. & Wiseman P.J.	Wellington	2004/05
10th	52	Lees W.K. & Chatfield E.J.	Christchurch	1982/83

Sri Lanka

1st	102	Mahanama R.S. & Hathurusinghe U.C.	Colombo	1992/93
2nd	138	Mahanama R.S. & Gurusinha A.P.	Moratuwa	1992/93
3rd	184	Atapattu M.S. & Jayawardene D.P.M.D.	Napier	2004/05
4th	192	Gurusinha A.P. & Tillakaratne H.P.	Dunedin	1994/95
5th	133	Jayawardene D.P.M.D. & Tillakaratne H.P.	Colombo	2002/03
6th	109	Madugalle R.S. & Ranatunga A.	Colombo	1983/84
	109	Kuruppu D.S.B.P. & Madugalle R.S.	Colombo	1986/87
7th	137	Kaluwitharana R.S. & Vaas W.P.J.U.C.	Dunedin	1996/97
8th	89	Samaraweera T.T. & Chandana U.D.U.	Wellington	2004/05
9th	44	Sangakkara K.C. & Malinga S.L.	Christchurch	2006/07
10th	71	Kaluwitharana R.S. & Muralitharan M.	Colombo	1997/98

NEW ZEALAND v ZIMBABWE

New Zealand

1st	214	Spearman C.M. & Twose R.G.	Auckland	1995/96
2nd	127	Latham R.T. & Jones A.H.	Bulawayo	1992/93
3rd	137	Vincent L. & Fleming S.P.	Bulawayo	2005/06
4th	243	Horne M.J. & Astle N.J.	Auckland	1997/98
5th	222	Astle N.J. & McMillan C.D.	Wellington	2000/01
6th	120	Fleming S.P. & McCullum B.B.	Harare	2005/06
7th	108	McMillan C.D. & Nash D.J.	Wellington	1997/98
8th	144	Cairns C.L. & Nash D.J.	Harare	2000/01
9th	78	Parore A.C. & Vettori D.L.	Bulawayo	2000/01
10th	27	McMillan C.D. & Doull S.B.	Auckland	1997/98

Zimbabwe

1st	156	Rennie G.J. & Flower G.W.	Harare	1997/98
2nd	107	Arnott K.J. & Campbell A.D.R.	Harare	1992/93
3rd	70	Flower A. & Whittall G.J.	Bulawayo	1997/98
4th	130	Rennie G.J. & Flower A.	Wellington	2000/01
5th	131	Flower A. & Whittall G.J.	Harare	2000/01
6th	151	Whittall G.J. & Streak H.H.	Harare	2000/01
7th	91	Whittall G.J. & Strang P.A.	Hamilton	1995/96
8th	94	Campbell A.D.R. & Streak H.H.	Wellington	1997/98
9th	46	Crocker G.J. & Burmester M.G.	Harare	1992/93
10th	40	Whittall G.J. & Matambanadzo E.	Bulawayo	1997/98

NEW ZEALAND v BANGLADESH

New Zealand

1st	104	Richardson M.H. & Horne M.J.	Wellington	2001/02
2nd	90	Redmond A.J. & Ryder J.D.	Chittagong	2008/09
3rd	204	Fleming S P & Styris S B	Chittagong	2004/05
4th	137	Ryder J.D. & McCullum B.B.	Mirpur	2008/09
5th	190	Richardson M.H. & McMillan C.D.	Hamilton	2001/02
6th	89	McMillan C.D. & Cairns C.L.	Hamilton	2001/02
7th	81	McCullum B.B. & Vettori D.L.	Wellington	2007/08
8th	57	McCullum B.B. & Franklin J.E.C.	Dhaka	2004/05
9th	29	Vettori D.L. & Patel J.S.	Chittagong	2008/09
10th	31	Wiseman P.J. & Butler I.G.	Dhaka	2004/05

Bangladesh

1st	161	Tamim Iqbal & Zunaed Siddique	Dunedin	2007/08
2nd	38	Tamim Iqbal & Habibul Bashar	Dunedin	2007/08
3rd	60	Habibul Bashar & Aminul Islam	Hamilton	2001/02
4th	115	Rajin Saleh & Mohammad Ashraful	Dhaka	2004/05
5th	144	Mehrab Hossain & Mushfiqur Rahim	Chittagong	2008/09
6th	56	Mushfiqur Rahim & Shakib Al Hasan	Chittagong	2008/09
7th	78	Shakib Al Hasan & Masrafe bin Mortaza	Mirpur	2008/09
8th	39	Mushfiqur Rahman & Mohammad Rafique	Chittagong	2004/05
9th	49	Khaled Masud & Masrafe bin Mortaza	Wellington	2001/02
10th	45	Tapash Baisya & Enamul Haque	Chittagong	2004/05

CAREER RECORDS

Averages

	M	I	NO	HS	Runs	Ave	100	50	Ct	St	Wkts	Runs	Ave	Best	5WI	10WM
Adams A.R.	1	2	0	11	18	9.00	—	—	1	—	6	105	17.50	3-44	—	—
Alabaster J.C.	21	34	6	34	272	9.71	—	—	7	—	49	1863	38.02	4-46	—	—
Allcott C.F.W.	6	7	2	33	113	22.60	—	—	3	—	6	541	90.17	2-102	—	—
Allott G.I.	10	15	7	8*	27	3.37	—	—	2	—	19	1111	58.47	4-74	—	—
Anderson R.W.	9	18	0	92	423	23.50	—	3	1	—	—	—	—	—	—	—
Anderson W.M.	1	2	0	4	5	2.50	—	—	1	—	—	—	—	—	—	—
Andrews B.	2	3	2	17	22	22.00	—	—	1	—	2	154	77.00	2-40	—	—
Astle N.J.	81	137	10	222	4702	37.02	11	24	70	—	51	2143	42.01	3-27	—	—
Badcock F.T.	7	9	2	64	137	19.57	—	2	1	—	16	610	38.13	4-80	—	—
Barber R.T.	1	2	0	12	17	8.50	—	—	1	—	—	—	—	—	—	—
Bartlett G.A.	10	18	1	40	263	15.47	—	—	8	—	24	792	33.00	6-38	1	—
Barton P.T.	7	14	0	109	285	20.36	1	1	4	—	—	—	—	—	—	—
Beard D.D.	4	7	2	31	101	20.20	—	—	2	—	9	302	33.56	3-22	—	—
Beck J.E.F.	8	15	0	99	394	26.27	—	3	—	—	—	—	—	—	—	—
Bell M.D.	18	32	2	107	729	24.30	2	3	19	—	—	—	—	—	—	—
Bell W.	2	3	3	21*	21	—	—	—	1	—	2	235	117.50	1-54	—	—
Bilby G.P.	2	4	0	28	55	13.75	—	—	3	—	—	—	—	—	—	—
***Blain** T.E.	11	20	3	78	456	26.82	—	2	19	2	—	—	—	—	—	—
Blair R.W.	19	34	6	64*	189	6.75	—	1	5	—	43	1515	35.23	4-85	—	—
Blunt R.C.	9	13	1	96	330	27.50	—	1	5	—	12	472	39.33	3-17	—	—
Bolton B.A.	2	3	0	33	59	19.67	—	—	1	—	—	—	—	—	—	—
Bond S.E.	17	18	7	41*	139	12.63	—	—	6	—	79	1769	22.39	6-51	4	1
Boock S.L.	30	41	8	37	207	6.27	—	—	14	—	74	2564	34.64	7-87	4	—
Bracewell B.P.	6	12	2	8	24	2.40	—	—	1	—	14	585	41.78	3-110	—	—
Bracewell J.G.	41	60	11	110	1001	20.42	1	4	31	—	102	3653	35.81	6-32	4	1
Bradburn G.E.	7	10	2	30*	105	13.12	—	—	6	—	6	460	76.66	3-134	—	—
Bradburn W.P.	2	4	0	32	62	15.50	—	—	2	—	—	—	—	—	—	—
Brown V.R.	2	3	1	36*	51	25.50	—	—	3	—	1	176	176.00	1-17	—	—
Burgess M.G.	50	92	6	119*	2684	31.21	5	14	34	—	6	212	35.33	3-23	—	—
Burke C.	1	2	0	3	4	2.00	—	—	—	—	2	30	15.00	2-30	—	—
Burtt T.B.	10	15	3	42	252	21.00	—	—	2	—	33	1170	35.45	6-162	3	—
Butler I.G.	8	10	2	26	76	9.50	—	—	4	—	24	884	36.83	6-46	1	—
Butterfield L.A.	1	2	0	0	0	0.00	—	—	—	—	0	24	—	—	—	—
Cairns B.L.	43	65	8	64	928	16.28	—	2	30	—	130	4279	32.91	7-74	6	1
Cairns C.L.	62	104	5	158	3320	33.53	5	22	14	—	218	6410	29.40	7-27	13	1
Cameron F.J.	19	30	20	27*	116	11.60	—	—	2	—	62	1849	29.82	5-34	3	—
Cave H.B.	19	31	5	22*	229	8.81	—	—	8	—	34	1467	43.15	4-21	—	—
Chapple M.E.	14	27	1	76	497	19.12	—	3	10	—	1	84	84.00	1-24	—	—
Chatfield E.J.	43	54	33	21*	180	8.57	—	—	7	—	123	3958	32.17	6-73	3	1
Cleverley D.C.	2	4	3	10*	19	19.00	—	—	—	—	0	130	—	—	—	—
Collinge R.O.	35	50	13	68*	533	14.41	—	2	10	—	116	3393	29.25	6-63	3	—
†**Colquhoun** I.A.	2	4	2	1*	1	0.50	—	—	4	—	—	—	—	—	—	—
Coney J.V.	52	85	14	174*	2668	37.57	3	16	64	—	27	966	35.77	3-28	—	—
***Congdon** B.E.	61	114	7	176	3448	32.22	7	19	44*	—	59	2154	36.51	5-65	1	—
Cowie J.	9	13	4	45	90	10.00	—	—	3	—	45	969	21.53	6-40	4	1
Cresswell G.F.	3	5	3	12*	14	7.00	—	—	—	—	13	292	22.46	6-168	1	—
Cromb I.B.	5	8	2	51*	123	20.50	—	1	1	—	8	442	55.25	3-113	—	—
Crowe J.J.	39	65	4	128	1601	26.24	3	6	41	—	0	9	—	—	—	—
Crowe M.D.	77	131	11	299	5444	45.36	17	18	71	—	14	676	48.28	2-25	—	—

	M	I	NO	HS	Runs	Ave	100	50	Ct	St	Wkts	Runs	Ave	Best	5WI	10WM
Cumming C.D.	11	19	2	74	441	25.94	—	1	3	—	—	—	—	—	—	—
Cunis R.S.	20	31	8	51	295	12.83	—	1	1	—	51	1887	37.00	6-76	1	—
D'Arcy J.W.	5	10	0	33	136	13.60	—	—	—	—	—	—	—	—	—	—
de Groen R.P.	5	10	4	26	45	7.50	—	—	—	—	11	505	45.90	3-40	—	—
Davis H.T.	5	7	4	8*	20	6.66	—	—	4	—	17	499	29.35	5-63	1	—
Dempster C.S.	10	15	4	136	723	65.73	2	5	2	—	0	10	—	—	—	—
Dempster E.W.	5	8	2	47	106	17.67	—	—	1	—	2	219	109.50	1-24	—	—
†**Dick** A.E.	17	30	4	50*	370	14.73	—	1	47	4	—	—	—	—	—	—
Dickinson G.R.	3	5	0	11	31	6.20	—	—	3	—	8	245	30.63	3-66	—	—
Donnelly M.P.	7	12	1	206	582	52.91	1	4	7	—	0	20	—	—	—	—
Doull S.B.	32	50	11	46	570	14.61	—	—	16	—	98	2872	29.30	7-65	6	—
Dowling G.T.	39	77	3	239	2306	31.16	3	11	23	—	1	19	19.00	1-19	—	—
Drum C.J.	5	5	2	4	10	3.33	—	—	4	—	16	482	30.12	3-36	—	—
Dunning J.A.	4	6	1	19	38	7.60	—	—	2	—	5	493	98.60	2-35	—	—
***Edgar** B.A.	39	68	4	161	1958	30.59	3	12	14*	—	0	3	—	—	—	—
***Edwards** G.N.	8	15	0	55	377	25.13	—	3	7*	—	—	—	—	—	—	—
Elliott G.D.	3	5	1	9	27	6.75	—	—	2	—	2	129	64.50	1-15	—	—
Emery R.W.G.	2	4	0	28	46	11.50	—	—	—	—	2	52	26.00	2-52	—	—
Fisher F.E.	1	2	0	14	23	11.50	—	—	—	—	1	78	78.00	1-78	—	—
Fleming S.P.	111	189	10	274*	7172	40.06	9	46	172	—	—	—	—	—	—	—
Flynn D.R.	11	20	5	95	550	36.66	—	3	4	—	—	—	—	—	—	—
Foley H.	1	2	0	2	4	2.00	—	—	—	—	—	—	—	—	—	—
Franklin J.E.C.	26	36	6	122*	644	21.46	1	2	10	—	80	2612	32.65	6-119	3	—
Franklin T.J.	21	37	1	101	828	23.00	1	4	8	—	—	—	—	—	—	—
Freeman D.L.	2	2	0	1	2	1.00	—	—	—	—	1	169	169.00	1-91	—	—
Fulton P.G.	8	12	1	75	272	24.72	—	1	8	—	—	—	—	—	—	—
Gallichan N.	1	2	0	30	32	16.00	—	—	—	—	3	113	37.67	3-99	—	—
Gedye S.G.	4	8	0	55	193	24.13	—	2	—	—	—	—	—	—	—	—
†**Germon** L.K.	12	21	3	55	382	21.22	—	1	27	2	—	—	—	—	—	—
Gillespie M.R.	3	5	1	16*	25	6.25	—	—	—	—	11	380	34.54	5-136	1	—
Gillespie S.R.	1	1	0	28	28	28.00	—	—	—	—	1	79	79.00	1-79	—	—
Gray E.J.	10	16	0	50	248	15.50	—	1	6	—	17	886	52.11	3-73	—	—
Greatbatch M.J.	41	71	5	146*	2021	30.62	3	10	27	—	0	0	—	—	—	—
†**Guillen** S.C.	3	6	0	41	98	16.33	—	—	4	1	—	—	—	—	—	—
Guptill M.J.	3	5	0	49	136	27.20	—	—	—	—	—	—	—	—	—	—
Guy J.W.	12	23	2	102	440	20.95	1	3	2	—	—	—	—	—	—	—
Hadlee D.R.	26	42	5	56	530	14.32	—	1	8	—	71	2389	33.65	4-30	—	—
Hadlee R.J.	86	134	19	151*	3124	27.16	2	15	39	—	431	9611	22.29	9-52	36	9
Hadlee W.A.	11	19	1	116	543	30.17	1	2	6	—	—	—	—	—	—	—
Harford N.S.	8	15	0	93	229	15.27	—	2	—	—	—	—	—	—	—	—
†**Harford** R.I.	3	5	2	6	7	2.33	—	—	11	—	—	—	—	—	—	—
Harris C.Z.	23	42	4	71	777	20.44	—	5	14	—	16	1170	73.12	2-16	—	—
Harris P.G.Z.	9	18	1	101	378	22.24	1	1	6	—	0	14	—	—	—	—
Harris R.M.	2	3	0	13	31	10.33	—	—	—	—	—	—	—	—	—	—
Hart M.N.	14	24	4	45	353	17.65	—	—	9	—	29	1438	49.58	5-77	1	—
†**Hart** R.G.	11	19	3	57*	260	16.25	—	1	29	1	—	—	—	—	—	—
Hartland B.R.	9	18	0	52	303	16.83	—	1	5	—	—	—	—	—	—	—
Haslam M.J.	4	2	1	3	4	4.00	—	—	2	—	2	245	122.50	1-33	—	—
Hastings B.F.	31	56	6	117*	1510	30.20	4	7	23	—	0	9	—	—	—	—
Hayes J.A.	15	22	7	19	73	4.87	—	—	3	—	30	1217	40.57	4-36	—	—
Henderson M.	1	2	1	6	8	8.00	—	—	1	—	2	64	32.00	2-38	—	—
†**Hopkins** G.J.	1	2	0	15	27	13.50	—	—	3	—	—	—	—	—	—	—
Horne M.J.	35	65	2	157	1788	28.38	4	5	17	—	0	26	—	—	—	—
Horne P.A.	4	7	0	27	71	10.14	—	—	3	—	—	—	—	—	—	—

	M	I	NO	HS	Runs	Ave	100	50	Ct	St	Wkts	Runs	Ave	Best	5WI	10WM
Hough K.W.	2	3	2	31*	62	62.00	—	—	1	—	6	175	29.17	3-79	—	—
How J.M.	19	35	1	92	772	22.70	—	4	18	—	0	4	—	—	—	—
Howarth G.P.	47	83	5	147	2531	32.44	6	11	29	—	3	271	90.33	1-13	—	—
Howarth H.J.	30	42	18	61	291	12.13	—	1	33	—	86	3178	36.95	5-34	2	—
†**James** K.C.	11	13	2	14	52	4.73	—	—	11	5	—	—	—	—	—	—
Jarvis T.W.	13	22	1	182	625	29.76	1	2	3	—	0	3	—	—	—	—
Jones A.H.	39	74	8	186	2922	44.27	7	11	25	—	1	194	194.00	1-40	—	—
Jones R.A.	1	2	0	16	23	11.50	—	—	—	—	—	—	—	—	—	—
Kennedy R.J.	4	5	1	22	28	7.00	—	—	2	—	6	380	63.33	3-28	—	—
Kerr J.L.	7	12	1	59	212	19.27	—	1	4	—	—	—	—	—	—	—
Kuggeleijn C.M.	2	4	0	7	7	1.75	—	—	1	—	1	67	67.00	1-50	—	—
Larsen G.R.	8	13	4	26*	127	14.11	—	—	5	—	24	689	28.70	3-57	—	—
Latham R.T.	4	7	0	119	219	31.28	1	—	5	—	0	6	—	—	—	—
†**Lees** W.K.	21	37	4	152	778	23.57	1	1	52	7	0	4	—	—	—	—
Leggat I.B.	1	1	0	0	0	0.00	—	—	2	—	0	6	—	—	—	—
Leggat J.G.	9	18	2	61	351	21.94	—	2	—	—	—	—	—	—	—	—
Lissette A.F.	2	4	2	1*	2	1.00	—	—	1	—	3	124	41.33	2-73	—	—
Loveridge G.R.	1	1	1	4*	4	—	—	—	—	—	—	—	—	—	—	—
Lowry T.C.	7	8	0	80	223	27.88	—	2	8	—	0	5	—	—	—	—
***McCullum** B.B.	44	72	4	143	2222	32.67	3	13	132	9	—	—	—	—	—	—
McEwan P.E.	4	7	1	40*	96	16.00	—	—	5	—	0	13	—	—	—	—
MacGibbon A.R.	26	46	5	66	814	19.85	—	3	13	—	70	2160	30.86	5-64	1	—
McGirr H.M.	2	1	0	51	51	51.00	—	1	—	—	1	115	115.00	1-65	—	—
McGregor S.N.	25	47	2	111	892	19.82	1	3	9	—	—	—	—	—	—	—
McIntosh T.G.	5	9	1	136	257	32.12	1	—	3	—						
McLeod E.G.	1	2	1	16	18	18.00	—	—	—	—	0	5	—	—	—	—
†**McMahon** T.G.	5	7	4	4*	7	2.33	—	—	7	1	—	—	—	—	—	—
McMillan C.D.	55	91	10	142	3116	38.46	6	19	22	—	28	1257	44.89	3-48	—	—
McRae D.A.N.	1	2	0	8	8	4.00	—	—	—	—	0	44	—	—	—	—
Marshall H.J.H.	13	19	2	160	652	38.35	2	2	1	—	0	4	—	—	—	—
Marshall J.A.H.	7	11	0	52	218	19.81	—	1	5	—	—	—	—	—	—	—
Martin C.S.	48	68	33	12*	80	2.28	—	—	11	—	160	5357	33.48	6-54	8	1
Mason M.J.	1	2	0	3	3	1.50	—	—	—	—	0	105	—	—	—	—
Matheson A.M.	2	1	0	7	7	7.00	—	—	2	—	2	136	68.00	2-7	—	—
Meale T.	2	4	0	10	21	5.25	—	—	—	—	—	—	—	—	—	—
Merritt W.E.	6	8	1	19	73	10.43	—	—	2	—	12	617	51.42	4-104	—	—
Meuli E.M.	1	2	0	23	38	19.00	—	—	—	—	—	—	—	—	—	—
†**Milburn** B.D.	3	3	2	4*	8	8.00	—	—	6	2	—	—	—	—	—	—
Miller L.S.M.	13	25	0	47	346	13.84	—	—	1	—	0	1	—	—	—	—
Mills J.E.	7	10	1	117	241	26.78	1	—	1	—	—	—	—	—	—	—
Mills K.D.	19	30	5	57	289	11.56	—	1	4	—	44	1453	33.02	4-16	—	—
Moir A.M.	17	30	8	41*	327	14.86	—	—	2	—	28	1418	50.64	6-155	2	—
Moloney D.A.R.	3	6	0	64	156	26.00	—	1	3	—	0	9	—	—	—	—
†**Mooney** F.L.H.	14	22	2	46	343	17.15	—	—	22	8	0	0	—	—	—	—
***Morgan** R.W.	20	34	1	97	734	22.24	—	5	12*	—	5	609	121.80	1-16	—	—
Morrison B.D.	1	2	0	10	10	5.00	—	—	1	—	2	129	64.50	2-129	—	—
Morrison D.K.	48	71	26	42	379	8.42	—	—	14	—	160	5549	34.68	7-89	10	—
Morrison J.F.M.	17	29	0	117	656	22.62	1	3	9	—	2	71	35.50	2-52	—	—
Motz R.C.	32	56	3	60	612	11.55	—	3	9	—	100	3148	31.48	6-63	5	—
Murray B.A.G.	13	26	1	90	598	23.92	—	5	21	—	1	0	0.00	1-0	—	—
Murray D.J.	8	16	1	52	303	20.20	—	1	6	—	—	—	—	—	—	—
Nash D.J.	32	45	14	89*	729	23.51	—	4	13	—	93	2649	28.48	6-27	3	1
Newman J.	3	4	0	19	33	8.25	—	—	—	—	2	254	127.00	2-76	—	—
O'Brien I.E.	17	25	4	19*	122	5.80	—	—	3	—	52	1661	31.94	6-75	1	—

	M	I	NO	HS	Runs	Ave	100	50	Ct	St	Wkts	Runs	Ave	Best	5WI	10WM
O'Connor S.B.	19	27	9	20	105	5.83	–	–	6	–	53	1724	32.52	5-51	1	–
O'Sullivan D.R.	11	21	4	23*	158	9.29	–	–	2	–	18	1221	67.83	5-148	1	–
Oram J.D.P.	31	55	10	133	1667	37.04	5	5	14	–	60	1871	31.18	4-41	–	–
Overton G.W.F.	3	6	1	3*	8	1.60	–	–	1	–	9	258	28.67	3-65	–	–
Owens M.B.	8	12	6	8*	16	2.66	–	–	3	–	17	585	34.44	4-99	–	–
Page M.L.	14	20	0	104	492	24.60	1	2	6	–	5	231	46.20	2-21	–	–
Papps M.H.W.	8	16	1	86	246	16.40	–	2	11	–	–	–	–	–	–	–
Parker J.M.	36	63	2	121	1498	24.56	3	5	30	–	1	24	24.00	1-24	–	–
Parker N.M.	3	6	0	40	89	14.83	–	–	2	–	–	–	–	–	–	–
***Parore** A.C.	78	128	19	110	2865	26.28	2	14	197	7	–	–	–	–	–	–
Patel D.N.	37	66	8	99	1200	20.68	–	5	15	–	75	3154	42.05	6-50	3	–
Patel J.S.	7	8	2	27*	70	11.66	–	–	2	–	26	900	34.61	5-110	1	–
Petherick P.J.	6	11	4	13	34	4.86	–	–	4	–	16	685	42.81	3-90	–	–
†**Petrie** E.C.	14	25	5	55	258	12.90	–	1	25	–	–	–	–	–	–	–
Playle W.R.	8	15	0	65	151	10.07	–	1	4	–	–	–	–	–	–	–
Pocock B.A.	15	29	0	85	665	22.93	–	6	5	–	0	20	–	–	–	–
Pollard V.	32	59	7	116	1266	24.35	2	7	19	–	40	1853	46.33	3-3	–	–
Poore M.B.	14	24	1	45	355	15.43	–	–	1	–	9	367	40.78	2-28	–	–
Priest M.W.	3	4	0	26	56	14.00	–	–	–	–	3	158	52.66	2-42	–	–
Pringle C.	14	21	4	30	175	10.29	–	–	3	–	30	1389	46.30	7-52	1	1
Puna N.	3	5	3	18*	31	15.50	–	–	1	–	4	240	60.00	2-40	–	–
Rabone G.O.	12	20	2	107	562	31.22	1	2	5	–	16	635	36.69	6-68	1	–
Redmond A.J.	7	14	1	83	299	23.00	–	2	5	–	3	62	20.66	2-47	–	–
Redmond R.E.	1	2	0	107	163	81.50	1	1	–	–	–	–	–	–	–	–
Reid J.F.	19	31	3	180	1296	46.28	6	2	9	–	0	7	–	–	–	–
***Reid** J.R.	58	108	5	142	3428	33.28	6	22	43*	1	85	2835	33.35	6-60	1	–
Richardson M.H.	38	65	3	145	2776	44.77	4	19	26	–	1	21	21.00	1-16	–	–
Roberts A.D.G.	7	12	1	84*	254	23.09	–	1	4	–	4	182	45.50	1-12	–	–
Roberts A.W.	5	10	1	66*	248	27.56	–	3	4	–	7	209	29.86	4-101	–	–
Robertson G.K.	1	1	0	12	12	12.00	–	–	–	–	1	91	91.00	1-91	–	–
Rowe C.G.	1	2	0	0	0	0.00	–	–	1	–	–	–	–	–	–	–
Rutherford K.R.	56	99	8	107*	2465	27.08	3	18	32	–	1	161	161.00	1-38	–	–
Ryder J.D.	9	16	2	201	771	55.07	2	4	8	–	4	156	39.00	2-7	–	–
Scott R.H.	1	1	0	18	18	18.00	–	–	–	–	1	74	74.00	1-74	–	–
Scott V.J.	10	17	1	84	458	28.63	–	3	7	–	0	14	–	–	–	–
Sewell D.G.	1	1	1	1*	1	–	–	–	–	–	0	90	–	–	–	–
Shrimpton M.J.F.	10	19	0	46	265	13.95	–	–	2	–	5	158	31.60	3-35	–	–
Sinclair B.W.	21	40	1	138	1148	29.44	3	3	8	–	2	32	16.00	2-32	–	–
Sinclair I.M.	2	4	1	18*	25	8.33	–	–	1	–	1	120	120.00	1-79	–	–
***Sinclair** M.S.	32	54	5	214	1595	32.55	3	4	31	–	0	13	–	–	–	–
Smith F.B.	4	6	1	96	237	47.40	–	2	1	–	–	–	–	–	–	–
Smith H.D.	1	1	0	4	4	4.00	–	–	–	–	1	113	113.00	1-113	–	–
†**Smith** I.D.S.	63	88	17	173	1815	25.56	2	6	168	8	0	5	–	–	–	–
Snedden C.A.	1	–	–	–	–	–	–	–	–	–	0	46	–	–	–	–
Snedden M.C.	25	30	8	33*	327	14.86	–	–	7	–	58	2199	37.91	5-68	1	–
Southee T.G.	5	9	2	77*	127	18.14	–	1	1	–	12	575	47.91	5-55	1	–
Sparling J.T.	11	20	2	50	229	12.72	–	1	3	–	5	327	65.40	1-9	–	–
Spearman C.M.	19	37	2	112	922	26.34	1	3	20	–	–	–	–	–	–	–
Stead G.R.	5	8	0	78	278	34.75	–	2	2	–	0	1	–	–	–	–
Stirling D.A.	6	9	2	26	108	15.42	–	–	1	–	13	601	46.23	4-88	–	–
Styris S.B.	29	48	4	170	1586	36.04	5	6	23	–	20	1015	50.75	3-28	–	–
Su'a M.L.	13	18	5	44	165	12.69	–	–	8	–	36	1377	38.25	5-73	2	–
Sutcliffe B.	42	76	8	230*	2727	40.10	5	15	20	–	4	344	86.00	2-38	–	–
Taylor B.R.	30	50	6	124	898	20.41	2	2	10	–	111	2953	26.60	7-74	4	–

	M	I	NO	HS	Runs	Ave	100	50	Ct	St	Wkts	Runs	Ave	Best	5WI	10WM
Taylor D.D.	3	5	0	77	159	31.80	—	1	2	—	—	—	—	—	—	—
Taylor L.R.P.L.	17	31	1	154*	1184	39.46	4	4	27	—	0	14	—	—	—	—
Thomson K.	2	4	1	69	94	31.33	—	1	—	—	1	9	9.00	1-9	—	—
Thomson S.A.	19	35	4	120*	958	30.90	1	5	7	—	19	953	50.15	3-63	—	—
†**Tindill** E.W.T.	5	9	1	37*	73	9.13	—	—	6	1	—	—	—	—	—	—
Troup G.B.	15	18	6	13*	55	4.58	—	—	2	—	39	1454	37.28	6-95	1	1
Truscott P.B.	1	2	0	26	29	14.50	—	—	1	—	—	—	—	—	—	—
Tuffey D.R.	22	30	7	35	263	11.43	—	—	12	—	66	2057	31.16	6-54	2	—
Turner G.M.	41	73	6	259	2991	44.64	7	14	42	—	0	5	—	—	—	—
Twose R.G.	16	27	2	94	628	25.12	—	6	5	—	3	130	43.33	2-36	—	—
Vance R.H.	4	7	0	68	207	29.57	—	1	—	—	—	—	—	—	—	—
Vaughan J.T.C.	6	12	1	44	201	18.27	—	—	4	—	11	450	40.90	4-27	—	—
Vettori D.L.	92	137	23	137*	3220	28.24	3	19	47	—	293	9831	33.55	7-87	18	3
Vincent L.	23	40	1	224	1332	34.15	3	9	19	—	0	2	—	—	—	—
Vivian G.E.	5	6	0	43	110	18.33	—	—	3	—	1	107	107.00	1-14	—	—
Vivian H.G.	7	10	0	100	421	42.10	1	5	4	—	17	633	37.24	4-58	—	—
†**Wadsworth** K.J.	33	51	4	80	1010	21.49	—	5	92	4	—	—	—	—	—	—
Walker B.G.K.	5	8	2	27*	118	19.66	—	—	—	—	5	399	79.80	2-92	—	—
Wallace W.M.	13	21	0	66	439	20.90	—	5	5	—	0	5	—	—	—	—
Walmsley K.P.	3	5	0	5	13	2.60	—	—	—	—	9	391	43.44	3-70	—	—
†**Ward** J.T.	8	12	6	35*	75	12.50	—	—	16	1	—	—	—	—	—	—
Watson W.	15	18	6	11	60	5.00	—	—	4	—	40	1387	34.67	6-78	1	—
Watt L.	1	2	0	2	2	1.00	—	—	—	—	—	—	—	—	—	—
Webb M.G.	3	2	0	12	12	6.00	—	—	—	—	4	471	117.75	2-114	—	—
Webb P.N.	2	3	0	5	11	3.67	—	—	2	—	—	—	—	—	—	—
Weir G.L.	11	16	2	74*	416	29.71	—	3	3	—	7	209	29.86	3-38	—	—
White D.J.	2	4	0	18	31	7.75	—	—	—	—	0	5	—	—	—	—
Whitelaw P.E.	2	4	2	30	64	32.00	—	—	—	—	—	—	—	—	—	—
Wiseman P.J.	25	34	8	36	366	14.07	—	—	11	—	61	2903	47.59	5-82	2	—
Wright J.G.	82	148	7	185	5334	37.82	12	23	38	—	0	5	—	—	—	—
Young B.A.	35	68	4	267*	2034	31.78	2	12	54	—	—	—	—	—	—	—
Yuile B.W.	17	33	6	64	481	17.81	—	1	12	—	34	1213	35.68	4-43	—	—

Note: There have now been 69 dismissals made by substitutes: M.J. Greatbatch (5), J.G. Bracewell, J.J. Crowe, T.W. Jarvis (4), C.Z. Harris (3), J.M. How, J.A.H. Marshall, D.R. O'Sullivan, A.C. Parore, K.R. Rutherford, G.E. Vivian (2), J.C. Alabaster, R.W. Anderson, S.E. Bond, S.L. Boock, G.E. Bradburn, C. Burke, C. Cachopa, R.O. Collinge, B.E. Congdon, M.D. Crowe, H.T. Davis, C.J. Drum, E.W. Dempster, G.T. Dowling, S.W. Eathorne, B.A. Edgar, G.N. Edwards, S.G. Gedye, M.N. Hart, M.A. Hastings, N.K.W. Horsley, I.B. Leggat, T.G. McMahon, P.E. McEwan, M.N. McKenzie, H.J.H. Marshall, M.J. Mason, S.M. Mills, R.C. Motz, S.B. O'Connor, N.M. Parker, J.S. Patel, M.W. Priest, T.D. Ritchie, L. Vincent, B.G.K. Walker catches and B.E. Congdon a stumping. The latter is one of only two instances in tests of a substitute making a stumping.

† all test appearances were as wicketkeeper.
A.C. Parore had 67 tests as wicketkeeper, B.B. McCullum 43, T.E. Blain 9, G.N. Edwards 4, B.A. Edgar and J.R. Reid one each.

** record includes catches taken while keeping wicket as follows: A.C. Parore 194, B.B. McCullum 131, T.E. Blain 18, B.A. Edgar 4, J.R. Reid 2, B.E. Congdon, R.W. Morgan and M.S. Sinclair one each. Edwards' catches were all made while keeping wicket.*

Vettori's record includes one match for ICC World XI.

SUMMARY OF TEST CAREER RECORDS

Most Matches

Fleming S.P.	111	Martin C.S.	48	Parker J.M.	36
Vettori D.L.	92	Howarth G.P.	47	Collinge R.O.	35
Hadlee R.J.	86	McCullum B.B.	44	Young B.A.	35
Wright J.G.	82	Cairns B.L.	43	Horne M.J.	35
Astle N.J.	81	Chatfield E.J.	43	Wadsworth K.J.	33
Parore A.C.	78	Sutcliffe B.	42	Motz R.C.	32
Crowe M.D.	77	Turner G.M.	41	Pollard V.	32
Smith I.D.S.	63	Bracewell J.G.	41	Doull S.B.	32
Cairns C.L.	62	Greatbatch M.J.	41	Nash D.J.	32
Congdon B.E.	61	Dowling G.T.	39	Sinclair M.S.	32
Reid J.R.	58	Edgar B.A.	39	Hastings B.F.	31
Rutherford K.R.	56	Crowe J.J.	39	Oram J.D.P.	31
McMillan C.D	55	Jones A.H.	39	Howarth H.J.	30
Coney J.V.	52	Richardson M.H.	38	Taylor B.R.	30
Burgess M.G.	50	Patel D.N.	37	Boock S.L.	30
Morrison D.K.	48				

Most Runs

Fleming S.P.	7172	Sutcliffe B.	2727	Crowe J.J.	1601
Crowe M.D.	5444	Burgess M.G.	2684	Sinclair M.S.	1595
Wright J.G.	5334	Coney J.V.	2668	Styris S.B.	1586
Astle N.J.	4702	Howarth G.P.	2531	Hastings B.F.	1510
Congdon B.E.	3448	Rutherford K.R.	2465	Parker J.M.	1498
Reid J.R.	3428	Dowling G.T.	2306	Vincent L.	1332
Cairns C.L.	3320	McCullum B.B.	2222	Reid J.F.	1296
Vettori D.L.	3220	Young B.A.	2034	Pollard V.	1266
Hadlee R.J.	3124	Greatbatch M.J.	2021	Patel D.N.	1200
McMillan C.D.	3116	Edgar B.A.	1958	Taylor L.R.P.L.	1184
Turner G.M.	2991	Smith I.D.S.	1815	Sinclair B.W.	1148
Jones A.H.	2922	Horne M.J.	1788	Wadsworth K.J.	1010
Parore A.C.	2865	Oram J.D.P.	1667	Bracewell J.G.	1001
Richardson M.H.	2776				

Most Wickets

Hadlee R.J.	431	Doull S.B.	98	Tuffey D.R.	66
Vettori D.L.	293	Nash D.J.	93	Cameron F.J.	62
Cairns C.L.	218	Howarth H.J.	86	Wiseman P.J.	61
Morrison D.K.	160	Reid J.R.	85	Oram J.D.P.	60
Martin C.S.	160	Franklin J.E.C.	80	Congdon B.E.	59
Cairns B.L.	130	Bond S.E.	79	Snedden M.C.	58
Chatfield E.J.	123	Patel D.N.	75	O'Connor S.B.	53
Collinge R.O.	116	Boock S.L.	74	O'Brien I.E.	52
Taylor B.R.	111	Hadlee D.R.	71	Cunis R.S.	51
Bracewell J.G.	102	MacGibbon A.R.	70	Astle N.J.	51
Motz R.C.	100				

Most Catches

Fleming S.P.	172	Turner G.M.	42	Howarth H.J.	33
Crowe M.D.	71	Reid J.R.	41	Rutherford K.R.	32
Astle N.J.	70	Crowe J.J.	41	Bracewell J.G.	31
Coney J.V.	64	Hadlee R.J.	39	Parker J.M.	30
Young B.A.	54	Wright J.G.	38	Cairns B.L.	30
Vettori D.L.	47	Burgess M.G.	34	Sinclair M.S.	30
Congdon B.E.	43				

Most Wicketkeeping Dismissals

	Ct	St	Total
Parore A.C.	194	7	201
Smith I.D.S.	168	8	176
McCullum B.B.	131	9	140
Wadsworth K.J.	92	4	96
Lees W.K.	52	7	59
Dick A.E.	47	4	51

Test Captains

		RESULTS				TOSS	
		P	W	L	D	W	L
Fleming S.P.	1996/97 to 2006/07	80	28	27	25	37	43
Reid J.R.	1955/56 to 1965	34	3	18	13	17	17
Howarth G.P.	1979/80 to 1984/85	30	11	7	12	17	13
Dowling G.T.	1967/68 to 1971/72	19	4	7	8	10	9
Vettori D.L.	2007/08 to 2008/09	19	4	9	6	12	7
Rutherford K.R.	1992/93 to 1994/95	18	2	11	5	12	6
Congdon B.E.	1971/72 to 1974/75	17	1	7	9	4	13
Crowe M.D.	1990/91 to 1993/94	16	2	7	7	8	8
Coney J.V.	1984/85 to 1986/87	15	5	4	6	8	7
Wright J.G.	1987/88 to 1990	14	3	3	8	8	6
Germon L.K.	1995/96 to 1996/97	12	1	5	6	6	6
Turner G.M.	1975/76 to 1976/77	10	1	6	3	2	8
Burgess M.G.	1977/78 to 1980/81	10	1	6	3	4	6
Cave H.B.	1955/56	9	0	5	4	5	4
Hadlee W.A.	1945/46 to 1950/51	8	0	2	6	4	4
Lowry T.C.	1929/30 to 1931	7	0	2	5	5	2
Page M.L.	1931/32 to 1937	7	0	3	4	4	3
Crowe J.J.	1986/87 to 1987/88	6	0	1	5	3	3
Rabone G.O.	1953/54 to 1954/55	5	0	4	1	2	3
Sutcliffe B.	1951/52 to 1953/54	4	0	3	1	4	0
Sinclair B.W.	1965/66 to 1967/68	3	0	1	2	3	0
Nash D.J.	1998/99	3	0	1	2	3	0
Wallace W.M.	1952/53	2	0	1	1	0	2
Chapple M.E.	1965/66	1	0	0	1	0	1
Parker J.M.	1976/77	1	0	0	1	0	1
Smith I.D.S.	1990/91	1	0	0	1	1	0
Totals		**351**	**66**	**140**	**145**	**179**	**162**

Test Debuts

New Zealand has now played 351 test matches. In 200 there have been no new test caps. In the other 151 the records are:

11 players making debut 1929/30 v England at Christchurch (NZ's first test match)
6 players making debut 1937 v England at Lord's (NZ's first test since 1932/33)
6 players making debut 1945/46 v Australia at Wellington (NZ's first test after Second World War)
6 players making debut 1946/47 v England at Christchurch (test after one above)
5 players making debut 1961/62 v South Africa at Durban

Of the 12 players who made their debuts in the 1945/46 and 1946/47 tests above, seven did not appear again. In eight successive tests at least one player made his test debut – South Africa 1963/64 (3), Pakistan 1964/65 (3), India 1964/65 (2). In nine successive tests there were no new caps – England 1969 (2), India 1969/70 (3), Pakistan 1969/70 (3), England 1970/71 (1) and South Africa 1998/99 (1), England 1999 (4), India 1999/00 (3), West Indies 1999/00 (1).

Youngest/Oldest Test Players

YOUNGEST PLAYERS			Bat	Bowl
18 years 10 days	Vettori D.L. v England at Wellington	1996/97	3* & 2*	2-98
18 years 197 days	Freeman D.L. v England at Christchurch	1932/33	1	0-78
18 years 267 days	Vivian H.G. v England at The Oval	1931	3 & 51	2-96
18 years 295 days	Collinge R.O. v Pakistan at Wellington	1964/65	0*	2-51 & 3-43
18 years 316 days	Bracewell B.P. v England at The Oval	1978	0 & 0	2-46 & 1-26
19 years 5 days	Vivian G.E. v India at Calcutta	1964/65	1 & 43	0-37 & 1-14
19 years 102 days	Southee T.G. v England at Napier	2007/08	5 & 77*	5-55 & 0-84
19 years 145 days	Beck J.E.F. v South Africa at Johannesburg	1953/54	16 & 7	
19 years 154 days	Rutherford K.R. v West Indies at Port of Spain	1984/85	0 & 0	
19 years 157 days	Crowe M.D. v Australia at Wellington	1981/82	9	0-14
19 years 163 days	Parore A.C. v England at Birmingham	1990	12* & 20	4ct/1st
19 years 164 days	Cairns C.L. v Australia at Perth	1989/90	1 & 28	0-60
19 years 173 days	Pollard V. India at Madras	1964/65	3	3-90 & 1-32
19 years 186 days	Playle W.R. v England at Birmingham	1958	4 & 8	
19 years 252 days	Donnelly M.P. v England at Lord's	1937	0 & 21	
19 years 340 days	Sewell D.G. v Zimbabwe at Bulawayo	1997/98	1*	0-81 & 0-9
19 years 344 days	Sparling J.T. v England at Leeds	1958	9* & 18	1-78

OLDEST PLAYERS *(age on last day of final test)*

41 years 294 days	Alabaster J.C. v West Indies at Port of Spain	1971/72	18	0-49 & 1-5
41 years 196 days	Sutcliffe B. v England at Birmingham	1965	4* & 53	
40 years 198 days	Congdon B.E. v England at Lord's	1978	2 & 3	0-12

OLDEST PLAYER ON DEBUT

38 years 101 days	McGirr H.M.† v England at Auckland	1929/30		0-46

† he made 51 in his first test innings in his second test

YOUNGEST CENTURY MAKER

19 years 121 days†	Vivian H.G. 100 v South Africa at Wellington	1931/32

† world record at that time

OLDEST CENTURY MAKERS

41 years 109 days	Sutcliffe B. 151* v India at Calcutta	1964/65
39 years 12 days	Congdon B.E. 107* v Australia at Christchurch	1976/77

YOUNGEST CAPTAIN

23 years 319 days	Fleming S.P. v England at Christchurch	1996/97	62 & 11
25 years 252 days	Parker J.M. v Pakistan at Karachi	1976/77	24 & 16

OLDEST CAPTAIN *(age on last day of final test)*

37 years 40 days	Reid J.R. v England at Leeds	1965	54 & 5	
36 years 359 days	Congdon B.E. v England at Christchurch	1974/75	38	0-27
36 years 88 days	Wallace W.M. v South Africa at Auckland	1952/53	23	
36 years 5 days	Wright J.G. v England at Birmingham	1990	24 & 46	

LONGEST INTERVAL BETWEEN TEST APPEARANCES

14 years 28 days Cleverley D.C. — v South Africa at Christchurch 1/3/32
v Australia at Wellington 29/3/46

Only A.J. Traicos (22 years 222 days), G. Gunn (17 years 316 days), Younis Ahmed (17 years 111 days) and J.M.M. Commaille (14 years 95 days) have a longer interval between tests but Cleverley is unique in that the above matches were his only two tests.

NEW ZEALAND LIMITED-OVERS RECORDS

This section of the *Almanack* is devoted to limited-overs matches in New Zealand (other than one-day internationals) and has been compiled from the following games:

1. 766 matches in national competitions (Shell Cup, State Shield, etc) from 1971/72 to 2008/09.

2. 55 matches between provincial sides and overseas teams from 1970/71 to 2007/08.

1970/71	Wellington v MCC
	Otago v MCC
	Central Districts v MCC
1972/73	Central Districts v Pakistan
1973/74	Wellington v Australia
	Central Districts v Australia
1975/76	Wellington v India
1977/78	Northern Districts v England XI
1978/79	Auckland v Pakistan
	Canterbury v Pakistan
1979/80	Auckland XI v West Indies
	Central Districts v West Indies
1981/82	Northern Districts v Australia
	Central Districts v Australia
1983/84	Otago v England XI
1984/85	Wellington v New South Wales
1985/86	Auckland v Australia
1986/87	Auckland v West Indies
	Central Districts v South Australia *(4 matches)*
1987/88	Wellington v England
	Auckland v Victoria *(2 matches)*
	Wellington v Queensland
	Canterbury v Queensland
	Otago v Queensland
1988/89	Auckland v Pakistan
1991/92	Auckland v England
	Auckland v Australia
	Northern Districts v Zimbabwe *(2 matches)*
1993/94	Canterbury v New South Wales
1994/95	Auckland v West Indies
	Central Districts v India
	Wellington v South Africa
	Canterbury v Sri Lanka
1996/97	Central Districts v Sri Lanka
1997/98	Canterbury v Bangladesh
1998/99	Northern v Pakistan A
2000/01	Wellington v New South Wales
	Canterbury v Zimbabwe
2001/02	Northern Districts v England *(2 matches)*
2003/04	Wellington v Pakistan
	Northern Districts v South Africa
2004/05	Central Districts v Sri Lanka
2007/08	Northern Districts v Bangladesh *(2 matches)*
	Auckland v Bangladesh
	Canterbury v England *(2 matches)*

3. Three matches in the Data General competition in 1986/87.

4. Six matches in the Shell Shield competition in 1997/98.

5. 30 other matches not involving provincial sides.

1972/73	New Zealand Under 23 XI v Pakistan
1976/77	Australia v Invitation XIs *(2 matches)*
1981/82	North Island v South Island
1982/83	Sri Lanka v NZ Minor Associations *(2 matches)*
1992/93	New Zealand President's XI v Australia
1993/94	North Island v South Island
	Sir Ron Brierley XI v Pakistan
1994/95	North Island v South Island
	Sir Ron Brierley XI v West Indies
	New Zealand Academy XI v Sri Lanka
	New Zealand Academy XI v Australian Academy XI
1996/97	New Zealand Academy XI v England
1997/98	New Zealand Academy XI v Zimbabwe
1998/99	New Zealand A v Pakistan A *(3 matches)*
	New Zealand Academy XI v South Africa
1999/00	New Zealand Academy XI v England A *(2 matches)*
	New Zealand A v England A *(3 matches)*
2000/01	North Island Selection XI v Sri Lanka
2003/04	South Island v North Island
	New Zealand A v Sri Lanka A *(2 matches)*
2004/05	New Zealand v FICA World XI *(3 matches)*
	North Island v South Island
2008/09	New Zealand A v England Lions *(2 matches)*

TEAM RECORDS

Highest Totals

376-3	Central Districts v Otago	New Plymouth	1996/97
373-6	New Zealand A v England Lions	Palmerston North	2008/09
354-5	Central Districts v Canterbury	Christchurch	2003/04
341-5	Auckland v Northern Districts	Auckland	2007/08
339-5	Central Districts v Otago	Hastings	1998/99
338	England Lions v New Zealand A	Palmerston North	2008/09
332-5	Northern Districts v Canterbury	Christchurch	2006/07
329-5	Canterbury v Northern Districts	Christchurch	1995/96
328-4	New Zealand A v Sri Lanka A	Lincoln	2003/04

Lowest Totals

48	Pakistan v Auckland	Auckland	1988/89
58	Central Districts v Wellington	Wellington	2001/02
64	Otago v Wellington	Alexandra	1984/85
64	Otago v Central Districts	Invercargill	2004/05
66	Wellington v Canterbury	Wellington	1996/97
67	Otago v Central Districts	Invercargill	2000/01
67	Central Districts v Canterbury	Christchurch	2002/03
70	Auckland v Northern Districts	Pukekohe	1977/78

Most Extras in an Innings

55	Northern Districts (271-8)	v Wellington (228)	Hamilton	2002/03
51	NZ Academy XI (183)	v England A (184-4)	Lincoln	1999/00
48	Wellington (211-7)	v Otago (208-8)	Wellington	1996/97
45	Wellington (251-8)	v Otago (250-6)	Alexandra	1997/98
45	England A (219-7)	v New Zealand A (216)	Auckland	1999/00

Fewest Extras in an Innings

1	Canterbury (205-6)	v Wellington (203)	Timaru	1986/87
2	Pakistan (216-4)	v NZ Under 23 XI	Rotorua	1972/73
2	Otago (114)	v Canterbury (113)	Christchurch	1979/80
2	Auckland (163-4)	v Otago (162)	Oamaru	1981/82
2	Auckland (105)	v Otago (214-9)	Dunedin	1993/94
2	Otago (279-5)	v Central Districts (275-7)	Palmerston North	2006/07

Tied Match

Wellington v South Africa	Wellington	1994/95
Northern Districts v Auckland	Hamilton	2005/06

Close Finishes

RUNS *(winning team listed first)*

1	Northern Districts v Canterbury	Hamilton	1982/83
1	Northern Districts v Zimbabwe	Pukekohe	1991/92
1	Auckland v Central Districts	Auckland	1994/95
1	Otago v Auckland	Alexandra	1995/96
1	Central Districts v Wellington	Wellington	1996/97
1	Northern Districts v Wellington *(D/L)*	Taupo	2004/05
1	Otago v Northern Districts	Taupo	2005/06

ONE WICKET *(winning team listed first)*

Wellington v Auckland	Wellington	1973/74
Otago v Canterbury	Christchurch	1979/80
Central Districts v Australia	New Plymouth	1981/82
Canterbury v Central Districts	Christchurch	1986/87
Otago v Northern Districts	Gisborne	1986/87
Auckland v Northern Districts	Hamilton	1989/90
Otago v Auckland	Auckland	1990/91
Wellington v Otago	Alexandra	1992/93
Central Districts v Wellington	Masterton	1993/94
Wellington v Northern Districts	Wellington	1996/97
Central Districts v Canterbury	Napier	1996/97
Wellington v Northern Districts	Whangarei	1999/00
Auckland v Northern Districts	Auckland	1999/00
Otago v Wellington	Dunedin	2000/01
Central Districts v Wellington	Waikanae	2000/01
Canterbury v Auckland	Auckland	2001/02
Otago v Northern Districts	Invercargill	2003/04
Northern Districts v Wellington	Wellington	2008/09
Wellington v Otago	Invercargill	2008/09

SCORES LEVEL *(won by team listed first, having lost fewer wickets)*

Otago (223-5) v Wellington (223-9)	Dunedin	1979/80
Canterbury (182-7) v Auckland (182-9)	Christchurch	1983/84
Canterbury (136-9) v Auckland (136)	Ashburton	1985/86
Queensland (174-8) v Wellington (174)	Wellington	1987/88
Wellington (227-8) v Auckland (227)	Wellington	1995/96
Canterbury (238-6) v Auckland (238-7)	Auckland	1995/96

Large Victories

RUNS *(winning team listed first)*

200	Central Districts v Otago	Hastings	1998/99
200	Central Districts v Otago	Invercargill	2004/05
197	South Africa v New Zealand Academy XI	Alexandra	1998/99
189	New Zealand A v Pakistan A	Mt Maunganui	1998/99
186	Wellington v Auckland	Wellington	1971/72
153	Otago v Wellington	Alexandra	1982/83
152	Canterbury v Central Districts	Napier	1995/96
152	Otago v Auckland	Auckland	2004/05
151	Wellington v Northern Districts	Mt Maunganui	1997/98

TEN WICKETS *(winning team listed first)*

Northern Districts (71-0) v Auckland (70)	Pukekohe	1977/78
West Indies (132-0) v Central Districts (130)	New Plymouth	1979/80
Canterbury (120-0) v Auckland (119)	Christchurch	1987/88
Auckland (81-0) v Central Districts (78)	New Plymouth	1988/89
Wellington (205-0) v Canterbury (202-7)	Wellington	1994/95
Auckland (164-0) v Central Districts (163)	Auckland	1998/99

Most Run Outs

INNINGS

5	Wellington v Auckland	Wellington	1974/75
5	Northern Districts v Wellington	Hamilton	1992/93
5	Central Districts v Northern Districts	Hamilton	2000/01
5	Otago v Canterbury	Alexandra	2004/05

MATCH

7	Wellington v Auckland	Wellington	1974/75
7	Auckland v Canterbury	Auckland	1999/00

INDIVIDUAL RECORDS

Highest Scores

177	Pyke J.K.	South Australia v Central Districts	Palmerston North	1986/87
170	McCullum B.B.	Otago v Auckland	Auckland	2007/08
161	Hartland B.R.	Canterbury v Northern Districts	Timaru	1993/94
152*	Marshall J.A.H.	Northern Districts v Canterbury	Christchurch	2006/07
149	Nevin C.J.	Wellington v Central Districts	Wellington	1997/98
149	Flynn D.R.	Northern Districts v Canterbury	Christchurch	2007/08
147*	Edgar B.A.	Wellington v Northern Districts	Gisborne	1981/82
145	Vincent L.	Auckland v Central Districts	Napier	1999/00
143	Cairns C.L.	Canterbury v Auckland	Christchurch	1994/95
143	Flynn D.R.	Northern Districts v Wellington	Whangarei	2007/08
140	Scott D.G.	Auckland v Northern Districts	Hamilton	1986/87
140	Kelly D.P.	Central Districts v Wellington	Waikanae	1999/00

Fastest Centuries

Balls				
52	McCullum B.B.	Otago v Auckland	Auckland	2007/08
54	Fleming S.P.	New Zealand v FICA World XI	Christchurch	2004/05
65	de Silva P.A.	Auckland v Canterbury	Auckland	1996/97
72	Howell L.G.	Central Districts v Otago	New Plymouth	1996/97
77	McMillan C.D.	Canterbury v Central Districts	New Plymouth	2001/02
78	Astle N.J.	Canterbury v Central Districts	Christchurch	2001/02
79	Hick G.A.	Northern Districts v Canterbury	Rangiora	1987/88

Fastest Fifties

Balls				
19	McGlashan P.D.	Northern Districts v Auckland	Hamilton	2007/08
20	Cairns C.L.	Canterbury v Northern Districts	Timaru	2002/03
22	Maynard M.P.	Otago v Auckland	Alexandra	1997/98
22	Napier G.R.	England Lions v New Zealand A	Palmerston North	2008/09
23	Greatbatch M.J.	Central Districts v Otago	New Plymouth	1996/97
25	Mascarenhas A.D.	Otago v Central Districts	New Plymouth	2008/09

Note: I.D.S. Smith reached fifty from 24 balls for Auckland v Central Districts at Auckland, 1989/90 but the game was abandoned and restarted the following day and none of the performances in the game are included in any records).

Most Wickets in an Innings

7-0-23-7	Watson W.	Auckland v Otago	Auckland	1984/85
8-1-28-7	Penn A.J.	Wellington v Northern Districts	Mt Maunganui	2000/01
7.1-0-49-7	Marshall E.J.	Otago v Auckland	Dunedin	1993/94
10-5-12-6	Barrett B.J.	Northern Districts v Otago	Gisborne	1986/87
5.5-0-12-6	Cairns C.L.	New Zealand v FICA World XI	Hamilton	2004/05
9.3-1-25-6	Mason M.J.	Central Districts v Auckland	Auckland	2003/04
9.5-3-26-6	Vaughan J.T.C.	Auckland v Otago	Auckland	1995/96
10-2-26-6	Su'a M.L.	Auckland v Central Districts	New Plymouth	1995/96
7.7-2-31-6	Intikhab Alam	Pakistan v NZ Under 23 XI	Rotorua	1972/73
10-1-37-6	Cairns C.L.	Canterbury v Wellington	Christchurch	1996/97
9.3-0-43-6	Wisneski W.A.	Canterbury v Auckland	Christchurch	1996/97
10-1-45-6	Bennett H.K.	Canterbury v Auckland	Auckland	2007/08
10-1-49-6	Penn A.J.	Central Districts v Northern Districts	Napier	1996/97

Most Expensive Bowling

10-0-93-2	Presland C.M.	Northern Districts v Auckland	Gisborne	1982/83
10-0-89-2	Joseph R.H.	England Lions v New Zealand A	Palmerston North	2008/09
9-0-85-1	Kennedy R.J.	Otago v Canterbury	Christchurch	1996/97
10-1-85-0	Kennedy R.J.	Otago v Central Districts	New Plymouth	1996/97
9-1-84-0	Styris S.B.	Northern Districts v Auckland	Auckland	2000/01
10-0-83-2	Welch G.	Wellington v Central Districts	New Plymouth	1997/98
10-0-82-2	Bennett H.K.	Canterbury v Auckland	Rangiora	2007/08
8-0-81-1	Martin C.S.	Auckland v Otago	Auckland	2007/08
10-0-80-3	Blair B.R.	Otago v Central Districts	Oamaru	1982/83
9-0-80-0	Rushton N.W.	Otago v Canterbury	Timaru	2003/04

ALSO NOTE *(8-ball overs)*

1-0-18-0	Payton D.H.	Central Districts v Wellington	Wellington	1973/74
1-0-18-1	Redpath I.R.	Australia v Central Districts	New Plymouth	1973/74
2-0-29-0	Child M.J.	Northern Districts v Central Districts	Palmerston North	1975/76
3-0-37-0	Dunning B.	Northern Districts v Canterbury	Christchurch	1977/78
4-0-42-1	Maingay C.T.	Auckland v Wellington	Wellington	1971/72
5-0-48-0	Coles M.J.	Wellington v Canterbury	Christchurch	1975/76
6-0-56-0	Cater S.B.	Wellington v Auckland	Auckland	1977/78
6-0-56-0	Gilmour G.J.	Australia v Invitation XI	Christchurch	1976/77
7-0-68-1	Aldridge C.W.	Northern Districts v Auckland	Auckland	1978/79

ALSO NOTE *(6-ball overs)*

1-0-22-0	Pryor C.R.	Auckland v Wellington	Wellington	1998/99
1.5-0-27-0	Houghton M.V.	Wellington v Auckland	Auckland	2007/08
2-0-26-0	Roberts S.J.	Canterbury v Wellington	Ohoka	1990/91
2.2-0-29-0	Harvie M.J.	Otago v Wellington	Wellington	2006/07
3-0-42-1	McMillan C.D.	Canterbury v Central Districts	Napier	1996/97
3.1-0-57-0	Muralitharan M.	FICA World XI v New Zealand	Christchurch	2004/05
4-0-46-0	Trott I.J.L.	Otago v Canterbury	Dunedin	2005/06
5-0-55-0	McClenaghan M.J.	Central Districts v Wellington	Wellington	2007/08
6-0-65-0	de Silva D.S.	Sri Lanka v Minor Associations	Wanganui	1982/83
7-0-71-2	Aldridge G.W.	Northern Districts v Wellington	Taupo	2004/05

Most Economical Bowling

10-7-5-2	Boock S.L.	Otago v Central Districts	Alexandra	1986/87
10-5-6-2	Larsen G.R.	Wellington v Otago	Alexandra	1992/93
*8-3-7-2	Williams J.C.	Auckland v Northern Districts	Auckland	1971/72
10-6-8-1	Hills P.W.	Otago v Auckland	Oamaru	1981/82
10-6-8-2	Nuttall A.J.	Canterbury v Wellington	Christchurch	1988/89
10-4-8-0	Duff S.W.	Central Districts v Wellington	New Plymouth	1989/90
10-5-8-3	Vaughan J.T.C.	Auckland v Central Districts	Waikanae	1993/94
10-5-8-1	Harris C.Z.	Canterbury v Auckland	Christchurch	1995/96
*7-0-9-0	Dunning B.	Northern Districts v Canterbury	Christchurch	1976/77
10-6-9-1	Boock S.L.	Otago v Canterbury	Christchurch	1979/80
10-4-9-1	de Mel A.L.F.	Sri Lanka v Minor Associations	Wanganui	1982/83
10-5-9-2	Astle N.J.	Canterbury v Northern Districts	Christchurch	1991/92
10-4-9-2	Astle N.J.	Canterbury v Wellington	Christchurch	1993/94
10-3-9-1	de Groen R.P.	Northern Districts v Central Districts	Levin	1995/96
10-6-9-2	McCullum N.J.	Otago v Auckland	Auckland	2000/01
*7-1-10-2	Kirk C.M.	Canterbury v Otago	Christchurch	1973/74
10-5-10-3	McIntyre J.M.	Auckland v Canterbury	Auckland	1980/81
10-4-10-2	Pigott A.C.S.	Wellington v Northern Districts	Tauranga	1983/84

10-6-10-0	Bracewell J.G.	Auckland v Canterbury	Auckland	1986/87
10-7-10-4	Duers K.G.	Zimbabwe v Northern Districts	Cambridge	1991/92
10-3-10-2	Williams B.R.	Wellington v Northern Districts	Gisborne	1993/94
10-3-10-3	Larsen G.R.	Wellington v Canterbury	Rangiora	1994/95

* *8-ball overs*

(Note: C.M. Brown had figures of 10-5-6-2 for Auckland v Otago at Dunedin, 1993/94 but the game was abandoned and none of the performances in the game are included in any records).

Hat-tricks

7-0-23-7	Watson W.	Auckland v Otago	Auckland	1984/85
10-0-48-4	Briasco P.S.	Central Districts v Auckland	Napier	1989/90
10-1-40-3	Walker M.D.J.	Wellington v Otago	Dunedin	2000/01

Wicketkeeping

DISMISSALS

	(ct/st)				
6	(5/1)	Murray D.A.	West Indies v Central Districts	New Plymouth	1979/80
6	(6/0)	McSweeney E.B.	Wellington v Auckland	Wellington	1982/83
6	(6/0)	McSweeney E.B.	Wellington v Northern Districts	Wellington	1988/89
6	(6/0)	McRae G.P.	Central Districts v Wellington	Masterton	1994/95

THREE STUMPINGS IN AN INNINGS

Milburn B.D.	Otago v Wellington	Alexandra	1982/83
Rixon S.J.	NSW v Wellington	Wellington	1984/85
Dyer G.C.	NSW v Wellington	Wellington	1986/87

Fielding

CATCHES

5	Wilson J.W.	Otago v Auckland	Dunedin	1993/94
4	Redmond R.E.	Auckland v Otago	Auckland	1972/73
4	Sampson H.C.	Otago v Canterbury	Christchurch	1974/75
4	Howarth G.P.	Invitation XI v Australia	Auckland	1976/77
4	Wiltshire J.R.	Auckland v Northern Districts	Auckland	1978/79
4	Dickeson C.W.	Northern Districts v Canterbury	Hamilton	1980/81
4	Cooper B.G.	Northern Districts v Central Districts	Palmerston North	1982/83
4	Hore A.J.	Otago v Canterbury	Christchurch	1998/99

HISTORY OF THE LIMITED-OVER COMPETITION IN NEW ZEALAND

2008/09 was the 38th season of limited over competition between the six New Zealand first-class sides. In that time there have been several changes both in sponsorship and format.

For the first six seasons a knock-out competition was sponsored by the New Zealand Motor Corporation. Each innings was limited to 40 eight-ball overs during the initial two seasons, reduced to 35 thereafter. In 1977/78 and 1978/79 the sponsors changed and the teams competed for the Gillette Cup. In the first season 30 eight-ball overs were used but the limit reverted to 35 the following year. There was no sponsorship for the competition in 1979/80, known simply as the National Knock-out, where 50 six-ball overs was the limit for each innings.

In 1980/81. the Shell Cup, previously contested for as part of the first-class season, became the limited-over prize and the contest was run on a league basis for the first time with each side playing the other once.

In keeping with the previous limited-over competitions, a final was arranged, this time between the top two teams of the league table, points gained being disregarded at this stage. Fifty six-ball overs was the limit on each innings.

From 1985/86 the competition was held in its entirety, prior to the Shell Trophy series with no final. From 1989/90 the top four teams in the league table went on to semi-final play-offs, previous points being disregarded. The top two teams gained home ground advantage, the venue for the final being decided in a similar manner.

From 1993/94 to 1998/99 the top two sides played each other, with the winner going into the grand final. The loser then played the winner of the game between third and fourth to find the other finalist. From 1999/00, the leading team after the round robin went straight to the final with the second and third-placed sides meeting in a semi-final to find the other finalist. The finals became a best-of-three series.

In 2001/02, with a change of sponsor, the competition was renamed the State Shield. The format remained unaltered except the final reverted to a single game.

Winners of Limited-over Competitions

NEW ZEALAND MOTOR CORPORATION KNOCK-OUT

1971/72	Canterbury
1972/73	Auckland
1973/74	Wellington
1974/75	Wellington
1975/76	Canterbury
1976/77	Canterbury

GILLETTE CUP

1977/78	Canterbury
1978/79	Auckland

NATIONAL KNOCK-OUT

1979/80	Northern Districts

SHELL CUP

1980/81	Auckland
1981/82	Wellington
1982/83	Auckland
1983/84	Auckland
1984/85	Central Districts
1985/86	Canterbury
1986/87	Auckland
1987/88	Otago
1988/89	Wellington
1989/90	Auckland
1990/91	Wellington
1991/92	Canterbury
1992/93	Canterbury
1993/94	Canterbury
1994/95	Northern Districts
1995/96	Canterbury
1996/97	Canterbury
1997/98	Northern Districts
1998/99	Canterbury
1999/00	Canterbury
2000/01	Central Districts

STATE SHIELD

2001/02	Wellington
2002/03	Northern Districts
2003/04	Central Districts
2004/05	Northern Districts
2005/06	Canterbury
2006/07	Auckland
2007/08	Otago
2008/09	Northern Districts

Table of Results

1971/72 – 2008/09

	P	*W*	*L*	*T*	*NR*
Auckland	259*	120	120	1	18
Canterbury	269	152	104	–	13
Central Districts	252	106	127	–	19
Northern Districts	261	122	131	1	7
Otago	246	91	144	–	11
Wellington	263	144	107	–	12

** The Auckland and Central Districts totals include a match won by the toss of a coin against Central Districts and Northern Districts respectively.*

Northern Districts v Otago in 1980/81, Auckland v Wellington in 1985/86, Canterbury v Auckland, Auckland v Central Districts and Wellington v Otago in 1991/92, Central Districts v Auckland and Auckland v Wellington in 1996/97, Canterbury v Northern Districts in 1997/98, Central Districts v Canterbury in 1999/00 and Central Districts v Otago, Northern Districts, Canterbury and Auckland and Auckland v Canterbury in 2000/01, Central Districts v Auckland, Auckland v Wellington and Central Districts v Canterbury in 2006/07 and Canterbury v Otago in 2007/08 were abandoned without a ball being bowled. Wellington v Auckland in 1984/85 and Northern Districts v Canterbury 1988/89 were abandoned after one innings had been completed. The semi-final between Canterbury and Central Districts 1993/94 was due to be replayed after a match had been started and abandoned. However, no play at all was possible in the scheduled replay.

INTER-PROVINCIAL RECORDS

	Highest Score	***Lowest Score***	***Highest Individual Score***	***Best Bowling***
Auckland	341-5 v N.D. 2007/08	70 v N.D. 1977/78	L. Vincent 145 v C.D. 1999/00	W. Watson 7-0-23-7 v Otago 1984/85
Canterbury	329-5 v N.D. 1995/96	75 v Otago 1973/74	B.R. Hartland 161 v N.D. 1993/94	C.L. Cairns 10-1-37-6 v Wellington 1996/97
Central Districts	376-3 v Otago 1996/97	58 v Wellington 2001/02	D.P. Kelly 140 v Wellington 1999/00	M.J. Mason 9.3-1-25-6 v Auckland 2003/04
Northern Districts	332-5 v Canterbury 2006/07	76 v C.D. 1987/88	J.A.H. Marshall 152* v Canterbury 2006/07	B.J. Barrett 10-5-12-6 v Otago 1986/87
Otago	321-5 v CD 2007/08	64 v Wellington/CD 1984/85 2004/05	B.B. McCullum 170* v Auckland 2007/08	E.J. Marshall 7.1-0-49-7 v Auckland 1993/94
Wellington	308-9 v Canterbury 2003/04	66 v Canterbury 1996/97	C.J. Nevin 149 v CD 1997/98	A.J. Penn 8-1-28-7 v ND 2000/01

	Most Economical Bowling	*Most Expensive Bowling*	*Most Catches/ Stumpings in an innings*
Auckland	J.T.C. Vaughan 10-5-8-3 v C.D. 1993/94 J.C. Williams 8-3-7-2 (8 ball overs) v N.D. 1971/72	C.S. Martin 8-0-81-1 v Otago 2007/08	R.A. Dykes 5c v Wellington 1973/74 L. Vincent 5c v Otago 2002/03
Canterbury	A.J. Nuttall 10-6-8-2 v Wellington 1988/89 C.Z. Harris 10-5-8-1 v Auckland 1995/96	H.K. Bennett 10-0-82-2 v Auckland 2007/08	L.K. Germon 5c v Otago 1988/89
Central Districts	S.W. Duff 10-4-8-0 v Wellington 1989/90	C.O. Findlay 10-0-76-2 v Canterbury 1998/99	G.P. McRae 6c v Wellington 1994/95
Northern Districts	R.P. de Groen 10-3-9-1 v C.D. 1995/96	C.M. Presland 10-0-93-2 v Auckland 1982/83	M.J.E. Wright 5c v Auckland 1982/83
Otago	S.L. Boock 10-7-5-2 v C.D. 1986/87	R.J. Kennedy 9-0-85-1 v Canterbury 1996/97 R.J. Kennedy 10-1-85-0 v C.D. 1996/97	B.D. Milburn 5c v C.D. 1982/83 J.W. Wilson 5c v Auckland 1993/94
Wellington	G.R. Larsen 10-5-6-2 v Otago 1992/93	G. Welch 10-0-83-2 v CD 1997/98	E.B. McSweeney 6c v Auckland 1982/83 E.B. McSweeney 6c v N.D. 1988/89

RECORD PARTNERSHIPS

AUCKLAND

1st	166*	Young B.A. & Pocock B.A.	v Central Districts	Auckland	1998/99
2nd	156	Hitchcock P.A. & Jones R.A.	v Canterbury	Auckland	2006/07
3rd	242	Jones R.A. & Nicol R.J.	v Northern Districts	Auckland	2007/08
4th	157	Nicol R.J. & Barnes A.C.	v Otago	Auckland	2003/04
5th	171	Vivian G.E. & Reid J.F.	v Wellington	Auckland	1977/78
6th	109	Lynch S.M. & Vaughan J.T.C.	v Otago	Auckland	1996/97
7th	87	Mills K.D. & Hitchcock P.A.	v Central Districts	Auckland	2004/05
8th	† 121	Canning T.K. & Morgan R.G.	v Otago	Alexandra	2000/01
9th	59	Mills J.M. & Haslam M.J.	v Wellington	Wellington	1998/99
10th	48	Tuffey D.R. & Hira R.M.	v Otago	Auckland	2007/08

CANTERBURY

1st	168	Papps M.H.W. & Astle N.J.	v Wellington	Timaru	2004/05
2nd	189	Hartland B.R. & Howell L.G.	v Northern Districts	Timaru	1993/94
3rd	174	McMillan C.D. & Latham R.T.	v Central Districts	Christchurch	1994/95
4th	† 221	Howell L.G. & Stead G.R.	v Otago	Oamaru	1997/98
5th	† 198	Cairns C.L. & Germon L.K.	v Wellington	Christchurch	1992/93
6th	142	Cairns C.L. & Fleming S.P.	v Central Districts	Napier	1993/94
7th	74	Redmond A.J. & Wisneski W.A.	v Wellington	Wellington	2001/02
8th	91	Harris C.Z. & Wiseman P.J.	v Central Districts	Christchurch	2003/04
9th	53	Howell L.G. & Petrie R.G.	v Wellington	Wellington	1991/92
10th	34*	Anderson C.J. & Burson R.D.	v Otago	Oamaru	2001/02

CENTRAL DISTRICTS

1st	161	Worker G.H.& Ingram P.J.	v Northern Districts	Palmerston Nth	2008/09
2nd	172	How J.M. & Taylor L.R.P.L.	v Northern Districts	Masterton	2004/05
3rd	156	Oram J.D.P. & Douglas M.W.	v Otago	Hastings	1998/99
4th	132	Sinclair M.S. & Oram J.D.P.	v Auckland	Auckland	2003/04
5th	153*	Harden R.J. & Blain T.E.	v Canterbury	Christchurch	1990/91
6th	103	Sandbrook I.P. & Griggs B.B.J.	v Canterbury	Nelson	2002/03
7th	109	Sulzberger G.P. & Furlong C.J.M.	v Otago	Palmerston Nth	1997/98
8th	82	Thompson E.P. & Sinclair M.S.	v Otago	New Plymouth	2008/09
9th	92	Loveridge G.R. & Penn A.J.	v Canterbury	Napier	1996/97
10th	50	Garner C.D. & Alcock A.J.	v Otago	Oamaru	1993/94

NORTHERN DISTRICTS

1st	168	Marshall J.A.H. & Vettori D.L.	v Wellington	Hamilton	2002/03
2nd	† 240	Watling B-J. & Flynn D.R.	v Wellington	Whangarei	2007/08
3rd	210	Flynn D.R. & Marshall J.A.H.	v Canterbury	Christchurch	2007/08
4th	123	Parore A.C. & Thomson S.A.	v Canterbury	Mt Maunganui	1995/96
5th	137	Nash D.J. & Bradburn G.E.	v Otago	Taupo	1997/98
6th	† 196	Williamson K.S. & McGlashan P.D.	v Canterbury	Hamilton	2008/09
7th	96	Styris S.B. & McGlashan P.D.	v Central Districts	Masterton	2004/05
8th	75	Dickeson C.W. & Child M.J.	v Auckland	Pukekohe	1980/81
9th	68*	Hart R.G. & Styris S.B.	v Wellington	Wellington	1996/97
10th	† 62	Aldridge G.W. & Butler I.G.	v Canterbury	Hamilton	2003/04

OTAGO

1st	154	Hore A.J. & Lawson R.A.	v Wellington	Wellington	2001/02
2nd	134*	Richardson M.H. & Lamont M.J.	v Auckland	Auckland	1998/99
3rd	194	McCullum B.B. & Cumming C.D.	v Auckland	Auckland	2007/08
4th	190	Trott I.J.L. & Broom N.T.	v Northern Districts	Hamilton	2005/06
5th	130	McKenzie M.N. & McGlashan P.D.	v Northern Districts	Rotorua	2002/03
6th	129	Trott I.J.L. & McCullum N.L.	v Auckland	Alexandra	2005/06
7th	103*	Richardson M.H. & Campbell P.A.	v Central Districts	New Plymouth	1996/97
8th	93	McSkimming W.C. & Morland N.D.	v Central Districts	New Plymouth	2002/03
9th	54	Butler I.G. & de Boorder D.C.	v Northern Districts	Hamilton	2008/09
10th	56*	McSkimming W.C. & Sewell D.G.	v Northern Districts	Oamaru	2000/01

WELLINGTON

1st	† 205*	Aiken J.M. & Douglas M.W.	v Canterbury	Wellington	1994/95
2nd	173	Weenink S.W. & Wells J.D.	v Central Districts	Wellington	1996/97
3rd	† 244*	Fleming S.P. & Twose R.G.	v Otago	Wellington	2000/01
4th	162	Parlane N.R. & Elliott G.D.	v Northern Districts	Wellington	2008/09
5th	127	Twose R.G. & Kerr R.J.	v Northern Districts	Wellington	1996/97
6th	109	Nevin C.J. & Franklin J.E.C.	v Northern Districts	Wellington	2005/06
7th	† 130*	Bell M.D. & Mather S.R.	v Northern Districts	Mt Maunganui	1997/98
8th	98*	Taylor B.R. & Collinge R.O.	v Central Districts	Lower Hutt	1971/72
9th	† 98	Doull L.J. & Williams B.R.	v Otago	Alexandra	1993/94
10th	36*	Jefferson M.R. & R.J. Kennedy	v Canterbury	Christchurch	1999/00

† *record for all teams*

DOMESTIC ONE-DAY CAREER RECORDS

BATTING		*M*	*In*	*NO*	*HS*	*Runs*	*Ave*	*100s*	*50s*
Parlane M.E.	*ND, W*	139	138	10	132	3909	30.53	5	22
Harris C.Z.	*C*	137	126	42	107	3796	45.19	1	23
Sinclair M.S.	*CD*	112	109	15	110	3399	36.15	1	28
Astle N.J.	*C*	99	90	12	131	3285	42.11	8	16
Nevin C.J.	*W*	129	122	9	149	3124	27.64	5	14
Marshall J.A.H.	*ND*	92	89	8	152*	3042	37.55	4	20
Howell L.G.	*C. CD, A, ND*	105	105	14	134*	3022	33.20	5	22
Fleming S.P.	*C, W*	81	75	11	131	2960	46.25	6	21
Bell M.D.	*ND, W*	125	119	9	124	2947	26.79	4	14
Jones R.A.	*A, W*	118	117	6	108	2877	25.91	1	15
Barnes A.C.	*A*	114	112	11	116	2866	28.37	2	20
Twose R.G.	*ND, CD, W*	95	93	9	124*	2769	32.96	6	16
Papps M.H.W.	*C*	73	73	6	137*	2738	40.86	6	15
McMillan C.D.	*C*	88	84	12	125	2550	35.41	7	9
Cumming C.D.	*C , O*	99	94	5	112	2479	27.85	3	14
Spearman C.M.	*A, CD*	90	90	1	126	2421	27.20	1	17
Gaffaney C.B.	*O*	107	104	7	101*	2357	24.29	1	11
Douglas M.W.	*CD, W*	101	98	8	121	2326	25.84	2	10
Cairns C.L.	*ND, C*	91	82	13	143	2300	33.33	3	10
Young B.A.	*ND, A*	85	83	8	101*	2284	30.45	1	15
Richardson M.H.	*A, O*	76	74	7	128*	2283	34.07	3	14
Styris S.B.	*ND, A*	86	79	19	123	2282	38.03	1	16
Lawson R.A.	*O*	90	87	7	83*	2241	28.01	–	16
Latham R.T.	*C*	84	80	4	108	2206	29.02	1	9
Stewart S.L.	*C*	73	72	5	120	2200	32.83	3	9

		M	In	NO	HS	Runs	Ave	100s	50s
Crowe M.D.	A, CD, W	57	56	5	125	2171	42.56	5	12
Bailey M.D.	ND	103	101	14	76*	2159	24.81	—	11
Parlane N.R.	ND, W	94	87	6	105	2125	26.23	1	13
Stead G.R.	C	99	87	12	101*	2081	27.74	2	9
Bradburn G.E.	ND	121	110	15	80*	2048	21.55	—	5
Hopkins G.J.	ND, C, O, A	110	95	16	130*	2042	25.84	1	8

BOWLING		M	O	M	R	W	Ave	R/O	Best
Harris C.Z.	C	137	1091.3	72	4014	134	29.95	3.67	4-28
Tait A.R.	ND	90	757.4	75	3138	128	24.51	4.14	4-29
Hitchcock P.A.	A, W	88	698.5	38	3391	125	27.12	4.85	5-10
Petrie R.G.	C, W	100	736	58	3146	119	26.43	4.27	5-24
Aldridge G.W.	ND	81	618	42	2901	117	24.79	4.69	5-34
Martin C.S.	C, A	81	678.5	61	3169	116	27.31	4.67	5-43
Priest M.W.	C	89	724.5	69	2668	106	25.16	3.68	5-26
Yovich J.A.F.	ND	93	508.2	26	2684	106	25.32	5.28	4-44
Mason M.J.	CD	73	576	65	2398	104	23.05	4.16	6-25
Cairns C.L.	ND, C	91	587.2	39	2412	103	23.41	4.10	6-37
Astle N.J.	C	99	728.2	86	2479	102	24.30	3.40	4-14
McSkimming W.C.	O	79	643.5	55	2936	101	29.06	4.56	5-9
Tuffey D.R.	ND, A	88	720.1	55	3224	101	31.92	4.48	4-33
Styris S.B.	ND, A	86	586.4	46	2538	100	25.38	4.33	4-19

MOST ECONOMICAL BOWLING *(qualification 100 overs)*

		O	M	R	W	Ave	R/O
Hadlee R.J.	C	174.4	33	440	29	15.17	2.51
Boock S.L.	O	338.2	74	947	47	20.12	2.79
McIntyre J.M.	A	118	25	335	15	22.33	2.83
Webb R.J.	O	117.4	16	344	20	17.20	2.92
Mallender N.A.	O	458.4	83	1356	72	18.83	2.95
Chatfield E.J.	W	305	68	902	50	18.04	2.95

FIELDING		Ct	St	Total
Nevin C.J.	W	157	12	169
Hart R.G.	ND	117	30	147
Hopkins G.J.	ND, C, O, A	112	20	132
McSweeney E.B.	CD, W	97	26	123
Germon L.K.	C, O	88	18	106
Griggs B.B.J.	CD	97	6	103
Blain T.E.	CD, C	62	15	77
Young R.A.	A	63	12	75
Croy M.G.	O	64	9	73
Harris C.Z.	C	72	—	72
McGlashan P.D.	CD, O, ND	61	10	71
Bell M.D.	ND, W	62	—	62
Vincent L.	A	57	3	60
Sinclair M.S.	CD	58	1	59
Young B.A.	ND, A	46	12	58
Bradburn G.E.	ND	57	—	57
Hart M.N.	ND	55	—	55
Douglas M.W.	CD, W	47	5	52

NEW ZEALAND ONE-DAY INTERNATIONAL RECORDS

TEAM RECORDS

Results

1972/73	Pakistan	Christchurch	NZ 187	P 165	*NZ won by 22 runs*
1973	England	Swansea	NZ 158	E 159-3	*England won by 7 wickets*
	England	Manchester	E 167-8		*abandoned*
1973/74	Australia	Dunedin	NZ 194-9	A 195-3	*Australia won by 7 wickets*
	Australia	Christchurch	A 265-5	NZ 234-6	*Australia won by 31 runs*
1974/75	England	Melbourne	NZ 262-8	E 196	*NZ won by 66 runs*
	England	Dunedin	E 136	NZ 15-0	*abandoned*
	England	Wellington	NZ 227	E 35-1	*abandoned*
1975	East Africa	Birmingham	NZ 309-5	EA 128-8	*NZ won by 181 runs*
World Cup	England	Nottingham	E 266-6	NZ 186	*England won by 80 runs*
	India	Manchester	I 230-9	NZ 233-6	*NZ won by 4 wickets*
	West Indies	The Oval	NZ 158	WI 159-5	*West Indies won by 5 wickets*
1975/76	India	Christchurch	I 154	NZ 155-1	*NZ won by 9 wickets*
	India	Auckland	NZ 236-8	I 156	*NZ won by 80 runs*
1976/77	Pakistan	Sialkot	NZ 198-8	P 197-9	*NZ won by 1 run*
1978	England	Scarborough	E 206-8	NZ 187-8	*England won by 19 runs*
	England	Manchester	E 278-5	NZ 152	*England won by 126 runs*
1979	Sri Lanka	Nottingham	SL 189	NZ 190-1	*NZ won by 9 wickets*
World Cup	India	Leeds	I 182	NZ 183-2	*NZ won by 8 wickets*
	West Indies	Nottingham	WI 244-7	NZ 212-9	*West Indies won by 32 runs*
	England	Manchester	E 221-8	NZ 212-9	*England won by 9 runs*
1979/80	West Indies	Christchurch	WI 203-7	NZ 207-9	*NZ won by 1 wicket*
1980/81	Australia	Adelaide	A 217-9	NZ 219-7	*NZ won by 3 wickets*
	Australia	Sydney	A 289-3	NZ 195	*Australia won by 94 runs*
	Australia	Melbourne	NZ 156	A 159-6	*Australia won by 4 wickets*
	India	Perth	I 162	NZ 157	*India won by 5 runs*
	India	Brisbane	I 204	NZ 205-7	*NZ won by 3 wickets*
	India	Adelaide	I 230-7	NZ 224	*India won by 6 runs*
	India	Melbourne	I 112-9	NZ 113-0	*NZ won by 10 wickets*
	Australia	Sydney	NZ 220-8	A 219-7	*NZ won by 1 run*
	India	Brisbane	NZ 242-9	I 220	*NZ won by 22 runs*
	Australia	Sydney	A 180	NZ 23-1	*abandoned*
	Australia	Sydney	NZ 233-6	A 155	*NZ won by 78 runs*
	Australia	Melbourne	NZ 126	A 130-3	*Australia won by 7 wickets*
	Australia	Melbourne	A 235-4	NZ 229-8	*Australia won by 6 runs*
	Australia	Sydney	NZ 215-8	A 218-4	*Australia won by 6 wickets*
1980/81	India	Auckland	NZ 218-6	I 140-9	*NZ won by 78 runs*
	India	Hamilton	NZ 210-8	I 153	*NZ won by 57 runs*

1981/82	Australia	Auckland	NZ 240-6	A 194	*NZ won by 46 runs*
	Australia	Dunedin	NZ 159-9	A 160-4	*Australia won by 6 wickets*
	Australia	Wellington	NZ 74	A 75-2	*Australia won by 8 wickets*
1982/83	Australia	Melbourne	NZ 181	A 182-2	*Australia won by 8 wickets*
	England	Melbourne	NZ 239-8	E 237-8	*NZ won by 2 runs*
	England	Brisbane	E 267-6	NZ 213	*England won by 54 runs*
	Australia	Sydney	NZ 226-8	A 179	*NZ won by 47 runs*
	England	Sydney	NZ 199	E 200-2	*England won by 8 wickets*
	Australia	Melbourne	NZ 246-6	A 188	*NZ won by 58 runs*
	England	Adelaide	E 296-5	NZ 297-6	*NZ won by 4 wickets*
	Australia	Adelaide	NZ 200-9	A 153	*NZ won by 47 runs*
	England	Perth	E 88-7	NZ 89-3	*NZ won by 7 wickets*
	Australia	Perth	A 191-9	NZ 164	*Australia won by 27 runs*
	Australia	Sydney	NZ 193-7	A 155-4	*Australia won on faster scoring rate*
	Australia	Melbourne	A 302-8	NZ 153	*Australia won by 149 runs*
1982/83	England	Auckland	E 184	NZ 187-4	*NZ won by 6 wickets*
	England	Wellington	NZ 295-6	E 192	*NZ won by 103 runs*
	England	Christchurch	NZ 211-8	E 127	*NZ won by 84 runs*
	Sri Lanka	Dunedin	NZ 183-8	SL 118-9	*NZ won by 65 runs*
	Australia	Sydney	NZ 138-8	A 124	*NZ won by 14 runs*
	Sri Lanka	Napier	SL 167-8	NZ 168-3	*NZ won by 7 wickets*
	Sri Lanka	Auckland	NZ 304-5	SL 188-6	*NZ won by 116 runs*
1983	England	The Oval	E 322-6	NZ 216	*England won by 106 runs*
World Cup	Pakistan	Birmingham	NZ 238-9	P 186	*NZ won by 52 runs*
	Sri Lanka	Bristol	SL 206	NZ 209-5	*NZ won by 5 wickets*
	England	Birmingham	E 234	NZ 238-8	*NZ won by 2 wickets*
	Sri Lanka	Derby	NZ 181	SL 184-7	*Sri Lanka won by 3 wickets*
	Pakistan	Nottingham	P 261-3	NZ 250	*Pakistan won by 11 runs*
1983/84	England	Christchurch	E 188-9	NZ 134	*England won by 54 runs*
	England	Wellington	NZ 135	E 139-4	*England won by 6 wickets*
	England	Auckland	E 209-9	NZ 210-3	*NZ won by 7 wickets*
1983/84	Sri Lanka	Colombo	NZ 234-6	SL 130	*NZ won by 104 runs*
	Sri Lanka	Moratuwa	SL 157-8	NZ 116	*Sri Lanka won by 41 runs*
	Sri Lanka	Colombo	NZ 201-8	SL 115	*NZ won by 86 runs*
1984/85	Sri Lanka	Colombo	NZ 171-6	SL 174-6	*Sri Lanka won by 4 wickets*
	Sri Lanka	Moratuwa	SL 114-9	NZ 118-3	*NZ won by 7 wickets*
	Pakistan	Peshawar	P 191-5	NZ 145	*Pakistan won by 46 runs*
	Pakistan	Faisalabad	P 157-5	NZ 152-7	*Pakistan won by 5 runs*
	Pakistan	Sialkot	NZ 187-9	P 153-8	*NZ won by 34 runs*
	Pakistan	Multan	NZ 213-8	P 214-9	*Pakistan won by 1 wicket*
1984/85	Pakistan	Napier	NZ 277-6	P 167-9	*NZ won by 110 runs*
	Pakistan	Hamilton	P 221-4	NZ 222-6	*NZ won by 4 wickets*
	Pakistan	Christchurch	NZ 264-8	P 251	*NZ won by 13 runs*
	Pakistan	Auckland	P 189		*abandoned*
1984/85	West Indies	Sydney	NZ 57-2		*abandoned*
World Championship of Cricket	Sri Lanka	Melbourne	NZ 223	SL 172	*NZ won by 51 runs*
	India	Sydney	NZ 206	I 207-3	*India won by 7 wickets*
	West Indies	Sydney	NZ 138-9	WI 139-4	*West Indies won by 6 wickets*

1984/85	West Indies	Antigua	WI 231-8	NZ 208-8	*West Indies won by 23 runs*
	West Indies	Port of Spain	NZ 51-3	WI 55-4	*West Indies won by 6 wickets*
	West Indies	Berbice	WI 259-5	NZ 129	*West Indies won by 130 runs*
	West Indies	Port of Spain	NZ 116	WI 117-0	*West Indies won by 10 wickets*
	West Indies	Bridgetown	WI 265-3	NZ 153-8	*West Indies won by 112 runs*
1985/86	Australia	Melbourne	NZ 161-7		*abandoned*
	India	Brisbane	NZ 259-9	I 263-5	*India won by 5 wickets*
	Australia	Sydney	NZ 152	A 153-6	*Australia won by 4 wickets*
	India	Perth	I 113	NZ 115-7	*NZ won by 3 wickets*
	Australia	Perth	NZ 159-6	A 161-6	*Australia won by 4 wickets*
	India	Melbourne	I 238-8	NZ 239-5	*NZ won by 5 wickets*
	India	Adelaide	NZ 172	I 174-5	*India won by 5 wickets*
	Australia	Adelaide	NZ 276-7	A 70	*NZ won by 206 runs*
	Australia	Sydney	A 239-7	NZ 140	*Australia won by 99 runs*
	India	Launceston	I 202-9	NZ 168-9	*India won by 21 runs (target adjusted)*
1985/86	Australia	Dunedin	NZ 186-6	A 156	*NZ won by 30 runs*
	Australia	Christchurch	NZ 258-7	A 205	*NZ won by 53 runs*
	Australia	Wellington	NZ 229-9	A 232-7	*Australia won by 3 wickets*
	Australia	Auckland	A 231	NZ 187-9	*Australia won by 44 runs*
1985/86	Sri Lanka	Colombo	SL 137-9	NZ 140-4	*NZ won by 6 wickets*
	Pakistan	Colombo	NZ 214-8	P 217-6	*Pakistan won by 4 wickets*
	India	Sharjah	NZ 132-8	I 134-7	*India won by 3 wickets*
	Pakistan	Sharjah	NZ 64	P 66-0	*Pakistan won by 10 wickets*
1986	England	Leeds	NZ 217-8	E 170	*NZ won by 47 runs*
	England	Manchester	NZ 284-5	E 286-4	*England won by 6 wickets*
1986/87	West Indies	Dunedin	WI 237-9	NZ 142	*West Indies won by 95 runs*
	West Indies	Auckland	NZ 213	WI 217-4	*West Indies won by 6 wickets*
	West Indies	Wellington	*abandoned without a ball being bowled*		
	West Indies	Christchurch	NZ 191-9	WI 192-0	*West Indies won by 10 wickets*
1987/88 *World Cup*	Zimbabwe	Hyderabad	NZ 242-7	Z 239	*NZ won by 3 runs*
	India	Bangalore	I 252-7	NZ 236-8	*India won by 16 runs*
	Australia	Indore	A 199-4	NZ 196-9	*Australia won by 3 runs*
	Zimbabwe	Calcutta	Z 227-5	NZ 228-6	*NZ won by 4 wickets*
	Australia	Chandigarh	A 251-8	NZ 234	*Australia won by 17 runs*
	India	Nagpur	NZ 221-9	I 224-1	*India won by 9 wickets*
1987/88	Australia	Perth	NZ 232-9	A 231	*NZ won by 1 run*
	Sri Lanka	Sydney	SL 174	NZ 178-4	*NZ won by 6 wickets*
	Australia	Melbourne	A 216	NZ 210-9	*Australia won by 6 runs*
	Sri Lanka	Adelaide	SL 241	NZ 242-6	*NZ won by 4 wickets*
	Sri Lanka	Hobart	NZ 199-7	SL 200-6	*Sri Lanka won by 4 wickets*
	Sri Lanka	Brisbane	SL 164-8	NZ 167-6	*NZ won by 4 wickets*
	Australia	Brisbane	NZ 176-5	A 177-5	*Australia won by 5 wickets*
	Australia	Sydney	A 221-8	NZ 143	*Australia won by 78 runs*
	Australia	Melbourne	NZ 177	A 180-2	*Australia won by 8 wickets*
	Australia	Sydney	NZ 168-5	A 169-4	*Australia won by 6 wickets*

1987/88	England	Dunedin	NZ 204	E 207-5	*England won by 5 wickets*
	England	Christchurch	NZ186-8	E 188-4	*England won by 6 wickets*
	England	Napier	E 219	NZ 223-3	*NZ won by 7 wickets*
	England	Auckland	E 208	NZ 211-6	*NZ won by 4 wickets*
1987/88	India	Sharjah	I 267-6	NZ 194-8	*India won by 73 runs*
	Sri Lanka	Sharjah	NZ 258-8	SL 159	*NZ won by 99 runs*
	Sri Lanka	Sharjah	NZ 249-7	SL 206-9	*NZ won by 43 runs*
	India	Sharjah	I 250-7	NZ 198	*India won by 52 runs*
1988/89	India	Visakhapatnam	NZ 196-9	I 197-6	*India won by 4 wickets*
	India	Cuttack	NZ 160-7	I 161-5	*India won by 5 wickets*
	India	Indore	I 222-6	NZ 169-9	*India won by 53 runs*
	India	Baroda	NZ 278-3	I 282-8	*India won by 2 wickets*
	India	Jammu	*abandoned without a ball being bowled*		
1988/89	Pakistan	Dunedin	P 170-9	NZ 174-2	*NZ won by 8 wickets*
	Pakistan	Christchurch	P 170-7	NZ 171-3	*NZ won by 7 wickets*
	Pakistan	Wellington	P 253-6	NZ 254-4	*NZ won by 6 wickets*
	Pakistan	Auckland	NZ 249	P 251-3	*Pakistan won by 7 wickets*
	Pakistan	Hamilton	P 138-9	NZ 139-3	*NZ won by 7 wickets*
1989/90	India	Dunedin	NZ 246-6	I 138	*NZ won by 108 runs*
	Australia	Christchurch	A 244-8	NZ 94	*Australia won by 150 runs*
	India	Wellington	I 221	NZ 220	*India won by 1 run*
	Australia	Auckland	A 239-6	NZ 167-2	*Australia won on faster scoring rate*
	Australia	Auckland	NZ 162	A 164-2	*Australia won by 8 wickets*
1989/90	Australia	Sharjah	A 258-5	NZ 195-7	*Australia won by 63 runs*
	Bangladesh	Sharjah	NZ 338-4	B 177-5	*NZ won by 161 runs*
	Pakistan	Sharjah	NZ 74	P 75-2	*Pakistan won by 8 wickets*
1990	England	Leeds	E 295-6	NZ 298-6	*NZ won by 4 wickets*
	England	The Oval	NZ 212-6	E 213-4	*England won by 6 wickets*
1990/91	Pakistan	Lahore	P 196-8	NZ 177	*Pakistan won by 19 runs*
	Pakistan	Peshawar	NZ 127	P 128-2	*Pakistan won by 8 wickets*
	Pakistan	Sialkot	P 223-2	NZ 118	*Pakistan won by 105 runs*
1990/91	Australia	Sydney	A 236-9	NZ 174-7	*Australia won by 61 runs target reduced*
	England	Adelaide	NZ 199-6	E 192-9	*NZ won by 7 runs*
	Australia	Adelaide	NZ 208-7	A 210-4	*Australia won by 6 wickets*
	England	Perth	NZ 158	E 161-6	*England won by 4 wickets*
	Australia	Melbourne	A 263-7	NZ 224-8	*Australia won by 39 runs*
	England	Sydney	E 194	NZ 161	*England won by 33 runs*
	England	Brisbane	E 203-6	NZ 204-2	*NZ won by 8 wickets*
	Australia	Hobart	NZ 194-6	A 193	*NZ won by 1 run*
	Australia	Sydney	NZ 199-7	A 202-4	*Australia won by 6 wickets*
	Australia	Melbourne	NZ 208-6	A 209-3	*Australia won by 7 wickets*
1990/91	Sri Lanka	Napier	SL 177-8	NZ 178-5	*NZ won by 5 wickets*
	Sri Lanka	Auckland	NZ 242-5	SL 201	*NZ won by 41 runs*
	Sri Lanka	Dunedin	NZ 272-6	SL 165	*NZ won by 107 runs*
	England	Christchurch	E 230-7	NZ 216-8	*England won by 14 runs*
	England	Wellington	NZ 196-8	E 187	*NZ won by 9 runs*
	England	Auckland	NZ 224-7	E 217	*NZ won by 7 runs*

Season	Opponent	Venue	Team 1	Team 2	Result
1991/92	England	Auckland	NZ 178-7	E 179-3	*England won by 7 wickets*
	England	Dunedin	NZ 186-7	E 188-7	*England won by 3 wickets*
	England	Christchurch	E 255-7	NZ 184-8	*England won by 71 runs*
1991/92 *World Cup*	Australia	Auckland	NZ 248-6	A 211	*NZ won by 37 runs*
	Sri Lanka	Hamilton	SL 206-9	NZ 210-4	*NZ won by 6 wickets*
	South Africa	Auckland	SA 190-7	NZ 191-3	*NZ won by 7 wickets*
	Zimbabwe	Napier	NZ 163-3	Z 105-7	*NZ won by 49 runs target reduced*
	West Indies	Auckland	WI 203-7	NZ 206-5	*NZ won by 5 wickets*
	India	Dunedin	I 230-6	NZ 231-6	*NZ won by 4 wickets*
	England	Wellington	E 200-8	NZ 201-3	*NZ won by 7 wickets*
	Pakistan	Christchurch	NZ 166	P 167-3	*Pakistan won by 7 wickets*
	Pakistan	Auckland	NZ 262-7	P 264-6	*Pakistan won by 4 wickets*
1992/93	Zimbabwe	Bulawayo	NZ 244-7	Z 222-9	*NZ won by 22 runs*
	Zimbabwe	Harare	Z 271-6	NZ 272-6	*NZ won by 4 wickets*
1992/93	Sri Lanka	Colombo	NZ 166-9	SL 41-2	*abandoned*
	Sri Lanka	Colombo	NZ 190-7	SL 192-2	*SL won by 8 wickets*
	Sri Lanka	Colombo	SL 262-6	NZ 231	*SL won by 31 runs*
1992/93	Pakistan	Wellington	P 158-8	NZ 108	*Pakistan won by 50 runs*
	Pakistan	Napier	P 136-8	NZ 137-4	*NZ won by 6 wickets*
	Pakistan	Auckland	P 139	NZ 140-4	*NZ won by 6 wickets*
1992/93	Australia	Dunedin	A 258-4	NZ 129	*Australia won by 129 runs*
	Australia	Christchurch	NZ 196-8	A 197-9	*Australia won by 1 wicket*
	Australia	Wellington	NZ 214	A 126	*NZ won by 88 runs*
	Australia	Hamilton	A 247-7	NZ 250-7	*NZ won by 3 wickets*
	Australia	Auckland	A 232-8	NZ 229-8	*Australia won by 3 runs*
1993/94	South Africa	Adelaide	*abandoned without a ball being bowled*		
	Australia	Adelaide	NZ 135	A 136-2	*Australia won by 8 wickets*
	Australia	Melbourne	A 202-5	NZ 199-9	*Australia won by 3 runs*
	South Africa	Hobart	SA 147-7	NZ 148-6	*NZ won by 4 wickets*
	South Africa	Brisbane	NZ 256-7	SA 219-8	*NZ won by 9 runs target reduced*
	Australia	Sydney	NZ 198-9	A 185	*NZ won by 13 runs*
	South Africa	Perth	NZ 150	SA 151-5	*SA won by 5 wickets*
	Australia	Melbourne	A 217-3	NZ 166	*Australia won by 51 runs*
1993/94	Pakistan	Dunedin	NZ 122-9	P 123-5	*Pakistan won by 5 wickets*
	Pakistan	Auckland	P 146	NZ 110	*Pakistan won by 36 runs*
	Pakistan	Wellington	P 213-6	NZ 202-8	*Pakistan won by 11 runs*
	Pakistan	Auckland	P 161-9	NZ 161	*Tie*
	Pakistan	Christchurch	P 145-9	NZ 146-3	*NZ won by 7 wickets*
	India	Napier	NZ 240-5	I 212-9	*NZ won by 28 runs*
	India	Auckland	NZ 142	I 143-3	*India won by 7 wickets*
	India	Wellington	I 255-5	NZ 243-9	*India won by 12 runs*
	India	Christchurch	I 222-6	NZ 223-4	*NZ won by 6 wickets*
1993/94	Australia	Sharjah	NZ 207-9	A 208-3	*Australia won by 7 wickets*
	Sri Lanka	Sharjah	NZ 217-8	SL 215-9	*NZ won by 2 runs*
	Pakistan	Sharjah	P 328-2	NZ 266-7	*Pakistan won by 62 runs*
1994	England	Birmingham	E 224-8	NZ 182	*England won by 42 runs*
	England	Lord's	*abandoned without a ball being bowled*		

1994/95	West Indies	Goa	WI 123	NZ 25-1	*abandoned*
	India	Baroda	NZ 269-4	I 271-3	*India won by 7 wickets*
	West Indies	Guwahati	WI 306-6	NZ 171-9	*West Indies won by 135 runs*
	India	Delhi	I 289-3	NZ 182	*India won by 107 runs*
1994/95	South Africa	Cape Town	SA 203-8	NZ 134	*South Africa won by 69 runs*
	Sri Lanka	Bloemfontein	SL 288-4	NZ 66-1	*abandoned*
	South Africa	Verwoerdburg	SA 314-7	NZ 233	*South Africa won by 81 runs*
	Pakistan	Port Elizabeth	NZ 201	P 206-5	*Pakistan won by 5 wickets*
	Sri Lanka	East London	NZ 255-4	SL 257-5	*Sri Lanka won by 5 wickets*
	Pakistan	East London	NZ 172	P 175-5	*Pakistan won by 5 wickets*
1994/95	West Indies	Auckland	NZ 167-6	WI 149-1	*West Indies won by 9 wickets target reduced*
	West Indies	Wellington	WI 246-7	NZ 205	*West Indies won by 41 runs*
	West Indies	Christchurch	NZ 146	WI 149-1	*West Indies won by 9 wickets*
1994/95	India	Napier	I 160	NZ 162-6	*NZ won by 4 wickets*
	Australia	Auckland	A 254-5	NZ 227-9	*Australia won by 27 runs*
	South Africa	Christchurch	NZ 249-7	SA 203	*NZ won by 46 runs*
	Australia	Auckland	NZ 137-9	A 138-4	*Australia won by 6 wickets*
1994/95	Sri Lanka	Christchurch	NZ 271-6	SL 238	*NZ won by 33 runs*
	Sri Lanka	Hamilton	NZ 280-6	SL 117-6	*NZ won by 57 runs target reduced*
	Sri Lanka	Auckland	SL 250-6	NZ 199	*Sri Lanka won by 51 runs*
1995/96	India	Jamshedpur	I 236	NZ 237-2	*NZ won by 8 wickets*
	India	Amritsar	NZ 145	I 146-4	*India won by 6 wickets*
	India	Goa	*abandoned without a ball being bowled*		
	India	Pune	NZ 235-6	I 236-5	*India won by 5 wickets*
	India	Nagpur	NZ 348-8	I 249	*NZ won by 99 runs*
	India	Bombay	NZ 126	I 128-4	*India won by 6 wickets*
1995/96	Pakistan	Dunedin	P 189-9	NZ 169	*Pakistan won by 20 runs*
	Pakistan	Christchurch	P 232-9	NZ 236-9	*NZ won by 1 wicket*
	Pakistan	Wellington	P 261-4	NZ 207	*Pakistan won by 54 runs*
	Pakistan	Auckland	NZ 244-8	P 212	*NZ won by 32 runs*
1995/96	Zimbabwe	Auckland	NZ 278-5	Z 204	*NZ won by 74 runs*
	Zimbabwe	Wellington	Z 181-9	NZ 184-4	*NZ won by 6 wickets*
	Zimbabwe	Napier	Z 267-7	NZ 246	*Zimbabwe won by 21 runs*
1995/96	England	Ahmedabad	NZ 239-6	E 228-9	*NZ won by 11 runs*
World Cup	Holland	Baroda	NZ 307-8	H 188-7	*NZ won by 119 runs*
	South Africa	Faisalabad	NZ 177-9	SA 178-5	*Sth Africa won by 5 wickets*
	UAE	Faisalabad	NZ 276-8	UAE 167-9	*NZ won by 109 runs*
	Pakistan	Lahore	P 281-5	NZ 235	*Pakistan won by 46 runs*
	Australia	Madras	NZ 286-9	A 289-4	*Australia won by 6 wickets*
1995/96	West Indies	Kingston	NZ 243	WI 247-9	*West Indies won by 1 wicket*
	West Indies	Port of Spain	WI 238-7	NZ 239-6	*NZ won by 4 wickets*
	West Indies	Port of Spain	NZ 219-8	WI 225-3	*West Indies won by 7 wickets*
	West Indies	Georgetown	NZ 158	WI 154	*NZ won by 4 runs*
	West Indies	Arnos Vale	NZ 241-8	WI 242-3	*West Indies won by 7 wickets*

1996/97	Sri Lanka	Sharjah	NZ 206-8	SL 177	*NZ won by 29 runs*
	Pakistan	Sharjah	NZ 197	P 198-6	*Pakistan won by 4 wickets*
	Sri Lanka	Sharjah	NZ 169-8	SL 169	*Tie*
	Pakistan	Sharjah	NZ 192	P 196-6	*Pakistan won by 4 wickets*
	Pakistan	Sharjah	P 160	NZ 119	*Pakistan won by 41 runs*
1996/97	Pakistan	Gujranwala	P 228-8	NZ 217	*Pakistan won by 11 runs*
	Pakistan	Sialkot	P 277-9	NZ 231	*Pakistan won by 46 runs*
	Pakistan	Karachi	P 234-4	NZ 235-3	*NZ won by 7 wickets*
1996/97	England	Christchurch	NZ 222-6	E 226-6	*England won by 4 wickets*
	England	Auckland	NZ 253-8	E 134-4	*England won by 6 wickets target reduced*
	England	Napier	NZ 237	E 237-8	*Tie*
	England	Auckland	NZ 153	E 144	*NZ won by 9 runs*
	England	Wellington	NZ 228-8	E 200	*NZ won by 28 runs*
1996/97	Sri Lanka	Auckland	*abandoned without a ball being bowled*		
	Sri Lanka	Christchurch	NZ 201-9	SL 202-4	*Sri Lanka won by 6 wickets*
	Sri Lanka	Wellington	NZ 201	SL 132	*NZ won by 69 runs*
1996/97	Pakistan	Mohali	NZ 285-7	P 263-9	*NZ won by 22 runs*
	India	Bangalore	NZ 220-9	I 221-2	*India won by 8 wickets*
	Sri Lanka	Hyderabad	SL 214	NZ 162	*Sri Lanka won by 52 runs*
1997/98	Zimbabwe	Bulawayo	Z 233-8	NZ 233-9	*Tie*
	Zimbabwe	Harare	NZ 185-7	Z 188-7	*Zimbabwe won by 3 wickets*
	Zimbabwe	Harare	NZ 294-7	Z 211	*NZ won by 83 runs*
1997/98	South Africa	Adelaide	NZ 224-6	SA 177	*NZ won by 47 runs*
	Australia	Adelaide	NZ 260-7	A 263-7	*Australia won by 3 wickets*
	South Africa	Hobart	SA 174-9	NZ 173-7	*South Africa won by 1 run*
	Australia	Melbourne	NZ 141	A 142-4	*Australia won by 6 wickets*
	South Africa	Brisbane	SA 300-6	NZ 298-9	*South Africa won by 2 runs*
	Australia	Sydney	A 250	NZ 119	*Australia won by 131 runs*
	South Africa	Perth	SA 233-7	NZ 166	*South Africa won by 67 runs*
	Australia	Melbourne	A 251-4	NZ 253-6	*NZ won by 4 wickets*
1997/98	Zimbabwe	Hamilton	NZ 248-7	Z 208	*NZ won by 40 runs*
	Zimbabwe	Wellington	Z 138	NZ 139-2	*NZ won by 8 wickets*
	Australia	Christchurch	NZ 212-7	A 215-3	*Australia won by 7 wickets*
	Australia	Wellington	A 297-6	NZ 231	*Australia won by 66 runs*
	Australia	Napier	A 236	NZ 240-3	*NZ won by 7 wickets*
	Australia	Auckland	NZ 223-7	A 193	*NZ won by 30 runs*
	Zimbabwe	Christchurch	Z 228-7	NZ 227-9	*Zimbabwe won by 1 run*
	Zimbabwe	Napier	Z 207-8	NZ 211-1	*NZ won by 9 wickets*
	Zimbabwe	Auckland	NZ 231-9	Z 229-9	*NZ won by 2 runs*
1997/98	India	Sharjah	I 220-9	NZ 205	*India won by 15 runs*
	Australia	Sharjah	NZ 159	A 160-4	*Australia won by 6 wickets*
	India	Sharjah	I 181	NZ 183-6	*NZ won by 4 wickets*
	Australia	Sharjah	NZ 259-5	A 261-5	*Australia won by 5 wickets*
1997/98	Sri Lanka	Colombo	NZ 200-9	SL 201-3	*Sri Lanka won by 7 wickets*
	India	Colombo	NZ 219-8	I 131-3	*abandoned*
	Sri Lanka	Galle	*abandoned without a ball being bowled*		
	India	Galle	*abandoned without a ball being bowled*		
	India	Colombo	NZ 128-5		*abandoned*
	Sri Lanka	Colombo	SL 293-4	NZ 206	*Sri Lanka won by 87 runs*

1998/99	Zimbabwe	Dhaka	Z 258-7	NZ 260-5	*NZ won by 5 wickets*
ICC Knockout	Sri Lanka	Dhaka	NZ 188	SL 191-5	*Sri Lanka won by 5 wickets*
1998/99	India	Taupo	I 257-5	NZ 200-5	*NZ won by 5 wickets (D/L)*
	India	Napier	NZ 213	I 214-8	*India won by 2 wickets*
	India	Wellington	I 208-4	NZ 89-2	*abandoned*
	India	Auckland	NZ 207-7	I 208-5	*India won by 5 wickets*
	India	Christchurch	NZ 300-8	I 230	*NZ won by 70 runs*
1998/99	South Africa	Dunedin	SA 211	NZ 215-7	*NZ won by 3 wickets*
	South Africa	Christchurch	NZ 220-9	SA 224-3	*SA won by 7 wickets*
	South Africa	Auckland	SA 212-7	NZ 215-3	*NZ won by 7 wickets*
	South Africa	Napier	NZ 257-8	SA 10-0	*abandoned*
	South Africa	Napier	NZ 191	SA 194-8	*SA won by 2 wickets*
	South Africa	Auckland	SA 290-5	NZ 147	*SA won by 143 runs*
	South Africa	Wellington	SA 249-4		*abandoned*
1999 ***World Cup***	Bangladesh	Chelmsford	B 116	NZ 117-4	*NZ won by 6 wickets*
	Australia	Cardiff	A 213-8	NZ 214-5	*NZ won by 5 wickets*
	West Indies	Southampton	NZ 156	WI 158-3	*WI won by 7 wickets*
	Pakistan	Derby	P 269-8	NZ 207-8	*Pakistan won by 62 runs*
	Scotland	Edinburgh	S 121	NZ 123-4	*NZ won by 6 wickets*
	Zimbabwe	Leeds	Z 175	NZ 70-3	*abandoned*
	South Africa	Birmingham	SA 287-5	NZ 213-8	*SA won by 74 runs*
	India	Nottingham	I 251-6	NZ 253-5	*NZ won by 5 wickets*
	Pakistan	Manchester	NZ 241-7	P 242-1	*Pakistan won by 9 wickets*
1999/00	India	Rajkot	NZ 349-9	I 306	*NZ won by 43 runs*
	India	Hyderabad	I 376-2	NZ 202	*India won by 174 runs*
	India	Gwalior	I 261-5	NZ 247-8	*India won by 14 runs*
	India	Guwahati	NZ 236-9	I 188	*NZ won by 48 runs*
	India	Delhi	NZ 179-9	I 181-3	*India won by 7 wickets*
1999/00	West Indies	Auckland	WI 268-7	NZ 250-7	*NZ won by 3 wickets (D/L)*
	West Indies	Taupo	WI 192	NZ 194-3	*NZ won by 7 wickets*
	West Indies	Napier	WI 159	NZ 160-6	*NZ won by 4 wickets*
	West Indies	Wellington	WI 171-9	NZ 172-2	*NZ won by 8 wickets*
	West Indies	Christchurch	NZ 302-6	WI 282	*NZ won by 20 runs*
1999/00	Australia	Wellington	A 119-1	NZ	*Abandoned*
	Australia	Auckland	NZ 122	A 123-5	*Australia won by 5 wickets*
	Australia	Dunedin	A 310-4	NZ 260	*Australia won by 50 runs*
	Australia	Christchurch	A 349-6	NZ 301-9	*Australia won by 48 runs*
	Australia	Napier	NZ 243-9	A 245-5	*Australia won by 5 wickets*
	Australia	Auckland	A 191	NZ 194-3	*NZ won by 7 wickets*
2000/01	Pakistan	Singapore	P 191-6	NZ 179	*Pakistan won by 12 runs*
	South Africa	Singapore	NZ 158	SA 159-2	*SA won by 8 wickets*
2000/01	Zimbabwe	Harare	Z 183-8	NZ 184-3	*NZ won by 7 wickets*
	Zimbabwe	Bulawayo	Z 273-5	NZ 252	*Zimbabwe won by 21 runs*
	Zimbabwe	Bulawayo	NZ 264-8	Z 268-4	*Zimbabwe won by 6 wkts*
2000/01	Zimbabwe	Nairobi	NZ 265-7	Z 201	*NZ won by 64 runs*
ICC Knockout	Pakistan	Nairobi	P 252	NZ 255-6	*NZ won by 4 wickets*
	India	Nairobi	I 264-6	NZ 265-6	*NZ won by 4 wickets*

2000/01	South Africa	Potchefstroom	SA 191-2	NZ	*abandoned*
	South Africa	Benoni	NZ 194-8	SA 197-4	*SA won by 6 wkts*
	South Africa	Centurion	SA 324-4	NZ 189	*SA won by 115 runs (D/L)*
	South Africa	Kimberley	NZ 287-6	SA 289-5	*SA won by 5 wickets*
	South Africa	Durban	NZ 114-5	SA 158-4	*SA won by 6 wickets(D/L)*
	South Africa	Cape Town	NZ 256-9	SA 258-7	*SA won by 3 wickets*
2000/01	Zimbabwe	Taupo	Z 300-7	NZ 210	*Zimbabwe won by 70 runs (D/L)*
	Zimbabwe	Wellington	Z 236-7	NZ 237-2	*NZ won by 8 wickets*
	Zimbabwe	Auckland	NZ 273-9	Z 274-9	*Zimbabwe won by 1 wicket*
2000/01	Sri Lanka	Napier	SL 213-8	NZ 152	*Sri Lanka won by 61 runs*
	Sri Lanka	Wellington	NZ 205-8	SL 209-7	*Sri Lanka won by 3 wickets*
	Sri Lanka	Auckland	NZ 181	SL 182-1	*Sri Lanka won by 9 wickets*
	Sri Lanka	Hamilton	NZ 182-9	SL 155-5	*Sri Lanka won by 3 runs (D/L)*
	Sri Lanka	Christchurch	NZ 282-6	SL 269	*NZ won by 13 runs*
2000/01	Pakistan	Auckland	NZ 149	P 150-4	*Pakistan won by 6 wickets*
	Pakistan	Napier	P 135	NZ 136-4	*NZ won by 6 wickets*
	Pakistan	Wellington	P 243-9	NZ 215	*Pakistan won by 28 runs*
	Pakistan	Christchurch	NZ 284-5	P 146	*NZ won by 138 runs*
	Pakistan	Dunedin	P 285	NZ 290-6	*NZ won by 4 wickets*
2000/01	Sri Lanka	Sharjah	SL 269-9	NZ 163	*Sri Lanka won by 106 runs*
	Pakistan	Sharjah	NZ 266-7	P 270-2	*Pakistan won by 8 wickets*
	Pakistan	Sharjah	NZ 127	P 131-3	*Pakistan won by 7 wickets*
	Sri Lanka	Sharjah	NZ 248-6	SL 169-8	*NZ won by 79 runs*
2001/02	Sri Lanka	Colombo	SL 220	NZ 204-9	*Sri Lanka won by 16 runs*
	India	Colombo	NZ 211-8	I 127	*NZ won by 84 runs*
	Sri Lanka	Colombo	NZ 236-8	SL 240-5	*Sri Lanka won by 5 wickets*
	India	Colombo	NZ 200	I 133	*NZ won by 67 runs*
	Sri Lanka	Colombo	SL 221-6	NZ 115-9	*Sri Lanka won by 106 runs*
	India	Colombo	NZ 264-7	I 267-3	*India won by 7 wickets*
2001/02	Australia	Melbourne	NZ 199-8	A 176	*NZ won by 23 runs*
	South Africa	Hobart	SA 257-7	NZ 231-9	*SA won by 26 runs*
	Australia	Sydney	NZ 235-9	A 212	*NZ won by 23 runs*
	South Africa	Brisbane	SA 241	NZ 244-6	*NZ won by 4 wickets*
	Australia	Adelaide	NZ 242-5	A 165	*NZ won by 77 runs*
	South Africa	Adelaide	SA 253-5	NZ 160	*SA won by 93 runs*
	Australia	Melbourne	NZ 245-8	A 248-8	*Australia won by 2 wickets*
	South Africa	Perth	SA 270-5	NZ 203-8	*SA won by 67 runs*
	South Africa	Melbourne	NZ 190	SA 191-2	*SA won by 8 wickets*
	South Africa	Sydney	NZ 175	SA 173-4	*SA won by 6 wickets (D/L)*
2001/02	England	Christchurch	E 196	NZ 198-6	*NZ won by 4 wickets*
	England	Wellington	NZ 244-8	E 89	*NZ won by 155 runs*
	England	Napier	E 244-5	NZ 201	*England won by 43 runs*
	England	Auckland	E 193-6	NZ 189	*England won by 33 runs (D/L)*
	England	Dunedin	E 218-8	NZ 223-5	*NZ won by 5 wickets*
2001/02	Sri Lanka	Sharjah	NZ 218-8	SL 207	*NZ won by 11 runs*
	Pakistan	Sharjah	P 288-6	NZ 237-8	*Pakistan won by 51 runs*
	Sri Lanka	Sharjah	SL 243-9	NZ 197-9	*Sri Lanka won by 46 runs*
	Pakistan	Sharjah	NZ 213-9	P 217-2	*Pakistan won by 8 wickets*
2001/02	Pakistan	Karachi	P 275-6	NZ 122	*Pakistan won by 153 runs*
	Pakistan	Rawalpindi	NZ 277-5	P 278-7	*Pakistan won by 3 wickets*
	Pakistan	Lahore	P 278-5	NZ 212	*Pakistan won by 66 runs*

2001/02	West Indies	Kingston	NZ 176	WI	*abandoned*
	West Indies	Gros Islet	NZ 248-7	WI 250-4	*West Indies won by 6 wickets*
	West Indies	Gros Islet	NZ 210-7	WI 211-3	*West Indies won by 7 wickets*
	West Indies	Port of Spain	NZ 212-5	WI 202-9	*NZ won by 9 runs (D/L)*
	West Indies	Arnos Vale	NZ 291-8	WI 292-6	*West Indies won by 4 wickets*
2002/03	Australia	Colombo	A 296-7	NZ 132	*Australia won by 164 runs*
Champions Trophy	Bangladesh	Colombo	NZ 244-9	B 77	*NZ won by 167 runs*
2002/03	India	Auckland	I 108	NZ 109-7	*NZ won by 3 wickets*
	India	Napier	NZ 254-9	I 219	*NZ won by 35 runs*
	India	Christchurch	I 108	NZ 109-5	*NZ won by 5 wickets*
	India	Queenstown	I 122	NZ 123-3	*NZ won by 7 wickets*
	India	Wellington	NZ 168	I 169-8	*India won by 2 wickets*
	India	Auckland	NZ 199-9	I 200-9	*India won by 1 wicket*
	India	Hamilton	I 122	NZ 125-4	*NZ won by 6 wickets*
2002/03	Sri Lanka	Bloemfontein	SL 272-7	NZ 225	*Sri Lanka won by 47 runs*
World	West Indies	Port Elizabeth	NZ 241-7	WI 221	*NZ won by 20 runs*
Cup	South Africa	Johannesburg	SL 306-6	NZ 229-1	*NZ won by 9 wickets (D/L)*
	Kenya	Nairobi			*NZ forfeited the match*
	Bangladesh	Kimberley	B 198-7	NZ 199-3	*NZ won by 7 wickets*
	Canada	Benoni	C 196	NZ 197-5	*NZ won by 5 wickets*
	Zimbabwe	Bloemfontein	Z 252-7	NZ 253-4	*NZ won by 6 wickets*
	Australia	Port Elizabeth	A 208-9	NZ 112	*Australia won by 96 runs*
	India	Centurion	NZ 146	I 150-3	*India won by 7 wickets*
2002/03	Pakistan	Dambulla	P 116	NZ 117-3	*NZ won by 7 wickets*
	Sri Lanka	Dambulla	NZ 139	SL 143-5	*Sri Lanka won by 5 wickets*
	Sri Lanka	Dambulla	NZ 156-8	SL 147	*NZ won by 9 runs*
	Pakistan	Dambulla	P 203-9	NZ 181	*Pakistan won by 22 runs*
	Pakistan	Dambulla	P 198	NZ 200-6	*NZ won by 4 wickets*
2003/04	India	Chennai	I 141-3	NZ	*abandoned*
	Australia	Faridabad	NZ 97	A 101-2	*Australia won by 8 wickets*
	Australia	Pune	NZ 258-9	A 259-8	*Australia won by 2 wickets*
	India	Cuttack	I 246-6	NZ 249-6	*NZ won by 4 wickets*
	Australia	Guwahati	A 225-7	NZ 181	*Australia won by 44 runs*
	India	Hyderabad	I 353-5	NZ 208	*India won by 145 runs*
2003/04	Pakistan	Lahore	NZ 291-5	P 292-7	*Pakistan won by 3 wickets*
	Pakistan	Lahore	P 281-6	NZ 157	*Pakistan won by 124 runs*
	Pakistan	Faisalabad	P 314-7	NZ 263-7	*Pakistan won by 51 runs*
	Pakistan	Rawalpindi	NZ 183	P 184-3	*Pakistan won by 7 wickets*
	Pakistan	Rawalpindi	P 277-4	NZ 228-6	*Pakistan won by 49 runs*
2003/04	Pakistan	Auckland	P 229-7	NZ 230-6	*NZ won by 4 wickets*
	Pakistan	Queenstown	NZ 235-8	P 236-4	*Pakistan won by 6 wickets*
	Pakistan	Christchurch	P 255-9	NZ 259-3	*NZ won by 7 wickets*
	Pakistan	Napier	P 126	NZ 127-2	*NZ won by 8 wickets*
	Pakistan	Wellington	NZ 307-8	P 303	*NZ won by 4 runs*
2003/04	South Africa	Auckland	NZ 225-8	SA 226-5	*SA won by 5 wickets*
	South Africa	Christchurch	SA 253-8	NZ 255-5	*NZ won by 5 wickets*
	South Africa	Wellington	NZ 254-5	SA 249-7	*NZ won by 5 runs*
	South Africa	Dunedin	SA 259-7	NZ 264-4	*NZ won by 6 wickets*
	South Africa	Auckland	NZ 193-8	SA 175-5	*NZ won by 2 runs (D/L)*
	South Africa	Napier	SA 186-9	NZ 190-5	*NZ won by 5 wickets*

2004	England	Manchester	*abandoned without a ball being bowled*		
	West Indies	Birmingham	WI 122-4	NZ 97-2	*abandoned*
	England	Chester-le-Street	E 101	NZ 103-3	*NZ won by 7 wickets*
	West Indies	Cardiff	WI 216	NZ 220-5	*NZ won by 5 wickets*
	England	Bristol	E 237-7	NZ 241-4	*NZ won by 6 wickets*
	West Indies	Southampton	*abandoned without a ball being bowled*		
	West Indies	Lord's	NZ 266	WI 159	*NZ won by 107 runs*
2004	USA	The Oval	NZ 347-4	USA 137	*NZ won by 210 runs*
Champions Trophy	Australia	The Oval	NZ 198	A 199-3	*Australia won by 7 wickets*
2004/05	Bangladesh	Chittagong	NZ 224	B 86	*NZ won by 138 runs*
	Bangladesh	Dhaka	B 146	NZ 148-7	*NZ won by 3 wickets*
	Bangladesh	Dhaka	NZ 250-7	B 167-7	*NZ won by 83 runs*
2004/05	Australia	Melbourne	A 246-9	NZ 247-6	*NZ won by 4 wickets*
	Australia	Sydney	A 261-7	NZ 244	*Australia won by 17 runs*
	Australia	Brisbane	*abandoned without a ball being bowled*		
2004/05	Sri Lanka	Auckland	SL 141	NZ 144-3	*NZ won by 7 wickets*
2004/05	Australia	Wellington	A 236-7	NZ 226	*Australia won by 10 runs*
	Australia	Christchurch	A 314-6	NZ 208	*Australia won by 106 runs*
	Australia	Auckland	A 264-5	NZ 178	*Australia won by 86 runs*
	Australia	Welllington	NZ 233	A 236-3	*Australia won by 7 wickets*
	Australia	Napier	A 347-5	NZ 225-8	*Australia won by 122 runs*
2005/06	Zimbabwe	Bulawayo	NZ 397-5	Z 205	*NZ won by 192 runs*
	India	Bulawayo	NZ 215	I 164	*NZ won by 51 runs*
	Zimbabwe	Harare	NZ 238	Z 211	*NZ won by 27 runs*
	India	Harare	NZ 278-9	I 279-4	*India won by 6 wickets*
	India	Harare	I 276	NZ 278-4	*NZ won by 6 wickets*
2005/06	South Africa	Bloemfontein	NZ 249-8	SA 250-8	*SA won by 2 wickets*
	South Africa	Cape Town	SA 201-9	NZ 182	*SA won by 19 runs*
	South Africa	Port Elizabeth	NZ 243-9	SA 245-6	*SA won by 4 wickets*
	South Africa	Durban	SA 79-2	NZ	*Abandoned*
	South Africa	Centurion	NZ 215	SA 140-5	*SA won by 5 wickets (D/L)*
2005/06	Australia	Auckland	A 252-8	NZ 105	*Australia won by 147 runs*
	Australia	Wellington	A 322-5	NZ 320	*Australia won by 2 runs*
	Australia	Christchurch	A 331-7	NZ 332-8	*NZ won by 2 wickets*
2005/06	Sri Lanka	Queenstown	SL 164	NZ 166-3	*NZ won by 7 wickets*
	Sri Lanka	Christchurch	SL 255-7	NZ 256-5	*NZ won by 5 wickets*
	Sri Lanka	Wellington	NZ 224-9	SL 203	*NZ won by 21 runs*
	Sri Lanka	Napier	SL 273-6	NZ 253	*Sri Lanka won by 20 runs*
2005/06	West Indies	Wellington	NZ 288-9	WI 207	*NZ won by 81 runs*
	West Indies	Queenstown	WI 200-9	NZ 204-7	*NZ won by 3 wickets*
	West Indies	Christchurch	NZ 276-6	WI 255	*NZ won by 21 runs*
	West Indies	Napier	NZ 324-6	WI 233-8	*NZ won by 91 runs*
	West Indies	Auckland	NZ 233	WI 234-7	*West Indies won by 3 wickets*
2006/07	South Africa	Mumbai	NZ 195	SA 108	*NZ won by 87 runs*
Champions Trophy	Sri Lanka	Mumbai	NZ 165	SL 166-3	*Sri Lanka won by 7 wkts*
	Pakistan	Mohali	NZ 274-3	P 223	*NZ won by 51 runs*
	Australia	Mohali	A 240-9	NZ 206	*Australia won by 34 runs*
2006/07	Sri Lanka	Napier	NZ 285-8	SL 289-3	*Sri Lanka won by 7 wickets*
	Sri Lanka	Queenstown	SL 224-7	NZ 228-9	*NZ won by 1 wicket*
	Sri Lanka	Christchurch	SL 112	NZ 110-6	*NZ won by 4 wickets (D/L)*

	Sri Lanka	Auckland	SL 262-3	NZ 73	*Sri Lanka won by 189 runs*
	Sri Lanka	Hamilton	*abandoned without a ball being bowled*		
2006/07	Australia	Hobart	A 289-8	NZ 184	*Australia won by 105 runs*
	England	Hobart	NZ 205-9	E 206-7	*England won by 3 wickets*
	Australia	Sydney	NZ 218	A 224-8	*Australia won by 2 wickets*
	England	Adelaide	NZ 210	E 120	*NZ won by 90 runs*
	Australia	Perth	A 343-5	NZ 335-5	*Australia won by 8 runs*
	England	Perth	NZ 318-7	E 260-8	*NZ won by 58 runs*
	Australia	Melbourne	NZ 290-7	A 291-5	*Australia won by 5 wickets*
	England	Brisbane	E 270-7	NZ 256-8	*England won by 14 runs*
2006/07	Australia	Wellington	A 148	NZ 149-0	*NZ won by 10 wickets*
	Australia	Auckland	A 336-4	NZ 340-5	*NZ won by 5 wickets*
	Australia	Hamilton	A 346-5	NZ 350-9	*NZ won by 1 wicket*
2006/07	England	Gros Islet	E 209-7	NZ 210-4	*NZ won by 6 wickets*
World Cup	Kenya	Gros Islet	NZ 331-7	K 183	*NZ won by 148 runs*
	Canada	Gros Islet	NZ 363-5	C 249	*NZ won by 114 runs*
	West Indies	Antigua	WI 177	NZ 179-3	*NZ won by 7 wickets*
	Bangladesh	Antigua	B 174	NZ 178-1	*NZ won by 9 wickets*
	Ireland	Guyana	NZ 263-8	I 134	*NZ won by 129 runs*
	Sri Lanka	Grenada	NZ 219-7	SL 222-4	*Sri Lanka won by 6 wickets*
	South Africa	Grenada	SA 193-7	NZ 196-5	*NZ won by 5 wickets*
	Australia	Grenada	A 348-6	NZ 133	*Australia won by 215 runs*
	Sri Lanka	Kingston	SL 289-5	NZ 208	*Sri Lanka won by 81runs*
2007/08	South Africa	Durban	NZ 248-6	SA 249-8	*South Africa won by 2 wickets*
	South Africa	Port Elizabeth	SA 209-9	NZ 210-3	*NZ won by 7 wickets*
	South Africa	Cape Town	NZ 238-8	SA 242-5	*South Africa won by 5 wickets*
2007/08	Australia	Adelaide	NZ 254-7	A 255-3	*Australia won by 7 wickets*
	Australia	Sydney	NZ 30-3		*abandoned*
	Australia	Hobart	A 282-6	NZ 168	*Australia won by 114 runs*
2007/08	Bangladesh	Auckland	B 201	NZ 203-4	*NZ won by 6 wickets*
	Bangladesh	Napier	NZ 335-5	B 181-6	*NZ won by 102 runs (D/L)*
	Bangladesh	Queenstown	B 93	NZ 95-0	*NZ won by 10 wickets*
2007/08	England	Wellington	E 130	NZ 131-4	*NZ won by 6 wickets*
	England	Hamilton	E 158	NZ 165-0	*NZ won by 10 wickets (D/L)*
	England	Auckland	NZ 234-9	E 229-4	*England won by 6 wickets (D/L)*
	England	Napier	E 340-6	NZ 340-7	*Tie*
	England	Christchurch	E 242-7	NZ 213-6	*NZ won by 34 runs (D/L)*
2008	England	Chester-le-Street	E 307-5	NZ 193	*England won by 114 runs*
	England	Birmingham	E 162	NZ 127-2	*abandoned*
	England	Bristol	NZ 182	E 160	*NZ won by 22 runs*
	England	The Oval	E 245	NZ 246-9	*NZ won by 1 wicket*
	England	Lord's	NZ 266-5	E 215	*NZ won by 51 runs*
	Ireland	Aberdeen	NZ 402-2	I 112	*NZ won by 290 runs*
	Scotland	Aberdeen	S 101	NZ 102-2	*NZ won by 8 wickets*
2008/09	Bangladesh	Mirpur	NZ 201-9	B 202-3	*Bangladesh won by 7 wickets*
	Bangladesh	Mirpur	NZ 212-9	B 137	*NZ won by 75 runs*
	Bangladesh	Chittagong	NZ 249-7	B 170	*NZ won by 79 runs*
2008/09	West Indies	Queenstown	WI 129-5		*abandoned*
	West Indies	Christchurch	NZ 152-8	WI 158-5	*West Indies by 5 wks (D/L)*
	West Indies	Wellington	WI 128	NZ 129-3	*NZ won by 7 wickets*
	West Indies	Auckland	NZ 275-4	WI 64-0	*abandoned*
	West Indies	Napier	WI 293-9	NZ 211-5	*NZ won by 9 runs (D/L)*

2008/09	Australia	Perth	A 181	NZ 182-8	*NZ won by 2 wickets*
	Australia	Melbourne	A 225-5	NZ 226-4	*NZ won by 6 wickets*
	Australia	Sydney	A 301-9	NZ 269	*Australia won by 32 runs*
	Australia	Adelaide	NZ 244-8	A 247-4	*Australia won by 6 wickets*
	Australia	Brisbane	A 168-4	NZ 123-6	*abandoned*
2008/09	India	Napier	I 273-4	NZ 162	*India won by 53 runs (D/L)*
	India	Wellington	I 188-4		*abandoned*
	India	Christchurch	I 392-4	NZ 334	*India won by 58 runs*
	India	Hamilton	NZ 270-5	I 201-0	*India won by 84 runs (D/L)*
	India	Auckland	I 149	NZ 151-2	*NZ won by 8 wickets*

Summary of Results

	Played	*Won*	*Lost*	*Tie*	*Abandoned*
v Australia	117	32	80	—	5
v India	80	36	39	—	5
v Pakistan	78	29	47	1	1
v England	70	35	29	2	4
v Sri Lanka	68	34	30	1	3
v West Indies	51	20	24	—	7
v South Africa	50	17	29	—	4
v Zimbabwe	28	19	7	1	1
v Bangladesh	14	13	1	—	—
v Canada	2	2	—	—	—
v Ireland	2	2	—	—	—
v Scotland	2	2	—	—	—
v East Africa	1	1	—	—	—
v Holland	1	1	—	—	—
v UAE	1	1	—	—	—
v USA	1	1	—	—	—
v Kenya	1	1	—	—	—
TOTALS	**567**	**246**	**286**	**5**	**30**

In addition, New Zealand forfeited their match against Kenya, at Nairobi, 2002/03

One-day International Captains

		Results					*Toss*	
		P	*W*	*L*	*Tie*	*NR*	*W*	*L*
Fleming S.P.	1996/97 to 2006/07	218	98	106	1	13	106	112
Howarth G.P.	1979/80 to 1984/85	60	31	26	—	3	23	37
Vettori D.L.	2004/05 to 2008/09	49	27	15	1	6	32	17
Crowe M.D.	1989/90 to 1992/93	44	21	22	—	1	26	18
Rutherford K.R.	1993/94 to 1994/95	37	10	24	1	2	19	18
Germon L.K.	1995/96 to 1996/97	36	15	19	2	—	19	17
Wright J.G.	1982/83 to 1990	31	16	15	—	—	20	11
Coney J.V.	1984/85 to 1986/87	25	8	16	—	1	12	13
Crowe J.J.	1985/86 to 1987/88	16	4	12	—	—	7	9
Turner G.M.	1974/75 to 1976/77	8	5	2	—	1	5	3
Burgess M.G.	1978 to 1980/81	8	2	6	—	—	6	2
McMillan C.D.	2000/01 to 2001/02	8	2	6	—	—	3	5
Congdon B.E.	1972/73 to 1974/75	7	2	3	—	2	4	3
Nash D.J.	1998/99	7	3	3	—	1	4	3
Cairns C.L.	2001/02 to 2003/04	7	1	6	—	—	4	3
Larsen G.R.	1993/94	3	1	2	—	—	2	1
Jones A.H.	1992/93	2	—	2	—	—	1	1
McCullum B.B.	2008/09	1	—	1	—	—	1	—
TOTAL		**567**	**246**	**286**	**5**	**30**	**294**	**273**

Other One-day Internationals Played in New Zealand

1989/90	Christchurch	A	187-9	I	169	*Australia won by 18 runs*
	Hamilton	I	211-8	A	212-3	*Australia won by 7 wickets*
1991/92	New Plymouth	Z	312-4	SL	313-7	*Sri Lanka won by 3 wickets*
World Cup	Wellington	SA	195	SL	198-7	*Sri Lanka won by 3 wickets*
	Christchurch	SA	200-8	WI	136	*South Africa won by 64 runs*
	Hamilton	I	203-7	Z	104-1	*India won by 55 runs**
	Wellington	I	197	WI	195-5	*West Indies won by 5 wickets**
1994/95	Wellington	SA	123	A	124-7	*Australia won by 3 wickets*
	Hamilton	SA	223-6	I	209-9	*South Africa won by 14 runs*
	Dunedin	A	250-6	I	252-5	*India won by 5 wickets*

** target reduced*

Highest Totals

For

402-2	v Ireland	Aberdeen	2008
397-5	v Zimbabwe	Bulawayo	2005/06
363-5	v Canada	Gros Islet	2006/07
350-9	v Australia	Hamilton	2006/07
349-9	v India	Rajkot	1999/00
348-8	v India	Nagpur	1995/96
347-4	v USA	The Oval	2004
340-5	v Australia	Auckland	2006/07
340-7	v England	Napier	2007/08
338-4	v Bangladesh	Sharjah	1989/90
335-5	v Australia	Perth	2006/07
335-5	v Bangladesh	Napier	2007/08
334	v India	Christchurch	2008/09
332-8	v Australia	Christchurch	2005/06
331-7	v Kenya	Gros Islet	2006/07
324-6	v West Indies	Napier	2005/06
320	v Australia	Wellington	2005/06
318-7	v England	Perth	2006/07
309-5	v East Africa	Birmingham	1975
307-5	v Holland	Baroda	1995/96
307-8	v Pakistan	Wellington	2003/04
304-5	v Sri Lanka	Auckland	1982/83
302-6	v West Indies	Christchurch	1999/00
301-9	v Australia	Christchurch	1999/00
300-8	v India	Christchurch	1998/99

Against

392-4	by India	Christchurch	2008/09
376-2	by India	Hyderabad	1999/00
353-5	by India	Hyderabad	2003/04
349-6	by Australia	Christchurch	1999/00
348-6	by Australia	Grenada	2006/07
347-5	by Australia	Napier	2004/05
346-5	by Australia	Hamilton	2006/07
343-5	by Australia	Perth	2006/07
340-6	by England	Napier	2007/08
336-4	by Australia	Auckland	2006/07
331-7	by Australia	Christchurch	2005/06

328-2	by Pakistan	Sharjah	1993/94
324-4	by South Africa	Centurion	2000/01
322-6	by England	The Oval	1983
322-5	by Australia	Wellington	2005/06
314-7	by South Africa	Verwoerdburg	1994/95
314-7	by Pakistan	Faisalabad	2003/04
314-6	by Australia	Christchurch	2004/05
310-4	by Australia	Dunedin	1999/00
307-5	by England	Chester-le-Street	2008
306-6	by West Indies	Guwahati	1994/85
306-6	by South Africa	Johannesburg	2002/03
306	by India	Rajkot	1999/00
303	by Pakistan	Wellington	2003/04
302-8	by Australia	Melbourne	1982/83
301-9	by Australia	Sydney	2008/09
300-6	by South Africa	Brisbane	1997/98
300-7	by Zimbabwe	Taupo	2000/01

Zimbabwe scored 312-4 against Sri Lanka 313-7 at New Plymouth, 1991/92

Lowest Totals

For

64	v Pakistan	Sharjah	1985/86
73	v Sri Lanka	Auckland	2006/07
74	v Australia	Wellington	1981/82
74	v Pakistan	Sharjah	1989/90
94	v Australia	Christchurch	1989/90
97	v Australia	Faridabad	2003/04

Against

70	by Australia	Adelaide	1985/86
77	by Bangladesh	Colombo	2002/03
86	by Bangladesh	Chittagong	2004/05
89	by England	Wellington	2001/02
93	by Bangladesh	Queenstown	2007/08

Highest Match Aggregates

726	New Zealand v India	Christchurch	2008/09
696	New Zealand v Australia	Hamilton	2006/07
680	New Zealand v England	Napier	2007/08
678	Australia v New Zealand	Perth	2006/07
676	New Zealand v Australia	Auckland	2006/07
663	New Zealand v Australia	Christchurch	2005/06
655	India v New Zealand	Rajkot	1999/00
650	New Zealand v Australia	Christchurch	1999/00

Lowest Match Aggregates

130	New Zealand v Pakistan	Sharjah	1985/86
149	New Zealand v Australia	Wellington	1981/82
149	New Zealand v Pakistan	Sharjah	1989/90
188	New Zealand v Bangadesh	Queenstown	2007/08
198	New Zealand v Australia	Faridabad	2003/04

INDIVIDUAL RECORDS

Centuries

172	Vincent L.	v Zimbabwe	Bulawayo	2005/06
171*	Turner G.M.	v East Africa	Birmingham	1975
166	McCullum B.B.	v Ireland	Aberdeen	2008
161	Marshall J.A.H.	v Ireland	Aberdeen	2008
145*	Astle N.J.	v USA	The Oval	2004
141	Styris S.B.	v Sri Lanka	Bloemfontein	2002/03
140	Turner G.M.	v Sri Lanka	Auckland	1982/83
139	How J.M.	v England	Napier	2007/08
134*	Fleming S.P.	v South Africa	Johannesburg	2002/03
130	Harris C.Z.	v Australia	Madras	1995/96
128*	Taylor L.R.P.L.	v Sri Lanka	Napier	2006/07
122*	Astle N.J.	v England	Dunedin	2001/02
122*	Guptill M.J.	v West Indies	Auckland	2008/09
120	Astle N.J.	v Zimbabwe	Auckland	1995/96
120	Astle N.J.	v India	Rajkot	1999/00
119	Astle N.J.	v Pakistan	Dunedin	2000/01
118*	Sinclair M.S.	v Sri Lanka	Sharjah	2000/01
118*	Astle N.J.	v West Indies	Christchurch	2005/06
117	Astle N.J.	v Pakistan	Mohali	1996/97
117	Sinclair M.S.	v Pakistan	Sharjah	2000/01
117	Astle N.J.	v India	Colombo	2001/02
117	Taylor L.R.P.L.	v Australia	Auckland	2006/07
117	McMillan C.D.	v Australia	Hamilton	2006/07
116*	Fleming S.P.	v Australia	Melbourne	1997/98
115*	Fleming S.P.	v Pakistan	Christchurch	2003/04
115*	Astle N.J.	v India	Harare	2005/06
115	Cairns C.L.	v India	Christchurch	1998/99
115	Elliott G.D.	v Australia	Sydney	2008/09
114*	Turner G.M.	v India	Manchester	1975
114	Astle N.J.	v India	Nagpur	1995/96
112	Fulton P.G.	v Sri Lanka	Napier	2005/06
111*	Fleming S.P.	v Australia	Napier	1997/98
111*	Styris S.B.	v Sri Lanka	Grenada	2006/07
111	Greatbatch M.J.	v England	The Oval	1990
108	Rutherford K.R.	v India	Baroda	1994/95
108	Parore A.C.	v South Africa	Verwoerdburg	1994/95
108	Astle N.J.	v India	Colombo	2001/02
108	Fleming S.P.	v South Africa	Christchurch	2003/04
107*	Crowe M.D.	v India	Jamshedpur	1995/96
106*	Fleming S.P.	v West Indies	PortofSpain	1995/96
106	Fleming S.P.	v England	Brisbane	2006/07
105*	Crowe M.D.	v England	Auckland	1983/84
105	McMillan C.D.	v Pakistan	Rawalpindi	2001/02
105	Ryder J.D.	v India	Christchurch	2008/09
104*	Astle N.J.	v Zimbabwe	Napier	1997/98
104*	McMillan C.D.	v Pakistan	Christchurch	2000/01
104	Wadsworth K.J.	v Australia	Christchurch	1973/74
104	Crowe M.D.	v India	Dunedin	1989/90
104	Astle N.J.	v Australia	Napier	1999/00
103	Cairns C.L.	v India	Pune	1995/96

103	Twose R.G.	v South Africa	Cape Town	2000/01
103	Taylor L.R.P.L.	v Bangladesh	Chittagong	2008/09
102*	Edgar B.A.	v Australia	Melbourne	1980/81
102*	Greatbatch M.J.	v England	Leeds	1990
102*	Rutherford K.R.	v Sri Lanka	East London	1994/95
102*	Cairns C.L.	v India	Nairobi	2000/01
102*	Cairns C.L.	v South Africa	Brisbane	2001/02
102*	Astle N.J.	v Zimbabwe	Bloemfontein	2002/03
102*	Fleming S.P.	v Bangladesh	Antigua	2006/07
102	Vincent L.	v West Indies	Napier	2005/06
101*	Marshall H.J.H.	v Pakistan	Faisalabad	2003/04
101*	Styris S.B.	v Pakistan	Auckland	2003/04
101*	Oram J.D.P.	v Australia	Perth	2006/07
101	Congdon B.E.	v England	Wellington	1974/75
101	Wright J.G.	v England	Napier	1987/88
101	Astle N.J.	v England	Ahmedabad	1995/96
101	Styris S.B.	v Australia	Christchurch	2005/06
101	Vincent L.	v Canada	Gros Islet	2006/07
100*	Crowe M.D.	v Australia	Auckland	1991/92
100*	Astle N.J.	v South Africa	Auckland	1998/99

Successive Centuries

Greatbatch M.J. (2) 102* and 111 v England 1990

Most Successive Fifties

Jones A.H. (6) 57 v India and 55*, 62*, 67, 82, 63* v Pakistan 1988/89

Five Wickets in an Innings

9-3-19-6	Bond S.E.	v India	Bulawayo	2005/06
10-2-23-6	Bond S.E.	v Australia	Port Elizabeth	2002/03
7-0-25-6	Styris S.B.	v West Indies	Port of Spain	2001/02
6-2-7-5	Vettori D.L.	v Bangladesh	Queenstown	2007/08
10-2-22-5	Hart M.N.	v West Indies	Goa	1994/95
8.4-1-22-5	Adams A.R.	v India	Queenstown	2002/03
7-1-23-5	Collinge R.O.	v India	Christchurch	1975/76
9.3-2-23-5	Bond S.E.	v Australia	Wellington	2006/07
10.1-4-25-5	Hadlee R.J.	v Sri Lanka	Bristol	1983
9.2-2-25-5	Bond S.E.	v Australia	Adelaide	2001/02
10-2-25-5	Mills K.D.	v South Africa	Durban	2007/08
8.3-4-26-5	Hadlee R.J.	v Australia	Sydney	1980/81
10-3-26-5	Oram J.D.P.	v India	Auckland	2002/03
11-3-28-5	Cairns B.L.	v England	Scarborough	1978
9.2-1-30-5	Vettori D.L.	v West Indies	Lord's	2004
9-1-32-5	Hadlee R.J.	v India	Perth	1980/81
10-2-32-5	Hadlee R.J.	v England	Christchurch	1983/84
10-1-32-5	Latham R.T.	v Australia	Auckland	1992/93
10-1-34-5	Chatfield E.J.	v Australia	Adelaide	1980/81
10-0-34-5	Morrison D.K.	v Sri Lanka	Sharjah	1996/97
9.4-1-36-5	Oram J.D.P.	v USA	The Oval	2004
10-0-38-5	Hadlee R.J.	v Pakistan	Dunedin	1988/89

10-0-39-5	O'Connor S.B.	v Zimbabwe	Wellington	1997/98
10-0-42-5	Harris C.Z.	v Pakistan	Sialkot	1996/97
7.4-0-4-25	Cairns C.L.	v Australia	Napier	1997/98
10-1-42-5	Franklin J.E.C.	v England	ChesterleStreet	2004
11-1-45-5	Pringle C.	v England	Birmingham	1994
10-0-46-5	Morrison D.K.	v Pakistan	Christchurch	1995/96
9.2-0-46-5	O'Connor S.B.	v Pakistan	Nairobi	2000/01

Most Economical Bowling

10-4-8-1	Chatfield E.J.	v Sri Lanka	Dunedin	1982/83
12-6-10-0	Hadlee R.J.	v East Africa	Birmingham	1975
10-6-10-0	Cairns B.L.	v Sri Lanka	Dunedin	1982/83
10-2-11-2	Tuffey D.R.	v India	Christchurch	2002/03
10-5-12-2	Larsen G.R.	v South Africa	Hobart	1993/94
10-2-12-1	Harris C.Z.	v Pakistan	Napier	2000/01
10-5-13-0	Chatfield E.J.	v India	Adelaide	1985/86
10-3-14-2	Snedden M.C.	v Pakistan	Hamilton	1988/89
10-5-14-1	Larsen G.R.	v Zimbabwe	Wellington	1995/96
10-4-14-4	Vettori D.L.	v Sri Lanka	Dambulla	2002/03
10-3-14-3	Vettori D.L.	v USA	The Oval	2004
10-2-15-2	Chatfield E.J.	v England	Dunedin	1987/88
10-2-15-1	Watson W.	v England	Christchurch	1990/91
10-3-15-3	Allott G.I.	v Scotland	Edinburgh	1999
10-3-15-1	Harris C.Z.	v West Indies	Wellington	1999/00
10-4-15-2	Bond S.E.	v Bangladesh	Antigua	2006/07

Most Expensive Bowling

12-1-105-2	Snedden M.C.	v England	The Oval	1983
10-0-105-0	Southee T.G.	v India	Christchurch	2008/09
9-0-85-0	Drum C.J.	v India	Hyderabad	1999/00
11-0-84-0	Cairns B.L.	v England	Manchester	1978
10-0-83-2	Gillespie M.R.	v Australia	Hamilton	2006/07
10-0-80-1	Canning T.K.	v Australia	Napier	2004/05
10-0-80-0	Tuffey D.R.	v Australia	Auckland	2006/07
†7-0-77-1	Congdon B.E.	v Australia	Christchurch	1973/74
10-0-77-0	Oram J.D.P.	v Australia	Sydney	2004/05
10-0-76-1	Snedden M.C.	v England	Brisbane	1982/83
10-0-76-1	Troup G.B.	v England	Adelaide	1982/83
10-0-76-0	Cairns C.L.	v Australia	Christchurch	1999/00
10-0-76-1	Hamilton L.J.	v Australia	Napier	2004/05
10-1-76-1	Gillespie M.R.	v Australia	Perth	2006/07
10-0-75-1	Chatfield E.J.	v Pakistan	Christchurch	1984/85
10-0-75-0	de Groen R.P.	v Sri Lanka	Bloemfontein	1994/95

† 8-ball overs

Hat-tricks

9-1-35-3	Morrison D.K.	v India	Napier	1993/94
10-0-61-4	Bond S.E.	v Australia	Hobart	2006/07

Most Wicketkeeping Dismissals in an Innings

*5	Parore A.C.	v West Indies	Goa	1994/95
†5	McCullum B.B.	v India	Napier	2002/03
5	McCullum B.B	v India	Christchurch	2002/03
5	McCullum B.B.	v South Africa	Napier	2003/04
5	Hopkins G.J.	v Ireland	Aberdeen	2008
4	Lees W.K.	v India	Leeds	1979
4	Lees W.K.	v Australia	Sydney	1982/83
4	Parore A.C.	v Pakistan	Napier	1992/93
4	Blain T.E.	v South Africa	Hobart	1993/94
4	Germon L.K.	v Sri Lanka	Sharjah	1996/97
*4	Germon L.K.	v England	Wellington	1996/97
†4	Parore A.C.	v West Indies	Wellington	1999/00
4	McCullum B.B.	v Sri Lanka	Dambulla	2002/03
4	McCullum B.B.	v Pakistan	Dambulla	2002/03
†4	McCullum B.B.	v Zimbabwe	Harare	2005/06
4	McCullum B.B.	v England	Gros Islet	2006/07
4	McCullum B.B.	v West Indies	Antigua	2006/07

*† includes one stumping * includes two stumpings*

Most Catches in an Innings by a Fielder

4	Bracewell J.G. *(sub)*	v Australia	Adelaide	1980/81
4	Rutherford K.R.	v India	Napier	1994/95
4	Harris C.Z.	v India	Colombo	2001/02
4	Fleming S.P.	v England	Adelaide	2006/07

WALTER HADLEE TROPHIES

Awarded for the most meritorious batting and bowling performances by a New Zealand player in one-day internationals under the board's jurisdiction and other one-day matches as designated from time to time by the Board of Control.

BATTING

1988/89	Jones A.H.
1989/90	Crowe M.D.
1990/91	Crowe M.D.
1991/92	Crowe M.D.
1992/93	Crowe M.D.
1993/94	Thomson S.A.
1994/95	Parore A.C.
1995/96	Astle N.J.
1996/97	Fleming S.P.
1997/98	Harris C.Z.
1998/99	Astle N.J.
1999/00	Astle N.J.
2000/01	Twose R.G.
2001/02	Astle N.J.
2002/03	Fleming S.P.
2003/04	Fleming S.P.
2004/05	Marshall H.J.H.
2005/06	Astle N.J.
2006/07	Styris S.B.
2007/08	McCullum B.B.

BOWLING

1988/89	Snedden M.C.
1989/90	Snedden M.C.
1990/91	Pringle C.
1991/92	Patel D.N.
1992/93	Larsen G.R.
1993/94	Pringle C.
1994/95	Pringle C.
1995/96	Larsen G.R.
1996/97	Harris C.Z.
1997/98	Cairns C.L.
1998/99	Allott G.I.
1999/00	Allott G.I.
2000/01	Tuffey D.R.
2001/02	Bond S.E.
2002/03	Bond S.E.
2003/04	Tuffey D.R.
2004/05	Vettori D.L.
2005/06	Bond S.E.
2006/07	Bond S.E.
2007/08	Mills K.D.

RECORD PARTNERSHIPS

New Zealand v All Countries

For				
1st	274	Marshall J.A.H. & McCullum B.B. v Ireland	Aberdeen	2008
2nd	156	Vincent L. & Astle N.J. v West Indies	Napier	2005/06
3rd	180	Parore A.C. & Rutherford K.R. v India	Baroda	1994/95
4th	168	Germon L.K. & Harris C.Z. v Australia	Madras	1995/96
5th	148	Twose R.G. & Cairns C.L. v Australia	Cardiff	1999
6th	165	McMillan C.D.& McCullum B.B. v Australia	Hamilton	2006/07
7th	115	Parore A.C. & Germon L.K. v Pakistan	Sharjah	1996/97
8th	79	Styris S.B. & Vettori D.L. v Zimbabwe	Harare	2005/06
9th	83	Mills K.D. & Southee T.G. v India	Christchurch	2008/09
10th	65	Snedden M.C. & Chatfield E.J. v Sri Lanka	Derby	1983
Against				
1st	201	Tharanga W.U. & Jayasuriya S.T. for Sri Lanka	Napier	2006/07
	201*	Gambhir G. & Sehwag V. for India	Hamilton	2008/09
2nd	331	Tendulkar S.R. & Dravid R.S. for India	Hyderabad	1999/00
3rd	190*	Tavare C.J. & Lamb A.J. for England	Sydney	1982/83
4th	161	Yousuf Youhana & Younis Khan for Pakistan	Karachi	2001/02
5th	220	Symonds A. & Clarke M.J. for Australia	Wellington	2005/06
6th	136*	Clarke M.J. & Hussey M.E.K. for Australia	Auckland	2004/05
7th	108	Rameez Raja & Anil Dalpat for Pakistan	Christchurch	1984/85
8th	117	Houghton D.L. & Butchart I.P. for Zimbabwe	Hyderabad	1987/88
9th	118	Yadav Jai P. & Pathan I.K. for India	Bulawayo	2005/06
10th	67*	Morkel J.A. & Ntini M. for South Africa	Napier	2003/04

New Zealand v England

New Zealand				
1st	165*	Ryder J.D. & McCullum B.B.	Hamilton	2007/08
2nd	104	Fleming S.P. & Marshall H.J.H.	Bristol	2004
3rd	160	Howarth G.P. & Crowe M.D.	Auckland	1983/84
4th	100	Astle N.J. & McMillan C.D.	Dunedin	2001/02
5th	138*	Styris S.B. & Oram J.D.P.	Gros Islet	2006/07
6th	122	Rutherford K.R. & Harris C.Z.	Christchurch	1990/91
7th	74	Oram J.D.P. & Vettori D.L.	Auckland	2007/08
8th	68	Congdon B.E. & Cairns B.L.	Scarborough	1978
9th	63	Hadlee R.J. & Troup G.B.	Brisbane	1982/83
10th	30	Hart M.N. & Morrison D.K.	Birmingham	1994
England				
1st	193	Gooch G.A. & Athey C.W.J.	Manchester	1986
2nd	113	Gooch G.A. & Smith R.A.	Leeds	1990
3rd	190*	Tavare C.J. & Lamb A.J.	Sydney	1982/83
4th	136	Pietersen K.P. & Collingwood P.D.	Chester-le-Street	2008
5th	113	Gower D.I. & Randall D.W.	Brisbane	1982/83
6th	69	Shah O.A. & Wright L.J.	Christchurch	2007/08
7th	65	Collingwood P.D. & Swann G.P.	Bristol	2008
8th	76	Nixon P.A. & Plunkett L.E.	Perth	2006/07
9th	23	Shah O.A. & Sidebottom R.J.	Lord's	2008
10th	27	Gough D. & Caddick A.R.	Wellington	1996/97

New Zealand v Australia

New Zealand

1st	149*	Vincent L. & Fleming S.P.	Wellington	2006/07
2nd	151	Vincent L. & Fulton P.G.	Melbourne	2006/07
3rd	121	Astle N.J. & Twose R.G.	Dunedin	1999/00
4th	168	Germon L.K. & Harris C.Z.	Madras	1995/96
5th	148	Twose R.G. & Cairns C.L.	Cardiff	1999
6th	165	McMillan C.D.& McCullum B.B.	Hamilton	2006/07
7th	103	Oram J.D.P. & Vettori D.L.	Mohali	2006/07
8th	72	Harris C.Z. & Vettori D.L.	Melbourne	2001/02
9th	74*	McCullum B.B. & Vettori D.L.	Christchurch	2005/06
10th	50	Mills K.D. & Bond S.E.	Colombo	2002/03

Australia

1st	189	Waugh M.E. & Gilchrist A.C.	Christchurch	1999/00
2nd	200	Hayden M.L. & Ponting R.T.	Perth	2006/07
3rd	135	Ponting R.T. & Clarke M.J.	Adelaide	2007/08
4th	154	Ponting R.T. & Hodge B.J.	Melbourne	2006/07
5th	220	Symonds A. & Clarke M.J.	Wellington	2005/06
6th	136*	Clarke M.J. & Hussey M.E.K.	Auckland	2004/05
7th	74	Lehmann D.S. & Hogg G.B.	Sydney	2004/05
8th	97	Bevan M.G. & Bichel A.J.	Port Elizabeth	2002/03
9th	46	Marsh R.W. & Lawson G.F.	Adelaide	1980/81
10th	31	Martyn D.R. & McGrath G.D.	Auckland	1999/00

New Zealand v India

New Zealand

1st	166	Ryder J.D. & McCullum B.B.	Christchurch	2008/09
2nd	138	Astle N.J. & Fleming S.P.	Colombo	2001/02
3rd	180	Parore A.C. & Rutherford K.R.	Baroda	1994/95
4th	152	Crowe M.D. & Rutherford K.R.	Dunedin	1989/90
5th	147	Twose R.G. & Cairns C.L.	Pune	1995/96
6th	122	Cairns C.L. & Harris C.Z.	Nairobi	2000/01
7th	79	Burgess M.G. & Cairns B.L.	Adelaide	1980/81
8th	43	Nash D.J. & Vettori D.L.	Colombo	2001/02
9th	39	Snedden M.C. & Watson W.	Nagpur	1987/88
10th	52*	Tuffey D.R. & Bond S.E.	Auckland	2002/03

India

1st	201*	Gambhir G. & Sehwag V.	Hamilton	2008/09
2nd	331	Tendulkar S.R. & Dravid R.S.	Hyderabad	1999/00
3rd	158	Sidhu N.S. & Amarnath M.	Sharjah	1987/88
4th	135*	Tendulkar S.R. & Dhoni M.S.	Christchurch	2008/09
5th	92	Vengsarkar D.B. & Patil S.M.	Brisbane	1980/81
6th	127	Azharuddin M. & Sharma A.K.	Baroda	1988/89
7th	55	Abid Ali S. & Madan Lal S.	Manchester	1975
8th	82*	Kapil Dev & More K.S.	Bangalore	1987/88
9th	118	Yadav Jai P. & Pathan I.K.	Bulawayo	2005/06
10th	24	Kumble A.R. & Prasad B.K.V.	Rajkot	1999/00

New Zealand v Pakistan

New Zealand				
1st	193	Fleming S.P. & Astle N.J.	Dunedin	2000/01
2nd	148	Fleming S.P. & Marshall H.J.H.	Christchurch	2003/04
3rd	135	Astle N.J. & Twose R.G.	Nairobi	2000/01
4th	157	Marshall H.J.H. & McMillan C.D.	Wellington	2003/04
5th	108*	Crowe M.D. & Smith I.D.S.	Wellington	1988/89
6th	112*	McMillan C.D. & Harris C.Z.	Christchurch	2000/01
7th	115	Parore A.C. & Germon L.K.	Sharjah	1996/97
8th	48*	Harris C.Z. & Larsen G.R.	Sharjah	1993/94
9th	59	Lees W.K. & Bracewell J.G.	Nottingham	1983
10th	33	Germon L.K. & Morrison D.K.	Wellington	1995/96
Pakistan				
1st	199	Yasir Hameed & Imran Farhat	Rawalpindi	2003/04
2nd	263	Aamer Sohail & InzamamulHaq	Sharjah	1993/94
3rd	157*	Saeed Anwar & InzamamulHaq	Sharjah	2000/01
4th	161	Yousuf Youhana & Younis Khan	Karachi	2001/02
5th	108*	Ijaz Ahmed & Wasim Akram	Karachi	1996/97
6th	94	InzamamulHaq & Abdul Razzaq	Wellington	2003/04
7th	108	Rameez Raja & Anil Dalpat	Christchurch	1984/85
8th	65*	Abdul Razzaq & Mohammad Sami	Lahore	2003/04
9th	31*	Salim Malik & Mushtaq Ahmed	Gujranwala	1996/97
10th	39	Shoaib Akhtar & Mohammad Sami	Napier	2003/04

New Zealand v West Indies

New Zealand				
1st	136	How J.M. & Astle N.J.	Wellington	2005/06
2nd	156	Vincent L. & Astle N.J.	Napier	2005/06
3rd	170	Astle N.J. & Twose R.G.	Christchurch	1999/00
4th	139	McMillan C.D. & Vincent L.	Arnos Vale	2001/02
5th	99	Astle N.J. & Marshall H.J.H.	Christchurch	2005/06
6th	122*	Astle N.J. & Styris S.B.	Port of Spain	2001/02
7th	111	Parore A.C. & Patel D.N.	Kingston	1995/96
8th	63*	Vettori D.L. & Franklin J.E.C.	Queenstown	2005/06
9th	44*	Harris C.Z. & Vaughan J.T.C.	Arnos Vale	1995/96
10th	48*	Nash D.J. & Pringle C.	Guwahati	1994/95
West Indies				
1st	192*	Greenidge C.G. & Haynes D.L.	Christchurch	1986/87
2nd	184	Haynes D.L. & Gomes H.A.	Bridgetown	1984/85
3rd	186	Lara B.C. & Simmons P.V.	Arnos Vale	1995/96
4th	120	Hooper C.L. & Richards I.V.A.	Dunedin	1986/87
5th	91	Adams J.C. & Holder R.I.C.	Port of Spain	1995/96
6th	50	Chanderpaul S. & Hinds W.W.	Auckland	2005/06
7th	98	Sarwan R.R. & Jacobs R.D.	Port Elizabeth	2002/03
8th	48	Perry N.O. & Dillon M.	Napier	1999/00
9th	77	Sarwan R.R. & Bradshaw I.D.R.	Christchurch	2005/06
10th	27	Miller N.O. & Edwards F.H.	Wellington	2008/09

New Zealand v Sri Lanka

New Zealand

1st	132	Turner G.M. & Edgar B.A.	Auckland	1982/83
2nd	151	Astle N.J. & Taylor L.R.P.L.	Napier	2006/07
3rd	136	Parore A.C. & Rutherford K.R.	East London	1994/95
4th	97	Reid J.F. & Crowe J.J.	Colombo	1983/84
5th	75	Astle N.J. & Greatbatch M.J.	Sharjah	1996/97
6th	95	Blain T.E. & Hadlee R.J.	Hobart	1987/88
7th	85*	Harris C.Z. & Vincent L.	Christchurch	2000/01
8th	64*	Styris S.B. & Franklin J.E.C.	Grenada	2006/07
9th	47*	Cairns B.L. & Boock S.L.	Colombo	1983/84
10th	65	Snedden M.C. & Chatfield E.J.	Derby	1983

Sri Lanka

1st	201	Tharanga W.U. & Jayasuriya S.T.	Napier	2006/07
2nd	170	Jayasuriya S.T. & Tillakaratne H.P.	Bloemfontein	2002/03
3rd	184	Jayasuriya S.T. & Jayawardene D.P.M.D.	Sharjah	2000/01
4th	127	Kaluwitharana R.S. & Ranatunga A.	Dhaka	1998/99
5th	110	Atapattu M.S. & Arnold R.P.	Colombo	2001/02
6th	103*	Arnold R.P. & Perera A.S.A.	Colombo	2001/02
7th	52	de Alwis R.G. & Ratnayeke J.R.	Sydney	1987/88
8th	56	de Silva D.S. & Ratnayeke J.R.	Napier	1982/83
9th	45*	Ranatunga A. & de Silva D.S.	Moratuwa	1983/84
10th	29	de Silva D.S. & John V.	Melbourne	1984/85

New Zealand v Zimbabwe

New Zealand

1st	204	Vincent L. & Fleming S.P.	Bulawayo	2005/06
2nd	121	Vincent L. & McMillan C.D.	Bulawayo	2005/06
3rd	152	Spearman C.M. & Twose R.G.	Harare	2000/01
4th	130	Crowe M.D. & Rutherford K.R.	Harare	1992/93
5th	95	Twose R.G. & McMillan C.D.	Nairobi	2000/01
6th	75	Cairns C.L. & Harris C.Z.	Hamilton	1997/98
7th	50	Harris C.Z. & Parore A.C.	Christchurch	1997/98
8th	79	Styris S.B. & Vettori D.L.	Harare	2005/06
9th	55	Harris C.Z. & Larsen G.R.	Bulawayo	1997/98
10th	28	Franklin J.E.C. & Martin C.S.	Taupo	2000/01

Zimbabwe

1st	124	Flower A. & Flower G.W.	Harare	1992/93
2nd	91	Campbell A.D.R. & Carlisle S.V.	Wellington	2000/01
3rd	154	Carlisle S.V. & Flower A.	Taupo	2000/01
4th	123	Rennie G.J. & Campbell A.D.R.	Harare	1997/98
5th	70	Flower A. & Whittall G.J.	Christchurch	1997/98
6th	82	Flower A. & Viljoen D.P.	Auckland	2000/01
7th	68	Taibu T. & Streak H.H.	Bloemfontein	2002/03
8th	117	Houghton D.L. & Butchart I.P.	Hyderabad	1987/88
9th	54*	Strang P.A. & Rennie J.A.	Napier	1997/98
10th	23	Strang B.C. & Whittall A.R.	Harare	1997/98

New Zealand v South Africa

New Zealand

1st	114	Greatbatch M.J. & Latham R.T.	Auckland	1991/92
2nd	154	McCullum B.B. & How J.M.	Port Elizabeth	2007/08
3rd	126	Marshall H.J.H. & Styris S.B.	Dunedin	2003/04
4th	150	Twose R.G. & Cairns C.L.	Cape Town	2000/01
5th	106	Parore A.C. & Thomson S.A.	Centurion	1994/95
6th	124	McMillan C.D. & Harris C.Z.	Adelaide	1997/98
7th	84*	Cairns C.L. & Parore A.C.	Brisbane	2001/02
8th	69	Parore A.C. & Nash D.J.	Brisbane	1997/98
9th	47*	Parore A.C. & Vettori D.L.	Perth	2001/02
10th	29*	Parore A.C. & Bond S.E.	Hobart	2001/02

South Africa

1st	176	Kirsten G. & Gibbs H.H.	Birmingham	1999
2nd	172	Kirsten G. & Kallis J.H.	Kimberley	2000/01
3rd	139*	Kallis J.H. & Dippenaar H.H.	Melbourne	2001/02
4th	145	Kallis J.H. & Cullinan D.J.	Auckland	1998/99
5th	138	Rhodes J.N. & Boucher M.V.	Perth	2001/02
6th	97*	Rhodes J.N. & Pollock S.M.	Perth	2001/02
7th	65	Kemp J.M. & Pollock S.M.	Bloemfontein	2005/06
8th	69*	Klusener L. & Abrahams S.	Cape Town	2000/01
9th	22*	Pollock S.M. & Ntini M.	Christchurch	2003/04
10th	67*	Morkel J.A. & Ntini M.	Napier	2003/04

New Zealand v Bangladesh

New Zealand

1st	158	Crowe M.D. & Wright J.G.	Sharjah	1989/90
2nd	134*	Fleming S.P. & Marshall H.J.H.	Antigua	2006/07
3rd	125	How J.M. & Taylor L.R.P.L.	Chittagong	2008/09
4th	61*	Styris S.B. & Cairns C.L.	Kimberley	2002/03
5th	89	Taylor L.R.P.L. & Oram J.D.P.	Napier	2007/08
6th	49	Styris S.B. & Cairns C.L.	Chittagong	2004/05
7th	70	Oram J.D.P. & Vettori D.L.	Mirpur	2008/09
8th	41	Oram J.D.P. & Mills K.D.	Mirpur	2008/09
9th	33	Cairns C.L. & Adams A.R.	Chittagong	2004/05
10th	45*	Oram J.D.P. & Patel J.S.	Mirpur	2008/09

Bangladesh

1st	63	Tamim Iqbal & Zunaed Siddique	Napier	2007/08
2nd	67	Zunaed Siddique & Mushfiqur Rahim	Mirpur	2008/09
3rd	109	Zunaed Siddique & Mohammad Ashraful	Mirpur	2008/09
4th	40	Aftab Ahmed & Tushar Imran	Napier	2007/08
5th	34	Mohammad Ashraful & Akram Khan	Kimberley	2002/03
6th	56	Rajin Saleh & Khalid Masud	Dhaka	2004/05
7th	29	Khalid Masud & Alok Kapali	Dhaka	2004/05
8th	70*	Khalid Masud & Mohammad Rafique	Kimberley	2002/03
9th	26*	Naeem Islam & Shahadat Hossain	Chittagong	2008/09
10th	34	Mohammad Rafique & Syed Rasel	Antigua	2006/07

CAREER RECORDS

Averages

	M	In	NO	HS	Runs	Ave	100	50	Ct	St	Balls	Runs	Wkts	Ave	5WI	Best	R/100B	B/W
Adams A.R.	42	34	10	45	419	17.45	–	–	8	–	1885	1643	53	31.00	1	5-22	87	35
Allott G.I.	31	11	6	7*	17	3.40	–	–	5	–	1528	1207	52	23.21	–	4-35	78	29
Anderson R.W.	2	2	1	12	16	16.00	–	–	1	–	–	–	–	–	–	–	–	–
Astle N.J.	223	217	14	145*	7090	34.92	16	41	83	–	4850	3809	99	38.47	–	4-43	78	48
Bailey M.D.	1	–	–	–	–	–	–	–	–	–	–	–	–	–	–	–	–	–
Bell M.D.	7	7	0	66	133	19.00	–	1	1	–	–	–	–	–	–	–	–	–
Blain T.E.	38	38	11	49*	442	16.37	–	–	37	1	–	–	–	–	–	–	–	–
Blair B.R.	14	14	2	29*	174	12.50	–	–	4	–	30	34	1	34.00	–	1-7	113	30
Bond S.E.	67	28	14	31*	200	14.28	–	–	15	–	3446	2416	125	19.32	4	6-19	70	27
Boock S.L.	14	7	4	12	30	10.00	–	–	5	–	700	513	15	34.20	–	3-28	73	46
Bracewell B.P.	1	1	1	0*	0	–	–	–	–	–	66	41	1	41.00	–	1-41	62	66
Bracewell J.G.	53	43	12	43	512	16.51	–	–	19	–	2447	1884	33	57.09	–	2-3	76	74
Bradburn G.E.	11	10	3	30	60	8.57	–	–	2	–	385	318	6	53.00	–	2-18	82	64
Broom N.T.	8	8	2	29	107	17.83	–	–	–	–	–	–	–	–	–	–	–	–
Brown V.R.	3	3	0	32	44	14.66	–	–	2	–	66	75	1	75.00	–	1-24	113	66
Bulfin C.E.	4	2	1	7*	9	9.00	–	–	1	–	102	109	0	–	–	–	106	–
Burgess M.G.	26	20	0	47	336	16.80	–	–	8	–	74	69	1	69.00	–	1-10	93	74
Butler I.G.	18	8	4	24	30	7.50	–	–	6	–	713	675	17	39.70	–	3-41	94	41
Cairns B.L.	78	65	6	60	987	16.73	–	2	19	–	4015	2717	89	30.47	1	5-28	67	45
Cairns C.L.	*215	193	25	115	4950	29.46	4	26	66	–	8168	6594	201	32.80	1	5-42	80	40
Canning T.K.	4	4	1	23*	52	17.33	–	–	1	–	204	203	5	40.60		2-30	100	41
Chatfield E.J.	115	48	37	19*	118	10.72	–	–	19	–	6129	3666	142	25.81	1	5-34	59	43
Collinge R.O.	16	10	4	19	53	8.83	–	–	1	–	915	517	19	27.21	1	5-23	56	48
Coman P.G.	3	3	0	38	62	20.66	–	–	2	–	–	–	–	–	–	–	–	–
Coney J.V.	88	80	19	66*	1874	30.72	–	8	40	–	2931	2039	54	37.75	–	4-46	69	54
Congdon B.E.	12	10	3	101	373	54.71	1	2	1	–	501	322	8	40.25	–	2-17	64	62
Crowe J.J.	75	71	12	88*	1518	25.72	–	7	28	–	6	1	0	–	–	–	16	–
Crowe M.D.	143	140	18	107*	4704	38.55	4	34	66	–	1296	954	29	32.89	–	2-9	73	44
Cumming C.D.	13	13	1	45*	161	13.41	–	–	6	–	18	17	0	–	–	–	94	–
Davis H.T.	11	6	4	7*	13	6.50	–	–	2	–	432	436	11	39.63	–	4-35	100	39
de Groen R.P.	12	8	3	7*	12	2.40	–	–	2	–	549	478	8	59.75	–	2-34	87	68
Diamanti B.J.	1	1	1	26*	26	–	–	–	1	–	12	25	0	–	–	–	208	–
Douglas M.W.	6	6	0	30	55	9.16	–	–	2	–	–	–	–	–	–	–	–	–
Doull S.B.	42	27	13	22	172	12.28	–	–	10	–	1745	1459	36	40.52	–	4-25	83	48
Drum C.J.	5	2	2	7*	9	–	–	–	1	–	216	261	4	65.25	–	2-31	120	54
Edgar B.A.	64	64	5	102*	1814	30.74	1	10	12	–	12	5	0	–	–	–	41	–
Edwards G.N.	7	7	0	41	164	23.42	–	–	7	–	6	5	1	5.00	–	1-5	83	6
Elliott G.D.	21	13	5	115	421	52.62	1	2	4	–	374	318	13	24.46	–	3-14	85	28
Fleming S.P.	*280	269	21	134*	8037	32.40	8	49	133	–	29	28	1	28.00	–	1-8	96	29
Flynn D.R.	16	13	2	35	167	15.18	–	–	4	–	6	6	0	–	–	–	100	–
Franklin J.E.C.	65	44	15	45*	508	17.51	–	–	19	–	2804	2392	64	27.37	1	5-42	85	43
Franklin T.J.	3	3	0	21	27	9.00	–	–	–	–	–	–	–	–	–	–	–	–
Fulton P.G.	49	46	5	112	1334	32.53	1	8	17	–	–	–	–	–	–	–	–	–
Germon L.K.	37	31	5	89	519	19.96	–	3	21	9	–	–	–	–	–	–	–	–
Gillespie M.R.	32	14	8	28	93	15.50	–	–	6	–	1521	1369	37	37.00	–	4-58	90	41
Gillespie S.R.	19	11	5	18*	70	11.66	–	–	7	–	963	736	23	32.00	–	4-30	76	41
Gray E.J.	10	7	1	38	98	16.33	–	–	3	–	386	286	8	35.75	–	2-26	74	48
Greatbatch M.J.	84	83	5	111	2206	28.28	2	13	35	–	6	5	0	–	–	–	83	–
Guptill M.J.	12	11	3	122*	448	56.00	1	3	3	–	–	–	–	–	–	–	–	–
Hadlee B.G.	2	2	1	19	26	26.00	–	–	–	–	–	–	–	–	–	–	–	–
Hadlee D.R.	12	8	2	20	56	9.33	–	–	3	–	683	410	23	17.82	–	4-34	60	29
Hadlee R.J.	115	98	17	79	1751	21.61	–	4	27	–	6182	3407	158	21.56	5	5-25	55	39
Hamilton L.J.	2	2	2	2*	3	–	–	–	–	–	108	143	1	143.00	–	1-76	132	108
Harris C.Z.	250	213	62	130	4379	29.00	1	16	96		10667	7613	203	37.50	1	5-42	71	53
Hart M.N.	13	8	0	16	61	7.62	–	–	7	–	572	373	13	28.69	1	5-22	65	44
Hart R.G.	2	1	0	0	0	0.00	–	–	1	–	–	–	–	–	–	–	–	–
Hart R.T.	1	1	0	3	3	3.00	–	–	–	–	–	–	–	–	–	–	–	–
Hartland B.R.	16	16	1	68*	311	20.73	–	2	5	–	–	–	–	–	–	–	–	–
Haslam M.J.	1	1	0	9	9	–	–	–	–	–	30	28	1	28.00	–	1-28	93	30
Hastings B.F.	12	10	1	37	176	19.55	–	–	4	–	–	–	–	–	–	–	–	–

	M	In	NO	HS	Runs	Ave	100	50	Ct	St	Balls	Runs	Wkts	Ave	5WI	Best	R/100B	B/W
Hayes R.L.	1	1	0	13	13	13.00	–	–	–	–	42	31	0	–	–	–	73	–
Hitchcock P.A.	14	7	3	11*	41	10.25	–	–	4	–	558	468	12	39.00	–	3-30	83	46
Hopkins G.J.	12	5	0	25	41	8.20	–	–	16	–	–	–	–	–	–	–	–	–
Horne M.J.	50	48	0	74	980	20.41	–	5	12	–	–	–	–	–	–	–	–	–
Horne P.A.	4	4	0	18	50	12.50	–	–	–	–	–	–	–	–	–	–	–	–
How J.M.	31	28	1	139	930	34.44	1	7	13	–	–	–	–	–	–	–	–	–
Howarth G.P.	71	66	5	76	1384	22.72	–	6	16	–	90	68	3	22.67	–	1-4	75	30
Howarth H.J.	10	6	3	11	21	7.00	–	–	3	–	556	304	14	27.71	–	3-24	54	39
Howell L.G.	12	12	0	68	287	23.92	–	4	2	–	–	–	–	–	–	–	–	–
Jones A.H.	87	87	9	93	2784	35.69	–	25	23	–	306	216	4	54.00	–	2-42	70	76
Jones R.A.	5	5	0	63	168	33.60	–	1	–	–	–	–	–	–	–	–	–	–
Kennedy R.J.	7	4	3	8*	17	17.00	–	–	1	–	312	283	5	56.60	–	2-36	90	62
Kuggeleijn C.M.	16	11	2	40	142	15.77	–	–	9	–	817	604	12	50.33	–	2-31	74	68
Larsen G.R.	121	70	27	37	629	14.62	–	–	23	–	6368	4000	113	35.39	–	4-24	62	56
Latham R.T.	33	33	4	60	583	20.10	–	1	11	–	450	386	11	35.09	1	5-32	85	40
Lees W.K.	31	24	5	26	215	11.31	–	–	28	2	–	–	–	–	–	–	–	–
McCullum B.B.	153	127	22	166	2987	28.44	1	15	165	13	–	–	–	–	–	–	–	–
McEwan P.E.	17	15	0	41	204	13.60	–	–	1	–	420	353	6	58.83	–	2-29	84	70
McGlashan P.D.	4	2	1	56*	63	63.00	–	1	8	–	–	–	–	–	–	–	–	–
McKechnie B.J.	14	8	4	27	54	13.50	–	–	2	–	818	495	19	26.05	–	3-23	60	43
McMillan C.D.	197	183	16	117	4707	28.18	3	28	44	–	1879	1717	49	35.04	–	3-20	91	38
McSweeney E.B.	16	14	5	18*	73	8.11	–	–	14	3	–	–	–	–	–	–	–	–
Marshall H.J.H.	66	62	9	101*	1454	27.43	1	12	18	–	–	–	–	–	–	–	–	–
Marshall J.A.H.	10	10	0	161	250	25.00	1	1	–	–	–	–	–	–	–	–	–	–
Martin C.S.	20	7	2	3	8	1.60	–	–	7	–	948	804	18	44.66	–	3-62	84	52
Mason M.J.	25	6	3	13*	22	7.33	–	–	4	–	1119	956	30	31.86	–	4-24	85	37
Millmow J.P.	5	1	1	0*	0	–	–	–	1	–	270	232	4	58.00	–	2-22	85	67
Mills K.D.	102	56	23	54	545	16.51	–	1	27	–	5042	3936	149	26.41	1	5-25	78	33
Morrison D.K.	96	43	24	20*	171	9.00	–	–	19	–	4586	3470	126	27.53	2	5-34	75	36
Morrison J.F.M.	19	16	3	55	301	23.15	–	1	6	–	283	199	8	24.87	–	3-24	70	35
Murray D.J.	1	1	0	3	3	3.00	–	–	–	–	–	–	–	–	–	–	–	–
Nash D.J.	81	53	13	42	624	15.60	–	–	25	–	3416	2622	64	40.96	–	4-38	76	53
Nevin C.J.	37	36	0	74	732	20.33	–	4	16	3	–	–	–	–	–	–	–	–
O'Brien I.E.	10	2	2	3*	3	–	–	–	1	–	453	488	14	34.85	–	3-68	107	32
O'Connor S.B.	38	13	6	8	24	3.42	–	–	11	–	1487	1397	46	30.36	2	5-39	93	32
O'Sullivan D.R.	3	2	1	1*	2	2.00	–	–	–	–	168	123	2	61.50	–	1-38	73	84
Oram J.D.P.	130	94	12	101	2022	24.65	1	11	39	–	5506	4050	131	30.91	2	5-26	73	42
Owens M.B.	1	1	0	0	0	0.00	–	–	–	–	48	37	0	–	–	–	77	–
Papps M.H.W.	6	6	2	92*	207	51.75	–	2	1	–	–	–	–	–	–	–	–	–
Parker J.M.	25	21	0	66	280	13.33	–	1	11	1	16	10	1	10.00	–	1-10	62	16
Parker N.M.	1	1	0	0	0	0.00	–	–	1	–	–	–	–	–	–	–	–	–
Parore A.C.	179	161	32	108	3314	25.68	1	14	116	25	–	–	–	–	–	–	–	–
Patel D.N.	75	63	10	71	623	11.75	–	1	23	–	3251	2260	45	50.22	–	3-22	69	72
Patel J.S.	38	12	6	34	72	12.00	–	–	11	–	1766	1469	42	34.97	–	3-11	83	42
Penn A.J.	5	3	1	15	23	11.50	–	–	1	–	159	201	1	201.00	–	1-50	126	159
Petrie R.G.	12	8	3	21	65	13.00	–	–	2	–	660	449	12	37.41	–	2-25	68	55
Pollard V.	3	2	0	55	67	33.50	–	1	1	–	–	–	–	–	–	–	–	–
Priest M.W.	18	14	4	24	103	10.30	–	–	2	–	752	590	8	73.75	–	2-27	78	94
Pringle C.	64	41	19	34*	193	8.77	–	–	7	–	3314	2459	103	23.87	1	5-45	74	32
Redmond R.E.	2	1	0	3	3	3.00	–	–	–	–	–	–	–	–	–	–	–	–
Reid J.F.	25	24	1	88	633	27.16	–	4	5	–	–	–	–	–	–	–	–	–
Reid R.B.	9	9	0	64	248	27.55	–	2	3	–	7	13	1	13.00	–	1-13	185	7
Richardson M.H.	4	4	0	26	42	10.50	–	–	1	–	–	–	–	–	–	–	–	–
Roberts A.D.G.	1	1	0	16	16	16.00	–	–	1	–	56	30	1	30.00	–	1-30	53	56
Roberts S.J.	2	1	1	1*	1	–	–	–	–	–	42	47	0	–	–	–	111	–
Robertson G.K.	10	6	0	17	49	8.16	–	–	2	–	498	321	6	53.50	–	2-29	64	83
Rutherford K.R.	121	115	9	108	3143	29.65	2	18	41	–	389	323	10	32.30	–	2-39	83	38
Ryder J.D.	17	15	1	105	555	39.64	1	2	5	–	244	267	8	33.37	–	3-29	109	30
Sinclair M.S.	54	50	4	118*	1304	28.34	2	8	17	–	–	–	–	–	–	–	–	–
Smith I.D.S.	98	77	16	62*	1055	17.29	–	3	81	5	–	–	–	–	–	–	–	–
Snedden M.C.	93	54	19	64	535	15.28	–	1	19	–	4525	3237	114	28.39	–	4-34	71	39
Southee T.G.	21	10	3	32	96	13.71	–	–	1	–	1026	923	26	35.50	–	4-38	90	39
Spearman C.M.	51	50	0	86	936	18.72	–	5	15	–	3	6	0	–	–	–	–	–
Stirling D.A.	6	5	2	13*	21	7.00	–	–	3	–	246	207	6	34.33	–	2-29	84	41

	M	In	NO	HS	Runs	Ave	100	50	Ct	St	Balls	Runs	Wkts	Ave	5WI	Best	R/100B	B/W
Stott L.W.	1	—	—	—	—	—	—	—	1	—	72	48	3	16.00	—	3-48	66	24
Styris S.B.	157	135	21	141	3715	32.58	4	23	61	—	5313	4204	122	34.45	1	6-25	79	43
Su'a M.L.	12	7	2	12*	24	4.80	—	—	1	—	463	367	9	40.77	—	4-59	79	51
Sulzberger G.P.	3	2	1	6*	9	9.00	—	—	—	—	132	102	3	34.00	—	1-28	77	44
Tait A.R.	5	5	2	13*	35	11.66	—	—	—	—	120	88	3	29.33	—	2-37	73	40
Taylor B.R.	2	1	0	22	22	22.00	—	—	1	—	114	62	4	15.50	—	3-25	54	28
Taylor L.R.P.L.	63	57	11	128*	1770	38.47	3	10	36	—	30	32	0	—	—	—	106	—
Thompson E.P.	1	—	—	—	—	—	—	—	—	—	24	42	0	—	—	—	175	—
Thomson S.A.	56	52	10	83	964	22.95	—	5	18	—	2121	1602	42	38.14	—	3-14	75	50
Troup G.B.	22	12	8	39	101	25.25	—	—	2	—	1180	791	32	23.97	—	4-19	67	36
Tuffey D.R.	80	41	20	20*	154	7.33	—	—	19	—	3674	2910	91	31.97	—	4-24	79	40
Turner G.M.	41	40	6	171*	1598	47.00	3	9	13	—	6	0	0	—	—	—	—	—
Twose R.G.	87	81	11	103	2717	38.81	1	20	37	—	272	237	4	59.25	—	2-31	87	68
Vance R.H.	8	8	0	96	248	31.00	—	1	4	—	—	—	—	—	—	—	—	—
Vaughan J.T.C.	18	16	7	33	162	18.00	—	—	4	—	696	524	15	34.93	—	4-33	75	46
Vettori D.L.	† 239	144	46	83	1497	15.27	—	3	65	—	11234	7819	241	32.44	2	5-7	69	46
Vincent L.	102	99	10	172	2414	27.12	3	11	41	—	20	25	1	25.00	—	1-0	125	20
Vivian G.E.	1	1	0	14	14	14.00	—	—	—	—	—	—	—	—	—	—	—	—
Wadsworth K.J.	14	11	1	104	302	30.20	1	—	15	3	—	—	—	—	—	—	—	—
Walker B.G.K.	11	7	4	16*	47	15.66	—	—	5	—	438	417	8	52.12	—	2-43	95	54
Walker M.D.J.	3	1	0	10	10	10.00	—	—	2	—	132	119	4	29.75	—	4-49	90	33
Walmsley K.P.	2	—	—	—	—	—	—	—	—	—	120	117	2	58.60	—	1-53	97	60
Watson W.	61	24	13	21	86	7.81	—	—	9	—	3251	2247	74	30.36	—	4-27	69	43
Webb P.N.	5	5	1	10*	38	9.50	—	—	3	—	—	—	—	—	—	—	—	—
Webb R.J.	3	1	1	6*	6	—	—	—	—	—	161	105	4	26.25	—	2-28	65	40
White D.J.	3	3	0	15	37	12.33	—	—	1	—	—	—	—	—	—	—	—	—
Wilson J.W.	6	6	1	44*	103	20.60	—	—	4	—	242	260	4	65.00	—	2-21	107	61
Wiseman P.J.	15	7	5	16	45	22.50	—	—	2	—	450	368	12	30.66	—	4-45	81	37
Wisneski W.A.	3	2	1	6	10	10.00	—	—	1	—	114	123	0	—	—	—	107	—
Wright J.G.	149	148	1	101	3891	26.46	1	24	51	—	24	8	0	—	—	—	33	—
Young B.A.	74	73	5	74	1668	24.52	—	9	28	—	—	—	—	—	—	—	—	—

** includes one match for ICC World XI*
† includes four matches for ICC World XI

SUMMARY OF ONE-DAY INTERNATIONAL CAREER RECORDS

Most Matches

Fleming S.P.	280	Parore A.C.	179	Rutherford K.R.	121
Harris C.Z.	250	Styris S.B.	157	Larsen G.R.	121
Vettori D.L.	239	McCullum B.B.	153	Chatfield E.J.	115
Astle N.J.	223	Wright J.G.	149	Hadlee R.J.	115
Cairns C.L.	215	Crowe M.D.	143	Mills K.D.	102
McMillan C.D.	197	Oram J.D.P.	130	Vincent L.	102

Most Runs

		Ave
Fleming S.P.	8037	32.40
Astle N.J.	7090	34.92
Cairns C.L.	4950	29.46
McMillan C.D.	4707	28.18
Crowe M.D.	4704	38.55
Harris C.Z.	4379	29.00
Wright J.G.	3891	26.46
Styris S.B.	3715	32.58
Parore A.C.	3314	25.68
Rutherford K.R.	3143	29.65
McCullum B.B.	2987	28.44
Jones A.H.	2784	35.69
Twose R.G.	2717	38.81
Vincent L.	2414	27.12
Greatbatch M.J.	2206	28.28
Oram J.D.P.	2022	24.65
Coney J.V.	1874	30.72
Edgar B.A.	1814	30.74
Taylor L.R.P.L.	1770	38.47
Hadlee R.J.	1751	21.61
Young B.A.	1668	24.52
Turner G.M.	1598	47.00
Crowe J.J.	1518	25.72
Vettori D.L.	1497	15.27
Marshall H.J.H.	1454	27.43
Howarth G.P.	1384	22.72
Sinclair M.S.	1304	28.34
Fulton P.G.	1334	32.53
Smith I.D.S.	1055	17.29

Most Wickets

		Ave
Vettori D.L.	241	32.44
Harris C.Z.	203	37.50
Cairns C.L.	201	32.80
Hadlee R.J.	158	21.56
Mills K.D.	149	26.41
Chatfield E.J.	142	25.81
Oram J.D.P.	131	30.91
Morrison D.K.	126	27.53
Bond S.E.	125	19.32
Styris S.B.	122	34.49
Snedden M.C.	114	28.39
Larsen G.R.	113	35.39
Pringle C.	103	23.87

Most Economical Bowling

(qualification 600 balls)

	Balls bowled	Runs conceded	Runs conceded per 100 balls
Hadlee R.J.	6182	3407	55.11
Collinge R.O.	915	517	56.50
Chatfield E.J.	6129	3666	59.81
Hadlee D.R.	683	410	60.02
McKechnie B.J.	818	495	60.51
Larsen G.R.	6368	4000	62.81
Troup G.B.	1180	791	67.03
Cairns B.L.	4015	2717	67.67
Petrie R.G.	660	449	68.03
Watson W.	3251	2247	69.11

Best Strike Rates

(qualification 600 balls)

	Balls bowled	Wickets	Balls per wicket
Bond S.E.	3446	125	27.56
Allott G.I.	1528	52	29.38
Hadlee D.R.	683	23	29.69
Pringle C.	3314	103	32.17
O'Connor S.B.	1487	46	32.33
Mills K.D.	5042	149	33.83
Adams A.R.	1885	53	35.56
Morrison D.K.	4586	126	36.39
Troup G.B.	1180	32	36.87
Mason M.J.	1119	30	37.30

Register of New Zealand One-day Cricketers Who Have Not Played Test Cricket

	Born	Type	
Bailey Mark David	26/11/1970 Hamilton	RHB	RM
Blair Bruce Robert	27/12/1957 Dunedin	LHB	RM
Broom Neil Trevor	20/11/1983 Christchurch	RHB	RM
Bulfin Carl Edwin	19/8/1973 Blenheim	RHB	RFM
Canning Tamahau Karangatukituki	7/4/1977 Adelaide, Australia	RHB	RFM
Coman Peter George	13/4/1943 Christchurch	RHB	
Diamanti Brendon John	30/4/1981 Blenheim	RHB	RM
Douglas Mark William	20/10/1968 Nelson	LHB	
Hadlee Barry George	14/12/1941 Christchurch	RHB	
Hamilton Lance John	5/4/1973 Papakura	RHB	LFM
Hart Ronald Terence	7/11/1961 Lower Hutt	RHB	
Hayes Roydon Leslie	9/5/1971 Paeroa	RHB	RFM
Hitchcock Paul Anthony	23/1/1975 Whangarei	RHB	RM
Howell Llorne Gregory	8/7/1972 Napier	RHB	
McGlashan Peter Donald	22/6/1979 Napier	RHB	WK
McKechnie Brian John	6/11/1953 Gore	RHB	RM
McSweeney Ervin Bruce	8/3/1957 Wellington	RHB	WK
Millmow Jonathan Paul	22/9/1967 Wellington	RHB	RFM
Nevin Christopher John	3/8/1975 Dunedin	RHB	WK
Penn Andrew Jonathan	27/7/1974 Wanganui	RHB	RFM
Petrie Richard George	23/8/1967 Christchurch	RHB	RFM
Reid Richard Bruce	3/12/1958 Lower Hutt	RHB	
Roberts Stuart James	22/3/1965 Christchurch	RHB	RFM
Stott Leslie Warren	8/12/1946 Rochdale, England	RHB	RM
Sulzberger Glen Paul	14/3/1973 Kaponga	LHB	ROB
Tait Alex Ross	13/6/1972 Paparoa	RHB	RM
Thompson Ewen Paul	17/12/1979 Warkworth	LHB	LFM
Webb Richard John	15/9/1952 Invercargill	RHB	RFM
Walker Matthew David John	17/1/1977 Opunake	RHB	RM
Wilson Jeffrey William	24/10/1973 Invercargill	RHB	RFM
Wisneski Warren Anthony	19/2/1969 New Plymouth	RHB	RM

NEW ZEALAND TWENTY20 INTERNATIONAL RECORDS

TEAM RECORDS

Results

2004/05	Australia	Auckland	A 214-5	NZ 170	*Australia won by 44 runs*
2005/06	South Africa	Johannesburg	SA 133	NZ 134-5	*NZ won by 5 wickets*
2005/06	West Indies	Auckland	WI 126-7	NZ 126-8	*NZ won bowl-out*
2006/07	Sri Lanka	Wellington	NZ 162-8	SL 62-1	*Sri Lanka won by 18 runs (D/L)*
	Sri Lanka	Auckland	SL 115	NZ 116-5	*NZ won by 5 wickets*
2007/08	Kenya	Durban	K 73	NZ 74-1	*NZ won by 9 wickets*
	Sri Lanka	Johannesburg	NZ 164-7	SL 168-3	*Sri Lanka won by 7 wickets*
	India	Johannesburg	NZ 190	I 180-9	*NZ won by 10 runs*
	England	Durban	NZ 164-9	E 159-8	*NZ won by 5 runs*
	South Africa	Durban	NZ 153-8	SA 158-4	*South Africa won by 6 wickets*
	Pakistan	Cape Town	NZ 143-8	P 147-4	*Pakistan won by 6 wickets*
	South Africa	Johannesburg	NZ 129-7	SA131-7	*South Africa won by 3 wickets*
2007/08	Australia	Perth	A 186-6	NZ 132	*Australia won by 54 runs*
2007/08	England	Auckland	E 184-8	NZ 152	*England won by 32 runs*
	England	Christchurch	E 193-8	NZ 143-8	*England won by 50 runs*
2008	England	Manchester	NZ 123-9	E 127-1	*England won by 9 wickets*
2008/09	West Indies	Auckland	NZ 155-7	WI 155-8	*West Indies won eliminator*
	West Indies	Hamilton	NZ 191-9	WI 155-7	*NZ won by 36 runs*
	Australia	Sydney	A 150-7	NZ 149-5	*Australia won by 1 run*
	India	Christchurch	I 162-8	NZ 166-3	*NZ won by 7 wickets*
	India	Wellington	I 149-6	NZ 150-5	*NZ won by 5 wickets*
2009	Scotland	The Oval	S 89-4	NZ 90-3	*NZ won by 7 wickets*
	South Africa	Lord's	SA 128-7	NZ 127-5	*South Africa won by 1 run*
	Ireland	Nottingham	NZ 198-5	I 115	*NZ won by 83 runs*
	Pakistan	The Oval	NZ 99	P 100-4	*Pakistan won by 6 wickets*
	Sri Lanka	Nottingham	SL 158-5	NZ 110	*Sri Lanka won by 48 runs*

Summary of Results

	Played	*Won*	*Lost*	*NR*
v England	4	1	3	–
v South Africa	4	1	3	–
v Sri Lanka	4	1	3	–
v Australia	3	–	3	–
v West Indies	3	2	1	–
v India	3	3	–	–
v Pakistan	2	–	2	–
v Kenya	1	1	–	–
v Ireland	1	1	–	–
v Scotland	1	1	–	–
Total	**26**	**11**	**15**	**–**

Highest Totals

198-5	v Ireland	Nottingham	2009
191-9	v West Indies	Hamilton	2008/09
190	v India	Johannesburg	2007/08

Highest Individual Scores

69*	McCullum B.B.	v India	Wellington	2008/09
66*	Oram J.D.P.	v Australia	Perth	2007/08
66	Styris S.B.	v Australia	Auckland	2004/05
63	Taylor L.R.P.L.	v West Indies	Auckland	2008/09
63	Redmond A.J.	v Ireland	Nottingham	2009
62	Taylor L.R.P.L.	v Sri Lanka	Johannesburg	2007/08
62	Ryder J.D.	v West Indies	Hamilton	2008/09
61	Oram J.D.P.	v England	Auckland	2007/08
61	McCullum B.B.	v Australia	Sydney	2008/09

Four Wickets in an Innings

2.5-0-7-4	Gillespie M.R.	v Kenya	Durban	2007/08
4-0-20-4	Vettori D.L.	v India	Johannesburg	2007/08

CAREER RECORDS

	M	*In*	*NO*	*HS*	*Runs*	*Ave*	*100s*	*50s*	*Ct*	*St*	*O*	*M*	*R*	*W*	*Ave*	*R/O*	*Best*
A.R.Adams	4	2	1	7	13	13.00	-	-	1	-	12.5	0	105	3	35.00	8.18	2-20
N.J.Astle	4	4	1	40*	74	24.66	-	-	3	-	6.5	0	50	4	12.50	7.32	3-20
S.E.Bond	9	6	1	8*	19	3.80	-	-	1	-	34.3	1	244	12	20.33	7.07	2-12
N.T.Broom	5	3	0	36	42	14.00	-	-	2	-							
I.G.Butler	8	2	2	2*	3	-	-	-	-	-	25	0	199	11	18.09	7.96	3-19
C.L.Cairns	2	2	0	2	3	1.50	-	-	1	-	8	0	52	1	52.00	6.50	1-28
B.J.Diamanti	1	-	-	-	-	-	-	-	-	-	2	0	19	0	-	9.50	-
G.D.Elliott	1	1	1	23*	23	-	-	-	-	-	1	0	11	1	11.00	11.00	1-11
S.P.Fleming	5	5	0	38	110	22.00	-	-	2	-							
D.R.Flynn	4	4	0	23	37	9.25	-	-	2	-	1	0	7	0	-	7.00	-
J.E.C.Franklin	9	8	3	20	73	14.60	-	-	4	-	17	0	117	3	39.00	6.88	3-23
P.G.Fulton	11	11	1	25	118	11.80	-	-	3	-							
M.R.Gillespie	11	6	4	7	21	10.50	-	-	1	-	35	3	255	10	25.50	7.29	4-7
M.J.Guptill	8	7	1	45*	153	25.50	-	-	2	-							
P.A.Hitchcock	1	1	0	13	13	13.00	-	-	-	-	3	0	43	2	21.50	14.33	2-43
G.J.Hopkins	1	1	0	6	6	6.00	-	-	-	-							
J.M.How	5	5	0	31	56	11.20	-	-	1	-							
H.J.H.Marshall	3	3	0	8	12	4.00	-	-	1	-							
J.A.H.Marshall	3	2	0	13	14	7.00	-	-	-	-							
C.S.Martin	6	1	1	5*	5	-	-	-	1	-	23	1	193	7	27.57	8.39	2-14
M.J.Mason	3	1	0	2	2	2.00	-	-	-	-	9	0	65	2	32.50	7.22	1-18
B.B.McCullum	26	26	4	69*	689	31.31	-	5	17	3							
N.L.McCullum	9	5	2	10*	21	7.00	-	-	1	-	16.1	0	107	6	17.83	6.65	3-15
P.D.McGlashan	7	5	0	8	22	4.40	-	-	4	-							
C.D.McMillan	8	7	1	57	187	31.16	-	1	3	-							
K.D.Mills	13	10	3	33*	110	15.71	-	-	3	-	49.3	0	436	13	33.53	8.84	3-44
I.E.O'Brien	4	-	-	-	-	-	-	-	-	-	13	0	116	6	19.33	8.92	2-30
J.D.P.Oram	18	17	4	66*	352	27.07	-	2	7	-	40	0	360	3	120.00	9.00	1-14
J.S.Patel	11	4	1	5	9	3.00	-	-	4	-	33.1	1	269	16	16.81	8.11	3-20
A.J.Redmond	3	3	0	63	101	33.66	-	1	-	-							
J.D.Ryder	7	7	0	62	166	23.71	-	1	3	-	10	0	68	2	34.00	6.80	1-2
M.S.Sinclair	2	2	0	0	0	0.00	-	-	-	-							
T.G.Southee	7	3	1	12*	15	7.50	-	-	3	-	28	0	252	8	31.50	9.00	2-22
S.B.Styris	20	19	2	66	353	20.76	-	1	5	-	28.3	0	218	7	31.14	7.70	2-33
L.R.P.L.Taylor	20	19	2	63	374	22.00	-	2	15	-							
E.P.Thompson	1	1	1	1*	1	-	-	-	-	-	3	1	18	1	18.00	6.00	1-18
D.R.Tuffey	1	1	1	5*	5	-	-	-	-	-	4	0	50	1	50.00	12.50	1-50
D.L.Vettori	16	12	3	17*	67	7.44	-	-	6	-	64	0	352	25	14.08	5.50	4-20
L.Vincent	9	9	0	42	174	19.33	-	-	1	-							
J.W.Wilson	1	1	0	18	18	18.00	-	-	-	-	4	0	43	0	-	10.75	-

MINOR CRICKET

HIGHEST TEAM TOTALS

922-9	Australians v South Canterbury	Temuka	1913/14
741	Murphy's Pipe Works v Petone	Wellington	1919/20
709	Australians v Southland	Invercargill	1913/14
701-6 dec	Murphy's Pipe Works v Seatoun	Wellington	1919/20
686	Nelson City v Buller	Nelson	1954/55
683	Hamilton Old Boys v Eastern Suburbs	Hamilton	2007/08
681	New Zealand v Northern Districts (NSW)	West Maitland	1925/26
653-9 dec	Hawkes Bay v Wairarapa	Napier	1946/47
† 650-9 dec	Manawatu v South Canterbury	Palmerston North	1993/94
† 649	Nelson v Wairarapa	Nelson	1984/85
† 643	Nelson v North Canterbury	Nelson	1984/85
† 641-7	Nelson v Taranaki	Nelson	1983/84
633-7 dec	North v Returned Soldiers	Wellington	1917/18
† 633-9	Wellington City v Bay of Plenty	Mt Maunganui	1997/98
† 632	Nelson v Waikato	Nelson	1963/64
629-7 dec	Midland II v Railways	Wellington	1921/22
623	North Canterbury v South Canterbury	Christchurch	1907/08
619-3	Cornwall U19 v Sri Lanka CC U19	Auckland	1997/98
611	Australian Academy XI v NZ Academy XI	Lincoln	1999/00
609	Napier United A v Napier United B	Napier	1898/99
603-7 dec	Tinwald v Ashburton A	Ashburton	1927/28
603-7 dec	Australians v Wairarapa	Masteron	1949/50
603-8 dec	New South Wales v South Canterbury	Timaru	1923/24
602-9 dec	New Zealand v Melbourne CC	Christchurch	1926/27
† 602	Nelson v Hawkes Bay	Nelson	1959/60

† denotes Hawke Cup/U-Bix Cup/Fuji Xerox Cup Challenge match

HIGHEST INDIVIDUAL SCORES

400	C.D. Knight	Cornwall U19 v Sri Lanka CC U19	Auckland	1997/98
378	B-J. Watling	Hamilton Old Boys v Eastern Suburbs	Hamilton	2007/08
358	S. Goulding	St Bedes v Sydenham	Christchurch	2006/07
354	J.N. Crawford	Australians v South Canterbury	Temuka	1913/14
343*	J. Gray	Sydenham v Christ's College	Christchurch	1917/18
335	W.W. Armstrong	Melbourne CC v Southland	Invercargill	1905/06
334*	Harold B. Lusk	West Christchurch v St Albans	Christchurch	1915/16
324*	D.N. Hakaraia	Waitakere U17 v Howick Pakuranga U17	Auckland	1999/00
311	H.M. Butterworth	School B v Wanganui	Wanganui	1914/15
303*	M.D. Bell	ND U20 v Wellington U20	Wanganui	1994/95
300*	W.J. Hendy	Auckland Suburban Association v Christchurch HSOB	Christchurch	1925/26

HIGHEST PARTNERSHIPS

	Wkt				
518	2nd	A. Young & F.L. McMahon	Wanderers v Taruheru	Gisborne	1910/11
441	1st	J.E. Mills & H.D. Gillespie	Eden v University	Auckland	1924/25
437*	2nd	R. Eden & M.R. Eden	Wanderers v Wakefield	Nelson	1922/23
394	1st	R.S. Scragg & J.V. Hill	CD A v Otago A	P. North	2001/02
393	1st	M.E.L. Lane & J. Lane	Marlborough v Buller	Blenheim	1992/93
391	4th	T.P.L. Reaney & H. Hawthorne	Hawkes Bay v Wairarapa	Napier	1946/47
375	2nd	A.C. Barnes & S.M. Lynch	Cornwall v Waitakere	Auckland	1996/97
374*	1st	T.D. Astle & K.R. Ambler	Canterbury U19 v Auckland U19	Lincoln	2004/05
360	1st	G. Marshall & H.C. Wilson	Napier United A v Napier United B	Napier	1898/99
360	1st	B. Sutcliffe & F.J. Craig	Takapuna Grammar v Mt Albert Grammar	Devonport	1942/43